AF883166

Art & Architecture Thesaurus

THE GETTY ART HISTORY INFORMATION PROGRAM

The Art and Architecture Thesaurus is a program of The Getty Art History Information Program

Art & Architecture Thesaurus

Toni Petersen
DIRECTOR

Volume 2
Part III: Alphabetical Display

Published on behalf of
The Getty Art History Information Program

OXFORD UNIVERSITY PRESS

New York · 1990 · *Oxford*

Oxford University Press

Oxford New York Toronto
Delhi Bombay Calcutta Madras Karachi
Petaling Jaya Singapore Hong Kong Tokyo
Nairobi Dar es Salaam Cape Town
Melbourne Auckland

and associated companies in
Berlin Ibadan

Published by Oxford University Press, Inc.,
200 Madison Avenue, New York, New York 10016

Library of Congress Cataloging-in-Publication Data
Art & architecture thesaurus / Toni Petersen, director.
p.
21½x28 cm.
Half t.p.: The Getty Art History Information Program.
Includes bibliographical references.
Contents: v. 1, pt. 1. Introduction. pt. 2. Hierarchical displays — v. 2. Alphabetical display, A and–Knotted — v. 3. Alphabetical display, Knotting–Zutujil.
ISBN 0-19-506403-8 (set)
1. Subject headings—Art. 2. Art—Abstracting and indexing. 3. Subject headings—Architecture. 4. Architecture—Abstracting and indexing. I. Petersen, Toni. II. Getty Art History Information Program. III. J. Paul Getty Trust. IV. Title: Art and architecture thesaurus.
Z695.1.A7A76 1990 89-26479
025.4'97—dc20 CIP

9 8 7 6 5 4 3 2 1

Printed in the United States of America
on acid-free paper

Art &
Architecture
Thesaurus

PART III: Alphabetical Display

1-story
USE **single-story**

10th Dynasty
USE **Tenth Dynasty**

11th Dynasty
USE **Eleventh Dynasty**

1200 Style
USE **Early Gothic**

12th Dynasty
USE **Twelfth Dynasty**

136 armchairs
TG.80
ALT **136 armchair**
UF armchairs, 136
CN V.TG.AFU.AFU.ALO.AFU.AFU.AFU.JCO

13th Dynasty
USE **Thirteenth Dynasty**

14-carat gold
USE **fourteen-carat gold**

14th Dynasty
USE **Fourteenth Dynasty**

15th Dynasty
USE **Fifteenth Dynasty**

16th Dynasty
USE **Sixteenth Dynasty**

17th Dynasty
USE **Seventeenth Dynasty**

18-carat gold
USE **eighteen-carat gold**

18th Dynasty
USE **Eighteenth Dynasty**

19th Dynasty
USE **Nineteenth Dynasty**

1st Dynasty
USE **First Dynasty**

20th Dynasty
USE **Twentieth Dynasty**

21st Dynasty
USE **Twenty-first Dynasty**

22nd Dynasty
USE **Twenty-second Dynasty**

23rd Dynasty
USE **Twenty-third Dynasty**

24-carat gold
USE **gold**

24th Dynasty
USE **Twenty-fourth Dynasty**

25th Dynasty
USE **Twenty-fifth Dynasty**

26th Dynasty
USE **Twenty-sixth Dynasty**

27th Dynasty
USE **Twenty-seventh Dynasty**

28th Dynasty
USE **Twenty-eighth Dynasty**

29th Dynasty
USE **Twenty-ninth Dynasty**

2nd Dynasty
USE **Second Dynasty**

3-bay barns
USE **English barns**

3-story
USE **three-story**

30th Dynasty
USE **Thirtieth Dynasty**

35mm cameras
TB.290 (L)
ALT **35mm camera**
UF cameras, 35mm
cameras, thirty-five millimeter
thirty-five millimeter cameras
CN V.TB.AFU.ARI.CLM.ARI.AFU.AFU.AFU.AFU

3rd Dynasty
USE **Third Dynasty**

4th Dynasty
USE **Fourth Dynasty**

5th Dynasty
USE **Fifth Dynasty**

6th Dynasty
USE **Sixth Dynasty**

7th Dynasty
USE **Seventh Dynasty**

8th Dynasty
USE **Eighth Dynasty**

9th Dynasty
USE **Ninth Dynasty**

A and I services
USE **abstracting and indexing services**

à deux crayons
KT.190
SN A drawing technique, usually employing red chalk and black chalk or charcoal.
UF aux deux crayons
crayons, à deux
CN K.KT.AFU.ALO.DUC.BZY.ALO.AFU

A-frame houses
RK.245 (B)
ALT **A-frame house**
UF houses, A-frame
CN V.RK.AFU.ALO.ALO.AXC.ALO.AFU.CLM.AFU

A-shaped trestles
USE **A trestles**

A trestles
TG.842
ALT **A trestle**
UF A-shaped trestles
trestles, A
trestles, A-shaped
CN V.TG.ALO.BCW.AFU.AFU

à trois crayons
KT.191
SN A drawing technique usually employing a combination of red, black, and white chalks on a yellowish or off-white paper; especially common in the 18th century. (LAD)
UF aux trois crayons
couleurs, trois
crayons, à trois
crayons, trois
trois couleurs
trois crayons
CN K.KT.AFU.ALO.DUC.BZY.ALO.ALO

Ababua
USE **Babwa**

abaca
USE **Manila hemp**

abaci
RT.133 (N)
ALT **abacus**
SN Uppermost members of the capitals of columns; often plain square slabs, but sometimes molded or otherwise enriched. (HAS)
CN V.RT.AFU.AFU.AFU.AXC.BIQ.ALO.ARI.ALO.AFU

abaci (sideboards)
TG.587
ALT **abacus (sideboard)**
SN Ancient Roman sideboards, generally having a tablelike lower member and an upper member with shelving; used to display highly prized ornaments. (RICHTE)
CN V.TG.AFU.AFU.AXC.ALO.CRG.AFU

abalone
MT.944 (L)
CN M.MT.AFU.AFU.ALO.AFU.DUC.AFU

abamuri
USE **buttresses**

abandoned buildings
USE **derelict buildings**

abandoned farms
RG.5 (L)
ALT **abandoned farm**
UF farms, abandoned
CN V.RG.AFU.AFU.AFU.AFU.AFU

Abash-adar
USE **Bashadar**

Abasian boxwood
USE **boxwood**

abat-jours
RT.908
ALT **abat-jour**
SN Use for beveled apertures in a wall or in a roof to admit light from above and for windows, usually high in position, with the base of the opening beveled so that light may fall directly on areas below.
CN V.RT.AFU.ARI.AFU.AFU.BOK.AFU.AFU.AFU

abat-voix
USE **sounding boards**

abatement, noise
USE **noise control**

abatement, smoke
USE **smoke abatement**

abattoirs
USE **slaughterhouses**

Abbasid (Dynasty)
FL.3426 (A,L)
CN F.FL.ALO.BIQ.AFU.AFU

Abbevillian
FL.2450
UF Chellean
CN F.FL.ALO.AXC.AFU.AFU.AFU

abbey churches
RK.1105 (A,B)
ALT **abbey church**
UF churches, abbey
churches, conventual
conventual churches
CN V.RK.AFU.ALO.ALO.FCS.BIQ.ALO.ARI.AFU

abbeys
RG.195 (A,L,B,R)
ALT **abbey**
SN Designates independent and canonically erected monasteries, ruled by an abbot if occupied by monks and by an abbess if occupied by nuns.
CN V.RG.AFU.AFU.DUC.BIQ.AFU

abbots
HG.216 (L,R)
ALT **abbot**
SN The superiors of monastic abbeys for men. (W)
CN H.HG.AFU.AXC.AXC.BIQ.AFU.ARI.AFU

abbots' chairs
USE **Glastonbury chairs**

Abbotsford
FL.3283
UF Baronial
CN F.FL.ALO.BCW.ALO.AXC.CXA.AFU

ABC
USE **Minimal**

\`Abd-al-\`Aziz
USE **Abdülâziz**

\`Abd-al-Hamid I
USE **Abdülhamid I**

\`Abd-al-Hamid II
USE **Abdülhamid II**

\`Abd-al-Majid I
USE **Abdülmecid I**

Abdül Aziz
USE **Abdülâziz**

Abdül Hamid I
USE **Abdülhamid I**

Abdül-Hamid II
USE **Abdülhamid II**

Abdül hamit II
USE **Abdülhamid II**

Abdül Mecid I
USE **Abdülmecid I**

Abdülâziz
FL.3513
UF \`Abd-al-\`Aziz
Abdül Aziz
CN F.FL.ALO.BIQ.AFU.FOG.AFU.HCQ

Abdülhamid I
FL.3508
UF \`Abd-al-Hamid I
Abdül Hamid I
CN F.FL.ALO.BIQ.AFU.FOG.AFU.FZU

Abdülhamid II
FL.3515
UF \`Abd-al-Hamid II
Abdül-Hamid II
Abdül hamit II
Abdülhamit II
CN F.FL.ALO.BIQ.AFU.FOG.AFU.HOE

Abdülhamit II
USE **Abdülhamid II**

Abdülmecid I
FL.3512
UF \`Abd-al-Majid I
Abdül Mecid I
CN F.FL.ALO.BIQ.AFU.FOG.AFU.GWW

Abelam
FL.3647 (L)
CN F.FL.ALO.BOK.ALO.BCW.ALO.BCW.AFU.AFU

abherents
USE **parting compounds**

Abies
USE **fir**

Abies amabilis
USE **silver fir**

Abies balsamea
USE **balsam fir**

Abies Fraseri
USE **Fraser's balsam fir**

Abies humilis
USE **Fraser's balsam fir**

Abigarrado
USE **cursive**

Abipón
FL.1636 (L)
CN F.FL.ALO.ALO.ARI.ARI.AXC.AFU

ablution fountains
RT.1212
ALT **ablution fountain**
UF fountains, ablution
CN V.RT.AFU.BUE.ALO.AFU

Abnaki
FL.1288 (L)
UF Kennebec
Wabanaki
CN F.FL.ALO.ALO.ARI.AFU.ARI.AFU

abolitionists
HG.756 (L)
ALT **abolitionist**
CN H.HG.AFU.BCW.HZS.BUE.AFU

Aboriginal
USE **Australian Aboriginal**

Aboriginal, Australian
USE **Australian Aboriginal**

abrading
USE **abrasion**

Abraham of Kütahya style Iznik pottery
USE **Kütahya ware**

abrasion
KT.601
ALT **abraded**
SN Material-removing process usually accomplished by the action of mineral particles against a surface.
UF abrading
CN K.KT.AFU.ALO.FUA.AFU

abrasion-resistant materials
MT.2788
UF materials, abrasion-resistant
CN M.MT.AFU.BCW.AFU

abrasive blasting
USE **abrasive cleaning**

abrasive cleaning
KT.66
SN Cleaning method that removes soil, discolorations, or coatings through the action of certain materials which impact and abrade the surface under pressure. (GRIMMR)
UF abrasive blasting
blast-cleaning
blasting, abrasive
cleaning, abrasive
CN K.KT.AFU.ALO.BIQ.AFU

abrasive paper
TB.500
UF paper, abrasive

CN V.TB.AFU.ARI.EWY.ALO.AFU

abrasive wheels
USE **grinding wheels**

abrasives
MT.2292 (L)
SN Any hard, sharp material that wears away a softer, less resistant surface when the two are rubbed together. (HORNB)
CN M.MT.AFU.ARI.AFU

abreuvoirs
TF.617
ALT **abreuvoir**
SN Joints filled with mortar and located between masonry units. (MEANS)
CN V.TF.ALO.ARI.ALO.AFU.AFU

Abron
USE **Brong**

ABS
USE **acrylonitrile-butadiene-styrene copolymer**

ABS plastic
USE **acrylonitrile-butadiene-styrene copolymer**

Absaroke
USE **Crow**

absolute alcohol
MT.2687
UF alcohol, absolute
alcohol, anhydrous
anhydrous alcohol
CN M.MT.AFU.ARI.HZS.AFU.BOK.AFU.AXC.AFU

absolutism
USE **despotism**

absorbent materials
MT.2789
UF materials, absorbent
CN M.MT.AFU.BCW.ALO

absorbent paper
MT.1925 (L)
UF paper, absorbent
CN M.MT.AFU.AFU.ARI.ALO.ALO.AXC.ARI.AFU

absorption
KT.6 (L)
SN The process by which a liquid, or a mixture of gases and liquids, is drawn into and tends to fill permeable pores in a porous solid material; usually accompanied by a physical change, chemical change, or both. (DAC)
CN K.KT.AFU.ALO.AFU

absorption fields
USE **leaching fields**

absorption, sound
USE **sound absorption**

Abstract
FL.3289 (L,R)
SN Use with reference to 20th-century art; in other contexts use **abstraction.**
CN F.FL.ALO.BCW.ALO.AXC.DCU.AFU

Abstract Expressionist
FL.3713 (L,R)
ALT **Abstract Expressionism**
UF American-Type painting
Expressionist, Abstract
CN F.FL.ALO.BUE.ARI.AFU

Abstract Imagist
FL.3714
SN Use for certain Abstract Expressionist paintings. Use **Color-field** to encompass Abstract Imagist painting and the works of the 1960s derived from it.
UF Imagist, Abstract
CN F.FL.ALO.BUE.ARI.AFU.AFU

Abstract Impressionist
FL.3716 (L)
ALT **Abstract Impressionism**
UF Impressionist, Abstract
CN F.FL.ALO.BUE.ARI.ALO

Abstract, Perceptual
USE **Op art**

abstracting
KG.65 (L)
SN Production of a document surrogate which summarizes the subject matter or describes other essential qualities of the document. For the process of making visual forms less representational, use **abstraction.**
CN K.KG.AFU.AFU.AXC.AFU

abstracting and indexing services
HG.866 (L)
ALT **abstracting and indexing service**
SN Information services which provide access to documents in a specific subject field or fields by means of abstracts and indexes issued periodically on paper, in microform, or as machine-readable databases, available by subscription or fee. (ALAG)
UF A and I services
indexing and abstracting services
services, A and I
services, abstracting and indexing
services, indexing and abstracting
CN H.HG.ALO.DIO.AFU.AFU

abstraction
BM.185
SN Use for the general concept and approach. For the 20th-century movement and its products, use **Abstract.**
CN B.BM.AFU.AFU.AXC.CLM.AFU

Abstraction Lyrique
USE **Tachiste**

abstraction, biomorphic
USE **biomorphic abstraction**

Abstraction, Chromatic
USE **Color-field**

abstraction, classical
USE **geometric abstraction**

abstraction, creative
USE **biomorphic abstraction**

abstraction, geometric
USE **geometric abstraction**

Abstraction, Lyrical
USE **Lyrical Abstraction**

Abstraction, Post-painterly
USE **Color-field**

abstracts
VW.79 (L)
ALT **abstract**
SN Brief summaries that provide the essential points of written works.
UF précis
CN V.VW.AFU.AFU.AFU.FCS.AFU

Abua
FL.235 (L)
CN F.FL.ALO.AFU.AXC.AFU.ALO.AFU.AFU

abutments
RT.60 (L)
ALT **abutment**
UF butments
CN V.RT.AFU.AFU.AFU.AXC.AFU

abutting joints
TF.574
ALT **abutting joint**
SN Joints between two pieces of wood in which the direction of the grain of one piece is at an angle (usually 90 degrees) to the grain in the other. (DAC)
UF joints, abutting
CN V.TF.ALO.AFU.ALO

Acacia
MT.1199 (L)
UF arabic tree, gum
gum arabic tree
tree, gum arabic
CN M.MT.AFU.AFU.ALO.BIQ.DCU.AFU.AFU.AFU.HCQ.AFU

Acacia (black locust)
USE **black locust**

Acacia dealbata
USE **silver wattle**

Acacia gum
USE **gum arabic**

Acacia koa
USE **koa**

Acacia melanoxylon
USE **Australian locust**

Acacia, false
USE **black locust**

academic architecture
BM.222 (R)
SN Conforming to the architectural theories of the European and American academies of architecture.
UF architecture, academic
CN B.BM.AFU.ARI.AXC.AFU

academic art
BM.230 (R)
SN Conforming to the official standards and principles of taste of European and American art academies.
UF art, academic
CN B.BM.AFU.ARI.BCW.AFU

academic libraries
RK.700
ALT **academic library**
UF libraries, academic
CN V.RK.AFU.ALO.ALO.CRG.AXC.ALO.AFU

academicism
BM.504 (R)
CN B.BM.BIQ.AXC.AFU

academies
HG.800 (L)
ALT **academy**
CN H.HG.ALO.AFU

academies of art
USE **art schools**

academies (schools)
USE **schools**

academies, art
USE **art schools**

academies, military
USE **military academies**

academies, naval
USE **naval schools**

academy board
MT.1917
SN Heavy, smooth cardboard coated with a ground that has sufficient roughness for the application of oil paint. (MAYER)
UF board, academy
CN M.MT.AFU.AFU.ARI.ALO.ALO.AXC.ALO.BIQ.AFU.BCW.AFU

Acadian houses
USE **Creole cottages**

acanthus
DG.51 (R)
SN Use for the conventionalized decorative motif based on the deeply serrated and scalloped leaves and curving stems of the acanthus plant. (IDO)
UF bear's breech
bear's foot
brank-ursine
breech, bear's
foot, bear's
CN D.DG.AFU.AFU.DIO.AFU

acapau
USE **partridgewood**

acaroid resin
MT.1499
SN A gum resin from the base of the tufted trunk leaves of various species of Xanthorrhoea trees of Australia and Tasmania. (MH)
UF accroides
accroides, gum
Botany Bay gum
gum accroides
gum, Botany Bay
gum, yacca
resin, acaroid
xanthorrhoea
yacca gum
CN M.MT.AFU.AFU.ALO.BOK.CFS.AFU

accelerated cement
MT.38 (B)
SN Cement that will set hard in three days. (MH)
UF cement, accelerated
cement, rapid-hardening
rapid-hardening cement
CN M.MT.AFU.AFU.AFU.ALO.AFU.ALO.AFU

acceleration
BM.894 (L)
CN B.BM.CFS.AXC.BIQ.AFU.AXC.AFU

acceleration lanes
RM.483
ALT **acceleration lane**
UF lanes, acceleration
CN V.RM.ALO.ALO.ALO.ALO.BUE.AFU

accelerators
MT.2294
SN Any substances which hasten a reaction. (MAYER)
CN M.MT.AFU.ARI.ALO.AFU

accelerators, circular
USE **cyclotrons**

accelerators, linear
USE **linear accelerators**

accelerators, magnetic resonance
USE **cyclotrons**

accelerators, particle
USE **particle accelerators**

accent lighting
USE **directional lighting**

access
BM.199 (A,L,B)
CN B.BM.AFU.ALO.AFU

access doors
RT.861
ALT **access door**
SN Doors, usually small, provided through a finished construction, as into a duct, or behind a wall; used to provide a means of inspection of equipment or services housed within. (DAC)
UF doors, access
CN V.RT.AFU.ARI.AFU.AFU.AFU.ALO.ARI.AFU.ALO.AFU

access floors
RT.741
ALT **access floor**
SN A system of flooring consisting of completely removable and interchangeable floor panels which are supported on adjustable pedestals or stringers to allow free access to the area underneath. (DAC)
UF flooring systems, raised
floors, access
raised flooring systems
CN V.RT.AFU.ALO.AFU.BIQ.AFU.AFU

access roads
RK.1548 (L,B)
ALT **access road**
SN Use for public roads giving direct access to the land, premises, or highways on one or both sides.
UF access roads, highway
approach roads
highway access roads
roads, access
roads, approach
roads, highway access
CN V.RK.ALO.ALO.BIQ.ARI.ALO.AFU

access roads, highway
USE **access roads**

access, handicapped
USE **barrier-free design**

accession catalogs
VW.104
ALT **accession catalog**
SN Records of the stock added to a collection; may be in book form, on cards, or online.
UF catalogs, accession
CN V.VW.AFU.AFU.AFU.FZU.ALO.ALO.AFU

accession files
USE **accession records**

accession lists
USE **accession registers**

accession records
VW.766
ALT **accession record**
SN Records documenting additions to a collection; whether acquired by transfer under a legally based procedure, or by deposit, purchase, gift, or bequest. (ICA)
UF accession files
files, accession
records, accession
CN V.VW.AFU.ARI.AFU.AFU

accession registers
VW.767
ALT **accession register**
SN Lists of additions to the holdings of a collection, usually in chronological order by date of receipt and giving the titles of the accessions. (ICA)
UF accession lists
lists, accession
registers, accession
CN V.VW.AFU.ARI.AFU.AFU.AFU

accessioning
KG.69
ALT **accessioned**
SN Recording the entry of items into a collection in the order of acquisition. (W)
CN K.KG.AFU.AFU.AXC.AXC.AFU

accessories, bathroom
USE **bathroom hardware**

accessories, washroom
USE **bathroom hardware**

accident reports
VW.450
ALT **accident report**
UF reports, accident
CN V.VW.AFU.AFU.ALO.FIM.AFU.AFU.AFU

accidental color
USE **reflected color**

accolades
RT.804
ALT **accolade**
SN Ornamental treatments used over arches, doors, or windows, composed of two ogee curves meeting in the middle. (HAS)
CN V.RT.AFU.ALO.AFU.BOK.AFU.ALO.BZY.AFU

accordion doors
USE **folding doors**

account books
VW.840 (N,R)
ALT **account book**
SN Books in which financial accounts are kept. (GAHLM)
UF books, account
CN V.VW.AFU.ARI.AFU.BIQ.CXA.AFU.AFU

account books, household
USE **housebooks**

accountants
HG.393 (L)
ALT **accountant**
CN H.HG.AFU.AXC.BOK.AFU.AFU

accounting
KG.164 (L,B)
SN Collecting data (usually in monetary terms) about economic activity, processing those data, and reporting them for the use of interested decision-makers. (PG)
CN K.KG.AFU.ALO.AFU.AFU

accounting, cost
USE **cost accounting**

accounts
VW.841
ALT **account**
SN Documents in which monies or goods received and paid or given out are recorded in order to permit periodic totaling. (ICA)
CN V.VW.AFU.ARI.AFU.BIQ.CXA.AFU.ALO

accounts, churchwardens'
USE **churchwardens' accounts**

accrediting
KG.143 (L)
ALT **accredited**
SN Officially recognizing an institution as maintaining standards that render them eligible for membership in an association of similar institutions. (W)
CN K.KG.AFU.AFU.BIQ.ARI.AFU

accretions
USE **additions**

accroides
USE **acaroid resin**

accroides, gum
USE **acaroid resin**

accruals
USE **additions**

Acer
USE **maple**

Acer macrophyllum
USE **bigleaf maple**

Acer mono
USE **Japanese maple**

Acer negundo
USE **box elder**

Acer nigrum
USE **black maple**

Acer rubrum
USE **red maple**

Acer saccharinum
USE **silver maple**

Acer saccharum
USE **sugar maple**

Aceraceae
USE **maple**

acetal
MT.2117 (L)
SN Highly crystalline resins that are among the strongest and stiffest of the thermoplastics. (MH12)
UF acetal resin
polyether
polyformaldehyde resin
polyformaldehydes
polyoxide
resin, acetal
resin, polyformaldehyde
CN M.MT.AFU.AFU.ARI.BUE.ALO.AXC.AFU.AFU

acetal resin
USE **acetal**

acetal, polyvinyl
USE **polyvinyl acetal**

acetate butyrate, cellulose
USE **butyrate**

acetate, amyl
USE **amyl acetate**

acetate, butyl
USE **butyl acetate**

acetate, cellulose
USE **cellulose acetate**

acetate, ethyl
USE **ethyl acetate**

acetate, isopropyl
USE **isopropyl acetate**

acetate, N-butyl
USE **butyl acetate**

acetate, normal butyl
USE **butyl acetate**

acetate, polyvinyl
USE **polyvinyl acetate**

acetic acid
MT.294 (L)
UF acid, acetic
acid, ethanoic
ethanoic acid
CN M.MT.AFU.AFU.AFU.BOK.AFU.AFU

acetone
MT.2697 (L)
UF dimethyl ketone
ketone, dimethyl
CN M.MT.AFU.ARI.HZS.AFU.BOK.ARI.AFU

acetone, methyl
USE **methyl acetone**

acetylene black
USE **carbon black**

acetylene torches
TB.104 (N)
ALT **acetylene torch**
SN Torches operated by compressed acetylene gas and oxygen; used in welding and metal-cutting. (DAC)
UF torches, acetylene
CN V.TB.AFU.ARI.ALO.ARI.BCW.AFU

Achaemenid
FL.3014 (A,L,B)
CN F.FL.ALO.AXC.ARI.BIQ.AFU.ARI

Achagua
FL.1628 (L)
CN F.FL.ALO.ALO.ARI.ARI.ARI.AFU

Acheulian
FL.2451 (L)
CN F.FL.ALO.AXC.AFU.AFU.ALO

Achi
FL.261
CN F.FL.ALO.AFU.AXC.AFU.ALO.ARI.AXC.AFU

Acholi
FL.673
CN F.FL.ALO.AFU.AXC.AXC.BOK.AFU

Achomawi
FL.1247 (L)
CN F.FL.ALO.ALO.ARI.AFU.ALO.AFU

acid
MT.293 (L)
CN M.MT.AFU.AFU.AFU.BOK.AFU

acid-biting
KT.442
SN In printmaking, the process in which strong mixtures of nitric acid and water or gum arabic are applied directly on unprotected ink film, dissolving the surface through corrosive action. (TBL)
CN K.KT.AFU.ALO.DUC.DUC.ALO.AFU

acid copper chromate
MT.2643
UF chromate, acid copper
copper chromate, acid
CN M.MT.AFU.ARI.HCQ.ALO.AFU.AFU

acid igneous rock
MT.583
SN Igneous rock containing a high percentage of silica.
UF igneous rock, acid
rock, acid igneous
CN M.MT.AFU.AFU.AFU.DCU.AFU.AFU.AFU.AFU.AFU

acid rain
BM.437 (A,L)
SN Form of precipitation (rain, snow, sleet, or hail) containing high levels of sulfuric or nitric acids. (COLENC)
UF rain, acid
CN B.BM.AXC.BCW.ALO.AFU

acid resist
USE **resist**

acid resistance
BM.937 (B)
UF resistance, acid
CN B.BM.CFS.AXC.BZY.AFU

acid-resistant materials
MT.2791
UF materials, acid-resistant
CN M.MT.AFU.BCW.ARI.AFU

acid, acetic
USE **acetic acid**

acid, carbolic
USE **carbolic acid**

acid, ethanoic
USE **acetic acid**

acid, fatty
USE **fatty acid**

acid, hydrochloric
USE **hydrochloric acid**

acid, hydrofluoric
USE **hydrofluoric acid**

acid, muriatic
USE **hydrochloric acid**

acid, nitric
USE **nitric acid**

acid, sulfuric
USE **sulfuric acid**

acidity
BM.940
SN Use generally for the degree of acid content of a substance. Use particularly with reference to solutions having a PH value less than 7. (MH)
CN B.BM.CFS.AXC.BZY.ARI.AFU

acknowledgments
VW.294 (L)
ALT **acknowledgment**
SN Written recognitions of acts or achievements. (WCOL)
CN V.VW.AFU.AFU.ALO.AFU

Acoma
FL.1467 (L)
CN F.FL.ALO.ALO.ARI.AFU.CFS.CRG.AFU.AFU

acoustic equipment
TB.538 (N)
SN Encompasses objects used in the study of sound and for transmitting sound.
UF equipment, acoustic
CN V.TB.AFU.AXC.ALO.AFU

acoustic insulating materials
USE **acoustical insulation**

acoustical ceilings
RT.719 (B)
ALT **acoustical ceiling**
SN Ceilings covered with a material designed to absorb sound.
UF ceilings, acoustical
CN V.RT.AFU.ALO.AFU.ALO.AFU

acoustical engineering
KD.213 (L)
UF engineering, acoustical
engineering, sonic
engineering, sound
sonic engineering
sound engineering
CN K.KD.AFU.ARI.BIQ.AFU

acoustical engineers
HG.625
ALT **acoustical engineer**
UF acousticians
engineers, acoustical
engineers, sonic
engineers, sound
sonic engineers
sound engineers
CN H.HG.AFU.AXC.BZY.BCW.AFU

acoustical insulation
MT.2403 (L)
SN Insulation used in a building to resist passage of sound waves. (STEIN)
UF acoustic insulating materials
insulating materials, acoustic
insulation, acoustical
insulation, sound
materials, acoustic insulating
sound insulation
CN M.MT.AFU.ARI.BZY.BCW.AFU

acoustical plaster
MT.2451
SN Finishing plaster designed to correct sound reverberations or reduce noise intensity. (STEIN)
UF plaster, acoustical
CN M.MT.AFU.ARI.CRG.AFU.AXC.ALO.AFU

acoustical properties
BM.938 (L)
UF properties, acoustical
CN B.BM.CFS.AXC.BZY.ALO

acoustical tile
MT.2278
SN Any tile composed of materials having the property of absorbing sound waves. (PUTNAM)
UF tile, acoustical
CN M.MT.AFU.ALO.IFM.AFU

acousticians
USE **acoustical engineers**

acoustics
KD.281 (A,L,B,R)
CN K.KD.AFU.ARI.CLM.AXC.AFU

acoustics, architectural
USE **architectural acoustics**

acquiring
USE **procuring**

acquisition
KG.70
SN Obtaining materials for a library, documentation center, archive, or other collection, including selection, ordering, and obtaining by exchange or gift. (LG)
CN K.KG.AFU.AFU.AXC.AXC.ALO

acra red
USE **quinacridone red**

acridone red
USE **quinacridone red**

acropolises
RG.290 (B)
ALT **acropolis**
SN The higher and usually fortified sections of ancient Greek cities, typically containing temples and some public buildings and used as places of refuge.
CN V.RG.ALO.ALO.AFU

acroteria
RT.1048 (A,L)
ALT **acroterion**
SN The figures or ornaments at the lower angles or apex of a pediment, generally supported on plinths. (DINSMR)
CN V.RT.AFU.BCW.AFU

acrylate resin
USE **acrylic**

acrylic
MT.2118 (L,B,R)
SN Colorless, transparent, thermoplastic synthetic resin made by the polymerization of acrylic derivatives; used for adhesives, protective coatings, finishes, and as a paint medium.
UF acrylate resin
acrylic plastic
acrylic resin
plastic, acrylic
PMMA
resin, acrylate
resin, acrylic
CN M.MT.AFU.AFU.ARI.BUE.ALO.AXC.AFU.ALO

acrylic color
USE **acrylic paint**

acrylic paint
MT.2533
UF acrylic color
acrylic resin paint
color, acrylic
paint, acrylic
paint, acrylic resin
resin paint, acrylic
CN M.MT.AFU.ARI.CRG.ALO.BCW.AFU.BIQ.ALO.AFU

acrylic plastic
USE **acrylic**

acrylic resin
USE **acrylic**

acrylic resin paint
USE **acrylic paint**

acrylonitrile-butadiene-styrene copolymer
MT.2124 (B)
UF ABS
ABS plastic
copolymer, acrylonitrile-butadiene-styrene
plastic, ABS
CN M.MT.AFU.AFU.ARI.BUE.ALO.AXC.AFU.ARI

Action painting
FL.3715 (R)
UF Gestural painting
painting, Action
painting, Gestural
CN F.FL.ALO.BUE.ARI.AFU.ALO

action playgrounds
USE **adventure playgrounds**

activation analysis, neutron
USE **neutron activation analysis**

active solar heating
RT.1397
UF solar heating, active
CN V.RT.ALO.BCW.AFU.AFU.ARI.AXC.AFU

activists
HG.748
ALT **activist**
CN H.HG.AFU.BCW.HZS.AFU

actors
HG.66 (L,R)
ALT **actor**
SN Persons who portray roles in dramatic productions to interpret character or present characterization to an audience. (DOT)
UF actresses
CN H.HG.AFU.AXC.AXC.AFU.AFU.AFU.BIQ.AFU

actresses
USE **actors**

acts, legislative
USE **legislative acts**

actuaries
HG.394 (L)
ALT **actuary**
SN Persons trained in mathematics and statistics whose business it is to calculate insurance and annuity premiums, reserves, and dividends. (W)
CN H.HG.AFU.AXC.BOK.AFU.ALO

acute arches
USE **lancet arches**

Adam Style
FL.3311 (B,R)
UF Adamesque
CN F.FL.ALO.BCW.ALO.AXC.DIO.ALO.AFU

Adamesque
USE **Adam Style**

Adampa
USE **Adangme**

Adangme
FL.300 (L)
UF Adampa
CN F.FL.ALO.AFU.AXC.AFU.ARI.ALO.AFU

adaptability
BM.200 (B)
CN B.BM.AFU.ALO.ALO

adaptable furniture
USE **adjustable furniture**

adaptive reuse
BM.213 (A,B)
UF conversion of buildings
reuse, adaptive
CN B.BM.AFU.ALO.CFS.AFU

Adarawa
FL.390
CN F.FL.ALO.AFU.AXC.AFU.AXC.AXC.AFU

addenda
VW.4
ALT **addendum**
SN Printed matter included with or added to a text after it has been set.
CN V.VW.AFU.AFU.AFU.AFU

addendum drawings
USE **clarification drawings**

additions
VB.90 (A,B)
ALT **addition**
SN Use for parts added onto an object or structure. In architecture, if a modification does not substantially increase a structure's volume, use **alterations.** With regard to printed matter, use **addenda.**
UF accretions
accruals
extensions (additions)
CN V.VB.ALO.BOK.AFU

additive color
USE **additive mixture**

additive color mixture
USE **additive mixture**

additive color processes
KT.312
SN Photographic processes that record a color image by making three records of the scene on a monochrome plate or film, each record filtered for one of the three primary colors (red, green, and blue). The image is viewed by reassembling in register each of the separate records, each record being shown by the light of its own record, that is, the red record is displayed with red light.
UF additive processes (photography)
CN K.KT.AFU.ALO.DUC.DIO.ALO.AFU

additive mixture
BM.126
SN Mixture of colored light, so called because as the colors are combined the mixture becomes successively lighter. (PREBLE)
UF additive color
additive color mixture
color, additive
mixture, additive
CN B.BM.AFU.AFU.ARI.BOK.ALO.ALO.AFU.ALO.AFU

additive processes (photography)
USE **additive color processes**

additives
MT.2293 (A,L)
UF admixtures
CN M.MT.AFU.ARI.ALO

address books
VW.484 (N)
ALT **address book**
SN Books listing names with residences, usually in alphabetical order. (GAHLM)
UF books, address
CN V.VW.AFU.ALO.AFU.AFU.AFU.AFU

addresses
USE **speeches**

Adena
FL.878 (L)
CN F.FL.ALO.ALO.ALO.AFU.ALO.ALO.BCW.AFU

adhering
USE **adhesion**

adhesion
KT.22 (L)
SN The joining of two surfaces, by means of a viscous, sticky composition such as glue or through physical or chemical force. (DAC)
UF adhering
CN K.KT.AFU.ALO.BCW.AFU

adhesive anchors
TF.289
ALT **adhesive anchor**
UF anchors, adhesive
CN V.TF.AFU.AFU.AFU.ALO.AFU.AFU.AFU

adhesive tape
MT.2357 (L)
SN A tape coated on one side with an adhesive mixture. (W)
UF tape, adhesive
CN M.MT.AFU.ARI.ARI.ALO.AFU

adhesive, vegetable
USE **vegetable glue**

adhesives
MT.2336 (L,B)
UF agents, bonding
bonding agents
bonding materials
materials, bonding
CN M.MT.AFU.ARI.ARI

adhesives, organic
USE **organic adhesives**

adhocism
BM.188 (B)
SN Term coined by the architectural historian Charles Jencks to describe design which comes about, not by formulating new solutions to problems, but by combining pre-existing elements to achieve a new result. (THDAT)
CN B.BM.AFU.AFU.AXC.CLM.ALO

adinkra
MT.1880
SN Ashanti stamped cloth. (PC)
UF adinkra cloth
cloth, adinkra
CN M.MT.AFU.AFU.ARI.ALO.ALO.ALO.ARI.AFU

adinkra cloth
USE **adinkra**

adire
MT.1885
SN Yoruba indigo dyed cloth. (PC)
CN M.MT.AFU.AFU.ARI.ALO.ALO.ALO.ARI.BCW.AFU

Adirondack chairs
TG.22
ALT **Adirondack chair**
SN Angular chairs with slatted seats and backs; not known to have originated in the Adirondacks. (GILBOR)
UF chairs, Adirondack
CN V.TG.AFU.AFU.ALO.AFU.AFU.AFU.AFU

Adja
FL.304 (L)
CN F.FL.ALO.AFU.AXC.AFU.ARI.ALO.ARI.AFU

adjudicating
KG.4 (L)
SN Settling disputes by legal process. (RLG7)
CN K.KG.AFU.AFU.AFU.AFU

adjustable ball hinges
TF.95
ALT **adjustable ball hinge**
SN Hinges so designed that, when the door is closed, only a ball-type knuckle is exposed. Such hinges have an adjustment for vertical control within limited scope. (STEIN)
UF ball hinges, adjustable
hinges, adjustable ball
CN V.TF.AFU.AFU.AFU.AFU.CLM.AFU.AFU

adjustable furniture
TG.789 (B)
UF adaptable furniture
furniture, adaptable
furniture, adjustable
CN V.TG.AFU.ARI.AFU

adjustable inserts
TF.378
ALT **adjustable insert**
UF inserts, adjustable
CN V.TF.AFU.AFU.AFU.ALO.AFU.BZY.AFU

adjustable keys
TF.528
ALT **adjustable key**
SN Keys for sliding-door locks, having a stem or shank adjustable in length to adapt the key to doors of various thicknesses. (STEIN)
UF extension keys
keys, adjustable
keys, extension
CN V.TF.AFU.ALO.ARI.AFU.AFU

adjustable pipe hangers
TF.338
ALT **adjustable pipe hanger**
UF hangers, adjustable pipe
pipe hangers, adjustable
CN V.TF.AFU.AFU.AFU.ALO.AFU.BOK.AFU.AFU

adjustable wrenches
TB.770 (N)
ALT **adjustable wrench**
SN Wrenches with one fixed jaw and one adjustable jaw; generally refers to wrenches with crescent-shaped jaws.
UF crescent wrenches
wrenches, adjustable
wrenches, crescent
CN V.TB.AFU.BCW.BIQ.AXC.ALO.BIQ.AFU

adjusters, casement
USE **casement stays**

adjusting nuts
TF.451
ALT **adjusting nut**
SN Threaded nuts, used for alignment of an object, that are often coupled with a locking nut to secure them in position. (MEANS)
UF nuts, adjusting
CN V.TF.AFU.AFU.AFU.ALO.AFU.CLM.AFU

adjusting screws
TF.474
ALT **adjusting screw**
SN Screws, used for alignment of an object, that are often coupled with a locking nut to secure them in position. (MEANS)
UF screws, adjusting
CN V.TF.AFU.AFU.AFU.ALO.AFU.DIO.AFU.BCW.AFU

administering
KG.139 (L,B,R)
SN Supervising and managing the business affairs and human and material resources of a person, group, organization, or enterprise. Distinct from **managing** primarily in that it includes policy formulation as well as implementation.
UF administrating
CN K.KG.AFU.AFU.BIQ.AFU

administrating
USE **administering**

administration buildings
RK.915 (B)
ALT **administration building**
UF administrative buildings
administrative facilities
administrative office buildings
administrative services buildings
buildings, administration
buildings, administrative office
buildings, administrative services
facilities, administrative
office buildings, administrative
CN V.RK.AFU.ALO.ALO.DZW.ALO.AFU

administration, letters of
USE **letters of administration**

administration, museum
USE **museum administration**

administrative buildings
USE **administration buildings**

administrative facilities
USE **administration buildings**

administrative office buildings
USE **administration buildings**

administrative papers
USE **administrative records**

administrative records
VW.768
ALT **administrative record**
SN Records that relate to budget, personnel, supply, and similar facilitative operations within an organization. (ICA)
UF administrative papers
housekeeping records
papers, administrative
records, administrative
records, housekeeping
CN V.VW.AFU.ARI.AFU.ALO

administrative regulations
VW.1000 (L)
ALT **administrative regulation**
SN Regulations issued by a governmental agency, having the force of law, to interpret or implement the provisions of a statute. For acts of a legislature declaring, commanding, or prohibiting something, and that constitute the law use **statutes.** (BLACKS)
UF regulations, administrative
CN V.VW.AFU.ARI.ALO.BCW.AFU.AFU.AFU.CLM.AFU

administrative services buildings
USE **administration buildings**

administrators
HG.650 (L)
ALT **administrator**
CN H.HG.AFU.AXC.CFS.AFU

administrators, public
USE **public administrators**

admiralty bronze
USE **admiralty metal**

admiralty charts
USE **marine charts**

Admiralty Islands
USE **Manus**

admiralty metal
MT.374
SN Alloy consisting of about 70% copper, 1% tin, and the remainder zinc. (MH)
UF admiralty bronze
bronze, admiralty
metal, admiralty
CN M.MT.AFU.AFU.AFU.BZY.AFU.AFU.AFU.ALO.ARI.BCW.AFU

admission
USE **admitting**

admission tickets
VW.628
ALT **admission ticket**
SN Paper slips or cards indicating that the holder has paid for or is entitled to entrance or admission. (AHD)
UF tickets, admission
CN V.VW.AFU.ALO.AFU.DUC.AFU

admitting
KG.141
SN Authorizing entrance as in admission to an institution or program. (RLG7)
UF admission
CN K.KG.AFU.AFU.BIQ.ALO

admixture, air-entraining
USE **air-entraining agents**

admixtures
USE **additives**

admixtures, water-reducing
USE **water reducers**

adobe
MT.125 (A,B)
SN Brick composed of a mixture of clay, some sand, and straw or similar binder.
UF adobe brick
brick, adobe
CN M.MT.AFU.AFU.AFU.AXC.ALO.AFU.AXC.AFU.ALO.AFU

adobe brick
USE **adobe**

adolescents
USE **teenagers**

Adoptionism
BM.694 (L,R)
SN Doctrine that Jesus became son of God by exhaltation that was not his at birth. (W)
CN B.BM.BZY.ALO.ARI.AFU

ADs
USE **assessment districts**

adsorption
KT.7 (L)
SN The taking up of the molecules of gases, dissolved substances, or liquids by the surfaces of solids and liquids with which they are in contact. (W)
CN K.KT.AFU.ALO.ALO

adult day care centers
RK.1190 (A,L)
ALT **adult day care center**
SN Use for alternatives to nursing homes providing for aged and disabled members, if their needs are appropriate, a structured program of activities, meals, and medical and psychological services during daytime hours only; members spend evenings in their own homes.
UF adult day health centers
centers, adult day care
centers, adult day health
day care centers, adult
health centers, adult day
CN V.RK.AFU.ALO.ALO.FUA.ALO.AFU

adult day health centers
USE **adult day care centers**

adult education centers
USE **continuing education centers**

adults
HG.3 (L)
ALT **adult**
SN Persons aged 18 years or older. (TSIT)
CN H.HG.AFU.AFU.AFU

Aduma
USE **Duma**

adventure playgrounds
RK.1495 (B)
ALT **adventure playground**
SN Use for supervised play areas featuring exercise-oriented equipment often built and freely arranged by children from readily available loose materials, such as crates, tires, and ropes.
UF action playgrounds

junk playgrounds
playgrounds, action
playgrounds, adventure
playgrounds, junk
playgrounds, Robinson Crusoe
Robinson Crusoe playgrounds
workyards
CN V.RK.ALO.ALO.BCW.BUE.AFU

adversaria
USE **marginalia**

advertisements for bidders
USE **bidding announcements**

advertisements, bid
USE **bidding announcements**

advertising
KD.109 (L,B,R)
CN K.KD.AFU.ALO.ARI.AFU

advertising campaigns
KM.3 (L)
UF campaigns, advertising
CN K.KM.AFU.AFU.AFU

advertising cards
USE **business cards**

advertising design
KT.95
UF design, advertising
CN K.KT.AFU.ALO.CFS.AFU

advertising fliers
VW.604 (L)
ALT **advertising flier**
UF advertising handbills
fliers, advertising
handbills, advertising
CN V.VW.AFU.ALO.AFU.BUE.AFU

advertising handbills
USE **advertising fliers**

advertising photography
KT.292 (L,R)
UF commercial photography
photography, advertising
photography, commercial
photography, product
product photography
CN K.KT.AFU.ALO.DUC.DIO.AFU.AFU

advice centers
USE **information centers**

advice, letters of
USE **letters of advice**

advising
USE **counseling**

advisors
HG.706 (L)
ALT **advisor**
SN Use for persons who give advice either nonprofessionally, or in an official or professional context, usually on an ongoing basis. For persons called on for professional advice regarding matters in their field of special knowledge or training, usually for specific projects or problems, use **consultants.**
CN H.HG.AFU.BCW.AFU

advisors, investment
USE **investment advisors**

advocating
KG.33
SN Representing and supporting the interests of a person, group, project, or program. (RLG7)
CN K.KG.AFU.AFU.ALO.AFU

adyta
RM.336
ALT **adytum**
SN Use for small inner rooms adjacent to or within the naos, found in some ancient temples.
CN V.RM.AFU.DIO.AXC.ALO.AXC.AFU

Adyukru
USE **Ajukru**

adze-hatchets
TB.891
ALT **adze-hatchet**
SN Two-bladed tools with the larger blade in the shape of a hatchet and the smaller shaped like an adz, as distinguished from **hatchet-adzes** in which the adz-shaped blade is the larger.
CN V.TB.AFU.BCW.CFS.ALO.AFU.DCU.AFU

adzes
TB.116 (L,N)
ALT **adz**
SN Long-handled tools with a curved blade set perpendicular to the handle; used for dressing lumber. (MEANS)
CN V.TB.AFU.ARI.AXC.ALO.AFU

adzes, bunging
USE **bunging adzes**

adzes, carpenter's
USE **carpenter's adzes**

adzes, cleaving
USE **cleaving adzes**

adzes, cooper's
USE **cooper's adzes**

adzes, dished
USE **hollowing adzes**

adzes, dubbing
USE **lipped adzes**

adzes, gouge
USE **hollowing adzes**

adzes, guttering
USE **guttering adzes**

adzes, hollowing
USE **hollowing adzes**

adzes, lipped
USE **lipped adzes**

adzes, saucer
USE **hollowing adzes**

adzes, ship carpenter's
USE **shipwright's adzes**

adzes, shipwright's
USE **shipwright's adzes**

adzes, spout
USE **guttering adzes**

adzes, stowing
USE **trussing adzes**

adzes, trussing
USE **trussing adzes**

adzes, wheelwright's
USE **wheelwright's adzes**

Adzhina-Tepe
FL.1787
CN F.FL.ALO.ARI.AFU.AXC.AFU

aedes
RK.1133
SN Use only in ancient Roman contexts when distinguishing a sacred precinct (called a temple) from the building within the precinct housing a cult image or the treasure of a deity.
UF aedes sacrae
CN V.RK.AFU.ALO.ALO.FCS.BIQ.BZY.ALO.AFU

aedes sacrae
USE **aedes**

aediculae
RT.46 (R)
ALT **aedicula**
SN Use for niches, often intended for sculpture, or for frameworks around doors or windows formed of columns, corbeling, or pilasters, supporting a pediment or canopy.
UF edicules
tabernacles (aediculae)
CN V.RT.AFU.AFU.AFU.ARI.AFU

Aegean
FL.2529 (L,B)
CN F.FL.ALO.AXC.ALO.AFU

aegicranes
DG.20
ALT **aegicrane**
SN Motifs representing the head of a ram or goat; used originally in Greek and Roman temple decoration and later in classicizing styles. (LDDO)
CN D.DG.AFU.AFU.BCW.AFU

Aeneolithic
USE **Eneolithic**

aeolian landforms
RD.197
ALT **aeolian landform**
SN Landforms whose constituents have been carried and laid down by air currents. (WAYTA)
UF aeolian sediments
eolian landforms
landforms, aeolian
sediments, aeolian
CN V.RD.ARI.AFU.AXC.AFU.AFU.AXC

aeolian sediments
USE **aeolian landforms**

Aeolic
FL.2587
UF Proto-Aeolic
Proto-Ionic
Pseudo-Ionic
CN F.FL.ALO.AXC.ALO.AFU.ALO.ARI.AFU

Aeolic capitals
RT.117
ALT **Aeolic capital**
SN Use for a broad range of capital designs found in the Mediterranean world prior to the Classical period and generally characterized by paired, vertically rising volutes.
UF capitals, Aeolic
CN V.RT.AFU.AFU.AFU.AXC.BIQ.ALO.ARI.AFU.AFU

aeraria
RK.969
ALT **aerarium**
SN Use for ancient Roman public treasury buildings.
CN V.RK.AFU.ALO.ALO.ERE.AFU.AFU

aerated concrete
USE **air-entrained concrete**

aerial charts
USE **aeronautical charts**

aerial ladders
TB.479 (L)
ALT **aerial ladder**
SN Extension ladders capable of reaching very high places; often mounted on a vehicle such as a fire truck. (DAC)
UF ladders, aerial
CN V.TB.AFU.ARI.ERE.ALO.AFU

aerial mosaics
USE **photomosaic maps**

aerial perspective
KT.270
SN Use for the means of suggesting pictorial depth by decreasing clarity of outline and intensity of color.
UF atmospheric perspective
perspective, aerial
perspective, atmospheric
CN K.KT.AFU.ALO.DUC.DCU.BIQ.AFU

aerial perspectives
USE **bird's-eye perspectives**

aerial photogrammetry
KT.509 (L)
UF aerial photographic surveying
photogrammetry, aerial
photographic surveying, aerial
CN K.KT.AFU.ALO.EFQ.ALO.AFU

aerial photographic surveying
USE **aerial photogrammetry**

aerial photographs
VJ.94 (L)
ALT **aerial photograph**
SN Use for photographs of the earth taken from aircraft. For photographs taken from beyond the earth's atmosphere, use **space photographs.** For photographs of celestial bodies or astronomical phenomena, use **astrophotographs.**
UF air photographs
photographs, aerial
CN V.VJ.AFU.ARI.AFU.AFU

aerial photography
KT.393 (L,B,R)
SN Use for the activity of photographing from aircraft. When emphasis is on the view achieved by photographing from aircraft or other high locations, use **aerial views.** For photography beyond the earth's atmosphere, use **space photography**; for photography of celestial phenomena, use **astronomical photography.**
UF air photography
balloon photography
photography, aerial
photography, air
photography, balloon
CN K.KT.AFU.ALO.DUC.DIO.ARI.ARI.BZY.AFU

aerial transport
USE **air transport**

aerial views
VB.20 (L,B)
ALT **aerial view**
SN Use to designate views achieved by photographing from an aircraft or other high location. When emphasizing the photograph itself, use **aerial photographs.** For nonphotographic depictions having high viewpoints, use **bird's-eye views** or **bird's-eye perspectives.**
UF air views
views, aerial
CN V.VB.AFU.AFU.BOK.ALO.AFU

aerial views (perspective drawings)
USE **bird's-eye perspectives**

aerodromes
USE **airports**

aerodynamical laboratories
RK.1160 (A,L,B)
ALT **aerodynamical laboratory**
UF laboratories, aerodynamical
CN V.RK.AFU.ALO.ALO.FIM.ALO.AFU.AFU

aerodynamics
BM.890 (A,L,R)
CN B.BM.CFS.AXC.BIQ.AFU.AFU

aeronautical charts
VW.211 (L)
ALT **aeronautical chart**
SN Maps designed primarily for use in air navigation, giving surface features of aeronautical importance. (GAHLM)
UF aerial charts
aeronautical maps
charts, aerial
charts, aeronautical
maps, aeronautical
CN V.VW.AFU.AFU.AFU.FZU.AXC.AFU.ARI.AXC.DIO.ALO.AFU

aeronautical engineering
KD.215
SN Branch of aerospace engineering dealing with the design, development, and production of aircraft that function within the atmosphere, and their related systems. (RHDEL2)
UF engineering, aeronautical
CN K.KD.AFU.ARI.BIQ.ALO.AFU

aeronautical engineers
HG.627 (L)
ALT **aeronautical engineer**
UF engineers, aeronautical
CN H.HG.AFU.AXC.BZY.BCW.ALO.AFU

aeronautical laboratories
RK.1161 (A,L,B)
ALT **aeronautical laboratory**
UF laboratories, aeronautical
CN V.RK.AFU.ALO.ALO.FIM.ALO.AFU.ALO

aeronautical maps
USE **aeronautical charts**

aeronautical museums
RK.403 (A,L)
ALT **aeronautical museum**
UF air and space museums
aviation museums
museums, aeronautical
museums, air and space
museums, aviation
CN V.RK.AFU.ALO.ALO.BCW.AXC.ARI.AXC.BZY.AFU

aeronautical schools
RK.802 (B)
ALT **aeronautical school**
UF aviation schools
schools, aeronautical
schools, aviation
CN V.RK.AFU.ALO.ALO.CXA.ARI.ALO.AFU

aeronautics
KD.195 (L)
SN Science and practice of flight. (RHDEL2)
CN K.KD.AFU.ARI.AFU

Aeropainting
USE **Aeropittura**

Aeropittura
FL.3404
UF Aeropainting
CN F.FL.ALO.BCW.ALO.AXC.DIO.BOK.BCW.AFU

aerosol
MT.2209 (L)
SN Includes a suspension of liquid or fine solid particles in air, and any substance dispersed from a pressurized container.
CN M.MT.AFU.ALO.AFU

aerospace engineering
KD.214
SN Branch of engineering that deals with the design, development, testing, and production of aircraft, spacecraft, missiles, rocket propulsion systems, and other equipment operating both within and beyond the earth's atmosphere. (RHDEL2)
UF engineering, aerospace
CN K.KD.AFU.ARI.BIQ.ALO

aerospace engineers
HG.626 (L)
ALT **aerospace engineer**
UF engineers, aerospace
CN H.HG.AFU.AXC.BZY.BCW.ALO

Aesculus
USE **buckeye**

Aesculus californica
USE **California buckeye**

Aesculus flava
USE **yellow buckeye**

Aesculus hippocastanum
USE **horse chestnut**

Aesculus octandra
USE **yellow buckeye**

Aesculus pavia
USE **dwarf buckeye**

Aesthetic Movement
FL.3312 (A,L,R)
UF Aestheticism (art movement)
CN F.FL.ALO.BCW.ALO.AXC.DIO.ALO.ALO

aesthetic urge
USE **Kunstwollen**

aesthetic, machine
USE **machine aesthetic**

aestheticians
HG.207
ALT **aesthetician**
SN Specialists in aesthetics. (W)
CN H.HG.AFU.AXC.AXC.BCW.AFU

aestheticism
BM.505
SN A theory of art which maintains that the philosophy of art is separate from any other philosophy and that art can be judged only by its own standards. (THDAT)
CN B.BM.BIQ.AXC.ALO

Aestheticism (art movement)
USE **Aesthetic Movement**

aesthetics
KD.62 (A,L,B,R)
UF art, philosophy of
esthetics
philosophy of art
CN K.KD.AFU.AFU.BOK.AFU

Afanasievo
FL.2121
UF Afanasyevskaya
CN F.FL.ALO.ARI.ARI.AFU.AFU

Afanasyevskaya
USE **Afanasievo**

Afar
FL.615 (L)
UF Danakil
CN F.FL.ALO.AFU.AXC.AXC.ARI.AFU

afara
USE **limba**

affection
USE **love**

affidavits
VW.877 (L)
ALT **affidavit**
SN Sworn statements in writing; especially made upon oath before an authorized magistrate or officer. (GAHLM)
CN V.VW.AFU.ARI.AFU.BOK.BOK.AFU

affordable housing
RG.68 (A)
SN Designates housing for people who are unable to purchase or rent homes through normal marketplace mechanisms; includes such options as low cost housing, low income housing, shelters for the homeless, or mobile homes.
UF housing, affordable
CN V.RG.AFU.AFU.BOK.AXC.AFU

Afghan
FL.3588 (L,B)
CN F.FL.ALO.BIQ.AFU.IFM.ARI.AFU

Afikpo
FL.262
CN F.FL.ALO.AFU.AXC.AFU.ALO.ARI.AXC.ALO

Afo
FL.207
CN F.FL.ALO.AFU.AXC.AFU.AFU.ALO.ALO.AFU

Afrasiab
FL.1822
UF Afrosiab
Samarqand
CN F.FL.ALO.ARI.AFU.AXC.ELK.CLM.AFU

African
FL.35 (B,R)
CN F.FL.ALO.AFU

African American
FL.1721 (L,R)
UF Afro-American
Black (style)
Negro
CN F.FL.ALO.ALO.BCW.AFU.AFU

African Americans
HG.779 (L,R)
ALT **African American**
UF Afro-Americans
Americans, African
Blacks
Negroes
CN H.HG.AFU.BOK.ARI.AFU

African blackwood
MT.1301
UF blackwood, African
congo-wood
Dalbergia melanoxylin
ebony, Senegal
Senegal ebony
CN M.MT.AFU.AFU.ALO.BIQ.DCU.AFU.AFU.AFU.LCM.AXC.AFU

African cedar
MT.1359
UF cedar, African
Juniperus procera
CN M.MT.AFU.AFU.ALO.BIQ.DCU.AFU.AFU.ALO.BUE.AFU

African mahogany
MT.1209
UF khaya
mahogany, African
CN M.MT.AFU.AFU.ALO.BIQ.DCU.AFU.AFU.AFU.HTY.AFU

Africano, marmor
USE **marmor Africano**

Afro-American
USE **African American**

Afro-Americans
USE **African Americans**

Afro-Portuguese
FL.172
UF Sherbro (Afro-Portuguese)
CN F.FL.ALO.AFU.ARI.AFU

Afrosiab
USE **Afrasiab**

afterimages
BM.149 (L)
SN Visual sensation occurring after the external cause has disappeared.
CN B.BM.AFU.AFU.ARI.BOK.BZY.AFU

agal-agal
USE **agar-agar**

Agano
FL.2013 (L)
CN F.FL.ALO.ARI.ALO.ALO.ALO.ALO.ALO.AFU

agar
USE **agar-agar**

agar-agar
MT.1043 (L)
SN Gelatinous extract from seaweed. (MH)
UF agal-agal
agar
CN M.MT.AFU.AFU.ALO.BIQ.BUE.AFU

agate
MT.546 (L)
SN A natural mixture of crystalline and colloidal silica, but consisting mainly of the mineral chalcedony. (MH)
CN M.MT.AFU.AFU.AFU.CFS.AFU.GRC.AFU.ARI.AFU

Agate Basin
FL.754 (L)
CN F.FL.ALO.ALO.ALO.AFU.AFU.ARI.ALO.ARI.ALO.AFU

age discrimination
BM.1104 (L)
UF ageism
discrimination, age
CN B.BM.CRG.BCW.ARI.AFU

Age, Bronze
USE **Bronze Age**

age, golden
USE **golden age**

Age, Iron
USE **Iron Age**

age, spirit of the
USE **Zeitgeist**

Age, Stone
USE **Stone Age**

aged
HG.4 (A,L,B)
UF aging persons
citizens, senior
elderly persons
old people
older persons
senior citizens
CN H.HG.AFU.AFU.ALO

aged, housing for the
USE **housing for the elderly**

ageism
USE **age discrimination**

agencies
HG.812
ALT **agency**
SN Organizations serving the public; also administrative units of government. Use a more specific term if possible.
CN H.HG.ALO.ARI

agencies, employment
USE **employment agencies**

agencies, funding
USE **funding agencies**

agencies, granting
USE **funding agencies**

agencies, library service
USE **library service agencies**

agencies, travel
USE **travel agencies**

agendas
VW.769
ALT **agenda**
SN Documents, often in list form, stating things to be done, as items of business or discussions to be brought up at a meeting; includes programs consisting of such items. (GAHLM)
CN V.VW.AFU.ARI.AFU.ALO.AFU

agents
USE **commercial agents**

agents, air-entraining
USE **air-entraining agents**

agents, antifoaming
USE **antifoaming agents**

agents, antistatic
USE **antistatic agents**

agents, binding
USE **binders**

agents, bonding
USE **adhesives**

agents, cleaning
USE **cleaning compounds**

agents, commercial
USE **commercial agents**

agents, curing
USE **curing agents**

agents, dispersing
USE **dispersing agents**

agents, emulsifying
USE **emulsifiers**

agents, estate
USE **real estate agents**

agents, fireproofing
USE **fireproofing agents**

agents, foaming
USE **foaming agents**

agents, house
USE **real estate agents**

agents, insurance
USE **insurance agents**

agents, mold release
USE **mold release agents**

agents, permeability
USE **permeability agents**

agents, real estate
USE **real estate agents**

agents, release
USE **parting compounds**

agents, rust removing
USE **rust removing agents**

agents, stabilizing
USE **stabilizers**

agents, surface-active
USE **surface-active agents**

agents, suspending
USE **suspending agents**

agents, travel
USE **travel agents**

agents, water-reducing
USE **water reducers**

agents, wetting
USE **wetting agents**

Ages, Dark
USE **Dark Ages**

Ages, Dark (Medieval)
USE **Migration period**

Agfacolor (TM)
KT.367
CN K.KT.AFU.ALO.DUC.DIO.ALO.DZW.AFU.AFU

agglomerations
RD.17 (L)
ALT **agglomeration**
SN Use for large, unplanned clusterings of urban populations, that, as a result of urban sprawl, have outgrown local governmental boundaries.
CN V.RD.AFU.AFU.ALO.BIQ

agglutinant
USE **agglutinin**

agglutinin
MT.2369 (L)

SN A substance that causes the union of separate materials or particles into a group or mass; includes glues or adhesives that serve this function in making aqueous paints, pastel crayons, and inks for drawing.
UF agglutinant
CN M.MT.AFU.ARI.BIQ.AFU

aggregate, coarse
USE **coarse aggregate**

aggregate, fine
USE **fine aggregate**

aggregate, heavyweight
USE **heavyweight aggregate**

aggregate, lightweight
USE **lightweight aggregate**

aggregates
MT.2295 (L,B)
SN Inert granular materials such as natural sand, manufactured sand, or gravel that when bound together into a conglomerate mass form concrete or mortar. (DAC)
CN M.MT.AFU.ARI.ALO.ALO

Aghem
USE **Wum**

Aghlabid
FL.3430
CN F.FL.ALO.BIQ.AFU.ALO

agiasteria
USE **sanctuaries**

aging persons
USE **aged**

agitation propaganda
USE **agitprop**

agitprop
BM.220 (R)
SN Derived from agitation propaganda, meaning intended to inspire political action. With reference to visual art, use for the specific art movement arising in Soviet Russia following the Bolshevik revolution.
UF agitation propaganda
CN B.BM.AFU.ARI.ARI.AFU

Agkhand ware
FL.3563
UF ware, Agkhand
CN F.FL.ALO.BIQ.AFU.HIK.BCW.AFU

Agni
USE **Anyi**

agnosticism
BM.695 (L)
SN Doctrine affirming that the existence of God is possible, but denying that there are any sufficient reasons for holding either that God does or does not exist. (W)
CN B.BM.BZY.ALO.ARI.ALO

agoras
RK.1580 (A,B)
ALT **agora**
SN In ancient Greek settlements, open spaces used as marketplaces or general public meeting places.
CN V.RK.ALO.ARI.AFU

agreements
VW.878 (L)
ALT **agreement**
SN Writing made to evidence the terms and conditions, or the fact, of an accord or arrangement. (GAHLM)
UF articles of agreement
CN V.VW.AFU.ARI.AFU.BOK.BOK.ALO

agreements, apprenticeship
USE **articles of apprenticeship**

agreements, collective labor
USE **collective labor agreements**

agreements, cost plus fee
USE **cost plus fee agreements**

agreements, international
USE **international agreements**

agreements, master
USE **collective labor agreements**

agreements, owner-contractor
USE **owner-contractor agreements**

agreements, partnership
USE **partnership agreements**

agricultural buildings
RK.41 (B)
ALT **agricultural building**
SN Use for buildings used for the science or art of cultivating the soil, harvesting crops, or raising livestock, not used for human habitation, employment, or processing, and not used by the public.
UF agricultural facilities
agricultural works
buildings, agricultural
facilities, agricultural
works, agricultural
CN V.RK.AFU.ALO.ALO.AFU.AFU

agricultural facilities
USE **agricultural buildings**

agricultural laboratories
RK.1162 (A,L,B)
ALT **agricultural laboratory**
UF laboratories, agricultural
CN V.RK.AFU.ALO.ALO.FIM.ALO.AFU.ARI

agricultural land
RD.282
UF agricultural landscape
land, agricultural
landscape, agricultural
CN V.RD.ARI.ALO.AFU.AFU

agricultural landscape
USE **agricultural land**

agricultural settlements
RD.47
ALT **agricultural settlement**
UF agricultural villages
farming villages
settlements, agricultural
villages, agricultural
villages, farming
CN V.RD.AFU.AXC.AFU

agricultural villages
USE **agricultural settlements**

agricultural works
USE **agricultural buildings**

agriculture
KD.196 (L,R)
SN Science or art of cultivating the soil, harvesting crops, and raising livestock. (W)
CN K.KD.AFU.ARI.ALO

agriculture museums
RK.393 (L)
ALT **agriculture museum**
UF farm museums
museums, agriculture
museums, farm
CN V.RK.AFU.ALO.ALO.BCW.AXC.ARI.AXC.AFU

agriculturists
HG.360 (L)
ALT **agriculturist**
SN Persons trained in the theory or science of agriculture. (W)
UF agronomists
CN H.HG.AFU.AXC.BIQ.ALO.AXC.AFU

agronomists
USE **agriculturists**

AGT
USE **personal rapid transit**

Aguada
FL.1191
CN F.FL.ALO.ALO.ALO.ARI.BIQ.AFU

Ägyptischblau
USE **Egyptian blue**

Ahmad I
USE **Ahmed I**

Ahmad II
USE **Ahmed II**

Ahmadnagar
FL.2252 (L)
CN F.FL.ALO.ARI.AXC.ALO.AFU.BZY.AFU.AFU

Ahmed I
FL.3496
UF Ahmad I

Ahmet I
CN F.FL.ALO.BIQ.AFU.FOG.AFU.DIO

Ahmed II
FL.3502
UF Ahmad II
Ahmet II
CN F.FL.ALO.BIQ.AFU.FOG.AFU.ERE

Ahmed III
FL.3504
UF Ahmet III
CN F.FL.ALO.BIQ.AFU.FOG.AFU.FCS

Ahmet I
USE **Ahmed I**

Ahmet II
USE **Ahmed II**

Ahmet III
USE **Ahmed III**

Aht
USE **Nootka**

Ahtena
FL.1225 (L)
UF Atnah
Atnatana
CN F.FL.ALO.ALO.ARI.AFU.AFU.ARI.AFU

Ai-Hanum
FL.1788
UF Ai-Khanum
CN F.FL.ALO.ARI.AFU.AXC.ALO

Ai-Khanum
USE **Ai-Hanum**

aid, federal
USE **federal aid**

aid, student
USE **student aid**

aids, audiovisual
USE **audiovisual materials**

aids, finding
USE **finding aids**

aids, visual
USE **visual materials**

aiguilles
TB.585
ALT **aiguille**
SN Slender drills used for boring or drilling a blasthole in rock. (DAC)
CN V.TB.AFU.BCW.BCW.ALO.CLM.AFU

Aija
USE **Recuay**

ailerons
RT.635
ALT **aileron**
SN Half gables, such as those that close the end of a penthouse roof or the aisle of a church. (HAS)
CN V.RT.AFU.AFU.AFU.BIQ.BUE.ALO.AFU.AXC.AFU.AFU

Aimoré
USE **Botocudo**

air and space museums
USE **aeronautical museums**

air art
BM.255 (L,R)
SN A genre, appearing first in the late 1960s, encompassing structures and activities that exploit the possibilities of compressed air, or the natural force of the wind, usually in association with plastic envelopes.
UF art, air
CN B.BM.AFU.ARI.BCW.FOG.AFU

air barriers
USE **air infiltration barriers**

air bases
RG.124 (A,L)
ALT **air base**
UF Air Force bases
bases, air
military air bases
CN V.RG.AFU.AFU.BZY.AFU.AFU

air bases, naval
USE **naval air bases**

air brick
MT.92 (B)
SN A perforated brick or perforated metal unit of brick size which is built into a wall for ventilation. (DAC)
UF brick, air
brick, ventilating
ventilating brick
CN M.MT.AFU.AFU.AFU.AXC.ALO.AFU.ALO.AFU

air cleaners
USE **air filters**
air washers

air conditioners
TB.85 (N)
ALT **air conditioner**
SN Devices for controlling the temperature, humidity, and sometimes the purity of the air in an interior space. (RHDEL2)
UF conditioners, air
CN V.TB.AFU.ARI.ALO.AFU

air conditioning
RT.1383 (A,L,B)
SN Systems in which air is treated to control its temperature, humidity, cleanliness, or distribution to meet the requirements of the occupants of the conditioned space.
UF air conditioning systems
systems, air conditioning
CN V.RT.ALO.BCW.AFU.AFU.AFU

air conditioning locks
TF.254
ALT **air conditioning lock**
UF locks, air conditioning
CN V.TF.AFU.AFU.AFU.AFU.DIO.BIQ.ALO.BCW.AFU

air conditioning systems
USE **air conditioning**

air conditioning, central
USE **central air conditioning**

air conditioning, incremental
USE **incremental air conditioning**

air conditioning, unit
USE **unit air conditioning**

air cooling
RT.1387
UF cooling systems
systems, cooling
CN V.RT.ALO.BCW.AFU.AFU.ALO

air-cooling coils
USE **cooling coils**

air curtains
RT.834 (A,L,B,R)
ALT **air curtain**
SN Streams of high-velocity, temperature-controlled air which are directed downward across an opening to prevent transfer of heat across it, thus making it possible to air condition a space having an open entrance.
UF air doors
doors, air
CN V.RT.AFU.ARI.AFU.AFU.AFU.ALO.AFU

air diffusers
RT.1432
ALT **air diffuser**
SN Outlets in an air supply duct for distributing and blending air in an enclosure. Usually round, square, or rectangular units mounted in suspended ceilings. (MEANS)
UF diffusers, air
CN V.RT.ALO.BCW.AFU.ALO.ARI.AFU

air distribution systems
RT.1433
ALT **air distribution system**
SN That part of a ventilation system which includes supply and return air ducts and plenum chambers. (STEIN)
UF systems, air distribution
CN V.RT.ALO.BCW.AFU.ALO.ARI.ALO

air doors
USE **air curtains**

air-dried lumber
MT.1434
SN Any lumber from which sap has been removed by seasoning. (PUTNAM)

UF air-seasoned lumber
dry-lumber
dry wood
lumber, air-dried
lumber, air-seasoned
lumber, dry
wood, dry
CN M.MT.AFU.AFU.ALO.BIQ.DCU.ALO.BOK.ALO.ARI.AFU

air drills
USE **pneumatic drills**

air ducts
RT.1434 (L)
ALT **air duct**
SN Includes any tubes or conduits for conveying air in enclosed spaces or corridors within a wall or other structure used for conveying air.
UF ducts, air
CN V.RT.ALO.BCW.AFU.ALO.ARI.ARI

air-entrained concrete
MT.211 (A,L,B)
SN Concrete containing minute air bubbles that improve its workability and frost resistance. (MEANS)
UF aerated concrete
cellular concrete
concrete, aerated
concrete, air-entrained
concrete, cellular
CN M.MT.AFU.AFU.AFU.BCW.AFU.ARI.AFU

air-entraining admixture
USE **air-entraining agents**

air-entraining agents
MT.2304
SN Additions to natural cement, concrete, or mortar that cause entrained air to be incorporated into the concrete. (STEIN)
UF admixture, air-entraining
agents, air-entraining
air-entraining admixture
CN M.MT.AFU.ARI.ALO.ARI

air filters
RT.1435 (L)
ALT **air filter**
SN Devices for removing undesirable gaseous or solid particles from ambient air. (MEANS)
UF air cleaners
cleaners, air
filters, air
CN V.RT.ALO.BCW.AFU.ALO.ARI.AXC

Air Force bases
USE **air bases**

air forces
HG.815 (L)
ALT **air force**
CN H.HG.ALO.AXC.AFU

air hammers
USE **jackhammers**

air handlers
USE **air-handling units**

air-handling units
RT.1438
ALT **air-handling unit**
SN Devices, such as fans or blowers, that distribute a conditioned air supply to a room or space.
UF air handlers
handlers, air
CN V.RT.ALO.BCW.AFU.ALO.ARI.BCW

air-heating coils
USE **heating coils**

air infiltration barriers
MT.2383 (A)
SN Use for plastic sheeting, building paper, or similar material that wraps the walls of a building beneath the outermost surface, serving to diminish the infiltration and exfiltration of air.
UF air barriers
barriers, air
barriers, air infiltration
CN M.MT.AFU.ARI.BZY.AFU

air-inflated structures
RT.405 (L)
ALT **air-inflated structure**
SN Use for pneumatic structures in which building elements are inflated; for pneumatic structures supported by pressurization of the habitable space, use **air-supported structures.**
UF inflatable structures
structures, air-inflated
structures, inflatable
CN V.RT.AFU.AFU.AFU.BIQ.ALO.AFU.AFU

air locks
RM.209
ALT **air lock**
SN Spaces designed to isolate an air conditioned space from another space to which it is connected.
UF locks, air
CN V.RM.AFU.DIO.ALO.DIO.AFU

air photographs
USE **aerial photographs**

air photography
USE **aerial photography**

air pollution
BM.430 (A,L,B)
UF atmospheric pollution
pollution, air
pollution, atmospheric
CN B.BM.AXC.BCW.AFU.AFU

air pollution, indoor
USE **indoor air pollution**

air pressure
BM.931
UF pressure, air
CN B.BM.CFS.AXC.BUE.AFU

air purification
KG.123 (L)
UF purification of air
purification, air
CN K.KG.AFU.AFU.BCW.ALO.BZY.AFU

air quality
BM.202 (L)
UF quality, air
CN B.BM.AFU.ALO.ARI

air quality, indoor
USE **indoor air quality**

air raid shelters
RM.143 (A,L,N,B)
ALT **air raid shelter**
UF bomb shelters
shelters, air raid
shelters, bomb
CN V.RM.AFU.DIO.ALO.BZY.AFU

air rights
BM.443 (A,L,B)
SN Development rights to the space above a piece of real estate property; the owner of the land may sell or lease these rights to another party.
UF airspace (law)
airspace rights
rights, air
rights, airspace
CN B.BM.BCW.AFU

air-seasoned lumber
USE **air-dried lumber**

air shafts
RM.282 (B)
ALT **air shaft**
SN Use for very small courts that are enclosed within the walls of a building and supply ventilation to windows. Prefer **light courts** for somewhat larger courts supplying significant light as well as ventilation, or courts supplying only light.
UF air wells
shafts, air
CN V.RM.AFU.DIO.ARI.ALO.DIO.AFU

air-supported furniture
USE **inflatable furniture**

air-supported structures
RT.406 (A,L,B,R)
ALT **air-supported structure**
SN Use for pneumatic structures supported by pressurization of the habitable space; for pneumatic structures in which building elements are inflated, use **air-inflated structures.**
UF expandable structures
structures, air-supported
structures, expandable
CN V.RT.AFU.AFU.AFU.BIQ.ALO.AFU.ALO

air terminals
USE **airport terminals**

air transport
BM.1147 (L,B)
UF aerial transport
transport, air
CN B.BM.DCU.AFU.AFU

air views
USE **aerial views**

air washers
RT.1410
ALT **air washer**
SN Parts of air conditioning systems in which the air is freed from dust and given the desired humidity by means of a spray of water. (W)
UF air cleaners
washers, air
CN V.RT.ALO.BCW.AFU.ALO.AFU.AFU

air wells
USE **air shafts**

airbrush technique
USE **airbrushing**

airbrushing
KT.238 (L,N)
ALT **airbrushed**
SN A method of painting by means of a small, finely controllable mechanical paint sprayer; used also in the retouching of photographs. (THDAT)
UF airbrush technique
CN K.KT.AFU.ALO.DUC.CXA.ALO.AFU.DIO.AFU

aircraft hangars
USE **hangars**

airers, linen
USE **clotheshorses**
towel racks

airfields
RK.1504 (L,B)
ALT **airfield**
SN Use for areas prepared for the landing and takeoff of aircraft; may or may not be provided with associated buildings, equipment, or other installations. (DODDIC)
UF fields, landing
landing fields
CN V.RK.ALO.ALO.BIQ.AFU.AFU

airline maps
VW.212 (L)
ALT **airline map**
UF maps, airline
CN V.VW.AFU.AFU.AFU.FZU.AXC.AFU.ARI.AXC.DIO.ALO.AFU.AFU

airport buildings
RK.1233 (A,L,B)
ALT **airport building**
UF buildings, airport
CN V.RK.AFU.ALO.ALO.GLI.AFU.AFU

airport control towers
USE **control towers**

airport runways
USE **runways**

airport terminals
RK.1234 (A,L,B)
ALT **airport terminal**
UF air terminals
buildings, terminal (airports)
terminal buildings (airports)
terminals, air
terminals, airport
CN V.RK.AFU.ALO.ALO.GLI.AFU.AFU.AFU

airports
RG.218 (A,L,N,B,R)
ALT **airport**
UF aerodromes
CN V.RG.AFU.AFU.EFQ.AFU.AFU

airspace (law)
USE **air rights**

airspace rights
USE **air rights**

airstrips
RK.1508 (L,B)
ALT **airstrip**
SN Use for runways without normal airport facilities.
UF landing strips
strips, landing
CN V.RK.ALO.ALO.BIQ.AFU.AXC.AFU

airtightness
BM.977 (A,L)
ALT **airtight**
SN Use for the condition of being impervious to air penetration, or nearly so.
CN B.BM.CFS.AXC.BZY.BZY.AFU

aisles
RM.85 (A,B,R)
ALT **aisle**
SN Includes both passages between sections of seats and the side divisions of buildings where the interior is divided into parts by columns or piers.
CN V.RM.AFU.DIO.ALO.ARI.AFU

aisles, apse
USE **ambulatories**

aiwans
USE **iwans**

Aizo
FL.305
CN F.FL.ALO.AFU.AXC.AFU.ARI.ALO.ARI.ALO

Ajmer
FL.2286
CN F.FL.ALO.ARI.AXC.ALO.AFU.BZY.BCW.BCW.AFU

Ajukru
FL.292 (L)
UF Adyukru
CN F.FL.ALO.AFU.AXC.AFU.ARI.AFU.ALO.AFU

Ak-Beshim
FL.1789
CN F.FL.ALO.ARI.AFU.AXC.ARI

Ak Koyunlu
USE **Akkoyunlu**

Ak-Kuyunli
USE **Akkoyunlu**

Akamba
USE **Kamba**

Akan
FL.281 (L)
CN F.FL.ALO.AFU.AXC.AFU.ARI.AFU.AFU

Akan, Coastal
USE **Coastal Akan**

Akbar
FL.2231
CN F.FL.ALO.ARI.AXC.ALO.AFU.BIQ.ALO.AFU.AXC

Akem
USE **Akyem**

Akikuyu
USE **Kikuyu**

Akita Ranga School
FL.2050 (L)
CN F.FL.ALO.ARI.ALO.ALO.ALO.ARI.ALO

Akkadian
FL.2967 (L)
CN F.FL.ALO.AXC.ARI.BCW.AFU.AXC

Akkoyunlu
FL.3578 (L)
UF Ak Koyunlu
Ak-Kuyunli
Aq Qoyunlu
CN F.FL.ALO.BIQ.AFU.IFM.AFU

Akmak
FL.804
CN F.FL.ALO.ALO.ALO.AFU.ALO.AFU.ALO.ALO.ALO.AFU

Aksum
USE **Axum**

Akuapem
USE **Akwapim**

Akwamu
FL.283
CN F.FL.ALO.AFU.AXC.AFU.ARI.AFU.AFU.AFU.AFU

Akwapim
FL.284
UF Akuapem

CN F.FL.ALO.AFU.AXC.AFU.ARI.AFU.AFU.AFU.ALO

Akye
USE **Attie**

Akyem
FL.282 (L)
UF Akem
CN F.FL.ALO.AFU.AXC.AFU.ARI.AFU.AFU.AFU

`Ala'-ad-Din `Ali
FL.3469
CN F.FL.ALO.BIQ.AFU.DUC.BOK

`Ala'-ad-Din b. Khalil
FL.3467
CN F.FL.ALO.BIQ.AFU.DUC.BCW

`Ala'-ad-Din Khalil
FL.3466
CN F.FL.ALO.BIQ.AFU.DUC.AXC

Alabama cream marble
MT.819
UF cream marble, Alabama
marble, Alabama cream
CN M.MT.AFU.AFU.AFU.DCU.AFU.ARI.ARI.ARI.BOK.AFU

Alabama limestone
MT.663
UF limestone, Alabama
CN M.MT.AFU.AFU.AFU.DCU.AFU.ALO.AFU.ALO.ALO.AFU.AFU.ALO.AFU

alabaster
MT.521 (A,L,B)
SN Fine-grained marblelike variety of gypsum. (MH)
CN M.MT.AFU.AFU.AFU.CFS.AFU.DUC.AFU

alabaster (color)
USE **pale yellowish pink**
yellowish gray

Alacaluf
FL.1688 (L)
UF Alikaluf
Alikuluf
Alookooloop
Alukoelúf
CN F.FL.ALO.ALO.ARI.ARI.BOK.AFU

Aladian
USE **Alagya**

alae
RM.28
ALT **ala**
SN Alcoves or small room openings off the atrium of an ancient Roman house. (HAS)
CN V.RM.AFU.DIO.AFU.AFU.AFU

Alagya
FL.293 (L)
UF Aladian
Alangua
Alladians
CN F.FL.ALO.AFU.AXC.AFU.ARI.AFU.ALO.ALO

Alamannic
FL.3105 (L,R)
UF Alemannic
CN F.FL.ALO.BCW.ALO.ALO.AFU.BOK.ALO.ALO.AFU

alamedas
RK.1577
ALT **alameda**
SN Use both for shaded promenades, often with plantings and seating areas, in Spanish-speaking countries and for public gardens or parks with similar characteristics in the southwest United States.
CN V.RK.ALO.ALO.BUE.BCW.AFU

Alamgir
USE **Aurangzeb**

Alangua
USE **Alagya**

Alani
FL.1804 (R)
UF Alans
CN F.FL.ALO.ARI.AFU.AXC.DCU.AFU

Alans
USE **Alani**

alarm systems, fire
USE **fire alarm systems**

alarm systems, intermission
USE **intermission alarm systems**

alarm systems, local fire
USE **local fire alarm systems**

alarm systems, proprietary fire
USE **proprietary fire alarm systems**

Alaskan Eskimo, North
USE **Inupiaq**

Alaskan pine
USE **western hemlock**

albanene tracing paper
USE **tracing vellum**

Albanian
FL.3036 (L,B)
CN F.FL.ALO.BCW.AFU.AFU

Albany slip clay
MT.60
SN Clay used by potters to produce a natural black or brown glaze on stoneware. (W)
UF clay, Albany slip
slip clay, Albany
CN M.MT.AFU.AFU.AFU.AXC.AFU.AFU.BOK.AFU

Alberene stone
MT.876
SN A bluish gray stone quarried in Virginia; commonly used for building trim and for chemical labaratory tables and sinks; hard varieties employed for stair treads and flooring. (MH)
UF stone, Alberene
CN M.MT.AFU.AFU.AFU.DCU.AFU.ARI.BZY.AFU

Albizia lebbeck
USE **East India walnut**

Albizia odoratissima
USE **Ceylon rosewood**

albumen
MT.912
UF egg white
CN M.MT.AFU.AFU.ALO.AFU.AFU.AFU

albumen photoprints
USE **albumen prints**

albumen print process
USE **albumen process**

albumen prints
VJ.45
ALT **albumen print**
SN Use for photographic prints having albumen as the binder; always black-and-white, though they may be toned to a monochrome hue.
UF albumen photoprints
albumen silver prints
photoprints, albumen
prints, albumen
prints, albumen silver
prints, silver albumen
silver albumen prints
silver prints, albumen
CN V.VJ.AFU.AFU.ARI.ARI.AXC.AFU

albumen process
KT.317
SN Use for photographic processes in which albumen is used as the binder. Common for photographic prints and occasionally for lantern slides, but rarely used for negatives on glass.
UF albumen print process
albumen silver process
silver albumen process
CN K.KT.AFU.ALO.DUC.DIO.ALO.ALO

albumen silver prints
USE **albumen prints**

albumen silver process
USE **albumen process**

albumin
MT.911 (L)
SN The water-soluble and alcohol-soluble protein obtained from blood, eggs, or milk; used in adhesives, textile and paper finishes, leather coatings, varnishes, and as a clarifying agent for tannins and in-oil emulsions. (MH)

CN M.MT.AFU.AFU.ALO.AFU.AFU

albumin glue
MT.2345
UF albumin, animal blood
animal blood albumin
glue, albumin
CN M.MT.AFU.ARI.ARI.AFU.ALO.ALO.AFU.AFU

albumin, animal blood
USE **albumin glue**

albums
VW.485 (L,N)
ALT **album**
SN Books of blank leaves in which literary extracts, quotations, poems, drawings, photographs, or other items are written, inserted, or fixed. (LG)
CN V.VW.AFU.ALO.AFU.AFU.AFU.ALO

albums, autograph
USE **autograph albums**

albums, photograph
USE **photograph albums**

albums, postcard
USE **postcard albums**

albums, presentation
USE **presentation albums**

albums, souvenir
USE **souvenir albums**

albums, stamp
USE **stamp albums**

albums, view
USE **view albums**

alcazars
RK.444
ALT **alcazar**
SN Use for Spanish or Moorish castles, fortresses, or fortified palaces.
CN V.RK.AFU.ALO.ALO.BIQ.BIQ.AFU

alchemy
KD.301 (L,R)
SN Medieval chemical science and philosophy aiming to transmute base metals into gold. (W)
CN K.KD.AFU.BIQ.AFU

alcohol
MT.2681 (L)
UF spirit
CN M.MT.AFU.ARI.HZS.AFU.BOK.AFU

alcohol, absolute
USE **absolute alcohol**

alcohol, amyl
USE **amyl alcohol**

alcohol, anhydrous
USE **absolute alcohol**

alcohol, butyl
USE **butyl alcohol**

alcohol, denatured
USE **denatured alcohol**

alcohol, diacetone
USE **diacetone alcohol**

alcohol, ethyl
USE **ethyl alcohol**

alcohol, grain
USE **ethyl alcohol**

alcohol, industrial
USE **methyl alcohol**

alcohol, isopropyl
USE **isopropyl alcohol**

alcohol, methyl
USE **methyl alcohol**

alcohol, normal butyl
USE **butanol**

alcohol, polyvinyl
USE **polyvinyl alcohol**

alcohol, wood
USE **methyl alcohol**

alcove beds
USE **box beds**

alcoves
RM.27 (A,R)
ALT **alcove**
SN Use to designate small recessed spaces off of larger rooms.
UF nooks
recesses
CN V.RM.AFU.DIO.AFU.AFU

alcoves, dining
USE **dining alcoves**

alder
MT.1092 (L)
UF Alnus
CN M.MT.AFU.AFU.ALO.BIQ.DCU.AFU.AFU.AFU.ALO

alder, American green
USE **American green alder**

alder, black
USE **common alder**

alder, common
USE **common alder**

alder, European green
USE **European green alder**

alder, Formosan
USE **seaside alder**

alder, red
USE **red alder**

alder, seaside
USE **seaside alder**

alehouses
USE **pubs**

Alemannic
USE **Alamannic**

aleois
USE **loopholes**

aleppo oak
MT.1229 (L)
UF oak, aleppo
Quercus infectoria
CN M.MT.AFU.AFU.ALO.BIQ.DCU.AFU.AFU.AFU.IRA.AFU

alettes
RT.193
ALT **alette**
SN The wings of piers on both sides of an engaged column. (DAC)
CN V.RT.AFU.AFU.AFU.AXC.CRG.ALO.AFU

Aleut
FL.784
CN F.FL.ALO.ALO.ALO.AFU.ALO.AFU.AFU.AFU

Alexandria blue
USE **Egyptian blue**

alfa
USE **esparto**

algae
RD.259 (L,B)
ALT **alga**
CN V.RD.ARI.AFU.BCW.ALO.ALO.AFU.AFU

algal limestone
MT.653
UF limestone, algal
CN M.MT.AFU.AFU.AFU.DCU.AFU.ALO.AFU.ALO.ALO.AFU.AFU.AFU.AFU

Algaroba
USE **mesquite**

algebra
KD.251 (L)
CN K.KD.AFU.ARI.CFS.AFU

algicides
MT.2374 (L)
ALT **algicide**
CN M.MT.AFU.ARI.BOK.AFU

Algonkin
FL.1218 (L,R)
CN F.FL.ALO.ALO.ARI.AFU.AFU.ALO.AFU

algorithms
BM.756
CN B.BM.CFS.ARI.AFU

Ali Kosh
FL.3005
CN F.FL.ALO.AXC.ARI.BIQ.AFU.AFU.BIQ

aligning punches
USE **drift punches**

alignment
BM.47
ALT **aligned**
UF alinement
CN B.BM.AFU.AFU.ARI.AFU.AFU

Alikaluf
USE **Alacaluf**

Alikuluf
USE **Alacaluf**

alinement
USE **alignment**

aliphatic hydrocarbons
MT.2667
UF hydrocarbons, aliphatic
CN M.MT.AFU.ARI.HZS.AFU.BIQ.AFU

alizari
USE **madder**

alizarin
MT.1538 (L)
SN An orange or red crystalline compound formerly prepared from madder and now made synthetically from anthraquinone; used primarily in making red pigments. (W)
UF dihydroxy anthraquinone
CN M.MT.AFU.AFU.ARI.AFU.AFU.AFU.AFU.ALO.AFU

alizarin crimson
USE **alizarin madder**

alizarin madder
MT.1703
UF alizarin crimson
crimson, alizarin
lake, madder
madder lake
madder, alizarin
madder, rose (alizarin)
madder, synthetic
rose madder (alizarin madder)
synthetic madder
CN M.MT.AFU.AFU.ARI.AFU.AFU.ALO.ALO.BCW.AXC.AFU

alizarin violet
MT.1723
SN A transparent violet pigment made from synthetic purpurin, not sufficiently permanent for artists' use, since it turns dark or blackish on long exposure to light. (MAYER)
UF madder lake, violet
violet madder lake
violet, alizarin
CN M.MT.AFU.AFU.ARI.AFU.AFU.ALO.ALO.BIQ.AXC.AFU

alizarin yellow
MT.1798
SN A dull, brownish, translucent yellow pigment. (MAYER)
UF yellow, alizarin
CN M.MT.AFU.AFU.ARI.AFU.AFU.ALO.ALO.BUE.AXC.AFU

alizarine pink
USE **deep pink**
strong pink

alkali
MT.303
SN A caustic hydroxide characterized by its ability to neutralize acids and form soluble soaps with fatty acids. (MH)
CN M.MT.AFU.AFU.AFU.BOK.ALO

alkaline glaze
MT.2558
SN A ceramic glaze whose flux is an alkali. (MAYER)
UF glaze, alkaline
CN M.MT.AFU.ARI.CRG.ARI.ARI.AFU.AFU.AFU

alkanet
MT.1520
SN A red natural dyestuff from the alkanet root. (MAYER)
CN M.MT.AFU.AFU.ARI.AFU.AFU.AFU.AFU.AFU.AXC.AFU

alkyd plastic
USE **alkyd resin**

alkyd resin
MT.2159 (L)
UF alkyd plastic
plastic, alkyd
resin, alkyd
CN M.MT.AFU.AFU.ARI.BUE.ALO.AXC.ALO.AFU

alkyd, oil-modified
USE **oil-modified alkyd**

alla prima
KT.221 (L)
SN A method of oil painting in which the final effects are achieved in the initial application of paint as opposed to covering the canvas layer by layer. (MAYER)
UF au premier coup
direct painting
painting, direct
CN K.KT.AFU.ALO.DUC.CXA.ALO.AFU.AFU

Alladians
USE **Alagya**

allées couvertes
USE **gallery graves**

allegory
BM.14 (L,R)
CN B.BM.AFU.AFU.AFU.BZY.AFU

Allen head screws
USE **Allen screws**

Allen head wrenches
USE **Allen wrenches**

Allen screws
TF.468
ALT **Allen screw**
SN Screws with a hexagonal recess to receive an Allen wrench. (MEANS)
UF Allen head screws
screws, Allen
CN V.TF.AFU.AFU.AFU.ALO.AFU.DIO.AFU.AFU

Allen wrenches
TB.773 (N)
ALT **Allen wrench**
SN Wrenches which consist of a steel bar, hexagonal in section, bent to form a right angle; used for Allen screws. (DAC)
UF Allen head wrenches
wrenches, Allen
wrenches, Allen head
CN V.TB.AFU.BCW.BIQ.AXC.ALO.BIQ.ALO

alleys
RK.1528 (A,L,B,R)
ALT **alley**
CN V.RK.ALO.ALO.BIQ.ARI.AFU.ALO.AFU.AFU

alleys, blind
USE **blind alleys**

alleys, bowling
USE **bowling alleys**

alleys, skittle
USE **skittle alleys**

alligator shears
USE **lever shears**

allocating
USE **funding**

allotment gardens
RK.1438 (B)
ALT **allotment garden**
SN Garden areas which have been divided into plots, or allotments, for assignment or rental to individuals for cultivation; may also be used for the resulting gardens on those plots.
UF allotments
gardens, allotment
CN V.RK.ALO.AFU.AFU.BCW.AFU.AFU

allotments
USE **allotment gardens**

allover patterns
DG.95
ALT **allover pattern**
SN Use for patterns that extend broadly over a surface. For a continuous pattern that proceeds more directionally, use **running ornament.**
UF overall patterns

patterns, allover
patterns, overall
CN D.DG.AFU.ARI.AFU.AFU

alloy constructional steel
USE **high-strength low-alloy steel**

alloy steels
USE **steel alloys**

alloy, aluminum-silicon
USE **aluminum-silicon alloy**

alloy, aluminum-zinc
USE **aluminum-zinc alloy**

alloy, Koeller's
USE **Koeller's alloy**

alloy, monel
USE **monel**

alloys
MT.335 (L,B)
SN Substances having metallic properties, consisting of two or more metallic elements or of metallic and nonmetallic elements, which are miscible with each other when molten, and have not separated into distinct layers when solid. (HORNB)
UF alloys, metal
metal alloys
CN M.MT.AFU.AFU.AFU.BZY.AFU.AFU.AFU

alloys, aluminum
USE **aluminum alloys**

alloys, bearing
USE **Babbitt metal**

alloys, chromium
USE **chromium alloys**

alloys, copper
USE **copper alloys**

alloys, copper-beryllium
USE **copper-beryllium alloys**

alloys, copper-nickel
USE **copper-nickel alloys**

alloys, copper-silicon
USE **copper-silicon alloys**

alloys, copper-tin
USE **copper-tin alloys**

alloys, copper-zinc
USE **copper-zinc alloys**

alloys, ferrous
USE **iron alloys**

alloys, gold
USE **gold alloys**

alloys, iron
USE **iron alloys**

alloys, lead
USE **lead alloys**

alloys, lead-antimony-tin
USE **white metal**

alloys, metal
USE **alloys**

alloys, nickel
USE **nickel alloys**

alloys, nickel-copper
USE **copper-nickel alloys**

alloys, nonferrous
USE **nonferrous alloys**

alloys, plastic
USE **plastic alloys**

alloys, silver
USE **silver alloys**

alloys, steel
USE **steel alloys**

alloys, steel-aluminum
USE **steel-aluminum alloys**

alloys, tin
USE **tin alloys**

alloys, zinc
USE **zinc alloys**

allusion
BM.4
CN B.BM.AFU.AFU.AFU.AFU

alluvial fans
RD.188 (L)
ALT **alluvial fan**
SN Designates sloping, fan-shaped masses of sediment deposited by a watercourse at the place where it leaves a constricted course or upland and emerges into a broad valley or a plain.
UF fans, alluvial
CN V.RD.ARI.AFU.AXC.AFU.AFU.ARI.AFU

allyl plastic
USE **allyl resin**

allyl resin
MT.2161
UF allyl plastic
plastic, allyl
resin, allyl
CN M.MT.AFU.AFU.ARI.BUE.ALO.AXC.ALO.ALO

Alma
FL.944
CN F.FL.ALO.ALO.ALO.AFU.ALO.ARI.BIQ.BCW.AXC.AFU.AFU

Alma plain
FL.945
UF plain, Alma
CN F.FL.ALO.ALO.ALO.AFU.ALO.ARI.BIQ.BCW.AXC.AFU.AFU.AFU

Alma rough
FL.946
UF rough, Alma
CN F.FL.ALO.ALO.ALO.AFU.ALO.ARI.BIQ.BCW.AXC.AFU.AFU.ALO

almanacs
VW.389 (L,R)
ALT **alamanac**
SN Publications, usually annuals, containing a variety of useful facts of miscellaneous nature, or statistical information; originally included projections of coming days, months, and holidays. (LG)
CN V.VW.AFU.AFU.ALO.EWY.AFU

almemars
USE **bemas**

Almerian
FL.2486
CN F.FL.ALO.AXC.AFU.BCW.AFU

almeries
USE **aumbries**

almimbars
USE **minbars**

Almohad
FL.3431 (L)
CN F.FL.ALO.BIQ.AFU.ARI

almond
MT.1285 (L)
CN M.MT.AFU.AFU.ALO.BIQ.DCU.AFU.AFU.AFU.KLE.AFU

almond oil
MT.2032
SN A colorless or pale yellow bland and nearly odorless nondrying fatty oil used as an emollient. (W)
UF oil, almond
CN M.MT.AFU.AFU.ARI.ARI.AXC.ARI.AFU

almond-shaped
DC.113
CN D.DC.AFU.ARI.FCS.AFU

almoners cupboards
USE **livery cupboards**

Almoravid
FL.3432 (L)
CN F.FL.ALO.BIQ.AFU.AXC

almshouses
RK.784 (A,L,B,R)
ALT **almshouse**
UF farms, poor
poor farms
poorhouses
workhouses (almshouses)
CN V.RK.AFU.ALO.ALO.CXA.ALO.ALO.AFU

Alnus
USE **alder**

Alnus cremastogyne
MT.1093
CN M.MT.AFU.AFU.ALO.BIQ.DCU.AFU.AFU.AFU.ALO.AFU

Alnus crispa
USE **American green alder**

Alnus glutinosa
USE **common alder**

Alnus maritima
USE **seaside alder**

Alnus oregona
USE **red alder**

Alnus pendula
MT.1094
CN M.MT.AFU.AFU.ALO.BIQ.DCU.AFU.AFU.AFU.ALO.ALO

Alnus rubra
USE **red alder**

Alnus viridis
USE **European green alder**

Alookooloop
USE **Alacaluf**

alpaca
MT.1816 (L)
SN A fabric made from the fine woollike hair of the alpaca, an animal of the llama family. (MH)
CN M.MT.AFU.AFU.ARI.ALO.AFU.AFU.AFU.AFU

alpine architecture
USE **hillside architecture**

Alsea
FL.1334 (L)
CN F.FL.ALO.ALO.ARI.AFU.BIQ.AFU

Altai
FL.2140
UF Altaitsy
Altay
CN F.FL.ALO.ARI.ARI.ALO.AFU

Altaitsy
USE **Altai**

altar canopies
USE **baldachins**

altar frontals
RT.1218 (N,B,R)
ALT **altar frontal**
SN Ornamental hangings or panels for the front of an altar. (HAS)
UF antependia
frontals
frontals, altar
CN V.RT.AFU.BUE.ALO.ALO.ALO.AFU

altar rails
RT.1224 (B)
ALT **altar rail**
SN Low rails or barriers in front of the altar, separating the officiating clergy from the other worshippers. (HAS)
UF rails, altar
CN V.RT.AFU.BUE.ALO.ARI.AFU

altar screens
RT.1249 (L,B,R)
ALT **altar screen**
SN Use for screens that separate the altar area from the space behind it. Distinct from **reredoses**, which relate visually to the altar and may form part of the inner side of an altar screen.
UF screens, altar
CN V.RT.AFU.BUE.ALO.ARI.CXA.AFU

altar slabs
USE **mensas**

altar stones
USE **mensas**

altar tombs
RK.482
ALT **altar tomb**
SN Use for tombs or tomb monuments whose location or decoration resembles that of altars.
UF high tombs
tombs, altar
tombs, high
CN V.RK.AFU.ALO.ALO.BOK.BUE.AFU.AFU

altarpieces
RT.1226 (A,N,R)
ALT **altarpiece**
SN Devotional works of art on, above, or behind the altar of a Christian church. (THDAT)
CN V.RT.AFU.BUE.ALO.ARI.ALO

altars
RT.1214 (A,L,N,B,R)
ALT **altar**
SN Use both for tablelike constructions upon which religious sacrifice is offered and for certain large, freestanding structures used for religious ceremonies.
CN V.RT.AFU.BUE.ALO.ALO.AFU

altars, fire
USE **fire altars**

altars, high
USE **high altars**

altars, main
USE **high altars**

altars, side
USE **side altars**

Altay
USE **Altai**

alteration
KT.8
ALT **altered**
CN K.KT.AFU.ALO.ARI

alterations
VB.91 (A,L,B,R)
ALT **alteration**
SN Use for modifications to an object or structure. Refers especially to the physical evidence of the change. In architecture, use **additions** if the change increases the structure's volume; **alterations** if it does not.
CN V.VB.ALO.BOK.ALO

altered photographs
USE **manipulated photographs**

altered prints (photographs)
USE **manipulated photographs**

alternative schools
USE **free schools**

alternative technology
USE **appropriate technology**

Altoperuvian
FL.1708
CN F.FL.ALO.ALO.AXC.ALO.AFU.AFU

altstadts
USE **old towns**

Alukoelúf
USE **Alacaluf**

aluminate cement
USE **aluminous cement**

aluminizing
KT.816
SN The application of an aluminum coating such as to iron and steel sheet. (HORNB)
CN K.KT.AFU.ALO.HOE.BCW.ALO.ALO.AFU

aluminous cement
MT.8 (B)
SN Cement made with bauxite and containing a high percentage of alumina; valued for its fast setting and high strength properties. (MH12)
UF aluminate cement
cement, aluminate
cement, aluminous
cement, high alumina
cement, high speed
HAC
high alumina cement
high speed cement
CN M.MT.AFU.AFU.AFU.ALO.AFU.AFU.AFU

aluminum
MT.429 (A,L,B,R)
CN M.MT.AFU.AFU.AFU.BZY.AFU.AFU.ARI.AFU

aluminum alloys
MT.363 (L,B)
UF alloys, aluminum
CN M.MT.AFU.AFU.AFU.BZY.AFU.AFU.AFU.ALO.AFU

aluminum bronze
MT.369 (L)
SN A copper-aluminum alloy with aluminum as the chief alloying element. (MH)
UF bronze, aluminum
CN M.MT.AFU.AFU.AFU.BZY.AFU.AFU.AFU.ALO.ARI.AFU

aluminum (color)
USE **light gray**
medium gray

aluminum hydrate white
MT.1743
UF white, aluminum hydrate
CN M.MT.AFU.AFU.ARI.AFU.AFU.ALO.ALO.BOK.ALO.AFU

aluminum oxide
USE **corundum**

aluminum paint
MT.2511
SN Paint containing aluminum alloys effective in preventing discoloration of painted surfaces from mildew. (PUTNAM)
UF paint, aluminum
CN M.MT.AFU.ARI.CRG.ALO.BCW.AFU.AFU

aluminum-silicon alloy
MT.364
SN Refers to alloys with from 5 to 22% silicon characterized by ease of casting, corrosion resistance, lightness, and ease of welding. (MH)
UF alloy, aluminum-silicon
CN M.MT.AFU.AFU.AFU.BZY.AFU.AFU.AFU.ALO.AFU.AFU

aluminum stearate white
MT.1744
UF white, aluminum stearate
CN M.MT.AFU.AFU.ARI.AFU.AFU.ALO.ALO.BOK.ALO.ALO

aluminum-zinc alloy
MT.365 (L)
UF alloy, alumin[illegible]-zinc
CN M.MT.AFU.AFU.AFU.BZY.AFU.AFU.AFU.ALO.AFU.ALO

aluminum, structural
USE **structural aluminum**

alumni directories
VW.407 (L)
ALT **alumni directory**
SN Directories of names, addresses, and other data about former students of schools, colleges, or universities. (AHD)
UF directories, alumni
CN V.VW.AFU.AFU.ALO.EWY.AXC.AFU.AFU

Alunda
USE **Lunda**

alveated domes
USE **beehive domes**

Amahuaca
FL.1568 (L)
UF Ipitinere
Sayaco
CN F.FL.ALO.ALO.ARI.ARI.AFU.AFU

amalgam-gilding
KT.713
SN Technique of applying gold leaf in which gold is mixed with mercury and applied to the surface of the object; the object is then heated to dispel the mercury. (SCHNEI)
UF fire gilding
gilding, amalgam
gilding, fire
CN K.KT.AFU.ALO.GRC.CRG.ALO.AFU

amalgam-silvering
KT.718
SN Technique of applying silver leaf in which silver is mixed with mercury and applied to the surface of the object; the object is then heated to dispel the mercury. (SCHNEI)
CN K.KT.AFU.ALO.GRC.CRG.ARI.AFU

Aman-Kutan
FL.1764
CN F.FL.ALO.ARI.AFU.AFU.AFU

amaranth
USE **purpleheart**

Amargosa
FL.900
CN F.FL.ALO.ALO.ALO.AFU.ALO.ARI.AFU.AFU

Amarna age
USE **Amarna period**

Amarna period
FL.2819
UF Amarna age
CN F.FL.ALO.AXC.ALO.ARI.AFU.BUE.BCW

amateur art
BM.231 (L,R)
SN Includes any art created by nonprofessional artists practicing for pleasure or self-expression. For nonprofessional art valued for the roughness or rawness of its artistic impulse, use **art brut.**
UF art, amateur
CN B.BM.AFU.ARI.BCW.ALO

amateurism
BM.340 (L,R)
CN B.BM.ALO.ALO.CLM.AFU

amateurs
HG.762
ALT **amateur**
SN Persons who engage in a particular pursuit, study, or science as a pastime rather than as a profession. (W)
CN H.HG.AFU.BIQ.AFU

amatl
USE **bark cloth**

Amatle
FL.1024
CN F.FL.ALO.ALO.ALO.ALO.AFU.ALO.ARI.AFU.ALO.BUE

Amba
FL.507 (L)
UF Baamba
CN F.FL.ALO.AFU.AXC.ALO.ALO.BIQ.AFU.AFU.AFU

Ambamba
USE **Mbamba**

amber
MT.1494 (L,R)
CN M.MT.AFU.AFU.ALO.BOK.BOK.AFU

amber (color)
USE **dark orange yellow**
deep orange yellow
light yellow
moderate orange yellow
moderate yellow

amber gold
USE **grayish yellow**
light yellowish brown

Amber (painting style)
FL.2287
UF Jaipur
CN F.FL.ALO.ARI.AXC.ALO.AFU.BZY.BCW.BCW.ALO

amber yellow
USE **brilliant yellow**
light yellow

amber, light
USE **dark orange yellow**
moderate orange yellow

amber, Prussian
USE **succinite**

Ambete
USE **Mbete**

ambient energy
USE **solar power**

ambient light photography
USE **available light photography**

ambiente
USE **environmental art**

Ambo
FL.576 (L)
UF Ovambo

CN F.FL.ALO.AFU.AXC.ARI.BIQ.AFU

ambones
USE **ambos**

ambos
RT.1243 (A,R)
ALT **ambon**
SN In Early Christian churches, pulpits in the nave for reading the Gospels or the Epistles. In present-day Balkan and Greek churches, large pulpits or reading desks. (HAS)
UF ambones
CN V.RT.AFU.BUE.ALO.ARI.CLM.AFU.AFU

ambries
USE **aumbries**

ambrotype
KT.321 (L)
SN A variant of the wet collodion process to produce a direct-positive camera original. The collodion is coated on glass, the image underexposed and then underdeveloped, the glass backed with black lacquer or black cloth, and the whole mounted in a case or frame. Occasionally, the image was made on ruby glass.
CN K.KT.AFU.ALO.DUC.DIO.ALO.BCW.AFU

ambrotypes
VJ.29 (L,N,R)
ALT **ambrotype**
SN Photographs produced by mounting a negative (made by a variant of the wet collodion process) that is on glass with a dark backing, which makes the image appear as a positive.
UF collodion glass positives
glass-collodion positives
glass positives, collodion
positives, collodion glass
positives, glass-collodion
CN V.VJ.AFU.AFU.ARI.AFU.AFU

Ambrym
FL.3672 (L)
CN F.FL.ALO.BOK.ALO.BUE.AFU

ambulance stations
RK.736 (A,B)
ALT **ambulance station**
UF stations, ambulance
CN V.RK.AFU.ALO.ALO.CXA.ALO.AFU.AFU.AFU

ambulantes
USE **tables ambulantes**

ambulatories
RM.301
ALT **ambulatory**
SN Semicircular or polygonal circulation spaces enclosing an apse or a straight-ended sanctuary. (PDARC)
UF aisles, apse
apse aisles
deambulatories
CN V.RM.AFU.DIO.AXC.ALO.AFU.AFU

Ameca
USE **Ameca-Zacoalco**

Ameca-Zacoalco
FL.1069
UF Ameca
CN F.FL.ALO.ALO.ALO.ALO.AFU.ALO.BCW.ARI.AFU

amendments
VW.770 (L)
ALT **amendment**
SN Any writing made or proposed as an addition to or improvement of some principal writing; in legislation, refers to modifications or alterations in a bill or enacted law. (BLACKS)
CN V.VW.AFU.ARI.AFU.ALO.ALO

Amer
FL.695
UF Beni Amer
CN F.FL.ALO.AFU.AXC.BCW.ARI.AFU

American
FL.713 (L,B,R)
SN Use in the context of or associated specifically with the modern political entity of the United States of America.
UF U.S.
CN F.FL.ALO.ALO.AFU.ARI.AFU

American arbor vitae
MT.1334 (L)
UF arbor-vitae
arbor vitae, American
thuja accidentalis
thuya occidentalis
CN M.MT.AFU.AFU.ALO.BIQ.DCU.AFU.AFU.ALO.ALO.AFU

American ash
USE **white ash**

American aspen
MT.1274
SN A wood used chiefly for match stems and making excelsior; also for some inside construction work. (MH)
UF American poplar
aspen (American aspen)
aspen, American
aspen, quaking
poplar, American
Populus tremuloides
quaking aspen
CN M.MT.AFU.AFU.ALO.BIQ.DCU.AFU.AFU.AFU.KFK.ALO.AFU

American basswood
USE **linden**

American beech
MT.1105
UF beech, American
Fagus grandifolia
CN M.MT.AFU.AFU.ALO.BIQ.DCU.AFU.AFU.AFU.BCW.AFU

American black cherry
USE **black cherry**

American black walnut
USE **black walnut**

American bond
USE **common bond**

American cherry
USE **black cherry**

American chestnut
MT.1132 (L)
UF American sweet chestnut
Castanea dentata
chestnut, American
chestnut, American sweet
sweet chestnut, American
CN M.MT.AFU.AFU.ALO.BIQ.DCU.AFU.AFU.AFU.CLM.AFU

American Colonial
FL.1703 (L)
SN Style of furniture, architecture, and domestic articles built or made in the United States in the Colonial period or somewhat later.(RHDEL2) Popular term; when possible prefer a more specific style term such as **Georgian.**
UF American, Early
Colonial North American
Colonial, American
Early American
North American, Colonial
CN F.FL.ALO.ALO.AXC.AFU.AFU

American Deco
USE **Art Deco**

American elm
MT.1145 (L)
SN Fine-grain, durable wood used chiefly for ax handles, and for parts requiring a combination of strength, bending qualities, and ability to withstand rough usage. (MH)
UF American white elm
elm, American
elm, American white
elm, white
Ulmus americana
white elm
white elm, American
CN M.MT.AFU.AFU.ALO.BIQ.DCU.AFU.AFU.AFU.DCU.AFU

American Federal
USE **Federal**

American film
MT.2229
SN An invention of George Eastman, a photographic material consisting of a gelatino-bromide emulsion over plain gelatin; first appeared in 1888 on a paper support and later on ni-

trocellulose film. (HCOP)
UF film, American
CN M.MT.AFU.ALO.CXA.AFU

American green alder
MT.1095
UF alder, American green
Alnus crispa
green alder, American
CN M.MT.AFU.AFU.ALO.BIQ.DCU.AFU.AFU.AFU.ALO.ARI

American hop hornbeam
MT.1184
UF hop hornbeam, American
hornbeam, American hop
ironwood (American hop hornbeam)
Ostrya virginiana
CN M.MT.AFU.AFU.ALO.BIQ.DCU.AFU.AFU.AFU.EWY.ALO.AFU

American horse chestnut
USE **buckeye**

American Indian
USE **Native American**

American ivorytypes
USE **ivorytypes**

American limewood
USE **linden**

American plane
USE **sycamore**

American poplar
USE **American aspen**

American Renaissance
USE **Renaissance Revival**

American sassafras
MT.1307
UF Sassafras albidum
sassafras, American
CN M.MT.AFU.AFU.ALO.BIQ.DCU.AFU.AFU.AFU.LIG.AFU

American Scene
FL.1748 (R)
SN Movement of American figurative painting active from the 1920s to the 1940s, committed to the establishment of a genuinely American art by the realistic depiction of contemporary American life and the repudiation of contemporary nonrealist styles introduced by the Armory Show.
UF painting, American Scene
Scene, American
CN F.FL.ALO.ALO.BCW.AFU.CFS.AFU

American sweet chestnut
USE **American chestnut**

American sycamore
USE **sycamore**

American-Type painting
USE **Abstract Expressionist**

American vermilion
USE **chrome red**

American walnut
USE **black walnut**

American white ash
USE **white ash**

American white elm
USE **American elm**

American, Central
USE **Central American**

American, Early
USE **American Colonial**

American, Latin
USE **Latin American**

American, Native
USE **Native American**

American, North
USE **North American**

American, South
USE **South American**

Americans, African
USE **African Americans**

Americans, Hispanic
USE **Latinos**

Americans, Mexican
USE **Mexican Americans**

Amerindian
USE **Native American**

amethyst
MT.543 (L)
SN A violet or purple transparent quartz. (MH)
CN M.MT.AFU.AFU.AFU.CFS.AFU.GRC.AFU.AFU

amethyst (color)
USE **dark purple**
grayish purple
grayish reddish purple
moderate purple

amethyst violet
USE **vivid purple**

amethyst, light
USE **moderate purple**

Amhara
FL.637 (L)
CN F.FL.ALO.AFU.AXC.AXC.AXC.AFU

Amherst sandstone
MT.724
SN A stone from Ohio, containing up to 95% silica with 4% aluminum oxide, and colored gray and buff with iron oxides. (MH)
UF sandstone, Amherst
CN M.MT.AFU.AFU.AFU.DCU.AFU.ALO.AFU.ARI.AFU.ALO.BIQ.AFU

Ami School
FL.2049
CN F.FL.ALO.ARI.ALO.ALO.ALO.ARI.AFU

amianto
MT.851
UF amiantus, lapis
lapis amiantus
CN M.MT.AFU.AFU.AFU.DCU.AFU.ARI.BOK.AFU

amiantus, lapis
USE **amianto**

amino resin
MT.2162 (L)
UF aminoplastics
resin, amino
CN M.MT.AFU.AFU.ARI.BUE.ALO.AXC.ALO.ARI

aminoaldehyde resin
MT.2165
UF resin, aminoaldehyde
CN M.MT.AFU.AFU.ARI.BUE.ALO.AXC.ALO.ARI.ALO.AFU

aminoplastics
USE **amino resin**

Amish
BM.631 (L,B,R)
UF Old Order Amish
CN B.BM.BZY.AFU.ALO.ARI.AFU

ammonia
MT.306 (L)
CN M.MT.AFU.AFU.AFU.BOK.ARI

ammonia water
MT.2711
UF ammonia, aqua
ammonia, aqueous
aqua ammonia
aqueous ammonia
hartshorn, spirit of
spirit of hartshorn
water, ammonia
CN M.MT.AFU.ARI.HZS.ALO.AFU.AFU

ammonia, aqua
USE **ammonia water**

ammonia, aqueous
USE **ammonia water**

ammoniacal copper arsenate
MT.2644
UF copper arsenate, ammoniacal
CN M.MT.AFU.ARI.HCQ.ALO.AFU.ALO

Amol ware
FL.3428
UF ware, Amol
CN F.FL.ALO.BIQ.AFU.AFU.AFU.AFU

Amorgos group
FL.2543
CN F.FL.ALO.AXC.ALO.AFU.AFU.ALO.AFU.AFU.BIQ

amortization
BM.369 (L)
SN Gradual reduction of a financial obligation by payment of a part of the principal, contribution to a sinking fund, or the gradual depreciation of an asset.
CN B.BM.ARI.AFU

amortizements
RT.717
ALT **amortizement**
SN Sloping tops of buttresses or projecting piers.
CN V.RT.AFU.ALO.AFU.AFU

amphiprostyle
DC.84
CN D.DC.AFU.ARI.ERE.BIQ.AFU

amphitheaters
RK.936 (A,L,B,R)
ALT **amphitheater**
UF coliseums
CN V.RK.AFU.ALO.ALO.EFQ.ARI.BCW.AFU.ARI.AFU

Amratian
FL.2780
UF Early Naqada
Naqada I
CN F.FL.ALO.AXC.ALO.ARI.AFU.AFU.ALO.ALO

Amuq B ware
FL.2933
UF ware, Amuq B
CN F.FL.ALO.AXC.ARI.AXC.ALO.BIQ.AFU

amusement arcades
RK.1033 (B)
ALT **amusement arcade**
UF arcades, amusement
CN V.RK.AFU.ALO.ALO.EWY.AXC.ARI.AFU

amusement parks
RG.152 (A,L,B,R)
ALT **amusement park**
UF parks, amusement
CN V.RG.AFU.AFU.DOI.AFU

amusement rides
RK.1003 (L,N)
ALT **amusement ride**
UF rides
rides, amusement
CN V.RK.AFU.ALO.ALO.EWY.AFU.AFU

Amuzgo
FL.1510 (L)
CN F.FL.ALO.ALO.ARI.ALO.AXC.AFU

amyl acetate
MT.2692
UF acetate, amyl
CN M.MT.AFU.ARI.HZS.AFU.BOK.ALO.AFU

amyl alcohol
MT.2682
UF alcohol, amyl
CN M.MT.AFU.ARI.HZS.AFU.BOK.AFU.AFU

amylin
USE **dextrine**

An-yang
USE **Anyang (Shang style)**

anaglyphs
VJ.102 (R)
ALT **anaglyph**
SN Stereoscopic photographs in which the two images are in contrasting colors and produce a three-dimensional effect when viewed through colored filters. (W)
CN V.VJ.AFU.ARI.AFU.BOK.AFU

analogy
BM.19 (L)
CN B.BM.AFU.AFU.AFU.CFS.AFU

analysis
USE **analyzing**

analysis, chemical
USE **chemical analysis**

analysis, content
USE **subject analysis**

analysis, cost benefit
USE **cost benefit analysis**

analysis, discourse
USE **pragmatics**

analysis, literary
USE **literary criticism**

analysis, needs
USE **needs assessment**

analysis, neutron activation
USE **neutron activation analysis**

analysis, plastic
USE **plastic design**

analysis, radioactivation
USE **neutron activation analysis**

analysis, site
USE **site analysis**

analysis, stability
USE **structural stability**

analysis, stress
USE **structural analysis**

analysis, structural
USE **structural analysis**

analysis, subject
USE **subject analysis**

analysis, systems
USE **systems analysis**

analysis, terrain
USE **terrain analysis**

analysis, trace element
USE **trace element analysis**

analysis, ultimate-strength
USE **plastic design**

analysts, handwriting
USE **graphologists**

analysts, systems
USE **systems analysts**

analytical bibliography
BM.309 (L)
SN The study of the history of book production and the description of books as physical objects,(LG) including study of the relationships of varying texts or multiple editions of a work. (W)
UF bibliography, analytical
bibliography, critical
bibliography, descriptive
bibliography, historical
critical bibliography
descriptive bibliography
historical bibliography
CN B.BM.AFU.AXC.EFQ.AFU

Analytical Cubist
FL.3293
ALT **Analytical Cubism**
UF Cubist, Analytical
Cubist, Facet
Facet Cubist
CN F.FL.ALO.BCW.ALO.AXC.DCU.ARI.AFU

analyzing
KG.5 (A,L)
SN Examining an object, action, material, or concept in detail by separating it into its fundamental elements or component parts.
UF analysis
CN K.KG.AFU.AFU.AFU.ALO

anamorphic lenses
USE **wide-angle lenses**

anamorphoses
VB.3 (R)
ALT **anamorphosis**
SN Images so executed as to give a distorted shape to the object represented but which, if viewed from a certain point or reflected in a curved mirror, show the object in true proportion. (OCA)
CN V.VB.AFU.AFU.AFU

Anan'ino
FL.1780
CN F.FL.ALO.ARI.AFU.ARI.AFU

Anang
FL.241 (L)
CN F.FL.ALO.AFU.AXC.AFU.ALO.AFU.BCW.AFU

Anangula
FL.785
CN F.FL.ALO.ALO.ALO.AFU.ALO.AFU.AFU.ALO

anarchism
BM.553 (L,R)
CN B.BM.BOK.BZY.AFU

anarchists
HG.749 (L)
ALT **anarchist**
SN Persons who promote disorder or excite revolt against any established rule, law, or custom. (RHDEL2)
CN H.HG.AFU.BCW.HZS.ALO

Anasazi
FL.956 (A,L)
UF Basketmaker-Pueblo
CN F.FL.ALO.ALO.ALO.AFU.ALO.ARI.BIQ.BOK.AFU

anastatic printing
KT.469
SN A relief printing process in which all but the printing area of the plate is etched, leaving in relief only the lines and areas to be inked. (MAYER)
UF etching, zinc
printing, anastatic
zinc etching
CN K.KT.AFU.ALO.DUC.DUC.ALO.BCW.ARI.AFU

anastylosis
KT.632
SN The reconstruction of a monument or other structure from fallen parts. (W)
CN K.KT.AFU.ALO.FZU.BCW.AFU

Anatolian
FL.2847 (L)
CN F.FL.ALO.AXC.ARI.AFU

Anatolian Seljuq
USE **Seljuk of Rum**

anatomical illustration
KT.211 (R)
UF illustration, anatomical
CN K.KT.AFU.ALO.DUC.CLM.BOK.AFU.AFU

anatomical illustrations
VB.51 (R)
ALT **anatomical illustration**
SN Use for depictions that are intended to instruct the observer about structures or details of anatomy. Distinct from **anatomical studies**, in which an artist explores an anatomical structure to improve his/her understanding of it.
UF illustrations, anatomical
CN V.VB.AFU.ALO.AXC.ALO.ARI.AFU.AFU

anatomical models
VB.104 (L,N,R)
ALT **anatomical model**
UF models, anatomical
CN V.VB.ALO.BUE.ARI.AFU

anatomical studies
VB.59
ALT **anatomical study**
SN Use for exploratory works, usually drawings, done by an artist to improve his/her understanding of a structure or detail of anatomy. Distinct from **anatomical illustrations**, which are intended to instruct the observer about anatomy.
UF anatomy studies
studies, anatomical
CN V.VB.AFU.ALO.BOK.AFU

anatomists
HG.381 (L)
ALT **anatomist**
SN People who study anatomy.
CN H.HG.AFU.AXC.BIQ.ALO.BCW.AFU

anatomy
KD.201 (L,B,R)
SN Discipline concerned with the structure, function, and development of the cells, tissues, and organs constituting the animal body. (PG)
CN K.KD.AFU.ARI.ARI.AFU

anatomy studies
USE **anatomical studies**

Anau
FL.1769
CN F.FL.ALO.ARI.AFU.ALO.AFU

anchor bolts
TF.308
ALT **anchor bolt**
SN Threaded bolts, usually embedded in a foundation, for securing a sill, framework, or machinery. (MEANS)
UF bolts, anchor
bolts, foundation
bolts, hold-down
foundation bolts
hold-down bolts
CN V.TF.AFU.AFU.AFU.ALO.AFU.ALO.AFU.AFU

anchor davits
USE **davits**

anchor hinges
TF.133
ALT **anchor hinge**
UF hinges, anchor
CN V.TF.AFU.AFU.AFU.AFU.CLM.ALO.AFU

anchor plates
TF.290
ALT **anchor plate**
SN Plates attached to an object to which accessories or structural members may be attached by welding, screwing, nailing, or bolting. (MEANS)
UF plates, anchor
CN V.TF.AFU.AFU.AFU.ALO.AFU.AFU.ALO

anchor ties
TF.498
ALT **anchor tie**
SN Fasteners used to secure the parts of a wall to some stable object, such as another wall. (PUTNAM)
UF ties, anchor
CN V.TF.AFU.AFU.AFU.ALO.AFU.EWY.AFU

anchors (fasteners)
TF.288 (L)
ALT **anchor (fastener)**
SN Metal ties or plates used to fasten together timbers or masonry.
CN V.TF.AFU.AFU.AFU.ALO.AFU.AFU

anchors, adhesive
USE **adhesive anchors**

anchors, beam
USE **beam anchors**

anchors, buck
USE **buck anchors**

anchors, dog
USE **dogs (woodworking tools)**

anchors, double end
USE **double end anchors**

anchors, dovetail wire
USE **dovetail wire anchors**

anchors, dowel
USE **dowel anchors**

anchors, drive
USE **drive anchors**

anchors, furring
USE **slot anchors**

anchors, joist
USE **joist anchors**

anchors, joist (beam anchors)
USE **beam anchors**

anchors, lewis bolt
USE **lewis bolt anchors**

anchors, plate
USE **sill anchors**

anchors, rawlplug
USE **rawl plugs**

anchors, rod
USE **rod anchors**

anchors, screw
USE **screw anchors**

anchors, sill
USE **sill anchors**

anchors, slot
USE **slot anchors**

anchors, stone
USE **stone anchors**

anchors, strap
USE **strap anchors**

anchors, wall
USE **beam anchors**

anchors, Z
USE **Z anchors**

ancient
FL.2 (A,L,B,R)
CN F.FL.AFU.AFU

Ancient Elamite
USE **Old Elamite**

ancillaries
USE **outbuildings**

ancones
RT.322
ALT **ancone**
SN Use for consoles supporting an entablature or cornice over the aperture of a door or window. (RS)
UF elbows (ancones)
CN V.RT.AFU.AFU.AFU.BCW.AXC.ALO.AFU

andaman marblewood
USE **marblewood**

Andaqui
FL.1653 (L)
CN F.FL.ALO.ALO.ARI.ARI.BCW.AFU

Ande
USE **Campa**

andesite
MT.612
SN An extrusive, usually dark grayish rock consisting essentially of oligoclase or andesine feldspar with angite, homblende, hypersthene, or biotite. (W)
CN M.MT.AFU.AFU.AFU.DCU.AFU.AFU.AFU.AFU.ARI.AFU

Andhra
FL.2196 (L)
UF Andhra-Satavahana
Satvahana
CN F.FL.ALO.ARI.AXC.ALO.AFU.ARI.AXC

Andhra-Satavahana
USE **Andhra**

Andhra, Later
USE **Later Andhra**

Andoke
FL.1654 (L)
CN F.FL.ALO.ALO.ARI.ARI.BCW.ALO

Andorobo
USE **Dorobo**

andra
RM.389
ALT **andron**
SN Use for the parts of ancient Greek houses used only by men.
CN V.RM.AFU.DIO.BCW.AFU

Andra, Early
USE **Early Andra**

Andronovo
FL.2123
CN F.FL.ALO.ARI.ARI.AFU.ARI

Andumbo
USE **Ndumbo**

anechoic chambers
USE **anechoic rooms**

anechoic rooms
RM.396
ALT **anechoic room**
SN Rooms with sound-absorbent walls, especially designed for acoustic experiments. (W)
UF anechoic chambers
chambers, anechoic
rooms, anechoic
CN V.RM.AFU.DIO.BIQ.AFU

Angas
FL.225 (L)
CN F.FL.ALO.AFU.AXC.AFU.AFU.ALO.ARI.AFU

angel beds
USE **lits à la duchesse**

angel canopies
USE **canopies (bed components)**

angel lights
RT.970
ALT **angel light**
SN Small triangular lights between subordinate arches of the tracery of a window, found especially in the English Perpendicular Style. (HAS)
UF lights, angel
CN V.RT.AFU.ARI.AFU.AFU.BOK.ALO.ARI.AFU

anger
BM.572 (L,R)
UF rage
wrath
CN B.BM.BUE.ARI.AFU

Angevin Gothic
FL.3139
UF Gothic, Angevin
CN F.FL.ALO.BCW.ALO.ALO.AFU.BOK.ARI.BIQ.ALO.AFU

angiospermae
USE **flowers**

angiportus
RK.1529
SN Designates narrow, ancient Roman lanes, often leading to a dead end.
CN V.RK.ALO.ALO.BIQ.ARI.AFU.ALO.AFU.AFU.AFU

Angkor Thom
FL.2354
CN F.FL.ALO.ARI.BCW.ALO.ARI.ALO.AFU

Angkor Vat
FL.2357
CN F.FL.ALO.ARI.BCW.ALO.ARI.ALO.ALO

Angkorean
FL.2331 (A,L,B)
UF Khmer (Angkorean)
CN F.FL.ALO.ARI.BCW.ALO.ARI

angle arches, obtuse
USE **drop arches**

angle bars
USE **angles (rolled sections)**

angle bonds
TF.499
ALT **angle bond**
SN In masonry work, brick or metal ties used to bind the angles or corners of the walls together. (PUTNAM)
UF bonds, angle
CN V.TF.AFU.AFU.AFU.ALO.AFU.EWY.ALO

angle braces
RT.205
ALT **angle brace**
SN Any bars fixed across the inside of an angle in a framework in order to stiffen the framework. (PUTNAM)
UF angle ties
braces, angle
ties, angle
CN V.RT.AFU.AFU.AFU.AXC.DOI.AFU.AFU

angle braces (hand drills)
USE **hand drills**

angle brackets
RT.320
ALT **angle bracket**
SN Projecting brackets which are not at right angles to the wall. (DAC)
UF brackets, angle
CN V.RT.AFU.AFU.AFU.BCW.AXC.AFU

angle brick
MT.69
SN Any brick having an oblique shape to fit an oblique salient corner. (DAC)
UF brick, angle
CN M.MT.AFU.AFU.AFU.AXC.ALO.AFU.AFU.AFU.AFU

angle buttresses
RT.74
ALT **angle buttress**
SN Use for paired buttresses set at right angles, forming the corner of a structure.
UF buttresses, angle
CN V.RT.AFU.AFU.AFU.AXC.AXC.AFU.AFU

angle capitals
RT.118
ALT **angle capital**
SN Capitals at corner columns, especially Ionic capitals whose four volutes project equally on the diagonals instead of being in two parallel planes. (HAS)
UF capitals, angle
capitals, corner
corner capitals
CN V.RT.AFU.AFU.AFU.AXC.BIQ.ALO.ARI.AFU.ALO

angle chairs
USE **corner chairs**

angle cleats
TF.328
ALT **angle cleat**
SN Short sections of angle iron used to attach structural members, such as precast panels, to structural steel. (MEANS)
UF angle clips
cleats, angle
clips, angle
CN V.TF.AFU.AFU.AFU.ALO.AFU.ARI.AFU

angle clips
USE **angle cleats**

angle columns
RT.101
ALT **angle column**
SN Use for columns at the corner of a building or portico.
UF columns, angle
CN V.RT.AFU.AFU.AFU.AXC.BIQ.AFU.ALO.AFU

angle dozers
TB.34
ALT **angle dozer**
SN Bulldozers whose blades are set on an angle. (DAC)
UF angling dozers
dozers, angle
dozers, angling
CN V.TB.AFU.ARI.AFU.ARI.AFU.AFU

angle floats
TB.593
ALT **angle float**
SN Trowels with two surfaces meeting at a right angle; used to finish plaster or concrete in a corner. (MEANS)
UF floats, angle
CN V.TB.AFU.BCW.BCW.ALO.DIO.AFU

angle irons
USE **angles (rolled sections)**

angle joints
TF.573
ALT **angle joint**
SN Joints formed where two construction members meet at an angle. (PUTNAM)
UF joints, angle
CN V.TF.ALO.AFU.AFU

angle paddles
TB.564
ALT **angle paddle**
SN Hand tools used to finish a plastered surface. (DAC)
UF paddles, angle
CN V.TB.AFU.BCW.BCW.ALO.AFU

angle planes
TB.565
ALT **angle plane**
SN Plastering tools used to prepare surfaces for a finish coat by knocking down high spots, cleaning angles, and scraping. (PUTNAM)
UF planes, angle
CN V.TB.AFU.BCW.BCW.ALO.ALO

angle plows
TB.566
ALT **angle plow**
SN Plastering tools primarily used on inside corners to apply pressure to finish setting materials. (PUTNAM)
UF plows, angle
CN V.TB.AFU.BCW.BCW.ALO.ARI

angle rafters
USE **hip rafters**

angle ridges
USE **hip rafters**

angle saws
USE **dovetail saws**

angle stairs
USE **quarter-turn stairs**

angle ties
USE **angle braces**

angle trowels
USE **margin trowels**

angle views
USE **oblique views**

angles (mathematics)
BM.762 (L)
ALT **angled**
CN B.BM.CFS.ARI.AXC.AFU

angles (rolled sections)
RT.709
ALT **angle (rolled section)**
SN Metal beams with an L-shaped section.
UF angle bars
angle irons
bars, angle
irons, angle
CN V.RT.AFU.AFU.ALO.ARI.AFU

Anglican
BM.632 (L,B)
SN Use with regard to the Church of England; with regard to the Episcopal Church in America, use **Episcopal.**
CN B.BM.BZY.AFU.ALO.ARI.ALO

Anglican (Episcopal)
USE **Episcopal**

angling dozers
USE **angle dozers**

angling lodges
USE **fishing lodges**

Anglo-Chinoise
USE **Chinoiserie**

Anglo-Japanese
USE **Japonaiserie**

Anglo-Norman
FL.3118 (A)
CN F.FL.ALO.BCW.ALO.ALO.AFU.BOK.ARI.AFU

Anglo-Saxon
FL.3120 (A,L,B)
CN F.FL.ALO.BCW.ALO.ALO.AFU.BOK.ARI.ALO.AFU

Angoni
USE **Ngoni**

angora
MT.1817
CN M.MT.AFU.AFU.ARI.ALO.AFU.AFU.AFU.ALO

Angostura
FL.755
CN F.FL.ALO.ALO.ALO.AFU.AFU.ARI.ALO.ARI.ALO.ALO

angular
DC.55
CN D.DC.AFU.ARI.AFU

angular perspectives
USE **two-point perspectives**

Anguru
USE **Lomwe**

anhydrite white
MT.1745
UF white, anhydrite
CN M.MT.AFU.AFU.ARI.AFU.AFU.ALO.ALO.BOK.ALO.ARI

anhydrous alcohol
USE **absolute alcohol**

anhydrous gypsum plaster
MT.2440
UF class C gypsum plaster
gypsum plaster, anhydrous

gypsum plaster, class C
plaster, anhydrous gypsum
plaster, class C gypsum
CN M.MT.AFU.ARI.CRG.AFU.AXC.AFU.AXC.AFU

anhydrous lime
USE **quicklime**

aniconism
BM.342 (R)
SN Use generally for opposition to the use of idols. For more vehement movements against religious images, use **iconoclasm.**
CN B.BM.ALO.ALO.CLM.ALO

anilin
USE **aniline dye**

aniline black
MT.1579 (L)
UF black, aniline
CN M.MT.AFU.AFU.ARI.AFU.AFU.ALO.ALO.AFU.ARI.AFU

aniline black (color)
USE **dark grayish purple**
dark purplish gray

aniline blue, dark
USE **dark grayish blue**
dark grayish purple

aniline dye
MT.1539 (L)
SN Dye produced from aniline, a poisonous, oily liquid.(WCOL) Used to make the earliest synthetic dyes. (MAYER)
UF anilin
dye, aniline
CN M.MT.AFU.AFU.ARI.AFU.AFU.AFU.AFU.ALO.ALO

aniline printing
USE **aniline process**

aniline process
KT.318 (L)
SN A photographic process usually used for reproducing technical drawings. The image is formed using aniline dyes and appears blue-black.
UF aniline printing
printing, aniline
CN K.KT.AFU.ALO.DUC.DIO.ALO.ARI

aniline purple
USE **mauve**

aniline violet
USE **light violet**
mauve

aniline yellow
USE **deep yellow**

animal blood albumin
USE **albumin glue**

animal cemeteries
USE **pet cemeteries**

animal fiber
MT.1815 (L)
UF fiber, animal
CN M.MT.AFU.AFU.ARI.ALO.AFU.AFU.AFU

animal glue
USE **animal size**

animal homes
USE **animal shelters**

animal hospitals
USE **veterinary hospitals**

animal housing
RK.77 (A,L,B)
UF animal shelters (farm structures)
buildings, livestock
housing, animal
livestock buildings
shelters, animal (farm structures)
CN V.RK.AFU.ALO.ALO.AFU.ALO

animal materials
MT.910 (L)
SN Use for materials of animal origin.
UF materials, animal
CN M.MT.AFU.AFU.ALO.AFU

animal oil
MT.1983 (L)
UF oil, animal
CN M.MT.AFU.AFU.ARI.ARI.AFU.AFU

animal painters
HG.107 (L)
ALT **animal painter**
UF painters, animal
CN H.HG.AFU.AXC.AXC.AFU.AFU.ALO.AXC.CXA.AFU.AFU

animal parks
USE **wild animal parks**

animal pigment
MT.1556 (L)
UF pigment, animal
CN M.MT.AFU.AFU.ARI.AFU.AFU.ALO.AFU.ALO.AFU.AFU

animal pounds
USE **animal shelters**

animal-powered engines
TB.388 (L)
ALT **animal-powered engine**
UF engines, animal-powered
CN V.TB.AFU.ARI.DOI.ALO.AFU

animal sculptors
HG.137 (L)
ALT **animal sculptor**
UF sculptors, animal
CN H.HG.AFU.AXC.AXC.AFU.AFU.ALO.AXC.DZW.AFU

animal shelters
RK.786 (L,B)
ALT **animal shelter**
UF animal homes
animal pounds
estrays
homes, animal
pounds
pounds, animal
shelters, animal
CN V.RK.AFU.ALO.ALO.CXA.ALO.ALO.ALO

animal shelters (farm structures)
USE **animal housing**

animal size
MT.2729 (L)
SN An animal glue or gelatin used for surface-sizing the higher grades of paper. (W)
UF animal glue
glue, animal
size, animal
CN M.MT.AFU.ARI.IFM.BOK.AFU

Animal Style
FL.3019
CN F.FL.ALO.AXC.ARI.BIQ.ALO.AFU

animal wax
MT.2188
UF wax, animal
CN M.MT.AFU.AFU.ARI.BZY.AFU

Animalier
FL.3372 (L)
CN F.FL.ALO.BCW.ALO.AXC.DIO.BCW.BCW.AFU

animation
KT.172 (L,R)
ALT **animated**
CN K.KT.AFU.ALO.DUC.AFU

animation, computer
USE **computer animation**

animators
HG.82 (L)
ALT **animator**
SN Persons who contribute to the production of an animated cartoon or other animation, as by making drawings. (W)
CN H.HG.AFU.AXC.AXC.AFU.AFU.ALO.AFU

anime
USE **East African copal**

animism
BM.696 (L,R)
CN B.BM.BZY.ALO.ARI.ARI

anisometric projections
USE **trimetric drawings**

ankhs
DG.6
ALT **ankh**
SN Figures like a cross having a loop instead of an upper vertical, used especially in ancient Egypt as a symbol of life. (W)

UF ansate crosses
crosses, ansate
crosses, Egyptian
cruces ansatae
Egyptian crosses
keys of life
life, keys of
CN D.DG.AFU.AFU.ARI.AFU

Ankole
USE Nkole

Ankwe
USE Goemai

annals
USE **chronicles**

Annamese
FL.2435
CN F.FL.ALO.ARI.BCW.BUE.ALO.AFU

annatto
MT.1761 (L)
UF orlean
terra orellana
CN M.MT.AFU.AFU.ARI.AFU.AFU.ALO.
ALO.BUE.ALO.AFU

annealing
KT.732
ALT **annealed**
SN Process by which materials, such as metal and glass, are softened and made workable by heating. (THDAT)
CN K.KT.AFU.ALO.GWW.ARI.AFU

annexes
RM.2
ALT **annex**
SN Use for subsidiary supplementary structures, whether additions to a main building or separate from it, but usually visibly distinct and often with a separate entrance.
CN V.RM.AFU.AFU

annexing
KG.177 (L)
SN Including or appropriating an area within the limits of a governmental unit. (W)
CN K.KG.AFU.ALO.ARI.AFU

anniversaries
KM.6 (L)
CN K.KM.AFU.ALO.AFU

annotated bibliographies
VW.255
ALT **annotated bibliography**
SN Bibliographies with notes added to the entries to elucidate, evaluate, or describe the subject and contents of the entries.
UF bibliographies, annotated
CN V.VW.AFU.AFU.AFU.FZU.BCW.AFU.
ALO.AFU

annotations
VW.304 (B)
ALT **annotation**
SN Notes added as comment or explanation to manuscripts, catalogs, reading lists, or other printed works. (GAHLM)
UF notations
CN V.VW.AFU.AFU.ALO.BCW.AFU

announcements
VW.314 (N)
ALT **announcement**
SN Printed or published statements or notices that inform the reader of an event or other news.
UF notices
CN V.VW.AFU.AFU.ALO.BOK.AFU

announcements of bidding
USE **bidding announcements**

announcements, bidding
USE **bidding announcements**

announcements, business
USE **business announcements**

announcers
HG.281
ALT **announcer**
SN Persons who introduce television or radio programs, often act as masters of ceremonies, make commercial announcements, and read brief items such as news summaries and sports reviews. (W)
CN H.HG.AFU.AXC.BCW.ALO.AFU.
AFU

annual indexes
VW.434
ALT **annual index**
UF indexes, annual
CN V.VW.AFU.AFU.ALO.EWY.BOK.
ALO.AFU

annual reports
VW.457 (L)
ALT **annual report**
SN Documentation summarizing the activities of an organization over the course of a year.
UF reports, annual
CN V.VW.AFU.AFU.ALO.FIM.AFU.ALO.
AXC

annual reports of corporations
USE **corporation reports**

annuals
VW.612 (L)
ALT **annual**
SN Use generally for yearly publications.
CN V.VW.AFU.ALO.AFU.CXA.AFU.AFU

annuals (plants)
RD.265 (L)
ALT **annual (plant)**
SN Designates plants that complete their cycle from seed to seed in a single year. (ALLABY)
CN V.RD.ARI.AFU.BCW.ALO.ALO.ALO.
AFU.AFU

annular
DC.56
SN Ringlike; composed of ringlike sections. (THDAT)
UF ring-shaped
CN D.DC.AFU.ARI.ALO

annular bits
USE **tenon-cutting bits**

annular moldings
USE **roll moldings**

annular nails
USE **ring-shank nails**

annular ring nails
USE **ring-shank nails**

annular vaults
RT.538
ALT **annular vault**
SN Barrel vaults in the shape of a ring. (HAS)
UF vaults, annular
CN V.RT.AFU.AFU.AFU.BIQ.BOK.AFU.
ALO.AFU.AFU

annulated columns
RT.85
ALT **annulated column**
SN Use for columns or clusters of shafts encircled by rings, common in Medieval architecture.
UF columns, annulated
CN V.RT.AFU.AFU.AFU.AXC.BIQ.AFU.
AFU.AFU

annulets
RT.776
ALT **annulet**
SN Small moldings encircling a shaft and usually square or angular in section. (HAS)
UF bandelets
CN V.RT.AFU.ALO.AFU.BOK.AFU.AFU.
AXC.AXC.AFU

anodizing
KT.839 (L,B)
ALT **anodized**
SN Process in which the surface of a metal is coated with a protective or decorative layer through electrolytic action.
CN K.KT.AFU.ALO.HOE.BCW.ALO.
BCW.AFU

anonymous architecture
USE **vernacular architecture**

ansate crosses
USE **ankhs**

antae
RT.189
ALT **anta**
SN Piers produced by the thickening of walls at their termination. (W)

CN V.RT.AFU.AFU.AFU.AXC.CRG.AFU.
ALO.AFU

Antandroy
FL.555 (L)
CN F.FL.ALO.AFU.AXC.ARI.ARI.AFU

Antanosy
FL.556
CN F.FL.ALO.AFU.AXC.ARI.ARI.ALO

antecabinets
USE **anterooms**

antechambers
USE **anterooms**

antechoirs
RM.302
ALT **antechoir**
SN Spaces of a divided choir farthest from the sanctuary. (W)
UF choirs, fore
fore choirs
CN V.RM.AFU.DIO.AXC.ALO.AFU.ALO

antecourts
USE **forecourts**

antefixes
RT.1049 (N)
ALT **antefixe**
SN Use for small ornaments at the ridge or eaves of a roof, in classical architecture and derivatives, that close or conceal the open end of a row of roofing tiles.
CN V.RT.AFU.BCW.ALO

antemurals
USE **outworks**

antenna systems, television
USE **television antenna systems**

antependia
USE **altar frontals**

anterooms
RM.133
ALT **anteroom**
SN Rooms preceding or serving as a lobby or means of access to another and more important room. (RS)
UF antecabinets
antechambers
CN V.RM.AFU.DIO.ALO.BOK.AFU

anthemions
DG.52
ALT **anthemion**
SN Use for series of conventionalized flower and foliage motifs, usually palmettes alternating with lotus, or other similar forms having lobe or leaf shapes radiating from a base. Sometimes used for individual such motifs. Found in Greek and later classicizing styles.
UF honeysuckle motifs
motifs, honeysuckle
CN D.DG.AFU.AFU.DIO.ALO

anthocyanin
MT.1558 (L)
CN M.MT.AFU.AFU.ARI.AFU.AFU.ALO.
AFU.ALO.AFU.ALO.AFU

anthologies
VW.10 (L)
ALT **anthology**
SN Collections of choice extracts, from the writings of one author, or various authors, and usually having a common characteristic such as subject matter or literary form. (LG)
CN V.VW.AFU.AFU.AFU.AXC.AFU

anthracene green
USE **moderate bluish green**

anthracene purple
USE **dark grayish purple**
dark purplish red

anthracene violet
USE **moderate violet**

anthracene violet, dark
USE **dark purple**

anthracite
MT.993 (L)
UF anthracite coal
coal, anthracite
CN M.MT.AFU.AFU.ALO.ARI.AFU

anthracite coal
USE **anthracite**

anthropological archaeologists
HG.256
ALT **anthropological archaeologist**
UF archaeologists, anthropological
CN H.HG.AFU.AXC.BCW.AFU.ALO.
AFU

anthropological archaeology
KD.102
UF archaeology, anthropological
CN K.KD.AFU.ALO.ALO.AFU

anthropological linguistics
KD.34 (L)
SN Study of speech communities, particularly those with no writing system, by the application of anthropological and linguistic techniques. (ERIC)
UF anthropology, linguistic
linguistic anthropology
linguistics, anthropological
CN K.KD.AFU.AFU.AXC.AFU.AFU.AFU

anthropologists
HG.251 (L)
ALT **anthropologist**
CN H.HG.AFU.AXC.BCW.AFU.AFU

anthropologists, cultural
USE **social anthropologists**

anthropologists, physical
USE **physical anthropologists**

anthropologists, social
USE **social anthropologists**

anthropology
KD.90 (L,R)
CN K.KD.AFU.ALO.AFU

anthropology museums
RK.413 (L,B)
ALT **anthropology museum**
UF museums, anthropology
CN V.RK.AFU.ALO.ALO.BCW.AXC.ARI.
CFS.AFU

anthropology of religion
KD.75
UF religion, anthropology of
CN K.KD.AFU.AFU.BUE.AFU.AFU

anthropology, cultural
USE **social anthropology**

anthropology, demographic
USE **demographic anthropology**

anthropology, linguistic
USE **anthropological linguistics**

anthropology, philosophical
USE **philosophical anthropology**

anthropology, physical
USE **physical anthropology**

anthropology, psychological
USE **ethnopsychology**

anthropology, social
USE **social anthropology**

anthropology, structural
USE **structural anthropology**

anthropometrics
USE **anthropometry**

anthropometry
KD.97 (L,B)
SN Study of human body measurements on a comparative basis. (W)
UF anthropometrics
CN K.KD.AFU.ALO.AFU.BIQ.AFU

anthropomorphic
DC.114
SN Resembling a human form. (RHDEL2)
CN D.DC.AFU.ARI.FCS.ALO

anthropomorphism
BM.506 (A,L,R)
SN Interpretation of what is not human in terms of human characteristics. (W)
CN B.BM.BIQ.AXC.ARI

anthroposophy
BM.710 (L,R)
SN 20th-century spiritual and mystical doctrine centering on human development, deriving mainly from the religious ideology theosophy.
CN B.BM.BZY.ALO.ARI.DOI.AFU

Anti
USE **Campa**

anti-art
BM.189
SN Use to describe work which has the character of art, but which mocks or challenges preconceptions about the nature of art. (THDAT)
CN B.BM.AFU.AFU.AXC.CLM.ARI

Anti-form
USE **Post-Minimal**

anti-freeze solutions
USE **antifreeze**

antiabrasion layer
USE **supercoat**

antibacterial paint
USE **antifouling paint**

anticorrosives
USE **corrosion inhibitors**

antifoamers
USE **antifoaming agents**

antifoaming agents
MT.2305 (L)
UF agents, antifoaming
antifoamers
CN M.MT.AFU.ARI.ALO.AXC

antifouling paint
MT.2539 (L)
UF antibacterial paint
mold-resistant paint
paint, antibacterial
paint, antifouling
paint, mold-resistant
CN M.MT.AFU.ARI.CRG.ALO.BCW.ARI.AFU

antifreeze
MT.2306 (L)
UF anti-freeze solutions
antifreeze compounds
compounds, antifreeze
solutions, anti-freeze
CN M.MT.AFU.ARI.ALO.BCW

antifreeze compounds
USE **antifreeze**

antifriction bolts
USE **antifriction latch bolts**

antifriction latch bolts
TF.549
ALT **antifriction latch bolt**
UF antifriction bolts
bolts, antifriction latch
latch bolts, antifriction
CN V.TF.AFU.ALO.AXC.AFU.AFU

antimony
MT.431 (L)
SN Bluish white metal used in alloys and widely used in pigments. (MH)
UF Sb
stibium
CN M.MT.AFU.AFU.AFU.BZY.AFU.AFU.ARI.ALO

antimony orange
MT.1696 (L)
UF antimony red
orange, antimony
red, antimony
CN M.MT.AFU.AFU.ARI.AFU.AFU.ALO.ALO.BCW.ARI.AFU

antimony oxide
MT.1728
UF oxide, antimony
CN M.MT.AFU.AFU.ARI.AFU.AFU.ALO.ALO.BOK.AFU.AFU

antimony red
USE **antimony orange**

antimony vermilion
MT.1682
UF vermilion, antimony
CN M.MT.AFU.AFU.ARI.AFU.AFU.ALO.ALO.BCW.AFU.AXC.AFU

antimony white
MT.1729
UF timonox
white, antimony
CN M.MT.AFU.AFU.ARI.AFU.AFU.ALO.ALO.BOK.AFU.ALO

antimony yellow
USE **Naples yellow**
moderate orange yellow

antioxidants
MT.2307 (L)
SN Substances that oppose or inhibit oxidation. (W)
CN M.MT.AFU.ARI.ALO.BIQ

antiparabemata
RM.305
ALT **antiparabema**
SN Chapels at the west end of Byzantine churches, especially of the Armenian type.
CN V.RM.AFU.DIO.AXC.ALO.AFU.AXC.AFU

Antiplano
USE **Puná**

antiquarianism
BM.343 (R)
SN Interest in or devotion to things of the past, especially of ancient times. The term implies admiration of a style or object simply because it is old. (MAYER)
CN B.BM.ALO.ALO.CLM.ARI

antiquaries
HG.707 (B)
ALT **antiquary**
SN Experts on, or students or collectors of, antiquities. (RHDEL2)
CN H.HG.AFU.BCW.ALO

antique green (marble)
USE **verd antique**

antique porphyry, red
USE **red antique porphyry**

antique shops
USE **antique stores**

antique stores
RK.150 (A,L)
ALT **antique store**
UF antique shops
shops, antique
stores, antique
CN V.RK.AFU.ALO.ALO.ALO.ARI.BIQ.AFU.AFU

Antique, Late
USE **Late Antique**

Antique, the
BM.286
SN Use generally to mean belonging to or after the manner of ancient Greece or Rome. Use specifically to refer to those aspects of classical art, particularly the representation of the human figure in ancient sculpture and also the use of ornament in ancient art, when they are used as models of perfection in other periods.
UF the Antique
CN B.BM.AFU.AXC.AFU

antiques
VB.83 (L)
ALT **antique**
CN V.VB.ALO.AFU

antiquing
KT.257
ALT **antiqued**
SN The process of finishing or refinishing so as to give the appearance of age to an object. (W)
CN K.KT.AFU.ALO.DUC.CXA.ALO.BCW.ALO.AFU

antisemitism
BM.1105 (L,R)
CN B.BM.CRG.BCW.ARI.ALO

antiseptics
MT.2376 (L)
ALT **antiseptic**
CN M.MT.AFU.ARI.BOK.ALO.AFU

antistatic agents
MT.2364 (L)
SN Materials that prevent build-up or promote discharge of static electricity, as in films or textiles. (MH)
UF agents, antistatic
CN M.MT.AFU.ARI.AXC

antler
MT.913 (L,R)
CN M.MT.AFU.AFU.ALO.AFU.ALO

Antonine
FL.2723 (R)
CN F.FL.ALO.AXC.ALO.ALO.AFU.AXC.ALO.BOK

Antwerp blue
MT.1610
SN Pale variety of Prussian blue. (MAYER)
UF blue, Antwerp
blue, Haarlem
blue, mineral
Haarlem blue
mineral blue
CN M.MT.AFU.AFU.ARI.AFU.AFU.ALO.ALO.ALO.AXC.AXC.AFU

Antwerp blue (color)
USE **dark blue**
grayish blue

Anuradhapura
FL.2305
CN F.FL.ALO.ARI.AXC.ARI.AFU

anvil cutters
USE **hardies**

anvil tongs
USE **pickup tongs**

anvils
TB.647 (N)
ALT **anvil**
SN Heavy, usually steel or iron blocks on which metal is shaped by hand hammering or forging. (W)
CN V.TB.AFU.BCW.BIQ.AFU.ALO.AFU.AFU

anvils, bench
USE **bench anvils**

anvils, stake
USE **stakes**

anxiety
BM.573 (L,R)
CN B.BM.BUE.ARI.ALO

Anyang (Nigerian)
FL.236
UF Banyangi
CN F.FL.ALO.AFU.AXC.AFU.ALO.AFU.ALO

Anyang (Shang style)
FL.1858
UF An-yang
Yinxu
CN F.FL.ALO.ARI.ALO.AFU.AFU.ALO.BCW.ALO.AFU

Anyi
FL.285 (L)
UF Agni
CN F.FL.ALO.AFU.AXC.AFU.ARI.AFU.AFU.ALO

Ao Kutani
FL.2026
UF Green Kutani
Kutani, Ao
Kutani, Green
CN F.FL.ALO.ARI.ALO.ALO.ALO.ALO.ALO.CFS.AFU

Aoba
USE **Oba**

Aona
USE **Ona**

Aowin
FL.286 (L)
UF Brisa
CN F.FL.ALO.AFU.AXC.AFU.ARI.AFU.AFU.ALO.AFU

Apache
FL.1448 (L)
CN F.FL.ALO.ALO.ARI.AFU.CFS.AFU

Apache, Chiricahua
USE **Chiricahua Apache**

Apache, Eastern
USE **Eastern Apache**

Apache, Jicarilla
USE **Jicarilla Apache**

Apache, Kiowa
USE **Kiowa Apache**

Apache, Lipan
USE **Lipan Apache**

Apache, Mescalero
USE **Mescalero Apache**

Apache, Mohave
USE **Yavapai**

Apache, Western
USE **Western Apache**

Apalai
FL.1569 (L)
CN F.FL.ALO.ALO.ARI.ARI.AFU.ALO

apartment buildings
USE **apartment houses**

apartment hotels
RK.361 (A,B)
ALT **apartment hotel**
SN Hotels providing apartments, usually furnished, to long-term tenants and including some services not available to the general public. (DDT)
UF hotels, apartment
hotels, residential
residential hotels
CN V.RK.AFU.ALO.ALO.AXC.AXC.AFU

apartment houses
RK.362 (A,L,B,R)
ALT **apartment house**
UF apartment buildings
blocks of flats
buildings, apartment
flats, blocks of
houses, apartment
CN V.RK.AFU.ALO.ALO.AXC.AXC.ALO

apartment houses, cooperative
USE **cooperative apartment houses**

apartments
RM.264 (A,L,N,B)
ALT **apartment**
SN Use for rooms or sets of rooms used as dwellings and located in private houses, hotels, or within apartment houses.
CN V.RM.AFU.DIO.ARI.ALO.BIQ.AFU

apartments, bachelor
USE **studio apartments**

apartments, cooperative
USE **cooperative apartment houses**

apartments, duplex
USE **duplex apartments**

apartments, efficiency
USE **studio apartments**

apartments, garden
USE **garden apartments**

apartments, model
USE **model apartments**

apartments, railroad
USE **railroad flats**

apartments, studio
USE **studio apartments**

apatite
MT.487 (L)
SN A mineral commonly used as a source of phosphorus, containing up to 20% phosphorus pentoxide with iron oxide and lime. (MH)
CN M.MT.AFU.AFU.AFU.CFS.AFU.AFU

Apennine
FL.2700
UF Extra Terramaricolan
CN F.FL.ALO.AXC.ALO.ALO.AFU.AFU.AFU

aperture cards
VW.669
ALT **aperture card**
SN Cards with one or more openings into each of which is mounted a frame cut from a strip of microfilm. (LG)
UF cards, aperture
cards, image
cards, peephole
image cards
peephole cards
CN V.VW.AFU.ALO.AFU.DZW.AXC.ALO.AFU

Aphrodisian
FL.2760
UF School of Aphrodisias
CN F.FL.ALO.AXC.ALO.ALO.ALO.BZY.AFU.AFU

apiaries
RK.78 (N,B)
ALT **apiary**
UF bee houses
houses, bee
mellaria
CN V.RK.AFU.ALO.ALO.AFU.ALO.AFU

apocalyptic art
BM.232 (L,R)
SN Use for any art which deals with the final doom or ultimate destiny of the world, including that in the Biblical story of Armaggedon in the Book of Revelation.
UF art, apocalyptic
CN B.BM.AFU.ARI.BCW.ARI

apodyteria
RM.73
ALT **apodyterium**
SN Rooms in Greek or Roman baths, or in palaestrae, where the bathers or those taking part in gymnastic exercises undressed and dressed. (HAS)
UF gymnasteria
CN V.RM.AFU.DIO.ALO.ALO.BOK.AFU

Apono
USE **Punu**

apophyges
RT.144
ALT **apophyge**
SN In columns, concave sweep where the shaft springs from the base or terminates in the capital; also, hollows or scotias beneath the echinus of some Archaic Doric capitals.
UF apotheses
conges
scapes
CN V.RT.AFU.AFU.AFU.AXC.BIQ.ALO.AXC.ALO.AFU

apothecae
RM.185
ALT **apotheca**
SN Use for ancient Greek or Roman storerooms.
CN V.RM.AFU.DIO.ALO.DCU.AFU

apothecaries
USE **drugstores**

apotheses
USE **apophyges**

Appalachee
FL.887
CN F.FL.ALO.ALO.ALO.AFU.ALO.ALO.BOK.AFU

apparatus, drying
USE **dryers**

apparatus, photographic
USE **photographic equipment**

appareilles
RT.1173
ALT **appareille**
SN Use for the slopes of or ascents to the platforms of bastions.
CN V.RT.AFU.BUE.AFU.ALO.ALO.AFU

appentices
RM.3
ALT **appentice**
SN Use to designate minor structures built against the sides of buildings with roofs of single slope. For freestanding structures of this type, use **lean-tos.**
UF pentices
pents
CN V.RM.AFU.ALO

apple, common
USE **applewood**

apple, wild
USE **applewood**

applewood
MT.1261
UF apple, common
apple, wild
common apple
malus
Pyrus malus
wild apple
CN M.MT.AFU.AFU.ALO.BIQ.DCU.AFU.AFU.AFU.JOC.AFU

application forms
VW.117
ALT **application form**
SN Forms used by persons requesting assistance, authorization, employment, admission, or other action.
UF forms, application
CN V.VW.AFU.AFU.AFU.FZU.ARI.AFU

applications, job
USE **job applications**

applications, marriage
USE **marriage applications**

applied arts
USE **decorative arts**

applied linguistics
KD.33 (L)
SN Application of the findings of linguistic science to practical language problems, such as language teaching, lexicography, translation, and speech therapy. (ERIC)
UF linguistics, applied
CN K.KD.AFU.AFU.AXC.AFU.AFU

applied mathematics
KD.252
UF mathematics, applied
CN K.KD.AFU.ARI.CFS.ALO

applied moldings
RT.754
ALT **applied molding**
SN Moldings which are nailed, laid on, or otherwise fastened to the work rather than cut into the solid material. (HAS)
UF moldings, applied
moldings, planted
planted moldings
CN V.RT.AFU.ALO.AFU.BOK.AFU.AFU.AFU

applied physics
KD.283
UF physics, applied
CN K.KD.AFU.ARI.CLM.AXC.ALO

applied science
USE **technology**

applied work
USE **appliqué**

appliqué
KT.558 (L,R)
ALT **appliquéd**
UF applied work
appliquéing
CN K.KT.AFU.ALO.ELK.DUC.ALO.AFU

appliquéing
USE **appliqué**

appointing
KG.150 (L)
SN Naming to or placing in an office or position. (RHDEL2)
CN K.KG.AFU.AFU.BIQ.BUE.AFU

appointment books
VW.494
ALT **appointment book**
SN Books for recording engagements; usually containing calendars.
UF books, appointment
books, date
date books
CN V.VW.AFU.ALO.AFU.AFU.AFU.ARI

apportioning
KG.178 (L)
ALT **apportioned**
CN K.KG.AFU.ALO.ARI.ALO

appraisals
VW.814 (L,B)
ALT **appraisal**
SN Printed or written statements of evaluation or estimate of the market or other value, cost, utility or other attribute of land, buildings, works of art, or other objects of property, by qualified persons.
CN V.VW.AFU.ARI.AFU.BIQ.AFU

appraisers
HG.398 (L)
ALT **appraiser**
SN Persons who engage in appraising.
UF evaluators
CN H.HG.AFU.AXC.BOK.ALO

appraising
KG.44 (L,B)

SN Determining an item's market value, as done by the estimate of an authorized person.
UF valuation
CN K.KG.AFU.AFU.ARI.AFU

appreciation, art
USE **art appreciation**

apprehension
USE **perception**

apprentices
HG.774 (L,B,R)
ALT **apprentice**
SN Persons who learn by practical experience under skilled workers a trade or art, usually for a prescribed period of time and for a prescribed compensation. (W)
CN H.HG.AFU.BIQ.CLM.AFU

apprenticeship agreements
USE **articles of apprenticeship**

apprenticeship, articles of
USE **articles of apprenticeship**

approach roads
USE **access roads**

approaches, bridge
USE **bridge approaches**

appropriate technology
BM.1134 (L,B)
UF alternative technology
intermediate technology
technology, alternative
technology, appropriate
technology, intermediate
CN B.BM.CXA.AFU.AFU

approved schools
USE **reformatories**

approximate symmetry
BM.94
SN The use of similar forms around a center of balance. The forms may give a feeling of equal relationships, but are varied to prevent visual monotony.
UF dynamic symmetry
symmetry, approximate
symmetry, dynamic
CN B.BM.AFU.AFU.ARI.AFU.FOG.AFU

apricot
MT.1286 (L)
CN M.MT.AFU.AFU.ALO.BIQ.DCU.AFU.AFU.AFU.KLE.ALO

apricot gum
MT.1049
SN A clear, pale gum that exudes from apricot trees. (MAYER)
UF gum, apricot
CN M.MT.AFU.AFU.ALO.BIQ.BUE.AXC.AFU

apron pieces
RT.1099
ALT **apron piece**
SN Horizontal wood beams, fixed into a wall and projecting horizontally, that support the ends of carriage pieces and joists at the landings of wood staircases.
UF pieces, apron
pieces, pitching
pitching pieces
CN V.RT.AFU.BIQ.AXC.ALO.AFU

apron pieces (furniture components)
USE **aprons (furniture components)**

apron stages
USE **forestages**

aprons (furniture components)
TG.807 (N)
ALT **apron (furniture component)**
SN Extensions below the bottom edge of the seat of a chair, or frame of a table or cabinet. (BEARD)
UF apron pieces (furniture components)
lambrequins
pieces, apron (furniture components)
skirts (furniture components)
CN V.TG.ALO.AFU

aprons (stages)
USE **forestages**

apse aisles
USE **ambulatories**

apses
RM.254 (A,L,B,R)
ALT **apse**
SN Use for semicircular or polygonal extensions off of a larger space; common in Roman basilicas and Christian churches.
UF tribunes (apses)
CN V.RM.AFU.DIO.ARI.ALO.AFU

apses, counter
USE **counter apses**

apsidal buildings
RK.16 (A,B)
ALT **apsidal building**
UF buildings, apsidal
CN V.RK.AFU.ALO.AFU.ALO.AFU

apsidioles
RM.255
ALT **apsidiole**
SN Small apses, especially those which project from a larger apse.
CN V.RM.AFU.DIO.ARI.ALO.AFU.AFU

Apulian
FL.2632 (L)
CN F.FL.ALO.AXC.ALO.AFU.ALO.AXC.ALO.BIQ.AFU

Aq Qoyunlu
USE **Akkoyunlu**

aqua
USE **light bluish green**
light greenish blue

aqua ammonia
USE **ammonia water**

aqua blue
USE **light greenish blue**
very light greenish blue

aqua blue, light
USE **pale blue**
very light greenish blue

aqua blue, pale
USE **very pale blue**

aqua fortis
MT.2721
SN Latin for nitric acid, a colorless to reddish liquid, which is highly corrosive and caustic, having a wide variety of uses for pickling metals, etching, and in the manufacture of plastics and dyestuffs. (MH)
CN M.MT.AFU.ARI.IFM.ARI.AFU

aqua gray
USE **bluish gray**
grayish blue
light bluish gray
pale green

aqua green
USE **light bluish green**
light greenish blue

aqua green, bright
USE **brilliant bluish green**
light bluish green
very light bluish green

aqua green, light
USE **pale green**
very light bluish green

aqua green, pale
USE **very light bluish green**
very pale green

aqua regia
MT.299
SN Acid used for dissolving or testing gold and platinum; consisting of three parts hydrochloric acid and one part nitric acid. (MH)
CN M.MT.AFU.AFU.AFU.BOK.AFU.AXC.AFU

aqua, bright
USE **brilliant bluish green**
light bluish green
light greenish blue
very light greenish blue

aqua, light
USE **pale blue**
pale green
very light greenish blue

aqua, pale
USE **very pale blue**
very pale green

aquamarine
MT.491
CN M.MT.AFU.AFU.AFU.CFS.AFU.AXC.AFU

aquamarine (color)
USE **light greenish blue**
pale blue

aquamarine green
USE **moderate bluish green**

aquarelle
KT.240
SN Use for watercolor painting done in transparent washes of color as distinguished from the opaque method using gouache.
CN K.KT.AFU.ALO.DUC.CXA.ALO.ALO.AFU

aquariums
RK.372 (A,L,N,B,R)
ALT **aquarium**
UF aquariums, public
public aquariums
CN V.RK.AFU.ALO.ALO.BCW.AFU.AFU

aquariums, marine
USE **marine aquariums**

aquariums, public
USE **aquariums**

aquariums, saltwater
USE **marine aquariums**

Aquarius symbols
DG.74 (R)
ALT **Aquarius symbol**
CN D.DG.AFU.AFU.ERE.AFU

aquatint
KT.457 (L,R)
SN An etching process in which a mordant acid is made to bite both lines and tonal areas in the plate. (PDAT)
CN K.KT.AFU.ALO.DUC.DUC.ALO.BCW.AFU.AXC.AFU

aquatint etching, lift-ground
USE **lift-ground**

aquatint (photography)
USE **photoaquatint**

aquatint photogravure
USE **photoaquatint**

aquatint process
USE **photoaquatint**

aquatint, lift-ground
USE **lift-ground**

aquatint, sugar-lift
USE **lift-ground**

aqueduct bridges
USE **aqueducts**

aqueducts
RK.570 (A,L,B,R)
ALT **aqueduct**
SN Use for artificial water channels for carrying water over long distances, usually by means of gravity, and for bridgelike structures that carry the channel or canal across a valley, river, or other obstacle.
UF aqueduct bridges
aqueducts, canal
bridges, aqueduct
bridges, canal
canal aqueducts
canal bridges
CN V.RK.AFU.ALO.ALO.CFS.ALO.BCW.AFU

aqueducts, canal
USE **aqueducts**

aqueous ammonia
USE **ammonia water**

Aquia Creek sandstone
MT.725
UF Aquia sandstone
sandstone, Aquia
sandstone, Aquia Creek
CN M.MT.AFU.AFU.AFU.DCU.AFU.ALO.AFU.ARI.AFU.ALO.BIQ.ALO

Aquia sandstone
USE **Aquia Creek sandstone**

aquifers
RD.143 (L)
ALT **aquifer**
CN V.RD.ARI.AFU.AFU.AFU.ALO.AFU

arabesques
DG.103 (A,L,R)
SN Decorative patterns of stylized foliage characterized by a continuous stem which splits regularly, producing a series of counterpoised, leafy, secondary stems.(AIW) Used also generally for allover patterns of fanciful foliate scrollwork.
UF rumi
waqwaq
CN D.DG.AFU.ARI.ALO.AFU

Arabian
FL.2880 (L,B)
CN F.FL.ALO.AXC.ARI.ALO

Arabic arches
USE **horseshoe arches**

arabic tree, gum
USE **Acacia**

arabic, gum
USE **gum arabic**

arable land
RD.283
UF land, arable
CN V.RD.ARI.ALO.AFU.AFU.AFU

arachis oil
USE **peanut oil**

arae
RK.1084
ALT **ara**
SN Ancient Roman altars.
CN V.RK.AFU.ALO.ALO.FCS.AFU.AFU

Aranda
USE **Arunta**

Arapaho
FL.1369 (L)
CN F.FL.ALO.ALO.ARI.AFU.BOK.AFU

arariba
USE **balaustre**

Araucanian
FL.1617 (L)
UF Mapuche
CN F.FL.ALO.ALO.ARI.ARI.ALO.ALO.AFU

Arawak
FL.1562 (L)
CN F.FL.ALO.ALO.ARI.ALO.BUE.AFU

arbitrating
KG.8 (L,B)
SN Determining disputes, as done by one or more outside, disinterested parties. (OCLD)
CN K.KG.AFU.AFU.AFU.ARI

arbitrators
HG.313 (L,B)
ALT **arbitrator**
CN H.HG.AFU.AXC.BCW.ALO.BIQ.AFU

arbitrators, industrial
USE **industrial arbitrators**

arbor-vitae
USE **American arbor vitae**

arbor vitae, American
USE **American arbor vitae**

arboretums
RK.1417 (A,L,B,R)
ALT **arboretum**
CN V.RK.ALO.AFU.AFU.ALO.AFU

arbors
RK.1329 (A,R)
ALT **arbor**
SN Designates light, open structures formed from trees, shrubs, or vines closely planted and twined together to be self-supporting or supported on a latticework frame.
CN V.RK.AFU.ALO.ARI.AFU.AFU

arc brazing
KT.791
SN Brazing with an electric arc, that is, the electrical discharge between two electrodes.
UF brazing, arc
CN K.KT.AFU.ALO.HOE.BCW.ALO.AFU.AFU.AFU.AFU

arc welders
USE **arc welding machines**

arc welding
KT.801 (L,B)
SN The joining of metal parts by fusion in which the necessary heat is produced by means of an electric arc, that is, the electrical discharge between two electrodes. (DAC)
UF electric arc welding
electrical arc welding
welding, arc
welding, electric arc
CN K.KT.AFU.ALO.HOE.BCW.ALO.AFU.ALO.ALO.AFU

arc-welding equipment
USE **arc welding machines**

arc welding machines
TB.742 (L,N)
ALT **arc welding machine**
UF arc welders
arc-welding equipment
electric welders
equipment, arc-welding
machines, arc welding
welders, arc
welders, electric
CN V.TB.AFU.BCW.BIQ.AXC.AFU.AFU

arc welding, shielded metal
USE **shielded metal arc welding**

arcades
RT.47 (A,L,N,B,R)
ALT **arcade**
SN Use both for lines of arches raised on columns or piers, and for covered walks with such lines of arches along one or both sides.
CN V.RT.AFU.AFU.AFU.ARI.ALO

arcades (shopping arcades)
USE **shopping arcades**

arcades, amusement
USE **amusement arcades**

arcades, blank
USE **blind arcades**

arcades, blind
USE **blind arcades**

arcades, interlacing
USE **interlacing arcades**

arcades, penny
USE **penny arcades**

arcades, shopping
USE **shopping arcades**

arcades, surface
USE **blind arcades**

arcades, video
USE **video arcades**

arcae
TG.446
ALT **arca**
SN Chests for the safe-keeping of valuables usually made of wood and sheathed in iron; of a type made in the ancient and Medieval periods. (RICHTE)
UF arcula
capsa
cista
loculus
scrinium
CN V.TG.AFU.AFU.AXC.ALO.AXC.AFU

arch blocks
USE **voussoirs**

arch braces
RT.210
ALT **arch brace**
SN Curved braces, usually in pairs, used to support a roof frame and give the effect of an arch. (DAC)
UF braces, arch
CN V.RT.AFU.AFU.AFU.AXC.DOI.AFU.ALO

arch brick
USE **compass brick**

arch bridges
RK.1274 (L)
ALT **arch bridge**
SN Bridges in which the main supporting elements are arches. (W)
UF bridges, arch
CN V.RK.AFU.ALO.ALO.GLI.ALO.AFU.AFU.AFU

arch buttresses
USE **flying buttresses**

arch dams
RK.522 (L)
ALT **arch dam**
SN Use for dams resisting water pressure by use of the arch principle and having, in plan, the form of a single arch abutted by natural rock formation.
UF dams, arch
CN V.RK.AFU.ALO.ALO.CFS.AFU.ARI.AFU.AFU

arch ribs
USE **transverse ribs**

arch-trusses, bowstring
USE **bowstring trusses**

archaeological illustration
KT.203 (L)
UF illustration, archaeological
CN K.KT.AFU.ALO.DUC.CLM.AFU

archaeological museums
RK.394 (A,L,B)
ALT **archaeological museum**
UF museums, archaeological
CN V.RK.AFU.ALO.ALO.BCW.AXC.ARI.AXC.ALO

archaeological sites
RG.204
ALT **archaeological site**
UF sites, archaeological
CN V.RG.AFU.AFU.DZW.AFU

archaeological societies
HG.893 (L,B)
ALT **archaeological society**
UF societies, archaeological
CN H.HG.ALO.DUC.AFU

archaeological surveying
KT.118 (L)
UF surveying, archaeological
CN K.KT.AFU.ALO.CXA.ARI.AFU

archaeological trails
USE **heritage trails**

archaeologists
HG.255 (A,L)
ALT **archaeologist**
CN H.HG.AFU.AXC.BCW.AFU.ALO

archaeologists, anthropological
USE **anthropological archaeologists**

archaeologists, industrial
USE **industrial archaeologists**

archaeology
KD.101 (A,L,B,R)
CN K.KD.AFU.ALO.ALO

archaeology, anthropological
USE **anthropological archaeology**

archaeology, classical
USE **classical archaeology**

archaeology, industrial
USE **industrial archaeology**

archaeology, marine
USE **underwater archaeology**

archaeology, submarine
USE **underwater archaeology**

archaeology, underwater
USE **underwater archaeology**

archaeomagnetic dating
USE **paleomagnetic dating**

archaeometry
KD.103 (L,R)
SN Branch of archaeology that deals with the dating of archaeological specimens through scientific techniques, such as radiocarbon dating and amino-acid dating. (RHDEL2)
UF archeometry
CN K.KD.AFU.ALO.ALO.ALO

Archaic
FL.2573
CN F.FL.ALO.AXC.ALO.AFU.AFU.ARI.AXC

Archaic (North American)
FL.730
CN F.FL.ALO.ALO.ALO.AFU.AFU.ALO

Archaic painted ware
USE **Archaic ware**
Hassuna Archaic ware

Archaic period (Egyptian)
USE **Early Dynastic (Egyptian)**

Archaic (Preclassic)
USE **Preclassic**

Archaic ware
FL.3023
UF Archaic painted ware
painted ware, Archaic
ware, Archaic
ware, Archaic painted
CN F.FL.ALO.AXC.ARI.BIQ.ALO.AXC.AFU

Archaic ware, Hassuna
USE **Hassuna Archaic ware**

Archaic, Boreal
USE **Boreal Archaic**

Archaic, Desert
USE **Desert Tradition**

Archaic, Early
USE **Early Archaic**

Archaic, Eastern
USE **Eastern Archaic**

Archaic, Late
USE **Late Archaic**

Archaic, Middle
USE **Middle Archaic**

Archaic, Northern
USE **Northern Archaic**

Archaic, Western
USE **Western Archaic**

archaism
BM.344 (L,R)
CN B.BM.ALO.ALO.CLM.AXC

Archaistic
FL.2682
CN F.FL.ALO.AXC.ALO.AFU.ALO.BCW.ALO.AFU

archangel fir
USE **Scotch pine**

archbishop-electors
HG.217
ALT **archbishop-elector**
CN H.HG.AFU.AXC.AXC.BIQ.AFU.ARI.ALO

archbishoprics
USE **archdioceses**

archbishops
HG.218 (L,R)
ALT **archbishop**
SN Bishops of the highest rank, who preside over archdioceses. (RHDEL2)
CN H.HG.AFU.AXC.AXC.BIQ.AFU.ARI.ARI

archdioceses
RG.254 (L)
ALT **archdiocese**
UF archbishoprics
CN V.RG.ALO.AFU.AFU.BIQ.AFU

arched
DC.57
CN D.DC.AFU.ARI.ARI

arched barrel roofs
USE **barrel roofs**

arched butments
USE **flying buttresses**

arched buttresses
USE **flying buttresses**

arched stretchers
USE **saltire stretchers**

archeometry
USE **archaeometry**

archery ranges
RG.148
ALT **archery range**
UF ranges, archery
CN V.RG.AFU.AFU.DIO.ARI.AFU

arches
RT.217 (A,L,N,B,R)
ALT **arch**
SN Structural elements, typically curved, spanning openings and transmitting vertical loads to either side of the opening; also, structural elements or freestanding structures that resemble arches or act structurally like arches.
CN V.RT.AFU.AFU.AFU.BCW.AFU.AFU

arches, acute
USE **lancet arches**

arches, Arabic
USE **horseshoe arches**

arches, back
USE **back arches**

arches, barrel
USE **semicircular arches**

arches, bell
USE **bell arches**

arches, blind
USE **blind arches**

arches, blunt
USE **blunt arches**

arches, broken
USE **broken arches**

arches, Byzantine
USE **horseshoe arches**

arches, camber
USE **camber arches**

arches, catenary
USE **catenary arches**

arches, chancel
USE **chancel arches**

arches, circular
USE **semicircular arches**

arches, cloistered
USE **cloister vaults**

arches, compass-headed
USE **semicircular arches**

arches, composite
USE **four-centered arches**

arches, concentric
USE **concentric arches**

arches, contrasted
USE **ogee arches**

arches, corbel
USE **corbel arches**

arches, counter
USE **counter arches**

arches, crescent
USE **horseshoe arches**

arches, cusped
USE **cusped arches**

arches, depressed
USE **drop arches**

arches, diaphragm
USE **diaphragm arches**

arches, discharging
USE **relieving arches**

arches, drop
USE **drop arches**

arches, Dutch
USE **Dutch arches**

arches, elliptical
USE **elliptical arches**

arches, equilateral
USE **equilateral arches**

arches, equilateral pointed
USE **equilateral arches**

arches, extradosed
USE **extradosed arches**

arches, flat
USE **flat arches**

arches, Florentine
USE **Florentine arches**

arches, foiled
USE **cusped arches**

arches, four-centered
USE **four-centered arches**

arches, four-centered Tudor
USE **Tudor arches**

arches, French
USE **Dutch arches**

arches, gauged
USE **gauged arches**

arches, Gothic
USE **pointed arches**

arches, honorific
USE **memorial arches**

arches, horseshoe
USE **horseshoe arches**

arches, inflected
USE **inverted arches**

arches, inverted
USE **inverted arches**

arches, Italian pointed
USE **Italian pointed arches**

arches, jack
USE **flat arches**

arches, keel
USE **ogee arches**

arches, lancet
USE **lancet arches**

arches, lobed
USE **cusped arches**

arches, memorial
USE **memorial arches**

arches, miter
USE **miter arches**

arches, monumental
USE **memorial arches**

arches, Moorish
USE **horseshoe arches**

arches, oblique
USE **oblique arches**

arches, obtuse angle
USE **drop arches**

arches, ogee
USE **ogee arches**

arches, ogival
USE **ogee arches**

arches, one-centered
USE **one-centered arches**

arches, peak
USE **pointed arches**

arches, pier
USE **pier arches**

arches, pointed
USE **pointed arches**

arches, pointed segmental
USE **pointed segmental arches**

arches, primitive
USE **miter arches**

arches, proscenium
USE **proscenium arches**

arches, pseudo-four-centered
USE **pseudo-four-centered arches**

arches, pseudo-three-centered
USE **pseudo-three-centered arches**

arches, raking
USE **rampant arches**

arches, rampant
USE **rampant arches**

arches, rear
USE **back arches**

arches, recessed
USE **back arches**

arches, relieving
USE **relieving arches**

arches, ribbed
USE **ribbed arches**

arches, rigid
USE **rigid arches**

arches, rising
USE **rampant arches**

arches, rollock
USE **rowlock arches**

arches, Roman
USE **semicircular arches**

arches, rough
USE **relieving arches**

arches, round
USE **semicircular arches**

arches, rowlock
USE **rowlock arches**

arches, rubble
USE **rustic arches**

arches, rustic
USE **rustic arches**

arches, safety
USE **relieving arches**

arches, scoinson
USE **back arches**

arches, sconcheon
USE **back arches**

arches, segment
USE **segmental arches**

arches, segmental
USE **segmental arches**

arches, semicircular
USE **semicircular arches**

arches, semielliptical
USE **elliptical arches**

arches, shouldered
USE **shouldered arches**

arches, single-center
USE **one-centered arches**

arches, skew
USE **oblique arches**

arches, sluing
USE **splayed arches**

arches, soldier
USE **soldier arches**

arches, splayed
USE **splayed arches**

arches, squinch
USE **squinches**

arches, stepped
USE **stepped arches**

arches, stilted
USE **stilted arches**

arches, straight
USE **flat arches**

arches, straining
USE **straining arches**

arches, surbased
USE **surbased arches**

arches, surmounted
USE **surmounted arches**

arches, three-centered
USE **three-centered arches**

arches, three-hinged
USE **three-hinged arches**

arches, three-pinned
USE **three-hinged arches**

arches, transverse
USE **transverse arches**

arches, triangular
USE **miter arches**

arches, triumphal
USE **triumphal arches**

arches, triumphal (church components)
USE **chancel arches**

arches, trumpet
USE **squinches**

arches, Tudor
USE **Tudor arches**

arches, two-centered
USE **two-centered arches**

arches, two-centered segmental
USE **pointed segmental arches**

arches, two-hinged
USE **two-hinged arches**

archil
USE **orchil**

architect-consultant contracts
VW.894
ALT **architect-consultant contract**
UF contracts, architect-consultant
CN V.VW.AFU.ARI.AFU.BOK.BOK.ALO.ALO.ARI.AFU

architect-designed furniture
USE **architectural furniture**

architect-designed houses
RK.283 (L,B)
ALT **architect-designed house**
UF houses, architect-designed
CN V.RK.AFU.ALO.ALO.AXC.ALO.ARI.AFU

architect's models
USE **architectural models**

architect's tables
USE **drawing tables**

architects
HG.83 (A,L,B,R)
ALT **architect**
CN H.HG.AFU.AXC.AXC.AFU.AFU.ALO.ALO

architects' homes
USE **architects' houses**

architects' houses
RK.324 (A,B)
ALT **architects' house**
UF architects' homes
homes, architects'
houses, architects'
CN V.RK.AFU.ALO.ALO.AXC.ALO.BOK.AFU

architects' marks
VW.740 (B,R)
ALT **architect's mark**
UF marks, architects'
CN V.VW.AFU.ALO.ALO.AFU.AXC.AXC.AFU

architects' office buildings
USE **architects' offices**

architects' offices
RK.916 (A,B)
ALT **architect's office**
UF architects' office buildings
office buildings, architects'
offices, architects'
CN V.RK.AFU.ALO.ALO.DZW.ALO.ALO

architects, associated
USE **associated architects**

architects, government
USE **government architects**

architects, landscape
USE **landscape architects**

architects, marine
USE **naval architects**

architects, naval
USE **naval architects**

architects, official
USE **government architects**

architects, project
USE **project architects**

architects, public
USE **government architects**

architects, supervising
USE **supervising architects**

architectural acoustics
KD.282 (A,L)
UF acoustics, architectural
CN K.KD.AFU.ARI.CLM.AXC.AFU.AFU

architectural associations
USE **architectural societies**

architectural bronze
MT.376
SN Bronze with a high copper content used for construction purposes.
UF art bronze
bronze, architectural
bronze, art
CN M.MT.AFU.AFU.AFU.BZY.AFU.AFU.AFU.ALO.ARI.BCW.ALO.AFU

architectural canopies
USE **canopies**

architectural centers
RK.384 (A,B)
ALT **architectural center**
SN Use for buildings constructed as resource and information centers for documents, exhibitions, and other events and data of relevance to architects.
UF centers, architectural
CN V.RK.AFU.ALO.ALO.BCW.AXC.ARI.AFU.AFU.AFU

architectural clubs
USE **architectural societies**

architectural criticism
KD.22 (A,L,B,R)
UF criticism, architectural
CN K.KD.AFU.AFU.AFU.ALO.AFU

architectural critics
HG.163 (A,B)
ALT **architectural critic**
UF critics, architectural
CN H.HG.AFU.AXC.AXC.AFU.ALO.AFU

architectural design
KT.96 (A,L,B)
UF design, architectural
CN K.KT.AFU.ALO.CFS.ALO

architectural detailing
USE **architectural drawing**

architectural draftsmen
HG.622 (B)
ALT **architectural draftsman**
SN Draftsmen who draw architectural and structural features of buildings, delineate designs and details, and confirm compliance with building codes. (DOT)
UF architectural draughtsmen
draftsmen, architectural
draughtsmen, architectural
CN H.HG.AFU.AXC.BZY.AXC.AFU

architectural draughtsmen
USE **architectural draftsmen**

architectural drawing
KT.188 (A,L,B,R)
UF architectural detailing
detailing, architectural
drawing, architectural
CN K.KT.AFU.ALO.DUC.BZY.AFU.AFU

architectural drawings
VD.145 (A,L,N,B)
ALT **architectural drawing**
SN Use for drawings of architecture and drawings for architectural projects, whether the project was executed or not.
UF drawings, architectural
CN V.VD.AFU.BIQ.AFU

architectural education
KD.129 (A,B,R)
UF architectural training
education, architectural
training, architectural
CN K.KD.AFU.ALO.BOK.ALO.AFU

architectural elements
RT.1 (A)
ALT **architectural element**
UF elements, architectural
CN V.RT.AFU

architectural engineering
KD.218 (A,L,B,R)
UF engineering, architectural
CN K.KD.AFU.ARI.BIQ.AXC.AFU

architectural firms
HG.846 (L)
ALT **architectural firm**
UF firms, architectural
CN H.HG.ALO.BOK.AFU.ALO.AFU.AFU

architectural follies
USE **follies**

architectural furniture
TG.790
SN Use for furniture designed by architects or to match or accord with the architectural features of the rooms for which it is intended.
UF architect-designed furniture

furniture, architect-designed
furniture, architectural
CN V.TG.AFU.ARI.ALO

architectural glass
MT.269
UF glass, architectural
CN M.MT.AFU.AFU.AFU.BIQ.AFU.AXC.AFU

architectural guidebooks
VW.510 (L)
ALT **architectural guidebook**
UF guidebooks, architectural
CN V.VW.AFU.ALO.AFU.AFU.AFU.BZY.ARI.AFU

architectural hardware
USE **finish hardware**

architectural historians
HG.164 (A,L)
ALT **architectural historian**
UF historians, architectural
CN H.HG.AFU.AXC.AXC.AFU.ALO.ALO

architectural history
KD.23 (A,L,B,R)
SN Study of the development over time of the human built environment.
UF architecture, history of
history of architecture
history, architectural
CN K.KD.AFU.AFU.AFU.ALO.ALO

architectural libraries
RK.707 (L,B)
ALT **architectural library**
UF libraries, architectural
CN V.RK.AFU.ALO.ALO.CRG.AXC.ARI.AFU

architectural lighting
RT.1365 (A,L)
UF decorative lighting
lighting, architectural
lighting, decorative
lighting, outline
outline lighting
CN V.RT.ALO.AXC.ALO.AFU

architectural materials
USE **building materials**

architectural models
VB.106 (A,L,N,B,R)
ALT **architectural model**
UF architect's models
models, architectural
CN V.VB.ALO.BUE.ARI.ALO

architectural museums
RK.383 (A,L,B)
ALT **architectural museum**
UF museums, architectural
CN V.RK.AFU.ALO.ALO.BCW.AXC.ARI.AFU.AFU

architectural orders
RT.50 (A,L,B,R)
ALT **architectural order**
SN In classical architecture, a particular ensemble of column with its entablature, having standardized details. (HAS)
UF classical orders
orders, architectural
orders, classical
CN V.RT.AFU.AFU.AFU.ARI.ARI

architectural photographers
HG.118 (A)
ALT **architectural photographer**
UF photographers, architectural
CN H.HG.AFU.AXC.AXC.AFU.AFU.ALO.AXC.DOI.AFU

architectural photography
KT.293 (A,L,B,R)
UF photography, architectural
CN K.KT.AFU.ALO.DUC.DIO.AFU.ALO

architectural presentation drawings
USE **presentation drawings**

architectural records
VW.789
ALT **architectural record**
SN Records documenting the design and construction of buildings or other structures.
UF records, architectural
CN V.VW.AFU.ARI.AFU.ARI

architectural renderings
USE **renderings**

architectural schools
RK.803 (A,L,B,R)
ALT **architectural school**
UF architecture, schools of
schools of architecture
schools, architectural
CN V.RK.AFU.ALO.ALO.CXA.ARI.ALO.ALO

architectural societies
HG.894 (A,B)
ALT **architectural society**
UF architectural associations
architectural clubs
associations, architectural
clubs, architectural
societies, architectural
CN H.HG.ALO.DUC.ALO

Architectural Style
USE **Second Style**

architectural stylebooks
USE **domestic stylebooks**

architectural surveys
VW.365 (A,B)
ALT **architectural survey**
UF historic structure surveys
surveys, architectural
surveys, historic structure
CN V.VW.AFU.AFU.ALO.DCU.AFU.AFU

architectural theory
BM.316 (A,B,R)
UF architecture, philosophy of
philosophy of architecture
theory, architectural
CN B.BM.AFU.AXC.ELK.AFU

architectural training
USE **architectural education**

architecture
KD.15 (A,L,B,R)
SN Art or science of designing and building structures, especially habitable structures, in accordance with principles determined by aesthetic and practical or material considerations.(W) Refers also to the structures created.
CN K.KD.AFU.AFU.AFU.AFU.ALO.AFU

architecture feinte
USE **fictive architecture**

architecture parlante
USE **mimetic buildings**

architecture, academic
USE **academic architecture**

architecture, alpine
USE **hillside architecture**

architecture, anonymous
USE **vernacular architecture**

architecture, bank
USE **banks**

architecture, cave
USE **cave architecture**

architecture, church
USE **churches**

architecture, community
USE **participatory design**

architecture, domestic
USE **dwellings**

architecture, ecclesiastical
USE **religious buildings**

architecture, fantastic
USE **fantastic architecture**

architecture, fictive
USE **fictive architecture**

architecture, folk
USE **vernacular architecture**

architecture, futuristic
USE **visionary architecture**

architecture, grotto
USE **cave architecture**

architecture, grouped domestic
USE **cluster housing**

architecture, hillside
USE **hillside architecture**

architecture, history of
USE **architectural history**

architecture, imaginary
USE **fantastic architecture**

architecture, indigenous
USE **vernacular architecture**

architecture, industrial
USE **industrial buildings**

architecture, landscape
USE **landscape architecture**

architecture, liturgical
USE **religious buildings**

architecture, marine
USE **naval architecture**

architecture, military
USE **military buildings**

architecture, mountain
USE **hillside architecture**

architecture, museum
USE **museums**

architecture, naval
USE **naval architecture**

architecture, non-pedigreed
USE **vernacular architecture**

architecture, organic
USE **organic architecture**

architecture, philosophy of
USE **architectural theory**

architecture, primitive
USE **primitive architecture**

architecture, programmatic
USE **mimetic buildings**

architecture, religious
USE **religious buildings**

architecture, rock-cut
USE **rock-cut architecture**

architecture, schools of
USE **architectural schools**

architecture, spontaneous
USE **vernacular architecture**

architecture, temporary
USE **temporary buildings**

architecture, trompe-l'oeil
USE **fictive architecture**

architecture, vernacular
USE **vernacular architecture**

architecture, visionary
USE **visionary architecture**

architrave cornices
RT.329
ALT **architrave cornice**
SN Entablatures in which the cornice rests directly on the architrave, the frieze being omitted. (DAC)
UF cornices, architrave
CN V.RT.AFU.AFU.AFU.BCW.BZY.AFU.AFU

architraves
RT.331
ALT **architrave**
SN Includes the lowermost element of a classical entablature, and similar features when carried around doorways or other openings.
UF epistyles
CN V.RT.AFU.AFU.AFU.BCW.BZY.ALO.AFU

archival calendars
VW.338 (L)
ALT **archival calendar**
SN Lists of descriptions of individual documents in a collection or of a specified kind, usually arranged in chronological order.
UF calendars, archival
CN V.VW.AFU.AFU.ALO.CXA.ALO.AFU

archival catalogs
VW.339 (L)
ALT **archival catalog**
UF catalogs, archival
CN V.VW.AFU.AFU.ALO.CXA.ALO.ALO

archival finding aids
USE **finding aids**

archival guides
VW.340
ALT **archival guide**
SN Includes finding aids that give a general account of the holdings of one or more archives, including background history, usually arranged by record group, thereunder by series; also, finding aids that describe the holdings of one or more archives relating to particular subjects or to specified types documents. (ICA)
UF guides, archival
CN V.VW.AFU.AFU.ALO.CXA.ALO.ARI

archival inventories
VW.341 (L)
ALT **archival inventory**
SN Finding aids, whose normal unit of entry is the series. Usually include a brief history and description of the organization that produced the records, descriptive lists of each record series, and sometimes supplementary information, such as selective indexes. (SAA)
UF inventories, archival
CN V.VW.AFU.AFU.ALO.CXA.ALO.AXC

archival processing
KT.405
SN Photographic processing designed to preserve a print or negative for as long as possible by protecting it against deterioration due to chemical reactions. (WHP) For activities involving the arrangement and description of archival materials use **processing** plus terms for the form of material being processed.
CN K.KT.AFU.ALO.DUC.DIO.ARI.AXC.AFU

archival registers
VW.342
ALT **archival register**
SN Finding aids developed at the Library of Congress to describe groups of papers, collections, and records by giving their provenance and conditions of administration, their scope and general content, including span and bulk dates, biographical notes about the person, group, or organization whose material it is, its arrangement, a container or folder listing, and, on occasion, selective document indexes. (SAA)
UF registers, archival
CN V.VW.AFU.AFU.ALO.CXA.ALO.BCW

archive repositories
USE **repositories**

archives
RK.685 (A,L,B,R)
ALT **archive**
CN V.RK.AFU.ALO.ALO.CRG.AFU

archives rooms
RM.149
ALT **archives room**
UF rooms, archives
CN V.RM.AFU.DIO.ALO.CFS.AFU

archives, family
USE **family papers**

archiving
KG.71
ALT **archived**
SN Filing or collecting (as records or documents) in an archive or other repository. (W)
CN K.KG.AFU.AFU.AXC.AXC.ARI

archivists
HG.269 (L)
ALT **archivist**
SN Persons concerned with collecting, evaluating, systemizing, preserving, and making available for reference public records and documents of historical significance. (DOT)
CN H.HG.AFU.AXC.BCW.AFU.BOK.ALO.AFU

archivolts
RT.286 (R)
ALT **archivolt**
SN Molded or decorated bands around an arch.
CN V.RT.AFU.AFU.AFU.BCW.AFU.ALO.AFU

archways
RT.993 (N)
ALT **archway**
SN Use for passageways under arches.
CN V.RT.AFU.ARI.AFU.ARI.AFU

arcs doubleaux
USE **transverse ribs**

arcs formerets
USE **wall ribs**

arctic climate
USE **polar climate**

Arctic Inuit, Western
USE **Western Arctic Inuit**

arcula
USE **arcae**

area
BM.802
CN B.BM.CFS.ARI.AXC.BUE.AFU

area code maps, telephone
USE **telephone area code maps**

area drains
RT.1456
ALT **area drain**
SN Receptacles designed to collect surface or rainwater from open areas. (STEIN)
UF drains, area
CN V.RT.ALO.BCW.ALO.ARI.AXC.AFU

area, vanishing
USE **vanishing area**

areas, commercial
USE **business districts**

areas, development
USE **development areas**

areas, growth
USE **growth centers**

areas, historic
USE **historic districts**

areas, metropolitan
USE **metropolitan areas**

areas, picnic
USE **picnic areas**

areas, recreation
USE **recreation areas**

areas, residential
USE **residential districts**

areas, spoil
USE **spoil banks**

Areas, Standard Metropolitan Statistical
USE **Standard Metropolitan Statistical Areas**

areas, statistical
USE **statistical areas**

areas, unincorporated
USE **unincorporated areas**

areas, urban
USE **urban areas**

areas, wilderness
USE **wilderness areas**

areaways
RM.40 (L)
ALT **areaway**
SN Open subsurface spaces around a basement window or doorway, adjacent to the foundation walls. (PUTNAM)
CN V.RM.AFU.DIO.AFU.BCW.AFU

arena theaters
RK.933 (L,B)
ALT **arena theater**
UF arenas (theaters)
theaters-in-the-round
theaters, arena
CN V.RK.AFU.ALO.ALO.EFQ.ARI.BCW.AFU.AFU

arenaceous limestone
USE **siliceous limestone**

arenaceous rock
USE **sandstone**

Arenal
FL.1021
CN F.FL.ALO.ALO.ALO.ALO.AFU.ALO.ARI.AFU.ALO.BCW

arenas
RK.1047 (B)
ALT **arena**
SN Use both for buildings housing central stages, rings, or areas used for sports or other entertainment events and for the central open spaces of ancient amphitheaters.
UF arenas, sports
coliseums
sports arenas
CN V.RK.AFU.ALO.ALO.EWY.AXC.BIQ.AFU.AFU

arenas (theaters)
USE **arena theaters**

arenas, sports
USE **arenas**

Arequipa
FL.1711
CN F.FL.ALO.ALO.AXC.ALO.AFU.ARI.AFU

Arévalo
FL.1017
CN F.FL.ALO.ALO.ALO.ALO.AFU.ALO.ARI.AFU.ALO.AFU

Argentine
FL.717 (L,B)
CN F.FL.ALO.ALO.AFU.AXC.AFU

argentotype
USE **kallitype**

argillaceous limestone
MT.679
SN Limestone containing 10 to 50% clay. (STEIN)
UF limestone, argillaceous
CN M.MT.AFU.AFU.AFU.DCU.AFU.ALO.AFU.ALO.ALO.AFU.ALO.AFU

argillaceous rock
MT.640
SN Rock, especially limestone and sandstone, containing clay.
UF pelites
rock, argillaceous
CN M.MT.AFU.AFU.AFU.DCU.AFU.ALO.AFU.AFU

argillaceous sandstone
MT.708
UF sandstone, argillaceous
CN M.MT.AFU.AFU.AFU.DCU.AFU.ALO.AFU.ARI.AFU.ALO.AFU

argillite
MT.641 (L)
SN Compact argillaceous rock that is cemented by silica. (W)
CN M.MT.AFU.AFU.AFU.DCU.AFU.ALO.AFU.AFU.AFU

Argive Minyan ware
FL.2659
UF Minyan ware, Argive
ware, Argive Miyan
CN F.FL.ALO.AXC.ALO.AFU.ALO.AXC.AXC.BOK.AFU

Argive School
FL.2683
CN F.FL.ALO.AXC.ALO.AFU.ALO.BCW.ALO.ALO

argon
MT.4 (L)
SN Inert gaseous element used in metalworking and as a filler for electric incandescent and fluorescent light bulbs.
CN M.MT.AFU.AFU.AFU.AFU

argon-potassium dating
USE **potassium-argon dating**

Aries symbols
DG.75
ALT **Aries symbol**
CN D.DG.AFU.AFU.ERE.ALO

Arikara
FL.1370 (L)
UF Ree
CN F.FL.ALO.ALO.ARI.AFU.BOK.ALO

aristo paper
MT.1947
UF aristotype papers
aristotypie
paper, aristo

papers, aristotype
CN M.MT.AFU.AFU.ARI.ALO.ALO.AXC.ARI.BOK.AXC.AFU

aristocracy
HG.888 (L,R)
CN H.HG.ALO.DOI.ALO.ARI.AFU

Aristotelianism
BM.507 (R)
SN Philosophy incorporating essential features of the thinking of Aristotle. (W)
CN B.BM.BIQ.AXC.AXC

aristotype
KT.319 (L)
SN Used loosely for various photographic processes employing silver chloride printing-out paper with either gelatin or collodion as the binder; popular from the late 1880s to the early 20th century. At one time a trade name, but the term fell into generic use.
CN K.KT.AFU.ALO.DUC.DIO.ALO.AXC

aristotype papers
USE **aristo paper**

aristotypes
VJ.46
ALT **aristotype**
CN V.VJ.AFU.AFU.ARI.ARI.AXC.ALO

aristotypie
USE **aristo paper**

Arita
FL.2014
CN F.FL.ALO.ARI.ALO.ALO.ALO.ALO.ALO.ALO

arithmetic
KD.253 (L,R)
CN K.KD.AFU.ARI.CFS.ARI

arithmetic progressions
BM.819 (L)
SN Sequences or series of mathematical objects or quantities, in which each entry is determined from its predecessors by some algorithm. (MHDSTT)
UF arithmetic series
progressions, arithmetic
series, arithmetic
CN B.BM.CFS.ARI.CLM.AFU

arithmetic series
USE **arithmetic progressions**

Arizona flagstone
MT.718
UF flagstone, Arizona
CN M.MT.AFU.AFU.AFU.DCU.AFU.ALO.AFU.ARI.AFU.ALO.AXC.AFU

ark chests
USE **arks**

arkose
USE **feldspathic sandstone**

arks
TG.397 (L,R)
ALT **ark**
SN Various forms of chests, coffers, and other covered receptacles generally made of strong and durable construction and used to store articles of great value, such as the Torah scrolls in synagogues.
UF ark chests
Arks of the Law
arks, holy
chests, ark
holy arks
shrines, Torah
Torah shrines
CN V.TG.AFU.AFU.AXC.ALO.AFU

Arks of the Law
USE **arks**

arks, holy
USE **arks**

arm chairs, continuous
USE **continuous-bow Windsor armchairs**

arm pads
TG.820
ALT **arm pad**
UF elbow pads
manchettes
pads, arm
pads, elbow
CN V.TG.ALO.ALO.ALO.AFU

arm posts
USE **arm supports**

arm rails
TG.821
ALT **arm rail**
UF rails, arm
CN V.TG.ALO.ALO.ALO.ALO

arm stumps
USE **arm supports**

arm supports
TG.822
ALT **arm support**
SN Vertical or curved uprights supporting the front end of chair arms.
UF arm posts
arm stumps
posts, arm
stumps, arm
supports, arm
CN V.TG.ALO.ALO.ALO.ARI

armada chests
TG.457
ALT **armada chest**
SN 19th-century term for heavy iron-bound coffers used for the storage of valuables; generally of German make and rarely dating from before the 17th century. (DDA)
UF chests, armada
CN V.TG.AFU.AFU.AXC.ALO.AXC.CLM.AFU

armadios
TG.499
ALT **armadio**
SN Italian cupboards, originally, a cassone with doors instead of a lid, but later (16th century) developing into a two-tiered piece similar to the English press cupboard. Generally having massive architecural decoration, including pilasters supporting a monumental cornice; frequently made for sacristies.
CN V.TG.AFU.AFU.AXC.ALO.BUE.AFU

armaria
TG.500
ALT **armarium**
SN Ancient Roman cupboards, generally having a rectangular case, mounted on feet, with doors reaching more or less from top to bottom, a gabled or flat top, and interior shelving. (RICHTE)
CN V.TG.AFU.AFU.AXC.ALO.BUE.ALO

armarios
TG.501
ALT **armario**
SN Spanish term for cupboards. (PAYNE)
CN V.TG.AFU.AFU.AXC.ALO.BUE.ARI

armchairs
TG.23 (N)
ALT **armchair**
SN Term applied to a wide variety of chairs with arms, to distinguish them from side chairs which have no arms.
UF chaises à bras
CN V.TG.AFU.AFU.ALO.AFU.AFU.AFU.ALO

armchairs, 136
USE **136 armchairs**

armchairs, cabriole
USE **cabriole chairs**

armchairs, continuous-bow Windsor
USE **continuous-bow Windsor armchairs**

armchairs, great
USE **great chairs**

armchairs, Plona folding
USE **Plona folding armchairs**

armchairs, Windsor low-back
USE **low-back Windsor chairs**

armchairs, Winsor continuous-bow
USE **continuous-bow Windsor armchairs**

armed forces
HG.814
UF armed services
forces, armed

military, the
services, armed
CN H.HG.ALO.AXC

armed services
USE **armed forces**

Armenian bole
USE **red bole**

Armenian stone
USE **azurite**

armies
HG.816 (L)
ALT **army**
CN H.HG.ALO.AXC.ALO

armoires
TG.598 (N,R)
ALT **armoire**
SN Use with reference to French-styled wardrobes for the storage of clothing or linens.
UF buffets (armoires)
CN V.TG.AFU.AFU.AXC.ALO.CXA.AFU

armoires à deux corps
TG.599
ALT **armoire à deux corps**
SN French case furniture consisting of two cupboards, set one above the other, each with two doors, the front and sides of the upper cupboard being recessed. They generally have an architectural framework with pilasters and a crowning pediment. (DDA)
CN V.TG.AFU.AFU.AXC.ALO.CXA.AFU.AFU

armoires à encoignure
USE **encoignures**

armoires à livres
USE **bibliothèques**

armoires-bibliothèque
USE **bibliothèques**

armoires bonnetières
USE **bonnetières**

armoires d'encoignure
USE **encoignures**

armoires dressoirs
USE **dressers**

armoires en bibliothèque
USE **bibliothèques**

armoires, mural
USE **hanging cupboards**

armor plates
TF.17
ALT **armor plate**
SN Metal plates which protect the lower part of a door from kicks and scratches; similar to kickplates but covering the door to a greater height, usually 39 inches (1 meter) or more from the bottom of the door. (DAC)
UF plates, armor
CN V.TF.AFU.AFU.AFU.AFU.AFU.CFS.AFU

armored cable
MT.2218
UF cable, armored
cable, metal-clad
metal-clad cable
CN M.MT.AFU.ALO.BCW.AFU

armorers
HG.510 (L)
ALT **armorer**
SN Persons that make armor or arms, or that repair, assemble, and test firearms. (W)
CN H.HG.AFU.AXC.BUE.ARI.CFS.ARI.AFU

armorers' marks
VW.741 (L,R)
ALT **armorer's mark**
UF marks, armorers'
CN V.VW.AFU.ALO.ALO.AFU.AXC.AXC.ALO

armorial porcelain
FL.3287
UF porcelain, armorial
CN F.FL.ALO.BCW.ALO.AXC.CXA.AXC.AFU

armories
RK.875 (A,L,N,B,R)
ALT **armory**
SN Distinguished from **arsenals** by being used both for military training and storage of arms and equipment.
CN V.RK.AFU.ALO.ALO.DIO.AXC.AFU

armrests
USE **arms (furniture components)**

arms (furniture components)
TG.809
ALT **arm (furniture component)**
SN Supports for the elbow and forearm used in seating furniture. (W)
UF armrests
elbows
CN V.TG.ALO.ALO.AFU

arms, coats of
USE **coats of arms**

arms, hollowed
USE **hollowed arms**

arms, knuckled
USE **knuckled arms**

arms, open
USE **open arms**

arms, roll-over
USE **rolled arms**

arms, rolled
USE **rolled arms**

arms, scroll-over
USE **scrolled arms**

arms, scrolled
USE **scrolled arms**

arms, swan
USE **swan arms**

arms, swan-neck
USE **swan arms**

arms, tablet
USE **tablet-arm chairs**
writing arms

arms, voluted
USE **scrolled arms**

arms, writing
USE **writing arms**

army bases
RG.126 (L)
ALT **army base**
UF army posts
bases, army
CN V.RG.AFU.AFU.BZY.AFU.ALO

army camps
RG.132 (B)
ALT **army camp**
UF camps, army
CN V.RG.AFU.AFU.BZY.ALO.AFU

army housing
USE **military housing**

army posts
USE **army bases**

Arnaudon's green
USE **chromium oxide green**

Arnhem Land
FL.3615 (L)
CN F.FL.ALO.BOK.AFU.ALO.AFU

Arnoaldi
FL.2737
CN F.FL.ALO.AXC.ALO.ALO.ALO.BIQ.AFU

aromatic hydrocarbons
MT.2671
SN One of four main types of hydrocarbons found in crude oil belonging to the class of organic compounds that have an unsaturated ring of carbon atoms, considered generally more volatile and active than oliphatic hydrocarbons. (GOTTS)
UF aromatic solvents
hydrocarbons, aromatic
solvents, aromatic
CN M.MT.AFU.ARI.HZS.AFU.BIQ.ALO

aromatic solvents
USE **aromatic hydrocarbons**

arrangers
HG.72
ALT **arranger**

SN Persons who transcribe music for voices or instruments for which it was not originally written or adapt it to a style suitable to a particular group of performers. (W)
CN H.HG.AFU.AXC.AXC.AFU.AFU.AFU.BIQ.BIQ.AFU

arrangers, makeup
USE **makeup arrangers**

Arretine pottery
USE **Arretine ware**

Arretine ware
FL.2756 (L)
UF Arretine pottery
pottery, Arretine
ware, Arretine
CN F.FL.ALO.AXC.ALO.ALO.ALO.BUE.ALO.BIQ.ALO.AFU

arricciato
USE **arriccio**

arriccio
MT.2455
SN In the preparation of a wall for fresco, the second coat of plaster, over the roughcast and under the intonaco. (PDAT)
UF arricciato
brown coat
CN M.MT.AFU.ARI.CRG.AFU.AXC.ARI.AFU

arrière-voussures
USE **back arches**

arris gutters
RT.1460
ALT **arris gutter**
SN V-shaped wooden gutters fixed to the eaves of a building. (HAS)
UF gutters, arris
CN V.RT.ALO.BCW.ALO.ARI.BCW.AFU

arris tile
MT.2279
SN Any angularly shaped tile. (HAS)
UF tile, arris
CN M.MT.AFU.ALO.IFM.ALO

arrondissements
RG.244
ALT **arrondissement**
SN Administrative subdivisions of French departments and some French cities.
CN V.RG.ALO.AFU.AFU.ALO.AFU

arrow feet
USE **therm feet**

arrow loops
USE **loopholes**

arrow spindles
TG.987
ALT **arrow spindle**
UF spindles, arrow
CN V.TG.ALO.HCQ.AFU

arrowroot
MT.1062 (L)
SN A nutritive starch obtained from the rootstock of the arrowroot plant. (W)
UF arrowroot starch
starch, arrowroot
CN M.MT.AFU.AFU.ALO.BIQ.BUE.BUE.AFU

arrowroot starch
USE **arrowroot**

arroyos
RD.190 (L)
ALT **arroyo**
SN Use for flat-bottomed and often steep-walled dry watercourses occupied by streams only after heavy rains; common in the southwest United States.
CN V.RD.ARI.AFU.AXC.AFU.AFU.ARI.ALO

Arsacid
USE **Parthian**

arsenals
RK.856 (A,L,B,R)
ALT **arsenal**
SN Distinguished from **armories** by being exclusively a repository or magazine for arms and military equipment.
CN V.RK.AFU.ALO.ALO.DIO.AFU.AFU

arsenate, chromated copper
USE **chromated copper arsenate**

arsenate, pale cobalt
USE **pale cobalt arsenate**

arsenic orange
USE **realgar**

arsenic yellow
USE **orpiment**

art
KD.18 (A,L,B,R)
SN Use with reference to the fine arts or the fine and decorative arts together. Refers also to the objects, images, and other works created in the areas of the fine and decorative arts. With reference to the visual and performing arts together, use **arts.**
CN K.KD.AFU.AFU.AFU.AFU.ALO.ALO

art academies
USE **art schools**

art appreciation
KD.130 (L,R)
UF appreciation, art
CN K.KD.AFU.ALO.BOK.ALO.ALO

Art Autre
USE **Art Informel**

art bronze
USE **architectural bronze**

art brut
BM.233 (L,R)
SN Use for art where the artistic impulse appears in a raw, uncivilized state, particularly work created by people isolated from society such as prisoners and the mentally ill. Use **amateur art** when referring to any art created by nonprofessionals.
UF art of the insane
art, outsider
art, psychiatric
art, psychotic
art, raw
brut, art
insane, art of the
l'art brut
outsider art
psychiatric art
psychotic art
raw art
CN B.BM.AFU.ARI.BCW.AXC

art centers
RK.1195 (A,L,B)
ALT **art center**
UF art centers, community
centers, art
community art centers
CN V.RK.AFU.ALO.ALO.FUA.AXC.AFU

art centers, community
USE **art centers**

art colleges
USE **art schools**

art colonies
USE **artists' colonies**

art commissions
HG.833 (L,R)
ALT **art commission**
SN Governmental agencies having administrative, legislative, or judicial powers concerning the arts.
UF arts agencies, state
commissions, art
state arts agencies
CN H.HG.ALO.BIQ.AFU

Art Concret
USE **Concrete art**

art criticism
KD.24 (L,R)
UF criticism, art
CN K.KD.AFU.AFU.AFU.ALO.ARI

art critics
HG.165 (A,L,R)
ALT **art critic**
UF critics, art
CN H.HG.AFU.AXC.AXC.AFU.ALO.ARI

Art Deco
FL.3251 (A,L,B,R)
UF American Deco
Art Décoratif
Art Moderne
Deco, American

Deco, Art
Jazz Modern
Modern, Jazz
Moderne
Style Moderne
CN F.FL.ALO.BCW.ALO.AXC.AFU

Art Décoratif
USE **Art Deco**

art directors
HG.90
ALT **art director**
SN Persons who formulate concepts and supervise workers engaged in executing layout designs for art work and copy to be presented by visual communications media, such as magazines, books, newspapers, television, film, posters, and packaging. (DOT)
UF directors, art
CN H.HG.AFU.AXC.AXC.AFU.AFU.ALO.ARI

art education
KD.131 (L,B,R)
UF education, art
CN K.KD.AFU.ALO.BOK.ALO.ARI

art furniture
TG.791
SN Term applied in the 1860s to furniture produced by firms which employed leading designers and architects. Designs tended toward simple forms with hand-carved and painted decoration.
UF furniture, art
CN V.TG.AFU.ARI.ARI

art galleries
RK.137 (A,L,B,R)
ALT **art gallery**
SN Use only for stores in which works of art are displayed for sale.
UF art galleries, commercial
commercial art galleries
galleries (art galleries)
galleries, art
CN V.RK.AFU.ALO.ALO.ALO.ARI.AFU

art galleries (museums)
USE **art museums**

art galleries, commercial
USE **art galleries**

art historians
HG.166 (A,L,R)
ALT **art historian**
UF historians, art
CN H.HG.AFU.AXC.AXC.AFU.ALO.AXC

art history
KD.25 (L,B,R)
SN Study of man-made visual forms in periods from prehistory to the present, including their use in communication, decoration, and aesthetic and intellectual stimulation.
UF history of art
history, art
CN K.KD.AFU.AFU.AFU.ALO.AXC

Art in motion
USE **Kinetic**

Art Informel
FL.3717 (R)
UF Art Autre
Informal art
L'Art Informel
CN F.FL.ALO.BUE.ARI.ARI

art libraries
RK.708 (L,B,R)
ALT **art library**
UF libraires, art
CN V.RK.AFU.ALO.ALO.CRG.AXC.ARI.ALO

art market
BM.370 (L,R)
SN Use for the contemporary buying and selling of art. For the exchange of art as a commodity before the 20th century, use **art trade.**
UF market, art
CN B.BM.ARI.ALO

art metalworking
KT.778 (L)
UF metalworking, art
CN K.KT.AFU.ALO.HOE.BCW.AFU.AFU

Art Moderne
USE **Art Deco**

art museums
RK.382 (A,L,B)
ALT **art museum**
UF art galleries (museums)
fine arts museums
galleries (art museums)
galleries, art (museums)
galleries, picture
museums, art
museums, fine arts
picture galleries
CN V.RK.AFU.ALO.ALO.BCW.AXC.ARI.AFU

art museums, folk
USE **folk art museums**

Art Nouveau
FL.3252 (A,L,B,R)
UF Arte Joven
Modern Style (Art Nouveau)
Modernismo
Nieuwe Kunst
Palingstijl
Quaint Style
Style Guimard
Yachting Style
CN F.FL.ALO.BCW.ALO.AXC.ALO

art objects
VB.84 (L,B,R)
ALT **art object**
SN Use for works of the fine or decorative arts when their qualities as discrete and coherent individual objects are emphasized, e.g., in relation to conservation or inventorying. When the aesthetic nature of works is emphasized, use **works of art.**
UF objects, art
objets d'art
objets de vertu
CN V.VB.ALO.ALO

art of the insane
USE **art brut**

Art Povera
USE **Arte Povera**

art restoration laboratories
USE **conservation laboratories**

art schools
RK.804 (A,L,B,R)
ALT **art school**
UF academies of art
academies, art
art academies
art colleges
art, academies of
art, schools of
colleges, art
schools of art
schools, art
CN V.RK.AFU.ALO.ALO.CXA.ARI.ALO.ARI

art theory
BM.319 (R)
UF theory, art
CN B.BM.AFU.AXC.ELK.ALO

art therapy
KD.26 (L)
SN Study and practice of the therapeutic use of images and objects, to foster nonverbal communication, creativity, and physical interaction, and to uncover verbal associations and interpretations, helping to identify and understand patients' emotional, motor, and perceptual disfunctions.
UF creative arts therapy
therapy, art
therapy, creative arts
CN K.KD.AFU.AFU.AFU.ALO.BCW

art trade
BM.413 (R)
SN Use for the exchange of art as a commodity before the 20th century. For contemporary buying and selling of art, use **art market.**
UF trade, art
CN B.BM.ARI.FIM.AFU

art, academic
USE **academic art**

art, academies of
USE **art schools**

art, air
USE **air art**

art, amateur
USE **amateur art**

art, apocalyptic
USE **apocalyptic art**

art, cave
USE **cave art**

art, children's
USE **children's art**

art, commercial
USE **commercial art**

art, community
USE **community art**

art, computer
USE **computer art**

art, Concrete
USE **Concrete art**

art, copy
USE **copy art**

art, correspondence
USE **correspondence art**

art, court
USE **court art**

art, didactic
USE **didactic art**

art, Direct
USE **Direct art**

art, dissident
USE **dissident art**

art, earth
USE **land art**

art, eco
USE **land art**

art, ecological
USE **land art**

art, environmental
USE **environmental art**

art, environmental (land art)
USE **land art**

art, ethnic
USE **ethnic art**

art, fantastic
USE **fantastic art**

art, figurative
USE **figurative art**

art, folk
USE **folk art**

art, funerary
USE **funerary art**

art, land
USE **land art**

art, laser
USE **laser art**

art, light
USE **light art**

art, mail
USE **correspondence art**

art, Matter
USE **Matter art**

art, monumental
USE **monumental art**

art, mourning
USE **funerary art**

art, municipal
USE **public art**

art, naive
USE **naive art**

art, nonconformist
USE **dissident art**

art, nonfigurative
USE **nonrepresentational art**

art, nonrepresentational
USE **nonrepresentational art**

art, objective
USE **figurative art**

art, Op
USE **Op art**

art, Optical
USE **Op art**

art, outsider
USE **art brut**

art, peasant
USE **folk art**

art, performance
USE **performance art**

art, philosophy of
USE **aesthetics**

art, postal
USE **correspondence art**

art, primitive
USE **primitive art**

art, Procedural
USE **Process art**

art, Process
USE **Process art**

art, psychiatric
USE **art brut**

art, psychotic
USE **art brut**

art, public
USE **public art**

art, raw
USE **art brut**

art, representational
USE **figurative art**

art, reprographic
USE **copy art**

art, schools of
USE **art schools**

art, sequential
USE **serial art**

art, serial
USE **serial art**

art, series
USE **serial art**

art, street
USE **street art**

art, Systems
USE **Systems art**

art, unofficial
USE **dissident art**

art, video
USE **video art**

art, visionary
USE **fantastic art**

art, works of
USE **works of art**

art, xerographic
USE **copy art**

art, Xerox
USE **copy art**

Arte Joven
USE **Art Nouveau**

Arte Metafisica
USE **Metaphysical**

Arte Povera
FL.3719 (L,R)
UF Art Povera
CN F.FL.ALO.BUE.ARI.AXC

artefacts
USE **artifacts**

arterial roads
USE **arterial streets**
arterials

arterial streets
RK.1542 (B)
ALT **arterial street**
SN Urban thoroughfares handling major portions of traffic, often larger than most streets and having medians;(EAA) use primarily when referring to the flow of traffic within a transportation system.

UF arterial roads
roads, arterial
streets, arterial
CN V.RK.ALO.ALO.BIQ.ARI.AFU.ALO.
ARI.AFU

arterials
RK.1549 (B)
ALT **arterial**
SN Intercity roads, usually with entrances at restricted locations and channelized intersections, designed to move large volumes of traffic; use only with reference to the flow of traffic within a transportation system.
UF arterial roads
roads, arterial
CN V.RK.ALO.ALO.BIQ.ARI.ALO.ALO

artesian wells
RK.595 (L)
ALT **artesian well**
SN Wells bored into a confined aquifer which overflow the wellhead, because the water level of the aquifer lies above the level of the wellhead; the water rises under its own pressure through the borehole. (W)
UF wells, artesian
CN V.RK.AFU.ALO.ALO.CFS.ALO.BCW.
CXA.ALO.AFU

articles
VW.5
ALT **article**
SN Literary compositions prepared for publication as an independent portion of a magazine, newspaper, encyclopedia, or other work. (GAHLM)
CN V.VW.AFU.AFU.AFU.ALO

articles of agreement
USE **agreements**

articles of apprenticeship
VW.916
ALT **article of apprenticeship**
SN Written agreements between masters and minors under which a minor agrees to work for a master for a stated period of time in return for instruction in a trade by a master. (BLACKS)
UF agreements, apprenticeship
apprenticeship agreements
apprenticeship, articles of
CN V.VW.AFU.ARI.AFU.BOK.BOK.BZY.
AFU

articles of association
USE **articles of incorporation**

articles of incorporation
VW.902 (L)
ALT **article of incorporation**
SN Written agreements embodying the purposes or other conditions of the association of a number of persons for the pursuit of a joint enterprise; especially those duly executed and filed with a state's administrative authorities so as to have the force of a charter under general incorporation law. (GAHLM)
UF articles of association
association, articles of
incorporation, articles of
CN V.VW.AFU.ARI.AFU.BOK.BOK.ARI

articulation
BM.48
SN Use when referring to the manner in which contiguous shapes are joined or formed in architectural or decorative designs or in works of art; also, the clarification of an architectural design by emphasizing certain elements of the structure.
UF spatial articulation
CN B.BM.AFU.AFU.ARI.AFU.ALO

artifacts
VB.85
ALT **artifact**
SN Objects made, modified, or used by man. (HOLHZR)
UF artefacts
realia
CN V.VB.ALO.ARI

artificial asphalt
MT.970
SN A term applied to the bituminous residue from coal distillation mechanically mixed with sand or limestone. (MH)
UF asphalt, artificial
CN M.MT.AFU.AFU.ALO.ALO.AFU.AFU
.AFU

artificial inorganic black pigment
MT.1576
UF black pigment, artificial inorganic
black pigment, synthetic inorganic
inorganic black pigment, artificial
inorganic black pigment, synthetic
pigment, artificial inorganic black
pigment, synthetic inorganic black
synthetic inorganic black pigment
CN M.MT.AFU.AFU.ARI.AFU.AFU.ALO.
ALO.AFU.ALO

artificial inorganic blue pigment
MT.1593
UF blue pigment, artificial inorganic
blue pigment, synthetic inorganic
inorganic blue pigment, artificial
inorganic blue pigment, synthetic
pigment, artificial inorganic blue
pigment, synthetic inorganic blue
synthetic inorganic blue pigment
CN M.MT.AFU.AFU.ARI.AFU.AFU.ALO.
ALO.ALO.ARI

artificial inorganic brown pigment
MT.1624
UF brown pigment, artificial inorganic
brown pigment, synthetic inorganic
inorganic brown pigment, artificial
inorganic brown pigment, synthetic
pigment, artificial inorganic brown
pigment, synthetic inorganic brown
synthetic inorganic brown pigment
CN M.MT.AFU.AFU.ARI.AFU.AFU.ALO.
ALO.ARI.ARI

artificial inorganic green pigment
MT.1647
UF green pigment, artificial inorganic
green pigment, synthetic inorganic
inorganic green pigment, artificial
inorganic green pigment, synthetic
pigment, artificial inorganic green
pigment, synthetic inorganic green
synthetic inorganic green pigment
CN M.MT.AFU.AFU.ARI.AFU.AFU.ALO.
ALO.AXC.ARI

artificial inorganic pigment
MT.1550
UF artificial mineral pigment
inorganic pigment, artificial
mineral pigment, artificial
pigment, artificial inorganic
pigment, artificial mineral
CN M.MT.AFU.AFU.ARI.AFU.AFU.ALO.
AFU.AFU.AFU

artificial inorganic red pigment
MT.1695
UF inorganic red pigment, artificial
inorganic red pigment, synthetic
pigment, artificial inorganic red
pigment, synthetic inorganic red
red pigment, artificial inorganic
red pigment, synthetic inorganic
synthetic inorganic red pigment
CN M.MT.AFU.AFU.ARI.AFU.AFU.ALO.
ALO.BCW.ARI

artificial inorganic violet pigment
MT.1718
UF inorganic violet pigment, artificial
inorganic violet pigment, synthetic
pigment, artificial inorganic violet
pigment, synthetic inorganic violet
synthetic inorganic violet pigment
violet pigment, artificial inorganic
violet pigment, synthetic inorganic
CN M.MT.AFU.AFU.ARI.AFU.AFU.ALO.
ALO.BIQ.ARI

artificial inorganic yellow pigment
MT.1769
UF inorganic yellow pigment, artificial
inorganic yellow pigment, synthetic
pigment, artificial inorganic yellow
pigment, synthetic inorganic yellow
synthetic inorganic yellow pigment
yellow pigment, artificial inorganic
yellow pigment, synthetic inorganic
CN M.MT.AFU.AFU.ARI.AFU.AFU.ALO.
ALO.BUE.ARI

artificial islands
RK.1347 (A,L)
ALT **artificial island**
UF islands, artificial

CN V.RK.AFU.ALO.ARI.AXC.AFU

artificial ivory
MT.2800
SN Material made to imitate ivory; usually consisting of celluloid, a synthetic resin, or, before 1881, ceramic.
UF ivory, artificial
CN M.MT.AFU.BCW.CFS.AFU

artificial ivorytypes
USE **ivorytypes**

artificial light
BM.847 (L,B)
UF artificial lighting
light, artificial
lighting, artificial
CN B.BM.CFS.AXC.ALO.AFU.ALO.AFU.AFU

artificial lighting
USE **artificial light**

artificial mineral pigment
USE **artificial inorganic pigment**

artificial mounds
USE **mounds**

artificial negatives
USE **clichés-verre**

artificial organic black pigment
USE **synthetic organic black pigment**

artificial organic blue pigment
USE **synthetic organic blue pigment**

artificial organic green pigment
USE **synthetic organic green pigment**

artificial organic pigment
USE **synthetic organic pigment**

artificial organic red pigment
USE **synthetic organic red pigment**

artificial organic violet pigment
USE **synthetic organic violet pigment**

artificial organic yellow pigment
USE **synthetic organic yellow pigment**

artificial perspective
USE **linear perspective**

artificial resins
USE **plastics**

artificial rubber
USE **elastomers**

artificial ruins
RK.1334
ALT **artificial ruin**
UF ruins, artificial
ruins, sham
sham ruins
CN V.RK.AFU.ALO.ARI.AFU.ARI.AFU

artificial ski slopes
RK.1077 (B)
ALT **artificial ski slope**
SN Usually small structures with artificial surfaces, often plastic, upon which to practice skiing. (HSRBD)
UF ski slopes, artificial
CN V.RK.AFU.ALO.ALO.EWY.BIQ.AFU

artificial stone
MT.2801 (A,L,B)
UF stone, artificial
CN M.MT.AFU.BCW.CFS.ALO

artificial ultramarine
USE **strong blue**
strong purplish blue

artificial ultramarine blue
MT.1594
UF blue, artificial ultramarine
blue, French
blue, Gmelin's
blue, lime (artificial ultramarine blue)
blue, new
blue, permanent
blue, royal
blue, ultramarine (artificial)
French blue
French ultramarine
Gmelin's blue
lime blue (artificial ultramarine blue)
new blue
outremer
permanent blue
royal blue
Ultramarinblau
ultramarine blue, artificial
ultramarine, French
CN M.MT.AFU.AFU.ARI.AFU.AFU.ALO.ALO.ALO.ARI.AFU

artificial vermilion
USE **grayish purplish red**

Artigue process
KT.350
SN A variant of the carbon process to produce contact prints; the image is formed from a pigment, usually carbon black, in a colloid suspension that has been made light-sensitive with bichromates. Marketed under the name Charbon Velours.
UF Artigueotype
Charbon Velours
CN K.KT.AFU.ALO.DUC.DIO.ALO.DIO.AFU.AFU.AFU

Artigueotype
USE **Artigue process**

Artisan Mannerist
FL.3201 (B)
ALT **Artisan Mannerism**
UF Mannerist, Artisan
CN F.FL.ALO.BCW.ALO.ARI.BIQ.BIQ.AFU.ALO.AFU

artisans
USE **craftsmen**

artisans' marks
VW.742 (L,R)
ALT **artisan's mark**
UF craftsmen's marks
marks, artisans'
marks, craftsmen's
CN V.VW.AFU.ALO.ALO.AFU.AXC.AXC.ARI

artist's tables
USE **drawing tables**

artistic dissenters
USE **dissident artists**

artistic masterpiece
USE **masterpiece**

artists
HG.91 (A,L,B,R)
ALT **artist**
SN Use specifically for people who produce work in the visual arts. For those in the performing arts, use **performing artists.**
CN H.HG.AFU.AXC.AXC.AFU.AFU.ALO.AXC

artists-in-residence
HG.92
ALT **artist-in-residence**
SN Artists officially associated with an organization.
CN H.HG.AFU.AXC.AXC.AFU.AFU.ALO.AXC.AFU

artists' colonies
RD.71 (A,L,R)
ALT **artist's colony**
UF art colonies
colonies, art
colonies, artists'
CN V.RD.AFU.BIQ.AFU

artists' colormen
HG.550
ALT **artist's colorman**
SN Persons who develop and supply artists' colors.
UF color makers
colormen, artists'
makers, color
CN H.HG.AFU.AXC.BUE.AXC.AFU

artists' contracts
VW.895 (L,R)
ALT **artist's contract**
UF contracts, artists'
CN V.VW.AFU.ARI.AFU.BOK.BOK.ALO.ALO.ARI.ALO

artists' houses
RK.325 (B,R)
ALT **artist's house**
UF artists' residences
houses, artists'
residences, artists'
CN V.RK.AFU.ALO.ALO.AXC.ALO.BOK.ALO

artists' marks
VW.743 (L,R)
ALT **artist's mark**
UF marks, artists'
CN V.VW.AFU.ALO.ALO.AFU.AXC.AXC.AXC

artists' materials
MT.2365 (L,R)
UF materials, artists'
CN M.MT.AFU.ARI.BCW

artists' residences
USE **artists' houses**

artists' rights
BM.444
SN Use with regard to legal protection for the work of visual artists, including copyright, protection from mutilation, and royalty payments.
UF rights, artists'
CN B.BM.BCW.ALO

artists' sketchbooks
VW.519 (R)
ALT **artist's sketchbook**
UF sketchbooks, artists'
CN V.VW.AFU.ALO.AFU.AFU.AFU.DCU.AFU

artists, benday
USE **benday artists**

artists, commercial
USE **commercial artists**

artists, conceptual
USE **conceptual artists**

artists, display
USE **display designers**

artists, dissident
USE **dissident artists**

artists, doll
USE **dollmakers**

artists, environmental
USE **environmental artists**

artists, fashion
USE **fashion illustrators**

artists, fiber
USE **fiber artists**

artists, folk
USE **folk artists**

artists, graphic (draftsmen)
USE **draftsmen**

artists, graphic (printmakers)
USE **printmakers**

artists, performance
USE **performance artists**

artists, performing
USE **performing artists**

artists, tattoo
USE **tattoo artists**

artists, woodblock
USE **wood engravers**

arts
KD.4 (L,R)
SN Use broadly for the areas of activity that encompass both performing and visual arts. With reference to the fine arts or the fine and decorative arts together, use **art.**
CN K.KD.AFU.AFU.AFU.AFU

arts agencies, state
USE **art commissions**

Arts and Crafts
FL.3313 (A,L,B,R)
ALT **Arts and Crafts Movement**
CN F.FL.ALO.BCW.ALO.AXC.DIO.ALO.ARI

arts centers, performing
USE **performing arts centers**

arts, applied
USE **decorative arts**

arts, decorative
USE **decorative arts**

arts, dramatic
USE **drama**

arts, fine
USE **fine arts**

arts, forbidden
USE **forbidden arts**

arts, graphic (printmaking)
USE **printmaking**

arts, illiberal
USE **mechanical arts**

arts, liberal
USE **liberal arts**

arts, liberal (Medieval studies)
USE **liberal arts (Medieval studies)**

arts, mechanical
USE **mechanical arts**

arts, minor
USE **decorative arts**

arts, performing
USE **performing arts**

arts, popular
USE **popular culture**

arts, theater
USE **theater**

arts, visual
USE **visual arts**

artworks
USE **works of art**

Arua
FL.1570
CN F.FL.ALO.ALO.ARI.ARI.AFU.ARI

Arunta
FL.3611 (L)
UF Aranda
CN F.FL.ALO.BOK.AFU.AFU.AFU

Arusha
FL.642 (L)
CN F.FL.ALO.AFU.AXC.AXC.BCW.AFU

Arusi
FL.616
UF Galla
CN F.FL.ALO.AFU.AXC.AXC.ARI.ALO

Aryan
USE **Vedic**

Aryavarta
USE **Nagara**

arzica
USE **weld**

as-built drawings
VD.91
ALT **as-built drawing**
SN Designates drawings that reflect a structure as it was actually built. May be a drawing that appears to correspond to the final structure or working drawings updated during construction.
UF drawings, as-built
CN V.VD.AFU.ALO.AFU

Asante
USE **Ashanti**

asarota
RT.816
ALT **asarotum**
SN Painted pavements used by the ancient Romans before their use of mosaic work. (DAC)
CN V.RT.AFU.ALO.AFU.BZY.ALO.AFU

asbestine
MT.563
SN Finely fibrous variety of talc used especially as a filler for rubber and paper and as an extender and white pigment in paint. (W)
CN M.MT.AFU.AFU.AFU.CFS.AFU.HCQ.AFU

asbestos
MT.488 (A,L,B)
SN General name for several varieties of fibrous minerals, the fibers of which are valued for their heat-resistant and chemical-resistant properties. (MH)
CN M.MT.AFU.AFU.AFU.CFS.AFU.ALO

asbestos-cement
MT.9 (L,B)
CN M.MT.AFU.AFU.AFU.ALO.AFU.AFU.ALO

asbestos curtains
TB.403
ALT **asbestos curtain**
SN Curtains which close the stage of a theater from the auditorium in case of fire, preventing the spread of flame and smoke; usually fabricated of woven asbestos and steel wire. (DAC)
UF curtains, asbestos
curtains, fire
curtains, safety
fire curtains
safety curtains
CN V.TB.AFU.ARI.DUC.AFU

Ascension Day
KM.78 (L,R)
SN The day 40 days after Easter observed in commemoration of Christ's ascension into heaven. (WCOL)
CN K.KM.AFU.CFS.ARI.AFU

aseismic design
USE **earthquake-resistant construction**

ash dumps
USE **ashpits**

ash glaze
MT.2559
SN Ceramic glaze, utilizing wood or vegetable ashes as the fluxing ingredient. (MAYER)
UF glaze, ash
CN M.MT.AFU.ARI.CRG.ARI.ARI.AFU.AFU.AFU.AFU

ash-leafed maple
USE **box elder**

ash (residue)
MT.2043 (L,B)
SN Earthy or mineral residue that remains after combustible substances have been thoroughly burned. (W)
UF ash, fly
fly ash
CN M.MT.AFU.AFU.ARI.AXC.AFU

Ash Wednesday
KM.79
SN The first day of Lent. (WCOL)
CN K.KM.AFU.CFS.ARI.ALO

ash (wood)
MT.1100 (L)
CN M.MT.AFU.AFU.ALO.BIQ.DCU.AFU.AFU.AFU.ARI

ash, American
USE **white ash**

ash, American white
USE **white ash**

ash, blue ultramarine
USE **moderate blue**

ash, bone
USE **bone white**

ash, Canadian
USE **white ash**

ash, common
USE **European ash**

ash, European
USE **European ash**

ash, fly
USE **ash (residue)**

ash, mountain
USE **mountain ash**

ash, ultramarine
USE **ultramarine blue**

ash, ultramarine grey
USE **light greenish gray**

ash, white
USE **white ash**

Ashanti
FL.287 (L)
UF Asante
CN F.FL.ALO.AFU.AXC.AFU.ARI.AFU.AFU.ARI

Ashberry metal
MT.409
SN Pewter for tableware, containing some nickel and aluminum. (MH)
UF metal, Ashberry
CN M.MT.AFU.AFU.AFU.BZY.AFU.AFU.AFU.ALO.BUE.ALO.AFU

Ashcan School
FL.1750 (L,R)
CN F.FL.ALO.ALO.BCW.AFU.CFS.ALO

ashes, blue
USE **Bremen blue**

Ashikaga
USE **Muromachi**

Ashira
USE **Shira**

ashlar
MT.901 (B)
SN Small dimension stone with a flat faced surface, usually square or rectangular.
UF ashlar masonry
masonry, ashlar
CN M.MT.AFU.AFU.AFU.DCU.ARI.AFU.AFU.AFU

ashlar brick
MT.100
UF brick, ashlar
brick, rock-faced
rock-faced brick
CN M.MT.AFU.AFU.AFU.AXC.ALO.AFU.ALO.BIQ.AFU

ashlar masonry
USE **ashlar**

Ashluslay
FL.1637 (L)
CN F.FL.ALO.ALO.ARI.ARI.AXC.ALO

Ashogo
USE **Tsogo**

Ashoka
USE **Asóka**

ashpits
RT.1152
ALT **ashpit**
SN Chambers located below the fireplace or firebox for the collection and removal of ashes.
UF ash dumps
cleanouts
dumps, ash
CN V.RT.AFU.BOK.ALO.ALO.AFU

ashtray stands
USE **smokers**

Asian
FL.1761 (L,B,R)
UF Oriental
CN F.FL.ALO.ARI

Asian, Central
USE **Central Asian**

Asian, East
USE **East Asian**

Asian, South
USE **South Asian**

Asian, Southeast
USE **Southeast Asian**

Asiatic bases
RT.113
ALT **Asiatic base**
SN Use for bases of Ionic columns following a pattern developed in Asia Minor, with an upper torus surmounting a disk generally composed of shallow scotias, both elements being usually horizontally fluted.
UF bases, Asiatic
CN V.RT.AFU.AFU.AFU.AXC.BIQ.ALO.AFU

Asiatic boxwood
USE **boxwood**

Asmat
FL.3629 (L)
CN F.FL.ALO.BOK.ALO.BCW.AFU.AFU.AFU

Asóka
FL.2194
UF Ashoka
CN F.FL.ALO.ARI.AXC.ALO.AFU.ARI.ALO.AFU

aspect
USE **orientation (architecture)**

aspen
MT.1275 (L)
UF Populus tremula
CN M.MT.AFU.AFU.ALO.BIQ.DCU.AFU.AFU.AFU.KFK.ALO.ALO

aspen (American aspen)
USE **American aspen**

aspen, American
USE **American aspen**

aspen, big toothed
USE **big toothed aspen**

aspen, quaking
USE **American aspen**

asphalt
MT.968 (A,L,B)
CN M.MT.AFU.AFU.ALO.ALO.AFU

asphalt cement
MT.10 (L)
UF cement, asphalt
CN M.MT.AFU.AFU.AFU.ALO.AFU.AFU.ARI

asphalt concrete
MT.197 (A,L)
SN High-quality, thoroughly controlled hot mixture of asphalt cement and well-graded, high-quality aggregate, thoroughly compacted into a uniform dense mass. (STEIN)
UF asphaltic concrete
concrete, asphalt
concrete, asphaltic
CN M.MT.AFU.AFU.AFU.BCW.AFU.AFU.AFU

asphalt emulsion mixtures
USE **emulsified asphalt**

asphalt oil
USE **petroleum asphalt**

asphalt, artificial
USE **artificial asphalt**

asphalt, emulsified
USE **emulsified asphalt**

asphalt, lake
USE **lake asphalt**

asphalt, liquid
USE **liquid asphalt**

asphalt, native
USE **natural asphalt**

asphalt, natural
USE **natural asphalt**

asphalt, oil
USE **petroleum asphalt**

asphalt, paving
USE **paving asphalt**

asphalt, petroleum
USE **petroleum asphalt**

asphalt, rapid-curing
USE **rapid-curing asphalt**

asphalt, rock
USE **rock asphalt**

asphalt, slow-curing
USE **slow-curing asphalt**

asphalters
HG.582
ALT **asphalter**
SN Persons who lay down asphalt. (OED)
CN H.HG.AFU.AXC.BZY.AFU.AFU

asphaltic concrete
USE **asphalt concrete**

asphaltum
MT.1615
UF bitumen (brown pigment)
CN M.MT.AFU.AFU.ARI.AFU.AFU.ALO.ALO.ARI.ALO.AFU

asphaltum (color)
USE **dark grayish yellowish brown**

assassinations
KM.138 (L)
SN Murders of high public officials or other prominent persons, whether by persons acting alone or in conspiracy with others. (DOAP)
CN K.KM.AFU.DOI.ALO.ALO.AFU

assayers
HG.334 (L)
ALT **assayer**
SN Chemists who analyze the value and quantity of metals in ores and alloys. (W)
CN H.HG.AFU.AXC.BIQ.AFU.AFU.ARI.AFU

assemblage
KT.534 (L)
SN A 20th-century technique of creating a three-dimensional work of art by combining various elements, especially found objects; may include elements painted, carved, or modeled by the artist. (MAYER)
CN K.KT.AFU.ALO.ELK.DIO.ALO.AFU

assemblers
HG.440
ALT **assembler**
SN Persons who assemble component parts of an item of manufacture. (W)
CN H.HG.AFU.AXC.BUE.ALO.AFU

assemblies, column and beam
USE **post-and-beam structures**

assembling
KT.21
ALT **assembled**
CN K.KT.AFU.ALO.BCW

assembling bolts
TF.309
ALT **assembling bolt**
SN Threaded bolts for holding together temporarily parts of a structure during riveting. (DAC)
UF bolts, assembling
CN V.TF.AFU.AFU.AFU.ALO.AFU.ALO.AFU.ALO

assembly buildings
USE **assembly halls**

assembly drawings
VD.112
ALT **assembly drawing**
UF drawings, assembly
major assemblies
CN V.VD.AFU.ALO.DCU.AFU

assembly drawings, minor
USE **minor assembly drawings**

assembly facilities
USE **assembly halls**

assembly halls
RK.1186 (A,L,B)
ALT **assembly hall**
UF assembly buildings
assembly facilities
buildings, assembly
facilities, assembly
halls (assembly halls)
halls, assembly
halls, public
public halls
CN V.RK.AFU.ALO.ALO.FUA.AFU

assembly plants
RK.615 (B)
ALT **assembly plant**
SN Factories where parts for a complete unit are put together, as in automobile manufacturing. (RHDEL2)
UF plants, assembly
CN V.RK.AFU.ALO.ALO.CLM.ALO.ALO.AFU.AFU

assembly rooms
RM.122 (A,B)
ALT **assembly room**
SN Use for rooms, primarily of the 18th century, in which social gatherings and balls (commonly referred to as assemblies) were held.
UF rooms, assembly
CN V.RM.AFU.DIO.ALO.BIQ.AFU

assessing
KG.179
ALT **assessed**
SN Determining the value of property for taxation purposes.
CN K.KG.AFU.ALO.ARI.ARI

assessment districts
RG.242
ALT **assessment district**
UF ADs
districts, assessment
CN V.RG.ALO.AFU.AFU.AFU

assessment, needs
USE **needs assessment**

assimilation (color)
BM.124

SN Phenomenon of visual preception which occurs when interlocking areas of contrasting colors are combined on the retina and perceived as a mixed color.
CN B.BM.AFU.AFU.ARI.BOK.ALO.ALO.AFU.AFU

Assiniboin
FL.1371 (L)
UF Stoney
CN F.FL.ALO.ALO.ARI.AFU.BOK.ARI

assistants
HG.763 (B)
ALT **assistant**
SN Persons who act as subordinates to another or as an official in a subordinate capacity. (W)
UF hands
helpers
mates
CN H.HG.AFU.BIQ.ALO

assisting
KG.46 (L)
SN Providing direct economic or financial aid. (RLG7)
CN K.KG.AFU.AFU.ARI.ALO

associated architects
HG.84
ALT **associated architect**
SN Architects working with other architects in a temporary agreement or partnership of joint venture. (STEIN)
UF architects, associated
CN H.HG.AFU.AXC.AXC.AFU.AFU.ALO.ALO.AFU

association buildings
USE **societies' buildings**

association, articles of
USE **articles of incorporation**

associations
HG.818 (L,B,R)
ALT **association**
CN H.HG.ALO.BCW

associations, architectural
USE **architectural societies**

associations, civic
USE **community organizations**

associations, professional
USE **professional associations**

associations, trade
USE **trade associations**

associations, voluntary
USE **voluntary associations**

assurance, quality
USE **quality control**

Assyrian
FL.2977 (L,B)
CN F.FL.ALO.AXC.ARI.BCW.AFU.BUE

Assyrian Colony period
FL.2853
UF Old Assyrian Colony period
CN F.FL.ALO.AXC.ARI.AFU.AFU.ALO

Assyrian, Late
USE **Late Assyrian**

Assyrian, Middle
USE **Middle Assyrian**

Assyrian, Old
USE **Old Assyrian**

Assyro-Babylonian
FL.2984 (A,L)
SN Use for art or architecture that is not distinctly Assyrian or Babylonian but has characteristics of both.
CN F.FL.ALO.AXC.ARI.BCW.ALO.AFU

astragal ends
TG.893
ALT **astragal end**
UF ends, astragal
ends, ovolo
ovolo ends
CN V.TG.ALO.DUC.AFU

astragal planes
USE **bead planes**

astragals
RT.784 (B)
ALT **astragal**
SN Small moldings having a rounded, convex section. (RS)
UF bagnettes
baguets
chaplets
CN V.RT.AFU.ALO.AFU.BOK.AFU.AFU.AXC.BCW.AFU

Astrolabe Bay
FL.3636
CN F.FL.ALO.BOK.ALO.BCW.ALO.AFU

astrological charts
VW.235 (L)
ALT **astrological chart**
UF charts, astrological
CN V.VW.AFU.AFU.AFU.FZU.AXC.ALO.AFU

astrology
KD.302 (L,R)
CN K.KD.AFU.BIQ.ALO

astronautical charts
VW.179 (L)
ALT **astronautical chart**
SN Charts used for navigation beyond the earth's atmosphere, including interplanetary or interstellar space.
UF charts, astronautical
CN V.VW.AFU.AFU.AFU.FZU.AXC.AFU.ARI.AXC.AFU

astronautical museums
RK.404 (A,L)
ALT **astronautical museum**
UF museums, astronautical
CN V.RK.AFU.ALO.ALO.BCW.AXC.ARI.AXC.BZY.AFU.AFU

astronomers
HG.326 (L,R)
ALT **astronomer**
CN H.HG.AFU.AXC.BIQ.AFU.AFU.AFU

astronomical charts
VW.180 (L,R)
ALT **astronomical chart**
UF celestial charts
charts, astronomical
charts, celestial
charts, star
maps, star
star charts
star maps
CN V.VW.AFU.AFU.AFU.FZU.AXC.AFU.ARI.AXC.ALO

astronomical museums
RK.415 (L)
ALT **astronomical museum**
UF museums, astronomical
CN V.RK.AFU.ALO.ALO.BCW.AXC.ARI.CFS.ALO

astronomical observatories
RK.1173 (A,L,B)
ALT **astronomical observatory**
UF observatories, astronomical
CN V.RK.AFU.ALO.ALO.FIM.ALO.ALO.AFU

astronomical photographs
USE **astrophotographs**

astronomical photography
KT.294 (L)
SN Use for techniques to record images of subjects located outside the atmosphere of the earth and certain phenomena associated with the ionosphere, such as aurorae and meteor showers. For the taking of photographs from beyond the earth's atmosphere, use **space photography.** For photography of the earth from aircraft, use **aerial photography.**
UF astrophotography
celestial photography
photography, astronomical
photography, celestial
CN K.KT.AFU.ALO.DUC.DIO.AFU.ARI

astronomy
KD.259 (A,L,R)
CN K.KD.AFU.ARI.CLM.AFU

astrophotographs
VJ.126
ALT **astrophotograph**
SN Use for photographs taken of celestial bodies or astronomical phenomena. For photographs taken from beyond the earth's atmosphere, use **space photographs.** For photographs of the earth taken from aircraft, use **aerial photographs.**

UF astronomical photographs
celestial photographs
photographs, astronomical
photographs, celestial
CN V.VJ.AFU.AXC.AFU

astrophotography
USE **astronomical photography**

astrophysics
KD.260 (L)
SN Study of astronomical phenomena in terms of the underlying physical processes. (PG)
CN K.KD.AFU.ARI.CLM.AFU.AFU

Asturian
FL.2475 (L)
CN F.FL.ALO.AXC.AFU.AXC.AFU

Asuka
FL.1974
UF Suiko
CN F.FL.ALO.ARI.ALO.ALO.AFU.AXC.AFU

asylum camps, first
USE **refugee camps**

asylum locks
TF.228
ALT **asylum lock**
SN Locks used on doors of psychiatric institutions providing special protection against tampering. (STEIN)
UF locks, asylum
CN V.TF.AFU.AFU.AFU.AFU.DIO.BIQ.ALO.AFU

asylums
RK.787 (A,L,B,R)
ALT **asylum**
UF homes (institutions)
CN V.RK.AFU.ALO.ALO.CXA.ALO.ALO.ARI

asylums, insane
USE **psychiatric hospitals**

asylums, orphan
USE **orphanages**

asymmetry
BM.49 (B,R)
ALT **asymmetrical**
CN B.BM.AFU.AFU.ARI.AFU.ARI

Atabeg
FL.3433
CN F.FL.ALO.BIQ.AFU.BCW

Atacama
USE **Atacameño**

Atacaman
USE **Atacameño**

Atacameño
FL.1183 (L)
UF Atacama
Atacaman
Chincha-Atacaman
CN F.FL.ALO.ALO.ALO.ARI.BCW.AFU

ataduras
RT.795
ALT **atadura**
SN In Mayan architecture, facade moldings on the exterior of a building; characteristic of the Puuc style. (HAS)
CN V.RT.AFU.ALO.AFU.BOK.AFU.ALO.AFU

Atakapa
FL.1430
CN F.FL.ALO.ALO.ARI.AFU.BZY.AFU

Atarco
FL.1159
CN F.FL.ALO.ALO.ALO.ARI.AXC.AFU.BCW.AFU

Atchana ware
FL.2934
UF Billa ware
Hurrian ware
Mitannian pottery
pottery, Mitannian
ware, Atchana
ware, Billa
ware, Hurrian
CN F.FL.ALO.AXC.ARI.AXC.ALO.BIQ.ALO

ateliers
USE **studios**
workshops

ateliers (work spaces)
USE **studios (work spaces)**
workshops (work spaces)

Aterian
FL.39
CN F.FL.ALO.AFU.AFU.AFU.AFU.AFU

Athabaskan
FL.1226
CN F.FL.ALO.ALO.ARI.AFU.AFU.ARI.ALO

atheism
BM.697 (L)
SN Doctrine that there is neither God nor any other deity. (W)
CN B.BM.BZY.ALO.ARI.AXC

athenaeums
RK.1202
ALT **athenaeum**
CN V.RK.AFU.ALO.ALO.FZU.AFU

athéniennes
TG.626
ALT **athénienne**
SN Ornate, multifunctional tripods, especially those in the style of antique bronzes from Herculaneum; common in Neoclassical French furniture.
CN V.TG.AFU.AFU.BIQ.BCW.AFU.BCW.ALO.AFU

athletic clubs
RK.1026 (A,L,B)
ALT **athletic club**
UF clubs, athletic
clubs, health
clubs, sports
health clubs
sports clubs
CN V.RK.AFU.ALO.ALO.EWY.AXC.ALO.AFU

athletic facilities
USE **sports complexes**

athletic fields
RK.1477 (A,L,B)
ALT **athletic field**
UF fields, athletic
fields, playing
grounds, sports
playfields
playing fields
sports grounds
CN V.RK.ALO.ALO.BCW.AFU

athletics buildings
USE **sports buildings**

athracene violet, dark
USE **dark grayish purple**

Atie
USE **Attie**

Atisha Style
USE **Kadam School**

atlantes
RT.62 (A,R)
ALT **atlante**
SN Figures of men used as supports or apparent supports. (RS)
UF telamones
CN V.RT.AFU.AFU.AFU.AXC.ALO.AFU

Atlantic cedar
MT.1335
UF atlas cedar
cedar, Atlantic
cedar, atlas
Cedrus atlantica
CN M.MT.AFU.AFU.ALO.BIQ.DCU.AFU.AFU.ALO.ALO.ALO

Atlantic white cedar
USE **white cypress**

atlas cedar
USE **Atlantic cedar**

atlases
VW.123 (L,R)
ALT **atlas**
SN Volumes of maps, with or without descriptive text, which may be issued to supplement or accompany texts or be published independently. (LG)
CN V.VW.AFU.AFU.AFU.FZU.AXC.AFU.AFU

atlases, city
USE **city atlases**

atlases, county
USE **county atlases**

atlases, historical
USE **historical atlases**

atlases, insurance
USE **fire insurance maps**

atlases, national
USE **national atlases**

atlases, regional
USE **regional atlases**

atlases, state
USE **state atlases**

atlases, statistical
USE **statistical atlases**

atlases, urban
USE **city atlases**

atlases, world
USE **world atlases**

Atlatongo
USE **Aztec II**

atmospheric perspective
USE **aerial perspective**

atmospheric pollution
USE **air pollution**

atmospheric pressure
BM.932 (L)
UF pressure, atmospheric
CN B.BM.CFS.AXC.BUE.ALO

atmospheric sciences
USE **meteorology**

Atnah
USE **Ahtena**

Atnatana
USE **Ahtena**

atolls
RD.221 (L)
ALT **atoll**
SN Designates circular, elliptical, or horseshoe-shaped islands or a ring of such islands, usually formed by coral reefs and enclosing a lagoon.
CN V.RD.ARI.AFU.AXC.AFU.ALO.AXC.ALO.AFU

atom smashers
USE **particle accelerators**

atomic bomb shelters
USE **nuclear bomb shelters**

atomic energy
USE **nuclear power**

atomic furnaces
USE **nuclear reactors**

atomic piles
USE **nuclear reactors**

atomic power plants
USE **nuclear power plants**

atomic power stations
USE **nuclear power plants**

atomic test sites
USE **nuclear test sites**

Atonement, Day of
USE **Yom Kippur**

atramentum
MT.2496
UF ink, Roman
Roman ink
CN M.MT.AFU.ARI.CRG.ALO.ALO.AFU

atrium houses
RK.257 (A,L,B)
ALT **atrium house**
SN Use for ancient Roman houses or similarly styled houses containing internal courtyards with impluvia but without colonnades; for houses with internal courtyards having colonnades, use **peristyle houses.**
UF houses, atrium
CN V.RK.AFU.ALO.ALO.AXC.ALO.AFU.CRG.AFU.AFU

atriums (church courtyards)
RM.46 (L,B,R)
ALT **atrium (church courtyard)**
SN Use for the colonnaded forecourts of early Christian churches.
CN V.RM.AFU.DIO.AFU.BCW.ARI.ARI.AFU

atriums (interior spaces)
RM.257 (L,B,R)
ALT **atrium (interior space)**
SN Use for many-storied, skylit spaces in or between high-rise buildings, common since 1960.
CN V.RM.AFU.DIO.ARI.ALO.ALO

atriums (Roman halls)
RM.41 (A,L,B,R)
ALT **atrium (Roman hall)**
SN Use for the main inner halls of Roman houses having a compluvium (opening in the roof) for rainwater and an impluvium (rectangular basin) to collect the water.
CN V.RM.AFU.DIO.AFU.BCW.ALO

Atsahuaca
FL.1604
CN F.FL.ALO.ALO.ARI.ARI.ALO.AFU.AFU

Atsina
FL.1372 (L)
UF Gros Ventre
CN F.FL.ALO.ALO.ARI.AFU.BOK.AXC

Atsugewi
FL.1248 (L)
UF Pit River Indians
CN F.FL.ALO.ALO.ARI.AFU.ALO.ALO

attached
DC.26
CN D.DC.AFU.ALO.ARI.AFU

attached columns
USE **engaged columns**

attachments, flash
USE **flash attachments**

attendance lists
VW.253
ALT **attendance list**
UF lists, attendance
CN V.VW.AFU.AFU.AFU.FZU.BCW.AFU.AFU

attendance records
VW.778
ALT **attendance record**
UF records, attendance
CN V.VW.AFU.ARI.AFU.ALO.BZY.AFU

Attic
FL.2614
CN F.FL.ALO.AXC.ALO.AFU.ALO.AXC.ALO.AXC.AFU

Attic bases
RT.114
ALT **Attic base**
SN Use for bases consisting of a scotia between an upper and lower torus, usually found on the Ionic order.
UF bases, Attic
CN V.RT.AFU.AFU.AFU.AXC.BIQ.ALO.ALO

attic stories
USE **attics (exterior stories)**

attics (exterior stories)
RM.410 (A,L,B)
ALT **attic (exterior story)**
SN Use to designate the exterior walled portions of buildings, above the uppermost cornice, whether fenestrated or not.
UF attic stories
CN V.RM.AFU.DUC.AFU

attics (interior spaces)
RM.258 (A,L,B)
ALT **attic (interior space)**
SN Use for spaces under sloping roofs, between the roof and the ceiling of the uppermost story.
UF cocklofts
garrets
CN V.RM.AFU.DIO.ARI.ALO.ARI

Attie
FL.294 (L)
UF Akye
Atie
Kuroba
CN F.FL.ALO.AFU.AXC.AFU.ARI.AFU.ALO.ARI

attiring houses
USE **tiring houses**

attorney, powers of
USE **powers of attorney**

attorneys
USE **lawyers**

attribution
BM.287 (L)
UF reattribution
CN B.BM.AFU.AXC.ALO

au premier coup
USE **alla prima**

Aua
FL.3677
UF Dourour
Durour
CN F.FL.ALO.BOK.ARI.AFU

Aubusson
FL.3210 (R)
CN F.FL.ALO.BCW.ALO.ARI.BIQ.BIQ.ARI.ALO.AFU

auction catalogs
VW.108 (L)
ALT **auction catalog**
SN Catalogs of objects, manuscripts, books, or other items offered for sale at auction.
UF catalogs, auction
CN V.VW.AFU.AFU.AFU.FZU.ALO.ALO.ARI.AFU.AFU

auction galleries
USE **auction houses**

auction houses
RK.138 (A)
ALT **auction house**
UF auction galleries
galleries, auction
houses, auction
CN V.RK.AFU.ALO.ALO.ALO.ARI.ALO

auctioneers
HG.399 (L)
ALT **auctioneer**
SN Persons who conduct the sale of goods at public auction usually as agents on commission. (W)
CN H.HG.AFU.AXC.BOK.ARI

auctions
KM.148 (L,R)
SN Public sales of property to the highest bidder, as by successive increased bids. (W)
CN K.KM.AFU.ELK.AFU

audience halls
USE **presence chambers**

audio cartridges
USE **audio cassettes**

audio cassettes
VW.633
ALT **audio cassette**
UF audio cartridges
cartridges, audio
cassettes, audio
CN V.VW.AFU.ALO.AFU.DZW.AFU.AFU.AFU.AFU

audio recordings
USE **sound recordings**

audio tapes
VW.632 (L,N,B)
ALT **audio tape**
SN Sound recordings on magnetic tape. (ICA)
UF phonotapes
recordings, tape
sound tapes
tape recordings
tapes, audio
tapes, sound
CN V.VW.AFU.ALO.AFU.DZW.AFU.AFU.AFU

audio-visual materials centers
USE **audiovisual centers**

audiovisual aids
USE **audiovisual materials**

audiovisual centers
RM.221 (L,B)
ALT **audiovisual center**
SN Instructional areas with equipment for storage and use of audiovisual aids. (ERIC)
UF audio-visual materials centers
centers, audiovisual
centers, instructional materials
educational media centers
instructional materials centers
media centers, educational
CN V.RM.AFU.DIO.ALO.DOI.AFU

audiovisual librarians
HG.306
ALT **audiovisual librarian**
SN Library personnel who plan audiovisual programs and administer libraries of film and audiovisual materials. (DOT)
UF film librarians
librarians, audiovisual
librarians, film
CN H.HG.AFU.AXC.BCW.ALO.BCW.ALO.AFU

audiovisual materials
VW.630 (L,B,R)
ALT **audiovisual material**
SN Use broadly for nonprint materials, such as slides, transparencies, films, or filmstrips, that make use of sight and sound to convey information, refers especially to such materials when used for instruction.
UF aids, audiovisual
audiovisual aids
audiovisual records
materials, audiovisual
materials, nonbook
materials, nonprint
nonbook materials
nonprint materials
records, audiovisual
CN V.VW.AFU.ALO.AFU.DZW.AFU

audiovisual records
USE **audiovisual materials**

audit reports
USE **audits**

auditing
KG.9 (L)
SN Reviewing a practice or set of practices to certify that they are being conducted in accordance with established principles. (RLG7)
CN K.KG.AFU.AFU.AFU.AXC

auditoriums
RM.60 (A,L,B)
ALT **auditorium**
SN Use for either rooms or entire buildings designed for a variety of activities such as would occur on a stage before a seated audience; for rooms or buildings used only for theatrical performances, use **theaters**; for rooms with fixed seating designed for lectures use **lecture halls.**
CN V.RM.AFU.DIO.ALO.AFU.AFU

auditoriums (theater spaces)
USE **theater auditoriums**

auditoriums, theater
USE **theater auditoriums**

auditors
HG.395 (L)
ALT **auditor**
SN Persons authorized to examine and verify accounts. (W)
CN H.HG.AFU.AXC.BOK.AFU.ARI

audits
VW.815 (L)
ALT **audit**
SN Final reports following formal examinations of account. (W)
UF audit reports
reports, audit
CN V.VW.AFU.ARI.AFU.BIQ.ALO

auger bits
TB.1098 (L)
ALT **auger bit**
SN Bits having a square tapered shank fitted into and rotated by a brace; used for drilling holes in wood. (DAC)
UF bits, auger
CN V.TB.ALO.ARI.AFU

auger bits, ship
USE **ship auger bits**

augers
TB.117 (L,N)
ALT **auger**
SN Hand tools with a long steel bit, usually not larger than 1 inch in diame-

ter, with a wood handle that is usually set perpendicular to the bit; used for boring holes in wood.
CN V.TB.AFU.ARI.AXC.ALO.ALO

augers, breast
USE **breast augers**

augers, burn
USE **burn augers**

augers, cylinder
USE **cylinder augers**

augers, downcutting
USE **nose augers**

augers, nose
USE **nose augers**

augers, pipe
USE **nose augers**

augers, pod
USE **shell augers**

augers, pump
USE **taper augers**

augers, raft
USE **raft augers**

augers, screw
USE **spiral augers**

augers, shell
USE **shell augers**

augers, shell (nose augers)
USE **nose augers**

augers, ship (bits)
USE **ship auger bits**

augers, snail
USE **shell augers**

augers, spiral
USE **spiral augers**

augers, tap
USE **taper augers**

augers, taper
USE **taper augers**

augers, taper shell
USE **taper augers**

augers, twist
USE **spiral augers**

augers, twist (bits)
USE **spiral bits**

augite
MT.489
SN Mineral occurring in igneous rocks such as basalt. (W)
CN M.MT.AFU.AFU.AFU.CFS.AFU.ARI

Augustan
FL.2718
CN F.FL.ALO.AXC.ALO.ALO.AFU.AXC.ALO.ALO

aumbries
TG.502 (L,R)
ALT **aumbry**
SN Medieval term for enclosed cupboards or storage niches enclosed by doors; often a receptacle for provisions to be given away as alms. The term remained in use chiefly for the aumbries, enclosed in or hung on a wall, near the altar in churches in which sacramental vessels were kept. When referring to such forms enclosed by doors from the 17th century on, use **cupboards.**
UF almeries
ambries
close cupboards
cupboards, close
CN V.TG.AFU.AFU.AXC.ALO.BUE.AXC

aural hospitals
RK.762 (A,L,B)
ALT **aural hospital**
UF hospitals, aural
CN V.RK.AFU.ALO.ALO.CXA.ALO.AFU.BCW.ALO.AFU

Aurangabad
FL.2253
CN F.FL.ALO.ARI.AXC.ALO.AFU.BZY.AFU.ALO

Aurangzeb
FL.2234
UF Alamgir
CN F.FL.ALO.ARI.AXC.ALO.AFU.BIQ.ALO.AFU.BOK

aureolin
USE **cobalt yellow**

aureolin (color)
USE **brilliant yellow**
strong yellow
vivid yellow

Auricular
FL.3184
UF Knorpelwork
Kwabornament
Lobate
CN F.FL.ALO.BCW.ALO.ARI.BIQ.BCW.AFU

Aurignacian
FL.2465 (L)
CN F.FL.ALO.AXC.AFU.ARI.ALO.AFU

Auripigment
USE **orpiment**

Aurora
FL.1023
CN F.FL.ALO.ALO.ALO.ALO.AFU.ALO.ARI.AFU.ALO.BOK

Aurora yellow
USE **cadmium yellow**

Ausonian
FL.2701
CN F.FL.ALO.AXC.ALO.ALO.AFU.AFU.ALO

austenitic stainless steel
MT.352 (L)
SN Stainless steel containing up to 30% chromium and 20% nickel; used chiefly in aircraft and other transport equipment because of its high strength and corrosion resistance. (MH)
UF stainless steel, austenitic
steel, austenitic stainless
CN M.MT.AFU.AFU.AFU.BZY.AFU.AFU.AFU.AFU.ALO.AFU.ALO.AFU.ALO.AFU

Austral Island
FL.3688
UF Tubuai Island
CN F.FL.ALO.BOK.AXC.AFU

Australian
FL.3609 (L,B)
CN F.FL.ALO.BOK.AFU

Australian Aboriginal
FL.3610 (A,L,R)
UF Aboriginal
Aboriginal, Australian
CN F.FL.ALO.BOK.AFU.AFU

Australian blackwood
USE **Australian locust**

Australian locust
MT.1201
SN A wood employed for cabinetwork, reddish brown to black in color and beautifully grained; similar to rosewood. (MH)
UF Acacia melanoxylon
Australian blackwood
blackwood, Australian
blackwood, Tasmanian
locust, Australian
Tasmanian blackwood
CN M.MT.AFU.AFU.ALO.BIQ.DCU.AFU.AFU.AFU.HCQ.ALO

Austrian
FL.3037 (L,B)
CN F.FL.ALO.BCW.AFU.ALO

Austrian black pine
USE **Austrian pine**

Austrian oak
MT.1230
UF oak, Austrian
CN M.MT.AFU.AFU.ALO.BIQ.DCU.AFU.AFU.AFU.IRA.ALO

Austrian pine
MT.1371 (L)
UF Austrian black pine
black pine
black pine, Austrian
pine, Austrian
pine, Austrian black
pine, black
CN M.MT.AFU.AFU.ALO.BIQ.DCU.AFU

.AFU.ALO.CXA.AFU

authenticating
KG.10 (L)
SN Determining the legitimacy of a document or other artifact, or validating a document, as done by an authorized person.
CN K.KG.AFU.AFU.AFU.BCW

authenticity
BM.1154 (L)
UF genuineness
CN B.BM.DIO.AFU

author catalogs
VW.98
ALT **author catalog**
SN Catalogs of works arranged alphabetically by authors' names or by other persons responsible for the intellectual content of the works, such as editors or translators.
UF catalogs, author
CN V.VW.AFU.AFU.AFU.FZU.ALO.AFU.AXC.AFU

author indexes
VW.440
ALT **author index**
SN Indexes consisting of the names of authors.
UF indexes, author
CN V.VW.AFU.AFU.ALO.EWY.BOK.ARI.AFU

authority control
KG.93
SN Establishing, maintaining, and applying consistent spellings and forms of proper names and terms used as the descriptive and access language for collections of documents and objects.
UF authority work
control, authority
control, terminological
control, vocabulary
terminological control
vocabulary control
work, authority
CN K.KG.AFU.AFU.AXC.CRG.AFU

authority files
VW.589 (L)
ALT **authority file**
SN Documentation of the form of names or subject headings used in a catalog, inventory, or information retrieval system.
UF files, authority
CN V.VW.AFU.ALO.AFU.BIQ.ALO.AFU

authority files, name
USE **name authority files**

authority files, subject
USE **subject authority files**

authority work
USE **authority control**

authorizing
KG.142
SN Giving sanction to an action or object, as done by a valid authority.
CN K.KG.AFU.AFU.BIQ.ARI

authors
HG.179 (L,R)
ALT **author**
SN Persons who write or otherwise compose books, articles, poems, plays, or other works which involve literary composition and are intended for publication. (W)
UF writers
CN H.HG.AFU.AXC.AXC.ARI.AFU.AFU

authorship
BM.26 (L)
CN B.BM.AFU.AFU.ALO.AFU

auto courts
USE **motor courts**

Auto-destructive
FL.3749
UF Self-destructive
CN F.FL.ALO.BUE.ARI.HIK.AFU

autobiographies
VW.297 (L)
ALT **autobiography**
SN Biographies of individuals written by themselves.
CN V.VW.AFU.AFU.ALO.ARI.AFU

autobiography
BM.278
CN B.BM.AFU.ARI.BIQ.BOK.AFU.AFU

autobody shops
USE **body shops**

Autochrome process
KT.313 (L)
SN An additive color process using a color screen with an irregular pattern formed from dyed starch grains. The screen was coated on a glass plate and a panchromatic black-and-white emulsion coated on top of the screen. The image is exposed through the glass and viewed from the emulsion side.
UF Lumière process
CN K.KT.AFU.ALO.DUC.DIO.ALO.AFU.AFU

Autochromes
VJ.67
ALT **Autochrome**
SN Photographs made by the Autochrome process.
CN V.VJ.AFU.AFU.ARI.AXC.BCW.AFU

autodromes
USE **automobile racetracks**

autograph albums
VW.486 (L,N,R)
ALT **autograph album**
SN Books, loose-leaf binders, or other volumes containing blank leaves, on which persons have written sentiments, quotations, or signatures. (GAHLM)
UF albums, autograph
autograph books
books, autograph
CN V.VW.AFU.ALO.AFU.AFU.AFU.ALO.AFU

autograph books
USE **autograph albums**

autographs
VW.7 (L)
ALT **autograph**
SN Documents, such as letters, notes, and manuscripts, written in, and usually signed with, the writer's own hand.
CN V.VW.AFU.AFU.AFU.ARI

autographs (signatures)
USE **signatures**

automated guideway transit
USE **people-movers**
personal rapid transit

automated guideway works
USE **personal rapid transit**

automated peoplemovers
USE **personal rapid transit**

automatic cameras
USE **electric eye cameras**

automatic doors
USE **mechanically operated doors**

automatic drills
USE **push drills**

automatic elevators
RT.1317 (L)
ALT **automatic elevator**
UF elevators, automatic
CN V.RT.ALO.ALO.AFU.ARI.ALO.ARI.AFU

automation
BM.1138 (L)
CN B.BM.CXA.ALO.AFU

automation, office
USE **office automation**

automatism
BM.569 (L,R)
ALT **automatist**
CN B.BM.BUE.AFU

Automats (TM)
RK.112 (B)
ALT **Automat (TM)**
UF restaurants, self-service
self-service restaurants
CN V.RK.AFU.ALO.ALO.ALO.AFU.AXC.

AFU

automobile dealerships
USE **automobile showrooms**

automobile factories
RK.616 (A,B)
ALT **automobile factory**
UF factories, automobile
CN V.RK.AFU.ALO.ALO.CLM.ALO.ALO.AFU.AFU.AFU

automobile graveyards
RK.1470 (L)
ALT **automobile graveyard**
UF automobile junkyards
graveyards, automobile
junkyards, automobile
CN V.RK.ALO.ALO.AXC.AFU.AFU.AFU

automobile junkyards
USE **automobile graveyards**

automobile museums
RK.405 (L)
ALT **automobile museum**
UF automotive museums
car museums
museums, automobile
museums, car
CN V.RK.AFU.ALO.ALO.BCW.AXC.ARI.AXC.BZY.ALO

automobile racetracks
RG.177 (L,B,R)
ALT **automobile racetrack**
UF autodromes
racetracks, automobile
speedways
CN V.RG.AFU.AFU.DOI.CFS.ALO.AFU

automobile service stations
USE **service stations**

automobile showrooms
RM.100 (A,L,B)
ALT **automobile showroom**
SN Includes both places where automobiles are displayed and entire dealership complexes including the sales-and-service building and surrounding lot.
UF automobile dealerships
dealerships, automobile
showrooms, automobile
CN V.RM.AFU.DIO.ALO.AXC.ARI.AFU

automotive museums
USE **automobile museums**

autoradiography
KT.389 (L,R)
SN Process of producing an image on a photographic film or plate by the radiations from a radioactive substance in an object which is in close contact with the emulsion. (W)
UF radioautography
CN K.KT.AFU.ALO.DUC.DIO.ARI.ARI.BIQ.AFU

autotype
USE **carbon process**

autowalks
USE **moving walkways**

autumn
BM.1037 (L,R)
UF fall
CN B.BM.CFS.AXC.CRG.ARI.AFU

aux deux crayons
USE **à deux crayons**

aux trois crayons
USE **à trois crayons**

auxiliaries
USE **auxiliary views**

auxiliary cartoons
VD.116
ALT **auxiliary cartoon**
UF cartoons, auxiliary
CN V.VD.AFU.ALO.DCU.ALO.AFU

auxiliary dead latches
TF.174
ALT **auxiliary dead latch**
UF auxiliary latch bolts
auxiliary latches
bolts, auxiliary latch
bolts, trigger
dead latches, auxiliary
deadlocking latch bolts
deadlocking latches
latches, auxiliary dead
latches, deadlocking
trigger bolts
CN V.TF.AFU.AFU.AFU.AFU.DIO.BCW.AFU.AFU

auxiliary drawings
USE **auxiliary views**

auxiliary fire alarm systems
RT.1506
ALT **auxiliary fire alarm system**
SN Use for fire alarm systems that transmit an alarm over a municipal system to the fire station.
UF fire alarm systems, auxiliary
systems, auxiliary fire alarm
CN V.RT.ALO.BIQ.AFU.AFU.AFU.AFU

auxiliary latch bolts
USE **auxiliary dead latches**

auxiliary latches
USE **auxiliary dead latches**

auxiliary rim locks
TF.218
ALT **auxiliary rim lock**
SN Surface-mounted locks in addition to the main lock on a door. (MEANS)
UF locks, auxiliary rim
rim locks, auxiliary
CN V.TF.AFU.AFU.AFU.AFU.DIO.BIQ.AFU.DZW.AFU

auxiliary sections
VD.74
ALT **auxiliary section**
SN Use for oblique sections that are intended to show true shape of an oblique plane in the structure or object.
UF sections, auxiliary
CN V.VD.AFU.AFU.BIQ.ALO.BIQ.BCW.AFU

auxiliary views
VD.21
ALT **auxiliary view**
SN Use for orthographic drawings projected at an angle other than the usual plan, section, or elevation, in order to show true shape of an oblique plane.
UF auxiliaries
auxiliary drawings
drawings, auxiliary
views, auxiliary
CN V.VD.AFU.AFU.BIQ.ALO.AFU

available light photography
KT.400 (L)
UF ambient light photography
existing light photography
low-light photography
photography, ambient light
photography, available light
photography, existing light
photography, low-light
CN K.KT.AFU.ALO.DUC.DIO.ARI.ARI.CFS.AFU

avalanche control
USE **avalanche protection**

avalanche protection
KG.114 (L)
UF avalanche control
control, avalanche
protection, avalanche
CN K.KG.AFU.AFU.BCW.ALO.AFU

avalanches
KM.102 (L,B)
SN Large masses of snow, earth, ice, rock, or other material in swift motion down a mountainside. (W)
CN K.KM.AFU.CXA.AFU

avant-corps
USE **pavilions (building divisions)**

avant-garde
BM.345 (L,R)
SN Use to describe attitudes, ideas, or works of art or architecture, especially from the late 19th to the mid-20th century, that depart from the existing norm in an original and experimental way.
CN B.BM.ALO.ALO.CLM.BCW

Avar
FL.3103 (L,R)
CN F.FL.ALO.BCW.ALO.ALO.AFU.BOK.ALO.AFU

aventurine
MT.559 (R)
SN Form of quartz crystal that comes from the Ural mountains and from India, made synthetically for costume jewelry under the name of goldstone. (MH)
CN M.MT.AFU.AFU.AFU.CFS.AFU.GRC.AFU.BCW.AFU

avenues
RK.1531 (L,B)
ALT **avenue**
SN Use for wide, straight, usually tree-lined roads or approaches.
CN V.RK.ALO.ALO.BIQ.ARI.AFU.ALO.AFU.ALO

average
USE **mean**

aviaries
RK.80 (A,L,N,B,R)
ALT **aviary**
SN Houses, enclosures, or large cages for confining live birds;(W) distinguished from **birdhouses** which house birds but do not confine them.
CN V.RK.AFU.ALO.ALO.AFU.ALO.ALO

aviation museums
USE **aeronautical museums**

aviation schools
USE **aeronautical schools**

Avignon berry
USE **buckthorn berry**

awards
VW.295 (A,L,N,B,R)
ALT **award**
SN Documents or tokens indicating that which is awarded, as a prize or honor; usually given in recognition of some act.
UF certificates of award
prizes
CN V.VW.AFU.AFU.ALO.ALO

awards, contract
USE **contract awards**

awe
BM.574 (L)
CN B.BM.BUE.ARI.ARI

awls
TB.383 (N)
ALT **awl**
SN Sharp metal points with wood handles; used to make small holes in wood or leather. (BLACKB)
CN V.TB.AFU.ARI.DIO.AFU

awls, burning
USE **burning awls**

awls, chisel-end marking
USE **scribe awls**

awls, flooring
USE **bradawls**

awls, marking
USE **scribe awls**

awls, peg
USE **peg awls**

awls, scratch
USE **scribe awls**

awls, scribe
USE **scribe awls**

awning hardware
TF.503
UF hardware, awning
CN V.TF.AFU.AFU.ALO.AFU

awning windows
RT.941
ALT **awning window**
SN Windows that have one or more top-hinged, out-swinging sashes. (STEIN)
UF top hung windows
windows, awning
windows, top hung
CN V.RT.AFU.ARI.AFU.AFU.BOK.AFU.AFU.EWY.ALO.ALO.AFU

ax chairs
TG.31
ALT **ax chair**
UF chairs, ax
CN V.TG.AFU.AFU.ALO.AFU.AFU.AFU.ARI

axed brick
MT.130
SN A brick that has been shaped with an ax and not trimmed when laid. (DAC)
UF brick, axed
brick, rough-axed
rough-axed brick
CN M.MT.AFU.AFU.AFU.AXC.ALO.AFU.AXC.ALO.AFU.AFU

axes
TB.118 (L,N,R)
ALT **ax**
SN Cutting tools that consist of a relatively heavy edged head fixed to a handle, the edge or edges being parallel to the handle so as to be suited for striking. (W)
CN V.TB.AFU.ARI.AXC.ALO.ARI

axes (mathematics)
BM.763
CN B.BM.CFS.ARI.AXC.ALO

axes, barking
USE **barking axes**

axes, beginning
USE **beginning axes**

axes, boatbuilder's
USE **shipwright's axes**

axes, carpenter's
USE **shipwright's axes**

axes, chip
USE **chip axes**

axes, cross
USE **twivels**

axes, dill
USE **froes**

axes, felling
USE **felling axes**

axes, fire
USE **fire axes**

axes, fireman's
USE **fire axes**

axes, fitting
USE **beginning axes**

axes, goosewing
USE **goosewing axes**

axes, hewing
USE **broadaxes**

axes, jedding
USE **cavils**

axes, lath
USE **froes**

axes, lopping
USE **lopping axes**

axes, marking
USE **marking axes**

axes, mason's
USE **axhammers**

axes, mast
USE **mast axes**

axes, mast and spar
USE **mast axes**

axes, mastmaker's
USE **mast axes**

axes, mortising
USE **mortising axes**

axes, pole (froes)
USE **froes**

axes, post
USE **mortising axes**

axes, rending
USE **froes**

axes, ship
USE **shipwright's axes**

axes, ship carpenter's
USE **shipwright's axes**

axes, shipbuilder's
USE **shipwright's axes**

axes, shipwright's
USE **shipwright's axes**

axes, snedding
USE **lopping axes**

axes, spar
USE **mast axes**

axes, split
USE **froes**

axes, topping
USE **lopping axes**

axhammers
TB.602 (N)
ALT **axhammer**
SN Axes having two cutting edges, or one cutting edge and one hammer face; used for dressing or spalling rough stone. (PUTNAM)
UF axes, mason's
mason's axes
CN V.TB.AFU.BCW.BCW.ALO.EFQ.AFU

axial balance
USE **axial symmetry**

axial loads
BM.1005 (L)
UF loads, axial
CN B.BM.CFS.AXC.CLM.ALO.ARI.AFU

axial perspective
KT.271
SN Use for a perspective system in which parallels converge to points on a vertical axis.
UF herringbone perspective
perspective, axial
perspective, herringbone
CN K.KT.AFU.ALO.DUC.DCU.BIQ.ALO

axial-plan
DC.78
UF longitudinal-plan
CN D.DC.AFU.ARI.ERE.AFU

axial sections
USE **longitudinal sections**

axial stress
BM.917
SN Tension and compression forces that are collinear with the long axes of structural members. (DS)
UF normal forces
stress, axial
CN B.BM.CFS.AXC.BIQ.ARI.BCW.AFU

axial symmetry
BM.95
SN Balanced arrangement of compositional units on either side of a central axis.
UF axial balance
axiality
balance, axial
symmetry, axial
CN B.BM.AFU.AFU.ARI.AFU.FOG.ALO

axiality
USE **axial symmetry**

axiology
KD.63 (L,R)
SN Study of values, primarily of intrinsic values (as those in ethics, aesthetics, and religion), but also of instrumental values (as those in economics), particularly with reference to the manner in which they can be known or experienced, their nature and kinds, and their ontological status. (W)
UF philosophy of value
theory of value
value theory
value, philosophy of
value, theory of
CN K.KD.AFU.AFU.BOK.ALO

axis, vanishing
USE **vanishing axis**

axonometric drawings
VD.10
ALT **axonometric drawing**
SN Use for drawings in which projectors are parallel, and at least one of the three spatial axes is inclined to the plane of projection. In modern architectural parlance, sometimes used only for strictly orthographic drawings with the object tilted to the plane.
UF axonometric projections
drawings, axonometric
drawings, paraline
paraline drawings
projections, axonometric
CN V.VD.AFU.AFU.BIQ.AFU

axonometric projection
KT.281
SN Historically, has meant projection in which projectors are parallel, and at least one of the three spatial axes is inclined to the plane of projection. In modern architectural parlance, sometimes used only for strictly orthographic projection with the object tilted to the plane.
UF projection, axonometric
CN K.KT.AFU.ALO.DUC.DCU.BOK.ALO.AFU

axonometric projections
USE **axonometric drawings**

Axum
FL.149
UF Aksum
CN F.FL.ALO.AFU.ALO.AXC.AFU

ayatollahs
HG.213
ALT **ayatollah**
CN H.HG.AFU.AXC.AXC.BIQ.AFU.AFU

Ayios Onouphrios ware
FL.2665
UF ware, Ayios Onouphrios
CN F.FL.ALO.AXC.ALO.AFU.ALO.AXC.BCW.AFU

Aymará
FL.1618 (L)
CN F.FL.ALO.ALO.ARI.ARI.ALO.ALO.ALO

Ayudhya
FL.2403
UF Ayuthya School
Ayutthaya
CN F.FL.ALO.ARI.BCW.BOK.AFU.AFU

Ayuthya School
USE **Ayudhya**

Ayutthaya
USE **Ayudhya**

Ayyubid
FL.3435 (L)
CN F.FL.ALO.BIQ.AFU.BIQ

Azande
USE **Zande**

Azanian
FL.150
CN F.FL.ALO.AFU.ALO.AXC.ALO

Azilian
FL.2476
CN F.FL.ALO.AXC.AFU.AXC.ALO

Aztalan
FL.814
CN F.FL.ALO.ALO.ALO.AFU.ALO.ALO.AFU.AFU

Aztatlán
FL.1065
CN F.FL.ALO.ALO.ALO.ALO.AFU.ALO.BCW.AFU

Aztec
FL.999 (A,L,B,R)
UF Mexica
CN F.FL.ALO.ALO.ALO.ALO.AFU.ALO.AFU.ALO.AFU

Aztec I
FL.994
UF Culhucán
Mazapán
Tula-Mazapán
CN F.FL.ALO.ALO.ALO.ALO.AFU.ALO.AFU.AFU.DIO

Aztec II
FL.995
UF Atlatongo
Tenayuca
CN F.FL.ALO.ALO.ALO.ALO.AFU.ALO.AFU.AFU.DOI

Aztec III
FL.996
UF Tenochtitlán
CN F.FL.ALO.ALO.ALO.ALO.AFU.ALO.AFU.AFU.DUC

Aztec IV
FL.997
UF Teocalco
Tlatelolco
CN F.FL.ALO.ALO.ALO.ALO.AFU.ALO.AFU.AFU.DZW

Aztec paper
USE **bark cloth**

azulejo
MT.190 (B)
SN Earthenware tile of Spanish manufacture, painted and enameled in rich colors. (HAS)
CN M.MT.AFU.AFU.AFU.AXC.ALO.ALO.ALO.AFU.ARI.AFU

azure
USE **ultramarine blue**

azure blue
USE **smalt**

azure cobalt
USE **cobalt blue**

azurite
MT.1582
UF Armenian stone
azzurro della magna
Bergblau
bleu Paul Véronèse
blue malachite
blue, copper
blue, mountain (azurite)
cendre
chessylite
copper blue
malachite, blue
mountain blue (azurite)
stone, Armenian
CN M.MT.AFU.AFU.ARI.AFU.AFU.ALO.ALO.ALO.AFU.AFU

azurite blue
USE **grayish blue**
moderate greenish blue
moderate purplish blue

azurro ultramarino
USE **ultramarine blue**

azzurro della magna
USE **azurite**

B & Bs
USE **bed-and-breakfasts**

B-and-Bs
USE **bed-and-breakfasts**

Baamba
USE **Amba**

Babanki
USE **Banki**

Babbits
USE **Babbitt metal**

Babbitt metal
MT.407 (L)
SN The original name for tin-antimony-copper alloys used for machinery bearings, but the term now applies to almost any bearing alloy with either a tin or lead base. (MH)
UF alloys, bearing
Babbits
bearing alloys
metal, Babbitt
CN M.MT.AFU.AFU.AFU.BZY.AFU.AFU.AFU.ALO.BUE.AFU

Babembe
USE **Bembe (Lower Zaire)**

Babeo
FL.520
CN F.FL.ALO.AFU.AXC.ALO.ALO.BIQ.AFU.ALO.AFU.AFU

Baboma
USE **Boma**

babool gum
USE **gum arabic**

babul gum
USE **gum arabic**

Babunda
USE **Mbun**

Babur
FL.2229
CN F.FL.ALO.ARI.AXC.ALO.AFU.BIQ.ALO.AFU.ALO

Babwa
FL.519
UF Ababua
Boa
CN F.FL.ALO.AFU.AXC.ALO.ALO.BIQ.AFU.ALO.AFU

baby blue
USE **bluish gray**
light bluish gray
pale blue
very light blue
very light greenish blue
very pale blue

baby books
VW.495 (L)
ALT **baby book**
UF books, baby
CN V.VW.AFU.ALO.AFU.AFU.AFU.AXC

baby pink
USE **light pink**
light yellowish pink
moderate yellowish pink
pale purplish pink

Babylonian
FL.2985 (L,B,R)
CN F.FL.ALO.AXC.ARI.BCW.ALO.ALO

Babylonian, Early
USE **Old Babylonian**

Babylonian, Old
USE **Old Babylonian**

Bacham
USE **Cham (Bamileke)**

Bachama
FL.226 (L)
CN F.FL.ALO.AFU.AXC.AFU.AFU.ALO.ARI.ALO

bachelor apartments
USE **studio apartments**

bachelor's chests
TG.476
ALT **bachelor's chest**
SN Chests of drawers having a folding top which, when open, serves as a writing board; of a type made in 18th-century England.
UF chests, bachelor's
CN V.TG.AFU.AFU.AXC.ALO.BCW.AFU

bacini
RT.629
ALT **bacino**
SN Ceramic basins pressed into walls as ornament.
CN V.RT.AFU.AFU.AFU.BIQ.BUE.ALO.AFU.ARI.AFU

back
USE **rear**

back arches
RT.278
ALT **back arch**
SN Use for arches that carry the interior face of a wall over an opening when the exterior face is carried by other means, such as a lintel.
UF arches, back
arches, rear
arches, recessed
arches, scoinson
arches, sconcheon
arrière-voussures
rear arches
rear vaults
recessed arches
scoinson arches
sconcheon arches
vaults, rear
CN V.RT.AFU.AFU.AFU.BCW.AFU.AFU.ARI.AFU

back boards
USE **backboards**

back catches
TF.41
ALT **back catch**
UF catches, back
CN V.TF.AFU.AFU.AFU.AFU.BCW.AFU

back checks
USE **door checks**

back clips
TF.329
ALT **back clip**
SN Special clips used on the back of gypsum board in certain applica-

tions, as in some demountable partitions, to hold the board in place by insertion into slots or other receptacles in the framing. (MEANS)
UF clips, back
CN V.TF.AFU.AFU.AFU.ALO.AFU.ARI.ALO

back elevations
USE **rear elevations**

back gutters
RT.1461
ALT **back gutter**
SN Gutters installed on the uphill side of a chimney on a sloping roof; used to divert water around the chimney. (HAS)
UF gutters, back
CN V.RT.ALO.BCW.ALO.ARI.BCW.ALO

back hearths
RT.1156
ALT **back hearth**
UF hearths, back
hearths, inner
inner hearths
CN V.RT.AFU.BOK.ALO.ALO.AXC.AFU

back nuts
TF.452
ALT **back nut**
SN Threaded nuts which help to create a watertight joint, as on the long thread of a pipe connector, and whose one dished side accepts a grommet. (MEANS)
UF nuts, back
CN V.TF.AFU.AFU.AFU.ALO.AFU.CLM.ALO

back painting
USE **reverse painting on glass**
verre églomisé

back posts
USE **back rails**

back rails
TG.831
ALT **back rail**
SN Extensions of back legs which support the chair back.
UF back posts
posts, back
rails, back
uprights
CN V.TG.ALO.AXC.ALO.AFU

back splats
USE **splats**

back stamps
VW.727
ALT **back stamp**
UF stamps, back
CN V.VW.AFU.ALO.ALO.AFU.AXC.ARI.AFU

back-stool chairs
USE **backstools**

backboards
TG.824
ALT **backboard**
SN The board or boards that make up the back of a piece of case furniture and sometimes extend above the top. (KETCH)
UF back boards
boards, back
CN V.TG.ALO.ARI

backchoirs
USE **retrochoirs**

backflap hinges
TF.96
ALT **backflap hinge**
SN Hinges in two leaves, screwed to the face of a door which is not thick enough to permit the use of butt hinges. (PUTNAM)
UF flap hinges
hinges, backflap
CN V.TF.AFU.AFU.AFU.AFU.CLM.AFU.ALO

backgammon tables
TG.743
ALT **backgammon table**
SN Gaming tables with tops marked as boards for playing backgammon.
UF tables, backgammon
CN V.TG.AFU.AFU.BIQ.BOK.ALO.CRG.AFU

background
BM.56
SN In pictorial arts, that part of the composition that appears to be farthest from the viewer. (MAYER)
CN B.BM.AFU.AFU.ARI.AFU.BCW.ALO.AFU

background brushes
TB.327
ALT **background brush**
SN Soft camel hair brushes used in lab work, photography, and photoengraving. (QUICK)
UF brushes, background
CN V.TB.AFU.ARI.CLM.ARI.ALO.AFU.AFU

backhoes
TB.39 (L,N)
ALT **backhoe**
SN Excavating machines used for cutting trenches with a boom-mounted bucket which is drawn through the ground toward the machine.
UF drag shovels
pull shovels
shovels, drag
shovels, pull
CN V.TB.AFU.ARI.AFU.ARI.ARI.AFU

backing brick
MT.93
SN A relatively low-quality brick used behind face brick or other masonry. (DAC)
UF backup brick
brick, backing
brick, backup
CN M.MT.AFU.AFU.AFU.AXC.ALO.AFU.ALO.ALO

backing drawknives
TB.901 (N)
ALT **backing drawknife**
SN Drawknives with a slight downward thrust of the handles for cutting outside curves, such as on the outside of barrel staves. (SALAM)
UF drawknives, backing
CN V.TB.AFU.BCW.CFS.ALO.AFU.DOI.ARI.AFU

backing-out punches
TB.669 (N)
ALT **backing-out punch**
SN Punches mounted on a handle; often used in conjunction with square and round punches in farriers' work.
UF pin punches (backing-out punches)
punches, backing-out
punches, pin (backing-out punches)
CN V.TB.AFU.BCW.BIQ.AFU.ALO.BZY.AFU

backplates
TF.260
ALT **backplate**
SN Plates that serve as mounts for knobs or pulls and intervene between them and the cabinetry to which they are attached. (DITTRI)
CN V.TF.AFU.AFU.AFU.AFU.DZW.AFU

backs
TG.827
ALT **back**
CN V.TG.ALO.AXC.AFU

backs, chimney
USE **firebacks**

backs, mirrored
USE **mirrored backs**

backs, scrolled
USE **scrolled backs**

backsaws
TB.987 (N)
ALT **backsaw**
SN Small handsaws whose back edge is stiffened with a steel or brass strip; used in finish carpentry for cutting mitered joints and other joinery work. (MEANS)
UF saws, back
CN V.TB.AFU.BCW.CFS.ALO.AFU.EWY.AFU

backsaws, fancy
USE **bead saws**

Backstein Gothic
USE **Backsteingotik**

Backsteingotik
FL.3144
UF Backstein Gothic
Gothic, Backstein
CN F.FL.ALO.BCW.ALO.ALO.AFU.BOK.ARI.BOK.AFU.AFU

backstools
TG.32
ALT **backstool**
SN Chairs in the form of a four-legged stool to which a back has been added. The term first appeared in the 16th century and was sometimes used in the 17th and 18th centuries for a chair without arms. (DDA)
UF back-stool chairs
chairs, back-stool
chairs, low back (backstools)
chaises à demoiselle
chaises à vertugadin
low back chairs (backstools)
CN V.TG.AFU.AFU.ALO.AFU.AFU.AFU.AXC

backstools, upholstered joined
USE **farthingale chairs**

backup brick
USE **backing brick**

backwaters
RD.168 (L)
ALT **backwater**
SN Areas of virtually stagnant water that are joined to a stream but relatively unaffected by its current. (DNE)
CN V.RD.ARI.AFU.ARI.AFU

Bactrian
FL.1790 (L)
CN F.FL.ALO.ARI.AFU.AXC.AXC

Bad Painting
USE **Neo-Expressionist**

Badarian
FL.2779
UF Tasian
CN F.FL.ALO.AXC.ALO.ARI.AFU.AFU.ALO.AFU

baddeleyite
USE **zirconium oxide**

badger planes
TB.913 (N)
ALT **badger plane**
SN Large wood hand planes, the mouths of which are cut obliquely from side to side, so that they can work close to a corner. (DAC)
UF planes, badger
planes, rabbet (badger planes)
rabbet planes (badger planes)
CN V.TB.AFU.BCW.CFS.ALO.AFU.DUC.ALO.AFU

badgers
TB.570
ALT **badger**
SN Tools used inside a pipe or culvert to remove excess mortar or deposits. (DAC)
CN V.TB.AFU.BCW.BCW.ALO.BCW

badigeon
MT.2592
SN Stiff paste used to stop small defects in stone. (MAYER)
CN M.MT.AFU.ARI.DZW.AFU

Badin
FL.826
CN F.FL.ALO.ALO.ALO.AFU.ALO.ALO.ALO.AFU

Badjok
USE **Chokwe**

badminton courts
RK.1009 (B)
ALT **badminton court**
UF courts, badminton
CN V.RK.AFU.ALO.ALO.EWY.ALO.AFU

Badr-al-Din Mahmud
FL.3465
CN F.FL.ALO.BIQ.AFU.DUC.ARI

Baehr Hopewell
FL.833
UF Hopewell, Baehr
CN F.FL.ALO.ALO.ALO.AFU.ALO.ALO.ARI.AFU.AFU

Baffin Island Inuit
FL.1207
UF Baffinland Eskimo
Eskimo, Baffinland
Inuit, Baffin Island
Nunatsiaqmiut
CN F.FL.ALO.ALO.ARI.AFU.AFU.AFU.ALO.AFU.AFU

Baffinland Eskimo
USE **Baffin Island Inuit**

Bafia
USE **Fia**

Bafo
FL.186
UF Fo
CN F.FL.ALO.AFU.AXC.AFU.AFU.AFU.ALO.AFU

Bafum
USE **Fum**

Bafumungu
USE **Fumu**

bag tables
USE **work tables**

Baga
FL.344
CN F.FL.ALO.AFU.AXC.AFU.ARI.BIQ.BUE.AFU

Bagam
FL.180
UF Gam
CN F.FL.ALO.AFU.AXC.AFU.AFU.AFU.AFU.AFU

Baganda
USE **Ganda**

bagasse
MT.1823 (L)
SN The residue left after grinding sugarcane and extracting the juice, employed in making paper and fiber building boards. (MH)
UF bagasse, sugar cane
sugar cane bagasse
CN M.MT.AFU.AFU.ARI.ALO.AFU.AFU.ALO.AFU

bagasse, sugar cane
USE **bagasse**

bagatelle boards
USE **bagatelle tables**

bagatelle tables
TG.710
ALT **bagatelle table**
UF bagatelle boards
bagatelles
boards, bagatelle
tables, bagatelle
CN V.TG.AFU.AFU.BIQ.BOK.ALO.ALO.AFU

bagatelles
USE **bagatelle tables**

baggage rooms
RM.186
ALT **baggage room**
SN Rooms for receiving, checking, and handling luggage. (RS)
UF rooms, baggage
CN V.RM.AFU.DIO.ALO.DCU.ALO

Baggara
FL.691 (L)
CN F.FL.ALO.AFU.AXC.BCW.AFU

bagh
RK.1400
SN Use for Islamic formal gardens.
CN V.RK.ALO.AFU.AFU.AFU.ARI.AFU

Baghdad School
FL.3438
CN F.FL.ALO.BIQ.AFU.BIQ.AFU.AFU.AFU

Bagirmi
FL.367 (L)
CN F.FL.ALO.AFU.AXC.AFU.AXC.ALO.AFU

bagnettes
USE **astragals**

bags, pounce
USE **pounce bags**

baguets
USE **astragals**

baguettes
USE **bead moldings**

Baham
USE **Cham (Bamileke)**

Bahía
FL.1117
CN F.FL.ALO.ALO.ALO.ARI.ALO.ARI.ALO

Baholoholo
USE **Holoholo**

Bahuana
USE **Huana**

bahuts
TG.458
ALT **bahut**
SN Medieval French term for portable coffers or chests used for personal luggage, covered in leather and studded with nails and usually having a rounded top. Eventually they took the form of a chest mounted on feet, used for storing goods. The current French form is a decorative high chest or cabinet with an arched or curved top.
UF coffres à bahut
CN V.TG.AFU.AFU.AXC.ALO.AXC.CLM.ALO

Bahzad School
USE **Bihzad School**

Bai miao
FL.1926
UF Pai miao
CN F.FL.ALO.ARI.ALO.AFU.AFU.AXC.ALO.AFU

bail bonds
VW.904
ALT **bail bond**
SN Bonds executed by defendants or those legally liable for debt, that state defendants will appear in court when required and that in the event defendants fail to appear, the signers of the bonds will pay to the court the amount of money specified. (BLACKS)
UF bonds, bail
CN V.VW.AFU.ARI.AFU.BOK.BOK.AXC.AFU

bail pulls
TF.70
ALT **bail pull**
UF pulls, bail
CN V.TF.AFU.AFU.AFU.AFU.CFS.BCW.AFU.AFU

bailey bridges
RK.1295 (L,B)
ALT **bailey bridge**
SN Use for temporary bridges designed for rapid construction of prefabricated, interchangeable, steel-truss panels bolted together.
UF bridges, bailey
CN V.RK.AFU.ALO.ALO.GLI.ALO.AFU.ARI.AFU

baileys
RT.1167
ALT **bailey**
SN Use for the outer walls of Medieval castles or the courts those walls form.
UF ballia
bayles
CN V.RT.AFU.BUE.AFU.AFU

baileys, inner
USE **inner baileys**

baileys, outer
USE **outer baileys**

Baining
FL.3622 (L)
CN F.FL.ALO.BOK.ALO.ARI.AFU

Bainov phase
FL.2134
CN F.FL.ALO.ARI.ARI.AFU.BIQ.BCW.AFU

baize
MT.1857
SN Coarsely woven woolen or cotton cloth napped to imitate felt and dyed in solid colors. (W)
CN M.MT.AFU.AFU.ARI.ALO.ALO.ALO.ALO.AFU

Bajokwe
USE **Chokwe**

Bajun
FL.609 (L)
UF Bajuni
CN F.FL.ALO.AFU.AXC.AXC.ALO.BUE.AFU

Bajuni
USE **Bajun**

baked brick
USE **fired brick**

Bakedi
USE **Teso**

Bakelite (TM)
MT.2172 (L,R)
SN The original name for phenol plastics, but now usually covers a range of different plastics.
CN M.MT.AFU.AFU.ARI.BUE.ALO.AXC.ALO.BIQ.AFU

baker's shops
USE **bakeries**

Bakerewe
USE **Kerewe**

bakeries
RK.151 (A,L,B,R)
ALT **bakery**
UF baker's shops
shops, baker's
CN V.RK.AFU.ALO.ALO.ALO.ARI.BIQ.AFU.ALO

bakers
HG.441 (L,R)
ALT **baker**
SN Persons who specialize in the making of breads, cakes, cookies, and pastries. (W)
CN H.HG.AFU.AXC.BUE.ALO.ALO

Bakete
USE **Kete**

Bakheng
FL.2358
UF Phnom Bakhen
CN F.FL.ALO.ARI.BCW.ALO.ARI.ALO.ARI

Bakongo
USE **Kongo**

Bakongo Kingdom
USE **Kongo Kingdom**

Bakosi
USE **Kossi**

Bakota
USE **Kota**

Bakuba
USE **Kuba**

Bakuba Kingdom
USE **Kuba Kingdom**

Bakusu
USE **Kusu**

Bakwele
USE **Kwele**

Bakwese
USE **Kwese**

Bakwiri
USE **Kpe**

Bal-bris
FL.2177
UF Bal'bris
Nepalese School
CN F.FL.ALO.ARI.AXC.AFU.BOK.AFU.AFU

Bal'bris
USE **Bal-bris**

Balali
USE **Lali**

Balalyk-Tepe
FL.1792
CN F.FL.ALO.ARI.AFU.AXC.BCW

balance
BM.50 (L,R)
SN Use for the impression of visual equilibrium in a composition.
UF equilibrium (composition)

CN B.BM.AFU.AFU.ARI.AFU.AXC

balance sheets
VW.842 (L)
ALT **balance sheet**
SN Statements of the financial condition, as of a corporation, at a given date showing the equality of total assets to total libilities plus net worth, or of total liabilities to total assets plus deficit. (W)
UF sheets, balance
CN V.VW.AFU.ARI.AFU.BIQ.CXA.AFU.ARI

balance, axial
USE **axial symmetry**

balance, radial
USE **radial symmetry**

balance, symmetrical
USE **bilateral symmetry**

balanced steps
RT.1118
ALT **balanced step**
SN Series of winders arranged so that the small ends of the steps are not much narrower than the parallel steps of the same stair. (PUTNAM)
UF dancing steps
dancing winders
steps, balanced
steps, dancing
winders, dancing
CN V.RT.AFU.BIQ.AXC.ALO.BIQ.AFU.BCW.AFU

balaustre
MT.1103
UF arariba
canarywood
centrolobium
CN M.MT.AFU.AFU.ALO.BIQ.DCU.AFU.AFU.AFU.AXC

Balawaste
FL.1811
CN F.FL.ALO.ARI.AFU.AXC.ELK.AFU

balconets
RM.31 (R)
ALT **balconet**
SN Use to designate very small balconies, usually not large enough to stand on and consisting of little more than a protective railing.
UF balconnettes
CN V.RM.AFU.DIO.AFU.ALO.AFU

balconies
RM.30 (A,L,N,B,R)
ALT **balcony**
SN Use for railed platforms projecting from the exterior walls of buildings. Use also for similar interior features, when small. For larger platforms which extend the length of one side of a room or are recessed behind an arcade, use **galleries.**
CN V.RM.AFU.DIO.AFU.ALO

balconnettes
USE **balconets**

baldacchinos
USE **baldachins**

baldachins
RT.414 (A,N,B,R)
ALT **baldachin**
UF altar canopies
baldacchinos
baldaquins
canopies, altar
CN V.RT.AFU.AFU.AFU.BIQ.ARI.AFU.AFU.AFU.ALO.AFU

baldachins (furniture components)
USE **canopies (bed components)**

baldaquins
USE **baldachins**

balection moldings
USE **bolection moldings**

Balega
USE **Lega**

Balesa
USE **Lese**

Bali
USE **Li**

Balinese
FL.2373 (L)
ALT **Bali**
CN F.FL.ALO.ARI.BCW.ARI.ALO.AFU

balks
RT.292
ALT **balk**
SN Use for large, square timbers, especially in older English construction.
CN V.RT.AFU.AFU.AFU.BCW.ALO.AFU.AFU

ball-and-claw feet
USE **claw-and-ball feet**

ball and spear pulls
TF.71
ALT **ball and spear pull**
SN Hand-forged pulls mounted with plates shaped like balls with single spear points projecting from them; similar to onion pulls. (DITTRI)
UF pulls, ball and spear
CN V.TF.AFU.AFU.AFU.AFU.CFS.BCW.AFU.ALO

ball-bearing hinges
TF.98
ALT **ball-bearing hinge**
SN Butt hinges having ball bearings positioned between the knuckles to reduce friction. (MEANS)
UF hinges, ball-bearing
CN V.TF.AFU.AFU.AFU.AFU.CLM.AFU.ARI.AFU

ball breakers
USE **wrecking balls**

ball-burnishing
KT.688
SN Smoothing or brightening of surfaces by means of metal pellets, balls, or other metal shapes in a rotating container. (STEIN)
CN K.KT.AFU.ALO.GRC.BCW.ARI.AFU.AFU

ball catches
TF.42
ALT **ball catch**
SN Catches whose strike holds a communicating projection or finger by means of the pressure exerted by one or two spring-loaded balls. (DITTRI)
UF catches, ball
CN V.TF.AFU.AFU.AFU.AFU.BCW.ALO

ball clay
MT.53 (L)
SN A kind of ceramic clay of exceptionally small particle size and, consequently, very good plasticity; used to impart plasticity to other clay bodies. (MAYER)
UF clay, ball
CN M.MT.AFU.AFU.AFU.AXC.AFU.AFU.AFU

ball cocks
TF.280
ALT **ball cock**
SN Float valves incorporating a spherical float; used to control the height of water. (MEANS)
UF cocks, ball
CN V.TF.AFU.AFU.AFU.AFU.EWY.ALO.AFU

ball courts
RK.1010
ALT **ball court**
SN Use only to designate the generally I-shaped playing area and associated viewing platforms of the ancient Mesoamerican ritual ball game.
UF courts, ball
pok-ta-poks
tlachtlis
CN V.RK.AFU.ALO.ALO.EWY.ALO.ALO

ball feet
TG.897
ALT **ball foot**
SN Spherical feet, used mainly on tables and case furniture in the second half of the 17th century. (TOMLIN)
UF feet, ball
CN V.TG.ALO.DZW.AFU.AFU

ball hinges, adjustable
USE **adjustable ball hinges**

ball joints
TF.642

ALT **ball joint**
SN Flexible mechanical joints that allow the axis of one part to be set at an angle to the other by virtue of the design of the two components. One possesses a fixed spherical shell to accommodate the ball-shaped end of the other. (MEANS)
UF joints, ball
CN V.TF.ALO.ARI.ARI.AFU

ball-peen hammers
TB.460 (N)
ALT **ball-peen hammer**
SN Hammers having a hemispherical peen, the end opposite the hammering face.
UF hammers, ball-peen
CN V.TB.AFU.ARI.ELK.AFU.ALO.AFU

ball-point pens
TB.268 (L,N)
ALT **ball-point pen**
SN Pens having as the writing point a small ball that rotates in its socket and inks itself by contact with an inner magazine of ink. (W)
UF pens, ball-point
CN V.TB.AFU.ARI.CLM.AFU.ALO.DOI.AFU

ball valves
TF.278
ALT **ball valve**
SN Spherically shaped gate valves which provide a very tight shut-off for fluids in a high-pressure piping system. (MEANS)
UF valves, ball
CN V.TF.AFU.AFU.AFU.AFU.EWY.AFU

ballast
MT.2297
SN Heavy material, such as water, sand, or iron, used to increase weight, as in a machine. (STEIN)
CN M.MT.AFU.ARI.ALO.ALO.AFU.AFU

ballasters
USE **balusters**

ballet
KD.7 (L,B,R)
CN K.KD.AFU.AFU.AFU.AFU.AFU.AFU.AFU

ballflowers
DG.54
ALT **ballflower**
SN Motifs consisting of three- or four-petal flowers, usually nearly closed over a ball, frequently occurring in hollow moldings in English Gothic architecture. (RS)
CN D.DG.AFU.AFU.DIO.ARI

ballia
USE **baileys**

ballnut
USE **mockernut hickory**

balloon-back chairs
TG.122
ALT **balloon-back chair**
SN Chairs with open backs and usually horizontal splats with the top rail and uprights rounded to give an overall balloon shape to the back. (FAIRB)
UF chairs, balloon-back
CN V.TG.AFU.AFU.ALO.AFU.AFU.AFU.NIE.AFU

balloon-back Windsor chairs
TG.97
ALT **balloon-back Windsor chair**
SN Windsor chairs with a bowlike back comprised of three sawn pieces of wood containing a central vertical back splat, sometimes spindles; common in the mid-19th century. (EVANS)
UF chairs, balloon-back Windsor
Windsor chairs, balloon-back
CN V.TG.AFU.AFU.ALO.AFU.AFU.AFU.MLC.AFU

balloon frame construction
USE **balloon frames**

balloon frames
RT.38 (B)
ALT **balloon frame**
SN Wooden frameworks in which all vertical structural elements of the exterior bearing walls and partitions consist of single studs which extend the full height of the frame.
UF balloon frame construction
balloon framing
construction, balloon frame
frame construction, balloon
frames, balloon
CN V.RT.AFU.AFU.AFU.ALO.AXC.AFU

balloon framing
USE **balloon frames**

balloon photography
USE **aerial photography**

balloon structures
USE **pneumatic structures**

balloon views
USE **bird's-eye views**

ballots
VW.771 (L,N)
ALT **ballot**
SN Sheets of paper, cards, or other devices used to cast a vote or announce a slate of candidates. (GMGPC)
UF ballots, election
election ballots
election tickets
papers, voting
tickets, election
voting papers
CN V.VW.AFU.ARI.AFU.ALO.ARI

ballots, election
USE **ballots**

ballrooms
RM.123 (A,B)
ALT **ballroom**
CN V.RM.AFU.DIO.ALO.BIQ.ALO

balls (foot components)
TG.932 (R)
ALT **ball (foot component)**
CN V.TG.ALO.DZW.ALO.AFU

balls (parties)
KM.130 (L,R)
CN K.KM.AFU.DIO.AFU

balls, breaker
USE **wrecking balls**

balls, headache
USE **wrecking balls**

balls, wrecking
USE **wrecking balls**

balm of gilead
MT.1281
UF balsam, hybrid
gilead, balm of
hybrid balsam
Populus candicans
Populus gileadensis
CN M.MT.AFU.AFU.ALO.BIQ.DCU.AFU.AFU.AFU.KFK.ARI.AFU

balnea
RK.781
ALT **balneum**
SN Use for public or private ancient Roman baths or bath buildings of ordinary size. For the great ancient Roman baths, use **thermae.**
CN V.RK.AFU.ALO.ALO.CXA.ALO.AFU.BZY.AFU

Baloi
USE **Loi**

Balombo
USE **Lumbu**

Balovale
USE **Lwena**

balsa wood
MT.1332 (L)
UF Ochroma lagopus
wood, balsa
CN M.MT.AFU.AFU.ALO.BIQ.DCU.AFU.AFU.ALO.AFU

balsam
MT.1467 (L)
UF oleoresin
CN M.MT.AFU.AFU.ALO.BOK.AFU

balsam fir
MT.1350 (L)
UF Abies balsamea
fir, balsam
CN M.MT.AFU.AFU.ALO.BIQ.DCU.AFU.AFU.ALO.BIQ.AFU

balsam of Peru
USE **Peru balsam**

balsam poplar
MT.1282
UF poplar, balsam
Populus balsamifera
Populus tacamahaca
tacamahac
CN M.MT.AFU.AFU.ALO.BIQ.DCU.AFU.AFU.AFU.KFK.ARI.ALO

balsam poplar, western
USE **black cottonwood**

balsam, Canada
USE **Canada balsam**

balsam, copaiba
USE **copaiba balsam**

balsam, hybrid
USE **balm of gilead**

balsam, Maracaibo
USE **Maracaibo balsam**

balsam, para
USE **para balsam**

balsam, Peru
USE **Peru balsam**

balsam, tolu
USE **tolu balsam**

baltei
RT.134
ALT **balteus**
SN Bands in the middle of the bolster of Ionic capitals; also bands joining the volutes of Ionic capitals. (HAS)
CN V.RT.AFU.AFU.AFU.AXC.BIQ.ALO.ARI.ALO.ALO

Baltic chests
USE **Nonsuch chests**

Baltic pine
USE **Scotch pine**

Baltic redwood
USE **Scotch pine**

Balualua
USE **Lwalwa**

Baluba
USE **Luba**

Balumbu
USE **Lumbu**

baluster columns
RT.86 (A)
ALT **baluster column**
SN Short, thick-set columns shaped somewhat like balusters with short, massive shafts.
UF baluster shafts
columns, baluster
shafts, baluster
CN V.RT.AFU.AFU.AFU.AXC.BIQ.AFU.AFU.ALO

baluster legs
TG.945
ALT **baluster leg**
UF baluster turned legs
bulbous legs
legs, baluster
legs, baluster turned
legs, bulbous
turned legs, baluster
CN V.TG.ALO.FIM.AFU.AFU.AFU

baluster shafts
USE **baluster columns**

baluster turned legs
USE **baluster legs**

balusters
RT.1040 (L,N,R)
ALT **baluster**
SN Short vertical members used to support a stair handrail or coping, often circular in section with a vase-shaped outline. Used also in furniture, as on the backs of chairs.
UF ballasters
banisters
CN V.RT.AFU.AXC.ALO.AFU.ARI.AFU

balusters (capital components)
USE **bolsters**

balustrades
RT.1037 (A,B,R)
ALT **balustrade**
SN Parapets or low screens composed of balusters and carrying a rail or other horizontal member that is usually heavy in proportion to the balusters themselves. (RS)
CN V.RT.AFU.AXC.ALO.AFU.AFU

Bamana
FL.374 (L)
CN F.FL.ALO.AFU.AXC.AFU.AXC.ARI.AFU

Bambala (Western Zaire)
USE **Mbala (Western Zaire)**

Bambete
USE **Mbete**

Bambole
USE **Mbole**

bamboo
MT.1027 (A,L,B,R)
CN M.MT.AFU.AFU.ALO.BIQ.AXC.AFU

bamboo, split
USE **split bamboo**

Bamenjo
FL.181 (L)
UF Menjo
CN F.FL.ALO.AFU.AXC.AFU.AFU.AFU.AFU.ALO

Bamileke
FL.179 (L)
UF Mileke
CN F.FL.ALO.AFU.AXC.AFU.AFU.AFU.AFU

Bamum
FL.195 (L)
UF Mum
Mun
CN F.FL.ALO.AFU.AXC.AFU.AFU.AFU.ARI.AFU

Ban Chieng
FL.2404
UF Ban Jieyang
CN F.FL.ALO.ARI.BCW.BOK.AFU.ALO

Ban Jieyang
USE **Ban Chieng**

Banana
USE **Masa**

banc lits
USE **settle beds**

bancelles (banquettes)
USE **banquettes**

banco
MT.54
CN M.MT.AFU.AFU.AFU.AXC.AFU.AFU.ALO

bancos
USE **benches**

Band ceramics
USE **Bandkeramik**

band patterns (running ornament)
USE **running ornament**

band saws
TB.134 (L,N)
ALT **band saw**
SN Power saws with a continuous piece of flexible steel running around two pulleys and with teeth on one or both sides;(MEANS) used primarily to cut wood, but with the proper blade may be used to cut metal.
UF endless saws
ribbon saws
saws, band
saws, endless
saws, ribbon
CN V.TB.AFU.ARI.AXC.ALO.CLM.AFU

band shells
RK.922 (A,B)
ALT **band shell**
SN Concave, acoustically resonant structures at the back of outdoor bandstands. (RHDEL2)
UF orchestra shells
shells, band
shells, orchestra
CN V.RK.AFU.ALO.ALO.EFQ.AFU

banded columns
RT.87
ALT **banded column**
SN Use for columns with drums alternately larger and smaller, or plainer and richer.
UF columns, banded
columns, ringed
columns, rusticated
ringed columns
rusticated columns
CN V.RT.AFU.AFU.AFU.AXC.BIQ.AFU.AFU.ARI

Banded ware
USE **Bandkeramik**

Banded ware, Incised
USE **Stichbandkeramik**

bandelets
USE **annulets**

Bandi
USE **Gbande**

banding
DG.107
SN Decorative border of contrasting woods cut at varying angles to the grain, such as for finishing the edges and rims of furniture.
CN D.DG.AFU.ARI.ALO.ARI.AFU

banding planes
TB.914 (N)
ALT **banding plane**
SN Wide planes with a rabbet taken out of one side and a blade that cuts flush with the rabbet; used for cutting wide bands of particular depths, the depth determined by the depth of the rabbet and the width determined by the width of the blade. (MERCER)
UF planes, banding
CN V.TB.AFU.BCW.CFS.ALO.AFU.DUC.ALO.ALO

banding, cross
USE **cross banding**

banding, feather
USE **feather banding**

banding, herringbone
USE **feather banding**

banding, straight
USE **straight banding**

Bandkeramik
FL.2502 (L)
UF Band ceramics
Banded ware
ceramics, Band
ware, Banded
CN F.FL.ALO.AXC.AFU.BCW.DCU.AFU

bandmasters
HG.74 (L)
ALT **bandmaster**
CN H.HG.AFU.AXC.AXC.AFU.AFU.AFU.BIQ.BIQ.ALO.AFU

bands, cloud
USE **cloud bands**

bands, fret
USE **frets**

bands, undulate
USE **undulate bands**

bandsmen
HG.73 (L)
ALT **bandsman**
SN Members of a band of musicians. (W)
CN H.HG.AFU.AXC.AXC.AFU.AFU.AFU.BIQ.BIQ.ALO

bandstands
RK.923 (L,B)
ALT **bandstand**
CN V.RK.AFU.ALO.ALO.EFQ.ALO

Bandwurmstil
USE **Jugendstil**

bandy legs
USE **cabriole legs**

Bangi
FL.526
CN F.FL.ALO.AFU.AXC.ALO.ALO.BIQ.ALO.AFU

Bangkok
FL.2422
UF Ratanakosin
CN F.FL.ALO.ARI.BCW.BOK.AFU.DUC

Bangomo
USE **Ngom**

Bangor limestone
MT.664
UF limestone, Bangor
CN M.MT.AFU.AFU.AFU.DCU.AFU.ALO.AFU.ALO.ALO.AFU.AFU.ALO.ALO

Bangua
USE **Ngwa**

Bangwa
USE **Ngwa**

banister-back chairs
TG.123
ALT **banister-back chair**
UF banister chairs
chairs, banister
chairs, banister-back
CN V.TG.AFU.AFU.ALO.AFU.AFU.AFU.NIE.ALO

banister-back chairs, harp
USE **lyre-back chairs**

banister chairs
USE **banister-back chairs**

banister planes
USE **capping planes**
handrail planes

banisters
USE **balusters**
handrails

Banjabi
USE **Nzebi**

bank architecture
USE **banks**

bank barns
RK.54
ALT **bank barn**
UF barns, bank
CN V.RK.AFU.ALO.ALO.AFU.AFU.AFU.ARI.AFU

bank barns, German
USE **Pennsylvania bank barns**

bank barns, Pennsylvania
USE **Pennsylvania bank barns**

bank buildings
USE **banks**

bank checks
USE **checks**

bank drafts
VW.827 (L)
ALT **bank draft**
SN Orders for the payment of money drawn by one party on another. (LCSH)
UF drafts (negotiable instruments)
drafts, bank
CN V.VW.AFU.ARI.AFU.BIQ.CFS.AFU

bank lobbies
USE **banking rooms**

bank statements
VW.822 (L,N)
ALT **bank statement**
SN The statements, usually monthly, rendered by a bank to a depositor. (GAHLM)
UF statements, back
CN V.VW.AFU.ARI.AFU.BIQ.BUE.AFU

bankbooks
VW.816 (N)
ALT **bankbook**
SN Books held by depositors in which a bank enters a record of the depositor's transactions. (RHDEL2)
UF passbooks
CN V.VW.AFU.ARI.AFU.BIQ.ARI

banker-marks
USE **masons' marks**

banker masons
HG.598
ALT **banker mason**
SN Persons who perform the final preparation work on stone masonry blocks. (W)
UF masons, banker
CN H.HG.AFU.AXC.BZY.AFU.DIO.AFU

bankers
HG.400 (L)
ALT **banker**
CN H.HG.AFU.AXC.BOK.AXC

Banki
FL.196
UF Babanki
CN F.FL.ALO.AFU.AXC.AFU.AFU.AFU.ARI.ALO

banking
KG.166 (L)
CN K.KG.AFU.ALO.AFU.ALO

banking halls
USE **banking rooms**

banking rooms
RM.222
ALT **banking room**
SN Use for rooms in banks open to the public for doing business and generally containing the tellers' stations, writing desks, and sometimes also officers' platforms.
UF bank lobbies
banking halls
halls, banking
lobbies, bank
rooms, banking
CN V.RM.AFU.DIO.ALO.DOI.ALO

Banko
FL.2018
CN F.FL.ALO.ARI.ALO.ALO.ALO.ALO.ALO.ARI

bankruptcy proceedings
VW.868
ALT **bankruptcy proceeding**
UF proceedings, bankruptcy
CN V.VW.AFU.ARI.AFU.BOK.AFU

bankruptcy, petitions for
USE **petitions for bankruptcy**

banks
RK.127 (A,L,B,R)
ALT **bank**
UF architecture, bank
bank architecture
bank buildings
buildings, bank
CN V.RK.AFU.ALO.ALO.ALO.ALO.AFU

banks (benches)
USE **benches**

banks (riverbanks)
USE **riverbanks**

Banks Island
FL.3673 (L)
CN F.FL.ALO.BOK.ALO.BUE.ALO

banks, blood
USE **blood banks**

banks, branch
USE **branch banks**

banks, drive-in
USE **drive-in banks**

banks, Federal Reserve
USE **Federal Reserve banks**

banks, loading
USE **loading docks**

banks, mobile
USE **mobile banks**

banks, savings
USE **savings banks**

banks, spoil
USE **spoil banks**

Bankutshu
USE **Nkutshu**

banner screens
USE **pole screens**

Bannock
FL.1308 (L)
CN F.FL.ALO.ALO.ARI.AFU.AXC.AFU

banquet cameras
TB.306
ALT **banquet camera**
SN Cameras with wide-angle lenses capable of producing oversized, wide-angle images of great depth and clarity.
UF cameras, banquet
CN V.TB.AFU.ARI.CLM.ARI.AFU.AFU.ALO.BIQ.AFU

banquet halls
RM.105 (B)
ALT **banquet hall**
SN Large rooms, halls, or apartments designed or used for festive or state functions.
UF banquet rooms
halls, banquet
rooms, banquet
CN V.RM.AFU.DIO.ALO.BCW.AFU

banquet rooms
USE **banquet halls**

banquet tables
USE **dining tables**

banquettes
TG.278
ALT **banquette**
SN Small benches usually with upholstered seats; in form they resemble a tabouret lengthened and supported on six or more legs. (DDA)
UF bancelles (banquettes)
CN V.TG.AFU.AFU.ALO.ALO.AFU.AFU.AFU

banquettes (defensive wall components)
RT.1186
ALT **banquette (defensive wall component)**
SN Steps made on the ramparts of works near the parapets, for the troops to stand upon, in order to fire over the parapet. (UMD)
CN V.RT.AFU.BUE.AFU.BCW.ALO.AFU

banquettes (pouffes)
USE **pouffes**

banquettes (sidewalks)
USE **sidewalks**

banquettes d'embrasure
USE **banquettes de croisée**

banquettes de croisée
TG.293
ALT **banquette de croisée**
SN Banquettes made to stand in the embrasure of a window. (DDA)
UF banquettes d'embrasure
CN V.TG.AFU.AFU.ALO.ALO.AFU.ALO.BCW.AFU

Bantéai Chhmar
USE **Banteay Chmar**

Banteay Chmar
FL.2359
UF Bantéai Chhmar
CN F.FL.ALO.ARI.BCW.ALO.ARI.ALO.AXC

Banteay Srei
FL.2360
CN F.FL.ALO.ARI.BCW.ALO.ARI.ALO.BCW

Bantu Kavirondo
FL.674 (L)
UF Kavirondo
CN F.FL.ALO.AFU.AXC.AXC.BOK.ALO

Banyamituku
USE **Metoko**

Banyangi
USE **Anyang (Nigerian)**

Banyankole
USE **Nkole**

Banyoro
USE **Nyoro**

Banyun
FL.336
CN F.FL.ALO.AFU.AXC.AFU.ARI.BIQ.AFU

Banza
USE **Mbanza**

baolis
RK.596 (A)
ALT **baoli**
SN Use for well constructions of India, often architecturally embellished, with steps deeply cut down to a water-drawing area.
UF stepped wells
wavs
wells, stepped
CN V.RK.AFU.ALO.ALO.CFS.ALO.BCW

.CXA.ALO.ALO

Baoulé
USE **Baulé**

Bapende
USE **Pende**

Baphuon
FL.2355
CN F.FL.ALO.ARI.BCW.ALO.ARI.ALO.AFU.AFU

baptism
KM.29 (L,R)
CN K.KM.AFU.ARI.AXC.AFU

baptismal certificates
VW.964 (L,N)
ALT **baptismal certificate**
SN Certificates which record the administration of the sacrament of baptism for an individual; often substituted for birth records that are unobtainable. (GAHLM)
UF certificates, baptismal
CN V.VW.AFU.ARI.ALO.ALO.AFU.AFU

baptismal fonts
USE **fonts**

baptismal registers
VW.969
ALT **baptismal register**
SN Registers which record the administration of the sacrament of baptism; often substituted for birth records that are unobtainable. (GAHLM)
UF registers, baptismal
CN V.VW.AFU.ARI.ALO.ALO.AFU.BCW.AFU

Baptist
BM.633 (L,B)
CN B.BM.BZY.AFU.ALO.ARI.ARI

baptisteries
RK.1093 (A,L,B,R)
ALT **baptistery**
SN Use for separate buildings or parts of buildings containing a font for the baptismal rite.
CN V.RK.AFU.ALO.ALO.FCS.BIQ.AFU

baptizing
KG.212
SN Ceremonially immersing in or applying water to someone as an initiation rite or sacrament of the Christian church. (RHDEL2)
CN K.KG.AFU.ALO.BIQ.AFU

bar-back chairs
TG.151
ALT **bar-back chair**
UF chairs, bar-back
CN V.TG.AFU.AFU.ALO.AFU.AFU.AFU.NIE.DOI.AFU

bar-back sofas
USE **chair-back settees**

bar clamps
USE **joiner's clamps**

bar feet
USE **runner feet**

bar graphs
VW.246
ALT **bar graph**
UF graphs, bar
CN V.VW.AFU.AFU.AFU.FZU.AXC.AXC.AFU

bar handles
TF.56
ALT **bar handle**
UF handles, bar
CN V.TF.AFU.AFU.AFU.AFU.CFS.AFU

bar joists
USE **open web joists**

bar mitzvahs
KM.30 (L)
CN K.KM.AFU.ARI.AXC.ALO

bar stools
USE **barstools**

bar tracery
RT.1017
SN Openwork of molded mullions that divide a window into lights in decorative patterns; common in the Gothic style.
UF tracery, bar
CN V.RT.AFU.ARI.ALO.BZY.AFU.AFU

Bara
FL.557 (L)
CN F.FL.ALO.AFU.AXC.ARI.ARI.ARI

Baradostian
FL.3000
CN F.FL.ALO.AXC.ARI.BIQ.AFU.AFU.AFU

Barat, Irian
USE **Irian Jaya**

Barawa
FL.211
CN F.FL.ALO.AFU.AXC.AFU.AFU.ALO.ALO.AXC.AFU

Barbacoa
FL.1655
CN F.FL.ALO.ALO.ARI.ARI.BCW.ARI

Barbarian
USE **Migration period**

barbed dowel pins
TF.459
ALT **barbed dowel pin**
SN Short, headless pins with a sharp point on one end and barbs between the two ends, used largely for fastening the mortise-and-tenon joints in a window sash and for door work. (PUTNAM)
UF dowel pins, barbed
pins, barbed dowel
CN V.TF.AFU.AFU.AFU.ALO.AFU.CXA.ALO.AFU

barbed nails
TF.420
ALT **barbed nail**
UF nails, barbed
CN V.TF.AFU.AFU.AFU.ALO.AFU.CFS.AFU.DIO.AFU

barbed wire
MT.482 (L)
UF wire, barbed
CN M.MT.AFU.AFU.AFU.BZY.ALO.BZY.AFU

barber's chairs
TG.162 (L,N)
ALT **barber's chair**
UF chairs, barber's
CN V.TG.AFU.AFU.ALO.AFU.AFU.ALO.AFU

barber's chairs (corner chairs)
USE **corner chairs**

barbershops
RK.189 (A,L,B)
ALT **barbershop**
CN V.RK.AFU.ALO.ALO.ALO.AXC.AFU

barbicans
RT.1201 (A,B)
ALT **barbican**
SN Outworks in Medieval fortifications, such as gate towers, but more frequently an advance work used to flank the approach to a gateway. (RS)
CN V.RT.AFU.BUE.AFU.BZY.AFU

barbières
USE **shaving stands**

Barcelona chairs
TG.34
ALT **Barcelona chair**
UF chairs, Barcelona
CN V.TG.AFU.AFU.ALO.AFU.AFU.AFU.BCW

bardiglio
MT.781
SN An Italian marble commonly having a dark gray or bluish ground traversed by veins and occurring in its principal varieties in the neighborhood of Carrara and Corsica. (W)
CN M.MT.AFU.AFU.AFU.DCU.AFU.ARI.ARI.ARI.ALO.AFU

bardiglio 'scuro
MT.782
CN M.MT.AFU.AFU.AFU.DCU.AFU.ARI.ARI.ARI.ALO.AFU.AFU

bardiglio fiorito
MT.783
CN M.MT.AFU.AFU.AFU.DCU.AFU.ARI.ARI.ARI.ALO.AFU.ALO

Bare Island
FL.866
CN F.FL.ALO.ALO.ALO.AFU.ALO.ALO.AXC.AFU

barge rafters
USE **bargeboards**

barge spikes
USE **boat spikes**

barge stones
RT.643
ALT **barge stone**
SN Stones which form the sloping top of a gable built of masonry. (HAS)
UF stones, barge
CN V.RT.AFU.AFU.AFU.BIQ.BUE.ALO.AFU.AXC.ALO.AFU

bargeboards
RT.495 (N,B)
ALT **bargeboard**
SN Boards which hang from the projecting end of a roof, covering the gables; often elaborately carved and ornamented. (HAS)
UF barge rafters
fascia rafters
fly rafters
gableboards
rafters, barge
rafters, fascia
rafters, fly
vergeboards
CN V.RT.AFU.AFU.AFU.BIQ.ARI.ALO.AFU.CXA.ALO.AFU

Bargu
FL.350 (L)
UF Bariba
CN F.FL.ALO.AFU.AXC.AFU.AXC.AFU.AFU

bargueños
USE **vargueños**

Bari
FL.617 (L)
CN F.FL.ALO.AFU.AXC.AXC.ARI.ARI

Bariba
USE **Bargu**

barium carbonate
MT.1746 (L)
UF carbonate, barium
CN M.MT.AFU.AFU.ARI.AFU.AFU.ALO.ALO.BOK.ALO.AXC

barium chromate
USE **barium yellow**

barium chrome
USE **barium yellow**

barium sulfate
USE **blanc fixe**

barium yellow
MT.1770
UF barium chromate
barium chrome
baryta yellow
Barytgelb
chromate, barium
chrome, barium
jaune de baryte
lemon yellow
permanent yellow
ultramarine, yellow
yellow ultramarine
yellow, barium
yellow, baryta
yellow, lemon
yellow, permanent
CN M.MT.AFU.AFU.ARI.ARI.AFU.AFU.ALO.ALO.BUE.ARI.AFU

barium yellow (color)
USE **brilliant yellow**
light greenish yellow
moderate greenish yellow

barjairs
USE **bergères**

bark
MT.1018 (L)
CN M.MT.AFU.AFU.ALO.BIQ.AFU

bark cloth
MT.1843 (L,R)
UF amatl
Aztec paper
bark cloth, beaten
bark paper
bark paper, cannabis
bark paper, fig
beaten bark cloth
cannabis bark paper
cloth, bark
cloth, beaten bark
cloth, tapa
fiber paper, plant
fig bark paper
huun
kapa
paper, Aztec
paper, bark
paper, cannabis bark
paper, fig bark
paper, plant fiber
plant fiber paper
tapa
CN M.MT.AFU.AFU.ARI.ALO.ALO.AFU

bark cloth, beaten
USE **bark cloth**

bark mills
TB.799 (N)
ALT **bark mill**
SN Horse-powered mills used for grinding bark.
UF mills, bark
CN V.TB.AFU.BCW.CFS.AFU.ALO

bark paper
USE **bark cloth**

bark paper, cannabis
USE **bark cloth**

bark paper, fig
USE **bark cloth**

bark strip
MT.1019
UF strip, bark
CN M.MT.AFU.AFU.ALO.BIQ.AFU.AFU

barkers
TB.800 (L)
ALT **barker**
SN Machines used especially in pulp mills to remove bark from logs. (W)
UF barking machines
debarkers
machines, barking
CN V.TB.AFU.BCW.CFS.AFU.ARI

barking axes
TB.835 (N)
ALT **barking ax**
SN Axes used to split timber before removal of the bark. (SLOANE)
UF axes, barking
CN V.TB.AFU.BCW.CFS.ALO.AFU.AXC.AFU

barking chisels
TB.852 (N)
ALT **barking chisel**
SN Chisels used in the debarking of timber.
UF chisels, barking
chisels, peeling
peeling chisels
CN V.TB.AFU.BCW.CFS.ALO.AFU.BUE.AFU

barking drawknives
TB.902 (N)
ALT **barking drawknife**
SN Large drawknives of varying shapes with the blade's bevel facing down so that the knife will not dig into the timber as it is removing the bark. (SALAM)
UF drawknives, barking
CN V.TB.AFU.BCW.CFS.ALO.AFU.DOI.ARI.ALO

barking irons
TB.846 (N)
ALT **barking iron**
SN Tools with a round, semicircular, or spade-shaped blade often socketed and mounted on a wood handle; used for stripping bark from logs. (SALAM)
UF irons, barking
irons, peeling
irons, rinding
irons, wrong
peeling irons
rinding irons
spuds
wrong irons
CN V.TB.AFU.BCW.CFS.ALO.AFU.BCW

barking machines
USE **barkers**

barley straw
MT.1078
UF straw, barley
CN M.MT.AFU.AFU.ALO.BIQ.CRG.AFU

barn-door hangers
TF.341
ALT **barn-door hanger**
SN Hangers used for heavy exterior sliding or rolling doors, consisting of two pulleys secured to the top of the door in tandem, connected by a heavy metal strap. The door is moved by rolling along a horizontal track which either hangs from the lintel or is anchored to a parallel member projecting slightly from it. (MEANS)
UF hangers, barn-door
CN V.TF.AFU.AFU.AFU.ALO.AFU.BOK.ALO.AFU

barn-door latches
TF.181
ALT **barn-door latch**
UF latches, barn-door
CN V.TF.AFU.AFU.AFU.AFU.DIO.BCW.AFU.BOK.AFU

barn-door pulls
TF.86
ALT **barn-door pull**
SN Large cupped pulls for heavy doors. (STEIN)
UF pulls, barn-door
CN V.TF.AFU.AFU.AFU.AFU.CFS.BCW.ALO.AFU

barn-door rollers
TF.6
ALT **barn-door roller**
UF rollers, barn-door
CN V.TF.AFU.AFU.AFU.AFU.AFU.AFU

barn-door stays
TF.7
ALT **barn-door stay**
SN Small pulleys or wheels which facilitate and direct the movement of a sliding barn (or other) door by rolling along a horizontal track or rail. (MEANS)
UF stays, barn-door
CN V.TF.AFU.AFU.AFU.AFU.AFU.ALO

barn siding
USE **barnboard**

Barnack rag
USE **Barnack stone**

Barnack stone
MT.690
UF Barnack rag
rag, Barnack
stone, Barnack
CN M.MT.AFU.AFU.AFU.DCU.AFU.ALO.AFU.ALO.ALO.ALO.AFU.AFU

barnboard
MT.1458
UF barn siding
barnwood
siding, barn
CN M.MT.AFU.AFU.ALO.BIQ.DCU.ALO.DOI.AFU

barns
RK.42 (A,L,N,B,R)
ALT **barn**
SN Agricultural buildings with large, usually sliding doors, prominent roofs, and predominantly open spaces on the interior, primarily used as storage buildings for hay, grains, and farm equipment and shelters for livestock; does not include those structures, often termed barns, used for the processing of food and other agricultural produce, such as hop barns and tobacco barns.
CN V.RK.AFU.ALO.ALO.AFU.AFU.AFU

barns, 3-bay
USE **English barns**

barns, bank
USE **bank barns**

barns, carriage
USE **carriage houses**

barns, cattle
USE **cattle barns**

barns, coach
USE **carriage houses**

barns, connected
USE **connected barns**

barns, Connecticut
USE **English barns**

barns, continuous
USE **connected barns**

barns, cow
USE **dairy barns**

barns, crib
USE **crib barns**

barns, dairy
USE **dairy barns**

barns, Dutch
USE **Dutch barns**

barns, English
USE **English barns**

barns, German bank
USE **Pennsylvania bank barns**

barns, hop
USE **hop barns**

barns, horse
USE **horse barns**

barns, New England
USE **English barns**

barns, New England connected
USE **connected barns**

barns, New World Dutch
USE **Dutch barns**

barns, Pennsylvania bank
USE **Pennsylvania bank barns**

barns, Pennsylvania German
USE **Pennsylvania bank barns**

barns, Pennsylvania standard
USE **Pennsylvania bank barns**

barns, sheep
USE **sheep barns**

barns, sugar
USE **sugar houses**

barns, three-bay
USE **English barns**

barns, tithe
USE **tithe barns**

barns, tobacco
USE **tobacco barns**

barns, Yankee
USE **English barns**

barnwood
USE **barnboard**

barnyards
RK.1601
ALT **barnyard**
SN Yards connected to and associated with a barn; usually fenced livestock yards separated from general work and activity areas. (BIGHSE)
CN V.RK.ALO.ARI.CRG.AFU

Barocchetto
FL.3231
CN F.FL.ALO.BCW.ALO.ARI.BIQ.BIQ.BCW.AFU

Baronial
USE **Abbotsford**

Baronial, Scottish
USE **Scottish Baronial**

Baroque
FL.3172 (A,L,B,R)
CN F.FL.ALO.BCW.ALO.ARI.AXC

Baroque Revival
FL.3263 (R)
UF Baroque, High Edwardian
High Edwardian Baroque
Neo-Baroque
Revival, Baroque
CN F.FL.ALO.BCW.ALO.AXC.CLM.AFU

Baroque, Early
USE **Early Baroque**

Baroque, High
USE **High Baroque**

Baroque, High Edwardian
USE **Baroque Revival**

Baroque, Late
USE **Late Baroque**

Barotse
USE **Lozi**

Barozi
USE **Lozi**

Barozwi
USE **Rozwi**

barracks
RK.218 (A,L,B,R)
CN V.RK.AFU.ALO.ALO.AXC.AFU.AFU

barracks, disciplinary
USE **military prisons**

barrages
RK.526 (L,B)
ALT **barrage**
SN Artificial dams placed in a watercourse to increase the depth of water or to divert it into a channel for navigation or irrigation. (W)
CN V.RK.AFU.ALO.ALO.CFS.AFU.ARI.ALO.AFU

Barrancoid
USE **Los Barrancos**

Barre granite
MT.594
UF granite, Barre
CN M.MT.AFU.AFU.AFU.DCU.AFU.AFU.AFU.AFU.AFU.ARI.ALO.AFU.AFU

Barreales
FL.1192
CN F.FL.ALO.ALO.ALO.ARI.BIQ.ALO

barred keys
USE **pipe keys**

barrel arches
USE **semicircular arches**

barrel bolts
TF.550
ALT **barrel bolt**
SN Cylindrical bolts that are mounted on a plate having a raised case that contains the bolt and guides it into a recess in a jamb or some other suitable cylindrical socket. (DITTRI)
UF bolts, barrel
CN V.TF.AFU.ALO.AXC.AFU.ALO

barrel-burnishing
USE **barreling**

barrel ceilings
RT.720
ALT **barrel ceiling**
SN Ceilings of semicylindrical shape. (DAC)
UF ceilings, barrel
CN V.RT.AFU.ALO.AFU.ALO.ALO

barrel chairs
TG.35
ALT **barrel chair**
SN Chairs with a solid, rounded wood back, the cruder type being made by cutting away parts of a barrel. For easy chairs having a semicircular back use **circular easy chairs.**
UF chairs, barrel
chairs, tub
tub chairs
CN V.TG.AFU.AFU.ALO.AFU.AFU.AFU.BIQ

barrel chairs (circular easy chairs)
USE **circular easy chairs**

barrel drills
TB.181
ALT **barrel drill**
SN Tools consisting of a long drill bit which pierces a spool-shaped object; used in conjunction with a bow to drill holes in brass, iron, and steel. Most often used by clock- and watchmakers.
UF drills, barrel
CN V.TB.AFU.ARI.BIQ.ALO.AFU.AFU.AFU

barrel-finishing
USE **barreling**

barrel keys
USE **pipe keys**

barrel roofs
RT.439 (A)
ALT **barrel roof**
SN Roofs that are semicircular in section or, sometimes, roofs that incorporate a semicircular ceiling.
UF arched barrel roofs
barrel roofs, arched
barrel shell roofs
cradle roofs
roofs, arched barrel
roofs, barrel shell
roofs, cradle
roofs, wagon
wagon roofs
CN V.RT.AFU.AFU.AFU.BIQ.ARI.AFU.AFU.ALO.AFU

barrel roofs, arched
USE **barrel roofs**

barrel shell roofs
USE **barrel roofs**

barrel vaults
RT.537 (B)
ALT **barrel vault**
SN Masonry vaults of plain, semicircular cross section supported by parallel walls or arcades. (DAC)
UF barrel vaults, transverse
cradle vaults
transverse barrel vaults
tunnel vaults
vaults, barrel
vaults, cradle
vaults, transverse barrel
vaults, tunnel
vaults, wagonhead
wagon vaults
wagonhead vaults
CN V.RT.AFU.AFU.AFU.BIQ.BOK.AFU.ALO.AFU

barrel vaults, inclined
USE **inclined barrel vaults**

barrel vaults, rampant
USE **rampant barrel vaults**

barrel vaults, transverse
USE **barrel vaults**

barrel vaults, uncentered
USE **pitched-brick vaults**

barreling
KT.684
ALT **barreled**
SN Use both for application of paint to small articles by tumbling them in a barrel containing paint, and the process of improving the surface finish of objects by processing them in a barrel along with abrasive particles.
UF barrel-burnishing
barrel-finishing
burnishing, barrel
finishing, barrel
tumbling
CN K.KT.AFU.ALO.GRC.BCW.AFU

barriadas
RG.280
ALT **barriada**
SN Use for self-built shantytowns located on the outskirts of large cities in Latin America.
CN V.RG.ALO.AFU.ALO.BCW.ALO.AFU

barrier-free design
BM.204 (A,L,B)
UF access, handicapped
design, barrier-free
handicapped access
CN B.BM.AFU.ALO.AXC

barriers
RT.1034 (B)
ALT **barrier**
CN V.RT.AFU.AXC.AFU

barriers, air
USE **air infiltration barriers**

barriers, air infiltration
USE **air infiltration barriers**

barriers, fire
USE **fire walls**

barriers, vapor
USE **vapor barriers**

barrios
RG.274
ALT **barrio**
SN Use only to denote the Spanish-speaking quarters of cities or towns.
CN V.RG.ALO.AFU.ALO.BCW.AFU.AFU

barristers
HG.318 (L)
ALT **barrister**
SN Counsels admitted to plead at the bar and undertake the public trial of causes in the higher courts of law. (W)
CN H.HG.AFU.AXC.BCW.ALO.BIQ.AXC.AFU

Barrow culture
USE **Kurgan**

barrows
USE **burial mounds**

barrows, long
USE **burial mounds**

barrs
USE **stretchers**

bars
RK.103 (A,L,B,R)
ALT **bar**
SN Places with counters where beverages, usually liquors, and light meals are served to customers. (RHDEL2)
CN V.RK.AFU.ALO.ALO.ALO.AFU.AFU

bars (building materials)
MT.2384 (L)
CN M.MT.AFU.ARI.BZY.ALO

bars (taverns)
USE **taverns**

bars, angle
USE **angles (rolled sections)**

bars, channel
USE **channel beams**

bars, chimney
USE **chimney bars**

bars, claw
USE **claw bars**

bars, deformed
USE **deformed bars**

bars, glazing
USE **muntins**

bars, grab
USE **grab bars**

bars, meeting
USE **meeting rails**

bars, milk
USE **milk bars**

bars, pinch
USE **pinch bars**

bars, pry
USE **crowbars**

bars, pull
USE **pull bars**

bars, push
USE **push bars**

bars, reinforcing
USE **reinforcing bars**

bars, ripping
USE **pinch bars**

bars, sand
USE **sand bars**

bars, shutter
USE **shutter bars**

bars, snack
USE **snack bars**

bars, towel
USE **towel bars**

bars, transom
USE **transoms**

bars, turning
USE **chimney bars**

bars, water
USE **water bars**

bars, wrecking
USE **pinch bars**

barstools
TG.261 (N)
ALT **barstool**
SN High stools that are usually one of a row of such stools standing in front of a bar; often taking the form of a rounded seat fixed on a central post. (W)
UF bar stools
stools, bar
CN V.TG.AFU.AFU.ALO.AFU.ALO.ARI.AFU

bartizans
RT.1187
ALT **bartizan**
UF echauguettes
turrets, watch
watch turrets
CN V.RT.AFU.BUE.AFU.BCW.ALO.ALO

bartons
USE **farmyards**

Barwa chairs
TG.36
ALT **Barwa chair**
UF chairs, Barwa
CN V.TG.AFU.AFU.ALO.AFU.AFU.AFU.BOK

barwood
MT.1688
CN M.MT.AFU.AFU.ARI.AFU.AFU.ALO.ALO.BCW.ALO.AFU

baryta paper
MT.1943
SN Paper with a gelatin/barium sulfate surface preparation. (REILLY)
UF paper, baryta
CN M.MT.AFU.AFU.ARI.ALO.ALO.AXC.ARI.BOK.AFU

baryta white
USE **blanc fixe**

baryta yellow
USE **barium yellow**

barytes
USE **blanc fixe**

Barytgelb
USE **barium yellow**

bas-relief
KT.538 (A,L)
SN Use to describe a surface that has an image or design in relief that is relatively shallow.
UF basso rilievo
low relief
CN K.KT.AFU.ALO.ELK.DIO.ALO.AXC.AFU

Basa
USE **Bassa**

Basal Neolithic
FL.19
UF Neolithic, Basal
CN F.FL.AFU.BCW.ALO.AFU

Basalampasu
USE **Salampasu**

basalt
MT.607 (L)
SN A dense, hard, dark brown to black igneous rock, consisting of feldspar and augite and often containing crystals of green olivine; it occurs as trap or volcanic rock. (MH)
UF lapis basanites
CN M.MT.AFU.AFU.AFU.DCU.AFU.AFU.AFU.AFU.ALO.AFU

basalt glass
USE **tachylite**

Basari
FL.351 (L)
UF Bassari
CN F.FL.ALO.AFU.AXC.AFU.AXC.AFU.ALO

bascule bridges
RK.1278
ALT **bascule bridge**
SN Bridges in which sections of the span are pivoted upward by use of counterweights.
UF bridges, bascule
CN V.RK.AFU.ALO.ALO.GLI.ALO.AFU.AFU.AXC.AFU

base
USE **inert pigment**

base bid specifications
VW.794
ALT **base bid specification**
SN Specifications listing or describing only the materials, equipment, and methods of construction upon which a base bid must be predicated, exclusive of any alternate bids. (MEANS)
UF specifications, base bid
CN V.VW.AFU.ARI.AFU.ARI.AFU.ARI.AFU

base-courts
RM.43
ALT **base-court**
SN Use for the outer or lesser courts of mansions or castles.
UF basse-cours
CN V.RM.AFU.DIO.AFU.BCW.ARI.AFU

base flashing
RT.736
SN The flashing provided by upturned edges of a watertight membrane on a roof; or any metal or composition flashing at the joint between a roofing surface and a vertical surface, such as a wall or parapet. (DAC)
UF flashing, base
CN V.RT.AFU.ALO.AFU.BCW.AFU

base maps
VW.150 (L)
ALT **base map**
SN Outline maps showing the important natural and man-made features of an area, to which specific information may be added for any of various purposes.
UF maps, base
CN V.VW.AFU.AFU.AFU.FZU.AXC.AFU.ARI.AFU.BZY.AFU

base ring ware
FL.2900
UF ring ware, base
ware, base ring
CN F.FL.ALO.AXC.ARI.ARI.ALO.ALO.AFU

base, safety
USE **safety film**

baseball cards
VW.560 (L,N)
ALT **baseball card**
UF cards, baseball
CN V.VW.AFU.ALO.AFU.ARI.AFU

baseball fields
RK.1478 (B)
ALT **baseball field**
UF fields, baseball
CN V.RK.ALO.ALO.BCW.AFU.AFU

baseball stadiums
RK.1055 (A,B)
ALT **baseball stadium**
UF stadiums, baseball
CN V.RK.AFU.ALO.ALO.EWY.AXC.BIQ.AFU.BCW.AFU

baseboard heaters
USE **baseboard units**

baseboard heating
USE **baseboard units**

baseboard radiator units
USE **baseboard units**

baseboard units
RT.1428 (B)
ALT **baseboard unit**
SN Heating systems in which the heating elements are housed in special panels placed horizontally along the baseboards of a wall.
UF baseboard heaters
baseboard heating
baseboard radiator units
heaters, baseboard
heating, baseboard
radiator units, baseboard
units, baseboard
CN V.RT.ALO.BCW.AFU.ALO.ALO.AFU

baseboards
RT.649 (B)
ALT **baseboard**
SN Flat or molded projections from interior walls or partitions at the floor, covering the joint between the floor and the wall.
UF boards, skirting
skirting boards
skirtings
CN V.RT.AFU.AFU.AFU.BIQ.BUE.ALO.AFU.BCW.AFU

basement windows
RT.958
ALT **basement window**
SN Windows of a type commonly used in residential basements, usually having between one and three lights only.
UF windows, basement
CN V.RT.AFU.ARI.AFU.AFU.BOK.AFU.ARI.AFU

basements
RM.411 (A,L,B,R)
ALT **basement**
SN Use to designate stories wholly or partly underground. For similar spaces used solely for storage, particularly food, prefer **cellars.**
CN V.RM.AFU.DUC.ALO

Basengele
USE **Sengele**

bases
RT.66 (L)
ALT **base**
SN Use for those elements located at the bottom of objects and upon which the objects rest or are supported. For the lower, supporting structures of furniture, such as on case furniture and tables, use **bases (furniture components).**
CN V.RT.AFU.AFU.AFU.AXC.ARI.AFU

bases (artists' materials)
USE **supports (artists' materials)**

bases (furniture components)
TG.840
ALT **base (furniture component)**
SN Use for the lower supporting structures of furniture, such as on case furniture and tables.
CN V.TG.ALO.BCW

bases (military installations)
USE **military bases**

bases, air
USE **air bases**

bases, army
USE **army bases**

bases, Asiatic
USE **Asiatic bases**

bases, Attic
USE **Attic bases**

bases, extraterrestrial
USE **extraterrestrial bases**

bases, guided missile
USE **guided missile bases**

bases, lunar
USE **lunar bases**

bases, military
USE **military bases**

bases, missile
USE **guided missile bases**

bases, moon
USE **lunar bases**

bases, naval
USE **naval bases**

bases, naval air
USE **naval air bases**

bases, space
USE **extraterrestrial bases**

bases, submarine
USE **submarine bases**

Bashadar
FL.2141
UF Abash-adar
CN F.FL.ALO.ARI.ARI.ALO.AFU.AFU

Bashilele
USE **Lele**

basic igneous rock
MT.606
UF basic rock
igneous rock, basic

rock, basic
rock, basic igneous
CN M.MT.AFU.AFU.AFU.DCU.AFU.AFU.AFU.AFU.ALO

basic liquid epoxy
MT.2168
UF DGEBA
epoxy, basic liquid
liquid epoxy, basic
CN M.MT.AFU.AFU.ARI.BUE.ALO.AXC.ALO.BCW.AFU

basic rock
USE **basic igneous rock**

Basikasingo
USE **Kasingo**

Basilian
BM.651 (L)
CN B.BM.BZY.AFU.ALO.BCW.AFU

basilicas
RK.19 (A,L,B,R)
ALT **basilica**
SN Use for religious or secular buildings characterized by an oblong plan divided into a nave with two or more side aisles, the former higher and wider than the latter and lit by clerestory windows; usually terminated by an apse.
CN V.RK.AFU.ALO.AFU.ALO.ALO

basin stands
TG.658
ALT **basin stand**
SN Small stands for washing, often having a molded ring to hold the basin, small drawers below the frieze, and a shelf for a ewer beneath.
UF bowl stands
stands, basin
stands, bowl
stands, toilet
toilet stands
CN V.TG.AFU.AFU.BIQ.BCW.ALO.FCS.AFU

basin stands, corner
USE **corner basin stands**

basin stands, corner enclosed
USE **corner enclosed basin stands**

basin stands, enclosed
USE **enclosed basin stands**

basins, catch
USE **catch basins**

basins, sedimentation
USE **settling basins**

basins, settling
USE **settling basins**

basins, stilling
USE **stilling basins**

basins, storm water retention
USE **storm water retention basins**

basins, water retention
USE **storm water retention basins**

basket capitals
RT.119
ALT **basket capital**
SN Use for capitals having interlaced bands resembling the weave of a basket; common in Byzantine architecture.
UF capitals, basket
CN V.RT.AFU.AFU.AFU.AXC.BIQ.ALO.ARI.AFU.ARI

basket chairs
TG.37
ALT **basket chair**
SN Wicker chairs with arms that are a forward continuation of the back, usually with a cane-shaped base in lieu of legs.
UF chairs, basket
CN V.TG.AFU.AFU.ALO.AFU.AFU.AFU.BUE

basket makers
HG.551 (L)
ALT **basket maker**
CN H.HG.AFU.AXC.BUE.AXC.ALO

basket ware
FL.2935
UF ware, basket
CN F.FL.ALO.AXC.ARI.AXC.ALO.BIQ.ARI

basketball courts
RK.1011
ALT **basketball court**
UF courts, basketball
CN V.RK.AFU.ALO.ALO.EWY.ALO.ARI

Basketmaker
FL.957 (L)
CN F.FL.ALO.ALO.ALO.AFU.ALO.ARI.BIQ.BOK.ALO

Basketmaker-Pueblo
USE **Anasazi**

basketmaking
KT.513 (L,R)
UF basketry
CN K.KT.AFU.ALO.ELK.AFU

basketry
USE **basketmaking**

Basoga
USE **Soga (African)**

Basohli
FL.2271
CN F.FL.ALO.ARI.AXC.ALO.AFU.BZY.BCW.ARI.AFU

Basonge
USE **Songye**

Basongo Meno
USE **Nkutshu**

Bassa
FL.187 (L)
UF Basa
CN F.FL.ALO.AFU.AXC.AFU.AFU.AFU.ALO.ALO

Bassari
USE **Basari**

basse-cours
USE **base-courts**

basse-taille
KT.659
SN Use for the enameling process developed in Mughal, India which uses both translucent and opaque enamel applied over gold and silver and carved into a bas-relief.
CN K.KT.AFU.ALO.GRC.AFU.ALO.AFU

basset tables
TG.714
ALT **basset table**
SN Small card tables for playing bassette, a card game popular in Italy and France in the late 17th century and in England in the early 18th century.
UF tables, basset
CN V.TG.AFU.AFU.BIQ.BOK.ALO.AXC.AFU

bassinets
TG.330 (N)
ALT **bassinet**
SN Use for infants' beds, especially those with a hood over one end.
CN V.TG.AFU.AFU.ARI.AFU.AFU.AXC.AFU

basso rilievo
USE **bas-relief**

basswood
USE **linden**

basswood, American
USE **linden**

bast
MT.1824 (L)
UF bast fiber
fiber, bast
CN M.MT.AFU.AFU.ARI.ALO.AFU.AFU.ALO.ALO

bast fiber
USE **bast**

bastard cedar
USE **incense cedar**

bastel houses
RK.228
ALT **bastel house**
SN Use for partly fortified houses usually having a vaulted ground floor and generally found along the Scottish border.
UF houses, bastel

peel towers
peels
towers, peel
CN V.RK.AFU.ALO.ALO.AXC.ALO.AFU.AFU

bastides
RD.32
ALT **bastide**
SN Use for Medieval planned settlements built for defense and often laid out on an orthogonal grid.
CN V.RD.AFU.ALO.ALO.AFU.AFU

basting
KT.568
ALT **basted**
SN Sewing by hand or machine with loose, long stitches in order to hold the material in place during fittings or for final stitching. (W)
CN K.KT.AFU.ALO.ELK.DUC.ARI.AFU

bastioned forts
RK.448
ALT **bastioned fort**
UF forts, bastioned
CN V.RK.AFU.ALO.ALO.BIQ.BOK.AFU

bastions
RT.1171 (B)
ALT **bastion**
SN The projecting portions of the outer wall of a fortification.
CN V.RT.AFU.BUE.AFU.ALO.AFU

bastwork
MT.2745 (L)
CN M.MT.AFU.AXC.BCW.AFU

Basuku
USE **Suku**

Basuto
USE **Sotho**

bat
USE **brickbat**

bat printing
KT.865
ALT **bat printed**
SN Technique of applying glaze to pottery in which oil is applied to a printing plate, then transferred to the pottery by means of a gelatin plate. The pottery is then dusted with color material which adheres to the oiled areas. (SCHNEI)
UF printing, bat
CN K.KT.AFU.ALO.HOE.BOK.AXC.AFU

Batavia damar
MT.1487
UF damar, Batavia
CN M.MT.AFU.AFU.ALO.BOK.AXC.AFU

Bateke
USE **Teke**

batement lights
RT.971
ALT **batement light**
SN In English Gothic architecture, traceried windows, or subdivisions of windows, having a curved or inclined bottom caused by the arched heads of other lights below.
UF lights, batement
CN V.RT.AFU.ARI.AFU.AFU.BOK.ALO.ARI.ALO

Bateso
USE **Teso**

Batesville marble
MT.665
SN Limestone from Arkansas, gray or cream colored. (MAYER)
UF marble, Batesville
CN M.MT.AFU.AFU.AFU.DCU.AFU.ALO.AFU.ALO.ALO.AFU.AFU.ALO.ARI

Batetela
USE **Tetela**

bath chairs
TG.185
ALT **bath chair**
SN Type of elaborate wheelchair, sometimes glassed, especially those made in England in the mid-19th century and used at spas and seaside resorts.
UF chairs, bath
CN V.TG.AFU.AFU.ALO.AFU.AFU.ALO.CLM.ARI.AFU

bath mitzvahs
KM.31 (L)
CN K.KM.AFU.ARI.AXC.ARI

Bath oolite
USE **Bath stone**

Bath stone
MT.666
UF Bath oolite
oolite, Bath
stone, Bath
CN M.MT.AFU.AFU.AFU.DCU.AFU.ALO.AFU.ALO.ALO.AFU.AFU.ALO.AXC

bath, Smillie's
USE **Smillie's bath**

bathhouses
RK.1070 (A,B,R)
ALT **bathhouse**
SN Use only for structures containing dressing rooms or lockers for bathers, as at the seashore. For buildings housing public swimming and bathing facilities, use **public baths.**
UF bathing pavilions
houses, pool
pavilions, bathing
pool houses
CN V.RK.AFU.ALO.ALO.EWY.BCW.AFU

bathhouses (public baths)
USE **public baths**

bathing beaches
RG.154 (L,B,R)
ALT **bathing beach**
UF beaches, bathing
CN V.RG.AFU.AFU.DOI.ALO

bathing pavilions
USE **bathhouses**

Bathonga
USE **Thonga**

bathroom accessories
USE **bathroom hardware**

bathroom hardware
TF.504
UF accessories, bathroom
accessories, washroom
bathroom accessories
hardware, bathroom
washroom accessories
CN V.TF.AFU.AFU.ALO.ALO

bathroom hooks
TF.151
ALT **bathroom hook**
UF hooks, bathroom
CN V.TF.AFU.AFU.AFU.AFU.CXA.AFU

bathrooms
RM.66 (A,L,B)
ALT **bathroom**
SN Use for rooms containing a bathtub or shower, and usually a toilet and lavatory; for rooms containing only a toilet and lavatory, use **lavatories (rooms)**; for public facilities containing toilets and lavatories, use **rest rooms.**
UF baths
CN V.RM.AFU.DIO.ALO.ALO.AFU

baths
USE **bathrooms**
bathtubs
public baths

baths, Finnish
USE **saunas**

baths, mineral
USE **spas**

baths, public
USE **public baths**

baths, steam
USE **steam baths**

baths, swimming
USE **swimming pools**

baths, thermal
USE **steam baths**

baths, Turkish
USE **Turkish baths**

baths, vapor
USE **steam baths**

bathtubs
RT.1479 (L,N,B)

ALT **bathtub**
UF baths
tubs
CN V.RT.ALO.BCW.ALO.ARI.CFS.AFU

bathymetric charts
USE **bathymetric maps**

bathymetric maps
VW.216 (L)
ALT **bathymetric map**
UF bathymetric charts
charts, bathymetric
maps, bathymetric
CN V.VW.AFU.AFU.AFU.FZU.AXC.AFU.ARI.AXC.DIO.ALO.ALO.ALO.AFU

Bati
USE **Beti**

Batie
FL.182
CN F.FL.ALO.AFU.AXC.AFU.AFU.AFU.AFU.ARI

batik
KT.80 (L)
SN Resist dyeing in which wax is used as the resist.
CN K.KT.AFU.ALO.BOK.ALO.ALO.AFU

Batonga
USE **Tonga**

bâtons rompus
RT.808
ALT **bâton rompus**
SN Short, straight billets or portions of molding usually of rounded section forming the zigzag molding in Romanesque architecture. (W)
CN V.RT.AFU.ALO.AFU.BOK.ALO.AFU

batoons
USE **battens**

Batshioko
USE **Chokwe**

batt insulation
MT.2409
UF blanket insulation
insulation, batt
insulation, blanket
CN M.MT.AFU.ARI.BZY.BCW.ARI.AFU.ALO.AFU

batten joints
TF.681
ALT **batten joint**
UF joints, batten
CN V.TF.ALO.ARI.AXC.ARI.AFU

batten, board and
USE **board and batten**

battened columns
RT.102
ALT **battened column**
SN Columns consisting of two shafts rigidly connected to each other. (HAS)
UF columns, battened
CN V.RT.AFU.AFU.AFU.AXC.BIQ.AFU.ALO.ALO

battened walls
RT.572
ALT **battened wall**
SN Walls to which battens have been affixed. (HAS)
UF strapped walls
walls, battened
walls, strapped
CN V.RT.AFU.AFU.AFU.BIQ.BUE.AFU.AFU.AFU

battening
USE **battens**

battens
MT.1414
ALT **batten**
SN Thin, narrow strips of wood covering the joint between two parallel boards.
UF batoons
battening
CN M.MT.AFU.AFU.ALO.BIQ.DCU.ALO.AFU

battered walls
RT.573 (B)
ALT **battered wall**
SN Walls that are battered, that is, slope inward.
UF talus walls
walls, battered
walls, talus
CN V.RT.AFU.AFU.AFU.BIQ.BUE.AFU.AFU.ALO

batteries
RT.1176 (A,L)
ALT **battery**
SN Use for fixed platforms on which artillery is mounted.
CN V.RT.AFU.BUE.AFU.ARI

batters
USE **mauls**

Battle-ax
USE **Corded ware**

battledores
USE **hornbooks**

battlefield maps
VW.196 (L)
ALT **battlefield map**
UF maps, battlefield
CN V.VW.AFU.AFU.AFU.FZU.AXC.AFU.ARI.AXC.BUE.AFU

battlefields
RG.212 (A,L)
ALT **battlefield**
UF battlegrounds
CN V.RG.AFU.AFU.DZW.AXC.AFU

battlegrounds
USE **battlefields**

battlements
RT.1189 (A)
ALT **battlement**
SN Fortified parapets with alternate solid parts and openings.
UF castellations
crenelated parapets
crenellations
embattlements
parapets, crenelated
CN V.RT.AFU.BUE.AFU.BCW.ALO.ARI.AFU

Batwa
USE **Twa**

Batwana
USE **Tswana**

Bauhaus
FL.3381 (B,R)
CN F.FL.ALO.BCW.ALO.AXC.DIO.BIQ.AFU

Baulé
FL.288 (L)
UF Baoulé
CN F.FL.ALO.AFU.AXC.AFU.ARI.AFU.AFU.AXC

Baumer
FL.845
CN F.FL.ALO.ALO.ALO.AFU.ALO.ALO.ARI.ALO.AFU

bauxite, ferroginous
USE **laterite**

Bavili
USE **Vili**

bawdyhouses
USE **brothels**

bawns
RK.435
ALT **bawn**
SN Use for enclosure walls, usually fortified, around Irish castles and some Irish houses.
CN V.RK.AFU.ALO.ALO.BIQ.AFU

Bawongo
USE **Wongo**

Bawoyo
USE **Woyo**

Bawumbu
USE **Hum**
Wumu

bay laurel
USE **laurel**

bay windows
RT.909 (A,B)
ALT **bay window**
SN Windows, either single or in a series, forming a bay or recess in a room and projecting outward from the wall in a rectangular, curved, or

polygonal form. (W)
UF jut windows
windows, bay
windows, jut
CN V.RT.AFU.ARI.AFU.AFU.BOK.AFU.AFU.ALO

bay windows, square
USE square bay windows

Bayaka
USE Yaka

Bayanzi
USE Yanzi

Bayard's process
KT.330
SN A direct positive process to make photographic prints in which a physically developed, unfixed print containing exposed silver chloride is soaked in a solution of potassium iodide and is bleached in relation to exposure in the camera.
CN K.KT.AFU.ALO.DUC.DIO.ALO.BUE.AFU

Bayat
FL.3009
CN F.FL.ALO.AXC.ARI.BIQ.AFU.AFU.CFS

Bayazid I
FL.3485
UF Beyazit I
Beyazit, Lightning
Lightning Beyazit
CN F.FL.ALO.BIQ.AFU.FOG.AFU.AXC

Bayazid II
FL.3490
UF Beyazit II
CN F.FL.ALO.BIQ.AFU.FOG.AFU.BZY

bayles
USE baileys

Bayombe
USE Yombe

Bayon
FL.2356
CN F.FL.ALO.ARI.BCW.ALO.ARI.ALO.AFU.ALO

bayonet saws
USE saber saws

bayous
RD.169 (L)
ALT bayou
SN Denotes marshy creeks or other sluggish swampy watercourses, generally found along the lower Mississippi River and other alluvial lowlands.
CN V.RD.ARI.AFU.ARI.ALO

bays
RD.145 (L)
ALT bay
SN Denotes wide, open, curving indentations of a shoreline, larger than coves and smaller than gulfs.
CN V.RD.ARI.AFU.AFU.AFU.ALO.ALO.AFU

bays (building divisions)
RM.4
ALT bay (building division)
SN Use for repeated, similar divisions or compartments of a building or part of a building, as defined by recurring architectural features, such as arches, vaults, openings, or pilasters.
CN V.RM.AFU.ARI

bays (vault components)
USE vault bays

bays, vault
USE vault bays

Baysonqur
FL.3581
CN F.FL.ALO.BIQ.AFU.IFM.AFU.ARI

Baysonqur Style
USE Baysunghur Style

Baysunghur Style
FL.3574
UF Baysonqur Style
CN F.FL.ALO.BIQ.AFU.HTY.AFU.AFU.AFU

Baytown
FL.846
CN F.FL.ALO.ALO.ALO.AFU.ALO.ALO.ARI.ALO.ALO

baywood
USE South American mahogany

bazaars
RG.40 (L,B)
ALT bazaar
UF bazaars, Oriental
Oriental bazaars
suqs
CN V.RG.AFU.AFU.AXC.AFU.AFU

bazaars, Oriental
USE bazaars

Bäzäklik
FL.1812
CN F.FL.ALO.ARI.AFU.AXC.ELK.ALO

beach chairs
TG.205 (N)
ALT beach chair
UF chairs, beach
CN V.TG.AFU.AFU.ALO.AFU.AFU.ARI.AFU

beach clubs
RK.1030 (B)
ALT beach club
UF clubs, beach
CN V.RK.AFU.ALO.ALO.EWY.AXC.ALO.ALO

beach cobble
MT.883
UF cobble, beach
CN M.MT.AFU.AFU.AFU.DCU.ALO.ALO.AFU

beach houses
RK.305 (A,B)
ALT beach house
UF houses, beach
CN V.RK.AFU.ALO.ALO.AXC.ALO.AXC.ALO.AFU

beach ridges
RD.191 (L)
ALT beach ridge
SN Low ridges of stratified, unconsolidated sand and gravel created by the wave action of lakes or oceans and representing previous coastlines. (WAYTA)
UF ridges, beach
CN V.RD.ARI.AFU.AXC.AFU.AFU.ARI.ARI

beaches
RD.228 (A,L,B,R)
ALT beach
CN V.RD.ARI.AFU.AXC.AFU.ALO.AXC.BUE.AFU

beaches, bathing
USE bathing beaches

beacons
RT.1291 (L)
ALT beacon
CN V.RT.ALO.AFU.ALO.AFU

beacons, cemetery
USE lanterns of the dead

bead and reel moldings
RT.759
ALT bead and reel molding
SN Round convex moldings with disks alternating singly or in pairs with oblong beads. (W)
UF moldings, bead and reel
moldings, reel and bead
reel and bead moldings
CN V.RT.AFU.ALO.AFU.BOK.AFU.AFU.ARI.AFU

bead molding planes
USE bead planes

bead moldings
RT.785
ALT bead molding
SN Small, convex moldings of semicircular or greater profile. (HAS)
UF baguettes
beads (moldings)
chaplets
moldings, bead
roundels (moldings)
CN V.RT.AFU.ALO.AFU.BOK.AFU.AFU.AXC.BCW.ALO

bead planes
TB.952 (N)
ALT **bead plane**
SN Planes having a curved cutting edge which makes bead moldings along a wood surface.
UF astragal planes
bead molding planes
molding planes, bead
planes, astragal
planes, bead
planes, bead molding
CN V.TB.AFU.BCW.CFS.ALO.AFU.DUC.AXC.AFU.AFU

bead saws
TB.988 (N)
ALT **bead saw**
SN Small backsaws, 3 to 6 inches in length, with very fine teeth and very little set; used for fine work. (SALAM)
UF backsaws, fancy
fancy backsaws
saws, bead
CN V.TB.AFU.BCW.CFS.ALO.AFU.EWY.AFU.AFU

bead screws, stop
USE **stop bead screws**

beaded dovetail seams
TF.650
UF dovetail seams, beaded
seams, beaded dovetail
CN V.TF.ALO.ARI.ARI.BUE.AFU

beaded joints
TF.575
ALT **beaded joint**
UF joints, beaded
CN V.TF.ALO.AFU.ARI

beadhouses
RK.785
ALT **beadhouse**
SN Almshouses in which the residents were required to pray for the founder. (RHDEL2)
UF bedehouses
CN V.RK.AFU.ALO.ALO.CXA.ALO.ALO.AFU.AFU

beading (edging pattern)
DG.111 (L)
ALT **beaded (edging pattern)**
SN Enrichment consisting of a line of tiny beads; common on silver and furniture. (LDDO)
UF pearling
CN D.DG.AFU.ARI.ALO.ARI.ALO

beading (textiles)
USE **beadwork**

beadmaking
KT.514
CN K.KT.AFU.ALO.ELK.ALO

beads and quirks
USE **quirk beads**

beads (moldings)
USE **bead moldings**

beads, quirk
USE **quirk beads**

beadwork
KT.559 (L,R)
ALT **beaded**
SN Type of needlework in which patterns are produced by sewing beads to a cloth or parchment ground. (OCDA)
UF beading (textiles)
CN K.KT.AFU.ALO.ELK.DUC.ALO.ALO

beak irons
TB.1095 (N)
ALT **beak iron**
SN The tapered ends of anvils. (W)
UF bick irons
bickerns
irons, beak
irons, bick
CN V.TB.ALO.AFU.AFU

beak moldings
RT.777
ALT **beak molding**
SN Use for fillet moldings with the front portion pendant; for moldings with a beaked head ornamental motif, use **beakhead moldings.**
UF hawksbeak moldings
moldings, beak
moldings, hawksbeak
CN V.RT.AFU.ALO.AFU.BOK.AFU.AFU.AXC.AXC.ALO

Beaker
USE **Bell Beaker**
Funnel Beaker

beakhead moldings
RT.760
ALT **beakhead molding**
SN Use for moldings with bird, animal, or human heads biting a roll molding as the ornamental motif; for fillet moldings with the front portion pendant, use **beak moldings.**
UF bird's beak moldings
moldings, beakhead
moldings, bird's beak
CN V.RT.AFU.ALO.AFU.BOK.AFU.AFU.ARI.ALO

beakhorn stakes
TB.682
ALT **beakhorn stake**
SN Stakes or small bench anvils having a slender horn on one side. (W)
UF stakes, beakhorn
CN V.TB.AFU.BCW.BIQ.AFU.ALO.CXA.AFU

beaking joints
TF.576
ALT **beaking joint**
UF joints, beaking
CN V.TF.ALO.AFU.AXC

beam anchors
TF.291
ALT **beam anchor**
SN Metal ties for securing a beam, joist, or floor firmly to a wall. (MEANS)
UF anchors, beam
anchors, joist (beam anchors)
anchors, wall
joist anchors (beam anchors)
wall anchors
CN V.TF.AFU.AFU.AFU.ALO.AFU.AFU.ARI

beam-and-slab floor constructions
USE **one-way beam and slab systems**

beam and slab systems, two-way
USE **two-way beam and slab systems**

beam ceilings
RT.721
ALT **beam ceiling**
SN Ceilings having beams, either structural or decorative, that are visible. (DAC)
UF ceilings, beam
CN V.RT.AFU.ALO.AFU.ALO.ARI

beam compasses
TB.238 (N)
ALT **beam compass**
SN Instruments consisting of a long horizontal bar on which two movable heads slide, one of which carries a pencil, and the other a pin or tracer; used to draw large circles or arcs of circles for full-scale working drawings. (DAC)
UF compasses, beam
CN V.TB.AFU.ARI.CLM.AFU.ALO.ARI.AFU

beam hangers
TF.350
ALT **beam hanger**
SN Wires, straps, or other hardware devices used to hang the formwork for concrete beams.
UF beam saddles
hangers, beam
saddles, beam
CN V.TF.AFU.AFU.AFU.ALO.AFU.BOK.ARI.AFU.AFU

beam hangers, steel-to-steel
USE **steel-to-steel beam hangers**

beam saddles
USE **beam hangers**

beam systems, flat slab and
USE **two-way beam and slab systems**

beams
RT.290 (A,L,B)
ALT **beam**
SN Structural members whose primary function is to carry transverse loads.
CN V.RT.AFU.AFU.AFU.BCW.ALO

beams, box
USE **box beams**

beams, built-up
USE **built-up beams**

beams, candle
USE **candle beams**

beams, cased
USE **cased beams**

beams, channel
USE **channel beams**

beams, collar
USE **collar beams**

beams, compound
USE **built-up beams**

beams, continuous
USE **continuous beams**

beams, dragging
USE **dragon beams**

beams, dragon
USE **dragon beams**

beams, flitch
USE **flitch beams**

beams, flitch plate
USE **flitch beams**

beams, ground
USE **sill plates**

beams, hammer
USE **hammer beams**

beams, jesting
USE **jesting beams**

beams, plate
USE **plate girders**

beams, ridge
USE **ridgeboards**

beams, sandwich
USE **flitch beams**

beams, simple
USE **simple beams**

beams, straining
USE **straining beams**

beams, tie
USE **tie beams**

beams, wide-flange
USE **wide-flange beams**

beams, wind
USE **collar beams**

bean
MT.1067 (L)
CN M.MT.AFU.AFU.ALO.BIQ.CFS.AFU.AFU

bean pod, locust
USE **locust bean pod**

bean pulls
TF.72
ALT **bean pull**
SN Hand-forged pulls mounted with lima bean-shaped plates. (DITTRI)
UF pulls, bean
CN V.TF.AFU.AFU.AFU.AFU.CFS.BCW.AFU.ARI

bean tree
USE **catalpa**

bean tree, Indian
USE **catalpa**

beanbag chairs
TG.38
ALT **beanbag chair**
SN Large, soft frameless chairs resembling a beanbag; typically a cloth like plastic shell filled with plastic chips, that molds itself readily to the contour of the occupant. (RHDEL2)
UF chairs, beanbag
CN V.TG.AFU.AFU.ALO.AFU.AFU.AFU.BZY

bear's breech
USE **acanthus**

bear's foot
USE **acanthus**

bearing alloys
USE **Babbitt metal**

bearing stress
BM.918
SN Stress developed at the point of contact between two loaded structural members. (DS)
UF stress, bearing
CN B.BM.CFS.AXC.BIQ.ARI.BCW.ALO

bearing walls
USE **loadbearing walls**

beatae
USE **blessed**

beaten bark cloth
USE **bark cloth**

beaters (mauls)
USE **mauls**

beati
USE **blessed**

beatifications
KM.143 (L)
SN Official acts of the pope whereby deceased persons are declared to be enjoying the happiness of heaven and therefore proper subjects of religious honor. (RHDEL2)
CN K.KM.AFU.DZW.AFU

Beau-Brummel dressing tables
TG.734
ALT **Beau-Brummel dressing table**
SN Men's or ladies' dressing boxes on a tall stand with a lid that opens to reveal a fitted interior, usually with drawers beneath. Unlike other dressing tables, it has taller legs and lacks a full case of drawers beneath. (ANTIQS)
UF Beau-Brummel tables
Beau-Brummels
dressing tables, Beau-Brummel
tables, Beau-Brummel dressing
CN V.TG.AFU.AFU.BIQ.BOK.ALO.CLM.ARI.AFU

Beau-Brummel tables
USE **Beau-Brummel dressing tables**

Beau-Brummels
USE **Beau-Brummel dressing tables**

beautification
BM.1065
CN B.BM.CLM.ALO.AFU.AFU

beautification, highway
USE **roadside improvement**

beautification, urban
USE **urban beautification**

beauty
BM.488 (L,B,R)
UF thc Beautiful
CN B.BM.BIQ.AFU.AFU

beauty parlors
USE **beauty shops**

beauty salons
USE **beauty shops**

beauty shops
RK.190 (A,L,B)
ALT **beauty shop**
UF beauty parlors
beauty salons
hairdressers
hairdressing salons
parlors, beauty
salons, beauty
salons, hairdressing
shops, beauty
CN V.RK.AFU.ALO.ALO.ALO.AXC.ALO

beauty, line of
USE **Hogarth's line**

Beaux-Arts
FL.3278 (A,L,B,R)
CN F.FL.ALO.BCW.ALO.AXC.CRG.AFU

beaux étages
USE **piani nobili**

Beaver
FL.1227 (L)
UF Tsattine
CN F.FL.ALO.ALO.ARI.AFU.AFU.ARI.ARI

beaverboard
USE **fiberboard**

Becton white
USE **lithopone**

bed-and-breakfast inns
USE **bed-and-breakfasts**

bed-and-breakfasts
RK.945 (A,L)
ALT **bed-and-breakfast**
SN Inns, hotels, or private homes offering a room for the night and breakfast the next morning for one inclusive price. (RHDEL2)
UF B & Bs
B-and-Bs
bed-and-breakfast inns
inns, bed-and-breakfast
CN V.RK.AFU.ALO.ALO.ELK.AFU

bed bolt covers
TF.514
ALT **bed bolt cover**
UF bedstead bolt covers
bolt covers, bed
covers, bed bolt
CN V.TF.AFU.ALO.AFU.AFU

bed bolts
TF.321
ALT **bed bolt**
UF bedstead bolts
bolts, bed
CN V.TF.AFU.AFU.AFU.ALO.AFU.ALO.ALO.AFU

bed canopies
USE **canopies (bed components)**

bed chairs
TG.163 (N)
ALT **bed chair**
SN Chairs with backs which may be lowered and seats that are hinged to unfold or that can otherwise be extended to form beds.
UF chair-beds
CN V.TG.AFU.AFU.ALO.AFU.AFU.ALO.ALO

bed-chests
USE **press beds**

bed joints
TF.635
ALT **bed joint**
SN Joints between different courses or layers of bricks. (AGS6)
UF joints, bed
CN V.TF.ALO.ARI.ALO.ALO.AFU

bed keys
USE **bed wrenches**

bed mold planes
USE **cornice planes**

bed moldings
RT.338
ALT **bed molding**
SN Moldings of the cornices of entablatures situated beneath the corona and above the frieze.
UF bed molds
moldings, bed
molds, bed
CN V.RT.AFU.AFU.AFU.BCW.BZY.ALO.ALO.ALO.AFU

bed molds
USE **bed moldings**

bed-outshuts
RM.20 (A)
ALT **bed-outshut**
SN Use for small additions to houses, accommodating a bed, common in South Wales.
CN V.RM.AFU.CFS.AFU

bed pillars
USE **bedposts**

bed slats
TG.844
ALT **bed slat**
SN Boards supporting the bedsprings, usually extending from side to side of a bedstead. (W)
UF bed staffs
bed sticks
slats, bed
staffs, bed
sticks, bed
CN V.TG.ALO.BIQ.AFU

bed springs
USE **bedsprings**

bed staffs
USE **bed slats**

bed steps
TG.663 (N)
ALT **bed step**
SN Steps used to climb into a bed. (W)
UF steps, bed
CN V.TG.AFU.AFU.BIQ.BIQ.AFU

bed sticks
USE **bed slats**

bed tables
TG.708
ALT **bed table**
UF tables, bed
CN V.TG.AFU.AFU.BIQ.BOK.ALO.AFU

bed wrenches
TB.774
ALT **bed wrench**
SN Wrenches for adjusting the nuts and bolts of a bedstead. (W)
UF bed keys
keys, bed
wrenches, bed
CN V.TB.AFU.BCW.BIQ.AXC.ALO.BIQ.ARI

bedboards
TG.845
ALT **bedboard**
SN Stiff, thin, wide boards inserted usually between bedspring and mattress. (W)
CN V.TG.ALO.BIQ.ALO

bedchambers
USE **bedrooms**

beddles
USE **beetles (mallets)**

bedehouses
USE **beadhouses**

Bedford stone
MT.669
UF stone, Bedford
CN M.MT.AFU.AFU.AFU.DCU.AFU.ALO.AFU.ALO.ALO.AFU.AFU.ALO.BIQ.AFU

bedframes
TG.846
ALT **bedframe**
CN V.TG.ALO.BIQ.ARI

Bedja
USE **Beja**

Bedouin
FL.692 (A,L)
CN F.FL.ALO.AFU.AXC.BCW.ALO

bedposts
TG.847
ALT **bedpost**
SN Upright supports on a bedstead, such as those which support the tester on a high-post bed.
UF bed pillars
pillars, bed
CN V.TG.ALO.BIQ.AXC

bedroom pianos, convertible
USE **piano beds**

bedrooms
RM.161 (A,L,B)
ALT **bedroom**
UF bedchambers
chambers (bedrooms)
CN V.RM.AFU.DIO.ALO.CRG.AFU

beds
TG.321 (L,N,R)
ALT **bed**
SN A term signifying either the bedding (mattress and cover), or the bedsteads, or both. (DDA)
UF bedsteads
bedstocks
CN V.TG.AFU.AFU.ARI.AFU

beds à la duchesse
USE **lits à la duchesse**

beds, alcove
USE **box beds**

beds, angel
USE **lits à la duchesse**

beds, boat
USE **sleigh beds**

beds, bookcase
USE **bookcase beds**

beds, box
USE **box beds**

beds, bunk
USE **bunk beds**

beds, bureau
USE **bureau beds**

beds, cabinet
USE **cabinet beds**

beds, camp
USE **field beds**

beds, canopy
USE **canopy beds**

beds, canopy (tester beds)
USE **tester beds**

beds, cant
USE **field beds**

beds, chiffonier
USE **chiffonier beds**

beds, chiffonier folding
USE **chiffonier beds**

beds, closet
USE **press beds**

beds, concealed
USE **deception beds**

beds, convertible
USE **sofa beds**

beds, couch
USE **couch beds**

beds, crib
USE **cribs**

beds, cupboard
USE **box beds**
press beds

beds, davenport
USE **davenports**

beds, deception
USE **deception beds**

beds, dome
USE **dome beds**

beds, double
USE **double beds**

beds, duchesse
USE **lits à la duchesse**

beds, field
USE **field beds**

beds, folding
USE **folding beds**

beds, four-posted
USE **tester beds**

beds, French
USE **French beds**

beds, French (sleigh beds)
USE **sleigh beds**

beds, full
USE **double beds**

beds, gondola
USE **sleigh beds**

beds, gondola-shaped
USE **sleigh beds**

beds, Grecian
USE **sleigh beds**

beds, half-tester
USE **half-tester beds**

beds, Herrera
USE **Herrera beds**

beds, hideaway
USE **hideaway beds**

beds, high-post
USE **high-post beds**

beds, hollywood
USE **hollywood beds**

beds, hospital
USE **hospital beds**

beds, Jenny Lind
USE **spool beds**

beds, king-size
USE **king-size beds**

beds, library press
USE **library press beds**

beds, livery
USE **livery beds**

beds, low-post
USE **low-post beds**

beds, Murphy
USE **Murphy beds**

beds, pencil-post
USE **pencil-post beds**

beds, piano
USE **piano beds**

beds, piano folding
USE **piano beds**

beds, plantation
USE **tester beds**

beds, platform
USE **platform beds**

beds, post
USE **high-post beds**
low-post beds

beds, press
USE **press beds**

beds, queen-size
USE **queen-size beds**

beds, rest
USE **daybeds**

beds, river
USE **river beds**

beds, settee
USE **settle beds**

beds, settle
USE **settle beds**

beds, single
USE **twin beds**

beds, sleigh
USE **sleigh beds**

beds, slope
USE **field beds**

beds, sofa
USE **sofa beds**

beds, sparver
USE **sparver beds**

beds, sperver
USE **sparver beds**

beds, spindle
USE **spool beds**

beds, spool
USE **spool beds**

beds, state
USE **state beds**

beds, stump
USE **stump beds**

beds, suitcase
USE **suitcase beds**

beds, summer
USE **summer beds**

beds, swinging crib
USE **swinging cribs**

beds, table
USE **table beds**

beds, tall-post
USE **high-post beds**

beds, tent
USE **field beds**

beds, tester
USE **tester beds**

beds, three-quarter size
USE **three-quarter size beds**

beds, truckle
USE **trundle beds**

beds, trundle
USE **trundle beds**

beds, trunk
USE **trundle beds**

beds, turn-up
USE **folding beds**
press beds

beds, twin
USE **twin beds**

beds, water
USE **water beds**

bedside cabinets
USE **night tables**

bedside cupboards
USE **night tables**

bedside tables
USE **night tables**

bedsprings
TG.850 (N)
ALT **bedspring**
SN Springs supporting a mattress. (W)
UF bed springs
springs, bed
CN V.TG.ALO.BIQ.BCW

bedstands
USE **night tables**

bedstead bolt covers
USE **bed bolt covers**

bedstead bolts
USE **bed bolts**

bedsteads
USE **beds**

bedsteads, box
USE **box beds**

bedsteads, buroe
USE **bureau beds**

bedsteads, cabinet
USE **press beds**

bedsteads, cot
USE **cots**

bedsteads, crib
USE **cribs**

bedsteads, field
USE **field beds**

bedsteads, high-post
USE **high-post beds**

bedsteads, library press
USE **library press beds**

bedsteads, low-post
USE **low-post beds**

bedsteads, table
USE **table beds**

bedsteads, tent
USE **field beds**

bedsteads, turn up
USE **folding beds**

bedstocks
USE **beds**

bee houses
USE **apiaries**

beech
MT.1104 (L)
UF Fagus
CN M.MT.AFU.AFU.ALO.BIQ.DCU.AFU.AFU.AFU.BCW

beech, American
USE **American beech**

beech, black
USE **New Zealand beech**

beech, Chinese
USE **Chinese beech**

beech, common
USE **European beech**

beech, European
USE **European beech**

beech, Japanese
USE **Japanese beech**

beech, New Zealand
USE **New Zealand beech**

beech, Oriental
USE **Oriental beech**

beech, red
USE **red beech**

beech, Siebold's
USE **Siebold's beech**

beech, white
USE **white beech**

beehive coke ovens
USE **beehive ovens**

beehive domes
RT.390 (B)
ALT **beehive dome**
SN Use for domes in the form of a cone with curved sides.
UF alveated domes
domes, alveated
domes, beehive
CN V.RT.AFU.AFU.AFU.BIQ.AFU.AFU.AFU

beehive dwellings
USE **beehive houses**

beehive houses
RK.246 (B,R)
ALT **beehive house**
UF beehive dwellings
beehive huts
dwellings, beehive
houses, beehive
huts, beehive
CN V.RK.AFU.ALO.ALO.AXC.ALO.AFU.CLM.ALO

beehive huts
USE **beehive houses**

beehive kilns
USE **beehive ovens**

beehive ovens
TB.91 (N)
ALT beehive oven
SN Kilns used to convert coal into coke, characterized by a dome-shaped roof. (RHDEL2)
UF beehive coke ovens
beehive kilns
beehives (ovens)
coke ovens, beehive
kilns, beehive
ovens, beehive
CN V.TB.AFU.ARI.ALO.ARI.ALO.AFU.AFU

beehive tombs
USE **tholos tombs**

beehives
RK.79 (L,N,B,R)
ALT **beehive**
UF skeps
CN V.RK.AFU.ALO.ALO.AFU.ALO.AFU.AFU

beehives (ovens)
USE **beehive ovens**

beer cellars
RM.188 (A)
ALT **beer cellar**
SN Use for cellars in which beer is stored.
UF cellars, beer
CN V.RM.AFU.DIO.ALO.DCU.ARI.AFU

beer gardens
RK.109
ALT **beer garden**
SN Distinguished from other drinking establishments (e.g., bars, saloons) by being family-oriented, by having chairs and tables rather than a bar, by emphasizing food as much as beer, by having music, and by being more impersonal than saloons.
UF gardens, beer
CN V.RK.AFU.ALO.ALO.ALO.AFU.ALO

beer halls
RK.107 (A)
ALT **beer hall**
SN Use for establishments chiefly serving beer and usually offering entertainment.
UF halls, beer
CN V.RK.AFU.ALO.ALO.ALO.AFU.AFU.ARI.AFU

beer limestone
USE **beer stone**

beer stone
MT.658

UF beer limestone
limestone, beer
stone, beer
CN M.MT.AFU.AFU.AFU.DCU.AFU.ALO.AFU.ALO.ALO.AFU.AFU.AFU.BCW.AFU

Beersheba-Ghassulian
USE **Ghassulian**

beeswax
MT.2190 (L)
SN Natural wax produced by bees as a by-product of honey production; used chiefly in polishes, candles, leather dressings, adhesives, cosmetics, as a protective coating for etching, and occasionally to modify paint. (MH)
CN M.MT.AFU.AFU.ARI.BZY.AFU.AFU.AFU

beeswax, bleached
USE **bleached beeswax**

beeswax, bleached white
USE **bleached beeswax**

beeswax, unbleached
USE **unbleached beeswax**

beetles (mallets)
TB.1087 (N)
ALT **beetle (mallet)**
SN Large sledgehammers made of wood, used for driving pegs or wedges, knocking heavy wood beams into place, or in other applications where material might sustain damage if struck with a conventional sledgehammer. (MEANS)
UF beddles
bittels
bittles, wedge
commanders (mallets)
wedge bittles
CN V.TB.AFU.BCW.CFS.ALO.ARI.ALO.AFU

beginning axes
TB.836
ALT **beginning ax**
SN Axes used to make rough cuts before an adz is used to produce a curved surface in wood. (HUMMEL)
UF axes, beginning
axes, fitting
fitting axes
CN V.TB.AFU.BCW.CFS.ALO.AFU.AXC.ALO

béguinages
RG.189 (L)
ALT **béguinage**
SN Communal facilities established for the sisterhood of Béguines.
CN V.RG.AFU.AFU.DUC.AFU

behavior, deviant
USE **deviant behavior**

behavior, human
USE **human behavior**

behavior, proxemic
USE **spatial behavior**

behavior, spatial
USE **spatial behavior**

Behzad School
USE **Bihzad School**

beige
USE **grayish yellow**
light grayish brown
light grayish yellowish brown
light olive brown
pale yellow

beige brown
USE **grayish yellowish brown**

beige gray
USE **medium gray**
yellowish gray

beige, light
USE **grayish yellow**
light grayish yellowish brown

beige, light rose
USE **grayish yellowish pink**

beige, yellow
USE **light yellowish brown**
moderate yellowish brown

Beinschwarz
USE **bone black**

Beja
FL.694 (L)
UF Bedja
CN F.FL.ALO.AFU.AXC.BCW.ARI

Belbasi
FL.2850
CN F.FL.ALO.AXC.ARI.AFU.AFU.AFU.AFU

Beldibi
FL.2851
CN F.FL.ALO.AXC.ARI.AFU.AFU.AFU.ALO

belection moldings
USE **bolection moldings**

Belén
FL.1186
CN F.FL.ALO.ALO.ALO.ARI.BCW.ALO.AFU.AFU

Belfast trusses
USE **bowstring trusses**

belfries
RM.140 (A,L,N,B,R)
ALT **belfry**
SN Use for the rooms or spaces in which bells are hung in a tower; for the entire tower structure, use **bell towers.**
CN V.RM.AFU.DIO.ALO.BUE.AFU

belfries (bell towers)
USE **bell towers**

belfrys (sheds)
RK.1213
ALT **belfry (shed)**
SN Use only for vernacular British sheds for cattle, wagons, or farm equipment from the 16th to the 18th century.
CN V.RK.AFU.ALO.ALO.GFO.BIQ.AFU

Belgian
FL.3038 (L,B)
CN F.FL.ALO.BCW.AFU.ARI

Belgian black marble
MT.773
UF black marble, Belgian
marble, Belgian black
noir belge
CN M.MT.AFU.AFU.AFU.DCU.AFU.ARI.ARI.ARI.AFU.AFU

Belgian block
MT.908
SN A type of paving stone generally cut in a truncated, pyramidal shape; laid with the base of the pyramid down. (DAC)
UF block, Belgian
CN M.MT.AFU.AFU.AFU.DCU.ARI.AXC.AFU

Belgian marble
USE **rance**

Belgian trusses
USE **Fink trusses**

Belgischestil
USE **Jugendstil**

bell-and-spigot joints
TF.643
ALT **bell-and-spigot joint**
SN Commonly used joints in cast iron pipe. Each piece is made with an enlarged diameter or bell at one end into which the plain or spigot end of another piece is inserted. The joint is sealed by cement, oakum, lead, or rubber caulked into the bell around the spigot. (MEANS)
UF joints, bell-and-spigot
joints, spigot-and-socket
spigot-and-socket joints
CN V.TF.ALO.ARI.ARI.ALO

bell arches
RT.219
ALT **bell arch**
SN Use for round arches supported by large corbels with curved lower edges, giving the opening a bell-shaped outline.
UF arches, bell
CN V.RT.AFU.AFU.AFU.BCW.AFU.AFU.AFU.AFU

Bell Beaker
FL.2505 (L)
UF Beaker
CN F.FL.ALO.AXC.AFU.BCW.DCU.ALO

bell canopies
USE **bellcotes**

bell capitals
RT.120
ALT **bell capital**
UF capitals, bell
CN V.RT.AFU.AFU.AFU.AXC.BIQ.ALO.ARI.AFU.AXC

bell flower motifs
USE **husks (motifs)**

bell-founders
HG.511 (L)
ALT **bell-founder**
SN Founders, casters, or makers of bells. (OED)
CN H.HG.AFU.AXC.BUE.ARI.CFS.ARI.ALO

bell gables
USE **bellcotes**

bell houses
USE **bell towers**

bell metal
MT.377
SN Bronze used chiefly for casting large bells. Its standard composition is 78% copper and 22% tin but is varied to give varying tones.
UF metal, bell
CN M.MT.AFU.AFU.AFU.BZY.AFU.AFU.AFU.ALO.ARI.BCW.ALO.ALO

bell-shaped
DC.58
SN The shape, in full or in outline, of a cross section of an inverted cup with flaring rim and convex crown, very like a bell. (W)
CN D.DC.AFU.ARI.AXC

bell towers
RK.32 (A,L,N,B,R)
ALT **bell tower**
UF belfries (bell towers)
bell houses
houses, bell
kolokolnya
towers, bell
CN V.RK.AFU.ALO.AFU.ALO.DCU.AFU

Bella Bella
FL.1335 (L)
CN F.FL.ALO.ALO.ARI.AFU.BIQ.ALO

Bella Coola
FL.1336 (L)
UF Bellacoola
CN F.FL.ALO.ALO.ARI.AFU.BIQ.ARI

Bellacoola
USE **Bella Coola**

bellboys
USE **bellmen**

bellcotes
RT.472
ALT **bellcote**
SN Use for small, open structures erected on a roof, wall, or gable of a church or other structure, carrying and sheltering bells, often sanctus bells.
UF bell canopies
bell gables
canopies, bell
gables, bell
CN V.RT.AFU.AFU.AFU.BIQ.ARI.ALO.AFU.BUE.AFU

bellexion moldings
USE **bolection moldings**

bellflowers
USE **husks (motifs)**

bellhops
USE **bellmen**

bellmen
HG.37 (L)
ALT **bellman**
SN Hotel or club employees who escort guests to rooms, assist them with luggage, and run errands. (WCOL)
UF bellboys
bellhops
CN H.HG.AFU.AXC.ARI.AFU

belly knives
USE **hollowing drawknives**

belt conveyors
TB.366 (L,N,B)
ALT **belt conveyor**
SN Continuous belts passing over pulleys, providing a track on which loose materials or small articles are carried from one point to another. (PUTNAM)
UF conveyors, belt
CN V.TB.AFU.ARI.DCU.AFU.AFU.AFU

belt courses
USE **stringcourses**

belt highways
USE **beltways**

belt racks
TF.270
ALT **belt rack**
UF racks, belt
CN V.TF.AFU.AFU.AFU.AFU.EFQ.AFU

belt sanders
TB.521 (N)
ALT **belt sander**
SN Portable tools with power-driven, abrasive-coated continuous belts, used to smooth surfaces. (DAC)
UF sanders, belt
CN V.TB.AFU.ARI.EWY.ALO.CXA.AFU

belts (tool components)
TB.1096 (L)
ALT **belt (tool component)**
SN Continuous bands of tough, flexible material such as leather, fabric, rubber, or wire; used for transmitting motion and power from one pulley to another or for conveying materials. (W)
CN V.TB.ALO.ALO

belts, safety
USE **safety belts**

beltways
RK.1516 (L,B)
ALT **beltway**
UF belt highways
circumferential highways
highways, belt
highways, circumferential
ring roads
roads, ring
CN V.RK.ALO.ALO.BIQ.ARI.AFU.AFU.AFU

belvederes
RT.473 (N,B,R)
ALT **belvedere**
SN Use for rooftop pavilions intended as lookouts or for the enjoyment of a view. For unroofed platforms, use **widow's walks**; for rooftop structures that are primarily ornamental, use **cupolas.**
CN V.RT.AFU.AFU.AFU.BIQ.ARI.ALO.AFU.BUE.ALO

belvederes (gazebos)
USE **gazebos**

bemas
RT.744
ALT **bema**
SN Refers to raised speaking platforms usually those found in synagogues or in some Christian churches, but may also be used in pre-Christian contexts.
UF almemars
bimahs
tevahs
CN V.RT.AFU.ALO.AFU.BIQ.AFU.ARI.AFU

Bemba
FL.543 (L)
CN F.FL.ALO.AFU.AXC.ARI.AFU.AFU

Bembe (Lower Zaire)
FL.476 (L)
UF Babembe
CN F.FL.ALO.AFU.AXC.ALO.ALO.AXC.AFU

Bembe (Northeastern Zaire)
FL.508 (L)
UF Wabembe
CN F.FL.ALO.AFU.AXC.ALO.ALO.BIQ.AFU.AFU.ALO

Bena
FL.583 (L)
UF Wabena
CN F.FL.ALO.AFU.AXC.AXC.AFU.AFU

Bena Kanioka
USE **Kanioka**

Bena Luluwa
USE **Lulua**

Benacci
FL.2738
CN F.FL.ALO.AXC.ALO.ALO.ALO.BIQ.ALO

bench anvils
TB.648
ALT **bench anvil**
SN Anvils with two shaped ends. (HAND)
UF anvils, bench
CN V.TB.AFU.BCW.BIQ.AFU.ALO.AFU.AFU.AFU

bench chisels
TB.853
ALT **bench chisel**
SN A class of woodworking chisels. (BLACKB)
UF chisels, bench
CN V.TB.AFU.BCW.CFS.ALO.AFU.BUE.ALO

bench clamps
TB.1049
ALT **bench clamp**
SN Simple tools used in conjunction with a workbench which hold a piece of wood firmly in place in a V-shaped mouth.
UF clamps, bench
CN V.TB.AFU.BCW.CFS.ALO.ALO.BCW.AFU

bench dogs
TB.1062
ALT **bench dog**
SN Pegs or pins partially inserted into a hole at an edge or end of a workbench to help secure a piece of work or prevent it from sliding off the bench. (MEANS)
UF bench stops (bench dogs)
dogs, bench
stops, bench (bench dogs)
CN V.TB.AFU.BCW.CFS.ALO.ALO.BIQ.AFU

bench hooks
TB.1044 (N)
ALT **bench hook**
SN Devices, usually made of hardwood, used in carpentry to secure the work at the back of the workbench, in order to protect the surface of the workbench from being scarred or damaged by movement of the work. (MEANS)
UF hooks, bench
hooks, side
side hooks
CN V.TB.AFU.BCW.CFS.ALO.ALO.AFU

bench knives
TB.898 (N)
ALT **bench knife**
SN Adjustable stops with a projecting knife or hook that holds a piece of work on a workbench. (W)
UF knives, bench
CN V.TB.AFU.BCW.CFS.ALO.AFU.DOI.AFU

bench marks
VW.713 (L,N)
ALT **bench mark**
SN Marks on a fixed and enduring object, indicating a particular elevation and used as a reference, such as in topographic surveys and tidal observations. (BLACKS)
UF marks, bench
CN V.VW.AFU.ALO.ALO.AFU.AXC.ALO.AFU

bench planes
TB.932
ALT **bench plane**
SN A class of planes used for reducing, leveling, and smoothing wood. (BLACKB)
UF planes, bench
CN V.TB.AFU.BCW.CFS.ALO.AFU.DUC.ARI.AFU

bench plates
TB.651 (N)
ALT **bench plate**
UF plates, bench
CN V.TB.AFU.BCW.BIQ.AFU.ALO.ALO

bench saws
TB.996 (N)
ALT **bench saw**
SN Name given to the ensemble of a circular saw mounted on a bench.
UF benches, saw
saw benches
saws, bench
CN V.TB.AFU.BCW.CFS.ALO.AFU.EWY.ALO

bench shears
TB.722 (N)
SN Large shears used in sheet metal work typically having one handle bent to go into a hole in the top of the workbench so that they rest on the surface when in use. (RUSERW)
UF shears, bench
CN V.TB.AFU.BCW.BIQ.ARI.ALO.BIQ.AFU

bench stops
TB.1045 (N)
ALT **bench stop**
SN Adjustable apparatus, often made of metal, used to secure wood near the end of the workbench; usually used during planing.
UF stops, bench
CN V.TB.AFU.BCW.CFS.ALO.ALO.ALO

bench stops (bench dogs)
USE **bench dogs**

bench tables
RT.613
ALT **bench table**
SN Projecting courses of masonry at the foot of an interior wall, or around a column; generally wide enough to form a seat. (HAS)
UF tables, bench
CN V.RT.AFU.AFU.AFU.BIQ.BUE.ALO.AFU.ALO.AFU

bench vises
TB.225 (N)
ALT **bench vise**
SN Vises attached to a workbench to hold material while it is being worked. (PUTNAM)
UF vises, bench
CN V.TB.AFU.ARI.CFS.BOK.AFU

Bencharong
FL.2424
CN F.FL.ALO.ARI.BCW.BOK.ALO.AFU

benches
TG.276 (L,N,B,R)
ALT **bench**
SN Seats for two or more persons, generally without a back.
UF bancos
banks (benches)
CN V.TG.AFU.AFU.ALO.ALO.AFU

benches, bucket
USE **water benches**

benches, carpenter's
USE **workbenches**

benches, cradle
USE **cradle benches**

benches, deacons'
USE **deacon's benches**

benches, garden
USE **garden seats**

benches, mammy's
USE **cradle benches**

benches, meeting house
USE **deacon's benches**

benches, milk
USE **water benches**

benches, monk's (box benches)
USE **box settles**

benches, monk's (chair-tables)
USE **chair-tables**

benches, piano
USE **piano benches**

benches, picnic
USE **picnic benches**

benches, rocking
USE **cradle benches**

benches, saw
USE **bench saws**

benches, settle
USE **settles**

benches, wagon
USE **wagon seats**

benches, water
USE **water benches**

benches, window
USE **window seats**

bend hangers, bottom
USE **bottom bend hangers**

bend hangers, bottom and flange
USE **bottom and flange bend hangers**

benday artists
HG.141
ALT **benday artist**
SN Artists who apply benday tints (shadings in the form of dots of different intensities) to drawings or to zinc or aluminum plates with an inked screen or pattern.
UF artists, benday
CN H.HG.AFU.AXC.AXC.AFU.AFU.ALO.BCW.AFU.AFU

Bende (Igbo)
FL.263
CN F.FL.ALO.AFU.AXC.AFU.ALO.ARI.AXC.ARI

Bende (Kenya)
FL.643
CN F.FL.ALO.AFU.AXC.AXC.BCW.ALO

bended-back chairs
TG.125
ALT **bended-back chair**
SN Early 18th-century chairs with or without arms, having a vase-shaped splat in the back which was curved to give comfortable support to the back. (GLOAG)
UF chairs, bended-back
chairs, Hogarth
Hogarth chairs
CN V.TG.AFU.AFU.ALO.AFU.AFU.AFU.NIE.ARI

bending
KT.128 (L)
ALT **bent**
CN K.KT.AFU.ALO.DOI.AFU

bending stress
BM.919
SN Stress induced by loads perpendicular to the member. (STEIN)
UF stress, bending
CN B.BM.CFS.AXC.BIQ.ARI.BCW.ARI

bends
TG.862
ALT **bend**
SN Curving members which connect the front and back legs on an object, such as on a chair, cradle, or bench, allowing it to rock.
UF rockers (bends)
runners (bends)
CN V.TG.ALO.BOK

Benedictine
BM.652 (A,L)
CN B.BM.BZY.AFU.ALO.BCW.ALO

benefactors
USE **patrons**

Bengal cutch
USE **cutch**

Beni Amer
USE **Amer**

Benin
FL.93 (L)
CN F.FL.ALO.AFU.ALO.AFU.BUE.AFU

Benin, Early
USE **Early Benin**

Benin, Late
USE **Late Benin**

Benin, Middle
USE **Middle Benin**

Benizuri-e
FL.2076
CN F.FL.ALO.ARI.ALO.ALO.ALO.AXC.AFU

bent gouges
TB.882
ALT **bent gouge**
SN Gouges whose shank is either curved for its entire length or straight for most of its length with a sharp bend near the tip. (MAYER)
UF gouges, bent
gouges, spade
gouges, spoon
spade gouges
spoon gouges
CN V.TB.AFU.BCW.CFS.ALO.AFU.CXA.AFU

bent-wire chairs
USE **ice-cream parlor chairs**

bentonite
MT.61 (L)
SN An extremely fine natural clay formed by the disintegration of volcanic ash used mainly to increase the plasticity of a ceramic clay body and also to keep glazes in suspension and as an inert pigment or filler in various compounds. (MAYER)
CN M.MT.AFU.AFU.AFU.AXC.AFU.AFU.BOK.ALO

bents
RT.318
ALT **bent**
SN Frameworks usually designed to carry both a lateral and a vertical load that is transverse to the length of a framed structure.
CN V.RT.AFU.AFU.AFU.BCW.ARI

bentwood
MT.1409 (L,R)
SN Use to describe wood that is bent rather than cut into shape.
CN M.MT.AFU.AFU.ALO.BIQ.DCU.AFU.ALO.AFU

benzene
MT.2672 (L)
UF benzol
CN M.MT.AFU.ARI.HZS.AFU.BIQ.ALO.AFU

benzene, methyl
USE **toluene**

benzine
USE **naphtha**

benzoin
MT.1479 (L)
SN A balsamic resin, used chiefly in treating irritations of the skin, as a fixative in perfume, and as incense. (W)
CN M.MT.AFU.AFU.ALO.BOK.ALO

benzol
USE **benzene**

benzol black
USE **carbon black**

Beothuk
FL.1219 (L)
CN F.FL.ALO.ALO.ARI.AFU.AFU.ALO.ALO

bequests
BM.463 (L)
SN Gifts of personal property by will. (OCLD)
UF legacies
CN B.BM.BCW.CXA.AFU.ARI.AFU

Berber
FL.696 (L)
CN F.FL.ALO.AFU.AXC.BCW.AXC

Berëzovo phase
USE **Berëzovsk phase**

Berëzovsk phase
FL.2129
UF Berëzovo phase
CN F.FL.ALO.ARI.ARI.AFU.BIQ.AFU.ALO

Bergblau
USE **azurite**

Bergdama
FL.551
CN F.FL.ALO.AFU.AXC.ARI.ALO.AFU

bergère chairs
USE **bergères**

bergères
TG.24
ALT **bergère**
SN Upholstered armchairs, differing from other armchairs in being upholstered between the arms and seats. (PC)
UF barjairs
bergère chairs
cabriole bergères
chairs, bergère
fauteuils à panneaux
fauteuils en bergère
CN V.TG.AFU.AFU.ALO.AFU.AFU.AFU.ALO.AFU

bergères à joue
USE **bergères en confessional**

bergères à la reine
TG.133
ALT **bergère à la reine**
SN Bergères with flat backs; distinct from bergères with concave backs called **bergères en cabriolet.** (PC)
CN V.TG.AFU.AFU.ALO.AFU.AFU.AFU.NIE.BOK.AFU

bergères à oreilles
USE **bergères en confessional**

bergères en cabriolet
TG.127
ALT **bergère en cabriolet**
SN Bergères with concave backs; distinct from bergeres with flat backs called **bergères à la reine.** (PC)
CN V.TG.AFU.AFU.ALO.AFU.AFU.AFU.NIE.AXC.AFU

bergères en confessional
TG.61
ALT **bergère en confessional**
SN Large and deep armchairs with sides and wings. (PC)
UF bergères à joue
bergères à oreilles
confessionals (chairs)
CN V.TG.AFU.AFU.ALO.AFU.AFU.AFU.FZU.AFU

bergères en gondole
TG.70
ALT **bergère en gondole**
SN U-shaped armchairs, the upper rail of the back gently sloping down to the arms. Most popular during the Louis XV period. (PC)
CN V.TG.AFU.AFU.ALO.AFU.AFU.AFU.GWW.AFU

Bering Sea, Old
USE **Old Bering Sea**

Berlin blue
USE **Prussian blue**
dark blue

berms
RM.450 (A)
ALT **berm**
SN Use for banks of earth piled against exterior walls.
CN V.RM.ALO.AFU.CFS.AFU

berry
MT.1024 (L)
CN M.MT.AFU.AFU.ALO.BIQ.ARI.AFU

berry, Avignon
USE **buckthorn berry**

berry, buckthorn
USE **buckthorn berry**

berry, French
USE **buckthorn berry**

berry, Persian
USE **buckthorn berry**

berry, yellow
USE **buckthorn berry**

berths
RK.1597
ALT **berth**
SN Use for unoccupied, open water spaces alotted to vessels when alongside a landing place; when such spaces are set between adjacent piers or perpendicular to landing places, use **slips.** Use **docks** for open water spaces when occupied by vessels made fast to landing places.
CN V.RK.ALO.ARI.CLM.ALO.AFU

berths, building
USE **slipways**

Bertoia chairs
USE **diamond chairs**

beryl
MT.490 (L)
CN M.MT.AFU.AFU.AFU.CFS.AFU.AXC

beryl, golden
USE **golden beryl**

beryllium bronze
USE **copper-beryllium alloys**

beryllium copper
USE **copper-beryllium alloys**

Bété
FL.312 (L)
CN F.FL.ALO.AFU.AXC.AFU.ARI.ARI.AFU

Beti
FL.409 (L)
UF Bati
CN F.FL.ALO.AFU.AXC.ALO.AFU.ARI.AFU

béton
MT.198 (A,L)
SN Concrete consisting of lime, sand, and gravel. (DAC)
CN M.MT.AFU.AFU.AFU.BCW.AFU.AFU.ALO

bettering houses
USE **workhouses**

betting-houses
USE **betting parlors**

betting parlors
RK.191 (A)
ALT **betting parlor**
SN Designates licensed bookmaking establishments that take off-track bets, especially with relation to horse racing.
UF betting-houses
betting shops
parlors, betting
shops, betting
CN V.RK.AFU.ALO.ALO.ALO.AXC.ARI

betting shops
USE **betting parlors**

betty saws
USE **felloe saws**

Betula
USE **birch**

Betula alleghaniensis
USE **yellow birch**

Betula lenta
USE **sweet birch**

Betula lutea
USE **yellow birch**

Betula nana
USE **dwarf birch**

Betula nigra
USE **river birch**

Betula papyrifera
USE **paper birch**

Betula pendula
USE **silver birch**

Betula populifolia
USE **gray birch**

Betula pubescens
USE **downy birch**
European birch

Betula utilis
USE **Himalayan birch**

bevel locks, reverse
USE **reverse bevel locks**

bevel siding
USE **clapboard siding**

bevel squares
TB.444 (N)

ALT **bevel square**
SN Tools similar to the try square except that they have an adjustable blade which can be set at any angle. (MEANS)
UF bevels
bevels, sliding
bevels, T
bevels, tee
sliding bevels
squares, bevel
T bevels
tee bevels
CN V.TB.AFU.ARI.EFQ.ALO.BZY.AFU

beveled butt joints
USE **oblique joints**

beveled closer
USE **king closer**

beveling
KT.129
ALT **beveled**
SN Cutting or shaping the edge or end of a material to form an angle that is not a right angle. In the context of furniture, prefer **chamfering.**
CN K.KT.AFU.ALO.DOI.ALO

bevels
USE **bevel squares**

bevels, sliding
USE **bevel squares**

bevels, T
USE **bevel squares**

bevels, tee
USE **bevel squares**

beverage processing plants
RK.621 (L)
ALT **beverage processing plant**
UF plants, beverage processing
processing plants, beverage
CN V.RK.AFU.ALO.ALO.CLM.ALO .ALO.AFU.AXC.AFU

Beyazit I
USE **Bayazid I**

Beyazit II
USE **Bayazid II**

Beyazit, Lightning
USE **Bayazid I**

Bhaca
FL.568 (L)
CN F.FL.ALO.AFU.AXC.ARI.AXC.BIQ. AFU

Bhaktapur
USE **Bhatgaon**

Bharatpur
USE **Bhatgaon**

Bhatgaon
FL.2167
UF Bhaktapur
Bharatpur
CN F.FL.ALO.ARI.AXC.AFU.AXC.ALO. AFU

Bhoti
FL.2272
CN F.FL.ALO.ARI.AXC.ALO.AFU.BZY. BCW.ARI.ALO

Bhutanese
FL.2153 (L)
CN F.FL.ALO.ARI.AXC.AFU.AFU

bi-gum
USE **gum bichromate process**

bianco e giallo
USE **bianco e giallo antico**

bianco e giallo antico
MT.804
UF bianco e giallo
marble, phengites
marmor phengite
phengites marble
CN M.MT.AFU.AFU.AFU.DCU.AFU.ARI. ARI.ARI.BIQ.AFU

bianco sangiovanni
MT.1747
CN M.MT.AFU.AFU.ARI.AFU.AFU.ALO. ALO.BOK.ALO.BCW

bib taps
USE **faucets**

bibcocks
USE **faucets**

Bible paper
USE **India paper**

Bible records
VW.1061
ALT **Bible record**
SN Family records of births, baptisms, marriages, and deaths written on blank or printed formlike pages of Bibles. (GAHLM)
UF records, Bible
CN V.VW.AFU.ARI.ALO.CFS.AFU.AFU

Bibles
VW.537 (L,N,R)
ALT **Bible**
CN V.VW.AFU.ALO.AFU.AFU.ALO.BUE. AFU

Biblia pauperum
VW.538 (R)
ALT **Biblium pauperum**
SN Medieval picture books of scriptural subjects, with descriptive vernacular text. (LG)
CN V.VW.AFU.ALO.AFU.AFU.ALO.BUE. AFU.AFU

Biblical studies
KD.81 (L)
UF studies, Biblical
CN K.KD.AFU.AFU.BUE.ALO.AFU

bibliographers
HG.193 (L)
ALT **bibliographer**
SN Persons who compile lists of books, periodical articles, and audiovisual materials on specialized subjects, annotate bibliographies with physical descriptors, and analyze subject content of materials; also those who advise on the acquisition of materials in special subjects. (DOT)
CN H.HG.AFU.AXC.AXC.ARI.ALO.AFU

bibliographic databases
VW.646 (L)
ALT **bibliographic database**
UF databases, bibliographic
CN V.VW.AFU.ALO.AFU.DZW.ALO. ALO. AFU

bibliographic utilities
HG.867 (L)
ALT **bibliographic utility**
SN Organizations that maintain large online bibliographic databases and offer cataloging support and related products to libraries and other customers who access those databases on an online, time-sharing basis. (SAF6BU)
UF bibliographical services
services, bibliographical
utilities, bibliographic
CN H.HG.ALO.DIO.AFU.ALO

bibliographical services
USE **bibliographic utilities**

bibliographies
VW.254 (A,L,B,R)
ALT **bibliography**
SN Lists of books or other textual materials arranged in some logical order giving brief information about the works, such as author, date, publisher, and place of publication; may be works by a particular author, or on a particular topic.
UF book lists
lists, book
CN V.VW.AFU.AFU.AFU.FZU.BCW.AFU. ALO

bibliographies of bibliographies
VW.259 (L)
ALT **bibliography of bibliographies**
UF bibliographies, bibliographies of
CN V.VW.AFU.AFU.AFU.FZU.BCW.AFU. ALO.AXC.AFU

bibliographies, annotated
USE **annotated bibliographies**

bibliographies, bibliographies of
USE **bibliographies of bibliographies**

bibliographies, enumerative
USE **systematic enumerative bibliographies**

bibliographies, local
USE **local bibliographies**

bibliographies, national
USE **national bibliographies**

bibliographies, partial
USE **selective bibliographies**

bibliographies, select
USE **selective bibliographies**

bibliographies, selective
USE **selective bibliographies**

bibliographies, subject
USE **subject bibliographies**

bibliographies, systematic
USE **systematic enumerative bibliographies**

bibliographies, systematic enumerative
USE **systematic enumerative bibliographies**

bibliographies, trade
USE **trade bibliographies**

bibliography, analytical
USE **analytical bibliography**

bibliography, critical
USE **analytical bibliography**

bibliography, descriptive
USE **analytical bibliography**

bibliography, historical
USE **analytical bibliography**

bibliothecae
USE **libraries**

bibliothèques
TG.399
ALT **bibliothèque**
SN Cupboards containing bookshelves and closed with doors usually of glass or sometimes fitted with grilles. (PC)
UF armoires à livres
armoires-bibliothèque
armoires en bibliothèque
bibliothèques basses
CN V.TG.AFU.AFU.AXC.ALO.ALO.AFU

bibliothèques basses
USE **bibliothèques**

bibs
USE **faucets**

bibs, breast
USE **breastplates (tools)**

bice, blue
USE **blue verditer**

bice, green
USE **green earth**

bichromate prints, gum
USE **gum bichromate prints**

bichromate processes
KT.348
SN Processes for making photographic prints using a bichromate compound which, when exposed to light, causes its colloid binder to harden; unhardened areas are washed or abraded away. Pigments may be incorporated before exposure or during development. Though the expression dichromate is now preferred in chemistry, bichromate remains common usage in photography.
UF bichromated pigment processes
dichromate processes
CN K.KT.AFU.ALO.DUC.DIO.ALO.DIO.AFU

bichromate, gum
USE **gum bichromate process**

bichromated pigment processes
USE **bichromate processes**

bick irons
USE **beak irons**

bickerns
USE **beak irons**

biclinia
TG.387
ALT **biclinium**
CN V.TG.AFU.AFU.ARI.ALO.AFU

bicycle paths
USE **cycling paths**

bicycle sheds
RK.1214 (A,B)
ALT **bicycle shed**
UF bicycle shelters
cycle sheds
sheds, bicycle
sheds, cycle
shelters, bicycle
CN V.RK.AFU.ALO.ALO.GFO.BIQ.ALO

bicycle shelters
USE **bicycle sheds**

bicycle tracks
USE **cycling paths**
velodromes

bid advertisements
USE **bidding announcements**

bid bonds
VW.905
ALT **bid bond**
SN Surety bonds executed by the bidder on a construction project that serve as a guarantee that the bidder will enter into a contract within a specified time and furnish any required bonds ensuring completion of the work.
UF bonds, bid
bonds, proposal
proposal bonds
CN V.VW.AFU.ARI.AFU.BOK.BOK.AXC.ALO

bid calls
USE **bidding announcements**

bid forms
VW.807
ALT **bid form**
SN Forms, furnished to bidders, on which to submit their bids. (MEANS)
UF forms, bid
CN V.VW.AFU.ARI.AFU.AXC.AFU

bid instructions
USE **instructions to bidders**

bid invitations
USE **bidding announcements**

bid, invitation to
USE **bidding announcements**

bidders
HG.401
ALT **bidder**
CN H.HG.AFU.AXC.BOK.BCW

bidders, advertisments for
USE **bidding announcements**

bidders, instructions to
USE **instructions to bidders**

biddery
USE **bidri**

bidding
KG.49 (L,B)
UF competitive bidding
competitive tendering
tendering
CN K.KG.AFU.AFU.ARI.ARI

bidding announcements
VW.808
ALT **bidding announcement**
SN Documents advertising for bids to be submitted for a particular job.
UF advertisements for bidders
advertisements, bid
announcements of bidding
announcements, bidding
bid advertisements
bid calls
bid invitations
bid, invitation to
bidders, advertisments for
calls, bid
invitations to bid
invitations, bid
CN V.VW.AFU.ARI.AFU.AXC.ALO

bidding documents
VW.806
ALT **bidding document**
UF bidding requirements documents
documents, bidding
CN V.VW.AFU.ARI.AFU.AXC

bidding requirements documents
USE **bidding documents**

bidery metal
USE **bidri**

bidet stands
USE **bidets (box stools)**

bidets
RT.1480 (N,B)
ALT **bidet**
CN V.RT.ALO.BCW.ALO.ARI.CFS.ALO

bidets (box stools)
TG.235
ALT **bidet (box stool)**
SN Box stools with a china bowl and cover. Use **commode chairs** for chairs having a chamber pot.
UF bidet stands
stands, bidet
CN V.TG.AFU.AFU.ALO.AFU.ALO.AFU.AFU.AFU

bidets, portable
USE **portable bidets**

bidets, traveling
USE **traveling bidets**

bidonvilles
RG.281
ALT **bidonville**
SN Use for impoverished shantytowns, jerry-built of cut and flattened metal drums, located in France or North Africa.
CN V.RG.ALO.AFU.ALO.BCW.ALO.ALO

bidri
MT.425
SN An alloy formerly used in India that contained zinc, lead, and copper, fluxed with resins. It was finished with a velvety-black color by a solution of copper sulfate. (MH)
UF biddery
bidery metal
metal, bidery
tutenag
CN M.MT.AFU.AFU.AFU.BZY.AFU.AFU.AFU.ALO.BUE.AXC.AFU

bidriware
MT.472 (L)
SN Articles made from bidri, a metal alloy, that has been inlaid with gold or silver.
CN M.MT.AFU.AFU.AFU.BZY.ALO.AFU

bids
VW.809 (L,B)
ALT **bid**
SN Offers to perform a contract for work and labor or to supply materials or goods at a specified price. (BLACKS)
UF tenders
CN V.VW.AFU.ARI.AFU.AXC.ARI

Bidyogo
USE **Bijogo**

Biedermeier
FL.3253 (A,L,R)
CN F.FL.ALO.BCW.ALO.AXC.ARI

biege, light rose
USE **brownish pink**

biennials
RD.266 (L)
ALT **biennial**
CN V.RD.ARI.AFU.BCW.ALO.ALO.ALO.AFU.ALO

Big Game Hunting
USE **Paleo-Indian**

big houses
USE **plantation houses**

big shellbark hickory
MT.1173
UF Carya lactiniosa
hickory, big shellbark
hickory, king nut
king nut hickory
shellbark hickory, big
CN M.MT.AFU.AFU.ALO.BIQ.DCU.AFU.AFU.AFU.ELK.AFU

big toothed aspen
MT.1276 (L)
UF aspen, big toothed
Populus grandidentata
CN M.MT.AFU.AFU.ALO.BIQ.DCU.AFU.AFU.AFU.KFK.ALO.ARI

bigio antico
MT.784
UF marmor batthium
CN M.MT.AFU.AFU.AFU.DCU.AFU.ARI.ARI.ARI.ALO.ALO

bigio e nero antico
MT.785
UF marmor proconnesium
CN M.MT.AFU.AFU.AFU.DCU.AFU.ARI.ARI.ARI.ALO.ARI

bigio e nero di francia
MT.786
UF marmor celticum
CN M.MT.AFU.AFU.AFU.DCU.AFU.ARI.ARI.ARI.ALO.AXC

bigio morato
MT.787
UF mormor luculleum
CN M.MT.AFU.AFU.AFU.DCU.AFU.ARI.ARI.ARI.ALO.BCW

bigleaf maple
MT.1218
UF Acer macrophyllum
broadleaved maple
maple, bigleaf
maple, broadleaved
maple, Oregon
Oregon maple
CN M.MT.AFU.AFU.ALO.BIQ.DCU.AFU.AFU.AFU.IFM.AFU

Bihara
USE **New Britain**

Bihzad School
FL.3537
UF Bahzad School
Behzad School
CN F.FL.ALO.BIQ.AFU.GRC.AFU.AXC.AFU

Biisk phase
USE **Biysk phase**

Bijapur
FL.2254
CN F.FL.ALO.ARI.AXC.ALO.AFU.BZY.AFU.ARI

Bijogo
FL.337
UF Bidyogo
Bissago
CN F.FL.ALO.AFU.AXC.AFU.ARI.BIQ.ALO

Bikaner
FL.2288
CN F.FL.ALO.ARI.AXC.ALO.AFU.BZY.BCW.BCW.ARI

bike paths
USE **cycling paths**

bikeways
USE **cycling paths**

Bikom
USE **Kom**

Bilaspur
FL.2273
UF Kahlur
CN F.FL.ALO.ARI.AXC.ALO.AFU.BZY.BCW.ARI.ARI

bilateral symmetry
BM.96
SN Extreme regularity of balance achieved by the correspondence of identical compositional units on either side of a central axis.
UF balance, symmetrical
symmetrical balance
symmetry, bilateral
CN B.BM.AFU.AFU.ARI.AFU.FOG.ALO.AFU

bilection moldings
USE **bolection moldings**

bilingual dictionaries
USE **foreign-language dictionaries**

Billa ware
USE **Atchana ware**

billet moldings
RT.761
ALT **billet molding**
SN Common Norman or Romanesque moldings formed by a series of circular or square cylinders, disposed alternately with the notches in single

or multiple rows.
UF billets (moldings)
moldings, billet
CN V.RT.AFU.ALO.AFU.BOK.AFU.AFU.ARI.ARI

billet moldings, roll
USE **roll billet moldings**

billet moldings, round
USE **roll billet moldings**

billets (moldings)
USE **billet moldings**

billheads
VW.118
ALT **billhead**
SN Printed forms, characterized by a heading containing the name of a company or name and address, on which a statement of money due is recorded.
CN V.VW.AFU.AFU.AFU.FZU.ARI.ALO

billiard halls
USE **pool halls**

billiard parlors
USE **pool halls**

billiard rooms
RM.128 (A,B)
ALT **billiard room**
UF rooms, billiard
CN V.RM.AFU.DIO.ALO.BIQ.BCW.AFU.AFU

billiard tables
TG.709 (N)
ALT **billiard table**
SN Tables with a slate surface covered with cloth and surrounded by cushioned rails, on which the game of billiards is played. Distinct from pool tables which are similar in form but have six pockets.
UF tables, billiard
CN V.TG.AFU.AFU.BIQ.BOK.ALO.ALO

billing
KG.50 (L)
SN Issuing a list of charges payable. (RLG7)
CN K.KG.AFU.AFU.ARI.AXC

bills (invoices)
USE **invoices**

bills (legislative records)
VW.1025 (L)
ALT **bill (legislative record)**
SN Drafts of proposed laws introduced in a legislative body. (LG)
UF bills, legislative
legislative bills
CN V.VW.AFU.ARI.ALO.BCW.AFU.ARI.AFU.AFU

bills of fare
USE **menus**

bills of lading
VW.934 (L)
ALT **bill of lading**
SN Written receipts given by a carrier for goods accepted for transportation. (RHDEL2)
UF lading, bills of
CN V.VW.AFU.ARI.AFU.CFS.AFU

bills of material
USE **quantity surveys**

bills of quantity
USE **quantity surveys**

bills of sale
VW.861 (L)
ALT **bill of sale**
SN Formal instruments attesting to the transfer of ownership of personal property. (W)
CN V.VW.AFU.ARI.AFU.BIQ.CXA.AXC.AFU

bills, House of Commons
USE **House of Commons bills**

bills, House of Lords
USE **House of Lords bills**

bills, legislative
USE **bills (legislative records)**

bills, tax
USE **tax bills**

billys
USE **jumpers**

bimahs
USE **bemas**

Bimal
FL.618
CN F.FL.ALO.AFU.AXC.AXC.ARI.AXC

bin pulls
TF.87
ALT **bin pull**
UF pulls, bin
CN V.TF.AFU.AFU.AFU.AFU.CFS.BCW.ALO.ALO

Binburra
USE **white beech**

binders
MT.2368 (L,B,R)
SN Use for substances that produce or promote cohesion among loosely assembled materials, such as portland cement in portland cement concrete; also includes the substance in a photograph or photographic film that holds the final image material. For the combined material of photographic binder and image material, use **emulsion.**
UF agents, binding
binding agents
colloids, image-bearing
image-bearing colloids
mediums (photographic binders)
CN M.MT.AFU.ARI.BIQ

binders (bookbinders)
USE **bookbinders**

binders (joists)
USE **binding joists**

binders, synthetic
USE **synthetic binders**

binding agents
USE **binders**

binding joists
RT.302
ALT **binding joist**
SN Beams which support common joists of a wood floor above and ceiling joists below. (DAC)
UF binders (joists)
joists, binding
CN V.RT.AFU.AFU.AFU.BCW.ALO.AFU.BOK.AFU

binding of books
USE **bookbinding**

binding, Chinese
USE **Japanese binding**

binding, Japanese
USE **Japanese binding**

binding, saw-kerf
USE **saw-kerf binding**

bingo halls
RK.1036 (B)
ALT **bingo hall**
UF bingo parlors
halls, bingo
parlors, bingo
CN V.RK.AFU.ALO.ALO.EWY.AXC.ARI.ALO

bingo parlors
USE **bingo halls**

Binh Dinh
FL.2438
UF Thap-mam
CN F.FL.ALO.ARI.BCW.BUE.ALO.ALO.AFU.AFU

Bini
FL.248 (L)
CN F.FL.ALO.AFU.AXC.AFU.ALO.ALO.AFU

Bini-Portuguese
FL.173
CN F.FL.ALO.AFU.ARI.AFU.AFU

bins, grain
USE **grain bins**

biochemistry
KD.262 (L)
UF biological chemistry
chemistry, biological
CN K.KD.AFU.ARI.CLM.ALO.AFU

biographers
HG.180 (L)
ALT **biographer**
CN H.HG.AFU.AXC.AXC.ARI.AFU.AFU.AFU

biographical dictionaries
VW.397 (L)
ALT **biographical dictionary**
UF dictionaries, biographical
CN V.VW.AFU.AFU.ALO.EWY.ARI.ALO.AFU

biographical notes
USE **biographies**

biographical sketches
USE **biographies**

biographies
VW.296 (L)
ALT **biography**
SN Written accounts of the lives of individuals. (GAHLM)
UF biographical notes
biographical sketches
notes, biographical
sketches, biographical
CN V.VW.AFU.AFU.ALO.ARI

biographies, collective
USE **collective biographies**

biography
BM.277 (L,B,R)
CN B.BM.AFU.ARI.BIQ.BOK.AFU

biography files
VW.594
ALT **biography file**
SN Files of records, giving information about individuals. (LG)
UF files, biographical
CN V.VW.AFU.ALO.AFU.BIQ.ARI.AFU

biological chemistry
USE **biochemistry**

biological illustration
KT.210 (L,R)
UF illustration, biological
CN K.KT.AFU.ALO.DUC.CLM.BOK.AFU

biological illustrations
VB.50 (L,R)
ALT **biological illustration**
UF illustrations, biological
CN V.VB.AFU.ALO.AXC.ALO.ARI.AFU

biological laboratories
RK.1163 (A,L,B)
ALT **biological laboratory**
UF laboratories, biological
CN V.RK.AFU.ALO.ALO.FIM.ALO.AFU.AXC

biological sciences
KD.200
UF sciences, biological
CN K.KD.AFU.ARI.ARI

biologists
HG.327 (L)
ALT **biologist**
CN H.HG.AFU.AXC.BIQ.AFU.AFU.ALO

biologists, marine
USE **marine biologists**

biology
KD.202 (L,R)
CN K.KD.AFU.ARI.ARI.ALO

biology, molecular
USE **molecular biology**

Biombo
FL.430
CN F.FL.ALO.AFU.AXC.ALO.ALO.AFU.AFU.AFU

biomedical engineers
HG.628 (L)
ALT **biomedical engineer**
UF engineers, biomedical
CN H.HG.AFU.AXC.BZY.BCW.ARI

biometrics
KD.254 (L)
SN Statistical study of biological observations and phenomena. (W)
UF biometry
CN K.KD.AFU.ARI.CFS.AXC

biometry
USE **biometrics**

biomorphic abstraction
BM.186
UF abstraction, biomorphic
abstraction, creative
concretions, humor
creative abstraction
humor concretions
CN B.BM.AFU.AFU.AXC.CLM.AFU.AFU

biotechnology
BM.1135 (L,B)
SN Aspect of technology concerned with the application of biological and engineering data to problems relating to the mutual adjustment of man and machine. (W)
CN B.BM.CXA.AFU.ALO

bipacks
MT.2234
SN Color film formed of two separate emulsions bound in register. For film with an integral, two-layer emulsion, use **integral bipacks.**
CN M.MT.AFU.ALO.CXA.ALO.ARI.AFU

bipacks, integral
USE **integral bipacks**

birch
MT.1114 (L)
UF Betula
CN M.MT.AFU.AFU.ALO.BIQ.DCU.AFU.AFU.AFU.BIQ

birch, black
USE **river birch**
sweet birch

birch, canoe
USE **paper birch**

birch, cherry
USE **sweet birch**

birch, common
USE **silver birch**

birch, downy
USE **downy birch**

birch, dwarf
USE **dwarf birch**

birch, European
USE **European birch**

birch, gray
USE **gray birch**

birch, Himalayan
USE **Himalayan birch**

birch, mahogany
USE **sweet birch**

birch, paper
USE **paper birch**

birch, river
USE **river birch**

birch, silver
USE **silver birch**

birch, sweet
USE **sweet birch**

birch, white
USE **silver birch**

birch, yellow
USE **yellow birch**

bird refuges
USE **bird sanctuaries**

bird sanctuaries
RK.1454 (A,L)
ALT **bird sanctuary**
UF bird refuges
refuges, bird
sanctuaries, bird
CN V.RK.ALO.ALO.ALO.ALO.AFU

bird's beak moldings
USE **beakhead moldings**

bird's-eye maple
MT.1219
UF maple, bird's-eye
CN M.MT.AFU.AFU.ALO.BIQ.DCU.AFU.AFU.AFU.IFM.ALO

bird's eye marble
USE **coral limestone**

bird's-eye perspectives
VD.85
ALT **bird's-eye perspective**

SN Use for perspective drawings having a viewpoint well above normal eye level; for other nonphotographic depictions from a high viewpoint, where perspective is not used or is not emphasized, use **bird's-eye views.** For photographs taken from high locations, use **aerial views** or **aerial photographs.**
UF aerial perspectives
aerial views (perspective drawings)
bird's-eye views (perspective drawings)
perspectives, aerial
perspectives, bird's-eye
views, aerial (perspective drawings)
views, bird's-eye (perspective drawings)
CN V.VD.AFU.AFU.BIQ.ARI.BCW.AFU

bird's-eye views
VB.21
ALT **bird's-eye view**
SN Use with reference to nonphotographic depictions having a viewpoint well above normal eye level; if these are architectural drawings in precise perspective, use **bird's-eye perspectives.** For photographs, use **aerial views** or **aerial photographs.**
UF balloon views
views, balloon
views, bird's-eye
CN V.VB.AFU.AFU.BOK.ALO.ALO

bird's-eye views (perspective drawings)
USE **bird's-eye perspectives**

birdbaths
RM.430 (L,N,B)
ALT **birdbath**
CN V.RM.ALO.AFU.AFU

birdcage supports
USE **birdcages (furniture components)**

birdcage Windsor chairs
USE **square-back Windsor chairs**

birdcages (furniture components)
TG.863
ALT **birdcage (furniture component)**
SN Double-block devices with columns fitted between the top and the shaft of a tilt-top table that allows the top to tilt and rotate. (FAIRB)
UF birdcage supports
boxes (furniture components)
cages, squirrel (furniture components)
squirrel cages (furniture components)
supports, birdcage
CN V.TG.ALO.BUE

birdhouses
RK.81 (A,L,N)
ALT **birdhouse**
SN Enclosures, often resembling houses, built as resting, nesting, or feeding places for birds; distinguished from **aviaries** by the lack of emphasis on confinement.
CN V.RK.AFU.ALO.ALO.AFU.ALO.ARI

Birnick
FL.805
CN F.FL.ALO.ALO.ALO.AFU.ALO.AFU.ALO.ALO.ALO.ALO

Birnin Gazargamo
FL.108
CN F.FL.ALO.AFU.ALO.AFU.BUE.BOK.AFU

birth
KM.134 (L,R)
UF childbirth
CN K.KM.AFU.DOI.AFU

birth certificates
VW.948 (L,N)
ALT **birth certificate**
SN Formal documents certifying the date and place of persons' births and their parentage, as issued by an official in charge of such records. (BLACKS)
UF certificates, birth
CN V.VW.AFU.ARI.AFU.DCU.AFU.AFU

birth control clinics
RK.741 (L)
ALT **birth control clinic**
UF clinics, birth control
clinics, family planning
family planning clinics
CN V.RK.AFU.ALO.ALO.CXA.ALO.AFU.ALO.AFU

birth records
VW.947
ALT **birth record**
SN Official documentation concerning dates and places of persons' births, as well as parentage. (BLACKS)
UF records, birth
CN V.VW.AFU.ARI.AFU.DCU.AFU

birth registers
VW.949 (L)
ALT **birth register**
UF registers, birth
CN V.VW.AFU.ARI.AFU.DCU.AFU.ALO

birthday cards
VW.567
ALT **birthday card**
UF cards, birthday
CN V.VW.AFU.ALO.AFU.ARI.BOK.AFU

birthdays
KM.7
CN K.KM.AFU.ALO.AFU.AFU

birthstones
MT.571 (L)
CN M.MT.AFU.AFU.AFU.CFS.ALO.AFU

bisellia
TG.294
ALT **bisellium**
CN V.TG.AFU.AFU.ALO.ALO.ALO

bisexuality
BM.602 (L)
SN Sexuality characterized by romantic love or sexual desire toward members of either sex.
CN B.BM.BUE.CXA.AFU

bishoprics
USE **dioceses**

bishops
HG.219 (L,R)
ALT **bishop**
SN Clergymen of the highest order in Christian churches, usually charged with an administrative function such as the supervision of a diocese. (W)
CN H.HG.AFU.AXC.AXC.BIQ.AFU.ARI.AXC

bishops' palaces
RK.338 (L,B)
ALT **bishop's palace**
UF episcopal palaces
palaces, bishops'
palaces, episcopal
CN V.RK.AFU.ALO.ALO.AXC.ALO.BOK.BOK.ALO.AFU

bismuth white
MT.1730
UF Bougival white
pearl white
white, bismuth
white, Bougival
white, pearl
CN M.MT.AFU.AFU.ARI.AFU.AFU.ALO.ALO.BOK.AFU.ARI

bisque
USE **brownish pink**
grayish yellow
grayish yellowish pink
light grayish brown
light grayish yellowish brown
moderate yellowish pink
pale orange yellow
yellowish gray

Bissago
USE **Bijogo**

bister
MT.1617
UF brown lampblack
brown, soot
lampblack, brown
soot brown
CN M.MT.AFU.AFU.ARI.AFU.AFU.ALO.ALO.ARI.ALO.ALO

bistre
USE **dark orange yellow**
dark yellow
deep yellow
grayish brown
grayish yellow

grayish yellowish brown
light brown
light brownish gray
light grayish olive
light grayish yellowish brown
light yellowish brown
moderate greenish yellow
moderate olive brown
moderate orange yellow
moderate yellow
moderate yellowish brown
pale yellow
strong yellowish brown

bistre brown
USE **light brown**
light brownish gray
light olive
light olive brown
moderate yellowish brown
moderate yellowish pink

bistre, brown
USE **light grayish yellowish brown**
light olive brown

bistre, deep
USE **light olive brown**

bistre, gray
USE **light grayish yellowish brown**
light olive brown
light yellowish brown

bistre, olive
USE **light olive**
light olive brown
light olive gray

bistre, purplish
USE **brownish pink**

bit
USE **bitstone**

bit braces
USE **braces (woodworking tools)**

bit-hilani
RK.339
SN Designates ancient Near Eastern and Anatolian palaces having two long rooms fronted by a portico, often flanked by projecting ells; may also refer to some ancient entrance buildings or gatehouses.
CN V.RK.AFU.ALO.ALO.AXC.ALO.BOK.BOK.ALO.ALO

bit key locks
TF.195
ALT **bit key lock**
UF key locks, bit
locks, bit key
CN V.TF.AFU.AFU.AFU.AFU.DIO.BIQ.AFU.AFU

bit stocks
USE **braces (woodworking tools)**

bit tongs, right-angle
USE **side tongs**

bits
TB.1097 (L,N)
ALT **bit**
SN Tool components of varying sizes that fit into a brace or drill and are rotated to bore a hole. (MEANS)
UF bits, drill
cherries
drill bits
reamers (bits)
CN V.TB.ALO.ARI

bits (key components)
TF.545
ALT **bit (key component)**
SN Parts of keys which are inserted into a lock and engage the tumblers or bolt. (MEANS)
UF key bits
CN V.TF.AFU.ALO.ARI.ALO.AFU

bits, annular
USE **tenon-cutting bits**

bits, auger
USE **auger bits**

bits, brush
USE **brush bits**

bits, button
USE **button bits**

bits, center
USE **center bits**

bits, chair
USE **spoon bits**

bits, cock plug
USE **tenon-cutting bits**

bits, countersink
USE **countersink bits**

bits, crook
USE **crook-bit tongs**

bits, deck dowelling
USE **tenon-cutting bits**

bits, dowel
USE **spoon bits**

bits, drill
USE **bits**

bits, expansion
USE **expansion bits**

bits, flat
USE **flat tongs**

bits, forstner
USE **forstner bits**

bits, gimlet
USE **gimlet bits**

bits, gouge
USE **gouge bits**

bits, nose
USE **nose bits**

bits, pin
USE **spoon bits**

bits, pivot
USE **tenon-cutting bits**

bits, plug
USE **tenon-cutting bits**

bits, plug center
USE **tenon-cutting bits**

bits, quill
USE **spoon bits**

bits, reamer
USE **reamer bits**

bits, shell
USE **shell bits**

bits, ship auger
USE **ship auger bits**

bits, spiral
USE **spiral bits**

bits, spoon
USE **spoon bits**

bits, sprig
USE **bradawls**

bits, tenon-cutting
USE **tenon-cutting bits**

bits, twist
USE **spiral bits**

bits, wimble
USE **nose bits**

bitstone
MT.544
SN Coarse, crushed quartz (silica) used in making ceramics, spread beneath delicate articles to prevent their sticking or being blemished by contact during firing. (MAYER)
UF bit
CN M.MT.AFU.AFU.AFU.CFS.AFU.GRC.AFU.ALO

bittels
USE **beetles (mallets)**

bitternut hickory
MT.1174
UF Carya cordiformis
hickory, bitternut
CN M.MT.AFU.AFU.ALO.BIQ.DCU.AFU.AFU.AFU.ELK.ALO

bittles, wedge
USE **beetles (mallets)**

bitudobe
MT.126
CN M.MT.AFU.AFU.AFU.AXC.ALO.AFU.AXC.AFU.ALO.AFU.AFU

bitumen
MT.973 (L,B)
SN Natural asphalt that is clear of earthy matter. (MH12)
CN M.MT.AFU.AFU.ALO.ALO.AFU.AFU.ALO.AFU

bitumen (brown pigment)
USE **asphaltum**

bitumen (color)
USE **dark grayish yellowish brown**

bitumen process
USE **heliography**

bitumen, natural
USE **natural bitumen**

bituminised paper
USE **tar paper**

bituminous coal
MT.994 (L)
UF coal, bituminous
coal, soft
soft coal
CN M.MT.AFU.AFU.ALO.ARI.ALO

bituminous coatings
MT.2425
UF coatings, bituminous
CN M.MT.AFU.ARI.CRG.AFU.AFU

bituminous earth
USE **Van Dyke brown**

bituminous limestone
USE **carbonaceous limestone**

bituminous materials
MT.967 (L)
UF bituminous products
materials, bituminous
products, bituminous
CN M.MT.AFU.AFU.ALO.ALO

bituminous products
USE **bituminous materials**

bituminous rock
USE **rock asphalt**

Biysk phase
FL.2128
UF Biisk phase
CN F.FL.ALO.ARI.ARI.AFU.BIQ.AFU.AFU

Bizen
FL.2019 (L)
CN F.FL.ALO.ARI.ALO.ALO.ALO.ALO.ALO.AXC

Bka'gdams
USE **Kadam School**

black
DL.305 (L,R)
UF black, grayish
black, jet
black, lamp
black, slate
blackish green gray
blue, midnight
brown, iron
centroid color 267
charcoal (color)
dark navy
dull violet black
graphite (color)
grayish black
green gray, blackish
greenish slate black
iron brown
iron (color)
jet black
lamp black
midnight blue
navy, dark
slate black
violet black, dull
CN D.DL.AFU.ALO.ARI

black alder
USE **common alder**

black-and-white film
MT.2231
UF film, black-and-white
CN M.MT.AFU.ALO.CXA.ALO.AFU

black-and-white negatives
VJ.8
ALT **black-and-white negative**
SN Use for negatives whose images are usually composed of only gray tones, black, and white or clear areas; may include one hue as a result of process, toning, or discoloration.
UF negatives, black-and-white
CN V.VJ.AFU.AFU.AFU.AXC.AFU

black-and-white photographs
VJ.70
ALT **black-and-white photograph**
SN Use for the broad class of photographs whose images are composed of gray tones, black, and white, and sometimes one hue (which can result from chemical processes used, including toning, or from aging).
UF photographs, black-and-white
CN V.VJ.AFU.AFU.AXC.AFU

black-and-white photography
KT.378
UF photography, black-and-white
CN K.KT.AFU.ALO.DUC.DIO.ARI.AFU

black-and-white photoprints
USE **black-and-white prints (photographs)**

black-and-white prints (photographs)
VJ.42
ALT **black-and-white print (photograph)**
SN Use for photographic prints whose images are composed of gray tones, black, and white, and sometimes one hue (which can result from chemical processes used, including toning, from aging, or from a colored support).
UF black-and-white photoprints
photoprints, black-and-white
prints, black-and-white (photographs)
CN V.VJ.AFU.AFU.ARI.ARI.ARI.AFU

black-and-white slides
VJ.86
ALT **black-and-white slide**
SN Use for slides whose images are composed of gray tones, black, and clear areas; may include one hue as a result of process, toning, or discoloration.
UF slides, black-and-white
CN V.VJ.AFU.AFU.BCW.AXC.AFU

Black and White Style (architecture)
FL.3202
CN F.FL.ALO.BCW.ALO.ARI.BIQ.BIQ.AFU.ALO.ALO

Black and White Style (pottery)
FL.2642
CN F.FL.ALO.AXC.ALO.AFU.ALO.AXC.ARI.AFU

black-and-white transparencies
VJ.64
ALT **black-and-white transparency**
SN Use for transparencies whose images are composed of gray tones, black, and clear areas; may include one hue as a result of process, toning, or discoloration.
UF transparencies, black-and-white
CN V.VJ.AFU.AFU.ARI.AXC.AXC.AFU

black beech
USE **New Zealand beech**

black birch
USE **river birch**
sweet birch

Black Bobo
USE **Bobo-Fing**

black brown
USE **brownish gray**
dark grayish brown
grayish brown
grayish olive
light brownish gray
olive gray

black-burnished ware
FL.2990
UF ware, black-burnished
CN F.FL.ALO.AXC.ARI.BCW.ALO.BCW.AFU

black burnished ware (Helladic pottery)
FL.2652
UF burnished ware, black (Helladic pottery)
ware, black burnished (Helladic pottery)

CN F.FL.ALO.AXC.ALO.AFU.ALO.AXC.
AXC.AFU

black carbon ink
MT.2497
UF carbon ink, black
ink, black carbon
CN M.MT.AFU.ARI.CRG.ALO.ALO.ALO

black chalk
MT.45
SN Natural chalk containing carbon or shale and used for drawing especially since the Renaissance.
UF chalk, black
chalk, Italian
Italian chalk
CN M.MT.AFU.AFU.AFU.ARI.AFU

black cherry
MT.1288
UF American black cherry
American cherry
black cherry, American
cherry, American
cherry, American black
cherry, black
cherry, rum
Prunus serotina
rum cherry
CN M.MT.AFU.AFU.ALO.BIQ.DCU.AFU
.AFU.AFU.KLE.ARI.AFU

black cherry, American
USE **black cherry**

black cottonwood
MT.1283
UF balsam poplar, western
cottonwood, black
poplar, western balsam
Populus trichocarpa
western balsam poplar
CN M.MT.AFU.AFU.ALO.BIQ.DCU.AFU
.AFU.AFU.KFK.ARI.ARI

black ebony
MT.1139
UF Diospyros dendo
ebony, black
CN M.MT.AFU.AFU.ALO.BIQ.DCU.AFU
.AFU.AFU.CXA.AFU

Black-figure
FL.2643
CN F.FL.ALO.AXC.ALO.AFU.ALO.AXC.
ARI.ALO

black granite
USE **diabase**
diorite

black gum
MT.1159
UF black tupelo
gum, black
Nyssa sylvatica
tupelo, black
CN M.MT.AFU.AFU.ALO.BIQ.DCU.AFU
.AFU.AFU.DIO.AXC.ARI.AFU

black hemlock
USE **mountain hemlock**

black hickory
MT.1175
UF Carya texana
hickory, black
CN M.MT.AFU.AFU.ALO.BIQ.DCU.AFU
.AFU.AFU.ELK.ARI

black iron oxide
USE **Mars black**

black lead
USE **graphite (black pigment)**

black locust
MT.1202 (L)
UF Acacia (black locust)
Acacia, false
false Acacia
locust, black
locust, red
red locust
Robinia pseudoacacia
CN M.MT.AFU.AFU.ALO.BIQ.DCU.AFU
.AFU.AFU.HCQ.ARI

black lustrous ware
FL.2901
UF lustrous ware, black
ware, black lustrous
CN F.FL.ALO.AXC.ARI.ARI.ALO.ALO.
ALO

black maple
MT.1220
UF Acer nigrum
maple, black
CN M.MT.AFU.AFU.ALO.BIQ.DCU.AFU
.AFU.AFU.IFM.ARI

black marble
MT.772
UF marble, black
CN M.MT.AFU.AFU.AFU.DCU.AFU.ARI.
ARI.ARI.AFU

black marble, Belgian
USE **Belgian black marble**

black marble, Irish
USE **Irish black marble**

black marble, Rockingham royal
USE **Rockingham royal black marble**

black metal
USE **pewter**

black-mouthed ware
FL.2837
UF ware, black-mouthed
CN F.FL.ALO.AXC.ALO.ARI.ALO.AFU.
AFU

black oak
MT.1231 (L)
UF oak, black
Quercus velutina
CN M.MT.AFU.AFU.ALO.BIQ.DCU.AFU
.AFU.AFU.IRA.ARI

black oak, California
USE **California black oak**

black oil
MT.2013
SN Linseed oil cooked at a high temperature with as much white lead or litharge as will combine with it. (MAYER)
UF oil, black
CN M.MT.AFU.AFU.ARI.ARI.AXC.AFU.
BCW.AFU.AFU

black olive
USE **dark olive**

black-on-buff ware
FL.2991
UF ware, black-on-buff
CN F.FL.ALO.AXC.ARI.BCW.ALO.BCW.
ALO

black-on-red ware
FL.2866
UF ware, black-on-red
CN F.FL.ALO.AXC.ARI.AFU.ALO.ARI.
AFU

black-on-white, Mimbres
USE **Mimbres black-on-white**

black persimmon
USE **persimmon**

black pigment
MT.1564
UF pigment, black
CN M.MT.AFU.AFU.ARI.AFU.AFU.ALO.
ALO.AFU

black pigment, artificial inorganic
USE **artificial inorganic black pigment**

black pigment, artificial organic
USE **synthetic organic black pigment**

black pigment, organic
USE **organic black pigment**

black pigment, synthetic inorganic
USE **artificial inorganic black pigment**

black pigment, synthetic organic
USE **synthetic organic black pigment**

black pine
USE **Austrian pine**

black pine, Austrian
USE **Austrian pine**

black plum
USE **dark grayish purple**
dark purplish gray
purplish black

black poplar
MT.1271
UF black poplar, European
English poplar
European black poplar
Lombardy poplar
poplar, black

poplar, English
poplar, European black
poplar, Lombardy
Populus nigra
CN M.MT.AFU.AFU.ALO.BIQ.DCU.AFU.AFU.AFU.KFK.AFU.AFU

black poplar, European
USE **black poplar**

Black pottery
USE **Longshan**

black slate
MT.864
UF slate, black
CN M.MT.AFU.AFU.AFU.DCU.AFU.ARI.BUE.AFU.AFU.AFU

black-slip-and-combed ware
FL.2902
UF ware, black-slip-and-combed
CN F.FL.ALO.AXC.ARI.ARI.ALO.ALO.ARI

black spruce
MT.1397 (L)
UF Picea nigra
pine, spruce
spruce pine
spruce, black
CN M.MT.AFU.AFU.ALO.BIQ.DCU.AFU.AFU.ALO.DOI.AFU

Black (style)
USE **African American**

black-topped pottery
FL.2838
UF pottery, black-topped
CN F.FL.ALO.AXC.ALO.ARI.ALO.AFU.ALO

black-topped red ware
FL.2839
UF red ware, black-topped
ware, black-topped red
CN F.FL.ALO.AXC.ALO.ARI.ALO.AFU.ALO.AFU

black tupelo
USE **black gum**

black violet
USE **blackish purple**
dark grayish purple
dark purplish red
very dark purplish red

black walnut
MT.1322 (L)
UF American black walnut
American walnut
black walnut, American
Juglans nigra
walnut, American
walnut, American black
walnut, black
CN M.MT.AFU.AFU.ALO.BIQ.DCU.AFU.AFU.AFU.MQW.AXC.AFU

black walnut, American
USE **black walnut**

black watercolor
USE **Japanese ink**

black-white-red
FL.1175
CN F.FL.ALO.ALO.ALO.ARI.AXC.ALO.ALO.AFU

black willow
MT.1327 (L)
UF Salix nigra
willow, black
CN M.MT.AFU.AFU.ALO.BIQ.DCU.AFU.AFU.AFU.MWQ.AFU

black willow, western
USE **western black willow**

black, acetylene
USE **carbon black**

black, aniline
USE **aniline black**

black, aniline (color)
USE **dark grayish purple**
dark purplish gray

black, benzol
USE **carbon black**

black, blue
USE **bluish gray**
dark bluish gray
vine black

black, blue violet
USE **dark gray**
dark purplish gray

black, bluish
USE **bluish black**

black, bone
USE **bone black**

black, brownish
USE **brownish black**

black, carbon
USE **carbon black**

black, charcoal
USE **charcoal black**

black, cork
USE **vine black**

black, deep purplish
USE **dark purplish gray**

black, diamond
USE **carbon black**

black, drop
USE **bone black**
vine black

black, dull blue green
USE **blackish blue**
bluish black
dark grayish blue

black, dull greenish
USE **dark gray**
dark greenish gray

black, flame
USE **carbon black**

black, Frankfort
USE **bone black**

black, fruit stone
USE **fruit stone black**

black, gas
USE **carbon black**

black, German
USE **vine black**

black, gray
USE **greenish gray**
light brownish gray
light olive gray
medium gray
olive gray

black, grayish
USE **black**

black, green
USE **dark grayish green**
dark greenish gray

black, greenish
USE **greenish black**

black, ink
USE **dark bluish gray**

black, ivory
USE **ivory black**

black, jet
USE **black**

black, kernel
USE **peach black**

black, lamp
USE **black**

black, Mars
USE **Mars black**

black, oil
USE **carbon black**

black, olive
USE **olive black**

black, Paris
USE **Paris black**

black, peach
USE **peach black**

black, purplish
USE **purplish black**

black, reddish
USE **reddish black**

black, slate
USE **black**

black, Spanish
USE **vine black**

black, vegetable
USE **carbon black**
charcoal black

black, vine
USE **vine black**

black, violet
USE **dark grayish red**
dark purplish gray

black, yeast
USE **vine black**

blackamoors
USE **guéridons**

blackboard slate
MT.871
SN Select, unfading, black slate of uniform color and thickness with all edges ground and accurately squared so that joints can be made tight, smooth, and on the same plane. (HORNB)
UF slate, blackboard
CN M.MT.AFU.AFU.AFU.DCU.AFU.ARI.BUE.ALO.AFU

blackbutt
MT.1152
UF Eucalyptus pilulares
CN M.MT.AFU.AFU.ALO.BIQ.DCU.AFU.AFU.AFU.DIO.AFU

Blackfoot
FL.1373
CN F.FL.ALO.ALO.ARI.AFU.BOK.BCW

blackish blue
DL.225
UF black, dull blue green
blue green black, dull
blue, blackish
blue, dull
blue, dull greenish
blue, dull reddish
blue, graphite
blue, midnight
centroid color 188
dark navy
dull blue
dull blue green black
dull greenish blue
dull reddish blue
graphite blue
greenish blue, dull
greenish navy
indigo (color)
midnight blue
navy
navy, dark
navy, greenish
reddish blue, dull
slate (color)
CN D.DL.AFU.AFU.BZY.CFS

blackish brown
USE **brownish gray**
dark grayish brown
dark reddish gray

blackish green
DL.177
UF blue green, dark
bluish green, dull
centroid color 152
dark blue green
dark slate green
dull bluish green
dull green
green, dull
green, blackish
green, dark slate
green, dull bluish
hemlock (color)
slate green, dark
CN D.DL.AFU.AFU.BUE.CFS

blackish green blue
USE **dark greenish blue**

blackish green gray
USE **black**

blackish green, dull
USE **dark grayish green**

blackish purple
DL.281
UF black violet
blue, midnight
bluish violet, dull
brown, dark violet
centroid color 230
dark eggplant
dark navy
dark plum
dark violet brown
dull bluish violet
dull reddish violet
dull violet
eggplant, dark
logwood (color)
midnight blue
navy
navy, dark
plum, dark
purple, blackish
reddish violet, dull
violet brown, dark
violet, black
violet, dull
violet, dull bluish
violet, dull reddish
CN D.DL.AFU.AFU.CFS.CFS

blackish red
DL.45
UF brown, dull reddish
brown, lilac
brown, red
centroid color 21
dull reddish brown
grayish lilac
lilac brown
lilac, grayish
red brown
red, blackish
reddish brown dull
CN D.DL.AFU.AFU.ALO.BOK

blackish red purple
USE **dark purplish red**

blackish slate
USE **dark gray**

blackish violet
USE **dark violet**
grayish violet
moderate violet

blackish violet gray
USE **dark gray**
dark purplish gray

blackline prints
VW.691 (L)
ALT **blackline print**
SN Use for prints made on light-sensitized surfaces that produce black lines on neutral backgrounds.
UF blacklines
prints, blackline
CN V.VW.AFU.ALO.AFU.DZW.BIQ.CRG.AFU

blackline process
USE **ferrogallic process**

blacklines
USE **blackline prints**

Blacks
USE **African Americans**

blacksmith shops
USE **smithies**

blacksmithing
KT.783 (L,R)
CN K.KT.AFU.ALO.HOE.BCW.AFU.BCW.AFU

blacksmiths
HG.497 (L)
ALT **blacksmith**
SN Persons who make iron into tools, horseshoes, machine parts, and other objects by heating it in a forge and hammering it into shape on an anvil. (W)
CN H.HG.AFU.AXC.BUE.ARI.CFS.AFU.BCW.AFU

blackwood, African
USE **African blackwood**

blackwood, Australian
USE **Australian locust**

blackwood, Tasmanian
USE **Australian locust**

bladder green
USE **sap green**

blades
TB.1116 (L)
ALT **blade**
CN V.TB.ALO.AXC

blades (graders)
USE **graders**

blades (rafters)
USE **principal rafters**

blades, cleaving
USE **cleaving blades**

blades, razor
USE **razor blades**

blades, saw
USE **saw blades**

blanc baryte
USE **blanc fixe**

blanc d'argent
USE **white lead**

blanc de plomb
USE **white lead**

blanc de zinc
USE **zinc white**

blanc fixe
MT.1748
UF barium sulfate
baryta white
barytes
blanc baryte
Bologna stone
constant white
heavy spar
permanent white
Permanentweiss
process white
spar, heavy
stone, Bologna
sulfate, barium
white, baryta
white, constant
white, permenent
white, process
CN M.MT.AFU.AFU.ARI.AFU.AFU.ALO.ALO.BOK.ALO.BIQ

blanc titane
USE **titanium white**

blank arcades
USE **blind arcades**

blank doors
USE **false doors**

blank tracery
USE **blind tracery**

blank walls
RT.574
ALT **blank wall**
SN Walls whose whole surfaces are unbroken by a window, door, or other opening. (HAS)
UF blind walls
dead walls
walls, blank
walls, blind
walls, dead
CN V.RT.AFU.AFU.AFU.BIQ.BUE.AFU.AFU.ARI

blank windows
USE **false windows**

blanket chests
TG.447 (N)
ALT **blanket chest**
UF chests, blanket
CN V.TG.AFU.AFU.AXC.ALO.AXC.ALO

blanket insulation
USE **batt insulation**

blanket rails
TG.851
ALT **blanket rail**
UF rails, blanket
CN V.TG.ALO.BIQ.BIQ

blanking
KT.826 (L)
SN Cutting desired shapes out of a material such as metal to be used for forming or other manufacturing operations. (STEIN)
CN K.KT.AFU.ALO.HOE.BCW.ALO.ARI.AFU

blast-cleaning
USE **abrasive cleaning**

blast furnaces
RK.676 (L,N,B)
ALT **blast furnace**
SN Large, vertical structures for smelting iron from ore, using a solid fuel, designed so as to direct a continuous blast of air through the fuel to assure a high rate of combustion.
UF furnaces, blast
CN V.RK.AFU.ALO.ALO.CLM.ARI.AFU

blasters
HG.583
ALT **blaster**
SN Construction workers whose work is blasting with an explosive. (W)
UF shot-firers
CN H.HG.AFU.AXC.BZY.AFU.ALO

blasting
KT.108 (L,B)
ALT **blasted**
SN The process of loosening rock, or other hard-packed materials, with explosives. (MEANS)
CN K.KT.AFU.ALO.CLM.AFU

blasting, abrasive
USE **abrasive cleaning**

Blaugrünoxid
USE **blue-green oxide**

bleach
MT.2380
CN M.MT.AFU.ARI.BUE

bleach-out process
USE **silver-dye bleach process**

bleach process, dye
USE **silver-dye bleach process**

bleached beeswax
MT.2191
UF beeswax, bleached
beeswax, bleached white
bleached white beeswax
cera alba
wax, white (beeswax)
white beeswax, bleached
white wax (beeswax)
CN M.MT.AFU.AFU.ARI.BZY.AFU.AFU.AFU.AFU

bleached white beeswax
USE **bleached beeswax**

bleacheries
RK.682
ALT **bleachery**
UF bleachworks
CN V.RK.AFU.ALO.ALO.CLM.BIQ.AFU

bleaching
KT.76 (L)
ALT **bleached**
SN The process of whitening or lightening the color of something, especially by chemical means. (W)
CN K.KT.AFU.ALO.BOK.AFU

bleachworks
USE **bleacheries**

bleeding
KT.917
SN Refers to an underlayer of paint or other colorant seeping through to the surface.
UF bleeding through (paint)
CN K.KT.ALO.BZY.AFU

bleeding through (paint)
USE **bleeding**

Bleiglätte
USE **litharge**

Bleiweiss
USE **white lead**

blending
KT.61
ALT **blended**
SN Mingling or combining so that the separate constituents or the line of demarcation cannot be distinguished.(W) In painting, includes the gradation of color so that two hues or values merge imperceptibly. (MAYER)
CN K.KT.AFU.ALO.BCW.CFS.AFU

blessed
HG.776
UF beatae

beati
CN H.HG.AFU.BOK.AFU

blessing
KG.213 (L)
SN Consecrating or sanctifying by a holy rite; also, invoking God's favor upon a person. (RHDEL2)
CN K.KG.AFU.ALO.BIQ.ALO

bleu céleste
USE **cerulean blue**

bleu d'azur
USE **ultramarine blue**

bleu d'Egypte
USE **Egyptian blue**

bleu d'émail
USE **smalt**

bleu de cobalt
USE **cobalt blue**

bleu de mangane
USE **manganese blue**

bleu de Prusse
USE **Prussian blue**

bleu héliogène
USE **phthalocyanine blue**

bleu Paul Véronèse
USE **azurite**

blight
USE **urban blight**

blind
HG.787 (A,L,B,R)
SN People having no sight or such limited vision that hearing and touch are the chief means of perception. (ERIC)
CN H.HG.AFU.BOK.AXC.ALO.ALO.AFU

blind alleys
RK.1530
ALT **blind alley**
SN Restricted to alleyways open only at one end; for larger thoroughfares having access at only one end, use **dead-end streets** or **culs-de-sac.**
UF alleys, blind
CN V.RK.ALO.ALO.BIQ.ARI.AFU.ALO.AFU.AFU.ALO

blind arcades
RT.48
ALT **blind arcade**
SN Arcades closed at the back and serving only as decorative features.
UF arcades, blank
arcades, blind
arcades, surface
blank arcades
surface arcades
wall arcades
CN V.RT.AFU.AFU.AFU.ARI.ALO.AFU

blind arches
RT.220
ALT **blind arch**
SN Arches in which the opening is permanently closed by the wall construction. (DAC)
UF arches, blind
CN V.RT.AFU.AFU.AFU.BCW.AFU.AFU.AFU.ALO

blind catches
TF.43
ALT **blind catch**
UF catches, blind
CN V.TF.AFU.AFU.AFU.AFU.BCW.ARI

blind contour drawing
KT.194
SN The technique of drawing the contours of an object while looking at the object and not at the drawing.
UF contour drawing, blind
drawing, blind contour
CN K.KT.AFU.ALO.DUC.BZY.ALO.AXC.AFU

blind contour drawings
VD.131
ALT **blind contour drawing**
UF contour drawings, blind
drawings, blind contour
CN V.VD.AFU.AXC.BIQ.AFU.AFU

blind dovetail joints
TF.673
ALT **blind dovetail joint**
UF dovetail joints, blind
joints, blind dovetail
CN V.TF.ALO.ARI.AXC.ALO.ALO.AFU

blind drawers
TG.876
ALT **blind drawer**
UF drawers, blind
CN V.TG.ALO.DCU.AFU.AFU.AFU

blind hinges
USE **concealed hinges**

blind joints
TF.636
ALT **blind joint**
SN Use for concealed joints in masonry.
UF joints, blind
CN V.TF.ALO.ARI.ALO.ALO.ALO

blind tracery
RT.1023
SN Tracery applied to a surface without being pierced through.
UF blank tracery
tracery, blank
tracery, blind
CN V.RT.AFU.ARI.ALO.BZY.AFU.ALO

blind trumpets
USE **trumpet spirals**

blind walls
USE **blank walls**

blind windows
USE false windows

blindness
BM.727 (L,R)
CN B.BM.CFS.AFU.BCW.ALO.AFU

blinds (shelters)
RK.1182 (A)
ALT **blind (shelter)**
CN V.RK.AFU.ALO.ALO.FOG.AFU

blinds (shutters)
USE **shutters**

blister glaze
MT.2566
SN Ceramic glaze that produces a broken blister effect. Made by combining an ordinary glaze with grains of a material that will become gaseous under firing. (MAYER)
UF glaze, blister
CN M.MT.AFU.ARI.CRG.ARI.ARI.AFU.ARI.AFU

blistering
KT.918
ALT **blistered**
SN Bulging out from the main mass or surface, such as paint. (W)
CN K.KT.ALO.BZY.ALO

blitz-back saws
TB.989
ALT **blitz-back saw**
SN Back saws with removable interchangeable blades and a thumb hook at the toe. (SALAM)
UF blitz saws
saws, blitz
saws, blitz-back
CN V.TB.AFU.BCW.CFS.ALO.AFU.EWY.AFU.ALO

blitz saws
USE **blitz-back saws**

blizzards
KM.114 (L,R)
CN K.KM.AFU.CXA.BIQ.AFU

block
MT.2210 (L,B)
CN M.MT.AFU.ALO.ALO

block and spindle stretchers
TG.997
ALT **block and spindle stretcher**
UF block and turned stretchers
stretchers, block and spindle
stretchers, block and turned
CN V.TG.ALO.HIK.ALO.ALO.AFU

block and tackle
TB.79 (N,B)
SN Mechanisms or apparatus as ropes and pulley blocks; used for hoisting, lowering, and shifting objects or materials. (RHDEL2)
UF tackles

CN V.TB.AFU.ARI.AFU.BCW.BCW.ALO.AFU

block and turned stretchers
USE **block and spindle stretchers**

block bond
USE **stack bond**

block capitals
USE **cushion capitals**

block cornices
RT.334
ALT **block cornice**
SN Use for cornices of slight projection, with plain blocklike modillions and simple bed moldings.
UF cornices, block
CN V.RT.AFU.AFU.AFU.BCW.BZY.ALO.ALO.AFU.AFU

block cutters
USE **wood engravers**

block diagrams
VW.243
ALT **block diagram**
SN Diagrams using labeled blocks connected by straight lines to represent the relationship of parts or phases. (W)
UF diagrams, block
CN V.VW.AFU.AFU.AFU.FZU.AXC.ARI.AFU

block engravers
USE **wood engravers**

block feet
TG.899
ALT **block foot**
SN Feet on furniture in the shape of a cube, generally used with square untapered legs. (W)
UF feet, block
CN V.TG.ALO.DZW.AFU.ALO

block knives
TB.899 (N)
ALT **block knife**
UF knives, block
knives, stock
stock knives
CN V.TB.AFU.BCW.CFS.ALO.AFU.DOI.ALO

block planes
TB.933 (N)
ALT **block plane**
SN Small hand-held planes, either of wood or metal, with low-angled cutting blades; used for small work, to clean up rough spots, and especially to clean up end grain and miters.
UF planes, block
CN V.TB.AFU.BCW.CFS.ALO.AFU.DUC.ARI.AFU.AFU

block planes, straight
USE **strike blocks**

block plans
VD.40
ALT **block plan**
SN Use for plans of building sites with structures indicated by simple outlines or shapes.
UF plans, block
CN V.VD.AFU.AFU.BIQ.ALO.AXC.AFU.ALO.AFU

block printing
KT.470 (L,R)
SN Relief printmaking method in which shaped or textured printing elements are adhered to a board, inked, and then hand printed in the manner of a woodcut. (MAYER)
UF block printing, relief
printing, block
relief block printing
CN K.KT.AFU.ALO.DUC.DUC.ALO.BCW.ARI.ALO

block-printing, linoleum
USE **linocut**

block printing, relief
USE **block printing**

block printing, tile
USE **tile block printing**

block scrapers
TB.571
ALT **block scraper**
SN Flat, rigid pieces of steel having either plain or toothed edges; used for applications such as smoothing plaster and clay. (QUICK)
UF scrapers, block
CN V.TB.AFU.BCW.BCW.ALO.BIQ

block, Belgian
USE **Belgian block**

block, cinder
USE **cinder block**

block, clinker
USE **cinder block**

block, concrete
USE **concrete block**

block, glass
USE **glass block**

block, hollow
USE **hollow block**

blockboard
MT.1459 (B)
SN A plywood board in which veneer layers used in the core are replaced by blocks of wood, the direction of grain of the blocks running at right angles to that of the adjacent veneer. (W)
CN M.MT.AFU.AFU.ALO.BIQ.DCU.ALO.DOI.ALO

blocked columns
RT.88
ALT **blocked column**
SN Use for columns with shafts in which rectangular blocks alternate with circular drums.
UF columns, blocked
CN V.RT.AFU.AFU.AFU.AXC.BIQ.AFU.AFU.AXC

blockfront
DC.101
SN Use with reference to furniture pieces having a front the center of which recedes in a flattened curve between convex sections of similar flattened curves. (DDA)
UF swell'd front
CN D.DC.AFU.ARI.EWY.AFU

blockhouses
RK.863 (A,N)
ALT **blockhouse**
SN Fortified log structures with loopholes or ports in their sides which permit gunfire in all directions. (HAS)
CN V.RK.AFU.ALO.ALO.DIO.ALO.AFU

blocking chisels
TB.576
ALT **blocking chisel**
SN Any rugged, broad-edged stone mason's chisels. (MEANS)
UF bolsters (blocking chisels)
chisels, blocking
CN V.TB.AFU.BCW.BCW.ALO.BZY.AFU

blocks (city blocks)
USE **city blocks**

blocks of flats
USE **apartment houses**

blocks (pulley blocks)
USE **pulley blocks**

blocks, arch
USE **voussoirs**

blocks, city
USE **city blocks**

blocks, corner
USE **corner blocks**

blocks, dapping
USE **dapping blocks**

blocks, filing
USE **filing blocks**

blocks, holding
USE **holding blocks**

blocks, impost
USE **impost blocks**

blocks, miter
USE **miter blocks**

blocks, point
USE **point blocks**

blocks, pulley
USE **pulley blocks**

blocks, punch
USE **punch blocks**

blocks, sanding
USE **sanding blocks**

blocks, shaving
USE **shaving blocks**

blocks, skew
USE **kneelers (gable components)**

blocks, slab
USE **slab blocks**

blocks, strike
USE **strike blocks**

blocks, striking
USE **striking blocks**

blocks, tower
USE **skyscrapers**

blocks, whetting
USE **saw clamps**

blockwork breakwaters
RK.556
ALT **blockwork breakwater**
UF breakwaters, blockwork
CN V.RK.AFU.ALO.ALO.CFS.ALO.ALO.AFU.AFU

blood
MT.914 (L,R)
CN M.MT.AFU.AFU.ALO.AFU.ARI

blood banks
RM.289 (L)
ALT **blood bank**
SN Includes spaces in rooms as well as rooms and buildings where blood or blood plasma is collected, processed, stored, and distributed.
UF banks, blood
CN V.RM.AFU.DIO.AXC.AFU.AFU

Blood (Native American)
FL.1374 (L)
UF Kainah
CN F.FL.ALO.ALO.ARI.AFU.BOK.BCW.AFU

blood red
USE **moderate red**
strong red
vivid red

blood, dragon's
USE **dragon's blood**

bloodstone
MT.550
UF heliotrope
CN M.MT.AFU.AFU.AFU.CFS.AFU.GRC.AFU.ARI.ALO

bloodwood
MT.1153
CN M.MT.AFU.AFU.ALO.BIQ.DCU.AFU.AFU.AFU.DIO.ALO

bloom, peach
USE **peach bloom**

blot drawing
KT.192
SN A technique, usually in watercolor, in which the design is derived from an accidental mark or blot. (THDAT)
UF drawing, blot
CN K.KT.AFU.ALO.DUC.BZY.ALO.ARI

blot drawings
VD.123
ALT **blot drawing**
UF drawings, blot
CN V.VD.AFU.AXC.AFU

blotters
VW.843
ALT **blotter**
SN Books in which entries of transactions or occurrences are made as they take place, usually pending their transfer to permanent record books; such as a police blotter or general merchandise store blotter. (GAHLM)
CN V.VW.AFU.ARI.AFU.BIQ.CXA.AFU.AXC

blotting paper
MT.1926
UF paper, blotting
CN M.MT.AFU.AFU.ARI.ALO.ALO.AXC.ARI.AFU.AFU

blow joints
USE **blown joints**

blow molding
KT.146
ALT **blow molded**
SN Forming process whereby a hollow unit is formed and then forced, by internal pneumatic pressure, against a surrounding mold shaped to form a bottle or other container.(DIETZ) Usually used with reference to glass and plastics.
UF mold-blowing
molding, blow
CN K.KT.AFU.ALO.DOI.CRG.AFU

blow-up furniture
USE **inflatable furniture**

blowers
RT.1439 (L)
ALT **blower**
CN V.RT.ALO.BCW.AFU.ALO.ARI.BIQ

blowhorn stakes
TB.683 (N)
ALT **blowhorn stake**
SN Long, tapered stakes used for a variety of shaping tasks with sheet metal. (RUSERW)
UF stakes, blowhorn
CN V.TB.AFU.BCW.BIQ.AFU.ALO.CXA.ALO

blowlamps
USE **blowtorches**

blown glass
MT.255
UF glass, blown
CN M.MT.AFU.AFU.AFU.BIQ.AFU.ARI.AFU

blown joints
TF.644
ALT **blown joint**
SN Plumbing joints sealed with the use of a blowtorch. (MEANS)
UF blow joints
joints, blown
CN V.TF.ALO.ARI.ARI.ARI

blown oil
MT.1996
SN A thickened oil obtained by blowing a fatty acid (as linseed oil or fish oil); used in paints and varnishes as a drying oil and in lubricants. (W)
UF oil, blown
CN M.MT.AFU.AFU.ARI.ARI.ARI.AFU

blowtorches
TB.105 (N)
ALT **blowtorch**
UF blowlamps
CN V.TB.AFU.ARI.ALO.ARI.BCW.ALO

blowups
USE **enlargements**

blue
DL.212 (L,R)
CN D.DL.AFU.AFU.BZY

blue-and-green
FL.1927
CN F.FL.ALO.ARI.ALO.AFU.AFU.AXC.ALO.ALO

blue-and-white ware, Transitional
USE **Kraak porcelain**

blue ashes
USE **Bremen blue**

blue bice
USE **blue verditer**

blue black
USE **bluish gray**
dark bluish gray
vine black

blue brick
MT.98
SN A brick of high strength whose blue color results from firing in a kiln with a flame of low oxygen content. (DAC)
UF blue brick, Staffordshire
brick, blue
brick, sewer
brick, Staffordshire blue

sewer brick
Staffordshire blue brick
CN M.MT.AFU.AFU.AFU.AXC.ALO.AFU.ALO.BCW.AFU

blue brick, Staffordshire
USE **blue brick**

blue carmine
MT.1588
UF carmine, blue
CN M.MT.AFU.AFU.ARI.AFU.AFU.ALO.ALO.ALO.ALO.AFU

blue collar workers
HG.24 (L)
ALT **blue collar worker**
SN Wage earners performing manual work which usually calls for the wearing of work clothes or protective clothing on the job.
UF manual workers
workers, blue collar
workers, manual
CN H.HG.AFU.AXC.ALO.AFU

blue de tungstène
USE **tungsten blue**

blue frit
USE **Egyptian blue**

blue gray
USE **bluish gray**
light greenish gray
medium gray

blue green
USE **brilliant bluish green**
brilliant green
light bluish green
light green
light yellowish green
moderate bluish green
moderate green
strong bluish green
strong green
very light green
vivid bluish green

blue green black, dull
USE **blackish blue**
dark grayish blue

blue-green oxide
MT.1648
UF Blaugrünoxid
Grünblauoxid
oxide, blue-green
CN M.MT.AFU.AFU.ARI.AFU.AFU.ALO.ALO.AXC.ARI.AFU

blue green, bright
USE **brilliant green**
strong green
vivid green

blue green, dark
USE **blackish green**
dark grayish green
dark green
light bluish green
moderate bluish green
moderate greenish blue
strong bluish green
strong green
very dark green

blue green, dark grayish
USE **dark gray**
dark greenish gray

blue green, deep grayish
USE **grayish green**

blue green, grayish
USE **grayish green**
moderate bluish green

blue green, light
USE **brilliant green**
light bluish green
light green

blue green, moderate
USE **moderate bluish green**

blue green, pale
USE **pale green**
very pale green

blue gum
MT.1156 (L)
UF Eucalyptus globulus
gum, blue
CN M.MT.AFU.AFU.ALO.BIQ.DCU.AFU.AFU.AFU.DIO.AXC.AFU

blue lake
MT.1589
UF lacree
lake, blue
CN M.MT.AFU.AFU.ARI.AFU.AFU.ALO.ALO.ALO.ALO.ALO

blue lavender
USE **pale purplish blue**

blue mahoe
USE **mahoe**

blue malachite
USE **azurite**

blue ocher
MT.1583
UF ocher, blue
vivianite
CN M.MT.AFU.AFU.ARI.AFU.AFU.ALO.ALO.ALO.AFU.ALO

blue pigment
MT.1580
UF pigment, blue
CN M.MT.AFU.AFU.ARI.AFU.AFU.ALO.ALO.ALO

blue pigment, artificial inorganic
USE **artificial inorganic blue pigment**

blue pigment, artificial organic
USE **synthetic organic blue pigment**

blue pigment, inorganic
USE **inorganic blue pigment**

blue pigment, organic
USE **organic blue pigment**

blue pigment, synthetic inorganic
USE **artificial inorganic blue pigment**

blue pigment, synthetic organic
USE **synthetic organic blue pigment**

blue plum
USE **dark grayish purple**
dark violet
grayish violet

blue-printing
USE **blueprint process**

blue process prints
USE **blueprints**

blue shale
USE **bluestone**

blue slate
MT.865
UF slate, blue
CN M.MT.AFU.AFU.AFU.DCU.AFU.ARI.BUE.AFU.AFU.ALO

blue spruce
MT.1398
UF blue spruce, Colorado
Colorado blue spruce
Colorado spruce
Picea pangens
pine, spruce
spruce pine
spruce, blue
spruce, Colorado
spruce, Colorado blue
CN M.MT.AFU.AFU.ALO.BIQ.DCU.AFU.AFU.ALO.DOI.ALO

blue spruce, Colorado
USE **blue spruce**

blue turquoise
USE **brilliant greenish blue**
light greenish blue

blue ultramarine ash
USE **moderate blue**

blue verditer
MT.1595
UF bice, blue
blue bice
blue, Neuwieder
Kalkblau
Neuwieder blue
verditer
verditer, blue
CN M.MT.AFU.AFU.ARI.AFU.AFU.ALO.ALO.ALO.ARI.ALO

blue verditer (color)
USE **moderate blue**

blue violet
USE **light purplish blue**

vivid purplish blue
vivid violet

blue violet black
USE **dark gray**
dark purplish gray

blue violet, dark grayish
USE **grayish violet**

blue violet, deep
USE **vivid purplish blue**
vivid violet

blue violet, dull
USE **brilliant violet**
moderate violet
strong purplish blue
strong violet

blue violet, grayish
USE **light purplish blue**
moderate purplish blue
moderate violet
strong purplish blue
strong violet

blue violet, light
USE **vivid purplish blue**

blue violet, light grayish
USE **light purplish blue**

blue violet, pale
USE **brilliant purplish blue**

blue violet, pale grayish
USE **very pale purplish blue**

blue violet, soft
USE **brilliant violet**

blue, Alexandria
USE **Egyptian blue**

blue, Antwerp
USE **Antwerp blue**

blue, Antwerp (color)
USE **dark blue**
grayish blue

blue, aqua
USE **light greenish blue**
very light greenish blue

blue, artificial ultramarine
USE **artificial ultramarine blue**

blue, azure
USE **smalt**

blue, azurite
USE **grayish blue**
moderate greenish blue

blue, baby
USE **bluish gray**
light bluish gray
pale blue
very light blue
very light greenish blue
very pale blue

blue, Berlin
USE **Prussian blue**
dark blue

blue, blackish
USE **blackish blue**

blue, Bremen
USE **Bremen blue**

blue, Bremen (color)
USE **light greenish blue**
moderate bluish green

blue, bright
USE **brilliant blue**
brilliant greenish blue
light greenish blue
moderate greenish blue
strong blue
strong bluish green
strong greenish blue
vivid blue

blue, bright cerulean
USE **moderate blue**
strong greenish blue

blue, bright copen
USE **strong blue**

blue, bright greenish
USE **vivid greenish blue**

blue, bright open
USE **brilliant blue**

blue, bright peacock
USE **brilliant greenish blue**
strong greenish blue

blue, bright periwinkle
USE **light violet**

blue, bright reddish
USE **vivid purplish blue**

blue, bright teal
USE **dark greenish blue**
moderate greenish blue

blue, bright turquoise
USE **brilliant greenish blue**
strong bluish green
strong greenish blue

blue, brilliant greenish
USE **brilliant greenish blue**

blue, brilliant peacock
USE **strong greenish blue**

blue, brilliant purplish
USE **brilliant purplish blue**

blue, bronze
USE **Prussian blue**

blue, Brunswick
USE **Prussian blue**

blue, cendre
USE **cendre blue**

blue, cerulean
USE **cerulean blue**

blue, cerulean (color)
USE **light blue**
moderate blue
strong blue
strong greenish blue
vivid blue
vivid greenish blue

blue, Chinese
USE **Prussian blue**

blue, cobalt
USE **cobalt blue**

blue, cobalt (color)
USE **strong greenish blue**
vivid blue

blue, copen
USE **light blue**
moderate blue
strong blue

blue, copper
USE **Bremen blue**
azurite

blue, cornflower
USE **cornflower blue**

blue, cornflower (color)
USE **moderate purplish blue**

blue, cyan
USE **moderate bluish green**
moderate greenish blue

blue, cyanine
USE **dark purplish blue**
moderate purplish blue

blue, dark
USE **dark blue**

blue, dark aniline
USE **dark grayish blue**
dark grayish purple

blue, dark cerulean
USE **dark greenish blue**
grayish blue

blue, dark delft
USE **dark grayish blue**

blue, dark grayish
USE **dark grayish blue**

blue, dark greenish
USE **dark greenish blue**

blue, dark peacock
USE **dark greenish blue**

blue, dark purplish
USE **dark purplish blue**

blue, dark steel
USE **grayish blue**

blue, dark teal
USE dark grayish blue
dark greenish blue

blue, deep
USE deep blue

blue, deep cerulean
USE dark greenish blue
deep greenish blue
moderate blue
moderate greenish blue

blue, deep delft
USE grayish blue

blue, deep greenish
USE deep greenish blue

blue, deep peacock
USE dark greenish blue
moderate greenish blue

blue, deep purplish
USE deep purplish blue

blue, deep royal
USE dark blue
deep blue
deep purplish blue
moderate purplish blue

blue, deep sapphire
USE dark blue
deep blue
moderate purplish blue

blue, deep teal
USE dark bluish green
dark greenish blue
moderate greenish blue

blue, delft
USE dark blue
grayish blue
grayish purplish blue
moderate blue
pale purplish blue

blue, della robbia
USE moderate blue

blue, diamin azo
USE dark grayish purple
grayish violet

blue, dull
USE blackish blue
dark bluish gray
dark grayish blue
deep blue
grayish blue
grayish purplish blue
moderate blue
pale blue
pale purplish blue
strong blue

blue, dull greenish
USE blackish blue
dark grayish blue
grayish blue
pale blue
very pale blue

blue, dull reddish
USE blackish blue
dark grayish blue
grayish blue
grayish purplish blue
pale blue
pale purplish blue
very pale blue
very pale purplish blue

blue, dumont
USE smalt

blue, Egyptian
USE Egyptian blue

blue, French
USE artificial ultramarine blue
light purplish blue
strong purplish blue
vivid purplish blue

blue, gentian
USE moderate purplish blue

blue, genuine ultramarine
USE strong blue
vivid blue

blue, Gmelin's
USE artificial ultramarine blue

blue, granite
USE light gray

blue, graphite
USE blackish blue
dark grayish blue
dark purplish blue
grayish purplish blue

blue, gray
USE light bluish gray
light purplish gray
moderate blue
pale blue
pale purplish blue

blue, grayish
USE grayish blue

blue, grayish purplish
USE grayish purplish blue

blue, greenish
USE greenish blue

blue, Haarlem
USE Antwerp blue

blue, Hungary
USE cobalt blue
smalt

blue, indanthrone
USE indanthrone blue

blue, Indian
USE indigo

blue, indigo
USE dark grayish blue
grayish blue
grayish purplish blue
indigo

blue, ink
USE dark grayish blue

blue, intense
USE indigo
phthalocyanine blue

blue, irgazin
USE irgazin blue

blue, iron
USE dark gray
Prussian blue

blue, Italian
USE Egyptian blue

blue, king's
USE cobalt blue

blue, kingfisher
USE strong greenish blue

blue, lapis lazuli
USE deep blue
moderate blue

blue, lazuline
USE ultramarine blue

blue, Leithner's
USE Leithner's blue

blue, light
USE light blue

blue, light aqua
USE pale blue
very light greenish blue

blue, light cerulean
USE brilliant greenish blue
light blue
strong greenish blue

blue, light copen
USE light blue

blue, light cornflower
USE light purplish blue
light violet
moderate purplish blue
moderate violet

blue, light gray
USE grayish blue
pale blue

blue, light greenish
USE light greenish blue

blue, light methyl
USE brilliant blue

blue, light periwinkle
USE light purplish blue
light violet
very pale violet

blue, light purplish
USE **light purplish blue**

blue, light turquoise
USE **light greenish blue**
very light greenish blue

blue, lime
USE **lime blue**

blue, lime (artificial ultramarine blue)
USE **artificial ultramarine blue**

blue, logwood
USE **dark bluish gray**

blue, manganese
USE **manganese blue**

blue, Mayan
USE **Mayan blue**

blue, medium
USE **dark blue**
dark greenish blue
grayish purplish blue
moderate blue
moderate greenish blue

blue, medium teal
USE **moderate greenish blue**

blue, medium turquoise
USE **moderate greenish blue**

blue, methyl
USE **vivid blue**

blue, midnight
USE **black**
blackish blue
blackish purple
bluish black
dark bluish gray
dark purplish blue

blue, Milori
USE **Prussian blue**

blue, mineral
USE **Antwerp blue**

blue, moderate
USE **moderate blue**

blue, moderate greenish
USE **moderate greenish blue**

blue, moderate purplish
USE **moderate purplish blue**

blue, Monastral
USE **dark blue**
moderate purplish blue
phthalocyanine blue

blue, Monastral fast
USE **phthalocyanine blue**

blue, mountain
USE **Bremen blue**

blue, mountain (azurite)
USE **azurite**

blue, navy
USE **dark purplish blue**
grayish purplish blue
moderate purplish blue

blue, Neuwieder
USE **blue verditer**

blue, new
USE **artificial ultramarine blue**
cobalt blue

blue, olympia
USE **cobalt blue**

blue, pale
USE **pale blue**

blue, pale aqua
USE **very pale blue**

blue, pale cerulean
USE **light blue**
very light blue

blue, pale grayish
USE **very pale blue**

blue, pale periwinkle
USE **very pale purple**
very pale purplish blue

blue, pale purplish
USE **pale purplish blue**

blue, pale Windsor
USE **light blue**

blue, Paris
USE **Prussian blue**
strong blue

blue, paste
USE **Prussian blue**

blue, pastel
USE **grayish blue**
pale blue
very pale blue

blue, peacock
USE **dark greenish blue**
moderate greenish blue
strong greenish blue

blue, pearl
USE **light gray**

blue, periwinkle
USE **light purplish blue**
light violet

blue, permanent
USE **artificial ultramarine blue**
strong purplish blue

blue, phenyl
USE **vivid purplish blue**

blue, phthalocyanine
USE **phthalocyanine blue**

blue, Pompeian
USE **Egyptian blue**

blue, powder
USE **bluish gray**
deep blue
moderate blue
pale blue
pale purplish blue

blue, Pozzuoli
USE **Egyptian blue**

blue, Prussian
USE **Prussian blue**

blue, Prussian (color)
USE **dark greenish blue**
deep greenish blue
moderate blue
strong blue

blue, purplish
USE **purplish blue**

blue, reddish
USE **brilliant purplish blue**
dark purplish blue
deep purplish blue
light purplish blue
moderate purplish blue
strong purplish blue
very light purplish blue

blue, royal
USE **artificial ultramarine blue**
dark blue
deep blue
deep purplish blue
moderate blue
moderate purplish blue
strong blue
strong purplish blue
vivid blue
vivid purplish blue

blue, Sanders
USE **ultramarine blue**

blue, sapphire
USE **dark blue**
deep purplish blue
strong blue
strong purplish blue
vivid blue
vivid purplish blue

blue, Saunders
USE **ultramarine blue**

blue, Saxon
USE **smalt**

blue, slate
USE **dark bluish gray**
grayish blue
moderate bluish green

blue, smalt
USE **moderate blue**
vivid purplish blue

blue, steel
USE **Prussian blue**
grayish blue

blue, strong
USE **strong blue**

blue, strong greenish
USE **strong greenish blue**

blue, strong purplish
USE **strong purplish blue**

blue, teal
USE **dark grayish blue**
dark greenish blue
moderate greenish blue

blue, Thalo
USE **phthalocyanine blue**

blue, Thalo (color)
USE **dark greenish blue**
very dark greenish blue

blue, Thénard's
USE **cobalt blue**

blue, tungsten
USE **tungsten blue**

blue, Turnbull's
USE **Prussian blue**

blue, turquoise
USE **light bluish green**
light greenish blue
moderate greenish blue
strong greenish blue

blue, ultramarine
USE **ultramarine blue**

blue, ultramarine (artificial)
USE **artificial ultramarine blue**

blue, ultramarine (color)
USE **vivid blue**
vivid purplish blue

blue, Venetian
USE **Egyptian blue**

blue, very dark greenish
USE **very dark greenish blue**

blue, very light
USE **very light blue**

blue, very light greenish
USE **very light greenish blue**

blue, very light purplish
USE **very light purplish blue**

blue, very pale
USE **very pale blue**

blue, very pale purplish
USE **very pale purplish blue**

blue, Vestorian
USE **Egyptian blue**

blue, Vienna
USE **cobalt blue**

blue, violet
USE **strong purplish blue**

blue, vivid
USE **vivid blue**

blue, vivid cerulean
USE **strong greenish blue**

blue, vivid greenish
USE **vivid greenish blue**

blue, vivid peacock
USE **strong greenish blue**

blue, vivid purplish
USE **vivid purplish blue**

blue, vivid turquoise
USE **moderate greenish blue**
strong bluish green
strong greenish blue

blue, white
USE **light bluish gray**

bluebooks
USE **social registers**

blueline prints
VW.692 (N)
ALT **blueline print**
SN Use for prints made on light-sensitized surfaces that produce blue images on neutral backgrounds. For white images on blue backgrounds, use **blueprints.**
UF bluelines
prints, blueline
CN V.VW.AFU.ALO.AFU.DZW.BIQ.CRG .ALO

bluelines
USE **blueline prints**

blueprint process
KT.342 (L,B)
SN A photographic process using iron salts and producing an image in Prussian blue. For the resulting prints, use **blueprints** if they are reproductions of technical drawings, or **cyanotypes** if they are camera images or photograms.
UF blue-printing
cyanotype
ferroprussiate process
CN K.KT.AFU.ALO.DUC.DIO.ALO.CRG. AFU

blueprints
VW.677 (A,L,N)
ALT **blueprint**
SN Use for reproductive prints of architectural and other technical drawings having white images on blue backgrounds, produced by the blueprint process. For blue images on white backgrounds, use **blueline prints.** For blue-toned photographs produced by the blueprint process, use **cyanotypes.**
UF blue process prints
cyanotypes (reproductions)
iron process prints
prints, blue process
prints, iron process
prints, white line
white line prints
CN V.VW.AFU.ALO.AFU.DZW.BIQ.AFU

blueprints (photographs)
USE **cyanotypes**

bluestone
MT.709
UF blue shale
shale, blue
CN M.MT.AFU.AFU.AFU.DCU.AFU.ALO .AFU.ARI.AFU.ALO.AFU.AFU

bluestone, Hudson
USE **Hudson bluestone**

bluestone, North River
USE **North River bluestone**

Bluff-dweller
FL.884
CN F.FL.ALO.ALO.ALO.AFU.ALO.ALO. BIQ.AFU

bluffs
USE **cliffs**

bluish black
DL.230
UF black, bluish
black, dull blue green
blue, midnight
centroid color 193
dark navy
dull blue green black
midnight blue
navy, dark
CN D.DL.AFU.AFU.BZY.CXA

bluish gray
DL.227
UF aqua gray
baby blue
black, blue
blue black
blue gray
blue, baby
blue, powder
centroid color 191
gray, aqua
gray, blue
gray, bluish
gray, light Payne's
light Payne's gray
Payne's gray, light
pewter (color)
powder blue
slate (color)
CN D.DL.AFU.AFU.BZY.CRG

bluish gray green
USE **grayish green**
pale green

bluish gray green, dark
USE **dark bluish green**
dark grayish green

grayish green
moderate bluish green

bluish gray green, deep
USE grayish green

bluish gray, dark
USE dark bluish gray

bluish gray, light
USE light bluish gray

bluish green
DL.195
UF green, bluish
CN D.DL.AFU.AFU.BUE.DCU.ALO

bluish green, bright
USE vivid bluish green

bluish green, brilliant
USE brilliant bluish green

bluish green, dark
USE dark bluish green

bluish green, deep
USE deep bluish green

bluish green, dull
USE blackish green
dark grayish green
grayish green
pale green
very pale green

bluish green, light
USE light bluish green

bluish green, moderate
USE moderate bluish green

bluish green, strong
USE strong bluish green

bluish green, very dark
USE very dark bluish green

bluish green, very light
USE very light bluish green

bluish green, vivid
USE vivid bluish green

bluish lavender
USE light violet

bluish lavender, pale
USE very pale purple

bluish lavender, pale bluish
USE very pale violet

bluish olive
USE dark grayish olive green
dark olive green
deep olive green
grayish olive green
moderate olive green
strong olive green

bluish pink
USE brilliant purplish pink
dark purplish pink
deep purplish pink
grayish purplish pink
light grayish purplish red
light purplish pink
moderate purplish pink
pale purplish pink
strong purplish pink

bluish red
USE deep purplish red
moderate purplish red
strong purplish red
very deep purplish red

bluish red, dull
USE dark purplish red
moderate purplish red
very dark purplish red

bluish slate black
USE dark blue

bluish violet
USE brilliant violet
dark violet
deep violet
light violet
moderate violet
strong violet
very light violet
vivid purplish blue
vivid violet

bluish violet, bright
USE vivid violet

bluish violet, dark
USE dark violet
grayish purple
grayish violet

bluish violet, dark dull
USE dark purple
grayish violet
moderate violet

bluish violet, deep dull
USE grayish purplish blue
moderate violet
pale purplish blue
pale violet
strong violet

bluish violet, dull
USE blackish purple
brilliant violet
dark grayish purple
grayish violet
light violet
pale purple
strong violet
very pale purple
very pale violet

bluish violet, light
USE brilliant purplish blue
brilliant violet
strong purplish blue

bluish violet, light dull
USE light violet

bluish violet, pale
USE brilliant purplish blue

bluish white
DL.226
UF centroid color 189
white, bluish
CN D.DL.AFU.AFU.BZY.CLM

blunt arches
RT.231
ALT blunt arch
SN Use for pointed arches in which the curves are struck from two centers closer together than the width of the arch.
UF arches, blunt
CN V.RT.AFU.AFU.AFU.BCW.AFU.AFU.AFU.CRG.AFU

blunt nails
TF.421
ALT blunt nail
UF nails, blunt
CN V.TF.AFU.AFU.AFU.ALO.AFU.CFS.AFU.DIO.ALO

blus, azurite
USE moderate purplish blue

Boa
USE Babwa

board
MT.2212 (N,B)
CN M.MT.AFU.ALO.ARI

board and batten
MT.2398
SN Siding in which joints between vertically placed boards are covered by narrow strips of wood. (MEANS)
UF batten, board and
CN M.MT.AFU.ARI.BZY.AXC.AXC.AFU

board chairs
TG.39
ALT board chair
SN Simple chairs consisting of a slab seat, four stick legs, and a plank back inserted into a slot in the seat. (BOYCE)
UF chairs, board
chairs, plank
plank chairs
CN V.TG.AFU.AFU.ALO.AFU.AFU.AFU.CFS

board chests
TG.448
ALT board chest
SN Simple chests constructed of six boards butted, lapped, nailed, and hinged together; an economical alternative to joined chests. (FAIRB)
UF boarded chests
chests, board
chests, six-board
six-board chests
CN V.TG.AFU.AFU.AXC.ALO.AXC.ARI

board hammers
USE **drop hammers**

board insulation
USE **rigid insulation**

board knives
USE **utility knives**

board nails, gypsum
USE **gypsum board nails**

board saws
USE **pit saws**

board, academy
USE **academy board**

board, bristol
USE **bristol board**

board, building
USE **building board**

board, canvas
USE **canvas board**

board, coquille
USE **coquille board**

board, fiber
USE **fiberboard**

board, fiber building
USE **fiberboard**

board, flake
USE **particle board**

board, form
USE **form lumber**

board, gypsum
USE **gypsum board**

board, illustration
USE **illustration board**

board, ivory
USE **ivory board**

board, jute
USE **jute board**

board, mat
USE **mat board**

board, museum
USE **museum board**

board, paper
USE **cardboard**

board, particle
USE **particle board**

board, rag
USE **museum board**

board, Ross (TM)
USE **Ross board (TM)**

board, wood-pulp
USE **pulpboard**

boarded chests
USE **board chests**

boarding homes
USE **rest homes**

boarding houses
USE **lodging houses**

boarding schools
RK.795 (L,B)
ALT **boarding school**
SN Educational institutions at the elementary-secondary level in which students are in residence while enrolled in an instructional program. (ERIC)
UF residential schools
schools, boarding
schools, residential
CN V.RK.AFU.ALO.ALO.CXA.ARI.AFU.AFU

boardrooms
RM.62 (B)
ALT **boardroom**
SN Rooms that are designated for meetings of a board and usually contain a large conference table. (W)
CN V.RM.AFU.DIO.ALO.AFU.ALO.AFU

boards of directors
HG.834 (L)
ALT **board of directors**
UF corporations, directors of
directors of corporations
directors, boards of
CN H.HG.ALO.BIQ.ALO

boards of health
USE **health boards**

boards of trade
HG.835 (L,B)
ALT **board of trade**
SN Organizations that regulate, promote, supervise, or protect commercial or business enterprises. (W)
UF chambers of commerce
commerce, chambers of
trade, boards of
CN H.HG.ALO.BIQ.ARI

boards of trustees
HG.836
ALT **board of trustees**
UF boards, governing
governing boards
trustees, boards of
CN H.HG.ALO.BIQ.AXC

boards of zoning adjustment
USE **zoning boards**

boards (organizations)
HG.832
ALT **board (organization)**
SN Groups of persons appointed to or elected to sit in council for the management or investigation of a public or private business, trust, or other organization or institution. (W)
UF commissions (boards)
CN H.HG.ALO.BIQ

boards (stage floors)
USE **stage floors**

boards (tables)
USE **tables**

boards, back
USE **backboards**

boards, bagatelle
USE **bagatelle tables**

boards, candle
USE **candle slides**

boards, comb
USE **saddle boards**

boards, corner
USE **corner boards**

boards, counter
USE **counters**

boards, eaves
USE **eaves boards**

boards, end
USE **end boards**

boards, fascia
USE **eaves fascias**

boards, fat
USE **hawks**

boards, governing
USE **boards of trustees**

boards, health
USE **health boards**

boards, hunting
USE **huntboards**

boards, ironing
USE **ironing boards**

boards, ledger
USE **ledger boards**

boards, lever
USE **louver boards**

boards, louver
USE **louver boards**

boards, luffer
USE **louver boards**

boards, matched
USE **matched lumber**

boards, miter
USE **miter boards**

boards, park
USE **park commissions**

boards, public health
USE **health boards**

boards, ribbon
USE **ledger boards**

boards, saddle
USE **saddle boards**

boards, serving
USE **sideboards**

boards, skirting
USE **baseboards**

boards, snow
USE **snow guards**

boards, sounding
USE **sounding boards**

boards, spot
USE **hawks**

boards, table
USE **tables**

boards, window
USE **window sills**

boards, writing
USE **writing arms**

boards, zoning
USE **zoning boards**

boasters
TB.578
ALT **boaster**
SN Flat steel mason's chisels used in dressing stone. (MEANS)
CN V.TB.AFU.BCW.BCW.ALO.BZY.ALO

boat beds
USE **sleigh beds**

boat clubs
RK.1031 (B)
ALT **boat club**
UF clubs, boat
CN V.RK.AFU.ALO.ALO.EWY.AXC.ALO.ARI

boat davits
USE **davits**

boat foundations
USE **raft foundations**

boat lumber
MT.1439
SN A term commonly applied to wide boards (12 inches to 16 inches in width) of lightweight clear wood, such as cedar, redwood, or white pine. (PUTNAM)
UF lumber, boat
CN M.MT.AFU.AFU.ALO.BIQ.DCU.ALO.BOK.ARI.AFU.AFU

boat ramps
USE **launching ramps**

boat spikes
TF.487
ALT **boat spike**
SN Long, square spikes used in heavy timber construction. (PUTNAM)
UF barge spikes
spikes, barge
spikes, boat
CN V.TF.AFU.AFU.AFU.ALO.AFU.DUC.AFU

boatbuilder's axes
USE **shipwright's axes**

boathouses
RK.1268 (A,L)
ALT **boathouse**
SN A building usually built partly in the water for the housing or storing of boats. (W)
CN V.RK.AFU.ALO.ALO.GLI.AFU.BIQ.AFU

boatyards
USE **shipyards**

bob punches
USE **countersinks**

bobbin lace
MT.1871 (L)
SN Handmade lace made by intertwisting threads wound on bobbins and worked over a pillow on which the pattern is marked out by pins. (W)
UF bone lace
lace, bobbin
lace, bone
lace, pillow
pillow lace
CN M.MT.AFU.AFU.ARI.ALO.ALO.ALO.ALO.CXA.AFU

Bobo
FL.380 (L)
CN F.FL.ALO.AFU.AXC.AFU.AXC.ARI.ARI.AFU

Bobo-Fing
FL.381 (L)
UF Black Bobo
Bobo, Black
CN F.FL.ALO.AFU.AXC.AFU.AXC.ARI.ARI.AFU.AFU

Bobo-Ule
USE **Bwa**

Bobo, Black
USE **Bobo-Fing**

bobruns
USE **bobsled runs**

bobsled runs
RK.1078 (B)
ALT **bobsled run**
UF bobruns
runs, bobsled
CN V.RK.AFU.ALO.ALO.EWY.BIQ.ALO

bodied oil
MT.2007
SN A drying oil whose drying properties have been increased.
UF oil, bodied
CN M.MT.AFU.AFU.ARI.ARI.AXC.AFU.AFU

bodies of water
RD.125
ALT **body of water**
UF water, bodies of
CN V.RD.ARI.AFU.AFU.AFU

body color
MT.2524
SN Pigments that possess body or opacity. (PDAT)
UF color, body
CN M.MT.AFU.ARI.CRG.ALO.BCW.AFU.ALO.AXC.AFU

body plans
VD.30
ALT **body plan**
SN Drawings that are end elevations of ships, indicating curvature at certain points along the ship's length. When appearing with a half-breadth plan and a sheer plan, use **lines drawings** for the set.
UF plans, body
CN V.VD.AFU.AFU.BIQ.ALO.ALO.BIQ.AFU

body rub parlors
USE **massage parlors**

body shops
RK.612
ALT **body shop**
SN Factories or machine shops in which bodies of vehicles are manufactured or repaired. (RHDEL2)
UF autobody shops
shops, autobody
shops, body
CN V.RK.AFU.ALO.ALO.CLM.ALO.AFU.BCW.AFU

Boeotian
FL.2618
CN F.FL.ALO.AXC.ALO.AFU.ALO.AXC.ALO.AXC.ALO

bog iron ore
USE **limonite**

bog spruce
MT.1399
UF Picea mariana
spruce, bog
CN M.MT.AFU.AFU.ALO.BIQ.DCU.AFU.AFU.ALO.DOI.ARI

bogs
RD.170 (L)
ALT **bog**
SN Designates waterlogged spongy ground with a characteristic plantlife, such as sphagnum mosses, and in which vegetation is decaying, ultimately producing highly acidic peat. Distinct from **fens**, in which the water remains alkaline.
CN V.RD.ARI.AFU.ARI.ARI

bogs, peat
USE **peat bogs**

Bohemian earth
MT.1638
UF earth, Bohemian
CN M.MT.AFU.AFU.ARI.AFU.AFU.ALO.ALO.AXC.AFU.ALO.AFU

Bohemianism
BM.346 (L,R)
CN B.BM.ALO.ALO.CLM.BIQ

boiled linseed oil
USE **boiled oil**

boiled oil
MT.2012
UF boiled linseed oil
linseed oil, boiled
oil, boiled
oil, boiled linseed
CN M.MT.AFU.AFU.ARI.ARI.AXC.AFU.BCW.AFU

boiler houses
RK.607 (B)
ALT **boiler house**
UF houses, boiler
CN V.RK.AFU.ALO.ALO.CLM.ALO.AFU.AFU

boiler rooms
RM.219
ALT **boiler room**
SN Spaces provided for the boilers used for heating, ventilation, or power generation. (RS)
UF rooms, boiler
CN V.RM.AFU.DIO.ALO.DIO.BIQ.AFU

boilermakers
HG.512 (L)
ALT **boilermaker**
CN H.HG.AFU.AXC.BUE.ARI.CFS.ARI.ARI

boilers
RT.1411 (L,B)
ALT **boiler**
SN Heating appliances intended to supply hot water or steam for space heating or to supply power. (STEIN)
CN V.RT.ALO.BCW.AFU.ALO.AFU.ALO

boilers, hot water
USE **hot water boilers**

boilers, steam
USE **steam boilers**

boiling point
BM.983 (L)
CN B.BM.CFS.AXC.BZY.CFS.AFU

bois d'arc
USE **Osage orange**

boiserie
MT.2260 (R)
SN Wood paneling on interior walls, usually floor to ceiling; as a rule enriched by carving, gilding, painting, or sometimes inlaying. (DAC)
CN M.MT.AFU.ALO.ELK.AFU

Bokhara School
USE **Bukhara School**

Boki
FL.237
CN F.FL.ALO.AFU.AXC.AFU.ALO.AFU.ARI

Bol'shaia Rechka
FL.2127
CN F.FL.ALO.ARI.ARI.AFU.BIQ.AFU

bole, Armenian
USE **red bole**

bole, red
USE **red bole**

bole, white
USE **kaolinite**

bolection moldings
RT.796
ALT **bolection molding**
SN Moldings or groups of moldings separating two planes (as a stile from a panel) and projecting beyond the surface of both. (W)
UF balection moldings
belection moldings
bellexion moldings
bilection moldings
moldings, balection
moldings, belection
moldings, bellexion
moldings, bolection
moldings, raised
moldings, risen
raised moldings
risen moldings
CN V.RT.AFU.ALO.AFU.BOK.AFU.ALO.ALO

Bolia
FL.527 (L)
UF Lia
CN F.FL.ALO.AFU.AXC.ALO.ALO.BIQ.ALO.ALO

Bolidist
FL.3706
ALT **Bolidism**
CN F.FL.ALO.BUE.ALO.AFU

Bolivian
FL.718 (L,B)
CN F.FL.ALO.ALO.AFU.AXC.ALO

bollards
RM.431 (A,N,B)
ALT **bollard**
SN Use for low stone piers that hold the line of a moored boat or prevent passage by automobiles.
CN V.RM.ALO.AFU.ALO

Bologna stone
USE **blanc fixe**

bolsters
RT.135
ALT **bolster**
SN Use for the rolls, faced at either end with volutes, forming the sides of an Ionic capital.
UF balusters (capital components)
CN V.RT.AFU.AFU.AFU.AXC.BIQ.ALO.ARI.ALO.ARI

bolsters (blocking chisels)
USE **blocking chisels**

bolt anchors, lewis
USE **lewis bolt anchors**

bolt clippers
TB.723 (N)
SN Heavy hand shears used for cutting bolts in two. (SMITH)
UF clippers, bolt
CN V.TB.AFU.BCW.BIQ.ARI.ALO.BIQ.ALO

bolt clippers (bolt cutters)
USE **bolt cutters**

bolt covers, bed
USE **bed bolt covers**

bolt cutters
TB.730 (N)
ALT **bolt cutter**
SN Tools which take a variety of forms; used for cutting threads in metal pegs to make bolts.
UF bolt clippers (bolt cutters)
clippers, bolt (bolt cutters)
cutters, bolt
CN V.TB.AFU.BCW.BIQ.ARI.ALO.BUE.AFU

bolt tongs
TB.750 (N)
UF tongs, bolt
CN V.TB.AFU.BCW.BIQ.AXC.ALO.AXC.AFU

bolted joints
TF.577
ALT **bolted joint**
UF joints, bolted
CN V.TF.ALO.AFU.BCW

boltels
USE **roll moldings**

bolting
KT.50
ALT **bolted**
CN K.KT.AFU.ALO.BCW.BCW.AFU

bolts (latch and lock components)
TF.548
ALT **bolt (latch and lock component)**
SN The protruding parts of a lock that prevent a door from opening. (STEIN)
CN V.TF.AFU.ALO.AXC.AFU

bolts
TF.306 (L,N)
ALT **bolt**
SN Small metal rods used as fasteners having a head and often helical

threading and being usually secured by a nut or by riveting. (W)
CN V.TF.AFU.AFU.AFU.ALO.AFU.ALO

bolts, anchor
USE **anchor bolts**

bolts, antifriction latch
USE **antifriction latch bolts**

bolts, assembling
USE **assembling bolts**

bolts, auxiliary latch
USE **auxiliary dead latches**

bolts, barrel
USE **barrel bolts**

bolts, bed
USE **bed bolts**

bolts, bookcase
USE **bookcase bolts**

bolts, bottom
USE **bottom bolts**

bolts, box
USE **box bolts**

bolts, button-headed
USE **carriage bolts**

bolts, Canada
USE **box bolts**

bolts, cane
USE **cane bolts**

bolts, carriage
USE **carriage bolts**

bolts, chain
USE **chain bolts**

bolts, cremorne
USE **cremorne bolts**

bolts, dead
USE **dead bolts**

bolts, door
USE **door bolts**

bolts, double-door
USE **double-door bolts**

bolts, double throw
USE **double throw bolts**

bolts, Dutch-door
USE **Dutch-door bolts**

bolts, espagnolette
USE **espagnolette bolts**

bolts, expansion
USE **expansion bolts**

bolts, extension
USE **extension flush bolts**

bolts, extension flush
USE **extension flush bolts**

bolts, eye
USE **eye bolts**

bolts, fire exit
USE **panic bolts**

bolts, flush
USE **flush bolts**

bolts, foot
USE **foot bolts**

bolts, foundation
USE **anchor bolts**

bolts, gutter
USE **gutter bolts**

bolts, handrail
USE **handrail bolts**

bolts, hanger
USE **hanger bolts**

bolts, hinged latch
USE **swinging latch bolts**

bolts, hold-down
USE **anchor bolts**

bolts, joint
USE **handrail bolts**

bolts, knob
USE **knob latches**

bolts, lag
USE **lag bolts**

bolts, latch
USE **latch bolts**

bolts, lewis
USE **lewis bolt anchors**

bolts, live
USE **latch bolts**

bolts, machine
USE **machine bolts**

bolts, mortise
USE **mortise bolts**

bolts, necked
USE **necked bolts**

bolts, night
USE **night latches**

bolts, panic
USE **panic bolts**

bolts, panic (locks)
USE **panicproof locks**

bolts, rail
USE **handrail bolts**

bolts, self-latching
USE **self-latching bolts**

bolts, split dead
USE **split dead bolts**

bolts, square
USE **square bolts**

bolts, star expansion
USE **star expansion bolts**

bolts, stove
USE **stove bolts**

bolts, swinging latch
USE **swinging latch bolts**

bolts, thumb
USE **thumb bolts**

bolts, tie
USE **tie rods**

bolts, toggle
USE **toggle bolts**

bolts, tower
USE **tower bolts**

bolts, trigger
USE **auxiliary dead latches**

bolts, window spring
USE **window spring bolts**

Boma
FL.461 (L)
UF Baboma
CN F.FL.ALO.AFU.AXC.ALO.ALO.ARI.AFU

bomb shelters
USE **air raid shelters**

Bombay mastic
USE **mastic**

bombé
DC.102
SN Having rounded, outward bulging, or swelling sides and front, used with reference to furniture. (FAIRB)
UF kettle (bombé)
CN D.DC.AFU.ARI.EWY.ALO

bombing and gunnery ranges
USE **firing ranges**

bombproof building
USE **bombproof construction**

bombproof construction
KT.43 (A,L)
UF bombproof building
building, bombproof
construction, bombproof
CN K.KT.AFU.ALO.BCW.ARI.ALO.AFU

bomoi
RK.1085
ALT **bomos**
SN Ancient Greek altars to supreme gods. (OCD)
CN V.RK.AFU.ALO.ALO.FCS.AFU.ALO

bond breakers
MT.2628
SN A material, such as form oil, used to prevent adhesion of newly placed concrete to the forms, wall, or other support. (PUTNAM)

UF breakers, bond
CN M.MT.AFU.ARI.GLI.AFU

bond courses
RT.614
ALT **bond course**
SN Courses of bondstones that affix the facing masonry to the backing masonry. (DAC)
UF courses, bond
lockbands
CN V.RT.AFU.AFU.AFU.BIQ.BUE.ALO.AFU.ALO.ALO

bond paper
MT.1960
UF paper, bond
CN M.MT.AFU.AFU.ARI.ALO.ALO.AXC.ARI.CLM.AFU

bond, American
USE **common bond**

bond, block
USE **stack bond**

bond, common
USE **common bond**

bond, English
USE **English bond**

bond, Flemish
USE **Flemish bond**

bond, running
USE **running bond**

bond, stack
USE **stack bond**

bond, stretcher
USE **running bond**

bonded warehouses
RK.1229 (L)
ALT **bonded warehouse**
UF warehouses, bonded
CN V.RK.AFU.ALO.ALO.GFO.BZY.AFU

Bondei
FL.595 (L)
CN F.FL.ALO.AFU.AXC.AXC.ALO.AFU

bonders
USE **bondstones**

bonding agents
USE **adhesives**

bonding (financial)
KG.51 (L)
CN K.KG.AFU.AFU.ARI.BCW

bonding (joining)
KT.25 (L,B)
ALT **bonded**
SN Includes the process of binding or tying, usually by lapping one unit over another, as various masonry units, and holding or adhering together firmly by means of a binder or bond, as the fibers in paper. (W)
CN K.KT.AFU.ALO.BCW.ALO

bonding materials
USE **adhesives**

bonds (financial records)
VW.828 (L,N)
ALT **bond (financial record)**
SN Documents indicating debt, usually for the purpose of borrowing money, bearing interest, issued by a corporation, a government, or other agency. (GAHLM)
CN V.VW.AFU.ARI.AFU.BIQ.CFS.ALO

bonds (legal records)
VW.903 (L,N)
ALT **bond (legal record)**
SN Written evidence of an indebtedness, under seal, containing a promise to pay a specified sum of money at a fixed time in the future; or a promise to indemnity for a loss suffered under certain conditions. (GAHLM)
CN V.VW.AFU.ARI.AFU.BOK.BOK.AXC

bonds (masonry)
MT.2748 (B)
ALT **bond (masonry)**
SN The arrangements of, or patterns formed by, the exposed faces of laid masonry units. (MEANS)
CN M.MT.AFU.AXC.BIQ.AFU.AFU

bonds, angle
USE **angle bonds**

bonds, bail
USE **bail bonds**

bonds, bid
USE **bid bonds**

bonds, labor and material
USE **labor and material bonds**

bonds, payment
USE **payment bonds**

bonds, performance
USE **performance bonds**

bonds, proposal
USE **bid bonds**

bonds, subcontractor
USE **subcontractor bonds**

bonds, surety
USE **surety bonds**

bondstones
MT.2758
ALT **bondstone**
SN In stone masonry, stones usually set with their longest dimension perpendicular to the wall.
UF bonders
CN M.MT.AFU.AXC.BIQ.ALO.AFU

bone
MT.915 (A,L)
CN M.MT.AFU.AFU.ALO.AFU.AXC

bone ash
USE **bone white**

bone black
MT.1567 (L)
UF Beinschwarz
black, bone
black, drop
black, Frankfort
drop black
Frankfort black
noire d'os
CN M.MT.AFU.AFU.ARI.AFU.AFU.ALO.ALO.AFU.AFU.AFU.AFU

bone brown
MT.1618
UF brown, bone
CN M.MT.AFU.AFU.ARI.AFU.AFU.ALO.ALO.ARI.ALO.ARI

bone glue
MT.2346
UF glue, bone
CN M.MT.AFU.ARI.ARI.AFU.ALO.ALO.AFU.ALO

bone houses
USE **ossuaries**

bone lace
USE **bobbin lace**

bone white
MT.1749
UF ash, bone
bone ash
white, bone
CN M.MT.AFU.AFU.ARI.AFU.AFU.ALO.ALO.BOK.ALO.BOK

bonfire firing
KT.863
UF firing, bonfire
CN K.KT.AFU.ALO.HOE.BOK.ARI.AFU

Bongo
FL.619 (L)
CN F.FL.ALO.AFU.AXC.AXC.ARI.BCW

bonheurs-du-jour
TG.576
ALT **bonheur-du-jour**
SN Women's small writing tables with a gradin (cabinet) at the back; often elaborately decorated and occasionally fitted for toilet purposes as well as writing. (PC)
UF tables à gradin
CN V.TG.AFU.AFU.AXC.ALO.BZY.FUA.BUE.AFU

bonnet hip tile
MT.186
SN A tile that resembles a bonnet; used to cover the hip on a hip roof. (HAS)
UF cone hip tile
cone tile
hip tile, bonnet

hip tile, cone
tile, bonnet hip
tile, cone
tile, cone hip
CN M.MT.AFU.AFU.AFU.AXC.ALO.ALO.ALO.AFU.ALO.AXC.AFU.ARI.ARI.AFU

bonnet tops
TG.940
ALT **bonnet top**
SN Triangular closed backs forming the hood or top to a tall piece of case furniture. (FAIRB)
UF bonnet tops, closed
closed bonnet tops
hooded tops
tops, bonnet
tops, closed bonnet
tops, hooded
CN V.TG.ALO.EWY.AFU

bonnet tops, closed
USE **bonnet tops**

bonnetières
TG.420
ALT **bonnetière**
SN Tall, narrow, and deep cabinets to accommodate the elaborate bonnets peculiar to Normandy and Brittany in the 18th century. (ARONS)
UF armoires bonnetières
chapelières
coiffières (bonnetières)
CN V.TG.AFU.AFU.AXC.ALO.ARI.ALO.AFU

bonnets (chimney caps)
USE **chimney caps**

book cabinets
USE **bookcases**

book catalogs
VW.94 (L)
ALT **book catalog**
SN Catalogs containing the surrogate descriptions of books or other bibliographic material in a collection.
CN V.VW.AFU.AFU.AFU.FZU.ALO.AFU.AFU

book cupboards
TG.400
ALT **book cupboard**
SN Bookcases having solid, as opposed to glazed, doors.
UF cupboards, book
CN V.TG.AFU.AFU.AXC.ALO.ALO.ALO

book illustration
KT.204 (L,R)
UF illustration, book
CN K.KT.AFU.ALO.DUC.CLM.ALO

book illustrations
VB.43 (L,R)
ALT **book illustration**
UF illustrations, book
CN V.VB.AFU.ALO.AXC.AFU.AFU

book illustrators
HG.145
ALT **book illustrator**
UF illustrators, book
CN H.HG.AFU.AXC.AXC.AFU.AFU.ALO.BCW.AFU.ALO.ALO.AFU

book labels
USE **bookplates**

book lists
USE **bibliographies**

book paper
MT.1955
SN A paper suitable for printing books, magazines, and advertising matter including many grades of plain and coated papers but excluding newsprint. (W)
UF paper, book
CN M.MT.AFU.AFU.ARI.ALO.ALO.AXC.ARI.BUE.AFU

book presses (bookcases)
USE **bookcases**

book reviews
VW.308 (L)
ALT **book review**
SN Critical descriptions, evaluations, or analyses of a book, whether newly published or not.
UF reviews, book
CN V.VW.AFU.AFU.ALO.BCW.ARI.AFU

book shelves
USE **bookshelves**

book stands
USE **bookstands**

book tea chests
USE **tea chests**

book tile
MT.161
SN Flat, cellular roofing tile having two parallel edges, one of which is convex and the other concave, so that a number may be fit together edge-to-edge between rafters, joists, or the like. (RHDEL2)
UF tile, book
CN M.MT.AFU.AFU.AFU.AXC.ALO.ALO.ALO.AFU.AFU.AFU

bookbinders
HG.451 (L,R)
ALT **bookbinder**
UF binders (bookbinders)
bookmakers
CN H.HG.AFU.AXC.BUE.ALO.CFS.AFU

bookbinding
KT.515 (L,B,R)
UF binding of books
books, binding of
CN K.KT.AFU.ALO.ELK.ARI

bookbinding marks
VW.728 (R)
ALT **bookbinding mark**
UF marks, bookbinding
CN V.VW.AFU.ALO.ALO.AFU.AXC.ARI.ALO

bookcase and secretaries
USE **secretary-bookcases**

bookcase beds
TG.340
ALT **bookcase bed**
SN Deception beds which fold into a dummy bookcase. (GILBR2)
UF beds, bookcase
CN V.TG.AFU.AFU.ARI.AFU.AFU.BIQ.AFU.AFU

bookcase bolts
TF.322
ALT **bookcase bolt**
UF bolts, bookcase
CN V.TF.AFU.AFU.AFU.ALO.AFU.ALO.ALO.ALO

bookcases
TG.398 (A,L,N,B,R)
ALT **bookcase**
SN Cases for holding books generally having several shelves enclosed by doors; distinct from **bookshelves** which are open shelves for holding books.
UF book cabinets
book presses (bookcases)
cabinets, book
presses, book (bookcases)
CN V.TG.AFU.AFU.AXC.ALO.ALO

bookcases, circular
USE **revolving bookcases**

bookcases, counting-house
USE **counting-house bookcases**

bookcases, desks and
USE **desks and bookcases**

bookcases, dwarf
USE **dwarf bookcases**

bookcases, library
USE **library bookcases**

bookcases, movable
USE **moving libraries**

bookcases, portable library
USE **moving libraries**

bookcases, revolving
USE **revolving bookcases**

bookcases, rotary
USE **revolving bookcases**

bookcases, secretary
USE **desks and bookcases**

bookcases, secretary and
USE **secretary-bookcases**

bookcases, sectional
USE **sectional bookcases**

bookcases, sister's cylinder
USE **cylinder desks and bookcases**

bookcases, tiered
USE **revolving bookcases**

bookkeepers
HG.396 (L)
ALT **bookkeeper**
SN Those who keep accounts but are not formally trained in accounting.
CN H.HG.AFU.AXC.BOK.AFU.AXC

bookkeeping records
VW.839 (L)
ALT **bookkeeping record**
UF records, bookkeeping
CN V.VW.AFU.ARI.AFU.BIQ.CXA.AFU

bookkeeping registers
VW.844
ALT **bookkeeping register**
UF registers, bookkeeping
CN V.VW.AFU.ARI.AFU.BIQ.CXA.AFU.BCW

booklets
USE **pamphlets**

bookmakers
USE **bookbinders**

bookplates
VW.760 (L,N,R)
ALT **bookplate**
SN Labels pasted in books to mark their ownership, and sometimes to indicate their location in a library. (LG)
UF book labels
ex libris
labels, book
CN V.VW.AFU.ALO.ALO.ALO.AFU

books
VW.482 (L,N,R)
ALT **book**
SN Collections of wood or ivory tablets, or sheets of paper, parchment, or similar material, that are blank, written on, or printed, and are strung or bound together; commonly many folded and bound sheets containing continuous printing or writing; especially, when printed, a bound volume, or a volume of some size.
CN V.VW.AFU.ALO.AFU.AFU

books of hours
VW.539 (L,R)
ALT **book of hours**
SN Books containing the prescribed order of prayers, readings from the Scripture, and rites for the canonical hours. (RHDEL2)
UF hours, books of
CN V.VW.AFU.ALO.AFU.AFU.ALO.BUE.ALO

books, account
USE **account books**

books, address
USE **address books**

books, appointment
USE **appointment books**

books, autograph
USE **autograph albums**

books, baby
USE **baby books**

books, binding of
USE **bookbinding**

books, bridal
USE **bridal books**

books, carol
USE **carol books**

books, christening
USE **christening books**

books, coloring
USE **coloring books**

books, commonplace
USE **commonplace books**

books, date
USE **appointment books**

books, deed
USE **deed books**

books, design
USE **design books**

books, drawing
USE **drawing books**

books, emblem
USE **emblem books**

books, field
USE **field notes**

books, grade
USE **grade books**

books, guest
USE **guest registers**

books, household account
USE **housebooks**

books, letter
USE **letter books**

books, mass
USE **missals**

books, minute
USE **minute books**

books, model
USE **pattern books**

books, painting
USE **painting books**

books, pattern
USE **pattern books**

books, penmanship
USE **copybooks**

books, phone
USE **telephone directories**

books, picture
USE **picture books**

books, plan
USE **pattern books**

books, plat
USE **plat books**

books, prayer
USE **prayer books**

books, price
USE **price books**

books, prompt
USE **prompt books**

books, psalm
USE **psalters**

books, receipt
USE **cookbooks**

books, recipe
USE **cookbooks**

books, religious
USE **religious books**

books, sample
USE **sample books**

books, service
USE **choirbooks**

books, song
USE **song books**

books, specimen
USE **sample books**

books, tax warrant
USE **warrant books**

books, telephone
USE **telephone directories**

books, time
USE **time books**

books, visitors'
USE **visitors' books**

books, warrant
USE **warrant books**

booksellers
HG.427 (A,L)
ALT **bookseller**
CN H.HG.AFU.AXC.BOK.FCS.AFU

booksellers' catalogs
VW.112 (L)
ALT **bookseller's catalog**
UF catalogs, booksellers'
CN V.VW.AFU.AFU.AFU.FZU.ALO.ALO.ARI.ALO.AFU

bookshelves
TG.395 (B)
ALT **bookshelf**
SN Open shelves for holding books; distinct from **bookcases** which generally have several shelves enclosed by doors.
UF book shelves
shelves, book
shelves, standing (bookshelves)
standing shelves (bookshelves)
CN V.TG.AFU.AFU.AXC.AFU

bookshops
USE **bookstores**

bookstalls
RK.145 (B)
ALT **bookstall**
CN V.RK.AFU.ALO.ALO.ALO.ARI.BCW.AFU

bookstands
TG.628 (N,B)
ALT **bookstand**
UF book stands
dictionary stands
stands, book
stands, dictionary
CN V.TG.AFU.AFU.BIQ.BCW.ALO.AFU

bookstores
RK.152 (A,B)
ALT **bookstore**
UF bookshops
CN V.RK.AFU.ALO.ALO.ALO.ARI.BIQ.AFU.ARI

boomtowns
RD.48
ALT **boomtown**
SN Towns that have grown very rapidly as a result of sudden prosperity. (RHDEL2)
CN V.RD.AFU.AXC.ALO

boot camps
RG.137
ALT **boot camp**
UF camps, boot
CN V.RG.AFU.AFU.BZY.ARI.AFU

booths
RM.259
ALT **booth**
SN Use generally for small enclosures or stands, permanent or temporary, and freestanding or not, used for selling goods or to afford privacy to their occupants.
CN V.RM.AFU.DIO.ARI.ALO.AXC

booths, exhibition
USE **exhibition booths**

booths, phone
USE **telephone booths**

booths, telephone
USE **telephone booths**

bootjack feet
TG.900
ALT **bootjack foot**
UF feet, bootjack
CN V.TG.ALO.DZW.AFU.ARI

Borana
FL.620 (L)
CN F.FL.ALO.AFU.AXC.AXC.ARI.BIQ

borax
MT.495 (L)
SN A white or colorless crystalline mineral used in glass and ceramic enamel mixes, as a scouring and cleansing agent, as a flux in melting materials and in soldering, and as a source of Boron. (MH)
CN M.MT.AFU.AFU.AFU.CFS.AFU.BCW

bordellos
USE **brothels**

borders
DG.87 (L)
ALT **border**
CN D.DG.AFU.ALO.AFU

Boreal Archaic
FL.867
UF Archaic, Boreal
CN F.FL.ALO.ALO.ALO.AFU.ALO.ALO.AXC.ALO

boreal forests
USE **taigas**

bored locks
TF.196
ALT **bored lock**
SN Locks manufactured to fit into a circular hole in a door. (MEANS)
UF locks, bored
CN V.TF.AFU.AFU.AFU.AFU.DIO.BIQ.AFU.ALO

borers
HG.584
ALT **borer**
SN Workers who bore holes. (W)
CN H.HG.AFU.AXC.BZY.AFU.ARI

borers, cylindrical bung
USE **cylinder augers**

boring
USE **drilling**

boring machinery
TB.176 (L,N)
UF machinery, boring
CN V.TB.AFU.ARI.BIQ.AFU.AFU

Borjeño
FL.1285
CN F.FL.ALO.ALO.ARI.AFU.ALO.FZU.ARI.AFU

borjs
RK.300
ALT **borj**
SN Use for multistory, Islamic towerlike dwellings often seasonally occupied and located on the fringes of urban areas, especially in North Africa.
CN V.RK.AFU.ALO.ALO.AXC.ALO.AXC.AFU.ALO.AFU

Bornean
FL.2375 (L)
UF Kalimantan
CN F.FL.ALO.ARI.BCW.ARI.ALO.ALO

Borneo cedar
USE **Borneo mahogany**

Borneo mahogany
MT.1210
UF Borneo cedar
cedar, Borneo
mahogany, Borneo
seraya
CN M.MT.AFU.AFU.ALO.BIQ.DCU.AFU.AFU.AFU.HTY.ALO

Borneo rosewood
MT.1297
UF ringas
rosewood, Borneo
CN M.MT.AFU.AFU.ALO.BIQ.DCU.AFU.AFU.AFU.LCM.AFU

bornes
TG.308
ALT **borne**
SN French type of sofa, oval or round, with an upholstered pillar-like back in the center of the seat. Intended to stand in the center of the room. (PC)
UF canapés confidents à quatre places
canapés ronds
milieu de salon
CN V.TG.AFU.AFU.ALO.ALO.BZY.AFU

Bororo (African)
FL.392 (L)
CN F.FL.ALO.AFU.AXC.AFU.AXC.AXC.ALO.AFU

Bororo (South American)
FL.1673 (L)
CN F.FL.ALO.ALO.ARI.ARI.BIQ.AFU

borosilicate glass
MT.237
UF glass, borosilicate
CN M.MT.AFU.AFU.AFU.BIQ.AFU.AFU.AFU

boroughs
RG.245 (L)
ALT **borough**
SN Use for incorporated municipalities smaller than cities.
CN V.RG.ALO.AFU.AFU.ALO.ALO

borrow soil
MT.2053
SN Soil borrowed from another location to be used in construction. (PUTNAM)
UF soil, borrow
CN M.MT.AFU.AFU.ARI.BOK.AFU.AFU

borstals
USE **reformatories**

boskets
RK.1397
ALT **bosket**
SN Use for garden areas composed of ornamental groupings of trees pierced by walkways.
UF bosquets
CN V.RK.ALO.AFU.AFU.AFU.AFU

bosquets
USE **boskets**

Boss Style
FL.2516
CN F.FL.ALO.AXC.AFU.BIQ.ALO.AFU

bostan
USE **bustanim**

Boston chairs
TG.42
ALT **Boston chair**
SN High-back chairs with broad central splats, generally having leather-upholstered backs and seats; popular in 18th-century America.
UF Boston leather chairs
chairs, Boston
chairs, crook'd-back leather
chairs, crooked-back
chairs, leather (Boston chairs)
chairs, leather-upholstered (Boston chairs)
crook'd-back leather chairs
crooked-back chairs
leather chairs (Boston chairs)
leather chairs, Boston
leather chairs, crook'd-back
leather-upholstered chairs (Boston chairs)
CN V.TG.AFU.AFU.ALO.AFU.AFU.AFU.CLM

Boston leather chairs
USE **Boston chairs**

Boston rockers
TG.226
ALT **Boston rocker**
SN 19th-century American rocking chairs derived from Windsor chairs and having wooden seats which curve upwards to meet the spindles of the noticeably high, curved back with a scrolled top rail; usually grained or painted with fine ornamental detail.
UF Boston rocking chairs
chairs, Boston rocking
rockers, Boston
rocking chairs, Boston
CN V.TG.AFU.AFU.ALO.AFU.AFU.AXC.ARI.AFU

Boston rocking chairs
USE **Boston rockers**

botanical gardens
RK.1418 (A,L,B,R)
ALT **botanical garden**
SN Primarily outdoor areas where a variety of plants are grown and displayed for scientific, educational, or artistic purposes.
UF gardens, botanical
CN V.RK.ALO.AFU.AFU.ALO.ALO

botanical illustration
KT.212 (L,R)
UF illustration, botanical
CN K.KT.AFU.ALO.DUC.CLM.BOK.AFU.ALO

botanical illustrations
VB.52 (L,R)
ALT **botanical illustration**
UF illustrations, botanical
CN V.VB.AFU.ALO.AXC.ALO.ARI.AFU.ALO

botanical museums
RK.416 (L)
ALT **botanical museum**
UF museums, botanical
CN V.RK.AFU.ALO.ALO.BCW.AXC.ARI.CFS.ARI

botanical societies
USE **garden clubs**
horticultural societies

botanists
HG.328 (L)
ALT **botanist**
CN H.HG.AFU.AXC.BIQ.AFU.AFU.ALO.AFU

botany
KD.203 (L,R)
CN K.KD.AFU.ARI.ARI.ARI

Botany Bay gum
USE **acaroid resin**

Botecudos
USE **Botocudo**

bothies
RK.237
ALT **bothy**
SN Denotes certain Scottish huts.
CN V.RK.AFU.ALO.ALO.AXC.ALO.AFU.BOK.AFU

Botocudo
FL.1674 (L)
UF Aimoré
Botecudos
CN F.FL.ALO.ALO.ARI.ARI.BIQ.ALO

bottegas
USE **studios**
workshops

Böttger ware
FL.3226 (L,R)
UF ware, Böttger
CN F.FL.ALO.BCW.ALO.ARI.BIQ.BIQ.AXC.AFU.AFU

bottle cases
TG.449
ALT **bottle case**
UF cases, bottle
cases, liquor
liquor cases
CN V.TG.AFU.AFU.AXC.ALO.AXC.AXC

bottle drawers
USE **celleret drawers**

bottle makers' marks
VW.745 (L)
ALT **bottle maker's mark**
UF marks, bottle makers'
CN V.VW.AFU.ALO.ALO.AFU.AXC.AXC.BCW

bottle tickets
USE **wine labels**

bottled gas
USE **liquefied petroleum gas**

bottling plants
RK.622 (A,B)
ALT **bottling plant**
UF plants, bottling
CN V.RK.AFU.ALO.ALO.CLM.ALO.ALO.AFU.AXC.AFU.AFU

bottom
DC.14
CN D.DC.AFU.ALO.ALO.AFU

bottom and flange bend hangers
TF.351
ALT **bottom and flange bend hanger**
UF bend hangers, bottom and flange
hangers, bottom and flange bend
CN V.TF.AFU.AFU.AFU.ALO.AFU.BOK.ARI.AFU.ALO

bottom bend hangers
TF.352
ALT **bottom bend hanger**
UF bend hangers, bottom
hangers, bottom bend
CN V.TF.AFU.AFU.AFU.ALO.AFU.BOK.ARI.AFU.ARI

bottom bolts
TF.164
ALT **bottom bolt**
SN Vertically mounted bolts on the bottom of a door which slide into a socket in the floor. (MEANS)
UF bolts, bottom
CN V.TF.AFU.AFU.AFU.AFU.DIO.ARI.AFU

bottom double seams
TF.651
ALT **bottom double seam**
UF double seams, bottom
seams, bottom double
CN V.TF.ALO.ARI.ARI.BUE.ALO

bottom plates
USE **sill plates**

bottom rails
RT.881
ALT **bottom rail**
UF rails, bottom
CN V.RT.AFU.ARI.AFU.AFU.AFU.ALO.ARI.ALO.ALO.AFU

bottom seams, insert
USE **insert bottom seams**

bottom seams, lap
USE **lap bottom seams**

bottom seams, single
USE **single bottom seams**

boudeusses
TG.309
ALT **boudeusse**
SN 19th-century sofas with a central backrest on either side of which people can sit. (DDA)
UF dos-à-dos
CN V.TG.AFU.AFU.ALO.ALO.BZY.ALO

boudoir card photographs
USE **boudoir prints**

boudoir card photoprints
USE **boudoir prints**

boudoir midget mount card photoprints
USE **boudoir midget mounts**

boudoir midget mounts
VJ.75
ALT **boudoir midget mount**
SN Commercial card photographs whose mounts measure about 3 3/8 by 2 inches; primarily used for portraits. (SAPSP)
UF boudoir midget mount card photoprints
card photoprints, boudoir midget mount
midget mounts, boudoir
mounts, boudoir midget
CN V.VJ.AFU.AFU.BCW.AFU.AFU.AFU

boudoir prints
VJ.74
ALT **boudoir print**
SN Commercial card photographs on cards measuring 8 1/2 by 5 1/2 or 8 1/4 by 5 inches; popular from the 1870s to the 1890s. (SAPSP)
UF boudoir card photographs
boudoir card photoprints
card photographs, boudoir
photographs, boudoir card
photoprints, boudoir card
prints, boudoir
CN V.VJ.AFU.AFU.BCW.AFU.AFU

boudoirs
RM.166
ALT **boudoir**
SN Use for rooms adjacent to a lady's bedroom, serving as private sitting rooms and dressing rooms.
CN V.RM.AFU.DIO.ALO.CXA.AFU.AFU

Bougainville
FL.3663 (L)
CN F.FL.ALO.BOK.ALO.BOK.AFU

bougard marble
MT.788
UF marble, bougard
CN M.MT.AFU.AFU.AFU.DCU.AFU.ARI.ARI.ARI.ALO.BIQ

Bougival white
USE **bismuth white**

boulder
MT.881 (L)
CN M.MT.AFU.AFU.AFU.DCU.ALO.AFU

bouleuteria
RK.982
ALT **bouleuterion**
SN Use for the council chambers of ancient Greek cities; the place where the Boule, a senate, met.
CN V.RK.AFU.ALO.ALO.ERE.AFU.BCW.AFU

boulevards
RK.1532 (L,B)
ALT **boulevard**
SN Wide city streets characterized by rows of trees or other plantings decoratively laid out along the sides or in a median strip.
CN V.RK.ALO.ALO.BIQ.ARI.AFU.ALO.AFU.ARI

boulle marquetry
USE **boulle work**

boulle work
KT.707 (L,R)
SN Marquetry comprised of brass and tortoise shell, applied to furniture especially in the late 17th and early 18th centuries.
UF boulle marquetry
buhl
buhl work
marquetry, boulle
CN K.KT.AFU.ALO.GRC.CLM.AFU

boultines
USE **roll moldings**

boundaries
BM.470 (L,B)
CN B.BM.BCW.CXA.ALO.AFU

boundary maps
USE **cadastral maps**

boundary stones
RM.432 (L)
ALT **boundary stone**
UF stones, boundary
CN V.RM.ALO.AFU.ARI

boundary walls
RM.443
ALT **boundary wall**
SN Use for walls enclosing an area or defining a boundary.
UF bounding walls
walls, boundary
CN V.RM.ALO.AFU.BOK.AFU

bounding walls
USE **boundary walls**

Bouneparte chairs
USE **Trafalgar chairs**

bouquet stands
USE **plant stands**

bourgeoisie
HG.885 (L,R)
SN One of the social classes whose income derives from the profits of commerical and industrial enterprise, especially as distinguished from the landed gentry, wage earners, farmers, and the professions. (W)
CN H.HG.ALO.DOI.ALO.AFU.AFU

bourses
USE **exchanges**

boutiques
RK.182 (A,B)
ALT **boutique**
SN Use for small, upscale specialty shops generally specializing in fashionable clothing or accessories or a special collection of other merchandise; may also be used for individual departments within larger stores if featuring a similar line of goods. (RHDEL2)
CN V.RK.AFU.ALO.ALO.ALO.ARI.BIQ.ALO.CLM.AFU

bovedas (pitched-brick vaults)
USE **pitched-brick vaults**

Bovidean Pastoral phase
FL.70
CN F.FL.ALO.AFU.AFU.ARI.ARI

bow-back Windsor chairs
TG.98
ALT **bow-back Windsor chair**
SN Windsor chairs having a back of medium height consisting of spindles contained within a bent bow that is anchored in the seat; may or may not have arms. (EVANS)
UF chairs, bow-back Windsor
chairs, dining Windsor
chairs, oval-back Windsor
dining Windsor chairs
oval-back Windsor chairs
Windsor chairs, bow-back
Windsor chairs, dining
Windsor chairs, oval-back
CN V.TG.AFU.AFU.ALO.AFU.AFU.AFU.MLC.ALO

bow drills
TB.182 (N)
ALT **bow drill**
SN Drills rotated by a cord or string

wrapped tightly around it and strung to a bow. (RHDEL2)
UF drills, bow
drills, fiddle
drills, thong
fiddle drills
thong drills
CN V.TB.AFU.ARI.BIQ.ALO.AFU.AFU.ALO

bow saws
TB.1005 (N)
ALT **bow saw**
SN Hand saws with a thin blade held in place between the two ends of a frame. (MEANS)
UF saws, bow
saws, sweep
saws, turning
sweep saws
turning saws
CN V.TB.AFU.BCW.CFS.ALO.AFU.EWY.BCW.AFU

bow windows
RT.910
ALT **bow window**
SN Bay windows that are curved in plan.
UF compass windows
curved windows
windows, bow
windows, compass
windows, curved
CN V.RT.AFU.ARI.AFU.AFU.BOK.AFU.AFU.ALO.AFU

bowed legs
USE **cabriole legs**

bowfront
DC.103
CN D.DC.AFU.ARI.EWY.ARI

bowl capitals
RT.121
ALT **bowl capital**
UF capitals, bowl
CN V.RT.AFU.AFU.AFU.AXC.BIQ.ALO.ARI.AFU.BCW

bowl gouges
TB.883
ALT **bowl gouge**
SN Short bowl-shaped gouges. (BLACKB)
UF gouges, bowl
CN V.TB.AFU.BCW.CFS.ALO.AFU.CXA.ALO

bowl stands
USE **basin stands**

bowling alleys
RK.1058 (A,L,B)
ALT **bowling alley**
UF alleys, bowling
bowling lanes
lanes, bowling
CN V.RK.AFU.ALO.ALO.EWY.AXC.BIQ.ALO.AFU

bowling greens
RK.1487 (L,B)
ALT **bowling green**
SN Designates closely mown, level pieces of ground reserved for the game of lawn bowling.
UF greens, bowling
CN V.RK.ALO.ALO.BCW.ALO

bowling lanes
USE **bowling alleys**

bowls, cricket
USE **cricket fields**

bows (tools)
TB.1118
ALT **bow (tool)**
SN Tools that consist of a bent elastic rod with ends connected by a string; used for various purposes, as for giving reciprocating motion to a drill. (W)
CN V.TB.ALO.BCW

bowstring arch-trusses
USE **bowstring trusses**

bowstring trusses
RT.359 (B)
ALT **bowstring truss**
SN Trusses having one curved member in the shape of a bow (often circular or parabolic in shape) and a straight or cambered member which ties together the two ends of the bow. (DAC)
UF arch-trusses, bowstring
Belfast trusses
bowstring arch-trusses
trusses, Belfast
trusses, bowstring
CN V.RT.AFU.AFU.AFU.BCW.CLM.AFU.AFU.AFU.AFU

bowtells
USE **roll moldings**

box beams
RT.293 (A,L,B)
ALT **box beam**
SN Use for hollow beams of rectangular section, whether metal or wood.
UF beams, box
box girders
girders, box
CN V.RT.AFU.AFU.AFU.BCW.ALO.AFU.ALO

box beds
TG.323
ALT **box bed**
SN Beds enclosed with paneling on all sides but one, where there was a curtain over the opening; usually stood against the wall and, in some cases, were built into the wall or incorporated into the scheme of paneling. (THORN2)
UF alcove beds
beds, alcove
beds, box
beds, cupboard
bedsteads, box
box bedsteads
close-beds
cupboard beds
lits alcoves (box beds)
lits carrosses(box beds)
lits chapelles
lits clos
lits en forme d'armoire
lits fermés
wall-beds
CN V.TG.AFU.AFU.ARI.AFU.AFU.AFU

box bedsteads
USE **box beds**

box bolts
TF.552
ALT **box bolt**
UF bolts, box
bolts, Canada
Canada bolts
CN V.TF.AFU.ALO.AXC.AFU.ARI

box cameras
TB.291 (N)
ALT **box camera**
SN Early type of camera consisting of a lightproof box, with lens, shutter, and viewfinder, and employing film rather than a plate. (HCOP)
UF cameras, box
CN V.TB.AFU.ARI.CLM.ARI.AFU.AFU.AFU.ALO

box chivs
USE **howell planes**

box elder
MT.1221
UF Acer negundo
ash-leafed maple
elder, box
maple, ash-leafed
CN M.MT.AFU.AFU.ALO.BIQ.DCU.AFU.AFU.AFU.IFM.AXC

box frames
RT.39 (B)
ALT **box frame**
SN Structural frames composed of cells which may be side by side or in vertical tiers; the cross-walls act as bearing walls, carrying the loads to the foundations. (DAC)
UF cellular frames
construction, cross-wall
cross-wall construction
frames, box
frames, cellular
CN V.RT.AFU.AFU.AFU.ALO.AXC.ALO

box girders
USE **box beams**

box hammer tongs
TB.756

SN Tongs to hold hammers being reforged. The prong fits into one eye of the hammer, while the bottom piece keeps the head from twisting sideways. (SMITH)
UF tongs, box hammer
CN V.TB.AFU.BCW.BIQ.AXC.ALO.AXC.BIQ.AFU

box-head windows
USE **jib-headed windows**

box locks
USE **rim locks**

box nails
TF.388
ALT **box nail**
SN Nails similar to common nails with the same penny designation of length but having a shank smaller in diameter. (MEANS)
UF nails, box
CN V.TF.AFU.AFU.AFU.ALO.AFU.CFS.AFU.AFU

box pews
RT.1237
ALT **box pew**
SN Church pews screened and enclosed by a high back and sides. (HAS)
UF pews, box
CN V.RT.AFU.BUE.ALO.ARI.BZY.AFU.AFU

box scrapers
TB.1036
ALT **box scraper**
SN Scraping tools whose blade is perpendicular to the handle and set at the end of two parallel arms.
UF scrapers, box
CN V.TB.AFU.BCW.CFS.ALO.AFU.FIM.AFU

box settles
TG.284
ALT **box settle**
SN Settles with a box seat with a hinged lid which allows access to a storage space beneath.
UF benches, monk's (box benches)
chest-benches
monk's benches (box settles)
settles, box
settles, storage
storage settles
CN V.TG.AFU.AFU.ALO.ALO.AFU.AFU.BIQ.AFU

box springs
TG.852
ALT **box spring**
UF springs, box
CN V.TG.ALO.BIQ.BOK

box stalls
RM.345
ALT **box stall**
SN In barns or stables, individual compartments in which an animal may move about freely. (DAC)
UF boxes, loose
loose boxes
stalls, box
CN V.RM.AFU.DIO.AXC.ARI.ARI.AFU

box stools
TG.234
ALT **box stool**
SN Stools with the seat board hinged to the seat-rail in the form of a small lidded chest. (CHINNE)
UF stools, box
CN V.TG.AFU.AFU.ALO.AFU.ALO.AFU.AFU

box stoops
RM.56
ALT **box stoop**
SN High stoops making a quarter turn, reached by a flight of stairs along a building front. (DAC)
UF stoops, box
CN V.RM.AFU.DIO.AFU.BCW.BOK.AFU

box stretcher desks-on-frames
USE **desks-on-frames**

box stretchers
TG.998
ALT **box stretcher**
UF stretchers, box
CN V.TG.ALO.HIK.ALO.ALO.ALO

box strikes
TF.516
ALT **box strike**
SN Strikes with enclosed recesses to receive lock bolts. (MEANS)
UF strikes, box
CN V.TF.AFU.ALO.AFU.ALO.AFU

box tongs
TB.751 (N)
UF tongs, box
CN V.TB.AFU.BCW.BIQ.AXC.ALO.AXC.ALO

box vises
TB.1075
ALT **box vise**
UF vises, box
CN V.TB.AFU.BCW.CFS.ALO.ALO.CXA.AFU

box, common
USE **boxwood**

box, European
USE **boxwood**

boxes (audience spaces)
RM.349
ALT **box (audience space)**
UF boxes, theater
theater boxes
CN V.RM.AFU.DIO.AXC.AXC.AFU.AFU

boxes (furniture components)
USE **birdcages (furniture components)**

boxes, call
USE **telephone booths**

boxes, cases of
USE **cabinets**

boxes, fire alarm
USE **manual stations**

boxes, flower
USE **window boxes**

boxes, loose
USE **box stalls**

boxes, miter
USE **miter boxes**

boxes, outlet
USE **power outlets**

boxes, screw
USE **screw boxes**

boxes, sentry
USE **sentry boxes**

boxes, signal
USE **signal towers**

boxes, theater
USE **boxes (audience spaces)**

boxes, window
USE **window boxes**

boxing planes
USE **rabbet planes**

boxing shutters
USE **folding shutters**

boxwood
MT.1125 (L)
UF Abasian boxwood
Asiatic boxwood
box, common
box, European
boxwood, Abasian
boxwood, Asiatic
boxwood, common
boxwood, European
boxwood, Indian
Buxus sempervirens
common box
common boxwood
European box
European boxwood
Indian boxwood
CN M.MT.AFU.AFU.ALO.BIQ.DCU.AFU.AFU.AFU.BOK

boxwood, Abasian
USE **boxwood**

boxwood, Asiatic
USE **boxwood**

boxwood, common
USE **boxwood**

boxwood, European
USE **boxwood**

boxwood, Indian
USE **boxwood**

boxwood, Maracaibo
USE **Maracaibo boxwood**

boxwood, West Indian
USE **Maracaibo boxwood**

Boyela
USE **Yela**

Boylston
FL.868
CN F.FL.ALO.ALO.ALO.AFU.ALO.ALO.AXC.ARI

Boyo
FL.509
CN F.FL.ALO.AFU.AXC.ALO.ALO.BIQ.AFU.AFU.ARI

Bozo
FL.375 (L)
CN F.FL.ALO.AFU.AXC.AFU.AXC.ARI.AFU.AFU

bozzetti
VB.12 (R)
ALT **bozzetto**
SN Use for fairly developed sketches, most often three-dimensional sketches for sculpture, but may be painted or drawn sketches. With regard to sketches for architecture, use **preliminary sketches.** For rougher sculptural sketches, use **maquettes.**
CN V.VB.AFU.AFU.BCW.AXC.AFU

braced frames
RT.43
ALT **braced frame**
SN Use for building frames that use diagonal bracing in which the timbers are heavy enough to be mortised.
UF frames, braced
CN V.RT.AFU.AFU.AFU.ALO.AXC.BCW.AFU

braced tables
USE **sawbuck tables**

bracelets (foot components)
TG.933
ALT **bracelet (foot component)**
SN Modern American term for a band separating the leg and foot of a table or stand.
CN V.TG.ALO.DZW.ALO.ALO

braces
RT.204 (N)
ALT **brace**
SN Use for rigid stays, usually of wood or metal, and commonly in compression.
UF struts
CN V.RT.AFU.AFU.AFU.AXC.DOI.AFU

braces (woodworking tools)
TB.847 (N)
ALT **brace (woodworking tool)**
SN Hand tools with a handle, crank, and chuck; used for turning a bit or auger to drill a hole by hand. (DAC)
UF bit braces
bit stocks
braces, bit
braces, hand
breast stocks
breast wimbles
hand braces
stocks
stocks, bit
stocks, breast
sways
sweeps
whimbles
wimbles, breast
CN V.TB.AFU.BCW.CFS.ALO.AFU.BIQ

braces, angle
USE **angle braces**

braces, angle (hand drills)
USE **hand drills**

braces, arch
USE **arch braces**

braces, bit
USE **braces (woodworking tools)**

braces, bracket
USE **bracket feet**

braces, drill
USE **hand drills**

braces, gearing
USE **hand drills**

braces, hand
USE **braces (woodworking tools)**

braces, knee
USE **knee braces**

braces, medial
USE **medial braces**

braces, ratchet
USE **ratchet braces**

braces, smith's
USE **smith's braces**

braces, spur
USE **spurs**

braces, sweep
USE **medial braces**

braces, wind
USE **wind braces**

bracket braces
USE **bracket feet**

bracket capitals
RT.122
ALT **bracket capital**
SN Use for capitals extended by brackets, lessening the span between posts; found in Near Eastern, Islamic, Indian, and Spanish architecture. (HAS)
UF capitals, bracket
CN V.RT.AFU.AFU.AFU.AXC.BIQ.ALO.ARI.AFU.BIQ

bracket feet
TG.901
ALT **bracket foot**
SN Feet shaped like a bracket, in common use on case furniture in the first half of the 18th century. (TOMLIN)
UF braces, bracket
bracket braces
brackets (feet)
Chinese feet
feet, bracket
feet, Chinese
feet, Goddard
Goddard feet
CN V.TG.ALO.DZW.AFU.AXC

bracket feet, common
USE **French feet**

bracket feet, flaring
USE **French feet**

bracket feet, ogee
USE **ogee bracket feet**

bracket saws
USE **fretsaws**

bracket scaffolding
TB.489
SN Scaffolding supported by metal brackets which are temporarily attached to a building or column. (DAC)
UF bracket staging
scaffolding, bracket
staging, bracket
CN V.TB.AFU.ARI.ERE.ARI.AFU

bracket staging
USE **bracket scaffolding**

bracket tables
USE **console tables**

bracket tables, console
USE **eagle console tables**

Bracketed mode
USE **Italian Villa Style**

brackets
RT.319 (L,N,B)
ALT **bracket**
SN Use for elements, usually of generally triangular shape, that project from a wall, pier, or other structure and which serve to support vertical loads or strengthen an angle by transferring the load against the face of the structure from which they project;

sometimes more decorative than functional.
CN V.RT.AFU.AFU.AFU.BCW.AXC

brackets (consoles)
USE **consoles**

brackets (feet)
USE **bracket feet**

brackets, angle
USE **angle brackets**

brackets, handrail
USE **handrail brackets**

brackets, knee
USE **knee brackets**

brackets, shelf
USE **shelf brackets**

brad nails
USE **brads**

brad nails, flooring
USE **flooring nails**

brad pushers
TB.1046
ALT **brad pusher**
SN Special tools used to grip and insert brads in an inaccessible location. (MEANS)
UF brad squeezers
pushers, brad
squeezers, brad
CN V.TB.AFU.BCW.CFS.ALO.ALO.ARI

brad squeezers
USE **brad pushers**

bradawls
TB.831 (N)
ALT **bradawl**
SN Tools resembling ice picks, used to make holes for brads and wood screws. (MEANS)
UF awls, flooring
bits, sprig
flooring awls
sprig bits
CN V.TB.AFU.BCW.CFS.ALO.AFU.ARI.AFU

brads
TF.402 (N)
ALT **brad**
SN Slender, smooth nails each having a small deep head used for finish carpentry work. (MEANS)
UF brad nails
nails, brad
CN V.TF.AFU.AFU.AFU.ALO.AFU.CFS.AFU.DCU.AFU

brads, flat-head wire
USE **flat-head wire brads**

Brah Pahdona
USE **Pra Patom**

Brahmanism
BM.661 (L)
ALT **Brahmanic**
CN B.BM.BZY.AFU.AXC.AFU

braid
USE **braiding**

braiding
KT.543 (L)
ALT **braided**
SN Technique in which three or more warps are crossed diagonally and lengthwise over and under one or more of the other warps. A strand alternately serves as warp and weft. (SCHNEI)
UF braid
plaiting
CN K.KT.AFU.ALO.ELK.DUC.AFU.AFU

braille maps
VW.140
ALT **braille map**
SN Maps for the blind utilizing symbols and the braille system of writing. (CM)
UF maps, braille
CN V.VW.AFU.AFU.AFU.FZU.AXC.AFU.ARI.AFU.AFU

branch banks
RK.128 (L)
ALT **branch bank**
UF banks, branch
CN V.RK.AFU.ALO.ALO.ALO.ALO.AFU.AFU

branch libraries
RK.696 (L,B)
ALT **branch library**
SN Libraries in a system other than the main or central library. (ERIC)
UF libraries, branch
CN V.RK.AFU.ALO.ALO.CRG.AXC.AFU.ARI.AFU

branch mahogany
USE **crotch mahogany**

branch sewers
RK.548
ALT **branch sewer**
SN Sewers that receive sewage from a relatively small area and are connected to main sewers or manholes. (MEANS)
UF sewers, branch
CN V.RK.AFU.ALO.ALO.CFS.ALO.AFU.ALO.ALO.AFU

Brancovan
FL.3205 (R)
CN F.FL.ALO.BCW.ALO.ARI.BIQ.BIQ.ALO.AFU.AFU

branding irons
USE **brands**

brands
TB.357 (L,N)
ALT **brand**
SN Iron rods which terminate in a flat surface on which is a device or letter set in relief; used after heating to mark livestock, tools, or manufactured goods with indelible evidence of ownership.
UF branding irons
brands, burn
brands, marking
burn brands
irons, branding
marking brands
CN V.TB.AFU.ARI.CXA.AFU

brands, burn
USE **brands**

brands, marking
USE **brands**

brank-ursine
USE **acanthus**

brasil
USE **logwood**

brass
MT.385 (A,L,B,R)
CN M.MT.AFU.AFU.AFU.BZY.AFU.AFU.AFU.ALO.ARI.BIQ.AFU

brass (color)
USE **dark yellow**
moderate yellow

Brass (Ijo)
FL.267
CN F.FL.ALO.AFU.AXC.AFU.ALO.AXC.AFU.AFU

brass rubbing
KT.740 (L,R)
SN Copying an incised or carved metal surface by rubbing paper with graphite or other drawing material. (MAYER)
UF rubbing, brass
CN K.KT.AFU.ALO.HCQ.ALO.AFU

brass-smithing
KT.779 (L)
UF brasswork (brass-smithing)
smithing, brass
CN K.KT.AFU.ALO.HOE.BCW.AFU.ALO

brass, cartridge
USE **cartridge brass**

brass, naval
USE **naval brass**

brass, red
USE **red brass**

brass, tin
USE **naval brass**

brass, yellow
USE **cartridge brass**

brasseries
RK.113 (A,B)
ALT **brasserie**
SN Use for unpretentious restaurants serving fresh, simply prepared foods, beers, and ales in an informal, casual atmosphere.
CN V.RK.AFU.ALO.ALO.ALO.AFU.AXC.ALO

brasses (furniture hardware)
USE **furniture hardware**

brasswork
MT.2766 (L)
CN M.MT.AFU.AXC.BOK.AFU

brasswork (brass-smithing)
USE **brass-smithing**

brattishing
RT.1051
SN Ornamental cresting on the top of a screen or cornice, usually formed of leaves, Tudor flowers, or miniature battlements; found especially in English Late Gothic architecture. (PDARC)
CN V.RT.AFU.BCW.ARI.AFU

braze welding
KT.799 (L)
SN Method of welding whereby a groove, fillet, plug, or seat weld is made using a nonferrous filler metal having a melting point below that of base metals. (STEIN)
UF welding, braze
CN K.KT.AFU.ALO.HOE.BCW.ALO.AFU.ALO.AFU

braziers
HG.492 (R)
ALT **brazier**
SN Persons who work in brass. (W)
CN H.HG.AFU.AXC.BUE.ARI.CFS.AFU.AFU

Brazilian
FL.719 (L,B)
CN F.FL.ALO.ALO.AFU.AXC.ARI

Brazilian rosewood
MT.1298
UF Dalbergia nigra
jacaranda
jacaranda wood
pao rosa
rosewood, Brazilian
wood, jacaranda
CN M.MT.AFU.AFU.ALO.BIQ.DCU.AFU.AFU.AFU.LCM.ALO

Brazilian Style
FL.271 (A)
CN F.FL.ALO.AFU.AXC.AFU.ALO.BCW.AFU.AFU

brazilwood
MT.1127
UF Caesalpinia brasiliensis
Caesalpinia echinata
ébano
CN F.FL.ALO.AFU.AXC.AFU.ALO.BCW.AFU.AFU

brazing
KT.790 (L)
ALT **brazed**
SN Type of soldering which employs nonferrous alloys that melt at lower temperatures than the metals being joined. (QUICK)
CN K.KT.AFU.ALO.HOE.BCW.ALO.AFU.AFU.AFU

brazing, arc
USE **arc brazing**

brazing, dip
USE **dip brazing**

brazing, furnace
USE **furnace brazing**

brazing, induction
USE **induction brazing**

brazing, resistance
USE **resistance brazing**

brazing, torch
USE **torch brazing**

brazing, vacuum
USE **vacuum brazing**

bread and cheese cupboards
USE **livery cupboards**

break joints
TF.578
ALT **break joint**
SN Arrangements of modular structural units, such as masonry or plywood sheathing, so that the vertical joints of adjacent units do not line up. (MEANS)
UF broken joints
joints, break
joints, broken
joints, shift
joints, staggered
shift joints
staggered joints
CN V.TF.ALO.AFU.BIQ

breaker balls
USE **wrecking balls**

breakers, ball
USE **wrecking balls**

breakers, bond
USE **bond breakers**

breakers, circuit
USE **circuit breakers**

breakers, sun
USE **brise-soleils**

breakfast nooks
RM.106 (A)
ALT **breakfast nook**
SN Alcoves where light meals are taken; usually containing a built-in table and seating.
UF nooks, breakfast
CN V.RM.AFU.DIO.ALO.BCW.ALO

breakfast rooms
RM.107
ALT **breakfast room**
SN Small rooms for the morning meal; usually, but not always, adjoining the chief dining room; in northern climates often specially arranged with an eastern exposure to catch the morning sun. (RS)
UF rooms, breakfast
CN V.RM.AFU.DIO.ALO.BCW.ARI

breakfast tables
TG.711 (N)
ALT **breakfast table**
SN Moderate-sized tables lacking the raised edge of a tea table or the scale of a dining table and having drop leaves and sometimes a small drawer or two in the apron. (DOWNS)
UF tables, breakfast
CN V.TG.AFU.AFU.BIQ.BOK.ALO.ARI

breakfront
DC.104
SN Having a slightly projecting central section, used with reference to case furniture. (THDAT)
UF broken front
CN D.DC.AFU.ARI.EWY.AXC

breaking
KT.110
ALT **broken**
CN K.KT.AFU.ALO.CLM.ALO

breaks, thermal
USE **thermal breaks**

breakwaters
RK.555 (A,L,R)
ALT **breakwater**
SN Use for structures, usually located offshore, built to protect an area from waves.
L moles
CN V.RK.AFU.ALO.ALO.CFS.ALO.ALO.AFU

breakwaters, blockwork
USE **blockwork breakwaters**

breakwaters, mound
USE **mound breakwaters**

breast augers
TB.822
ALT **breast auger**
SN Augers having a wood stock with a shell or nose bit; turned by a wood bar passing through a hole in the top of the stock. (SALAM)
UF augers, breast

CN V.TB.AFU.BCW.CFS.ALO.AFU.ALO.AFU

breast bibs
USE **breastplates (tools)**

breast drills
TB.183
ALT **breast drill**
SN Manual rotary drills which have an attachment for applying pressure with the chest; used by carpenters for drilling horizontal holes. (MEANS)
UF drills, breast
CN V.TB.AFU.ARI.BIQ.ALO.AFU.AFU.ARI

breast stocks
USE **braces (woodworking tools)**

breast wimbles
USE **braces (woodworking tools)**

breastplates (tools)
TB.850 (N)
ALT **breastplate (tool)**
SN Pieces of hardwood against which a workman presses his breast in operating a breast drill or similar tool. (W)
UF bibs, breast
breast bibs
CN V.TB.AFU.BCW.CFS.ALO.AFU.BOK

breasts, chimney
USE **chimney breasts**

breastworks
RT.1180
ALT **breastwork**
SN Hastily constructed defensive walls about breast high. (DAC)
CN V.RT.AFU.BUE.AFU.BCW.AFU.AFU

breccia
MT.734
CN M.MT.AFU.AFU.AFU.DCU.AFU.ALO.ALO.ARI.AFU

breccia a semesanto
MT.748
CN M.MT.AFU.AFU.AFU.DCU.AFU.ARI.ARI.ALO.AFU.AFU

breccia corallina
MT.749
CN M.MT.AFU.AFU.AFU.DCU.AFU.ARI.ARI.ALO.AFU.ALO

breccia di Settebasi
MT.750
CN M.MT.AFU.AFU.AFU.DCU.AFU.ARI.ARI.ALO.AFU.ARI

breccia marble
MT.747
UF marble, breccia
CN M.MT.AFU.AFU.AFU.DCU.AFU.ARI.ARI.ALO.AFU

breccia marble, Egyptian
USE **Egyptian breccia marble**

breccia traccagnina
MT.751
CN M.MT.AFU.AFU.AFU.DCU.AFU.ARI.ARI.ALO.AFU.AXC

breccia, Potomac
USE **Potomac breccia**

breche violette marble
MT.752
UF marble, breche violette
CN M.MT.AFU.AFU.AFU.DCU.AFU.ARI.ARI.ALO.AFU.BCW

breech, bear's
USE **acanthus**

breeders, horse
USE **horse breeders**

breeders, livestock
USE **livestock breeders**

breeze
MT.2302 (B)
SN Residue from the making of coke or charcoal. Refers also to a construction material made partly of breeze. (W)
UF breeze, pan
pan breeze
CN M.MT.AFU.ARI.ALO.ALO.ALO.AFU.AFU

breeze, pan
USE **breeze**

breezeways
RM.243
ALT **breezeway**
SN Use for roofed passages connecting two parts of a house or a house and garage; common after 1930. Distinct from **dogtrots**, which occur in folk architecture and log houses.
CN V.RM.AFU.DIO.ARI.AFU.AFU

Bremen blue
MT.1596
UF ashes, blue
blue ashes
blue, Bremen
blue, copper
blue, mountain
copper blue
mountain blue
CN M.MT.AFU.AFU.ARI.AFU.AFU.ALO.ALO.ALO.ARI.ARI

Bremen blue (color)
USE **light greenish blue**
moderate bluish green

Brettstuhls
TG.40
ALT **Brettstuhl**
SN German variety of the board chair. (BOYCE)
CN V.TG.AFU.AFU.ALO.AFU.AFU.AFU.CFS.AFU

Breuer chairs
USE **Cesca chairs**
Wassily chairs

breviaries
VW.540 (L,R)
ALT **breviary**
SN Books containing all daily psalms, hymns, prayers, lessons, and other religious recitations necessary to enable a cleric to recite the daily Divine Office. (RHDEL2)
CN V.VW.AFU.ALO.AFU.AFU.ALO.BUE.ARI

breweries
RK.623 (A,L,B,R)
ALT **brewery**
CN V.RK.AFU.ALO.ALO.CLM.ALO.ALO.AFU.AXC.AFU.ALO

Brewster chairs
TG.29
ALT **Brewster chair**
SN Collector's term for 17th-century American turned great chairs styled after one that belonged to Elder William Brewster of Plymouth Colony. Such chairs have boldly turned posts and decorative spindles, but unlike Carver chairs they have spindles below the seat as well as in the back and below the arms.
UF chairs, Brewster
CN V.TG.AFU.AFU.ALO.AFU.AFU.AFU.ALO.ARI.AFU

brick
MT.66 (A,L,B,R)
CN M.MT.AFU.AFU.AFU.AXC.ALO.AFU

brick cement
MT.39
SN Waterproof cement used in masonry work. (DAC)
UF cement, brick
CN M.MT.AFU.AFU.AFU.ALO.AFU.ALO.ALO

brick chisels
USE **brick sets**

brick kilns
TB.96 (N,B)
ALT **brick kiln**
UF kilns, brick
CN V.TB.AFU.ARI.ALO.ARI.ALO.ALO.AFU

brick red
USE **dark red**
grayish red
moderate red
strong reddish orange

brick sets
TB.577 (N)
ALT **brick set**
SN Chisels or bolsters for cutting brick. (DAC)
UF brick chisels

chisels, brick
sets, brick
CN V.TB.AFU.BCW.BCW.ALO.BZY.AFU.AFU

brick slip
MT.70
SN A solid tile used to simulate brickwork. (DAC)
UF slip, brick
CN M.MT.AFU.AFU.AFU.AXC.ALO.AFU.AFU.AFU.ALO

brick stamps
VW.729 (L,R)
ALT **brick stamp**
UF stamps, brick
CN V.VW.AFU.ALO.ALO.AFU.AXC.ARI.ARI

brick trowels
TB.631
ALT **brick trowel**
SN Trowels having a flat, triangular steel blade in an offset handle, used to pick up and spread mortar. (DAC)
UF trowels, brick
CN V.TB.AFU.BCW.BCW.ALO.HCQ.AFU

brick, adobe
USE **adobe**

brick, air
USE **air brick**

brick, angle
USE **angle brick**

brick, arch
USE **compass brick**

brick, ashlar
USE **ashlar brick**

brick, axed
USE **axed brick**

brick, backing
USE **backing brick**

brick, backup
USE **backing brick**

brick, baked
USE **fired brick**

brick, blue
USE **blue brick**

brick, building
USE **building brick**

brick, bullnose
USE **bullnose brick**

brick, burned
USE **fired brick**

brick, burnt
USE **fired brick**

brick, calcium silicate
USE **calcium silicate brick**

brick, cant
USE **splay brick**

brick, capping
USE **capping brick**

brick, cellular
USE **cellular brick**

brick, clinker
USE **clinker brick**

brick, common
USE **building brick**

brick, compass
USE **compass brick**

brick, concrete
USE **concrete block**

brick, coping
USE **capping brick**

brick, copper
USE **copper brick**

brick, dogleg
USE **dogleg brick**

brick, Dutch
USE **clinker brick**

brick, economy
USE **jumbo brick**

brick, end-cut
USE **end-cut brick**

brick, engineering
USE **engineering brick**

brick, face
USE **face brick**

brick, facing
USE **face brick**

brick, featheredge
USE **compass brick**

brick, fire
USE **fire brick**

brick, fired
USE **fired brick**

brick, Flemish
USE **Flemish brick**

brick, floor
USE **floor brick**

brick, furring
USE **furring brick**

brick, gauged
USE **gauged brick**

brick, great
USE **great brick**

brick, handmade
USE **handmade brick**

brick, hard
USE **hard-burned brick**

brick, hard-burned
USE **hard-burned brick**

brick, hollow
USE **hollow brick**

brick, jumbo
USE **jumbo brick**

brick, key
USE **compass brick**

brick, kiln-burned
USE **fired brick**

brick, modular
USE **modular building brick**

brick, modular building
USE **modular building brick**

brick, molded
USE **molded brick**

brick, Norman
USE **Norman brick**

brick, paving
USE **paving brick**

brick, paviour
USE **paving brick**

brick, perforated
USE **perforated brick**

brick, pilaster
USE **pilaster brick**

brick, place
USE **place brick**

brick, plinth
USE **plinth brick**

brick, pressed
USE **pressed brick**

brick, radial
USE **compass brick**

brick, radiating
USE **compass brick**

brick, radius
USE **compass brick**

brick, refractory
USE **fire brick**

brick, rock-faced
USE **ashlar brick**

brick, Roman
USE **Roman brick**

brick, rough-axed
USE **axed brick**

brick, rustic
USE **rustic brick**

brick, saddle-back coping
USE **saddle-back coping brick**

brick, salmon
USE **place brick**

brick, sammel
USE **sammel brick**

brick, sand-faced
USE **sand-struck brick**

brick, sand-lime
USE **sand-lime brick**

brick, sand-struck
USE **sand-struck brick**

Brick, SCR
USE **SCR brick**

brick, sewer
USE **blue brick**

brick, side-cut
USE **side-cut brick**

brick, slop
USE **water-struck brick**

brick, soft
USE **soft brick**

brick, soft-burned
USE **soft brick**

brick, soft-mud
USE **soft-mud brick**

brick, solid
USE **solid brick**

brick, splay
USE **splay brick**

brick, squint
USE **squint brick**

brick, Staffordshire blue
USE **blue brick**

brick, stiff-mud
USE **stiff-mud brick**

brick, stock
USE **stock brick**

brick, stone
USE **hard-burned brick**

brick, sun-baked
USE **sun-dried brick**

brick, sun-dried
USE **sun-dried brick**

brick, sun-dried mud
USE **sun-dried brick**

brick, tax
USE **tax brick**

brick, unburnt
USE **sun-dried brick**

brick, underburned
USE **soft brick**

brick, unfired
USE **soft brick**
sun-dried brick

brick, ventilating
USE **air brick**

brick, voussoir
USE **compass brick**

brick, water-struck
USE **water-struck brick**

brick, well-burned
USE **hard-burned brick**

brick, wire-cut
USE **wire-cut brick**

brickbat
MT.2216
SN A fragment of a hard material; refers especially to a fragment of brick. (WCOL)
UF bat
header, snap
snap header
CN M.MT.AFU.ALO.AXC

bricklayer's scaffolding
TB.490
SN Scaffolding composed of framed wood squares which support a platform; limited to light and medium duty. (DAC)
UF scaffolding, bricklayer's
CN V.TB.AFU.ARI.ERE.ARI.ALO

bricklayers
HG.599 (A,L,R)
ALT **bricklayer**
CN H.HG.AFU.AXC.BZY.AFU.DIO.ALO

bricklaying
KT.576 (A,L,B)
CN K.KT.AFU.ALO.ERE.AFU

bricklaying profiles
TB.572 (B)
ALT **bricklaying profile**
SN Guides used to set out brick work or block work accurately. (DAC)
UF profiles, bricklaying
CN V.TB.AFU.BCW.BCW.ALO.BOK

brickmakers
HG.552 (L)
ALT **brickmaker**
CN H.HG.AFU.AXC.BUE.AXC.ARI

brickwork
MT.2754 (A,L,B)
CN M.MT.AFU.AXC.BIQ.AFU.ALO

brickworks
RK.626 (A,L,B)
ALT **brickwork**
CN V.RK.AFU.ALO.ALO.CLM.ALO.ALO.AFU.AXC.ALO

bridal books
VW.496 (L)
ALT **bridal book**
UF books, bridal
brides' books
CN V.VW.AFU.ALO.AFU.AFU.AFU.BCW

bridal chests
USE **dower chests**

brides' books
USE **bridal books**

bridewell houses
USE **workhouses**

bridewells
USE **workhouses**

bridge approaches
RM.467 (L)
ALT **bridge approach**
SN Embankments, trestles, or other structures that provide access at either end of a bridge. (W)
UF approaches, bridge
CN V.RM.ALO.ALO.ALO.AFU.AFU

bridge cranes
TB.62 (L)
ALT **bridge crane**
SN Cranes used in manufacturing or assembling heavy objects, composed of a bridge spanning two overhead rails and a hoisting device which moves laterally along the bridge. The bridge can move longitudinally along the rails. (MEANS)
UF cranes, bridge
CN V.TB.AFU.ARI.AFU.BCW.AXC.AFU

bridge cranes (gantry cranes)
USE **gantry cranes**

bridge failures
BM.1030 (A,L)
UF failures, bridge
CN B.BM.CFS.AXC.CLM.ALO.BZY.AFU

bridge trusses
RT.378
ALT **bridge truss**
SN Trusses designed for use in bridges as opposed to roofs.
UF trusses, bridge
CN V.RT.AFU.AFU.AFU.BCW.CLM.AFU.ALO.AFU

bridgeboards
USE **open strings**

bridges
RK.1272 (A,L,N,B,R)
ALT **bridge**
CN V.RK.AFU.ALO.ALO.GLI.ALO.AFU

bridges, aqueduct
USE **aqueducts**

bridges, arch
USE **arch bridges**

bridges, bailey
USE **bailey bridges**

bridges, bascule
USE **bascule bridges**

bridges, cable braced
USE **cable-stayed bridges**

bridges, cable-stayed
USE **cable-stayed bridges**

bridges, canal
USE **aqueducts**

bridges, cantilever
USE **cantilever bridges**

bridges, cold
USE **thermal bridges**

bridges, continuous
USE **continuous bridges**

bridges, covered
USE **covered bridges**

bridges, deck
USE **deck truss bridges**

bridges, deck truss
USE **deck truss bridges**

bridges, flying
USE **skybridges**

bridges, girder
USE **girder bridges**

bridges, heat
USE **thermal bridges**

bridges, lift
USE **lift bridges**

bridges, military
USE **military bridges**

bridges, movable
USE **movable bridges**

bridges, multispan
USE **multispan bridges**

bridges, pedestrian
USE **footbridges**

bridges, pile
USE **pile bridges**

bridges, pontoon
USE **pontoon bridges**

bridges, railroad
USE **railroad bridges**

bridges, railway
USE **railroad bridges**

bridges, road
USE **road bridges**

bridges, single span
USE **single span bridges**

bridges, skew
USE **skew bridges**

bridges, skywalk
USE **skybridges**

bridges, stayed
USE **cable-stayed bridges**

bridges, stayed girder
USE **cable-stayed bridges**

bridges, suspension
USE **suspension bridges**

bridges, swing
USE **swing bridges**

bridges, thermal
USE **thermal bridges**

bridges, toll
USE **toll bridges**

bridges, truss
USE **truss bridges**

bridges, vertical lift
USE **lift bridges**

bridging
RT.211
SN Braces or systems of braces, placed between joists, or the like, to stiffen them, hold them in place, and to help distribute the load. (DAC)
CN V.RT.AFU.AFU.AFU.AXC.DOI.AFU.ARI

bridging joists
USE **common joists**

bridging, cross
USE **cross bridging**

bridging, diagonal
USE **cross bridging**

bridle joints
TF.678
ALT **bridle joint**
SN Mortise-and-tenon joints used when two timbers are joined at an angle of less than 90 degrees. (MEANS)
UF joints, bridle
CN V.TF.ALO.ARI.AXC.ALO.BCW.AFU

bridle paths
RK.1573 (A,L)
ALT **bridle path**
SN Paths cleared and compacted, reserved for riding horses and barred to vehicles. (DAC)
UF bridle roads
bridle trails
bridle ways
paths, bridle
riding trails
roads, bridle
trails, bridle
trails, riding
ways, bridle
CN V.RK.ALO.ALO.BUE.AXC.AFU

bridle roads
USE **bridle paths**

bridle trails
USE **bridle paths**

bridle ways
USE **bridle paths**

briefs
VW.870 (L)
ALT **brief**
SN Concise statements of the arguments of a party to a case in dispute, submitted to the court or other body hearing the case. (GAHLM)
CN V.VW.AFU.ARI.AFU.BOK.ALO

briefs (papal)
VW.965 (L)
ALT **brief (papal)**
SN Documents issued by the pope to a religious community, or an individual, on matters of discipline. (LG)
UF papal briefs
CN V.VW.AFU.ARI.ALO.ALO.AFU.ALO

briefs (programs)
USE **programs**

brigantins
USE **field beds**

bright aqua
USE **brilliant bluish green**
light bluish green
light greenish blue
very light greenish blue

bright aqua blue
USE **light greenish blue**

bright aqua green
USE **brilliant bluish green**
light bluish green
very light bluish green

bright blue
USE **brilliant blue**
brilliant greenish blue
light greenish blue
moderate greenish blue
strong blue
strong bluish green
strong greenish blue
vivid blue

bright blue green
USE **brilliant green**
strong green
vivid green

bright bluish green
USE **vivid bluish green**

bright bluish red
USE **vivid purplish red**

bright bluish violet
USE **vivid violet**

bright cerulean blue
USE **moderate blue**
strong greenish blue

bright chartreuse
USE brilliant yellow green
strong yellow green
vivid yellow green

bright chartreuse yellow
USE strong greenish yellow
vivid greenish yellow

bright copen blue
USE strong blue

bright emerald green
USE brilliant bluish green
brilliant green
strong bluish green
strong green

bright fuchsia purple
USE deep purplish red
deep reddish purple
strong reddish purple

bright fuchsia rose
USE moderate purplish red

bright gold
USE deep yellow
vivid yellow

bright green
USE brilliant bluish green
brilliant green
deep green
deep yellowish green
moderate green
strong bluish green
strong green
strong yellowish green
vivid green
vivid yellowish green

bright green yellow
USE vivid yellow green

bright greenish blue
USE vivid greenish blue

bright greenish yellow
USE vivid greenish yellow

bright jade green
USE brilliant bluish green
strong bluish green
strong green

bright kelly green
USE brilliant green
strong green
strong yellowish green
vivid yellowish green

bright lavender
USE light purple
light violet
moderate purple
moderate violet

bright lemon yellow
USE vivid greenish yellow

bright lime green
USE brilliant yellow green
brilliant yellowish green
strong yellow green
vivid yellow green

bright mauve
USE light violet

bright navy
USE dark blue
deep blue
moderate blue
moderate purplish blue

bright olive green
USE light olive
moderate olive
moderate olive green
moderate yellow green

bright open blue
USE brilliant blue

bright orange
USE strong orange
vivid orange

bright peach
USE strong yellowish pink

bright peacock blue
USE brilliant greenish blue
strong greenish blue

bright periwinkle blue
USE light violet

bright red
USE strong red
vivid red

bright red violet
USE strong purple
strong reddish purple
vivid purple
vivid reddish purple

bright reddish blue
USE vivid purplish blue

bright reddish orange
USE vivid reddish orange

bright reddish violet
USE vivid reddish purple

bright reddish yellow
USE vivid orange yellow
vivid yellow

bright rose
USE deep pink
deep purplish pink
grayish purplish red
moderate purplish red
strong purplish red
strong red
vivid purplish red

bright rose violet
USE deep purplish pink

bright teal blue
USE dark greenish blue
moderate greenish blue

bright turquoise
USE brilliant bluish green
strong bluish green

bright turquoise blue
USE brilliant greenish blue
strong bluish green
strong greenish blue

bright turquoise green
USE brilliant bluish green
light bluish green
moderate bluish green
strong bluish green

bright ultramarine
USE strong blue
strong purplish blue
vivid blue
vivid purplish blue

bright violet
USE moderate purple
moderate violet
strong purple
vivid purple
vivid violet

bright yellow
USE brilliant orange yellow
light orange yellow
moderate orange yellow
strong orange yellow
vivid yellow

bright yellowish green
USE vivid yellow green
vivid yellowish green

bright yellowish orange
USE vivid orange yellow

bright yellowish red
USE vivid red
vivid reddish orange

brightness
BM.853
SN Use when referring generally to the relative degree of lightness or darkness given to a surface by the amount of light reflected from it. When referring to the degree of lightness or darkness of a color, use value (color).
UF lightness
CN B.BM.CFS.AXC.ALO.AFU.ALO.ALO.AFU

brightness (color)
USE value (color)

brillant yellow
USE Naples yellow

brilliant blue
DL.214
UF blue, bright
blue, bright open

blue, light methyl
bright blue
bright open blue
centroid color 177
light methyl blue
methyl blue, light
ultramarine
CN D.DL.AFU.AFU.BZY.ALO

brilliant bluish green
DL.197
UF aqua green, bright
aqua, bright
blue green
bluish green, brilliant
bright aqua
bright aqua green
bright emerald green
bright green
bright jade green
bright turquoise
bright turquoise green
centroid color 159
emerald green, brilliant
green, bright
green, bright aqua
green, bright emerald
green, bright jade
green, bright turquoise
green, brilliant bluish
green, turquoise
jade green, bright
turquoise (color)
turquoise green
turquoise green, bright
turquoise, bright
CN D.DL.AFU.AFU.BUE.DCU.ALO.ALO

brilliant green
DL.165
UF blue green
blue green, bright
blue green, light
bright blue green
bright emerald green
bright green
bright kelly green
centroid color 140
chrysocolla green
emerald (color)
emerald green (color)
emerald green, bright
emerald green, light
green, bright
green, bright emerald
green, bright kelly
green, brilliant
green, chrysocolla
green, emerald (color)
green, light emerald
green, Paris
green, viridian
kelly green, bright
light blue green
light emerald green
Paris green
viridian green
CN D.DL.AFU.AFU.BUE.ALO

brilliant greenish blue
DL.234
UF blue turquoise
blue, bright
blue, bright peacock
blue, bright turquoise
blue, brilliant greenish
blue, light cerulean
bright blue
bright peacock blue
bright turquoise blue
centroid color 168
cerulean blue, light
greenish blue, brilliant
light cerulean blue
peacock blue, bright
turquoise blue, bright
turquoise, blue
CN D.DL.AFU.AFU.BZY.DCU.AFU.ALO

brilliant greenish yellow
DL.136
UF centroid color 98
chartreuse
chartreuse yellow
chartreuse yellow, light
citron
green yellow
lemon yellow
lemon yellow, light
light chartreuse yellow
light lemon yellow
lime yellow
strontium yellow (color)
sulphur yellow
yellow, chartreuse
yellow, lemon
yellow, light chartreuse
yellow, light lemon
yellow, strontium (color)
yellow, sulphur
CN D.DL.AFU.AFU.BCW.CRG.ALO.ALO

brilliant orange
DL.62
UF cadmium orange (color)
centroid color 49
orange pink
orange, brilliant
orange, cadmium (color)
pink, orange
CN D.DL.AFU.AFU.ARI.ALO

brilliant orange yellow
DL.127
UF bright yellow
centroid color 67
Indian yellow (color)
ocher (color)
orange yellow, brilliant
orange, yellowish
reddish yellow
yellow, bright
yellow, brilliant orange
yellow, Indian (color)
yellow, reddish
yellowish orange
CN D.DL.AFU.AFU.BCW.CRG.AFU.ALO

brilliant peacock blue
USE **strong greenish blue**

brilliant purple
DL.268
UF centroid color 217
mauve (color)
purple, brilliant
rose purple
CN D.DL.AFU.AFU.CFS.ALO

brilliant purplish blue
DL.244
UF blue violet, pale
blue, brilliant purplish
blue, reddish
bluish violet, light
bluish violet, pale
centroid color 195
deep lavender blue
grayish violet blue, light
lavender blue
lavender blue, deep
light bluish violet
light grayish violet blue
pale blue violet
pale bluish violet
purplish blue, brilliant
reddish blue
ultramarine
violet blue, light grayish
violet, light bluish
violet, pale bluish
CN D.DL.AFU.AFU.BZY.DCU.ALO.ALO

brilliant purplish pink
DL.16
UF bluish pink
centroid color 246
pink, bluish
pink, brilliant purplish
purplish pink, brilliant
CN D.DL.AFU.AFU.AFU.CLM.AFU.AFU

brilliant scarlet
USE **iodine scarlet**

brilliant violet
DL.256
UF blue violet, dull
blue violet, soft
bluish violet
bluish violet, dull
bluish violet, light
centroid color 206
dull blue violet
dull bluish violet
lavender violet
light bluish violet
mauve (color)
soft blue violet
violet, bluish
violet, brilliant
violet, dull bluish
violet, light bluish
CN D.DL.AFU.AFU.BZY.DCU.ARI.ALO

brilliant yellow
DL.113
UF amber yellow

aureolin (color)
barium yellow (color)
buff, orange
canary yellow
centroid color 83
cobalt yellow (color)
gold, light
lemon yellow
light gold
Naples yellow (color)
ocher (color)
orange buff
orpiment (color)
reddish yellow
Turner's yellow (color)
yellow, amber
yellow, barium (color)
yellow, brilliant
yellow, canary
yellow, cobalt (color)
yellow, lemon
yellow, Naples (color)
yellow, reddish
yellow, Turner's (color)
CN D.DL.AFU.AFU.BCW.ALO

brilliant yellow green
DL.156
UF bright chartreuse
bright lime green
centroid color 116
chartreuse green
chartreuse, bright
chartreuse, light
green, bright lime
green, brilliant yellow
green, chartreuse
light chartreuse
lime green, bright
lime yellow
yellow green, brilliant
yellow, lime
CN D.DL.AFU.AFU.BOK.ALO

brilliant yellowish green
DL.186
UF bright lime green
centroid color 130
emerald (color)
emerald green (color)
green, bright lime
green, brilliant yellowish
green, emerald (color)
green, light lime
green, Paris
light lime green
lime green, bright
lime green, light
Paris green
yellowish green, brilliant
CN D.DL.AFU.AFU.BUE.DCU.AFU.ALO

brimstone
USE **sulfur**

Brisa
USE **Aowin**

brise-soleils
RT.967 (B)
ALT **brise-soleil**
SN Fixed or movable devices, such as louvers, designed to block the direct entrance of sun rays into buildings. (HAS)
UF breakers, sun
louvers, sun
shades, sun
sun breakers
sun louvers
sun shades
CN V.RT.AFU.ARI.AFU.AFU.BOK.ALO.AFU

bristles
MT.936 (L)
CN M.MT.AFU.AFU.ALO.AFU.CXA.AFU.ALO.AFU

bristol board
MT.1911
SN A high-grade white cardboard, supercalendered with China clay; also made by pasting together sheets of heavy ledger paper. (MH)
UF board, bristol
CN M.MT.AFU.AFU.ARI.ALO.ALO.AXC.ALO.BIQ.AFU.AFU

Bristol glaze
MT.2561
SN A low-fire glaze usually containing zinc oxide. (W)
UF glaze, Bristol
CN M.MT.AFU.ARI.CRG.ARI.ARI.AFU.AFU.ALO

britannia metal
MT.410 (R)
SN A type of pewter that usually contains copper. Its color is silvery white with a bluish tinge, or with a yellowish tinge if the copper content is high.
UF metal, britannia
CN M.MT.AFU.AFU.AFU.BZY.AFU.AFU.AFU.ALO.BUE.ALO.ALO

britannia metal, English
USE **English britannia metal**

British
FL.3039 (L,B)
CN F.FL.ALO.BCW.AFU.AXC

British gum
MT.2342
SN Grade of dextrin used as a paper adhesive and in the manufacture of gouache, watercolor, and other aqueous paints. (MAYER)
UF gum, British
CN M.MT.AFU.ARI.ARI.AFU.ALO.AFU.AFU

British oak
USE **English oak**

British Solomon Island
USE **Solomon Island**

brittle-painted ware
FL.2936
UF ware, brittle-painted
CN F.FL.ALO.AXC.ARI.AXC.ALO.BIQ.AXC

brittle ware
FL.2748
UF ware, brittle
CN F.FL.ALO.AXC.ALO.ALO.ALO.BUE.ALO.AFU

brittleness
BM.948 (L)
ALT **brittle**
CN B.BM.CFS.AXC.BZY.BOK.AFU

Brno chairs
TG.43
ALT **Brno chair**
UF chairs, Brno
CN V.TG.AFU.AFU.ALO.AFU.AFU.AFU.CRG

broach spires
RM.404
ALT **broach spire**
SN Octagonal spires rising from a square tower without an intervening parapet, the four angles of the tower being covered by corner segments of a pyramid seeming to penetrate the tower. (W)
UF spires, broach
CN V.RM.AFU.DOI.ALO.AFU.AFU

broaching
KT.603 (L)
SN Drilling or cutting out material left between adjacent holes in a row of closely spaced drill holes; process used especially in mining and quarrying. (W)
CN K.KT.AFU.ALO.FUA.ALO

broad glass
USE **cylinder glass**

broadaxes
TB.837 (N)
ALT **broadax**
SN Axes having a large, broad blade bevelled on one side, used for the rough dressing of timber. (DAC)
UF axes, hewing
hewing axes
CN V.TB.AFU.BCW.CFS.ALO.AFU.AXC.ARI

broadcasters
HG.282 (L)
ALT **broadcaster**
CN H.HG.AFU.AXC.BCW.ALO.AFU.ALO

broadcasters, radio
USE **radio broadcasters**

broadcasting
KD.110 (L,B)
CN K.KD.AFU.ALO.ARI.ALO

broadcasting stations
RK.202 (L,B)
ALT **broadcasting station**
SN If possible use a more specific term.
UF stations, broadcasting
CN V.RK.AFU.ALO.ALO.ARI.AFU.ARI.AFU

broadcasting studios
RM.223 (A,B)
ALT **broadcasting studio**
UF studios, broadcasting
CN V.RM.AFU.DIO.ALO.DOI.ARI

broadcasting, radio
USE **radio broadcasting**

broadcasting, television
USE **television broadcasting**

broadleaved maple
USE **bigleaf maple**

broadsheets
USE **broadsides**

broadsides
VW.558 (L,N,R)
ALT **broadside**
SN Use to designate single-sheet public notices that are usually printed on only one side; often chiefly textual rather than pictorial and meant to be read unfolded.
UF broadsheets
CN V.VW.AFU.ALO.AFU.ALO

brocade
KT.552 (L,R)
ALT **brocaded**
SN Distinguished from **embroidery** in that raised patterns are woven into the cloth instead of being stitched through it.
CN K.KT.AFU.ALO.ELK.DUC.AFU.BOK.AFU

Brocade Style
FL.2988
CN F.FL.ALO.AXC.ARI.BCW.ALO.AXC.AFU

brocatelle
KT.553
SN Use for brocade done in high relief.
CN K.KT.AFU.ALO.ELK.DUC.AFU.BOK.AFU.AFU

brocatelle marble
MT.805
UF marble, brocatelle
CN M.MT.AFU.AFU.AFU.DCU.AFU.ARI.ARI.ARI.BIQ.ALO

brocatello
MT.765
UF marmor schiston
CN M.MT.AFU.AFU.AFU.DCU.AFU.ARI.ARI.ALO.BOK.AFU

broccatellone
MT.753
CN M.MT.AFU.AFU.AFU.DCU.AFU.ARI.ARI.ALO.AFU.BIQ

brochs
RK.868 (A,L)
ALT **broch**
SN Use for circular stone towers having a double wall, found in Scotland and neighboring islands.
CN V.RK.AFU.ALO.ALO.DIO.ALO.AXC.AFU.AFU

brochures
USE **pamphlets**

broken
DC.59
SN Use in the sense of interrupted. For the sense of damaged, see **breaking**, alternative form **broken.**
UF discontinuous
CN D.DC.AFU.ARI.BCW

broken arches
RT.221
ALT **broken arch**
SN Use for arches interrupted by a central gap.
UF arches, broken
CN V.RT.AFU.AFU.AFU.BCW.AFU.AFU.AFU.ARI

broken front
USE **breakfront**

broken joints
USE **break joints**

broken-out sections
VD.68
ALT **broken-out section**
SN Use for orthographic drawings of the exterior of a structure or object with a small portion removed to show an interior detail. When a more substantial portion is removed, use **half sections** or **sectional elevations.**
UF sections, broken-out
CN V.VD.AFU.AFU.BIQ.ALO.BIQ.AFU

broken pediments
RT.673
ALT **broken pediment**
SN Pediments, common in Baroque and later classicizing styles, having a gap at the apex, sometimes occupied by a statue or ornament.
UF pediments, broken
CN V.RT.AFU.AFU.AFU.BIQ.BUE.ALO.ALO.BIQ.AFU

broken stone
USE **crushed stone**

brokers
HG.407 (L)
ALT **broker**
SN Middlemen who for a fee or commission negotiate contracts of purchase and sale between buyers and sellers. (W)
CN H.HG.AFU.AXC.BOK.BZY.AFU

broletti
RK.1000
ALT **broletto**
SN Use for town hall buildings in smaller Italian communities, especially in Lombardy.
CN V.RK.AFU.ALO.ALO.ERE.ALO.AFU.BIQ.AFU

bromide (silver bromide)
USE **silver bromide**

bromoil photoprints
USE **bromoil prints**

bromoil prints
VJ.56
ALT **bromoil print**
UF bromoil photoprints
photoprints, bromoil
prints, bromoil
CN V.VJ.AFU.AFU.ARI.ARI.AXC.BUE.ARI.AFU

bromoil process
KT.356
SN Use for the photographic process that is a variant of the oil process in which the developed silver in a gelatin print is used as a catalyst to tan the gelatin. The untanned highlights become saturated when the print is soaked in water and will resist a greasy ink, while the tanned shadows accept the ink. The original print may be the end product or may be used as a master for transferring the image to another support.
CN K.KT.AFU.ALO.DUC.DIO.ALO.DIO.AFU.BCW.AFU

Brong
FL.298 (L)
UF Abron
CN F.FL.ALO.AFU.AXC.AFU.ARI.AFU.ARI.AFU

bronze
MT.375 (A,L,B,R)
SN Generally applied to any copper alloy that has as the principal alloying element a metal other than zinc or nickel. (MH)
CN M.MT.AFU.AFU.AFU.BZY.AFU.AFU.AFU.ALO.ARI.BCW.ALO

Bronze Age
FL.26 (A,L,R)
UF Age, Bronze
CN F.FL.AFU.BCW.ARI

Bronze Age, Early
USE **Early Bronze Age**

Bronze Age, Late
USE **Late Bronze Age**

Bronze Age, Middle
USE **Middle Bronze Age**

bronze blue
USE **Prussian blue**

bronze brown
USE **brownish gray**

bronze (color)
USE **moderate olive brown**
moderate yellowish brown

bronze gold
USE **strong yellow**

bronze green
USE **chrome green**

bronze, admiralty
USE **admiralty metal**

bronze, aluminum
USE **aluminum bronze**

bronze, architectural
USE **architectural bronze**

bronze, art
USE **architectural bronze**

bronze, beryllium
USE **copper-beryllium alloys**

bronze, lead
USE **lead bronze**

bronze, manganese
USE **manganese bronze**

bronze, naval
USE **naval brass**

bronze, nickel
USE **nickel bronze**

bronze, ordnance
USE **lead bronze**

bronze, phosphor
USE **phosphor bronze**

bronze, silicon
USE **silicon bronze**

bronze, statuary
USE **statuary bronze**

bronze, steel
USE **phosphor bronze**

bronzers
HG.453
ALT **bronzer**
CN H.HG.AFU.AXC.BUE.ALO.CFS.ALO.AFU

bronzeworkers
HG.493
ALT **bronzeworker**
CN H.HG.AFU.AXC.BUE.ARI.CFS.AFU.ALO

bronzing
KT.711 (L)
ALT **bronzed**
SN The painting of a surface to give the appearance of bronze. In printmaking, refers to printing with metallic inks. (TBL)
UF hand-bronzing
CN K.KT.AFU.ALO.GRC.CRG.AFU

Brook's curves
TB.433 (N)
ALT **Brook's curve**
UF curves, Brook's
CN V.TB.AFU.ARI.EFQ.ALO.AFU.AFU

brooks
RD.140 (L,R)
ALT **brook**
SN Use for small streams, generally smaller than creeks.
UF rivulets
rivurets
CN V.RD.ARI.AFU.AFU.AFU.AFU.ARI.ALO.AFU

broom closets
RM.195
ALT **broom closet**
UF closets, broom
CN V.RM.AFU.DIO.ALO.DCU.BOK.AFU

broommakers
HG.553
ALT **broommaker**
CN H.HG.AFU.AXC.BUE.AXC.AXC

brooms
TB.347 (L,N)
ALT **broom**
CN V.TB.AFU.ARI.CRG.ALO.AFU

brooms, whisk
USE **whisk brooms**

brothels
RK.192 (A,L,R)
ALT **brothel**
UF bawdyhouses
bordellos
cat houses
houses of ill repute
houses of prostitution
houses, cat
houses, panel
houses, sporting
panel houses
sporting houses
whorehouses
CN V.RK.AFU.ALO.ALO.ALO.AXC.AXC

brotherhoods
HG.895 (L)
ALT **brotherhood**
CN H.HG.ALO.DUC.ARI

brown
DL.76 (L)
CN D.DL.AFU.AFU.AXC

brown bistre
USE **light grayish yellowish brown**
light olive brown

brown black
USE **brownish gray**

brown carmine
USE **dark red**
very deep red

brown coat
USE **arriccio**

brown hematite
USE **limonite**

brown iron oxide
MT.1626
UF brown, Mars
iron oxide, brown
Mars brown
CN M.MT.AFU.AFU.ARI.AFU.AFU.ALO.ALO.ARI.ARI.ALO

brown lake
USE **moderate red**

brown lampblack
USE **bister**

brown ocher
MT.1625
UF ocher, brown
CN M.MT.AFU.AFU.ARI.AFU.AFU.ALO.ALO.ARI.ARI.AFU

brown olive
USE **light olive brown**

brown-on-cream ware
FL.2867
UF ware, brown-on-cream
CN F.FL.ALO.AXC.ARI.AFU.ALO.ARI.ALO

brown orange
USE **brownish orange**
deep orange
grayish reddish orange
light brown
light yellowish brown
moderate orange
moderate orange yellow
moderate yellow
moderate yellowish pink
strong orange
strong orange yellow

brown ore
USE **limonite**

brown pigment
MT.1611
UF pigment, brown
CN M.MT.AFU.AFU.ARI.AFU.AFU.ALO.ALO.ARI

brown pigment, artificial inorganic
USE **artificial inorganic brown pigment**

brown pigment, inorganic
USE **inorganic brown pigment**

brown pigment, organic
USE **organic brown pigment**

brown pigment, synthetic inorganic
USE **artificial inorganic brown pigment**

brown pink
USE **Dutch pink**

brown purple
USE **grayish purple**

brown red
USE **grayish red**
grayish reddish brown
light grayish red
vivid red

brown-slipped ware
FL.2868
UF ware, brown-slipped
CN F.FL.ALO.AXC.ARI.AFU.ALO.ARI.ARI

brown violet
USE **dark purplish red**
grayish purplish red

brown, beige
USE **grayish yellowish brown**

brown, bistre
USE **light brown**
light brownish gray
light olive
light olive brown
moderate yellowish brown
moderate yellowish pink

brown, black
USE **brownish gray**
dark grayish brown
grayish brown
grayish olive
light brownish gray
olive gray

brown, blackish
USE **brownish gray**
dark grayish brown
dark reddish gray

brown, bone
USE **bone brown**

brown, bronze
USE **brownish gray**

brown, Caledonian
USE **burnt sienna**

brown, Cappagh
USE **umber**

brown, Cassel
USE **moderate brown**

brown, chestnut
USE **burnt umber**

brown, dark
USE **dark brown**

brown, dark grayish
USE **dark grayish brown**

brown, dark grayish reddish
USE **dark grayish reddish brown**

brown, dark grayish yellowish
USE **dark grayish yellowish brown**

brown, dark olive
USE **dark olive brown**

brown, dark reddish
USE **dark reddish brown**

brown, dark rose
USE **dark grayish red**
dark reddish gray

brown, dark violet
USE **blackish purple**
dark grayish purple
dark purplish red
very dark purplish red

brown, dark yellowish
USE **dark yellowish brown**

brown, deep
USE **deep brown**

brown, deep red
USE **grayish reddish brown**

brown, deep reddish
USE **deep reddish brown**

brown, deep yellowish
USE **deep yellowish brown**

brown, dull
USE **brownish pink**
dark grayish brown
grayish brown
light grayish brown

brown, dull reddish
USE **blackish red**
dark grayish red
dark grayish reddish brown
dark red
dark reddish brown
grayish red
grayish reddish brown
light grayish reddish brown
light reddish brown
very dark red

brown, dull yellowish
USE **dark grayish yellowish brown**
dark yellowish brown
grayish yellowish brown
light grayish yellowish brown
light yellowish brown
moderate yellowish brown

brown, ebony
USE **dark gray**
dark reddish gray
reddish black

brown, Egyptian
USE **mummy**

brown, garnet
USE **dark red**
deep red

brown, gold
USE **brownish orange**
strong brown

brown, golden
USE **deep yellowish brown**
moderate yellowish brown

brown, gray
USE **light brownish gray**
light grayish reddish brown
light olive brown
light olive gray

brown, grayish
USE **grayish brown**

brown, grayish reddish
USE **grayish reddish brown**

brown, grayish yellowish
USE **grayish yellowish brown**

brown, iron
USE **black**

brown, jacaranda
USE **burnt umber**

brown, light
USE **light brown**

brown, light copper
USE **strong brown**

brown, light grayish
USE **light grayish brown**

brown, light grayish reddish
USE **light grayish reddish brown**

brown, light grayish yellowish
USE **light grayish yellowish brown**

brown, light olive
USE **light olive brown**

brown, light reddish
USE **light reddish brown**

brown, light rose
USE **dark grayish red**
grayish red

brown, light yellowish
USE **light yellowish brown**

brown, lilac
USE **blackish red**
light brownish gray
reddish gray

brown, Mars
USE **brown iron oxide**
moderate brown

brown, mauve
USE **dark reddish gray**

brown, metallic
USE **deep brown**

deep reddish brown

brown, moderate
USE **moderate brown**

brown, moderate olive
USE **moderate olive brown**

brown, moderate reddish
USE **moderate reddish brown**

brown, moderate yellowish
USE **moderate yellowish brown**

brown, mummy
USE **dark yellowish brown**
grayish brown
grayish yellowish brown

brown, mustard
USE **moderate olive**

brown, ocher
USE **golden ocher**

brown, olive
USE **olive brown**

brown, orange
USE **brownish orange**
dark red
deep orange
grayish reddish orange
light brown
light grayish brown
light grayish yellowish brown
moderate brown
moderate reddish orange
strong brown
strong reddish brown

brown, pale
USE **light brown**
light grayish reddish brown
light grayish yellowish brown
light yellowish brown
moderate orange

brown, pale reddish
USE **light reddish brown**

brown, pale yellowish
USE **light grayish yellowish brown**

brown, purple
USE **grayish purple**

brown, red
USE **blackish red**
brownish orange
dark red
dark reddish orange
deep orange
grayish red
grayish yellowish pink
light brown
light grayish red
light reddish brown
moderate brown
moderate olive brown
moderate orange
moderate reddish brown
moderate reddish orange
moderate yellowish brown
pale yellowish pink
reddish gray
strong yellowish brown

brown, reddish
USE **reddish brown**

brown, rose
USE **dark grayish red**
deep purplish red
deep red
grayish red
grayish reddish brown
very deep purplish red
very deep red
vivid red

brown, Rubens'
USE **Van Dyke brown**

brown, sepia
USE **dark grayish yellowish brown**
dark olive brown
dark yellowish brown

brown, Sicilian
USE **raw umber**

brown, sienna
USE **moderate brown**

brown, soot
USE **bister**

brown, Spanish
USE **strong reddish brown**

brown, strong
USE **strong brown**

brown, strong reddish
USE **strong reddish brown**

brown, strong yellowish
USE **strong yellowish brown**

brown, taupe
USE **brownish gray**
dark grayish purple
grayish brown
grayish reddish brown

brown, transparent
USE **transparent brown**

brown, umber
USE **grayish brown**

brown, Van Dyke
USE **Van Dyke brown**

brown, Van Dyke (color)
USE **grayish brown**
moderate brown

brown, Verona
USE **transparent brown**

brown, Veronese
USE **transparent brown**

brown, very dark
USE **dark brown**
dark yellowish brown

brown, very dark grayish
USE **dark grayish yellowish brown**
moderate olive brown

brown, very pale
USE **brownish pink**
light grayish yellowish brown
light yellowish brown
pale orange yellow

brown, violet
USE **dark purplish red**
grayish purple
grayish red

brown, yellow
USE **brownish orange**
brownish pink
dark orange yellow
dark reddish orange
light brown
light olive
light reddish brown
moderate orange
strong brown
strong yellowish brown

brown, yellowish
USE **yellowish brown**

browning brushes
TB.574
ALT **browning brush**
SN Tools used to throw water on the surface of applied mortar to provide lubrication to the tools used to straighten the surface. (PUTNAM)
UF brushes, browning
CN V.TB.AFU.BCW.BCW.ALO.BUE.AFU

brownish black
DL.87
UF black, brownish
centroid color 65
CN D.DL.AFU.AFU.AXC.BUE

brownish gray
DL.85
UF black brown
blackish brown
bronze brown
brown black
brown, black
brown, blackish
brown, bronze
brown, taupe
centroid color 64
dark rose taupe
gray, brownish
gray, rose
gray, very dark
rose gray
rose taupe, dark
taupe
taupe brown
taupe, dark rose

very dark gray
CN D.DL.AFU.AFU.AXC.BOK

brownish gray, light
USE **light brownish gray**

brownish olive
USE **light olive brown**
moderate olive brown

brownish olive, dull
USE **dark olive brown**

brownish olive, light
USE **light olive brown**

brownish orange
DL.75
UF brown orange
brown, gold
brown, orange
brown, red
brown, yellow
centroid color 54
gold brown
gold ocher, transparent (color)
ocher, transparent gold (color)
orange brown
orange, brown
orange, brownish
raw sienna (color)
red brown
red, yellow
sienna, raw (color)
terra cotta (color)
terra sienna
transparent gold ocher (color)
yellow brown
yellow red
CN D.DL.AFU.AFU.ARI.BOK.ALO

brownish pink
DL.33
UF biege, light rose
bisque
bistre, purplish
brown, dull
brown, very pale
brown, yellow
buff
centroid color 33
dull brown
gray, lilac
light rose beige
lilac gray
pink, brownish
purplish bistre
rose beige, light
very pale brown
yellow brown
CN D.DL.AFU.AFU.AFU.CLM.ARI

brownish white
USE **yellowish white**

brownish yellow
USE **dark orange yellow**

brownline prints
VW.693
ALT **brownline print**
SN Use for prints made on light-sensitized surfaces that produce brown lines on neutral backgrounds. For white images on brown backgrounds, use **brownprints.** For brownline prints on translucent paper, use **sepia prints.**
UF brownlines
prints, brownline
CN V.VW.AFU.ALO.AFU.DZW.BIQ.CRG.ARI

brownlines
USE **brownline prints**

brownprints
VW.678
ALT **brownprint**
SN Use for prints made on light-sensitized surfaces that produce white images on brown backgrounds. For brown images on neutral backgrounds use **brownline prints** or **sepia prints.**
UF photoprints, Van Dyke
photoprints, Van Dyke brown
prints, Van Dyke (brownprints)
Van Dyke brown photoprints
Van Dyke photoprints
Van Dyke prints (brownprints)
CN V.VW.AFU.ALO.AFU.DZW.BIQ.ALO

brownstone
MT.719
CN M.MT.AFU.AFU.AFU.DCU.AFU.ALO.AFU.ARI.AFU.ALO.AXC.ALO

brownstones
RK.266 (B)
ALT **brownstone**
SN Dwellings, often row houses, faced with brownstone. (HAS)
CN V.RK.AFU.ALO.ALO.AXC.ALO.AFU.CRG.BIQ.AFU

Brunswick blue
USE **Prussian blue**

Brunswick green
MT.1664
UF green, Brunswick
green, Prussian
Prussian green
CN M.MT.AFU.AFU.ARI.AFU.AFU.ALO.ALO.AXC.BCW.AFU.AFU

brush bits
TB.1100
ALT **brush bit**
UF bits, brush
CN V.TB.ALO.ARI.ALO

brush graining
USE **graining**

brush technique
USE **brushwork**

brushes
TB.504 (L,N)
ALT **brush**
SN Implements made of natural or artificial bristles which are attached to a handle or back, used for cleaning or painting a surface. (DAC)
CN V.TB.AFU.ARI.EWY.ALO.ALO

brushes, background
USE **background brushes**

brushes, browning
USE **browning brushes**

brushes, dusting
USE **dusting brushes**

brushes, file
USE **file brushes**

brushes, fountain
USE **fountain brushes**

brushes, paint
USE **paintbrushes**

brushes, paperhanging
USE **wallpaper brushes**

brushes, rasp
USE **file brushes**

brushes, scrub
USE **scrub brushes**

brushes, wallpaper
USE **wallpaper brushes**

brushes, wire
USE **wire brushes**

brushmakers
HG.554
ALT **brushmaker**
CN H.HG.AFU.AXC.BUE.AXC.BCW

brushwork
KT.694 (L)
UF brush technique
CN K.KT.AFU.ALO.GRC.BUE.AFU

brut, art
USE **art brut**

Brutalist
FL.3707 (A,L,B,R)
ALT **Brutalism**
SN Includes late works of Le Corbusier and other architecture influenced by it, characterized by raw concrete and undisguised functional features.
UF Neo-Brutalist
New Brutalist
CN F.FL.ALO.BUE.ALO.ALO

bruzz chisels
USE **corner chisels**

Brya ebenus
USE **granadilla**

bryozoa limestone
MT.654
UF limestone, bryozoa
CN M.MT.AFU.AFU.AFU.DCU.AFU.ALO.AFU.ALO.ALO.AFU.AFU.AFU.ALO

Bubalus phase
FL.68
UF Hunter period
Large wild fauna phase
CN F.FL.ALO.AFU.AFU.ARI.AFU

Bubi
USE **Bulu**

Bucchero ware
FL.2744 (L)
UF pottery, Bucchero
ware, Bucchereo
CN F.FL.ALO.AXC.ALO.ALO.ALO.
BUE.AFU.AFU

buck anchors
TF.292
ALT **buck anchor**
UF anchors, buck
CN V.TF.AFU.AFU.AFU.ALO.AFU.
AFU.AXC

Buckelkeramik
USE **knobbed ware**

bucket benches
USE **water benches**

bucket loaders
TB.53
ALT **bucket loader**
UF loaders, bucket
CN V.TB.AFU.ARI.AFU.BCW.AFU

bucket loaders, chain
USE **chain bucket loaders**

buckets (construction equipment)
TB.55 (L)
ALT **bucket (construction equipment)**
SN Attachments for a materials-handling or excavating machine. (DAC)
CN V.TB.AFU.ARI.AFU.BCW.ALO

buckets, clamshell
USE **clamshell buckets**

buckets, dipper
USE **dippers**

buckets, dragline
USE **dragline buckets**

buckets, grab
USE **grab buckets**

buckeye
MT.1087
UF Aesculus
American horse chestnut
chestnut, American horse
horse chestnut, American
CN M.MT.AFU.AFU.ALO.BIQ.DCU.
AFU.AFU.AFU.AFU.AFU

buckeye, California
USE **California buckeye**

buckeye, dwarf
USE **dwarf buckeye**

buckeye, Ohio
USE **Ohio buckeye**

buckeye, sweet
USE **yellow buckeye**

buckeye, yellow
USE **yellow buckeye**

buckle tongs
USE **sliding tongs**

buckling
KT.886 (L)
ALT **buckled**
SN Failure of a structural member caused by lateral or torsional instability.
CN K.KT.ALO.AFU

buckling, elastic
USE **elastic buckling**

buckling, inelastic
USE **inelastic buckling**

buckling, lateral
USE **lateral buckling**

bucks, door
USE **door bucks**

bucks, rough
USE **door bucks**

bucksaws
TB.1007 (N)
ALT **bucksaw**
SN Saws with a fixed blade set in an H-shaped frame, used mainly for cutting across the grain of lumber and firewood.
UF saws, buck
saws, woodcutter's
woodcutter's saws
CN V.TB.AFU.BCW.CFS.ALO.AFU.
EWY.BCW.ALO

buckskin
MT.955 (L)
CN M.MT.AFU.AFU.ALO.AFU.DZW.
AXC.AFU

buckthorn berry
MT.1521
UF Avignon berry
berry, Avignon
berry, buckthorn
berry, French
berry, Persian
berry, yellow
French berry
Persian berry
yellow berry
CN M.MT.AFU.AFU.ARI.AFU.AFU.
AFU.AFU.AFU.AXC.ALO

buckthorn lake
USE **Persian berries lake**

bucranes
USE **bucrania**

bucrania
DG.21
ALT **bucranium**
SN Motifs representing the head or skull of an ox, often garlanded, common in classical style friezes. (HAS)
UF bucranes
CN D.DG.AFU.AFU.BCW.ALO

Buddhism
BM.610 (A,L,B,R)
ALT **Buddhist**
CN B.BM.BZY.AFU.AFU

Buddhism, Ch'an
USE **Ch'an**

Buddhism, Hinayana
USE **Hinayana**

Buddhism, Mahayana
USE **Mahayana**

Buddhism, Pali
USE **Theravada**

Buddhism, Southern
USE **Theravada**

Buddhism, Theravada
USE **Theravada**

Buddhism, Vajrayana
USE **Vajrayana**

Buddhism, Zen
USE **Zen**

budgeting
KG.52
SN Planning, coordinating, and allocating financial resources and expenditures.
CN K.KG.AFU.AFU.ARI.BIQ

budgets
VW.817 (L)
ALT **budget**
CN V.VW.AFU.ARI.AFU.BIQ.AXC

Budu
FL.521
UF Mabudu
CN F.FL.ALO.AFU.AXC.ALO.ALO.
BIQ.AFU.ALO.ALO

bufetes
TG.736
ALT **bufete**
SN Small Spanish tables, usually in a lady's room. (BURR2)
CN V.TG.AFU.AFU.BIQ.BOK.ALO.
CLM.AXC.AFU

bufetillos
TG.567
ALT **bufetillo**
SN Castilian name for small writing tables with hidden places for jewels and other valuables. (BUENO)
CN V.TG.AFU.AFU.AXC.ALO.BZY.
FUA.AFU

buff
USE **brownish pink**
dark orange yellow
grayish yellow
light grayish yellowish brown
light orange
light yellowish brown
moderate orange
moderate orange yellow
moderate yellow
moderate yellowish pink
pale orange yellow
pale yellow
pale yellowish pink
yellowish gray
yellowish white

buff ware
FL.3024
UF ware, buff
CN F.FL.ALO.AXC.ARI.BIQ.ALO.AXC.ALO

buff ware, gritty
USE **gritty buff ware**

buff ware, red-washed
USE **red-washed buff ware**

buff yellow
USE **moderate yellow**

buff, cream
USE **pale yellow**

buff, dull
USE **grayish yellowish pink**
moderate orange yellow
pale orange yellow
pale yellowish pink

buff, light
USE **pale orange yellow**
pale yellow

buff, orange
USE **brilliant yellow**
light orange yellow
light yellow
moderate orange yellow
moderate yellow
moderate yellowish pink
strong yellow

buff, pale pinkish
USE **pale orange yellow**

buff, yellow
USE **grayish yellow**
light yellowish brown
moderate orange yellow
pale orange yellow
pale yellow

buffer zones
RG.286 (L)
ALT **buffer zone**
SN Strips established to separate and protect one type of land use from another (e.g., industry versus housing). (LOC)
UF zones, buffer
CN V.RG.ALO.AFU.ALO.BIQ.AFU

buffers
TB.708 (N)
ALT **buffer**
SN Tools used for cutting horseshoe nails. (KNIGHT)
UF clinch cutters
cutters, clinch
CN V.TB.AFU.BCW.BIQ.ARI.ALO.ALO.AFU

buffet stools
TG.239
ALT **buffet stool**
SN 16th-century English and early 17th-century American stools, usually upholstered and covered with sumptuous fabric and fringe.(FORMAN) Term also applied to a variety of small, low stools generally with socketed legs.
UF cricket stools (buffet stools)
stools, buffet
stools, cricket (buffet stools)
CN V.TG.AFU.AFU.ALO.AFU.ALO.AFU.ALO

buffets (armoires)
USE **armoires**

buffets (sideboard tables)
USE **sideboard tables**

buffets (sideboards)
TG.588
ALT **buffet (sideboard)**
SN Term used loosely for a variety of serving cupboards or tables since the 16th century, now generally called **sideboards.** (FAIRB)
CN V.TG.AFU.AFU.AXC.ALO.CRG.ALO

buffing
USE **polishing**

buffing compositions
MT.2576
SN Materials used for buffing or polishing metals, originally of dolomitic lime with from 18 to 25% saponifiable grease as a bond. (MH)
UF compositions, buffing
CN M.MT.AFU.ARI.CRG.AXC.AFU

buffs
TB.508
ALT **buff**
SN Devices, such as sticks or blocks, having a soft absorbant surface; used to apply polishing material. (W)
CN V.TB.AFU.ARI.EWY.ALO.ARI

buggies (equipment)
TB.545
ALT **buggy (equipment)**
SN Devices for transporting concrete. (DAC)
UF carts, concrete
concrete carts
CN V.TB.AFU.BCW.ALO.AFU

Buhagana
USE **Macuna**

buhl
USE **boulle work**

buhl saws
TB.1011 (N)
ALT **buhl saw**
SN Fretsaws having a very deep frame and a short blade; used for inlay work. (DISSTO)
UF inlaying saws
saws, buhl
saws, inlaying
CN V.TB.AFU.BCW.CFS.ALO.AFU.EWY.BCW.BCW.AFU

buhl work
USE **boulle work**

builder-designed houses
RK.284 (B)
ALT **builder-designed house**
UF houses, builder-designed
CN V.RK.AFU.ALO.ALO.AXC.ALO.ARI.ALO

builders
HG.585 (A,B)
ALT **builder**
CN H.HG.AFU.AXC.BZY.AFU.AXC

builders' finish hardware
USE **finish hardware**

builders' guides
VW.528
ALT **builder's guide**
UF carpenters' handbooks
guides, builders'
handbooks, carpenters'
CN V.VW.AFU.ALO.AFU.AFU.ALO.BCW.AFU

builders' hardware
USE **finish hardware**

building
USE **construction**

building berths
USE **slipways**

building board
MT.2213 (L,B)
SN Multipurpose structural insulating board. (STEIN)
UF board, building
CN M.MT.AFU.ALO.ARI.AFU

building board, fiber
USE **fiberboard**

building brick
MT.94
SN Brick made from natural clay and having no special surface treatment. (W)
UF brick, building

brick, common
common brick
CN M.MT.AFU.AFU.AFU.AXC.ALO.AFU.ALO.ARI

building brick, modular
USE **modular building brick**

building caretakers
USE **caretakers**

building codes
VW.1002 (A,L,B)
ALT **building code**
SN Laws, ordinances, or government regulations concerning fitness for habitation setting forth standards and requirements for the construction, maintenance, operation, occupancy, use, or appearance of buildings, premises, and dwelling units. (BLACKS)
UF building laws
building regulations
codes, building
laws, building
regulations, building
CN V.VW.AFU.ARI.ALO.BCW.AFU.AFU.AFU.CLM.ALO.AFU

building diagnostics
KG.16 (A)
SN Judging how well a building performs its functions, through an understanding of the building's purpose, present use, environment, and history.
UF diagnostics, building
CN K.KG.AFU.AFU.AFU.BZY.AFU

building envelopes
BM.480
SN Use for the three-dimensional space within which a structure is permitted to be built on a zoning lot;(LOFZ) used especially in relation to zoning regulations concerned with land use and access to light and air.
UF bulk envelopes
envelopes, building
envelopes, bulk
CN B.BM.BCW.DUC.AFU

building equipment
USE **construction equipment**

building evaluation
USE **post-occupancy evaluation**

building failures
BM.1031 (A)
UF failures, building
CN B.BM.CFS.AXC.CLM.ALO.BZY.ALO

building heating systems
USE **heating systems**

building land
USE **building sites**

building laws
USE **building codes**

building lines
BM.481 (L,B)
SN Lines on a land plot beyond which the law forbids the erection of a building. (PUTNAM)
UF lines, building
CN B.BM.BCW.DUC.ALO

building lots
USE **lots**

building materials
MT.2382 (A,L,B,R)
UF architectural materials
construction materials
materials, architectural
materials, building
materials, construction
CN M.MT.AFU.ARI.BZY

building paper
MT.1927 (L)
SN Paper used for insulation, as in walls, roofs, and between floors. (W)
UF paper, building
paper, sheathing
sheathing paper
CN M.MT.AFU.AFU.ARI.ALO.ALO.AXC.ARI.ALO

building pathology
KG.17
SN Use for the evaluation of building performance in terms of technical and physical aspects of structures after construction, such as structural integrity, mechanical system performance, and properties of materials. (PC)
UF pathology, building
CN K.KG.AFU.AFU.AFU.BZY.AFU.AFU

building permits
VW.378 (L)
ALT **building permit**
SN Permits required by local governmental bodies for new building, or for major alteration or expansion of existing structures. Applications, building plans, estimated costs, and a fee are usually required before a permit is issued. (BLACKS)
UF lining petitions
permits, building
petitions, lining
CN V.VW.AFU.AFU.ALO.DUC.AXC.AFU

building plots
USE **building sites**

building programs
VW.69 (A)
ALT **building program**
SN Written statements setting forth design objectives, constraints, and criteria for a building project, including space requirements and relationships, site requirements, and other considerations. (MEANS)
UF programs, building
CN V.VW.AFU.AFU.AFU.ELK.AFU

building regulations
USE **building codes**

building sand
MT.2069
SN Selected sand used for concrete, for mortar, for laying bricks, and for plastering. (MH)
UF sand, building
CN M.MT.AFU.AFU.ARI.BOK.ALO.BOK.AFU

building sections
USE **longitudinal sections**

building security
USE **burglary protection**

building sites
RG.207 (A,L,B)
ALT **building site**
UF building land
building plots
construction sites
land, building
plots, building
sites, building
sites, construction
CN V.RG.AFU.AFU.DZW.ALO

building slips
USE **slipways**

building stone
MT.899 (L)
SN Any stone used for building.
UF stone, building
CN M.MT.AFU.AFU.AFU.DCU.ARI.AFU

building surveys
VW.364 (B)
ALT **building survey**
UF surveys, building
CN V.VW.AFU.AFU.ALO.DCU.AFU

building systems
RT.1281
ALT **building system**
UF systems, building
CN V.RT.ALO

building, bombproof
USE **bombproof construction**

building, stormproof
USE **stormproof construction**

buildings
RK.4 (A,L,B,R)
ALT **building**
SN Use for structures, generally enclosed, that are used or intended to be used for sheltering an activity or occupancy.
CN V.RK.AFU.AFU.AFU.AFU

buildings, abandoned
USE **derelict buildings**

buildings, administration
USE **administration buildings**

buildings, administrative office
USE **administration buildings**

buildings, administrative services
USE **administration buildings**

buildings, agricultural
USE **agricultural buildings**

buildings, airport
USE **airport buildings**

buildings, apartment
USE **apartment houses**

buildings, apsidal
USE **apsidal buildings**

buildings, assembly
USE **assembly halls**

buildings, association
USE **societies' buildings**

buildings, athletics
USE **sports buildings**

buildings, bank
USE **banks**

buildings, business
USE **commercial buildings**

buildings, capitol
USE **capitols**

buildings, church
USE **churches**

buildings, civic
USE **public buildings**

buildings, commercial
USE **commercial buildings**

buildings, communications
USE **communications buildings**

buildings, community
USE **community centers**

buildings, computer
USE **computer centers**

buildings, containment
USE **reactor containment buildings**

buildings, conventual
USE **convents**

buildings, cultural
USE **cultural centers**

buildings, demountable
USE **demountable buildings**

buildings, derelict
USE **derelict buildings**

buildings, earth sheltered
USE **earth sheltered buildings**

buildings, educational
USE **schools**

buildings, embassy
USE **embassy buildings**

buildings, employees'
USE **employees' buildings**

buildings, energy efficient
USE **energy efficient buildings**

buildings, entertainment
USE **entertainment buildings**

buildings, exhibition
USE **exhibition buildings**

buildings, experimental
USE **experimental buildings**

buildings, exposition
USE **exhibition buildings**

buildings, factory
USE **factories**

buildings, fair
USE **exhibition buildings**

buildings, farm
USE **farm buildings**

buildings, floating
USE **floating buildings**

buildings, foundation
USE **societies' buildings**

buildings, fraternal
USE **fraternal lodges**

buildings, funerary
USE **funerary buildings**

buildings, government
USE **public buildings**

buildings, government office
USE **government office buildings**

buildings, health care
USE **health facilities**

buildings, heritage
USE **historic buildings**

buildings, high
USE **skyscrapers**

buildings, high-rise
USE **high-rise buildings**

buildings, historic
USE **historic buildings**

buildings, horticultural
USE **horticultural buildings**

buildings, illegal
USE **illegal buildings**

buildings, industrial
USE **industrial buildings**

buildings, intelligent
USE **intelligent buildings**

buildings, landmark
USE **landmark buildings**

buildings, legislative
USE **legislative buildings**

buildings, listed
USE **landmark buildings**

buildings, livestock
USE **animal housing**

buildings, local authority
USE **municipal buildings**

buildings, local government
USE **municipal buildings**

buildings, loft
USE **loft buildings**

buildings, low-energy
USE **energy efficient buildings**

buildings, low-rise
USE **low-rise buildings**

buildings, masonic
USE **masonic buildings**

buildings, medium-rise
USE **mid-rise buildings**

buildings, mercantile
USE **mercantile buildings**

buildings, mid-rise
USE **mid-rise buildings**

buildings, military
USE **military buildings**

buildings, mimetic
USE **mimetic buildings**

buildings, mine
USE **mine buildings**

buildings, mobile
USE **portable buildings**

buildings, movable
USE **portable buildings**

buildings, multipurpose
USE **multipurpose buildings**

buildings, multistory
USE **multistory buildings**

buildings, municipal
USE **municipal buildings**

buildings, office
USE **office buildings**

buildings, organizations'
USE **societies' buildings**

buildings, out-patient
USE **clinics**

buildings, parliament
USE **parliament buildings**

buildings, personnel
USE **employees' buildings**

buildings, physical education
USE **physical education buildings**

buildings, portable
USE **portable buildings**

buildings, public
USE **public buildings**

buildings, public safety
USE **public safety buildings**

buildings, railway
USE **railway buildings**

buildings, reactor containment
USE **reactor containment buildings**

buildings, recreation
USE **recreation buildings**

buildings, religious
USE **religious buildings**

buildings, research
USE **research buildings**

buildings, residential
USE **dwellings**

buildings, revolving
USE **revolving buildings**

buildings, service station
USE **service stations**

buildings, slab
USE **slab blocks**

buildings, smart
USE **intelligent buildings**

buildings, societies'
USE **societies' buildings**

buildings, society and association
USE **societies' buildings**

buildings, solar
USE **solar buildings**

buildings, spa
USE **spas**

buildings, sports
USE **sports buildings**

buildings, store
USE **stores**

buildings, sun-heated
USE **solar buildings**

buildings, tall
USE **skyscrapers**

buildings, temporary
USE **temporary buildings**

buildings, terminal (airports)
USE **airport terminals**

buildings, textile mill
USE **textile mills**

buildings, tower
USE **tower buildings**

buildings, transportable
USE **portable buildings**

buildings, transportation
USE **transportation buildings**

buildings, underground
USE **underground buildings**

buildings, underwater
USE **underwater buildings**

buildings, welfare
USE **welfare buildings**

buildings, windowless
USE **windowless buildings**

built-in furniture
TG.792 (A,L,B)
UF fitted furniture
furniture, built-in
furniture, fitted
CN V.TG.AFU.ARI.AXC

built-up beams
RT.294
ALT **built-up beam**
SN Use for solid beams, whether of metal, wood, or concrete, which are made up of separate parts fastened together.
UF beams, built-up
beams, compound
compound beams
CN V.RT.AFU.AFU.AFU.BCW.ALO.AFU.ARI

built-up roofing
MT.2394
SN Continuous roof covering of laminations or piles of saturated or coated felts, alternated with layers of bitumen and surfaced with mineral aggregate or asphaltic materials. (STEIN)
UF composition roofing
roofing, built-up
roofing, composition
CN M.MT.AFU.ARI.BZY.AXC.ALO.AFU

Bujinga
USE **Nanga**

Buka
FL.3664
CN F.FL.ALO.BOK.ALO.BOK.ALO

Bukhara School
FL.3600
UF Bokhara School
CN F.FL.ALO.BIQ.AFU.IRA.AFU.AFU

bulb plants
USE **bulbs**

bulbous domes
USE **onion domes**

bulbous feet
USE **bun feet**

bulbous legs
USE **baluster legs**

bulbs
RD.267 (L)
ALT **bulb**
SN Plants with swollen, underground food-storage organs ringed with fleshy scale-like leaves enclosing next year's buds.
UF bulb plants
plants, bulb
CN V.RD.ARI.AFU.BCW.ALO.ALO.ALO.AFU.ARI

Bulgarian
FL.3043 (L,B)
CN F.FL.ALO.BCW.AFU.BCW

Buli
FL.496 (L)
UF Long-faced Style
Luba, Northern
Northern Luba
CN F.FL.ALO.AFU.AXC.ALO.ALO.BCW.BCW.AFU

bulk envelopes
USE **building envelopes**

bulkheads
RT.588 (A,N)
ALT **bulkhead**
SN Walls used to resist pressure caused by rock or water, such as to separate land and water areas. (BROOKS)
CN V.RT.AFU.AFU.AFU.BIQ.BUE.AFU.ALO.AXC.AFU

bulky color
USE **volume color**

bull floats
TB.594
ALT **bull float**
SN Wood, aluminum, or magnesium boards mounted on poles; used to spread and smooth freshly placed, horizontal concrete surfaces. (MEANS)
UF floats, bull
CN V.TB.AFU.BCW.BCW.ALO.DIO.ALO

bull header
MT.2761
SN In masonry, a brick having one rounded corner, usually laid with the short face exposed to form the brick sill under and beyond a window frame; also used as a quoin or around doorways. (PUTNAM)
UF header, bull
CN M.MT.AFU.AXC.BIQ.ALO.ALO.AFU

bull laurel
USE **magnolia graniflora**

bull's-eye windows
USE **oculi**

bulldozers
TB.33 (L,N,B)
ALT **bulldozer**
SN Tractors with caterpillar treads, used to push away debris for clearing an area. (PUTNAM)
UF dozers
CN V.TB.AFU.ARI.AFU.ARI.AFU

bullet catches
TF.44
ALT **bullet catch**
SN Door latches employing a spring-loaded steel ball. The loaded ball holds the door closed but rolls free when the door is pulled. (MEANS)
UF catches, bullet
CN V.TF.AFU.AFU.AFU.AFU.BCW.AXC

bullet-resistant glass
MT.286
UF bulletproof glass
glass, bullet-resistant
glass, bulletproof
CN M.MT.AFU.AFU.AFU.BIQ.AFU.AXC.CXA.AFU

bulletins
USE **newsletters**

bulletins, church
USE **church bulletins**

bulletins, news
USE **news bulletins**

bulletproof glass
USE **bullet-resistant glass**

bullnose brick
MT.71
UF brick, bullnose
CN M.MT.AFU.AFU.AFU.AXC.ALO.AFU.AFU.AFU.ARI

bullnose planes
TB.923 (N)
ALT **bullnose plane**
SN Small planes whose mouths can be adjusted for coarse or fine work; used in corners and other difficult to reach places. (PUTNAM)
UF bullnose rabbet planes
planes, bullnose
planes, bullnose rabbet
rabbet planes, bullnose
CN V.TB.AFU.BCW.CFS.ALO.AFU.DUC.ALO.BUE.AFU

bullnose rabbet planes
USE **bullnose planes**

bullnose steps
RT.1113
ALT **bullnose step**
SN Steps, usually the lowest in a flight, having one or both ends rounded to a semicircle and projecting beyond the face of the stair string and the newel. (HAS)
UF steps, bullnose
CN V.RT.AFU.BIQ.AXC.ALO.BIQ.AFU.AFU.AFU

bullrings
RK.1060 (B)
ALT **bullring**
CN V.RK.AFU.ALO.ALO.EWY.AXC.BIQ.ALO.ALO

bulls
VW.966 (L)
ALT **bull**
SN Formal documents issued by the pope that are sealed with a bulla (a round, usually lead, seal) or sealed with a red-ink imprint of the device on the bulla.
UF papal bulls
CN V.VW.AFU.ARI.ALO.ALO.AFU.ARI

Bulom
USE **Sapi-Portuguese**
Sherbro

bulrush
MT.1032
CN M.MT.AFU.AFU.ALO.BIQ.AXC.AXC.AFU

Bulu
FL.410 (L)
UF Bubi
CN F.FL.ALO.AFU.AXC.ALO.AFU.ARI.ALO

bulwarks
USE **ramparts**

bumpers
USE **door bumpers**

bumpers, door
USE **door bumpers**

bun feet
TG.904
ALT **bun foot**
SN Flattened ball feet, used on furniture from the mid-17th century. (BEARD)
UF bulbous feet
feet, bulbous
feet, bun
feet, onion
onion feet
pieds d'oignon
CN V.TG.ALO.DZW.AFU.BCW

buna N
USE **nitrile elastomer**

bunas
USE **styrene-butadiene rubber**

Bunda
USE **Mbun**

Bundelkhand
FL.2267 (L)
CN F.FL.ALO.ARI.AXC.ALO.AFU.BZY.BCW.AFU.AFU

Bundi
FL.2289
CN F.FL.ALO.ARI.AXC.ALO.AFU.BZY.BCW.BCW.AXC

bundle piers
RT.186
ALT **bundle pier**
UF bundle pillars
piers, bundle
pillars, bundle
CN V.RT.AFU.AFU.AFU.AXC.CRG.AFU.AFU.AFU

bundle pillars
USE **bundle piers**

bung borers, cylindrical
USE **cylinder augers**

bung floggers
USE **bungstarts**

bungalows
RK.229 (A,L,B,R)
ALT **bungalow**
CN V.RK.AFU.ALO.ALO.AXC.ALO.AFU.ALO

bunging adzes
TB.810 (N)
ALT **bunging adz**
SN Tools similar to rounding adzes, but used for rougher work, including, but not limited to, cross-cutting bungs and stock for bungs. (SALAM)
UF adzes, bunging
CN V.TB.AFU.BCW.CFS.ALO.AFU.AFU.AFU

bungstarters
USE **bungstarts**

bungstarts
TB.1088 (N)
ALT **bungstart**
UF bung floggers
bungstarters
floggers, bung
CN V.TB.AFU.BCW.CFS.ALO.ARI.ALO.ALO

Bunjin-ga
USE **Nanga**

Bunjinga
USE **Nanga**

bunk beds
TG.324 (L,N)
ALT **bunk bed**
SN Beds for two people with one sleeping place above the other in the manner of tiered bunks. (W)
UF beds, bunk
lits superposés
CN V.TG.AFU.AFU.ARI.AFU.AFU.ALO

bunkers
RK.864 (A)
ALT **bunker**
SN Fortification chambers mostly below

ground level built of reinforced concrete or similar material and usually provided with embrasures; also, dugouts that are reinforced (as with logs or bags of sand) and usually have firing slits. (W)
CN V.RK.AFU.ALO.ALO.DIO.ALO.ALO

bunkhouses
RK.219
ALT **bunkhouse**
SN Rough buildings often with bunk beds, used for sleeping quarters, as for ranch hands, migratory workers, and campers. (RHDEL2)
CN V.RK.AFU.ALO.ALO.AXC.AFU.ALO

Bunzlau pottery
FL.3387 (R)
UF pottery, Bunzlau
CN F.FL.ALO.BCW.ALO.AXC.DIO.BIQ.BCW.AFU

buon fresco
USE **fresco painting**

bur oak
MT.1233 (L)
UF mossy-cup oak
oak, bur
oak, mossy-cup
Quercus macrocarpa
CN M.MT.AFU.AFU.ALO.BIQ.DCU.AFU.AFU.AFU.IRA.AXC

bur reed
MT.1033
UF reed, bur
CN M.MT.AFU.AFU.ALO.BIQ.AXC.AXC.ALO

Bura
FL.227
CN F.FL.ALO.AFU.AXC.AFU.AFU.ALO.ARI.ARI

bureau beds
TG.341
ALT **bureau bed**
SN Deception beds concealed in a carcase that outwardly resembles a bureau. (GILBR2)
UF beds, bureau
bedsteads, buroe
buroe bedsteads
CN V.TG.AFU.AFU.ARI.AFU.AFU.BIQ.AFU.ALO

bureau-bookcases
TG.530
ALT **bureau-bookcase**
SN Use for English desks with a steeply sloping lid (usually a 45 degree angle) surmounted by a bookcase. (BEARD) For similar American examples use **desks and bookcases.**
UF desks, secretary
scrutoires (bureau-bookcases)
secretary desks
CN V.TG.AFU.AFU.AXC.ALO.BZY.BCW.AFU

bureau-cabinets
USE **fall-front desks**

bureau dressing tables
USE **bureau tables**

bureau tables
TG.523
ALT **bureau table**
SN Kneehole writing or dressing tables. (GILBR2)
UF bureau dressing tables
buroe dressing tables
combined dressing tables and desks
combined writing and dressing tables
desks, kneehole (bureau tables)
dressing tables and desks, combined
dressing tables, bureau
kneehole desks (bureau tables)
kneehole tables (bureau tables)
tables and desks, combined dressing
tables, bureau
tables, bureau dressing
tables, combined writing and dressing
tables, kneehole (bureau tables)
writing and dressing tables, combined
CN V.TG.AFU.AFU.AXC.ALO.BZY.AFU

bureaucrats
HG.661
ALT **bureaucrat**
CN H.HG.AFU.AXC.CFS.ALO

bureaus
TG.537
ALT **bureau**
SN English desks having a lid sloping at an acute angle (usually 45 degrees) that folds out as a writing surface, above drawers. (BEARD)
CN V.TG.AFU.AFU.AXC.ALO.BZY.BUE.ALO.AFU

bureaus (chests of drawers)
USE **chests of drawers**

bureaus, cheval
USE **cheval dressers**

bureaus, cylinder
USE **bureaux à cylindre**

bureaus, information
USE **information centers**

bureaux (kneehole desks)
USE **kneehole desks**

bureaux (writing tables)
USE **writing tables**

bureaux à cylindre
TG.527
ALT **bureau à cylindre**
SN Large French desks popular in the late Louis XV and the Louis XVI periods with a roll top in the shape of a quarter cylinder. This type was occasionally imitated in other countries, besides France, particularly in Germany and Scandinavia in the last decade of the 18th century and virtually every western country during the 19th and 20th centuries. (PC)
UF bureaus, cylinder
bureaux à la Kaunitz
bureaux à panse
bureaux à rouleau
cylinder bureaus
secrétaires à cylindre
secrétaires à panse
secrétaires à rouleau
CN V.TG.AFU.AFU.AXC.ALO.BZY.ARI.AFU

bureaux à dos d'âne
USE **bureaux en pente**

bureaux à gradin
TG.570
ALT **bureau à gradin**
SN Bureaux plats with a set of drawers or pigeonholes along one side of the top. (DDA)
CN V.TG.AFU.AFU.AXC.ALO.BZY.FUA.ARI.AFU

bureaux à la Bourgogne
USE **secrétaires à la Bourgogne**

bureaux à la Kaunitz
USE **bureaux à cylindre**

bureaux à panse
USE **bureaux à cylindre**

bureaux à rouleau
USE **bureaux à cylindre**

bureaux de dame
TG.577
ALT **bureau de dame**
CN V.TG.AFU.AFU.AXC.ALO.BZY.FUA.BUE.ALO

bureaux debout
TG.556
ALT **bureau debout**
SN French form of standing desk, sometimes having a pupitre. (PC)
CN V.TG.AFU.AFU.AXC.ALO.BZY.EFQ.AFU

bureaux en pente
TG.538
ALT **bureau en pente**
SN Slant-front desks generally intended for a woman's use. (PC)
UF bureaux à dos d'âne
bureaux en tombeau
secrétaires à dessus brisé
secrétaires à pupitre
secrétaires en pente
secrétaires en tombeau
CN V.TG.AFU.AFU.AXC.ALO.BZY.BUE.ALO.ALO

bureaux en pupitre
TG.568

ALT **bureau en pupitre**
SN Writing tables with a pop up reading stand. (PC)
CN V.TG.AFU.AFU.AXC.ALO.BZY.FUA.ALO

bureaux en tombeau
USE **bureaux en pente**

bureaux Mazarins
TG.542
ALT **bureau Mazarin**
SN Bureaux with two tiers of drawers flanking a kneehole recess, some forms intended to be used as writing desks, others as dressing tables; of a type popular in France during the second half of the 17th century. (PC)
CN V.TG.AFU.AFU.AXC.ALO.BZY.BZY.AFU

bureaux plats
TG.569
ALT **bureau plat**
SN Large flat-top writing tables, usually with drawers in the frieze. (PC)
CN V.TG.AFU.AFU.AXC.ALO.BZY.FUA.ARI

bureaux, dressing
USE **dressing tables**

burglar-proofing
USE **burglary protection**

burglary protection
KG.112 (A,L,B)
UF building security
burglar-proofing
housing security
protection, burglary
security, building
security, housing
CN K.KG.AFU.AFU.BCW.AFU.AFU

burgomaster chairs
USE **corner chairs**

burgomeister chairs
USE **corner chairs**

Burgundian
FL.3106 (A,L,R)
CN F.FL.ALO.BCW.ALO.ALO.AFU.BOK.ALO.ALO.ALO

Burgundy pitch
MT.1469
UF pitch, Burgundy
CN M.MT.AFU.AFU.ALO.BOK.AFU.AFU.AFU

Burgundy turpentine
MT.1468
UF turpentine, Burgundy
CN M.MT.AFU.AFU.ALO.BOK.AFU.AFU

Burgundy violet
USE **manganese violet**

burial chambers
RM.385 (A)
ALT **burial chamber**
UF chambers, burial
CN V.RM.AFU.DIO.AXC.BCW.AFU

burial grounds
USE **cemeteries**

Burial Mound I
FL.764
CN F.FL.ALO.ALO.ALO.AFU.AFU.AXC.ALO.AFU.AFU

Burial Mound II
FL.765
CN F.FL.ALO.ALO.ALO.AFU.AFU.AXC.ALO.AFU.ALO

Burial Mound period
FL.763
CN F.FL.ALO.ALO.ALO.AFU.AFU.AXC.ALO.AFU

burial mounds
RK.457 (A,L)
ALT **burial mound**
SN Use for piles of earth erected over grave sites; for piles of stones built over grave sites, use **cairns**; for piles of earth used generally and not over burials, use **mounds.**
UF barrows
barrows, long
conical mounds
kurgans
long barrows
mounds, burial
mounds, conical
tumuli
CN V.RK.AFU.ALO.ALO.BOK.AFU

burial records
VW.951
ALT **burial record**
UF records, burial
CN V.VW.AFU.ARI.AFU.DCU.ALO.AFU

burial registers
VW.970
ALT **burial register**
UF registers, burial
CN V.VW.AFU.ARI.ALO.ALO.AFU.BCW.ALO

buried cable maps
VW.203 (L)
ALT **buried cable map**
UF maps, buried cable
CN V.VW.AFU.AFU.AFU.FZU.AXC.AFU.ARI.AXC.CRG.AFU

buried cities
RD.40 (A,L)
ALT **buried city**
UF cities, buried
CN V.RD.AFU.ARI.ARI.AFU

burins
USE **gravers**

burl veneer
MT.2284
UF veneer, burl
CN M.MT.AFU.ALO.IRA.AFU

burlap
MT.1858 (L,B)
UF gunny
hessian
CN M.MT.AFU.AFU.ARI.ALO.ALO.ALO.ALO.ALO

burled walnut
MT.1318
UF walnut, burled
CN M.MT.AFU.AFU.ALO.BIQ.DCU.AFU.AFU.AFU.MQW.AFU

Burmese
FL.2308 (L,B)
CN F.FL.ALO.ARI.BCW.AFU

burn augers
TB.823 (N)
ALT **burn auger**
SN Augers whose points are heated to burn holes in wood and then twisted to enlarge the holes.
UF augers, burn
CN V.TB.AFU.BCW.CFS.ALO.AFU.ALO.ALO

burn brands
USE **brands**

burn care units
RM.293 (L)
ALT **burn care unit**
CN V.RM.AFU.DIO.AXC.AFU.AXC.AFU

burned brick
USE **fired brick**

burning awls
TB.832
ALT **burning awl**
SN Awls used for burning holes in wood, often to remove sap from trees. (SLOANE)
UF awls, burning
CN V.TB.AFU.BCW.CFS.ALO.AFU.ARI.ALO

burning in (painting)
KT.242
ALT **burned-in (painting)**
SN The stage of encaustic painting in which the surface of a painting is heated so that the colors may be manipulated and blended.
UF inustion
CN K.KT.AFU.ALO.DUC.CXA.ALO.ALO.ALO.AFU

burning in (photography)
KT.406
ALT **burned-in (photography)**
SN Use for the mechanical process employed in the darkroom to darken a portion of a print, by means of additional exposure. (HCOP)
CN K.KT.AFU.ALO.DUC.DIO.ARI.AXC.ALO

burnished ware, black (Helladic pottery)
USE **black burnished ware (Helladic pottery)**

burnished ware, dark-faced
USE **dark-faced burnished ware**

burnished ware, gray
USE **gray burnished ware**

burnished ware, gray (Syrian)
USE **Syrian gray-black ware**

burnished ware, red
USE **red burnished ware**

burnished ware, red-black
USE **Khirbet Kerak ware**

burnished ware, red-pattern
USE **red-pattern burnished ware**

burnishers
TB.509 (N)
ALT **burnisher**
SN Implements with a hard smooth rounded end or surface; used for smoothing and polishing. (MAYER)
CN V.TB.AFU.ARI.EWY.ALO.AXC

burnishing
KT.687 (L)
ALT **burnished**
SN Making shiny or lustrous by rubbing with a tool that compacts or smooths. (W)
CN K.KT.AFU.ALO.GRC.BCW.ARI.AFU

burnishing (photography)
KT.407
ALT **burnished (photography)**
SN Method of obtaining a glossy surface on collodion prints by pressing them between rollers.
CN K.KT.AFU.ALO.DUC.DIO.ARI.AXC.ARI

burnishing, barrel
USE **barreling**

burnt brick
USE **fired brick**

burnt carmine
MT.1619
SN A deep brownish purple pigment made by carefully roasting or charring carmine. (MAYER)
UF carmine, burnt
CN M.MT.AFU.AFU.ARI.AFU.AFU.ALO.ALO.ARI.ALO.AXC

burnt daga
MT.2055
UF daga, burnt
CN M.MT.AFU.AFU.ARI.BOK.AFU.ALO.AFU

burnt green earth
USE **transparent brown**

burnt Italian earth
USE **dark reddish orange**

burnt Italian ocher
USE **dark reddish orange**

burnt lime
USE **quicklime**

burnt ocher
MT.1627
UF gebrannter Ocker
ocher, burnt
ocre brûlée
CN M.MT.AFU.AFU.ARI.AFU.AFU.ALO.ALO.ARI.ARI.ARI

burnt ocher (color)
USE **moderate reddish orange**

burnt-oil varnish
USE **litho varnish**

burnt sienna
MT.1629
UF brown, Caledonian
Caledonian brown
gebrannte Siena
Italian earth
sienna, burnt
terre de Sienne brûlée
CN M.MT.AFU.AFU.ARI.AFU.AFU.ALO.ALO.ARI.ARI.AXC.AFU

burnt sienna (color)
USE **dark reddish orange**
strong reddish brown

burnt terre verte
USE **transparent brown**

burnt umber
MT.1632
UF brown, chestnut
brown, jacaranda
chestnut brown
euchrome
jacaranda brown
terre d'ombre brûlée
umber, burnt
Umbra gebrannt
CN M.MT.AFU.AFU.ARI.AFU.AFU.ALO.ALO.ARI.ARI.BCW.AFU

burnt umber (color)
USE **grayish reddish brown**
moderate brown

buroe bedsteads
USE **bureau beds**

buroe dressing tables
USE **bureau tables**

Burr arch trusses
RT.360
ALT **Burr arch truss**
SN Trusses, patented in the early 19th century by Theodore Burr, combining a wood arch with a series of metal king-post trusses.
UF trusses, Burr arch
CN V.RT.AFU.AFU.AFU.BCW.CLM.AFU.AFU.AFU.ALO

bursting strength
BM.959
SN Ability of a material, usually in sheet form, to withstand hydrostatic pressure without rupture. (MH)
UF strength, bursting
CN B.BM.CFS.AXC.BZY.BOK.CLM.AFU

burying-grounds
USE **cemeteries**

bus lanes
RM.484 (L)
ALT **bus lane**
UF lanes, bus
CN V.RM.ALO.ALO.ALO.ALO.BUE.ALO

Bus Mordeh
FL.3004
CN F.FL.ALO.AXC.ARI.BIQ.AFU.AFU.BCW

bus rapid transit
USE **bus transit systems**

bus route maps
VW.209
ALT **bus route map**
UF maps, bus route
CN V.VW.AFU.AFU.AFU.FZU.AXC.AFU.ARI.AXC.DIO.AFU

bus shelters
RK.1248 (A,B)
ALT **bus shelter**
SN Use for minimal structures providing weather protection for patrons at bus stops; for more substantial buildings along bus routes, usually with sales and service facilities, use **bus stations.**
UF shelters, bus
CN V.RK.AFU.ALO.ALO.GLI.AFU.ARI.AFU

bus stations
RK.1249 (A,L,B)
ALT **bus station**
SN Use only for intermediate stops along bus routes, usually containing sales and service facilities; use **bus shelters** for structures at bus stops affording weather protection but having no sales or service facilties; use **bus terminals** only to refer to buildings or other structures located at bus route endpoints.
UF stations, bus
CN V.RK.AFU.ALO.ALO.GLI.AFU.ARI.ALO

bus stops
RM.470
ALT **bus stop**
CN V.RM.ALO.ALO.ALO.ALO.AFU

bus systems
USE **bus transit systems**

bus terminals
RK.1250 (A,L)
ALT **bus terminal**
SN Use only to refer to buildings or other structures placed at the end-points of bus routes; use **bus stations** only for intermediate stops along bus routes; use **bus shelters** for structures at bus stops affording weather protection but having no sales or service facilities.
UF motor bus terminals
terminals, bus
terminals, motor bus
CN V.RK.AFU.ALO.ALO.GLI.AFU.ARI.ARI

bus transit
USE **bus transit systems**

bus transit systems
RD.95
ALT **bus transit system**
UF bus rapid transit
bus systems
bus transit
motor bus systems
rapid transit, bus
systems, bus
systems, bus transit
systems, motor bus
transit systems, bus
transit, bus
CN V.RD.ALO.ARI.AFU.AFU.AFU.AFU

busducts
USE **busways**

bush
RD.297
UF bushland
CN V.RD.ARI.ALO.ALO.BIQ.AFU

bushhammers
TB.603 (N)
ALT **bushhammer**
SN Chunky hammers with two striking surfaces covered with rows of pyramidal metal teeth or points; used in stone carving. (MAYER)
UF hammers, bush
CN V.TB.AFU.BCW.BCW.ALO.EFQ.ALO

bushland
USE **bush**

Bushmen
USE **San**

Bushong
USE **Kuba Kingdom**

Bushongo
USE **Kuba Kingdom**
Mbala (Kuba Folk Style)

business
KG.163 (L,R)
SN Use for the broad area of commercial or mercantile activity involving the exchange of commodities, services, or financial resources.(W) For the activity of buying, selling, or bartering commodities, use **trade.**
UF commerce
CN K.KG.AFU.ALO.AFU

business announcements
VW.315 (L)
ALT **business announcement**
UF announcements, business
CN V.VW.AFU.AFU.ALO.BOK.AFU.AFU

business buildings
USE **commercial buildings**

business cards
VW.561 (L,N,R)
ALT **business card**
SN Small cards bearing the name and address of a business concern and one of its representatives, and often some descriptive or advertising matter. (GAHLM)
UF advertising cards
cards, advertising
cards, business
cards, show
cards, trade
cards, tradesmen's
show cards
trade cards
tradesmen's cards
CN V.VW.AFU.ALO.AFU.ARI.ALO

business centers
USE **central business districts**

business colleges
RK.806 (B)
ALT **business college**
SN Schools for training students in the clerical aspects of business and commerce, such as typing and bookkeeping. (RHDEL2)
UF colleges, business
colleges, commercial
commercial colleges
CN V.RK.AFU.ALO.ALO.CXA.ARI.ALO.AXC.AFU

business directories
USE **commercial directories**

business districts
RG.266 (B)
ALT **business district**
UF areas, commercial
commercial areas
commercial districts
commercial zones
districts, business
districts, commercial
zones, commercial
CN V.RG.ALO.AFU.ALO.AFU

business districts, central
USE **central business districts**

business enterprises
HG.841 (L)
ALT **business enterprise**
UF business organizations
businesses
commercial enterprises
enterprises
enterprises, business
enterprises, commercial
organizations, business
CN H.HG.ALO.BOK

business facilities
USE **commercial buildings**

business letters
VW.17 (L)
ALT **business letter**
UF letters, business
CN V.VW.AFU.AFU.AFU.BIQ.AFU.ARI.AFU

business organizations
USE **business enterprises**

business records
VW.961 (L,R)
ALT **business record**
SN Records generated by a commercial or industrial enterprise. (GAHLM)
UF company records
records, business
records, company
CN V.VW.AFU.ARI.ALO.AFU

business schools
RK.805
ALT **business school**
UF commercial schools
schools, business
schools, commercial
CN V.RK.AFU.ALO.ALO.CXA.ARI.ALO.AXC

businesses
USE **business enterprises**

businessmen
HG.403 (L)
ALT **businessman**
SN Persons who transact business, especially business executives. (W)
CN H.HG.AFU.AXC.BOK.BIQ

busta
RK.462
ALT **bustum**
SN Ancient Roman enclosures for cremation and for deposition of cremation urns.
CN V.RK.AFU.ALO.ALO.BOK.ARI.AFU.AFU.AFU

bustan
USE **bustanim**

bustanim
RK.1440 (A)
UF bostan
bustan
CN V.RK.ALO.AFU.AFU.BCW.ALO.AFU

busways
RT.1348 (L)

ALT **busway**
SN Electric conduits prefabricated in sections and containing heavy conductors for transmission of large currents at relatively low voltage. (W)
UF busducts
CN V.RT.ALO.ARI.ALO.CRG.AFU

butane
MT.1012 (L)
CN M.MT.AFU.AFU.ALO.BCW.ALO.ALO.AFU

butanol
MT.2684 (L)
UF alcohol, normal butyl
butyl alcohol, normal
normal butyl alcohol
CN M.MT.AFU.ARI.HZS.AFU.BOK.AFU.ALO.AFU

butcher paper
MT.1958
UF paper, butcher
CN M.MT.AFU.AFU.ARI.ALO.ALO.AXC.ARI.CFS.AFU

butler's desks
TG.477
ALT **butler's desk**
SN Chests of drawers with a secretary drawer at the top. (MONTGO)
UF desks, butler's
CN V.TG.AFU.AFU.AXC.ALO.BCW.ALO

butler's pantries
RM.202
ALT **butler's pantry**
SN Service rooms between kitchens and dining rooms, typically equipped with counters, a sink, and storage space for china and silver. (RHDEL2)
UF pantries, butler's
CN V.RM.AFU.DIO.ALO.DCU.CLM.AFU

butlers (cellerets)
USE **cellerets**

butments
USE **abutments**

butments, arched
USE **flying buttresses**

butt chisels
TB.854
ALT **butt chisel**
SN Chisels with a short blade; used especially for setting hinges on doors and door frames. (MEANS)
UF chisels, butt
CN V.TB.AFU.BCW.CFS.ALO.AFU.BUE.ALO.AFU

butt hinges
TF.97
ALT **butt hinge**
SN Hinges mortised into the edge of a door and the edge of the jamb against which the edge of the door will butt when closed. (DITTRI)
UF butts
hinges, butt
CN V.TF.AFU.AFU.AFU.AFU.CLM.AFU.ARI

butt hinges, capped
USE **capped butt hinges**

butt hinges, loose-joint
USE **loose-joint hinges**

butt hinges, pocket
USE **pocket butt hinges**

butt hinges, rising
USE **rising hinges**

butt joints
TF.579
ALT **butt joint**
SN Square joints between two members at right angles to each other. The contact surface of the outstanding member is cut square and fits flush to the surface of the other member. (MEANS)
UF end joints
joints, butt
joints, end
CN V.TF.ALO.AFU.BOK

butt joints, beveled
USE **oblique joints**

butt joints, oblique
USE **oblique joints**

butt stiles
USE **hinge stiles**

butter cupboards
USE **livery cupboards**

butterfly chairs
USE **Hardoy chairs**

butterfly hinges
TF.104
ALT **butterfly hinge**
SN Surface-mounted cabinet hinges that have the appearance of a butterfly when opened out flat. (DITTRI)
UF hinges, butterfly
CN V.TF.AFU.AFU.AFU.AFU.CLM.AFU.AXC

butterfly joints
TF.692
ALT **butterfly joint**
UF joints, butterfly
CN V.TF.ALO.ARI.AXC.ARI.BUE.AFU

butterfly roofs
RT.412 (L,B)
ALT **butterfly roof**
SN Use for roofs sloping downward from eaves on either side to a central valley.
UF butterfly-shell roofs
roofs, butterfly
roofs, butterfly-shell
CN V.RT.AFU.AFU.AFU.BIQ.ARI.AFU.AFU.AFU.AFU

butterfly-shell roofs
USE **butterfly roofs**

butterfly tables
TG.671
ALT **butterfly table**
UF tables, butterfly
CN V.TG.AFU.AFU.BIQ.BOK.AFU.AXC.AFU

butteries
USE **pantries**

buttering trowels
TB.632
ALT **buttering trowel**
SN Small trowels used to spread mortar on brick before it is laid. (DAC)
UF trowels, buttering
CN V.TB.AFU.BCW.BCW.ALO.HCQ.ALO

butternut
MT.1323 (L)
UF walnut, white
white walnut
CN M.MT.AFU.AFU.ALO.BIQ.DCU.AFU.AFU.AFU.MQW.AXC.ALO

buttery hatches
RT.902
ALT **buttery hatch**
SN Half-doors giving entrance to a buttery and over which are served out the contents of the buttery. (RS)
UF hatches, buttery
CN V.RT.AFU.ARI.AFU.AFU.AXC.AFU

buttes
RD.208
ALT **butte**
SN Use for erosional landforms that are carved from flat-lying sediment or rocks having resistant top layers and characterized as conspicuous, isolated flat-topped hills with relatively steep sides; smaller in extent than mesas.
CN V.RD.ARI.AFU.AXC.AFU.ALO.AFU.BCW

button bits
TB.1101
ALT **button bit**
SN Bits used to inscribe, smooth, and cut out circles from thin bone plates in the production of buttons. (MERCER)
UF bits, button
CN V.TB.ALO.ARI.ARI

button-headed bolts
USE **carriage bolts**

button pulls
TF.73
ALT **button pull**
UF pulls, button
CN V.TF.AFU.AFU.AFU.AFU.CFS.BCW.AFU.AXC

buttonball
USE **sycamore**

buttonwood
USE **sycamore**

buttress dams
RK.523 (L)
ALT **buttress dam**
UF dams, buttress
CN V.RK.AFU.ALO.ALO.CFS.AFU.ARI.AFU.ALO

buttress piers
RT.190
ALT **buttress pier**
SN Use for piers serving both as buttresses and as regular supporting and dividing elements.
UF piers, buttress
CN V.RT.AFU.AFU.AFU.AXC.CRG.AFU.ALO.ALO

buttresses
RT.72 (A,L,N,B,R)
ALT **buttress**
UF abamuri
CN V.RT.AFU.AFU.AFU.AXC.AXC

buttresses, angle
USE **angle buttresses**

buttresses, arch
USE **flying buttresses**

buttresses, arched
USE **flying buttresses**

buttresses, clasping
USE **clasping buttresses**

buttresses, diagonal
USE **diagonal buttresses**

buttresses, flying
USE **flying buttresses**

buttresses, hanging
USE **hanging buttresses**

buttresses, lateral
USE **lateral buttresses**

buttresses, setback
USE **setback buttresses**

butts
USE **butt hinges**

butts, skew
USE **kneelers (gable components)**

butyl acetate
MT.2693
SN A colorless liquid ester of acetic acid that has a fruity odor and is used as a solvent, especially in cellulose nitrate lacquers. (W)
UF acetate, butyl
acetate, N-butyl
acetate, normal butyl
butyl acetate, normal
N-butyl acetate
normal butyl acetate
CN M.MT.AFU.ARI.HZS.AFU.BOK.ALO.ALO

butyl acetate, normal
USE **butyl acetate**

butyl alcohol
MT.2683 (L)
SN Any of four flammable liquid alcohols derived from the butanes and used chiefly in organic synthesis and as solvents often in the form of their esters. (W)
UF alcohol, butyl
CN M.MT.AFU.ARI.HZS.AFU.BOK.AFU.ALO

butyl alcohol, normal
USE **butanol**

butyl lactate
MT.2661
SN A volatile solvent or diluent used in lacquers and other industrial coating materials as a retardant, to delay setting or drying. (MAYER)
UF lactate, butyl
CN M.MT.AFU.ARI.HZS.AFU.AFU

butyl rubber
MT.2082 (L)
UF elastomer, isobutylene-isoprene
isobutylene-isoprene elastomer
rubber, butyl
CN M.MT.AFU.AFU.ARI.BUE.AFU.AFU.AFU

butyral, polyvinyl
USE **polyvinyl butyral**

butyrate
MT.2125
SN Made by the esterification of cellulose with acetic acid and butyric acid in the presence of a catalyst; particularly valued for coatings, insulating types, varnishes, and lacquers. (MH)
UF acetate butyrate, cellulose
butyrate, cellulose acetate
CAB
cellulose acetate butyrate
CN M.MT.AFU.AFU.ARI.BUE.ALO.AXC.AFU.AXC

butyrate, cellulose acetate
USE **butyrate**

Buvayhid
USE **Buyid**

Buwaihid
USE **Buyid**

Buwayhid
USE **Buyid**

Buxus sempervirens
USE **boxwood**

Buye
USE **Hemba**

buyers
HG.404 (L)
ALT **buyer**
SN Persons who have charge of the selection, purchasing, pricing, and display of goods. (W)
UF purchasers
CN H.HG.AFU.AXC.BOK.BOK

buyers' guides
VW.349
ALT **buyer's guide**
UF guides, buyers'
CN V.VW.AFU.AFU.ALO.CXA.BIQ.AFU

Buyid
FL.3441 (L)
UF Buvayhid
Buwaihid
Buwayhid
CN F.FL.ALO.BIQ.AFU.BOK

buying
USE **purchasing**

Buzi
USE **Loma**

buzz saws
USE **circular saws**

Bwa
FL.382 (L)
UF Bobo-Ule
CN F.FL.ALO.AFU.AXC.AFU.AXC.ARI.ARI.AFU.ALO

Bwaka
USE **Ngbaka**

Bwende
FL.477
CN F.FL.ALO.AFU.AXC.ALO.ALO.AXC.ALO

bylaws
VW.772 (L,B)
ALT **bylaw**
SN Laws, ordinances, or regulations made by a public or private corporation, association, or unincorporated society for the regulation of its own local or internal affairs, for its dealings with others, or for the government of its members. (GAHLM)
CN V.VW.AFU.ARI.AFU.ALO.AXC

bylaws (municipal)
USE **ordinances**

bypass roads
USE **bypasses**

bypasses
RK.1550 (L,B)
ALT **bypass**
UF bypass roads
roads, bypass
CN V.RK.ALO.ALO.BIQ.ARI.ALO.ARI

byres
USE **dairy barns**

Byzantine
FL.3068 (A,L,B,R)
CN F.FL.ALO.BCW.ALO.AFU.ALO

Byzantine arches
USE **horseshoe arches**

Byzantine Renaissance
USE **Palaeologan**

Byzantine Revival
FL.3264 (R)
UF Neo-Byzantine
Revival, Byzantine
CN F.FL.ALO.BCW.ALO.AXC.CLM.ALO

Byzantine, Early
USE **Early Byzantine**

Byzantine, Late
USE **Late Byzantine**

Byzantine, Middle
USE **Middle Byzantine**

C-14 dating
USE **radiocarbon dating**

C-clamps
TB.1050 (N)
ALT **C-clamp**
SN Clamps in the shape of the letter C in which force is applied by rotating a threaded shaft through one jaw of the C to force the work against the other jaw; frequently used in carpentry and joinery. (MEANS)
UF circle clamps
circle-end clamps
clamps, C
clamps, circle
clamps, circle-end
clamps, G
clamps, gee
G-clamps
gee clamps
CN V.TB.AFU.BCW.CFS.ALO.ALO.BCW.ALO

C-scrolls
DG.65
ALT **C-scroll**
SN Ornamental scrolls that coil in only one direction, i.e., not reversing direction, as do S-scrolls.
CN D.DG.AFU.AFU.DOI.AFU

CA
USE **cellulose acetate**

CAB
USE **butyrate**

Cabahiba
USE **Parintintin**

Caballine phase
USE **Horse phase**

cabañas
RK.1071 (A)
ALT **cabaña**
CN V.RK.AFU.ALO.ALO.EWY.BCW.AFU.AFU

cabarets
RK.925 (A,L,B,R)
ALT **cabaret**
SN Use for cafélike facilities often with a dance floor or small stage and featuring entertainment generally of a improvisational, satirical, or topical nature.
CN V.RK.AFU.ALO.ALO.EFQ.ARI.AFU

cabin camps
USE **motor courts**

cabin door hooks
TF.152
ALT **cabin door hook**
SN Use for heavy hooks and eyes, generally used on marine installations. Distinguished from **cabin hooks,** which are generally used on cabinets.
UF door hooks, cabin
hooks, cabin door
CN V.TF.AFU.AFU.AFU.AFU.CXA.ALO

cabin hooks
TF.153
ALT **cabin hook**
SN Use for small hooks and eyes, generally used on cabinets. Distinguished from **cabin door hooks,** which are generally used on marine installations.
UF hooks, cabin
CN V.TF.AFU.AFU.AFU.AFU.CXA.ARI

cabinet beds
TG.342
ALT **cabinet bed**
UF beds, cabinet
CN V.TG.AFU.AFU.ARI.AFU.AFU.BIQ.AFU.ARI

cabinet bedsteads
USE **press beds**

cabinet card photographs
USE **cabinet photographs**

cabinet card photoprints
USE **cabinet photographs**

cabinet cards
USE **cabinet photographs**

cabinet chairs
TG.174
ALT **cabinet chair**
SN Form of late 19th-century commode chair, often associated with invalids, having a chamber pot concealed within a small cabinet under the seat; such cabinets usually have a door in the back so the chamber pot can be removed without disturbing the patient. (PC)
UF cabinet commode chairs
chairs, cabinet commode
commode chairs, cabinet
CN V.TG.AFU.AFU.ALO.AFU.AFU.ALO.BIQ.AFU

cabinet commode chairs
USE **cabinet chairs**

cabinet files
TB.874
ALT **cabinet file**
SN Single-cut files which are half-round on one side and flat on the other. (DAC)
UF files, cabinet
CN V.TB.AFU.BCW.CFS.ALO.AFU.CFS.AFU

cabinet knobs
TF.65
ALT **cabinet knob**
UF cupboard knobs
drawer knobs
knobs, cabinet
knobs, cupboard
knobs, drawer
CN V.TF.AFU.AFU.AFU.AFU.CFS.AXC.ALO.AFU

cabinet latches
TF.183
ALT **cabinet latch**
UF latches, cabinet
CN V.TF.AFU.AFU.AFU.AFU.DIO.BCW.ALO.AFU

cabinet locks
TF.247
ALT **cabinet lock**
SN Spring bolts or magnetic latches, usually found on cabinets. (MEANS)
UF locks, cabinet
CN V.TF.AFU.AFU.AFU.AFU.DIO.BIQ.ALO.ARI.AFU

cabinet locks, push-pull
USE **push-pull cabinet locks**

cabinet nests of drawers
USE **cabinets of drawers**

cabinet oblique drawings
VD.15
ALT **cabinet oblique drawing**
SN Use for drawings in oblique projection in which a vertical plane is parallel to the plane of projection (drawing surface), and receding planes are drawn at half the scale of that vertical plane.
UF cabinet projections
drawings, cabinet oblique
oblique drawings, cabinet
projections, cabinet
CN V.VD.AFU.AFU.BIQ.AFU.ARI.AFU.AFU

cabinet office secretaries
USE **Wooton cabinet office secretaries**

cabinet officers
HG.662 (L)

ALT **cabinet officer**
UF officers, cabinet
CN H.HG.AFU.AXC.CFS.ARI

cabinet photographs
VJ.76 (L,N,R)
ALT **cabinet photograph**
SN Use for card photographs on mounts measuring 4 1/4 by 6 1/2 inches.
UF cabinet card photographs
cabinet card photoprints
cabinet cards
cabinet prints
card photographs, cabinet
card photoprints, cabinet
cards, cabinet
photographs, cabinet
photoprints, cabinet card
prints, cabinet
CN V.VJ.AFU.AFU.BCW.AFU.ALO

cabinet prints
USE **cabinet photographs**

cabinet projections
USE **cabinet oblique drawings**

cabinet rasps
TB.981
ALT **cabinet rasp**
SN Rasps which are half-round on one side and flat on the other.
UF cabinet rasps, half-round
half-round cabinet rasps
rasps, cabinet
rasps, half-round cabinet
CN V.TB.AFU.BCW.CFS.ALO.AFU.EFQ.AFU

cabinet rasps, half-round
USE **cabinet rasps**

cabinet saws
TB.1018
ALT **cabinet saw**
SN Saws with a reversible handle and a blade which has teeth on either side; one set is fine and the other coarse.
UF saws, cabinet
CN V.TB.AFU.BCW.CFS.ALO.AFU.EWY.BUE.AFU

cabinet scrapers
TB.1037
ALT **cabinet scraper**
SN Flat steel blades used to smooth wood surfaces after planing, or for scraping paint. (DAC)
UF planes, scraper
scraper planes
scrapers, cabinet
CN V.TB.AFU.BCW.CFS.ALO.AFU.FIM.ALO

cabinet stands
TG.618
ALT **cabinet stand**
SN Low tables, often with a raised rim around the edge, intended to support a cabinet, chest, or other piece of case furniture. Intended to stand against a wall, and thus usually undecorated on one side. (BOYCE)
UF cabinet tables
casket stands
stands, cabinet
stands, casket
tables, cabinet
CN V.TG.AFU.AFU.BIQ.BCW.AFU.AFU

cabinet tables
USE **cabinet stands**

cabinet windows
RT.955
ALT **cabinet window**
UF windows, cabinet
CN V.RT.AFU.ARI.AFU.AFU.BOK.AFU.ALO.ALO.AFU

cabinet-workers
USE **cabinetmakers**

cabinets, map
USE **map cabinets**

cabinetmakers
HG.558 (A,L,B,R)
ALT **cabinetmaker**
UF cabinet-workers
CN H.HG.AFU.AXC.BUE.AXC.BUE.AFU

cabinetmakers' marks
VW.746 (R)
ALT **cabinetmaker's mark**
UF marks, cabinetmakers'
CN V.VW.AFU.ALO.ALO.AFU.AXC.AXC.BIQ

cabinetmaking
KT.524 (L,R)
SN The making of fine furniture and intricate woodwork. Use **carpentry** for constructing buildings and other structures with wood, including installation of floors, windows, and other trim work. Use **woodworking** broadly for the activity of fashioning in wood.
CN K.KT.AFU.ALO.ELK.BUE.AFU

cabinets
TG.409 (N,R)
ALT **cabinet**
SN Case furniture consisting of a set of small drawers or pigeonholes, fronted by one or more doors, and intended for the storage and sometimes the display of small objects. (DDA)
UF boxes, cases of
cases of boxes
CN V.TG.AFU.AFU.AXC.ALO.ARI

cabinets (rooms)
RM.165 (A,L)
ALT **cabinet (room)**
SN Use for small, private rooms, usually adjacent to bedrooms in great houses, serving as sitting and dressing rooms and often containing collections of art objects.
UF closets (rooms)
CN V.RM.AFU.DIO.ALO.CXA.AFU

cabinets and stands
USE **cabinets on stands**

cabinets and writing tables, lady's
USE **lady's cabinet dressing tables**

cabinets of drawers
TG.411
ALT **cabinet of drawers**
UF cabinet nests of drawers
drawers, cabinets of
drawers, pedestals with
nests of drawers, cabinet
pedestals with drawers
CN V.TG.AFU.AFU.AXC.ALO.ARI.AFU.AFU

cabinets on stands
TG.412
ALT **cabinet on stand**
UF cabinets and stands
stands, cabinets and
stands, cabinets on
CN V.TG.AFU.AFU.AXC.ALO.ARI.AFU.ALO

cabinets, bedside
USE **night tables**

cabinets, book
USE **bookcases**

cabinets, china
USE **china cabinets**

cabinets, coin
USE **medal cabinets**

cabinets, corner
USE **corner cabinets**

cabinets, dental
USE **dental cabinets**

cabinets, drop-front
USE **fall-front desks**

cabinets, drying
USE **print dryers**

cabinets, filing
USE **filing cabinets**

cabinets, gun
USE **gun cabinets**

cabinets, hanging
USE **hanging cabinets**

cabinets, Hoosier
USE **Hoosier cabinets**

cabinets, jewel
USE **jewel cabinets**

cabinets, kitchen
USE **kitchen cabinets**

cabinets, lady's
USE **cheverets**
lady's writing tables

cabinets, lyre-shaped
USE **lyre-shaped cabinets**

cabinets, medal
USE **medal cabinets**

cabinets, music
USE **music cabinets**

cabinets, piano roll
USE **pianola roll cabinets**

cabinets, pianola
USE **pianola roll cabinets**

cabinets, pianola roll
USE **pianola roll cabinets**

cabinets, print
USE **print cabinets**

cabinets, record
USE **record cabinets**

cabinets, shell
USE **shell cabinets**

cabinets, smoker's
USE **smoking stands**

cabinets, spice
USE **spice cabinets**

cabinets, thread
USE **thread cabinets**

cabinets, utility
USE **utility cabinets**

cabinets, wax work
USE **wax museums**

cabinets, Welsh
USE **tridarns**

cabinetwork
USE **joinery**

cabins
RK.230 (A,L,N,B,R)
ALT **cabin**
CN V.RK.AFU.ALO.ALO.AXC.ALO.
AFU.ARI

cabins, log
USE **log cabins**

cabins, slave
USE **slave quarters**

cabins, tourist
USE **tourist cabins**

cable
MT.2217 (L)
UF rope, wire
wire rope
CN M.MT.AFU.ALO.BCW

cable braced bridges
USE **cable-stayed bridges**

cable car railways
USE **cable railroads**

cable laying
KT.578
CN K.KT.AFU.ALO.ERE.ALO.AFU

cable moldings
RT.763
ALT **cable molding**
SN Bead or torus moldings resembling a rope or cable.
UF moldings, cable
moldings, rope
rope moldings
CN V.RT.AFU.ALO.AFU.BOK.AFU.
AFU.ARI.AXC

cable net structures
RT.17 (L,B)
ALT **cable net structure**
SN Use for suspension structures in which a field of crossed cables, of different and often reverse curvatures, make up the primary roof surface.
UF cable nets
double curvature net structures
net structures
net structures, cable
net structures, double curvature
nets (net structures)
nets, cable
structures, cable net
structures, net
CN V.RT.AFU.AFU.AFU.ALO.AFU.AFU

cable nets
USE **cable net structures**

cable railroads
RD.100 (A,L)
ALT **cable railroad**
SN Use for light rail transit in which railroad-type vehicles are pulled by a moving continuous cable or belt, usually located beneath the railway.
UF cable car railways
cable railway works
cable railways
cable transportation
cableways
railroads, cable
railways, cable car
transportation, cable
CN V.RD.ALO.ARI.AFU.AFU.ALO.
AFU.AFU

cable railway works
USE **cable railroads**

cable railways
USE **cable railroads**

cable releases
TB.308 (N)
ALT **cable release**
SN Long, flexible, cable-like plungers that permit the photographer to release the shutter without touching the camera. (SWED)
UF releases, cable
CN V.TB.AFU.ARI.CLM.ARI.AFU.ALO.
AFU

cable-stayed bridges
RK.1296 (L)
UF bridges, cable braced
bridges, cable-stayed
bridges, stayed
bridges, stayed girder
cable braced bridges
stayed bridges
stayed girder bridges
CN V.RK.AFU.ALO.ALO.GLI.ALO.
AFU.ARI.ALO

cable-stayed structures
RT.18
ALT **cable-stayed structure**
SN Cable structures that use vertical or sloping compression masts from which straight cables run to critical points or horizontally spanning members.
UF stayed cable structures
structures, cable-stayed
structures, stayed cable
CN V.RT.AFU.AFU.AFU.ALO.AFU.ALO

cable structures
RT.16 (L)
ALT **cable structure**
SN Use for structures in which cables are essential to the system of support, as by suspension or staying.
UF structures, cable
CN V.RT.AFU.AFU.AFU.ALO.AFU

cable transportation
USE **cable railroads**

cable, armored
USE **armored cable**

cable, metal-clad
USE **armored cable**

cabled fluting
DG.113
SN Fluting in which the lower part of each groove is filled with a solid convex form. (PDARC)
UF fluting, cabled
fluting, ribbed
ribbed fluting
CN D.DG.AFU.ARI.ALO.ARI.ARI.AFU

cablegrams
USE **telegrams**

cables (column components)
USE **cabling**

cables, electric
USE **electric cables**

cableways
USE **cable railroads**

cabling
RT.145
SN The convex fillings of the lower part of the flutes of classical columns or pilasters. (HAS)

UF cables (column components)
rudenture
CN V.RT.AFU.AFU.AFU.AXC.BIQ.
ALO.AXC.ALO.ALO

cabochons
DG.3
ALT **cabochon**
SN Motifs consisting of a smooth, convex circular or oval ornament; much used during the 16th and 17th centuries and revived in kidney shape on the cabriole knees of chairs and tables in the mid-18th century. (EDWARD)
CN D.DG.AFU.AFU.AFU

cabriole armchairs
USE **cabriole chairs**

cabriole bergères
USE **bergères**

cabriole chairs
TG.44 (N)
ALT **cabriole chair**
SN Chairs with a stuffed oval or cartouche-shaped back; of a type popular in the late 18th century.
UF armchairs, cabriole
cabriole armchairs
cabrioles
cabriolets
chairs, cabriole
chairs, French (cabriole chairs)
French chairs (cabriole chairs)
CN V.TG.AFU.AFU.ALO.AFU.AFU.
AFU.CXA

cabriole legs
TG.946
ALT **cabriole leg**
SN Legs with a double curve, convex above concave, introduced about 1700. (TOMLIN)
UF bandy legs
bowed legs
cabrioles
legs, bandy
legs, bowed
legs, cabriole
CN V.TG.ALO.FIM.AFU.AFU.ALO

cabriole seats
USE **cabriole sofas**

cabriole sofas
TG.310
ALT **cabriole sofa**
SN Period term for late 18th- and early 19th-century sofas having a high-pitch back.
UF cabriole seats
seats, cabriole
sofas, cabriole
CN V.TG.AFU.AFU.ALO.ALO.BZY.ARI

cabrioles
USE **cabriole chairs**
cabriole legs

cabriolet hammers
TB.531
ALT **cabriolet hammer**
SN Hammers with very small narrow faces used in upholstery for show-wood or neat work. (SALAM)
UF cabriolet hammers, coach trimmer's
coach trimmer's cabriolet hammers
French upholsterer's hammers
hammers, cabriolet
hammers, coach trimmer's cabriolet
hammers, French upholsterer's
CN V.TB.AFU.ARI.FCS.AFU

cabriolet hammers, coach trimmer's
USE **cabriolet hammers**

cabriolets
USE **cabriole chairs**

cabstands
USE **taxi stands**

cachou
USE **cutch**

cacqueteuses
USE **caquetoires**

cacquetoires
USE **caquetoires**

CAD
USE **computer-aided design**

cadastral maps
VW.153 (A,L)
ALT **cadastral map**
SN Maps showing boundaries of subdivisions of land for purposes of describing and recording ownership. (DOD)
UF boundary maps
cadastral plans
cadastral surveys
land ownership maps
maps, boundary
maps, cadastral
maps, land ownership
maps, property
maps, real estate
maps, real property
maps, tax
plans, cadastral
plans, property
property maps
property plans
real estate maps
real property maps
surveys, cadastral
tax maps
CN V.VW.AFU.AFU.AFU.FZU.AXC.
AFU.ARI.AFU.CLM.AFU

cadastral plans
USE **cadastral maps**

cadastral surveys
USE **cadastral maps**

caddies, tea
USE **tea caddies**

caddies, tea (tea tables)
USE **tea tables**

Caddo
FL.852 (L)
CN F.FL.ALO.ALO.ALO.AFU.ALO.
ALO.ARI.ARI.AFU

Caddo, Fulton
USE **Fulton Caddo**

Caddo, Gibson
USE **Gibson Caddo**

cadmium
MT.432 (L)
SN A silvery-white crystalline metal element, very ductile, and which can be rolled or beaten into thin sheets; resembles tin but is harder. (MH)
CN M.MT.AFU.AFU.AFU.BZY.AFU.
AFU.ARI.ARI

cadmium carmine
USE **strong red**

cadmium green
MT.1649
UF green, cadmium
CN M.MT.AFU.AFU.ARI.AFU.AFU.
ALO.ALO.AXC.ARI.ALO

cadmium orange
MT.1772
UF cadmium yellow, orange
Kadmiumgelb orange
orange cadmium yellow
orange, cadmium
yellow, orange cadmium
CN M.MT.AFU.AFU.ARI.AFU.AFU.
ALO.ALO.BUE.ARI.ALO.AFU

cadmium orange (color)
USE **brilliant orange**
strong orange
vivid orange

cadmium purple
USE **deep red**
moderate red

cadmium red
MT.1697
UF Kadmiumrot
red, cadmium
red, selenium
rouge de cadmium
selenium red
CN M.MT.AFU.AFU.ARI.AFU.AFU.
ALO.ALO.BCW.ARI.ALO

cadmium red (color)
USE **moderate red**
strong red
vivid red
vivid reddish orange

cadmium red lithopone
MT.1698

UF lithopone, cadmium red
red lithopone, cadmium
CN M.MT.AFU.AFU.ARI.AFU.AFU.
ALO.ALO.BCW.ARI.ALO.AFU

cadmium vermilion
USE **moderate red**
strong red

cadmium yellow
MT.1771
UF Aurora yellow
jaune de cadmium
Kadmiumgelb
yellow, Aurora
yellow, cadmium
CN M.MT.AFU.AFU.ARI.AFU.AFU
.ALO.ALO.BUE.ARI.ALO

cadmium yellow (color)
USE **moderate orange**
moderate orange yellow
strong orange
strong orange yellow

cadmium yellow lithopone
MT.1773
UF cadmopone
lithopone, cadmium yellow
yellow lithopone, cadmium
CN M.MT.AFU.AFU.ARI.AFU.AFU.
ALO.ALO.BUE.ARI.ALO.ALO

cadmium yellow, deep
USE **deep cadmium yellow**

cadmium yellow, lemon
USE **lemon cadmium yellow**

cadmium yellow, middle
USE **middle cadmium yellow**

cadmium yellow, orange
USE **cadmium orange**

cadmium yellow, pale
USE **pale cadmium yellow**

cadmium, light
USE **vivid yellow**

cadmopone
USE **cadmium yellow lithopone**

Caduveo
FL.1638
CN F.FL.ALO.ALO.ARI.ARI.AXC.ARI

Caen limestone
USE **Caen stone**

Caen stone
MT.667
UF Caen limestone
kane stone
limestone, Caen
stone, Caen
stone, kane
CN M.MT.AFU.AFU.AFU.DCU.AFU.
ALO.AFU.ALO.ALO.AFU.AFU.
ALO.BCW

Caeretan
FL.2600
CN F.FL.ALO.AXC.ALO.AFU.ALO.
AXC.ALO.AFU.AFU

caeruleum
USE **cerulean blue**

Caesalpinia brasiliensis
USE **brazilwood**

Caesalpinia echinata
USE **brazilwood**

Caesalpinia sappan
USE **sappanwood**

Caesarian
FL.2714
CN F.FL.ALO.AXC.ALO.ALO.AFU.
AXC.AFU.ALO

café chairs
USE **ice-cream parlor chairs**

café tables
USE **ice-cream tables**

cafés
RK.114 (A,L,B,R)
ALT **café**
SN Designates informal eating facilities with plated table service, a limited food-oriented menu generally of simply prepared items and coffee, and a social atmosphere emphasizing bustle and noise.
CN V.RK.AFU.ALO.ALO.ALO.AFU.
AXC.ARI

cafés (coffeehouses)
USE **coffeehouses**

cafés, outdoor
USE **outdoor cafés**

cafeterias
RM.108 (A,L,B)
ALT **cafeteria**
UF restaurants, self-service
self-service restaurants
CN V.RM.AFU.DIO.ALO.BCW.AXC

Caga
USE **Chagga**

cages
RM.32
ALT **cage**
SN Use for any boxlike enclosures having openwork of bars, wires, or the like used to confine or protect its occupant, or to admit light or ventilation.
CN V.RM.AFU.DIO.AFU.ARI

cages, squirrel (furniture components)
USE **birdcages (furniture components)**

Cahokia
FL.847
CN F.FL.ALO.ALO.ALO.AFU.ALO.
ALO.ARI.ALO.ARI

Cahuilla
FL.1249 (L)
UF Coahuila
Kawia
CN F.FL.ALO.ALO.ARI.AFU.ALO.ARI

Caingang
FL.1675 (L)
UF Caiuá
Cayuá
Kaingua
CN F.FL.ALO.ALO.ARI.ARI.BIQ.ARI

cairns
RK.1357 (L)
ALT **cairn**
SN Designates piles of stones heaped up for landmarks, monuments, memorials, or as coverings over tombs. For piles of earth, generally, use **mounds**; for piles of earth used specifically over tombs, use **burial mounds.**
CN V.RK.AFU.ALO.ARI.AXC.ARI.ARI.
AFU

caisson foundations
USE **pier foundations**

caisson piles
RT.160
ALT **caisson pile**
SN Piles formed by driving a metal tube into the ground, excavating within the tube, and filling with concrete.
UF piles, caisson
CN V.RT.AFU.AFU.AFU.AXC.BUE.
ALO.ALO.AFU.AFU.AFU

caissons
RT.153 (L)
ALT **caisson**
SN Use for watertight boxes or cylinders serving to hold out water during excavation for foundations, and becoming part of the foundation after excavation is complete.
CN V.RT.AFU.AFU.AFU.AXC.BUE.
AFU.ALO.AFU

caissons (coffers)
USE **coffers (ceiling components)**

Caiuá
USE **Caingang**

Cakchiquel
FL.1532 (L)
CN F.FL.ALO.ALO.ARI.ALO.BIQ.AFU.
AFU

cake stands
USE **muffin stands**

Calamari
FL.1656
CN F.FL.ALO.ALO.ARI.ARI.BCW.AXC

Calapooya
USE **Kalapuya**

calc sinter
USE **travertine**

calcareous clay
USE **marl**

calcareous rock
USE **carbonate rock**

calcareous sandstone
MT.714
UF firestone
malmstone
sandstone, calcareous
CN M.MT.AFU.AFU.AFU.DCU.AFU.ALO.AFU.ARI.AFU.ALO.ALO

calcareous tufa
USE **travertine**

Calchaqui
USE **Diaguita**

calcimine
MT.2514
UF kalsomine
CN M.MT.AFU.ARI.CRG.ALO.BCW.AFU.ALO.AFU.AFU

calcined gypsum
MT.522
UF gypsum, calcined
CN M.MT.AFU.AFU.AFU.CFS.AFU.DUC.ALO

calcite
MT.496 (L)
CN M.MT.AFU.AFU.AFU.CFS.AFU.BIQ

calcite marble
MT.744
SN Crystalline variety of limestone containing not more than 5% magnesium carbonate. (STEIN)
UF marble, calcite
CN M.MT.AFU.AFU.AFU.DCU.AFU.ARI.ARI.AFU.AFU

calcium silicate brick
MT.42
UF brick, calcium silicate
silicate brick, calcium
CN M.MT.AFU.AFU.AFU.ALO.ALO.AFU

calcium sulphate
USE **gypsum**

calculators
TB.140 (L,N,R)
ALT **calculator**
SN Small electronic or mechanical devices that perform calculations, requiring manual action for each individual operation. (RHDEL2)
UF calculators, desk
calculators, office
desk calculators
office calculators
CN V.TB.AFU.ARI.BCW.AFU

calculators, desk
USE **calculators**

calculators, office
USE **calculators**

calculators, pocket
USE **pocket calculators**

calculus
KD.255 (L)
CN K.KD.AFU.ARI.CFS.BCW

caldaria
RM.74
ALT **caldarium**
SN The vapor baths or hot plunges in Roman baths. (HAS)
CN V.RM.AFU.DIO.ALO.ALO.BOK.ALO

Caledonian brown
USE **burnt sienna**

Caledonian white
MT.1731
UF white, Caledonian
CN M.MT.AFU.AFU.ARI.AFU.AFU.ALO.ALO.BOK.AFU.AXC

calefactories
RM.167
ALT **calefactory**
CN V.RM.AFU.DIO.ALO.CXA.ALO

calendars
VW.87 (L,N,R)
ALT **calendar**
SN Use for tabular registers of days. (WCOL)
CN V.VW.AFU.AFU.AFU.FZU.AFU

calendars, archival
USE **archival calendars**

calendars, court
USE **dockets**

calendars, devotional
USE **devotional calendars**

calendars, perpetual
USE **perpetual calendars**

calendars, project
USE **project calendars**

calendars, religious
USE **religious calendars**

calendars, trial
USE **dockets**

calendering
KT.156
ALT **calendered**
SN The process of giving paper a smooth surface by running it between rollers under strong pressure. (MAYER)
CN K.KT.AFU.ALO.DOI.DIO.AFU

Calene ware
FL.2634
UF ware, Calene
CN F.FL.ALO.AXC.ALO.AFU.ALO.AXC.ALO.BIQ.ALO

caliche
MT.648
SN Cemented deposits of calcium carbonate materials. (MH)
CN M.MT.AFU.AFU.AFU.DCU.AFU.ALO.AFU.ALO.AFU

calico
MT.1848 (R)
SN Cotton cloth with patterns printed in one or more colors. In the 18th and 19th centuries referred to printed cloth from India, now refers generally to cotton prints with small, stylized patterns. (NYLAN)
CN M.MT.AFU.AFU.ARI.ALO.ALO.ALO.AFU.ALO.AFU

calico marble
USE **Potomac breccia**

calico rock
USE **Potomac breccia**

California black oak
MT.1232 (L)
UF black oak, California
oak, California black
Quercus kelloggii
CN M.MT.AFU.AFU.ALO.BIQ.DCU.AFU.AFU.AFU.IRA.ARI.AFU

California buckeye
MT.1088 (L)
UF Aesculus californica
buckeye, California
CN M.MT.AFU.AFU.ALO.BIQ.DCU.AFU.AFU.AFU.AFU.AFU.AFU

California live oak
USE **coast live oak**

California redwood
USE **redwood**

California white oak
MT.1234
UF oak, California white
oak, valley
Quercus lobata
valley oak
white oak, California
CN M.MT.AFU.AFU.ALO.BIQ.DCU.AFU.AFU.AFU.IRA.BCW

California Yuman
FL.1274
UF Yuman, California
CN F.FL.ALO.ALO.ARI.AFU.ALO.FZU.AFU

Californian, Early period
USE **Early period Californian**

Californian, Late period
USE **Late period Californian**

Californian, Middle period
USE **Middle period Californian**

Calima
FL.1109 (L)
CN F.FL.ALO.ALO.ALO.ARI.AFU.AFU

Caliphate, Orthodox
USE **Orthodox Caliphate**

calite
USE **perlite**

calk joints
TF.645
ALT **calk joint**
UF joints, calk
CN V.TF.ALO.ARI.ARI.AXC

calking compounds
USE **caulking compounds**

call boxes
USE **telephone booths**

calligraphers
HG.143 (L,B)
ALT **calligrapher**
UF penmen
CN H.HG.AFU.AXC.AXC.AFU.AFU.ALO.BCW.AFU.ALO.AFU

calligraphers' marks
VW.747 (L)
ALT **calligrapher's mark**
UF marks, calligraphers'
CN V.VW.AFU.ALO.ALO.AFU.AXC.AXC.BOK

calligraphic lettering pens
USE **lettering pens**

calligraphy
KT.484 (A,L,B,R)
CN K.KT.AFU.ALO.DUC.EWY.AFU

calling card tables
USE **card stands**

calling cards
USE **visiting cards**

callitype
USE **kallitype**

calls, bid
USE **bidding announcements**

calottes
RT.391
ALT **calotte**
SN Use for those low, plaster domes that constitute the ceiling of a room.
CN V.RT.AFU.AFU.AFU.BIQ.AFU.AFU.ALO

calotype
KT.362 (L)
SN Use for Talbot's patented process to make negatives on paper; the image is formed from silver iodide coated on the base without a binder and is developed. In the mid-20th century, sometimes used incorrectly for any salted paper or paper negative process. Distinguished from **photogenic drawing,** in which the image was printed out.
UF Talbotype
CN K.KT.AFU.ALO.DUC.DIO.ALO.DUC.AFU

calotype negatives
USE **calotypes**

calotype photonegatives
USE **calotypes**

calotype photoprints
USE **salted paper prints**

calotype positives
USE **salted paper prints**

calotype prints
USE **salted paper prints**

calotypes
VJ.11 (R)
ALT **calotype**
SN Use for negatives on paper made by Talbot's patented calotype process, a developing-out process. Distinguished from Talbot's **photogenic drawings,** in which the image was printed out. For most prints made from these negatives, use **salted paper prints.** In the mid-20th century, sometimes used incorrectly for any other paper negatives or salted paper prints.
UF calotype negatives
calotype photonegatives
negatives, calotype
Talbotypes
CN V.VJ.AFU.AFU.AFU.BCW.AFU

Calukya
USE **Chalukyan**

Calvary crosses
DG.11
ALT **Calvary cross**
SN Latin crosses set upon three steps or upon a mount. (W)
UF crosses, Calvary
crosses, passion
passion crosses
CN D.DG.AFU.AFU.ARI.BCW.AFU

Camacan
FL.1676
CN F.FL.ALO.ALO.ARI.ARI.BIQ.AXC

camaieu
KT.253
SN Technique of painting or decorating in several shades of a single hue.
UF en camaieu
CN K.KT.AFU.ALO.DUC.CXA.ALO.BCW.AFU

camas de bilros
TG.357
ALT **cama de bilros**
SN Portuguese tester beds with turned elements and carvings on the headboard; generally having turned posts and either a plain or pagoda-shaped tester. Of a type made in the 16th century. (HAYWAR)
CN V.TG.AFU.AFU.ARI.AFU.AFU.BZY.ALO.AFU

camber arches
RT.253
ALT camber arch
SN Use for flat arches with the intrados very slightly curved.
UF arches, camber
CN V.RT.AFU.AFU.AFU.BCW.AFU.AFU.AFU.ELK.AXC.AFU

camber windows
RT.915
ALT **camber window**
SN Windows very slightly arched at the top.
UF windows, camber
CN V.RT.AFU.ARI.AFU.AFU.BOK.AFU.AFU.ARI

Cambodian
FL.2316 (L,B)
CN F.FL.ALO.ARI.BCW.ALO

camel
USE **light grayish yellowish brown**
light olive brown
light yellowish brown
moderate yellowish brown

camel hair
MT.931
SN The fine, tough, soft hair from the mane and back of the camel used for artists' brushes and for industrial stripping brushes; also, the fine body hair, or camel wool, used as a textile fiber. (MH)
UF hair, camel
CN M.MT.AFU.AFU.ALO.AFU.CXA.AFU.AFU.AFU

camelback trusses
USE **crescent trusses**

cameo prints
VJ.78
ALT **cameo print**
SN Cartes-de-visite which are raised, like medallions, by pressure to the back. (HCOP)
UF prints, cameo
CN V.VJ.AFU.AFU.BCW.AFU.ARI.AFU

cameotypes
VJ.107
ALT **cameotype**
SN Small vignette daguerreotypes, sometimes mounted like jewels. (WOODB)
UF crayon daguerreotypes
daguerreotypes, crayon
daguerreotypes, vignette
vignette daguerreotypes

CN V.VJ.AFU.ARI.ALO.AFU

camera lenses
USE **photographic lenses**

camera operators
USE **cameramen**

camera originals
USE **direct positives**

cameraless photographs
USE **photograms**

cameramen
HG.60
ALT **camerman**
SN Operators of motion picture or television cameras.(W) For persons who oversee all the aspects of photography in a filmmaking or television project, use **cinematographers.**
UF camera operators
operators, camera
CN H.HG.AFU.AXC.AXC.AFU.AFU.AFU.AFU

cameramen, lighting
USE **cinematographers**

cameras
TB.288 (L,N,R)
ALT **camera**
SN Lightproof boxes fitted with a lens through the aperture of which the image of an object is recorded on light-sensitive material. (W)
CN V.TB.AFU.ARI.CLM.ARI.AFU.AFU

cameras, 35mm
USE **35mm cameras**

cameras, automatic
USE **electric eye cameras**

cameras, banquet
USE **banquet cameras**

cameras, box
USE **box cameras**

cameras, circuit
USE **panoramic cameras**

cameras, cirkut
USE **panoramic cameras**

cameras, electric eye
USE **electric eye cameras**

cameras, field
USE **view cameras**

cameras, flatbed
USE **view cameras**

cameras, miniature
USE **miniature cameras**

cameras, motion-picture
USE **motion-picture cameras**

cameras, movie
USE **motion-picture cameras**

cameras, moving-picture
USE **motion-picture cameras**

cameras, panoramic
USE **panoramic cameras**

cameras, pinhole
USE **pinhole cameras**

cameras, rangefinder
USE **rangefinder cameras**

cameras, reflex
USE **reflex cameras**

cameras, single lens reflex
USE **single lens reflex cameras**

cameras, stereo
USE **stereoscopic cameras**

cameras, stereoscopic
USE **stereoscopic cameras**

cameras, subminiature
USE **subminiature cameras**

cameras, television
USE **television cameras**

cameras, thirty-five millimeters
USE **35mm cameras**

cameras, twin-lens
USE **twin-lens cameras**

cameras, view
USE **view cameras**

cames
RT.968 (R)
ALT **came**
SN Slender rods of cast lead, with or without grooves, used in casements and stained glass windows. (HAS)
CN V.RT.AFU.ARI.AFU.AFU.BOK.ALO.ALO

Camirian
USE **Rhodian**

camis
USE **jamis**

camouflage
BM.106 (L,B,R)
CN B.BM.AFU.AFU.ARI.BOK.AFU

camp beds
USE **field beds**

camp ceilings
RT.722
ALT **camp ceiling**
SN Use for ceilings, usually within the roof of a building, characterized by sloping sides and a flat center.
UF ceilings, camp
ceilings, cum
ceilings, tent
ceilings, tray
cum ceilings
tent ceilings
tray ceilings
CN V.RT.AFU.ALO.AFU.ALO.AXC

camp chairs
TG.219
ALT **camp chair**
SN Light folding chairs, usually with canvas seats and backs. (RHDEL2)
UF chairs, camp
CN V.TG.AFU.AFU.ALO.AFU.AFU.AXC.AFU.AFU

camp furniture
TG.799
SN Portable furniture intended for use outdoors. (INNO)
UF furniture, camp
CN V.TG.AFU.ARI.BZY.AFU

camp sites
RK.1488 (L,B)
ALT **camp site**
SN Use for individual locations, within organized campgrounds or as isolated sites, set aside or otherwise marked for camping.
UF sites, camp
CN V.RK.ALO.ALO.BCW.ARI

Campa
FL.1605 (L)
UF Ande
Anti
CN F.FL.ALO.ALO.ARI.ARI.ALO.AFU.ALO

campaign chests
TG.450 (N)
ALT **campaign chest**
SN Popular name for low chests of drawers having handles on each end for lifting.
UF chests, campaign
CN V.TG.AFU.AFU.AXC.ALO.AXC.BCW

campaign furniture
TG.800
UF furniture, campaign
CN V.TG.AFU.ARI.BZY.ALO

campaign trim
TF.39
SN Use for the decorative hardware used on chests and trunks.
UF trim, campaign
CN V.TF.AFU.AFU.AFU.AFU.AXC

campaigning
KG.145
SN Engaging in or conducting a systematic course of aggressive activities for some special purpose. (RHDEL2)
CN K.KG.AFU.AFU.BIQ.AXC

campaigns
KM.2
CN K.KM.AFU.AFU

campaigns, advertising
USE **advertising campaigns**

campaigns, political
USE **political campaigns**

campan marble
MT.806
UF marble, campan
CN M.MT.AFU.AFU.AFU.DCU.AFU.ARI.ARI.ARI.BIQ.ARI

Campanian
FL.2635
CN F.FL.ALO.AXC.ALO.AFU.ALO.AXC.ALO.BIQ.ARI

campaniles
RK.33 (A,L,B)
SN Use for Italian bell towers, usually of a church and usually freestanding.
CN V.RK.AFU.ALO.AFU.ALO.DCU.AFU.AFU

campeachy lake
MT.1590
UF lake, campeachy
CN M.MT.AFU.AFU.ARI.AFU.AFU.ALO.ALO.ALO.ALO.ARI

campeachy wood
USE **logwood**

camper trailers
USE **travel trailers**

campers
USE **camping trailers**
motor homes
travel trailers

campgrounds
RG.155 (L)
ALT **campground**
SN Use for areas comprised of individual camp sites and providing facilities and conveniences for camping.
CN V.RG.AFU.AFU.DOI.ARI

camphor
MT.997 (L)
SN The white resin of the Cinnamomum camphora, an evergreen tree with laurel-like leaves; used for hardening nitrocellulose plastics, but is also used in pharmaceuticals, disinfectants, explosives, and chemicals. (MH)
CN M.MT.AFU.AFU.ALO.AXC.AFU

camphor laurel
USE **camphorwood**

camphor tree
USE **camphorwood**

camphorwood
MT.1129 (L)
UF camphor laurel
camphor tree
laurel, camphor
tree, camphor
CN M.MT.AFU.AFU.ALO.BIQ.DCU.AFU.AFU.AFU.BZY

Campignian
FL.2477
CN F.FL.ALO.AXC.AFU.AXC.ARI

camping trailers
RK.351 (L,N)
ALT **camping trailer**
SN Use for automobile-drawn, wheeled recreational mobile dwellings with a folding shelter of canvas or other fabric.
UF campers
tent trailers
trailers, camping
trailers, tent
CN V.RK.AFU.ALO.ALO.AXC.ARI.AFU

camps
RG.156 (A,L,B,R)
ALT **camp**
CN V.RG.AFU.AFU.DOI.AXC

camps (military)
USE **military camps**

camps, army
USE **army camps**

camps, boot
USE **boot camps**

camps, cabin
USE **motor courts**

camps, church
USE **church camps**

camps, concentration
USE **concentration camps**

camps, day
USE **day camps**

camps, detention
USE **concentration camps**

camps, fishing
USE **fishing lodges**

camps, hunting
USE **hunting lodges**

camps, internment
USE **concentration camps**

camps, labor
USE **labor camps**

camps, logging
USE **lumber camps**

camps, lumber
USE **lumber camps**

camps, military
USE **military camps**

camps, military training
USE **military training camps**

camps, nudist
USE **nudist camps**

camps, prison
USE **prison camps**

camps, refugee
USE **refugee camps**

camps, religious
USE **religious camps**

camps, school
USE **school camps**

camps, summer
USE **summer camps**

camps, trailer
USE **trailer camps**

camps, work
USE **prison camps**

campstools
TG.266 (N)
ALT **campstool**
SN Small, folding stools with a detachable seat of canvas or leather. (GLOAG)
CN V.TG.AFU.AFU.ALO.AFU.ALO.AXC.AFU.AFU

campus planning
KD.169 (A,L,B,R)
UF planning, campus
CN K.KD.AFU.ALO.DUC.AFU

campuses
RG.52 (A)
ALT **campus**
CN V.RG.AFU.AFU.BIQ.AFU

Canaanean
USE **Canaanite**

Canaanite
FL.2926 (L)
UF Canaanean
CN F.FL.ALO.AXC.ARI.AXC.ALO.AFU

Canabal
USE **Tojolabal**

Canada balsam
MT.1470
UF balsam, Canada
CN M.MT.AFU.AFU.ALO.BOK.AFU.ALO

Canada bolts
USE **box bolts**

Canada hemlock
USE **eastern hemlock**

Canadian
FL.714 (L,B)
CN F.FL.ALO.ALO.AFU.ARI.ALO

Canadian ash
USE **white ash**

Canadian spruce
USE **red spruce**
white spruce

Çanakkale
USE **Chanak Kalé**

canal aqueducts
USE **aqueducts**

canal bridges
USE **aqueducts**

Canaliño
FL.901
CN F.FL.ALO.ALO.ALO.AFU.ALO.ARI.AFU.ALO

canals
RK.518 (A,L,B,R)
ALT **canal**
SN Use for artificial navigable waterways.
CN V.RK.AFU.ALO.ALO.CFS.AFU.ALO

canals, interoceanic
USE **interoceanic canals**

canals, sea level
USE **interoceanic canals**

canapés
TG.311
ALT **canapé**
CN V.TG.AFU.AFU.ALO.ALO.BZY.AXC

canapés à confident
TG.312
ALT **canapé à confident**
UF canapés à la maintenon
canapés en confident
confidents (canapés à confident)
duchesses avec encoignures
CN V.TG.AFU.AFU.ALO.ALO.BZY.AXC.AFU

canapés à confident (confidantes)
USE **confidantes**

canapés à corbeille
TG.313
ALT **canapé à corbeille**
SN Canapés whose backs gently curve forward and downward to form the arms. (PC)
CN V.TG.AFU.AFU.ALO.ALO.BZY.AXC.ALO

canapés à la maintenon
USE **canapés à confident**

canapés à marquise
USE **marquises**

canapés confidents à quatre places
USE **bornes**

canapés de l'amitié
USE **marquises**

canapés en confident
USE **canapés à confident**

canapés en lit
USE **sofa beds**

canapés-lits
USE **sofa beds**

canapés ronds
USE **bornes**

Cañar
FL.1639 (L)
CN F.FL.ALO.ALO.ARI.ARI.AXC.AXC

Cañari
FL.1606 (L)
CN F.FL.ALO.ALO.ARI.ARI.ALO.AFU.ARI

canary
USE **light greenish yellow**
moderate yellow

canary whitewood
USE **tulipwood**

canary yellow
USE **brilliant yellow**
light yellow
vivid yellow

canarywood
USE **balaustre**

cancellation marks
VW.714
ALT **cancellation mark**
UF deletion marks
marks, cancellation
marks, deletion
CN V.VW.AFU.ALO.ALO.AFU.AXC.ALO.ALO

Cancer symbols
DG.76
ALT **Cancer symbol**
CN D.DG.AFU.AFU.ERE.ARI

canchas
RK.1012 (B,R)
ALT **cancha**
UF courts, jai alai
courts, pelota
frontons
jai alai courts
pelota courts
CN V.RK.AFU.ALO.ALO.EWY.ALO.AXC

Candelaria
FL.1193
CN F.FL.ALO.ALO.ALO.ARI.BIQ.ARI

candelilla wax
MT.2205
SN A brown vegetable wax obtained from a weed native to Texas and Mexico used to impart hardness to mixtures of waxes and other compounds. (MAYER)
UF wax, candelilla
CN M.MT.AFU.AFU.ARI.BZY.AXC.AFU

Candella
FL.2215 (L)
UF Chandella
CN F.FL.ALO.ARI.AXC.ALO.AFU.AXC.BZY

candle beams
RT.296
ALT **candle beam**
SN Use for fixed beams holding candles in a church.
UF beams, candle
CN V.RT.AFU.AFU.AFU.BCW.ALO.AFU.AXC

candle boards
USE **candle slides**

candle slides
TG.985
ALT **candle slide**
SN Small slides above the slant top in desks to support candlesticks.
UF boards, candle
candle boards
slides, candle
CN V.TG.ALO.GWW.AFU

candlemaking
KT.519 (L)
CN K.KT.AFU.ALO.ELK.AXC

candlenut oil
MT.2008
UF lumbang oil
oil, candlenut
oil, lumbang
CN M.MT.AFU.AFU.ARI.ARI.AXC.AFU.ALO

candlestands
TG.630 (N,R)
ALT **candlestand**
SN Portable stands with a very small top intended to hold a candle or lamp; usually having a round or shaped top supported on a central pillar and with a tripod base. (MONTGO)
CN V.TG.AFU.AFU.BIQ.BCW.ALO.ALO

candlestands, ratchet
USE **ratchet candlestands**

candlestands, ratchet-base
USE **ratchet candlestands**

Candy Creek
FL.888
CN F.FL.ALO.ALO.ALO.AFU.ALO.ALO.BOK.ALO

cane
MT.1021
CN M.MT.AFU.AFU.ALO.BIQ.ALO

cane bolts
TF.553
ALT **cane bolt**
UF bolts, cane
CN V.TF.AFU.ALO.AXC.AFU.AXC

canella
USE **imbuia**

canephores
RT.64 (L)
ALT **canephore**
CN V.RT.AFU.AFU.AFU.AXC.ALO.ALO.AFU

canework
MT.2739
CN M.MT.AFU.AXC.AFU

caning
KT.761
ALT **caned**
SN Process of weaving with split rattan such as for seats or backs of chairs. (W)
CN K.KT.AFU.ALO.HOE.AFU

cannabis bark paper
USE **bark cloth**

cannel coal
MT.995 (L)
UF coal, cannel
CN M.MT.AFU.AFU.ALO.ARI.ARI

canneries
RK.630 (A,L,B)
ALT **cannery**
CN V.RK.AFU.ALO.ALO.CLM.ALO.ALO.AFU.AXC.BCW.AFU

canoe birch
USE **paper birch**

canonizations
KM.144 (L,R)
SN Official placements of deceased persons within the canon of saints. (RHDEL2)
CN K.KM.AFU.DZW.ALO

canons
HG.220 (L)
ALT **canon**
SN Clergy of a large church living as a community under a rule; also Medieval clergymen belonging to the chapter or the staff of a cathedral or collegiate church. (W)
CN H.HG.AFU.AXC.AXC.BIQ.AFU.ARI.BCW

cañons
USE **canyons**

canopies
RT.413 (A,L,N,B,R)
ALT **canopy**
SN Use for small, decorative, rooflike structures, often suspended. Use also for exterior roofs over entrances.
UF architectural canopies
canopies, architectural
CN V.RT.AFU.AFU.AFU.BIQ.ARI.AFU.AFU.AFU.ALO

canopies (bed components)
TG.853 (A)
ALT **canopy (bed component)**
SN Use for rooflike components suspended over the head of a bed by means of a cord attached to the ceiling; usually a cone-shaped or domed bowl with a valance all around, and with two or three curtains long enough to reach and encompass the foot of the bed.(THORN2) Use **testers** for rooflike components supported above the bed by posts.
UF angel canopies
baldachins (furniture components)
bed canopies
canopies, angel
canopies, bed
impériales
pavillons (canopies)
CN V.TG.ALO.BIQ.BUE

canopies (testers)
USE **testers**

canopies, altar
USE **baldachins**

canopies, angel
USE **canopies (bed components)**

canopies, architectural
USE **canopies**

canopies, bed
USE **canopies (bed components)**

canopies, bell
USE **bellcotes**

canopies, half
USE **half-testers**

canopy beds
TG.325 (N)
ALT **canopy bed**
SN Use for beds with suspended canopies, cone-shaped or domed and with curtains that reach and encompass the foot of the bed.(THORN2) Use **tester beds** for beds having a rooflike component supported on posts.
UF beds, canopy
CN V.TG.AFU.AFU.ARI.AFU.AFU.ARI

canopy beds (tester beds)
USE **tester beds**

canopy trees
RD.278
ALT **canopy tree**
UF trees, canopy
CN V.RD.ARI.AFU.BCW.ALO.ALO.ALO.ARI.ALO.AFU

Canosa
FL.2636
CN F.FL.ALO.AXC.ALO.AFU.ALO.AXC.ALO.BIQ.AXC

cans, chimney
USE **chimney pots**

cant beds
USE **field beds**

cant brick
USE **splay brick**

cant chisels
USE **forming chisels**

cant hooks
TB.1067 (N)
ALT **cant hook**
SN Wooden levers with metal hooks on their shafts, used to roll logs; later combined with the jam pike to become peavies.
UF hooks, cant
CN V.TB.AFU.BCW.CFS.ALO.ALO.BZY.AFU

cant moldings
RT.770
ALT **cant molding**
SN Beveled moldings, either having a beveled back for nailing into a corner or angle, or one whose face or profile is a cant or oblique surface. (RS)
UF moldings, cant
CN V.RT.AFU.ALO.AFU.BOK.AFU.AFU.AXC.AFU

canted corners
TG.868
ALT **canted corner**
SN Corners on furniture that have wide chamfers at the junctions of front and sides. (COLLEC)
UF corners, canted
CN V.TG.ALO.CRG.AFU

canted moldings
USE **raking moldings**

canted vaults
USE **pitched-brick vaults**

canted walls
RT.575
ALT **canted wall**
SN Walls built at an angle to the face of another wall. (PUTNAM)
UF walls, canted
CN V.RT.AFU.AFU.AFU.BIQ.BUE.AFU.AFU.AXC

canteens (lunchrooms)
USE **lunchrooms**

canteens (post exchanges)
USE **post exchanges**

canteens (recreation centers)
USE **recreation centers**

canterburies
TG.607 (N)
ALT **canterbury**
SN Use for small racks with partitions intended to hold sheet music, books, or loose papers.
UF canterbury music cases
cases, canterbury music
music cases, canterbury
CN V.TG.AFU.AFU.BIQ.AFU

canterburies (stands)
TG.619
ALT **canterbury (stand)**
SN 18th-century term for English stands

in the form of a deep partitioned tray on legs intended to be placed near a table to hold plates and cutlery.
UF canterburies, supper
supper canterburies
supper trays (canterburies)
trays, supper (canterburies)
CN V.TG.AFU.AFU.BIQ.BCW.AFU.ALO

canterburies, supper
USE **canterburies (stands)**

canterbury music cases
USE **canterburies**

cantilever bridges
RK.1297 (A,L)
ALT **cantilever bridge**
UF bridges, cantilever
CN V.RK.AFU.ALO.ALO.GLI.ALO.AFU.ARI.ARI

cantilever construction
KT.28 (B)
ALT **cantilevered**
SN Construction employing a horizontally projecting member unsupported at one end.
UF construction, cantilever
CN K.KT.AFU.ALO.BCW.ARI.AFU.AFU

cantilevered chairs
USE **Cesca chairs**

cantilevered footings
RT.172
ALT **cantilevered footing**
UF footings, cantilevered
CN V.RT.AFU.AFU.AFU.AXC.BUE.ARI.ALO.AFU.AFU

cantilevered side chairs
USE **Cesca chairs**

cantilevered stairs
USE **flying stairs**

cantilevers
RT.323
ALT **cantilever**
SN Any members fixed at one end and free at the other and under a load.
CN V.RT.AFU.AFU.AFU.BCW.BCW

Canton
FL.1928
CN F.FL.ALO.ARI.ALO.AFU.AFU.AXC.ALO.ARI

Canton porcelain
USE **Chinese export porcelain**

cantonment towns
USE **cantonments**

cantonments
RG.133 (B)
ALT **cantonment**
SN Use for encampments formed by troops for long stays while on a campaign, especially during winter.
UF cantonment towns
towns, cantonment
CN V.RG.AFU.AFU.BZY.ALO.ALO

cantons
HG.802 (R)
ALT **canton**
CN H.HG.ALO.ALO.AFU

cantons (wall components)
RT.667 (R)
ALT **canton (wall component)**
SN Corners of a building decorated with a projecting masonry course, a pilaster, or similar feature. (HAS)
CN V.RT.AFU.AFU.AFU.BIQ.BUE.ALO.ALO.AFU

cantoriae
USE **choir lofts**

cantors
HG.214 (L)
ALT **cantor**
SN Synagogue officials who sing or chant liturgical music and lead the congregation in prayer. (W)
CN H.HG.AFU.AXC.AXC.BIQ.AFU.ALO

canvas
MT.1859 (L,B,R)
SN A firm, closely woven cloth of plain weave made in various weights, usually of linen, hemp, or cotton, and used especially for clothing, sails, tarpaulins, and awnings.(W) Also used for painting supports.
CN M.MT.AFU.AFU.ARI.ALO.ALO.ALO.ALO.ARI

canvas board
MT.1918
SN Common gray cardboard or pasteboard to which a white cotton cloth, prepared for oil painting, has been glued or pasted. (MAYER)
UF board, canvas
CN M.MT.AFU.AFU.ARI.ALO.ALO.AXC.ALO.BIQ.AFU.BCW.ALO

canyons
RD.192 (L,R)
ALT **canyon**
SN Deep, steep-sided land depressions, often having a river at the bottom; common to arid and semi-arid areas; distinct from **valleys**, which tend to have a flattish landscape rather than high, precipitous slopes; distinct from **gorges**, which tend to be smaller, narrower, and more rocky.
UF cañons
CN V.RD.ARI.AFU.AXC.AFU.AFU.ARI.AXC

cap flashing
USE **counter flashing**

cap moldings
RT.797
ALT **cap molding**
SN Moldings which embellish the top of a piece of simple trim or casing, such as the top of a dado, baseboard, or window casing.
UF moldings, cap
CN V.RT.AFU.ALO.AFU.BOK.AFU.ALO.ARI

cap screws
TF.481
ALT **cap screw**
SN Threaded fasteners that screw into a threaded hole rather than into a nut. Cap screws are specified by diameter, length, and thread pitch. (MEANS)
UF screws, cap
CN V.TF.AFU.AFU.AFU.ALO.AFU.DIO.AFU.CFS.AFU

cap strip seams
TF.652
ALT **cap strip seam**
UF seams, cap strip
strip seams, cap
CN V.TF.ALO.ARI.ARI.BUE.ARI

cape chisels
TB.705 (N)
ALT **cape chisel**
SN Long, cold chisels having long tapers and narrow cutting edges; used for cutting keyways and the like. (DAC)
UF chisels, cape
chisels, cope
cope chisels
CN V.TB.AFU.BCW.BIQ.ARI.ALO.AFU.AFU.AFU

Cape Indians
USE **Makah**

capes (landforms)
RD.219 (L)
ALT **cape (landform)**
CN V.RD.ARI.AFU.AXC.AFU.ALO.AXC.AFU

capital
BM.371 (L)
SN Accumulated goods and financial resources devoted to the production of other goods or to generating income. (WCOL)
UF capital goods
goods, capital
CN B.BM.ARI.ARI

capital cities
RD.22 (A,L,B,R)
ALT **capital city**
UF capitals (cities)
cities, capital
CN V.RD.AFU.ALO.AFU.AFU

capital goods
USE **capital**

capital plant
USE **infrastructure**

capitalism
BM.381 (L,R)
SN Economic system characterized by private or corporate ownership of capital goods, by investments that are determined by private decision rather than state control, and by prices, production, and the distribution of goods that are determined mainly by competition in a free market. (WCOL)
CN B.BM.ARI.BUE.AFU

capitals
RT.116 (A,L,B,R)
ALT **capital**
UF chapiters
CN V.RT.AFU.AFU.AFU.AXC.BIQ.ALO.ARI.AFU

capitals (cities)
USE **capital cities**

capitals, Aeolic
USE **Aeolic capitals**

capitals, angle
USE **angle capitals**

capitals, basket
USE **basket capitals**

capitals, bell
USE **bell capitals**

capitals, block
USE **cushion capitals**

capitals, bowl
USE **bowl capitals**

capitals, bracket
USE **bracket capitals**

capitals, chalice
USE **chalice capitals**

capitals, corner
USE **angle capitals**

capitals, crocket
USE **crocket capitals**

capitals, cubiform
USE **cushion capitals**

capitals, cushion
USE **cushion capitals**

capitals, lotus
USE **lotus capitals**

capitals, lotus bud
USE **lotus capitals**

capitals, palm
USE **palm capitals**

capitals, papyriform
USE **papyrus capitals**

capitals, papyrus
USE **papyrus capitals**

capitals, pillow
USE **cushion capitals**

capitals, protomai
USE **protomai capitals**

capitals, scalloped
USE **scalloped capitals**

capitals, vaulting
USE **vaulting capitals**

capitol buildings
USE **capitols**

capitols
RK.983 (A,L,B,R)
ALT **capitol**
SN Use only for buildings in the United States occupied by a legislature; may also house one or more of the other branches of government.
UF buildings, capitol
capitol buildings
capitols, state
state capitols
statehouses
CN V.RK.AFU.ALO.ALO.ERE.AFU.BCW.ALO

capitols, state
USE **capitols**

capitular records
USE **church records**

Cappadocian ware
FL.2869 (L)
UF ware, Cappadocian
CN F.FL.ALO.AXC.ARI.AFU.ALO.ARI.AXC

Cappagh brown
USE **umber**

capped butt hinges
TF.105
ALT **capped butt hinge**
UF butt hinges, capped
hinges, capped butt
CN V.TF.AFU.AFU.AFU.AFU.CLM.AFU.BCW

capping brick
MT.95
UF brick, capping
brick, coping
coping brick
CN M.MT.AFU.AFU.AFU.AXC.ALO.AFU.ALO.AXC

capping planes
TB.953 (N)
ALT **capping plane**
SN Planes used in conjunction with a set of handrail planes; the former cuts the top of the handrail and the latter cuts the sides. (SALAM)
UF banister planes
planes, banister
planes, capping
planes, stair
planes, stairbuilder's
stair planes
stairbuilder's planes
CN V.TB.AFU.BCW.CFS.ALO.AFU.DUC.AXC.AFU.ALO

capping planes (handrail planes)
USE **handrail planes**

capricci
VB.70 (R)
ALT **capriccio**
SN Scenes of accurately rendered buildings grouped in an arbitrary, imaginary arrangement. Distinct from **vedute ideate,** in which scenes are realistically conceived but the elements are completely imaginary. Use especially with reference to 18th-century Italian paintings and prints.
CN V.VB.AFU.AXC.AFU

Capricious Style
USE **Third Style**

Capricorn symbols
DG.77
ALT **Capricorn symbol**
CN D.DG.AFU.AFU.ERE.AXC

caps (lock components)
TF.561
ALT **cap (lock component)**
UF covers (lock components)
CN V.TF.AFU.ALO.AXC.ALO

caps (pedestal components)
RT.180
ALT **cap (pedestal component)**
SN Use for the topmost projecting element of a pedestal classically divided by tripartation.
UF surbases
CN V.RT.AFU.AFU.AFU.AXC.CFS.ALO.AFU

caps, chimney
USE **chimney caps**

caps, lens
USE **lens caps**

caps, newel
USE **newel caps**

capsa
USE **arcae**

Capsian
FL.42
CN F.FL.ALO.AFU.AFU.AFU.ALO.AFU

capstan expanding tables
USE **capstan tables**

capstan tables
TG.667
ALT **capstan table**
SN Tables with a circular top which expands on an iron frame to allow eight extra leaves to be inserted.

Patented by Robert Jupe in 1835. (COLLAR)
UF capstan expanding tables
drum tables
expanding tables, capstan
tables, capstan
tables, capstan expanding
tables, drum
CN V.TG.AFU.AFU.BIQ.BOK.AFU.AFU

captain's chairs
USE **low-back Windsor chairs**

captain's walks
USE **widow's walks**

caput mortuum
USE **Indian red**

caqueteuses
USE **caquetoires**

Caquetío
FL.1571
CN F.FL.ALO.ALO.ARI.ARI.AFU.AXC

caquetoires
TG.45
ALT **caquetoire**
SN Small, low armchairs, or backstools, often upholstered, which have a wide front, a very narrow back, and a trapezoidal seat.
UF cacqueteuses
cacquetoires
caqueteuses
CN V.TG.AFU.AFU.ALO.AFU.AFU.AFU.DCU

caquetoires (chauffeuses)
USE **chauffeuses**

car lots, used
USE **used car lots**

car museums
USE **automobile museums**

car parks
USE **parking garages**

car parks, multi-storey
USE **parking garages**

Cara
FL.1657 (L)
CN F.FL.ALO.ALO.ARI.ARI.BCW.BCW

caraboard
MT.2416
SN A building material consisiting of an overlap siding split from several species of deciduous trees and nailed directly to the roof-bearing walls' studs; perhaps uniquely Cameroonian. (OLIVER)
CN M.MT.AFU.ARI.BZY.BOK.AFU

caracoles
USE **spiral stairs**

Carajá
FL.1629 (L)
UF Karajá
CN F.FL.ALO.ALO.ARI.ARI.ARI.ALO

Carancahua Indians
USE **Karankawa**

caravan sites
USE **trailer camps**

caravans
RK.352 (L,B)
ALT **caravan**
SN Use for covered nonmotorized vehicles equipped as traveling living quarters; for motorized counterparts use **motor homes.**
UF gypsy wagons
wagons, gypsy
CN V.RK.AFU.ALO.ALO.AXC.ARI.ALO

caravanserais
RK.946 (A,L,B)
ALT **caravanserai**
SN Use for stations along caravan routes providing overnight accommodations and facilities for caravans and individuals and their animals; generally characterized by large central courtyards, a single entrance and, often, shops.
UF choultries
dharmsalas
CN V.RK.AFU.ALO.ALO.ELK.ALO

Caraway
FL.827
CN F.FL.ALO.ALO.ALO.AFU.ALO.ALO.ALO.ALO

carbitol
MT.2662
SN A commercially prepared high-boiling ether alcohol used especially as an organic solvent. (W)
CN M.MT.AFU.ARI.HZS.AFU.ALO

carbolic acid
MT.296 (L)
UF acid, carbolic
phenol
CN M.MT.AFU.AFU.AFU.BOK.AFU.ALO

carbolic oil
USE **middle oil**

carbolineum
MT.2637
SN A heavy, oily substance distilled from an anthracene-oil or creosote-oil fraction of coal tar, sometimes chlorinated or otherwise treated, and used as a wood preservative, disinfectant, or insecticide. (W)
CN M.MT.AFU.ARI.HCQ.AFU.AFU

carbon-14 dating
USE **radiocarbon dating**

carbon bisulfide
USE **carbon disulfide**

carbon black
MT.1566 (L)
UF acetylene black
benzol black
black, acetylene
black, benzol
black, carbon
black, diamond
black, flame
black, gas
black, oil
black, vegetable
diamond black
flame black
gas black
noir de bougie
oil black
vegetable black
CN M.MT.AFU.AFU.ARI.AFU.AFU.ALO.ALO.AFU.AFU.AFU

carbon copies
VW.679 (L)
ALT **carbon copy**
SN Copies of documents created simultaneously with the original manuscript or typescript by the use of an intermediate sheet of paper coated with carbon. (ICA)
UF copies, carbon
CN V.VW.AFU.ALO.AFU.DZW.BIQ.ARI

carbon dioxide
MT.998 (L)
CN M.MT.AFU.AFU.ALO.AXC.ALO

carbon disulfide
MT.2663 (L)
SN Compound made by heating together carbon and sulfur; used as a solvent for rubber and other products. (MH)
UF carbon bisulfide
CN M.MT.AFU.ARI.HZS.AFU.ARI

carbon ink, black
USE **black carbon ink**

carbon monoxide
MT.999 (L)
CN M.MT.AFU.AFU.ALO.AXC.ARI

carbon paper
MT.1931 (L)
UF paper, carbon
CN M.MT.AFU.AFU.ARI.ALO.ALO.AXC.ARI.ARI

carbon photoprints
USE **carbon prints**

carbon print process
USE **carbon process**

carbon prints
VJ.53
ALT **carbon print**
SN Use for photographic prints made by the carbon process.
UF carbon photoprints
photoprints, carbon

prints, carbon
CN V.VJ.AFU.AFU.ARI.ARI.AXC.BUE.AFU

carbon process
KT.349 (L)
SN A bichromate process to produce photographic prints using a carbon pigment to form the image. The most widely used carbon process was J.W. Swan's, introduced in 1864, which used sheets of pigmented gelatin that were transferred in processing to a paper support.
UF autotype
carbon print process
print process, carbon
CN K.KT.AFU.ALO.DUC.DIO.ALO.DIO.AFU.AFU

carbon steel
MT.344 (L)
UF carbon steel, plain
carbon steel, straight
ordinary steel
plain carbon steel
steel, carbon
steel, ordinary
steel, plain carbon
steel, straight carbon
straight carbon steel
CN M.MT.AFU.AFU.AFU.BZY.AFU.AFU.AFU.AFU.ALO.AFU.AFU

carbon steel, plain
USE **carbon steel**

carbon steel, straight
USE **carbon steel**

carbon tetrachloride
MT.2676 (L)
CN M.MT.AFU.ARI.HZS.AFU.BIQ.ARI.AFU

carbonaceous limestone
MT.682
UF bituminous limestone
limestone, bituminous
limestone, carbonaceous
CN M.MT.AFU.AFU.AFU.DCU.AFU.ALO.AFU.ALO.ALO.AFU.ALO.ALO

carbonate ore
USE **siderite**

carbonate rock
MT.647 (L)
UF calcareous rock
rock, calcareous
rock, carbonate
CN M.MT.AFU.AFU.AFU.DCU.AFU.ALO.AFU.ALO

carbonate, barium
USE **barium carbonate**

carborundum cloth
USE **carborundum paper**

carborundum paper
TB.501
SN Abrasive cloth or paper made by covering the material with powdered carborundum held in place by some adhesive such as glue. (PUTNAM)
UF carborundum cloth
cloth, carborundum
paper, carborundum
CN V.TB.AFU.ARI.EWY.ALO.AFU.AFU

carborundum stones
TB.510
ALT **carborundum stone**
SN Abrasive stones, made of carborundum; used for sharpening tools such as plane irons and chisels. (PUTNAM)
UF stones, carborundum
CN V.TB.AFU.ARI.EWY.ALO.BCW

carbro process
KT.357 (L)
SN A carbon process to produce photographic prints in which the carbon transfer tissue is made sensitive when placed in contact with a developed silver bromide print. Distinguished from the **carbon process** by the chemical method for hardening the carbon transfer tissue and by the use of a silver bromide print, which allows carbro prints to be made from smaller negatives.
UF ozobrome
ozobrome process
ozotype
CN K.KT.AFU.ALO.DUC.DIO.ALO.DIO.ALO

carbro tri-color
USE **three-color carbro process**

carbro trichrome
USE **three-color carbro process**

carcase furniture
USE **case furniture**

carcase grooving planes
USE **dado planes**

carcases
TG.864
ALT **carcase**
SN The body or main structure of furniture to which veneers are applied. (BEARD)
CN V.TG.ALO.BZY

carcass saws
TB.995 (N)
ALT **carcass saw**
SN Thin saws with approximately 11 teeth per inch, stiffened with a metal rib along the top to prevent buckling; used to smooth cut the edges of tenons, dovetails, or miter fittings; a modern variety of the tenon saw.
UF saws, carcass
CN V.TB.AFU.BCW.CFS.ALO.AFU.EWY.AFU.BOK.AFU

card catalogs
VW.95 (L)
ALT **card catalog**
UF catalogs, card
CN V.VW.AFU.AFU.AFU.FZU.ALO.AFU.ALO

card files
VW.585
ALT **card file**
SN Any files employing the use of cards. (GAHLM)
UF files, card
CN V.VW.AFU.ALO.AFU.BIQ.AFU.AFU

card frames
TF.18
ALT **card frame**
SN Small frames that attach to a door surface for insertion of a name card or plate. (MEANS)
UF card holders
card plates
frames, card
holders, card
plates, card
CN V.TF.AFU.AFU.AFU.AFU.AFU.CFS.ALO

card holders
USE **card frames**

card indexes
VW.426 (L)
ALT **card index**
SN Indexes recorded on cards of uniform size, arranged alphabetically, numerically, or by some other order. (ICA)
UF indexes, card
CN V.VW.AFU.AFU.ALO.EWY.BOK.AFU.AFU

card keys
TF.529
ALT **card key**
UF keys, card
CN V.TF.AFU.ALO.ARI.AFU.ALO

card photographs
VJ.73
ALT **card photograph**
SN Photographic prints made by a variety of processes on commercially produced cardboard mounts of standard sizes. (GMGPC)
UF photographs, card
CN V.VJ.AFU.AFU.BCW.AFU

card photographs (cartes-de-visite)
USE **cartes-de-visite**

card photographs, boudoir
USE **boudoir prints**

card photographs, cabinet
USE **cabinet photographs**

card photographs, imperial
USE **imperial prints**

card photographs, promenade
USE **promenade prints**

card photographs, victoria
USE **victoria prints**

card photoprints, boudoir midget mount
USE **boudoir midget mounts**

card photoprints, cabinet
USE **cabinet photographs**

card plates
USE **card frames**

card receivers
USE **card stands**

card stands
TG.633 (N)
ALT **card stand**
SN Small stands with a dished top intended to hold calling cards; of a type made in the late 19th century.
UF calling card tables
card receivers
card tables, calling
receivers, card
stands, card
tables, calling card
CN V.TG.AFU.AFU.BIQ.BCW.ALO.ARI

card stereographs
USE **stereographs**

card tables
TG.713 (L,N)
ALT **card table**
SN Tables with a smooth undecorated top, generally intended to be used for playing cards; often having a folding top and may have inset pockets to hold coins or counters. Distinguished from **gaming tables** which have tops marked as boards for playing chess, backgammon, or other games.
UF tables, card
CN V.TG.AFU.AFU.BIQ.BOK.ALO.AXC

card tables, calling
USE **card stands**

card tables, tripod
USE **tripod card tables**

cardboard
MT.1910 (L,N,B)
UF board, paper
paper board
paperboard
CN M.MT.AFU.AFU.ARI.ALO.ALO.AXC.ALO.BIQ.AFU

cardinals
HG.221 (L,R)
ALT **cardinal**
CN H.HG.AFU.AXC.AXC.BIQ.AFU.ARI.BIQ

cardines
RK.1544
ALT **cardo**
SN Designates the north-south streets used in laying out ancient Roman countryside tracts and associated towns and thus, by extension, the main north-south streets, distinguished by greater width and scale of appointments, of planned Roman towns.
CN V.RK.ALO.ALO.BIQ.ARI.AFU.ALO.ARI.ALO.AFU

carding
KT.636 (L)
SN Preparing fibers for spinning by cleansing, disentangling, and collecting together, by the use of a card; used to prepare fibers of relatively short length. (W)
CN K.KT.AFU.ALO.GFO.AFU

cardrooms
RM.129
ALT **cardroom**
SN Use for rooms equipped for card playing.
CN V.RM.AFU.DIO.ALO.BIQ.BCW.AFU.ALO

cards
VW.559 (L,R)
ALT **card**
CN V.VW.AFU.ALO.AFU.ARI

cards, advertising
USE **business cards**

cards, aperture
USE **aperture cards**

cards, baseball
USE **baseball cards**

cards, birthday
USE **birthday cards**

cards, business
USE **business cards**

cards, cabinet
USE **cabinet photographs**

cards, calling
USE **visiting cards**

cards, catalog
USE **catalog cards**

cards, Chanukah
USE **Hanukkah cards**

cards, Christmas
USE **Christmas cards**

cards, cigarette
USE **cigarette cards**

cards, credit
USE **credit cards**

cards, dance
USE **dance cards**

cards, Easter
USE **Easter cards**

cards, greeting
USE **greeting cards**

cards, Hanukkah
USE **Hanukkah cards**

cards, I.D.
USE **identity cards**

cards, IBM (TM)
USE **punched cards**

cards, identification
USE **identity cards**

cards, identity
USE **identity cards**

cards, image
USE **aperture cards**

cards, library
USE **library cards**

cards, mass
USE **mass cards**

cards, memorial
USE **memorial cards**

cards, peephole
USE **aperture cards**

cards, playing
USE **playing cards**

cards, postal
USE **postal cards**

cards, punched
USE **punched cards**

cards, readers'
USE **library cards**

cards, report
USE **report cards**

cards, show
USE **business cards**

cards, sure
USE **cartes-de-visite**

cards, time
USE **time cards**

cards, trade
USE **business cards**

cards, tradesmen's
USE **business cards**

cards, visiting
USE **visiting cards**

care facilities, extended
USE **extended care facilities**

care facilities, long-term
USE **extended care facilities**

care, day
USE **day care**

career guidance
USE **vocational guidance**

caretakers
HG.40
ALT **caretaker**
SN Persons placed usually as occupants in charge of the upkeep, repair, and protection of the house, estate, or farm of owners who may be absent. (W)
UF building caretakers
caretakers, building
CN H.HG.AFU.AXC.ARI.ARI.AFU

caretakers, building
USE **caretakers**

Carib
FL.1563 (L)
UF Karinye
CN F.FL.ALO.ALO.ARI.ALO.BUE.ALO

Caribbean
FL.707 (B)
CN F.FL.ALO.ALO.AFU.ALO

Caribou Eskimo
USE **Caribou Inuit**

Caribou Inuit
FL.1208
UF Caribou Eskimo
Eskimo, Caribou
Inuit, Caribou
CN F.FL.ALO.ALO.ARI.AFU.AFU.AFU.ALO.AFU.ALO

caricatures
VB.4 (A,L,B,R)
ALT **caricature**
SN Use for representations, often portraits, that exaggerate certain features or characteristics to humorous or ludicrous effect.
CN V.VB.AFU.AFU.ALO

caricaturists
HG.93 (L)
ALT **caricaturist**
CN H.HG.AFU.AXC.AXC.AFU.AFU.ALO.AXC.ALO

Carijona
FL.1572 (L)
UF Omagua
Umaua
CN F.FL.ALO.ALO.ARI.ARI.AFU.BCW

Caripuna
FL.1573
CN F.FL.ALO.ALO.ARI.ARI.AFU.BIQ

Carlovingian
USE **Carolingian**

Carlton House desks
USE **Carlton House tables**

Carlton House tables
TG.571
ALT **Carlton House table**
SN Writing tables with a low superstructure consisting of two or three tiers of small drawers rising from the back and curving around the sides. Presumably named in the late 18th century after the Prince Regent's Carlton House. (DDA)
UF Carlton House desks
Carlton tables
desks, Carlton House
drawing and writing tables, lady's
lady's drawing and writing tables
tables, Carlton
tables, Carlton House
tables, lady's drawing and writing
CN V.TG.AFU.AFU.AXC.ALO.BZY.FUA.AXC

Carlton tables
USE **Carlton House tables**

carmine
MT.1689
UF carmine lake
crimson
Florentine lake
Karmin
Karminlack
lacque carminée
lake, carmine
lake, Florentine
lake, Munich
lake, Vienna
Munich lake
Vienna lake
CN M.MT.AFU.AFU.ARI.AFU.AFU.ALO.ALO.BCW.ALO.ALO

carmine (cochineal)
USE **cochineal**

carmine (color)
USE **dark pink**
deep purplish red
deep red
grayish red
moderate purplish red
moderate red
strong purplish red
strong red
vivid pink
vivid purplish red
vivid red

carmine lake
USE **carmine**
moderate purplish red
moderate red
strong purplish red
strong red
vivid red

carmine rose
USE **deep purplish pink**
grayish red
moderate purplish red
moderate red
strong purplish red
strong red
vivid red

carmine, blue
USE **blue carmine**

carmine, brown
USE **dark red**
very deep red

carmine, burnt
USE **burnt carmine**

carmine, cadmium
USE **strong red**

carmine, dark
USE **vivid red**

carmine, madder
USE **moderate purplish red**
moderate red

carmine, rose
USE **moderate purplish red**
strong purplish red
vivid purplish red

carmine, violet
USE **violet carmine**

carmine, violet (color)
USE **dark purplish red**
dark reddish purple

carmine, yellow
USE **yellow carmine**

carnauba wax
MT.2206 (L)
SN The hardest of the vegetable waxes, obtained from the leaves of the Brazilian palm; used in compounds of waxes and other materials to impart hardness and durability. (MAYER)
UF wax, carnauba
CN M.MT.AFU.AFU.ARI.BZY.AXC.ALO

Carnegie libraries
RK.697 (B)
ALT **Carnegie library**
SN Use for libraries, found in the United States and Great Britain, originally funded by Andrew Carnegie.
UF libraries, Carnegie
CN V.RK.AFU.ALO.ALO.CRG.AXC.AFU.ARI.ALO

carnelian
MT.547
UF cornelian
CN M.MT.AFU.AFU.AFU.CFS.AFU.GRC.AFU.ARI.AFU.AFU

Carnival
KM.10 (L)
SN Use specifically for the festivals,

merry-making, and revelry held a few days before Lent. For traveling amusement enterprises consisting of sideshows, games of chance, rides, and such entertainments, use **carnivals.**
UF Fastnacht
Mardi Gras
CN K.KM.AFU.ALO.ARI.AFU

carnivals
KM.54 (L)
SN Use for traveling amusement enterprises, consisting of sideshows, games of chance, rides, and such entertainments. For the festivals, merry-making, and revelry held a few days before Lent, use **Carnival.**
CN K.KM.AFU.BOK.AFU

carol books
VW.556
ALT **carol book**
UF books, carol
CN V.VW.AFU.ALO.AFU.AFU.ALO.CFS.AFU

Carolean
USE **Restoration (period)**

Caroline Island
FL.3678 (L)
CN F.FL.ALO.BOK.ARI.ALO

Carolingian
FL.3090 (A,L,B,R)
UF Carlovingian
Carolingian Renaissance
CN F.FL.ALO.BCW.ALO.ALO.AFU.AFU.ALO

Carolingian Renaissance
USE **Carolingian**

carols (carrels)
USE **carrels**

carotene
MT.1559 (L)
CN M.MT.AFU.AFU.ARI.AFU.AFU.ALO.AFU.ALO.AFU.ALO.ALO

carpenter's adzes
TB.811 (N)
ALT **carpenter's adz**
SN Long handled adzes whose blade is beveled on the inside; later adzes have polls on the head which are used as a maul.
UF adzes, carpenter's
CN V.TB.AFU.BCW.CFS.ALO.AFU.AFU.ALO

carpenter's axes
USE **shipwright's axes**

carpenter's benches
USE **workbenches**

Carpenter's Gothic
FL.1722 (A,B)
UF Carpenteresque
Gothic, Carpenter's
CN F.FL.ALO.ALO.BCW.AFU.ALO

carpenter's mallets
TB.1089 (N)
ALT **carpenter's mallet**
UF mallets, carpenter's
CN V.TB.AFU.BCW.CFS.ALO.ARI.ALO.ARI

carpenter's pincers
USE **farrier's pincers**

carpenter's squares
TB.445 (L,N)
ALT **carpenter's square**
SN Flat, metal, L-shaped tools that constitute an accurate right angle and are engraved with divisions and markings useful to a carpenter in laying out and erecting framing. (MEANS)
UF framing squares
squares (carpenter's squares)
squares, carpenter's
squares, framing
squares, steel
steel squares
CN V.TB.AFU.ARI.EFQ.ALO.BZY.ALO

Carpenteresque
USE **Carpenter's Gothic**

carpenters
HG.586 (A,L,B)
ALT **carpenter**
CN H.HG.AFU.AXC.BZY.AFU.BCW

carpenters' handbooks
USE **builders' guides**

carpentry
KT.879 (L,B,R)
SN The art of building with wood, especially in the construction of buildings and other structures, including the installation of floors, windows, and other trim work. For the making of fine furniture and intricate woodwork, use **cabinetmaking.** For the activity of working in wood more generally, use **woodworking.**
CN K.KT.AFU.ALO.HOE.BUE.AFU.AFU

carpet holders, stair
USE **stair carpet holders**

carpet tacks
TF.494
ALT **carpet tack**
UF tacks, carpet
CN V.TF.AFU.AFU.AFU.ALO.AFU.ERE.AFU

Carpinus betulus
USE **European hornbeam**

carports
RM.244 (L)
ALT **carport**
CN V.RM.AFU.DIO.ARI.AFU.ALO

Carrara marble
MT.822
UF marble, Carrara
CN M.MT.AFU.AFU.AFU.DCU.AFU.ARI.ARI.ARI.BOK.ALO

Carrara structural glass
MT.270
UF glass, Carrara structural
structural glass, Carrara
CN M.MT.AFU.AFU.AFU.BIQ.AFU.AXC.AFU.AFU

carreau
MT.162
CN M.MT.AFU.AFU.AFU.AXC.ALO.ALO.ALO.AFU.AFU.ALO

carrefours
USE **intersections**

carrels
RM.150 (B)
ALT **carrel**
SN Small individual compartments, alcoves, or furniture, such as in libraries, used for semiprivate study. (DAC)
UF carols (carrels)
stalls (carrels)
CN V.RM.AFU.DIO.ALO.CFS.ALO

carrene
USE **methylene chloride**

carriage barns
USE **carriage houses**

carriage bolts
TF.310
ALT **carriage bolt**
SN Threaded bolts having a round smooth head; prevented from rotating in their holes by a square neck directly under the head. (MEANS)
UF bolts, button-headed
bolts, carriage
button-headed bolts
CN V.TF.AFU.AFU.AFU.ALO.AFU.ALO.AFU.ARI

carriage chairs
TG.172
ALT **carriage chair**
SN Adjustable highchairs which may be converted into a carriage or walker.
UF chairs, carriage
combination highchair and carriages
highchair and carriages, combination
CN V.TG.AFU.AFU.ALO.AFU.AFU.ALO.BCW.AFU.AFU

carriage cradles
TG.332
ALT **carriage cradle**
SN Cradles with two front wheels for transport.
UF carriages, cradles and
cradles and carriages
cradles, carriage

CN V.TG.AFU.AFU.ARI.AFU.AFU.AXC.
ALO.AFU

carriage houses
RK.1224 (A,B)
ALT **carriage house**
UF barns, carriage
barns, coach
carriage barns
carriage sheds
chaise houses
coach barns
coach houses
houses, carriage
houses, chaise
houses, coach
sheds, carriage
stables (carriage houses)
CN V.RK.AFU.ALO.ALO.GFO.BUE.AFU

carriage pieces
RT.1100
ALT **carriage piece**
SN Inclined beams which support the steps or add support between the strings of a wooden staircase, usually between the wall and outer string. (DAC)
UF horses (stair components)
pieces, carriage
rough strings
strings, rough
CN V.RT.AFU.BIQ.AXC.ALO.ALO

carriage porches
USE **porte-cocheres**

carriage sheds
USE **carriage houses**

carriages (stair components)
USE **strings**

carriages, cradles and
USE **carriage cradles**

carriageways
USE **roadways**

Carrier
FL.1228 (L)
UF Takulli
CN F.FL.ALO.ALO.ARI.AFU.AFU.ARI.
AXC

carrousels
USE **merry-go-rounds**

carstone
MT.737 (L)
UF gingerbread stone
stone, gingerbread
CN M.MT.AFU.AFU.AFU.DCU.AFU.
ALO.ALO.ARI.ALO.AFU

carte-de-visite photographs
USE **cartes-de-visite**

cartes-de-visite
VJ.77 (L,N,R)
ALT **carte-de-visite**
SN Use for card photographs on mounts measuring about 4 by 2 1\2 inches. Primarily used for portraiture and functioning as calling cards; flourished from the 1860s to the 1880s.
UF card photographs (cartes-de-visite)
cards, sure
carte-de-visite photographs
photographs, carte-de-visite
sure cards
CN V.VJ.AFU.AFU.BCW.AFU.ARI

cartes de visite (visiting cards)
USE **visiting cards**

carthame
USE **safflower (red pigment)**

Carthusian
BM.654 (A,L)
CN B.BM.BZY.AFU.ALO.BCW.ARI

cartoccios
USE **cartouches**

cartograms
VW.141
ALT **cartogram**
SN Highly abstracted, simplified maps, which demonstrate a single idea or a specific type of data, often statistical, in a diagrammatic way. (LG)
CN V.VW.AFU.AFU.AFU.FZU.AXC.
AFU.ARI.AFU.ALO

cartographers
HG.261 (L,R)
ALT **cartographer**
UF mapmakers
CN H.HG.AFU.AXC.BCW.AFU.BCW.
AFU

cartographic materials
VW.122
SN Any materials representing, in whole or part, the earth or any celestial body at any scale. (AACR2)
UF cartographic records
materials, cartographic
records, cartographic
CN V.VW.AFU.AFU.AFU.FZU.AXC.AFU

cartographic records
USE **cartographic materials**

cartography
KT.174 (L,B,R)
UF chartography
mapping (cartography)
CN K.KT.AFU.ALO.DUC.ALO

cartonniers
TG.421
ALT **cartonnier**
SN Pieces of furniture fitted with pigeonholes or compartments to hold boxes made either as independent pieces of furniture or as pieces to be placed on top of a bureau plat. (PC)
CN V.TG.AFU.AFU.AXC.ALO.ARI.
ALO.ALO

cartoon strips
USE **comics**

cartooning
KT.175 (L)
SN The activity of creating cartoons, that is, pictorial parodies.
CN K.KT.AFU.ALO.DUC.ARI

cartoonists
HG.94 (L)
ALT **cartoonist**
SN Persons who draw cartoons (humorous images).
CN H.HG.AFU.AXC.AXC.AFU.AFU.
ALO.AXC.ARI

cartoons (humorous images)
VB.34 (L,R)
ALT **cartoon (humorous image)**
SN Pictorial parodies using caricature, analogy, and ludicrous juxtaposition to comment on such things as contemporary events, social habits, or political trends. (ENCYB)
CN V.VB.AFU.ALO.AFU

cartoons (working drawings)
VD.115 (R)
ALT **cartoon (working drawing)**
SN Use for full-size preparatory drawings made for the purpose of transferring a design to the working surface of a painting, tapestry, or other large work.
CN V.VD.AFU.ALO.DCU.ALO

cartoons, auxiliary
USE **auxiliary cartoons**

cartoons, editorial
USE **editorial cartoons**

cartoons, political
USE **political cartoons**

cartouches
DG.88
ALT **cartouche**
SN Ornamental enframements (as for an inscription, monogram, or coat of arms) or ornately framed tablets, often bearing inscriptions.
UF cartoccios
CN D.DG.AFU.ALO.ALO

cartridge brass
MT.386
UF brass, cartridge
brass, yellow
yellow brass
CN M.MT.AFU.AFU.AFU.BZY.AFU.
AFU.AFU.ALO.ARI.BIQ.AFU.AFU

cartridge paper
MT.1901
SN Fifty- to eighty-pound Manila paper, waxed on one side, originally used for muzzle-loading cartridges, but now employed where a stiff, waterproof material is needed. (MH)
UF paper, cartridge

CN M.MT.AFU.AFU.ARI.ALO.ALO.
AXC.AFU.AXC.ALO.AFU

cartridges, audio
USE **audio cassettes**

cartridges, video
USE **videocassettes**

cartridges, video tape
USE **videocassettes**

carts, concrete
USE **buggies (equipment)**

carts, tea
USE **tea wagons**

cartularies
VW.268 (L)
ALT **cartulary**
SN Registers, usually in volume form, of copies of charters, title deeds, and other documents of significance belonging to a person, family, or institution. (ICA)
UF chartularies
CN V.VW.AFU.AFU.AFU.FZU.BCW.
AFU.BIQ.AFU

cartunnel kilns
USE **tunnel kilns**

Carver chairs
TG.30
ALT **Carver chair**
SN Collector's term for 17th-century American turned great chairs styled after one that belonged to John Carver, Governor of Massachusetts Bay Colony. Such chairs have boldly turned posts and decorative spindles, but unlike Brewster chairs they have spindles only in the back and below the arms, and not below the seat.
UF chairs, Carver
CN V.TG.AFU.AFU.ALO.AFU.AFU.
AFU.ALO.ARI.ALO

carver's mallets
TB.1090 (N)
ALT **carver's mallet**
SN Mallets whose head is a well-rounded truncated cone mounted upside down on a short handle. The shape enables the carver to strike the chisel from any angle without altering the hand's position on the tool. (SALAM)
UF mallets, carver's
CN V.TB.AFU.BCW.CFS.ALO.ARI.ALO.
AXC

carver's punches
TB.974 (N)
ALT **carver's punch**
SN Steel punches with a decorative face, used for marking wood to give texture. (SALAM)
UF punches, carver's
CN V.TB.AFU.BCW.CFS.ALO.AFU.
DZW.AFU

carvers
HG.442
ALT **carver**
SN Persons who engage in carving.
CN H.HG.AFU.AXC.BUE.ALO.ARI

carving
KT.86 (L,R)
ALT **carved**
SN The act of shaping wood, stone, or another material by cutting or incising.
CN K.KT.AFU.ALO.BUE.AFU

carving gouges
TB.884 (N)
ALT **carving gouge**
SN Gouges sharpened both outside and inside; the larger outside bevel is used for hardwoods, and the smaller inside bevel for softwoods. (SALAM)
UF gouges, carving
CN V.TB.AFU.BCW.CFS.ALO.AFU.
CXA.ARI

carving, chip
USE **chip carving**

carving, direct
USE **direct carving**

carving, gem
USE **lapidary**

Carya
USE **hickory**

Carya amara
USE **pignut hickory**

Carya cordiformis
USE **bitternut hickory**

Carya glabra
USE **pignut hickory**

Carya illinoensis
USE **pecan**

Carya illoinesis
USE **pecan**

Carya lactiniosa
USE **big shellbark hickory**

Carya ovata
USE **shagbark hickory**

Carya texana
USE **black hickory**

Carya tomentosa
USE **mockernut hickory**

caryatids
RT.63 (A,L,B,R)
ALT **caryatid**
SN Supporting members serving the function of a pier, column, or pilaster and carved or molded into the form of a draped female human figure.
CN V.RT.AFU.AFU.AFU.AXC.ALO.ALO

Carystian marble
USE **cipollino**

Casali's green
USE **viridian**

Casas Grandes
FL.928
CN F.FL.ALO.ALO.ALO.AFU.ALO.
ARI.BIQ.AFU

cascades
RM.451 (R)
ALT **cascade**
SN Use for man-made stepped waterfalls, whether naturalistic or architectural in form.
UF waterfalls (man-made)
CN V.RM.ALO.AFU.CFS.ALO

cascadis fir
USE **silver fir**

case files
VW.595
ALT **case file**
SN Files relating to a specific action, event, person, place, project, or other subject. (ICA)
UF dossiers
files, case
CN V.VW.AFU.ALO.AFU.BIQ.ARI.ALO

case furniture
TG.396
SN Furniture that encloses a space and is generally boxlike in structure; intended for storage or display.
UF carcase furniture
case pieces
cases (furniture)
furniture, carcase
furniture, case
pieces, case
CN V.TG.AFU.AFU.AXC.ALO

case-hardening
KT.843 (L)
ALT **case-hardened**
SN Producing a hard surface layer on steel, as by carbonizing, cyaniding, and flame hardening. (DAC)
CN K.KT.AFU.ALO.HOE.BCW.ALO.
BCW.AXC.AFU

case histories
VW.329
ALT **case history**
UF histories, case
CN V.VW.AFU.AFU.ALO.CRG.AFU

case method
BM.1157 (L)
UF case teaching
method, case
teaching, case
CN B.BM.DIO.ARI.AFU

case pieces
USE **case furniture**

case teaching
USE **case method**

Casearia praecox
USE **Maracaibo boxwood**

casebooks
VW.523
ALT **casebook**
SN Books containing records of cases illustrative of general principles or typifying significant situations; used for reference or instruction. (GAHLM)
CN V.VW.AFU.ALO.AFU.AFU.ALO.AFU

cased beams
RT.297
ALT **cased beam**
SN Use for beams enclosed in finished millwork.
UF beams, cased
cased-in timbers
timbers, cased-in
CN V.RT.AFU.AFU.AFU.BCW.ALO.AFU.BCW

cased concrete piles
USE **cased piles**

cased glass
MT.256 (R)
SN Glass formed of two or more fused layers of different colors; the top layer may be cut, permitting a lower layer to show through. (DAC)
UF glass, cased
CN M.MT.AFU.AFU.AFU.BIQ.AFU.ARI.ALO

cased-in timbers
USE **cased beams**

cased photographs
VJ.108
ALT **cased photograph**
SN Use to describe photographs, usually daguerreotypes, ambrotypes, or tintypes, mounted in sturdy, boxlike cases.
UF photographs, cased
CN V.VJ.AFU.ARI.ALO.ALO

cased piles
RT.161
ALT **cased pile**
SN Use for concrete piles that are driven together with their steel casing, which is later removed and replaced by a permanent casing. (STEIN)
UF cased concrete piles
piles, cased
CN V.RT.AFU.AFU.AFU.AXC.BUE.ALO.ALO.AFU.AFU.ALO

cased posts
RT.197
ALT **cased post**
SN Use for interior posts or columns encased in finished millwork.
UF posts, cased
CN V.RT.AFU.AFU.AFU.AXC.DCU.AFU.AFU

casein
MT.916 (L)
SN Protein material precipitated from skimmed milk by the action of either rennet or diluted acid; used in the manufacture of plastics.(STEIN) Also used as a binding or adhesive material, and by artists as a paint emulsion.
CN M.MT.AFU.AFU.ALO.AFU.BCW

casein color
USE **casein paint**

casein glue
MT.2347
SN A cold-work, water-resistant paste made from casein by dispersion with a mild base such as ammonia. (MH)
UF glue, casein
CN M.MT.AFU.ARI.ARI.AFU.ALO.ALO.AFU.ARI

casein paint
MT.2519
UF casein color
casein tempera
color, casein
paint, casein
tempera, casein
CN M.MT.AFU.ARI.CRG.ALO.BCW.AFU.ALO.ARI.AFU

casein plastic
MT.2166
UF plastic, casein
CN M.MT.AFU.AFU.ARI.BUE.ALO.AXC.ALO.AXC

casein tempera
USE **casein paint**

casemates
RT.1174
ALT **casemate**
CN V.RT.AFU.BUE.AFU.ALO.ALO.ALO

casement adjusters
USE **casement stays**

casement doors
USE **French doors**

casement fasteners
USE **casement-window fasteners**

casement hinges
TF.134
ALT **casement hinge**
UF hinges, casement
CN V.TF.AFU.AFU.AFU.AFU.CLM.ALO.ALO

casement stays
TF.57
ALT **casement stay**
SN Braces or bars used to hold a casement window open in any of several positions. (MEANS)
UF adjusters, casement
casement adjusters
stays, casement
CN V.TF.AFU.AFU.AFU.AFU.CFS.ALO

casement-window fasteners
TF.45
ALT **casement-window fastener**
UF casement fasteners
fasteners, casement-window
CN V.TF.AFU.AFU.AFU.AFU.BCW.BCW

casement windows
RT.939 (A,B)
ALT **casement window**
SN Windows having a sash that opens on hinges attached to the upright side of the frame.
UF side hung windows
windows, casement
windows, side hung
CN V.RT.AFU.ARI.AFU.AFU.BOK.AFU.AFU.EWY.ALO.AFU

cases (furniture)
USE **case furniture**

cases (kassen)
USE **kassen**

cases (lock components)
TF.562
ALT **case (lock component)**
SN Lock housings. (MEANS)
CN V.TF.AFU.ALO.AXC.ARI

cases of boxes
USE **cabinets**

cases, bottle
USE **bottle cases**

cases, canterbury music
USE **canterburies**

cases, china
USE **china cabinets**

cases, display
USE **showcases**

cases, exhibit
USE **exhibit cases**

cases, high
USE **high chests of drawers**

cases, library
USE **library bookcases**

cases, liquor
USE **bottle cases**

cases, low
USE **low chests**

cases, medal
USE **medal cabinets**

cash journals
USE **cashbooks**

cashbooks
VW.845
ALT **cashbook**
SN Books of original entry in which a record is kept of all cash receipts, disbursements, or both. (GAHLM)
UF cash journals
journals, cash
CN V.VW.AFU.ARI.AFU.BIQ.CXA.AFU.BIQ

casing nails
TF.404
ALT **casing nail**
SN Wire nails with a flaring head, used for outside finish and also for nailing floors. (PUTNAM)
UF nails, casing
CN V.TF.AFU.AFU.AFU.ALO.AFU.CFS.AFU.DCU.ALO

casings
USE **jambs**

casings, door
USE **doorframes**

casinos
RK.1037 (A,L,B)
ALT **casino**
SN Use for public entertainment buildings for meeting, dancing, and general recreation, often with eating and drinking facilities, music, and game rooms; for similar buildings equipped with gambling devices, use **gambling casinos.**
CN V.RK.AFU.ALO.ALO.EWY.AXC.ARI.ARI

casinos, gambling
USE **gambling casinos**

casket stands
USE **cabinet stands**

caskets (chests)
TG.451 (L)
ALT **casket (chest)**
SN Small, usually ornamental, chests or boxes (as for jewels or other valuables). (W)
CN V.TG.AFU.AFU.AXC.ALO.AXC.BIQ

cassapanche
TG.279
ALT **cassapanca**
SN Italian wood benches with a chest under the seat, often in the form of a cassone with an upright back. (DDA)
CN V.TG.AFU.AFU.ALO.ALO.AFU.AFU.ALO

cassava
MT.1063 (L)
UF mandioca
manihot esculenta
manihot utilissima
manioc
tapioca
tapioca plant
yuca
CN M.MT.AFU.AFU.ALO.BIQ.BUE.BUE.ALO

Cassel brown
USE **moderate brown**

Cassel earth
USE **moderate brown**
Van Dyke brown

Cassel yellow
USE **Turner's yellow**

cassettes, audio
USE **audio cassettes**

cassettes, video tape
USE **videocassettes**

Cassite
USE **Kassite**

cassoni
TG.452 (R)
ALT **cassone**
SN Italian 15th- and 16th-century chests, sometimes richly decorated; frequently intended as dower chests. (DDA)
CN V.TG.AFU.AFU.AXC.ALO.AXC.BOK

cassoons
USE **coffers (ceiling components)**

cast-in-place piles
RT.159
ALT **cast-in-place pile**
SN Concrete piles that are poured at their permanent location.
UF formed piles, in situ
in situ formed piles
piles, cast-in-place
CN V.RT.AFU.AFU.AFU.AXC.BUE.ALO.ALO.AFU.AFU

cast iron
MT.337 (A,L,B,R)
CN M.MT.AFU.AFU.AFU.BZY.AFU.AFU.AFU.AFU.AFU

cast plate glass
USE **rolled glass**

cast shadows
BM.863
UF shadows, cast
CN B.BM.CFS.AXC.ALO.AFU.ALO.ALO.BZY.AFU

Castanea
USE **chestnut**

Castanea crenata
USE **Japanese chestnut**

Castanea dentata
USE **American chestnut**

Castanea mollissima
USE **Chinese chestnut**

Castanea sativa
USE **European chestnut**

Castanea vesca
USE **European chestnut**

caste
BM.1127 (L)
CN B.BM.CRG.BUE.AFU

castellations
USE **battlements**

castelli
RD.33
ALT **castellum**
SN Small, ancient Roman fortified towns or outposts.
CN V.RD.AFU.ALO.ALO.AFU.ALO

castelli aquae
RK.577
ALT **castellum aquae**
SN Use for Roman water distribution structures, usually reservoirs, constructed at locations where water delivered by an aqueduct is diverted to various points in town.
CN V.RK.AFU.ALO.ALO.CFS.ALO.BCW.BIQ.AFU

Castelli maiolica
FL.3233 (R)
UF maiolica, Castelli
majolica, Castelli
CN F.FL.ALO.BCW.ALO.ARI.BIQ.BIQ.BCW.ALO.AFU

casters (people)
HG.443
ALT **caster (person)**
SN Persons who engage in casting.
CN H.HG.AFU.AXC.BUE.ALO.AXC

casting
KT.130 (L,R)
ALT **cast**
SN The act or process of making casts or impressions or of shaping in a mold, as in making pottery or in forming metal objects by pouring molten metal into a mold. (W)
CN K.KT.AFU.ALO.DOI.ARI

casting plaster
MT.2443
SN Type of plaster of Paris especially prepared to have the properties most desirable for casting and carving; it is very fine-grained, absorbent, brilliantly white, slow setting, and capable of taking fine detail. (MAYER)
UF plaster, casting
CN M.MT.AFU.ARI.CRG.AFU.AXC.AFU.AXC.ARI.AFU

casting, cavityless
USE **lost-wax process**

casting, centrifugal
USE **centrifugal casting**

casting, continuous
USE **continuous casting**

casting, die
USE **die casting**

casting, full mold
USE **lost-wax process**

casting, investment
USE **lost-wax process**

casting, lost pattern
USE **lost-wax process**

casting, sand
USE **sand casting**

casting, slip
USE **slip casting**

casting, vaporization
USE **lost-wax process**

casting, wax
USE **lost-wax process**

castings
MT.2219
CN M.MT.AFU.ALO.BIQ

castles
RK.436 (A,L,N,B,R)
ALT **castle**
SN Use for buildings or groups of buildings intended primarily to serve as a fortified residence of a prince or nobleman. (AVERY)
CN V.RK.AFU.ALO.ALO.BIQ.ALO

castles, moated
USE **moated castles**

castor oil
MT.2033 (L)
UF oil, castor
CN M.MT.AFU.AFU.ARI.ARI.AXC.ARI.ALO

castors
TF.51 (N)
ALT **castor**
SN Use for wheels set in a swivel and added to the feet on furniture to allow easy movement. Distinguished from **foot sockets** which serve to protect the feet on furniture as well as to allow easy movement.
CN V.TF.AFU.AFU.AFU.AFU.BIQ

castra
RG.134
ALT **castrum**
SN Use for permanent ancient Roman military encampments laid out on a grid; may also designate later castles, forts, or fortified towers.
CN V.RG.AFU.AFU.BZY.ALO.ARI

casts (molds)
USE **molds**

cat houses
USE **brothels**

cat's eye damar
USE **Mata Kuching damar**

cat's paws
USE **tack pulls**

catacombs
RG.27 (A,L,B,R)
ALT **catacomb**
SN Underground systems of passages used as cemeteries, generally unsystematic and irregular in plan with networks of galleries and multiple levels over extensive areas. (TOYNBE)
UF coemeteria
CN V.RG.AFU.AFU.ALO.AFU.AFU

catafalques
RK.458 (A,N,R)
ALT **catafalque**
SN Use for raised structures, often canopied, on which the coffin or effigy of a deceased person lies or is carried in state.
CN V.RK.AFU.ALO.ALO.BOK.ALO

Çatal West ware
FL.2870
UF ware, Çatal West
CN F.FL.ALO.AXC.ARI.AFU.ALO.ARI.BCW

Catalan vaults
USE **pitched-brick vaults**

catalin
MT.2173
SN A thermosetting plastic made of a cast phenol-formaldehyde resin and having high compressive strength and ready machinability. (MH)
CN M.MT.AFU.AFU.ARI.BUE.ALO.AXC.ALO.BIQ.ALO

catalog cards
VW.562 (L)
ALT **catalog card**
UF cards, catalog
CN V.VW.AFU.ALO.AFU.ARI.ARI

catalogers
HG.307 (L)
ALT **cataloger**
CN H.HG.AFU.AXC.BCW.ALO.BCW.ALO.ALO

cataloging
KG.72 (L,B)
ALT **cataloged**
CN K.KG.AFU.AFU.AXC.AXC.AXC

cataloging, descriptive
USE **descriptive cataloging**

catalogs
VW.92 (L,N,R)
ALT **catalog**
SN Enumerations of items, usually arranged systematically, with descriptive details; may be in book form, on cards, or online.
CN V.VW.AFU.AFU.AFU.FZU.ALO

catalogs, accession
USE **accession catalogs**

catalogs, archival
USE **archival catalogs**

catalogs, auction
USE **auction catalogs**

catalogs, author
USE **author catalogs**

catalogs, booksellers'
USE **booksellers' catalogs**

catalogs, card
USE **card catalogs**

catalogs, classed
USE **classified catalogs**

catalogs, classified
USE **classified catalogs**

catalogs, commercial
USE **commercial catalogs**

catalogs, dictionary
USE **dictionary catalogs**

catalogs, exhibition
USE **exhibition catalogs**

catalogs, loose-leaf
USE **loose-leaf catalogs**

catalogs, mail order
USE **mail order catalogs**

catalogs, manufacturers'
USE **manufacturers' catalogs**

catalogs, online
USE **online catalogs**

catalogs, publishers'
USE **publishers' catalogs**

catalogs, sale
USE **sale catalogs**

catalogs, sheaf
USE **loose-leaf catalogs**

catalogs, subject
USE **subject catalogs**

catalogs, systematic
USE **classified catalogs**

catalogs, trade
USE **commercial catalogs**

catalogs, union
USE **union catalogs**

catalogues raisonnés
VW.105 (R)
ALT **catalogue raisonné**
UF oeuvre catalogues
CN V.VW.AFU.AFU.AFU.FZU.ALO.ALO.ALO

catalpa
MT.1130 (L)
UF bean tree
bean tree, Indian
Indian bean tree
tree, bean
tree, Indian bean
CN M.MT.AFU.AFU.ALO.BIQ.DCU.AFU.AFU.AFU.CFS

catalysts
MT.2419 (L)
CN M.MT.AFU.ARI.CFS

cataracts
RD.164 (L,R)
ALT **cataract**
SN Large, often high, thundering waterfalls; may also be used to designate a series of rapids.
CN V.RD.ARI.AFU.AFU.ALO.BIQ.AFU

catch basins
RT.1452
ALT **catch basin**
SN Receptacles that separate and retain greases, oil, dirt, gravel, and all other substances lighter or heavier than the liquid waste that bears them, such as to prevent their entrance into the house sewer. (STEIN)
UF basins, catch
CN V.RT.ALO.BCW.ALO.ARI.AFU

catches
TF.40
ALT **catch**
SN Use for holding devices that rely on a roller, magnet, or friction as the means of closure. Distinguished from latches which rely on some form of horizontal bar, such as a bolt, rod, or hook.
CN V.TF.AFU.AFU.AFU.AFU.BCW

catches, back
USE **back catches**

catches, ball
USE **ball catches**

catches, blind
USE **blind catches**

catches, bullet
USE **bullet catches**

catches, cupboard
USE **cupboard catches**

catches, friction
USE **friction catches**

catches, magnetic
USE **magnetic catches**

catches, magnetic push
USE **magnetic push catches**

catches, roller
USE **roller latches**

catches, screen-door
USE **screen-door latches**

catches, transom
USE **transom catches**

catechisms
VW.541 (L,R)
ALT **catechism**
CN V.VW.AFU.ALO.AFU.AFU.ALO.BUE.AXC

catechu
USE **cutch**

catenary arches
RT.222
ALT **catenary arch**
SN Arches constructed on the principle of the catenary, the shape assumed by a cord suspended at its ends from two supports in equilibrium under given forces.
UF arches, catenary
CN V.RT.AFU.AFU.AFU.BCW.AFU.AFU.AFU.AXC

cathedrae
TG.165 (A,L,B,R)
ALT **cathedra**
SN Ancient Roman chairs with a rounded backboard resting on vertical stiles and curved legs. (RICHTE)
CN V.TG.AFU.AFU.ALO.AFU.AFU.ALO.ARI.AFU

cathedral ceilings
RT.723
ALT **cathedral ceiling**
UF ceilings, cathedral
CN V.RT.AFU.ALO.AFU.ALO.BCW

cathedral cities
RD.23
ALT **cathedral city**
UF cathedral towns
cities, cathedral
towns, cathedral
CN V.RD.AFU.ALO.AFU.ALO

cathedral closes
USE **closes**

cathedral records
USE **church records**

Cathedral Style
USE **Troubadour**

cathedral towns
USE **cathedral cities**

cathedrals
RK.1106 (A,L,B,R)
ALT **cathedral**
CN V.RK.AFU.ALO.ALO.FCS.BIQ.ALO.ARI.ALO

cathedrals, double
USE **double churches**

cathedrals, twin
USE **double churches**

Catherine-wheel windows
USE **rose windows**

Catholic Reformation
USE **Counter-Reformation**

Catholicism
BM.628 (L,B)
ALT **Catholic**
UF Roman Catholicism
CN B.BM.BZY.AFU.ALO.AFU

catladders
USE **catwalks**

catlinite
MT.55
UF pipestone
CN M.MT.AFU.AFU.AFU.AXC.AFU.AFU.ARI

Catloltx
USE **Comox**

Catlow
FL.906
CN F.FL.ALO.ALO.ALO.AFU.ALO.ARI.ALO.AFU

Catoquina Indians
USE **Catukina**

catslide houses
USE **saltbox houses**

catsteps
USE **crowsteps**

catsup gables
USE **crow-stepped gables**

cattle barns
RK.48 (L,B)
ALT **cattle barn**
SN Barns for beef cattle; for dairy cow housing, use **dairy barns**; for primarily open shelters for bovines, use **cow sheds.**
UF barns, cattle
cattle housing
housing, cattle
CN V.RK.AFU.ALO.ALO.AFU.AFU.AFU.ALO.AFU

cattle housing
USE **cattle barns**

cattle manure
USE **cow manure**

cattle ranches
RG.24 (A,L)
ALT **cattle ranch**
UF ranches, cattle
CN V.RG.AFU.AFU.AFU.BIQ.AFU

cattle sheds
USE cow sheds

Catukina
FL.1574 (L)
UF Catoquina Indians
CN F.FL.ALO.ALO.ARI.ARI.AFU.BOK

catwalks
RT.1063
ALT catwalk
SN Narrow fixed walkways providing access to an otherwise inaccessable area or to lighting units; generally used above the ceiling of an auditorium or theater, or around a stage house. (DAC)
UF catladders
duckboards
CN V.RT.AFU.BIQ.AFU

caulicoles
RT.136
ALT caulicole
SN Ornamental stalks rising between the leaves of a Corinthian capital, from which the volutes spring. (HAS)
CN V.RT.AFU.AFU.AFU.AXC.BIQ.ALO.ARI.ALO.AXC

caulk, latex
USE latex caulk

caulking
USE caulking compounds

caulking chisels
USE caulking irons

caulking compounds
MT.2650 (A,L,B)
UF calking compounds
caulking
caulking materials
compounds, caulking
materials, caulking
CN M.MT.AFU.ARI.HTY.AFU

caulking irons
TB.511 (N)
ALT caulking iron
SN Steel tools resembling chisels, most often characterized by a large, thick, flat blade cast as a single piece with a narrower handle and striking surface; used in conjunction with a caulking mallet to drive various materials into seams and crevices to make joints water- and airtight.
UF caulking chisels
caulking tools
chisels, caulking
irons, caulking
tools, caulking
CN V.TB.AFU.ARI.EWY.ALO.BIQ

caulking mallets
TB.469 (N)
ALT caulking mallet
SN Long-headed wooden mallets used for driving caulking irons. (SALAM)
UF mallets, caulking
mallets, ship-carpenter's
ship-carpenter's mallets
CN V.TB.AFU.ARI.ELK.ARI.AFU

caulking materials
USE caulking compounds

caulking tools
USE caulking irons

cauls
TB.1047
ALT caul
SN Tools used in forming veneer to the shape of a curved surface. (PUTNAM)
CN V.TB.AFU.BCW.CFS.ALO.ALO.AXC

cauponae
RK.957
ALT caupona
CN V.RK.AFU.ALO.ALO.ELK.BIQ.AFU

causeuses
USE marquises

causeways
RK.1564 (L)
ALT causeway
SN Use for roads or pathways raised above surrounding low, wet, or uneven ground.
CN V.RK.ALO.ALO.BIQ.ARI.AXC.AFU

caustic lime
USE quicklime

caustic potash
USE potassium hydroxide

caustic soda
USE sodium hydroxide

cavalier oblique drawings
VD.16
ALT cavalier oblique drawing
SN Use for drawings in oblique projection in which the vertical plane is parallel to the plane of projection (drawing surface), and all three spatial axes are drawn to the same scale.
UF cavalier perspectives
cavalier projections
drawings, cavalier oblique
military perspectives
oblique drawings, cavalier
perspectives, cavalier
perspectives, military
projections, cavalier
CN V.VD.AFU.AFU.BIQ.AFU.ARI.AFU.ALO

cavalier perspectives
USE cavalier oblique drawings

cavalier projections
USE cavalier oblique drawings

cavaliers
RT.1177
ALT cavalier
SN Raised portions of a fortress for commanding adjacent defenses or for the placement of weapons. (HAS)
CN V.RT.AFU.BUE.AFU.AXC

cave architecture
RK.1348 (A,L)
UF architecture, cave
architecture, grotto
grotto architecture
CN V.RK.AFU.ALO.ARI.AXC.ALO

cave art
BM.234
UF art, cave
CN B.BM.AFU.ARI.BCW.BCW

cave churches
RK.1107 (A,L,B)
ALT cave church
UF churches, cave
churches, monolithic
churches, rock
monolithic churches
rock churches
CN V.RK.AFU.ALO.ALO.FCS.BIQ.ALO.ARI.ARI

cave drawings
VD.121 (L)
ALT cave drawing
UF drawings, cave
CN V.VD.AFU.ARI.AFU

cave dwellings
RK.306 (L,B)
ALT cave dwelling
UF cave houses
dwellings, cave
houses, cave
CN V.RK.AFU.ALO.ALO.AXC.ALO.AXC.ALO.ALO

cave houses
USE cave dwellings

cave temples
RK.1138 (A,L,B)
ALT cave temple
UF temples, cave
CN V.RK.AFU.ALO.ALO.FCS.BIQ.BZY.ARI.AFU

caveae
RM.350
ALT cavea
CN V.RM.AFU.DIO.AXC.AXC.AFU.ALO

Cavernas
USE Paracas Cavernas

caverns
RD.233 (A,L,R)
ALT cavern
SN Use for large, subterranean, naturally formed chambers, with entrances from the surface.
CN V.RD.ARI.AFU.AXC.ALO.AFU

caves
RD.234 (A,L,B,R)

ALT **cave**
CN V.RD.ARI.AFU.AXC.ALO.ALO

caves, chaitya
USE **chaityas**

caves, storm
USE **storm cellars**

cavetto cornices
RT.335
ALT **cavetto cornice**
SN Cornices consisting of a large cavetto molding, sometimes decorated.
UF cornices, cavetto
cornices, gorge
Egyptian gorges
gorge cornices
gorges, Egyptian
CN V.RT.AFU.AFU.AFU.BCW.BZY.ALO.ALO.AFU.ALO

cavetto moldings
RT.771
ALT **cavetto molding**
SN Moldings with a rounded concave surface. (HAS)
UF cove moldings
gorge moldings
hollow moldings
moldings, cavetto
moldings, cove
moldings, gorge
moldings, hollow
moldings, throat
throat moldings
trochili
CN V.RT.AFU.ALO.AFU.BOK.AFU.AFU.AXC.ALO

cavils
TB.568 (N)
ALT **cavil**
SN Axes having a flat face for knocking off projecting angular points and a pointed peen for reducing a surface to a desired form. (DAC)
UF axes, jedding
jedding axes
kevils
CN V.TB.AFU.BCW.BCW.ALO.AXC.AFU

cavity walls
RT.576 (B)
ALT **cavity wall**
SN Walls, usually of masonry, consisting of two wythes separated by a continuous air space. (DAC)
UF hollow masonry walls
hollow walls
masonry walls, hollow
walls, cavity
walls, hollow
walls, hollow masonry
CN V.RT.AFU.AFU.AFU.BIQ.BUE.AFU.AFU.BCW

cavityless casting
USE **lost-wax process**

Cawahib
USE **Parintintin**

Cayapó
FL.1575 (L)
UF Kayapo
CN F.FL.ALO.ALO.ARI.ARI.AFU.BUE

Cayuá
USE **Caingang**

Cayuga
FL.1293 (L)
CN F.FL.ALO.ALO.ARI.AFU.ARI.BCW.AFU

Cayuse
FL.1405 (L)
CN F.FL.ALO.ALO.ARI.AFU.BUE.AFU

CBDs
USE **central business districts**

CCUs
USE **coronary care units**

CDs (compact disks)
USE **compact disks**

cedar
MT.1333 (L,R)
UF Cedrus
CN M.MT.AFU.AFU.ALO.BIQ.DCU.AFU.AFU.ALO.ALO

cedar green
USE **chrysocolla**

cedar, African
USE **African cedar**

cedar, Atlantic
USE **Atlantic cedar**

cedar, Atlantic white
USE **white cypress**

cedar, atlas
USE **Atlantic cedar**

cedar, bastard
USE **incense cedar**

cedar, Borneo
USE **Borneo mahogany**

cedar, Central American
USE **Spanish cedar**

cedar, Chinese
USE **toon**

cedar, cigar-box
USE **Spanish cedar**

cedar, Himalayan
USE **deodar**

cedar, incense
USE **incense cedar**

cedar, Lebanon
USE **Lebanon cedar**

cedar, Oregon
USE **Port Orford cedar**

cedar, Paraguayan
USE **Paraguayan cedar**

cedar, pencil
USE **red cedar**

cedar, Port Orford
USE **Port Orford cedar**

cedar, red
USE **red cedar**

cedar, southern white
USE **white cypress**

cedar, Spanish
USE **Spanish cedar**

cedar, white
USE **Port Orford cedar**

cedar, yellow
USE **yellow cypress**

Cedrela braziliensis
USE **Paraguayan cedar**

Cedrela odorata
USE **Spanish cedar**

Cedrela sinensis
USE **toon**

Cedrela toona
USE **toon**
Cedrus
USE **cedar**

Cedrus atlantica
USE **Atlantic cedar**

Cedrus deodara
USE **deodar**

Cedrus libani
USE **Lebanon cedar**

ceika
USE **kapok**

ceiling hooks
TF.154 (N)
ALT **ceiling hook**
SN Hooks that fasten to the ceiling or to the underside of shelves. (BROWNL)
UF hooks, ceiling
CN V.TF.AFU.AFU.AFU.AFU.CXA.AXC

ceiling joists
RT.304
ALT **ceiling joist**
SN Joists which carry a ceiling; also small beams to which the ceiling of a room is attached.
UF joists, ceiling
CN V.RT.AFU.AFU.AFU.BCW.ALO.AFU.BOK.ALO.AFU

ceiling plans, reflected
USE **reflected ceiling plans**

ceilings
RT.718 (A,L,B,R)
ALT **ceiling**
SN The overhead surfaces of rooms.
UF plafonds
CN V.RT.AFU.ALO.AFU.ALO

ceilings, acoustical
USE **acoustical ceilings**

ceilings, barrel
USE **barrel ceilings**

ceilings, beam
USE **beam ceilings**

ceilings, camp
USE **camp ceilings**

ceilings, cathedral
USE **cathedral ceilings**

ceilings, coffered
USE **coffered ceilings**

ceilings, compartment
USE **compartment ceilings**

ceilings, cove
USE **cove ceilings**

ceilings, cum
USE **camp ceilings**

ceilings, domed
USE **domed ceilings**

ceilings, drop
USE **suspended ceilings**

ceilings, false
USE **suspended ceilings**

ceilings, luminous
USE **luminous ceilings**

ceilings, suspended
USE **suspended ceilings**

ceilings, tent
USE **camp ceilings**

ceilings, tray
USE **camp ceilings**

celadon
MT.2562
CN M.MT.AFU.ARI.CRG.ARI.ARI.AFU.AFU.ARI

celadon (color)
USE **very pale green**

celadon gray
USE **grayish yellow green**
pale green

celadon green
USE **grayish yellow green**
green earth
moderate yellowish green
pale green

Celebes
USE **Sulawesi**

celebrating
KG.217
SN Observing, honoring, or commemorating with ceremonies, festivities, or wide public praise. (RHDEL2)
CN K.KG.AFU.ALO.BOK.AFU

celebrations
KM.5 (R)
CN K.KM.AFU.ALO

celestial charts
USE **astronomical charts**

celestial globes
VW.136 (L,R)
ALT **celestial globe**
UF globes, celestial
CN V.VW.AFU.AFU.AFU.FZU.AXC.AFU.ALO.AFU

celestial photographs
USE **astrophotographs**

celestial photography
USE **astronomical photography**

celite
USE **diatomaceous earth**

cellae
USE **naoi**

cellarets, wine
USE **wine coolers**

cellarette drawers
USE **celleret drawers**

cellarettes
USE **cellerets**

cellarettes, wine
USE **cellerets**

cellars
RM.187 (A,L,B)
ALT **cellar**
SN Use for rooms, wholly or mostly below ground level, used for storage, particularly of food; for similar areas serving utility purposes or as living spaces, use **basements.**
CN V.RM.AFU.DIO.ALO.DCU.ARI

cellars, beer
USE **beer cellars**

cellars, cyclone
USE **storm cellars**

cellars, root
USE **root cellars**

cellars, storm
USE **storm cellars**

cellars, tornado
USE **storm cellars**

cellars, wine
USE **wine cellars**

celleret drawers
TG.880
ALT **celleret drawer**
UF bottle drawers
cellarette drawers
drawers, bottle
drawers, cellarette
drawers, celleret
CN V.TG.ALO.DCU.AFU.ALO.AFU

celleret sideboards
TG.589
ALT **celleret sideboard**
SN Sideboards with a place at one end to hold bottles of wine and at the other end either a plain drawer or a drawer lined with lead, in which glasses could be washed.
UF sideboards, celleret
CN V.TG.AFU.AFU.AXC.ALO.CRG.ARI

cellerets
TG.453 (N)
ALT **celleret**
SN Use for small chests or cabinets, usually with locks and often fitted with side handles, designed to store bottles of wine or liquor. For metal-lined tubs or stands for cooling wine bottles, use **wine coolers.**
UF butlers (cellerets)
cellarettes
cellarettes, wine
cellerettes
chests, wine
gardes du vin
guardivines
sarcophagi (cellerets)
wine cellarettes
wine chests
CN V.TG.AFU.AFU.AXC.ALO.AXC.BUE

cellerettes
USE **cellerets**

cellosolve
USE **ethylene glycol monoethyl ether**

cells
RM.261
ALT **cell**
SN Single rooms usually housing only one person within a building having numerous similar rooms, as in a convent or in a prison. (W)
CN V.RM.AFU.DIO.ARI.ALO.BCW

cells (vault components)
USE **vaulting cells**

cells, vault
USE **vaulting cells**

cells, vaulting
USE **vaulting cells**

cellular brick
MT.87
UF brick, cellular
CN M.MT.AFU.AFU.AFU.AXC.ALO.AFU.AFU.ALO.AFU

cellular concrete
USE **air-entrained concrete**

cellular frames
USE **box frames**

cellular glass
MT.257 (L)
UF cellulated glass
expanded glass
foamed glass
glass, cellular
glass, cellulated
glass, expanded
glass, foamed
CN M.MT.AFU.AFU.AFU.BIQ.AFU.
ARI.ARI

cellular materials
MT.2220
UF materials, cellular
CN M.MT.AFU.ALO.BOK

cellular plastic
USE **plastic foam**

cellulated glass
USE **cellular glass**

celluloid
MT.2133 (L)
SN A tough, highly flammable but not usually explosive synthetic thermoplastic composed essentially of cellulose nitrate and camphor or other plasticizer. (W)
CN M.MT.AFU.AFU.ARI.BUE.ALO.
AXC.AFU.BCW.ARI.AFU

cellulose
MT.1044 (L)
CN M.MT.AFU.AFU.ALO.BIQ.BUE.ALO

cellulose acetate
MT.2127
UF acetate, cellulose
CA
CN M.MT.AFU.AFU.ARI.BUE.ALO.
AXC.AFU.BCW.AFU

cellulose acetate butyrate
USE **butyrate**

cellulose cement
MT.2352
UF cement, cellulose
CN M.MT.AFU.ARI.ARI.AFU.ALO.
ALO.ALO.AFU

cellulose diacetate
MT.2128
UF diacetate, cellulose
CN M.MT.AFU.AFU.ARI.BUE.ALO.
AXC.AFU.BCW.AFU.AFU

cellulose ether
MT.2130
UF ether, cellulose
CN M.MT.AFU.AFU.ARI.BUE.ALO.
AXC.AFU.BCW.ALO

cellulose nitrate
USE **nitrocellulose**

cellulose triacetate
MT.2129
SN Fully esterified cellulose acetate containing three acetyl groups per glucose unit. (NEBLET)
UF triacetate (cellulose triacetate)
triacetate, cellulose
CN M.MT.AFU.AFU.ARI.BUE.ALO.
AXC.AFU.BCW.AFU.ALO

cellulose, ethyl
USE **ethyl cellulose**

cellulosic
MT.2126
UF cellulosic plastic
plastic, cellulosic
CN M.MT.AFU.AFU.ARI.BUE.ALO.
AXC.AFU.BCW

cellulosic plastic
USE **cellulosic**

celters
USE **testers**

Celtic
FL.2522 (A,L,B,R)
UF Keltic
CN F.FL.ALO.AXC.AFU.BOK.ALO.AFU

Celtic crosses
DG.7
ALT **Celtic cross**
SN Crosses having a ring or halo about the intersection. (IDO)
UF crosses of Iona
crosses, Celtic
crosses, Iona
crosses, Irish
crosses, ring
crosses, wheel (Celtic crosses)
crosses, wheel-head
Iona crosses
Irish crosses
ring crosses
wheel crosses (Celtic crosses)
wheel-head crosses
CN D.DG.AFU.AFU.ARI.ALO

Celtic trumpet motifs
USE **trumpet spirals**

celtis
USE **hackberry**

Celtis australis
USE **European hackberry**

Celtis mississippiensis
USE **Mississippi hackberry**

Celtis sinensis
USE **Chinese hackberry**

celures
USE **testers**

cement
MT.6 (L,B,R)
SN A material, usually in powder form that can be made into a paste when mixed with water, that is used as a construction material as an ingredient of mortar and concrete. (W)
CN M.MT.AFU.AFU.AFU.ALO.AFU

cement clinker
USE **clinker**

cement-coated nails
TF.389
ALT **cement-coated nail**
SN Nails which are coated with cement in order to increase friction and holding power. (MEANS)
UF nails, cement-coated
CN V.TF.AFU.AFU.AFU.ALO.AFU.CFS.
AFU.ALO

cement color
MT.1809
UF color, cement
CN M.MT.AFU.AFU.ARI.AFU.ALO.AFU

cement kilns
TB.97 (L)
ALT **cement kiln**
SN Kilns used to fire cement to less than complete melting. (MHDSTT)
UF kilns, cement
CN V.TB.AFU.ARI.ALO.ARI.ALO.
ALO.ALO

cement mixers
USE **concrete mixers**

cement mortar
MT.2596
UF mortar, cement
CN M.MT.AFU.ARI.DZW.ARI.AFU.AFU

cement plants
RK.627 (L)
ALT **cement plant**
UF plants, cement
CN V.RK.AFU.ALO.ALO.CLM.ALO.
ALO.AFU.AXC.ARI

cement stone
USE **hydraulic limestone**

cement, accelerated
USE **accelerated cement**

cement, aluminate
USE **aluminous cement**

cement, aluminous
USE **aluminous cement**

cement, asphalt
USE **asphalt cement**

cement, brick
USE **brick cement**

cement, cellulose
USE **cellulose cement**

cement, expanding
USE **expanding cement**

cement, expansive
USE **expanding cement**

cement, extra-rapid-hardening
USE **high-early-strength cement**

cement, flooring
USE **gypsum cement**

cement, glass reinforced
USE **glass reinforced cement**

cement, granite-powder
USE **granite-powder cement**

cement, gypsum
USE **gypsum cement**

cement, high alumina
USE **aluminous cement**

cement, high-early
USE **high-early-strength cement**

cement, high-early-strength
USE **high-early-strength cement**

cement, high speed
USE **aluminous cement**

cement, hydraulic
USE **natural cement**

cement, hydraulic lime
USE **natural cement**

cement, joint
USE **Spackle (TM)**

cement, Keene's
USE **Keene's cement**

cement, low-heat
USE **low-heat cement**

cement, Mack's
USE **Mack's cement**

cement, magnesia
USE **magnesia cement**

cement, Martin's
USE **Martin's cement**

cement, masonry
USE **masonry cement**

cement, moderate portland
USE **modified portland cement**

cement, modified portland
USE **modified portland cement**

cement, natural
USE **natural cement**

cement, neat
USE **neat cement**

cement, oxychloric
USE **oxychloric cement**

cement, Parian
USE **Parian cement**

cement, polymer-impregnated
USE **polymer-impregnated cement**

cement, portland
USE **portland cement**

cement, portland blast-furnace
USE **portland slag cement**

cement, portland blast-furnace-slag
USE **portland slag cement**

cement, portland normal
USE **standard portland cement**

cement, portland-pozzolan
USE **portland-pozzolan cement**

cement, portland slag
USE **portland slag cement**

cement, pozzolan
USE **pozzolan cement**

cement, pozzuolana
USE **pozzolan cement**

cement, rapid-hardening
USE **accelerated cement**

cement, Roman
USE **natural cement**
pozzolan cement

cement, slag
USE **slag cement**

cement, soil
USE **soil cement**

cement, sorel
USE **oxychloric cement**

cement, standard portland
USE **standard portland cement**

cement, sulfate-resistant
USE **sulfate-resistant cement**

cement, sulfate-resisting
USE **sulfate-resistant cement**

cement, sulfoaluminate
USE **expanding cement**

cement, sulfur
USE **sulfur cement**

cement, sulphur
USE **sulfur cement**

cement, supersulphate
USE **sulfur cement**

cement, type I portland
USE **standard portland cement**

cement, type II portland
USE **modified portland cement**

cement, type III
USE **high-early-strength cement**

cement, type III portland
USE **high-early-strength cement**

cement, type IV
USE **low-heat cement**

cement, type V portland
USE **sulfate-resistant cement**

cement, waterproof
USE **natural cement**

cemeteries
RG.25 (A,L,B,R)
ALT **cemetery**
UF burial grounds
burying-grounds
graveyards
grounds, burial
CN V.RG.AFU.AFU.ALO

cemeteries, animal
USE **pet cemeteries**

cemeteries, military
USE **national cemeteries**
war cemeteries

cemeteries, national
USE **national cemeteries**

cemeteries, pet
USE **pet cemeteries**

cemeteries, war
USE **war cemeteries**

cemetery beacons
USE **lanterns of the dead**

cendre
USE **azurite**

cendre blue
MT.1584
UF blue, cendre
CN M.MT.AFU.AFU.ARI.AFU.AFU.ALO.ALO.ALO.AFU.ARI

cenotaphs
RK.477 (A,B,R)
ALT **cenotaph**
SN Sepulchral monuments erected to a person or persons buried elsewhere. (PDARC)
CN V.RK.AFU.ALO.ALO.BOK.BOK.AFU

censoring
KG.66
ALT **censored**
SN Altering, deleting, or banning completely a report, document, art work, or any item bearing a message, information, or image which the censoring body wants to suppress.
CN K.KG.AFU.AFU.AXC.ALO

censorship
BM.1094 (L,R)
CN B.BM.CRG.BCW.AFU

census districts
USE **census tracts**

census maps
VW.199 (L)
ALT **census map**
UF maps, census
CN V.VW.AFU.AFU.AFU.FZU.AXC.

AFU.ARI.AXC.CFS.AFU

census records
VW.812
ALT **census record**
SN Official, usually periodic, lists of persons or property with varying degrees of descriptive detail. (ICA)
UF census returns
census schedules
censuses
records, census
returns, census
schedules, census
CN V.VW.AFU.ARI.AFU.BCW

census returns
USE **census records**

census schedules
USE **census records**

census tracts
RG.262 (L)
ALT **census tract**
UF census districts
districts, census
tracts, census
CN V.RG.ALO.AFU.AFU.BZY.AFU

censuses
USE **census records**

center bits
TB.1102 (N)
ALT **center bit**
SN Tools used to start holes or make shallow borings in wood. They are held by braces and consist of a sharp point (or threaded center spur), a projecting scoring edge, and a sharp lip for cutting away the wood inside the circumference. (DAC)
UF bits, center
CN V.TB.ALO.ARI.AXC

center bits, plug
USE **tenon-cutting bits**

center cities
USE **inner cities**

center of projection
BM.153
SN Use for the implied location of the viewer's eye in a perspective construction.
UF projection, center of
CN B.BM.AFU.AFU.ARI.BOK.CFS.AFU

center tables
TG.773 (N)
ALT **center table**
SN Tables of any shape, finished on all sides and used in the center of a room for any purpose. (ARON)
UF tables, center
CN V.TG.AFU.AFU.BIQ.BOK.ARI.
AFU.AFU

centerbead molding planes
USE **centerboard planes**

centerboard planes
TB.954 (N)
ALT **centerboard plane**
SN Planes that cut a bead or some other simple shape, and that are provided with a fence so that the molding can be cut in the middle of a piece of work. (SALAM)
UF centerbead molding planes
molding planes, centerbead
planes, centerbead molding
planes, centerboard
CN V.TB.AFU.BCW.CFS.ALO.AFU.
DUC.AXC.AFU.ARI

centered
DC.27
CN D.DC.AFU.ALO.ARI.ALO

centers
BM.764
CN B.BM.CFS.ARI.AXC.ARI

centers for the performing arts
USE **performing arts centers**

centers, adult day care
USE **adult day care centers**

centers, adult day health
USE **adult day care centers**

centers, adult education
USE **continuing education centers**

centers, advice
USE **information centers**

centers, architectural
USE **architectural centers**

centers, art
USE **art centers**

centers, audiovisual
USE **audiovisual centers**

centers, business
USE **central business districts**

centers, child care
USE **day care centers**

centers, civic
USE **civic centers**

centers, college community
USE **student unions**

centers, commercial
USE **central business districts**

centers, community
USE **community centers**

centers, community recreation
USE **community centers**

centers, computer
USE **computer centers**

centers, conference
USE **convention centers**

centers, continuing education
USE **continuing education centers**

centers, convention
USE **convention centers**

centers, cultural
USE **cultural centers**

centers, data processing
USE **computer centers**

centers, data processing service
USE **computer centers**

centers, day care
USE **day care centers**

centers, design
USE **design centers**

centers, detention
USE **detention centers**

centers, documentation
USE **documentation centers**

centers, emergency medical
USE **emergency medical centers**

centers, growth
USE **growth centers**

centers, health
USE **health facilities**
medical centers

centers, immunization
USE **vaccination centers**

centers, information
USE **information centers**

centers, information (organizations)
USE **information services**

centers, instructional materials
USE **audiovisual centers**
learning resource centers

centers, juvenile detention
USE **detention centers**

centers, learning resource
USE **learning resource centers**

centers, medical
USE **medical centers**

centers, municipal
USE **civic centers**

centers, nature
USE **nature centers**

centers, parish
USE **parish houses**

centers, performing arts
USE **performing arts centers**

centers, physical training
USE **physical education buildings**

centers, pilgrimage
USE **pilgrimage centers**

centers, play
USE **playgrounds**

centers, poison control
USE **poison control centers**

centers, recreation
USE **recreation centers**

centers, rehabilitation
USE **rehabilitation centers**

centers, research
USE **research centers**

centers, school media
USE **learning resource centers**

centers, science
USE **science museums**

centers, senior
USE **senior centers**

centers, shopping
USE **shopping centers**

centers, social
USE **community centers**

centers, sports
USE **sports complexes**

centers, student
USE **student unions**

centers, tourist information
USE **information centers**

centers, transport
USE **terminals**

centers, urban
USE **central cities**

centers, vaccination
USE **vaccination centers**

centers, village community
USE **community centers**

centers, visitors'
USE **visitors' centers**

centers, welfare
USE **welfare buildings**

centers, youth
USE **youth centers**

central
DC.28
CN D.DC.AFU.ALO.ARI.ARI

central air conditioning
RT.1384
UF air conditioning, central
central systems
CN V.RT.ALO.BCW.AFU.AFU.AFU.AFU

Central American
FL.704 (L,B,R)
UF American, Central
CN F.FL.ALO.ALO.AFU.AFU

Central American cedar
USE **Spanish cedar**

Central Asian
FL.1762 (L)
UF Asian, Central
Transoxiana
CN F.FL.ALO.ARI.AFU

central business districts
RG.291 (A,L,B)
ALT **central business district**
SN Designates the high density cores of cities, where activities are principally retail, commercial, service, and often governmental.
UF business centers
business districts, central
CBDs
centers, business
centers, commercial
commercial centers
districts, central business
downtowns
CN V.RG.ALO.ALO.ALO

central cities
RG.292
ALT **central city**
SN Largest core areas within the incorporated limits of metropolitan areas; often used to distinguish the center from the suburban or newer outlying sections of metropolitan areas; generally excludes the central business district and inner city sections.
UF centers, urban
urban centers
CN V.RG.ALO.ALO.ARI

Central Ge
FL.1677
UF Ge, Central
CN F.FL.ALO.ALO.ARI.ARI.BIQ.BCW

Central Indian
FL.2266
UF Indian, Central
CN F.FL.ALO.ARI.AXC.ALO.AFU.BZY.BCW.AFU

Central Javanese
FL.2378
UF Javanese, Central
CN F.FL.ALO.ARI.BCW.ARI.ALO.AXC.AFU

central perspective
USE **one-point perspective**

central perspectives
USE **one-point perspectives**

central-plan
DC.79
UF centralized-plan
centrally planned
CN D.DC.AFU.ARI.ERE.ALO

central projection
KT.279
SN Technique for representing three-dimensional objects in two dimensions using projecting lines that converge toward one or more points rather than running parallel, as in one-point, two-point, and three-point perspective.
UF perspective projection
projection, central
projection, perspective
CN K.KT.AFU.ALO.DUC.DCU.BOK.AFU

central systems
USE **central air conditioning**

central towers
USE **crossing towers**

centralized-plan
USE **central-plan**

centrally planned
USE **central-plan**

centrifugal casting
KT.134 (L)
SN A method of casting by the lost-wax process using a machine in which the mold revolves so that its cavity is filled with molten metal by centrifugal action and pressure. (MAYER)
UF casting, centrifugal
CN K.KT.AFU.ALO.DOI.ARI.ARI.AFU

centrifugal force
BM.895 (L)
SN Force that tends to impel matter outward from a center of rotation. (WCOL)
UF force, centrifugal
CN B.BM.CFS.AXC.BIQ.AFU.AXC.ALO

centripetal force
BM.896 (L)
SN Force that keeps an object moving in a circular path and that is directed inward toward the center of rotation. (WCOL)
UF force, centripetal
CN B.BM.CFS.AXC.BIQ.AFU.AXC.ARI

centripetal spring chairs
TG.224
ALT **centripetal spring chair**
SN Reclining chairs with a spring concealed under the seat which allows the chairs to recline and then snap into place; attributed to the American Chair Company, Troy, NY, about 1850. (HAYWAR)
UF chairs, centripetal spring
spring chairs, centripetal
CN V.TG.AFU.AFU.ALO.AFU.AFU.AXC.ALO.AFU

centroid color 1
USE **vivid pink**

centroid color 10
USE **pinkish gray**

centroid color 100
USE **deep greenish yellow**

centroid color 101
USE **light greenish yellow**

centroid color 102
USE **moderate greenish yellow**

centroid color 103
USE **dark greenish yellow**

centroid color 104
USE **pale greenish yellow**

centroid color 105
USE **grayish greenish yellow**

centroid color 106
USE **light olive**

centroid color 107
USE **moderate olive**

centroid color 108
USE **dark olive**

centroid color 109
USE **light grayish olive**

centroid color 11
USE **vivid red**

centroid color 110
USE **grayish olive**

centroid color 111
USE **dark grayish olive**

centroid color 112
USE **light olive gray**

centroid color 113
USE **olive gray**

centroid color 114
USE **olive black**

centroid color 115
USE **vivid yellow green**

centroid color 116
USE **brilliant yellow green**

centroid color 117
USE **strong yellow green**

centroid color 118
USE **deep yellow green**

centroid color 119
USE **light yellow green**

centroid color 12
USE **strong red**

centroid color 120
USE **moderate yellow green**

centroid color 121
USE **pale yellow green**

centroid color 122
USE **grayish yellow green**

centroid color 123
USE **strong olive green**

centroid color 124
USE **deep olive green**

centroid color 125
USE **moderate olive green**

centroid color 126
USE **dark olive green**

centroid color 127
USE **grayish olive green**

centroid color 128
USE **dark grayish olive green**

centroid color 129
USE **vivid yellowish green**

centroid color 13
USE **deep red**

centroid color 130
USE **brilliant yellowish green**

centroid color 131
USE **strong yellowish green**

centroid color 132
USE **deep yellowish green**

centroid color 133
USE **very deep yellowish green**

centroid color 134
USE **very light yellowish green**

centroid color 135
USE **light yellowish green**

centroid color 136
USE **moderate yellowish green**

centroid color 137
USE **dark yellowish green**

centroid color 138
USE **very dark yellowish green**

centroid color 139
USE **vivid green**

centroid color 14
USE **very deep red**

centroid color 140
USE **brilliant green**

centroid color 141
USE **strong green**

centroid color 142
USE **deep green**

centroid color 143
USE **very light green**

centroid color 144
USE **light green**

centroid color 145
USE **moderate green**

centroid color 146
USE **dark green**

centroid color 147
USE **very dark green**

centroid color 148
USE **very pale green**

centroid color 149
USE **pale green**

centroid color 15
USE **moderate red**

centroid color 150
USE **grayish green**

centroid color 151
USE **dark grayish green**

centroid color 152
USE **blackish green**

centroid color 153
USE **greenish white**

centroid color 154
USE **light greenish gray**

centroid color 155
USE **greenish gray**

centroid color 156
USE **dark greenish gray**

centroid color 157
USE **greenish black**

centroid color 158
USE **vivid bluish green**

centroid color 159
USE **brilliant bluish green**

centroid color 16
USE **dark red**

centroid color 160
USE **strong bluish green**

centroid color 161
USE **deep bluish green**

centroid color 162
USE **very light bluish green**

centroid color 163
USE **light bluish green**

centroid color 164
USE **moderate bluish green**

centroid color 165
USE **dark bluish green**

centroid color 166
USE **very dark bluish green**

centroid color 167
USE **vivid greenish blue**

centroid color 168
USE **brilliant greenish blue**

centroid color 169
USE **strong greenish blue**

centroid color 17
USE **very dark red**

centroid color 170
USE **deep greenish blue**

centroid color 171
USE **very light greenish blue**

centroid color 172
USE **light greenish blue**

centroid color 173
USE **moderate greenish blue**

centroid color 174
USE **dark greenish blue**

centroid color 175
USE **very dark greenish blue**

centroid color 176
USE **vivid blue**

centroid color 177
USE **brilliant blue**

centroid color 178
USE **strong blue**

centroid color 179
USE **deep blue**

centroid color 18
USE **light grayish red**

centroid color 180
USE **very light blue**

centroid color 181
USE **light blue**

centroid color 182
USE **moderate blue**

centroid color 183
USE **dark blue**

centroid color 184
USE **very pale blue**

centroid color 185
USE **pale blue**

centroid color 186
USE **grayish blue**

centroid color 187
USE **dark grayish blue**

centroid color 188
USE **blackish blue**

centroid color 189
USE **bluish white**

centroid color 19
USE **grayish red**

centroid color 190
USE **light bluish gray**

centroid color 191
USE **bluish gray**

centroid color 192
USE **dark bluish gray**

centroid color 193
USE **bluish black**

centroid color 194
USE **vivid purplish blue**

centroid color 195
USE **brilliant purplish blue**

centroid color 196
USE **strong purplish blue**

centroid color 197
USE **deep purplish blue**

centroid color 198
USE **very light purplish blue**

centroid color 199
USE **light purplish blue**

centroid color 2
USE **strong pink**

centroid color 20
USE **dark grayish red**

centroid color 200
USE **moderate purplish blue**

centroid color 201
USE **dark purplish blue**

centroid color 202
USE **very pale purplish blue**

centroid color 203
USE **pale purplish blue**

centroid color 204
USE **grayish purplish blue**

centroid color 205
USE **vivid violet**

centroid color 206
USE **brilliant violet**

centroid color 207
USE **strong violet**

centroid color 208
USE **deep violet**

centroid color 209
USE **very light violet**

centroid color 21
USE **blackish red**

centroid color 210
USE **light violet**

centroid color 211
USE **moderate violet**

centroid color 212
USE **dark violet**

centroid color 213
USE **very pale violet**

centroid color 214
USE **pale violet**

centroid color 215
USE **grayish violet**

centroid color 216
USE **vivid purple**

centroid color 217
USE **brilliant purple**

centroid color 218
USE **strong purple**

centroid color 219
USE **deep purple**

centroid color 22
USE **reddish gray**

centroid color 220
USE **very deep purple**

centroid color 221
USE **very light purple**

centroid color 222
USE **light purple**

centroid color 223
USE **moderate purple**

centroid color 224
USE **dark purple**

centroid color 225
USE **very dark purple**

centroid color 226
USE **very pale purple**

centroid color 227
USE **pale purple**

centroid color 228
USE **grayish purple**

centroid color 229
USE **dark grayish purple**

centroid color 23
USE **dark reddish gray**

centroid color 230
USE **blackish purple**

centroid color 231
USE **purplish white**

centroid color 232
USE **light purplish gray**

centroid color 233
USE **purplish gray**

centroid color 234
USE **dark purplish gray**

centroid color 235
USE **purplish black**

centroid color 236
USE **vivid reddish purple**

centroid color 237
USE **strong reddish purple**

centroid color 238
USE **deep reddish purple**

centroid color 239
USE **very deep reddish purple**

centroid color 24
USE **reddish black**

centroid color 240
USE **light reddish purple**

centroid color 241
USE **moderate reddish purple**

centroid color 242
USE **dark reddish purple**

centroid color 243
USE **very dark reddish purple**

centroid color 244
USE **pale reddish purple**

centroid color 245
USE **grayish reddish purple**

centroid color 246
USE **brilliant purplish pink**

centroid color 247
USE **strong purplish pink**

centroid color 248
USE **deep purplish pink**

centroid color 249
USE **light purplish pink**

centroid color 25
USE **vivid yellowish pink**

centroid color 250
USE **moderate purplish pink**

centroid color 251
USE **dark purplish pink**

centroid color 252
USE **pale purplish pink**

centroid color 253
USE **grayish purplish pink**

centroid color 254
USE **vivid purplish red**

centroid color 255
USE **strong purplish red**

centroid color 256
USE **deep purplish red**

centroid color 257
USE **very deep purplish red**

centroid color 258
USE **moderate purplish red**

centroid color 259
USE **dark purplish red**

centroid color 26
USE **strong yellowish pink**

centroid color 260
USE **very dark purplish red**

centroid color 261
USE **light grayish purplish red**

centroid color 262
USE **grayish purplish red**

centroid color 263
USE **white**

centroid color 264
USE **light gray**

centroid color 265
USE **medium gray**

centroid color 266
USE **dark gray**

centroid color 267
USE **black**

centroid color 27
USE **deep yellowish pink**

centroid color 28
USE **light yellowish pink**

centroid color 29
USE **moderate yellowish pink**

centroid color 3
USE **deep pink**

centroid color 30
USE **dark yellowish pink**

centroid color 31
USE **pale yellowish pink**

centroid color 32
USE **grayish yellowish pink**

centroid color 33
USE **brownish pink**

centroid color 34
USE **vivid reddish orange**

centroid color 35
USE **strong reddish orange**

centroid color 36
USE **deep reddish orange**

centroid color 37
USE **moderate reddish orange**

centroid color 38
USE **dark reddish orange**

centroid color 39
USE **grayish reddish orange**

centroid color 4
USE **light pink**

centroid color 40
USE **strong reddish brown**

centroid color 41
USE **deep reddish brown**

centroid color 42
USE **light reddish brown**

centroid color 43
USE **moderate reddish brown**

centroid color 44
USE **dark reddish brown**

centroid color 45
USE **light grayish reddish brown**

centroid color 46
USE **grayish reddish brown**

centroid color 47
USE **dark grayish reddish brown**

centroid color 48
USE **vivid orange**

centroid color 49
USE **brilliant orange**

centroid color 5
USE **moderate pink**

centroid color 50
USE **strong orange**

centroid color 51
USE **deep orange**

centroid color 52
USE **light orange**

centroid color 53
USE **moderate orange**

centroid color 54
USE **brownish orange**

centroid color 55
USE **strong brown**

centroid color 56
USE **deep brown**

centroid color 57
USE **light brown**

centroid color 58
USE **moderate brown**

centroid color 59
USE **dark brown**

centroid color 6
USE **dark pink**

centroid color 60
USE **light grayish brown**

centroid color 61
USE **grayish brown**

centroid color 62
USE **dark grayish brown**

centroid color 63
USE **light brownish gray**

centroid color 64
USE **brownish gray**

centroid color 65
USE **brownish black**

centroid color 66
USE **vivid orange yellow**

centroid color 67
USE **brilliant orange yellow**

centroid color 68
USE **strong orange yellow**

centroid color 69
USE **deep orange yellow**

centroid color 7
USE **pale pink**

centroid color 70
USE **light orange yellow**

centroid color 71
USE **moderate orange yellow**

centroid color 72
USE **dark orange yellow**

centroid color 73
USE **pale orange yellow**

centroid color 74
USE **strong yellowish brown**

centroid color 75
USE **deep yellowish brown**

centroid color 76
USE **light yellowish brown**

centroid color 77
USE **moderate yellowish brown**

centroid color 78
USE **dark yellowish brown**

centroid color 79
USE **light grayish yellowish brown**

centroid color 8
USE **grayish pink**

centroid color 80
USE **grayish yellowish brown**

centroid color 81
USE **dark grayish yellowish brown**

centroid color 82
USE **vivid yellow**

centroid color 83
USE **brilliant yellow**

centroid color 84
USE **strong yellow**

centroid color 85
USE **deep yellow**

centroid color 86
USE **light yellow**

centroid color 87
USE **moderate yellow**

centroid color 88
USE **dark yellow**

centroid color 89
USE **pale yellow**

centroid color 9
USE **pinkish white**

centroid color 90
USE **grayish yellow**

centroid color 91
USE **dark grayish yellow**

centroid color 92
USE **yellowish white**

centroid color 93
USE **yellowish gray**

centroid color 94
USE **light olive brown**

centroid color 95
USE **moderate olive brown**

centroid color 96
USE **dark olive brown**

centroid color 97
USE **vivid greenish yellow**

centroid color 98
USE **brilliant greenish yellow**

centroid color 99
USE **strong greenish yellow**

centrolobium
USE **balaustre**

Centuripe
FL.2637
CN F.FL.ALO.AXC.ALO.AFU.ALO.AXC.ALO.BIQ.BCW

cera alba
USE **bleached beeswax**

cera colla
MT.2370
SN A Medieval term for an emulsion of glue solution and molten beeswax; called for in old recipes as an ingredient of aqueous paint binders. (MAYER)
CN M.MT.AFU.ARI.BIQ.ALO

cera flava
USE **unbleached beeswax**

ceramic color
MT.1811
UF color, ceramic
color, porcelain
porcelain color
CN M.MT.AFU.AFU.ARI.AFU.ALO.ALO

ceramic engineering
USE **ceramic science**

ceramic glaze
MT.2556
UF glaze, ceramic
CN M.MT.AFU.ARI.CRG.ARI.ARI.AFU

ceramic metals
USE **cermets**

ceramic process
KT.352 (L)
SN Use for a variant of the dusting-on process in which the pigment is a vitrifiable powder, available in a wide range of colors, that is fired onto porcelain, earthenware, china, or the like; more broadly, use for any process to form an image on porcelain, china, earthenware, or similar material.
UF china process
enamel process
porcelain process
CN K.KT.AFU.ALO.DUC.DIO.ALO.DIO.AFU.ALO.AFU

ceramic science
KD.246
UF ceramic engineering
engineering, ceramic
science, ceramic
CN K.KD.AFU.ARI.BZY.AFU

ceramic tile
MT.159 (A)
SN Tile made from clay or a mixture of clay and other ceramic materials. (STEIN)
UF tile, ceramic
CN M.MT.AFU.AFU.AFU.AXC.ALO.ALO.ALO.AFU

ceramic ware
USE **ceramics**

ceramics
MT.144 (L,R)
ALT **ceramic**
UF ceramic ware
keramics
ware, ceramic
CN M.MT.AFU.AFU.AFU.AXC.ALO.ALO.AFU

ceramics, Band
USE **Bandkeramik**

ceramists
HG.472 (R)
ALT **ceramist**
SN Persons who engage in ceramic arts, manufacturing, or technology. (W)
CN H.HG.AFU.AXC.BUE.ARI.AFU

Cerbat
FL.952
CN F.FL.ALO.ALO.ALO.AFU.ALO.ARI.BIQ.BIQ.AFU

ceremonies
KM.11 (L,R)
SN Formal acts or series of acts typically conducted elaborately, solemnly, and as prescribed by the ritual or protocol of religious, state, court, social, or tribal procedure. (W)
CN K.KM.AFU.ARI

ceresin
MT.2200 (L)
SN Pure white or slightly yellowish mineral wax; suitable substitute for beeswax as an ingredient of polishes and protective coatings of sculptures. (MAYER)
CN M.MT.AFU.AFU.ARI.BZY.ALO.ALO.AFU

cerise
USE **deep purplish red**
vivid purplish red

cerise pink
USE **strong purplish red**

cermets
MT.473 (L)
UF ceramic metals
metals, ceramic
CN M.MT.AFU.AFU.AFU.BZY.ALO.ALO

cerography
KT.176 (L)
SN The art of making characters or designs in or with wax. (W)
UF printing, wax
wax printing
CN K.KT.AFU.ALO.DUC.AXC

cerography (wax painting)
USE **encaustic painting**

Cerro Mangote
FL.1086
CN F.FL.ALO.ALO.ALO.ALO.ALO.ALO.AFU.AFU

Cerro Sechín
FL.1140
UF Sechín
CN F.FL.ALO.ALO.ALO.ARI.AXC.AFU.ARI.AFU

certificates
VW.299
ALT **certificate**
SN Documents giving authoritative recognition of a fact, qualification, or promise.
CN V.VW.AFU.AFU.ALO.AXC

certificates of award
USE **awards**

certificates of compliance
USE **certificates of occupancy**

certificates of incorporation
VW.911 (L)
ALT **certificate of incorporation**
SN Documents issued by the Secretary of State or other state official, establishing a corporation. (GAHLM)
UF incorporation, certificates of
CN V.VW.AFU.ARI.AFU.BOK.BOK.BCW

certificates of occupancy
VW.300
ALT **certificate of occupancy**
SN Documents officially certifying that premises conform to provisions of the zoning ordinance and building code and may be used or occupied; granted for new construction or for alteration or additions to existing structures. (LOFZ)
UF certificates of compliance
compliance, certificates of
occupancy permits
occupancy, certificates of
permits, occupancy
CN V.VW.AFU.AFU.ALO.AXC.AFU

certificates of origin
VW.301 (L)
ALT **certificate of origin**
SN Certificates attesting to the country of manufacture of a commodity, often required by the customs office before importation. (RHDEL2)
UF origin, certificates of
CN V.VW.AFU.AFU.ALO.AXC.ALO

certificates of stock
USE **stock certificates**

certificates, baptismal
USE **baptismal certificates**

certificates, birth
USE **birth certificates**

certificates, copyright
USE **copyright certificates**

certificates, death
USE **death certificates**

certificates, hypothecation
USE **hypothecation certificates**

certificates, marriage
USE **marriage certificates**

certificates, share
USE **stock certificates**

certificates, stock
USE **stock certificates**

certified checks
VW.830
ALT **certified check**
SN Checks of a depositor on a bank, on which the bank has noted its acceptance or certification with date and the signature of a bank official; the bank is then liable to pay the amount to the proper party. (BLACKS)
UF checks, certified
CN V.VW.AFU.ARI.AFU.BIQ.CFS.ARI.AFU

certifying
KG.144 (B)
SN Officially attesting that something is valid or meets a standard, or, with regard to people, that a standard degree of qualification has been met.
CN K.KG.AFU.AFU.BIQ.ARI.ALO

certose
USE **charterhouses**

cerulean
USE **light blue**
light purplish blue

cerulean blue
MT.1598
UF bleu céleste
blue, cerulean
caeruleum
ceruleum
coelin
Coelinblau
coeruleum
CN M.MT.AFU.AFU.ARI.AFU.AFU.ALO.ALO.ALO.ARI.AXC

cerulean blue (color)
USE **light blue**
moderate blue
strong blue
strong greenish blue
vivid blue
vivid greenish blue

cerulean blue, bright
USE **moderate blue**
strong greenish blue

cerulean blue, dark
USE **dark greenish blue**
grayish blue

cerulean blue, deep
USE **dark greenish blue**
deep greenish blue
moderate blue
moderate greenish blue

cerulean blue, light
USE **brilliant greenish blue**
light blue
strong greenish blue

cerulean blue, pale
USE **light blue**
very light blue

cerulean blue, vivid
USE **strong greenish blue**

ceruleum
USE **cerulean blue**

ceruse
USE **white lead**

ceruse of tin
USE **tin white**

Cesca chairs
TG.46
ALT **Cesca chair**
UF Breuer chairs
cantilevered chairs
cantilevered side chairs
chairs, Breuer
chairs, cantilevered
chairs, Cesca
side chairs, cantilevered
CN V.TG.AFU.AFU.ALO.AFU.AFU.AFU.DIO

cesspools
RT.1453 (L,B)
ALT **cesspool**
SN Covered pits into which raw sewage is discharged, the liquid portion seeping or leaching into the sur-

rounding porous soil, and the solids being retained in the pit to undergo partial decomposition before removal. (STEIN)
CN V.RT.ALO.BCW.ALO.ARI.ALO

Ceylon rosewood
MT.1299
UF Albizia odoratissima
rosewood, Ceylon
CN M.MT.AFU.AFU.ALO.BIQ.DCU.AFU.AFU.AFU.LCM.ARI

Ceylonese
USE **Sri Lankan**

CFCs
USE **chlorofluorocarbons**

Ch'an
BM.617 (L)
UF Buddhism, Ch'an
Ch'an Buddhism
Chan
Meditation, School of
School of Meditation
CN B.BM.BZY.AFU.AFU.BCW.AFU

Ch'an Buddhism
USE **Ch'an**

Ch'en
USE **Chen**

Ch'i, Northern
USE **Northern Qi**

Ch'i, Southern
USE **Southern Qi**

Ch'ien-lung
USE **Qianlong**

Ch'in
USE **Qin**

Ch'ing
USE **Qing**

Ch'ing-lien-kang
USE **Qingliangang**

Ch'ing-pai ware
USE **Qingbai ware**

Ch'iu-tzu
USE **Kuça**

Ch'un-ch'iu
USE **Spring and Autumn Annals**

Ch'ung-chêng
USE **Chongzhen**

Chad Civilization
USE **Sao Empire**

Chagga
FL.644 (L)
UF Caga
Wachaga
CN F.FL.ALO.AFU.AXC.AXC.BCW.ARI

chahar bagh
RK.1401
SN Use for quadripartite Islamic gardens.
CN V.RK.ALO.AFU.AFU.AFU.ARI.AFU.AFU

chahar taqs
RK.1135
ALT **chahar taq**
SN Use for Zoroastrian fire temples of the Sassanian period.
UF char taqs
tchahar taqs
CN V.RK.AFU.ALO.ALO.FCS.BIQ.BZY.ALO.ALO.AFU

chaifs
USE **howell planes**

Chaima
FL.1630
CN F.FL.ALO.ALO.ARI.ARI.ARI.ARI

chain
MT.2222 (L,N)
CN M.MT.AFU.ALO.BUE

chain bolts
TF.161
ALT **chain bolt**
SN Locks with a spring bolt at the top of the door that can be operated by pulling an attached chain. (MEANS)
UF bolts, chain
CN V.TF.AFU.AFU.AFU.AFU.DIO.AFU

chain bucket loaders
TB.54
ALT **chain bucket loader**
SN Mobile loaders that use a series of small buckets on a roller chain to elevate excavated dirt or rock to the dumping point. (STEIN)
UF bucket loaders, chain
loaders, chain bucket
CN V.TB.AFU.ARI.AFU.BCW.AFU.AFU

chain conveyors
TB.367 (L)
ALT **chain conveyor**
UF conveyors, chain
CN V.TB.AFU.ARI.DCU.AFU.AFU.ALO

chain courses
RT.615
ALT **chain course**
SN Bond courses of stone headers fastened together continuously by metal clamps. (RS)
UF courses, chain
CN V.RT.AFU.AFU.AFU.BIQ.BUE.ALO.AFU.ALO.ARI

chain door fasteners
TF.162
ALT **chain door fastener**
SN Chains that can be secured by a slide bolt between a door stile and a door jamb to allow the door to be opened slightly while remaining securely fastened. (MEANS)
UF door fasteners, chain
fasteners, chain door
CN V.TF.AFU.AFU.AFU.AFU.DIO.ALO

chain link fences
RM.435
ALT **chain link fence**
SN Fences made of heavy steel wire fabric which is interwoven in such a way as to provide a continuous mesh without ties or knots, except at the ends. (DAC)
UF fences, chain link
CN V.RM.ALO.AFU.BCW.AFU

chain moldings
RT.764
ALT **chain molding**
SN Moldings carved with a motif resembling a chain. (DAC)
UF moldings, chain
CN V.RT.AFU.ALO.AFU.BOK.AFU.AFU.ARI.BCW

chain-pipe vises
TB.767
ALT **chain-pipe vise**
SN Portable vises used to hold pipes in the jaw by means of a chain. (DAC)
UF vises, chain-pipe
CN V.TB.AFU.BCW.BIQ.AXC.ALO.BCW.AFU

chain pipe wrenches
USE **chain tongs**

chain saws
TB.997 (L,N)
ALT **chain saw**
SN Power-driven saws, usually hand-held, with a protruding arm that carries an endless chain into which the cutting teeth are set. (DAC)
UF saws, chain
CN V.TB.AFU.BCW.CFS.ALO.AFU.EWY.ARI

chain stores
RK.169 (L)
ALT **chain store**
UF stores, chain
CN V.RK.AFU.ALO.ALO.ALO.ARI.BIQ.ALO.AFU

chain tongs
TB.775 (N)
SN Plumber's tongs used for turning pipes, consisting of a lever arm which has sharp teeth that engage the pipe and a short adjustable chain which is wrapped around the pipe to hold it securely. (DAC)
UF chain pipe wrenches
pipe wrenches, chain
tongs, chain
wrenches, chain pipe
CN V.TB.AFU.BCW.BIQ.AXC.ALO.BIQ.AXC

chaînes
RT.630
ALT **chaîne**
SN Type of wall decorations consisting of vertical bands of rusticated masonry which divide the surface into panels or bays; common in 17th-century French domestic architecture. (HAS)
CN V.RT.AFU.AFU.AFU.BIQ.BUE.ALO. AFU.ARI.ALO

chains, sash
USE **sash chains**

chair-back settees
TG.301
ALT **chair-back settee**
SN Small sofas formed of two or three combined chair backs, with arms, backs, and legs similar to those of the open-back chairs of the particular period. (FAIRB)
UF bar-back sofas
chairs, double
Darby and Joan settees
double chairs
settees, chair-back
settees, Darby and Joan
sofas, bar-back
CN V.TG.AFU.AFU.ALO.ALO.BUE.AFU

chair-beds
USE **bed chairs**

chair bits
USE **spoon bits**

chair-lift stations
USE **ski-lift stations**

chair lifts
RT.1297 (N)
ALT **chair lift**
SN Use for inclined lifts installed in buildings, usually on a staircase, and including a chair in which the passenger sits.
UF lifts, chair
CN V.RT.ALO.ALO.AFU.AFU.ALO.AFU

chair lifts (ski lifts)
USE **ski lifts**

chair rails
RT.650
ALT **chair rail**
SN Horizontal strips, usually of wood, affixed to walls at a height which prevents the backs of chairs from damaging the wall surface.
UF rails, chair
CN V.RT.AFU.AFU.AFU.BIQ.BUE.ALO. AFU.BCW.ALO

chair-tables
TG.47 (N)
ALT **chair-table**
SN Armchairs with large backs which are hinged so that they can be swung forward to rest on the arms, converting the piece into a table. Chairs of this type were made from the Middle Ages to the late 17th century in Europe and until the late 19th century in America. (DDA)
UF benches, monk's (chair-tables)
chairs, monk's (chair-tables)
monk's benches (chair-tables)
monk's chairs (chair-tables)
monk's seats
seats, monk's
table-chairs
CN V.TG.AFU.AFU.ALO.AFU.AFU.AFU. DOI

chair vises
TB.1076
ALT **chair vise**
UF vises, chair
CN V.TB.AFU.BCW.CFS.ALO.ALO.CXA. ALO

chair web saws
USE **web saws**

chairmakers
HG.560 (A,L)
ALT **chairmaker**
CN H.HG.AFU.AXC.BUE.AXC.BUE.ALO

chairs
TG.20 (A,L,N,B,R)
ALT **chair**
SN Seats for one person with a back or a back and arms. Distinct from **stools** which have no back. (DDA)
CN V.TG.AFU.AFU.ALO.AFU.AFU

chairs, abbots'
USE **Glastonbury chairs**

chairs, Adirondack
USE **Adirondack chairs**

chairs, angle
USE **corner chairs**

chairs, ax
USE **ax chairs**

chairs, back-stool
USE **backstools**

chairs, balloon-back
USE **balloon-back chairs**

chairs, balloon-back Windsor
USE **balloon-back Windsor chairs**

chairs, banister
USE **banister-back chairs**

chairs, banister-back
USE **banister-back chairs**

chairs, bar-back
USE **bar-back chairs**

chairs, barber's
USE **barber's chairs**

chairs, barber's (corner chairs)
USE **corner chairs**

chairs, Barcelona
USE **Barcelona chairs**

chairs, barrel
USE **barrel chairs**

chairs, barrel (circular easy chairs)
USE **circular easy chairs**

chairs, Barwa
USE **Barwa chairs**

chairs, basket
USE **basket chairs**

chairs, bath
USE **bath chairs**

chairs, beach
USE **beach chairs**

chairs, beanbag
USE **beanbag chairs**

chairs, bended-back
USE **bended-back chairs**

chairs, bent-wire
USE **ice-cream parlor chairs**

chairs, bergère
USE **bergères**

chairs, Bertoia
USE **diamond chairs**

chairs, birdcage Windsor
USE **square-back Windsor chairs**

chairs, board
USE **board chairs**

chairs, Boston
USE **Boston chairs**

chairs, Boston rocking
USE **Boston rockers**

chairs, Bouneparte
USE **Trafalgar chairs**

chairs, bow-back Windsor
USE **bow-back Windsor chairs**

chairs, Breuer
USE **Cesca chairs**
Wassily chairs

chairs, Brewster
USE **Brewster chairs**

chairs, Brno
USE **Brno chairs**

chairs, burgomeister
USE **corner chairs**

chairs, butterfly
USE **Hardoy chairs**

chairs, cabinet commode
USE **cabinet chairs**

chairs, cabriole
USE **cabriole chairs**

chairs, Grecian rocking
USE **Lincoln rockers**

chairs, grotto
USE **grotto chairs**

chairs, gunstock Windsor
USE **gunstock Windsor chairs**

chairs, half-round
USE **corner chairs**

chairs, hall
USE **hall chairs**

chairs, hammock
USE **hammock chairs**

chairs, Hardoy
USE **Hardoy chairs**

chairs, harp-back
USE **lyre-back chairs**

chairs, harp banister-back
USE **lyre-back chairs**

chairs, harpsicord
USE **music chairs**

chairs, Harvard
USE **great chairs**

chairs, heart and shield back
USE **hcart-back chairs**

chairs, heart-back
USE **heart-back chairs**

chairs, hearts and crown
USE **hearts and crown chairs**

chairs, high-back Windsor
USE **high-back Windsor chairs**

chairs, high (tall chairs)
USE **tall chairs**

chairs, hip-joint
USE **X-chairs**

chairs, Hitchcock
USE **Hitchcock chairs**

chairs, Hogarth
USE **bended-back chairs**

chairs, hoop-back Windsor
USE **sack-back Windsor chairs**

chairs, hunting
USE **hunting chairs**

chairs, ice-cream parlor
USE **ice-cream parlor chairs**

chairs, India
USE **India chairs**

chairs, invalid's
USE **invalid's chairs**

chairs, iron-wire
USE **ice-cream parlor chairs**

chairs, kitchen
USE **kitchen chairs**

chairs, klismos
USE **klismoi**

chairs, ladder-back
USE **slat-back chairs**

chairs, lady's
USE **lady's chairs**

chairs, lath-back Windsor
USE **lath-back Windsor chairs**

chairs, lattice-back
USE **lattice-back chairs**

chairs, leather (Boston chairs)
USE **Boston chairs**

chairs, leather-upholstered (Boston chairs)
USE **Boston chairs**

chairs, leather-upholstered (Cromwellian chairs)
USE **Cromwellian chairs**

chairs, library (reading chairs)
USE **reading chairs**

chairs, Lincoln rocking
USE **Lincoln rockers**

chairs, lolling
USE **lolling chairs**

chairs, loop-back Windsor
USE **sack-back Windsor chairs**

chairs, lounge
USE **chaises longues**

chairs, low back (backstools)
USE **backstools**

chairs, low-back Windsor
USE **low-back Windsor chairs**

chairs, lug
USE **easy chairs**

chairs, lunette-back
USE **lunette-back chairs**

chairs, lyre-back
USE **lyre-back chairs**

chairs, marquise
USE **marquises**

chairs, Martha Washington
USE **lolling chairs**

chairs, Mendlesham
USE **Mendlesham chairs**

chairs, Mendlesham Windsor
USE **Mendlesham chairs**

chairs, monk's (chair-tables)
USE **chair-tables**

chairs, monk's (sillónes fraileros)
USE **fraileros**

chairs, Morris
USE **Morris chairs**

chairs, MR
USE **MR chairs**

chairs, music
USE **music chairs**

chairs, necessary
USE **commode chairs**

chairs, necessity
USE **commode chairs**

chairs, Nelson's
USE **Trafalgar chairs**

chairs, nursing
USE **nursing chairs**

chairs, occasional
USE **side chairs**

chairs, office
USE **office chairs**

chairs, open-arm
USE **elbow chairs**

chairs, oval-back
USE **oval-back chairs**

chairs, oval-back Windsor
USE **bow-back Windsor chairs**

chairs, page's
USE **porter's chairs**

chairs, panel-back
USE **wainscot chairs**

chairs, parlor
USE **parlor chairs**

chairs, pattern
USE **pattern chairs**

chairs, pedestal
USE **pedestal chairs**

chairs, pew
USE **pew chairs**

chairs, piano
USE **music chairs**

chairs, pillow back Windsor
USE **high-back Windsor chairs**

chairs, plank
USE **board chairs**

chairs, platform rocking
USE **platform rockers**

chairs, Plia folding
USE **Plia folding chairs**

chairs, pompador
USE **lady's chairs**

chairs, porter's
USE **porter's chairs**

chairs, preaching
USE **preaching chairs**

chairs, press-back
USE **press-back chairs**

chairs, pretzel-back
USE **pretzel-back chairs**

chairs, pulpit
USE **preaching chairs**

chairs, reading
USE **reading chairs**

chairs, reception
USE **reception chairs**

chairs, reclining
USE **reclining chairs**

chairs, revolving
USE **swivel chairs**

chairs, ribbon-back
USE **ribbon-back chairs**

chairs, riding
USE **chamber horses**

chairs, rocking
USE **rocking chairs**

chairs, rod-back Windsor
USE **square-back Windsor chairs**

chairs, roll-top Windsor
USE **roll-top Windsor chairs**

chairs, round (corner chairs)
USE **corner chairs**

chairs, round-top Windsor
USE **sack-back Windsor chairs**

chairs, roundabout
USE **corner chairs**

chairs, rout
USE **rout chairs**

chairs, S
USE **S chairs**

chairs, sack-back Windsor
USE **sack-back Windsor chairs**

chairs, saddle cheek
USE **easy chairs**

chairs, safari
USE **director's chairs**

chairs, Savonarola
USE **Savonarola chairs**

chairs, Savonarola cross
USE **Savonarola chairs**

chairs, scissors
USE **X-chairs**

chairs, secretary's
USE **typewriter chairs**

chairs, sedan
USE **sedan chairs**

chairs, shaving
USE **corner chairs**

chairs, sheaf-back
USE **sheaf-back chairs**

chairs, shell
USE **diamond chairs**

chairs, shield-back
USE **shield-back chairs**

chairs, shop
USE **tall chairs**

chairs, side
USE **side chairs**

chairs, single
USE **side chairs**

chairs, single bow Windsor
USE **single rod-back Windsor chairs**

chairs, single rod-back Windsor
USE **single rod-back Windsor chairs**

chairs, six-back
USE **slat-back chairs**

chairs, slat-back
USE **slat-back chairs**

chairs, slat-back Windsor
USE **slat-back Windsor chairs**

chairs, sleeping
USE **sleeping chairs**

chairs, Sleepy Hollow
USE **Sleepy Hollow chairs**

chairs, sling
USE **sling chairs**

chairs, slipper
USE **slipper chairs**

chairs, smoking
USE **smoking chairs**

chairs, soda
USE **ice-cream parlor chairs**

chairs, soda fountain
USE **ice-cream parlor chairs**

chairs, Spanish back
USE **square-back chairs**

chairs, spindle-back
USE **spindle-back chairs**

chairs, splat-back Windsor
USE **splat-back Windsor chairs**

chairs, spoon-back
USE **spoon-back chairs**

chairs, square-back
USE **square-back chairs**

chairs, square-back Windsor
USE **square-back Windsor chairs**

chairs, square easy
USE **square easy chairs**

chairs, stackable
USE **stacking chairs**

chairs, stacking
USE **stacking chairs**

chairs, state
USE **state chairs**

chairs, steamer
USE **deck chairs**

chairs, stenographer's
USE **typewriter chairs**

chairs, step
USE **step chairs**

chairs, step-ladder
USE **step chairs**

chairs, stick-back
USE **spindle-back chairs**

chairs, stick (sedan chairs)
USE **sedan chairs**

chairs, straight-back easy
USE **square easy chairs**

chairs, strapple
USE **smoking chairs**

chairs, student
USE **student chairs**

chairs, swan
USE **swan chairs**

chairs, swan easy
USE **swan chairs**

chairs, swept-leg
USE **Trafalgar chairs**

chairs, swing rocking
USE **platform rockers**

chairs, swivel
USE **swivel chairs**

chairs, tablet
USE **tablet-arm chairs**

chairs, tablet-arm
USE **tablet-arm chairs**

chairs, tablet top
USE **Trafalgar chairs**

chairs, tablet-top Windsor
USE **tablet-top Windsor chairs**

chairs, tall
USE **tall chairs**

chairs, three-seated
USE **indiscrets**

chairs, touring
USE **touring chairs**

chairs, Trafalgar
USE **Trafalgar chairs**

chairs, trellis-back
USE **lattice-back chairs**

chairs, tub
USE **barrel chairs**
circular easy chairs

chairs, tub-back easy
USE **circular easy chairs**

chairs, turkey work (Cromwellian chairs)
USE **Cromwellian chairs**

chairs, Turkish
USE **Turkish chairs**

chairs, Turkish frame
USE **Turkish chairs**

chairs, turned three-square great
USE **great chairs**

chairs, typewriter
USE **typewriter chairs**

chairs, urn back
USE **shield-back chairs**

chairs, vase back
USE **shield-back chairs**

chairs, vesper
USE **prie-dieus**

chairs, wainscot
USE **wainscot chairs**

chairs, Wassily
USE **Wassily chairs**

chairs, Waterloo
USE **Trafalgar chairs**

chairs, Wellington
USE **Trafalgar chairs**

chairs, Westport
USE **Westport chairs**

chairs, wheatsheaf-back
USE **sheaf-back chairs**

chairs, wheel-back
USE **wheel-back chairs**

chairs, window
USE **window chairs**

chairs, Windsor
USE **Windsor chairs**

chairs, Windsor rocking
USE **Windsor rocking chairs**

chairs, Windsor rod-back
USE **square-back Windsor chairs**

chairs, wing
USE **easy chairs**

chairs, wing-back
USE **easy chairs**

chairs, womb
USE **womb chairs**

chairs, writing-arm Windsor
USE **writing-arm Windsor chairs**

chairs, writing (corner chairs)
USE **corner chairs**

chairs, X-shaped
USE **X-chairs**

chairs, Y
USE **Y chairs**

chaise houses
USE **carriage houses**

chaises à bras
USE **armchairs**

chaises à dame
USE **chauffeuses**

chaises à demoiselle
USE **backstools**
chauffeuses

chaises à femme
USE **chauffeuses**

chaises à la d'artois
TG.142
ALT **chaise à la d'artois**
SN French chairs with oval or medallion-shaped backs, the frames being carved in the center of the top with a ribbon bow. (WATSON)
CN V.TG.AFU.AFU.ALO.AFU.AFU.AFU.NIE.CRG.AFU

chaises à la dauphine
USE **perroquets**

chaises à la reine
TG.134
ALT **chaise à la reine**
SN Upholstered chairs with flat backs; distinct from those with concave backs called **chaises en cabriolet.** (PC)
UF sieges à la reine
CN V.TG.AFU.AFU.ALO.AFU.AFU.AFU.NIE.BOK.ALO

chaises à médaillon
TG.143
ALT **chaise à médaillon**
CN V.TG.AFU.AFU.ALO.AFU.AFU.AFU.NIE.CRG.ALO

chaises à porteur
USE **sedan chairs**

chaises à vertugadin
USE **backstools**
chauffeuses

chaises caquetoires
USE **voyeuses**

chaises chauffeuses
USE **chauffeuses**

chaises curules
USE **sellae curulis**

chaises de table
USE **fauteuils de bureau**

chaises du four
USE **chauffeuses**

chaises en cabriolet
TG.128
ALT **chaise en cabriolet**
SN Upholstered chairs with slightly concave backs to fit the contours of the human body; distinct from those with flat backs called **chaises à la reine.** (PC)
CN V.TG.AFU.AFU.ALO.AFU.AFU.AFU.NIE.AXC.ALO

chaises en voyeuse
USE **voyeuses**

chaises longues
TG.48 (N)
ALT **chaise longue**
SN Chairs having a full-length leg rest and usually arms, designed for lounging. For similar chairs used outdoors, use **deck chairs.**
UF chairs, lounge
dormeuses (chaises longues)
lounge chairs
loungers
CN V.TG.AFU.AFU.ALO.AFU.AFU.AFU.DUC

chaises percées
USE **commode chairs**

chaitya caves
USE **chaityas**

chaitya halls
USE **chaityas**

chaityas
RK.1140
ALT **chaitya**
SN Use for Buddhist rock-cut shrines or sanctuaries.
UF caves, chaitya
chaitya caves
chaitya halls
CN V.RK.AFU.ALO.ALO.FCS.BOK.AFU

Chaka
USE **Saka**

chalcedony
MT.545 (R)
SN A submicroscopic variety of fibrous quartz, generally translucent and containing variable amounts of opal; reacts with alkali in portland cement. (DAC)
CN M.MT.AFU.AFU.AFU.CFS.AFU.GRC.AFU.ARI

Chalcidian
FL.2619
CN F.FL.ALO.AXC.ALO.AFU.ALO.AXC.ALO.AXC.ARI

Chalcolithic
FL.20 (L)
UF Copper Age

Cuprolithic
CN F.FL.AFU.BCW.ALO.ALO

Chalcolithic, Early
USE **Early Chalcolithic**

Chalcolithic, Late
USE **Late Chalcolithic**

Chalcolithic, Middle
USE **Middle Chalcolithic**

Chaldean
FL.2982
CN F.FL.ALO.AXC.ARI.BCW.AFU.BZY.AFU

chalets
RK.231 (A,N)
ALT **chalet**
SN Use both for Swiss herdsmen's houses, usually of wood with exposed structural members and overhanging upper floors, and for any house built in the Swiss style.
CN V.RK.AFU.ALO.ALO.AXC.ALO.AFU.AXC

chalice capitals
RT.123
ALT **chalice capital**
SN Use for capitals in the shape of a chalice, that is, with a trumpetlike flare at the top; the shape may be partially obscured by ornamentation.
UF capitals, chalice
CN V.RT.AFU.AFU.AFU.AXC.BIQ.ALO.ARI.AFU.BOK

Chalice Style
FL.2607
CN F.FL.ALO.AXC.ALO.AFU.ALO.AXC.ALO.ARI.AFU.AFU

chalk
MT.44 (L,N,B)
SN A fine-grained limestone, or soft, earthy form of calcium carbonate; used chiefly in putty, crayons, paints, rubber goods, linoleum, and as a pigment and abrasive. (MH12)
UF chalk, natural
English white
lime white
natural chalk
white, lime
whiting
CN M.MT.AFU.AFU.AFU.ARI

chalk holders
USE **portcrayons**

chalk sticks
TB.235
ALT **chalk stick**
UF sticks, chalk
CN V.TB.AFU.ARI.CLM.AFU.ALO.AFU

chalk, black
USE **black chalk**

chalk, fabricated
USE **fabricated chalk**

chalk, French
USE **French chalk**

chalk, Italian
USE **black chalk**

chalk, natural
USE **chalk**

chalk, natural red
USE **red chalk**

chalk, precipitated
USE **precipitated chalk**

chalk, red
USE **red chalk**

Chalukyan
FL.2208 (L)
UF Calukya
CN F.FL.ALO.ARI.AXC.ALO.AFU.AXC.ALO

Cham (Bamileke)
FL.183
UF Bacham
Baham
CN F.FL.ALO.AFU.AXC.AFU.AFU.AFU.AFU.AXC

Cham (Vietnamese)
FL.2436 (L)
UF Champa
CN F.FL.ALO.ARI.BCW.BUE.ALO.ALO

Chamacoco
FL.1640 (L)
CN F.FL.ALO.ALO.ARI.ARI.AXC.BCW

Chamaecyparis nootkatensis
USE **yellow cypress**

Chamaecyparis thyoides
USE **white cypress**

Chamba (Nigerian)
FL.203
CN F.FL.ALO.AFU.AXC.AFU.AFU.ALO.AFU.AFU

Chamba (Pahari)
FL.2274
CN F.FL.ALO.ARI.AXC.ALO.AFU.BZY.BCW.ARI.AXC

chamber chairs
USE **commode chairs**

Chamber (Fancy)
USE **Fancy**

chamber horses
TG.169
ALT **chamber horse**
SN Devices which allow the motions of horse exercise to be simulated indoors, consisting of springs encased in a concertinalike leather envelope, framed in mahogany. (GLOAG)
UF chairs, exercising
chairs, riding
exercising chairs
exercising machines, horse
horse exercising machines
horses, chamber
machines, horse exercising
riding chairs
CN V.TG.AFU.AFU.ALO.AFU.AFU.ALO.AXC

chamber kilns
TB.92 (L)
ALT **chamber kiln**
SN Kilns consisting of a series of adjacent chambers in a ring or oval through which fire moves, taking several days to make a circuit. (MHDSTT)
UF kilns, chamber
CN V.TB.AFU.ARI.ALO.ARI.ALO.AFU.ALO

chamber tables
TG.731
ALT **chamber table**
SN Contemporary name for plain dressing or writing tables in the 18th century. (GILBR2)
UF tables, chamber
CN V.TG.AFU.AFU.BIQ.BOK.ALO.CLM.AFU

chamber tombs
RK.483
ALT **chamber tomb**
SN Use for communal burial places, cut into rock or hillslopes or constructed of masonry, whose chamber may or may not have an entry passage, usually covered by a mound.
UF tombs, chamber
CN V.RK.AFU.ALO.ALO.BOK.BUE.AFU.ALO

chamber tombs, megalithic
USE **megalithic chamber tombs**

chambers
RM.381
ALT **chamber**
SN Use for the recessed part of an upper stage in an Elizabethan theater.
UF inner stages
stages, inner
CN V.RM.AFU.DIO.AXC.AXC.ALO.BUE.ALO.AFU

chambers (bedrooms)
USE **bedrooms**

chambers (rooms)
USE **rooms**

chambers of commerce
USE **boards of trade**

chambers, anechoic
USE **anechoic rooms**

chambers, burial
USE **burial chambers**

chambers, plenum
USE **plenum chambers**

chambers, presence
USE **presence chambers**

Chambri
FL.3648 (L)
UF Tchambuli
CN F.FL.ALO.BOK.ALO.BCW.ALO.BCW.AFU.ALO

chamfer knives
TB.903 (N)
ALT **chamfer knife**
SN Draw knives used to cut an oblique surface.
UF knives, chamfer
CN V.TB.AFU.BCW.CFS.ALO.AFU.DOI.ARI.ARI

chamfer spokeshaves
TB.1040
ALT **chamfer spokeshave**
SN Spokeshaves which cut a chamfer on the edge of a piece of wood.
UF spokeshaves, chamfer
CN V.TB.AFU.BCW.CFS.ALO.AFU.FUA.AFU

chamfering
KT.136
ALT **chamfered**
SN In the context of furniture, refers to cutting or shaping the edge or end of a material to form an angle that is not a right angle. In other contexts, prefer **beveling.**
CN K.KT.AFU.ALO.DOI.AXC

chamfers, swelled
USE **wave moldings**

chammy
USE **chamois**

chamois
MT.956 (L)
SN Soft, pliable leather originally made from the skins of the chamois, Antilopa rupicapra, a small deer. (MH)
UF chammy
shammy
shamoy
CN M.MT.AFU.AFU.ALO.AFU.DZW.AXC.ALO

chamois (color)
USE **grayish yellow**
moderate yellow

chamois (yellow ocher)
USE **yellow ocher**

Champa
USE **Cham (Vietnamese)**

champlevé
KT.660 (L,R)
SN Enameling that is accomplished by carving away troughs or cells in metal, leaving a raised line that forms the outline of the design. The enamel is laid in the cells, fired, and then filed and polished. (QUICK)
CN K.KT.AFU.ALO.GRC.AFU.ALO.ALO

Chamula
FL.1543 (L)
CN F.FL.ALO.ALO.ARI.ALO.BIQ.AFU.CLM.AFU

Chan
USE **Ch'an**

Chan-Kuo
USE **Warring States**

Chaná
FL.1689 (L)
CN F.FL.ALO.ALO.ARI.ARI.BOK.ALO

Chanak Kalé
FL.3519
UF Çanakkale
Chanak Kalessi
Chanakkale
CN F.FL.ALO.BIQ.AFU.FOG.ALO.AFU

Chanak Kalessi
USE **Chanak Kalé**

Chanakkale
USE **Chanak Kalé**

Chanapata
FL.1145
CN F.FL.ALO.ALO.ALO.ARI.AXC.AFU.ARI.BIQ

Chancay
FL.1166 (L)
CN F.FL.ALO.ALO.ALO.ARI.AXC.AFU.BIQ.ARI

chancel arches
RT.279
ALT **chancel arch**
SN Use for the arch marking the separation of chancel from nave.
UF arches, chancel
arches, triumphal (church components)
triumphal arches (church components)
CN V.RT.AFU.AFU.AFU.BCW.AFU.AFU.ARI.ALO

chancel enclosures
USE **chancel screens**

chancel screens
RT.1250 (R)
ALT **chancel screen**
SN Use for partitions in Christian churches separating the chancel from the body of the church. For partitions that separate the choir from other areas use **choir screens.**
UF chancel enclosures
enclosures, chancel
screens, chancel
CN V.RT.AFU.BUE.ALO.ARI.CXA.ALO

chancelleries
USE **embassy buildings**

chancels
RM.303 (A,R)
ALT **chancel**
SN Use for spaces in Christian churches containing the altar and reserved for the use of the clergy. Includes the choir area when present. Use **choirs** for spaces in Christian churches reserved for the singers.
CN V.RM.AFU.DIO.AXC.ALO.AFU.ARI

chanceries
USE **embassy buildings**

chancery documents
VW.1004
ALT **chancery document**
UF documents, chancery
CN V.VW.AFU.ARI.ALO.BCW.AFU.AFU.ALO.AFU

Chandella
USE **Candella**

chandleries
RM.191
ALT **chandlery**
SN Storage places for candles and other lighting devices.
UF chandries
CN V.RM.AFU.DIO.ALO.DCU.AXC

chandries
USE **chandleries**

Chané
FL.1641 (L)
CN F.FL.ALO.ALO.ARI.ARI.AXC.BIQ

change keys
USE **master keys**

change order drawings
VD.94
ALT **change order drawing**
UF drawings, change order
CN V.VD.AFU.ALO.ARI.AFU

change orders
VW.791
ALT **change order**
SN Written and signed legal documents authorizing a change from the original plans, specifications, or other contract documents, or authorizing a change in the cost of the project. (MEANS)
UF orders, change
orders, variation
variation orders
CN V.VW.AFU.ARI.AFU.ARI.AFU.AFU

change, population
USE **population change**

changes (key components)
TF.546
ALT **change (key component)**
CN V.TF.AFU.ALO.ARI.ALO.ALO

changing rooms
USE **dressing rooms**

channel bars
USE **channel beams**

channel beams
RT.710
ALT **channel beam**
SN Use for metal sections having a C- or U-shaped profile.
UF bars, channel
beams, channel
channel bars
channel irons
channel sections
irons, channel
sections, channel
CN V.RT.AFU.AFU.ALO.ARI.ALO

channel inserts
TF.379
ALT **channel insert**
UF continuous inserts
inserts, channel
inserts, continuous
CN V.TF.AFU.AFU.AFU.ALO.AFU.BZY.ALO

channel irons
USE **channel beams**

channel saddle hangers
TF.357
ALT **channel saddle hanger**
UF hangers, channel saddle
saddle hangers, channel
CN V.TF.AFU.AFU.AFU.ALO.AFU.BOK.ARI.ALO.AFU.AFU

Channel School
USE **Channel Style**

channel sections
USE **channel beams**

Channel Style
FL.3134
UF Channel School
CN F.FL.ALO.BCW.ALO.ALO.AFU.BOK.ARI.AXC

channeled ware
FL.145
UF ware, channeled
CN F.FL.ALO.AFU.ALO.ARI.BOK.AFU

channels
RD.157 (L)
ALT **channel**
SN Components of bodies of water characterized as being relatively long and narrow and axially located in relation to the waterway, such as used to designate the deepest part of streambeds where the main current runs, or stretches of sea between two land areas and linking two seas.
CN V.RD.ARI.AFU.AFU.ALO.AFU

chantries
RM.306 (A,L)
ALT **chantry**
SN Use for chapels, altars, or other parts of a church endowed for chanting of masses.
UF chantry chapels
chapels, chantry
CN V.RM.AFU.DIO.AXC.ALO.AFU.AXC.ALO

chantry chapels
USE **chantries**

Chanukah
USE **Hanukkah**

Chanukah cards
USE **Hanukkah cards**

chapbooks
VW.497 (L,R)
ALT **chapbook**
CN V.VW.AFU.ALO.AFU.AFU.AFU.BIQ

chapelières
USE **bonnetières**

chapels
RM.304 (A,L,B,R)
ALT **chapel**
SN Includes both freestanding chapels and rooms or recesses serving as chapels in churches or other buildings.
CN V.RM.AFU.DIO.AXC.ALO.AFU.AXC

chapels of ease
RK.1101 (B)
ALT **chapel of ease**
SN Churches built within the bounds of a parish for the attendance of those who cannot reach the parish church conveniently. (DAC)
CN V.RK.AFU.ALO.ALO.FCS.BIQ.ALO.ALO.AFU

chapels royal
USE **royal chapels**

chapels, chantry
USE **chantries**

chapels, court
USE **royal chapels**

chapels, domestic
USE **private chapels**

chapels, funeral
USE **funeral chapels**

chapels, lady
USE **lady chapels**

chapels, monumental
USE **sepulchral chapels**

chapels, mortuary
USE **sepulchral chapels**

chapels, palace
USE **royal chapels**

chapels, private
USE **private chapels**

chapels, royal
USE **royal chapels**

chapels, sepulchral
USE **sepulchral chapels**

chapiters
USE **capitals**

chaplains
HG.222 (L)
ALT **chaplain**
SN Clergymen officially attached to the army or navy, to some public institution, or to a family or court. (W)
CN H.HG.AFU.AXC.AXC.BIQ.AFU.ARI.BOK

chaplets
USE **astragals**
bead moldings

chapter houses
RK.1187 (A,R)
ALT **chapter house**
SN Designates assembly halls for the business meetings of religious or fraternal organizations.
UF halls, synodal
houses, chapter
synodal halls
CN V.RK.AFU.ALO.ALO.FUA.AFU.AFU

chaptrels
RT.124
ALT **chaptrel**
SN Use for engaged capitals, particularly the capitals of pilasters and vaulting shafts.
CN V.RT.AFU.AFU.AFU.AXC.BIQ.ALO.ARI.AFU.BUE

char taqs
USE **chahar taqs**

Charbon Velours
USE **Artigue process**

charcoal
MT.1045 (L,R)
CN M.MT.AFU.AFU.ALO.BIQ.BUE.ARI

charcoal black
MT.1570
UF black, charcoal
black, vegetable
vegetable black
CN M.MT.AFU.AFU.ARI.AFU.AFU.ALO.ALO.AFU.AFU.AFU.ALO

charcoal (color)
USE **black**
dark grayish blue

dark grayish brown
dark grayish purple
dark purplish gray

charcoal gray
USE **dark gray**

charcoal paper
MT.1933
UF paper, charcoal
CN M.MT.AFU.AFU.ARI.ALO.ALO.AXC.ARI.AXC.AFU

charcoal pencils
TB.262
ALT **charcoal pencil**
SN Pencils with lead of finely ground, highly compacted charcoal. Less messy, but not as versatile as charcoal sticks. (HAND)
UF pencils, charcoal
CN V.TB.AFU.ARI.CLM.AFU.ALO.DIO.AFU

charcoal sticks
TB.236
ALT **charcoal stick**
SN Black crayons made of charred twigs of wood, usually willow, or pieces of vine.(MAYER) Also used for sticks of compressed charcoal.
UF charcoal, vine
sticks, charcoal
vine charcoal
CN V.TB.AFU.ARI.CLM.AFU.ALO.ALO

charcoal, vine
USE **charcoal sticks**

charcoal, wood
USE **wood charcoal**

charettes
KM.47 (A)
SN The intense final effort made by architectural students to complete their solutions to a given architectural problem in an allotted time or the period in which such an effort is made. (W)
CN K.KM.AFU.BCW.AFU

charge plates
USE **credit cards**

chargehands
USE **foremen**

charges
USE **fees**

charges (heraldic motifs)
USE **heraldic motifs**

Chariot sub-period
FL.72
CN F.FL.ALO.AFU.AFU.ARI.AXC.AFU

charitable institutions
USE **charities**
welfare buildings

charitable societies
HG.896 (L)
ALT **charitable society**
UF societies, charitable
CN H.HG.ALO.DUC.AXC

charities
HG.859 (L,R)
ALT **charity**
SN Organizations or institutions engaged in the free assistance of the poor, the suffering, or the distressed. (W)
UF charitable institutions
institutions, charitable
CN H.HG.ALO.CXA.AFU

Charles X
USE **Restauration**

Charlton white
USE **lithopone**

charnel houses
USE **ossuaries**

Charrúa
FL.1690 (L)
CN F.FL.ALO.ALO.ARI.ARI.BOK.ARI

charter rolls
VW.1005
ALT **charter roll**
UF rolls, charter
CN V.VW.AFU.ARI.ALO.BCW.AFU.AFU.ALO.AFU.AFU

charterhouses
RG.196 (R)
ALT **charterhouse**
UF certose
chartreuses
CN V.RG.AFU.AFU.DUC.BIQ.ALO

charters
VW.912
ALT **charter**
SN Documents, usually sealed, granting specific rights, setting forth aims and principles of a newly established entity, and often embodying formal agreements and authorizing special privileges or exemptions. (ICA)
CN V.VW.AFU.ARI.AFU.BOK.BOK.BIQ

chartography
USE **cartography**

chartophylacia
RK.686
ALT **chartophylacium**
SN In Medieval ecclesiastical contexts, places for the safekeeping of records and other valuable documents.
CN V.RK.AFU.ALO.ALO.CRG.AFU.AFU

chartreuse
USE **brilliant greenish yellow**
light greenish yellow
moderate greenish yellow
moderate yellow green
strong greenish yellow
strong yellow green

chartreuse green
USE **brilliant yellow green**
dark greenish yellow
vivid yellow green

chartreuse yellow
USE **brilliant greenish yellow**
light greenish yellow
moderate greenish yellow
strong greenish yellow

chartreuse yellow, bright
USE **strong greenish yellow**
vivid greenish yellow

chartreuse yellow, light
USE **brilliant greenish yellow**
light greenish yellow
moderate greenish yellow
strong greenish yellow

chartreuse, bright
USE **brilliant yellow green**
strong yellow green
vivid yellow green

chartreuse, light
USE **brilliant yellow green**
light yellow green

chartreuse, pale
USE **light yellow green**
pale yellow green

chartreuse, vivid
USE **vivid yellow green**

chartreuses
USE **charterhouses**

charts
VW.234
ALT **chart**
CN V.VW.AFU.AFU.AFU.FZU.AXC.ALO

charts (maps)
USE **maps**

charts, admiralty
USE **marine charts**

charts, aerial
USE **aeronautical charts**

charts, aeronautical
USE **aeronautical charts**

charts, astrological
USE **astrological charts**

charts, astronautical
USE **astronautical charts**

charts, astronomical
USE **astronomical charts**

charts, bathymetric
USE **bathymetric maps**

charts, celestial
USE **astronomical charts**

charts, climatic
USE **climatic charts**

charts, coastal
USE **coastal charts**

charts, color
USE **color charts**

charts, hydrographic
USE **nautical charts**

charts, isogonic
USE **isogonic charts**

charts, marine
USE **marine charts**

charts, nautical
USE **nautical charts**

charts, navigation
USE **navigation charts**

charts, organizational
USE **organizational charts**

charts, pilot
USE **navigation charts**

charts, plotting
USE **plotting charts**

charts, polar
USE **polar charts**

charts, portolan
USE **portolanos**

charts, portulan
USE **portolanos**

charts, progress
USE **progress schedules**

charts, river
USE **river charts**

charts, sea
USE **marine charts**

charts, solar
USE **solar charts**

charts, star
USE **astronomical charts**

chartularies
USE **cartularies**

chasers
TB.731
ALT **chaser**
SN Threading tools, many-toothed or with a single cut edge, shaped especially for cutting or finishing external or internal threads; usually used in conjunction with a lathe. (PUTNAM)
CN V.TB.AFU.BCW.BIQ.ARI.ALO.BUE.ALO

chases
RM.210
ALT chase
SN Use for continuous recesses or grooves built into walls to receive pipes, ducts, and other elements.
UF chases, pipe
chases, wall
pipe chases
wall chases
CN V.RM.AFU.DIO.ALO.DIO.ALO

chases, pipe
USE **chases**

chases, wall
USE **chases**

chashitsu
USE **teahouses**

Chasidism
USE **Hasidism**

chasing
KT.833 (L,R)
ALT **chased**
SN The process of adding detail or ornament on metal by indenting with a hammer and tools without a cutting edge. (W)
UF chasing, metal
metal chasing
CN K.KT.AFU.ALO.HOE.BCW.ALO.AXC.AFU

chasing, metal
USE **chasing**

Chasseen
FL.2487
UF Chassey
CN F.FL.ALO.AXC.AFU.BCW.ALO

Chassey
USE **Chasseen**

Château Style
FL.1731
UF Châteauesque
CN F.FL.ALO.ALO.BCW.AFU.BUE.AFU

Châteauesque
USE **Château Style**

châteaus
USE **châteaux**

châteaux
RK.290 (A,L,B,R)
ALT **château**
SN Use for large country houses in France, which prior to the 16th century were usually fortified.
UF châteaus
CN V.RK.AFU.ALO.ALO.AXC.ALO.AXC.AFU.AFU.AFU.AFU

châtelets
RK.437
ALT **châtelet**
SN Use for small French castles.
CN V.RK.AFU.ALO.ALO.BIQ.ALO.AFU

Châtelperronian
FL.2466
CN F.FL.ALO.AXC.AFU.ARI.ALO.ALO

Chatino
FL.1511 (L)
CN F.FL.ALO.ALO.ARI.ALO.AXC.ALO

chatônes
TF.405
ALT **chatône**
CN V.TF.AFU.AFU.AFU.ALO.AFU.CFS.AFU.DCU.ARI

Chaudor
USE **Chodor**

chauffeuses
TG.51
ALT **chauffeuse**
SN Upholstered chairs with low seats and very high backs placed either beside or in front of the fire.
UF caquetoires (chauffeuses)
chaises à dame
chaises à demoiselle
chaises à femme
chaises à vertugadin
chaises chauffeuses
chaises du four
coins de feu
remailloteuse
sièges à langer
sièges de nourrice
CN V.TG.AFU.AFU.ALO.AFU.AFU.AFU.DZW

Chavín
FL.1141 (L)
CN F.FL.ALO.ALO.ALO.ARI.AXC.AFU.ARI.ALO

Chavín horizon
FL.1173 (L)
CN F.FL.ALO.ALO.ALO.ARI.AXC.ALO.AFU

Chavín, Kotosh
USE **Kotosh Chavín**

chay
MT.1522
SN The root of an East Indian herb that yields a red dye. (W)
CN M.MT.AFU.AFU.ARI.AFU.AFU.AFU.AFU.AFU.AXC.ARI

Che
USE **Zhe**

check dams
RK.527
ALT **check dam**
UF dams, check
CN V.RK.AFU.ALO.ALO.CFS.AFU.ARI.ALO.ALO

check pattern
USE **checker pattern**

check planes
USE **rabbet planes**

check stamping
KT.159
ALT **check stamped**
SN The decorating of pottery with small, impressed squares, produced by a paddle or stamp. (JANA)
UF stamping, check
CN K.KT.AFU.ALO.DOI.DÙC.AFU

check stubs
VW.818
ALT **check stub**
UF counterfoils
stubs, check
CN V.VW.AFU.ARI.AFU.BIQ.BCW

checkbooks
VW.819
ALT **checkbook**
SN Books containing blank checks on a bank. (GAHLM)
CN V.VW.AFU.ARI.AFU.BIQ.BIQ

checker pattern
DG.123
ALT **checkered**
SN A pattern of alternating squares or lozenges of contrasting color or texture. (THDAT)
UF check pattern
checkers (pattern)
checkerwork
checks (pattern)
chequer pattern
pattern, checker
CN D.DG.AFU.ARI.ALO.BIQ.AFU

checker tables
USE **chess tables**

checkers (pattern)
USE **checker pattern**

checkers (people)
HG.708
ALT **checker (person)**
SN Persons responsible for checking that a product or service meets required standards.
CN H.HG.AFU.BCW.ARI

checkerwork
USE **checker pattern**

checking floor hinges
TF.136
ALT **checking floor hinge**
SN Hinges containing a spring for closing a compression chamber in which the liquid escapes slowly, thus retarding the closing action to prevent slamming of the door. (STEIN)
UF floor hinges, checking
hinges, checking floor
CN V.TF.AFU.AFU.AFU.AFU.CLM.ALO.ARI.AFU

checklists
VW.263 (B)
ALT **checklist**
SN Lists in which items can be compared, scheduled, verified, or identified. (AHD)
CN V.VW.AFU.AFU.AFU.FZU.BCW.AFU.ARI

checkrooms
RM.192
ALT **checkroom**
SN Rooms at which baggage, parcels, clothing, or other personal articles are deposited with a clerk for temporary storage.
CN V.RM.AFU.DIO.ALO.DCU.BCW

checks
VW.829 (L)
ALT **check**
SN Bills of exchange or written orders drawn on a bank or the Treasury of the United States to pay on demand a specified sum of money to a named person, to his order, or to bearer, out of money on deposit to the credit of the writer. (GAHLM)
UF bank checks
CN V.VW.AFU.ARI.AFU.BIQ.CFS.ARI

checks (furniture backs)
USE **wings (furniture components)**

checks (pattern)
USE **checker pattern**

checks, back
USE **door checks**

checks, certified
USE **certified checks**

checks, door
USE **door checks**

checks, travelers'
USE **travelers' checks**

chedi
USE **stupas**

cheeks, chimney
USE **chimney cheeks**

cheeks, fireplace
USE **fireplace cheeks**

Chehalis
FL.1337 (L)
CN F.FL.ALO.ALO.ARI.AFU.BIQ.AXC

Chellean
USE **Abbevillian**

Chelles-Acheul
FL.51
CN F.FL.ALO.AFU.AFU.ALO.AFU.ALO

Chemehuevi
FL.1309 (L)
CN F.FL.ALO.ALO.ARI.AFU.AXC.ALO

chemical analysis
KT.11 (L)
UF analysis, chemical
CN K.KT.AFU.ALO.AXC.AFU

chemical cleaning
KT.69
UF cleaning, chemical
CN K.KT.AFU.ALO.BIQ.ALO

chemical engineering
KD.216 (L)
SN Discipline in which chemistry, physics, and mathematics are combined with basic engineering principles to solve environmental, biomedical, societal, or technological problems arising in the application of chemistry. (PG)
UF engineering, chemical
CN K.KD.AFU.ARI.BIQ.ARI

chemical engineers
HG.629 (L)
ALT **chemical engineer**
UF engineers, chemical
CN H.HG.AFU.AXC.BZY.BCW.AXC

chemical inhibitors
USE **inhibitors**

chemical laboratories
RK.1164 (A,L,B)
ALT **chemical laboratory**
UF laboratories, chemical
CN V.RK.AFU.ALO.ALO.FIM.ALO.AFU.BCW

chemical pollution
BM.438 (L)
UF pollution, chemical
CN B.BM.AXC.BCW.ALO.ALO

chemical properties
BM.939
UF properties, chemical
CN B.BM.CFS.AXC.BZY.ARI

chemical-resistant materials
MT.2790
UF materials, chemical-resistant
CN M.MT.AFU.BCW.ARI

chemical-resistant paint
MT.2540
UF paint, chemical-resistant
CN M.MT.AFU.ARI.CRG.ALO.BCW.ARI.ALO

chemicals, petroleum
USE **petrochemicals**

chemist's shops
USE **drugstores**

chemistry
KD.261 (L,R)
CN K.KD.AFU.ARI.CLM.ALO

chemistry, biological
USE **biochemistry**

chemistry, inorganic
USE **inorganic chemistry**

chemistry, organic
USE **organic chemistry**

chemists
HG.333 (L)
ALT **chemist**
CN H.HG.AFU.AXC.BIQ.AFU.AFU.ARI

Chen
FL.1879 (L)
UF Ch'en
CN F.FL.ALO.ARI.ALO.AFU.AFU.ALO.BUE.AFU.ALO.AXC

Chen-la
FL.2320
CN F.FL.ALO.ARI.BCW.ALO.AFU.ALO

Chen-Yen
BM.618
UF Mi Tsung
True Word sect (China)
CN B.BM.BZY.AFU.AFU.BCW.ALO

cheneaux
RT.1052
ALT **cheneau**
SN Use for cresting occurring above the eaves or cornices of buildings, or an ornamental gutter.
CN V.RT.AFU.BCW.ARI.ALO

Chenes
FL.1039
UF Los Chenes
CN F.FL.ALO.ALO.ALO.ALO.AFU.ALO.ARI.ALO.AFU.AFU

Cheng chou
USE **Zhengzhou**

Cheng chow
USE **Zhengzhou**

Cheng-te
USE **Zhengde**

Chengchou
USE **Zhengzhou**

Chenghua
FL.1901
CN F.FL.ALO.ARI.ALO.AFU.AFU.ALO.DIO.AXC

chequer pattern
USE **checker pattern**

Cherokee
FL.1431 (L)
CN F.FL.ALO.ALO.ARI.AFU.BZY.ALO

cherries
USE **bits**

cherry
MT.1287 (L)
CN M.MT.AFU.AFU.ALO.BIQ.DCU.AFU.AFU.AFU.KLE.ARI

cherry birch
USE **sweet birch**

cherry gum
MT.1050
UF cherry-tree gum
gum, cherry
gum, cherry-tree
gum, plum
plum gum
CN M.MT.AFU.AFU.ALO.BIQ.BUE.AXC.ALO

cherry pickers
TB.60
ALT **cherry picker**
SN Machines for lifting men or materials on a platform at the end of an extendable boom, usually mounted on a carrier with wheels to provide mobility. (DAC)
CN V.TB.AFU.ARI.AFU.BCW.ARI

cherry-tree gum
USE **cherry gum**

cherry, American
USE **black cherry**

cherry, American black
USE **black cherry**

cherry, black
USE **black cherry**

cherry, English
USE **English cherry**

cherry, rum
USE **black cherry**

cherry, sour
USE **sour cherry**

cherry, sweet
USE **sweet cherry**

cherry, wild
USE **sweet cherry**

chert
MT.551 (L,B)
SN Fine-grain, dense rock consisting of chalcedony or opal. (DAC)
CN M.MT.AFU.AFU.AFU.CFS.AFU.GRC.AFU.ARI.ARI

cherty limestone
USE **siliceous limestone**

chess tables
TG.744
ALT **chess table**
SN Tables with tops marked as a board for playing chess or checkers.
UF checker tables
tables, checker
tables, chess
CN V.TG.AFU.AFU.BIQ.BOK.ALO.CRG.ALO

chessboard plan
USE **grid plan**

chessylite
USE **azurite**

chest-benches
USE **box settles**

chest lifts
USE **drawer pulls**

chest pulls
USE **drawer pulls**

chesterfields
TG.314
ALT **chesterfield**
SN Well-stuffed upholstered sofas with no wood showing. (DDA)
CN V.TG.AFU.AFU.ALO.ALO.BZY.BCW

chestnut
MT.1131 (L)
UF Castanea
CN M.MT.AFU.AFU.ALO.BIQ.DCU.AFU.AFU.AFU.CLM

chestnut brown
USE **burnt umber**

chestnut oak
MT.1235 (L)
UF oak, chestnut
CN M.MT.AFU.AFU.ALO.BIQ.DCU.AFU.AFU.AFU.IRA.BIQ

chestnut, American
USE **American chestnut**

chestnut, American horse
USE **buckeye**

chestnut, American sweet
USE **American chestnut**

chestnut, Chinese
USE **Chinese chestnut**

chestnut, common horse
USE **horse chestnut**

chestnut, European
USE **European chestnut**

chestnut, horse
USE **horse chestnut**

chestnut, Indian rose
USE **gangaw**

chestnut, Italian
USE **European chestnut**

chestnut, Japanese
USE **Japanese chestnut**

chestnut, Spanish
USE **European chestnut**

chestnut, sweet
USE **European chestnut**

chests
TG.445 (L,N,B,R)
ALT **chest**
SN Large boxes with hinged lids intended for the storage of textiles, clothing and other articles. (GEWARD)
CN V.TG.AFU.AFU.AXC.ALO.AXC

chests of drawers
TG.475 (L,N)
ALT **chest of drawers**
SN Type of case furniture usually having four drawers but sometimes made with three, five or more; generally supported on feet and sometimes resting directly on the floor. Use **commodes** for similar case pieces generally supported on short legs. Use **chests with drawers** for chests with one or more tiers of drawers below a deep storage space.
UF bureaus (chests of drawers)
chests, dressing (chests of drawers)
drawers, chests of
dressers (chests of drawers)
dressing chests (chests of drawers)
CN V.TG.AFU.AFU.AXC.ALO.BCW

chests of drawers on frames
USE **chests on frames**

chests of drawers, double
USE **chests-on-chests**

chests of drawers, high
USE **high chests of drawers**

chests of drawers, kneehole
USE **kneehole desks**

chests of drawers, low
USE **low chests**

chests of drawers, tall
USE **chiffoniers**

chests-on-chests
TG.478 (L,N)
ALT **chest-on-chest**
SN Two-part chests of drawers, one stacked on top of the other. (NEF)
UF chests of drawers, double
chests upon chests
chests, chests upon
chests, double
double chests
double chests of drawers
drawers, double chests of
CN V.TG.AFU.AFU.AXC.ALO.BCW.ARI

chests on frames
TG.479 (N)
ALT **chest on frame**
SN Chests of drawers which sit on a framed stand. (NEF)
UF chests of drawers on frames
frames, chests of drawers on
frames, chests on
CN V.TG.AFU.AFU.AXC.ALO.BCW.AXC

chests over drawers
USE **chests with drawers**

chests upon chests
USE **chests-on-chests**

chests with drawers
TG.454
ALT **chest with drawers**
SN Chests with one or two tiers of drawers below a deep storage space; precursor to chests of drawers. Use **chests of drawers** for case furniture having two or more drawers but lacking a deep storage space. (NEF)
UF chests over drawers
drawers, chests with
CN V.TG.AFU.AFU.AXC.ALO.AXC.BZY

chests, ark
USE **arks**

chests, armada
USE **armada chests**

chests, bachelor's
USE **bachelor's chests**

chests, Baltic
USE **Nonsuch chests**

chests, blanket
USE **blanket chests**

chests, board
USE **board chests**

chests, book tea
USE **tea chests**

chests, bridal
USE **dower chests**

chests, campaign
USE **campaign chests**

chests, chests upon
USE **chests-on-chests**

chests, clothes
USE **clothes chests**

chests, commode
USE **commodes**

chests, double
USE **chests-on-chests**

chests, dower
USE **dower chests**

chests, dressing (chests of drawers)
USE **chests of drawers**

chests, dug-out
USE **dug-out chests**

chests, French commode dressing
USE **commode dressing tables**

chests, half
USE **low chests**

chests, high
USE **high chests of drawers**

chests, hope
USE **dower chests**

chests, kneehole
USE **kneehole desks**

chests, lobby
USE **lobby chests**

chests, low
USE **low chests**

chests, marriage
USE **dower chests**

chests, medicine
USE **medicine chests**

chests, mule
USE **mule chests**

chests, Nonsuch
USE **Nonsuch chests**

chests, Rudd dressing
USE **Rudd dressing chests**

chests, sea
USE **sea chests**

chests, ship
USE **sea chests**

chests, six-board
USE **board chests**

chests, spice
USE **spice chests**

chests, sugar
USE **sugar chests**

chests, tea
USE **tea chests**

chests, tilting
USE **tilting chests**

chests, wedding
USE **dower chests**

chests, wine
USE **cellerets**

cheval bureaus
USE **cheval dressers**

cheval dressers
TG.480
ALT **cheval dresser**
SN Chests of drawers having a full length mirror on one side and drawers on the other.
UF bureaus, cheval
cheval bureaus
dressers, cheval
CN V.TG.AFU.AFU.AXC.ALO.BCW.BCW

cheval fire screens
TG.5
ALT **cheval fire screen**
SN Fire screens with a sliding panel set between two standards on four legs; distinguished from **pole screens** which have a tripod base and shaft which supports the fire screen.
UF cheval screens
fire screens, cheval
fire screens, horse
horse fire screens
screens, cheval
screens, cheval fire

screens, horse fire
CN V.TG.AFU.AFU.AFU.AFU.AFU

cheval screens
USE **cheval fire screens**

cheverets
TG.572
ALT **cheveret**
SN 18th-century English writing tables with oblong tops, shallow drawers below, and four slender tapering legs joined with a shelf; often made in satinwood. (DDA)
UF cabinets, lady's
lady's cabinets
sheverets
CN V.TG.AFU.AFU.AXC.ALO.BZY.FUA.BCW

cheves
USE **howell planes**

chevets
RM.314 (A)
ALT **chevet**
SN Use for the combination of apse, ambulatory, and usually radial chapels of a church, especially French Gothic.
CN V.RM.AFU.DIO.AXC.ALO.AFU.BCW

chevets (headboards)
USE **headboards**

chevets (night tables)
USE **night tables**

chevrons
DG.24
ALT **chevron**
SN Simple geometric forms composed of Vs used singly, in a vertical series, or in a string to form a zigzag. (LDDO)
UF dancettes
CN D.DG.AFU.AFU.BIQ.AFU

Chewa
FL.544 (L)
CN F.FL.ALO.AFU.AXC.ARI.AFU.ALO

Cheyenne
FL.1376 (L,R)
CN F.FL.ALO.ALO.ARI.AFU.BOK.BIQ

Cheyenne, Northern
USE **Northern Cheyenne**

Cheyenne, Southern
USE **Southern Cheyenne**

Chia-ch'ing
USE **Jiaqing**

Chia-ching
USE **Jiajing**

Chian
FL.2606
UF Chiot
Naukratite
CN F.FL.ALO.AXC.ALO.AFU.ALO.AXC.ALO.ARI.AFU

chian turpentine
USE **turpentine**

Chiang Mai
FL.2420
UF Chieng Mai
Jiang Hmai
CN F.FL.ALO.ARI.BCW.BOK.AFU.DIO

chiaroscuro
KT.263 (L,R)
SN The technique of contrasting light and dark within a picture, especially one in which the forms are largely determined, not by sharp outlines, but by the meeting of lighter and darker areas.
UF clairobscur
CN K.KT.AFU.ALO.DUC.DCU.AFU

chiaroscuro drawings
USE **three-tone drawings**

Chiavari chairs
TG.153
ALT **Chiavari chair**
UF chairs, Chiavari
CN V.TG.AFU.AFU.ALO.AFU.AFU.AFU.NIE.DUC.AFU

Chibcha
FL.1658 (L)
UF Mosca
Muisca
CN F.FL.ALO.ALO.ARI.ARI.BCW.BIQ

Chicago Imagist
FL.3720 (R)
ALT **Chicago Imagism**
UF Imagist (Chicago Imagist)
Imagist, Chicago
CN F.FL.ALO.BUE.ARI.BCW

Chicago windows
RT.916
ALT **Chicago window**
SN Windows occupying the full width of a bay and divided into a large fixed sash flanked by a narrow movable sash on each side. (PDARC)
UF windows, Chicago
CN V.RT.AFU.ARI.AFU.AFU.BOK.AFU.AFU.AXC

Chicanel
FL.1012
CN F.FL.ALO.ALO.ALO.ALO.AFU.ALO.ARI.AFU.AFU.ARI

Chicanos
USE **Mexican Americans**

Chichimec
FL.1499 (L)
CN F.FL.ALO.ALO.ARI.ALO.ARI.AFU

Chickasaw
FL.1432 (L)
CN F.FL.ALO.ALO.ARI.AFU.BZY.ARI

chicken-coop Windsor chairs
USE **square-back Windsor chairs**

chicken coops
USE **chicken houses**

chicken hatcheries
RK.91 (L)
ALT **chicken hatchery**
UF hatcheries, chicken
CN V.RK.AFU.ALO.ALO.AFU.ALO.CFS.AFU.AFU

chicken houses
RK.90 (A,L,B)
ALT **chicken house**
UF chicken coops
chicken sheds
coops, chicken
hen houses
houses, chicken
houses, hen
sheds, chicken
CN V.RK.AFU.ALO.ALO.AFU.ALO.CFS.AFU

chicken sheds
USE **chicken houses**

chicken wire
MT.483
UF wire, chicken
CN M.MT.AFU.AFU.AFU.BZY.ALO.BZY.ALO

chieftains
HG.691
ALT **chieftain**
CN H.HG.AFU.AXC.CFS.CRG.AFU

Chieng Mai
USE **Chiang Mai**

Chiengsen
USE **Northern Thai**

chiens-assis
RT.476
ALT **chien-assis**
SN Small, unglazed dormer windows used to provide light and ventilation in an attic or space below a sloping roof; especially used in Medieval buildings. (HAS)
CN V.RT.AFU.AFU.AFU.BIQ.ARI.ALO.AFU.BUE.AXC.AFU

chiffonier beds
TG.343
ALT **chiffonier bed**
SN Deception beds which fold into a dummy chiffonier.
UF beds, chiffonier
beds, chiffonier folding
chiffonier folding beds
folding beds, chiffonier
CN V.TG.AFU.AFU.ARI.AFU.AFU.BIQ.AFU.AXC

chiffonier folding beds
USE **chiffonier beds**

chiffoniers
TG.481 (N)
ALT **chiffonier**
SN Tall chests of drawers with a mirror on top; common in late 19th and early 20th century.
UF chests of drawers, tall
drawers, tall chests of
tall chests of drawers
CN V.TG.AFU.AFU.AXC.ALO.BCW.BIQ

chiffonièrs (chiffonnières)
USE **chiffonnières**

chiffoniers (sideboards)
TG.590
ALT **chiffonier (sideboard)**
SN Anglicized name from French for a small cupboard with a top forming a sideboard.(BEARD) For small, low chests of drawers use **chiffoniéres.**
CN V.TG.AFU.AFU.AXC.ALO.CRG.AXC

chiffonnières
TG.482 (N)
ALT **chiffonnière**
SN 18th-century French term for a piece of furniture for the storage of stuffs (chiffons) and small articles of clothing. It is usually, but not necessarily, a small, low chest of drawers, narrower than the normal commode. (DDA) For small cupboards with a top forming a sideboard use **chiffoniers (sideboards).**
UF chiffonièrs (chiffonnières)
CN V.TG.AFU.AFU.AXC.ALO.BCW.BOK

chiffonnières (table)
USE **tables en chiffonnière**

chifforobes
TG.483
ALT **chifforobe**
SN Use for chests of drawers having a wardrobe cabinet built alongside.
CN V.TG.AFU.AFU.AXC.ALO.BCW.BUE

chifforobes (wardrobes)
USE **wardrobes**

chika
MT.2062
SN Any kind of earth, especially clay, that is mixed with water to make mortar in Ethiopia. (OLIVER)
CN M.MT.AFU.AFU.ARI.BOK.ALO.AFU

Chilcotin
FL.1229 (L)
UF Tsilkotin
CN F.FL.ALO.ALO.ARI.AFU.AFU.ARI.BCW

child care centers
USE **day care centers**

child's chairs
TG.170
ALT **child's chair**
UF chairs, child's
CN V.TG.AFU.AFU.ALO.AFU.AFU.ALO.BCW

child's table chairs
USE **highchairs**

childbirth
USE **birth**

children
HG.6 (L,R)
ALT **child**
CN H.HG.AFU.AFU.ARI.AFU

children (offspring)
USE **offspring**

children's art
BM.235 (L,R)
SN Art produced by children.
UF art, children's
CN B.BM.AFU.ARI.BCW.BIQ

children's films
VW.675 (L)
ALT **children's film**
SN Films produced primarily for children. (LCSH)
UF films, children's
CN V.VW.AFU.ALO.AFU.DZW.BCW.AFU

children's gardens
RK.1419 (A,L,B)
ALT **children's garden**
UF gardens, children's
CN V.RK.ALO.AFU.AFU.ALO.ARI

children's homes
USE **orphanages**

children's hospitals
RK.763 (A,L,B)
ALT **children's hospital**
UF hospitals, children's
hospitals, pediatric
pediatric hospitals
CN V.RK.AFU.ALO.ALO.CXA.ALO.AFU.BCW.ALO.ALO

children's hostels
USE **orphanages**
youth hostels

children's libraries
RK.709 (A,L,B)
ALT **children's library**
UF libraries, children's
CN V.RK.AFU.ALO.ALO.CRG.AXC.ARI.ARI

children's museums
RK.378 (A,L)
ALT **children's museum**
UF junior museums
museums, children's
museums, junior
CN V.RK.AFU.ALO.ALO.BCW.AXC.AFU

children's nurseries
USE **nurseries (rooms)**

children's parks
USE **playgrounds**

children's playgrounds
USE **playgrounds**

children's playhouses
RK.1024 (A,L)
ALT **children's playhouse**
UF playhouses (recreation buildings)
playhouses, children's
CN V.RK.AFU.ALO.ALO.EWY.AXC.AFU

children's villages
RG.37 (L,B)
ALT **children's village**
SN Use for residential treatment centers, often in a rural setting, which provide medical and counseling services for children with emotional problems.
UF villages, children's
CN V.RG.AFU.AFU.ARI

children's zoological gardens
USE **children's zoos**

children's zoos
RG.230 (A,L)
ALT **children's zoo**
UF children's zoological gardens
gardens, children's zoological
zoos, children's
CN V.RG.AFU.AFU.ELK.AFU

Chilean
FL.720 (L,B)
CN F.FL.ALO.ALO.AFU.AXC.AXC

Chilean Diaguite
FL.1187
UF Diaguite, Chilean
CN F.FL.ALO.ALO.ALO.ARI.BCW.ALO.AFU.ALO

chilled water systems
RT.1388
ALT **chilled water system**
UF systems, chilled water
water systems, chilled
CN V.RT.ALO.BCW.AFU.AFU.ALO.AFU

Chimalhuacán
FL.986
CN F.FL.ALO.ALO.ALO.ALO.AFU.ALO.AFU.AFU.BOK

chimney backs
USE **firebacks**

chimney bars
RT.1136
ALT **chimney bar**
SN Metal bars that support the masonry above fireplace openings.
UF bars, chimney
bars, turning
turning bars
CN V.RT.AFU.BOK.AFU.ALO.AFU

chimney breasts
RT.1137 (A,N,B,R)
ALT **chimney breast**
SN The front portions of fireplaces that

project out into the room, often ornamented.
UF breasts, chimney
chimney pieces
pieces, chimney
CN V.RT.AFU.BOK.AFU.ALO.ALO

chimney cans
USE **chimney pots**

chimney caps
RT.1138
ALT **chimney cap**
SN Abaci or cornices forming a crowning termination of a chimney. (HAS)
UF bonnets (chimney caps)
caps, chimney
CN V.RT.AFU.BOK.AFU.ALO.ARI

chimney cheeks
RT.1139
ALT **chimney cheek**
SN Use for the sides of a fireplace opening that support the mantelpiece.
UF cheeks, chimney
CN V.RT.AFU.BOK.AFU.ALO.AXC

chimney corners
USE **inglenooks**

chimney crickets
RT.1140 (A)
ALT **chimney cricket**
SN Small false roofs built over the main roof behind a chimney; used to provide protection against water leakage where the chimney penetrates the roof. (HAS)
UF crickets
crickets, chimney
CN V.RT.AFU.BOK.AFU.ALO.BCW

chimney flues
USE **flues**

chimney heads
USE **chimney pots**

chimney hoods
RT.1141
ALT **chimney hood**
SN Coverings that protect chimney openings.
UF hoods, chimney
CN V.RT.AFU.BOK.AFU.ALO.BIQ

chimney hooks
TF.155
ALT **chimney hook**
UF hooks, chimney
CN V.TF.AFU.AFU.AFU.AFU.CXA.BCW

chimney linings
USE **flue linings**

chimney pieces
USE **chimney breasts**

chimney pots
RT.1142 (A,N,B)
ALT **chimney pot**
UF cans, chimney
chimney cans
chimney heads
heads, chimney
pots, chimney
CN V.RT.AFU.BOK.AFU.ALO.BOK

chimney stacks
RT.1133 (B)
ALT **chimney stack**
SN Groups of chimneys, usually carried up together. (HAS)
UF chimney tuns
stacks, chimney
tuns, chimney
CN V.RT.AFU.BOK.AFU.AFU.AFU

chimney throats
RT.1144
ALT **chimney throat**
SN The narrowest portions of a chimney flue, between the gathering, or upward contraction above the fireplace, and the flue proper; often where the damper is located. (HAS)
UF chimney waists
fireplace throats
throats, chimney
throats, fireplace
waists, chimney
CN V.RT.AFU.BOK.AFU.ALO.BUE

chimney tuns
USE **chimney stacks**

chimney waists
USE **chimney throats**

chimney wings
RT.1145
ALT **chimney wing**
SN The sides of a fireplace chimney above the opening that close in toward the chimney throat or damper opening.
UF wings, chimney
CN V.RT.AFU.BOK.AFU.ALO.BZY

chimneys
RT.1132 (A,L,N,B,R)
ALT **chimney**
CN V.RT.AFU.BOK.AFU.AFU

Chimú
FL.1167 (L)
CN F.FL.ALO.ALO.ALO.ARI.AXC.AFU.BIQ.AXC

Chin
USE **Jin**

Chin (Six Dynasties)
USE **Jin (Six Dynasties)**

Chin, Eastern
USE **Eastern Jin**

Chin, Later
USE **Later Jin**

Chin, Western
USE **Western Jin**

china cabinets
TG.422 (N)
ALT **china cabinet**
SN Use for glass-fronted cabinets used to hold and display china.
UF cabinets, china
cases, china
china cases
china closets (cabinets)
china presses
closets, china (cabinets)
presses, china
CN V.TG.AFU.AFU.AXC.ALO.ARI.ALO.ARI

china cases
USE **china cabinets**

China-clay
USE **kaolin**

China clay
USE **kaolinite**

china closets (cabinets)
USE **china cabinets**

China grass
USE **ramie**

china presses
USE **china cabinets**

china process
USE **ceramic process**

china shelves
TG.603
ALT **china shelf**
SN Open hanging shelves for displaying china, often with lattice work on the sides. (GILBR2)
UF shelves, china
CN V.TG.AFU.AFU.AXC.ARI

China silk
USE **Chinese silk**

China stone
USE **petuntze**

china tables
TG.761
ALT **china table**
SN Use for those tea tables with a raised edge or gallery to protect china against damage.
UF dished-top tables
dished tops
fret tables
galleried tables
tables, china
tables, dished-top
tables, fret
tables, galleried
tops, dished
CN V.TG.AFU.AFU.BIQ.BOK.ALO.FOG.AFU

China trade porcelain
USE **Chinese export porcelain**

China wood oil
USE **tung oil**

chinaberry
MT.1342
CN M.MT.AFU.AFU.ALO.BIQ.DCU.AFU.AFU.ALO.ARI

chinampas
RD.284 (L)
SN Mexican artificial fields made arable by piling onto the planting areas silt dredged from a criss-crossing series of irrigation canals plus organic wastes.
CN V.RD.ARI.ALO.AFU.AFU.ALO

Chinantec
FL.1512 (L)
CN F.FL.ALO.ALO.ARI.ALO.AXC.ARI

Chinatowns
RG.275 (L)
ALT **Chinatown**
CN V.RG.ALO.AFU.ALO.BCW.AFU.ALO

Chinautla
FL.1026
CN F.FL.ALO.ALO.ALO.ALO.AFU.ALO.ARI.AFU.ALO.CFS

Chincha
FL.1168
CN F.FL.ALO.ALO.ALO.ARI.AXC.AFU.BIQ.BCW

Chincha-Atacaman
USE **Atacameño**

chincing irons
TB.415 (N)
ALT **chincing iron**
SN Tools used by coopers to insert a cooper's flag between the head and staves of a barrel after the head is in place. (W)
UF irons, chincing
CN V.TB.AFU.ARI.DZW.AFU

Chine sur commande
USE **Compagnie des Indes ware**

chiné technique
KT.78
SN Technique of dyeing threads of a fabric in different colors so as to produce an image. (SCHNEI)
CN K.KT.AFU.ALO.BOK.ALO.AFU

Chinese
FL.1832 (A,L,B,R)
CN F.FL.ALO.ARI.ALO.AFU

Chinese beech
MT.1106
UF beech, Chinese
Fagus englerana
CN M.MT.AFU.AFU.ALO.BIQ.DCU.AFU.AFU.AFU.BCW.ALO

Chinese binding
USE **Japanese binding**

Chinese blue
USE **Prussian blue**

Chinese cedar
USE **toon**

Chinese chairs
TG.137
ALT **Chinese chair**
SN Term used by Chippendale and others for fret-back chairs incorporating Chinese frets.
UF chairs, Chinese
chairs, Chinese Chippendale
Chinese Chippendale chairs
Chippendale chairs, Chinese
CN V.TG.AFU.AFU.ALO.AFU.AFU.AFU.NIE.BUE.AFU

Chinese chestnut
MT.1133 (L)
UF Castanea mollissima
chestnut, Chinese
CN M.MT.AFU.AFU.ALO.BIQ.DCU.AFU.AFU.AFU.CLM.ALO

Chinese Chippendale
FL.3337
UF Chippendale, Chinese
CN F.FL.ALO.BCW.ALO.AXC.DIO.ALO.BUE.AFU.AFU

Chinese Chippendale chairs
USE **Chinese chairs**

Chinese elm
MT.1146
UF elm, Chinese
Ulmus parrifolia
CN M.MT.AFU.AFU.ALO.BIQ.DCU.AFU.AFU.AFU.DCU.ALO

Chinese export porcelain
FL.1942 (L,R)
SN Porcelain made and decorated in China to European order, as distinct from porcelain in native taste. (SAVAGE)
UF Canton porcelain
China trade porcelain
Chinese Lowestoft
export porcelain, Chinese
Lowestoft, Chinese
Lowestoft, Oriental
Oriental Lowestoft
porcelain, Canton
porcelain, China trade
porcelain, Chinese export
trade porcelain, China
CN F.FL.ALO.ARI.ALO.AFU.AFU.AXC.ARI.AFU

Chinese feet
USE **bracket feet**

Chinese frets
DG.125
ALT **Chinese fret**
SN Frets characterized by elongated, right-angled meanderlike elements, originating in Chinese art and adapted to Chinoiserie in Europe in the 18th century.
UF frets, Chinese
CN D.DG.AFU.ARI.ALO.BIQ.ALO.AFU

Chinese fretwork
DG.128
SN A type of openwork pattern originating in Chinese art and adapted to Chinoiserie in Europe in the 18th century.
UF Chinese lattice
Chinese paling
Chinese railing
fretwork, Chinese
lattice, Chinese
paling, Chinese
railing, Chinese
CN D.DG.AFU.ARI.ALO.BIQ.ARI.AFU

Chinese gardens
RK.1398 (L)
ALT **Chinese garden**
UF gardens, Chinese
CN V.RK.ALO.AFU.AFU.AFU.ALO

Chinese green
USE **lokao**

Chinese hackberry
MT.1168
UF Celtis sinensis
hackberry, Chinese
CN M.MT.AFU.AFU.ALO.BIQ.DCU.AFU.AFU.AFU.DZW.AFU

Chinese ink
MT.2498
UF ink, Chinese
CN M.MT.AFU.ARI.CRG.ALO.ALO.ARI

Chinese insect wax
MT.2194
SN Fairly hard, yellowish white wax produced by insects that are cultivated by humans; used for general purposes and as a substitute for beeswax. (AHMT)
UF insect wax, Chinese
wax, Chinese insect
CN M.MT.AFU.AFU.ARI.BZY.AFU.AFU.ALO

Chinese lattice
USE **Chinese fretwork**

Chinese Lowestoft
USE **Chinese export porcelain**

Chinese nails
TF.390
ALT **Chinese nail**
UF nails, Chinese
CN V.TF.AFU.AFU.AFU.ALO.AFU.CFS.AFU.ARI

Chinese paling
USE **Chinese fretwork**

Chinese railing
USE **Chinese fretwork**

Chinese red
USE chrome red

Chinese silk
MT.1819 (L)
SN Lightweight silk of plain weave.
UF China silk
petkin
silk, Chinese
CN M.MT.AFU.AFU.ARI.ALO.AFU.AFU.AFU.ARI.AFU

Chinese toon
USE toon

Chinese vermilion
MT.1683
UF vermilion, Chinese
CN M.MT.AFU.AFU.ARI.AFU.AFU.ALO.ALO.BCW.AFU.AXC.ALO

Chinese vermilion (color)
USE vivid red

Chinese white
USE zinc white

Chinese yellow
USE orpiment

Chinese, Cochin
USE Cochin Chinese

Ching-T'u
BM.619 (L)
UF Pure Land sect (China)
CN B.BM.BZY.AFU.AFU.BCW.ARI

chinkapin oak
USE chinquapin oak

Chinoiserie
FL.3185 (A,B,R)
UF Anglo-Chinoise
CN F.FL.ALO.BCW.ALO.ARI.BIQ.BCW.ALO

Chinook
FL.1338 (L)
CN F.FL.ALO.ALO.ARI.AFU.BIQ.BCW

chinquapin oak
MT.1238
UF chinkapin oak
oak, chinkapin
oak, chinquapin
CN M.MT.AFU.AFU.ALO.BIQ.DCU.AFU.AFU.AFU.IRA.BOK

chintz
MT.1846 (L,R)
SN Cloth, usually cotton or linen, dyed in a number of colors and usually glazed.
CN M.MT.AFU.AFU.ARI.ALO.ALO.ALO.AFU.AFU

Chios mastic
USE mastic

Chiot
USE Chian

chip axes
TB.119
ALT chip ax
SN Small axes for chipping wood or stone into shape. (DAC)
UF axes, chip
CN V.TB.AFU.ARI.AXC.ALO.ARI.AFU

chip carving
KT.881
ALT chip carved
SN Hand carving of wood by cutting chips with a knife or other instrument usually in simple geometric designs. (W)
UF carving, chip
CN K.KT.AFU.ALO.HOE.BUE.AFU.ALO.AFU

chip planes
USE splint planes

chipboard
MT.1464 (L,B)
CN M.MT.AFU.AFU.ALO.BIQ.DCU.ALO.DOI.BCW.AFU

Chipewyan
FL.1230 (L)
UF Yellowknife
CN F.FL.ALO.ALO.ARI.AFU.AFU.ARI.BIQ

Chippendale
FL.3336 (L,R)
UF Director Style
CN F.FL.ALO.BCW.ALO.AXC.DIO.ALO.BUE.AFU

Chippendale chairs, Chinese
USE Chinese chairs

Chippendale, Chinese
USE Chinese Chippendale

chippers
TB.801 (L,N)
ALT chipper
SN Machines for reducing something, such as pulpwood, to chips. (W)
CN V.TB.AFU.BCW.CFS.AFU.AXC

Chippewa
USE Ojibwa

chipping
KT.894
ALT chipped
SN The separation of small pieces or fragments from an object or surface, such as masonry.
CN K.KT.ALO.BCW.AFU

Chiricahua Apache
FL.1449 (L)
UF Apache, Chiricahua
CN F.FL.ALO.ALO.ARI.AFU.CFS.AFU.AFU

Chiricahua Cochise
FL.930
UF Cochise, Chiricahua
CN F.FL.ALO.ALO.ALO.AFU.ALO.ARI.BIQ.ALO.AFU

Chiricahua stage Mogollon
FL.936
UF Mogollon, Chiricahua stage
CN F.FL.ALO.ALO.ALO.AFU.ALO.ARI.BIQ.BCW.AFU

Chiriguano
FL.1576 (L)
CN F.FL.ALO.ALO.ARI.ARI.AFU.BZY

Chiripa, Early
USE Early Chiripa

Chiripa, Late
USE Late Chiripa

Chiriqui
FL.1093
UF Chiriqui, Classic
Classic Chiriqui
CN F.FL.ALO.ALO.ALO.ALO.ALO.ALO.AFU.BUE

Chiriqui, Classic
USE Chiriqui

chiropractic
KD.238 (L)
SN Study of the processes of human health and disease, giving special attention to spinal mechanics, musculoskeletal, neurological, vascular, nutritional, and environmental relationships. (PG)
CN K.KD.AFU.ARI.BUE.AFU

chiropractors
HG.382 (L)
ALT chiropractor
CN H.HG.AFU.AXC.BIQ.ALO.BCW.ALO

chisel-end marking awls
USE scribe awls

chisel nails
TF.422
ALT chisel nail
UF nails, chisel
CN V.TF.AFU.AFU.AFU.ALO.AFU.CFS.AFU.DIO.ARI

chisel planes
USE edge planes

chisels
TB.120 (L,N)
ALT chisel
SN Metal hand tools with a cutting edge at one end, usually driven by a hammer or mallet; used in dressing, shaping, or working wood, stone, or metal. (MEANS)
CN V.TB.AFU.ARI.AXC.ALO.AXC

chisels, barking
USE barking chisels

chisels, bench
USE **bench chisels**

chisels, blocking
USE **blocking chisels**

chisels, brick
USE **brick sets**

chisels, bruzz
USE **corner chisels**

chisels, butt
USE **butt chisels**

chisels, cant
USE **forming chisels**

chisels, cape
USE **cape chisels**

chisels, caulking
USE **caulking irons**

chisels, claw
USE **claw chisels**

chisels, cold
USE **cold chisels**

chisels, cope
USE **cape chisels**

chisels, corner
USE **corner chisels**

chisels, dogleg
USE **corner chisels**

chisels, fishtail
USE **fishtail tools**

chisels, floor
USE **floor chisels**

chisels, forming
USE **forming chisels**

chisels, framing
USE **framing chisels**

chisels, heading
USE **mortise chisels**

chisels, hinge
USE **hinge chisels**

chisels, hot
USE **hot chisels**

chisels, joiner's
USE **paring chisels**

chisels, mortise
USE **mortise chisels**

chisels, paring
USE **paring chisels**

chisels, peeling
USE **barking chisels**

chisels, pitching
USE **pitching chisels**

chisels, plugging
USE **plugging chisels**

chisels, pocket
USE **sash chisels**

chisels, ripping
USE **ripping chisels**

chisels, sash
USE **sash chisels**

chisels, skew
USE **skew chisels**

chisels, socket
USE **socket chisels**

chisels, spline
USE **spline chisels**

chisels, splitting
USE **splitting chisels**

chisels, stonecutter's
USE **tooth chisels**

chisels, tooth
USE **tooth chisels**

chisels, turning
USE **turning chisels**

Chitimacha
FL.1433 (L)
UF Shetinasha
CN F.FL.ALO.ALO.ARI.AFU.BZY.AXC

Chitrasena
USE **Mahendravarman**

chits
USE **froes**

chiv planes
USE **howell planes**

chives
USE **howell planes**

chivs, box
USE **howell planes**

chloride, chromated zinc
USE **chromated zinc chloride**

chloride, methylene
USE **methylene chloride**

chloride, polyvinyl
USE **polyvinyl chloride**

chloride, polyvinylidene
USE **polyvinylidene chloride**

chloride, silver
USE **silver chloride**

chlorinated hydrocarbons
MT.2675
SN Highly toxic materials used as solvents for fats, waxes, oils, and plastic.
UF hydrocarbons, chlorinated
CN M.MT.AFU.ARI.HZS.AFU.BIQ.ARI

chlorite
MT.497 (L)
SN Any of a group of monoclinic minerals of extensive occurrence that are essentially hydrous silicates of aluminum, ferrous iron, and magnesium, which are associated with and resemble the micas and are usually green in color. (W)
CN M.MT.AFU.AFU.AFU.CFS.AFU.BOK

chloro-copper phthalocyanine
USE **phthalocyanine green**

chlorofluorocarbons
MT.1000 (L)
UF CFCs
Freon (TM)
CN M.MT.AFU.AFU.ALO.AXC.AXC

Chlorophora excelsa
USE **iroko**

chlorophyll
MT.1560 (L)
CN M.MT.AFU.AFU.ARI.AFU.AFU.ALO.AFU.ALO.AFU.ALO.ARI

chloroprene rubber
USE **neoprene**

Chocho
FL.1513 (L)
CN F.FL.ALO.ALO.ARI.ALO.AXC.AXC

Chocó
FL.1659 (L)
UF Cholo
Noaname
CN F.FL.ALO.ALO.ARI.ARI.BCW.BOK

Choctaw
FL.1434 (L)
CN F.FL.ALO.ALO.ARI.AFU.BZY.BCW

Chodor
FL.3589
UF Chaudor
CN F.FL.ALO.BIQ.AFU.IFM.ARI.ALO

Choga Mami Transitional
FL.3025
UF Transitional, Choga Mami
CN F.FL.ALO.AXC.ARI.BIQ.ALO.AXC.ARI

choir enclosures
USE **choir screens**

choir lofts
RM.34
ALT **choir loft**
SN Galleries appropriated to a choir. (W)
UF cantoriae
lofts, choir
CN V.RM.AFU.DIO.AFU.AXC.AFU

choir screens
RT.1253 (A,L,R)
ALT **choir screen**
SN Use for partitions in Christian

churches dividing the choir from other areas. For partitions that separate the chancel from the body of the church, use **chancel screens**. (DAC)
UF choir enclosures
enclosures, choir
screens, choir
CN V.RT.AFU.BUE.ALO.ARI.CXA.ARI

choir stalls
RT.1258 (A,L,B,R)
ALT **choir stall**
SN Fixed seats with high backs in the choir area of a church, for choristers.
UF stalls (choir stalls)
stalls, choir
CN V.RT.AFU.BUE.ALO.ARI.DIO.AFU

choirbooks
VW.524 (L,R)
ALT **choirbook**
UF books, service
service books
CN V.VW.AFU.ALO.AFU.AFU.ALO.ALO

choirs
RM.315 (A,L,R)
ALT **choir**
SN Use for spaces in Christian churches reserved for the singers. Use **chancels** for spaces containing the choir and altar area. (HAS)
CN V.RM.AFU.DIO.AXC.ALO.AFU.BIQ

choirs, fore
USE **antechoirs**

Choiseul
FL.3665 (L)
CN F.FL.ALO.BOK.ALO.BOK.ARI

Chokwe
FL.452 (L)
UF Badjok
Bajokwe
Batshioko
Cokwe
Jokwe
Kioko
Kiokwe
Quioco
Tuchokwe
CN F.FL.ALO.AFU.AXC.ALO.ALO.ALO.AFU

Chola
FL.2217 (A,L)
UF Cola
CN F.FL.ALO.ARI.AXC.ALO.AFU.AXC.CLM

Cholo
USE **Chocó**

Chona I
USE **Monomotapa**

Chona II
USE **Mambo**

Chongzhen
FL.1908
UF Ch'ung-chêng
CN F.FL.ALO.ARI.ALO.AFU.AFU.ALO.DIO.CLM

Chono
FL.1691 (L)
CN F.FL.ALO.ALO.ARI.ARI.BOK.AXC

Chontal
FL.1514 (L)
CN F.FL.ALO.ALO.ARI.ALO.AXC.BCW

Chontal de Oaxaca
USE **Tequislatec**

Chontales
FL.1075
CN F.FL.ALO.ALO.ALO.ALO.ALO.AFU.AFU

Chontaquiro
USE **Piro**

Chonyi
FL.602
CN F.FL.ALO.AFU.AXC.AXC.ALO.BOK.AFU

choosing
USE **selecting**

Chopi
FL.579 (L)
CN F.FL.ALO.AFU.AXC.ARI.BOK.AFU

Chopunnish
USE **Nez Percé**

choragic monuments
RK.905
ALT **choragic monument**
SN In ancient Greece, monuments erected by leaders or winners of certain choral competitions; often quite elaborate.
UF monuments, choragic
CN V.RK.AFU.ALO.ALO.DOI.ALO.AFU

Chorasmia
USE **Khorezm**

chords
RT.385
ALT **chord**
SN Principal members of trusses that extend the length of the truss, primarily to resist bending. (DAC)
CN V.RT.AFU.AFU.AFU.BCW.CLM.ALO.AFU

choreographers
HG.61 (L)
ALT **choreographer**
CN H.HG.AFU.AXC.AXC.AFU.AFU.AFU.ALO

Choris
FL.798
CN F.FL.ALO.ALO.ALO.AFU.ALO.AFU.ALO.ALO.AFU.AFU

chorochromatic maps
VW.142
ALT **chorochromatic map**
SN Maps in which aerial distribution is shown by distinctive colors or tints; most geological, soil and political maps are of this type. (LG)
UF maps, chorochromatic
CN V.VW.AFU.AFU.AFU.FZU.AXC.AFU.ARI.AFU.ARI

chorographic maps
VW.143
ALT **chorographic map**
SN Any maps representing large regions, such as countries or continents, on a small scale.
UF maps, chorographic
CN V.VW.AFU.AFU.AFU.FZU.AXC.AFU.ARI.AFU.AXC

choroschematic maps
VW.144
ALT **choroschematic map**
SN Maps in which small, semipictorial symbols such as dots or lines are used over the area of the map to represent distribution, without indication of quantity, of land utilization, or vegetation. (LG)
UF maps, choroschematic
CN V.VW.AFU.AFU.AFU.FZU.AXC.AFU.ARI.AFU.BCW

Chorotega
USE **Mangue**

Chorotegan
FL.1076 (L)
UF Manguean
CN F.FL.ALO.ALO.ALO.ALO.ALO.AFU.ALO

Chorotí
FL.1642 (L)
UF Yofuaha
CN F.FL.ALO.ALO.ARI.ARI.AXC.BOK

Chorrera
FL.1115
CN F.FL.ALO.ALO.ALO.ARI.ALO.ARI

chortens
RK.1149
ALT **chorten**
SN Use for Tibetan stupas, generally charaterized by bulbous domes set on square bases and surmounted by a spire of tiered disklike shapes.
CN V.RK.AFU.ALO.ALO.FCS.BUE.AFU

Chosen
FL.2115
CN F.FL.ALO.ARI.ALO.ARI.AFU.BCW

Chou
USE **Xia**

Chou, Eastern
USE **Eastern Zhou**

Chou, Late
USE **Late Zhou**

Chou, Later
USE **Later Zhou**

Chou, Northern
USE **Northern Zhou**

Chou, Western
USE **Western Zhou**

Choukoutien
FL.1836
CN F.FL.ALO.ARI.ALO.AFU.AFU.AFU.
AFU.AFU

choultries
USE **caravanserais**

chrismatories
RT.1229
ALT **chrismatory**
SN Niches close to a church font which hold the consecrated oil for baptism. (HAS)
CN V.RT.AFU.BUE.ALO.ARI.ARI

christening books
VW.542
ALT **christening book**
UF books,.christening
CN V.VW.AFU.ALO.AFU.AFU.ALO.BUE.
BCW

christenings
KM.18 (L)
SN Ceremonial namings of people, animals, or things, such as ships.
CN K.KM.AFU.ARI.ARI.AFU

Christian, Early
USE **Early Christian**

Christianity
BM.627 (L,R)
ALT **Christian**
CN B.BM.BZY.AFU.ALO

Christmas
KM.80 (L,R)
CN K.KM.AFU.CFS.ARI.ARI

Christmas cards
VW.568 (L)
ALT **Christmas card**
UF cards, Christmas
CN V.VW.AFU.ALO.AFU.ARI.BOK.ALO

chroma
USE **intensity**

chromate, acid copper
USE **acid copper chromate**

chromate, barium
USE **barium yellow**

chromated copper arsenate
MT.2645
UF arsenate, chromated copper
copper arsenate, chromated
CN M.MT.AFU.ARI.HCQ.ALO.AFU.ARI

chromated zinc chloride
MT.2646
UF chloride, chromated zinc
zinc chloride, chromated
CN M.MT.AFU.ARI.HCQ.ALO.AFU.AXC

Chromatic Abstraction
USE **Color-field**

chromatics
USE **color**

chrome
USE **chromium**

chrome green
MT.1663
UF bronze green
cinnabar green
green, bronze
green, chrome
green, cinnabar
green, nitrate
green, oil
green, royal
green, Victoria
green, zinnober
nitrate green
oil green
royal green
verde chrome
vert de chrome
vert de cinabre
Victoria green
zinnober green
Zinnobergrün
CN M.MT.AFU.AFU.ARI.AFU.AFU.ALO.
ALO.AXC.BCW.AFU

chrome green (color)
USE **moderate green**
strong green
very dark yellowish green

chrome green, deep
USE **dark yellowish green**

chrome green, light
USE **dark yellowish green**

chrome green, medium
USE **dark green**
dark yellowish green

chrome green, zinc
USE **zinc chrome green**

chrome ocher
USE **golden ocher**

chrome orange
USE **chrome red**
vivid orange
vivid reddish orange

chrome oxide
USE **chromium oxide green**

chrome red
MT.1669
UF American vermilion
Chinese red
chrome orange
Chromrot
Derby red
orange, chrome
Persian red
red, Chinese
red, chrome
red, Derby
red, Persian
red, Victoria
red, Vienna
rouge de chrome
vermilion, American
Victoria red
Vienna red
CN M.MT.AFU.AFU.ARI.AFU.AFU.ALO.
ALO.BCW.AFU.AFU

chrome steel
MT.349 (L)
UF steel, chrome
CN M.MT.AFU.AFU.AFU.BZY.AFU.AFU.
AFU.AFU.ALO.AFU.ALO.AFU

chrome-vanadium steel
MT.350 (L)
UF steel, chrome-vanadium
CN M.MT.AFU.AFU.AFU.BZY.AFU.AFU.
AFU.AFU.ALO.AFU.ALO.AFU.AFU

chrome yellow
MT.1778 (L)
UF Chromgelb
jaune de chrome
Leipzig yellow
Paris yellow
yellow, chrome
yellow, Leipzig
yellow, Paris
CN M.MT.AFU.AFU.ARI.AFU.AFU.
ALO.ALO.BUE.ARI.ARI

chrome yellow (color)
USE **strong orange yellow**
vivid orange yellow
vivid yellow

chrome yellow, deep
USE **moderate orange yellow**

chrome yellow, light
USE **strong yellow**

chrome, barium
USE **barium yellow**

chrome, deep
USE **strong orange yellow**

chrome, strontium
USE **strontium yellow**

chrome, zinc
USE **zinc yellow**

Chromgelb
USE **chrome yellow**

chromium
MT.433 (L)
SN An elementary metal, used in stainless steels, heat-resistant alloys, high-

strength alloy steels, and for wear-resistant electroplating. (MH)
UF chrome
CN M.MT.AFU.AFU.AFU.BZY.AFU.AFU.ARI.AXC

chromium alloys
MT.367 (L)
UF alloys, chromium
CN M.MT.AFU.AFU.AFU.BZY.AFU.AFU.AFU.ALO.ALO

chromium oxide
USE **moderate yellowish green**

chromium oxide green
MT.1650
UF Arnaudon's green
chrome oxide
chromium, oxide of
Chromoxidgrün
Dingler's green
green, Arnaudon's
green, chromium oxide
green, Dingler's
green, Plessy's
green, Reading
green, Schnitzer's
oxide of chromium
oxide verte de chrome opaque
Plessy's green
Reading green
Schnitzer's green
CN M.MT.AFU.AFU.ARI.AFU.AFU.ALO.ALO.AXC.ARI.ARI

chromium oxide green, transparent
USE **viridian**

chromium, oxide of
USE **chromium oxide green**

chromogenic development processes
USE **chromogenic processes**

chromogenic processes
KT.366
SN Photographic processes in which subtractive dyes form from the reaction of the oxidation product of the developing agent (resulting from the development of the latent image) with a coupler, contained either in the film or in the developing solution. (HAIST)
UF chromogenic development processes
color coupler processes
color dye coupler processes
dye coupler processes
dye coupling processes
CN K.KT.AFU.ALO.DUC.DIO.ALO.DZW.AFU

chromolithography
KT.463 (L,R)
SN Multicolored lithography made by using a separate stone or plate for each color. (THDAT)
UF color lithography
CN K.KT.AFU.ALO.DUC.DUC.ALO.BCW.ALO.AFU.AFU

chromophotography
USE **color photography**

chromotypography
USE **color printing**

Chromoxidgrün
USE **chromium oxide green**

Chromoxidhydratgrün
USE **viridian**

Chromrot
USE **chrome red**

chroniclers
HG.182
ALT **chronicler**
CN H.HG.AFU.AXC.AXC.ARI.AFU.AFU.ALO

chronicles
VW.330 (L,R)
ALT **chronicle**
SN Chronological records of historical events. (AHD)
UF annals
CN V.VW.AFU.AFU.ALO.CRG.ALO

chronology
BM.1155 (L,R)
SN Use generally for a sequence or list of events in the order of time of their occurrence or appearance. In art or literary history, use specifically for the sequence of major events in the life of a painter, architect, writer, or other artist, including dates of the production of major works; use also for tables or lists detailing the sequence of development of major artistic works.
CN B.BM.DIO.ALO

chronometer locks
USE **time locks**

chronophotographs
VJ.95
ALT **chronophotograph**
SN Use for photographs that record movement or change in a series of images, regardless of the amount of time intervening. For a series of images capturing an action, as of a human figure or animal, use **motion photographs.**
CN V.VJ.AFU.ARI.AFU.ALO

chronophotography
KT.381 (L,R)
SN Use for the making of chronophotographs, recording motion or change with a series of photographic images, either discrete photographs taken sequentially or a single exposure capturing movement. (W)
UF motion photography
motion study photography
photochronography
photography, motion
photography, motion study
photography, sequential
photography, serial
sequential photography
serial photography
CN K.KT.AFU.ALO.DUC.DIO.ARI.ARI.AFU

chrysocolla
MT.1636
UF cedar green
gold solder
green, cedar
solder, gold
CN M.MT.AFU.AFU.ARI.AFU.AFU.ALO.ALO.AXC.AFU.AFU

chrysocolla (color)
USE **moderate yellowish green**

chrysocolla green
USE **brilliant green**
strong green

chrysolite
USE **olivine**

chrysolith
USE **olivine**

chrysoprase
MT.552
SN An apple-green variety of chalcedony valued as a gem. (W)
CN M.MT.AFU.AFU.AFU.CFS.AFU.GRC.AFU.ARI.AXC

chucks
TB.1119 (L,N)
ALT **chuck**
SN Devices with adjustable jaws used for centering and holding a cutting bit or a drill bit. (DAC)
CN V.TB.ALO.BIQ

Chugach
FL.1199 (L)
CN F.FL.ALO.ALO.ARI.AFU.AFU.AFU.AFU.AFU

Chuguji
FL.2099
CN F.FL.ALO.ARI.ALO.ALO.ALO.BCW.AFU

Chukchi
FL.2149 (L)
UF Chukotan
CN F.FL.ALO.ARI.ARI.ALO.BCW.AFU

Chukotan
USE **Chukchi**

chullpas
RK.488
ALT **chullpa**
SN Use for tombs built as round or rectangular towerlike structures of stone or adobe found predominantly in pre-Inca Peru and Bolivia.

UF tomb towers
towers, tomb
CN V.RK.AFU.ALO.ALO.BOK.BUE.AFU.ARI

Chumash
FL.1250 (L)
UF Chumashan
CN F.FL.ALO.ALO.ARI.AFU.ALO.AXC

Chumashan
USE **Chumash**

Chun ware
USE **Jun ware**

Chung-yuan
USE **Chungwan**

Chungwan
FL.1844
UF Chung-yuan
CN F.FL.ALO.ARI.ALO.AFU.AFU.AFU.ARI.ALO.AFU

Chunqiu
USE **Spring and Autumn Annals**

Chuntaquiro
USE **Piro**

church and state
BM.531 (L,R)
CN B.BM.BOK.AFU

church architecture
USE **churches**

church buildings
USE **churches**

church bulletins
VW.967 (L)
ALT **church bulletin**
UF bulletins, church
CN V.VW.AFU.ARI.ALO.ALO.AFU.AXC

church camps
RG.160 (L)
ALT **church camp**
UF camps, church
CN V.RG.AFU.AFU.DOI.AXC.ARI.AFU

church halls
USE **parish houses**

church historians
HG.245 (L)
ALT **church historian**
UF historians, church
CN H.HG.AFU.AXC.AXC.BIQ.ALO.AFU

church history
KD.82 (L)
UF history, church
CN K.KD.AFU.AFU.BUE.ALO.ALO

church houses
USE **parish houses**

church records
VW.962 (L)
ALT **church record**
UF capitular records
cathedral records
records, capitular
records, cathedral
records, church
CN V.VW.AFU.ARI.ALO.ALO

church registers
VW.968 (L)
ALT **church register**
UF records, vestry
registers, church
vestry records
CN V.VW.AFU.ARI.ALO.ALO.AFU.BCW

church schools
USE **parochial schools**

church symbolism
USE **religious symbolism**

church towers
RM.418 (L,B,R)
ALT **church tower**
UF towers, church
CN V.RM.AFU.DZW.AFU

churches
RK.1094 (A,L,B,R)
ALT **church**
UF architecture, church
buildings, church
church architecture
church buildings
kirks
tabernacles (churches)
CN V.RK.AFU.ALO.ALO.FCS.BIQ.ALO

churches, abbey
USE **abbey churches**

churches, cave
USE **cave churches**

churches, collegiate
USE **collegiate churches**

churches, conventual
USE **abbey churches**

churches, double
USE **double churches**

churches, hall
USE **hall churches**

churches, mast
USE **stave churches**

churches, mission
USE **mission churches**

churches, monastic
USE **monastic churches**

churches, monolithic
USE **cave churches**

churches, parish
USE **parish churches**

churches, pilgrimage
USE **pilgrimage churches**

churches, rock
USE **cave churches**

churches, rock-cut
USE **rock-cut churches**

churches, stave
USE **stave churches**

churches, twin
USE **double churches**

churchwardens' accounts
VW.974 (L)
ALT **churchwarden's account**
UF accounts, churchwardens'
records, vestry
vestry records
CN V.VW.AFU.ARI.ALO.ALO.ALO.AFU

churchyards
RG.31 (A,L,B,R)
ALT **churchyard**
SN Yards which belong to churches and are used as burial grounds. (W)
CN V.RG.AFU.AFU.ALO.ALO.AFU

Churrigueresque
FL.3243 (A)
CN F.FL.ALO.BCW.ALO.ARI.BIQ.BIQ.BUE.AFU

Chust
FL.1781
CN F.FL.ALO.ARI.AFU.ARI.ALO

chutes
RM.211 (B)
ALT **chute**
SN Inclined or vertical troughs or shafts, for conveying materials of any kind to a lower level. (RS)
CN V.RM.AFU.DIO.ALO.DIO.ARI

chutes, clothes
USE **laundry chutes**

chutes, coal
USE **coal chutes**

chutes, drop
USE **drop chutes**

chutes, garbage
USE **refuse chutes**

chutes, laundry
USE **laundry chutes**

chutes, letter
USE **mail chutes**

chutes, mail
USE **mail chutes**

chutes, refuse
USE **refuse chutes**

chutes, rubbish
USE **refuse chutes**

chutes, trash
USE **refuse chutes**

Chêng-chou
USE **Zhengzhou**

Cibachrome (TM)
KT.372
SN A subtractive color process for making prints and transparencies using a silver-dye bleach process. Also marketed under the name Cilchrome.
UF Cilchrome
CN K.KT.AFU.ALO.DUC.DIO.ALO.DZW.ALO.AFU

Ciboney
FL.1564 (L)
CN F.FL.ALO.ALO.ARI.ALO.BUE.ARI

ciboria
RT.1230 (A,L,B,R)
ALT **ciborium**
SN Roofed structures with four or more columns built over an altar. (NCE)
CN V.RT.AFU.BUE.ALO.ARI.AXC

cigar-box cedar
USE **Spanish cedar**

cigarette cards
VW.563 (L,N,R)
ALT **cigarette card**
SN Cards containing pictures of birds, baseball players, celebrities, or other popular culture subjects packaged by manufacturers of cigarettes with their product during the 19th and early 20th centuries.
UF cards, cigarette
CN V.VW.AFU.ALO.AFU.ARI.AXC

cigarette tables
USE **smokers**

Cilchrome
USE **Cibachrome (TM)**

cills
USE **sills**

cimas
USE **cymas**

cimbiae
USE **shaft rings**

cimeliarchs
RM.206
ALT **cimeliarch**
SN Rooms for keeping the valuables of a church. (RHDEL2)
CN V.RM.AFU.DIO.ALO.DCU.DCU.AFU

cinctures
RT.69
ALT **cincture**
SN Rings or annular fillets at the top or bottom of the shaft of a column of classical design. (RS)
CN V.RT.AFU.AFU.AFU.AXC.ARI.ALO.AFU

cinder
MT.2044
SN The incombustible residue of something burnt. (W)
CN M.MT.AFU.AFU.ARI.AXC.ALO

cinder block
MT.233 (A,L)
UF block, cinder
block, clinker
clinker block
CN M.MT.AFU.AFU.AFU.BCW.ALO.AFU.AFU

cinder concrete
MT.199
SN A lightweight concrete made with cinder as the coarse aggregate. (DAC)
UF concrete, cinder
CN M.MT.AFU.AFU.BCW.AFU.AFU.ARI

cinema
USE **film (performing arts)**

cinemas
USE **movie theaters**

cinemas, drive-in
USE **drive-in theaters**

cinematographers
HG.119 (L)
ALT **cinematographer**
SN Persons who oversee all the aspects of photography in a television or filmmaking project, especially the lighting; they are particularly charged with achieving the photographic images and effects desired by the director. For operators of motion picture or television cameras, use **cameramen.**
UF cameramen, lighting
lighting cameramen
CN H.HG.AFU.AXC.AXC.AFU.AFU.ALO.AXC.DOI.ALO

cinematography
KT.295 (L)
SN Science of motion picture photography. (W)
CN K.KT.AFU.ALO.DUC.DIO.AFU.AXC

cineraria
RG.32
ALT **cinerarium**
SN Use for places reserved for depositing ashes or ash urns of the dead.
CN V.RG.AFU.AFU.ALO.ALO.ALO

cinnabar green
USE **chrome green**

cinnabar (vermilion)
USE **vermilion**

Cinquecentismo
USE **Stile Umberto**

cinquefoils
DG.25
ALT **cinquefoil**
SN Figures of five equal arcs or lobes, separated by cusps. (IDO)
UF quintfoils
CN D.DG.AFU.AFU.BIQ.ALO

ciphers
USE **monograms**

cipollino
MT.807
UF Carystian marble
marble, Carystian
marmor Carystium
CN M.MT.AFU.AFU.AFU.DCU.AFU.ARI.ARI.ARI.BIQ.AXC

cippi
RK.881
ALT **cippus**
SN Use for small Roman, Etruscan, or Greek stelae or stone pillars, usually inscribed, marking, for example, events, boundaries, or grave sites.
CN V.RK.AFU.ALO.ALO.DOI.AFU.ALO.AFU

cirage
KT.254
SN Painting in monochrome, done in yellow tones. (THDAT)
CN K.KT.AFU.ALO.DUC.CXA.ALO.BCW.AFU.AFU

circle clamps
USE **C-clamps**

circle-end clamps
USE **C-clamps**

circle shears
TB.724 (N)
SN Term used for regular hand shears with a slight curve to their blade or mechanical shears, both of which are used to cut a circle out of sheet metal.
UF shears, circle
CN V.TB.AFU.BCW.BIQ.ARI.ALO.BIQ.ARI

circles
BM.768 (L,B,R)
ALT **circular**
CN B.BM.CFS.ARI.AXC.BCW.AFU.AFU

circles (road junctions)
USE **traffic circles**

circles, color
USE **color wheels**

circles, interlocking
USE **interlocking circles**

circles, stone
USE **cromlechs**

circles, traffic
USE **traffic circles**

circles, turning
USE **traffic circles**

circuit breakers
RT.1336 (L,N)
ALT **circuit breaker**
SN Reusable electrical devices for discontinuing current flow during abnormal conditions.
UF breakers, circuit
circuit-breakers, electric
electric circuit-breakers
CN V.RT.ALO.ARI.ALO.AFU

circuit-breakers, electric
USE **circuit breakers**

circuit cameras
USE **panoramic cameras**

circuit interruptors, ground-fault
USE **ground-fault circuit interruptors**

circuits
RT.1337 (L)
ALT **circuit**
UF circuits, electric
electric circuits
CN V.RT.ALO.ARI.ALO.ALO

circuits, electric
USE **circuits**

circular accelerators
USE **cyclotrons**

circular arches
USE **semicircular arches**

circular bookcases
USE **revolving bookcases**

circular easy chairs
TG.63
ALT **circular easy chair**
SN 18th-century term for easy chairs having a semicircular back forming a single upholstered piece with the wings and arms. For chairs with a solid, rounded wooden back or those made from cutting away parts of a barrel, use **barrel chairs.**
UF barrel chairs (circular easy chairs)
chairs, barrel (circular easy chairs)
chairs, circular easy
chairs, tub
chairs, tub-back easy
easy chairs, circular
easy chairs, tub-back
tub-back easy chairs
tub chairs
CN V.TG.AFU.AFU.ALO.AFU.AFU.AFU.FZU.ARI

circular engine houses
USE **roundhouses**

circular-front
DC.105
CN D.DC.AFU.ARI.EWY.BCW

circular graphs
VW.247
ALT **circular graph**
UF graphs, circular
graphs, pie
pie graphs
CN V.VW.AFU.AFU.AFU.FZU.AXC.AXC.ALO

circular letters
VW.18 (L)
ALT **circular letter**
SN Letters intended for circulation, either widely or throughout a particular group. (GAHLM)
UF letters, circular
CN V.VW.AFU.AFU.AFU.BIQ.AFU.ARI.ALO

circular notes
USE **letters of credit**

circular saws
TB.998 (L,N)
ALT **circular saw**
SN Thin steel disks, with teeth on their periphery, that rotate on a power-driven spindle; used either as hand tools or are table mounted. (MEANS)
UF buzz saws
saws, buzz
saws, circular
CN V.TB.AFU.BCW.CFS.ALO.AFU.EWY.AXC

circular saws, portable
USE **electric-portable saws**

circular stairs
USE **spiral stairs**

circulars (memorandums)
USE **memorandums**

circulation (architecture)
BM.205 (B)
SN Use with reference to traffic patterns through areas or buildings, including the means of travel through a building, such as doors, corridors, stairs, or elevators. (DAC)
CN B.BM.AFU.ALO.BCW

circulation
KG.75 (L)
ALT **circulating**
SN Lending items from a collection to outside users and keeping records of such loans.
CN K.KG.AFU.AFU.AXC.AXC.BCW

circulation librarians
HG.308
ALT **circulation librarian**
UF librarians, circulation
CN H.HG.AFU.AXC.BCW.ALO.BCW.ALO.ARI

circumcision
KM.32 (L,R)
CN K.KM.AFU.ARI.AXC.AXC

circumference
BM.803
SN Line that bounds a circular plane surface; the length of this line, equal to pi times the diameter. (W)
CN B.BM.CFS.ARI.AXC.BUE.ALO

circumferential highways
USE **beltways**

circuses
KM.58 (L,R)
CN K.KM.AFU.BOK.AXC.AFU

circuses (Roman arenas)
RK.1048 (A,L,B,R)
ALT **circus (Roman arena)**
SN Use for oblong ancient Roman enclosures which are curved at one end, with tiered seating on three sides, and built for chariot and horse racing.
CN V.RK.AFU.ALO.ALO.EWY.AXC.BIQ.AFU.ALO

cire perdue
USE **lost-wax process**

cirkut cameras
USE **panoramic cameras**

cirricule chairs
USE **curricles**

ciseleurs-doreurs
HG.475
ALT **ciseleur-doreur**
SN Craftsmen who gild the metal mounts on furniture. (HAYWAR)
CN H.HG.AFU.AXC.BUE.ARI.ARI.AFU

ciselure
KT.834
SN The final chasing or smoothing of a metal object. (THDAT)
CN K.KT.AFU.ALO.HOE.BCW.ALO.AXC.AFU.AFU

cist graves
RK.489
ALT **cist grave**
SN Use to designate boxlike graves, normally rectangular and meant for single burial, dug into the ground and often lined with stone slabs and covered.
UF cist tombs
cists
cistvaens
graves, cist
tombs, cist
CN V.RK.AFU.ALO.ALO.BOK.BUE.AFU.AXC

cist tombs
USE **cist graves**

cista
USE **arcae**

Cistercian
BM.655 (A,L)

CN B.BM.BZY.AFU.ALO.BCW.AXC

cisterns
RT.1454 (A,L,N,B,R)
ALT **cistern**
SN May range in size from covered tanks to artificial reservoirs in which rainwater is stored for use when required.
UF cisterns, water storage
water storage cisterns
CN V.RT.ALO.BCW.ALO.ARI.ARI

cisterns (wine coolers)
USE **wine coolers**

cisterns, water storage
USE **cisterns**

cisterns, wine
USE **wine coolers**

cists
USE **cist graves**

cistvaens
USE **cist graves**

citadels
RK.445 (B)
ALT **citadel**
CN V.RK.AFU.ALO.ALO.BIQ.BIQ.ALO

citation indexes
VW.435 (L)
ALT **citation index**
SN Indexes to published materials that have cited a particular work; often includes subject and author indexes as well.
UF indexes, citation
CN V.VW.AFU.AFU.ALO.EWY.BOK.ALO.ALO

cities
RD.11 (A,L,R)
ALT **city**
SN Distinctions among villages, towns, and cities are relative and vary according to their individual regional contexts. Generally, cities designate large or important communities with population, status, and internal complexity greater than most towns in the region.
UF communities, urban
urban communities
CN V.RD.AFU.AFU.ALO.AXC

cities of the future
USE **future cities**

cities, buried
USE **buried cities**

cities, capital
USE **capital cities**

cities, cathedral
USE **cathedral cities**

cities, center
USE **inner cities**

cities, colonial
USE **colonial cities**

cities, fortified
USE **fortified towns**

cities, future
USE **future cities**

cities, garden
USE **garden cities**

cities, history of
USE **urban history**

cities, ideal
USE **ideal cities**

cities, inner
USE **inner cities**

cities, linear
USE **linear cities**

cities, lost
USE **lost cities**

cities, mining
USE **mining towns**

cities, model
USE **model cities**

cities, pilgrimage
USE **pilgrimage centers**

cities, port
USE **ports**

cities, ruined
USE **ruined cities**

cities, satellite
USE **satellite cities**

cities, satellite (new towns)
USE **new towns**

cities, university
USE **university towns**

citizen participation
BM.532 (L,B)
UF community participation
participation, citizen
participation, community
CN B.BM.BOK.ALO

citizens, senior
USE **aged**

citizenship papers
VW.312
ALT **citizenship paper**
SN Documents which evidence the status of being a citizen, such as passports and birth certificates. (GAHLM)
UF papers, citizenship
CN V.VW.AFU.AFU.ALO.BIQ.AFU

citron
USE **brilliant greenish yellow**
grayish greenish yellow

citron green
USE **grayish greenish yellow**
moderate greenish yellow

citron yellow
USE **light greenish yellow**
moderate greenish yellow
zinc yellow

citron yellow, light
USE **light greenish yellow**

city atlases
VW.129 (L)
ALT **city atlas**
UF atlases, city
atlases, urban
urban atlases
CN V.VW.AFU.AFU.AFU.FZU.AXC.AFU.AFU.AFU.AXC.AFU

city beautification
USE **urban beautification**

City Beautiful Movement
FL.1732 (R)
CN F.FL.ALO.ALO.BCW.AFU.BUE.ALO

city blocks
RK.1581 (A,L)
ALT **city block**
SN Use for pieces of land within urban areas usually bounded on all sides by streets or other transportation routes, natural physical barriers, or public open space and not traversed by through streets. (LOFZ)
UF blocks (city blocks)
blocks, city
CN V.RK.ALO.ARI.ALO

city crosses
USE **market crosses**

city directories
VW.416 (L)
ALT **city directory**
UF directories, city
directories, local
local directories
CN V.VW.AFU.AFU.ALO.EWY.AXC.AFU.BOK.ALO

city forestry
USE **urban forestry**

city gates
RK.499 (A,R)
ALT **city gate**
UF gates, city
CN V.RK.AFU.ALO.ALO.BUE.AFU

city guidebooks
VW.506 (L)
ALT **city guidebook**
UF guidebooks, city
CN V.VW.AFU.ALO.AFU.AFU.AFU.BZY.ALO.AFU

city halls
RK.994 (A,L,B,R)
ALT **city hall**
SN Use for the chief public administration buildings of a city, generally housing the mayor's office and legislative chambers.
UF halls, city
CN V.RK.AFU.ALO.ALO.ERE.ALO.AFU.AFU

city lighting
USE **municipal lighting**

city maps
VW.226 (L)
ALT **city map**
UF maps, city
CN V.VW.AFU.AFU.AFU.FZU.AXC.AFU.ARI.AXC.DUC.ARI

city noise
BM.423 (L)
UF noise, city
noise, urban
urban noise
CN B.BM.AXC.ALO.AFU.AFU

city ordinances
USE **ordinances**

city parks
USE **urban parks**

city planners
HG.646 (A,L,B)
ALT **city planner**
UF planners, city
planners, town
planners, urban
town planners
urban planners
urbanists
CN H.HG.AFU.AXC.BZY.BIQ.AFU

city planning
KD.170 (A,L,B,R)
UF civic design
civic planning
design, civic
design, urban
planning, city
planning, civic
planning, town
planning, urban
town planning
urban design
urban planning
CN K.KD.AFU.ALO.DUC.ALO

city plans
VD.38
ALT **city plan**
SN Use for drawings of cities or towns in plan view.
UF plans, city
plans, town
town plans
CN V.VD.AFU.AFU.BIQ.ALO.AXC.AFU.AFU

city squares
USE **squares**

city transit
USE **local transit**

city transportation
USE **urban transportation**

city views
VB.71 (A)
ALT **city view**
SN Includes views of cities, towns, or villages.
UF cityscapes (views)
townscapes (views)
urban views
views, city
views, urban
CN V.VB.AFU.AXC.ALO

city walls
RK.440 (A,L,B,R)
ALT **city wall**
UF walls, city
CN V.RK.AFU.ALO.ALO.BIQ.ARI

city-wide parks
USE **urban parks**

city, linear
USE **linear development**

cityscapes
USE **townscapes**

cityscapes (views)
USE **city views**

civic associations
USE **community organizations**

civic buildings
USE **public buildings**

civic centers
RG.269 (A,L,B)
ALT **civic center**
SN Use for areas within a city where the prinicpal governmental and cultural buildings are grouped; may also denote building complexes or individual buildings housing such a range of functions, especially when the construction was financed by municipal funds.
UF centers, civic
centers, municipal
municipal centers
CN V.RG.ALO.AFU.ALO.ALO

civic design
USE **city planning**

civic groups
USE **community organizations**

civic improvement
BM.1064 (L)
UF improvement, civic
improvement, municipal
municipal improvement
CN B.BM.CLM.ALO.AFU

civic organizations
USE **community organizations**

civic planning
USE **city planning**

civil court records
VW.1015
ALT **civil court record**
UF records, civil court
CN V.VW.AFU.ARI.ALO.BCW.AFU.ALO.ALO.AFU

civil engineering
KD.217 (L,B,R)
SN Branch of engineering concerned primarily with public works such as highways, bridges, waterways, harbors, and water supply systems, but also private enterprises such as land drainage and railroad building. (W)
UF engineering, civil
CN K.KD.AFU.ARI.BIQ.AXC

civil engineers
HG.630 (A,L,B)
ALT **civil engineer**
UF engineers, civil
CN H.HG.AFU.AXC.BZY.BCW.BCW

civil law
KD.161 (L)
SN Body of private law that has developed from the Roman law in states where the legal system is substantially Roman but has been influenced by Germanic, ecclesiastical, and purely modern institutions. (W)
UF law, civil
CN K.KD.AFU.ALO.DOI.AFU

civil rights
BM.533 (L)
UF rights, civil
CN B.BM.BOK.ARI

civil servants
USE **government employees**

civil war
BM.1120 (L)
UF war, civil
CN B.BM.CRG.BCW.CLM.ARI.AFU

civilization
BM.328 (L)
CN B.BM.ALO.ALO.AFU

Civitavecchia
FL.2745
CN F.FL.ALO.AXC.ALO.ALO.ALO.BUE.AFU.ALO

Clactonian
FL.2452
CN F.FL.ALO.AXC.AFU.AFU.ARI

cladding
MT.474 (L,R)
SN Metal coating bonded to metal

objects by heat and pressure or by casting. (W)
UF cladding, metal
metal cladding
CN M.MT.AFU.AFU.AFU.BZY.ALO.ARI

cladding (siding)
USE **siding**

cladding, metal
USE **cladding**

claims
VW.871 (L)
ALT **claim**
SN Documents asserting a right,(OCLD) including titles to debts, privileges, or other things in possession of another; also includes titles to anything which another should give, concede, or confer on the claimant. (GAHLM)
CN V.VW.AFU.ARI.AFU.BOK.ARI

claims, insurance
USE **insurance claims**

clairobscur
USE **chiaroscuro**

Clallam
USE **Klallam**

clamp drills
USE **drill clamps**

clamp nails
TF.429
ALT **clamp nail**
SN Mechanical fasteners designed to bridge a joint and pull the two pieces tightly together as they are driven in place. (MEANS)
UF nails, clamp
CN V.TF.AFU.AFU.AFU.ALO.AFU.CFS. ALO.AFU

clamping-pliers
USE **sliding tongs**

clamping screws
TF.469
ALT **clamping screw**
SN Screws that in connection with wood or metal jaws may be used to provide a clamping force. (MEANS)
UF screws, clamping
CN V.TF.AFU.AFU.AFU.ALO.AFU. DIO.AFU.ALO

clamps
TB.214 (L,N)
ALT **clamp**
SN Mechanical devices commonly used to hold items together or firmly in place while other operations are being performed. (MEANS)
UF cramps
glauns
CN V.TB.AFU.ARI.CFS.AFU

clamps, bar
USE **joiner's clamps**

clamps, bench
USE **bench clamps**

clamps, C
USE **C-clamps**

clamps, circle
USE **C-clamps**

clamps, circle-end
USE **C-clamps**

clamps, combination
USE **universal clamps**

clamps, corner
USE **corner clamps**

clamps, dovetail
USE **dovetail clamps**

clamps, drill
USE **drill clamps**

clamps, G
USE **C-clamps**

clamps, gee
USE **C-clamps**

clamps, hand
USE **screw clamps**

clamps, handscrew
USE **screw clamps**

clamps, hexagon
USE **universal clamps**

clamps, joiner's
USE **joiner's clamps**

clamps, panel
USE **panel clamps**

clamps, picture-framing
USE **corner clamps**

clamps, sash
USE **sash clamps**

clamps, saw
USE **saw clamps**

clamps, screw
USE **screw clamps**

clamps, slat-bending
USE **slat-bending clamps**

clamps, spring
USE **spring clamps**

clamps, universal
USE **universal clamps**

clamps, web
USE **web clamps**

clamshell buckets
TB.56 (N)
ALT **clamshell bucket**
SN Buckets used on cranes or derricks for handling granular materials. Their jaw-like halves close and open by cable or hydraulic action. (DAC)
UF buckets, clamshell
clamshells
CN V.TB.AFU.ARI.AFU.BCW.ALO.AFU

clamshells
USE **clamshell buckets**

clans
HG.880 (L)
ALT **clan**
SN Groups of families and households, the heads of which claim descent from a common ancestor. (W)
CN H.HG.ALO.DOI.AFU.AFU

clap tables
USE **console tables**

clapboard siding
MT.2399 (A,B)
UF bevel siding
siding, bevel
siding, clapboard
siding, weatherboard
weatherboard siding
CN M.MT.AFU.ARI.BZY.AXC.AXC.ALO

clarification drawings
VD.95
ALT **clarification drawing**
SN Graphic interpretations of the drawings or other contractual documents issued by the architect. (DAC)
UF addendum drawings
drawings, addendum
drawings, clarification
CN V.VD.AFU.ALO.ARI.ALO

clasp knives
TB.126
ALT **clasp knife**
SN Large pocket knives whose blade or blades fold or shut into the handle. (W)
UF knives, clasp
CN V.TB.AFU.ARI.AXC.ALO.BUE.AFU. AFU

clasp nails
USE **cut nails**

clasping buttresses
RT.75
ALT **clasping buttress**
SN Use for buttresses which in plan are squares or rectangles penetrated by the corner of the building.
UF buttresses, clasping
CN V.RT.AFU.AFU.AFU.AXC.AXC.AFU. ALO

class B gypsum plaster
USE **retarded hemihydrate plaster**

class C gypsum plaster
USE **anhydrous gypsum plaster**

class D gypsum plaster
USE **Keene's cement**

class differences
USE **social classes**

class status
USE **social status**

class, laboring
USE **working class**

class, middle
USE **middle class**

class, working
USE **working class**

classed catalogs
USE **classified catalogs**

classes, social
USE **social classes**

classes, upper
USE **upper classes**

Classic
FL.967
CN F.FL.ALO.ALO.ALO.ALO.AFU.AFU.AXC

Classic Chiriqui
USE **Chiriqui**

classic cypress
MT.1344
UF Cupressus sempervirens
cypress, classic
cypress, Mediterranean
Mediterranean cypress
CN M.MT.AFU.AFU.ALO.BIQ.DCU.AFU.AFU.ALO.AXC.AFU

Classic Kerma
FL.160
UF Kerma, Classic
CN F.FL.ALO.AFU.ALO.AXC.AXC.AFU.AFU.ARI

Classic Maori
FL.3698
UF Maori, Classic
CN F.FL.ALO.BOK.AXC.BOK.AFU.AFU

Classic Revival
USE **Classical Revival**

Classic Veracruz
FL.1004
UF Veracruz, Classic
CN F.FL.ALO.ALO.ALO.ALO.AFU.ALO.ALO.AFU

Classic Veraguas
USE **Veraguas**

Classic, Early
USE **Early Classic**

Classic, Late
USE **Late Classic**

Classic, Middle
USE **Middle Classic**

Classical
FL.2577 (A)
CN F.FL.ALO.AXC.ALO.AFU.AFU.ARI.BCW

classical abstraction
USE **geometric abstraction**

classical archaeology
KD.104 (L)
UF archaeology, classical
CN K.KD.AFU.ALO.ALO.ARI

Classical Ife
FL.101
UF Ife, Classical
CN F.FL.ALO.AFU.ALO.AFU.BUE.BCW.AFU

classical orders
USE **architectural orders**

Classical Revival
FL.3265 (A,B)
SN Use for late 18th- to early 20th-century architecture and ornament based relatively closely on ancient classical forms. For other architecture and art of the late 18th and the 19th centuries that follow principles of classicism, use **Neoclassical.**
UF Classic Revival
Neoclassical Revival
Revival, Classic
Revival, Classical
Revival, Neoclassical
CN F.FL.ALO.BCW.ALO.AXC.CLM.ARI

Classical Revival (North American)
USE **Federal**

Classical, Early
USE **Early Classical**

Classical, High
USE **High Classical**

Classical, Late
USE **Late Classical**

classicism
BM.172 (A,L,R)
ALT **classicizing**
SN Includes any manifestation of the material culture of classical Greece and Rome. With reference to the period of late 18th- and 19th-century art and architecture which featured a return to classical principles, use **Neoclassical.** With reference to the period of architecture and ornament of the late 18th- to early 20th-century based relatively closely on ancient classical forms, use **Classical Revival.**
CN B.BM.AFU.AFU.AXC.AFU

classicists
HG.770 (L)
ALT **classicist**
SN Scholars of the ancient classical period or adherents of classicism in art or literature.
CN H.HG.AFU.BIQ.BUE.AFU

classics
KD.29 (L)
SN Area of study covering the civilizations of ancient Greece and Rome, including history, philosophy, language, literature, and to some extent art and archaeology. (PG)
CN K.KD.AFU.AFU.ALO

classification
USE **classifying**

classification yards
USE **marshalling yards**

classified catalogs
VW.96 (L)
ALT **classified catalog**
SN Subject catalogs in which entries are arranged by the class numbers of a classification schedule. (ALAG)
UF catalogs, classed
catalogs, classified
catalogs, systematic
classed catalogs
systematic catalogs
CN V.VW.AFU.AFU.AFU.FZU.ALO.AFU.ARI

classifying
KG.67 (L,B,R)
SN Arranging systematically in groups or categories according to established criteria. (WCOL)
UF classification
CN K.KG.AFU.AFU.AXC.ARI

classroom windows
RT.917
ALT **classroom window**
SN Windows designed to meet the requirements of school buildings, usually featuring a large fixed glass area and equipped with a means of controlling ventilation. (STEIN)
UF windows, classroom
CN V.RT.AFU.ARI.AFU.AFU.BOK.AFU.AFU.BCW

classrooms
RM.226 (A,B)
ALT **classroom**
SN Use for rooms devoted to formal instruction in schools.
UF schoolrooms
CN V.RM.AFU.DIO.ALO.DOI.AXC

Claudian stone
USE **Porta Santa marble**

claw-and-ball feet
TG.918
ALT **claw-and-ball foot**
SN A termination mainly used on cabri-

ole legs in the first half of the 18th century (though earlier examples occur), representing a bird's or dragon's claw clutching a ball. Of Oriental derivation. (TOMLIN)
UF ball-and-claw feet
eagle's feet
feet, ball-and-claw
feet, claw-and-ball
feet, eagle's
feet, talon and ball
talon and ball feet
CN V.TG.ALO.DZW.AFU.DCU.AFU.AFU

claw bars
TB.417
ALT **claw bar**
SN Steel bars that have a straight chisel point at one end, and are bent at the other end, which has a notch for pulling nails; used for general demolition work. (MEANS)
UF bars, claw
CN V.TB.AFU.ARI.DZW.ALO.AFU

claw chisels
TB.579
ALT **claw chisel**
SN Chisels with a serrated cutting edge; used in cutting stone. (DAC)
UF chisels, claw
CN V.TB.AFU.BCW.BCW.ALO.BZY.ARI

claw feet
TG.917
ALT **claw foot**
SN Feet, in the shape of claws, on a piece of furniture. (W)
UF feet, claw
CN V.TG.ALO.DZW.AFU.DCU.AFU

claw feet, rat
USE **rat claw feet**

claw feet, retracted
USE **retracted claw feet**

claw feet, winged
USE **winged claw feet**

claw hammers
TB.1079 (N)
ALT **claw hammer**
SN Hammers with a hardened face on one end of the head for driving nails, and curved forked tines on the other end for pulling out nails. (MEANS)
UF hammers, claw
CN V.TB.AFU.BCW.CFS.ALO.ARI.AFU.AFU

claw hatchets
TB.895 (N)
ALT **claw hatchet**
SN Medium-sized hatchets with a nail-pulling claw at the side of a nail-driving poll. (BLACKB)
UF hatchets, claw
CN V.TB.AFU.BCW.CFS.ALO.AFU.DCU.AXC.AFU

claw tables
USE **pillar and claw tables**

claw tools
USE **tooth chisels**

claws
USE **talons**

claws, nail
USE **tack pulls**

claws, tack
USE **tack pulls**

clay
MT.51 (A,L,B,R)
UF clay, native
native clay
CN M.MT.AFU.AFU.AFU.AXC.AFU

clay-and-hair mortar
MT.2598
UF mortar, clay-and-hair
CN M.MT.AFU.ARI.DZW.ARI.AFU.ALO.AFU

clay mortar
MT.2597
UF mortar, clay
CN M.MT.AFU.ARI.DZW.ARI.AFU.ALO

clay products
MT.65 (B)
UF products, clay
CN M.MT.AFU.AFU.AFU.AXC.ALO

clay shale
MT.646
UF shale, clay
CN M.MT.AFU.AFU.AFU.DCU.AFU.ALO.AFU.AFU.BCW.AFU

clay stone
MT.642
SN Fine-grain rocks largely composed of or derived by erosion of sedimentary silts and clays or any type of rock that contained clay. (STEIN)
UF siltstone (clay stone)
stone, clay
CN M.MT.AFU.AFU.AFU.DCU.AFU.ALO.AFU.AFU.ALO

clay tile, structural
USE **structural clay tile**

clay, Albany slip
USE **Albany slip clay**

clay, ball
USE **ball clay**

clay, calcareous
USE **marl**

clay, China
USE **kaolinite**

clay, Devonshire
USE **kaolin**

clay, gilders red
USE **red bole**

clay, native
USE **clay**

clay, pipe
USE **kaolinite**

clay, potter's
USE **potter's clay**

clay, refractory
USE **fireclay**

clay, slip
USE **slip**

Clazomenian
FL.2602 (L)
CN F.FL.ALO.AXC.ALO.AFU.ALO.AXC.ALO.ALO.AFU

clean rooms
RM.397 (L)
ALT **clean room**
SN Rooms in which efforts are made to keep contamination out, including atmospheric pollutants, by the use of air filters, mats, or other devices, as in assembly rooms for precision products or computer rooms.
UF rooms, clean
CN V.RM.AFU.DIO.BIQ.ALO

clean timber
USE **clear lumber**

cleaners (people)
HG.38
ALT **cleaner (person)**
CN H.HG.AFU.AXC.ARI.ALO

cleaners, air
USE **air filters**

cleaning
KT.65 (A,L,B)
ALT **cleaned**
CN K.KT.AFU.ALO.BIQ

cleaning agents
USE **cleaning compounds**

cleaning compounds
MT.2421 (L)
UF agents, cleaning
cleaning agents
compounds, cleaning
CN M.MT.AFU.ARI.CLM

cleaning-out planes
USE **cooper's stoup planes**

cleaning, abrasive
USE **abrasive cleaning**

cleaning, chemical
USE **chemical cleaning**

cleanouts
USE **ashpits**

clear glaze
MT.2564
UF glaze, clear
CN M.MT.AFU.ARI.CRG.ARI.ARI.AFU.ALO.AFU

clear lumber
MT.1438
UF clean timber
lumber, clear
timber, clean
CN M.MT.AFU.AFU.ALO.BIQ.DCU.ALO.BOK.ARI.AFU

clearance, slum
USE **slum clearance**

clearinghouses
HG.848
ALT **clearinghouse**
SN Organizations that serve as central agencies for the collection, organization, storage, and dissemination of documents and that perform referral services for researchers. (ALAG)
UF clearinghouses, information
information clearinghouses
CN H.HG.ALO.BUE.AFU

clearinghouses, information
USE **clearinghouses**

clearstories
USE **clerestories**

cleats
TG.865
ALT **cleat**
CN V.TG.ALO.CFS

cleats, angle
USE **angle cleats**

cleaving adzes
TB.812 (N)
ALT **cleaving adz**
SN Short-handled adzes used for splitting wood. (HAND)
UF adzes, cleaving
CN V.TB.AFU.BCW.CFS.ALO.AFU.AFU.ARI

cleaving blades
TB.583
ALT **cleaving blade**
SN Sharp steel bars used to split stone so that the facet angles can be measured. (HAND)
UF blades, cleaving
CN V.TB.AFU.BCW.BCW.ALO.CFS

cleaving irons
USE **froes**

cleaving wedges
USE **splitting wedges**

clench hammers
TB.1080 (N)
ALT **clench hammer**
SN Hammers with an octagonal or round face, chamfered neck, and a cross peen with thick rounded edges; used as an anvil when held behind the head of a rivet or nail to hold it in position while its point is hammered over. (SALAM)
UF flooring hammers
hammers, clench
hammers, flooring
hammers, roofing
roofing hammers
CN V.TB.AFU.BCW.CFS.ALO.ARI.AFU.ALO

clench nails, rose
USE **rose clench nails**

clerestories
RM.412
ALT **clerestory**
SN Upper zones of walls rising above adjacent roofs and pierced by windows so as to admit light to a high central room or space flanked by lower rooms or spaces.
UF clearstories
CN V.RM.AFU.DUC.ARI

clergy
HG.215 (L,R)
SN Religious officials or functionaries prepared and authorized to conduct religious services and attend to other religious duties. (W)
UF clerics
ecclesiastics
CN H.HG.AFU.AXC.AXC.BIQ.AFU.ARI

clerical workers
HG.33 (L)
ALT **clerical worker**
SN Workers occupied in preparing, transcribing, systematizing, and preserving written communications and records, distributing information, or collecting accounts, usually in an office environment. (ERIC)
UF office workers
workers, clerical
workers, office
CN H.HG.AFU.AXC.ALO.BOK.AFU

clerics
USE **clergy**

clerks of the works
HG.587 (B)
ALT **clerk of the works**
SN On-site clerical workers who keep records of the workers on a building project, deliveries made, and progress of the job; they make reports, receive and catalog samples, and keep a log of job activities. (STEIN)
CN H.HG.AFU.AXC.BZY.AFU.BIQ

clichés-verre
VJ.109 (L,R)
ALT **cliché-verre**
SN Photographic prints produced from a glass plate that has been drawn on or painted and is then used like a negative.
UF artificial negatives
factitious negatives
glass photoprints
glass prints
photoprints, glass
CN V.VJ.AFU.ARI.ALO.ARI

clients
HG.405
ALT **client**
SN Persons who engage the professional advice or services of another. (W)
CN H.HG.AFU.AXC.BOK.BUE

cliff dwellings
RK.307 (A,L,B)
ALT **cliff dwelling**
SN Houses built on ledges in the vertical sides of mesas, as in the American Southwest or similarly inaccesible locations.
UF dwellings, cliff
CN V.RK.AFU.ALO.ALO.AXC.ALO.AXC.ALO.ARI

cliffs
RD.235 (L)
ALT **cliff**
UF bluffs
CN V.RD.ARI.AFU.AXC.ALO.ARI

climate
BM.740 (L,B,R)
UF microclimate
CN B.BM.CFS.ALO.AXC.ALO.AFU

climate, arctic
USE **polar climate**

climate, desert
USE **desert climate**

climate, polar
USE **polar climate**

climate, tropical
USE **tropical climate**

climatic charts
VW.236
ALT **climatic chart**
UF charts, climatic
CN V.VW.AFU.AFU.AFU.FZU.AXC.ALO.ALO

climatic maps
VW.181 (L)
ALT **climatic map**
UF maps, climatic
CN V.VW.AFU.AFU.AFU.FZU.AXC.AFU.ARI.AXC.ARI

climbing cranes
TB.63

ALT **climbing crane**
SN Hoisting devices consisting of a horizontal boom, equipped with a winch and hoist line, and swung from the top of the vertical mast; used in the erection of high-rise buildings. (DAC)
UF cranes, climbing
CN V.TB.AFU.ARI.AFU.BCW.AXC.ALO

climbing plants
USE **vines**

clinch cutters
USE **buffers**

clinical laboratories
USE **medical laboratories**

clinics
RK.740 (A,L,B,R)
ALT **clinic**
UF buildings, out-patient
clinics, medical
clinics, out-patient
departments, out-patient
medical clinics
out-patient buildings
out-patient clinics
out-patient departments
policlinics
CN V.RK.AFU.ALO.ALO.CXA.ALO.AFU.ALO

clinics, birth control
USE **birth control clinics**

clinics, dental
USE **dental clinics**

clinics, family planning
USE **birth control clinics**

clinics, medical
USE **clinics**

clinics, mental health
USE **psychiatric clinics**

clinics, mobile
USE **mobile hospitals**

clinics, out-patient
USE **clinics**

clinics, psychiatric
USE **psychiatric clinics**

clinics, surgical
USE **surgical clinics**

clinker
MT.2045
UF cement clinker
clinker, cement
CN M.MT.AFU.AFU.ARI.AXC.ARI

clinker block
USE **cinder block**

clinker brick
MT.119 (L)
SN Very hard-burnt brick whose shape is distorted, owing to nearly complete vitrification; used for paving. (DAC)
UF brick, clinker
brick, Dutch
clinker, Dutch
Dutch brick
Dutch clinker
klinkart
CN M.MT.AFU.AFU.AFU.AXC.ALO.AFU.AXC.AFU.AFU.AFU.AFU

clinker, cement
USE **clinker**

clinker, Dutch
USE **clinker brick**

clip hangers
TF.343
ALT **clip hanger**
UF hangers, clip
CN V.TF.AFU.AFU.AFU.ALO.AFU.BOK.ALO.ALO.AFU

clip pullers
USE **clip tongs**

clip tongs
TB.752 (N)
SN Flat tongs whose faces are shaped to pull or grip wire; used in welding clips and in horseshoeing.
UF clip pullers
draw tongs
pullers, clip
tongs, clip
tongs, draw
CN V.TB.AFU.BCW.BIQ.AXC.ALO.AXC.ARI

clipped gable roofs
USE **jerkinhead roofs**

clippers, bolt
USE **bolt clippers**

clippers, bolt (bolt cutters)
USE **bolt cutters**

clippings
VW.581 (L)
ALT **clipping**
UF clippings, newspaper
clippings, press
cuttings
cuttings, press
newspaper clippings
press clippings
press cuttings
CN V.VW.AFU.ALO.AFU.AXC

clippings files
VW.586
ALT **clipping file**
SN Collections of cuttings from newspapers and periodicals, usually kept in folders in vertical files and arranged systematically. (LG)
UF cuttings files
files, clipping
files, cuttings
files, media
media files
CN V.VW.AFU.ALO.AFU.BIQ.AFU.ALO

clippings, newspaper
USE **clippings**

clippings, press
USE **clippings**

clips
TF.327
ALT **clip**
SN Small metal fastening devices. (MEANS)
CN V.TF.AFU.AFU.AFU.ALO.AFU.ARI

clips, angle
USE **angle cleats**

clips, back
USE **back clips**

clips, corner
USE **corner clips**

clips, nailing
USE **nailing clips**

clips, truss
USE **truss clips**

clipsham stone
MT.659
UF stone, clipsham
CN M.MT.AFU.AFU.AFU.DCU.AFU.ALO.AFU.ALO.ALO.AFU.AFU.AFU.BCW.ALO

cloacae
RK.549
ALT **cloaca**
SN Use for ancient Roman sewers. (BOETH)
CN V.RK.AFU.ALO.ALO.CFS.ALO.AFU.ALO.ALO.ALO

cloakrooms
RM.193 (B)
ALT **cloakroom**
SN Rooms in which coats or other garments may be placed during one's stay. (W)
UF coatrooms
CN V.RM.AFU.DIO.ALO.DCU.BIQ

cloath chairs
TG.64
ALT **cloath chair**
SN Chippendale's term for high backed easy chairs stuffed all over and upholstered in wool fabric. (GILBR2)
UF chairs, cloath
CN V.TG.AFU.AFU.ALO.AFU.AFU.AFU.FZU.AXC

clochans
RK.247
ALT **clochan**
SN Use for masonry, corbel-domed huts found from the Medieval period in

Ireland and possibly built to house hermit monks.
CN V.RK.AFU.ALO.ALO.AXC.ALO.AFU.CLM.ALO.AFU

clock and program systems
RT.1284
ALT **clock and program system**
SN Use for systems that bring several clocks into conformity, and may ring bells or alarms at scheduled intervals.
UF school clock and program systems
systems, clock and program
systems, school clock and program
CN V.RT.ALO.AFU.AFU.AFU

clock making
KT.520 (L)
CN K.KT.AFU.ALO.ELK.BCW

clock towers
RK.35 (A,L,B,R)
ALT **clock tower**
UF towers, clock
CN V.RK.AFU.ALO.AFU.ALO.DCU.ALO

clockmaker's files
TB.715
ALT **clockmaker's file**
UF files, clockmaker's
files, watchmaker's
watchmaker's files
CN V.TB.AFU.BCW.BIQ.ARI.ALO.ARI.AFU

clockmakers
HG.555 (L,R)
ALT **clockmaker**
SN Persons who make or repair clocks. (W)
CN H.HG.AFU.AXC.BUE.AXC.BIQ

cloisonné
KT.661 (L,R)
SN A technique of enameling in which the design is laid down in thin metal strips on a metal or porcelain ground, forming chambers (cloisons) to receive the vitreous enamel pastes. (PDAT)
UF shippo
CN K.KT.AFU.ALO.GRC.AFU.ALO.ARI

Cloisonnist
FL.3373 (R)
ALT **Cloisonnism**
CN F.FL.ALO.BCW.ALO.AXC.DIO.BCW.BCW.ALO

cloister gardens
RK.1428
ALT **cloister garden**
SN Use chiefly for Medieval gardens, generally found in monasteries, often formally arranged with planters and boxed sections.
UF gardens, cloister
CN V.RK.ALO.AFU.AFU.ARI.AFU

cloister garths
RM.44
ALT **cloister garth**
SN Open courtyards surrounded by cloisters, especially in a group of buildings of a monastery or college. (W)
UF garths
garths, cloister
CN V.RM.AFU.DIO.AFU.BCW.ARI.ALO

cloister vaults
RT.530
ALT **cloister vault**
SN Use for vaults shaped either like a pyramid or a frustrum but with sides that bow outward.
UF arches, cloistered
cloistered arches
cloistered vaults
coved vaults
vaults, cloister
vaults, cloistered
vaults, coved
CN V.RT.AFU.AFU.AFU.BIQ.BOK.AFU.AFU.AFU.ALO.AFU

cloistered arches
USE **cloister vaults**

cloistered vaults
USE **cloister vaults**

cloisters
RM.316 (A,L,B,R)
ALT **cloister**
SN Use for covered walks, walled on one side and usually arcaded on the other, and surrounding or partly surrounding an open area in a monastery or similar complex of Christian buildings; use for such features in secular buildings only when closely resembling the prototype.
CN V.RM.AFU.DIO.AXC.ALO.AFU.BOK

close-beds
USE **box beds**

close cupboards
USE **aumbries**

close range photography
USE **close-up photography**

close-stool chairs
USE **commode chairs**

close stools
TG.238
ALT **close stool**
UF necessary stools
stools, close
stools, necessary
CN V.TG.AFU.AFU.ALO.AFU.ALO.AFU.AFU.ALO

Close Style
FL.2653
CN F.FL.ALO.AXC.ALO.AFU.ALO.AXC.AXC.ALO

close-up photography
KT.394 (L)
UF close range photography
photography, close range
photography, close-up
CN K.KT.AFU.ALO.DUC.DIO.ARI.ARI.BZY.ALO

close-up views
VB.22
ALT **close-up view**
SN Use when emphasis is on the closeness of the camera to the subject, as distinct from **details,** where emphasis is on the partial nature of the view.
UF close-ups
views, close-up
CN V.VB.AFU.AFU.BOK.ALO.ARI

close-ups
USE **close-up views**

closed bonnet tops
USE **bonnet tops**

closed composition
BM.53
UF composition, closed
CN B.BM.AFU.AFU.ARI.AFU.BCW.AFU.AFU

closed eaves
RT.460
SN Use for eaves in which the supporting members are enclosed and therefore not visible.
UF eaves, closed
CN V.RT.AFU.AFU.AFU.BIQ.ARI.ALO.AFU.ALO.AFU.AFU

closed scorpers
TB.1033 (N)
ALT **closed scorper**
SN Two-handed scorpers having a semicircular blade about 4 inches wide and bent to bring the wood handles in line with the blade. (SALAM)
UF one-hand round shaves
round shaves, one-hand
scorpers, closed
shaves, one-hand round
CN V.TB.AFU.BCW.CFS.ALO.AFU.FCS.AFU

closed specifications
VW.795
ALT **closed specification**
UF specifications, closed
CN V.VW.AFU.ARI.AFU.ARI.AFU.ARI.ALO

closer
MT.111
UF closure
CN M.MT.AFU.AFU.AFU.AXC.ALO.AFU.ARI.AFU

closer, beveled
USE **king closer**

closer, king
USE **king closer**

closer, quarter
USE **quarter closer**

closer, queen
USE **queen closer**

closer, three-quarter
USE **king closer**

closers, door
USE **door checks**

closes
RG.255 (B)
ALT **close**
SN Use for the precincts, usually walled, around cathedrals and their dependent buildings.
UF cathedral closes
CN V.RG.ALO.AFU.AFU.BIQ.ALO

closet beds
USE **press beds**

closet hardware
TF.505
UF hardware, closet
CN V.TF.AFU.AFU.ALO.ARI

closet knobs
TF.66
ALT **closet knob**
SN A form of door hardware that consists of a single knob fastened to one end of a spindle, on the other end of which is a rose or plate used to secure the knob and spindle to the closet door. Distinguished from **doorknobs,** in which a pair of knobs on opposite ends of a spindle is used to release the door latch.
UF knobs, closet
CN V.TF.AFU.AFU.AFU.AFU.CFS.AXC.ALO.ALO

closets
RM.194 (L,B)
ALT **closet**
CN V.RM.AFU.DIO.ALO.DCU.BOK

closets (rooms)
USE **cabinets (rooms)**

closets, broom
USE **broom closets**

closets, china (cabinets)
USE **china cabinets**

closets, clothes
USE **clothes closets**

closets, electric
USE **electric closets**

closets, linen
USE **linen closets**

closure
USE **closer**

closure, king
USE **king closer**

closure, quarter
USE **quarter closer**

closure, queen
USE **queen closer**

cloth
MT.1844 (A,L)
SN Use generally for material composed of fiber that is woven, felted, beaten, or otherwise constructed.
UF fabric
CN M.MT.AFU.AFU.ARI.ALO.ALO.ALO

cloth presses
USE **clothes presses**

cloth, adinkra
USE **adinkra**

cloth, bark
USE **bark cloth**

cloth, beaten bark
USE **bark cloth**

cloth, carborundum
USE **carborundum paper**

cloth, crocus
USE **crocus cloth**

cloth, cut-pile
USE **cut-pile cloth**

cloth, drafting
USE **drafting cloth**

cloth, emery
USE **emery cloth**

cloth, jeweler's
USE **jeweler's cloth**

cloth, kente
USE **kente**

cloth, korhogo
USE **korhogo cloth**

cloth, mud
USE **mud cloth**

cloth, mud dyed
USE **mud cloth**

cloth, mud-resist
USE **mud cloth**

cloth, resist-dyed
USE **resist-dyed cloth**

cloth, starch-resist
USE **starch-resist cloth**

cloth, tapa
USE **bark cloth**

cloth, tie and dye
USE **tie and dye cloth**

cloth, tobacco
USE **tobacco cloth**

cloth, tracing
USE **tracing cloth**

cloth, wax
USE **wax resist cloth**

cloth, wax-printed
USE **wax resist cloth**

cloth, wax resist
USE **wax resist cloth**

clothes chests
TG.455
ALT **clothes chest**
UF chests, clothes
CN V.TG.AFU.AFU.AXC.ALO.AXC.CFS

clothes chutes
USE **laundry chutes**

clothes closets
RM.196 (L)
ALT **clothes closet**
UF closets, clothes
CN V.RM.AFU.DIO.ALO.DCU.BOK.ALO

clothes cupboards
USE **wardrobes**

clothes designers
USE **fashion designers**

clothes presses
TG.514 (R)
ALT **clothes press**
SN 18th-century term for large cupboards used to store clothes, having sliding shelves behind closed doors. For large case pieces fitted with hooks, pegs, or rods to hang clothes, use **wardrobes.**
UF cloth presses
presses à vêtements
presses, cloth
presses, clothes
CN V.TG.AFU.AFU.AXC.ALO.BUE.CXA.AFU

clothes presses, wing
USE **wing clothes presses**

clotheshorses
TG.612
ALT **clotheshorse**
SN Racks on which to hang wet laundry for drying.
UF airers, linen
drying racks
linen airers
racks, drying
CN V.TG.AFU.AFU.BIQ.AXC.AFU

clothing stores
RK.153 (A,B)
ALT **clothing store**
UF stores, clothing
CN V.RK.AFU.ALO.ALO.ALO.ARI.BIQ.AFU.AXC

cloud bands
DG.105
ALT **cloud band**
SN A running ornament consisting of a sinuous stylization of a cloud, common in Chinese art and in Oriental rugs. (W)
UF bands, cloud
CN D.DG.AFU.ARI.ALO.ALO

cloud scrolls
DG.145
ALT **cloud scroll**
SN Characteristic Chinese motifs of the Han Dynasty consisting of long, convoluted, ribbonlike forms with deep curls and curves constantly changing direction, and at such points widening into grotesque shapes. (IDO)
UF scrolls, cloud
CN D.DG.AFU.ARI.ALO.CRG.AFU

clout nails
TF.406
ALT **clout nail**
SN Nails each having a large flat head, round shank, and long flattened point; used on sheet metal and dry wallboard. (MEANS)
UF nails, clout
CN V.TF.AFU.AFU.AFU.ALO.AFU.CFS.AFU.DCU.AXC

clove oil
MT.1987
SN Additive used to retard the drying of paint. (GOTTS)
UF oil of clove
oil, clove
CN M.MT.AFU.AFU.ARI.ARI.AFU.ARI.AFU.AFU

cloven feet
USE **hoof feet**

cloven-hoof feet
USE **hoof feet**

clover crossings
USE **cloverleafs**

cloverleafs
RM.480 (L,B)
ALT **cloverleaf**
UF clover crossings
CN V.RM.ALO.ALO.ALO.ALO.BOK.AFU.AFU

Clovis
FL.745
CN F.FL.ALO.ALO.ALO.AFU.AFU.ARI.ALO.AFU.AFU

clowns
HG.67 (L,R)
ALT **clown**
CN H.HG.AFU.AXC.AXC.AFU.AFU.AFU.BIQ.ALO

club chairs
TG.52
ALT **club chair**
SN Heavily upholstered chairs having solid sides and low backs. (RHDEL2)
UF chairs, club
club divans
divans, club
CN V.TG.AFU.AFU.ALO.AFU.AFU.AFU.EFQ

club divans
USE **club chairs**

club feet
TG.906
ALT **club foot**
SN Plain, circular feet used to terminate the cabriole leg, particularly in the early 18th century.(TOMLIN) When such feet are set on a disk use **pad feet.**
UF feet, club
CN V.TG.ALO.DZW.AFU.BIQ

clubhouses
RK.1025 (A,L,R)
ALT **clubhouse**
SN Buildings occupied by a club or commonly used for club activities. (W)
UF lesches
CN V.RK.AFU.ALO.ALO.EWY.AXC.ALO

clubhouses, faculty
USE **faculty clubs**

clubs
HG.819 (A,L,B)
ALT **club**
SN Associations of persons for social and recreational purposes or for the promotion of some common object. (W)
CN H.HG.ALO.BCW.AFU

clubs, architectural
USE **architectural societies**

clubs, athletic
USE **athletic clubs**

clubs, beach
USE **beach clubs**

clubs, boat
USE **boat clubs**

clubs, country
USE **country clubs**

clubs, equestrian
USE **riding clubs**

clubs, faculty
USE **faculty clubs**

clubs, froe
USE **froe clubs**

clubs, frow
USE **froe clubs**

clubs, garden
USE **garden clubs**

clubs, health
USE **athletic clubs**

clubs, horseback riding
USE **riding clubs**

clubs, officers'
USE **officers' clubs**

clubs, polo
USE **polo clubs**

clubs, riding
USE **riding clubs**

clubs, sports
USE **athletic clubs**

clubs, tennis
USE **tennis clubs**

clubs, yacht
USE **yacht clubs**

clubs, youth
USE **youth centers**

Cluniac
BM.653 (A,L)
CN B.BM.BZY.AFU.ALO.BCW.ALO.AFU

cluster housing
RG.56 (A,L,B)
SN Dwellings grouped closely together to form relatively compact units, with the space between clusters usually allocated to pedestrian circulation and cooperative recreational use. (DAC)
UF architecture, grouped domestic
domestic architecture, grouped
grouped domestic architecture
housing, cluster
CN V.RG.AFU.AFU.BOK.AFU.AFU

cluster legs
TG.947
ALT **cluster leg**
SN Legs having the form of a cluster of columns or shafts. (RHDEL2)
UF legs, cluster
CN V.TG.ALO.FIM.AFU.AFU.ARI

clutch pencils
USE **mechanical pencils**

CN
USE **nitrocellulose**

co-ops
USE **cooperative apartment houses**
cooperative housing
cooperative stores

coach barns
USE **carriage houses**

coach framing hammers
USE **framing hammers**

coach houses
USE **carriage houses**

coach screws
USE **lag bolts**

coach trimmer's cabriolet hammers
USE **cabriolet hammers**

coach varnish
MT.2483
UF coachbuilder's varnish
varnish, coach
varnish, coachbuilder's
CN M.MT.AFU.ARI.CRG.AFU.BOK.ALO.AFU.AFU

coachbuilder's framing hammers
USE **framing hammers**

coachbuilder's varnish
USE **coach varnish**

coaches
HG.709 (L)
ALT **coach**
CN H.HG.AFU.BCW.AXC

coade stone
MT.2802 (A,B,R)
UF stone, coade
CN M.MT.AFU.BCW.CFS.ALO.AFU

Coahuila
USE **Cahuilla**

coakels
USE **spiral stairs**

coal
MT.992 (L,B,R)
CN M.MT.AFU.AFU.ALO.ARI

coal-burning power plants
USE **coal-fired power plants**

coal chutes
RM.212
ALT **coal chute**
UF chutes, coal
CN V.RM.AFU.DIO.ALO.DIO.ARI.AFU

coal-fired power plants
RG.116 (L)
ALT **coal-fired power plant**
SN Steam-producing, electric power generating plants using coal as the primary fuel.
UF coal-burning power plants
coal-fired steam electric power plants
plants, coal-fired power
power plants, coal-fired
steam electric power plants, coal-fired
CN V.RG.AFU.AFU.BUE.ARI.AXC.AFU

coal-fired steam electric power plants
USE **coal-fired power plants**

coal mines
RG.98 (L,B,R)
ALT **coal mine**
UF collieries
mines, coal
CN V.RG.AFU.AFU.BUE.AFU.ALO.AFU

coal oil
USE **kerosene**

coal tar
MT.988 (L)
UF tar, coal
CN M.MT.AFU.AFU.ALO.ALO.ALO.AFU

coal-tar color
USE **synthetic organic pigment**

coal tar creosote
MT.2639
UF creosote, coal tar
CN M.MT.AFU.ARI.HCQ.AFU.ALO.AFU

coal-tar dye
USE **synthetic organic pigment**

coal tar solvents
MT.2664
SN Volatile solvents obtained by the distillation of coal tar; industrial grades widely used as solvents for rubber and many resinous materials. (MAYER)
UF solvents, coal tar
CN M.MT.AFU.ARI.HZS.AFU.AXC

coal tips
USE **spoil banks**

coal, anthracite
USE **anthracite**

coal, bituminous
USE **bituminous coal**

coal, cannel
USE **cannel coal**

coal, soft
USE **bituminous coal**

coaming
RT.1001
SN Frames or curbs around an opening in a roof or floor, raised above the surrounding level to prevent the flow of water into the opening. (DAC)
CN V.RT.AFU.ARI.ALO.AFU

coarse aggregate
MT.2298
UF aggregate, coarse
CN M.MT.AFU.ARI.ALO.ALO.AFU.ALO

coarse-grain materials
MT.2253
UF materials, coarse-grain
CN M.MT.AFU.ALO.DOI.ARI

coarse stuff
MT.2436
UF stuff, coarse
CN M.MT.AFU.ARI.CRG.AFU.AXC.AFU.AFU

Coast Chavin
USE **Cupisnique**

coast live oak
MT.1244 (L)
UF California live oak
live oak, California
live oak, coast
oak, California live
oak, coast live
Quercus agrifolia
CN M.MT.AFU.AFU.ALO.BIQ.DCU.AFU.AFU.AFU.IRA.CRG.AFU

coast redwood
USE **Humboldt redwood**

Coast Salish
FL.912 (L)
UF Salish, Coast
CN F.FL.ALO.ALO.ALO.AFU.ALO.ARI.ARI.AFU

Coastal Akan
FL.291
UF Akan, Coastal
CN F.FL.ALO.AFU.AXC.AFU.ARI.AFU.ALO

coastal charts
VW.214
ALT **coastal chart**
SN Nautical charts used for navigation close to shore, such as for entering or leaving bays and harbors or for navigating inland waterways.
UF charts, coastal
CN V.VW.AFU.AFU.AFU.FZU.AXC.AFU.ARI.AXC.DIO.ALO.ALO.AFU

coastal defenses
USE **coastal fortifications**

coastal fortifications
RK.441 (L)
ALT **coastal fortification**
UF coastal defenses
fortifications, coastal
CN V.RK.AFU.ALO.ALO.BIQ.AXC

Coastal Tiahuanaco
USE **Pacheco**

coastal towns
RD.67 (A,B)
ALT **coastal town**
UF seaside towns
towns, coastal
towns, seaside
CN V.RD.AFU.BCW.BCW.AFU

coastal zone maps
VW.184
ALT **coastal zone map**
UF maps, coastal zone
CN V.VW.AFU.AFU.AFU.FZU.AXC.AFU.ARI.AXC.BCW.AFU

coasters, roller
USE **roller coasters**

coastguard stations
RK.1269 (B)
ALT **coastguard station**
UF stations, coastguard
CN V.RK.AFU.ALO.ALO.GLI.AFU.BIQ.ALO

coastlines
RD.229 (L,B)
ALT **coastline**
SN Use either generally for the lines forming boundaries between land and sea or specifically for the lines reached by the highest storm waves or the high-water marks of median tides; for strips of land bordering any large bodies of water, use **shores.**
UF coasts
shorelines
CN V.RD.ARI.AFU.AXC.AFU.ALO.AXC.BUE.ALO

coasts
USE **coastlines**
shores

coat, top
USE **supercoat**

coated paper
USE **prepared paper**

coating
KT.656 (L)
ALT **coated**
CN K.KT.AFU.ALO.GRC.AFU

coating, substratum
USE **subbing layer**

coating, zinc
USE **electrogalvanizing**

coatings
MT.2423 (A,L)
ALT **coating**
SN Use generally for any substances spread over a surface, usually for protection or decoration. (W)
UF surface-coatings
CN M.MT.AFU.ARI.CRG

coatings, bituminous
USE **bituminous coatings**

coatings, concrete
USE **concrete coatings**

coatings, paper
USE **paper coatings**

coatings, powder
USE **powder coatings**

coatrooms
USE **cloakrooms**

coats of arms
VW.700 (L,N,R)
ALT **coat of arms**
SN Use for devices that include the full display of armorial bearings: the escutcheon plus its adjuncts (helm, crest, mantling, motto, supporters).
UF arms, coats of
heraldic achievements
CN V.VW.AFU.ALO.ALO.AFU.AFU.AFU.AFU

cob
MT.192 (L,B)
CN M.MT.AFU.AFU.AFU.AXC.ALO.ARI

cobalt
USE **cobalt blue**

cobalt arsenate, pale
USE **pale cobalt arsenate**

cobalt blue
MT.1599
UF azure cobalt
bleu de cobalt
blue, cobalt
blue, Hungary
blue, king's
blue, new
blue, olympia
blue, Thénard's
blue, Vienna
cobalt
cobalt, azure
Hungary blue
king's blue
Kobaltblau
new blue
olympia blue
Thénard's blue
ultramarine, Vienna
Vienna blue
Vienna ultramarine
CN M.MT.AFU.AFU.ARI.AFU.AFU.ALO.ALO.ALO.ARI.BCW

cobalt blue (color)
USE **strong greenish blue**
vivid blue

cobalt green
MT.1651
UF Gellert green
green smalt
green, cobalt
green, Gellert
green, Rinman's
green, Saxony
green, zinc
Kobaltgrün
Rinman's green
Saxony green
smalt, green
vert de cobalt
zinc green
CN M.MT.AFU.AFU.ARI.AFU.AFU.ALO.ALO.AXC.ARI.AXC

cobalt green (color)
USE **moderate yellowish green**

cobalt phosphate, deep
USE **deep cobalt phosphate**

cobalt ultramarine
USE **strong greenish blue**

cobalt violet
MT.1719
UF Kobaltviolet
violet de cobalt
violet, cobalt
CN M.MT.AFU.AFU.ARI.AFU.AFU.ALO.ALO.BIQ.ARI.AFU

cobalt violet (color)
USE **moderate purple**
strong purple

cobalt yellow
MT.1779
UF aureolin
jaune de cobalt
Kobaltgelb
yellow, cobalt
CN M.MT.AFU.AFU.ARI.AFU.AFU.ALO.ALO.BUE.ARI.AXC

cobalt yellow (color)
USE **brilliant yellow**

cobalt, azure
USE **cobalt blue**

Cobbeos
USE **Cubeo**

cobble
USE **cobblestone**

cobble, beach
USE **beach cobble**

cobblers
USE **shoemakers**

cobblestone
MT.882 (A,L,B)
UF cobble
CN M.MT.AFU.AFU.AFU.DCU.ALO.ALO

Cochin Chinese
FL.2445
UF Chinese, Cochin
CN F.FL.ALO.ARI.BCW.BUE.ALO.ARI

cochineal
MT.1690 (L)
UF carmine (cochineal)
CN M.MT.AFU.AFU.ARI.AFU.AFU.ALO.ALO.BCW.ALO.ARI

cochineal (color)
USE **vivid red**

Cochise
FL.929 (L)
CN F.FL.ALO.ALO.ALO.AFU.ALO.ARI.BIQ.ALO

Cochise, Chiricahua
USE **Chiricahua Cochise**

Cochise, San Pedro
USE **San Pedro Cochise**

Cochise, Sulphur Spring
USE **Sulphur Spring Cochise**

Cochiti
FL.1468 (L)
CN F.FL.ALO.ALO.ARI.AFU.CFS.CRG.AFU.ALO

cock plug bits
USE **tenon-cutting bits**

cock's combs
TB.625
ALT **cock's comb**
SN Pieces of metal with a serrated edge; used to scratch plaster and create a rough gripping surface for the next coat. (MEANS)
UF combs, cock's
CN V.TB.AFU.BCW.BCW.ALO.GRC.AFU

Cockeysville marble
MT.823
UF marble, Cockeysville
CN M.MT.AFU.AFU.AFU.DCU.AFU.ARI.ARI.ARI.BOK.ARI

cockfight chairs
USE **reading chairs**

cockfighting chairs
USE **reading chairs**

cocking pieces
USE **sprockets**

cockle stairs
USE **spiral stairs**

cocklofts
USE **attics (interior spaces)**

cocks, ball
USE **ball cocks**

cocktail lounges
RM.109 (B)
ALT **cocktail lounge**
SN Public rooms as in hotels, clubs, or restaurants, where cocktails and other drinks are served. (W)
UF lounges, cocktail
CN V.RM.AFU.DIO.ALO.BCW.BCW

cocktail tables
TG.719
ALT **cocktail table**
UF tables, cocktail
CN V.TG.AFU.AFU.BIQ.BOK.ALO.BCW

Coclé
FL.1096
CN F.FL.ALO.ALO.ALO.ALO.ALO.ALO.ALO.AFU

Cocle, Early
USE **Conte Polychrome**

cocoacood
USE **granadilla**

cocobolo
MT.1302 (L)
UF Dalbergia retusa
Honduran rosewood
rosewood, Honduran
CN M.MT.AFU.AFU.ALO.BIQ.DCU.AFU.AFU.AFU.LCM.AXC.ALO

Cocomaricopa
USE **Maricopa**

Cocopa
FL.1455 (L)
CN F.FL.ALO.ALO.ARI.AFU.CFS.ALO

cocus wood
USE **granadilla**

code maps, zip
USE **zip code maps**

codes
VW.1001
ALT **code**
SN Systematically arranged and comprehensive collection of laws; any systematic collection of regulations and rules or procedure or conduct. (AHD)
CN V.VW.AFU.ARI.ALO.BCW.AFU.AFU.AFU.CLM.ALO

codes, building
USE **building codes**

codices
VW.656 (L)
ALT **codex**
SN Ancient and Medieval manuscripts in book form that replaced the scroll.
CN V.VW.AFU.ALO.AFU.DZW.ARI.AFU.AFU

Cody
FL.756
CN F.FL.ALO.ALO.ALO.AFU.AFU.ARI.ALO.ARI.ALO.ARI

coelin
USE **cerulean blue**

Coelinblau
USE **cerulean blue**

coemeteria
USE **catacombs**

coeruleum
USE **cerulean blue**

Coeur d'Alène
FL.1406
CN F.FL.ALO.ALO.ARI.AFU.BUE.ALO

coffee public houses
USE **coffeehouses**

coffee shops
RK.115 (A)
ALT **coffee shop**
SN Use for small, usually inexpensive, restaurants with a limited menu of light meals served at counters or tables.
UF shops, coffee
CN V.RK.AFU.ALO.ALO.ALO.AFU.AXC.AXC

coffee tables
TG.720 (N)
ALT **coffee table**
UF tables, coffee
CN V.TG.AFU.AFU.BIQ.BOK.ALO.BIQ

coffeehouses
RK.110 (A,L,B,R)
ALT **coffeehouse**
SN Use for public places serving coffee and other refreshments and inexpensive foods; often meeting places for lively political discussions, especially popular in Europe from the 17th to the 19th century.
UF cafés (coffeehouses)
coffee public houses
public houses, coffee
CN V.RK.AFU.ALO.ALO.ALO.AFU.ARI

cofferdams
RK.528 (L)
ALT **cofferdam**
SN Use for watertight enclosures from which water is pumped to expose an area in order to permit construction or repairs. (MEANS)
CN V.RK.AFU.ALO.ALO.CFS.AFU.ARI.ALO.ARI

coffered ceilings
RT.725 (A)
ALT **coffered ceiling**
SN Ceilings treated with coffers.
UF ceilings, coffered
CN V.RT.AFU.ALO.AFU.ALO.BIQ.AFU

coffering (ceiling components)
USE **coffers (ceiling components)**

coffers (ceiling components)
RT.727
ALT **coffer (ceiling component)**
SN Recessed panels, usually square or octagonal, set into ceilings, vaults, or soffits.
UF caissons (coffers)
cassoons
coffering (ceiling components)
lacunars
CN V.RT.AFU.ALO.AFU.ALO.BIQ.ALO.AFU

coffers (furniture)
TG.456 (L,B)
ALT **coffer (furniture)**
SN Small chests for the storage of valuables which may also serve as seats or tables.
UF coffres
coffrets
CN V.TG.AFU.AFU.AXC.ALO.AXC.CLM

coffers, traveling
USE **trussing coffers**

coffers, trussing
USE **trussing coffers**

coffin planes
USE **smoothing planes**

coffin stools
USE **joint stools**

coffre à bijoux
USE **jewel cabinets**

coffres
USE **coffers (furniture)**

coffres à bahut
USE **bahuts**

coffrets
USE **coffers (furniture)**

cog railroads
USE **rack railroads**

cogged joints
TF.582
ALT **cogged joint**
SN Joints consisting of two crossing pieces of wood, each piece notched to fit into the other. (MEANS)
UF joints, cogged
CN V.TF.ALO.AFU.BUE

cognition
BM.570 (L,R)
CN B.BM.BUE.ALO

cogs
TB.1120
ALT **cog**
SN Teeth on the rim of a wheel or gear. (W)
CN V.TB.ALO.BOK

cogwheels
USE **gears**

Cohonina
FL.953 (L)
CN F.FL.ALO.ALO.ALO.AFU.ALO.ARI.BIQ.BIQ.ALO

coiffeuses (chairs)
TG.53
ALT **coiffeuse (chair)**
SN French armchairs with the crest rail curving downward in the center to enable the hair to be dressed. (HAYWAR)
CN V.TG.AFU.AFU.ALO.AFU.AFU.AFU.ELK

coiffeuses
TG.739
ALT **coiffeuse**
SN Fitted dressing tables. The most typical 18th-century form has three rising flaps, the center one being fitted with a dressing mirror. (WATSON)
UF poudreuses
CN V.TG.AFU.AFU.BIQ.BOK.ALO.CLM.AXC.ARI.AFU

coiffières (bonnetières)
USE **bonnetières**

coigns
USE **quoins**

coil
MT.2223
CN M.MT.AFU.ALO.BZY

coil construction
USE **coiling**

coil method
USE **coiling**

coil-spring seats
TG.975
ALT **coil-spring seat**
SN Upholstered seats with interior springs of coiled wire.
UF coiled inner-spring seats
inner-spring seats, coiled
seats, coil-spring
CN V.TG.ALO.GLI.AFU.ARI.AFU

coiled inner-spring seats
USE **coil-spring seats**

coiling
KT.860
ALT **coiled**
SN Pottery technique in which the piece is built up from ropelike coils of clay, without the use of a potter's wheel.
UF coil construction
coil method
CN K.KT.AFU.ALO.HOE.BOK.AFU

coillons
USE **quoins**

coils
RT.1420
ALT **coil**
SN Piping or tubing employed in cooling or heating systems that serve as heat exchangers.
CN V.RT.ALO.BCW.AFU.ALO.AFU.BCW.AFU

coils, air cooling
USE **cooling coils**

coils, air heating
USE **heating coils**

coils, cooling
USE **cooling coils**

coils, dehumidifying
USE **dehumidifying coils**

coils, heating
USE **heating coils**

coin cabinets
USE **medal cabinets**

coin moldings
USE **money pattern**

coin operated laundries
USE **laundries**

coins de feu
USE **chauffeuses**

coins (encoignures)
USE **encoignures**

coins (wall components)
USE **quoins**

coir
MT.1825 (L)
SN Stiff, coarse fiber from the outer husk of the coconut;(W) used for making brushes, mats, cordage, and coarse cloths. (MH)
CN M.MT.AFU.AFU.ARI.ALO.AFU.AFU.ALO.ARI

coke ovens
TB.98 (A,L,N)
ALT **coke oven**
SN Closed refractory chambers in which coal is converted to coke by carbonization. (MHDSTT)
UF ovens, coke
CN V.TB.AFU.ARI.ALO.ARI.ALO.ALO.ARI

coke ovens, beehive
USE **beehive ovens**

cokels
USE **spiral stairs**

Cokwe
USE **Chokwe**

Cola
USE **Chola**

Colastiné
FL.1692
CN F.FL.ALO.ALO.ARI.ARI.BOK.BCW

colcothar
USE **Indian red**

cold
BM.843 (L)
CN B.BM.CFS.AXC.ALO.AFU.AFU.ALO.AXC.AFU

cold bridges
USE **thermal bridges**

cold chisels
TB.704 (N)
ALT **cold chisel**
SN Common form of chisel with a cutting edge of 60 degrees formed of tempered steel; used for cutting metal which has not been softened by heating. (DAC)
UF chisels, cold
CN V.TB.AFU.BCW.BIQ.ARI.ALO.AFU.AFU

cold cut varnish
USE **simple solution varnish**

cold joints
TF.611
ALT **cold joint**
SN Joints between two consecutive pours of concrete if the time elapsed between the first and second pours is such that the first pour has started to harden. (MEANS)
UF joints, cold
CN V.TF.ALO.ARI.AFU.AFU

cold-pressed oil
MT.1997
SN Any vegetable oil that has been extracted from seeds or nuts by pressing them without the aid of heat. (MAYER)
UF oil, cold-pressed
CN M.MT.AFU.AFU.ARI.ARI.ARI.ALO

cold pressure welding
USE **cold welding**

cold rooms
USE **cold storage rooms**

Cold Springs
FL.913
CN F.FL.ALO.ALO.ALO.AFU.ALO.ARI.ARI.ALO

cold storage coolers
USE **cold storage rooms**

cold storage rooms
RM.198
ALT **cold storage room**
SN Rooms kept at low temperatures for the storage of perishable items.
UF cold rooms
cold storage coolers
coolers, cold storage
rooms, cold storage
CN V.RM.AFU.DIO.ALO.DCU.BUE

cold welding
KT.813 (L)
ALT **cold welded**
SN The joining of metals at room temperature by subjecting to pressure. (DAC)
UF cold pressure welding
welding, cold
CN K.KT.AFU.ALO.HOE.BCW.ALO.AFU.ALO.BIQ.AFU

cold-working
KT.137 (L)
ALT **cold-worked**
SN The process of hammering metal into shape without the use of heat.
CN K.KT.AFU.ALO.DOI.BCW

coldwater flats
RM.267
ALT **coldwater flat**
SN Apartments provided with only cold running water, often in a building with no central heating. (RHDEL2)
UF flats, coldwater
CN V.RM.AFU.DIO.ARI.ALO.BIQ.AFU.ALO.AFU

Coles Creek
FL.855
CN F.FL.ALO.ALO.ALO.AFU.ALO.ALO.ARI.ARI.ALO

Colima
FL.1066
CN F.FL.ALO.ALO.ALO.ALO.AFU.ALO.BCW.ALO

coliseums
USE **amphitheaters**
arenas
stadiums

collage
KT.177 (L,R)
UF collage technique
CN K.KT.AFU.ALO.DUC.BCW

Collage Cubist
USE **Synthetic Cubist**

collage technique
USE **collage**

collagists
HG.95
ALT **collagist**
SN Artists who work in collage. (W)
CN H.HG.AFU.AXC.AXC.AFU.AFU.ALO.AXC.AXC

collagraph printing
KT.449 (L)
SN Intaglio printmaking process in which proofs are pulled from a block similar to that used in relief block printing, that is, a block on which the design or pattern is built up in the manner of collage. (MAYER)
UF printing, collagraph
CN K.KT.AFU.ALO.DUC.DUC.ALO.BCW.AFU.AFU

collapse design
USE **plastic design**

collar beam roofs
RT.449
ALT **collar beam roof**
SN Roofs supported by rafters tied together by collar beams. (DAC)
UF collar roofs
roofs, collar
roofs, collar beam
roofs, trussed rafter
trussed rafter roofs (collar beam roofs)
CN V.RT.AFU.AFU.AFU.BIQ.ARI.AFU.ALO.ARI.AFU

collar beams
RT.308
ALT **collar beam**
SN Horizontal members which tie together and stiffen two opposite rafters, usually at a point about halfway up the rafters in a collar beam roof. (HAS)
UF beams, collar
beams, wind
collar ties
collars (beams)
strutbeams
ties, collar
wind beams
CN V.RT.AFU.AFU.AFU.BCW.ALO.ALO.AFU

collar joints
TF.637
ALT **collar joint**
UF joints, collar
CN V.TF.ALO.ARI.ALO.ALO.ARI

collar roofs
USE **collar beam roofs**

collar ties
USE **collar beams**

collars (beams)
USE **collar beams**

collars, newel
USE **newel collars**

collected works
VW.9
ALT **collected work**
SN All the writings of an author, including those which have not been printed previously, published in one volume or a number of volumes in a uniform style of binding, usually with an inclusive title.
UF collections (document types)
works, collected
CN V.VW.AFU.AFU.AFU.AXC

collectibles
VB.86 (L,R)
ALT **collectible**
SN Objects collected by fanciers, especially items other than such traditionally collectible items as art, stamps, coins, and antiques. (W)
CN V.VB.ALO.AXC

collecting
KG.76 (L,R)
SN Gathering things in order to retain them. (RLG7)
CN K.KG.AFU.AFU.AXC.AXC.BIQ

collection developing
USE **collection development**

collection development
KG.77 (L)
SN Building a coherent and reliable collection over a number of years. (LG)
UF collection developing
development, collection
CN K.KG.AFU.AFU.AXC.AXC.BOK

collections
HG.847 (A,L,R)

ALT collection
CN H.HG.ALO.BUE

collections (document types)
USE collected works

collections management
KG.68
UF management, collections
CN K.KG.AFU.AFU.AXC.AXC

collections, corporate
USE corporate collections

collections, private
USE private collections

collections, visual
USE visual resource collections

collections, visual resource
USE visual resource collections

collective biographies
VW.298
ALT collective biography
SN Works consisting of separate accounts of lives of people. (LG)
UF biographies, collective
CN V.VW.AFU.AFU.ALO.ARI.ALO

collective farms
RG.16 (L,B)
ALT collective farm
SN Farms consisting of many small holdings collected into a single unit for joint operation by a community under public or state supervision.
UF farms, collective
CN V.RG.AFU.AFU.AFU.AFU.AXC.AFU

collective labor agreements
VW.879 (L)
ALT collective labor agreement
SN Bargaining agreements as to wages and conditions of work entered into by groups of employees, usually organized into a union on one side and one or more employers or corporations on the other side. (BLACKS)
UF agreements, collective labor
agreements, master
labor agreements, collective
master agreements
CN V.VW.AFU.ARI.AFU.BOK.BOK.ALO.AFU

collective settlements
RD.77 (A,L,R)
ALT collective settlement
UF collectives
communal settlements
settlements, collective
settlements, communal
CN V.RD.AFU.BOK.AFU

collectives
USE collective settlements

collectors
HG.710 (L,R)
ALT collector
CN H.HG.AFU.BCW.BCW

collectors' guides
VW.350
ALT collectors' guide
UF guides, collectors'
CN V.VW.AFU.AFU.ALO.CXA.BIQ.ALO

collectors' marks
VW.715 (L,R)
ALT collector's mark
UF marks, collectors'
CN V.VW.AFU.ALO.ALO.AFU.AXC.ALO.ARI

collectors, solar
USE solar collectors

collectors, tax
USE tax collectors

college community centers
USE student unions

college housing
USE student housing

college towns
RD.49 (L)
ALT college town
UF towns, college
CN V.RD.AFU.AXC.ARI

college unions
USE student unions

colleges
RK.842 (A,L,B)
ALT college
CN V.RK.AFU.ALO.ALO.CXA.ARI.AXC.BIQ.AFU

colleges, art
USE art schools

colleges, business
USE business colleges

colleges, commercial
USE business colleges

colleges, community
USE community colleges

colleges, dental
USE dental schools

colleges, junior
USE junior colleges

colleges, medical
USE medical schools

colleges, sixth-form
USE high schools

colleges, state
USE state colleges

colleges, teachers
USE teachers colleges

colleges, technical
USE polytechnics

colleges, veterinary
USE veterinary colleges

collegiate churches
RK.1108 (B)
ALT collegiate church
UF churches, collegiate
CN V.RK.AFU.ALO.ALO.FCS.BIQ.ALO.ARI.AXC

collets
TB.1121 (L)
ALT collet
SN Casings or sockets which hold a drill or other tool. (W)
CN V.TB.ALO.BUE

collieries
USE coal mines

collodion
MT.2134 (L)
SN Cellulose nitrate in a mixture of 60% ether and 40% alcohol for making fibers and film. (MH)
CN M.MT.AFU.AFU.ARI.BUE.ALO.AXC.AFU.BCW.ARI.ALO

collodion dry-plate process
USE dry collodion process

collodion glass positives
USE ambrotypes

collodion negatives, wet
USE wet collodion negatives

collodion pellicle
MT.2232
UF pellicle, collodion
CN M.MT.AFU.ALO.CXA.ALO.ALO

collodion photoprints
USE collodion prints

collodion prints
VJ.47
ALT collodion print
SN Use for photographic prints having collodion as the binder.
UF collodion photoprints
photoprints, collodion
prints, collodion
CN V.VJ.AFU.AFU.ARI.ARI.AXC.ARI

collodion processes
KT.320 (L,R)
SN Use for photographic processes in which collodion is the binder. A silver halide is the light sensitive agent, and the process may be used to produce positives (ambrotypes, tintypes) or negatives.
CN K.KT.AFU.ALO.DUC.DIO.ALO.BCW

collodion transfers
VJ.48
ALT collodion transfer
SN Collodion positives transferred from the glass plate to another support,

usually paper. (HCOP)
UF transfers, collodion
CN V.VJ.AFU.AFU.ARI.ARI.AXC.AXC

collodion wet plate photonegatives
USE **wet collodion negatives**

collodion wet process
USE **wet collodion process**

colloid
USE **gel**

colloidal concrete
MT.200 (L)
SN Concrete in which the aggregate is bound by a grout that has the ability to retain dispersed solid particles in suspension.
UF concrete, colloidal
CN M.MT.AFU.AFU.AFU.BCW.AFU.AFU.AXC

colloids, image-bearing
USE **binders**
emulsion

colloquiums
USE **symposia**

collotype
KT.435 (A,L,R)
SN A type of photolithography in which the printing plate is prepared using a bichromate process. Unhardened gelatin areas hold water and thus resist greasy ink; hardened areas accept ink and hold it in the characteristic wormlike pattern of cracks.
UF phototype
CN K.KT.AFU.ALO.DUC.DOI.AXC.AFU.AFU

collotype prints
USE **collotypes**

collotypes
VJ.25
ALT **collotype**
SN Photomechanical prints produced by the process called collotype.
UF collotype prints
prints, collotype
CN V.VJ.AFU.AFU.ALO.BIQ.AFU

Cologne earth
USE **Van Dyke brown**

Cologne spirits
USE **ethyl alcohol**

cololches
RT.81
ALT **cololche**
SN Thin wood poles used in Mayan building construction. (DWELL)
CN V.RT.AFU.AFU.AFU.AXC.BCW

Colombian
FL.721 (L,B)
CN F.FL.ALO.ALO.AFU.AXC.BCW

colonial cities
RD.24 (A)
ALT **colonial city**
SN Designates cities built in territories where no urban settlements existed before, generally created following an overall plan, and often established by an urban culture for purposes of local administration. (JOHNUG)
UF cities, colonial
CN V.RD.AFU.ALO.AFU.ARI

Colonial North American
USE **American Colonial**

Colonial Revival
FL.1723 (A,L,B,R)
UF Revival, Colonial
CN F.FL.ALO.ALO.BCW.AFU.ARI

Colonial Revival, Spanish
USE **Spanish Colonial Revival**

Colonial, American
USE **American Colonial**

Colonial, Dutch
USE **Dutch Colonial**

Colonial, French
USE **French Colonial**

Colonial, Portuguese
USE **Portuguese Colonial**

Colonial, Spanish
USE **Spanish Colonial**

colonies, art
USE **artists' colonies**

colonies, artists'
USE **artists' colonies**

colonies, penal
USE **penal colonies**

colonies, space
USE **space colonies**

colonization
BM.1045 (L,R)
SN Extension of political and economic control over an area by a foreign occupying state that usually has organizational and military superiority. (CCE)
CN B.BM.CLM.AFU.AFU.AFU.AFU

colonnades
RT.57 (A,B)
ALT **colonnade**
SN Use for rows of columns supporting an architrave and often one side of a roof. Includes spaces behind such a feature when they are long and used for circulation.
UF orthostyles
CN V.RT.AFU.AFU.AFU.ARI.AXC

colonnettes
RT.89
ALT **colonnette**
SN Use for conspicuously small columns.
CN V.RT.AFU.AFU.AFU.AXC.BIQ.AFU.AFU.BCW

colophons
VW.42 (L)
ALT **colophon**
SN Inscriptions usually placed at the end of books or manuscripts and usually containing facts relative to its production. (W)
CN V.VW.AFU.AFU.AFU.CRG.AFU

colophony
USE **rosin**

color
BM.108 (A,L,B,R)
SN Use to refer to perceived qualities that result from the response of vision to the wavelength of reflected or transmitted light. For individual chromatic colors and achromatic colors or neutrals, use **colors.**
UF chromatics
CN B.BM.AFU.AFU.ARI.BOK.ALO.AFU

color charts
VW.237
ALT **color chart**
UF charts, color
color diagrams
diagrams, color
CN V.VW.AFU.AFU.AFU.FZU.AXC.ALO.ARI

color circles
USE **color wheels**

color constancy
USE **constancy (color)**

color coupler processes
USE **chromogenic processes**

color diagrams
USE **color charts**

color dye coupler processes
USE **chromogenic processes**

Color-field
FL.3721 (L,R)
SN Encompasses both Abstract Imagist painting and works of the 1960s derived from it.
UF Abstraction, Chromatic
Abstraction, Post-painterly
Chromatic Abstraction
Post-painterly Abstraction
CN F.FL.ALO.BUE.ARI.BIQ

color film
MT.2233 (L)
UF film, color
CN M.MT.AFU.ALO.CXA.ALO.ARI

color filters
USE **light filters**

color lithography
USE **chromolithography**

color makers
USE **artists' colormen**

color measurement
USE **colorimetry**

color mixture
BM.125
UF colorant mixture
mixture, color
mixture, optical
optical mixture
CN B.BM.AFU.AFU.ARI.BOK.ALO.ALO.AFU.ALO

color mixture, subtractive
USE **subtractive mixture**

color negatives
VJ.9
ALT **color negative**
SN Use for photographic negatives that record on a single base the hue and lightness of a scene in complementary relation to the scene's perceived values; e.g., light blue is recorded as dark yellow. Use **color separation negatives** for images in which each color is recorded on a physically separate negative.
UF negatives, color
CN V.VJ.AFU.AFU.AFU.AXC.ALO

color photographs
VJ.71
ALT **color photograph**
SN Use for the broad class of photographs whose images are composed of more than one hue, plus the neutral tones. For photographs having a range of tones within one hue, use **black-and-white photographs.**
UF photographs, color
CN V.VJ.AFU.AFU.AXC.ALO

color photography
KT.379 (L,R)
UF chromophotography
heliochromy (color photography)
photography, color
CN K.KT.AFU.ALO.DUC.DIO.ARI.ALO

color photoprints
USE **color prints (photographs)**

color printing
KT.443 (L,R)
UF chromotypography
printing, color
CN K.KT.AFU.ALO.DUC.DUC.ALO.ALO

color prints (photographs)
VJ.43
ALT **color print (photograph)**
SN Use for photographic prints whose images are composed of more than one hue, plus the neutral tones. For prints having a range of tones within one hue, use **black-and-white prints (photographs).**
UF color photoprints
photoprints, color
prints, color (photographs)
CN V.VJ.AFU.AFU.ARI.ARI.ARI.ALO

color screen processes
USE **screen processes**

color separation
KT.444 (L)
SN The isolation of individual colors on separate printing plates or photographic negatives, so that a picture or design may be printed in multiple colors.
UF separation, color
CN K.KT.AFU.ALO.DUC.DUC.ALO.ALO.AFU

color separation negatives
VJ.4
ALT **color separation negative**
SN Use for negatives that record in monochrome the ranges of lightness of one hue per negative, usually in sets of three negatives. Each is used to make a plate or matrix for printing one color, in register with the others, to form a full-color print.
UF color separation photonegatives
negatives, color separation
negatives, separation
separation negatives
separation negatives, color
CN V.VJ.AFU.AFU.AFU.AFU

color separation photonegatives
USE **color separation negatives**

color separation phototransparencies
USE **color separation positives**

color separation positives
VJ.60
ALT **color separation positive**
SN Use for positive transparencies that record in monochrome the ranges of lightness of one hue per film, usually in sets of three films. Each is used to make a plate or matrix for printing one color, in register with the others, to form a full-color print.
UF color separation phototransparencies
color separation transparencies
positives, color separation
positives, separation
separation positives
transparencies, color separation
CN V.VJ.AFU.AFU.ARI.AXC.AFU

color separation transparencies
USE **color separation positives**

color shift
KT.907
SN Change in color brought about by either differential fade rates of dyes or by an imbalance of dyes in an image area. (CPEK)
UF shift, color
CN K.KT.ALO.BIQ.AFU

color slides
VJ.87 (L,R)
ALT **color slide**
SN Use for photographic slides whose images are composed of more than one hue, plus the neutral tones. For slides having a range of tones within one hue, use **black-and-white slides.**
UF slides, color
CN V.VJ.AFU.AFU.BCW.AXC.ALO

color transparencies
VJ.65
ALT **color transparency**
SN Use for transparencies whose images are composed of more than one hue, plus the neutral tones. For transparencies having a range of tones within one hue, use **black-and-white transparencies.**
UF positive color transparencies
transparencies, color
transparencies, positive color
CN V.VJ.AFU.AFU.ARI.AXC.AXC.ALO

color ware, lost
USE **lost color ware**

color wheels
VW.238
ALT **color wheel**
UF circles, color
color circles
wheels, color
CN V.VW.AFU.AFU.AFU.FZU.AXC.ALO.ARI.AFU

color, accidental
USE **reflected color**

color, acrylic
USE **acrylic paint**

color, additive
USE **additive mixture**

color, body
USE **body color**

color, bulky
USE **volume color**

color, casein
USE **casein paint**

color, cement
USE **cement color**

color, ceramic
USE **ceramic color**

color, coal-tar
USE **synthetic organic pigment**

color, dry
USE **dry color**

color, earth
USE **natural inorganic pigment**
color, film
USE **film color**

color, local
USE **local color**

color, luminous
USE **luminous color**

color, mass
USE **mass color**

color, metallic
USE **metallic pigment**

color, mortar
USE **mortar color**

color, oil
USE **oil paint**

Color, Party of
USE **Rubenism**

color, polymer
USE **polymer paint**

color, porcelain
USE **ceramic color**

color, poster
USE **poster color**

color, reflected
USE **reflected color**

color, surface
USE **local color**

color, symbolic
USE **symbolic color**

color, volume
USE **volume color**

Colorado blue spruce
USE **blue spruce**

Colorado spruce
USE **blue spruce**

Colorado yule statuary marble
MT.824
UF marble, Colorado yule statuary
statuary marble, Colorado yule
CN M.MT.AFU.AFU.AFU.DCU.AFU.ARI.ARI.ARI.BOK.AXC

colorant
MT.1511 (L)
UF coloring matter
matter, coloring
CN M.MT.AFU.AFU.ARI.AFU

colorant mixture
USE **color mixture**

colored ink
MT.2499
UF ink, colored
CN M.MT.AFU.ARI.CRG.ALO.ALO.AXC

colored pencils
TB.263 (N)
ALT **colored pencil**
UF pencils, colored
CN V.TB.AFU.ARI.CLM.AFU.ALO.DIO.ALO

colorers
HG.452
ALT **colorer**
SN Persons who color by hand or spray designs on cards, calendars, maps, and related articles, using colored inks and pens or airbrush, following instructions or working drawings. (DOT)
CN H.HG.AFU.AXC.BUE.ALO.CFS.ALO

colorimetry
KT.14 (L)
SN Use for the process of determining and specifying colors.
UF color measurement
measurement, color
CN K.KT.AFU.ALO.AXC.ALO

coloring
KT.75
ALT **colored**
CN K.KT.AFU.ALO.BOK

coloring books
VW.516 (L)
ALT **coloring book**
UF books, coloring
CN V.VW.AFU.ALO.AFU.AFU.AFU.CRG.AFU

coloring matter
USE **colorant**

coloring, hand
USE **hand coloring**

colorism
USE **Rubenism**

colormen, artists'
USE **artists' colormen**

colors
DL.1 (A,L,B,R)
SN Use to refer to individual chromatic colors in the spectrum and the achromatic colors or neutrals. With reference to theory and perception, use color.
CN D.DL.AFU

colors, complementary
USE **complementary colors**

colors, cool
USE **cool colors**

colors, primary
USE **primary colors**

colors, secondary
USE **secondary colors**

colors, show-card
USE **poster color**

colors, structural
USE **structural colors**
colors, warm
USE **warm colors**

colorwashing
KT.657
SN Applying a whitewash or a cold-water paint tinted with colored pigments. (W)
CN K.KT.AFU.ALO.GRC.AFU.AFU

colt feet
TG.922
ALT **colt foot**
SN Feet on baluster legs which end in a ball flanked by rings, over the beginning of another baluster facing downwards; resembling the foot of a colt. (KIRK)
UF colt's feet
feet, colt
CN V.TG.ALO.DZW.AFU.DCU.ALO

colt's feet
USE **colt feet**

columbaria
RG.28 (A,B)
ALT **columbarium**
SN Sepulchral chambers lined with rows of niches for cinerary urns.
CN V.RG.AFU.AFU.ALO.AFU.ALO

columbaria (dovecotes)
USE **dovecotes**

columbariums
USE **dovecotes**

Columbia
USE **Sinkiuse**

Columbian spirits
USE **methyl alcohol**

column and beam assemblies
USE **post-and-beam structures**

columnae caelatae
RT.90
ALT **columna caelata**
SN Columns found in ancient Greek architecture whose shafts are adorned by carving, as those of the Temple of Artemis at Ephesus. (RS)
CN V.RT.AFU.AFU.AFU.AXC.BIQ.AFU.AFU.BIQ

columnae rostratae
USE **rostral columns**

columnar
DC.60
SN Formed in columns; having the form of a column or shaft of a column. (W)
CN D.DC.AFU.ARI.BIQ

columnists
HG.286 (L)
ALT **columnist**

SN Journalists who analyze news and write columns or commentary based on personal knowledge and experience for publication or broadcast. (DOT)
CN H.HG.AFU.AXC.BCW.ALO.AFU.ARI.AFU

columns
RT.83 (A,L,N,B,R)
ALT **column**
SN Use for cylindrical, upright members, usually either giving support or appearing to give support; common also on furniture, especially as decorative elements. Use also for all uprights in steel frame or concrete frame structures. For square or rectangular members, either in masonry construction or classically treated, and for massive uprights in Medieval architecture, use **piers**; for wooden square uprights, use **posts.**
UF pillars
CN V.RT.AFU.AFU.AFU.AXC.BIQ.AFU

columns, angle
USE **angle columns**

columns, annulated
USE **annulated columns**

columns, attached
USE **engaged columns**

columns, baluster
USE **baluster columns**

columns, banded
USE **banded columns**

columns, battened
USE **battened columns**

columns, blocked
USE **blocked columns**

columns, coupled
USE **coupled columns**

columns, diminishing
USE **diminishing columns**

columns, doubled
USE **doubled columns**

columns, engaged
USE **engaged columns**

columns, flanked
USE **flanked columns**

columns, grouped
USE **grouped columns**

columns, half
USE **half columns**

columns, lally
USE **lally columns**

columns, median
USE **median columns**

columns, memorial
USE **memorial columns**

columns, mid-wall
USE **mid-wall columns**

columns, monolithic
USE **monolithic columns**

columns, monumental
USE **memorial columns**

columns, newspaper
USE **newspaper columns**

columns, ringed
USE **banded columns**

columns, rostral
USE **rostral columns**

columns, rusticated
USE **banded columns**

columns, serpent
USE **serpent columns**

columns, Solomonic
USE **spiral columns**

columns, spiral
USE **spiral columns**

columns, trinity
USE **trinity columns**

columns, twisted
USE **spiral columns**

columns, wreathed
USE **spiral columns**

columns, zoophoric
USE **zoophoric columns**

COM (microfiche)
USE **computer-output microfiche**

COM (microfilm)
USE **computer-output microfilms**

COM (microforms)
USE **computer-output microforms**

Comanche
FL.1380 (L)
CN F.FL.ALO.ALO.ARI.AFU.BOK.BOK

comb-back Windsor chairs
USE **high-back Windsor chairs**

comb boards
USE **saddle boards**

combination clamps
USE **universal clamps**

combination highchair and carriages
USE **carriage chairs**

combination locks
TF.197
ALT **combination lock**
UF dial locks
locks, combination
locks, dial
CN V.TF.AFU.AFU.AFU.AFU.DIO.BIQ.AFU.ARI

combination photoprints
USE **composite photographs**

combination planes
TB.911 (N)
ALT **combination plane**
SN Planes with a moveable fence and interchangeable blades; used for a variety of grooving and molding purposes. (KEBABI)
UF planes, combination
CN V.TB.AFU.BCW.CFS.ALO.AFU.DUC.AFU

combination pliers
TB.746 (N)
SN Any of several styles of pliers that can be used for cutting, swaging, or hammering, as well as for gripping. (MEANS)
UF half-round pliers
pliers, combination
pliers, half-round
CN V.TB.AFU.BCW.BIQ.AXC.ALO.AFU.AFU

combination printing
KT.408
SN Use for the technique of printing one photograph using images from more than one negative. For the technique of recording more than one image on a single sheet or frame of film, use **multiple exposure.**
CN K.KT.AFU.ALO.DUC.DIO.ARI.AXC.AXC

combination prints
USE **composite photographs**

combination windows
RT.918
ALT **combination window**
SN Windows equipped with removable or interchangeable screen and glass sections that make them suitable for either summer or winter use. (DAC)
UF windows, combination
CN V.RT.AFU.ARI.AFU.AFU.BOK.AFU.AFU.BIQ

combination writing table and dressing stands
USE **lady's cabinet dressing tables**

combined dressing tables and desks
USE **bureau tables**

combined escutcheon plates
TF.263
ALT **combined escutcheon plate**
SN Escutcheons cut for both knob and keyhole or cylinder. (BROWNL)
UF escutcheon plates, combined
plates, combined eschutcheon
CN V.TF.AFU.AFU.AFU.AFU.DZW.ALO.AFU

combined footings
RT.173
ALT **combined footing**
SN Use for footings that are slabs under two or more columns, one of the columns being internal rather than on the perimeter so that the footing cannot take a beamlike form.
UF footings, combined
CN V.RT.AFU.AFU.AFU.AXC.BUE.ARI.ALO.AFU.ALO

combined loads
BM.1006
SN Two or more different types of loads (such as dead load, live load, or wind load) occurring simultaneously on a structure. (DAC)
UF loads, combined
CN B.BM.CFS.AXC.CLM.ALO.ARI.ALO

combined sewerage system
USE **combined sewers**

combined sewers
RK.544 (L)
ALT **combined sewer**
SN Sewers that receive both storm water and sewage. (MEANS)
UF combined sewerage system
sewerage system, combined
sewers, combined
CN V.RK.AFU.ALO.ALO.CFS.ALO.AFU.ALO.AFU.AFU

combined store-door locks
TF.230
ALT **combined store-door lock**
UF locks, combined store-door
store-door locks, combined
CN V.TF.AFU.AFU.AFU.AFU.DIO.BIQ.ALO.ALO.AFU

combined stress
BM.920
SN Bending or twisting stress in a structural member combined with direct tension or compression. (MHDSTT)
UF stress, combined
CN B.BM.CFS.AXC.BIQ.ARI.BCW.AXC

combined writing and dressing tables
USE **bureau tables**

combing
KT.637
ALT **combed**
SN Preparing fiber for spinning by cleansing, disentangling, and collecting together by the use of a comb; used to prepare relatively long fibers. (W)
CN K.KT.AFU.ALO.GFO.ALO

combs, cock's
USE **cock's combs**

combs, threshold
USE **threshold combs**

combustion
KT.727 (L)
SN Use for the initial act or instance of burning and for the chemical processes in which light or heat are produced by the vigorous union of various substances with oxygen.
CN K.KT.AFU.ALO.GWW.AFU

come-alongs
TB.80 (N)
ALT **come-along**
SN Portable ratcheting winches consisting of a fastening device on one end and a hook attached to a cable at the other end. Operating a lever turns a drum which takes up the cable and exerts a pulling force on the hook. (MEANS)
UF hoists, ratchet
pullers, ratchet
ratchet hoists
ratchet pullers
CN V.TB.AFU.ARI.AFU.BCW.BCW.ALO.ALO

Comechingón
FL.1619 (L)
CN F.FL.ALO.ALO.ARI.ARI.ALO.ALO.ARI

comedians
HG.68 (L,R)
ALT **comedian**
CN H.HG.AFU.AXC.AXC.AFU.AFU.AFU.BIQ.ARI

comedy
BM.266 (L,R)
CN B.BM.AFU.ARI.BIQ.AFU

Comeya
USE **Kamia**

comfort
BM.595 (L,B)
SN Sense of ease and satisfaction of bodily wants, with freedom from pain and anxiety. (RHDEL2)
CN B.BM.BUE.CLM.AFU

comfort stations
RK.746 (L,R)
ALT **comfort station**
SN Buildings with toilets and lavatory facilities for public use. (RHDEL2)
UF comfort stations, public
pissoirs
public comfort stations
public toilets
stations, public comfort
toilets, public
CN V.RK.AFU.ALO.ALO.CXA.ALO.AFU.ARI

comfort stations, public
USE **comfort stations**

comic strips
USE **comics**

comics
VB.35 (L,R)
ALT **comic**
SN Groups of cartoons arranged in a narrative sequence. (W)
UF cartoon strips
comic strips
strips, cartoon
strips, comic
CN V.VB.AFU.ALO.AFU.AFU

comitia
RK.1188 (L)
ALT **comitium**
SN Use for ancient Roman places of political assembly for a variety of legal and administrative functions.
CN V.RK.AFU.ALO.ALO.FUA.AFU.ALO

commanders (mallets)
USE **beetles (mallets)**

commedia dell'arte
BM.267 (L,R)
SN Italian 16th- to 18th-century comedy performed by companies of actors trained to improvise dialogue, gesture, and movement from a written plot built around standardized situations and stock characters. (W)
CN B.BM.AFU.ARI.BIQ.ALO

commemorations
USE **memorials**

commencements
KM.13
SN Ceremonies at which degrees or diplomas are conferred by an educational institution. (W)
UF graduations
CN K.KM.AFU.ARI.AFU.AFU

commentaries
VW.303
ALT **commentary**
SN Use generally for document types that explain or critique another work, such as an analysis of a film, or an account of a work of literature.
CN V.VW.AFU.AFU.ALO.BCW

commerce
USE **business**

commerce, chambers of
USE **boards of trade**

commercial agents
HG.406 (L)
ALT **commercial agent**
UF agents
agents, commercial
CN H.HG.AFU.AXC.BOK.BZY

commercial areas
USE **business districts**

commercial art
BM.236 (L,R)
UF art, commercial
CN B.BM.AFU.ARI.BCW.BOK

commercial art galleries
USE **art galleries**

commercial artists
HG.140 (L)
ALT **commercial artist**
SN Designers whose work is commissioned for such uses as advertising, illustration, and the design, embellishment, or decoration of products. (MAYER)
UF artists, commercial
CN H.HG.AFU.AXC.AXC.AFU.AFU.ALO.BCW.AFU

commercial buildings
RK.101 (A,L,N,B,R)
ALT **commercial building**
SN Use broadly to refer to buildings associated with any aspect of the various activities and business relationships of industry and trade; when referring to structures associated with the purchase, sale, or exchange of goods in business, use **mercantile buildings.** (RHDEL2)
UF buildings, business
buildings, commercial
business buildings
business facilities
commercial facilities
facilities, business
facilities, commercial
CN V.RK.AFU.ALO.ALO.ALO

commercial catalogs
VW.106 (A,L,N)
ALT **commercial catalog**
UF catalogs, commercial
catalogs, trade
trade catalogs
CN V.VW.AFU.AFU.AFU.FZU.ALO.ALO.ARI

commercial centers
USE **central business districts**

commercial colleges
USE **business colleges**

commercial correspondence
VW.31 (L)
UF correspondence, commercial
CN V.VW.AFU.AFU.AFU.BIQ.ALO.AFU

commercial directories
VW.408
ALT **commercial directory**
UF business directories
directories, business
directories, commercial
directories, trade
trade directories
CN V.VW.AFU.AFU.ALO.EWY.AXC.AFU.ALO

commercial districts
USE **business districts**

commercial enterprises
USE **business enterprises**

commercial facilities
USE **commercial buildings**

commercial laundries
USE **laundries**

commercial letters of credit
USE **letters of credit**

commercial museums
USE **company museums**

commercial photography
USE **advertising photography**

commercial portraiture
KT.296
SN Use for the activity of taking portrait photographs as a livelihood.
UF photography, professional portrait
portrait photography, professional
portraiture, commercial
portraiture, studio
professional portrait photography
studio portraiture
CN K.KT.AFU.ALO.DUC.DIO.AFU.BCW

commercial schools
USE **business schools**

commercial specifications
VW.796
ALT **commercial specification**
UF specifications, commercial
CN V.VW.AFU.ARI.AFU.ARI.AFU.ARI.ARI

commercial strips
RG.236 (A,L,B)
ALT **commercial strip**
UF strips, commercial
CN V.RG.AFU.ALO.AFU

commercial zones
USE **business districts**

commissaries
USE **lunchrooms**
mess halls
post exchanges

commission merchants
HG.412 (L)
ALT **commission merchant**
UF merchants, commission
CN H.HG.AFU.AXC.BOK.CFS

commissioners
HG.663
ALT **commissioner**
CN H.HG.AFU.AXC.CFS.AXC

commissions
VW.373 (N)
ALT **commission**
SN Includes authorizations granting the power to perform a task or duty and documents appointing or hiring someone to perform a task.
CN V.VW.AFU.AFU.ALO.DUC.AFU

commissions (boards)
USE **boards (organizations)**

commissions, art
USE **art commissions**

commissions, military
USE **military commissions**

commissions, park
USE **park commissions**

commissions, planning
USE **planning commissions**

committee rooms
USE **conference rooms**

committees
HG.852 (L,B)
ALT **committee**
SN Groups of persons delegated to consider, investigate, or take action upon and usually to report concerning some matter or business. (W)
CN H.HG.ALO.BZY

commode chairs
TG.173
ALT **commode chair**
SN Term generally applied to a variety of chairs fitted with a chamber pot. Use **bidets** for box stools with a chamber pot.
UF chairs, chamber
chairs, close-stool
chairs, commode
chairs, necessary
chairs, necessity
chaises percées
chamber chairs
close-stool chairs
fauteuils de bidet
necessary chairs
necessity chairs
CN V.TG.AFU.AFU.ALO.AFU.AFU.ALO.BIQ

commode chairs, cabinet
USE **cabinet chairs**

commode chests
USE **commodes**

commode dressing chests, French
USE **commode dressing tables**

commode dressing tables
TG.732
ALT **commode dressing table**
UF chests, French commode dressing
commode dressing chests, French
commode tables
dressing chests, French commode
dressing tables, commode
French commode dressing chests
tables, commode
CN V.TG.AFU.AFU.BIQ.BOK.ALO.CLM.ALO

commode steps
RT.1112
ALT **commode step**
SN Steps at the foot of a flight of stairs

which have curved ends projecting beyond the string and surrounding the newel. (DAC)
UF steps, commode
CN V.RT.AFU.BIQ.AXC.ALO.BIQ.AFU.AFU

commode tables
USE **commode dressing tables**

commode tables, French
USE **commodes**

commodes
TG.484 (N)
ALT **commode**
SN Chests of drawers or cabinets of chair-rail height, made for display as well as storage and often quite elaborately decorated. Term is applied especially to French forms, and to English, American, and other styles to indicate a form inspired by French taste. (PC)
UF chests, commode
commode chests
commode tables, French
French commode tables
tables, French commode
CN V.TG.AFU.AFU.AXC.ALO.BCW.BZY

commodes à battants anterieurs
USE **commodes à vantaux**

commodes à encoignures
TG.485
ALT **commode à encoignures**
SN Commodes incorporating a tier of drawers flanked by open shelves or cupboards. (PC)
CN V.TG.AFU.AFU.AXC.ALO.BCW.BZY.AFU

commodes à la régence
TG.486
ALT **commode à la régence**
SN Term used in the 18th century for commodes with two tiers of drawers set on high legs; term later used for commodes with three or four tiers of drawers. (PC)
UF commodes en tombeau
CN V.TG.AFU.AFU.AXC.ALO.BCW.BZY.ALO

commodes à vantaux
TG.487
ALT **commode à vantaux**
SN Commodes with two cupboard doors instead of the more usual drawer front. Inside there may be drawers or open shelves. (PC)
UF commodes à battants anterieurs
CN V.TG.AFU.AFU.AXC.ALO.BCW.BZY.ARI

commodes en console
TG.488
ALT **commode en console**
SN Commodes which consist of a single drawer set on tall legs presumably intended to stand beneath a mirror. (WATSON)
UF commodes en table d'applique
CN V.TG.AFU.AFU.AXC.ALO.BCW.BZY.AXC

commodes en table d'applique
USE **commodes en console**

commodes en tombeau
USE **commodes à la régence**

commodes (washstands)
USE **washstands**

commodes, corner
USE **corner commodes**

commodes, petites
USE **petites commodes**

commodity exchanges
RK.134 (A,L)
ALT **commodity exchange**
SN Organized markets where future delivery contracts for graded commodities (as grains, cotton, sugar, coffee, wool) are bought and sold. (W)
UF exchanges, commodity
exchanges, produce
produce exchanges
CN V.RK.AFU.ALO.ALO.ALO.ALO.ALO.AFU

common alder
MT.1096
UF alder, black
alder, common
Alnus glutinosa
black alder
CN M.MT.AFU.AFU.ALO.BIQ.DCU.AFU.AFU.AFU.ALO.AXC

common apple
USE **applewood**

common ash
USE **European ash**

common beech
USE **European beech**

common birch
USE **silver birch**

common bond
MT.2749
SN Pattern bond in which a course of full-length headers occurs at regular intervals, usually every five or six courses; other courses are composed of only stretchers.
UF American bond
bond, American
bond, common
CN M.MT.AFU.AXC.BIQ.AFU.AFU.AFU

common box
USE **boxwood**

common boxwood
USE **boxwood**

common bracket feet
USE **French feet**

common brick
USE **building brick**

common dimension lumber
USE **dimension lumber**

common fig
USE **fig**

common hawthorn
USE **hawthorn**

common hemlock
USE **eastern hemlock**

common hornbeam
USE **European hornbeam**

common horse chestnut
USE **horse chestnut**

common joists
RT.303
ALT **common joist**
SN Use for the parallel joists on which the subfloor is directly laid.
UF bridging joists
joists, bridging
joists, common
CN V.RT.AFU.AFU.AFU.BCW.ALO.AFU.BOK.ALO

common land
RD.309
UF communal land
land, common
CN V.RD.ARI.ALO.AXC.AFU

common lands
USE **commons**

common laurel
USE **laurel**

common lime
MT.1312 (L)
UF common linden
lime, common
linden, common
Tilia europea
Tilia vulgaris
CN M.MT.AFU.AFU.ALO.BIQ.DCU.AFU.AFU.AFU.LZO.AFU

common lime (quicklime)
USE **quicklime**

common linden
USE **common lime**

common nails
TF.391
ALT **common nail**
SN General-use nails each having a head and a diamond-shaped point that are used where appearance is not important, as in framing.

(MEANS)
UF nails, common
CN V.TF.AFU.AFU.AFU.ALO.AFU.CFS.AFU.AXC

common pear
MT.1262
UF pear, common
Pyrus communis
CN M.MT.AFU.AFU.ALO.BIQ.DCU.AFU.AFU.AFU.JOC.ALO

common Persian walnut
USE **English walnut**

common persimmon
MT.1265 (L)
UF Diospyros virginiana
persimmon, common
CN M.MT.AFU.AFU.ALO.BIQ.DCU.AFU.AFU.AFU.JTW.AFU

common rafters
RT.498
ALT **common rafter**
SN Rafters which are at right angles to the eaves of a roof, extending from the plate to the ridgeboard.
UF intermediate rafters
rafters, common
rafters, intermediate
spars
CN V.RT.AFU.AFU.AFU.BIQ.ARI.ALO.ALO.AFU.AFU

common rooms
RM.168
ALT **common room**
SN Use for public lounges or similar rooms in such places as hotels and colleges.
UF rooms, common
CN V.RM.AFU.DIO.ALO.CXA.ARI

common spruce
MT.1400 (L)
UF deal, white
European spruce
fir, spruce
fir, white
Picea excelsa
pine, white
spruce fir
spruce, common
spruce, European
violin wood
white deal
white fir
white pine
wood, violin
CN M.MT.AFU.AFU.ALO.BIQ.DCU.AFU.AFU.ALO.DOI.AXC

commonplace books
VW.49 (L)
ALT **commonplace book**
SN Books in which noteworthy literary passages, cogent quotations, poems, comments, recipes, prescriptions, and other miscellaneous document types, are written. (GAHLM)
UF books, commonplace
CN V.VW.AFU.AFU.AFU.DCU.AFU

commons
RK.1583 (A,L,B,R)
ALT **common**
SN Use for expanses of land, paved or green, owned by the community as a whole. (DLA)
UF common lands
CN V.RK.ALO.ARI.ARI

commons, student
USE **student unions**

commonwealths
HG.821
ALT **commonwealth**
SN Groups of sovereign states and their dependencies associated by their own choice and linked with common objectives and interests. For the concept of nations or states, use **nations**. (RHDEL2)
CN H.HG.ALO.BCW.ALO

communal gardens
USE **community gardens**

communal housing
RG.89 (A,B)
UF communal residences
housing, communal
CN V.RG.AFU.AFU.BOK.BIQ.AFU

communal land
USE **common land**

communal living
BM.1128 (L)
SN Use for informal or formally organized cooperative living arrangements based on ideological, religious, or political affiliation. (LCSH)
UF communalism
living, communal
CN B.BM.CRG.BUE.ALO

communal residences
USE **communal housing**

communal restaurants
USE **soup kitchens**

communal settlements
USE **collective settlements**

communalism
USE **communal living**

communes
RD.78 (L,B)
ALT **commune**
SN Use for self-supporting and self-governing communities comprised of small groups of people living together with minimal interference from outsiders.
CN V.RD.AFU.BOK.AFU.AFU

communicating
KG.34 (L)
CN K.KG.AFU.AFU.ALO.ALO

communicating-door locks
TF.231
ALT **communicating-door lock**
UF connecting-door locks
locks, communicating-door
locks, connecting-door
CN V.TF.AFU.AFU.AFU.AFU.DIO.BIQ.ALO.ALO.ALO

communication systems
RT.1283
ALT **communication system**
SN Use for mechanical and electrical systems that relay information within buildings.
UF signal systems
systems, communication
systems, signal
CN V.RT.ALO.AFU.AFU

communication systems (infrastructural systems)
USE **telecommunication systems**

communication systems, police
USE **police communication systems**

communications
KD.108 (L,B,R)
CN K.KD.AFU.ALO.ARI

communications buildings
RK.198
ALT **communications building**
UF buildings, communications
communications facilities
facilities, communications
CN V.RK.AFU.ALO.ALO.ARI.AFU

communications facilities
USE **communications buildings**

communications museums
RK.390
ALT **communications museum**
UF museums, communications
CN V.RK.AFU.ALO.ALO.BCW.AXC.ARI.ALO

communion
KM.33 (L)
CN K.KM.AFU.ARI.AXC.BCW

communion rails
RT.1225 (B)
ALT **communion rail**
SN Altar rails at which communicants receive communion. (W)
UF rails, communion
CN V.RT.AFU.BUE.ALO.ARI.AFU.AFU

communion records
VW.972
ALT **communion record**
UF first communion records
records, communion
records, first communion

CN V.VW.AFU.ARI.ALO.ALO.AFU.BIQ

communion tables
TG.721 (L,R)
ALT **communion table**
UF tables, communion
CN V.TG.AFU.AFU.BIQ.BOK.ALO.BOK

communiques
VW.459
ALT **communique**
SN Official announcements. (AHD)
CN V.VW.AFU.AFU.ALO.FIM.ALO.AFU

communism
BM.382 (L,R)
SN Economic and political system in which land and capital goods are publicly owned, and the governing authorities control the means of production, prices, and distribution.
CN B.BM.ARI.BUE.ALO

communities, life care
USE **life care communities**

communities, new
USE **new towns**

communities, plant
USE **plant communities**

communities, religious
USE **religious communities**

communities, retirement
USE **retirement communities**

communities, satellite
USE **satellite cities**

communities, urban
USE **cities**

community architecture
USE **participatory design**

community art
BM.237 (R)
SN Includes art undertaken in conjunction with particular communities, often socially deprived, usually with the idea of producing an effect or inspiring response specifically within those communities, with no reference to widely established standards.(THDAT) For art intended to beautify and enrich public places, use **public art.**
UF art, community
CN B.BM.AFU.ARI.BCW.BUE

community art centers
USE **art centers**

community based residences
USE **group homes**

community buildings
USE **community centers**

community centers
RK.1189 (A,L,B)
ALT **community center**
UF buildings, community
centers, community
centers, community recreation
centers, social
centers, village community
community buildings
community centers, village
community recreation centers
recreation centers, community
social centers
village community centers
CN V.RK.AFU.ALO.ALO.FUA.ALO

community centers, college
USE **student unions**

community centers, village
USE **community centers**

community colleges
RK.843 (L)
ALT **community college**
UF colleges, community
CN V.RK.AFU.ALO.ALO.CXA.ARI.AXC.BIQ.AFU.AFU

community development
BM.1069 (A,L)
UF development, community
development, regional
regional development
CN B.BM.CLM.ALO.ALO.AFU

community development, rural
USE **rural development**

community gardens
RK.1437 (A,L,B)
ALT **community garden**
UF communal gardens
gardens, community
gardens, neighborhood
gardens, working-men's
neighborhood gardens
working-men's gardens
CN V.RK.ALO.AFU.AFU.BCW.AFU

community organizations
HG.907
ALT **community organization**
UF associations, civic
civic associations
civic groups
civic organizations
groups, civic
organizations, civic
organizations, community
CN H.HG.ALO.ELK.AFU

community parks
RK.1457
ALT **community park**
UF parks, community
CN V.RK.ALO.ALO.ARI.AFU.AFU

community participation
USE **citizen participation**

community recreation centers
USE **community centers**

community transit
USE **local transit**

commuter rail
USE **commuter railroads**

commuter rail service
USE **commuter railroads**

commuter rail transit
USE **commuter railroads**

commuter railroads
RD.110
ALT **commuter railroad**
SN Rapid rail transit systems linking suburban districts with central city terminals; generally not operating on exclusive rights of way.
UF commuter rail
commuter rail service
commuter rail transit
commuter service, railroad
rail service, commuter
rail, suburban
railroad commuter service
railroads, commuter
suburban rail
CN V.RD.ALO.ARI.AFU.ALO.AFU

commuter service, railroad
USE **commuter railroads**

Comnene
USE **Comnenian**

Comnenian
FL.3073 (R)
UF Comnene
CN F.FL.ALO.BCW.ALO.AFU.ALO.ALO.AFU

Comox
FL.1357 (L)
UF Catloltx
Sliammon
CN F.FL.ALO.ALO.ARI.AFU.BIQ.FCS.AFU

compact disks
VW.644
ALT **compact disk**
UF CDs (compact disks)
disks, compact
CN V.VW.AFU.ALO.AFU.DZW.ALO.AFU

compacting equipment
TB.24
UF equipment, compacting
CN V.TB.AFU.ARI.AFU.ALO

compaction
KT.138 (L)
SN The process of consolidating or compressing substances to form a more dense unit, such as packing of the solid particles in freshly mixed concrete, mortar, or other mixture.
UF tamping
CN K.KT.AFU.ALO.DOI.BIQ

compactors
TB.25 (N)
ALT **compactor**
SN Machines that use weight, vibration, or a combination of both, to achieve compaction. (DAC)
CN V.TB.AFU.ARI.AFU.ALO.AFU

Compagnie-des-Indes porcelain
USE **Compagnie des Indes ware**

Compagnie des Indes ware
FL.1943 (R)
UF Chine sur commande
Compagnie-des-Indes porcelain
East India porcelain
porcelain, Compagnie-des-Indes
porcelain, East India
ware, Compagnie des Indes
CN F.FL.ALO.ARI.ALO.AFU.AFU.AXC.ARI.AFU.AFU

companies
HG.842 (L)
ALT **company**
SN Use generally for associations of persons for carrying on commercial or industrial enterprises. (W)
CN H.HG.ALO.BOK.AFU

companies, incorporated
USE **corporations**

companions, lady's
USE **lady's writing tables**

Company
FL.2243
UF Company School
CN F.FL.ALO.ARI.AXC.ALO.AFU.BOK.AFU.AFU

company halls
USE **guildhalls**

company housing
USE **industrial housing**

company museums
RK.429 (L)
ALT **company museum**
UF commercial museums
museums, commercial
museums, company
CN V.RK.AFU.ALO.ALO.BCW.AXC.AXC.AFU

company records
USE **business records**

Company School
USE **Company**

company stores
RK.170 (L)
ALT **company store**
UF industrial stores
stores, company
stores, industrial
CN V.RK.AFU.ALO.ALO.ALO.ARI.BIQ.ALO.ALO

company towns
RD.50 (A,L,B)
ALT **company town**
SN Use for settlements whose inhabitants depend solely or chiefly on a single employer who also owns a substantial portion of the settlement's real estate and housing.
UF company villages
single company towns
towns, company
villages, company
CN V.RD.AFU.AXC.AXC

company villages
USE **company towns**

comparative government
KD.176 (L)
UF comparative politics
government, comparative
politics, comparative
CN K.KD.AFU.ALO.DZW.AFU

comparative literature
KD.54
UF literature, comparative
CN K.KD.AFU.AFU.BCW.AFU

comparative politics
USE **comparative government**

comparative religion
KD.76 (L)
UF religion, comparative
CN K.KD.AFU.AFU.BUE.AFU.ALO

comparing
KG.11 (L)
CN K.KG.AFU.AFU.AFU.BIQ

compartment ceilings
RT.728
ALT **compartment ceiling**
SN Ceilings divided into compartments or panels separated by moldings or ribs, particularly those in which the compartments or panels are not all uniform rectangles. (RS)
UF ceilings, compartment
CN V.RT.AFU.ALO.AFU.ALO.BOK

compartments, toilet
USE **toilet compartments**

compartments, vaulting
USE **vaulting cells**

compass brick
MT.72
UF arch brick
brick, arch
brick, compass
brick, featheredge
brick, key
brick, radial
brick, radiating
brick, radius
brick, voussoir
featheredge brick
key brick
radial brick
radiating brick
radius brick
voussoir brick
CN M.MT.AFU.AFU.AFU.AXC.ALO.AFU.AFU.AFU.AXC

compass-headed arches
USE **semicircular arches**

compass-headed roofs
USE **compass roofs**

compass maps
USE **portolanos**

compass planes
TB.942 (N)
ALT **compass plane**
SN Planes having a curved baseplate, either concave or convex, used for smoothing curved woodwork. (DAC)
UF compass smoothing planes
heel planes
planes, compass
planes, compass smoothing
planes, heel
roundsils
smoothing planes, compass
CN V.TB.AFU.BCW.CFS.ALO.AFU.DUC.ARI.ALO

compass roofs
RT.440
ALT **compass roof**
SN Use for timber roofs in which rafters, collar beams, and braces combine to suggest an arch; most common in Medieval architecture.
UF compass-headed roofs
cradle roofs
roofs, compass
roofs, compass-headed
roofs, cradle
CN V.RT.AFU.AFU.AFU.BIQ.ARI.AFU.AFU.ALO.ALO

compass saws
TB.1019 (N)
ALT **compass saw**
SN Hand saws having a narrow blade; used to cut small intricate shapes or circles of small radii. (DAC)
UF port saws
saws, compass
saws, port
CN V.TB.AFU.BCW.CFS.ALO.AFU.EWY.BUE.ALO

compass seats
TG.971
ALT **compass seat**
SN Period term used to describe chair seats which are rounded in the front and which sometimes have incurving sides, forming an outline like a horseshoe; most popular in America between the 1730s and 1760s, although in many areas persisting into the Federal period. (FAIRB)

UF compass-shaped seats
horseshoe seats
seats, compass
seats, horseshoe
CN V.TG.ALO.GLI.AFU.AFU

compass-shaped seats
USE **compass seats**

compass smoothing planes
USE **compass planes**

compass windows
USE **bow windows**

compasses
TB.237 (L)
ALT **compass**
SN Instruments for drawing circles and measuring the distance between two points; consisting of two pointed legs, movable on a joint or pivot, usually made so that one of the points can be detached for the insertion of a pen or an extension. (DAC)
CN V.TB.AFU.ARI.CLM.AFU.ALO.ARI

compasses, beam
USE **beam compasses**

compasses, drop bow
USE **drop bow compasses**

compasses, proportional
USE **proportional compasses**

compendiums
VW.11
ALT **compendium**
SN Works containing in a smaller document the substance or general principles of larger works, often serving as a supplement to the larger work.
UF digests (compendiums)
CN V.VW.AFU.AFU.AFU.BCW

compensating hubs
TF.567
ALT **compensating hub**
UF hubs, compensating
CN V.TF.AFU.ALO.AXC.BOK.AFU

compensation
BM.372 (L,B)
CN B.BM.ARI.AXC

compensation (restoring)
KT.626
SN Use broadly for painting conservation treatments, such as oiling and inpainting, intended to recreate the original appearance of the design in a defect that cannot be corrected. Use a more specific term if possible.
CN K.KT.AFU.ALO.FZU.AFU

competition designs
USE **competition drawings**

competition drawings
VD.92
ALT **competition drawing**
UF competition designs
designs, competition
drawings, competition
CN V.VD.AFU.ALO.ALO

competitions
KM.42 (A,L,B,R)
CN K.KM.AFU.AXC.AFU

competitive bidding
USE **bidding**

competitive tendering
USE **bidding**

compilers
HG.194
ALT **compiler**
SN Persons who assemble items of information. (W)
CN H.HG.AFU.AXC.AXC.ARI.ALO.ALO

complementary colors
BM.109
SN Two colors having maximum contrast with each other and which, when mixed, result in a neutral color.
UF colors, complementary
CN B.BM.AFU.AFU.ARI.BOK.ALO.AFU.AFU

complexes
RG.1 (B)
ALT **complex**
SN Aggregations of buildings, other structures, and open spaces, often multifunctional, and more extensive, and usually shaped over a longer period of time by more participants, than single built works.
CN V.RG.AFU

complexes, educational
USE **educational complexes**

complexes, industrial
USE **industrial complexes**

complexes, launch
USE **launch complexes**

complexes, office
USE **office complexes**

complexes, school
USE **educational complexes**

complexes, sports
USE **sports complexes**

complexity
BM.99 (L)
SN The state or quality of having many intricate or interrelated parts.
CN B.BM.AFU.AFU.ARI.ALO

compliance, certificates of
USE **certificates of occupancy**

compluvia
RT.994
ALT **compluvium**
SN Apertures in the center of roofs of atriums in Roman houses, sloping inward to discharge rainwater into a cistern or tank. (HAS)
CN V.RT.AFU.ARI.AFU.ARI.ALO

component drawings
USE **minor assembly drawings**

composers
HG.75 (L,R)
ALT **composer**
CN H.HG.AFU.AXC.AXC.AFU.AFU.AFU.BIQ.BIQ.ARI

Composite
FL.2740
CN F.FL.ALO.AXC.ALO.ALO.ALO.BOK.AFU

composite arches
USE **four-centered arches**

composite construction
KT.29 (A,L)
SN Use both for construction utilizing various different building materials and for the use of more than one type of construction method in a structure, such as a masonry building with a laminated wood beam roof.
UF construction, composite
CN K.KT.AFU.ALO.BCW.ARI.AFU.ALO

composite drawings
VD.3
ALT **composite drawing**
SN Use for drawings in which two or more related images (e.g., different views of the same structure, or a figure in various poses) are displayed together or fused into one.
UF drawings, composite
CN V.VD.AFU.AFU.AFU

composite green pigment
MT.1662
UF green pigment, composite
pigment, composite green
CN M.MT.AFU.AFU.ARI.AFU.AFU.ALO.ALO.AXC.BCW

composite materials
MT.2224 (L,B)
UF materials, composite
materials, sandwich
sandwich materials
CN M.MT.AFU.ALO.CFS

Composite order
RT.51 (A,B,R)
UF order, Composite
CN V.RT.AFU.AFU.AFU.ARI.ARI.AFU

composite photographs
VJ.117 (L)
ALT **composite photograph**
SN Use for photographic prints in which two or more negatives are printed as one unified image. For combinations of images, such as

photographs with architectural drawings, use **photomontages.** When pieces of photographs or other relatively flat materials are pasted together into less unified images, use **collages.**
UF combination photoprints
combination prints
composite photoprints
composites
composites, photo
photo composites
photographs, composite
photoprints, composite
prints, combination
CN V.VJ.AFU.ARI.ALO.BUE.AFU

composite photoprints
USE **composite photographs**

composite pigment
MT.1803
SN Any pigment that contains more than one basic ingredient, as cadmium-barium yellow, which contains both cadmium sulfide and barium sulfate coprecipitated. (MAYER)
UF pigment, composite
CN M.MT.AFU.AFU.ARI.AFU.AFU.ALO.ARI.AFU

Composite Style
USE **Fourth Style**

composite white
MT.1732
UF mixed white
permalba
superba
superba white
ultra white
white, composite
white, mixed
white, superba
white, ultra
CN M.MT.AFU.AFU.ARI.AFU.AFU.ALO.ALO.BOK.AFU.BCW

composites
USE **composite photographs**

composites, photo
USE **composite photographs**

composition
BM.52 (A,L,B,R)
SN Structure or arrangement of the internal elements of a work of art, such as a drawing, sculpture, or written or musical work.
CN B.BM.AFU.AFU.ARI.AFU.BCW.AFU

composition drawings
VD.149
ALT **composition drawing**
SN Use for fairly finished drawings of whole compositions, whether as pattern drawings, working drawings, or done after a finished work.
UF drawings, composition
CN V.VD.AFU.BIQ.ALO

composition leaf
USE **leaf**

composition roofing
USE **built-up roofing**

composition sketches
VB.8
ALT **composition sketch**
UF sketches, composition
CN V.VB.AFU.AFU.BCW.AFU

composition studies
VB.63
ALT **composition study**
UF studies, composition
CN V.VB.AFU.ALO.BOK.AXC.AFU

composition, closed
USE **closed composition**

composition, open
USE **open composition**

compositions, buffing
USE **buffing compositions**

compositors
HG.454
ALT **compositor**
SN Persons who assemble, set, proof, and generally prepare type and illustrations for printing. (W)
CN H.HG.AFU.AXC.BUE.ALO.CFS.ARI

compound beams
USE **built-up beams**

compound piers
RT.187
ALT **compound pier**
UF compound pillars
piers, compound
pillars, compound
CN V.RT.AFU.AFU.AFU.AXC.CRG.AFU.AFU.ALO

compound pillars
USE **compound piers**

compound vaults
RT.522
ALT **compound vault**
SN Use for vaults formed by the intersection of two or more simple vaults.
UF vaults, compound
CN V.RT.AFU.AFU.AFU.BIQ.BOK.AFU.AFU

compounds, antifreeze
USE **antifreeze**

compounds, caulking
USE **caulking compounds**

compounds, cleaning
USE **cleaning compounds**

compounds, organic
USE **organic compounds**

compounds, parting
USE **parting compounds**

compounds, sealing
USE **sealing compounds**

compreg
USE **impregnated wood**

compregnated wood
USE **impregnated wood**

comprehensive plans
VW.462 (A)
ALT **comprehensive plan**
SN Use with reference to land use control law, zoning, and urban redevelopment to describe the omnibus plans of cities or towns for housing, industry, commercial, and recreational facilities and their impact on environmental factors. (BLACKS)
UF general plans
master plans (reports)
plans, comprehensive
plans, general
plans, master (reports)
CN V.VW.AFU.AFU.ALO.FIM.ARI.AFU.AFU

comprehensive record schedules
USE **records schedules**

compressed wood
MT.1415 (L)
SN Wood which has been impregnated with resin and subjected to a high pressure to increase its density and strength. (DAC)
UF densified wood
pressed wood
wood, comressed
wood, densified
wood, pressed
CN M.MT.AFU.AFU.ALO.BIQ.DCU.ALO.ALO

compressibility
BM.949 (L)
SN Property by which a decrease of volume results when an external pressure is applied. (STEIN)
CN B.BM.CFS.AXC.BZY.BOK.ALO

compression molding
KT.147
SN Molding process used especially for plastics in which heat and pressure are brought to bear on the materials in the mold. (W)
UF molding, compression
CN K.KT.AFU.ALO.DOI.CRG.ALO

compressors
TB.386 (L,N)
ALT **compressor**
SN Machines that compress a refrigerant gas; used in air conditioning and refrigeration. (MEANS)
CN V.TB.AFU.ARI.DOI.AFU

compters
USE **debtor's prisons**

comptrollers
HG.397
ALT **comptroller**
SN Controllers of accounts or finances. (W)
UF controllers
CN H.HG.AFU.AXC.BOK.AFU.BCW

computation laboratories
USE **computer centers**

computational linguistics
KD.35 (L)
UF linguistics, computational
CN K.KD.AFU.AFU.AXC.AFU.AFU.ALO

computer-aided design
KT.98 (A,L)
UF CAD
computer drawing
design, computer-aided
drawing, computer
CN K.KT.AFU.ALO.CFS.ARI

computer animation
KT.173 (L)
UF animation, computer
CN K.KT.AFU.ALO.DUC.AFU.AFU

computer art
BM.256 (L,R)
UF art, computer
CN B.BM.AFU.ARI.BCW.FOG.ALO

computer-assisted maps
VW.171
ALT **computer-assisted map**
UF maps, computer-assisted
CN V.VW.AFU.AFU.AFU.FZU.AXC.AFU.ARI.ARI.AFU

computer buildings
USE **computer centers**

computer centers
RK.199 (A,L,B)
ALT **computer center**
UF buildings, computer
centers, computer
centers, data processing
centers, data processing service
computation laboratories
computer buildings
computer laboratories
computing centers
computing laboratories
data processing centers
data processing service centers
departments, electronic data processing
electronic data processing departments
laboratories, computation
CN V.RK.AFU.ALO.ALO.ARI.AFU.AFU

computer drawing
USE **computer-aided design**

computer drawings
VD.124
ALT **computer drawing**
UF computer-generated drawings
drawings, computer
drawings, computer-generated
CN V.VD.AFU.AXC.ALO

computer-generated drawings
USE **computer drawings**

computer graphics
KT.178 (A)
SN Use generally for computer processing in which the output is in pictorial form. (DOC)
UF graphics, computer
CN K.KT.AFU.ALO.DUC.BIQ

computer laboratories
USE **computer centers**

computer-output microfiche
VW.666
SN Computer output produced directly onto microfiche, without paper printout as an intermediary. (ICA)
UF COM (microfiche)
microfiche, computer-output
CN V.VW.AFU.ALO.AFU.DZW.AXC.AFU.AFU

computer-output microfilms
VW.667 (L)
ALT **computer-output microfilm**
SN Computer output produced directly onto microfilm, without paper printout as an intermediary. (ICA)
UF COM (microfilm)
microfilms, computer-output
CN V.VW.AFU.ALO.AFU.DZW.AXC.AFU.ALO

computer-output microforms
VW.665
ALT **computer-output microform**
SN Computer output produced directly on to microform, without paper printout as an intermediary. (ICA)
UF COM (microforms)
microforms, computer-output
CN V.VW.AFU.ALO.AFU.DZW.AXC.AFU

computer peripherals
USE **peripherals**

computer printouts
USE **printouts**

computer programmers
HG.356 (L)
ALT **computer programmer**
UF programmers, computer
CN H.HG.AFU.AXC.BIQ.ALO.AFU

computer programming
KG.83 (L,B)
UF programming (computers)
CN K.KG.AFU.AFU.AXC.BCW

computer programs
USE **software**

computer rooms
RM.141
ALT **computer room**
UF rooms, computer
CN V.RM.AFU.DIO.ALO.BUE.ALO

computer science
KD.210
SN Study of phenomena related to computers; it emphasizes the creation, analysis, and implementation of algorithms at all levels in the computer hierarchy, from circuits at the binary representation level to the more macroscopic description of algorithms by programming languages. (PG)
UF science, computer
CN K.KD.AFU.ARI.AXC

computer searching
USE **online searching**

computer storage devices
USE **storage devices**

computer terminals
TB.142 (L,N)
ALT **computer terminal**
SN Computer peripherals composed of a monitor or printing device and a keyboard, which are linked together to function as a single input/output unit.
UF terminals (computers)
terminals, computer
CN V.TB.AFU.ARI.BCW.ALO

computers
TB.143 (A,L,B,R)
ALT **computer**
SN Devices or systems capable of carrying out a sequence of operations in a distinctly and explicitly defined manner. (DOC)
UF hardware (computers)
CN V.TB.AFU.ARI.BCW.ARI

computers, home
USE **microcomputers**

computers, laptop
USE **laptop computers**

computers, personal
USE **microcomputers**

computers, portable
USE **portable computers**

computing centers
USE **computer centers**

computing laboratories
USE **computer centers**

computus manuscripts
VW.88 (R)
ALT **computus manuscript**

UF manuscripts, computus
CN V.VW.AFU.AFU.AFU.FZU.AFU.AFU

concave
DC.62
SN Hollowed out like the inner curve of a circle or sphere. (PUTNAM)
CN D.DC.AFU.ARI.BOK.AFU

concave joints
TF.625
ALT concave joint
SN Recessed masonry joints formed in mortar by the use of a curved steel jointing tool; effective in resisting rain penetration.
UF joints, concave
joints, rodded
rodded joints
CN V.TF.ALO.ARI.ALO.AFU.ARI.AXC.AFU

concave seats
USE **hollowed seats**

concealed beds
USE **deception beds**

concealed doors
USE **jib doors**

concealed hinges
TF.140
ALT concealed hinge
SN Use for door hinges that are visible when the door is open but concealed when the door is closed. Distinguished from **invisible hinges** which are completely concealed, from the outside, whether the door is open or closed.
UF blind hinges
hinges, blind
hinges, concealed
CN V.TF.AFU.AFU.AFU.AFU.CLM.ARI.AFU

concentrated loads
BM.1007
SN Loads acting on a very small area of a structure. (DAC)
UF loads, concentrated
CN B.BM.CFS.AXC.CLM.ALO.ARI.ARI

concentration camps
RG.48 (L,B,R)
ALT concentration camp
UF camps, concentration
camps, detention
camps, internment
detention camps
internment camps
CN V.RG.AFU.AFU.BCW.AFU

concentric
DC.29
CN D.DC.AFU.ALO.ARI.AXC

concentric arches
RT.248
ALT concentric arch
SN Use for arches laid in several courses whose curves have a common center.
UF arches, concentric
CN V.RT.AFU.AFU.AFU.BCW.AFU.AFU.AFU.ELK.AFU

Concept art
USE **Conceptual**

concept drawings
USE **conceptual drawings**

concept sketches
USE **conceptual drawings**

Conception, Immaculate
USE **Immaculate Conception**

Conceptual
FL.3722 (L,R)
UF Concept art
Conceptualist
Idea art
Possible art
Post-object art
CN F.FL.ALO.BUE.ARI.BOK

conceptual artists
HG.96
ALT conceptual artist
UF artists, conceptual
CN H.HG.AFU.AXC.AXC.AFU.AFU.ALO.AXC.BCW

conceptual drawings
VD.97
ALT conceptual drawing
SN Designates architectural drawings done early in the design process; often not to scale and may include diagrammatic elements.
UF concept drawings
concept sketches
conceptual sketches
drawings, conceptual
sketches, conceptual
CN V.VD.AFU.ALO.AXC.AFU

conceptual sketches
USE **conceptual drawings**

Conceptualist
USE **Conceptual**

concert halls
RK.926 (A,L,B,R)
ALT concert hall
UF halls, concert
halls, symphony
symphony halls
CN V.RK.AFU.ALO.ALO.EFQ.ARI.ALO

concertina doors
USE **folding doors**

concerts
KM.59 (L,R)
CN K.KM.AFU.BOK.AXC.ALO

conch domes
USE **umbrella domes**

Conchas
FL.1031
CN F.FL.ALO.ALO.ALO.ALO.AFU.ALO.ARI.AFU.ARI.AXC

Concho
FL.1456
CN F.FL.ALO.ALO.ARI.AFU.CFS.ARI

conchs
RT.657
ALT conch
SN Semicircular niches which are covered with a semidome. (HAS)
CN V.RT.AFU.AFU.AFU.BIQ.BUE.ALO.AFU.BIQ.AFU

concinnity
BM.101
SN Harmony or fitness in the adaptation of the parts of a whole to each other; often, studied elegance of design or arrangement. (W)
UF eurhythmy
CN B.BM.AFU.AFU.ARI.ARI.AFU

concord
USE **harmony**

concordances
VW.390 (L)
ALT concordance
SN Includes indexes to the location of words or phrases in a text and finding aids, in two columns, establishing the relationship between the past and present reference numbers of individual items.
CN V.VW.AFU.AFU.ALO.EWY.ALO

concourses
RM.86 (A)
ALT concourse
SN Use for open spaces or halls where crowds may gather, especially by chance coming together, as in a large railroad station.
CN V.RM.AFU.DIO.ALO.ARI.ALO

concrete
MT.195 (A,L,B,R)
SN A mixture of sand, gravel, crushed rock, or other aggregate, held together by a hardened paste of cement and water. (HORNB)
CN M.MT.AFU.AFU.AFU.BCW.AFU

Concrete art
FL.3291 (L,R)
UF Art Concret
art, Concrete
Konkrete Kunst
CN F.FL.ALO.BCW.ALO.AXC.DCU.ALO

concrete block
MT.232 (A,L,B)
UF block, concrete
brick, concrete
concrete brick
CN M.MT.AFU.AFU.AFU.BCW.ALO.AFU

concrete brick
USE **concrete block**

concrete carts
USE **buggies (equipment)**

concrete coatings
MT.2552 (L)
UF coatings, concrete
CN M.MT.AFU.ARI.CRG.ARI.AFU

concrete finishing machines
TB.548 (N)
ALT **concrete finishing machine**
SN Used both for large power-driven machines mounted on wheels that ride on steel pavement forms and for portable machines with large paddles used to float and finish concrete floors and slabs. (MEANS)
UF finishing machines, concrete
machines, concrete finishing
CN V.TB.AFU.BCW.ALO.ARI.AFU

concrete inserts
TF.380
ALT **concrete insert**
SN Devices such as pipe sleeves, threaded bolts, or nailing blocks that are attached to a concrete form before pouring the concrete. When the forms are removed, the inserts remain embedded in the concrete. (MEANS)
UF inserts, concrete
CN V.TF.AFU.AFU.AFU.ALO.AFU.BZY.ARI

concrete laying
USE **pouring concrete**

concrete mixers
TB.549 (L,N,B)
ALT **concrete mixer**
SN Machines that mix cement, aggregate, and water in a rotating drum to make concrete. (MEANS)
UF cement mixers
mixers, cement
mixers, concrete
CN V.TB.AFU.BCW.ALO.ARI.ALO

concrete nails
TF.430
ALT **concrete nail**
SN Steel nails each having a diamond point that has been hardened so that it can be driven into concrete without bending. (MEANS)
UF nails, concrete
CN V.TF.AFU.AFU.AFU.ALO.AFU.CFS.ALO.ALO

concrete paint
MT.2535
SN Paint used on concrete.
UF paint, concrete
CN M.MT.AFU.ARI.CRG.ALO.BCW.ALO.AFU

concrete pavers
TB.550
ALT **concrete paver**
SN Concrete mixers, usually mounted on crawler tracks, that mix and place concrete pavement on the subgrade. (STEIN)
UF pavers
pavers, concrete
CN V.TB.AFU.BCW.ALO.ARI.ALO.AFU

concrete placing
USE **pouring concrete**

concrete poetry
BM.312 (L,R)
SN Use for works that may be both literary and graphic in which meaning is conveyed by the patterns of letters, words, or symbols rather than by the conventional arrangement of words.
UF poetry, concrete
CN B.BM.AFU.AXC.EFQ.ARI.AFU

concrete products
MT.231 (L)
UF products, concrete
CN M.MT.AFU.AFU.AFU.BCW.ALO

concrete pumps
TB.551 (L)
ALT **concrete pump**
SN Pumps that force premixed concrete through a hose to a desired location. (MEANS)
UF pumps, concrete
CN V.TB.AFU.BCW.ALO.ARI.ARI

concrete saws
TB.554 (N)
ALT **concrete saw**
SN Power-operated saws used in grooving uncured concrete, to prevent cracking, or in cutting hard concrete slabs. (DAC)
UF saws, concrete
CN V.TB.AFU.BCW.ALO.AXC.AFU

concrete slabs
USE **slabs**

concrete spreaders
TB.552
ALT **concrete spreader**
SN Machines, usually carried on side forms or on rails parallel thereto, designed to spread concrete from heaps or to receive and spread concrete in a uniform layer. (STEIN)
UF spreaders, concrete
CN V.TB.AFU.BCW.ALO.ARI.AXC

concrete, aerated
USE **air-entrained concrete**

concrete, air-entrained
USE **air-entrained concrete**

concrete, asphalt
USE **asphalt concrete**

concrete, asphaltic
USE **asphalt concrete**

concrete, cellular
USE **air-entrained concrete**

concrete, cinder
USE **cinder concrete**

concrete, colloidal
USE **colloidal concrete**

concrete, cyclopean
USE **cyclopean concrete**

concrete, expanding
USE **expansive concrete**

concrete, expansive
USE **expansive concrete**

concrete, foamed
USE **foamed concrete**

concrete, foamed sand
USE **foamed sand concrete**

concrete, foamed slag
USE **foamed slag concrete**

concrete, frost-resistant
USE **frost-resistant concrete**

concrete, heat-resistant
USE **heat-resistant concrete**

concrete, high-strength
USE **high-strength concrete**

concrete, insulating
USE **insulating concrete**

concrete, lightweight
USE **lightweight concrete**

concrete, lime
USE **lime concrete**

concrete, no-fines
USE **no-fines concrete**

concrete, normal-weight
USE **normal-weight concrete**

concrete, polymer-cement
USE **polymer-impregnated cement**

concrete, polymer-impregnated
USE **polymer-impregnated concrete**

concrete, porous
USE **porous concrete**

concrete, post-tensioned prestressed
USE **post-tensioned prestressed concrete**

concrete, precast
USE **precast concrete**

concrete, prestressed
USE **prestressed concrete**

concrete, ready-mixed
USE **ready-mixed concrete**

concrete, reinforced
USE **reinforced concrete**

concrete, resin
USE **polymer-impregnated concrete**

concrete, rubble
USE **rubble concrete**

concrete, slag
USE **slag concrete**

concrete, sprayed
USE **gunite**

concrete, sulfate-resistant
USE **sulfate-resistant concrete**

concrete, Zonolite (TM)
USE **Zonolite concrete (TM)**

concreters
HG.588
ALT **concreter**
SN Persons who build or work with concrete. (W)
CN H.HG.AFU.AXC.BZY.AFU.BOK

concretework
MT.2741
CN M.MT.AFU.AXC.ALO

concreting
USE **pouring concrete**

concretion
USE **concretionary stone**

concretionary stone
MT.730
UF concretion
stone, concretionary
CN M.MT.AFU.AFU.AFU.DCU.AFU.ALO.ALO.AFU

concretions, humor
USE **biomorphic abstraction**

condemning
KG.180 (L,B)
ALT **condemned**
SN Use when real estate is legally declared unfit for habitation or use, usually accompanied by the appropriation of that property under the power of eminent domain. For the appropriating of real estate or other property as a punishment for breach of the law, use **confiscating.**
CN K.KG.AFU.ALO.ARI.AXC

condensation
BM.925 (L,B)
CN B.BM.CFS.AXC.BOK.AFU

condensers
RT.1424 (L)
ALT **condenser**
SN In refrigeration systems, the heat exchangers that remove heat from the refrigerant and transform a hot gas under pressure into a cool liquid. (MEANS)
CN V.RT.ALO.BCW.AFU.ALO.AFU.BCW.ALO

conditioners, air
USE **air conditioners**

condominiums
RG.91 (A,L)
ALT **condominium**
SN Multifamily dwellings in which each unit is individually owned and ownership of common areas and facilities is shared. (MEANS)
UF condos
CN V.RG.AFU.AFU.BOK.BIQ.ALO

condos
USE **condominiums**

conducting materials
USE **conductors**

conductivity, electrical
USE **electrical conductivity**

conductivity, thermal
USE **thermal conductivity**

conductors
MT.2579
UF conducting materials
materials, conducting
CN M.MT.AFU.ARI.CXA

conductors (music)
HG.76 (L)
ALT **conductor (music)**
SN Persons who conduct an orchestra, chorus, or other group of musical performers. (W)
UF directors (music)
directors, music (conductors)
music directors (conductors)
CN H.HG.AFU.AXC.AXC.AFU.AFU.AFU.BIQ.BIQ.AXC

conductors (piping)
RT.1468
ALT **conductor (piping)**
SN Any vertical pipes which convey rainwater, including those within a building. (DAC)
UF leaders, rainwater
rainwater leaders
CN V.RT.ALO.BCW.ALO.ARI.BZY.AFU

conductors, electric
USE **electric conductors**

conductors, lightning
USE **lightning rods**

conduits
RK.572 (L,R)
ALT **conduit**
CN V.RK.AFU.ALO.ALO.CFS.ALO.BCW.ALO

conduits (electric)
USE **electric conduits**

conduits, electric
USE **electric conduits**

cone hip tile
USE **bonnet hip tile**

cone tile
USE **bonnet hip tile**

cones
BM.790
ALT **conical**
CN B.BM.CFS.ARI.AXC.BCW.ALO.AFU

Conestoga
FL.1289 (L)
CN F.FL.ALO.ALO.ARI.AFU.ARI.ALO

confectioneries
RK.155 (A)
ALT **confectionery**
UF confectionery stores
confiseries
stores, confectionery
CN V.RK.AFU.ALO.ALO.ALO.ARI.BIQ.AFU.BCW

confectionery stores
USE **confectioneries**

conference centers
USE **convention centers**

conference facilities
USE **convention centers**

conference proceedings
USE **proceedings**

conference reports
USE **proceedings**

conference rooms
RM.61 (A,L,B)
ALT **conference room**
UF committee rooms
meeting rooms
rooms, committee
rooms, conference
rooms, meeting
CN V.RM.AFU.DIO.ALO.AFU.ALO

conferences
KM.97 (A,L,B,R)
UF congresses
conventions
CN K.KM.AFU.CRG.AFU

confessionals
RT.1231 (L,R)
ALT **confessional**
SN Small booths furnished with a seat for a priest and with a screen or latticed window through which the penitent may talk to the priest, who is hidden. (HAS)
UF shriving-seats
CN V.RT.AFU.BUE.ALO.ARI.BCW

confessionals (chairs)
USE **bergères en confessional**

confessors
HG.233 (L,R)
ALT confessor
SN Persons who hear confessions of others. (W)
CN H.HG.AFU.AXC.AXC.BIQ.AFU.ARI.DUC.AFU

confidantes
TG.315 (N)
ALT confidante
UF canapés à confident (confidantes)
confidents
tête-à-têtes
têtes (confidantes)
vis-à-vis
CN V.TG.AFU.AFU.ALO.ALO.BZY.BIQ

confidents
USE **confidantes**

confidents (canapés à confident)
USE **canapés à confident**

confidents à trois places
USE **indiscrets**

confirmation
KM.34 (L,R)
CN K.KM.AFU.ARI.AXC.BIQ

confirmed letters of credit
USE **letters of credit**

confiscating
KG.181 (L)
SN Seizing and appropriating real estate or other property to the public domain as a punishment for breach of the law. For the appropriation of real estate accompanying the declaration of its unfitness for habitation or use, use condemning.
CN K.KG.AFU.ALO.ARI.BCW

confiseries
USE **confectioneries**

conflict, social
USE **social conflict**

confraternities
HG.897 (L,R)
ALT confraternity
SN Groups of people united for a religious, charitable, or other purpose, or in a profession or occupation. (W)
UF sodalities
CN H.HG.ALO.DUC.BCW

Confucianism
BM.659 (L)
ALT Confucian
CN B.BM.BZY.AFU.ARI

Congdon
FL.925
CN F.FL.ALO.ALO.ALO.AFU.ALO.ARI.BCW.AFU

conges
USE **apophyges**

conglomerate
MT.736 (L)
SN Elastic sedimentary rock composed of rounded fragments varying from small pebbles to large boulders in a cement of calcareous material, iron oxide, silica, or hardened clay. (W)
CN M.MT.AFU.AFU.AFU.DCU.AFU.ALO.ALO.ARI.ALO

Congo copal
MT.1481
UF copal, Congo
CN M.MT.AFU.AFU.ALO.BOK.ARI.AFU

Congo Kingdom
USE **Kongo Kingdom**

congo-wood
USE **African blackwood**

Congregational
BM.634 (L,B)
CN B.BM.BZY.AFU.ALO.ARI.AXC

congress facilities
USE **convention centers**

Congress, Members of
USE **Members of Congress**

congresses
USE **conferences**

congressional committee records
VW.1034 (L)
ALT congressional committee record
UF records, congressional committee
CN V.VW.AFU.ARI.ALO.BCW.AFU.ARI.ALO.AFU.AFU

congressional committee reports
VW.1035 (L)
ALT congressional committee report
UF reports, congressional committee
CN V.VW.AFU.ARI.ALO.BCW.AFU.ARI.ALO.AFU.AFU.AFU

congressional districts
RG.249
ALT congressional district
UF districts, congressional
CN V.RG.ALO.AFU.AFU.ARI.AFU

congressional records
VW.1033
ALT congressional record
UF records, congressional
CN V.VW.AFU.ARI.ALO.BCW.AFU.ARI.ALO.AFU

Congressmen
USE **Members of the House of Representatives**

Congresspersons
USE **Members of the House of Representatives**

Congresswomen
USE **Members of the House of Representatives**

Coniagui
USE **Koniagui**

Conibo
FL.1577
CN F.FL.ALO.ALO.ARI.ARI.AFU.CFS

conical mounds
USE **burial mounds**

conical vaults
USE **expanding vaults**

connected barns
RK.56
ALT connected barn
SN Use for barns connected, often via intermediate outbuildings, to the main farmhouse.
UF barns, connected
barns, continuous
barns, New England connected
connected barns, New England
continuous barns
New England connected barns
CN V.RK.AFU.ALO.ALO.AFU.AFU.AFU.ARI.ALO

connected barns, New England
USE **connected barns**

Connecticut barns
USE **English barns**

connecting-door locks
USE **communicating-door locks**

connections
USE **joints**

connelly feet
USE **therm feet**

Connemara marble
MT.792
UF marble, Connemara
CN M.MT.AFU.AFU.AFU.DCU.AFU.ARI.ARI.ARI.ARI.AFU

connoisseurship
BM.288 (L,R)
CN B.BM.AFU.AXC.ARI

conoidal vaults
RT.545
ALT conoidal vault
SN Use for expanding vaults in which the smaller base is semicircular, the larger base semielliptical.
UF vaults, conoidal
CN V.RT.AFU.AFU.AFU.BIQ.BOK.AFU.ALO.ALO.AFU

conoidal vaults, convex
USE **convex conoidal vaults**

consecration
KM.35 (L)
CN K.KM.AFU.ARI.AXC.BOK

consents
VW.374 (B)
ALT consent

CN V.VW.AFU.AFU.ALO.DUC.ALO

conservation
KT.628 (A,L,B,R)
SN Use for the discipline of restoring, reconditioning, and preserving artifacts. For the preservation of historic buildings, structures, or sites, use **historic preservation.**
CN K.KT.AFU.ALO.FZU.ALO

conservation laboratories
RK.1165 (A,B)
ALT **conservation laboratory**
UF art restoration laboratories
laboratories, art restoration
laboratories, conservation
CN V.RK.AFU.ALO.ALO.FIM.ALO.AFU.BIQ

conservation scientists
USE **conservators**

conservation technicians
USE **conservators**

conservation, energy
USE **energy conservation**

conservationists
HG.750 (A,L)
ALT **conservationist**
SN Persons who advocate conservation of natural resources. (W)
CN H.HG.AFU.BCW.HZS.ARI

conservatism
BM.554 (L)
CN B.BM.BOK.BZY.ALO

Conservative Judaism
BM.670 (L)
ALT **Conservative Jewish**
CN B.BM.BZY.AFU.BOK.AFU

conservatories
RM.97 (L,B)
ALT **conservatory**
SN Greenhouses or mostly glazed rooms, devoted to growing and displaying plants and attached to a residence.
CN V.RM.AFU.DIO.ALO.AXC.AFU

conservatories (greenhouses)
USE **greenhouses**

conservatories of music
USE **music conservatories**

conservatories, music
USE **music conservatories**

conservators
HG.335
ALT **conservator**
SN Use for persons who repair, restore, or maintain the condition of objects.
UF conservation scientists
conservation technicians
scientists, conservation
technicians, conservation
CN H.HG.AFU.AXC.BIQ.AFU.AFU.AXC

console dessertes
TG.591
ALT **console desserte**
SN French sideboards with a drawer or drawers beneath the top and a shelf between the legs. Usually D-shaped in plan, but sometimes rectangular. Used for the serving of food. (PC)
UF dessertes
CN V.TG.AFU.AFU.AXC.ALO.CRG.BCW

consoles en acajou
USE **pier tables**

console tables
TG.694
ALT **console table**
SN Side tables with tops supported by a substructure consisting of two or more legs of console form, sometimes having marble tops and heavily carved substructures.
UF bracket tables
clap tables
consoles (tables)
tables, bracket
tables, clap
tables, console
CN V.TG.AFU.AFU.BIQ.BOK.AFU.DUC.AFU

console tables, eagle
USE **eagle console tables**

consoles
RT.321 (R)
ALT **console**
SN Use for projecting, scroll-shaped members serving as brackets or corbels.
UF brackets (consoles)
CN V.RT.AFU.AFU.AFU.BCW.AXC.ALO

consoles (tables)
USE **console tables**

consoles, key
USE **key consoles**

consolidated schools
RK.796 (L)
ALT **consolidated school**
UF schools, consolidated
CN V.RK.AFU.ALO.ALO.CXA.ARI.AFU.ALO

consolidation (masonry)
KT.644
SN Use for the processes involved in strenghtening masonry, particularly natural stone and concrete.
CN K.KT.AFU.ALO.GLI.AFU.AFU

consortia
HG.822 (L,B)
ALT **consortium**
SN Associations of individual groups formed to undertake an enterprise or project beyond the resources of any one member. (W)
UF consortiums
CN H.HG.ALO.BCW.ARI

consortiums
USE **consortia**

constables
HG.672 (L)
ALT **constable**
SN Public officers responsible for keeping the public peace and for certain petty judicial duties. (W)
CN H.HG.AFU.AXC.CFS.CFS.AFU

constancy
BM.130
SN The relative independence of perceived object color from changes in color of the light source. (GCT)
UF color constancy
constancy, color
CN B.BM.AFU.AFU.ARI.BOK.ALO.ALO.ALO.AFU

constancy, color
USE **constancy**

constant white
USE **blanc fixe**

Constantinian
FL.2727
CN F.FL.ALO.AXC.ALO.ALO.AFU.AXC.ARI.ALO

Constantinopolitan
FL.3081
UF Metropolitan (Byzantine)
CN F.FL.ALO.BCW.ALO.AFU.ALO.BCW.AFU

constituencies
USE **election districts**

constitutions
VW.773 (L)
ALT **constitution**
SN Documents embodying the fundamental organic law of government of a nation, state, society, or other organized body; laying down fundamental rules and principles for the conduct of affairs. (GAHLM)
CN V.VW.AFU.ARI.AFU.ALO.BCW

construction
KT.26 (A,L,B,R)
ALT **constructed**
SN Use for the process of creating something by combining parts or elements, and also for the manner in which the thing has been put together.
UF building
CN K.KT.AFU.ALO.BCW.ARI

construction drawings
VD.117
ALT **construction drawing**
UF construction plans

drawings, construction
drawings, operational
operational drawings
plans, construction
CN V.VD.AFU.ALO.DCU.ARI

construction equipment
TB.16 (A,L,N,B)
UF building equipment
equipment, building
equipment, construction
CN V.TB.AFU.ARI.AFU

construction joints
TF.612 (L)
ALT **construction joint**
SN Interfaces or meeting surfaces between two successive pours of concrete. (MEANS)
UF joints, construction
CN V.TF.ALO.ARI.AFU.ALO

construction loads
BM.1008
UF loads, construction
CN B.BM.CFS.AXC.CLM.ALO.ARI.AXC

construction materials
USE **building materials**

construction plans
USE **construction drawings**

construction sites
USE **building sites**

construction workers
HG.581 (A,L)
ALT **construction worker**
SN Use for all types of laborers employed in building construction, including skilled and unskilled workers.
UF workers, construction
CN H.HG.AFU.AXC.BZY.AFU

construction, balloon frame
USE **balloon frames**

construction, bombproof
USE **bombproof construction**

construction, cantilever
USE **cantilever construction**

construction, composite
USE **composite construction**

construction, cross-wall
USE **box frames**

construction, drywall
USE **drywall construction**

construction, earthquake-resistant
USE **earthquake-resistant construction**

construction, fire-resistive
USE **fire-resistive construction**

construction, fireproof
USE **fire-resistive construction**

construction, flat slab
USE **flat slab systems**

construction, frame
USE **frame construction**

construction, half-timber
USE **half-timber construction**

construction, lightweight
USE **lightweight construction**

construction, log
USE **log construction**

construction, log-end
USE **stovewood construction**

construction, modular
USE **modular construction**

construction, monocoque
USE **monocoque construction**

construction, plank-and-beam
USE **post-and-beam structures**

construction, post-and-beam
USE **post-and-beam structures**

construction, post-and-lintel
USE **post-and-beam structures**

construction, reinforced monocoque
USE **monocoque construction**

construction, sandwich
USE **sandwich construction**

construction, semi-monocoque
USE **monocoque construction**

construction, shell
USE **shell structures**

construction, stackwood
USE **stovewood construction**

construction, stormproof
USE **stormproof construction**

construction, stovewood
USE **stovewood construction**

construction, stressed-skin
USE **stressed skin structures**

construction, thesaurus
USE **thesaurus construction**

construction, two-way
USE **two-way structural systems**

construction, unit
USE **modular construction**

construction, wood frame
USE **frame construction**

constructional steel, alloy
USE **high-strength low-alloy steel**

Constructionist
FL.3723 (R)
ALT **Constructionism**
SN Use especially with reference to certain work in Britain in the 1950s; can also refer to certain American and European works of the 1930s and 1940s.
UF Structurist
CN F.FL.ALO.BUE.ARI.BUE

constructions, waffle flat plate
USE **waffle slabs**

Constructivist
FL.3412 (A,L,B,R)
ALT **Constructivism**
UF Productivist
CN F.FL.ALO.BCW.ALO.AXC.DIO.BZY.AFU

constructors
HG.610
ALT **constructor**
SN Naval officers supervising the construction and repair of ships. (W)
CN H.HG.AFU.AXC.BZY.AFU.FCS.AFU

Consulat
FL.3358 (R)
CN F.FL.ALO.BCW.ALO.AXC.DIO.BCW.ALO.AFU.AFU

consulates
RK.971 (A,L,B)
ALT **consulate**
SN Use for the official headquarters of foreign ministers appointed primarily to oversee and protect the home country's economic interests in a host country; when such headquarters are for ministers called ambassadors appointed to transact matters of international policy and business with a foreign government, use **embassy buildings.** For the official residences of foreign ministers in general; use **legations.**
CN V.RK.AFU.ALO.ALO.ERE.AFU.ALO.AFU

consuls
HG.673 (L)
ALT **consul**
SN Officials appointed by or with the authority of a government to reside in a foreign country in order to represent the interests of citizens of the appointing country. (W)
CN H.HG.AFU.AXC.CFS.CFS.ALO

consultants
HG.711 (L)
ALT **consultant**
SN Use for persons called on for professional advice or services regarding matters in the field of their special knowledge or training,(W) usually for specific projects or problems. For persons who give advice either professionally or nonprofessionally, usually on an ongoing basis, use **advisors.**
CN H.HG.AFU.BCW.BIQ

consulting
KG.35
SN Providing professional or expert advice. (WCOL)
CN K.KG.AFU.AFU.ALO.ARI

consumers
HG.413 (L,R)
ALT consumer
CN H.HG.AFU.AXC.BOK.CLM

consumption, energy
USE **energy consumption**

consumption, fuel
USE **fuel consumption**

contact photoprints
USE **contact prints**

contact printers
TB.328 (N)
ALT contact printer
SN Devices used for making contact prints, having a frame for holding printing paper and negatives together and a light source for making an exposure. (RHDEL2)
UF printers, contact
CN V.TB.AFU.ARI.CLM.ARI.ALO.ALO

contact printing
KT.409
SN Making photographic prints by placing a negative in contact with sensitized paper and exposing the sandwich to strong light, giving a print the same size as the negative. Many 19th-century printing processes employed contact printing because they required exposure to intense light.
UF printing, contact
CN K.KT.AFU.ALO.DUC.DIO.ARI.AXC.BCW

contact prints
VJ.110 (L)
ALT contact print
SN Prints made by interfacing a negative and a sheet of photographic paper and exposing the paper with raw light. (SWED)
UF contact photoprints
lumiprints
photoprints, contact
prints, contact
CN V.VJ.AFU.ARI.ALO.AXC

contact sheets
VJ.111
ALT contact sheet
SN Use for contact prints containing prints from more than one negative, usually from all the negatives on a roll of film.
UF prints, proof
proof prints
proof sheets
sheets, contact
sheets, proof
CN V.VJ.AFU.ARI.ALO.AXC.AFU

contadores
TG.413
ALT contador
SN Portuguese paneled cabinets on stands. (PAYNE)
CN V.TG.AFU.AFU.AXC.ALO.ARI.AFU.ALO.AFU

containment buildings
USE **reactor containment buildings**

containment buildings, reactor
USE **reactor containment buildings**

containment, cost
USE **cost control**

conté
USE **Conté crayon (TM)**

Conté crayon (TM)
MT.47
SN Hard crayons made of a mixture of graphite and clay in white, sepia, sanguine, and three grades of black. (W)
UF conté
crayon, Conté (TM)
CN M.MT.AFU.AFU.AFU.ARI.ALO.AFU

Conté crayons (TM)
TB.242
ALT Conté crayon (TM)
SN French crayons made of graphite and clay in the form of square sticks and wood-encased pencils; used in chalk and hard-pastel drawings and lithography. (MAYER)
UF crayons, Conté (TM)
CN V.TB.AFU.ARI.CLM.AFU.ALO.AXC.AFU

Conte Polychrome
FL.1090
UF Cocle, Early
Early Cocle
Polychrome, Conte
CN F.FL.ALO.ALO.ALO.ALO.ALO.ALO.AFU.BCW

content analysis
USE **subject analysis**

contests
KM.41 (L)
CN K.KM.AFU.AXC

contextualism
BM.317 (A)
CN B.BM.AFU.AXC.ELK.AFU.AFU

continental displacement
USE **continental drift**

continental drift
KM.104 (L)
UF continental displacement
displacement, continental
drift, continental
CN K.KM.AFU.CXA.ALO.AFU

continental log house
USE **log houses**

continental masses
USE **continents**

continents
RD.179 (L,R)
ALT continent
UF continental masses
CN V.RD.ARI.AFU.AXC.AFU.AFU.AFU.AFU

continuing education
KD.127 (L)
UF education, continuing
education, lifelong
learning, lifelong
lifelong education
lifelong learning
CN K.KD.AFU.ALO.BOK.AFU.AXC.AFU

continuing education centers
RK.850 (L)
ALT continuing education center
UF adult education centers
centers, adult education
centers, continuing education
CN V.RK.AFU.ALO.ALO.CXA.ARI.AXC.BOK

continuity
USE **rhythm**

continuous
USE **unbroken**

continuous-arm armchairs, Windsor
USE **continuous-bow Windsor armchairs**

continuous arm chairs
USE **continuous-bow Windsor armchairs**

continuous arm Windsor chairs
USE **continuous-bow Windsor armchairs**

continuous barns
USE **connected barns**

continuous beams
RT.316
ALT continuous beam
SN Use for beams with three or more supports.
UF beams, continuous
CN V.RT.AFU.AFU.AFU.BCW.ALO.ARI.AFU

continuous-bow Windsor armchairs
TG.99
ALT continuous-bow Windsor armchair
SN Windsor armchairs having a back of medium height consisting of back spindles contained within a bent bow that continues forward to form arms; frequently with a back brace. (EVANS)
UF arm chairs, continuous
armchairs, continuous-bow Windsor

armchairs, Winsor continuous-bow
chairs, continuous arm
chairs, continuous arm Windsor
continuous-arm armchairs, Windsor
continuous arm chairs
continuous arm Windsor chairs
Windsor armchairs, continuous-bow
Windsor chairs, continuous arm
Windsor continuous-arm armchairs
CN V.TG.AFU.AFU.ALO.AFU.AFU.AFU.MLC.ARI

continuous bridges
RK.1275 (L)
ALT **continuous bridge**
UF bridges, continuous
continuous span bridges
CN V.RK.AFU.ALO.ALO.GLI.ALO.AFU.AFU.ALO

continuous casting
KT.131 (L)
UF casting, continuous
CN K.KT.AFU.ALO.DOI.ARI.AFU

continuous footings
RT.174
ALT continuous footing
SN Use for footings that support a number of columns in a line or walk.
UF footings, continuous
footings, strap
footings, strip
strap footings
strip footings
CN V.RT.AFU.AFU.AFU.AXC.BUE.ARI.ALO.AFU.ARI

continuous girders
RT.299 (L)
ALT **continuous girder**
SN Girders with more than two supports. (DAC)
UF girders, continuous
CN V.RT.AFU.AFU.AFU.BCW.ALO.AFU.BIQ.AFU

continuous hinges
TF.106
ALT **continuous hinge**
UF hinges, continuous
piano hinges
CN V.TF.AFU.AFU.AFU.AFU.CLM.AFU.BIQ

continuous inserts
USE **channel inserts**

continuous kilns
USE **tunnel kilns**

continuous linear pattern
USE **running ornament**

continuous narration
USE **continuous representation**

continuous representation
BM.141
SN Pictorial narrative featuring two or more successive actions from the same story within one setting. A character may, therefore, appear more than once in the same painting or sculpture. (RHLPS)
UF continuous narration
narration, continuous
representation, continuous
CN B.BM.AFU.AFU.ARI.BOK.ARI

continuous span bridges
USE **continuous bridges**

contour
BM.69
SN The outer boundary of an object or shape, especially when it suggests volume or mass. (A-Z)
UF edge (contour)
CN B.BM.AFU.AFU.ARI.AFU.CLM.AFU

contour drawing
KT.193
UF contour line drawing
drawing, contour
CN K.KT.AFU.ALO.DUC.BZY.ALO.AXC

contour drawing, blind
USE **blind contour drawing**

contour drawing, cross
USE **cross-contour drawing**

contour drawings
VD.130
ALT **contour drawing**
SN Distinct from **outline drawings** in that the lines in contour drawings also follow major spatial edges within an outline; distinct from **contour maps**, which delineate contours at regular intervals of elevation; distinct from **cross-contour drawings**, in which the lines follow contours across the surface of the form.
UF drawings, contour
line drawing, contour
CN V.VD.AFU.AXC.BIQ.AFU

contour drawings, blind
USE **blind contour drawings**

contour line drawing
USE **contour drawing**

contour maps
VW.159
ALT **contour map**
SN Maps showing elevation and the configuration of the ground by the use of contour lines and usually lacking other detail.
UF maps, contour
CN V.VW.AFU.AFU.AFU.FZU.AXC.AFU.ARI.AFU.CXA.AFU

contour sanders
TB.522
ALT **contour sander**
SN Sanders shaped so that they can be used to smooth complex moldings. (HAND)
UF sanders, contour
sanding slips
slips, sanding
CN V.TB.AFU.ARI.EWY.ALO.CXA.ALO

contract awards
VW.872
ALT **contract award**
UF awards, contract
CN V.VW.AFU.ARI.AFU.BOK.AXC

contract documents
VW.790 (B)
ALT **contract document**
SN Use with specific reference to documents, such as drawings and specifications, associated with a construction project.
UF documents, contract
CN V.VW.AFU.ARI.AFU.ARI.AFU

contract drawings
VD.93
ALT **contract drawing**
SN Use for drawings that form part of a contract agreement and on the basis of which the contractor, architect, or artist is legally obliged to produce the drawings, building, painting, or other commissioned work.
UF drawings, contract
CN V.VD.AFU.ALO.ARI

contracting
KG.192 (L)
SN Hiring of another party by a government agency or business organization to perform parts of an operation, rather than performing the tasks themselves. (W)
UF contracting out
CN K.KG.AFU.ALO.BCW.AFU

contracting out
USE **contracting**

contraction
KT.913
SN The action or process of becoming smaller, shorter, or pressed together. (W)
CN K.KT.ALO.BUE.AFU

contraction joints
TF.603
ALT **contraction joint**
SN Joints that allow for contraction of two adjacent parts of a structure.
UF joints, contraction
CN V.TF.ALO.ALO.AFU

contractors
HG.616 (L,B)
ALT **contractor**
SN Persons who perform work or provide supplies on a large scale according to a contractual agreement. (W)
CN H.HG.AFU.AXC.BZY.ALO

contractors, general
USE **general contractors**

contractors, main
USE **general contractors**

contractors, prime
USE **prime contractors**

contracts
VW.880 (L,N,B)
ALT **contract**
SN Documents, enforceable by law, embodying agreements between two or more competent parties to do or not to do something, and specifying the terms and conditions of the agreement.
CN V.VW.AFU.ARI.AFU.BOK.BOK.ALO.ALO

contracts, architect-consultant
USE **architect-consultant contracts**

contracts, artists'
USE **artists' contracts**

contracts, cost plus fee
USE **cost plus fee agreements**

contracts, cost reimbursement
USE **cost reimbursement contracts**

contracts, discharges of
USE **discharges of contracts**

contracts, divided
USE **divided contracts**

contracts, firm price
USE **fixed-price contracts**

contracts, fixed-price
USE **fixed-price contracts**

contracts, government
USE **government contracts**

contracts, lump sum
USE **fixed-price contracts**

contracts, public
USE **government contracts**

contracts, separate
USE **separate contracts**

contracts, single
USE **single contracts**

contracts, turnkey
USE **turnkey contracts**

contrapposto
BM.163 (R)
SN Position of the depicted human body, balanced but asymmetrical, in which twisting or bending of the body's vertical axis results in hips, shoulders, and head turned or tipped in different directions.
CN B.BM.AFU.AFU.ARI.BOK.CRG.AFU

contrast, simultaneous
USE **simultaneous contrast**

contrasted arches
USE **ogee arches**

contributions
USE **donations**

control joints
TF.604
ALT **control joint**
SN Shallow grooves in masonry or concrete designed to control and guide stresses and resultant cracking or separation.
UF joints, control
CN V.TF.ALO.ALO.ALO

control rooms
RM.227 (A)
ALT **control room**
SN Use for rooms containing control equipment, common examples being in broadcasting studios, auditoriums, and theaters.
UF rooms, control
CN V.RM.AFU.DIO.ALO.DOI.BCW

control towers
RK.1235 (A,L,N,B)
ALT **control tower**
UF airport control towers
towers, control
traffic control towers (airports)
CN V.RK.AFU.ALO.ALO.GLI.AFU.AFU.ALO

control, authority
USE **authority control**

control, avalanche
USE **avalanche protection**

control, cost
USE **cost control**

control, environmental
USE **environmental policy**

control, eviction
USE **rent control**

control, flood
USE **flood control**

control, humidity
USE **humidity control**

control, inventory
USE **inventorying**

control, landslide
USE **landslide protection**

control, noise
USE **noise control**

control, pollution
USE **pollution control**

control, quality
USE **quality control**

control, rent
USE **rent control**

control, rent and eviction
USE **rent control**

control, terminological
USE **authority control**

control, vocabulary
USE **authority control**

controlled access highways
USE **limited access highways**

controllers
USE **comptrollers**

conurbations
RD.18 (L,B)
ALT **conurbation**
SN Extensive built-up urban areas that contain some isolated rural areas and are formed by the merging together of cities or towns that formerly were separate. For more extensive or comprehensive clusters of urban areas, use **megalopolises.**
CN V.RD.AFU.AFU.ALO.BIQ.AFU

convalescent homes
USE **convalescent hospitals**

convalescent hospitals
RK.764 (A,L,B,R)
ALT **convalescent hospital**
UF convalescent homes
homes, convalescent
hospitals, convalescent
CN V.RK.AFU.ALO.ALO.CXA.ALO.AFU.BCW.ALO.ARI

convectors
RT.1429
ALT **convector**
CN V.RT.ALO.BCW.AFU.ALO.ALO.ALO

convenience stores
RK.171 (A,L)
ALT **convenience store**
UF stores, convenience
CN V.RK.AFU.ALO.ALO.ALO.ARI.BIQ.ALO.ARI

conventicles
RM.317
ALT **conventicle**
SN Rooms or buildings used for secret or nonconformist worship.
CN V.RM.AFU.DIO.AXC.ALO.AFU.BUE

convention centers
RK.1193 (A,L,B)
ALT **convention center**
UF centers, conference
centers, convention
conference centers
conference facilities
congress facilities
convention facilities
convention halls
facilities, conference
facilities, congress

halls, convention
CN V.RK.AFU.ALO.ALO.FUA.ARI

convention facilities
USE **convention centers**

convention halls
USE **convention centers**

conventional locks
USE **mortise locks**

conventions
USE **conferences**

convents
RG.190 (A,L,B,R)
ALT **convent**
UF buildings, conventual
conventual buildings
nunneries
CN V.RG.AFU.AFU.DUC.ALO

conventual buildings
USE **convents**

conventual churches
USE **abbey churches**

conversation chairs
USE **voyeuses**

conversation-seats
USE **voyeuses**

conversion of buildings
USE **adaptive reuse**

conversion plants, ocean thermal energy
USE **ocean thermal energy conversion plants**

conversion tables
VW.250 (L)
ALT **conversion table**
UF tables, conversion
CN V.VW.AFU.AFU.AFU.FZU.AXC.BCW.AFU

conversion, data
USE **data conversion**

conversion, retrospective
USE **retrospective conversion**

convertible bedroom pianos
USE **piano beds**

convertible beds
USE **sofa beds**

convertible furniture
USE **folding furniture**

convertible lenses
TB.316
ALT **convertible lens**
SN Camera lenses that consist of several elements which can be used in various combinations to provide different focal lengths. (QUICK)
UF lenses, convertible
lenses, separable
separable lenses
CN V.TB.AFU.ARI.CLM.ARI.AFU.ALO.BOK.AFU

convertible sofas
USE **sofa beds**

convex
DC.63
SN Curved or rounded outward like the exterior curve of a circle or sphere.
CN D.DC.AFU.ARI.BOK.ALO

convex conoidal vaults
RT.546
ALT **convex conoidal vault**
SN Conoidal vaults with a curved ridge, the expansion being in a vertical direction only.
UF conoidal vaults, convex
vaults, convex conoidal
CN V.RT.AFU.AFU.AFU.BIQ.BOK.AFU.ALO.ALO.AFU.AFU

convex planes
USE **guttering planes**

conveyances
VW.924
ALT **conveyance**
SN Documents, such as deeds, by which title to property is conveyed from one person to another. (W)
UF conveyances, property
property conveyances
CN V.VW.AFU.ARI.AFU.BZY.AFU

conveyances, property
USE **conveyances**

conveying machinery
USE **conveyors**

conveying systems
RT.1293
ALT **conveying system**
UF systems, conveying
CN V.RT.ALO.ALO.AFU

conveyors
TB.365 (L,N,B)
ALT **conveyor**
SN Motor-driven machines, such as endless belts or a series of rollers, used for the continuous transport of material. (DAC)
UF conveying machinery
machinery, conveying
CN V.TB.AFU.ARI.DCU.AFU.AFU

conveyors, belt
USE **belt conveyors**

conveyors, chain
USE **chain conveyors**

conveyors, passenger
USE **moving walkways**

conveyors, roller
USE **roller conveyors**

conveyors, slat
USE **slat conveyors**

conveyors, vibrating
USE **vibrating conveyors**

convicting
KG.201
SN Proving, finding, or judging a person guilty of an offense or crime. (W)
CN K.KG.AFU.ALO.BCW.BOK.AFU

convicts
USE **prisoners**

convocations
KM.14
SN Assemblies of members of a college or university to observe a particular ceremony, such as the opening of the academic year or the announcing of prizes, awards, and honors. (W)
CN K.KM.AFU.ARI.AFU.ALO

Cook Island
FL.3689 (L,B)
UF Hervey Island
Tarawa Atoll
CN F.FL.ALO.BOK.AXC.ALO

cookbooks
VW.525 (L,R)
ALT **cookbook**
UF books, receipt
books, recipe
receipt books
recipe books
CN V.VW.AFU.ALO.AFU.AFU.ALO.ARI

cool colors
BM.110
SN Colors commonly associated with air, sky, and water, such as green, greenish blue, and violet, which suggest coolness and which normally appear to recede.
UF colors, cool
CN B.BM.AFU.AFU.ARI.BOK.ALO.AFU.ALO

Cool Realist
USE **Photorealist**

coolants
MT.2583
CN M.MT.AFU.ARI.DCU

coolers (wine coolers)
USE **wine coolers**

coolers, cold storage
USE **cold storage rooms**

coolers, wine
USE **wine coolers**

cooling
KT.728 (L)
ALT **cooled**
CN K.KT.AFU.ALO.GWW.ALO

cooling coils
RT.1421
ALT **cooling coil**
UF air-cooling coils
coils, air cooling
coils, cooling
CN V.RT.ALO.BCW.AFU.ALO.AFU.BCW.AFU.AFU

cooling systems
USE **air cooling**

cooling towers
RT.1414 (L,B)
ALT **cooling tower**
SN Outdoor structures frequently placed on roofs, through which warm water is circulated to cool it by evaporation and exposure to the air. (MEANS)
UF towers, cooling
CN V.RT.ALO.BCW.AFU.ALO.AFU.ARI

cooper's adzes
TB.813 (N)
ALT **cooper's adz**
SN Short handled tools where the handle is often wedged into the head to lean sharply towards the blade. (SALAM)
UF adzes, cooper's
CN V.TB.AFU.BCW.CFS.ALO.AFU.AFU.AXC

cooper's hollowing drawknives
USE **hollowing drawknives**

cooper's jointer planes
TB.936
ALT **cooper's jointer plane**
SN Planes as large as 5 to 6 feet in length which are turned upside down and mounted on legs. The wood to be planed is slid over the plane.
UF jointer planes, cooper's
long-jointer planes
planes, cooper's jointer
planes, long-jointer
CN V.TB.AFU.BCW.CFS.ALO.AFU.DUC.ARI.AFU.ARI.AFU

cooper's levellers
USE **sun-planes**

cooper's stoup planes
TB.943 (N)
ALT **cooper's stoup plane**
SN Coffin-shaped planes, similar to smoothing planes except that they are round in both planes on the bottom, with a 2 inch single or double iron made in different sizes to fit the barrel it is cleaning and smoothing. (SALAM)
UF cleaning-out planes
inside planes
planes, cleaning-out
planes, cooper's stoup
planes, inside
planes, round-both-ways
round-both-ways planes
CN V.TB.AFU.BCW.CFS.ALO.AFU.DUC.ARI.ARI

cooper's whittles
USE **hoop-notching knives**

cooperage
USE **coopering**

cooperative apartment houses
RK.363 (A,L)
ALT **cooperative apartment house**
SN Apartment houses owned and managed by a corporation in which shares are sold entitling shareholders to occupy individual units in the building. (RHDEL2)
UF apartment houses, cooperative
apartments, cooperative
co-ops
cooperative apartments
cooperatives
CN V.RK.AFU.ALO.ALO.AXC.AXC.ALO.AFU

cooperative apartments
USE **cooperative apartment houses**

cooperative housing
RG.92 (A,L,B)
SN Housing owned by a legal entity that permits a group of members to mutually own all, or agreed-upon parts, of the complex and to share mutually in the benefits derived by the group under provisions of the entity's rules. (DDT)
UF co-ops
housing, cooperative
CN V.RG.AFU.AFU.BOK.BIQ.ARI

cooperative stores
RK.172 (L,B)
ALT **cooperative store**
UF co-ops
stores, cooperative
CN V.RK.AFU.ALO.ALO.ALO.ARI.BIQ.ALO.AXC

cooperatives
USE **cooperative apartment houses**

coopered joints
TF.583
ALT **coopered joint**
SN Joints made on a curved surface similar to the joints made between the staves of a barrel. (MEANS)
UF joints, coopered
CN V.TF.ALO.AFU.BZY

coopering
KT.521 (L)
SN The construction of barrels or casks.
UF cooperage
CN K.KT.AFU.ALO.ELK.BIQ

coopers
HG.544 (L)
ALT **cooper**
SN Persons who make or repair wooden casks or tubs; also shipboard artisans who repair casks and other vessels. (W)
CN H.HG.AFU.AXC.BUE.ARI.DIO.AFU

coops, chicken
USE **chicken houses**

coordinating
KG.146
SN Causing discrete agents or agencies to work together. (RLG7)
CN K.KG.AFU.AFU.BIQ.BCW

coordination, dimensional
USE **modular coordination**

coordination, modular
USE **modular coordination**

Coos
FL.1339 (L)
UF Kusan
CN F.FL.ALO.ALO.ARI.AFU.BIQ.BIQ

Copador
FL.1080
CN F.FL.ALO.ALO.ALO.ALO.ALO.AFU.ARI

copaiba balsam
MT.1471 (L)
SN A viscous fluid oleoresin obtained from several species of tropical trees. (MAYER)
UF balsam, copaiba
CN M.MT.AFU.AFU.ALO.BOK.AFU.ARI

copal
MT.1480 (L)
SN A general name for fossil and other hard resins found in nearly all tropical countries and used in making varnishes, laquers, adhesives, and coatings. (MH)
CN M.MT.AFU.AFU.ALO.BOK.ARI

copal varnishes
MT.2487
UF varnishes, copal
CN M.MT.AFU.ARI.CRG.AFU.BOK.ALO.ARI.AFU

copal, Congo
USE **Congo copal**

copal, East African
USE **East African copal**

copal, kauri
USE **kauri**

copal, Manila
USE **Manila copal**

copal, Sierra Leone
USE **Sierra Leone copal**

copal, Zanzibar
USE **Zanzibar copal**

cope chisels
USE **cape chisels**

coped joints
TF.671
ALT **coped joint**
SN Intersections consisting of two pieces of molding where one is cut to fit the contour of the other. (MEANS)
UF joints, coped
joints, scribed
scribed joints
CN V.TF.ALO.ARI.AXC.ALO.AFU

copen blue
USE **light blue**
moderate blue
strong blue

copen blue, bright
USE **strong blue**

copen blue, light
USE **light blue**

Copena
FL.889
CN F.FL.ALO.ALO.ALO.AFU.ALO.ALO.BOK.ARI

copies
VB.114 (R)
ALT **copy**
SN Use for objects or documents made to resemble other, existing objects or documents. Implies less precise and faithful imitation than does the term **reproductions.** When copies are presented with intent to deceive, use **forgeries** or **counterfeits.** When more than one similar work is produced by the same maker, use **replicas** or **versions.** Use for photographs when the image is more than one generation removed from an original photographic image.
UF imitations
CN V.VB.ALO.BZY.AFU

copies, carbon
USE **carbon copies**

copies, electrostatic
USE **electrostatic copies**

copies, letterpress
USE **letterpress copies**

copies, master
USE **master copies**

copies, mimeograph
USE **mimeograph copies**

copies, multilith
USE **multigraphs**

copies, xerographic
USE **xerographic copies**

coping
RT.733
SN Protective caps, tops, or covers of a wall, parapet, or other structure, often of stone, terracotta, or metal. (DAC)
CN V.RT.AFU.ALO.AFU.ARI

coping brick
USE **capping brick**

coping saws
TB.1008 (N)
ALT **coping saw**
SN Light hand saws with a narrow blade mounted in a U-shaped frame with a handle; used to cut curves in wood. The blade may be rotated to keep the frame away from the work. (MEANS)
UF saws, coping
saws, scribing
scribing saws
CN V.TB.AFU.BCW.CFS.ALO.AFU.EWY.BCW.ARI

copolymer, acrylonitrile-butadiene-styrene
USE **acrylonitrile-butadiene-styrene copolymer**

copolymer, sytrene-butadiene
USE **styrene-butadiene rubber**

copolymer, tetrole
USE **furan**

copolymer, vinyl
USE **vinyl**

copper
MT.434 (A,L,B,R)
CN M.MT.AFU.AFU.AFU.BZY.AFU.AFU.ARI.BCW

copper (color)
USE **grayish reddish orange**
moderate orange
moderate reddish orange

Copper Age
USE **Chalcolithic**

copper alloys
MT.368 (L,B)
UF alloys, copper
CN M.MT.AFU.AFU.AFU.BZY.AFU.AFU.AFU.ALO.ARI

copper arsenate, ammoniacal
USE **ammoniacal copper arsenate**

copper arsenate, chromated
USE **chromated copper arsenate**

copper basic acetate
USE **verdigris**

copper-beryllium alloys
MT.370 (L)
SN Alloys of copper and beryllium containing usually not more than 3% beryllium. The alloys have a bronze-like, crystalline structure and are unsurpassed in their ability to withstand fatigue, wear, and corrosion and in their electrical conductivity at high temperatures.
UF alloys, copper-beryllium
beryllium bronze
beryllium copper
bronze, beryllium
copper, beryllium
CN M.MT.AFU.AFU.AFU.BZY.AFU.AFU.AFU.ALO.ARI.ALO

copper blue
USE **Bremen blue**
azurite

copper brick
MT.103 (B)
UF brick, copper
CN M.MT.AFU.AFU.AFU.AXC.ALO.AFU.ALO.BOK.AFU

copper brown, light
USE **strong brown**

copper chromate, acid
USE **acid copper chromate**

Copper Culture, Old
USE **Old Copper Culture**

copper enameling
KT.663 (L)
UF enameling, copper
CN K.KT.AFU.ALO.GRC.AFU.ALO.AXC

Copper Inuit
FL.1209
UF Inuit, Copper
CN F.FL.ALO.ALO.ARI.AFU.AFU.AFU.ALO.AFU.ARI

copper mines
RG.99 (L)
ALT **copper mine**
UF mines, copper
CN V.RG.AFU.AFU.BUE.AFU.ALO.ALO

copper-nickel alloys
MT.371 (L)
UF alloys, copper-nickel
alloys, nickel-copper
nickel-copper alloys
CN M.MT.AFU.AFU.AFU.BZY.AFU.AFU.AFU.ALO.ARI.ARI

copper ore, green
USE **malachite**

copper points
TB.255
ALT **copper point**
SN Points or styluses of copper used as drawing instruments. (GETTEN)
UF points, copper
CN V.TB.AFU.ARI.CLM.AFU.ALO.CLM.AFU

copper resinate
MT.1652
UF resinate, copper
CN M.MT.AFU.AFU.ARI.AFU.AFU.ALO.ALO.AXC.ARI.BCW

copper-silicon alloys
MT.372
UF alloys, copper-silicon
CN M.MT.AFU.AFU.AFU.BZY.AFU.AFU.AFU.ALO.ARI.AXC

copper-tin alloys
MT.373 (L)
UF alloys, copper-tin
CN M.MT.AFU.AFU.AFU.BZY.AFU.AFU.AFU.ALO.ARI.BCW

copper-zinc alloys
MT.384 (L)
UF alloys, copper-zinc
CN M.MT.AFU.AFU.AFU.BZY.AFU.AFU.AFU.ALO.ARI.BIQ

copper, beryllium
USE **copper-beryllium alloys**

coppers, soldering
USE **soldering irons**

coppersmithing
KT.780 (L)
CN K.KT.AFU.ALO.HOE.BCW.AFU.ARI

coppersmiths
HG.494 (L)
ALT **coppersmith**
SN Persons who work in copper, especially those who make objects such as kettles, coils, tubing, and fittings.
CN H.HG.AFU.AXC.BUE.ARI.CFS.AFU.ARI

copperwork
MT.2767 (L)
CN M.MT.AFU.AXC.BOK.ALO

Coptic
BM.643 (A,L,B,R)
SN Use with reference to the Egyptian Christian church; with reference specifically to the Early Medieval period in Egypt, use **Coptic (period)**.
CN B.BM.BZY.AFU.ALO.AXC.AFU

Coptic (period)
FL.2834 (A,L,B,R)
CN F.FL.ALO.AXC.ALO.ARI.AFU.CRG

copy art
BM.257 (L,R)
UF art, copy
art, reprographic
art, xerographic
art, Xerox
generative systems (copy art)
reprographic art
systems, generative (copy art)
xerographic art
Xerox art
CN B.BM.AFU.ARI.BCW.FOG.ARI

copybooks
VW.498 (L)
ALT **copybook**
SN Books in which copies, especially of penmanship, are written or printed for learners to imitate. (GAHLM)
UF books, penmanship
penmanship books
CN V.VW.AFU.ALO.AFU.AFU.AFU.BOK

copybooks (pattern books)
USE **pattern books**

copybooks, letterpress
USE **letterpress copybooks**

copying
KT.179 (L,B)
ALT **copied**
SN Use for any of various processes involved in the reproduction of documents or other artifacts. Use a more specific term if possible.
UF duplicating
duplicating processes
CN K.KT.AFU.ALO.DUC.BOK

copying processes, fluid
USE **spirit duplicating**

copying, electrostatic
USE **electrostatic printing**

copying, heat
USE **thermography**

copying, thermal
USE **thermography**

copying, thermic
USE **thermography**

copyists
HG.469 (L,R)
ALT **copyist**
SN People employed to make copies of hand-written documents.
CN H.HG.AFU.AXC.BUE.ALO.CRG.AFU

copyright
BM.466 (A,L,B,R)
SN Exclusive, legally secured right to reproduce (as by writing or printing), publish, and sell the matter and form of a literary, musical, or artistic work. (W)
CN B.BM.BCW.CXA.AFU.AXC.AFU

copyright certificates
VW.302
ALT **copyright certificate**
UF certificates, copyright
CN V.VW.AFU.AFU.ALO.AXC.ARI

coquillage
DG.4
SN Use for shell-like ornament, especially of the Rococo period.
CN D.DG.AFU.AFU.ALO

coquille board
MT.1913
SN An artist's white drawing board with stippled texture that produces a dotted drawing. (W)
UF board, coquille
CN M.MT.AFU.AFU.ARI.ALO.ALO.AXC.ALO.BIQ.AFU.ALO.AFU

coquilliers
TG.427
ALT **coquillier**
SN 18th-century French cabinets with small drawers designed to house a collection of shells; fashionable between 1730 and 1750. (HAYWAR)
CN V.TG.AFU.AFU.AXC.ALO.ARI.ALO.AXC.ARI.AFU

coquina
USE **coquina rock**

coquina rock
MT.660
SN Limestone composed of loosely cohering shell fragments cemented together by an infiltration of carbonate of lime. (STEIN)
UF coquina
rock, coquina
shellstone
CN M.MT.AFU.AFU.AFU.DCU.AFU.ALO.AFU.ALO.ALO.AFU.AFU.AFU.BCW.ARI

Cora
FL.1489 (L)
UF Nayarit (Cora)
CN F.FL.ALO.ALO.ARI.ALO.AFU.AFU

coral
MT.917 (L,R)
CN M.MT.AFU.AFU.ALO.AFU.BIQ

coral limestone
MT.655
UF bird's eye marble
coral rag
coral rock
coral stone
coraliferous limestone
corallian oolite
limestone, coral
limestone, coraliferous
marble, bird's eye
oolite, corallian
rag, coral
rock, coral
stone, coral
CN M.MT.AFU.AFU.AFU.DCU.AFU.ALO.AFU.ALO.ALO.AFU.AFU.AFU.ARI

coral rag
USE **coral limestone**

coral rock
USE **coral limestone**

coral stone
USE **coral limestone**

coral, star
USE **star coral**

coraliferous limestone
USE **coral limestone**

corallian oolite
USE **coral limestone**

corbel arches
RT.250
ALT **corbel arch**
SN Masonry constructions whose arch-like form is created by uniformly advancing courses from each springing until they meet at the span's midpoint; not true arches.
UF arches, corbel
CN V.RT.AFU.AFU.AFU.BCW.AFU.AFU.AFU.ELK.ALO

corbel courses
USE **corbel tables**

corbel gables
USE **crow-stepped gables**

corbel steps
USE **crowsteps**

corbel tables
RT.616
ALT **corbel table**
SN Masonry courses acting as a corbel, or ornaments of similar appearance. (HAS)
UF corbel courses
courses, corbel
tables, corbel
CN V.RT.AFU.AFU.AFU.BIQ.BUE.ALO.AFU.ALO.AXC

corbel vaults
RT.556
ALT **corbel vault**
SN Vaults constructed of corbels. (RS)
UF vaults, corbel
CN V.RT.AFU.AFU.AFU.BIQ.BOK.AFU.ARI.AFU.ARI.AFU

corbelling
USE **corbels**

corbels
RT.324 (A,L,B,R)
ALT **corbel**
SN In masonry, projections stepped progressively farther forward with height. (HAS)
UF corbelling
CN V.RT.AFU.AFU.AFU.BCW.BIQ

corbie gables
USE **crow-stepped gables**

corbiestepped gables
USE **crow-stepped gables**

corbiesteps
USE **crowsteps**

cord
MT.1973
CN M.MT.AFU.AFU.ARI.ALO.ALO.BIQ.AFU

cord marking
KT.861
ALT **cord marked**
SN A ceramic technique in which fine cord is wrapped around a paddle and pressed against an unfired clay vessel, leaving the cord imprint. (MUSER)
UF marking, cord
CN K.KT.AFU.ALO.HOE.BOK.ALO

Corded ware
FL.2488 (L)
UF Battle-ax
ware, Corded
CN F.FL.ALO.AXC.AFU.BCW.ARI

Cordilleran, Old
USE **Old Cordilleran**

cordons
USE **stringcourses**

cords, sash
USE **sash cords**

corduroy
MT.1861 (L)
CN M.MT.AFU.AFU.ARI.ALO.ALO.ALO.ALO.AXC

Corean
USE **Korean**

coremakers
HG.513 (L)
ALT **coremaker**
SN Persons who make sand cores for metal castings, clay cores for iron pipe, or metal cores for building tile. (W)
CN H.HG.AFU.AXC.BUE.ARI.CFS.ARI.AXC

cores (service cores)
USE **service cores**

coretti
RM.318
ALT **coretto**
SN Small galleries like the boxes of a theater, often inserted into the choir wall of Baroque churches. (BLUNT)
CN V.RM.AFU.DIO.AXC.ALO.AFU.BZY

Corinthian (architectural style)
FL.2588
CN F.FL.ALO.AXC.ALO.AFU.ALO.ARI.ALO

Corinthian (pottery style)
FL.2625
CN F.FL.ALO.AXC.ALO.AFU.ALO.AXC.ALO.BCW.AFU

Corinthian order
RT.52 (A,B,R)
UF order, Corinthian
CN V.RT.AFU.AFU.AFU.ARI.ARI.ALO

Corinthian, Early
USE **Early Corinthian**

Corinthian, Late
USE **Late Corinthian**

Corinthian, Middle
USE **Middle Corinthian**

cork
MT.1020 (A,L,B)
CN M.MT.AFU.AFU.ALO.BIQ.AFU.ALO

cork (blue pigment)
MT.1591 (L)
CN M.MT.AFU.AFU.ARI.AFU.AFU.ALO.ALO.ALO.ALO.AXC

cork black
USE **vine black**

corkboard
MT.1460
SN Construction board made by compressing granulated cork and subjecting it to heat so that the particles cement themselves together. (MH)
CN M.MT.AFU.AFU.ALO.BIQ.DCU.ALO.DOI.ARI

corkscrew stairs
USE **spiral stairs**

corn
MT.1068 (L)
CN M.MT.AFU.AFU.ALO.BIQ.CFS.AFU.ALO

corn houses
USE **corncribs**

corn oil
USE **maize oil**

corn palaces
RK.375 (L,R)
ALT **corn palace**
UF palaces, corn
CN V.RK.AFU.ALO.ALO.BCW.ALO

corn stalk, guinea
USE **guinea corn stalk**

corncribs
RK.97 (L,N)
ALT **corncrib**
SN Structures for storing corn, usually with slotted boards for ventilation, slanted walls for weather protection, and set on stilts to deter rodents. (BIGHSE)
UF corn houses
houses, corn
CN V.RK.AFU.ALO.ALO.AFU.ARI.AFU

cornelian
USE **carnelian**

corner
DC.15
CN D.DC.AFU.ALO.ALO.ALO

corner basin stands
TG.659
ALT **corner basin stand**
UF basin stands, corner
stands, corner basin

CN V.TG.AFU.AFU.BIQ.BCW.ALO.FCS.
AFU.AFU

corner blocks
TG.866
ALT **corner block**
SN Reinforcing blocks glued, nailed, or screwed into the corner of a chair or sofa frame to hold the leg and seat rail together. (FAIRB)
UF blocks, corner
CN V.TG.ALO.CLM

corner boards
RT.611
ALT **corner board**
SN Boards which are used as trim on the external corner of a wood frame structure and against which the ends of the siding are fitted. (HAS)
UF boards, corner
CN V.RT.AFU.AFU.AFU.BIQ.BUE.ALO.
AFU.AFU

corner cabinets
TG.414 (N)
ALT **corner cabinet**
SN Cabinets designed to fit into a corner of a room, usually by being triangular.
UF cabinets, corner
meubles de coin
CN V.TG.AFU.AFU.AXC.ALO.ARI.AFU.
ARI

corner capitals
USE **angle capitals**

corner chairs
TG.54 (N)
ALT **corner chair**
UF angle chairs
barber's chairs (corner chairs)
burgomaster chairs
burgomeister chairs
chairs, angle
chairs, barber's (corner chairs)
chairs, burgomeister
chairs, corner
chairs, half-round
chairs, round (corner chairs)
chairs, roundabout
chairs, shaving
chairs, writing (corner chairs)
fauteuils en encoignures
half-round chairs
round chairs (corner chairs)
roundabout chairs
roundabouts
shaving chairs
writing chairs (corner chairs)
CN V.TG.AFU.AFU.ALO.AFU.AFU.AFU.
ERE

corner chisels
TB.855 (N)
ALT **corner chisel**
SN Chisels having two cutting edges which meet at right angles; used to cut corners of mortises. (DAC)
UF bruzz chisels
chisels, bruzz
chisels, corner
chisels, dogleg
dogleg chisels
CN V.TB.AFU.BCW.CFS.ALO.AFU.BUE.
ALO.ALO

corner clamps
TB.1051 (N)
ALT **corner clamp**
SN Clamps used to join corners during gluing.
UF clamps, corner
clamps, picture-framing
picture-framing clamps
CN V.TB.AFU.BCW.CFS.ALO.ALO.BCW.
ARI

corner clips
TF.330
ALT **corner clip**
UF clips, corner
CN V.TF.AFU.AFU.AFU.ALO.AFU.ARI.
ARI

corner commodes
TG.489
ALT **corner commode**
UF commodes, corner
CN V.TG.AFU.AFU.AXC.ALO.BCW.BZY.
BCW

corner cupboards
TG.503 (L,N)
ALT **corner cupboard**
SN Freestanding, built-in, or hanging cupboards made to fit the shape of a room's corner. (PAIN)
UF corner dish dressers
corners (cupboards)
cupboards, corner
dish dressers, corner
dressers, corner dish
CN V.TG.AFU.AFU.AXC.ALO.BUE.BCW

corner dish dressers
USE **corner cupboards**

corner double seams
TF.653
ALT **corner double seam**
UF double seams, corner
seams, corner double
CN V.TF.ALO.ARI.ARI.BUE.AXC

corner drills
USE **hand drills**

corner enclosed basin stands
TG.660
ALT **corner enclosed basin stand**
UF basin stands, corner enclosed
enclosed basin stands, corner
stands, corner enclosed basin
CN V.TG.AFU.AFU.BIQ.BCW.ALO.FCS.
AFU.AFU.AFU

corner saws
USE **dovetail saws**

corner shelves
TG.496
ALT **corner shelf**
UF corner stands
shelves, corner
stands, corner
CN V.TG.AFU.AFU.AXC.ALO.BIQ

corner stands
USE **corner shelves**

corner tables
USE **handkerchief tables**

corner trowels
TB.633
ALT **corner trowel**
SN Plasterer's trowels having a V-shaped blade made for working corners. (PUTNAM)
UF trowels, corner
CN V.TB.AFU.BCW.BCW.ALO.HCQ.ARI

corner trowels, inside
USE **inside corner trowels**

corner trowels, outside
USE **outside corner trowels**

corners (cupboards)
USE **corner cupboards**

corners (encoignures)
USE **encoignures**

corners, canted
USE **canted corners**

corners, chimney
USE **inglenooks**

corners, hollow
USE **hollow corners**

corners, ovolo
USE **ovolo corners**

corners, sash plan
USE **ovolo corners**

cornerstones
RT.668 (B)
ALT **cornerstone**
SN Stones forming part of corners or angles in walls, especially lying at the foundation of a principal angle. (W)
UF pillar-stones
CN V.RT.AFU.AFU.AFU.BIQ.BUE.ALO.
ALO.ALO

cornflower blue
MT.1592
UF blue, cornflower
CN M.MT.AFU.AFU.ARI.AFU.AFU.ALO.
ALO.ALO.ALO.BCW

cornflower blue (color)
USE **moderate purplish blue**

cornflower blue, light
USE **light purplish blue**
light violet
moderate purplish blue
moderate violet

cornice lighting
RT.1376
UF lighting, cornice
CN V.RT.ALO.AXC.AXC.ALO.AFU

cornice planes
TB.962 (N)
ALT cornice plane
SN General term for wide molding planes with a simple or complicated profile. (SALAM)
UF bed mold planes
cornish planes
crown mold planes
crown planes
mold planes, bed
mold planes, crown
planes, bed mold
planes, cornice
planes, cornish
planes, crown
planes, crown mold
CN V.TB.AFU.BCW.CFS.ALO.AFU.DUC.AXC.ALO.AFU

cornices
RT.333 (A,L,B,R)
ALT cornice
SN The projecting, uppermost features of classical entablatures; use also for similar features crowning a wall, in any style.
CN V.RT.AFU.AFU.AFU.BCW.BZY.ALO.ALO.AFU

cornices, architrave
USE **architrave cornices**

cornices, block
USE **block cornices**

cornices, cavetto
USE **cavetto cornices**

cornices, gorge
USE **cavetto cornices**

cornices, open
USE **open eaves**

cornices, raking
USE **raking cornices**

Cornish granite
MT.595
UF granite, Cornish
CN M.MT.AFU.AFU.AFU.DCU.AFU.AFU.AFU.AFU.AFU.ARI.ALO.AFU.ALO

cornish planes
USE **cornice planes**

cornstalk
MT.1074 (L)
CN M.MT.AFU.AFU.ALO.BIQ.CLM.AFU

corona discharge photography
USE **Kirlian photography**

coronary care units
RM.294 (L)
ALT coronary care unit
UF CCUs
CN V.RM.AFU.DIO.AXC.AFU.AXC.ALO

coronas
RT.339
ALT corona
SN Overhanging vertical members of a cornice, supported by bed moldings and crowned by cymatia, usually with a drip to throw rainwater clear of the building. (HAS)
CN V.RT.AFU.AFU.AFU.BCW.BZY.ALO.ALO.ALO.ALO

coronation chairs
USE **thrones**

coronations
KM.19 (L,R)
CN K.KM.AFU.ARI.ARI.ALO

Corondá
FL.1693
CN F.FL.ALO.ALO.ARI.ARI.BOK.BIQ

coronets (architectural elements)
RT.631
ALT coronet (architectural element)
SN Use for ornamental features, resembling but never constituting pediments, over doors or windows.
CN V.RT.AFU.AFU.AFU.BIQ.BUE.ALO.AFU.ARI.ARI

corporate collections
HG.849 (A,L,R)
ALT corporate collection
UF collections, corporate
CN H.HG.ALO.BUE.ALO

corporate files
USE **corporation records**

corporate headquarters
RK.917 (A,L)
UF headquarters, corporate
CN V.RK.AFU.ALO.ALO.DZW.ALO.ARI

corporate libraries
RK.704 (L)
ALT corporate library
UF libraries, corporate
CN V.RK.AFU.ALO.ALO.CRG.AXC.ALO.ARI.AFU

corporate plazas
USE **shopping plazas**

corporation records
VW.979 (L)
ALT corporation record
SN Records evidencing the creation or existence of a corporate body, such as charters or articles of incorporation; also used generally to refer to records growing out of a corporate enterprise. (GAHLM)
UF corporate files
files, corporate
records, corporation
CN V.VW.AFU.ARI.ALO.ARI

corporation reports
VW.451 (L)
ALT corporation report
UF annual reports of corporations
corporations, annual reports of
reports, corporation
CN V.VW.AFU.AFU.ALO.FIM.AFU.AFU.ALO

corporations
HG.843 (L)
ALT corporation
SN Groups of persons, commonly formed as business enterprises, considered in law as legal persons having an existence and rights and duties distinct from those of the individuals who form it. For unincorporated groups of persons contractually associated as joint principals in business, use **partnerships.**
UF companies, incorporated
incorporated companies
CN H.HG.ALO.BOK.AFU.AFU

corporations, annual reports of
USE **corporation reports**

corporations, directors of
USE **boards of directors**

corps de logis
RM.5
ALT corp de logis
SN Use to designate the central portions of a building as opposed to the terminal or end pavilions or other outlying portions, especially found in French architecture or in buildings closely derived from French architecture.
CN V.RM.AFU.AXC

corrals
RK.83
ALT corral
CN V.RK.AFU.ALO.ALO.AFU.ALO.AXC

correction, optical
USE **optical correction**

correctional facilities
USE **correctional institutions**

correctional institutions
RK.714 (A,L)
ALT correctional institution
SN Use to denote any buildings or groups of buildings in which people accused or convicted of breaking the law may be confined and which may or may not attempt some form of reform or rehabilitative correction of offenders.
UF correctional facilities
facilities, correctional
houses of correction
institutions, correctional

institutions, penal
penal institutions
CN V.RK.AFU.ALO.ALO.CXA.AFU

correctional institutions, medium-security
USE **medium-security prisons**

correctional institutions, minimum-security
USE **minimum-security prisons**

correlation
BM.825 (L)
CN B.BM.CFS.ARI.CRG.ALO.AFU

correspondence
VW.12 (L,R)
SN Any forms of addressed and written communication sent and received, including letters, postcards, memoranda, notes, telegrams, or cables. (ICA)
CN V.VW.AFU.AFU.AFU.BIQ

correspondence art
BM.258 (L,R)
UF art, correspondence
art, mail
art, postal
envois (correspondence art)
mail art
postal art
postal sculpture
sculpture, postal
CN B.BM.AFU.ARI.BCW.FOG.AXC

correspondence, commercial
USE **commercial correspondence**

correspondence, legal
USE **legal correspondence**

correspondence, personal
USE **personal correspondence**

correspondence, private
USE **personal correspondence**

correspondents
HG.289 (L)
ALT **correspondent**
SN Persons employed by a newspaper or broadcasting company to contribute regular news reports or interpretations from a location distant from the home office. (W)
CN H.HG.AFU.AXC.BCW.ALO.AFU.ARI.ARI.AFU

correspondents, foreign
USE **foreign correspondents**

corridors
RM.89 (A,L,B)
ALT **corridor**
SN Use for passages affording entrance to the rooms of a building.
UF halls (corridors)
hallways
CN V.RM.AFU.DIO.ALO.ARI.AXC.AFU

corrosion
KT.895 (A,L,B)
ALT **corroded**
SN The deterioration of metal or other substances by chemical or electrochemical reaction resulting from exposure to weathering, moisture, chemicals, or other agents. (DAC)
CN K.KT.ALO.BCW.ALO

corrosion inhibitors
MT.2316 (L)
SN Materials used to prevent or retard the oxidation of metals. (MH)
UF anticorrosives
inhibitors, corrosion
CN M.MT.AFU.ARI.ALO.DCU.AFU

corrosion, electrochemical
USE **electrochemical corrosion**

corrosion, electrolytic
USE **electrochemical corrosion**

corrosion, galvanic
USE **electrochemical corrosion**

corrosive materials
MT.2792
UF materials, corrosive
CN M.MT.AFU.BCW.AXC

corrugated, Mimbres
USE **Mimbres corrugated**

Corsican pine
MT.1372 (L)
UF pine, Corsican
CN M.MT.AFU.AFU.ALO.BIQ.DCU.AFU.AFU.ALO.CXA.ALO

cortiles
USE **courtyards**

cortili
USE **courtyards**

corundum
MT.498 (L)
SN A very hard crystalline mineral, aluminum oxide, used chiefly as an abrasive. (MH)
UF aluminum oxide
CN M.MT.AFU.AFU.AFU.CFS.AFU.BUE

Cosmati work
KT.701
SN A type of decoration in mosaic and marble inlay, found especially in Rome from the 12th to the 14th centuries. (THDAT)
CN K.KT.AFU.ALO.GRC.BZY.AFU

cosmography
KD.64 (L)
SN Science that deals with the whole order of nature. (W)
CN K.KD.AFU.AFU.BOK.ARI

cosmology
KD.69 (L,R)
SN Branch of systematic philosophy that deals with the character of the universe as a cosmos, combining speculative metaphysics and scientific knowledge. (W)
CN K.KD.AFU.AFU.BOK.BOK.AFU

cost accounting
KG.165 (L,B)
UF accounting, cost
CN K.KG.AFU.ALO.AFU.AFU.AFU

cost analysis
USE **cost benefit analysis**

cost benefit analysis
KG.6 (L,B)
SN Systematic, quantitative appraisal of a project to determine whether its benefits justify its costs. (MGHDME)
UF analysis, cost benefit
cost analysis
engineering, value
value analysis
value engineering
CN K.KG.AFU.AFU.AFU.ALO.AFU

cost containment
USE **cost control**

cost control
KG.53 (L,B)
SN Using corrective measures through management and interpretation of cost benefit analyses to increase efficiency and economy of operation. (W)
UF containment, cost
control, cost
cost containment
cost reduction
reduction, cost
CN K.KG.AFU.AFU.ARI.BOK

cost estimates
USE **estimates**

cost plus contracts
USE **cost plus fee agreements**

cost plus fee agreements
VW.890
ALT **cost plus fee agreement**
SN Agreements or contracts under which the contractor or the architect is reimbursed for the direct and indirect costs of performance of the agreement and in addition is paid a fee for services. (GCIT)
UF agreements, cost plus fee
contracts, cost plus fee
cost plus contracts
cost plus fee contracts
CN V.VW.AFU.ARI.AFU.BOK.BOK.ALO.ALO.ALO.AFU

cost plus fee contracts
USE **cost plus fee agreements**

cost reduction
USE **cost control**

cost reimbursement contracts
VW.891
ALT **cost reimbursement contract**
UF contracts, cost reimbursement
CN V.VW.AFU.ARI.AFU.BOK.BOK.ALO.ALO.ALO.ALO

Costanoan
FL.1251 (L)
CN F.FL.ALO.ALO.ARI.AFU.ALO.BCW

costruzione legittima
USE **linear perspective**

costs
BM.377 (L,B)
SN Amount paid, given, or charged, or engaged to be paid or given, for anything bought or taken in barter or for service rendered. (W)
CN B.BM.ARI.BCW

costume design
KT.99 (L)
SN Designing clothing, accessories, and ensembles intended to create an appearance characteristic of a particular period, person, place, or thing,(WCOL) especially (but not exclusively) for theatrical performances. For the design of clothing and accessories for personal wear, use **fashion design.**
UF design, costume
design, dress (costume design)
dress design (costume design)
CN K.KT.AFU.ALO.CFS.AXC

costume designers
HG.150 (L)
ALT **costume designer**
SN Persons engaged in costume design.
UF costumers, theatrical
designers, costume
designers, dress (costume designers)
dress designers (costume designers)
theatrical costumers
CN H.HG.AFU.AXC.AXC.AFU.AFU.ALO.BCW.ALO

costume museums
RK.391 (L)
ALT **costume museum**
UF museums, costume
CN V.RK.AFU.ALO.ALO.BCW.AXC.ARI.ARI

costumers
TG.634
ALT **costumer**
CN V.TG.AFU.AFU.BIQ.BCW.ALO.AXC

costumers (people)
HG.62
ALT **costumer (person)**
SN Persons who make, sell, or rent costumes, as for stage or fancy dress events. (W)
CN H.HG.AFU.AXC.AXC.AFU.AFU.AFU.ARI

costumers, theatrical
USE **costume designers**

cot bedsteads
USE **cots**

cotes
USE **cottages**

cots
TG.337
ALT **cot**
SN Light beds, often collapsible and typically used for camping or by a child; generally made of canvas stretched on a frame. (W)
UF bedsteads, cot
cot bedsteads
CN V.TG.AFU.AFU.ARI.AFU.AFU.BCW

cottage courts
USE **motor courts**

cottage hospitals
RK.759 (B)
ALT **cottage hospital**
SN Use for health care facilities which, by their design, layout, or plan, are made to resemble cottages or a group of cottages rather than elaborate public buildings.
UF hospitals, cottage
CN V.RK.AFU.ALO.ALO.CXA.ALO.AFU.BCW.AFU.AFU

cottage industries
HG.856 (L)
ALT **cottage industry**
SN Use for industries carried on in the home by a self-employed worker and his/her family, often with the aid of a few apprentices.
UF industries, cottage
industries, village
village industries
CN H.HG.ALO.CLM.AFU

cottage latches
TF.184
ALT **cottage latch**
UF latches, cottage
CN V.TF.AFU.AFU.AFU.AFU.DIO.BCW.ALO.ALO

cottage roofs
USE **single-framed roofs**

Cottage Style
FL.1742
SN Mid-19th-century furniture style, characterized by simplicity of design with natural woods, unpolished or painted in pale colors. (IDO)
CN F.FL.ALO.ALO.BCW.AFU.BZY.AFU

cottages
RK.232 (A,L,N,B,R)
ALT **cottage**
UF cotes
CN V.RK.AFU.ALO.ALO.AXC.ALO.AFU.BCW

cottages ornés
RK.233 (B)
ALT **cottage orné**
SN Use for certain picturesque, small rustic houses, primarily of the late 18th and early 19th centuries in England, with an asymmetrical plan and wood siding.
UF fermes ornées
CN V.RK.AFU.ALO.ALO.AXC.ALO.AFU.BCW.AFU

cottages, Creole
USE **Creole cottages**

cottages, summer
USE **summer houses**

cottanello
MT.808
CN M.MT.AFU.AFU.AFU.DCU.AFU.ARI.ARI.ARI.BIQ.BCW

cotter pin hinges
TF.107
UF hinges, cotter pin
hinges, snipe
hinges, snipe-bill
snipe-bill hinges
snipe hinges
CN V.TF.AFU.AFU.AFU.AFU.CLM.AFU.BOK

cotter pins
TF.457 (N)
ALT **cotter pin**
SN Half-round metal strips bent into a pinlike shape whose ends can be flared after insertion through a slot or hole. (W)
UF kotter pins
pins, cotter
pins, kotter
CN V.TF.AFU.AFU.AFU.ALO.AFU.CXA.AFU

cotton
MT.1847 (L,R)
SN The white to yellowish fiber of the calyx, or blossom, of several species of plants of the genus Gossypium of the mallow family; used especially for making fabrics, cordage, and padding, and for producing cellulose for plastics and rayon. (MH)
CN M.MT.AFU.AFU.ARI.ALO.ALO.ALO.AFU.ALO

cotton gum
USE **tupelo**

cotton mills
RK.660 (L)
ALT **cotton mill**
UF mills, cotton
CN V.RK.AFU.ALO.ALO.CLM.ALO.ALO.AFU.AXC.DZW.AFU

cotton, java
USE **kapok**

cotton, silk
USE **kapok**

cottonseed oil
MT.2026 (L)
UF oil, cottonseed
CN M.MT.AFU.AFU.ARI.ARI.AXC.ALO.AFU

cottonwood
MT.1277 (L)
CN M.MT.AFU.AFU.ALO.BIQ.DCU.AFU.AFU.AFU.KFK.ALO.AXC

cottonwood, black
USE **black cottonwood**

cottonwood, eastern
USE **eastern cottonwood**

Cotzumalhuapa
FL.1036
CN F.FL.ALO.ALO.ALO.ALO.AFU.ALO.ARI.AFU.ARI.BZY

couch beds
TG.388
ALT **couch bed**
SN Term used by Chippendale for double-headed couches with a canopy. (GILBR2)
UF beds, couch
CN V.TG.AFU.AFU.ARI.ALO.ALO

couches
TG.386 (N)
ALT **couch**
SN Long seating forms with a back support and one end; primarily used for reclining rather than sitting. Distinct from **sofas** which have a back and two ends and are primarily used for sitting rather than reclining.
UF lounges (couches)
CN V.TG.AFU.AFU.ARI.ALO

couches (sofas)
USE **sofas**

couches à l'antique
USE **lits à l'antique**

couches, Grecian
USE **Grecian couches**

couching
KT.562 (L)
ALT **couched**
SN Embroidering a design by laying down a thread and fastening it with small stitches at regular intervals. (W)
CN K.KT.AFU.ALO.ELK.DUC.ALO.AXC.AFU

couching (papermaking)
KT.857
ALT **couched**
SN Use for the pressing of a wet sheet of newly made paper still on the mold onto a felt.
CN K.KT.AFU.ALO.HOE.BIQ.ALO.AFU

coulees
RD.193 (L)
ALT **coulee**
CN V.RD.ARI.AFU.AXC.AFU.AFU.ARI.BCW

couleurs, trois
USE **à trois crayons**

coulisses
BM.57
SN Elements in a pictorial composition like side-pieces in a stage set that lead the eye step-by-step back into depth.
CN B.BM.AFU.AFU.ARI.AFU.BCW.ALO.ALO

council housing
USE **public housing**

counseling
KG.36 (L)
SN Providing professional assistance to people in making decisions and coping with adjustment problems.
UF advising
CN K.KG.AFU.AFU.ALO.AXC

counselors
HG.295
ALT **counselor**
SN Persons whose profession is counseling.
CN H.HG.AFU.AXC.BCW.ALO.ALO

counselors, investment
USE **investment advisors**

counter apses
RM.256
ALT **counter apse**
SN Use for apses opposite other apses.
UF apses, counter
CN V.RM.AFU.DIO.ARI.ALO.AFU.ALO

counter arches
RT.274
ALT **counter arch**
SN Use for arches that counteract the thrust of another arch.
UF arches, counter
CN V.RT.AFU.AFU.AFU.BCW.AFU.AFU.ALO.AFU

counter boards
USE **counters**

counter culture
USE **radicalism**

counter-enameling
KT.664
SN A technique invented in the late 15th century in which both sides of an object are covered with enamel of the same thickness, which prevents the object from curling. (THDAT)
CN K.KT.AFU.ALO.GRC.AFU.ALO.BCW

counter flashing
RT.737
SN Strips of sheet metal, often built into masonry and turned down over other flashing; used to prevent water from entering the joints and exposed upturned edges of base flashing on a roof. (DAC)
UF cap flashing
cover flashing
flashing, counter
flashing, cover
flashing, dap
CN V.RT.AFU.ALO.AFU.BCW.ALO

Counter-Reformation
FL.3171 (L,R)
UF Catholic Reformation
CN F.FL.ALO.BCW.ALO.ARI.ARI

counter stools
TG.262
ALT **counter stool**
SN High stools that are usually one of a row of such stools fixed in front of a counter; often backless and having a revolving seat.
UF lunch counter stools
lunch stools
stools, counter
stools, lunch
stools, lunch counter
CN V.TG.AFU.AFU.ALO.AFU.ALO.ARI.ALO

counter tables
USE **counters**

counterbores
TB.184 (N)
ALT **counterbore**
SN Drills used to enlarge holes for the reception of a bolt or nut.
CN V.TB.AFU.ARI.BIQ.ALO.AFU.AFU.AXC

counterchange
DG.98
SN Interlocking patterns of similar shapes with alternating colors or tones;(LDDO) both figures and ground may be read as coherent patterns. (RGRS)
UF counterchange patterns
patterns, counterchange
CN D.DG.AFU.ARI.AFU.ALO

counterchange patterns
USE **counterchange**

counterfeiters
HG.713 (L)
ALT **counterfeiter**
CN H.HG.AFU.BCW.BOK.AFU

counterfeits
VB.117 (L)
ALT **counterfeit**
SN Use for reproductions of whole objects when the intention is to deceive; includes sculptures cast without the artist's permission.

CN V.VB.ALO.BZY.AFU.ALO.AFU

counterfoils
USE **check stubs**

counterpunches
TB.670
ALT **counterpunch**
SN Supports beneath metal being hammered or punched from above. (W)
CN V.TB.AFU.BCW.BIQ.AFU.ALO.BZY.ALO

counters
TG.497 (N)
ALT **counter**
SN Originally small tables or chests with the top marked for counting money, sometimes with a cupboard below.(DDA) Term later applied to large pieces such as those in stores or work areas, e.g., kitchens.
UF boards, counter
counter boards
counter tables
tables, counter
CN V.TG.AFU.AFU.AXC.ALO.BOK

counterscarps
RT.1202
ALT **counterscarp**
SN Use for the outer slopes of encircling defensive ditches, the inner slope being the scarp.
CN V.RT.AFU.BUE.AFU.BZY.ALO

countersink bits
TB.1103 (N)
ALT **countersink bit**
SN Bits used to cut a conical depression for recessing the head of a bolt, nut, or screw, so that it is flush with the surface.
UF bits, countersink
CN V.TB.ALO.ARI.BCW

countersinks
TB.512 (N)
ALT **countersink**
SN Hand tools that usually take the form of a triangular blade at the end of a shaft; used to make conical depressions for recessing the head of a bolt, nut, or screw so that it is flush with the surface.
UF bob punches
punches, bob
CN V.TB.AFU.ARI.EWY.ALO.BOK

countervaults
USE **inverted arches**

counterweights
RT.1329 (N)
ALT **counterweight**
CN V.RT.ALO.ALO.ALO.ARI.AFU

counterweights, sash
USE **sash weights**

counties
HG.803
ALT **county**
CN H.HG.ALO.ALO.ALO

counting desks
USE **counting-house desks**

counting-house bookcases
TG.401
ALT **counting-house bookcase**
SN Term used in the late 18th and early 19th centuries for relatively small and narrow bookcases, generally 3 feet wide and 3 feet high.
UF bookcases, counting-house
CN V.TG.AFU.AFU.AXC.ALO.ALO.ARI

counting-house chairs
USE **tall chairs**

counting-house desks
TG.524
ALT **counting-house desk**
SN 18th-century term for desks on frames set on high legs.
UF counting desks
counting-house desks, single
desks, counting
desks, counting-house
desks, single counting-house
single counting-house desks
CN V.TG.AFU.AFU.AXC.ALO.BZY.ALO

counting-house desks, double
USE **double counting-house desks**

counting-house desks, single
USE **counting-house desks**

countries
USE **nations**

country clubs
RG.164 (A,L,B)
ALT **country club**
UF clubs, country
CN V.RG.AFU.AFU.DOI.BCW

country elevators
USE **grain elevators**

country homes
USE **country houses**

country houses
RK.289 (A,L,B,R)
ALT **country house**
UF country homes
country residences
country seats
estates (country houses)
homes, country
houses, country
residences, country
seats, country
CN V.RK.AFU.ALO.ALO.AXC.ALO.AXC.AFU.AFU.AFU

country maps
USE **national maps**

country of origin marks
VW.722
ALT **country of origin mark**
UF marks, country of origin
CN V.VW.AFU.ALO.ALO.AFU.AXC.ALO.BZY.AFU

country planning
USE **rural planning**

country printers
USE **job printers**

country residences
USE **country houses**

country seats
USE **country houses**

country stores
USE **general stores**

county atlases
VW.130
ALT **county atlas**
UF atlases, county
CN V.VW.AFU.AFU.AFU.FZU.AXC.AFU.AFU.AFU.AXC.ALO

county courthouses
RK.979 (L,B)
ALT **county courthouse**
UF courthouses, county
CN V.RK.AFU.ALO.ALO.ERE.AFU.AXC.AFU.AFU

county directories
VW.417
ALT **county directory**
UF directories, county
CN V.VW.AFU.AFU.ALO.EWY.AXC.AFU.BOK.ARI

county government records
VW.1045 (L)
ALT **county government record**
UF records, county government
CN V.VW.AFU.ARI.ALO.BCW.ALO.AFU.AFU

county halls
RK.995 (A,B)
ALT **county hall**
UF halls, county
CN V.RK.AFU.ALO.ALO.ERE.ALO.AFU.ALO

county maps
VW.228
ALT **county map**
UF maps, county
CN V.VW.AFU.AFU.AFU.FZU.AXC.AFU.ARI.AXC.DUC.BCW

county museums
RK.430
ALT **county museum**
UF museums, county
CN V.RK.AFU.ALO.ALO.BCW.AXC.AXC.ALO

county seats
RD.26
ALT **county seat**
UF seats, county
CN V.RD.AFU.ALO.AFU.AXC.AFU

couple roofs
RT.450
ALT **couple roof**
SN Use for roofs without tie or collar beams, and depending on walls to resist thrust.
UF roofs, couple
CN V.RT.AFU.AFU.AFU.BIQ.ARI.AFU.ALO.ARI.ALO

coupled columns
RT.103
ALT **coupled column**
SN Use for columns set closer together than others in a line, or otherwise forming a visual unit; for columns with interpenetrating shafts, use **doubled columns.**
UF columns, coupled
CN V.RT.AFU.AFU.AFU.AXC.BIQ.AFU.ALO.ARI

coupled windows
RT.919
ALT **coupled window**
SN Two closely spaced windows which form a pair. (HAS)
UF gemel windows
paired windows
windows, coupled
windows, gemel
windows, paired
CN V.RT.AFU.ARI.AFU.AFU.BOK.AFU.AFU.BOK

Couri
FL.1104
CN F.FL.ALO.ALO.ALO.ALO.ARI.AFU

courie
USE **cowrie**

cours d'honneur
USE **forecourts**

courses
RT.612
ALT **course**
SN Layers of masonry units running horizontally in a wall or, much less commonly, curved over an arch. (HAS)
CN V.RT.AFU.AFU.AFU.BIQ.BUE.ALO.AFU.ALO

courses, belt
USE **stringcourses**

courses, bond
USE **bond courses**

courses, chain
USE **chain courses**

courses, corbel
USE **corbel tables**

courses, damp
USE **damp courses**

courses, dampproof
USE **damp courses**

courses, dogtooth
USE **dogtooth courses**

courses, golf
USE **golf courses**

courses, lacing
USE **lacing courses**

courses, lintel
USE **lintel courses**

courses, obstacle
USE **obstacle courses**

courses, oversailing
USE **oversailing courses**

courses, plinth
USE **plinth courses**

courses, putt-putt
USE **miniature golf courses**

courses, sill
USE **sill courses**

courses, Tom Thumb
USE **miniature golf courses**

courses, tumbling
USE **tumbling courses**

courses, vaulting
USE **vaulting courses**

court art
BM.238 (R)
SN Includes both art created by court artists and art produced for a royal court.
UF art, court
CN B.BM.AFU.ARI.BCW.BZY

court calendars
USE **dockets**

court chapels
USE **royal chapels**

court cupboards
TG.505
ALT **court cupboard**
SN Large but fairly low cupboards with an enclosed storage cabinet above and an open shelf or shelves below; a type made in 16th- and 17th-century England and 17th-century America. Distinct from **press cupboards** which have both the upper and lower sections enclosed.
UF cupboards, court
cupboards, plate
plate cupboards
CN V.TG.AFU.AFU.AXC.ALO.BUE.BIQ

court decisions
USE **decisions**

court records
USE **judicial records**

court reporters
USE **law reporters**

court rolls
USE **judicial records**

court style
BM.306
SN Official or approved style, as of art, architecture, or costume, established at a ruler's court.
UF palace style
style, court
style, palace
CN B.BM.AFU.AXC.DUC.AFU

Court Style, Kuba
USE **Kuba Court Style**

court, fives
USE **fives courts**

courthouses
RK.978 (A,L,N,B,R)
ALT **courthouse**
SN Use to designate buildings which contain rooms for courts of law and often judges' chambers and other offices.
UF courts, law
law courts
CN V.RK.AFU.ALO.ALO.ERE.AFU.AXC.AFU

courthouses, county
USE **county courthouses**

courtiers
HG.664 (L,R)
ALT **courtier**
SN Persons who frequent the court of a sovereign or are attendants at court. (OED)
CN H.HG.AFU.AXC.CFS.BCW

courting chairs
USE **love seats**

courtroom art
USE **courtroom illustrations**

courtroom illustrations
VB.47 (L)
ALT **courtroom illustration**
UF courtroom art
illustrations, courtroom
CN V.VB.AFU.ALO.AXC.ALO.AFU

courtrooms
RM.63
ALT **courtroom**
CN V.RM.AFU.DIO.ALO.AFU.ARI

courts
RK.1008
ALT **court**

SN Quadrangular spaces either walled or otherwise marked off for playing one of various games with a ball. (W)
CN V.RK.AFU.ALO.ALO.EWY.ALO

courts (courtyards)
USE **courtyards**

courts, auto
USE **motor courts**

courts, badminton
USE **badminton courts**

courts, ball
USE **ball courts**

courts, basketball
USE **basketball courts**

courts, cottage
USE **motor courts**

courts, croquet
USE **croquet courts**

courts, district
USE **district courts**

courts, handball
USE **handball courts**

courts, indoor tennis
USE **indoor tennis courts**

courts, jai alai
USE **canchas**

courts, law
USE **courthouses**

courts, lawn tennis
USE **tennis courts**

courts, light
USE **light courts**

courts, motor
USE **motor courts**

courts, pelota
USE **canchas**

courts, racquetball
USE **racquetball courts**

courts, shuffleboard
USE **shuffleboard courts**

courts, squash
USE **squash courts**

courts, tennis
USE **tennis courts**

courts, tourist
USE **motor courts**

courts, trailer
USE **trailer camps**

courts, volleyball
USE **volleyball courts**

courtyard houses
RK.256 (A,L,B)
ALT **courtyard house**
SN Houses with internal courtyards of any configuration or design. For houses with internal courtyards having impluvia but no colonnades, use **atrium houses**; for houses with internal courtyards with colonnades, use **peristyle houses.**
UF houses, courtyard
houses, patio
patio houses
CN V.RK.AFU.ALO.ALO.AXC.ALO.AFU.CRG.AFU

courtyards
RM.42 (A,L,B,R)
ALT **courtyard**
SN Use for uncovered areas, surrounded or partially surrounded by the walls of a building.
UF cortiles
cortili
courts (courtyards)
CN V.RM.AFU.DIO.AFU.BCW.ARI

couturiers
USE **fashion designers**

cove ceilings
RT.729
ALT **cove ceiling**
SN Ceilings having coving at the wall lines. (DAC)
UF ceilings, cove
CN V.RT.AFU.ALO.AFU.ALO.BUE

cove lighting
RT.1377
SN Interior lighting system comprised of light sources shielded by a ledge or in a recess, distributing light over the ceiling and upper and side walls. (STEIN)
UF lighting, cove
CN V.RT.ALO.AXC.AXC.ALO.ALO

cove molding planes
USE **cove planes**

cove moldings
USE **cavetto moldings**

cove planes
TB.955
ALT **cove plane**
SN Planes whose blades cut a quarter of a circle, or a cove; used for cutting the under edge of a table leaf or to produce decorative moldings. (HUMMEL)
UF cove molding planes
molding planes, cove
planes, cove
planes, cove molding
CN V.TB.AFU.BCW.CFS.ALO.AFU.DUC.AXC.AFU.AXC

coved vaults
USE **cloister vaults**

covenants
BM.450 (L,B)
SN Promises or undertakings of legal validity embodied in a contract under seal; also particular agreements contained in a deed or contract under seal which are incidental to the main purpose of the document. (W)
CN B.BM.BCW.BOK.AFU

covenants, restrictive
USE **restrictive covenants**

cover fillets
USE **cover moldings**

cover flashing
USE **counter flashing**

cover moldings
RT.798
ALT **cover molding**
UF cover fillets
cover strips
fillets, cover
moldings, cover
strips, cover
CN V.RT.AFU.ALO.AFU.BOK.AFU.ALO.AXC

cover strips
USE **cover moldings**

cover tile
MT.180
UF covering tile
tile, cover
tile, covering
CN M.MT.AFU.AFU.AFU.AXC.ALO.ALO.ALO.AFU.ALO.AXC.AFU.ALO.AFU

covered bridges
RK.1276 (A,L,N,B)
ALT **covered bridge**
UF bridges, covered
CN V.RK.AFU.ALO.ALO.GLI.ALO.AFU.AFU.ARI

covered joints
TF.584
ALT **covered joint**
UF joints, covered
joints, shiplap
shiplap joints
CN V.TF.ALO.AFU.CFS

covered walkways
RK.1569 (A,B)
ALT **covered walkway**
UF covered ways
walkways, covered
ways, covered
CN V.RK.ALO.ALO.BUE.AFU

covered ways
USE **covered walkways**

covered ways (fortification elements)
RT.1203

ALT **covered way (fortification element)**
SN Corridors running along the top of a counterscarp and protected by an embankment whose outer slope forms the glacis. (W)
UF covert-ways
ways, covered (fortification elements)
CN V.RT.AFU.BUE.AFU.BZY.ARI

covering power
BM.972
SN The ability of a paint or varnish to cover a surface in one coat.
UF power, covering
CN B.BM.CFS.AXC.BZY.BUE.ARI.AFU

covering tile
USE **cover tile**

covers (lock components)
USE **caps (lock components)**

covers, bed bolt
USE **bed bolt covers**

covers, manhole
USE **manhole covers**

covert-ways
USE **covered ways (fortification elements)**

coves
RD.146
ALT **cove**
SN Denotes small rounded indentations in a coastline, smaller than bays and generally characterized by a narrow entrance.
CN V.RD.ARI.AFU.AFU.AFU.ALO.ALO.ALO

coves (coving)
USE **coving**

coving
RT.651
SN Large concave moldings, or arched surfaces, located at the junction of a wall and ceiling.
UF coves (coving)
CN V.RT.AFU.AFU.AFU.BIQ.BUE.ALO.AFU.BCW.ARI

cow barns
USE **dairy barns**

cow dung
USE **cow manure**

cow manure
MT.920 (L)
UF cattle manure
cow dung
dung, cow
manure, cattle
manure, cow
CN M.MT.AFU.AFU.ALO.AFU.BOK.AFU

cow planes
USE **roughing planes**

cow sheds
RK.84 (B)
ALT **cow shed**
SN Use for open-sided structures, set against a barn or other large farm building, for sheltering bovines and for protecting manure piles from the weather to preserve their nutrients; for buildings designed for the housing of bovines, use either **cattle barns** or **dairy barns.**
UF cattle sheds
sheds, cattle
sheds, cow
CN V.RK.AFU.ALO.ALO.AFU.ALO.BCW

Cowichan
FL.1358 (L)
CN F.FL.ALO.ALO.ARI.AFU.BIQ.FCS.ALO

Cowlitz
FL.1340 (L)
CN F.FL.ALO.ALO.ARI.AFU.BIQ.BOK

cowls
RT.457 (R)
ALT **cowl**
SN Use for protective hoods or caps, serving to exclude precipitation and to direct exhausts, and often designed to rotate with the wind, such as found on vent pipes.
UF cowls, ventilating
ventilating cowls
CN V.RT.AFU.AFU.AFU.BIQ.ARI.ALO.AFU.AFU

cowls, ventilating
USE **cowls**

cowrie
MT.945 (L)
SN The shell of any of numerous marine gastropod mollusks of a family widely distributed in warm seas; beautifully polished, often brightly colored, and much used for ornament or as money. (W)
UF courie
CN M.MT.AFU.AFU.ALO.AFU.DUC.ALO

coyns
USE **quoins**

Coyotlatelco
FL.993
UF Xometla
CN F.FL.ALO.ALO.ALO.ALO.AFU.ALO.AFU.AFU.DCU

crabapple, prairie
USE **prairie crabapple**

crackers, skull
USE **wrecking balls**

cracking
KT.919 (A,L)
ALT **cracked**
SN Use for the fracturing in a material or object, usually along a single or branched path.
UF fissuring
CN K.KT.ALO.BZY.ARI

cradle benches
TG.280 (N)
ALT **cradle bench**
SN Popular American term for mid-19th-century benches on rockers, with detachable fences two thirds of their length so that a baby could lie on the seat without rolling off, while the mother sat beside it.
UF benches, cradle
benches, mammy's
benches, rocking
mamma's benches
mammy's benches
mammy's rockers
rockers, mammy's
rocking benches
rocking settees
settees, rocking
CN V.TG.AFU.AFU.ALO.ALO.AFU.AFU.ARI

cradle roofs
USE **barrel roofs**
compass roofs

cradle vaults
USE **barrel vaults**

cradles
TG.331 (L,N,R)
ALT **cradle**
SN Small beds for infants, usually on rockers. (RHDEL2)
CN V.TG.AFU.AFU.ARI.AFU.AFU.AXC.ALO

cradles and carriages
USE **carriage cradles**

cradles, carriage
USE **carriage cradles**

cradles, swinging
USE **swinging cradles**

craft knives
USE **utility knives**

crafts
BM.239 (L,B,R)
SN The activity, and its products, of forming handmade articles.
UF handicrafts
CN B.BM.AFU.ARI.BCW.CFS

Craftsman
FL.1726 (A)
CN F.FL.ALO.ALO.BCW.AFU.AXC

craftsmanship
BM.27 (A,L,B)
UF workmanship
CN B.BM.AFU.AFU.ALO.ALO

craftsmen
HG.438 (A,L,B,R)
ALT **craftsman**
SN Persons who practice or are highly skilled in a craft. (RHDEL2)
UF artisans
CN H.HG.AFU.AXC.BUE.AFU

craftsmen's marks
USE **artisans' marks**

cramps
USE **clamps**

crandall hammers
TB.604 (N)
ALT **crandall hammer**
SN Hand tools consisting of several sharp pointed bars fixed to the end of a handle in a hammerlike configuration: used for dressing stone. (MEANS)
UF hammers, crandall
CN V.TB.AFU.BCW.BCW.ALO.EFQ.ARI

cranemen
HG.589
ALT **craneman**
CN H.HG.AFU.AXC.BZY.AFU.BUE

cranes
TB.61 (L,N,B)
ALT **crane**
SN Machines for raising, shifting, or lowering heavy weights, usually by means of a projecting swinging arm. (MEANS)
CN V.TB.AFU.ARI.AFU.BCW.AXC

cranes, bridge
USE **bridge cranes**

cranes, bridge (gantry cranes)
USE **gantry cranes**

cranes, climbing
USE **climbing cranes**

cranes, crawler
USE **crawler cranes**

cranes, gantry
USE **gantry cranes**

cranes, locomotive
USE **locomotive cranes**

cranes, tower
USE **tower cranes**

cranes, traveling
USE **traveling cranes**

cranes, truck
USE **truck cranes**

cranes, truck-mounted
USE **truck cranes**

cranes, wall
USE **wall cranes**

cranes, wheel-mounted
USE **wheel-mounted cranes**

crannogs
RK.309 (L,R)
ALT **crannog**
SN Use for ancient dwellings built on artificial islands in lakes, common in Ireland, Scotland, and Britain.
CN V.RK.AFU.ALO.ALO.AXC.ALO.AXC.ALO.AXC.AFU

crapauds
TG.55
ALT **crapaud**
SN Heavily upholstered low armchairs, generally with fringe hiding the legs and woodwork; of a type first made in France in the 1840s.
CN V.TG.AFU.AFU.ALO.AFU.AFU.AFU.EWY

Crataegus
USE **hawthorn**

Crataegus monogyna
USE **hawthorn**

crate furniture
TG.802
SN Precut furniture parts, made of wood generally used for crates, sold in kits to be assembled by the purchaser into tables, chairs, and bookcases at low cost. Designed by Gerrit Rietveld in 1934. (PAGE)
UF furniture, crate
CN V.TG.AFU.ARI.BZY.ARI.AFU

crawl spaces
RM.216 (L)
ALT **crawl space**
SN Small spaces provided in a building in order to be able to gain access to plumbing, wiring, and other equipment.
UF spaces, crawl
CN V.RM.AFU.DIO.ALO.DIO.AXC

crawler cranes
TB.64
ALT **crawler crane**
SN Cranes consisting of a rotating superstructure with power plant, operating machinery, and boom mounted on a base equipped with crawler treads for travel; used to hoist and swing loads at various radii. (STEIN)
UF cranes, crawler
CN V.TB.AFU.ARI.AFU.BCW.AXC.ARI

crawler tractors
TB.37 (L)
ALT **crawler tractor**
SN Engine-driven vehicles that travel on segmented roller-chain tracks designed to reduce ground pressure and increase traction in loose footing. (DAC)
UF track-type tractors
tracklaying tractors
tractors, crawler
tractors, track-type
tractors, tracklaying
CN V.TB.AFU.ARI.AFU.ARI.ALO

crayon daguerreotypes
USE **cameotypes**

crayon enlargements
VJ.113
ALT **crayon enlargement**
SN A term for a type of photographic portrait popular in the years before World War I. Usually oval, finished with liberal airbrushing and colored with pastels. (HCOP)
UF enlargements, crayon
CN V.VJ.AFU.ARI.ALO.BCW.AFU

crayon holders
USE **portcrayons**

crayon, Conté (TM)
USE **Conté crayon (TM)**

crayons
TB.241 (L,N)
ALT **crayon**
SN A generic term for any drawing material made in stick form. (MAYER)
CN V.TB.AFU.ARI.CLM.AFU.ALO.AXC

crayons, Conté (TM)
USE **Conté crayons (TM)**

crayons, grease
USE **grease pencils**

crayons, lithographic
USE **lithographic crayons**

crayons, pastel
USE **pastels (crayons)**

crayons, wax
USE **wax crayons**

crazing
KT.920
ALT **crazed**
SN Use for fine, random cracks or fissures in the surface of hardened or dried material, such as concrete, plaster, or paint, caused by shrinkage; often used with reference to the surface of glazed objects.
CN K.KT.ALO.BZY.ARI.AFU

cream
USE **pale yellow**
yellowish white

cream blanc marble
MT.820
UF marble, cream blanc
CN M.MT.AFU.AFU.AFU.DCU.AFU.ARI.ARI.ARI.BOK.AFU.AFU

cream buff
USE **moderate yellow**
pale yellow

cream color
USE **light yellow**

cream-colored earthenware
USE **creamware**

cream marble, Alabama
USE **Alabama cream marble**

cream marble, madre
USE **madre cream marble**

creameries
USE **dairy plants**

creamware
MT.150 (L,R)
UF cream-colored earthenware
earthenware, cream-colored
CN M.MT.AFU.AFU.AFU.AXC.ALO.ALO.AFU.ALO.AFU.AFU

crease tile
USE **crest tile**

creasing stakes
TB.684 (N)
ALT **creasing stake**
SN T-shaped stakes with a grooved surface on one side and square end on the other; used in metalworking to shape corners and edges.
UF stakes, creasing
CN V.TB.AFU.BCW.BIQ.AFU.ALO.CXA.ARI

creation
BM.681 (L,R)
CN B.BM.BZY.ALO.AFU.AFU

Creationist
FL.1757
ALT **Creationism**
CN F.FL.ALO.ALO.BCW.ALO.AFU

creative ability
USE **creativity**

creative abstraction
USE **biomorphic abstraction**

creative arts therapy
USE **art therapy**

creativity
BM.28 (L,R)
UF creative ability
CN B.BM.AFU.AFU.ALO.ARI

creches
USE **day care centers**

credence tables
USE **credences**

credences
TG.722
ALT **credence**
SN Collector's term for small tables or shelves near the altar in a church, used for the eucharistic elements before consecration; obsolete term for a sideboard or side table. (DDA)
UF credence tables
credenzas (credences)
tables, credence
CN V.TG.AFU.AFU.BIQ.BOK.ALO.BUE

credences (credenzas)
USE **credenzas**

credences (cupboards)
USE **cupboards**

credentials
VW.311
ALT **credential**
SN Use to designate evidence of authority, status, rights, entitlement to privileges, or the like. (RHDEL2)
CN V.VW.AFU.AFU.ALO.BIQ

credenzas
TG.592 (N)
ALT **credenza**
SN Use for an originally Italian form of sideboard generally having two or three cupboard doors and drawers in the frieze; the bases are often molded and rest directly on the floor or on lion feet.
UF credences (credenzas)
CN V.TG.AFU.AFU.AXC.ALO.CRG.BIQ

credenzas (credences)
USE **credences**

credit
BM.378 (L)
SN The extent to which a person can receive money or goods for payment in the future. (W)
CN B.BM.ARI.BIQ

credit cards
VW.564 (L,N)
ALT **credit card**
SN Cards used to obtain money, goods, or services on credit. (BLACKS)
UF cards, credit
charge plates
plates, charge
CN V.VW.AFU.ALO.AFU.ARI.BCW

credit records
VW.855
ALT **credit record**
UF records, credit
CN V.VW.AFU.ARI.AFU.BIQ.CXA.ALO

credit unions
HG.823 (L)
ALT **credit union**
SN Cooperative associations that make small loans to their members at low interest rates. (W)
UF unions, credit
CN H.HG.ALO.BCW.AXC

credit, letters of
USE **letters of credit**

credit, traveler's letters of
USE **letters of credit**

Cree
FL.1220 (L,R)
CN F.FL.ALO.ALO.ARI.AFU.AFU.ALO.ARI

Cree, Plains
USE **Plains Cree**

Creek
FL.1435 (L)
UF Muskogee
CN F.FL.ALO.ALO.ARI.AFU.BZY.BIQ

creeks
RD.141 (L)
ALT **creek**
CN V.RD.ARI.AFU.AFU.AFU.AFU.ARI.ARI

creep
BM.950 (L)
SN Slow, continuous deformation or movement of structures and landscape features under sustained pressure or downward pull, such as by gravity. (MEANS)
CN B.BM.CFS.AXC.BZY.BOK.ARI

creepie stools
USE **cutty stools**

creepies
USE **cutty stools**

Cremation, Late
USE **Late Cremation**

crematories
RK.461 (A,L,B)
ALT **crematory**
CN V.RK.AFU.ALO.ALO.BOK.ARI.AFU.AFU

Cremnitz white
USE **white lead**

cremorne bolts
TF.233
ALT **cremorne bolt**
UF bolts, cremorne
CN V.TF.AFU.AFU.AFU.AFU.DIO.BIQ.ALO.ALO.ARI.AFU

crenelated parapets
USE **battlements**

crenelets
USE **embrasures (battlement components)**

crenellations
USE **battlements**

crenels
USE **embrasures (battlement components)**

Creole cottages
RK.234
ALT **Creole cottage**
SN Side-gabled vernacular buildings of simple massing, normally having their front walls moved inward to make an integral porch under a single steep roofline; the form was originally brought to Louisiana by French Canadian (Acadian) immigrants with a knowledge of long-span roof framing techniques.
UF Acadian houses
cottages, Creole
Creole houses
grenier houses
houses, Acadian
houses, Creole
houses, grenier
CN V.RK.AFU.ALO.ALO.AXC.ALO.AFU.BCW.ALO

Creole houses
USE **Creole cottages**

creosote
MT.2638 (L,B)
UF dead oil
oil, dead
oil, pitch
pitch oil
CN M.MT.AFU.ARI.HCQ.AFU.ALO

creosote, coal tar
USE **coal tar creosote**

crepe paper
MT.1904 (L)
UF paper, crepe
CN M.MT.AFU.AFU.ARI.ALO.ALO.AXC.ALO.AFU

crepidomas
RM.14
ALT **crepidoma**
SN Use for the stepped platforms of Classical temples.
UF krepidomas
CN V.RM.AFU.BOK.AFU

crescent arches
USE **horseshoe arches**

crescent moons
USE **crescents**

crescent stretchers
TG.999
ALT **crescent stretcher**
UF stretchers, crescent
CN V.TG.ALO.HIK.ALO.ALO.ARI

crescent trusses
RT.361
ALT **crescent truss**
SN Use for trusses whose upper and lower chords are both curved in the same direction but with different radii of curvature, so that they meet at the ends, giving a crescentlike appearance.
UF camelback trusses
curved trusses
trusses, camelback
trusses, crescent
trusses, curved
CN V.RT.AFU.AFU.AFU.BCW.CLM.AFU.AFU.AFU.ARI

crescent wrenches
USE **adjustable wrenches**

crescents
DG.42
ALT **crescent**
SN Motifs consisting of a curved segment of a circle, often suggesting a crescent moon.
UF crescent moons
moons, crescents
CN D.DG.AFU.AFU.CXA.AFU

crescents (row houses)
RK.267 (B)
ALT **crescent (row house)**
SN Use for row houses whose facades in plan follow the concave arc of a circle or ellipse.
CN V.RK.AFU.ALO.ALO.AXC.ALO.AFU.CRG.BIQ.ALO

cress tile
USE **crest tile**

crest pieces
USE **crest rails**

crest rails
TG.832
ALT **crest rail**
UF crest pieces
cresting rails
crossrails
pieces, crest
rails, crest
top-rails (crest rails)
CN V.TG.ALO.AXC.ALO.ALO

crest tile
MT.183
UF crease tile
cress tile
tile, crease
tile, cress
tile, crest
CN M.MT.AFU.AFU.AFU.AXC.ALO.ALO.ALO.AFU.ALO.AXC.AFU.ARI.AFU

cresting
RT.1050
SN Ornamental members or groups of members used to form a decorative finish at the top of the roof as an elaborate coping, the top of a pinnacle, or the like. (RS)
UF crests
CN V.RT.AFU.BCW.ARI

cresting rails
USE **crest rails**

crests
USE **cresting**

Cretan
FL.2584 (L)
CN F.FL.ALO.AXC.ALO.AFU.ALO.AFU

Creto-Mycenaean
FL.2585
CN F.FL.ALO.AXC.ALO.AFU.ALO.ALO

crewelwork
KT.563 (L,R)
SN Embroidery utilizing simple stitches and loosely twisted worsted yarn (crewel), usually worked into floral and scroll patterns on plain cloth.
CN K.KT.AFU.ALO.ELK.DUC.ALO.AXC.ALO

crib barns
RK.44
ALT **crib barn**
UF barns, crib
CN V.RK.AFU.ALO.ALO.AFU.AFU.AFU.AFU.AFU

crib beds
USE **cribs**

crib bedsteads
USE **cribs**

crib retaining walls
USE **cribbing**

cribbing
RT.148 (A,L)
SN Designates a framework of open bins filled with rocks or other pervious materials and used as retaining walls or to support a construction.
UF crib retaining walls
cribwork
retaining walls, crib
walls, crib retaining
CN V.RT.AFU.AFU.AFU.AXC.BOK

cribs
TG.334 (L,N)
ALT **crib**
SN Small bedsteads with a high enclosure and usually slatted sides for a child. (W)
UF beds, crib
bedsteads, crib
crib beds
crib bedsteads
CN V.TG.AFU.AFU.ARI.AFU.AFU.AXC.ARI

cribs, folding
USE **folding cribs**

cribs, portable
USE **folding cribs**

cribs, swinging
USE **swinging cribs**

cribwork
USE **cribbing**

cricket bowls
USE **cricket fields**

cricket fields
RK.1479 (A,L,B)
ALT **cricket field**
SN Use for the entire playing areas upon which the game of cricket is played.
UF bowls, cricket
cricket bowls
cricket grounds
cricket pitches
fields, cricket
grounds, cricket
pitches, cricket
CN V.RK.ALO.ALO.BCW.AFU.ALO

cricket grounds
USE **cricket fields**

cricket pitches
USE **cricket fields**

cricket stools
TG.240
ALT **cricket stool**
SN Applies to a variety of small stools, such as footstools, generally having splayed legs. (DADA)
UF splayed-leg stools
stools, cricket
CN V.TG.AFU.AFU.ALO.AFU.ALO.AFU.ARI

cricket stools (buffet stools)
USE **buffet stools**

cricket tables
TG.668
ALT **cricket table**
SN Joined tables with three legs; of a type made in 17th-century England. (CHINNE)
UF splay-leg tables
tables, cricket
tables, splay-leg
CN V.TG.AFU.AFU.BIQ.BOK.AFU.ALO

crickets
USE **chimney crickets**

crickets, chimney
USE **chimney crickets**

Crideb
USE **Sri Deb**

crime
BM.1095 (L,R)
CN B.BM.CRG.BCW.ALO

crime laboratories
RK.1166 (A,L)
ALT **crime laboratory**
UF laboratories, crime
CN V.RK.AFU.ALO.ALO.FIM.ALO.AFU.BOK

crime prevention
KG.111 (A,L,B)
UF prevention of crime
prevention, crime
CN K.KG.AFU.AFU.BCW.AFU

criminal court records
VW.1022 (L)
ALT **criminal court record**
UF records, criminal court
CN V.VW.AFU.ARI.ALO.BCW.AFU.ALO.ALO.ALO

criminal law
KD.162 (L,R)
SN Branch of jurisprudence that relates to crimes. (W)
UF law, criminal
law, penal
penal law
CN K.KD.AFU.ALO.DOI.ALO

criminals
HG.712 (L,R)
ALT **criminal**
CN H.HG.AFU.BCW.BOK

criminology
KD.116
SN Scientific study of offenders, of crime as a social phenomenon, and of the criminal justice system. (PG)
CN K.KD.AFU.ALO.AXC

crimping
KT.140
ALT **crimped**
SN Pinching together, often to make wavy or bent;(W) also the process of preparing wire for weaving into wire products. (STEIN)
CN K.KT.AFU.ALO.DOI.BOK

crimson
USE **carmine**
deep purplish red
vivid purplish red
vivid red

crimson (natural dye)
USE **madder**

crimson lake
MT.1691
SN Deep, transparent, ruby-red lake pigment with bluish undertone, made from kermes, a natural dyestuff of insect origin; carmine, a better pigment introduced in the 16th century, became its chief competitor. (MAYER)
UF Florentine lake
lake, crimson
lake, Florentine
CN M.MT.AFU.AFU.ARI.AFU.AFU.ALO.ALO.BCW.ALO.AXC

crimson lake (color)
USE **moderate red**

crimson madder
USE **vivid red**

crimson, alizarin
USE **alizarin madder**

crinkling
USE **wrinkling**

crinoidal limestone
MT.656
UF limestone, crinoidal
CN M.MT.AFU.AFU.AFU.DCU.AFU.ALO.AFU.ALO.ALO.AFU.AFU.AFU.AXC

cripple rafters
USE **jack rafters**

Cris
FL.2489
UF Cris-Koros
CN F.FL.ALO.AXC.AFU.BCW.AXC

Cris-Koros
USE **Cris**
Koros

critical bibliography
USE **analytical bibliography**

critical care units
USE **intensive care units**

critical theory
BM.1088 (L)
UF Frankfurt school of sociology
sociology, Frankfurt school of
theory, critical
CN B.BM.CRG.AFU

criticism
BM.293 (L)
CN B.BM.AFU.AXC.BCW

criticism of literature
USE **literary criticism**

criticism, architectural
USE **architectural criticism**

criticism, art
USE **art criticism**

criticism, historical
USE **historiography**

criticism, literary
USE **literary criticism**

critics
HG.197 (L,R)
ALT **critic**
SN Persons who write critical reviews of literary, musical, or artistic works and performances for broadcast or publication. (DOT)
CN H.HG.AFU.AXC.AXC.ARI.ALO.ARI

critics, architectural
USE **architectural critics**

critics, art
USE **art critics**

critics, literary
USE **literary critics**

critiques
KM.48
CN K.KM.AFU.BCW.ALO

crochet
KT.560 (L)
ALT **crocheted**
SN Needlework consisting of the interlocking of looped stitches formed with a single thread and a single hooked needle. (W)
UF crocheting
CN K.KT.AFU.ALO.ELK.DUC.ALO.ARI

crocheting
USE **crochet**

crocket capitals
RT.125
ALT **crocket capital**
SN Capitals having a series of crockets. (HAS)
UF capitals, crocket
CN V.RT.AFU.AFU.AFU.AXC.BIQ.ALO.ARI.AFU.BZY

crockets
RT.1053
ALT **crocket**
SN In Gothic architecture and derivatives, upward-oriented ornaments, often vegetal in form, regularly spaced along sloping or vertical edges of emphasized details such as spires, pinnacles, and gables. (HAS)
CN V.RT.AFU.BCW.AXC

crocodile shears
USE **lever shears**

crocus cloth
TB.513
SN Fabric coated with red iron oxide marketed in sheets and used for polishing metal. (MH)
UF cloth, crocus
CN V.TB.AFU.ARI.EWY.ALO.BUE

crofts
TG.573
ALT **croft**
SN Small writing cabinets of table height with small drawers in the support and a flap top with drop leaves; of a type invented in late 18th-century England by the Reverend Sir Herbert Croft.
CN V.TG.AFU.AFU.AXC.ALO.BZY.FUA.BIQ

croisettes
USE **crossettes**

cromlechs
RK.890 (A,L,B,R)
ALT **cromlech**
SN Use only for prehistoric circular enclosures of well-spaced large upright stones; if the ring of stones is bordered by a circular ditch and bank of earth, use **henges**. Use **megalithic chamber tombs** if the stone enclosure is capped by stones and covered by a mound of earth or stones.
UF circles, stone
peristaliths
stone circles
CN V.RK.AFU.ALO.ALO.DOI.AFU.ARI.AFU

Cromwellian chairs
TG.56
ALT **Cromwellian chair**
SN Collector's term for square low-back chairs, often without arms, having turned legs and stretchers; this type, covered in leather or Turkey work, long antedated the period of Cromwell but became widely popular in England in the mid-1600's.
UF chairs, Cromwellian
chairs, leather-upholstered (Cromwellian chairs)
chairs, turkey work (Cromwellian chairs)
leather-upholstered chairs (Cromwellian chairs)
turkey work chairs (Cromwellian chairs)
CN V.TG.AFU.AFU.ALO.AFU.AFU.AFU.FCS

crook-bit tongs
TB.753 (N)
SN Tongs with one straight jaw and one crooked jaw; used by blacksmiths.
UF bits, crook
crook bits
tongs, crook-bit
CN V.TB.AFU.BCW.BIQ.AXC.ALO.AXC.AXC

crook bits
USE **crook-bit tongs**

crook'd-back leather chairs
USE **Boston chairs**

crooked-back chairs
USE **Boston chairs**

cropland
RD.285
CN V.RD.ARI.ALO.AFU.AFU.ARI

cropping
KT.92
ALT **cropped**
SN The trimming or cutting away of edges, as portions of a photograph or printed page.
CN K.KT.AFU.ALO.BUE.BCW.AFU

croquet courts
RK.1013 (A)
ALT **croquet court**
UF courts, croquet
CN V.RK.AFU.ALO.ALO.EWY.ALO.BCW

croquis
USE **preliminary sketches**

crosettes
USE **crossettes**

cross axes
USE **twivels**

cross banding
DG.108
SN Decorative border of contrasting woods cut straight across the grain, generally used to finish edges and rims of furniture.
UF banding, cross
CN D.DG.AFU.ARI.ALO.ARI.AFU.AFU

cross bridging
RT.212
SN Diagonal bracing in pairs between adjacent floor joists to prevent the joists from twisting. (DAC)
UF bridging, cross
bridging, diagonal
diagonal bridging
herringbone strutting
strutting, herringbone
CN V.RT.AFU.AFU.AFU.AXC.DOI.AFU.ARI.AFU

cross chairs, Savonarola
USE **Savonarola chairs**

cross-contour drawing
KT.195
SN Drawing technique in which lines move in any direction across the form rather than along the edge of it. (KAUP)
UF contour drawing, cross
drawing, cross-contour
CN K.KT.AFU.ALO.DUC.BZY.ALO.AXC.ALO

cross-contour drawings
VD.132
ALT **cross-contour drawing**
SN Use for drawings in which lines follow contours of the form across the surface of the form; distinct from **contour drawings**, in which lines follow edges of the form.
UF drawings, cross-contour
CN V.VD.AFU.AXC.BIQ.AFU.ALO

cross-cultural psychology
USE **ethnopsychology**

cross gables
RT.636
ALT **cross gable**
SN Gables set parallel to the roof ridge. (HAS)
UF gables, cross
CN V.RT.AFU.AFU.AFU.BIQ.BUE.ALO.AFU.AXC.AFU.ALO

cross-hatching
KT.266
SN Hatching in which a network of lines

of darker value is made by drawing one set of hatchings over another. (A-Z)
CN K.KT.AFU.ALO.DUC.DCU.ARI.AFU

cross-legged stools
USE **folding stools**

cross legs, Grecian
USE **curule legs**

cross-lined pottery, white
USE **white cross-lined pottery**

cross-peen hammers
TB.461 (N)
ALT **cross-peen hammer**
SN Hammers having a wedge-shaped peen. (DAC)
UF hammers, cross-peen
CN V.TB.AFU.ARI.ELK.AFU.ALO.ALO

cross rails
USE **slats**

cross ribs
USE **transverse ribs**

cross-section paper
USE **graph paper**

cross sections
VD.69
ALT **cross section**
UF sections, cross
sections, transverse
transverse sections
CN V.VD.AFU.AFU.BIQ.ALO.BIQ.ALO

cross shaped stretchers, diagonal
USE **cross stretchers**

cross-springers
USE **diagonal ribs**

cross stretchers
TG.1000
ALT **cross stretcher**
SN X-shaped horizontal braces or rails connecting and supporting the legs of chairs, tables, and case pieces. (FAIRB)
UF cross shaped stretchers, diagonal
cruciform stretchers
diagonal cross shaped stretchers
diagonal-shaped stretchers
diagonal stretchers
stretchers, cross
stretchers, cruciform
stretchers, diagonal
stretchers, diagonal cross shaped
X-stretchers
CN V.TG.ALO.HIK.ALO.ALO.AXC

cross vaults
USE **groined vaults**

cross-wall construction
USE **box frames**

crossbeams
RT.309
ALT **crossbeam**
SN Use for large beams that span between the two walls or sides of a structure.
CN V.RT.AFU.AFU.AFU.BCW.ALO.ALO.ALO

crosscut saws
TB.1023 (L,N)
ALT **crosscut saw**
SN Large saws whose teeth are filed and set to cut across the grain of wood, providing more of a knife action in the cutting than ripsaws; designed for either one or two people.
UF long saws
saws, crosscut
saws, long
CN V.TB.AFU.BCW.CFS.ALO.AFU.EWY.BUE.ARI

crosscut saws, one-man
USE **one-man crosscut saws**

crosses
DG.5 (A,L,B,R)
ALT **cross**
SN Figures and symbols of great antiquity consisting of two intersecting lines or bars, with many variations in the shapes of the arms.
CN D.DG.AFU.AFU.ARI

crosses of eight points
USE **Maltese crosses**

crosses of Iona
USE **Celtic crosses**

crosses of Lorraine
DG.8 (L)
ALT **cross of Lorraine**
SN Crosses having two crossbars, a shorter one crossing above the center and a longer one below the center.
UF crosses, Lorraine
Lorraine crosses
CN D.DG.AFU.AFU.ARI.ARI

crosses, ansate
USE **ankhs**

crosses, Calvary
USE **Calvary crosses**

crosses, Celtic
USE **Celtic crosses**

crosses, city
USE **market crosses**

crosses, Egyptian
USE **ankhs**

crosses, Greek
USE **Greek crosses**

crosses, Iona
USE **Celtic crosses**

crosses, Irish
USE **Celtic crosses**

crosses, Latin
USE **Latin crosses**

crosses, long
USE **Latin crosses**

crosses, Lorraine
USE **crosses of Lorraine**

crosses, Maltese
USE **Maltese crosses**

crosses, market
USE **market crosses**

crosses, papal
USE **papal crosses**

crosses, passion
USE **Calvary crosses**

crosses, patriarchal
USE **patriarchal crosses**

crosses, pope's
USE **papal crosses**

crosses, preaching
USE **preaching crosses**

crosses, ring
USE **Celtic crosses**

crosses, roadside
USE **wayside crosses**

crosses, Saint Andrew's
USE **Saint Andrew's crosses**

crosses, St. Anthony's
USE **tau crosses**

crosses, tau
USE **tau crosses**

crosses, wayside
USE **wayside crosses**

crosses, weeping
USE **preaching crosses**

crosses, wheel
USE **wheel crosses**

crosses, wheel (Celtic crosses)
USE **Celtic crosses**

crosses, wheel-head
USE **Celtic crosses**

crossettes
RT.799
ALT **crossette**
SN Elaborated details projecting laterally at the corners of doors and window frames.
UF croisettes
crosettes
elbows (crossettes)
CN V.RT.AFU.ALO.AFU.BOK.AFU.ALO.BCW

crossing
USE **transverse**

crossing towers
RM.419 (A)
ALT **crossing tower**
SN Use for towers over the crossings of churches.
UF central towers
lantern towers
rood spires
rood steeples
rood towers
spires, rood
steeples, rood
towers, central
towers, crossing
towers, lantern
towers, rood
CN V.RM.AFU.DZW.AFU.AFU

crossings
RM.319 (L,B)
ALT **crossing**
SN Places in churches where a transept crosses the nave. (W)
CN V.RM.AFU.DIO.AXC.ALO.AFU.CFS

crossings (grade crossings)
USE **grade crossings**

crossings, level
USE **grade crossings**

crosslap joints
TF.685
ALT **crosslap joint**
SN Wood joints in which two pieces are each cut to half their thickness at the overlap, so that the total thickness of the system does not change. (MEANS)
UF joints, crosslap
CN V.TF.ALO.ARI.AXC.ARI.AXC.AFU

crossrails
USE **crest rails**

crossroads
USE **intersections**

crosswalks
RM.471
ALT **crosswalk**
SN Specially paved or marked paths for pedestrians crossing a street or road. (W)
CN V.RM.ALO.ALO.ALO.ALO.ALO

crosswise
USE **transverse**

crotch mahogany
MT.1213
UF branch mahogany
mahogany, branch
mahogany, crotch
CN M.MT.AFU.AFU.ALO.BIQ.DCU.AFU.AFU.AFU.HTY.ARI.AFU.AFU

croton oil
MT.2027 (L)
UF oil, croton
CN M.MT.AFU.AFU.ARI.ARI.AXC.ALO.ALO

Crow
FL.1381 (L)
UF Absaroke
CN F.FL.ALO.ALO.ARI.AFU.BOK.BUE

crow-stepped gables
RT.637 (B)
ALT **crow-stepped gable**
SN Gables having a stepped edge. (DAC)
UF catsup gables
corbel gables
corbie gables
corbiestepped gables
gables, catsup
gables, corbel
gables, corbie
gables, corbiestepped
gables, crow-stepped
gables, step
step gables
CN V.RT.AFU.AFU.AFU.BIQ.BUE.ALO.AFU.AXC.AFU.ARI

crowbars
TB.416 (L,N)
ALT **crowbar**
SN Steel bars with a flattened, forked, or chisel-shaped end which is sometimes slightly bent; used for heavy prying, and as a lever for moving heavy objects.
UF bars, pry
crows
pry bars
CN V.TB.AFU.ARI.DZW.ALO

crowding
USE **overcrowding**

crowding stress
USE **overcrowding**

crown glass
MT.258
UF disc-blown glass
glass, crown
glass, disc-blown
CN M.MT.AFU.AFU.AFU.BIQ.AFU.ARI.AXC

crown land
RD.310 (L)
SN Land in some countries and regions belonging to the British Commonwealth and held in the name of the sovereign.
UF land, crown
CN V.RD.ARI.ALO.AXC.ALO

crown mold planes
USE **cornice planes**

crown moldings
RT.800
ALT **crown molding**
SN The uppermost moldings, as on an interior wall, the top of a cornice, or on a piece of furniture.
UF moldings, crown
CN V.RT.AFU.ALO.AFU.BOK.AFU.ALO.BIQ

crown planes
USE **cornice planes**

crown posts
RT.511
ALT **crown post**
SN Any vertical members in a roof truss, especially a king post or a queen post.
UF posts, crown
CN V.RT.AFU.AFU.AFU.BIQ.ARI.ALO.ALO.ARI.AFU

crown saws
TB.135 (N)
ALT **crown saw**
SN Metal cylinders with teeth cut on one end; used for cutting cylindrical objects or discs from wood, horn, metal, and other materials. (SALAM)
UF cylinder saws
hole saws
round saws
saws, crown
saws, cylinder
saws, hole
saws, round
saws, sheave
saws, trepan
sheave saws
trepan saws
CN V.TB.AFU.ARI.AXC.ALO.CLM.ALO

crown steeples
RM.401
ALT **crown steeple**
SN Openwork spires, the upper portion being carried over an open area by crossed arches or buttresses.
UF steeples, crown
CN V.RM.AFU.DOI.AFU.AFU

crown tile
USE **ridge tile**

crowns (architectural elements)
RT.562
ALT **crown (architectural element)**
SN The highest points of arches or vaults.
CN V.RT.AFU.AFU.AFU.BIQ.BOK.ALO.AFU

crows
USE **crowbars**

crowsteps
RT.644
ALT **crowstep**
SN The component projections of a crow-stepped gable.
UF catsteps
corbel steps

corbiesteps
steps, corbel
CN V.RT.AFU.AFU.AFU.BIQ.BUE.ALO.AFU.AXC.ALO.ALO

CRTs
USE **monitors**

Crucero
FL.1032
CN F.FL.ALO.ALO.ALO.ALO.AFU.ALO.ARI.AFU.ARI.BCW

cruces ansatae
USE **ankhs**

cruces capitatae
USE **Latin crosses**

cruces commissae
USE **tau crosses**

cruces decussatae
USE **Saint Andrew's crosses**

cruces immissae
USE **Latin crosses**

cruciform stretchers
USE **cross stretchers**

crucks
RT.325 (A,L,R)
ALT **cruck**
SN Pairs of naturally curved timbers that rise from the outer walls to support the ridge beam; joined at the top and connected by one or two tie beams. (DAC)
UF crutches (frame components)
CN V.RT.AFU.AFU.AFU.BCW.BOK

crumbling
KT.898
ALT **crumbled**
CN K.KT.ALO.BCW.ARI

Crusader
FL.3101 (A,R)
SN European-influenced art and architecture of the eastern Mediterranean, from the 13th to the 15th century.
CN F.FL.ALO.BCW.ALO.ALO.AFU.BOK.AFU

crushed rock
USE **crushed stone**

crushed stone
MT.884 (L)
UF broken stone
crushed rock
rock, crushed
stone, broken
stone, crushed
CN M.MT.AFU.AFU.AFU.DCU.ALO.ARI

crushing
KT.111
ALT **crushed**
CN K.KT.AFU.ALO.CLM.ARI

crushing machinery
TB.111 (L)
UF machinery, crushing
CN V.TB.AFU.ARI.ARI.AFU

crushing plants
RK.628 (B)
ALT **crushing plant**
UF plants, crushing
CN V.RK.AFU.ALO.ALO.CLM.ALO.ALO.AFU.AXC.AXC

crusted ware
FL.2654
UF ware, crusted
CN F.FL.ALO.AXC.ALO.AFU.ALO.AXC.AXC.ARI

crutches (frame components)
USE **crucks**

cryptographers
HG.175 (L)
ALT **cryptographer**
CN H.HG.AFU.AXC.AXC.ALO.ALO.AFU

cryptoportici
RM.90 (L)
ALT **cryptoporticum**
SN Use for corridors or galleries in Roman architecture with windowlike openings, whether subterranean or above ground.
CN V.RM.AFU.DIO.ALO.ARI.AXC.ALO

crypts
RM.320 (A,L,B,R)
ALT **crypt**
SN Use for subterranean rooms or entire stories in churches, often serving as places of burial.
CN V.RM.AFU.DIO.AXC.ALO.AFU.CLM

crystal
MT.244 (L,R)
UF crystal glass
crystal glass, high-lead
crystal, lead
glass, crystal
glass, high-lead crystal
high-lead crystal glass
lead crystal
CN M.MT.AFU.AFU.AFU.BIQ.AFU.AFU.AXC.AFU

crystal glass
USE **crystal**

crystal glass, high-lead
USE **crystal**

crystal, lead
USE **crystal**

crystal, quartz
USE **quartz crystal**

crystal, rock
USE **quartz crystal**

crystalline glaze
MT.2567 (L)
UF glaze, crystalline
CN M.MT.AFU.ARI.CRG.ARI.ARI.AFU.ARI.ALO

crystallographers
HG.336 (L)
ALT **crystallographer**
CN H.HG.AFU.AXC.BIQ.AFU.AFU.BCW

crystals, snow
USE **snowflakes**

Cuadros
FL.1029
CN F.FL.ALO.ALO.ALO.ALO.AFU.ALO.ARI.AFU.ARI.ALO

Cuautepec
FL.982
CN F.FL.ALO.ALO.ALO.ALO.AFU.ALO.AFU.AFU.ARI.ARI

Cuban
FL.708 (L,B)
CN F.FL.ALO.ALO.AFU.ALO.AFU

Cuban mahogany
USE **South American mahogany**

Cuban pine
MT.1373 (L)
UF ocote
pine, Cuban
pine, pitch
pine, slash
pine, spruce
pine, swamp
Pinus caribaea
pitch pine
slash pine
spruce pine
swamp pine
CN M.MT.AFU.AFU.ALO.BIQ.DCU.AFU.AFU.ALO.CXA.ARI

Cubeo
FL.1578 (L)
UF Cobbeos
CN F.FL.ALO.ALO.ARI.ARI.AFU.CLM

cubes
BM.794 (L,R)
ALT **cubic**
CN B.BM.CFS.ARI.AXC.BCW.ALO.AXC.AFU

cubes, flash
USE **flash cubes**

cubicula
RM.162
ALT **cubiculum**
SN Ancient Roman bedrooms. (HAS)
CN V.RM.AFU.DIO.ALO.CRG.AFU.AFU

cubiform capitals
USE **cushion capitals**

Cubist
FL.3292 (A,L,R)

ALT **Cubism**
CN F.FL.ALO.BCW.ALO.AXC.DCU.ARI

Cubist-Realist
USE **Precisionist**

Cubist, Analytical
USE **Analytical Cubist**

Cubist, Collage
USE **Synthetic Cubist**

Cubist, Facet
USE **Analytical Cubist**

Cubist, Synthetic
USE **Synthetic Cubist**

Cubo-Futurist
FL.3414 (L,R)
ALT **Cubo-Futurism**
CN F.FL.ALO.BCW.ALO.AXC.DIO.BZY.ALO.AFU

Cubo-Realist
USE **Precisionist**

Cucuteni-Tripolye
USE **Tripolye**

cudbear
USE **orchil**

cudgels
USE **froe clubs**

cuenca
KT.868
SN A technique of decoration employed in Spain for tiles and other wares which superseded the cuerda seca method. It involved impressing the pattern on tiles to form ridges which prevented the colored glazes from intermingling. (SAVAGE)
CN K.KT.AFU.ALO.HOE.BOK.AXC.ARI.AFU

cuerda seca
KT.869
SN Tile decoration technique found in Spain in which outlines were drawn on the surface of the ware with a greasy substance colored with manganese, allowing glazes of several colors to be used without intermingling. The grease would disappear during firing. (SAVAGE)
CN K.KT.AFU.ALO.HOE.BOK.AXC.ARI.ALO

Cueva-Cuna
FL.1549
CN F.FL.ALO.ALO.ARI.ALO.BOK.AFU.AFU

cuffs (leg components)
TG.959
ALT **cuff (leg component)**
CN V.TG.ALO.FIM.ALO.AFU

Cuicatec
FL.1515 (L)
CN F.FL.ALO.ALO.ARI.ALO.AXC.BIQ

Cuicuilco
USE **Ticomán**

Cuicuru
USE **Kuikuru**

cul-de-fours
USE **semidomes**

Culhucán
USE **Aztec I**

cullonen
USE **white beech**

culs-de-sac
RK.1534 (L)
ALT **cul-de-sac**
SN Use for dead-end streets that have circular turn-around areas at their ends.
CN V.RK.ALO.ALO.BIQ.ARI.AFU.ALO.AFU.AXC.AFU

cultural anthropologists
USE **social anthropologists**

cultural anthropology
USE **social anthropology**

cultural buildings
USE **cultural centers**

cultural centers
RK.1194 (A,N,B)
ALT **cultural center**
UF buildings, cultural
centers, cultural
cultural buildings
CN V.RK.AFU.ALO.ALO.FUA.AXC

cultural landscapes
RD.280
ALT **cultural landscape**
SN Designates land and water areas significantly altered or modified by human actions; used in contrast to **natural landscapes,** that designate areas where human effects, if present, are not ecologically significant to the regions as a whole.
UF landscapes, cultural
CN V.RD.ARI.ALO

cultural patrimony
USE **cultural property**

cultural property
BM.460 (A,L)
UF cultural patrimony
heritage property
national treasure
patrimony, cultural
property, cultural
property, heritage
treasure, national
CN B.BM.BCW.CXA.AFU.AFU

culture
BM.326 (L,R)
CN B.BM.ALO.AFU

culture, counter
USE **radicalism**

culture, material
USE **material culture**

culture, popular
USE **popular culture**

culture, punk
USE **punk culture**

culverts
RK.541 (L,B)
ALT **culvert**
SN Use for drainage structures that extend across and beneath roadways, canals, embankments, or traveled ways other than bridges.
CN V.RK.AFU.ALO.ALO.CFS.ALO.AFU.AFU

cum ceilings
USE **camp ceilings**

Cumberland Fluted
FL.738
UF Fluted, Cumberland
CN F.FL.ALO.ALO.ALO.AFU.AFU.ARI.AFU.ALO

cumulative indexes
VW.436
ALT **cumulative index**
SN Indexes which combine separately published indexes into one sequence. (LG)
UF indexes, cumulative
CN V.VW.AFU.AFU.ALO.EWY.BOK.ALO.ARI

Cuna
FL.1548 (L)
CN F.FL.ALO.ALO.ARI.ALO.BOK.AFU

cunei
RM.351
ALT **cuneus**
SN Use for wedgeshaped sections of seats in ancient theaters.
CN V.RM.AFU.DIO.AXC.AXC.AFU.ARI

cunes
USE **quoins**

cup escutcheons
TF.264
ALT **cup escutcheon**
UF escutcheons, cup
CN V.TF.AFU.AFU.AFU.AFU.DZW.ALO.ALO

cup joints
TF.646
ALT **cup joint**
SN In plumbing, a socket joint formed between two similar pipes in the same line, by opening out the end of one pipe to receive the tapered end of the other. (PUTNAM)

UF joints, cup
CN V.TF.ALO.ARI.ARI.BCW

cupboard beds
USE **box beds**
press beds

cupboard catches
TF.46
ALT **cupboard catch**
UF catches, cupboard
CN V.TF.AFU.AFU.AFU.AFU.BCW.BIQ

cupboard knobs
USE **cabinet knobs**

cupboard locks
TF.249
ALT **cupboard lock**
UF locks, cupboard
CN V.TF.AFU.AFU.AFU.AFU.DIO.BIQ.ALO.ARI.ALO

cupboard turns
TF.52
ALT **cupboard turn**
UF turns, cupboard
CN V.TF.AFU.AFU.AFU.AFU.BOK

cupboards
TG.498 (A,L,N,B,R)
ALT **cupboard**
SN Originally a board or an open structure of shelves on which cups, especially silver, might be placed for storage or display; often used interchangeably with buffets and dressoirs in the Middle Ages. Beginning in the 15th century, doors were added. Today a generic term for all such receptacles enclosed by doors.
UF credences (cupboards)
huches
hutches
vaisseliers
CN V.TG.AFU.AFU.AXC.ALO.BUE

cupboards, almoners
USE **livery cupboards**

cupboards, bedside
USE **night tables**

cupboards, book
USE **book cupboards**

cupboards, bread and cheese
USE **livery cupboards**

cupboards, butter
USE **livery cupboards**

cupboards, close
USE **aumbries**

cupboards, clothes
USE **wardrobes**

cupboards, corner
USE **corner cupboards**

cupboards, court
USE **court cupboards**

cupboards, dole
USE **dole cupboards**

cupboards, food
USE **livery cupboards**

cupboards, hanging
USE **hanging cupboards**

cupboards, linen
USE **linen presses**

cupboards, livery
USE **livery cupboards**

cupboards, plate
USE **court cupboards**

cupboards, pot
USE **night tables**

cupboards, press
USE **press cupboards**

cupboards, spice
USE **spice cupboards**

cupboards, tridarn
USE **tridarns**

cupboards, wall
USE **hanging cupboards**

cupboards, Welsh
USE **tridarns**

Cupeño
FL.1252 (L)
CN F.FL.ALO.ALO.ARI.AFU.ALO.BIQ

Cupisnique
FL.1143 (L)
UF Coast Chavin
CN F.FL.ALO.ALO.ALO.ARI.AXC.AFU.ARI.AXC

cupolas
RT.474 (A,L,N,B,R)
ALT **cupola**
SN Use for small structures built on the ridges of roofs, particularly common in American architecture; when these structures are intended to be used as lookouts, prefer **belvederes.**
CN V.RT.AFU.AFU.AFU.BIQ.ARI.ALO.AFU.BUE.ARI

cupped nails
TF.407
ALT **cupped nail**
UF nails, cupped
CN V.TF.AFU.AFU.AFU.ALO.AFU.CFS.AFU.DCU.BCW

Cupressus
USE **cypress**

Cupressus lawsoniana
USE **Port Orford cedar**

Cupressus sempervirens
USE **classic cypress**

Cuprolithic
USE **Chalcolithic**

cups, force
USE **plungers**

curating
KG.78
SN Superintending or managing the collections, exhibits, research activities, and personnel of a museum, art gallery, zoo, or other place of exhibit; also, the superintending or managing of a single collection or subject of study in such an institution. (W)
UF curatorship
CN K.KG.AFU.AFU.AXC.AXC.BUE

curators
HG.202 (L)
ALT **curator**
SN Persons engaged in curating.
UF keepers (curators)
CN H.HG.AFU.AXC.AXC.AXC.AFU

curatorship
USE **curating**

curb joints
USE **knuckle joints**

curb rolls
USE **knuckle joints**

curb roofs
RT.421
ALT **curb roof**
SN Roofs in which the slope is broken, the lower slope being steeper than the upper slope; may be two-sided or four-sided roofs.
UF dual-pitched roofs
roofs, curb
roofs, dual-pitched
CN V.RT.AFU.AFU.AFU.BIQ.ARI.AFU.AFU.AFU.BOK.AFU

curbing
MT.905 (B)
UF curbstone
CN M.MT.AFU.AFU.AFU.DCU.ARI.ALO

curbs
RM.472 (L,B)
ALT **curb**
SN Raised edgings, as of stone or concrete, built along driveways, roads, or roofs, usually forming part of a gutter.
CN V.RM.ALO.ALO.ALO.ALO.ARI

curbs, seat
USE **fender stools**

curbstone
USE **curbing**

curcas oil
MT.2028
UF oil, curcas
CN M.MT.AFU.AFU.ARI.ARI.AXC.

ALO.ARI

curcuma
USE **turmeric**

curiae
RK.984
ALT **curia**
SN Council houses in Roman municipalities. (HAS)
CN V.RK.AFU.ALO.ALO.ERE.AFU.BCW.ARI

curing agents
MT.2308
UF agents, curing
CN M.MT.AFU.ARI.ALO.BOK

curing (leather)
KT.772
ALT **cured**
UF leather curing
CN K.KT.AFU.ALO.HOE.AXC.AFU

curling
KT.890
ALT **curled**
SN The distortion of an object originally linear or planar so that it is curved or coiled in shape. Use especially with reference to paper and to concrete slabs.
CN K.KT.ALO.ALO

curricles
TG.57
ALT **curricle**
SN Term used by Sheraton to describe armchairs having a semicicular back and elongated seat, whose shape suggests an open carriage.
UF chairs, cirricule
cirricule chairs
currieles
CN V.TG.AFU.AFU.ALO.AFU.AFU.AFU.FIM

curricula
VW.1064 (L)
ALT **curriculum**
CN V.VW.AFU.ARI.ALO.CRG.AFU

curricula vitae
USE **resumes**

currieles
USE **curricles**

curriers
HG.486
ALT **currier**
SN Persons who dress and color leather after it has been tanned. (RHDEL2)
CN H.HG.AFU.AXC.BUE.ARI.BZY.AFU

currying
KT.773
ALT **curried**
SN Applied to all the processes that improve the quality of leather after tanning. (SALAM)
CN K.KT.AFU.ALO.HOE.AXC.AFU.AFU

cursive
FL.1176
UF Abigarrado
cursive modeled
modeled, cursive
CN F.FL.ALO.ALO.ALO.ARI.AXC.ALO.ALO.ALO

cursive modeled
USE **cursive**

curtain walls
RT.585 (A,L,B)
ALT **curtain wall**
SN Nonbearing walls supported by the members of a rigid frame structure, such as a reinforced concrete or steel frame, and therefore serving to enclose but not to support.
UF enclosure walls
walls, curtain
walls, enclosure
walls, window
window walls
CN V.RT.AFU.AFU.AFU.BIQ.BUE.AFU.ALO.ARI.AFU

curtain walls (fortification elements)
RT.1181
ALT **curtain wall (fortification element)**
SN Use for the enclosing walls connecting bastions or towers in fortifications.
UF walls, curtain (fortifications elements)
CN V.RT.AFU.BUE.AFU.BCW.AFU.ALO

curtains, asbestos
USE **asbestos curtains**

curtains, fire
USE **asbestos curtains**

curtains, safety
USE **asbestos curtains**

curule chairs
USE **sellae curulis**

curule legs
TG.948
ALT **curule leg**
SN X-shaped legs based on Roman chair design, used on Federal and other classically inspired furnishings. (CTSB)
UF cross legs, Grecian
Grecian cross legs
legs, curule
legs, Grecian cross
legs, X-shaped
X-shaped legs
CN V.TG.ALO.FIM.AFU.AFU.AXC

curve tracers
USE **flexible curves**

curved
DC.61
CN D.DC.AFU.ARI.BOK

curved-back chairs en gondola
USE **gondola chairs**

curved dormers
RT.477
ALT **curved dormer**
SN Use for dormers with a roof terminating in an overhanging semiconical front; common in Victorian architecture.
UF dormers, curved
CN V.RT.AFU.AFU.AFU.BIQ.ARI.ALO.AFU.BUE.AXC.ALO

curved trusses
USE **crescent trusses**

curved windows
USE **bow windows**

curves
TB.432 (N,B)
ALT **curve**
SN Tools which take a variety of forms; used to guide draftsmen in drawing curved lines.
UF curves, drawing
drawing curves
CN V.TB.AFU.ARI.EFQ.ALO.AFU

curves, Brook's
USE **Brook's curves**

curves, drawing
USE **curves**

curves, flexible
USE **flexible curves**

curves, French
USE **French curves**

curves, irregular
USE **French curves**

curves, snake
USE **flexible curves**

curves, whiplash
USE **whiplash curves**

Curvilinear Decorated
FL.3126
UF Curvilinear Style (architecture style)
Decorated, Curvilinear
CN F.FL.ALO.BCW.ALO.ALO.AFU.BOK.ARI.ALO.AXC.AFU.ALO

curvilinear
DC.64 (A)
SN Consisting of or bounded by curved lines. With reference to furniture pieces, the fronts of which have alternating concave and convex curves, use **serpentine.** For other features, such as arches or moldings, composed of flowing, wavelike curves, use **undulating.**
CN D.DC.AFU.ARI.BUE

Curvilinear Style
FL.2593

UF Naturalistic Style
CN F.FL.ALO.AXC.ALO.AFU.ALO.
AXC.AFU.AFU

Curvilinear Style (architecture style)
USE **Curvilinear Decorated**

curvilinear tracery
USE **flowing tracery**

cushion capitals
RT.126
ALT **cushion capital**
SN Capitals resembling a cushion that is pressed down because of weight on it; also, cubic capitals with their lower angles rounded off, especially common in Medieval architecture.
UF block capitals
capitals, block
capitals, cubiform
capitals, cushion
capitals, pillow
cubiform capitals
pillow capitals
CN V.RT.AFU.AFU.AFU.AXC.BIQ.
ALO.ARI.AFU.CFS

cushioned friezes
USE **pulvinated friezes**

Cushite
USE **Kushite**

cusped arches
RT.223
ALT **cusped arch**
SN Arches which have cusps or foliations worked on the intrados. (DAC)
UF arches, cusped
arches, foiled
arches, lobed
foiled arches
lobed arches
CN V.RT.AFU.AFU.AFU.BCW.AFU.
AFU.AFU.BCW

cusps
RT.1054
ALT **cusp**
SN The intersection of two arcs or foils, as in tracery. (HAS)
CN V.RT.AFU.BCW.BCW

custodians
HG.39 (L)
ALT **custodian**
SN Persons officially entrusted with guarding and keeping things, such as property, artifacts, or records, or with custody or guardianship of people, such as prisoners, inmates, or wards. (W)
CN H.HG.AFU.AXC.ARI.ARI

customhouses
RK.974 (A,B,R)
ALT **customhouse**
UF customs posts
posts, customs
CN V.RK.AFU.ALO.ALO.ERE.AFU.
ARI.AFU

customs
BM.329 (L,R)
SN Usages, practices, or conventions that regulate social life. (W)
UF social customs
CN B.BM.ALO.ALO.ALO

customs posts
USE **customhouses**

customs records
VW.985
ALT **customs record**
UF records, custom
CN V.VW.AFU.ARI.ALO.BCW.AFU.
AFU.AFU.AFU

cut and straight hangers
TF.353
ALT **cut and straight hanger**
UF hangers, cut and straight
CN V.TF.AFU.AFU.AFU.ALO.AFU.
BOK.ARI.AFU.AXC

cut film
MT.2238
UF film, cut
film, sheet
sheet film
CN M.MT.AFU.ALO.CXA.ALO.AXC

cut nails
TF.392
ALT **cut nail**
SN Hard, wedge-shaped nails used for nailing hardwoods such as oak flooring. (MEANS)
UF clasp nails
nails, clasp
nails, cut
CN V.TF.AFU.AFU.AFU.ALO.AFU.CFS.
AFU.BCW

cut-pile cloth
MT.1862
UF cloth, cut-pile
kasai velvet
velvet, kasai
CN M.MT.AFU.AFU.ARI.ALO.ALO.
ALO.ALO.BCW

cut slating nails
TF.431
ALT **cut slating nail**
UF nails, cut slating
slating nails, cut
CN V.TF.AFU.AFU.AFU.ALO.AFU.CFS.
ALO.ARI

cut stone
USE **dimension stone**

cut strings
USE **open strings**

cutaway drawings
VD.4
ALT **cutaway drawing**
SN Use for drawings in which part of an object or structure is removed to show the interior. For orthographic drawings specifically, use **broken-out sections, half sections** (for objects), or **sectional elevations** (for structures).
UF cutaways
drawings, cutaway
CN V.VD.AFU.AFU.ALO

cutaways
USE **cutaway drawings**

cutch
MT.1620 (L)
SN Natural, nearly permanent dye obtained chiefly from various species of acacia and mimosa, used to produce shades of brown, black and olive; also employed in tanning leather. (MAYER)
UF Bengal cutch
cachou
catechu
cutch, Bengal
earth, Japan
Japan earth
katechu
CN M.MT.AFU.AFU.ARI.AFU.AFU.
ALO.ALO.ARI.ALO.BCW

cutch-grass
MT.1029 (L)
UF grass, quitch
quitch grass
CN M.MT.AFU.AFU.ALO.BIQ.AXC.ALO

cutch, Bengal
USE **cutch**

cuts
RK.1350
ALT **cut**
CN V.RK.AFU.ALO.ARI.AXC.ARI.AFU

cutter
MT.73
UF rubber (brick)
CN M.MT.AFU.AFU.AFU.AXC.ALO.
AFU.AFU.AFU.BCW

cutters, anvil
USE **hardies**

cutters, block
USE **wood engravers**

cutters, bolt
USE **bolt cutters**

cutters, clinch
USE **buffers**

cutters, dovetail
USE **dovetail cutters**

cutters, dowel
USE **peg cutters**

cutters, milling
USE **milling cutters**

cutters, peg
USE **peg cutters**

cutters, pinion
USE **pinion cutters**

cutters, pipe
USE **pipe cutters**

cutters, plug
USE **plug cutters**

cutters, side
USE **side cutters**

cutters, sprue
USE **sprue cutters**

cutters, wire
USE **wire cutters**

cutting
KT.85 (L)
ALT **cut**
CN K.KT.AFU.ALO.BUE

cutting oil
MT.1992
SN An oil or oily preparation used on cutting tools or on work being machined to aid in the cutting action.
UF oil, cutting
CN M.MT.AFU.AFU.ARI.ARI.ALO.AFU

cutting, electrochemical
USE **electrochemical cutting**

cutting, gem
USE **lapidary**

cutting, laser beam
USE **laser beam cutting**

cutting, thermal
USE **thermal cutting**

cuttings
USE **clippings**

cuttings files
USE **clippings files**

cuttings, press
USE **clippings**

cuttlefish ink
USE **sepia**

cutty stools
TG.241
ALT **cutty stool**
SN Low stools used in churches in Scotland before pews were introduced. (OCDA)
UF creepie stools
creepies
stools, creepie
stools, cutty
CN V.TG.AFU.AFU.ALO.AFU.ALO.AFU.AXC

cutwaters
RM.468
ALT **cutwater**
SN Structures built around or upstream from a bridge pier with an angle or edge to resist better the action of water, ice, or flotsam. (W)
CN V.RM.ALO.ALO.ALO.AFU.ALO

Cuzco
FL.1717 (L)
UF Cuzco Circle
CN F.FL.ALO.ALO.AXC.ALO.AFU.AXC.AFU

Cuzco Circle
USE **Cuzco**

cyan blue
USE **moderate bluish green**
moderate greenish blue

cyanine blue
USE **dark purplish blue**
moderate purplish blue

cyanotype
USE **blueprint process**

cyanotypes
VJ.49 (L)
ALT **cyanotype**
SN Use for blue-toned photographic prints produced by the blueprint process, not including reproductive prints of architectural or other technical drawings; for these, use **blueprints or blueline prints.**
UF blueprints (photographs)
CN V.VJ.AFU.AFU.ARI.ARI.AXC.BCW

cyanotypes (reproductions)
USE **blueprints**

cyberneticians
HG.337
ALT **cybernetician**
UF cyberneticists
CN H.HG.AFU.AXC.BIQ.AFU.AFU.BIQ

cyberneticists
USE **cyberneticians**

cybernetics
KD.211 (A,R)
SN Comparative study of control and communication processes of organisms and machines. (ERIC)
CN K.KD.AFU.ARI.BCW

Cycladic
FL.2536 (L,B,R)
CN F.FL.ALO.AXC.ALO.AFU.AFU.ALO.AFU

Cycladic white ware
FL.2594 (L)
UF ware, Cycladic white
white ware, Cycladic
CN F.FL.ALO.AXC.ALO.AFU.ALO.AXC.AFU.ALO

Cycladic, Early
USE **Early Cycladic**

Cycladic, Late
USE **Late Cycladic**

Cycladic, Middle
USE **Middle Cycladic**

cycle racing tracks
USE **velodromes**

cycle sheds
USE **bicycle sheds**

cycle tracks
USE **velodromes**

cycleways
USE **cycling paths**

cycling paths
RK.1574 (A,L,B)
ALT **cycling path**
UF bicycle paths
bicycle tracks
bike paths
bikeways
cycleways
cycling tracks
paths, bicycle
paths, cycling
tracks, bicycle
tracks, cycling
CN V.RK.ALO.ALO.BUE.AXC.ALO

cycling tracks
USE **cycling paths**

cyclone cellars
USE **storm cellars**

cyclones
KM.115 (L,B)
CN K.KM.AFU.CXA.BIQ.ALO

cyclopean concrete
MT.201
UF concrete, cyclopean
CN M.MT.AFU.AFU.AFU.BCW.AFU.AFU.BCW

cyclopean masonry
MT.2756
SN Stonework using large, irregular block of stone fitted closely together. (FOFDA)
UF masonry, cyclopean
CN M.MT.AFU.AXC.BIQ.AFU.ARI.AFU

cyclopedias
USE **encyclopedias**

cyclotrons
RK.1156 (L,N,B)
ALT **cyclotron**
SN Designates structures in which charged atomic particles are accelerated along a spiral path by means of alternating electric currents with a constant magnetic field.
UF accelerators, circular
accelerators, magnetic resonance
circular accelerators
magnetic resonance accelerators

phasotrons
CN V.RK.AFU.ALO.ALO.FIM.AFU.AFU

cylinder augers
TB.824
ALT **cylinder auger**
UF augers, cylinder
borers, cylindrical bung
bung borers, cylindrical
cylindrical bung borers
CN V.TB.AFU.BCW.CFS.ALO.AFU.ALO.ARI

cylinder bookcases, sister's
USE **cylinder desks and bookcases**

cylinder bureaus
USE **bureaux à cylindre**

cylinder desks
USE **cylinder fall desks**

cylinder desks and bookcases
TG.531
ALT **cylinder desk and bookcase**
SN Desks and bookcases with a hinged one-piece round lid or cover that resembles a section of a cylinder and which rolls up into the desk top; chiefly made in the late 18th and early 19th centuries.
UF bookcases, sister's cylinder
cylinder bookcases, sister's
cylinder-fall desks and bookcases
cylinder secretaries and bookcases
desks and bookcases, cylinder
desks and bookcases, cylinder-fall
secretaries and bookcases, cylinder
sister's cylinder bookcases
CN V.TG.AFU.AFU.AXC.ALO.BZY.BCW.ALO

cylinder desks, rotary
USE **rotary desks**

cylinder fall desks
TG.526
ALT **cylinder fall desk**
SN Desks with a hinged one-piece round lid or cover that resembles a section of a cylinder and which rolls up into the desk top.
UF cylinder desks
cylinder fall writing tables
cylinder-front desks
cylinder-top desks
cylindrical writing tables
desks, cylinder
desks, cylinder fall
writing tables, cylinder fall
CN V.TG.AFU.AFU.AXC.ALO.BZY.ARI

cylinder-fall desks and bookcases
USE **cylinder desks and bookcases**

cylinder fall writing tables
USE **cylinder fall desks**

cylinder-front desks
USE **cylinder fall desks**

cylinder glass
MT.259
UF broad glass
glass, broad
glass, cylinder
glass, muff
muff-blown glass
muff glass
CN M.MT.AFU.AFU.AFU.BIQ.AFU.ARI.BCW

cylinder locks
TF.198
ALT **cylinder lock**
SN Locks in which the keyhole and tumbler mechanism are contained in a cylinder or escutcheon separate from the lock case. (MEANS)
UF locks, cylinder
CN V.TF.AFU.AFU.AFU.AFU.DIO.BIQ.AFU.AXC

cylinder locks, mortise
USE **mortise locks**

cylinder saws
USE **crown saws**

cylinder screws
TF.470
ALT **cylinder screw**
SN Set screws that hold a cylinder in place to prevent the cylinder from being turned after installation. (BROWNL)
UF screws, cylinder
CN V.TF.AFU.AFU.AFU.ALO.AFU.DIO.AFU.ARI

cylinder secretaries and bookcases
USE **cylinder desks and bookcases**

cylinder-top desks
USE **cylinder fall desks**

cylinder writing tables, lady's
USE **lady's writing tables**

cylinders
BM.791 (L,R)
ALT **cylindrical**
CN B.BM.CFS.ARI.AXC.BCW.ALO.ALO

cylinders (lock components)
TF.563
ALT **cylinder (lock component)**
SN The housing containing the tumbler mechanism and the key way, which can be actuated only by the correct key. (BROWNL)
CN V.TF.AFU.ALO.AXC.AXC

cylinders, phonograph
USE **phonograph cylinders**

cylindrical bung borers
USE **cylinder augers**

cylindrical writing tables
USE **cylinder fall desks**

cyma rectas
RT.773
ALT **cyma recta**
SN Moldings of double curvature where the uppermost surface is concave and the lowermost is convex.
UF cymas, Doric
Doric cymas
CN V.RT.AFU.ALO.AFU.BOK.AFU.AFU.AXC.ARI.AFU

cyma reversas
RT.774
ALT **cyma reversa**
SN Moldings of double curvature where the uppermost surface is convex and the lowermost is concave.
UF cymas, Lesbian
Lesbian cymas
moldings, reverse ogee
ogee moldings, reverse
reverse ogee moldings
CN V.RT.AFU.ALO.AFU.BOK.AFU.AFU.AXC.ARI.ALO

cymas
RT.772
ALT **cyma**
SN Moldings having a profile of double curvature. (HAS)
UF cimas
doucines
moldings, ogee
moldings, talon
ogee moldings
simas
talon moldings
CN V.RT.AFU.ALO.AFU.BOK.AFU.AFU.AXC.ARI

cymas, Doric
USE **cyma rectas**

cymas, Lesbian
USE **cyma reversas**

cymatia
RT.340
ALT **cymatium**
SN Crowning moldings of a classical cornice, especially when in the form of a cyma, though they may also be an ovolo or cavetto molding. (HAS)
UF scimatia
CN V.RT.AFU.AFU.AFU.BCW.BZY.ALO.ALO.ALO.ARI

cyphers
USE **monograms**

cypher-back chairs
TG.145
ALT **cypher-back chair**
SN Chairs whose splats are pierced to form a cypher with the initials of their owners. (KANE)
UF chairs, cypher-back
CN V.TG.AFU.AFU.ALO.AFU.AFU.AFU.NIE.CXA.AFU

cypress
MT.1343 (L)
UF Cupressus
CN M.MT.AFU.AFU.ALO.BIQ.DCU.AFU.AFU.ALO.AXC

cypress, classic
USE **classic cypress**

cypress, lawson
USE **Port Orford cedar**

cypress, Mediterranean
USE **classic cypress**

cypress, white
USE **white cypress**

cypress, yellow
USE **yellow cypress**

Cypressus nootkatensis
USE **yellow cypress**

Cyprian green earth
MT.1639
UF green earth, Cyprian
CN M.MT.AFU.AFU.ARI.AFU.AFU.ALO.ALO.AXC.AFU.ALO.ALO

Cypriote
FL.2890 (L)
CN F.FL.ALO.AXC.ARI.ARI

Cypriote, Early
USE **Early Cypriote**

Cypriote, Late
USE **Late Cypriote**

Cypriote, Middle
USE **Middle Cypriote**

Cypro-Phoenician
FL.2898
CN F.FL.ALO.AXC.ARI.ARI.ALO.AFU

Cyprus umber
USE **umber**

Cyrenaic
USE **Laconian**

Cyrenaican
FL.693
CN F.FL.ALO.AFU.AXC.BCW.ALO.AFU

cyrtostyles
RM.252
ALT **cyrtostyle**
SN Circular, projecting, columned porticoes. (W)
UF sigmas
CN V.RM.AFU.DIO.ARI.AFU.BUE.AFU

czars
HG.692
ALT **czar**
SN Rulers of Russia before the 1917 revolution. (W)
UF tsars
CN H.HG.AFU.AXC.CFS.CRG.ALO

Czech
FL.3044 (L,B)
CN F.FL.ALO.BCW.AFU.BIQ

D'Entrecasteaux
FL.3639 (L)
CN F.FL.ALO.BOK.ALO.BCW.ALO.ARI.AFU

Dabban
FL.40
CN F.FL.ALO.AFU.AFU.AFU.AFU.ALO

dachas
RK.291
ALT **dacha**
SN Country houses, summer houses, or villas in Russia. (W)
CN V.RK.AFU.ALO.ALO.AXC.ALO.AXC.AFU.AFU.AFU.ALO

dacite
MT.584 (L)
CN M.MT.AFU.AFU.AFU.DCU.AFU.AFU.AFU.AFU.AFU.AFU

Dacron (TM)
MT.1840 (L)
UF fiber V
terylene
CN M.MT.AFU.AFU.ARI.ALO.AFU.ALO.AFU.AFU

Dada
FL.3295 (L,R)
ALT **Dadaism**
CN F.FL.ALO.BCW.ALO.AXC.DCU.AXC

daders
USE **twivels**

dado and rabbet joints
TF.668
ALT **dado and rabbet joint**
UF joints, dado and rabbet
CN V.TF.ALO.ARI.AXC.AFU.AFU.AFU

dado grooving planes
USE **dado planes**

dado joints
TF.667
ALT **dado joint**
SN Joints which are created by the end of a piece of wood fitting, usually at right angles, into a groove cut across the width of another piece to a depth of half its thickness. (MEANS)
UF joints, dado
CN V.TF.ALO.ARI.AXC.AFU.AFU

dado planes
TB.915 (N)
ALT **dado plane**
SN Planes whose iron is set on a skew; used to cut grooves across the grain of wood.
UF carcase grooving planes
dado grooving planes
grooving planes, carcase
grooving planes, dado
housing planes
planes, carcase grooving
planes, dado
planes, dado grooving
planes, housing
planes, trenching
raglets
trenching planes
CN V.TB.AFU.BCW.CFS.ALO.AFU.DUC.ALO.ARI

dado, tongue and rabbet joints
TF.669
ALT **dado, tongue and rabbet joint**
UF joints, dado, tongue and rabbet
CN V.TF.ALO.ARI.AXC.AFU.AFU.ALO

dadoes
RT.181
ALT **dado**
SN Use for the middle portion of a pedestal, between the base and the cap. Use also for the lower zone of an interior wall, when given a distinct treatment, as this treatment often resembles a pedestal in appearance.
UF dies (dadoes)
CN V.RT.AFU.AFU.AFU.AXC.CFS.ALO.ALO

Daedalic
FL.2685
CN F.FL.ALO.AXC.ALO.AFU.ALO.BCW.ALO.ARI

daga
MT.2054
SN Coarse, granular, sandlike substance that consists chiefly of clay, made into a mortar used in African building construction.
UF dagga
CN M.MT.AFU.AFU.ARI.BOK.AFU.ALO

daga, burnt
USE **burnt daga**

dagga
USE **daga**

Dagger period
FL.2509
CN F.FL.ALO.AXC.AFU.BIQ.AFU.AFU

daggers (tracery components)
RT.1027
ALT **dagger (tracery component)**
SN In late 13th- and early 14th-century Gothic tracery, lancet-shaped openings pointed at the foot, rounded or pointed at the head, and cusped inside.
CN V.RT.AFU.ARI.ALO.BZY.ALO.AFU

dagobas
RK.1150 (A,L)
ALT **dagoba**
SN Use for Ceylonese and Singhalese stupas, generally with a tripartite base and a dome surmounted by a

small pavilionlike structure and a spire.
CN V.RK.AFU.ALO.ALO.FCS.BUE.ALO

daguerreotype
KT.331 (L)
SN An early photographic process producing a direct positive image on a silver-coated copper plate.
UF daguerreotypy
CN K.KT.AFU.ALO.DUC.DIO.ALO.BUE.ALO

daguerreotype prints
USE **etched daguerreotype prints**

daguerreotype prints, etched
USE **etched daguerreotype prints**

daguerreotypes
VJ.30 (L,N,R)
ALT **daguerreotype**
SN Use for photographs made by the process called daguerreotype, usually mounted in cases.
CN V.VJ.AFU.AFU.ARI.AFU.ALO

daguerreotypes, crayon
USE **cameotypes**

daguerreotypes, vignette
USE **cameotypes**

daguerreotypy
USE **daguerreotype**

Dai Co Viet
USE **Vietnamese**

Dai-La
FL.2428
CN F.FL.ALO.ARI.BCW.BUE.AFU.AFU

Dai Viet
USE **Vietnamese**

Daibutsuyo
FL.1993
UF Great Buddha Style
Indian Style
Tenjiku-yo
Tenjiku yo
Tenjikuyo
CN F.FL.ALO.ARI.ALO.ALO.ALO.AFU.AFU

daily reports
VW.454
ALT **daily report**
UF reports, daily
CN V.VW.AFU.AFU.ALO.FIM.AFU.ALO.AFU

Daima
FL.97
CN F.FL.ALO.AFU.ALO.AFU.BUE.ALO

dairies
RK.57 (A,B)
ALT **dairy**
SN Use for farm buildings, generally of the 18th to early 19th century, where country ladies supervised the making and storing of dairy products. Distinguished from **dairy plants** by their lack of mechanization.
CN V.RK.AFU.ALO.ALO.AFU.AFU.ALO

dairies (mechanized)
USE **dairy plants**

dairy barns
RK.49 (L,B)
ALT **dairy barn**
SN Barns for dairy cows; for beef cattle housing, use **cattle barns**; for primarily open shelters, use **cow sheds**.
UF barns, cow
barns, dairy
byres
cow barns
CN V.RK.AFU.ALO.ALO.AFU.AFU.AFU.ALO.AFU.AFU

dairy farms
RG.8 (L,B)
ALT **dairy farm**
UF farms, dairy
CN V.RG.AFU.AFU.AFU.AFU.ARI.AFU

dairy plants
RK.631 (A,L,B)
ALT **dairy plant**
SN Use for buildings built after the early 19th century, not found only on farms, for the mechanized processing, storing, or selling of milk and milk products. Distinguished from **dairies** by the use of mechanization.
UF creameries
dairies (mechanized)
plants, dairy
CN V.RK.AFU.ALO.ALO.CLM.ALO.ALO.AFU.AXC.BCW.ALO

daisywheel printers
TB.168
ALT **daisywheel printer**
SN Serial impact printers in which the font is formed on the end of spring fingers that extend radially from a central hub. (DOC)
UF printers, daisywheel
CN V.TB.AFU.ARI.BCW.AXC.AXC.ALO.ARI.AFU.AFU

Dakota
FL.1397 (L,R)
UF Nadowessioux
Wahpekute
CN F.FL.ALO.ALO.ARI.AFU.BOK.FCS.AFU

Dakota, Santee
USE **Santee Dakota**

Dalbergia
MT.1300 (L)
CN M.MT.AFU.AFU.ALO.BIQ.DCU.AFU.AFU.AFU.LCM.AXC

Dalbergia latifolia
USE **East Indian rosewood**

Dalbergia melanoxylin
USE **African blackwood**

Dalbergia nigra
USE **Brazilian rosewood**

Dalbergia retusa
USE **cocobolo**

Dalton
FL.739
CN F.FL.ALO.ALO.ALO.AFU.AFU.ARI.AFU.ARI

Dalverzin
USE **Dalverzin-Tepe**

Dalverzin-Tepe
FL.1793
UF Dalverzin
CN F.FL.ALO.ARI.AFU.AXC.BIQ

damage
KT.891 (A,L,B)
ALT **damaged**
CN K.KT.ALO.ARI

damage reports
VW.452 (A)
ALT **damage report**
UF reports, damage
CN V.VW.AFU.AFU.ALO.FIM.AFU.AFU.ARI

damar
MT.1486
UF damar, gum
gum damar
CN M.MT.AFU.AFU.ALO.BOK.AXC

damar, Batavia
USE **Batavia damar**

damar, cat's eye
USE **Mata Kuching damar**

damar, gum
USE **damar**

damar, Mata Kuching
USE **Mata Kuching damar**

damar, Singapore
USE **Singapore damar**

damascening
KT.835 (L)
ALT **damascened**
SN Decorating metal, usually iron, with flat ornaments of precious metal, such as gold or silver.
CN K.KT.AFU.ALO.HOE.BCW.ALO.AXC.ALO

Damascus style Iznik pottery
USE **Damascus ware**

Damascus ware
FL.3521
UF Damascus style Iznik pottery
Iznik pottery, Damascus style
pottery, Damascus style Iznik
ware, Damascus

CN F.FL.ALO.BIQ.AFU.FOG.ALO.
ALO.AFU

damask
MT.1863 (R)
SN Reversible, figured fabric in which the design is worked in such a way that it appears on face and back in reverse positions. (WATS)
CN M.MT.AFU.AFU.ARI.ALO.ALO.
ALO.ALO.BIQ

damp courses
RT.617 (B)
ALT **damp course**
SN In masonry, impervious horizontal layers of material used to prevent upward capillary movement or downward seepage of water.
UF courses, damp
courses, dampproof
dampproof courses
CN V.RT.AFU.AFU.AFU.BIQ.BUE.
ALO.AFU.ALO.BCW

dampers
RT.1440 (B)
ALT **damper**
SN Use for devices, such as valves or gates, for controlling the flow of air in a ventilation system, or the flow of combustion gases in a chimney flue.
CN V.RT.ALO.BCW.AFU.ALO.ARI.BOK

dampness
BM.929 (A,L,B)
ALT **damp**
CN B.BM.CFS.AXC.BOK.ALO

dampproof courses
USE **damp courses**

dampproofing
USE **waterproofing**

dampproofing paint
MT.2541
UF paint, dampproofing
paint, vapor barrier
vapor barrier paint
CN M.MT.AFU.ARI.CRG.ALO.BCW.
ARI.ARI

dams
RK.520 (A,L,N,B,R)
ALT **dam**
CN V.RK.AFU.ALO.ALO.CFS.AFU.ARI

dams, arch
USE **arch dams**

dams, buttress
USE **buttress dams**

dams, check
USE **check dams**

dams, diversion
USE **diversion dams**

dams, earth-fill
USE **earth-fill dams**

dams, flood
USE **flood dams**

dams, gravity
USE **gravity dams**

dams, hydraulic fill
USE **earth-fill dams**

dams, hydroelectric
USE **hydroelectric dams**

dams, power
USE **hydroelectric dams**

dams, reinforced earth
USE **zoned earth dams**

dams, rock-fill
USE **rock-fill dams**

dams, rolled-fill
USE **rolled-fill dams**

dams, wing
USE **wing dams**

dams, zoned earth
USE **zoned earth dams**

Dan
FL.321 (L)
UF Gio
Yakuba
CN F.FL.ALO.AFU.AXC.AFU.ARI.
BCW.AFU

Dan Day chairs
USE **Mendlesham chairs**

Danakil
USE **Afar**

dance
KD.6 (L,R)
CN K.KD.AFU.AFU.AFU.AFU.AFU.AFU

dance cards
VW.565
ALT **dance card**
SN Cards listing, in order, the names of the partners with whom a woman has agreed to dance at a formal ball or party. (RHDEL2)
UF cards, dance
CN V.VW.AFU.ALO.AFU.ARI.BIQ

dance grounds
RG.205
ALT **dance ground**
SN Use for cleared and bounded areas, devoid of artifacts, and of unknown function found associated with hunter-gatherer camps, especially those of the North American Great Basin.
UF grounds, dance
CN V.RG.AFU.AFU.DZW.AFU.AFU

dance halls
RK.1039 (A,B)
ALT **dance hall**
SN Use for large rooms or buildings set aside for dancing, but which may be used for other social functions. Distinguished from **ballrooms** by their less formal nature.
UF halls, dance
CN V.RK.AFU.ALO.ALO.EWY.AXC.
ARI.AXC

dance, tap
USE **tap dance**

dancers
HG.69 (L,R)
ALT **dancer**
CN H.HG.AFU.AXC.AXC.AFU.AFU.
AFU.BIQ.AXC

dancettes
USE **chevrons**

dancing steps
USE **balanced steps**

dancing winders
USE **balanced steps**

Dandan Oilik
FL.1813
CN F.FL.ALO.ARI.AFU.AXC.ELK.ARI

dandyism
BM.347 (L,R)
SN Literary or artistic style often associated with the English and French decadents of the late 19th century, marked especially by precocity of language and refined emotionalism of subject matter. (W)
CN B.BM.ALO.ALO.CLM.BOK

Danger Cave
FL.907
CN F.FL.ALO.ALO.ALO.AFU.ALO.
ARI.ALO.ALO

Dani
FL.3630 (L)
UF Ndani
CN F.FL.ALO.BOK.ALO.BCW.AFU.
AFU.ALO

Danish
FL.3058 (L,B)
CN F.FL.ALO.BCW.AFU.DUC.AFU

Dante chairs
TG.117
ALT **Dante chair**
SN Collector's term for Italian Renaissance X-chairs with crossing assemblies only in the front and back. Their name is derived from association with the 14th-century poet Dante, although it is questionable that such chairs were actually used by him.
UF chairs, Dante
chairs, Dantesca
Dantesca chairs
sedia Dantesca
CN V.TG.AFU.AFU.ALO.AFU.AFU.
AFU.MWQ.AFU

Dantesca chairs
USE **Dante chairs**

Dantesque
FL.3402
CN F.FL.ALO.BCW.ALO.AXC.DIO.BOK.AXC.AFU

Danubian
FL.2490
CN F.FL.ALO.AXC.AFU.BCW.BCW

Danzig fir
USE **Scotch pine**

Danzig pine
USE **Scotch pine**

Daoguang
FL.1915 (L)
UF Tao-kuang
CN F.FL.ALO.ARI.ALO.AFU.AFU.ALO.DOI.BIQ

dap joints
TF.585
ALT **dap joint**
UF joints, dap
CN V.TF.ALO.AFU.CLM

Daphne ware
FL.2608
UF ware, Daphne
CN F.FL.ALO.AXC.ALO.AFU.ALO.AXC.ALO.ARI.ALO

dapping blocks
TB.653
ALT **dapping block**
SN Anvils used in conjunction with dapping punches for depressing metal.
UF blocks, dapping
CN V.TB.AFU.BCW.BIQ.AFU.ALO.ARI.AFU

dapping punches
TB.671
ALT **dapping punch**
SN Punches used in conjunction with dapping blocks for depressing metal.
UF punches, dapping
CN V.TB.AFU.BCW.BIQ.AFU.ALO.BZY.ARI

darbies
TB.595 (N)
ALT **darby**
SN Float tools which are about 4 feet long, usually made of wood or aluminum and having either one or two handles; used by concrete finishers and plasterers in preliminary floating and leveling operations. (MEANS)
UF derby slickers
floats, long
long floats
slickers, derby
CN V.TB.AFU.BCW.BCW.ALO.DIO.ARI

Darby and Joan settees
USE **chair-back settees**

Darfur
FL.168
CN F.FL.ALO.AFU.ALO.BCW.AFU

Darién
FL.1097
CN F.FL.ALO.ALO.ALO.ALO.ALO.ALO.ALO.ALO

Dark Ages
FL.3
SN Can be used for substantial periods of any cultures from which little reliable data are available.
UF Ages, Dark
CN F.FL.AFU.ALO

Dark Ages (Medieval)
USE **Migration period**

dark aniline blue
USE **dark grayish blue**
dark grayish purple

dark anthracene violet
USE **dark grayish purple**
dark purple

dark blue
DL.220
UF Antwerp blue (color)
Berlin blue
blue, Antwerp (color)
blue, Berlin
blue, dark
blue, deep royal
blue, deep sapphire
blue, delft
blue, medium
blue, Monastral
blue, royal
blue, sapphire
bluish slate black
bright navy
centroid color 183
dark green blue slate
dark navy
deep royal blue
deep sapphire blue
delft blue
green blue slate, dark
greenish navy
indigo (color)
kingfisher
light navy
medium blue
Monastral blue
navy
navy, bright
navy, dark
navy, greenish
navy, light
royal blue
royal blue, deep
sapphire blue
sapphire blue, deep
slate black, bluish
slate, dark green blue
CN D.DL.AFU.AFU.BZY.BOK

dark blue green
USE **blackish green**
dark grayish green
dark green
light bluish green
moderate bluish green
moderate greenish blue
strong bluish green
strong green
very dark green

dark bluish gray
DL.229
UF black, blue
black, ink
blue black
blue, dull
blue, logwood
blue, midnight
blue, slate
bluish gray, dark
centroid color 192
dark navy
dark Payne's gray
dull blue
dull violet black
gray, dark bluish
gray, dark Payne's
gray, teal
indigo (color)
ink black
logwood blue
midnight blue
navy, dark
Payne's gray, dark
slate (color)
slate blue
teal gray
violet black, dull
CN D.DL.AFU.AFU.BZY.CRG.ALO

dark bluish gray green
USE **dark bluish green**
dark grayish green
grayish green
moderate bluish green

dark bluish green
DL.203
UF blue, deep teal
bluish gray green, dark
bluish green, dark
centroid color 165
dark bluish gray green
dark jade gray
dark jade green
dark teal
dark teal green
deep teal
deep teal blue
deep teal green
gray green, dark bluish
gray, dark jade
green, dark bluish
green, dark jade
green, dark teal
green, deep teal

green, deep teal
green, teal
jade gray, dark
jade green, dark
teal
teal blue, deep
teal green
teal green, dark
teal green, deep
teal, dark
teal, deep
CN D.DL.AFU.AFU.BUE.DCU.ALO.BOK

dark bluish violet
USE **dark violet**
grayish purple
grayish violet

dark brown
DL.81
UF brown, dark
brown, very dark
centroid color 59
very dark brown
CN D.DL.AFU.AFU.AXC.BCW

dark-burnished ware
FL.2595
UF ware, dark-burnished
CN
F.FL.ALO.AXC.ALO.AFU.ALO.AXC.
AFU.ARI

dark carmine
USE **vivid red**

dark cerulean blue
USE **dark greenish blue**
grayish blue

dark delft blue
USE **dark grayish blue**

dark dull bluish violet
USE **dark purple**
grayish violet
moderate violet

dark dull violet blue
USE **grayish purplish blue**
grayish violet

dark dull yellow green
USE **grayish olive green**
moderate olive green

dark eggplant
USE **blackish purple**

dark emerald green
USE **deep green**
moderate bluish green

dark-faced burnished ware
FL.2937
UF burnished ware, dark-faced
ware, dark-faced burnished
CN F.FL.ALO.AXC.ARI.AXC.ALO.
BIQ.BCW

dark-faced incised ware
FL.2596
UF incised ware, dark-faced
ware, dark-faced incised
CN F.FL.ALO.AXC.ALO.AFU.ALO.
AXC.AFU.AXC

dark fuchsia
USE **strong reddish purple**

dark gray
DL.304
UF black, blue violet
black, dull greenish
blackish slate
blackish violet gray
blue green, dark grayish
blue violet black
blue, iron
brown, ebony
centroid color 266
charcoal gray
dark gray, medium
dark grayish blue green
dark neutral gray
dark violet gray
deep navy gray
deep neutral gray
deep violet gray
dull greenish black
dull violet black
ebony brown
ebony (color)
gray, charcoal
gray, dark
gray, dark neutral
gray, deep navy
gray, deep neutral
gray, iron
gray, lead
gray, medium dark
gray, navy
gray, steel
gray, teal
gray, very dark
grayish blue green, dark
greenish black, dull
greenish slate black
gunmetal (color)
gunmetal, light
india ink (color)
ink, india (color)
iron blue
iron gray
lead (color)
lead gray
light gunmetal
medium dark gray
navy gray
navy gray, deep
neutral gray, dark
neutral gray, deep
pewter (color)
rose taupe
slate black, greenish
slate color
slate (color)
slate gray
slate, blackish
steel (color)
steel gray
taupe, rose
teal gray
very dark gray
violet black, dull
violet gray, blackish
violet gray, dark
violet gray, deep
wrought iron (color)
CN D.DL.AFU.ALO.ALO.ARI

dark gray, medium
USE **dark gray**

dark grayish blue
DL.224
UF aniline blue, dark
black, dull blue green
blue green black, dull
blue, dark aniline
blue, dark delft
blue, dark grayish
blue, dark teal
blue, dull
blue, dull greenish
blue, dull reddish
blue, graphite
blue, indigo
blue, ink
blue, teal
centroid color 187
charcoal (color)
dark aniline blue
dark delft blue
dark green blue slate
dark navy
dark Payne's gray
dark teal
dark teal blue
delft blue, dark
dull blue
dull blue green black
dull greenish blue
dull reddish blue
dull violet black
graphite (color)
graphite blue
gray, dark Payne's
gray, Payne's
grayish blue, dark
green blue slate, dark
greenish blue, dull
indigo (color)
indigo blue
ink blue
midnight
navy
navy, dark
Payne's gray
Payne's gray, dark
reddish blue, dull
slate (color)
slate, dark green blue
teal blue
teal blue, dark
teal, dark
violet black, dull
CN D.DL.AFU.AFU.BZY.BZY.AFU

dark grayish blue green
USE **dark gray**
dark greenish gray

dark grayish blue violet
USE **grayish violet**

dark grayish brown
DL.84
UF black brown
blackish brown
brown, black
brown, blackish
brown, dark grayish
brown, dull
centroid color 62
charcoal (color)
dull brown
grayish brown, dark
CN D.DL.AFU.AFU.AXC.BIQ.ALO

dark grayish green
DL.176
UF black, green
blackish green, dull
blue green, dark
bluish gray green, dark
bluish green, dull
centroid color 151
dark blue green
dark bluish gray green
dark slate green
dull blackish green
dull bluish green
dull green
gray green, dark bluish
grayish green, dark
green black
green, dark grayish
green, dark slate
green, dull
green, dull blackish
green, dull bluish
green, hemlock
green, slate
hemlock green
slate (color)
slate green
slate green, dark
CN D.DL.AFU.AFU.BUE.BZY.AFU

dark grayish lavender
USE **pale violet**

dark grayish olive
DL.150
UF centroid color 111
grayish olive, dark
olive, dark grayish
CN D.DL.AFU.AFU.BIQ.AXC.ALO

dark grayish olive green
DL.211
UF bluish olive
centroid color 128
grayish olive green, dark
green, dark grayish olive
green, ivy
ivy green
olive green, dark grayish
olive, bluish
CN D.DL.AFU.AFU.BUE.DCU.ARI.BCW.AFU

dark grayish purple
DL.280
UF aniline black (color)
aniline blue, dark
anthracene purple
athracene violet, dark
black plum
black violet
black, aniline (color)
blue plum
blue, dark aniline
blue, diamin azo
bluish violet, dull
brown, dark violet
brown, taupe
centroid color 229
charcoal (color)
dark aniline blue
dark anthracene violet
dark madder violet
dark naphthalene violet
dark orchid taupe
dark violet brown
deep plum
diamin azo blue
dull bluish violet
dull reddish violet
dull violet
dull violet black
graphite (color)
grayish purple, dark
indigo (color)
madder violet, dark
Mars violet (color)
mauve taupe
mauve, rose
midnight
naphthalene violet, dark
navy
orchid taupe
orchid taupe, dark
plum (color)
plum, black
plum, deep
plum, red
purple, anthracene
purple, dark grayish
red plum
reddish violet, dull
rose mauve
slate purple
slate violet
taupe brown
taupe, dark orchid
taupe, mauve
taupe, orchid
violet black, dull
violet brown, dark
violet, black
violet, dark anthracene
violet, dark madder
violet, dark naphthalene
violet, dull
violet, dull bluish
violet, dull reddish
violet, Mars (color)
CN D.DL.AFU.AFU.CFS.BZY.AFU

dark grayish red
DL.43
UF black, violet
brown, dark rose
brown, dull reddish
brown, light rose
brown, rose
centroid color 20
dark Indian red
dark mauve taupe
dark rose brown
deep maroon
dull reddish brown
grayish red, dark
haematite red
Indian red, dark
light rose brown
maroon
maroon, deep
mauve taupe, dark
red, dark grayish
red, dark Indian
red, haematite
reddish brown, dull
rose brown
rose brown, dark
rose brown, light
taupe, dark mauve
violet black
CN D.DL.AFU.AFU.ALO.BIQ.AFU

dark grayish reddish brown
DL.97
UF brown, dark grayish reddish
brown, dull reddish
centroid color 47
deep maroon
dull reddish brown
maroon, deep
reddish brown, dark grayish
reddish brown, dull
CN D.DL.AFU.AFU.AXC.BZY.AFU.BIQ.ALO

dark grayish yellow
DL.121
UF centroid color 91
dull reddish yellow
dull yellow
grayish yellow, dark
parchment (color)
reddish yellow, dark
yellow, dark grayish
yellow, dull reddish
CN D.DL.AFU.AFU.BCW.BZY.AFU

dark grayish yellowish brown
DL.106
UF asphaltum (color)
bitumen (color)
brown, dark grayish yellowish
brown, dull yellowish
brown, sepia
brown, very dark grayish
centroid color 81

dull yellowish brown
grayish brown, very dark
sepia brown
sepia (color)
very dark grayish brown
yellowish brown, dark grayish
yellowish brown, dull
CN D.DL.AFU.AFU.AXC.BZY.ALO.
BIQ.ALO

dark green
DL.171
UF blue green, dark
centroid color 146
chrome green, medium
dark blue green
dark hunter green
dark jade green
dark slate green
forest green
green, dark
green, dark hunter
green, dark jade
green, dark slate
green, forest
green, hunter
green, medium chrome
hunter green
hunter green, dark
jade green, dark
medium chrome green
mint
slate green, dark
CN D.DL.AFU.AFU.BUE.BOK

dark green blue slate
USE **dark blue**
dark grayish blue

dark greenish blue
DL.240
UF blackish green blue
blue, bright teal
blue, dark cerulean
blue, dark greenish
blue, dark peacock
blue, dark teal
blue, deep cerulean
blue, deep peacock
blue, deep teal
blue, medium
blue, peacock
blue, Prussian (color)
blue, teal
blue, Thalo (color)
bright teal blue
centroid color 174
cerulean blue, dark
cerulean blue, deep
dark cerulean blue
dark peacock blue
dark teal blue
deep cerulean blue
deep peacock blue
deep teal blue
green blue, blackish
greenish blue, dark
medium blue
peacock blue
peacock blue, dark
peacock blue, deep
Prussian blue (color)
teal blue
teal blue, bright
teal blue, dark
teal blue, deep
Thalo blue (color)
CN D.DL.AFU.AFU.BZY.DCU.AFU.BOK

dark greenish gray
DL.181
UF black, dull greenish
black, green
blue green, dark grayish
centroid color 156
dark grayish blue green
dark ivy
deep slate green
deep slate olive
dull greenish black
gray, dark greenish
grayish blue green, dark
green black
greenish black, dull
greenish slate black
ivy
ivy, dark
slate (color)
slate black, greenish
slate green
slate green, deep
slate olive
slate olive, deep
CN D.DL.AFU.AFU.BUE.CRG.ALO

dark greenish olive
USE **grayish olive**
moderate olive

dark greenish yellow
DL.141
UF centroid color 103
chartreuse green
green, chartreuse
green, lime
greenish yellow, dark
light yellowish olive
lime green
olive yellow
olive, light yellowish
yellow, dark greenish
yellow, olive
yellowish olive, light
CN D.DL.AFU.AFU.BCW.CRG.ALO.BOK

dark header
USE **glazed header**

dark hunter green
USE **dark green**
very dark yellowish green

dark Indian red
USE **dark grayish red**
grayish red

dark ivy
USE **dark greenish gray**

dark jade gray
USE **dark bluish green**

dark jade green
USE **dark bluish green**
dark green
light bluish green
moderate bluish green

dark lavender
USE **light purple**

dark madder violet
USE **dark grayish purple**

dark maroon purple
USE **dark reddish purple**

dark mauve taupe
USE **dark grayish red**
dark purplish gray

dark naphthalene violet
USE **dark grayish purple**

dark navy
USE **black**
blackish blue
blackish purple
bluish black
dark blue
dark bluish gray
dark grayish blue
dark purplish blue
dark purplish gray
grayish blue

dark neutral gray
USE **dark gray**

dark nigrosin violet
USE **dark purple**

dark ocher
USE **light olive brown**

dark olive
DL.147
UF black olive
centroid color 108
drab, olive
ebony (color)
olive drab
olive, black
olive, dark
CN D.DL.AFU.AFU.BIQ.ARI

dark olive brown
DL.110
UF brown, dark olive
brown, sepia
brownish olive, dull
centroid color 96
dull brownish olive
olive brown, dark
olive, dull brownish
sepia (color)
sepia brown
CN D.DL.AFU.AFU.AXC.BZY.ARI.ARI

dark olive gray
USE **grayish olive**

grayish olive green
olive gray

dark olive green
DL.209
UF bluish olive
centroid color 126
green, dark olive
olive green, dark
olive, bluish
CN D.DL.AFU.AFU.BUE.DCU.ARI.AXC

dark-on-light painted ware
FL.2655
UF painted ware, dark-on-light
ware, dark-on-light painted
CN F.FL.ALO.AXC.ALO.AFU.ALO.AXC.AXC.AXC.AXC

dark orange yellow
DL.132
UF amber (color)
amber, light
bistre
brown, yellow
brownish yellow
buff
centroid color 72
dark yellowish orange
golden yellow
light amber
Mars yellow (color)
ocher, yellow (color)
orange yellow, dark
orange, dark yellowish
orange, yellowish
raw sienna (color)
reddish yellow
sienna, raw (color)
topaz (color)
yellow brown
yellow ocher (color)
yellow, brownish
yellow, dark orange
yellow, golden
yellow, Mars (color)
yellow, reddish
yellowish orange
yellowish orange, dark
CN D.DL.AFU.AFU.BCW.CRG.AFU.BOK

dark orchid taupe
USE **dark grayish purple**
dark purplish gray

dark Payne's gray
USE **dark bluish gray**
dark grayish blue

dark peacock blue
USE **dark greenish blue**

dark pink
DL.9
UF carmine (color)
centroid color 6
pink, dark
rose
vermilion (color)
CN D.DL.AFU.AFU.AFU.BIQ

dark plum
USE **blackish purple**
dark purplish gray

dark purple
DL.275
UF amethyst (color)
anthracene violet, dark
bluish violet, dark dull
centroid color 224
dark anthracene violet
dark dull bluish violet
dark nigrosin violet
dull bluish violet, dark
litho purple
nigrosin violet
nigrosin violet, dark
plum (color)
purple, dark
purple, litho
violet, dark anthracene
violet, dark dull bluish
violet, dark nigrosin
violet, nigrosin
CN D.DL.AFU.AFU.CFS.BOK

dark purple, dull
USE **deep reddish purple**

dark purplish blue
DL.250
UF blue, cyanine
blue, dark purplish
blue, graphite
blue, midnight
blue, navy
blue, reddish
centroid color 201
cyanine blue
dark navy
graphite blue
light navy
midnight blue
navy
navy blue
navy, dark
navy, light
purplish blue, dark
reddish blue
slate (color)
CN D.DL.AFU.AFU.BZY.DCU.ALO.BOK

dark purplish gray
DL.285
UF aniline black (color)
black plum
black, aniline (color)
black, blue violet
black, deep purplish
black, violet
blackish violet gray
blue violet black
centroid color 234
charcoal (color)
dark mauve taupe
dark navy
dark orchid taupe
dark plum
dark slate violet
deep purplish black
deep violet gray
dull violet black
gray, dark purplish
gray, taupe
mauve taupe
mauve taupe, dark
midnight blue
navy, dark
orchid taupe, dark
plum, black
plum, dark
purplish black, deep
purplish gray, dark
slate (color)
slate violet
slate violet, dark
taupe gray
taupe, dark mauve
taupe, dark orchid
taupe, mauve
violet black
violet black, dull
violet gray, blackish
violet gray, deep
CN D.DL.AFU.AFU.CFS.CRG.ALO

dark purplish pink
DL.21
UF bluish pink
centroid color 251
lilac, rose
mauve, orchid
orchid mauve
pink, bluish
pink, dark purplish
purplish pink, dark
rose
rose lilac
CN D.DL.AFU.AFU.AFU.CLM.AFU.BIQ

dark purplish red
DL.56
UF anthracene purple
black violet
blackish red purple
bluish red, dull
brown violet
brown, dark violet
brown, violet
carmine, violet (color)
centroid color 259
dark violet brown
deep lake
dull bluish red
dull violet
garnet (color)
lake, deep
lake, purple
lake, rose
magenta (color)
magenta rose
maroon
mauve, rose
plum violet
plum, red
plum, rose
purple lake

purple, anthracene
purple, red
purplish red, dark
red plum
red purple
red purple, blackish
red, dark purplish
red, dull bluish
rose lake
rose mauve
rose plum
rose, magenta
violet brown
violet brown, dark
violet carmine (color)
violet, black
violet, brown
violet, dull
violet, plum
CN D.DL.AFU.AFU.ALO.CFS.AFU.BCW

dark putty
USE **olive gray**

dark red
DL.40
UF brick red
brown carmine
brown, dull reddish
brown, garnet
brown, orange
brown, red
carmine, brown
centroid color 16
dull red
dull reddish brown
garnet (color)
garnet brown
garnet red
garnet, light
haematite red
lake (color)
light garnet
madder, purple
maroon
orange brown
purple madder
red brown
red, brick
red, dark
red, dull
red, garnet
red, haematite
red, rose
reddish brown, dull
rose red
ruby (color)
CN D.DL.AFU.AFU.ALO.BCW

dark red brown
USE **grayish reddish brown**

dark reddish brown
DL.94
UF brown, dark reddish
brown, dull reddish
centroid color 44
dull reddish brown
maroon
reddish brown, dark
reddish brown, dull
CN D.DL.AFU.AFU.AXC.BZY.AFU.BCW

dark reddish gray
DL.47
UF blackish brown
brown, blackish
brown, dark rose
brown, ebony
brown, mauve
centroid color 23
dark rose brown
dark rose taupe
ebony brown
gray, dark reddish
mauve taupe
reddish gray, dark
rose brown, dark
rose taupe
rose taupe, dark
rose, taupe
taupe rose
taupe, dark rose
taupe, mauve
taupe, rose
CN D.DL.AFU.AFU.ALO.BUE.AFU

dark reddish orange
DL.73
UF brown, red
brown, yellow
burnt Italian earth
burnt Italian ocher
burnt sienna (color)
centroid color 38
Indian red (color)
Mars orange
Mars red
ocher, burnt Italian
orange, dark reddish
orange, Mars
red brown
red, Indian (color)
red, Mars
red, yellowish
reddish orange, dark
sienna, burnt (color)
terra cotta (color)
vermilion (color)
yellow brown
yellowish red
CN D.DL.AFU.AFU.ARI.BOK.AFU.BCW

dark reddish purple
DL.295
UF carmine, violet (color)
centroid color 242
dark maroon purple
fuchsia purple
magenta (color)
maroon purple, dark
naphthalene violet
purple, dark maroon
purple, dark reddish
purple, fuchsia
reddish purple, dark
reddish violet
slate purple
violet carmine (color)
violet, naphthalene
violet, reddish
CN D.DL.AFU.AFU.CFS.DCU.AFU.BIQ

dark rose
USE **moderate purplish red**
moderate red

dark rose brown
USE **dark grayish red**
dark reddish gray

dark rose taupe
USE **brownish gray**
dark reddish gray

dark slate green
USE **blackish green**
dark grayish green
dark green
very dark green

dark slate violet
USE **dark purplish gray**
grayish purple

dark steel blue
USE **grayish blue**

dark teal
USE **dark bluish green**
dark grayish blue
grayish blue
very dark bluish green

dark teal blue
USE **dark grayish blue**
dark greenish blue

dark teal green
USE **dark bluish green**

dark terre verte
USE **grayish green**

dark violet
DL.262
UF blackish violet
blue plum
bluish violet
bluish violet, dark
centroid color 212
dark bluish violet
navy, reddish
plum (color)
plum purple
plum, blue
purple, plum
reddish navy
violet, blackish
violet, bluish
violet, dark
violet, dark bluish
CN D.DL.AFU.AFU.BZY.DCU.ARI.BOK

dark violet brown
USE **blackish purple**
dark grayish purple
dark purplish red
very dark purplish red

dark violet gray
USE **dark gray**

dark violet slate
USE **grayish blue**

dark viridian green
USE **moderate green**

dark yellow
DL.118
UF bistre
brass (color)
centroid color 88
mustard
olive yellow
reddish yellow
yellow, dark
yellow, olive
yellow, reddish
CN D.DL.AFU.AFU.BCW.BOK

dark yellowish brown
DL.103
UF brown, dark yellowish
brown, dull yellowish
brown, mummy
brown, sepia
brown, very dark
centroid color 78
dull yellowish brown
mummy brown
raw umber (color)
sepia brown
umber, raw (color)
very dark brown
yellowish brown, dark
yellowish brown, dull
CN D.DL.AFU.AFU.AXC.BZY.ALO.BCW

dark yellowish green
DL.193
UF centroid color 137
chrome green, deep
chrome green, light
chrome green, medium
deep chrome green
deep dull yellow green
dull green
dull yellow green, deep
green, dark yellowish
green, deep chrome
green, dull
green, light chrome
green, medium chrome
light chrome green
medium chrome green
yellow green, deep dull
yellowish green, dark
CN D.DL.AFU.AFU.BUE.DCU.AFU.BOK

dark yellowish orange
USE **dark orange yellow**

dark yellowish pink
DL.30
UF centroid color 30
pink, dark yellowish
rose
vermilion (color)
yellowish pink, dark
CN D.DL.AFU.AFU.AFU.CLM.ALO.BIQ

darkness
BM.854 (R)
CN B.BM.CFS.AXC.ALO.AFU.ALO.ALO.ALO

darkrooms
RM.398 (L,B)
ALT **darkroom**
SN Rooms freed from light or lighted by a safelight for handling and processing light-sensitive materials. (W)
UF darkrooms, photographic
photographic darkrooms
CN V.RM.AFU.DIO.BIQ.ARI

darkrooms, photographic
USE **darkrooms**

Darwinism, Social
USE **Social Darwinism**

dash, pebble
USE **pebble dash**

dash, rock
USE **pebble dash**

data conversion
KG.85
SN Changing the representation of data in a database from one form to another, as for instance changing the storage medium, data format, or the code in which the data is held.
UF conversion, data
CN K.KG.AFU.AFU.AXC.BIQ.AFU

data dictionaries
VW.354 (L)
ALT **data dictionary**
UF dictionaries, data
CN V.VW.AFU.AFU.ALO.CXA.BIQ.BCW.AFU

data files
USE **databases**

data processing
KG.84 (L)
UF electronic data processing
processing, data
processing, electronic data
CN K.KG.AFU.AFU.AXC.BIQ

data processing centers
USE **computer centers**

data processing service centers
USE **computer centers**

data retrieval
USE **information retrieval**

data search services
USE **information retrieval services**

database search services, online
USE **information retrieval services**

database searching
USE **online searching**

database vendors
USE **online vendors**

databases
VW.645 (A,L)
ALT **database**
SN Structured assemblies of logically related data, usually machine-readable data, designed to meet various applications but managed independently of them. (ICA)
UF data files
files, data
CN V.VW.AFU.ALO.AFU.DZW.ALO.ALO

databases, bibliographic
USE **bibliographic databases**

date books
USE **appointment books**

date marks
VW.716
ALT **date mark**
UF marks, date
CN V.VW.AFU.ALO.ALO.AFU.AXC.ALO.AXC

Datia
FL.2268
CN F.FL.ALO.ARI.AXC.ALO.AFU.BZY.BCW.AFU.ALO

dating
KT.496 (A,L)
ALT **dated**
SN Determining or fixing a date of origination, fabrication, composition, or occurrence. (W)
CN K.KT.AFU.ALO.EFQ.AFU

dating, archaeomagnetic
USE **paleomagnetic dating**

dating, C-14
USE **radiocarbon dating**

dating, carbon-14
USE **radiocarbon dating**

dating, fission track
USE **fission track dating**

dating, fluorine
USE **fluorine dating**

dating, hydration ring
USE **neutron activation analysis**

dating, K-Ar
USE **potassium-argon dating**

dating, nitrogen
USE **nitrogen dating**

dating, obsidian hydration
USE **obsidian hydration dating**

dating, paleomagnetic
USE **paleomagnetic dating**

dating, potassium-argon
USE **potassium-argon dating**

dating, radioactive
USE **radioactive dating**

dating, radiocarbon
USE **radiocarbon dating**

dating, radiometric
USE **radioactive dating**

dating, thermoluminescence
USE **thermoluminescence dating**

dating, tree ring
USE **dendrochronology**

daub
MT.2388
SN Material, such as plaster or mud, used with wattle as a building material.
CN M.MT.AFU.ARI.BZY.ARI

daub, wattle and
USE **wattle and daub**

daughters
HG.10 (L)
ALT **daughter**
CN H.HG.AFU.ALO.AFU.AFU

Daulatabad
FL.2255
UF Devagiri
CN F.FL.ALO.ARI.AXC.ALO.AFU.BZY.AFU.AXC

davenport beds
USE **davenports**

davenport desks
USE **davenports (desks)**

davenport tables
USE **sofa tables**

davenports
TG.317 (N)
ALT **davenport**
SN Large upholstered sofas, often convertible into beds. (W)
UF beds, davenport
davenport beds
CN V.TG.AFU.AFU.ALO.ALO.BZY.BOK.AFU

davenports (desks)
TG.528 (R)
ALT **davenport (desk)**
UF davenport desks
desks, davenport
devonports
CN V.TG.AFU.AFU.AXC.ALO.BZY.AXC

David's shields
USE **Stars of David**

davits
TB.65 (L,N)
ALT **davit**
SN Fixed or moveable cranes that project over the side of a ship or over a hatchway; used especially for hoisting ship's boats, anchors, or cargo. (W)
UF anchor davits
boat davits
davits, anchor
davits, boat
davits, hatch
hatch davits
CN V.TB.AFU.ARI.AFU.BCW.AXC.AXC

davits, anchor
USE **davits**

davits, boat
USE **davits**

davits, hatch
USE **davits**

dawn redwood
MT.1392
UF Metasequoia glyptostroboides
redwood, dawn
CN M.MT.AFU.AFU.ALO.BIQ.DCU.AFU.AFU.ALO.DCU.AFU

dawn, gray
USE **purplish gray**

Dawu
FL.77
CN F.FL.ALO.AFU.ALO.AFU.AFU

day
BM.1034 (L,R)
CN B.BM.CFS.AXC.CRG.AFU

day camps
RG.157 (L)
ALT **day camp**
UF camps, day
CN V.RG.AFU.AFU.DOI.AXC.AFU

day care
HG.876 (L)
SN Care of children or others unable to be left by themselves by persons other than their parents, family, or guardians on a partial or full day basis.
UF care, day
CN H.HG.ALO.DIO.BCW.AFU

day care centers
RK.833 (A,L,B)
ALT **day care center**
UF centers, child care
centers, day care
child care centers
creches
day nurseries
nurseries, day
CN V.RK.AFU.ALO.ALO.CXA.ARI.AXC.AFU.AFU

day care centers, adult
USE **adult day care centers**

day-glow paint
USE **fluorescent paint**

day nurseries
USE **day care centers**

Day of Atonement
USE **Yom Kippur**

day schools
RK.797
ALT **day school**
SN Use for schools, usually elementary or secondary, where classes are held only on weekdays and that do not provide any boarding facilities.
UF schools, day
CN V.RK.AFU.ALO.ALO.CXA.ARI.AFU.ARI

daybeds
TG.392 (N)
ALT **daybed**
SN Extended chairs, generally without arms, used for lounging with one backed end usually made to tilt; often supported on a stretcher frame with six or eight legs.
UF beds, rest
lits de repos
reading seats
rest beds
seats, reading
sultanes (lits de repos)
CN V.TG.AFU.AFU.ARI.ARI

daybooks
VW.847 (N)
ALT **daybook**
SN Volumes used in bookkeeping containing daily records of receipts and expenditures in the order of their occurrence. (GAHLM)
CN V.VW.AFU.ARI.AFU.BIQ.CXA.AFU.BOK.AFU

daylight
BM.848 (A,L,B)
SN Use with reference to the natural light of day; for the direct light of the sun specifically, use **sunlight.**
UF daylighting
light, natural
lighting, natural
natural light
natural lighting
CN B.BM.CFS.AXC.ALO.AFU.ALO.AFU.ALO

daylighting
USE **daylight**

De
FL.318
CN F.FL.ALO.AFU.AXC.AFU.ARI.AXC.AFU

De Stijl
FL.3350 (A,B,R)
UF Stijl, De
CN F.FL.ALO.BCW.ALO.AXC.DIO.AXC.AFU

deaccessioning
KG.79
ALT **deaccessioned**
SN Permanently removing an object from a collection.
CN K.KG.AFU.AFU.AXC.AXC.BZY

deacon's benches
TG.281
ALT **deacon's bench**
UF benches, deacons'
benches, meeting house
deacon's seats
meeting house benches
meeting house seats
seats, deacon's
seats, meeting house
CN V.TG.AFU.AFU.ALO.ALO.AFU.AFU.AXC

deacon's seats
USE **deacon's benches**

deacons
HG.223 (L,R)
ALT **deacon**
SN Subordinate officers in a Christian church. (W)
CN H.HG.AFU.AXC.AXC.BIQ.AFU.ARI.BUE

dead-blow mallets
TB.1091
ALT **dead-blow mallet**
SN Mallets whose heads are filled with lead shot so that there is no rebound to the blow. (HAND)
UF mallets, dead-blow
CN V.TB.AFU.BCW.CFS.ALO.ARI.ALO.BCW

dead bolts
TF.554
ALT **dead bolt**
SN Door locks that must be operated actively in both directions by turning a key or a thumb bolt. (MEANS)
UF bolts, dead
CN V.TF.AFU.ALO.AXC.AFU.BCW

dead bolts, split
USE **split dead bolts**

dead-end streets
RK.1533 (L)
ALT **dead-end street**
UF streets, dead-end
CN V.RK.ALO.ALO.BIQ.ARI.AFU.ALO.AFU.AXC

dead latches
USE **night latches**

dead latches, auxiliary
USE **auxiliary dead latches**

dead loads
BM.1009 (L)
SN Constant loads in structures that are due to the combined weight of its members, the supported structures, and permanent attachments or accessories. (W)
UF loads, dead
loads, static
static loads
CN B.BM.CFS.AXC.CLM.ALO.ARI.BCW

dead oil
USE **creosote**

dead walls
USE **blank walls**

deadlights
USE **fixed windows**

deadlocking latch bolts
USE **auxiliary dead latches**

deadlocking latches
USE **auxiliary dead latches**

deadlocks
TF.199
ALT **deadlock**
SN Use for locks with dead bolts only.
CN V.TF.AFU.AFU.AFU.AFU.DIO.BIQ.AFU.BCW

deaf
HG.788 (L,B)
SN People deprived of the functional use of the sense of hearing. (ERIC)
CN H.HG.AFU.BOK.AXC.ALO.ALO.ALO

deal, white
USE **common spruce**

deal, yellow
USE **Scotch pine**

dealers
HG.414 (R)
ALT **dealer**
SN Persons who buy and sell. (W)
CN H.HG.AFU.AXC.BOK.CRG

dealers' marks
VW.717
ALT **dealer's mark**
UF marks, dealers'
CN V.VW.AFU.ALO.ALO.AFU.AXC.ALO.BCW

dealerships, automobile
USE **automobile showrooms**

deambulatories
USE **ambulatories**

deaneries
RK.327 (A,L,B,R)
ALT **deanery**
CN V.RK.AFU.ALO.ALO.AXC.ALO.BOK.ARI.AFU

deans
HG.297 (L)
ALT **dean**
SN Persons who head one of the divisions, faculties, colleges, or schools of a university. (W)
CN H.HG.AFU.AXC.BCW.ALO.ARI.AFU

death
KM.135 (L,R)
CN K.KM.AFU.DOI.ALO

death certificates
VW.952 (L,N)
ALT **death certificate**
SN Certificates issued by public officials stating that a person has died; often include the cause of death and the signature of the attending or examining physician. (BLACKS)
UF certificates, death
CN V.VW.AFU.ARI.AFU.DCU.ALO.ALO

death notices
USE **obituaries**

death records
VW.950
ALT **death record**
SN Official records of deaths kept by public officials charged with registering deaths. (BLACKS)
UF records, death
CN V.VW.AFU.ARI.AFU.DCU.ALO

death registers
VW.953 (L,R)
ALT **death register**
UF necrologies
registers, death
CN V.VW.AFU.ARI.AFU.DCU.ALO.ARI

debarkers
USE **barkers**

debtor's prisons
RK.721 (A)
ALT **debtor's prison**
SN Use for local places of detention primarily for debtors.
UF compters
prisons, debtor's
CN V.RK.AFU.ALO.ALO.CXA.AFU.AXC.AFU.AFU

Decadence (artistic and literary movement)
USE **Decadent Movement**

Decadent Movement
FL.3256 (L,R)
UF Decadence (artistic and literary movement)
CN F.FL.ALO.BCW.ALO.AXC.BCW.AFU

Decadent period
USE **Late Postclassic**

decagons
BM.784
ALT **decagonal**
CN B.BM.CFS.ARI.AXC.BCW.AFU.BIQ.BIQ

decalcomania
KT.741 (L,R)
SN Includes the art or process of transferring pictures and designs from specially prepared paper onto a surface, such as glass, and the Surrealist painting technique in which one freshly painted or inked surface is pressed against another to form an image.
CN K.KT.AFU.ALO.HCQ.ALO.ALO

decanter labels
USE **wine labels**

decastyle
DC.85
CN D.DC.AFU.ARI.ERE.BIQ.ALO

decay
KT.899
ALT **decayed**
SN Use for the process of passing gradually from a comparatively sound or perfect state to one of unsoundness, imperfection, or dissolution. (W)
CN K.KT.ALO.BCW.AXC

decay, urban
USE **urban decay**

Deccani
FL.2251 (L)
UF Deccani School
Dekkhan
CN F.FL.ALO.ARI.AXC.ALO.AFU.BZY.AFU

Deccani School
USE **Deccani**

decentralization
BM.534 (L)
CN B.BM.BOK.AXC

deception beds
TG.339
ALT **deception bed**
SN Any of various kinds of concealed or disguised beds first designed in the 18th century. Such beds were among the many ingenious forms of late 19th-century patent furniture.
UF beds, concealed
beds, deception
concealed beds
CN V.TG.AFU.AFU.ARI.AFU.AFU.BIQ.AFU

deciduous trees
RD.275
ALT **deciduous tree**
UF trees, deciduous
CN V.RD.ARI.AFU.BCW.ALO.ALO.ALO.ARI.AFU.AFU

decision making
KG.12 (L)
CN K.KG.AFU.AFU.AFU.BOK

decisions
VW.1010
ALT **decision**
UF court decisions
determinations
judgements
CN V.VW.AFU.ARI.ALO.BCW.AFU.ALO.AFU.AFU

deck bridges
USE **deck truss bridges**

deck chairs
TG.206 (N)
ALT **deck chair**
SN Chairs usually with arms and having full-length leg rests, designed for lounging outdoors. Use chaises longues for similar forms used indoors.
UF chairs, deck
chairs, steamer
steamer chairs
CN V.TG.AFU.AFU.ALO.AFU.AFU.ARI.ALO

deck dowelling bits
USE **tenon-cutting bits**

deck nails
TF.432
ALT **deck nail**
UF nails, deck
CN V.TF.AFU.AFU.AFU.ALO.AFU.CFS.ALO.AXC

deck paint
MT.2536
SN Enamel with a high degree of resistance to mechanical wear, for use on such surfaces as porch floors. (STEIN)
UF paint, deck
CN M.MT.AFU.ARI.CRG.ALO.BCW.ALO.ALO

deck plans
VD.58
ALT **deck plan**
SN In shipbuilding, drawings showing layouts of decks.
UF plans, deck
CN V.VD.AFU.AFU.BIQ.ALO.AXC.ARI

deck span bridges
USE **deck truss bridges**

deck truss bridges
RK.1303
ALT **deck truss bridge**
SN Truss bridges having the roadway or track on top of the trusses. (WB)
UF bridges, deck
bridges, deck truss
deck bridges
deck span bridges
CN V.RK.AFU.ALO.ALO.GLI.ALO.AFU.ARI.BUE.AFU

deck trusses
USE **through trusses**

decking
RT.326
SN Self-supporting flooring or roofing unit that is able to span between structural members. (HORNB)
UF planking
planks (decking)
CN V.RT.AFU.AFU.AFU.BCW.BUE

deckling
KT.858
ALT **deckled**
SN Use for the process of decreasing the width of handmade paper by the use of detachable frames surrounding the papermaker's mold.
CN K.KT.AFU.ALO.HOE.BIQ.ALO.ALO

decks
RM.50 (A,L)
ALT **deck**
SN Use for uncovered wood or metal platforms, usually attached to structures and raised off the ground.
CN V.RM.AFU.DIO.AFU.BCW.AXC

decks, observation
USE **observation decks**

decks, sun
USE **sun decks**

Deckweiss
USE **lithopone**

declarations
VW.318 (L)
ALT **declaration**
SN Documents conveying formal statements intended to create, preserve, assert, or testify to a right. (OCLD)
CN V.VW.AFU.AFU.ALO.BOK.ALO

decline, population
USE **population decline**

Deco, American
USE **Art Deco**

Deco, Art
USE **Art Deco**

décollage
KT.185 (R)
SN The tearing away of parts of posters, or other objects, that have been applied in layers, so that selected portions of the underlayers contribute to the total image. The reverse of collage. (PDAT)
CN K.KT.AFU.ALO.DUC.BUE

deconsecration
KM.36
SN Act or ceremony of removing the sacred character of a thing or place. (WCOL)
CN K.KM.AFU.ARI.AXC.BOK.AFU

deconstruction
BM.290 (R)

SN Strategy of critical analysis arising in the mid-20th century, directed toward exposing unquestioned assumptions and internal contradictions in philiosophical and literary language. (OED)
CN B.BM.AFU.AXC.AXC.AFU

Deconstructivist
FL.3708 (A)
ALT **Deconstructivism**
CN F.FL.ALO.BUE.ALO.ARI

Decorated Style
FL.3124 (R)
UF Pointed, Second
Second Pointed
CN F.FL.ALO.BCW.ALO.ALO.AFU.BOK.ARI.ALO.AXC.AFU

Decorated, Curvilinear
USE **Curvilinear Decorated**

Decorated, Early
USE **Early Decorated**

Decorated, Geometrical
USE **Early Decorated**

decorating
USE **decoration**

decoration
KT.93 (A,L,B,R)
ALT **decorated**
SN Use for the overall approach to and techniques of embellishing architecture, furniture, or other objects. Use **ornament** in reference to specific forms, such as fluting, finials, or monograms, that embellish and are part of the building or object, but are not structurally essential to it.
UF decorating
CN K.KT.AFU.ALO.BZY

decoration, encaustic
USE **encaustic decoration**

decoration, foliate
USE **foliation**

decoration, graffito
USE **sgraffito**

decoration, interior
USE **interior decoration**

decoration, knulled
USE **gadrooning**

decoration, lobed
USE **gadrooning**

decoration, nulled
USE **gadrooning**

decoration, running
USE **running ornament**

Decorationist
USE **Pattern painting**

decorative arts
KD.19 (L,B,R)
SN Traditional Western designation for those arts involving the creation of works that serve utilitarian as well as aesthetic purposes, or involving the decoration and embellishment of utilitarian objects.
UF applied arts
arts, applied
arts, decorative
arts, minor
minor arts
CN K.KD.AFU.AFU.AFU.AFU.ALO.ALO.AFU

decorative arts museums
RK.385
ALT **decorative arts museum**
UF museums, decorative arts
CN V.RK.AFU.ALO.ALO.BCW.AXC.ARI.AFU.ALO

decorative glass
USE **figured glass**

decorative lighting
USE **architectural lighting**

decorators' show houses
RK.274
ALT **decorators' show house**
UF houses, show
show houses
CN V.RK.AFU.ALO.ALO.AXC.ALO.ALO.AFU

decorators, interior
USE **interior decorators**

decorum
BM.294 (R)
SN A critical concept concerning the qualities of congruence among the elements of a work of visual art, literature, or theater, and good taste in the work's relationship to external reality.
UF propriety
CN B.BM.AFU.AXC.BIQ

decrees
VW.319 (L)
ALT **decree**
SN Includes judicial decisions issued in an equity or probate court and doctrinal or disciplinary religious orders applying or interpreting articles of canon law.
UF edicts
CN V.VW.AFU.AFU.ALO.BOK.ARI

decretals
VW.320 (R)
ALT **decretal**
SN Letters of the pope determining some point or question in ecclesiastical law and possessing the force of law within the Roman Catholic Church. (BLACKS)
CN V.VW.AFU.AFU.ALO.BOK.ARI.AFU

decumani
RK.1545
ALT **decumanus**
SN Designates the east-west streets used in laying out ancient Roman countryside tracts and associated towns and thus, by extension, the main east-west streets, distinguished by greater width and scale of appointments, of planned Roman towns.
CN V.RK.ALO.ALO.BIQ.ARI.AFU.ALO.ARI.ALO.ALO

dedicatees
HG.777
ALT **dedicatee**
SN Persons to whom anything is dedicated. (OED)
CN H.HG.AFU.BOK.ALO

dedication to public use
BM.445 (L)
SN An appropriation or giving up of property to public use that precludes the owner from asserting any right of ownership inconsistent with the use for which the property is dedicated. (W)
UF public use, dedication to
use, dedication to public
CN B.BM.BCW.ARI

Dedication, Feast of
USE **Hanukkah**

dedications
VW.324 (L)
ALT **dedication**
SN Authors' notes prefixed to works, offering them to friends or patrons as marks of esteem, affection, or gratitude, or as pleas for patronage. (GAHLM)
CN V.VW.AFU.AFU.ALO.BUE

dedications (ceremonies)
KM.20 (L)
SN Acts or rites of dedicating something or someone to a special use or purpose, or to the memory of particular people or events.
CN K.KM.AFU.ARI.ARI.ARI

deed books
VW.526
ALT **deed book**
UF books, deed
CN V.VW.AFU.ALO.AFU.AFU.ALO.AXC

deed registers
VW.925
ALT **deed register**
UF registers, deed
CN V.VW.AFU.ARI.AFU.BZY.ALO

deeds
VW.927 (L,N)
ALT **deed**
SN Documents, usually executed under

seal, containing a conveyance, especially of real estate. (RHDEL2)
UF deeds, title
title deeds
CN V.VW.AFU.ARI.AFU.BZY.ARI

deeds, mortgage
USE **mortgage deeds**

deeds, title
USE **deeds**

deep bistre
USE **light olive brown**

deep blue
DL.216
UF blue, deep
blue, deep royal
blue, deep sapphire
blue, dull
blue, lapis lazuli
blue, powder
blue, royal
bright navy
centroid color 179
deep royal blue
deep sapphire blue
dull blue
indigo (color)
lapis lazuli blue
navy, bright
powder blue
royal blue
royal blue, deep
sapphire blue, deep
smalt (color)
ultramarine
CN D.DL.AFU.AFU.BZY.AXC

deep blue violet
USE **vivid purplish blue**
vivid violet

deep bluish gray green
USE **grayish green**

deep bluish green
DL.199
UF bluish green, deep
centroid color 161
deep turquoise green
green, deep bluish
green, deep turquoise
green, Prussian
Prussian green
turquoise green, deep
CN D.DL.AFU.AFU.BUE.DCU.ALO.AXC

deep brown
DL.78
UF brown, deep
brown, metallic
centroid color 56
metallic brown
CN D.DL.AFU.AFU.AXC.ALO

deep cadmium yellow
MT.1774
UF cadmium yellow, deep
jaune de cadmium foncé
Kadmiumgelb dunkel
orient yellow
yellow, deep cadmium
yellow, orient
CN M.MT.AFU.AFU.ARI.AFU.AFU.ALO.ALO.BUE.ARI.ALO.ARI

deep cerulean blue
USE **dark greenish blue**
deep greenish blue
moderate blue
moderate greenish blue

deep chrome
USE **strong orange yellow**

deep chrome green
USE **dark yellowish green**

deep chrome yellow
USE **moderate orange yellow**

deep cobalt phosphate
MT.1720
UF cobalt phosphate, deep
phosphate, deep cobalt
CN M.MT.AFU.AFU.ARI.AFU.AFU.ALO.ALO.BIQ.ARI.AFU.AFU

deep delft blue
USE **grayish blue**

deep dull bluish violet
USE **grayish purplish blue**
moderate violet
pale purplish blue
pale violet
strong violet

deep dull lavender
USE **pale purple**

deep dull yellow green
USE **dark yellowish green**
moderate olive green
moderate yellow green

deep emerald green
USE **moderate bluish green**
moderate green

deep etching
KT.459
SN The etching of an offset printing plate to such a degree that the printing area becomes slightly recessed and thereby productive of sharper definition and longer runs. (W)
UF etching, deep
CN K.KT.AFU.ALO.DUC.DUC.ALO.BCW.AFU.AXC.ALO

deep grayish blue green
USE **grayish green**

deep grayish lavender
USE **pale purple**
pale violet

deep grayish olive
USE **olive gray**

deep green
DL.167
UF bright green
centroid color 142
dark emerald green
emerald green, dark
green, bright
green, dark emerald
green, deep
CN D.DL.AFU.AFU.BUE.AXC

deep green blue gray
USE **grayish blue**

deep greenish blue
DL.236
UF blue, deep cerulean
blue, deep greenish
blue, Prussian (color)
centroid color 170
cerulean blue, deep
deep cerulean blue
green, Prussian
greenish blue, deep
Prussian blue (color)
Prussian green
CN D.DL.AFU.AFU.BZY.DCU.AFU.AXC

deep greenish yellow
DL.138
UF centroid color 100
greenish yellow, deep
lemon yellow
olive yellow
yellow, deep greenish
yellow, lemon
yellow, olive
CN D.DL.AFU.AFU.BCW.CRG.ALO.AXC

deep lake
USE **dark purplish red**

deep lavender
USE **light violet**

deep lavender blue
USE **brilliant purplish blue**

deep magenta
USE **vivid purplish red**

deep malachite green
USE **moderate yellowish green**

deep maroon
USE **dark grayish red**
dark grayish reddish brown

deep navy gray
USE **dark gray**

deep neutral gray
USE **dark gray**

deep olive
USE **grayish olive**
moderate olive

deep olive gray
USE **light olive gray**

deep olive green
DL.207
UF bluish olive
centroid color 124
green, deep olive
olive green, deep
olive, bluish
CN D.DL.AFU.AFU.BUE.DCU.ARI.ALO

deep orange
DL.64
UF brown orange
brown, orange
brown, red
centroid color 51
ocher (color)
orange brown
orange vermilion (color)
orange, brown
orange, deep
orange, xanthine
red brown
terra cotta (color)
vermilion, orange (color)
xanthine orange
CN D.DL.AFU.AFU.ARI.AXC

deep orange yellow
DL.129
UF amber (color)
centroid color 69
Mars yellow (color)
orange yellow, deep
orange, yellowish
reddish yellow
yellow, deep orange
yellow, Mars (color)
yellow, reddish
yellowish orange
CN D.DL.AFU.AFU.BCW.CRG.AFU.AXC

deep Payne's gray
USE **grayish blue**

deep peacock blue
USE **dark greenish blue**
moderate greenish blue

deep pink
DL.6
UF alizarine pink
bright rose
centroid color 3
deep rose
pink, alizarine
pink, deep
rose, bright
rose, deep
scarlet
CN D.DL.AFU.AFU.AFU.ARI

deep plum
USE **dark grayish purple**
moderate purplish red
very dark reddish purple

deep purple
DL.270
UF centroid color 219
purple, deep
red violet
CN D.DL.AFU.AFU.CFS.AXC

deep purplish black
USE **dark purplish gray**

deep purplish blue
DL.246
UF blue, deep purplish
blue, deep royal
blue, reddish
blue, royal
blue, sapphire
centroid color 197
deep royal blue
purplish blue, deep
reddish blue
royal blue
royal blue, deep
sapphire blue
CN D.DL.AFU.AFU.BZY.DCU.ALO.AXC

deep purplish pink
DL.18
UF bluish pink
bright rose
bright rose violet
carmine rose
centroid color 248
fuchsia pink
light orchid rose
lilac rose
orchid
orchid rose
orchid rose, light
pink, bluish
pink, deep purplish
pink, fuchsia
purplish pink, deep
rose
rose violet, bright
rose, bright
rose, carmine
rose, light orchid
rose, lilac
rose, orchid
violet, bright rose
CN D.DL.AFU.AFU.AFU.CLM.AFU.ARI

deep purplish red
DL.53
UF bluish red
bright fuchsia purple
brown, rose
carmine (color)
centroid color 256
cerise
crimson
fuchsia purple
fuchsia purple, bright
fuchsia red
magenta (color)
magenta rose
plum (color)
purple, bright fuchsia
purple, fuchsia
purplish red, deep
red, bluish
red, deep purplish
red, fuchsia
rose brown
rose violet
rose, magenta
ruby (color)
violet, rose
CN D.DL.AFU.AFU.ALO.CFS.AFU.ARI

deep red
DL.37
UF brown, garnet
brown, rose
cadmium purple
carmine (color)
centroid color 13
garnet brown
garnet red
lake, purple
purple lake
purple, cadmium
red, deep
red, garnet
red, rose
red, ruby
rose brown
rose red
ruby (color)
ruby red
CN D.DL.AFU.AFU.ALO.ARI

deep red brown
USE **grayish reddish brown**

deep reddish brown
DL.91
UF brown, deep reddish
brown, metallic
centroid color 41
dull red
garnet (color)
maroon
Mars violet (color)
metallic brown
metallic red
red oxide
red, dull
red, metallic
red, Venetian (color)
reddish brown, deep
Venetian red (color)
violet, Mars (color)
CN D.DL.AFU.AFU.AXC.BZY.AFU.ALO

deep reddish orange
DL.71
UF centroid color 36
lacquer red
lead, red (color)
orange, deep reddish
quinacridone red (color)
red lead (color)
red, lacquer
red, quinacridone (color)
red, yellowish
reddish orange, deep
vermilion (color)
yellowish red
CN D.DL.AFU.AFU.ARI.BOK.AFU.ARI

deep reddish purple
DL.291
UF bright fuchsia purple
centroid color 238
dark purple, dull
dull dark purple
fuchsia purple, bright
plum (color)
purple, bright fuchsia
purple, deep reddish
purple, dull dark
purple, red
purple, violet
red purple
red violet
reddish purple, deep
reddish violet
rose violet
violet purple
violet, red
violet, reddish
violet, rose
CN D.DL.AFU.AFU.CFS.DCU.AFU.ARI

deep rose
USE **deep pink**
moderate purplish red
moderate red

deep rose pink
USE **strong purplish pink**

deep royal blue
USE **dark blue**
deep blue
deep purplish blue
moderate purplish blue

deep sapphire blue
USE **dark blue**
deep blue
moderate purplish blue

deep-sea moorings
USE **moorings**

deep slate blue
USE **grayish blue**

deep slate green
USE **dark greenish gray**

deep slate olive
USE **dark greenish gray**

deep slate violet
USE **grayish purple**

deep teal
USE **dark bluish green**

deep teal blue
USE **dark bluish green**
dark greenish blue
moderate greenish blue

deep teal green
USE **dark bluish green**

deep turquoise green
USE **deep bluish green**
moderate bluish green

deep ultramarine
USE **moderate blue**
vivid blue
vivid purplish blue

deep violet
DL.258
UF bluish violet
centroid color 208
violet, bluish
violet, deep
CN D.DL.AFU.AFU.BZY.DCU.ARI.AXC

deep violet gray
USE **dark gray**
dark purplish gray
medium gray
purplish gray

deep yellow
DL.115
UF aniline yellow
bistre
bright gold
centroid color 85
gold, bright
lemon yellow
reddish yellow
yellow, aniline
yellow, deep
yellow, lemon
yellow, reddish
CN D.DL.AFU.AFU.BCW.AXC

deep yellow green
DL.158
UF centroid color 118
green, deep yellow
yellow green, deep
CN D.DL.AFU.AFU.BOK.AXC

deep yellowish brown
DL.100
UF brown, deep yellowish
brown, golden
centroid color 75
golden brown
yellowish brown, deep
CN D.DL.AFU.AFU.AXC.BZY.ALO.ALO

deep yellowish green
DL.188
UF bright green
centroid color 132
emerald (color)
green, bright
green, deep yellowish
green, kelly
kelly green
yellowish green, deep
CN D.DL.AFU.AFU.BUE.DCU.AFU.AXC

deep yellowish pink
DL.27
UF centroid color 27
light red
pink, deep yellowish
red, light
rose
vermilion (color)
yellowish pink, deep
CN D.DL.AFU.AFU.AFU.CLM.ALO.ARI

deer-hoof feet
USE **hoof feet**

defacement
BM.1101 (A,L)
SN Use for intentional injury to the surface or outer appearance of buildings or objects.
CN B.BM.CRG.BCW.ALO.ARI.AFU

defects
KT.892 (A,L,B)
ALT **defect**
SN Irregularities in the surface or structure of something that spoil appearance or cause weakness or failure. (W)
CN K.KT.ALO.AXC

defenders, public
USE **public defenders**

defensible space
BM.1089
SN Use for the concept of a residential environment in which inhabitants can enhance the quality of their lives, while providing security for their families, neighbors, and friends. (NEWMAN)
UF space, defensible
CN B.BM.CRG.ALO

defensive walls
RT.1179 (L)
ALT **defensive wall**
SN Use broadly for all sorts of walls constructed to resist attack.
UF walls, defensive
CN V.RT.AFU.BUE.AFU.BCW.AFU

definitive drawings
USE **design development drawings**

deflections
BM.911
CN B.BM.CFS.AXC.BIQ.ARI.AFU.AFU

deformations
BM.910 (L)
SN Any change of form, shape, or dimensions produced in a body by a stress or force without a breach of the continuity of its parts. (DAC)
CN B.BM.CFS.AXC.BIQ.ARI.AFU

deformed bars
MT.2386
SN Reinforcing bars made with lugs or ridges to produce a better bond between the bar and the concrete. (PUTNAM)
UF bars, deformed
CN M.MT.AFU.ARI.BZY.ALO.AFU.AFU

deformed joints
TF.586
ALT **deformed joint**

SN Joints made by deforming the members in order to make the connection. (DS)
UF joints, deformed
CN V.TF.ALO.AFU.CRG

Degenerate art
USE **Entartete Kunst**

degeneration
USE **deterioration**

dehumidification
KT.604 (B)
SN Removal of water vapor from air by chemical or physical methods. (CUT)
CN K.KT.AFU.ALO.FUA.ARI

dehumidifying coils
RT.1422
ALT **dehumidifying coil**
UF coils, dehumidifying
CN V.RT.ALO.BCW.AFU.ALO.AFU.BCW.AFU.ALO

deinstallation
USE **dismantling**

déjeuner tables
TG.712
ALT **déjeuner table**
SN Period term for small breakfast tables, made in early 19th century, intended to be used in ladies' boudoirs or morning rooms.
UF tables, déjeuner
CN V.TG.AFU.AFU.BIQ.BOK.ALO.ARI.AFU

Dekkhan
USE **Deccani**

delamination
KT.922
SN Condition of stone in which the outer surface splits apart into thin layers, called laminae, and peels off the face of the stone. (GRIMMR)
CN K.KT.ALO.BZY.AXC.AFU

Delaware
FL.1290 (L,R)
UF Lenape
Lenni Lenape
CN F.FL.ALO.ALO.ARI.AFU.ARI.ARI

deletion marks
USE **cancellation marks**

Delft
FL.3238
CN F.FL.ALO.BCW.ALO.ARI.BIQ.BIQ.BIQ.ALO.AFU

delft blue
USE **dark blue**
grayish blue
grayish purplish blue
moderate blue
pale purplish blue

delft blue, dark
USE **dark grayish blue**

delft blue, deep
USE **grayish blue**

delftware
MT.151
CN M.MT.AFU.AFU.AFU.AXC.ALO.ALO.AFU.ALO.AFU.ALO

Delhi Sultanate
FL.2225
UF Sultanate of Delhi
CN F.FL.ALO.ARI.AXC.ALO.AFU.BIQ.AFU

delicatessens
RK.156 (A,L)
ALT **delicatessen**
SN Use for stores selling foods already prepared or requiring little preparation for serving, such as cooked meats, cheeses, and salads, to be taken out or to be eaten on the premises.
CN V.RK.AFU.ALO.ALO.ALO.ARI.BIQ.AFU.BIQ

delineators
HG.623
ALT **delineator**
SN Use for draftsmen who execute technical drawings from others' designs.
CN H.HG.AFU.AXC.BZY.AXC.ALO

delivery of documents
USE **document delivery**

della robbia
USE **strong purplish blue**

della robbia blue
USE **moderate blue**

deltas
RD.189 (L)
ALT **delta**
SN Alluvial deposits at the mouths of rivers commonly forming nearly flat, fan-shaped plains of considerable area traversed by many separate branches of water. (W)
CN V.RD.ARI.AFU.AXC.AFU.AFU.ARI.AFU.AFU

demand responsive service
USE **paratransit**

demand responsive transportation
USE **paratransit**

demesnes
RD.311 (L)
ALT **demesne**
SN Land portions of estates kept in possession by the owner for personal use or the use of servants; manorial land not granted out or held by tenants.
CN V.RD.ARI.ALO.AXC.ARI

demi-canapés
USE **marquises**

demi-commodes
TG.490
ALT **demi-commode**
SN Small and narrow commodes.
CN V.TG.AFU.AFU.AXC.ALO.BCW.BZY.BIQ

demi-lune
DC.106
CN D.DC.AFU.ARI.EWY.BIQ

demicolumns
USE **half columns**

demilitarized zones
RG.287
ALT **demilitarized zone**
SN Defined areas in which the stationing or concentrating of military forces, or the retention or establishment of military installations of any description, is prohibited. (DODDIC)
UF zones, demilitarized
CN V.RG.ALO.AFU.ALO.BIQ.ALO

demilunes
USE **ravelins**

demimetopes
RT.352
ALT **demimetope**
SN Half, or incomplete, metopes in Doric friezes. (HAS)
CN V.RT.AFU.AFU.AFU.BCW.BZY.ALO.ARI.ALO.ALO.AFU

democracy
BM.539 (L,R)
CN B.BM.BOK.BOK.AFU.AFU

demographers
HG.258 (L)
ALT **demographer**
UF population specialists
specialists, population
CN H.HG.AFU.AXC.BCW.AFU.ARI

demographic anthropology
KD.91 (L)
UF anthropology, demographic
CN K.KD.AFU.ALO.AFU.AFU

demographic maps
USE **population maps**

demographics
BM.1042
CN B.BM.CLM.AFU

demography
KD.117 (L,B,R)
SN Statistical study of the characteristics of human populations especially with reference to size and density, growth, distribution, migration, and vital statistics, and the effect of all these on social and economic conditions. (W)
UF population studies

studies, population
CN K.KD.AFU.ALO.BCW

demolishers
USE **wreckers**

demolishing
USE **demolition**

demolition
KT.112 (L,B)
ALT **demolished**
UF demolishing
wrecking
CN K.KT.AFU.ALO.CLM.AXC

demolition permits
VW.379
ALT **demolition permit**
SN Permits granted by public officials authorizing the wrecking or destruction of property, especially by the use of explosives.
UF permits, demolition
CN V.VW.AFU.AFU.ALO.DUC.AXC.ALO

demonstration houses
USE **model houses**

demountable buildings
RK.1380 (A,L,B)
ALT **demountable building**
UF buildings, demountable
CN V.RK.AFU.ALO.AXC.BOK.AFU

demountable partitions
RT.606 (B)
ALT **demountable partition**
SN Nonloadbearing partitions made of prefabricated sections that can be readily disassembled and relocated.
UF partitions, demountable
partitions, relocatable
relocatable partitions
CN V.RT.AFU.AFU.AFU.BIQ.BUE.
AFU.ARI.AXC.AFU.AFU

denatured alcohol
MT.2688 (L)
SN Ethyl alcohol which has been rendered unfit for drinking; used as a diluent and cleaner. (MAYER)
UF alcohol, denatured
synasol
CN M.MT.AFU.ARI.HZS.AFU.BOK.
AFU.AXC.ALO

Denbigh
FL.806
CN F.FL.ALO.ALO.ALO.AFU.ALO.
AFU.ALO.ALO.ALO.ARI

dendrochronology
KT.500 (A,L,R)
SN The technique of dating events, intervals of time, and variations in environment understood by studying the sequence of and differences between rings of growth in trees and aged wood. (W)
UF dating, tree ring
tree ring dating
CN K.KT.AFU.ALO.EFQ.AFU.ALO

Dengese
USE **Ndengese**

denim
MT.1852 (L)
SN A heavy, twill-woven, warp-flush textile. (MH)
CN M.MT.AFU.AFU.ARI.ALO.ALO.
ALO.AFU.ARI

denominational schools
USE **parochial schools**

dens
RM.169
ALT **den**
SN Small, private, informal rooms in houses or apartments used for work, reading, or relaxation.
CN V.RM.AFU.DIO.ALO.CXA.AXC

densified wood
USE **compressed wood**

density
BM.942 (L,B)
CN B.BM.CFS.AXC.BZY.AXC

density of population
USE **population density**

density, population
USE **population density**

dental cabinets
TG.429
ALT **dental cabinet**
UF cabinets, dental
CN V.TG.AFU.AFU.AXC.ALO.ARI.
ALO.BCW

dental clinics
RK.742 (A,L,B)
ALT **dental clinic**
UF clinics, dental
CN V.RK.AFU.ALO.ALO.CXA.ALO.
AFU.ALO.ALO

dental colleges
USE **dental schools**

dental offices
RK.918 (A,L)
ALT **dental office**
UF dentists' offices
offices, dental
CN V.RK.AFU.ALO.ALO.DZW.ALO.AXC

dental schools
RK.807 (L,B)
ALT **dental school**
UF colleges, dental
dental colleges
schools, dental
CN V.RK.AFU.ALO.ALO.CXA.ARI.
ALO.BCW

dental sinks
RT.1485
ALT **dental sink**
UF sinks, dental
CN V.RT.ALO.BCW.ALO.ARI.CFS.
BIQ.AFU

dentils
RT.341
ALT **dentil**
SN Bands of small, square, toothlike blocks, usually along the underside of a cornice; a characteristic ornament of classical and classicizing styles.
CN V.RT.AFU.AFU.AFU.BCW.BZY.
ALO.ALO.ALO.AXC

dentist's chairs
TG.175 (N)
ALT **dentist's chair**
UF chairs, dentist's
CN V.TG.AFU.AFU.ALO.AFU.AFU.
ALO.BOK

dentistry
KD.239 (L)
CN K.KD.AFU.ARI.BUE.ALO

dentists
HG.383 (L,R)
ALT **dentist**
CN H.HG.AFU.AXC.BIQ.ALO.BCW.ARI

dentists' offices
USE **dental offices**

deodar
MT.1336
UF cedar, Himalayan
Cedrus deodara
Himalayan cedar
CN M.MT.AFU.AFU.ALO.BIQ.DCU.
AFU.AFU.ALO.ALO.ARI

Deogarh
FL.2290
CN F.FL.ALO.ARI.AXC.ALO.AFU.BZY.
BCW.BCW.BCW

department stores
RK.173 (A,L,B,R)
ALT **department store**
UF stores, department
CN V.RK.AFU.ALO.ALO.ALO.ARI.
BIQ.ALO.BCW

departments
HG.804
ALT **department**
CN H.HG.ALO.ALO.ARI

departments, electronic data processing
USE **computer centers**

departments, out-patient
USE **clinics**

depositions
VW.476 (L)
ALT **deposition**
SN Testimonies of witnesses, under oath or affirmation, before a person empowered to administer oaths.

(GAHLM)
CN V.VW.AFU.AFU.ALO.FZU.AFU

depositories
USE **repositories**

depository libraries
RK.710 (L)
ALT **depository library**
SN In Canada and the United States, libraries designated to receive all or selected government publications, with the provision that public access to the collections be provided.
UF libraries, depository
CN V.RK.AFU.ALO.ALO.CRG.AXC.ARI.AXC

deposits, fluvial
USE **fluvial landforms**

depots
USE **railroad stations**
stations

depots, ordnance
USE **ordnance depots**

depots, railway
USE **railroad stations**

depots, tram
USE **tram depots**

depreciation
BM.379 (L)
SN A decline in value or reduction of worth. (PUTNAM)
CN B.BM.ARI.BOK

depressed arches
USE **drop arches**

Deptford
FL.890
CN F.FL.ALO.ALO.ALO.AFU.ALO.ALO.BOK.AXC

depth
BM.804
CN B.BM.CFS.ARI.AXC.BUE.ARI

depth of field
BM.142 (L)
SN Range of distances, near and far, within which objects appear in sharp focus. (A-Z)
CN B.BM.AFU.AFU.ARI.BOK.AXC

Derby red
USE **chrome red**

derby slickers
USE **darbies**

derelict buildings
RK.1390 (A)
ALT **derelict building**
SN Designates abandoned or unoccupied buildings or groups of buildings that constitute potential public hazards.
UF abandoned buildings
buildings, abandoned
buildings, derelict
CN V.RK.AFU.ALO.BCW.AFU

derrickmen
HG.591
ALT **derrickman**
CN H.HG.AFU.AXC.BZY.AFU.BZY

derricks
TB.74 (L,N)
ALT **derrick**
SN Devices consisting of a vertical mast and a horizontal or sloping boom operated by cables to a separate engine or motor; used for hoisting and moving heavy loads or objects. (MEANS)
CN V.TB.AFU.ARI.AFU.BCW.BCW.AFU

derricks, gin pole
USE **gin pole derricks**

derricks, guy
USE **guy derricks**

derricks, pole
USE **pole derricks**

dervishes
HG.236 (L)
ALT **dervish**
SN Friars or monks of Islam.
CN H.HG.AFU.AXC.AXC.BIQ.AFU.AXC

desalination
KT.605
SN Removal of salts, as from water or soil.
CN K.KT.AFU.ALO.FUA.AXC

desalination facilities
USE **desalination plants**

desalination plants
RK.585
ALT **desalination plant**
UF desalination facilities
facilities, desalination
plants, desalination
CN V.RK.AFU.ALO.ALO.CFS.ALO.BCW.CRG.AFU

describing
KG.14 (L)
UF description
CN K.KG.AFU.AFU.AFU.BUE

description
USE **describing**

descriptive bibliography
USE **analytical bibliography**

descriptive cataloging
KG.73 (L)
SN Identifying and describing items in a library or other collection, and recording this information in the form of a catalog entry. (WYNAR)
UF cataloging, descriptive
CN K.KG.AFU.AFU.AXC.AXC.AXC.AFU

Desert Archaic
USE **Desert Tradition**

desert climate
BM.741 (L,B,R)
SN Climate characterized by very little precipitation and extreme hot to cold temperatures, with great changes in daily temperature except in coastal areas. (WB)
UF climate, desert
CN B.BM.CFS.ALO.AXC.ALO.AFU.AFU

Desert Tradition
FL.733
UF Archaic, Desert
Desert Archaic
CN F.FL.ALO.ALO.ALO.AFU.AFU.ALO.ALO.AFU

deserted medieval villages
USE **deserted villages**

deserted villages
RD.44
ALT **deserted village**
SN Use for western European abandoned settlements from the Middle Ages, usually buried and visible only on aerial photographs.
UF deserted medieval villages
villages, deserted
CN V.RD.AFU.ARI.ARI.ALO

deserts
RD.166 (L,R)
ALT **desert**
SN Dry, barren, treeless regions, so arid because of little rainfall that they support only sparse and widely spaced vegetation or no vegetation at all; usually sandy. (RHDEL2)
CN V.RD.ARI.AFU.ALO

design
KT.94 (A,L,B,R)
CN K.KT.AFU.ALO.CFS

design-and-build
USE **design-build**

design books
VW.527
ALT **design book**
UF books, design
CN V.VW.AFU.ALO.AFU.AFU.ALO.BCW

design-build
KG.193 (B)
SN A contracting arrangement in which a person or organization assumes responsibility under a single contract for both the design and construction of a project. (GCIT)
UF design-and-build
package deal
CN K.KG.AFU.ALO.BCW.AFU.AFU

design centers
RK.139 (A,B)
ALT **design center**

SN Use for buildings providing permanent showrooms, galleries, or other display spaces for designers' work or for vendors of products for the design professions.
UF centers, design
CN V.RK.AFU.ALO.ALO.ALO.ARI.ARI

design development drawings
VD.98
ALT **design development drawing**
SN Use for drawings done when an architectural design is more developed than at the stage of conceptual and schematic drawings but is not yet to the stage of working drawings.
UF definitive drawings
developed sketches
drawings, definitive
drawings, design development
sketches, developed
CN V.VD.AFU.ALO.AXC.ALO

design drawings
VD.96
ALT **design drawing**
SN Use for drawings intended to work out the scheme of a project, whether the project is expected to be executed or not; more finished than sketches.
UF designs (drawings)
drawings, design
CN V.VD.AFU.ALO.AXC

design drawings, schematic
USE **schematic drawings**

design guidelines
VW.344
ALT **design guideline**
UF guidelines, design
CN V.VW.AFU.AFU.ALO.CXA.ARI.AFU

design patents
VW.998 (L)
ALT **design patent**
UF patents, design
CN V.VW.AFU.ARI.ALO.BCW.AFU.AFU.AFU.CFS.AFU

design review
KG.30 (A)
UF review, design
CN K.KG.AFU.AFU.AFU.DUC.AFU

design, advertising
USE **advertising design**

design, architectural
USE **architectural design**

design, aseismic
USE **earthquake-resistant construction**

design, barrier-free
USE **barrier-free design**

design, civic
USE **city planning**

design, collapse
USE **plastic design**

design, computer-aided
USE **computer-aided design**

design, costume
USE **costume design**

design, dress (costume design)
USE **costume design**

design, dress (fashion design)
USE **fashion design**

design, earthquake-resistant
USE **earthquake-resistant construction**
seismic design

design, fashion
USE **fashion design**

design, graphic
USE **graphic design**

design, industrial
USE **industrial design**

design, interior
USE **interior design**

design, landscape
USE **landscape architecture**

design, limit-load
USE **plastic design**

design, limit-states
USE **plastic design**

design, modular
USE **modular coordination**

design, participatory
USE **participatory design**

design, plastic
USE **plastic design**

design, seismic
USE **seismic design**

design, theater
USE **theater design**

design, ultimate-load
USE **plastic design**

design, urban
USE **city planning**

designers
HG.139 (A,L,B)
ALT **designer**
CN H.HG.AFU.AXC.AXC.AFU.AFU.ALO.BCW

designers, clothes
USE **fashion designers**

designers, costume
USE **costume designers**

designers, display
USE **display designers**

designers, dress (costume designers)
USE **costume designers**

designers, dress (fashion designers)
USE **fashion designers**

designers, exhibition
USE **exhibition designers**

designers, fashion
USE **fashion designers**

designers, floral
USE **floral designers**

designers, graphic
USE **graphic designers**

designers, industrial
USE **industrial designers**

designers, interior
USE **interior designers**

designers, landscape
USE **landscape architects**

designers, theater
USE **theater designers**

designs
BM.32 (L)
SN Specific conceptual schemes for the organization or appearance of graphic works, objects, structures, or systems. For proposed undertakings or creations in general, including works of art or architecture, or for the actual carrying out of such proposals, use **projects.**
CN B.BM.AFU.AFU.ALO.AXC

designs (drawings)
USE **design drawings**

designs, competition
USE **competition drawings**

designs, geometric
USE **geometric patterns**

designs, preliminary
USE **preliminary drawings**

designs, presentation
USE **preparatory drawings**
presentation drawings

designs, proposed
USE **preparatory drawings**
presentation drawings

designs, theoretical
USE **theoretical drawings**

designs, unbuilt
USE **unbuilt projects**

designs, unexecuted
USE **unexecuted designs**

desk calculators
USE **calculators**

desk chairs
TG.176 (N)
ALT **desk chair**
UF chairs, desk
CN V.TG.AFU.AFU.ALO.AFU.AFU.ALO.BUE

desk locks
TF.250
ALT **desk lock**
UF locks, desk
CN V.TF.AFU.AFU.AFU.AFU.DIO.BIQ.ALO.ARI.ARI

desks
TG.522 (L,N,R)
ALT **desk**
SN Various forms of furniture for readers or writers, generally having a flat writing surface and often drawers and other compartments.
UF scriptoires
scrutoires (desks)
scrutoirs
CN V.TG.AFU.AFU.AXC.ALO.BZY

desks and bookcases
TG.529 (R)
ALT **desk and bookcase**
SN Desks surmounted by a bookcase with glazed or paneled doors. For similar English forms which have a steeply sloping lid, use **bureau-bookcases.**
UF bookcases, desks and
bookcases, secretary
desks, secretary
escritoires (desks and bookcases)
secretary bookcases
secretary-cabinets
secretary desks
CN V.TG.AFU.AFU.AXC.ALO.BZY.BCW

desks and bookcases, cylinder
USE **cylinder desks and bookcases**

desks and bookcases, cylinder-fall
USE **cylinder desks and bookcases**

desks-on-frames
TG.532
ALT **desk-on-frame**
SN Slant-front desks supported on low removable frames, popular in the Queen Anne period. (KETCH)
UF box stretcher desks-on-frames
CN V.TG.AFU.AFU.AXC.ALO.BZY.BIQ

desks-over-bookcases
TG.533
ALT **desk-over-bookcase**
SN Shallow desks with a slant front over a bookcase base. (CTSB)
UF desks, larkin
larkin desks
CN V.TG.AFU.AFU.AXC.ALO.BZY.BOK

desks, butler's
USE **butler's desks**

desks, Carlton House
USE **Carlton House tables**

desks, counting
USE **counting-house desks**

desks, counting-house
USE **counting-house desks**

desks, cylinder
USE **cylinder fall desks**

desks, cylinder fall
USE **cylinder fall desks**

desks, davenport
USE **davenports (desks)**

desks, double
USE **partner's desks**

desks, double counting-house
USE **double counting-house desks**

desks, drop-front
USE **fall-front desks**

desks, fall-front
USE **fall-front desks**

desks, gentleman's portable
USE **portable desks**

desks, Governor Winthrop
USE **Governor Winthrop desks**

desks, kneehole
USE **kneehole desks**

desks, kneehole (bureau tables)
USE **bureau tables**

desks, lady's
USE **lady's desks**

desks, lady's small writing
USE **lady's writing tables**

desks, larkin
USE **desks-over-bookcases**

desks, music
USE **reading desks**

desks, partner's
USE **partner's desks**

desks, pedestal
USE **pedestal desks**

desks, portable
USE **portable desks**

desks, portable writing
USE **portable desks**

desks, reading
USE **reading desks**

desks, rolltop
USE **rolltop desks**

desks, rotary
USE **rotary desks**

desks, rotary cylinder
USE **rotary desks**

desks, screen
USE **lady's screen writing tables**

desks, secretary
USE **bureau-bookcases**
desks and bookcases

desks, single counting-house
USE **counting-house desks**

desks, slant-front
USE **slant-front desks**

desks, spinet
USE **spinet desks**

desks, standing
USE **standing desks**

desks, straight-front
USE **fall-front desks**

desks, table
USE **portable desks**

desks, tambour
USE **tambour desks**

desks, traveling
USE **traveling desks**

desks, wall
USE **wall desks**

desks, Winthrop
USE **Governor Winthrop desks**

desks, Wooton
USE **Wooton desks**

desks, writing
USE **writing desks**

desks, writing (portable desks)
USE **portable desks**

despotism
BM.555 (L,R)
UF absolutism
tyranny
CN B.BM.BOK.BZY.ARI

dessertes
USE **console dessertes**

destitution
USE **poverty**

destroying
USE **destruction**

destruction
KT.107
ALT **destroyed**
UF destroying
CN K.KT.AFU.ALO.CLM

destruction of property
USE **vandalism**

detachable keys
TF.530

ALT **detachable key**
SN Keys so constructed that the bit or portion that actuates the tumblers may be detached from the shank or handle of the key for convenience in carrying. (STEIN)
UF keys, detachable
CN V.TF.AFU.ALO.ARI.AFU.ARI

detachable legs
TG.955
ALT **detachable leg**
UF legs, detachable
CN V.TG.ALO.FIM.AFU.ALO.AFU

detached
DC.30 (B)
UF separate
CN D.DC.AFU.ALO.ARI.BCW

detached houses
RK.259 (A)
ALT **detached house**
UF houses, detached
CN V.RK.AFU.ALO.ALO.AXC.ALO.AFU.CRG.ALO

detail assemblies
USE **subassembly drawings**

detail drawings
VD.150 (L)
ALT **detail drawing**
SN Use for drawings of construction or design details. For minute parts of a larger structure, object, or image, use **details.** For preparatory studies of pictorial or design details, use **detail studies.**
UF details (drawings)
drawings, detail
CN V.VD.AFU.BIQ.ARI

detail drawings (studies)
USE **detail studies**

detail drawings, standard
USE **standard detail drawings**

detail sketches
USE **detail studies**

detail studies
VB.64
ALT **detail study**
SN Use for preparatory studies of pictorial or design details. For minute parts of a larger structure, object, or image, use **details.** For drawings of architectural construction or design details, use **detail drawings.**
UF detail drawings (studies)
detail sketches
drawings, detail (studies)
sketches, detail
studies, detail
CN V.VB.AFU.ALO.BOK.AXC.ALO

detailing, architectural
USE **architectural drawing**

details
VB.92 (A,L,B)
ALT **detail**
SN Use for minute parts of a larger structure, object, or image. For architectural drawings of design or construction details, use **detail drawings.** For preparatory studies of pictorial or design details, use **detail studies.**
CN V.VB.ALO.BOK.ARI

details (drawings)
USE **detail drawings**

detection systems, fire
USE **fire detectors**

detectives
HG.716 (L)
ALT **detective**
CN H.HG.AFU.BCW.BUE

detectors, fire
USE **fire detectors**

detectors, flame
USE **flame detectors**

detectors, ionization
USE **ionization detectors**

detectors, photoelectric
USE **photoelectric detectors**

detectors, smoke
USE **smoke detectors**

detectors, temperature
USE **temperature detectors**

detention camps
USE **concentration camps**

detention centers
RK.731 (A,L,B)
ALT **detention center**
SN Use for places of relatively short confinement for youthful offenders pending transfer or trial.
UF centers, detention
centers, juvenile detention
detention centers, juvenile
detention facilities
detention homes
detention homes, juvenile
facilities, detention
homes, detention
homes, juvenile detention
juvenile detention centers
juvenile detention homes
CN V.RK.AFU.ALO.ALO.CXA.AFU.BCW.AFU

detention centers, juvenile
USE **detention centers**

detention facilities
USE **detention centers**

detention homes
USE **detention centers**

detention homes, juvenile
USE **detention centers**

detergents
MT.2422 (L)
SN Materials which have a cleansing action like soap, usually applies to synthetic chemicals, or soapless soaps. (MH)
UF detergents, synthetic
synthetic detergents
CN M.MT.AFU.ARI.CLM.AFU

detergents, synthetic
USE **detergents**

deterioration
KT.893 (L)
ALT **deteriorated**
SN Use broadly for the action or process of growing worse or becoming impaired in quality, state, or condition. (W)
UF degeneration
CN K.KT.ALO.BCW

deterioration, oxidative-reductive
USE **oxidative-reductive deterioration**

determinate structures
USE **statically determinate structures**

determinations
USE **decisions**

determinism
BM.508 (L)
SN Doctrine that all acts of will result from causes which determine them either in such a manner that people have no alternative course of action, or that the will is still free in the sense of being uncompelled. (W)
CN B.BM.BIQ.AXC.BCW

detoxification
KT.70
ALT **detoxified**
SN The act of removing the poison or effect of poison from something. (W)
CN K.KT.AFU.ALO.BIQ.ARI

Devagiri
USE **Daulatabad**

Developed Orientalizing
FL.2571
UF Orientalizing, Developed
CN F.FL.ALO.AXC.ALO.AFU.AFU.ARI.ARI.ALO

developed sketches
USE **design development drawings**

developers
HG.620
ALT **developer**
SN Individuals, companies, or corporations engaged in the development and improvement of land for construction purposes. (STEIN)
CN H.HG.AFU.AXC.BZY.ARI

developing (photography)
KT.410 (L)
ALT **developed**
SN Procedures for making a latent photographic image visible and then fixing it (making it insensitive to further changes from light).
UF development (photography)
CN K.KT.AFU.ALO.DUC.DIO.ARI.AXC.BIQ

developing-out paper
MT.1944
SN Photographic papers on which the image is brought out by development after exposure. (JCCOP)
UF development paper
DOP
paper, developing-out
paper, development
CN M.MT.AFU.AFU.ARI.ALO.ALO.AXC.ARI.BOK.ALO

developing tanks
TB.329
ALT **developing tank**
UF tanks, developing
CN V.TB.AFU.ARI.CLM.ARI.ALO.ARI

development (photography)
USE **developing (photography)**

development areas
RG.299
ALT **development area**
UF areas, development
CN V.RG.ALO.ARI.AFU

development paper
USE **developing-out paper**

development rights transfer
BM.446 (A,L)
SN Use for the transfer, usually by sale, of the right to construct a certain amount of building space, from one piece of property to another, adjacent or in the same area; often as a means of subsidizing the preservation of landmark buildings in built-up areas.
UF rights transfer, development
transfer of development rights
CN B.BM.BCW.AXC

development, collection
USE **collection development**

development, community
USE **community development**

development, economic
USE **economic development**

development, industrial
USE **industrialization**

development, infill
USE **infill**

development, land
USE **real estate development**

development, linear
USE **linear development**

development, real estate
USE **real estate development**

development, regional
USE **community development**

development, ribbon
USE **ribbon development**

development, rural
USE **rural development**

development, string
USE **ribbon development**

development, strip
USE **ribbon development**

development, urban
USE **urban development**

development, urban economic
USE **urban development**

development, water resources
USE **water resources development**

developmental sketches
USE **preliminary sketches**

developments
USE **housing developments**

developments, housing
USE **housing developments**

developments, mixed-use
USE **mixed-use developments**

developments, multiuse
USE **mixed-use developments**

developments, planned unit
USE **planned unit developments**

deversoria
RK.958
ALT **deversorium**
SN Use for private ancient Roman residences providing food and lodging for travelers en route to rural estates.
CN V.RK.AFU.ALO.ALO.ELK.BIQ.ALO

deviancy, social
USE **deviant behavior**

deviant behavior
BM.583 (L)
UF behavior, deviant
deviancy, social
social deviancy
CN B.BM.BUE.AXC.AFU

deviation, standard
USE **standard deviation**

devices
VW.698 (A,L,R)
ALT **device**
SN Use for representations, designs, or mottoes, or combinations of these, used to signify an individual, a group, or sometimes a commercial concern, and intended to convey a sense of lineage or quality.
CN V.VW.AFU.ALO.ALO.AFU.AFU

devices (motifs)
USE **motifs**

devices, computer storage
USE **storage devices**

devices, input
USE **input devices**

devices, output
USE **output devices**

devices, step-and-hook
USE **stepped frets**

devices, storage
USE **storage devices**

devices, typographical
USE **printers' marks**

devil floats
TB.626
ALT **devil float**
SN Hand-held flat tools with nails in each edge; used to scratch a coat of plaster prior to applying the next coat. (MEANS)
UF devils
floats, devil
floats, nail
nail floats
CN V.TB.AFU.BCW.BCW.ALO.GRC.ALO

devil's tails
USE **jumpers**

devils
USE **devil floats**

devils (jumpers)
USE **jumpers**

devonports
USE **davenports (desks)**

Devonshire clay
USE **kaolin**

devotional calendars
VW.91 (L)
ALT **devotional calendar**
UF calendars, devotional
CN V.VW.AFU.AFU.AFU.FZU.AFU.ARI.AFU

devotional chairs
USE **prie-dieus**

dew
BM.926
CN B.BM.CFS.AXC.BOK.AFU.AFU

dew point
BM.745 (L)
UF point, dew
CN B.BM.CFS.ALO.AXC.ALO.ALO

dewatering
KT.606
SN Use for the removal of water from a site to maintain a dry and stable condition during construction.
CN K.KT.AFU.ALO.FUA.BCW

dextrine
MT.2341 (L)
SN A group of compounds obtained from starch by the action of heat, acids, or enzymes.(W) Have strong adhesive properties and are used as pastes, particularly for envelopes, gummed paper, and postage stamps, for blending with gum arabic, in pyrotechnic compositions, and in textile finishing. (MH)
UF amylin
gum, starch
starch gum
CN M.MT.AFU.ARI.ARI.AFU.ALO.AFU

DGEBA
USE **basic liquid epoxy**

Dharanindravarman I
FL.2342
CN F.FL.ALO.ARI.BCW.ALO.ARI.AFU.CFS

Dharanindravarman II
FL.2344
CN
F.FL.ALO.ARI.BCW.ALO.ARI.AFU.CRG

dharmsalas
USE **caravanserais**

Dhlo Dhlo
FL.138
CN F.FL.ALO.AFU.ALO.ARI.BCW.AFU

di sotto in su
USE **sotto in su**

diabase
MT.609 (L)
SN Coarsely crystalline variety of basalt. (STEIN)
UF black granite
dolerite
granite, black
traprock
CN M.MT.AFU.AFU.AFU.DCU.AFU.AFU.AFU.AFU.ALO.ALO

diacetate, cellulose
USE **cellulose diacetate**

diacetone alcohol
MT.2685
SN Solvent for nitrocellulose, cellulose acetate, gums, and resins; also used in lacquers, thinners, and ink removers. (MH)
UF alcohol, diacetone
CN M.MT.AFU.ARI.HZS.AFU.BOK.AFU.ARI

diaconica
RM.330 (A)
ALT **diaconicon**
SN Sacristies in Orthodox Eastern and Byzantine churches.
UF parabemata
sceuophylacia
CN V.RM.AFU.DIO.AXC.ALO.AFU.DZW.AFU

diagnosing
KG.15 (L)
SN Identifying the condition of a person, object, or structure.
CN K.KG.AFU.AFU.AFU.BZY

diagnostics, building
USE **building diagnostics**

diagonal
DC.7
CN D.DC.AFU.ALO.AFU.AFU

diagonal bridging
USE **cross bridging**

diagonal buttresses
RT.76
ALT **diagonal buttress**
SN Use for buttresses extending at about a 45 degree angle from the corner of a building.
UF buttresses, diagonal
CN V.RT.AFU.AFU.AFU.AXC.AXC.AFU.ARI

diagonal cross shaped stretchers
USE **cross stretchers**

diagonal ribs
RT.685
ALT **diagonal rib**
SN Ribs along groins, used either to mask the groins or to support them.
UF cross-springers
groin ribs
ogives
ribs, diagonal
ribs, groin
CN V.RT.AFU.AFU.ALO.AFU.ARI.AFU

diagonal-shaped stretchers
USE **cross stretchers**

diagonal stretchers
USE **cross stretchers**

diagonal views
USE **oblique views**

diagrams
VW.242
ALT **diagram**
SN Graphic designs that explain rather than represent. (W)
UF diagrams, graphic
graphic diagrams
CN V.VW.AFU.AFU.AFU.FZU.AXC.ARI

diagrams, block
USE **block diagrams**

diagrams, color
USE **color charts**

diagrams, flow
USE **flowcharts**

diagrams, graphic
USE **diagrams**

diagrams, plan
USE **plans**

diagrams, planting
USE **planting plans**

diagrams, Venn
USE **Venn diagrams**

Diaguita
FL.1184 (L)
UF Calchaqui
CN F.FL.ALO.ALO.ALO.ARI.BCW.ALO

Diaguita, Northern
USE **Santa Maria (pottery style)**

Diaguite, Chilean
USE **Chilean Diaguite**

dial locks
USE **combination locks**

dialectic
BM.501 (A,L,R)
CN B.BM.BIQ.ARI.AFU

dialectical materialism
BM.1091 (L)
UF materialism, dialectical
CN B.BM.CRG.ARI.AFU

dialogues
VW.34 (L)
ALT **dialogue**
SN Written compositions in which two or more characters are represented as conversing. (WCOL)
CN V.VW.AFU.AFU.AFU.BOK

diameter
BM.805
CN B.BM.CFS.ARI.AXC.BUE.AXC

diamin azo blue
USE **dark grayish purple**
grayish violet

diamond
MT.502 (L)
SN A highly transparent and exceedingly hard crystalline stone of almost pure carbon; it is the hardest known substance. (MH)
CN M.MT.AFU.AFU.AFU.CFS.AFU.BZY

diamond black
USE **carbon black**

diamond chairs
TG.58
ALT **diamond chair**
UF Bertoia chairs
chairs, Bertoia

chairs, diamond
chairs, shell
shell chairs
CN V.TG.AFU.AFU.ALO.AFU.AFU.AFU.FOG

diamond mesh lath
MT.2413
UF expanded metal lath, flat
flat expanded metal lath
lath, diamond mesh
lath, flat expanded metal
mesh lath, diamond
metal lath, flat expanded
CN M.MT.AFU.ARI.BZY.BIQ.AFU

diamond mines
RG.100 (L)
ALT **diamond mine**
UF mines, diamond
CN V.RG.AFU.AFU.BUE.AFU.ALO.ARI

diamond nails
TF.423
ALT **diamond nail**
UF nails, diamond
CN V.TF.AFU.AFU.AFU.ALO.AFU.CFS.AFU.DIO.AXC

diamond-point engraving
KT.678
SN A technique for decorating glass, and sometimes porcelain, by scratching or stippling it with a diamond-tipped stylus. (THDAT)
UF engraving, diamond-point
CN K.KT.AFU.ALO.GRC.ARI.AFU

Diamond Vehicle
USE **Vajrayana**

diamonds (motifs)
USE **lozenges**

diamonds, paste
USE **paste (glass)**

diaper
USE **diaper patterns**

diaper pattern, petal
USE **scale pattern**

diaper patterns
DG.96
ALT **diaper pattern**
SN Designs consisting of repeated geometric allover patterning often forming a framework filled by such motifs as lozenges or formalized leaves. (LDDO)
UF diaper
diaper work
patterns, diaper
CN D.DG.AFU.ARI.AFU.AFU.AFU

diaper work
USE **diaper patterns**

diaphragm arches
RT.280
ALT **diaphragm arch**
SN Use for arches built across the nave of a church and supporting a flat wall above; for such arches when they support vaults, use **transverse arches.**
UF arches, diaphragm
CN V.RT.AFU.AFU.AFU.BCW.AFU.AFU.ARI.ARI

diaphragm walls
RM.445 (A)
ALT **diaphragm wall**
UF slurry-trenches
slurry-walls
walls, diaphragm
CN V.RM.ALO.AFU.BOK.ALO

diapositives
USE **transparencies**

diaries
VW.50 (L,N,R)
ALT **diary**
SN Use for books containing the daily, personal accounts of the writer's own experiences, attitudes, and observations. Use **journals** when referring to an individual's or an organization's account of daily occurrences or transactions.
CN V.VW.AFU.AFU.AFU.DCU.ALO

diaries, weather
USE **weather diaries**

diarists
HG.183
ALT **diarist**
SN Persons who keep a diary. (W)
CN H.HG.AFU.AXC.AXC.ARI.AFU.AFU.ARI

diatomaceous earth
MT.1750 (L)
UF celite
diatomite
earth, diatomaceous
earth, infusorial
infusorial earth
CN M.MT.AFU.AFU.ARI.AFU.AFU.ALO.ALO.BOK.ALO.BUE

diatomite
USE **diatomaceous earth**

diazo photoprints
USE **diazotypes**

diazo prints
USE **diazotypes**

diazo process
KT.325 (L)
SN Printing processes based on light-sensitive diazonium compounds, most often used to reproduce technical drawings.
UF diazotype (process)
CN K.KT.AFU.ALO.DUC.DIO.ALO.BIQ

diazo process prints
USE **diazotypes**

diazomata
RM.352
ALT **diazoma**
SN Passages or aisles in Greek theaters concentric with the outer wall. (RS)
CN V.RM.AFU.DIO.AXC.AXC.AFU.AXC

diazotype (process)
USE **diazo process**

diazotypes
VW.680 (L)
ALT **diazotype**
SN Prints produced using a duplicating process in which images are produced by the effect of light on diazonium-sensitized materials.(ICA) Used most often for architectural and other technical drawings.
UF diazo photoprints
diazo prints
diazo process prints
ozalids
prints, diazo
CN V.VW.AFU.ALO.AFU.DZW.BIQ.AXC

dichloromethane
USE **methylene chloride**

dichromate processes
USE **bichromate processes**

dichromatic processes
USE **two-color processes**

dictatorship
BM.540
SN A form of government in which a person or small clique has absolute power without effective constitutional limitations. (W)
CN B.BM.BOK.BOK.AFU.ALO

dictionaries
VW.391 (A,L,B,R)
ALT **dictionary**
SN Reference sources containing alphabetical lists of words with information given for each word; generally including meanings, pronunciation, etymology, and often usage guidance. (AHD)
CN V.VW.AFU.AFU.ALO.EWY.ARI

dictionaries of heraldry
USE **heraldic dictionaries**

dictionaries of synonyms
VW.398 (L)
ALT **dictionary of synonyms**
UF synonyms, dictionaries of
CN V.VW.AFU.AFU.ALO.EWY.ARI.ALO.ALO

dictionaries, bilingual
USE **foreign-language dictionaries**

dictionaries, biographical
USE **biographical dictionaries**

dictionaries, data
USE **data dictionaries**

dictionaries, etymological
USE **etymological dictionaries**

dictionaries, foreign-language
USE **foreign-language dictionaries**

dictionaries, heraldic
USE **heraldic dictionaries**

dictionaries, multilingual
USE **polyglot dictionaries**

dictionaries, pictorial
USE **picture dictionaries**

dictionaries, picture
USE **picture dictionaries**

dictionaries, polyglot
USE **polyglot dictionaries**

dictionaries, technical
USE **technical dictionaries**

dictionary catalogs
VW.97 (L)
ALT **dictionary catalog**
UF catalogs, dictionary
CN V.VW.AFU.AFU.AFU.FZU.ALO.AFU.AXC

dictionary stands
USE **bookstands**

didactic art
BM.240
UF art, didactic
CN B.BM.AFU.ARI.BCW.CLM

die casting
KT.132 (L)
ALT **die cast**
SN Metal casting technique in which a molten metal (as a zinc, lead, or aluminum alloy) is forced into a die. (W)
UF casting, die
CN K.KT.AFU.ALO.DOI.ARI.ALO

die stamping
KT.450
SN Use for the intaglio method in which an inked plate is printed under pressure resulting in a partially embossed image. (SAFF)
UF stamping, die
CN K.KT.AFU.ALO.DUC.DUC.ALO.BCW.AFU.ALO

Diegueño
FL.1275 (L)
UF Yahano
CN F.FL.ALO.ALO.ARI.AFU.ALO.FZU.AFU.AFU

dies (dadoes)
USE **dadoes**

dies (metalwork)
TB.732 (L,N,R)
ALT **die (metalwork)**
SN Tools used for cutting the threads of bolts, pipes, or other metal objects.
CN V.TB.AFU.BCW.BIQ.ARI.ALO.BUE.ARI

dies (stamps)
USE **stamps (tools)**

dietitians
HG.384 (L)
ALT **dietitian**
CN H.HG.AFU.AXC.BIQ.ALO.BCW.AXC

diffuse lighting, general
USE **general diffuse lighting**

diffusers, air
USE **air diffusers**

diffusion
KT.639 (L)
ALT **diffused**
SN Use for the process whereby particles intermingle and move from a region of higher to one of lower concentration, and for the transmission or reflection of light. Includes the effect of such processes, such as the softening of sharp outlines in a photograph.
CN K.KT.AFU.ALO.GFO.ARI.AFU

diffusion transfer prints
USE **instant camera photographs**

diffusion transfer prints, dye
USE **dye diffusion transfer prints**

diffusion transfer process
KT.326
SN Photographic process used primarily for instant or self-developing photographs in which the positive image is formed from undeveloped silver halides in the negative. The negative is placed in contact with a support in the presence of a developing agent, and the unexposed silver diffuses to the support to form the positive image. For making color instant camera photographs, it is dye couplers that are in the negative, in which case use **dye diffusion transfer process** or **internal dye diffusion transfer process.**
UF instant photography
photography, instant
CN K.KT.AFU.ALO.DUC.DIO.ALO.BOK

diffusion transfer process, internal dye
USE **internal dye diffusion transfer process**

diffusion transfer, dye
USE **dye diffusion transfer process**

digests (compendiums)
USE **compendiums**

digests (legal documents)
VW.873 (L)
ALT **digest (legal document)**
SN Systematically arranged summaries of laws, reported cases, decisions, and other legal documents. (GAHLM)
CN V.VW.AFU.ARI.AFU.BOK.BCW

digests (periodicals)
VW.620 (L)
ALT **digest (perdiodical)**
CN V.VW.AFU.ALO.AFU.CXA.AFU.BCW.AFU

diggers, post-hole
USE **post-hole diggers**

digging
USE **excavation**

digital maps
VW.172
ALT **digital map**
UF maps, digital
CN V.VW.AFU.AFU.AFU.FZU.AXC.AFU.ARI.ARI.AFU.AFU

digitizers
TB.151
ALT **digitizer**
SN Devices used to convert data to digital form for use in a computer. (RHDEL2)
UF quantizers
CN V.TB.AFU.ARI.BCW.AXC.AFU.AFU

digitizing tablets
USE **graphics tablets**

Digo
FL.603 (L)
CN F.FL.ALO.AFU.AXC.AXC.ALO.BOK.ALO

digs
USE **excavations**

dihydroxy anthraquinone
USE **alizarin**

dikes
RK.566 (A,L,B)
ALT **dike**
SN Use for embankments built along a river or sea and set at some distance from it to control or retain flood waters. For embankments built only to prevent flooding of low-lying land use **levees.**
UF dykes
CN V.RK.AFU.ALO.ALO.CFS.ALO.ARI.AFU

dikes, spur
USE **wing dams**

dikka
RT.1260
SN In mosques, high podiums on columns from which the celebrant's assistant repeats his Koran readings

and gestures for the more distant worshippers. (AK)
CN V.RT.AFU.BUE.ALO.AXC.AFU

dilettantism
BM.341 (L,R)
SN The quality or procedure characteristic of a person who cultivates an art or a branch of knowledge as a pastime without pursuing it professionally. (W)
CN B.BM.ALO.ALO.CLM.AFU.AFU

dill axes
USE **froes**

Dilmun
FL.2882
CN F.FL.ALO.AXC.ARI.ALO.AFU.AFU

Dilmun, Early
USE **Early Dilmun**

Dilmun, Late
USE **Late Dilmun**

Dilmun, Middle
USE **Middle Dilmun**

diluents
USE **thinners**

dime stores
USE **variety stores**

dimension lumber
MT.1440
SN Lumber cut to a particular size and stocked for the building industry; usually 2 to 5 inches thick and 5 to 12 inches wide. (DAC)
UF common dimension lumber
dimension lumber, common
dimension parts
dimension stock
dimension stuff
lumber, common dimension
lumber, dimension
parts, dimension
stock, dimension
stuff, dimension
CN M.MT.AFU.AFU.ALO.BIQ.DCU.ALO.BOK.ARI.ALO

dimension lumber, common
USE **dimension lumber**

dimension parts
USE **dimension lumber**

dimension stock
USE **dimension lumber**

dimension stone
MT.900 (L)
SN Stone finished to a specific size and squared to specific dimensions and thickness. (HORNB)
UF cut stone
stone, cut
stone, dimension
CN M.MT.AFU.AFU.AFU.DCU.ARI.AFU.AFU

dimension stuff
USE **dimension lumber**

dimensional coordination
USE **modular coordination**

dimensioning
KT.486
ALT **dimensioned**
SN Indicating on a drawing the actual dimensions of whatever is represented in the drawing.
CN K.KT.AFU.ALO.DUC.EWY.ALO.AFU

dimensions
USE **size**

dimethyl ketone
USE **acetone**

dimetric drawings
VD.11
ALT **dimetric drawing**
SN Use for drawings in which all three spatial axes are inclined, and two of those are equally inclined, to the plane of projection (drawing surface).
UF dimetric projections
drawings, dimetric
projections, dimetric
CN V.VD.AFU.AFU.BIQ.AFU.AFU

dimetric projection
KT.282
SN Axonometric projection in which only two spatial axes are equally inclined to the plane of projection (drawing surface).
UF projection, dimetric
CN K.KT.AFU.ALO.DUC.DCU.BOK.ALO.AFU.AFU

dimetric projections
USE **dimetric drawings**

Dimini
FL.2534
CN F.FL.ALO.AXC.ALO.AFU.AFU.AFU.ARI

diminishing columns
RT.91
ALT **diminishing column**
SN Use for columns with shafts smaller in radius at the top than at the bottom, particularly when the inward taper is a straight line, as opposed to exhibiting entasis.
UF columns, diminishing
CN V.RT.AFU.AFU.AFU.AXC.BIQ.AFU.AFU.BOK

dimity
MT.1849
SN Cotton cloth with corded stripes or check effects. (NYLAN)
CN M.MT.AFU.AFU.ARI.ALO.ALO.ALO.AFU.ALO.ALO

dimple based ware
FL.146
UF ware, dimple based
CN F.FL.ALO.AFU.ALO.ARI.BOK.ALO

diners
RK.116 (A,L,B,R)
ALT **diner**
CN V.RK.AFU.ALO.ALO.ALO.AFU.AXC.BCW

dinettes
RM.110
ALT **dinette**
SN Use for small dining areas, usually extensions of kitchens or pantries; for such areas when they are extensions of living rooms, use **dining alcoves.**
CN V.RM.AFU.DIO.ALO.BCW.BIQ

Ding ware
FL.1945
UF Ting ware
Ting yao
ware, Ding
ware, Ting
CN F.FL.ALO.ARI.ALO.AFU.AFU.AXC.ARI.ALO

Dingler's green
USE **chromium oxide green**

dining alcoves
RM.111 (B)
ALT **dining alcove**
SN Use for small dining areas when they are extensions of living rooms. Use **dinettes** when referring to similar structures that are extensions of kitchens or pantries.
UF alcoves, dining
dining recesses
recesses, dining
CN V.RM.AFU.DIO.ALO.BCW.BOK

dining chairs
TG.211 (N)
ALT **dining chair**
UF chairs, dining
dining-room chairs
CN V.TG.AFU.AFU.ALO.AFU.AFU.ARI.AXC.AFU

dining halls
RM.112 (A,B,R)
ALT **dining hall**
SN Use both for large dining rooms, as in a college, and for buildings containing a dining hall.
UF halls, dining
CN V.RM.AFU.DIO.ALO.BCW.BUE

dining recesses
USE **dining alcoves**

dining-room chairs
USE **dining chairs**

dining-room tables
USE **extension dining tables**

dining rooms
RM.115 (A,L,B,R)
ALT **dining room**
UF rooms, dining
CN V.RM.AFU.DIO.ALO.BCW.BZY

dining tables
TG.723 (N)
ALT **dining table**
UF banquet tables
tables, banquet
tables, dining
CN V.TG.AFU.AFU.BIQ.BOK.ALO.BZY

dining tables, expandable
USE **extension dining tables**

dining tables, extension
USE **extension dining tables**

dining tables, horseshoe
USE **horseshoe dining tables**

dining tables, imperial
USE **extension dining tables**

dining tables, long
USE **refectory tables**

dining tables, pillar and claw
USE **pillar and claw dining tables**

dining tables, telescope
USE **telescope tables**

dining tables, three-part
USE **three-part dining tables**

dining Windsor chairs
USE **bow-back Windsor chairs**

Dinka
FL.621 (L)
CN F.FL.ALO.AFU.AXC.AXC.ARI.BOK

diocesan records
VW.975 (L)
ALT **diocesan record**
SN Records of districts or churches under the jurisdiction of a bishop. (AHD)
UF records, diocesan
CN V.VW.AFU.ARI.ALO.ALO.ALO.ALO

diocesan schools
USE **parochial schools**

dioceses
RG.256 (L)
ALT **diocese**
UF bishoprics
CN V.RG.ALO.AFU.AFU.BIQ.ARI

Diocletian windows
RT.934
ALT **Diocletian window**
SN Semicircular windows divided by two upright mullions. (IGA)
UF therm windows
windows, Diocletian
windows, therm
CN V.RT.AFU.ARI.AFU.AFU.BOK.AFU.AFU.ERE.AFU

Diola
FL.338 (L)
CN F.FL.ALO.AFU.AXC.AFU.ARI.BIQ.ARI

dioptrics
USE **refraction**

diorite
MT.613 (L)
UF black granite
granite, black
CN M.MT.AFU.AFU.AFU.DCU.AFU.AFU.AFU.AFU.ARI.ALO

diorite, mica
USE **mica diorite**

diorite, porphyritic
USE **red antique porphyry**

diorite, quartz
USE **quartz diorite**

Diospyros
USE **ebony**

Diospyros dendo
USE **black ebony**

Diospyros ebenum
MT.1140
CN M.MT.AFU.AFU.ALO.BIQ.DCU.AFU.AFU.AFU.CXA.AFU.AFU

Diospyros kurzii
USE **marblewood**

Diospyros melanoxylos
MT.1141 (L)
CN M.MT.AFU.AFU.ALO.BIQ.DCU.AFU.AFU.AFU.CXA.ALO

Diospyros virginiana
USE **common persimmon**

dioxide, sulfur
USE **sulfur dioxide**

dip brazing
KT.792
SN Process whereby the metals to be joined are dipped into a bath of molten salt, which acts as both flux and a source of heat. (HORNB)
UF brazing, dip
CN K.KT.AFU.ALO.HOE.BCW.ALO.AFU.AFU.AFU.ALO

dipentene
MT.2703
SN A liquid terpene hydrocarbon found in many essential oils, usually obtained along with other terpenoids from certain turpentines and used chiefly as a solvent and dispersing agent (as for resins and varnishes). (W)
CN M.MT.AFU.ARI.HZS.AFU.BZY.AFU

diphroi
TG.242
ALT **diphros**
SN Ancient Greek stools without a back and having four turned legs, sometimes connected by stretchers.
CN V.TG.AFU.AFU.ALO.AFU.ALO.AFU.BCW

diphroi okladias
TG.267
ALT **diphros okladias**
SN Ancient Greek folding stools without a back and having crossed legs.
CN V.TG.AFU.AFU.ALO.AFU.ALO.AXC.AFU.ALO

diplomas
VW.1065 (L,N)
ALT **diploma**
SN Formal documents conferring some honor, degree, or privilege, especially those bearing record of graduation from or a degree conferred by an educational institution.
CN V.VW.AFU.ARI.ALO.CRG.ALO

diplomats
HG.674 (L,R)
ALT **diplomat**
CN H.HG.AFU.AXC.CFS.CFS.ARI

dipped seats
USE **hollowed seats**

dipper buckets
USE **dippers**

dippers
TB.57
ALT **dipper**
SN Type of bucket used on any of several kinds of excavating equipment.
UF buckets, dipper
dipper buckets
CN V.TB.AFU.ARI.AFU.BCW.ALO.ALO

dipteral
DC.86
SN Describes buildings surrounded by two rows of columns on all sides.
CN D.DC.AFU.ARI.ERE.BIQ.ARI

Diquis
FL.1098
CN F.FL.ALO.ALO.ALO.ALO.ALO.ALO.ALO.ARI

Direct art
FL.3724
UF art, Direct
CN F.FL.ALO.BUE.ARI.BZY

direct carving
KT.87
SN Sculptural process in which the sculptor forms the image by cutting away from the block of stone, generally without working from a model. The concept of the work evolves and develops during the carving process and adaptation may be made according to the character of the stone found within the block.

UF carving, direct
CN K.KT.AFU.ALO.BUE.AFU.AFU

direct image photographs
USE **direct positives**

direct lighting
RT.1354
UF lighting, direct
CN V.RT.ALO.AXC.AFU.AFU

direct painting
USE **alla prima**

direct positive processes
KT.329
SN Use for processes in which a positive-image photograph is formed in the camera without an intermediate negative, or for positive-to-positive processes.
CN K.KT.AFU.ALO.DUC.DIO.ALO.BUE

direct positives
VJ.28
ALT **direct positive**
SN Use for positive-image photographs produced in the camera without the intervening use of a negative, or produced by a positive-to-positive process.
UF camera originals
direct image photographs
originals, camera
photographs, direct image
photographs, unique image
positives, direct
unique image photographs
CN V.VJ.AFU.AFU.ARI.AFU

directional lighting
RT.1355
UF accent lighting
lighting, accent
lighting, directional
CN V.RT.ALO.AXC.AFU.ALO

directives
USE **guidelines**

Directoire
FL.3357 (L)
CN F.FL.ALO.BCW.ALO.AXC.DIO.BCW.ALO.AFU

Director Style
USE **Chippendale**

director's chairs
TG.59
ALT **director's chair**
UF chairs, director's
chairs, safari
safari chairs
CN V.TG.AFU.AFU.ALO.AFU.AFU.AFU.FUA

directories
VW.405 (A,L,R)
ALT **directory**
SN Enumerations of names, addresses, and other data about specific groups of persons or organizations. (AHD)
CN V.VW.AFU.AFU.ALO.EWY.AXC

directories, alumni
USE **alumni directories**

directories, business
USE **commercial directories**

directories, city
USE **city directories**

directories, commercial
USE **commercial directories**

directories, county
USE **county directories**

directories, elite
USE **social registers**

directories, international
USE **international directories**

directories, local
USE **city directories**

directories, manufacturers'
USE **manufacturers' registers**

directories, national
USE **national directories**

directories, post office
USE **post office directories**

directories, professional
USE **professional directories**

directories, regional
USE **regional directories**

directories, state
USE **state directories**

directories, street
USE **street directories**

directories, telephone
USE **telephone directories**

directories, trade
USE **commercial directories**

directors
HG.652
ALT **director**
SN Use for the official heads of organizations such as schools, institutions, or government bureaus, or those named to control a business. Distinct from **managers,** who control a portion of an institution or business.
CN H.HG.AFU.AXC.CFS.AFU.AFU.AFU

directors (music)
USE **conductors (music)**

directors (performing arts)
HG.63 (L)
ALT **director (performing arts)**
SN People who supervise the production of a stage show or motion picture. (WCOL)
CN H.HG.AFU.AXC.AXC.AFU.AFU.AFU.AXC

directors of corporations
USE **boards of directors**

directors, art
USE **art directors**

directors, boards of
USE **boards of directors**

directors, gallery
USE **gallery directors**

directors, music (conductors)
USE **conductors (music)**

dirt
USE **earth**

disabled
USE **handicapped**

disabled, housing for
USE **housing for the handicapped**

disappearing stairs
RT.1070
ALT **disappearing stair**
SN Specially constructed stairs which can be folded and swung upward into a space in the ceiling when not in use. (PUTNAM)
UF disappearing stairways
stairs, disappearing
stairways, disappearing
CN V.RT.AFU.BIQ.AXC.AFU.AFU.AFU

disappearing stairways
USE **disappearing stairs**

disaster housing
USE **emergency housing**

disbursing
KG.54
CN K.KG.AFU.AFU.ARI.BUE

disc-blown glass
USE **crown glass**

discharge photography, corona
USE **Kirlian photography**

discharges
VW.874
ALT **discharge**
SN Documents effecting the release of a right or obligation from its binding force; used especially in military and legal contexts.
UF releases (discharges)
CN V.VW.AFU.ARI.AFU.BOK.BIQ

discharges of contracts
VW.875 (L)
ALT **discharge of contract**
SN Documents attesting to the fulfillment of the terms or conditions of a contract.
UF contracts, discharges of
CN V.VW.AFU.ARI.AFU.BOK.BIQ.AFU

discharging arches
USE **relieving arches**

disciplinary barracks
USE **military prisons**

disciplines
KD.1
SN Branches of learning, professions, and areas of professional specialization.
CN K.KD.AFU

disciplining
USE **punishing**

discographies
VW.275 (L)
ALT **discography**
SN Selective or complete lists of phonographic recordings, typically of one composer, performer, or group of performers. (RHDEL2)
CN V.VW.AFU.AFU.AFU.FZU.BCW.ALO.AFU

discoloration
KT.906
ALT **discolored**
SN Any change in the color of an object. (W)
CN K.KT.ALO.BIQ

discontinuous
USE **broken**

discos
USE **discotheques**

discotheques
RK.1040 (A,L,B,R)
ALT **discotheque**
UF discos
CN V.RK.AFU.ALO.ALO.EWY.AXC.ARI.BCW

discount houses
RK.175 (L)
ALT **discount house**
SN Stores that sell merchandise at a price below the usual price. (RHDEL2)
UF discount stores
houses, discount
stores, discount
CN V.RK.AFU.ALO.ALO.ALO.ARI.BIQ.ALO.BIQ

discount stores
USE **discount houses**

discourse
USE **pragmatics**

discourse analysis
USE **pragmatics**

discourse grammar
USE **pragmatics**

discrimination
BM.1103 (L)
SN According of biased or differential treatment to people on the basis of the group, class, or category to which they belong.
CN B.BM.CRG.BCW.ARI

discrimination in housing
USE **housing discrimination**

discrimination, age
USE **age discrimination**

discrimination, housing
USE **housing discrimination**

discrimination, race
USE **race discrimination**

discrimination, sex
USE **sex discrimination**

discs (foot components)
TG.934
ALT **disc (foot component)**
CN V.TG.ALO.DZW.ALO.ARI

discs, video
USE **videodiscs**

disease
BM.716 (L,R)
CN B.BM.CFS.AFU.AFU

disegno
BM.320 (R)
CN B.BM.AFU.AXC.ELK.ARI

dish dressers
USE **dressers**

dish dressers, corner
USE **corner cupboards**

dished adzes
USE **hollowing adzes**

dished-top tables
USE **china tables**

dished tops
USE **china tables**

disinfectants
MT.2375 (L)
ALT **disinfectant**
SN Materials used for killing germs, bacteria, or spores. (MH)
UF germicides
CN M.MT.AFU.ARI.BOK.ALO

disinfecting
KT.71
SN To free from infection especially by destroying harmful microorganisms. (W)
CN K.KT.AFU.ALO.BIQ.AXC

disk feet
USE **pad feet**

disk film
MT.2239
UF film, disk
CN M.MT.AFU.ALO.CXA.ALO.BCW

disk sanders
TB.523 (N)
ALT **disk sander**
SN Power hand tools that have a rotating, circular abrasive disk; used for smoothing or polishing a surface. (MEANS)
UF sanders, disk
CN V.TB.AFU.ARI.EWY.ALO.CXA.ARI

diskettes
USE **floppy disks**

disks (magnetic disks)
USE **magnetic disks**

disks, compact
USE **compact disks**

disks, floppy
USE **floppy disks**

disks, laser
USE **optical disks**

disks, magnetic
USE **magnetic disks**

disks, optical
USE **optical disks**

disks, sanding
USE **sanding disks**

disks, video
USE **videodiscs**

Dismal River
FL.918
CN F.FL.ALO.ALO.ALO.AFU.ALO.ARI.AXC.AFU

dismantling
KT.113
UF deinstallation
CN K.KT.AFU.ALO.CRG

dispatches
VW.14
ALT **dispatch**
SN Messages, intended usually for special or expeditious transmittal or delivery, such as important official messages, or news items sent with promptness by correspondents to newspapers or news agencies. (GAHLM)
CN V.VW.AFU.AFU.AFU.BIQ.AFU.AFU

dispensaries
RK.743 (L,B)
ALT **dispensary**
CN V.RK.AFU.ALO.ALO.CXA.ALO.AFU.ALO.ARI

dispensaries (furniture)
TG.583
CN V.TG.AFU.AFU.AXC.ALO.CFS

dispensers, hand towel
USE **hand towel dispensers**

dispensers, soap
USE **soap dispensers**

dispersants
MT.2733
SN Materials that deflocculate or disperse finely ground materials by satisfying the surface energy requirements of the particles; used as slurry thinners or grinding agents. (STEIN)
CN M.MT.AFU.ARI.IFM.BUE.AFU

dispersing agents
MT.2309 (L)
UF agents, dispersing
CN M.MT.AFU.ARI.ALO.BUE

dispersion
KT.638 (L)
ALT **dispersed**
CN K.KT.AFU.ALO.GFO.ARI

displacement, continental
USE **continental drift**

display artists
USE **display designers**

display cases
USE **showcases**

display designers
HG.151
ALT **display designer**
SN Persons who plan and design displays to decorate streets, fairgrounds, buildings, and other places for celebrations, fairs, and special occasions. (DOT)
UF artists, display
designers, display
display artists
CN H.HG.AFU.AXC.AXC.AFU.AFU.ALO.BCW.ARI

display drawings
USE **presentation drawings**

display windows
USE **show-windows**

displaying
USE **exhibiting**

displays (monitors)
USE **monitors**

disposal fields
USE **leaching fields**

disposal of refuse
USE **refuse disposal**

disposal, refuse
USE **refuse disposal**

disposal, sewage
USE **sewage disposal**

disposal, solid waste
USE **refuse disposal**

disposal, waste
USE **waste disposal**

disposition schedules
USE **records schedules**

disposition schedules, records
USE **records schedules**

disproportion
BM.63
SN A lack of symmetry or proper relation. (W)
CN B.BM.AFU.AFU.ARI.AFU.BIQ

disseminating
USE **publicizing**

dissenters
HG.751 (L,R)
ALT **dissenter**
SN People who disagree with or take an opposing view to established, orthodox, or majority values or opinions, especially those of a church or political party. (RHDEL2)
UF nonconformists
CN H.HG.AFU.BCW.HZS.AXC

dissenters, artistic
USE **dissident artists**

dissertations
VW.1071 (L,B,R)
ALT **dissertation**
SN Written treatises, or the records of a discourse on a subject, usually prepared and presented as the final requirement for a degreee or diploma and typically based on independent research and giving evidence of the candidate's mastery of the subject and of scholarly method. (GAHLM)
CN V.VW.AFU.ARI.ALO.CRG.BOK.AFU

dissident art
BM.241 (L,R)
UF art, dissident
art, nonconformist
art, unofficial
nonconformist art
unofficial art
CN B.BM.AFU.ARI.BCW.CRG

dissident artists
HG.97 (L)
ALT **dissident artist**
UF artistic dissenters
artists, dissident
dissenters, artistic
CN H.HG.AFU.AXC.AXC.AFU.AFU.ALO.AXC.BIQ

distance
BM.765 (L)
CN B.BM.CFS.ARI.AXC.AXC

distance, middle
USE **middle ground**

distant views
VB.23
ALT **distant view**
UF views, distant
CN V.VB.AFU.AFU.BOK.ALO.AXC

distemper paint
MT.2513 (B)
UF glue paint
paint, distemper
paint, glue
CN M.MT.AFU.ARI.CRG.ALO.BCW.AFU.ALO.AFU

distilled water
MT.321 (L)
UF water, distilled
CN M.MT.AFU.AFU.AFU.BOK.BOK.ALO.AFU

distilleries
RK.624 (A,L,N,B)
ALT **distillery**
UF stills
CN V.RK.AFU.ALO.ALO.CLM.ALO.ALO.AFU.AXC.AFU.ARI

distortion
BM.143
CN B.BM.AFU.AFU.ARI.BOK.BCW

distributed loads
BM.1010 (B)
UF loads, distributed
CN B.BM.CFS.AXC.CLM.ALO.ARI.BIQ

distributing
KG.55 (L)
CN K.KG.AFU.AFU.ARI.BZY

distribution (statistics)
BM.826 (L)
CN B.BM.CFS.ARI.CRG.ALO.ALO

district courts
RK.980 (L)
ALT **district court**
UF courts, district
CN V.RK.AFU.ALO.ALO.ERE.AFU.AXC.AFU.ALO

districts
RG.239 (A,L)
ALT **district**
SN Territorial divisions as for administrative or electoral purposes, or settlement areas with distinguishing characteristics. (WCOL)
CN V.RG.ALO

districts, assessment
USE **assessment districts**

districts, business
USE **business districts**

districts, census
USE **census tracts**

districts, central business
USE **central business districts**

districts, commercial
USE **business districts**

districts, congressional
USE **congressional districts**

districts, election
USE **election districts**

districts, historic
USE **historic districts**

districts, historic preservation
USE **historic districts**

districts, industrial
USE **industrial districts**

districts, legislative
USE **legislative districts**

districts, park
USE **park districts**

districts, planning
USE **planning districts**

districts, preservation
USE **historic districts**

districts, retailing
USE **shopping districts**

districts, school
USE **school districts**

districts, shopping
USE **shopping districts**

districts, voting
USE **election districts**

districts, water
USE **water districts**

distyle in antis
DC.87
CN D.DC.AFU.ARI.ERE.BIQ.AXC

ditchers
USE **trenching machines**

ditches
RK.1351 (A,L)
ALT **ditch**
SN Long narrow excavations dug in the earth for defense, drainage, or irrigation. (WCOL)
CN V.RK.AFU.ALO.ARI.AXC.ARI.AFU.AFU

ditching machines
USE **trenching machines**

divans
TG.295 (N)
ALT **divan**
SN Long, low, upholstered seats of Turkish origin usually without backs or arms. (GLOAG)
CN V.TG.AFU.AFU.ALO.ALO.ARI

divans, club
USE **club chairs**

divergent spirals
USE **trumpet spirals**

diversion dams
RK.529 (L)
ALT **diversion dam**
SN Use for barriers built across waterways to turn aside all or some of the flow from its usual course into a pipe, trench, or channel, as to bypass construction work.
UF dams, diversion
CN V.RK.AFU.ALO.ALO.CFS.AFU.ARI.ALO.AXC

divided contracts
VW.882
ALT **divided contract**
SN Contracts in which the work of the job is divided into several prime contracts, such as general, mechanical, and electrical, rather than awarded to one contractor. (STEIN)
UF contracts, divided
CN V.VW.AFU.ARI.AFU.BOK.BOK.ALO.ALO.AFU.AFU

divided highways
RK.1517
ALT **divided highway**
UF dual highways
highways, divided
highways, dual
CN V.RK.ALO.ALO.BIQ.ARI.AFU.AFU.ALO

dividers (froes)
USE **froes**

dividers (interior walls)
USE **room dividers**

dividers, room
USE **room dividers**

dividers, space
USE **room dividers**

dividing engines
TB.427 (L,N)
ALT **dividing engine**
SN Machines for graduating or dividing a circle into a number of equal parts, or for cutting the circumference of a wheel into a number of teeth. (OED)
UF dividing machines
engines, dividing
machines, dividing
CN V.TB.AFU.ARI.EFQ.AFU.AFU

dividing machines
USE **dividing engines**

divinity
BM.682
SN The quality or state of being divine; the nature or essence of God. (W)
CN B.BM.BZY.ALO.AFU.ALO

divinity schools
USE **theological seminaries**

divisionism
USE **pointillism**

Divisionist
USE **Neo-Impressionist**

divorce records
VW.955 (L)
ALT **divorce record**
SN Records documenting the legal separation of husband and wife, effected by the judgment or decree of a court, and either totally dissolving the marriage relation, or suspending its effects so far as concerns the cohabitation of the parties. (BLACKS)
UF records, divorce
CN V.VW.AFU.ARI.AFU.DCU.ARI.AFU

Djaba
USE **Jaba**

djamis
USE **jamis**

Djebel
USE **Dzhebel Cave**

Djeitun
USE **Dzheytun**

Djemdet Nasr
USE **Jamdat Nasr**

Djenne
USE **Jenne**

Djibu
USE **Jibu**

Djubu
USE **Jibu**

Djukun
USE **Jukun**

do-it-yourself manuals
VW.361
ALT **do-it-yourself manual**
UF manuals, do-it-yourself
CN V.VW.AFU.AFU.ALO.CXA.BZY.AFU

docents
HG.203 (L)
ALT **docent**
SN Persons who conduct guided groups through a museum or art gallery and discuss and comment on the exhibits. (W)
UF guides (docents)
interpreters (docents)
CN H.HG.AFU.AXC.AXC.AXC.ALO

dockets
VW.597
ALT **docket**
SN Lists or registers of cases before a tribunal, usually kept by the clerk of the court, identifying the cases, with entries of action taken; used originally in connection with judicial proceedings, now also used in connec-

tion with quasi-judicial or administrative proceedings. (GAHLM)
UF calendars, court
calendars, trial
court calendars
trial calendars
CN V.VW.AFU.ALO.AFU.BIQ.ARI.ALO.AFU.AFU

docking plans
VD.157
ALT **docking plan**
SN Use for drawings giving the information necessary for preparing a dry dock for reception of a ship. May include profiles and sections.
UF plans, docking
CN V.VD.AFU.BIQ.BOK.AFU

docks
RK.1598 (A,L,N,B,R)
ALT **dock**
SN Use for the open water spaces occupied by vessels made fast to landing places. When such open spaces are unoccupied and are alongside a landing place, use **berths**; use slips when such water spaces are unoccupied and set between adjacent piers or perpendicular to landing places. Use **dockyards** for the group of landing places in ports or for port facilities as a whole.
CN V.RK.ALO.ARI.CLM.ALO.ALO

docks, dry
USE **dry docks**

docks, floating
USE **floating docks**

docks, graving
USE **dry docks**

docks, loading
USE **loading docks**

docks, wet
USE **wet docks**

dockyards
RG.224 (A,L,R)
ALT **dockyard**
CN V.RG.AFU.AFU.EFQ.ARI.AFU

doctors
USE **physicians**

doctors' offices
USE **medical offices**

doctors' surgeries
USE **medical offices**

document delivery
KG.87
SN Providing documents, published or unpublished, in hard copy or microform, upon request,(ALAG) either free of charge or for a fee.
UF delivery of documents
CN K.KG.AFU.AFU.AXC.BOK

document drawers
TG.881
ALT **document drawer**
UF drawers, document
CN V.TG.ALO.DCU.AFU.ALO.ALO

documentary photography
KT.297 (L,R)
SN Use for an approach to photography in which the subject is recorded with an emphasis on factual accuracy and with a high degree of objectivity by the photographer; often of a newsworthy event. May be intended to record, and ultimately influence, social conditions. (ICPEP)
UF photography, documentary
CN K.KT.AFU.ALO.DUC.DIO.AFU.BIQ

documentation centers
RK.688 (B)
ALT **documentation center**
SN Use for places where publications are received, preserved, abstracted, and indexed for bulletins and bibliographies which are produced for distribution. (LG)
UF centers, documentation
CN V.RK.AFU.ALO.ALO.CRG.ALO

documenting
KG.88 (L,B)
SN Use broadly for the gathering and recording of information. For the organizing and controlling of information, use **information management**.
CN K.KG.AFU.AFU.AXC.BUE

documents
VW.1 (L,R)
ALT **document**
SN Recorded information regardless of medium or characteristics. (SAA)
CN V.VW.AFU

documents, bidding
USE **bidding documents**

documents, chancery
USE **chancery documents**

documents, contract
USE **contract documents**

documents, legal
USE **legal documents**

documents, machine-readable
USE **machine-readable records**

documents, manorial
USE **manorial records**

documents, notarial
USE **notarial documents**

documents, official
USE **official documents**

documents, public
USE **government records**

dodecagons
BM.785
ALT **dodecagonal**
SN Polygons having 12 angles and 12 sides. (WCOL)
UF duodecagons
CN B.BM.CFS.ARI.AXC.BCW.AFU.BIQ.BOK

dodgers
TB.330
ALT **dodger**
SN Tools used for photographic dodging.
CN V.TB.AFU.ARI.CLM.ARI.ALO.AXC

dodging
KT.411
SN Use for photographic printing techniques in which light is obstructed or reduced in selective portions of the image, lessening exposure (and resulting density) in those areas.
CN K.KT.AFU.ALO.DUC.DIO.ARI.AXC.BOK

Doe
FL.596
CN F.FL.ALO.AFU.AXC.AXC.ALO.ALO

dog anchors
USE **dogs (woodworking tools)**

dog-eared fold joints
TF.647
ALT **dog-eared fold joint**
UF fold joints, dog-eared
joints, dog-eared fold
CN V.TF.ALO.ARI.ARI.BIQ

dog gates
RT.893 (A)
ALT **dog gate**
SN Swinging doors or flexible barriers which may be closed across stairs, doorways, or other indoor circulation points to restrain the free movement of dogs.
UF gates, dog
CN V.RT.AFU.ARI.AFU.AFU.ARI.ALO.AFU.AFU.AFU

dog irons
USE **dogs (woodworking tools)**

dog kennels
USE **kennels**

dog nails
TF.393
ALT **dog nail**
SN Large nails or spikes whose heads project over one side. (MEANS)
UF nails, dog
CN V.TF.AFU.AFU.AFU.ALO.AFU.CFS.AFU.BIQ

dog racetracks
USE **dog tracks**

dog tracks
RG.179 (B)
ALT **dog track**
UF dog racetracks
tracks, dog
CN V.RG.AFU.AFU.DOI.CFS.ALO.ALO

dog's paw feet
TG.927
ALT **dog's paw foot**
UF feet, dog's paw
CN V.TG.ALO.DZW.AFU.DCU.BIQ.AFU

doges
HG.693 (R)
ALT **doge**
SN Rulers and chief magistrates of the former republics of Venice and Genoa.
CN H.HG.AFU.AXC.CFS.CRG.ARI

doghouses
RK.85 (A,L,N)
ALT **doghouse**
CN V.RK.AFU.ALO.ALO.AFU.ALO.BIQ

dogleg brick
MT.74
UF brick, dogleg
CN M.MT.AFU.AFU.AFU.AXC.ALO.AFU.AFU.AFU.BIQ

dogleg chisels
USE **corner chisels**

dogleg stairs
RT.1084 (B)
ALT **dogleg stair**
SN Half-turn stairs which have no well hole between successive flights; the rail and balusters of the upper and under flights fall in the same vertical plane. (DAC)
UF stairs, dogleg
CN V.RT.AFU.BIQ.AXC.AFU.AFU.BUE.ALO.AFU

Dogon
FL.352 (L)
UF Habe
CN F.FL.ALO.AFU.AXC.AFU.AXC.AFU.ARI

Dogrib
FL.1231 (L)
UF Thlingchadine
CN F.FL.ALO.ALO.ARI.AFU.AFU.ARI.BOK

dogs (woodworking tools)
TB.1061 (N)
ALT **dog (woodworking tool)**
SN Simple metal devices, usually a bar with hooks at each end, used for binding two pieces of timber together. Also a general term for any device used for gripping, holding, or fastening an object.
UF anchors, dog
dog anchors
dog irons
irons, dog
CN V.TB.AFU.BCW.CFS.ALO.ALO.BIQ

dogs, bench
USE **bench dogs**

dogs, ring
USE **ring dogs**

dogs, shutter
USE **shutter dogs**

dogs, spoke
USE **spoke dogs**

dogtooth courses
RT.623
ALT **dogtooth course**
SN Stringcourses of bricks laid diagonally so that one corner projects from the face of the wall. (DAC)
UF courses, dogtooth
CN V.RT.AFU.AFU.AFU.BIQ.BUE.ALO.AFU.ALO.CFS.AFU

dogtooth moldings
RT.765
ALT **dogtooth molding**
SN Moldings enriched with a series of starlike, raised pyramidal forms; common especially in Early English Gothic architecture. (PDARC)
UF moldings, dogtooth
CN V.RT.AFU.ALO.AFU.BOK.AFU.AFU.ARI.BIQ

dogtrot houses
RK.261
ALT **dogtrot house**
SN Use for houses, generally of logs, in which two pens are separated by a passageway, and the whole is covered by a single roof.
UF dogtrot plan houses
houses, dogtrot
houses, possum-trot plan
possum-trot plan houses
CN V.RK.AFU.ALO.ALO.AXC.ALO.AFU.CRG.ARI.AFU

dogtrot plan houses
USE **dogtrot houses**

dogtrots
RM.245
ALT **dogtrot**
SN Use for passages, sharing a roof common with the rest of the building, connecting two parts of a log house of the American folk architecture tradition. Distinguished from **breezeways** by its folk architecture and log house context and its common roof.
CN V.RM.AFU.DIO.ARI.AFU.ARI

dogwood
MT.1137 (L)
CN M.MT.AFU.AFU.ALO.BIQ.DCU.AFU.AFU.AFU.CRG

Dokathismata type
FL.2677
CN F.FL.ALO.AXC.ALO.AFU.ALO.BCW.AFU.AFU

dokhmas
USE **towers of silence**

dole cupboards
TG.506
ALT **dole cupboard**
UF cupboards, dole
CN V.TG.AFU.AFU.AXC.ALO.BUE.BOK

dolerite
USE **diabase**

doll artists
USE **dollmakers**

dollmakers
HG.556 (L)
ALT **dollmaker**
UF artists, doll
doll artists
CN H.HG.AFU.AXC.BUE.AXC.BOK

dollmaking
KT.573 (L)
CN K.KT.AFU.ALO.ELK.DZW.AFU

dolmens
USE **megalithic chamber tombs**

dolomite
MT.685 (L)
SN A type of limestone whose calcium carbonate content approaches 45%; employed as a flux in melting iron, as a lining for basic steel furnaces, for the production of magnesium metal, for filtering, and as a construction stone. (MH)
CN M.MT.AFU.AFU.AFU.DCU.AFU.ALO.AFU.ALO.ALO.AFU.ALO.AXC.AFU

dolomitic limestone
USE **magnesian limestone**

dolphin feet
TG.923
ALT **dolphin foot**
SN Popular motif used as the terminal ornament on chair feet and table legs in the 17th, 18th, and 19th centuries. (IDO)
UF feet, dolphin
CN V.TG.ALO.DZW.AFU.DCU.ARI

dolphin supports
TG.991
ALT **dolphin support**
UF supports, dolphin
CN V.TG.ALO.HIK.AFU.AFU

dolphins
RK.1315
ALT **dolphin**
SN Use for multipurpose boating structures consisting of a group of piles

driven close together into the sea bottom and bound firmly into a single cluster.
CN V.RK.AFU.ALO.ALO.GLI.ARI.ARI.AFU

domain, eminent
USE **eminent domain**

domain, national
USE **public domain**

domain, public
USE **public domain**

domain, state
USE **public domain**

dome beds
TG.326
ALT **dome bed**
UF beds, dome
CN V.TG.AFU.AFU.ARI.AFU.AFU.ARI.AFU

dome beds, French
USE **French beds**

domed ceilings
RT.730
ALT **domed ceiling**
UF ceilings, domed
CN V.RT.AFU.ALO.AFU.ALO.BZY

domes
RT.389 (A,L,B,R)
ALT **dome**
SN Vaults in the form of a hemisphere, an approximate hemisphere, or a segment of a hemisphere.
CN V.RT.AFU.AFU.AFU.BIQ.AFU.AFU

domes (furniture components)
USE **hoods (furniture components)**

domes, alveated
USE **beehive domes**

domes, beehive
USE **beehive domes**

domes, bulbous
USE **onion domes**

domes, conch
USE **umbrella domes**

domes, geodesic
USE **geodesic domes**

domes, half
USE **semidomes**

domes, melon
USE **umbrella domes**

domes, onion
USE **onion domes**

domes, parachute
USE **umbrella domes**

domes, pendentive
USE **pendentive domes**

domes, pumpkin
USE **umbrella domes**

domes, ribbed
USE **ribbed domes**

domes, saucer
USE **saucer domes**

domes, Schwedler
USE **Schwedler domes**

domes, segmental
USE **saucer domes**

domes, Turkish
USE **onion domes**

domes, umbrella
USE **umbrella domes**

domestic architecture
USE **dwellings**

domestic architecture, grouped
USE **cluster housing**

domestic chapels
USE **private chapels**

domestic facilities
USE **dwellings**

domestic science
USE **home economics**

domestic stylebooks
VW.533
ALT **domestic stylebook**
UF architectural stylebooks
stylebooks, architectural
stylebooks, domestic
CN V.VW.AFU.ALO.AFU.AFU.ALO.BCW.BCW.AFU

domestics
HG.41 (L)
ALT **domestic**
SN Hired household servants. (RHDEL2)
CN H.HG.AFU.AXC.ARI.AXC

domical vaults
RT.532
ALT **domical vault**
SN Use for groined vaults in which the crown of the vault is higher than the crown of the transverse arches so that the ridge line is curved in elevation.
UF vaults, domical
CN V.RT.AFU.AFU.AFU.BIQ.BOK.AFU.AFU.AFU.ALO.ALO.AFU

domiciles
USE **dwellings**

Dominican
BM.656 (A,L)
CN B.BM.BZY.AFU.ALO.BCW.BCW

dominotiers
HG.523
ALT **dominotier**
SN Workmen in 15th-century France who made wallpapers printed from wood blocks and colored by hand. (MCCLEL)
CN H.HG.AFU.AXC.BUE.ARI.CRG.AFU

domus
RK.235
SN Use for ancient Roman single family dwellings.
CN V.RK.AFU.ALO.ALO.AXC.ALO.AFU.BIQ

domus ecclesiae
RK.1113 (R)
SN Use for the Early Christian meeting house and community center, derived from utilitarian domestic structures, serving the religious, administrative, and charitable needs of the congregation.
UF oikos ekklesias
tituli
CN V.RK.AFU.ALO.ALO.FCS.BIQ.ARI

donations
BM.464
SN Gifts or contributions to public or charitable causes. (WCOL)
UF contributions
CN B.BM.BCW.CXA.AFU.ARI.ALO

Dondo
FL.478
CN F.FL.ALO.AFU.AXC.ALO.ALO.AXC.ARI

Dong-duong
FL.2443
CN F.FL.ALO.ARI.BCW.BUE.ALO.ALO.AFU.AXC

Dong-Ju
FL.1929
CN F.FL.ALO.ARI.ALO.AFU.AFU.AXC.ALO.AXC

Dông-Son
FL.2370
CN F.FL.ALO.ARI.BCW.ARI.AFU.AFU

Dông-Son (Vietnamese)
FL.2429
UF Dongsonian (Vietnamese)
CN F.FL.ALO.ARI.BCW.BUE.AFU.ALO

Dongsonian (Vietnamese)
USE **Dông-Son (Vietnamese)**

donjons
USE **keeps**

donkey saws
USE **felloe saws**

donor lists
VW.276
ALT **donor list**
SN Lists documenting persons or organizations from which a repository or institution has received gifts or donations.

UF lists, donor
CN V.VW.AFU.AFU.AFU.FZU.BCW.
ALO.ALO

donors
HG.717
ALT **donor**
CN H.HG.AFU.BCW.BZY

doodles
VD.126 (L)
ALT doodle
UF scribbles
CN V.VD.AFU.AXC.ARI

doodling
KT.196
ALT **doodled**
CN K.KT.AFU.ALO.DUC.BZY.ALO.BCW

door bolts
TF.163
ALT **door bolt**
SN Sliding bars or rods used for locking a door. (MEANS)
UF bolts, door
CN V.TF.AFU.AFU.AFU.AFU.DIO.ARI

door bucks
RT.838
ALT **door buck**
SN Wood or metal surfaces, set in a wall, to which the finished doorframe is attached. (DAC)
UF bucks, door
bucks, rough
rough bucks
sub-bucks
CN V.RT.AFU.ARI.AFU.AFU.AFU.ALO.
ALO.ALO.AFU

door bumpers
TF.8 (N)
ALT **door bumper**
SN Devices placed on the wall or floor behind a door to limit the swing of the door. (MEANS)
UF bumpers
bumpers, door
CN V.TF.AFU.AFU.AFU.AFU.AFU.ARI

door casings
USE **doorframes**

door checks
TF.9
ALT **door check**
SN Devices used to retard the movement of a closing door and to guard against its slamming or banging, but also insures the closing of the door. (PUTNAM)
UF back checks
checks, back
checks, door
closers, door
door closers
CN V.TF.AFU.AFU.AFU.AFU.AFU.AXC

door closers
USE **door checks**

door edge pulls
TF.89
ALT **door edge pull**
UF edge pulls, door
pulls, door edge
CN V.TF.AFU.AFU.AFU.AFU.CFS.
BCW.ALO.ARI.AFU

door fasteners, chain
USE **chain door fasteners**

door fittings
USE **door hardware**

door fixtures
USE **door hardware**

door frames
USE **doorframes**

door hardware
TF.506 (A,B)
UF door fittings
door fixtures
fittings, door
fixtures, door
hardware, door
CN V.TF.AFU.AFU.ALO.AXC

door hinges, gravity
USE **rising hinges**

door holders
TF.10
ALT **door holder**
SN Devices used for holding a door open. (MEANS)
UF holders, door
CN V.TF.AFU.AFU.AFU.AFU.AFU.BCW

door holders, overhead
USE **overhead door holders**

door hoods
USE **doorheads**

door hooks, cabin
USE **cabin door hooks**

door jacks
TB.1064
ALT **door jack**
SN Frames for holding a wood door in place while it is off its hinges and being planed. (DAC)
UF jacks, door
CN V.TB.AFU.BCW.CFS.ALO.ALO.BOK

door jambs
RT.839 (B)
ALT **door jamb**
SN Vertical members on each side of a door. (HAS)
UF door trees
doorcheeks
doorposts
jambs, door
trees, door
CN V.RT.AFU.ARI.AFU.AFU.AFU.ALO.
ALO.ALO.ALO

door knobs
USE **doorknobs**

door knockers
TF.12 (L,N,R)
ALT **door knocker**
UF knockers
knockers, door
CN V.TF.AFU.AFU.AFU.AFU.AFU.BIQ

door leaves
RT.879
ALT **door leaf**
SN The separate elements that make up a folding or double door.
UF fores
leaves (door components)
leaves, door
CN V.RT.AFU.ARI.AFU.AFU.AFU.ALO.
ARI.ALO.AFU

door linings
USE **doorframes**

door locks
TF.229 (N)
ALT **door lock**
UF locks, door
CN V.TF.AFU.AFU.AFU.AFU.DIO.BIQ.
ALO.ALO

door plates
USE **doorplates**

door pulls
TF.88
ALT **door pull**
UF pulls, door
CN V.TF.AFU.AFU.AFU.AFU.CFS.BCW.
ALO.ARI

door rails
RT.880
ALT **door rail**
UF rails, door
CN V.RT.AFU.ARI.AFU.AFU.AFU.ALO.
ARI.ALO.ALO

door rings
TF.13
ALT **door ring**
SN Entrance doorbell devices activated by turning a bar or thumb piece located on the outside of an exterior door frame that communicates with a bell located somewhere inside the door frame. (DITTRI)
UF rings, door
CN V.TF.AFU.AFU.AFU.AFU.AFU.BOK

door silencers
TF.14
ALT **door silencer**
UF silencers, door
CN V.TF.AFU.AFU.AFU.AFU.AFU.BUE

door trees
USE **door jambs**

door windows
USE **French doors**

doorbells
RT.1285 (N)

ALT **doorbell**
CN V.RT.ALO.AFU.AFU.ALO

doorcheeks
USE **door jambs**

doorframes
RT.836 (A,N,B)
ALT **doorframe**
SN Assemblies built into a wall consisting of two upright members (doorjambs) and a horizontal member (doorhead), and providing support on which to hang the door. (DAC)
UF casings, door
door casings
door frames
door linings
doorway frames
frames, door
frames, doorway
linings, door
CN V.RT.AFU.ARI.AFU.AFU.AFU.ALO.ALO.AFU

doorheads
RT.840 (B)
ALT **doorhead**
SN Uppermost, horizontal member of a doorframe; also horizontal projections above a door. (DAC)
UF door hoods
hoods, door
CN V.RT.AFU.ARI.AFU.AFU.AFU.ALO.ALO.ALO.ARI

doorknobs
TF.15 (L,N)
ALT **doorknob**
SN A form of door hardware that consists of a pair of knobs on opposite ends of a spindle used to release a door latch. Distinguished from **closet knobs**, which have a knob on one end of the spindle and a rose or plate on the other.
UF door knobs
knobs, door
CN V.TF.AFU.AFU.AFU.AFU.AFU.BZY

doornails
TF.408
ALT **doornail**
UF nails, door
CN V.TF.AFU.AFU.AFU.ALO.AFU.CFS.AFU.DCU.BIQ

doorplates
TF.16 (N)
ALT **doorplate**
SN Plates that serve as a mount for a doorknob or lever door handle and intervene between them and the door. (DITTRI)
UF door plates
plates, door
CN V.TF.AFU.AFU.AFU.AFU.AFU.CFS

doorposts
USE **door jambs**

doors
RT.844 (A,L,N,B,R)
ALT **door**
SN Barriers which swing, slide, tilt, or fold to close a doorway, usually of solid and finished construction and usually leading to or separating interior spaces. Use also for similar features that close a container or a piece of case furniture. For barriers of less solid or finished construction, and usually separating two exterior spaces, use **gates**.
CN V.RT.AFU.ARI.AFU.AFU.AFU.ALO.ARI.AFU

doors, access
USE **access doors**

doors, accordion
USE **folding doors**

doors, air
USE **air curtains**

doors, automatic
USE **mechanically operated doors**

doors, blank
USE **false doors**

doors, casement
USE **French doors**

doors, concealed
USE **jib doors**

doors, concertina
USE **folding doors**

doors, double
USE **double doors**

doors, double acting
USE **swinging doors**

doors, Dutch
USE **Dutch doors**

doors, elevator
USE **elevator doors**

doors, false
USE **false doors**

doors, fire
USE **fire doors**

doors, fire-resistant
USE **fire doors**

doors, flush
USE **flush doors**

doors, folding
USE **folding doors**

doors, French
USE **French doors**

doors, garage
USE **garage doors**

doors, gib
USE **jib doors**

doors, hinged
USE **hinged doors**

doors, hollow-core
USE **hollow-core doors**

doors, jib
USE **jib doors**

doors, louver
USE **louver doors**

doors, mechanically operated
USE **mechanically operated doors**

doors, overhead
USE **overhead doors**

doors, panel
USE **panel doors**

doors, pivoted
USE **pivoted doors**

doors, pocket
USE **pocket doors**

doors, prospect
USE **prospect doors**

doors, revolving
USE **revolving doors**

doors, roll-up
USE **roll-up doors**

doors, rolling
USE **roll-up doors**

doors, screen
USE **screen doors**

doors, secret
USE **secret doors**

doors, sham
USE **false doors**

doors, shutter
USE **louver doors**

doors, slat
USE **louver doors**

doors, sliding
USE **sliding doors**

doors, solid
USE **solid-core doors**

doors, solid-core
USE **solid-core doors**

doors, soot
USE **soot doors**

doors, storm
USE **storm doors**

doors, swing
USE **swinging doors**

doors, swinging
USE **swinging doors**

doors, trap
USE **trap doors**

doors, weather
USE **storm doors**

doorsills
RT.883
ALT **doorsill**
SN Horizontal members, usually boards, covering the floor joint on the threshold of a door. (DAC)
UF saddles
CN V.RT.AFU.ARI.AFU.AFU.AFU.ALO.ARI.ALO.ARI

doorstones
RT.841
ALT **doorstone**
SN Stepstones at the threshold of a door. (DAC)
CN V.RT.AFU.ARI.AFU.AFU.AFU.ALO.ALO.ALO.AXC

doorstops
TF.23 (N)
ALT **doorstop**
SN Strips on the door frame against which the door closes.
CN V.TF.AFU.AFU.AFU.AFU.AFU.CLM

doorway frames
USE **doorframes**

doorways
RT.832 (A,L,B,R)
ALT **doorway**
SN Openings in walls containing doors that provide passage into rooms or buildings.
CN V.RT.AFU.ARI.AFU.AFU.AFU.AFU

dooryards
RK.1602
ALT **dooryard**
SN Use for the outside areas of farms adjacent to the main house, kitchen, and the main barn door.
CN V.RK.ALO.ARI.CRG.ALO

DOP
USE **developing-out paper**

Dorasque
FL.1551 (L)
CN F.FL.ALO.ALO.ARI.ALO.BOK.ALO

Doric
FL.2589
CN F.FL.ALO.AXC.ALO.AFU.ALO.ARI.ARI

Doric cymas
USE **cyma rectas**

Doric order
RT.53 (A,B,R)
UF order, Doric
CN V.RT.AFU.AFU.AFU.ARI.ARI.ARI

dormers
RT.475 (N)
ALT **dormer**
SN Structures projecting from a sloping roof usually housing a window or ventilating louver. (DAC)
UF dormers, roof
lucarnes
lutherns
roof dormers
CN V.RT.AFU.AFU.AFU.BIQ.ARI.ALO.AFU.BUE.AXC

dormers, curved
USE **curved dormers**

dormers, eyebrow
USE **eyebrow dormers**

dormers, gabled
USE **gabled dormers**

dormers, hipped
USE **hipped dormers**

dormers, pedimented
USE **pedimented dormers**

dormers, roof
USE **dormers**

dormers, shaped
USE **shaped dormers**

dormers, shed
USE **shed dormers**

dormers, stair
USE **stair dormers**

dormers, swept
USE **eyebrow dormers**

dormeuses (chaises longues)
USE **chaises longues**

dormitories
RK.220 (A,L,B,R)
ALT **dormitory**
UF halls, residence
residence halls
CN V.RK.AFU.ALO.ALO.AXC.AFU.ARI

dormitories (rooms)
RM.163
ALT **dormitory (room)**
SN Rooms containing a number of beds and serving as communal sleeping quarters, as in an institution, fraternity house, or passenger ship. (RHDEL2)
CN V.RM.AFU.DIO.ALO.CRG.ALO

Dorobo
FL.645 (L)
UF Andorobo
Ndorobo
Ogiek
Okiek
Torobo
Wandorobo
CN F.FL.ALO.AFU.AXC.AXC.BCW.AXC

Dorset
FL.792
CN F.FL.ALO.ALO.ALO.AFU.ALO.AFU.ALO.AFU.AFU

dos-à-dos
USE **boudeusses**

dosserets
USE **impost blocks**

dossiers
USE **case files**

dossiers (benches)
USE **hooded settles**

dot maps
VW.145
ALT **dot map**
SN Maps that indicate density of distribution by dots of uniform size, each dot representing a given quantity. (LG)
UF maps, dot
CN V.VW.AFU.AFU.AFU.FZU.AXC.AFU.ARI.AFU.BIQ

dot matrix printers
TB.169
ALT **dot matrix printer**
SN Printers that create each character from an array of dots that are usually formed by transferring ink by mechanical impact. (DOC)
UF printers, dot matrix
CN V.TB.AFU.ARI.BCW.AXC.AXC.ALO.ARI.AFU.ALO

dots
DG.26 (L)
CN D.DG.AFU.AFU.BIQ.ARI

dotted line pens
USE **dotting wheels**

dotting wheels
TB.278
ALT **dotting wheel**
SN Instruments composed of a pen attached to a wheel with interchangeable cogs used in conjunction with a straightedge to produce a stippled line of dots, dashes, or both; used for technical and working drawings.
UF dotted line pens
pens, dotted line
wheels, dotting
CN V.TB.AFU.ARI.CLM.AFU.ALO.DOI.BUE.AFU

double-acting doors
USE **swinging doors**

double-acting hinges
TF.108
ALT **double-acting hinge**
SN Hinges used on a swinging door that swings both ways. (MEANS)

UF hinges, double-acting
CN V.TF.AFU.AFU.AFU.AFU.CLM.
AFU.BUE

double-acting spring hinges
TF.127
ALT **double-acting spring hinge**
SN Double-acting hinges equipped with a spring to bring the door back in line with the frame. (DITTRI)
UF hinges, double-acting spring
spring hinges, double-acting
CN V.TF.AFU.AFU.AFU.AFU.CLM.
AFU.FOG.AFU

double beds
TG.382
ALT **double bed**
SN Beds which are 54 inches wide; large enough to accommodate two adults.
UF beds, double
beds, full
full beds
full size beds
CN V.TG.AFU.AFU.ARI.AFU.ALO.ALO

double-bitted keys
TF.531
ALT **double-bitted key**
UF keys, double-bitted
CN V.TF.AFU.ALO.ARI.AFU.AXC

double bow-back Windsor chairs
USE **double rod-back Windsor chairs**

double-cable structures
RT.19
ALT **double-cable structure**
SN Use for suspension structures supported by interconnected double cables of different curvature used in the same vertical plane.
UF structures, double-cable
CN V.RT.AFU.AFU.AFU.ALO.AFU.ARI

double cathedrals
USE **double churches**

double chairs
USE **chair-back settees**

double chests
USE **chests-on-chests**

double chests of drawers
USE **chests-on-chests**

double churches
RK.1096
ALT **double church**
SN Use for churches comprised of two complete sanctuaries, either placed one above the other or attached side by side.
UF cathedrals, double
cathedrals, twin
churches, double
churches, twin
double cathedrals
twin cathedrals
twin churches
CN V.RK.AFU.ALO.ALO.FCS.BIQ.
ALO.AFU.AFU

double-cleat ladders
TB.480
ALT **double-cleat ladder**
SN Similar to the single-cleat ladders, but wider, with an additional center rail which allows for two-way traffic of workmen ascending and descending. (DAC)
UF ladders, double-cleat
CN V.TB.AFU.ARI.ERE.ALO.ALO

double counting-house desks
TG.525
ALT **double counting-house desk**
UF counting-house desks, double
desks, double counting-house
CN V.TG.AFU.AFU.AXC.ALO.BZY.
ALO.AFU

double-creasing stakes
TB.685 (N)
ALT **double-creasing stake**
UF stakes, double-creasing
CN V.TB.AFU.BCW.BIQ.AFU.ALO.
CXA.ARI.AFU

double curvature net structures
USE **cable net structures**

double-deck elevators
RT.1307
ALT **double-deck elevator**
UF elevators, double-deck
CN V.RT.ALO.ALO.AFU.ARI.ALO.
AFU.AFU

double desks
USE **partner's desks**

double-door bolts
TF.165
ALT **double-door bolt**
UF bolts, double-door
CN V.TF.AFU.AFU.AFU.AFU.DIO.ARI.
ALO

double doors
RT.846
ALT **double door**
SN Two single doors or door leaves hung in the same frame. (DAC)
UF doors, double
CN V.RT.AFU.ARI.AFU.AFU.AFU.ALO.
ARI.AFU.AFU.AFU

double dwellings
USE **double houses**

double end anchors
TF.301
ALT **double end anchor**
UF anchors, double end
CN V.TF.AFU.AFU.AFU.ALO.AFU.
AFU.CRG.AFU

double-faced hammers
USE **framing hammers**

double frame windows
USE **double windows**

double-framed roofs
RT.447
ALT **double-framed roof**
SN Use for roofs in which the common rafters rest on purlins which transfer the loads to principal rafters or trusses.
UF double roofs
principal rafter roofs
roofs, double
roofs, double-framed
roofs, principal rafter
CN V.RT.AFU.AFU.AFU.BIQ.ARI.AFU.
ALO.ALO.ALO

double-gable roofs
RT.428
ALT **double-gable roof**
SN Roofs formed by the junction of two simple pitched roofs with a valley between them, resembling the letter M in section. (DAC)
UF gable roofs, parallel
M-roofs
parallel gable roofs
roofs, double-gable
roofs, parallel gable
roofs, trough
trough roofs
CN V.RT.AFU.AFU.AFU.BIQ.ARI.AFU.
AFU.AFU.BOK.AXC.AFU

double glazing, sealed
USE **double windows**

double-headed nails
TF.409
ALT **double-headed nail**
SN Nails having two heads, one above the other, used for temporary construction such as concrete forms and scaffolds. The nail can secure the work but still be easily extracted. (MEANS)
UF duplex nails
form nails
nails, double-headed
nails, duplex
nails, form
nails, scaffold
scaffold nails
CN V.TF.AFU.AFU.AFU.ALO.AFU.CFS.
AFU.DCU.BOK

double hip roofs
USE **mansard roofs**

double houses
RK.367 (A)
ALT **double house**
SN Use for houses with separate dwelling units for two individual families placed side-by-side and separated horizontally by party walls. When the units are set one above the other use **duplex houses.**
UF double dwellings

duplexes, horizontal
dwellings, double
horizontal duplexes
houses, double
houses, semidetached
houses, two-family
semidetached houses
two-family houses
CN V.RK.AFU.ALO.ALO.AXC.AXC.ARI

double-hung windows
RT.944
ALT **double-hung window**
SN Windows having two vertically sliding sashes, each closing a different part of the window; the weight of each sash is counter-balanced for ease of opening and closing. (DAC)
UF windows, double-hung
CN V.RT.AFU.ARI.AFU.AFU.BOK.AFU.AFU.EWY.ARI.AFU

double monasteries
RG.197
ALT **double monastery**
UF monasteries, double
CN V.RG.AFU.AFU.DUC.BIQ.ARI

double-pen houses
RK.260
ALT **double-pen house**
UF double-pens
houses, double-pen
CN V.RK.AFU.ALO.ALO.AXC.ALO.AFU.CRG.ARI

double-pens
USE **double-pen houses**

double-pile houses
RK.263
ALT **double-pile house**
UF houses, double-pile
CN V.RK.AFU.ALO.ALO.AXC.ALO.AFU.CRG.AXC

double pitch roofs
USE **gable roofs**

double pointed tacks
TF.495
ALT **double pointed tack**
UF tacks, double pointed
CN V.TF.AFU.AFU.AFU.AFU.ALO.AFU.ERE.ALO

double-printing
KT.747
SN Process of reprinting an image to overcome the problem of roller lap marks.
UF printing, double
printing, second
second printing
CN K.KT.AFU.ALO.HCQ.ALO.BIQ.AFU

double rabbet joints
TF.595
ALT **double rabbet joint**
UF joints, double rabbet
rabbet joints, double
CN V.TF.ALO.AFU.ELK.AFU

double return stairs
RT.1088
ALT **double return stair**
SN Stairs with one flight up from the lower floor to the landing and two flights from the landing to the next floor. (SCOTT)
UF stairs, double return
CN V.RT.AFU.BIQ.AXC.AFU.AFU.BZY.ALO.AFU

double rod-back Windsor chairs
TG.107
ALT **double rod-back Windsor chair**
SN Square-back Windsor chairs with two turned rods across the top, the upper rod either capping the back posts or framed between them. (EVANS)
UF chairs, double bow-back Windsor
chairs, double rod-back Windsor
double bow-back Windsor chairs
Windsor chairs, double bow-back
Windsor chairs, double rod-back
CN V.TG.AFU.AFU.ALO.AFU.AFU.AFU.MLC.CFS.AFU

double roofs
USE **double-framed roofs**

double seamers
TB.679
ALT **double seamer**
SN Closing machines that roll together the rims and lids of metal cans to make a hermetic seal. (W)
UF seamers, double
CN V.TB.AFU.BCW.BIQ.AFU.ALO.CLM.AFU

double seams, bottom
USE **bottom double seams**

double seams, corner
USE **corner double seams**

double sliding fire screens
TG.11
SN Fire screens constructed of two folding leaves with sliding panels. (GILBR2)
CN V.TG.AFU.AFU.AFU.AFU.BCW.AFU

double spiral stairs
RT.1076
ALT **double spiral stair**
SN Stairs in which two spiral stairs are intertwined, one of the most famous examples being the central staircase at the Château of Chambord.
UF spiral stairs, double
stairs, double spiral
CN V.RT.AFU.BIQ.AXC.AFU.AFU.BIQ.AFU

double strength window glass
MT.251
UF glass, double strength window
window glass, double strength
CN M.MT.AFU.AFU.AFU.BIQ.AFU.ALO.AXC.AFU

double style hangers
TF.372
ALT **double syle hanger**
UF hangers, double style
CN V.TF.AFU.AFU.AFU.ALO.AFU.BOK.ARI.ARI.AXC.ALO.AFU

double sun snakes
USE **swastikas**

double throw bolts
TF.556
ALT **double throw bolt**
SN Bolts that can be projected beyond their normal position, thus giving extra security. (BROWNL)
UF bolts, double throw
throw bolts, double
CN V.TF.AFU.ALO.AXC.AFU.BIQ

double whole plate
DC.126
SN A photographic plate size, about 8 1/2 by 13 inches.
CN D.DC.AFU.AXC.BIQ.AFU

double windows
RT.920 (L,B)
ALT **double window**
SN Two windows, one outside the other, as storm windows, used to provide improved thermal and noise insulation. (DAC)
UF double frame windows
double glazing, sealed
glazing, sealed double
heat insulation windows
sealed double glazing
windows, double
windows, double frame
windows, heat insulation
CN V.RT.AFU.ARI.AFU.AFU.BOK.AFU.AFU.BUE

doubled columns
RT.104
ALT **doubled column**
SN Use for pairs of columns which interlock as if the shaft of one were gripping the shaft of the other; for pairs of columns set close together so as to form a visual unit, use **coupled columns.**
UF columns, doubled
CN V.RT.AFU.AFU.AFU.AXC.BIQ.AFU.ALO.AXC

doucines
USE **cymas**

Douglas fir
MT.1352 (L)
UF Douglas pine
Douglas spruce
fir, Douglas
fir, red
fir, yellow
Oregon pine

pine, Douglas
pine, Oregon
pine, Puget Sound
Puget Sound pine
red fir
spruce, Douglas
yellow fir
CN M.MT.AFU.AFU.ALO.BIQ.DCU.
AFU.AFU.ALO.BIQ.ALO

Douglas pine
USE **Douglas fir**

Douglas spruce
USE **Douglas fir**

Dourour
USE **Aua**

dovecotes
RK.82 (A,L,B,R)
ALT **dovecote**
UF columbaria (dovecotes)
columbariums
houses, pigeon
pigeon houses
CN V.RK.AFU.ALO.ALO.AFU.ALO.
ARI.AFU

dovetail clamps
TB.215
ALT **dovetail clamp**
SN Devices, usually of iron, bent at the ends, or of dovetail form; used to hold together structural timbers or stone. (PUTNAM)
UF clamps, dovetail
CN V.TB.AFU.ARI.CFS.AFU.AFU

dovetail cutters
TB.871
ALT **dovetail cutter**
SN Rotary cutting tools used to shape dovetails. (DAC)
UF cutters, dovetail
CN V.TB.AFU.BCW.CFS.ALO.AFU.
BZY.AFU

dovetail joints
TF.672
ALT **dovetail joint**
SN Interlocking joints formed by a flaring or fanlike tenon and a mortise into which it fits tightly. (WCOL)
UF joints, dovetail
CN V.TF.ALO.ARI.AXC.ALO.ALO

dovetail joints, blind
USE **blind dovetail joints**

dovetail joints, shouldered
USE **shouldered dovetail joints**

dovetail saws
TB.990 (N)
ALT **dovetail saw**
SN Small backsaws, about 9 inches in length, with thin blades, fine teeth, and straight handles; used for accurate work, as in cabinetmaking and patternmaking.
UF angle saws
corner saws
saws, angle
saws, corner
saws, dovetail
CN V.TB.AFU.BCW.CFS.ALO.AFU.
EWY.AFU.ARI

dovetail seams
USE **plain dovetail seams**

dovetail seams, beaded
USE **beaded dovetail seams**

dovetail seams, flange
USE **flange dovetail seams**

dovetail templates
TB.454
ALT **dovetail template**
UF templates, dovetail
CN V.TB.AFU.ARI.EFQ.ALO.CRG.AFU

dovetail wire anchors
TF.302
ALT **dovetail wire anchor**
UF anchors, dovetail wire
wire anchors, dovetail
CN V.TF.AFU.AFU.AFU.ALO.AFU.
AFU.CRG.ALO

dowel
MT.2225 (L,N)
SN A pin of wood or metal used to hold or strengthen two pieces of timber where they join. (PUTNAM)
CN M.MT.AFU.ALO.CLM

dowel anchors
TF.293
ALT **dowel anchor**
UF anchors, dowel
CN V.TF.AFU.AFU.AFU.ALO.AFU.
AFU.BCW

dowel bits
USE **spoon bits**

dowel cutters
USE **peg cutters**

dowel pins
TF.458
ALT **dowel pin**
SN Special nails that are pointed at both ends and are used to fasten mortise-and-tenon joints. (MEANS)
UF pins, dowel
CN V.TF.AFU.AFU.AFU.ALO.AFU.
CXA.ALO

dowel pins, barbed
USE **barbed dowel pins**

dowel plates
USE **peg cutters**

dower chests
TG.460 (N)
ALT **dower chest**
SN Chests made to commemorate or anticipate a wedding; usually incorporating names and dates in their decoration. (PAIN)
UF bridal chests
chests, bridal
chests, dower
chests, hope
chests, marriage
chests, wedding
hope chests
marriage chests
wedding chests
CN V.TG.AFU.AFU.AXC.ALO.AXC.CRG

down
MT.925 (L)
CN M.MT.AFU.AFU.ALO.AFU.CFS.AFU

downcutting augers
USE **nose augers**

downfeed distribution
USE **downfeed systems**

downfeed systems
RT.1448
ALT **downfeed system**
UF downfeed distribution
systems, downfeed
CN V.RT.ALO.BCW.ALO.AFU.ALO.AFU

downtowns
USE **central business districts**
inner cities

downy birch
MT.1115
UF Betula pubescens
birch, downy
CN M.MT.AFU.AFU.ALO.BIQ.DCU.
AFU.AFU.AFU.BIQ.AFU

dowsing
KT.115 (L,B)
SN Use for the technique of detecting underground water or other substances or objects by feeling the motion of a divining rod.
CN K.KT.AFU.ALO.CXA.AFU

dozers
USE **bulldozers**

dozers, angle
USE **angle dozers**

dozers, angling
USE **angle dozers**

dozers, shovel
USE **shovel dozers**

dozers, tilting
USE **tilting dozers**

drab gray
USE **yellowish gray**

drab gray, pale
USE **light gray**
white

drab, light olive
USE **olive gray**

drab, olive
USE **dark olive**
grayish olive
olive gray

Draconian
FL.1188
CN F.FL.ALO.ALO.ALO.ARI.BCW.
ALO.AFU.ARI

draft shaves
USE **drawknives**

drafting
KT.197 (A,L)
ALT **drafted**
UF drawing, mechanical
drawing, precision
mechanical drawing
precision drawing
CN K.KT.AFU.ALO.DUC.BZY.ALO.BIQ

drafting cloth
MT.1864
SN Linen or cotton coated on one or both sides with starch or a mixture of starch and gelatine, producing a support of even transparency and strength. (ADAG)
UF cloth, drafting
CN M.MT.AFU.AFU.ARI.ALO.ALO.
ALO.ALO.BOK

drafting equipment
TB.231 (N)
UF equipment, drafting
CN V.TB.AFU.ARI.CLM.AFU.AFU.AFU

drafting machines
TB.246 (N)
ALT **drafting machine**
SN Devices which attach to a drawing table and combine the functions of a straightedge, T-square, triangle, and protractor; used by draftsmen, designers, architects, and engineers.
UF machines, drafting
CN V.TB.AFU.ARI.CLM.AFU.ALO.BCW

drafting tables
USE **drawing tables**

drafts (documents)
VW.35
ALT **draft**
SN Preliminary or tentative versions of documents.
CN V.VW.AFU.AFU.AFU.BUE

drafts (negotiable instruments)
USE **bank drafts**

drafts, bank
USE **bank drafts**

drafts, first
USE **first drafts**

drafts, rough
USE **first drafts**

draftsmen
HG.98
ALT **draftsman**
SN Persons skilled in drawing.
UF artists, graphic (draftsmen)
draughtsmen
graphic artists (draftsmen)
CN H.HG.AFU.AXC.AXC.AFU.AFU.
ALO.AXC.BOK

draftsmen (technical)
HG.621
ALT **draftsman (technical)**
SN Persons skilled in the creation of technical drawings, as of structures or machines. (W)
UF draughtsmen (technical)
CN H.HG.AFU.AXC.BZY.AXC

draftsmen, architectural
USE **architectural draftsmen**

drag shovels
USE **backhoes**

drag strips
RG.178
ALT **drag strip**
UF dragways
CN V.RG.AFU.AFU.DOI.CFS.ALO.
AFU.AFU

dragging
KT.222
ALT **dragged**
SN A technique of stroking oil color lightly over a rough surface so that it covers the high spots and leaves the depressions untouched, thus creating a broken area of color with irregular spots of the undercolor showing through.
UF scruffing
scuffing
CN K.KT.AFU.ALO.DUC.CXA.ALO.
AFU.ALO

dragging beams
USE **dragon beams**

dragging pieces
USE **dragon beams**

dragline buckets
TB.58 (N)
ALT **dragline bucket**
SN Bucket attachments for cranes; used for removing earth by pulling the bucket toward the crane. (DAC)
UF buckets, dragline
CN V.TB.AFU.ARI.AFU.BCW.ALO.ARI

dragon beams
RT.310
ALT **dragon beam**
SN Use for short angled beams reaching from the corner of the structure, at the level of the roof plate, to an angle brace, and serving to support the foot of a hip rafter.
UF beams, dragging
beams, dragon
dragging beams
dragging pieces
dragon pieces
pieces, dragging
pieces, dragon
CN V.RT.AFU.AFU.AFU.BCW.ALO.
ALO.ARI

dragon feet
TG.924
ALT **dragon foot**
UF feet, dragon
CN V.TG.ALO.DZW.AFU.DCU.AXC

dragon pieces
USE **dragon beams**

dragon ties
RT.206
ALT **dragon tie**
SN Angle braces which support one end of a dragon beam.
UF ties, dragon
CN V.RT.AFU.AFU.AFU.AXC.DOI.
AFU.AFU.AFU

dragon's blood
MT.1490 (L)
SN Group of red resins used in fine lacquers and varnishes. (MH)
UF blood, dragon's
CN M.MT.AFU.AFU.ALO.BOK.BCW

dragon's blood (color)
USE **grayish red**

drags (scratch tools)
TB.627
ALT **drag (scratch tool)**
SN Long serrated plates used to level and score plaster in preparation for the next coat. (MEANS)
CN V.TB.AFU.BCW.BCW.ALO.GRC.ARI

dragways
USE **drag strips**

drainage
BM.417 (A,L,B)
CN B.BM.AXC.AFU

drainage networks
USE **drainage systems**

drainage piping
RT.1469 (L)
SN The piping comprising the plumbing of a drainage system. (MEANS)
UF piping, drainage
CN V.RT.ALO.BCW.ALO.ARI.BZY.ALO

drainage systems
RD.87 (B)
ALT **drainage system**
UF drainage networks
networks, drainage
systems, drainage

CN V.RD.ALO.AFU

drainage systems, sanitary
USE **sanitary drainage systems**

drainage systems, storm
USE **storm water systems**

drainage tile
USE **draintile**

drainage, land
USE **land drainage**

drainage, sanitary
USE **sanitary drainage systems**

drainage, soil
USE **land drainage**

drainage, waste and vent piping
USE **DWV piping**

drains
RT.1455
ALT **drain**
SN Artificial channels by means of which liquid or other matter is drained or carried off. (W)
CN V.RT.ALO.BCW.ALO.ARI.AXC

drains, area
USE **area drains**

drains, fixture
USE **fixture drains**

drains, storm
USE **storm drains**

draintile
MT.166 (L)
UF drainage tile
field tile
tile, drainage
tile, field
CN M.MT.AFU.AFU.AFU.AXC.ALO.ALO.ALO.AFU.ALO.AFU

drake feet
USE **trifid feet**

drama
KD.55 (L,R)
SN Use for the academically oriented study of theater, comprising theater criticism, history, aesthetics, and the study of drama as a specialized form of literature. For the professionally oriented study and practice of theater, use **theater.**
UF arts, dramatic
dramatic arts
CN K.KD.AFU.AFU.BCW.ALO

drama, religious
USE **religious drama**

dramatic arts
USE **drama**

dramatists
USE **playwrights**

drapers
HG.160
ALT **draper**
CN H.HG.AFU.AXC.AXC.AFU.AFU.ALO.BCW.BZY.AFU

drapery holdbacks
TF.28
ALT **drapery holdback**
UF holdbacks, drapery
CN V.TF.AFU.AFU.AFU.AFU.ALO.AFU

drapery studies
VB.60
ALT **drapery study**
UF studies, drapery
CN V.VB.AFU.ALO.BOK.ALO

draught chairs
USE **easy chairs**

draught screens
USE **folding screens**

draughtsmen
USE **draftsmen**

draughtsmen (technical)
USE **draftsmen (technical)**

draughtsmen, architectural
USE **architectural draftsmen**

Dravidian
FL.2247 (A,L)
CN F.FL.ALO.ARI.AXC.ALO.AFU.BUE.AFU

draw leaf tables
USE **draw tables**

draw-out tables
USE **draw tables**

draw runners
USE **lopers**

draw slips
USE **lopers**

draw tables
TG.669
ALT **draw table**
SN Tables with flaps which may be drawn out from beneath the top to extend the length. Late 16th-century and early 17th-century hall tables are often of this type. (DDA)
UF draw leaf tables
draw-out tables
draw-top tables
drawer tables
drawing tables (draw tables)
tables, draw
tables, draw leaf
tables, draw-out
tables, draw-top
tables, drawer
tables, drawing (draw tables)
CN V.TG.AFU.AFU.BIQ.BOK.AFU.ARI

draw tongs
USE **clip tongs**

draw-top tables
USE **draw tables**

drawbenches
TB.743 (L)
ALT **drawbench**
SN Benches used in conjunction with drawplates for drawing long or tough lengths of wire. (HAND)
CN V.TB.AFU.BCW.BIQ.AXC.AFU.ALO

drawbridges
RK.1279 (A,L,R)
ALT **drawbridge**
SN Use for movable bridges in which one or more span sections can be pivoted upward by means of chains, cables, or other ropelike devices; if the sections are pivoted by counterweights, use **bascule bridges.**
CN V.RK.AFU.ALO.ALO.GLI.ALO.AFU.AFU.AXC.ALO

drawer knobs
USE **cabinet knobs**

drawer locks
TF.251
ALT **drawer lock**
UF locks, drawer
locks, till
till locks
CN V.TF.AFU.AFU.AFU.AFU.DIO.BIQ.ALO.ARI.AXC

drawer pulls
TF.91
ALT **drawer pull**
UF chest lifts
chest pulls
lifts, chest
pulls, chest
pulls, drawer
CN V.TF.AFU.AFU.AFU.AFU.CFS.BCW.ALO.AXC

drawer pulls, drop
USE **drop pulls**

drawer supports
TG.995
ALT **drawer support**
UF supports, drawer
CN V.TG.ALO.HIK.ALO.AFU

drawer tables
USE **draw tables**

drawers
TG.874
ALT **drawer**
UF furniture drawers
CN V.TG.ALO.DCU.AFU

drawers, blind
USE **blind drawers**

drawers, bottle
USE **celleret drawers**

drawers, cabinets of
USE cabinets of drawers

drawers, cellarette
USE celleret drawers

drawers, celleret
USE celleret drawers

drawers, chests of
USE chests of drawers

drawers, chests with
USE chests with drawers

drawers, document
USE document drawers

drawers, double chests of
USE chests-on-chests

drawers, dressing
USE dressing drawers

drawers, high chests of
USE high chests of drawers

drawers, kneehole chests of
USE kneehole desks

drawers, lipped
USE lipped drawers

drawers, low chests of
USE low chests

drawers, nests of
USE nests of drawers

drawers, pedestals with
USE cabinets of drawers

drawers, quadrant
USE quadrant drawers

drawers, secret
USE secret drawers

drawers, secretary
USE secretary drawers

drawers, tall chests of
USE chiffoniers

drawers, writing
USE secretary drawers

drawing
KT.187 (A,L,R)
UF graphic arts (drawing)
CN K.KT.AFU.ALO.DUC.BZY.AFU

drawing (metalwork)
KT.845 (L)
SN The stretching, spreading, or shaping of metal by passing through dies or by stamping successively, as with a series of dies or by hammeri
CN K.KT.AFU.ALO.HOE.BCW.ALO.BIQ.AFU

drawing and writing tables, lady's
USE Carlton House tables

drawing books
VW.529 (L,R)
ALT **drawing book**
UF books, drawing
CN V.VW.AFU.ALO.AFU.AFU.ALO.BCW.ALO

drawing curves
USE curves

drawing instruments
TB.232 (L,B)
ALT **drawing instrument**
UF drawing tools
instruments, drawing
tools, drawing
CN V.TB.AFU.ARI.CLM.AFU.AFU.ALO

drawing paper
MT.1932
UF paper, drawing
CN M.MT.AFU.AFU.ARI.ALO.ALO.AXC.ARI.AXC

drawing rooms
RM.170 (A)
ALT **drawing room**
SN Formal reception rooms, as in a home or hotel, or rooms to which one may retire for privacy or rest. (W)
UF rooms, drawing
CN V.RM.AFU.DIO.ALO.CXA.BCW

drawing tables
TG.729 (N)
ALT **drawing table**
SN Tables with surfaces adjustable for elevation and angles of incline.
UF architect's tables
artist's tables
drafting tables
tables, architect's
tables, artist's
tables, drafting
tables, drawing
CN V.TG.AFU.AFU.BIQ.BOK.ALO.CFS

drawing tables (draw tables)
USE draw tables

drawing techniques
KT.189 (L,R)
CN K.KT.AFU.ALO.DUC.BZY.ALO

drawing tools
USE drawing instruments

drawing, architectural
USE architectural drawing

drawing, blind contour
USE blind contour drawing

drawing, blot
USE blot drawing

drawing, computer
USE computer-aided design

drawing, contour
USE contour drawing

drawing, cross-contour
USE cross-contour drawing

drawing, fashion
USE fashion illustration

drawing, freehand
USE freehand drawing

drawing, gesture
USE gesture drawing

drawing, mechanical
USE drafting

drawing, photogenic
USE photogenic drawing

drawing, precision
USE drafting

drawings
VD.1 (A,L,N,B)
ALT **drawing**
SN Visible forms produced primarily by delineation, usually by the direct application of material or instrument to the surface of the support.
CN V.VD.AFU

drawings, addendum
USE clarification drawings

drawings, architectural
USE architectural drawings

drawings, as-built
USE as-built drawings

drawings, assembly
USE assembly drawings

drawings, auxiliary
USE auxiliary views

drawings, axonometric
USE axonometric drawings

drawings, blind contour
USE blind contour drawings

drawings, blot
USE blot drawings

drawings, cabinet oblique
USE cabinet oblique drawings

drawings, cavalier oblique
USE cavalier oblique drawings

drawings, cave
USE cave drawings

drawings, change order
USE change order drawings

drawings, chiaroscuro
USE three-tone drawings

drawings, clarification
USE clarification drawings

drawings, competition
USE competition drawings

drawings, component
USE **minor assembly drawings**

drawings, composite
USE **composite drawings**

drawings, composition
USE **composition drawings**

drawings, computer
USE **computer drawings**

drawings, computer-generated
USE **computer drawings**

drawings, conceptual
USE **conceptual drawings**

drawings, construction
USE **construction drawings**

drawings, contour
USE **contour drawings**

drawings, contract
USE **contract drawings**

drawings, cross-contour
USE **cross-contour drawings**

drawings, cutaway
USE **cutaway drawings**

drawings, definitive
USE **design development drawings**

drawings, design
USE **design drawings**

drawings, design development
USE **design development drawings**

drawings, detail
USE **detail drawings**

drawings, detail (studies)
USE **detail studies**

drawings, dimetric
USE **dimetric drawings**

drawings, display
USE **preparatory drawings**
presentation drawings

drawings, electrical
USE **electrical drawings**

drawings, elevation
USE **elevations**

drawings, elevation oblique
USE **elevation oblique drawings**

drawings, engineering
USE **technical drawings**

drawings, erection
USE **erection drawings**

drawings, exploded
USE **exploded drawings**

drawings, facade oblique
USE **elevation oblique drawings**

drawings, figure
USE **figure drawings**

drawings, freehand
USE **freehand drawings**

drawings, full-scale
USE **full-scale drawings**

drawings, full-size
USE **full-scale drawings**

drawings, general oblique
USE **general oblique drawings**

drawings, gesture
USE **gesture drawings**

drawings, gouache
USE **gouaches**

drawings, hard-line
USE **mechanical drawings**

drawings, HVAC
USE **HVAC drawings**

drawings, isometric
USE **isometric drawings**

drawings, layout
USE **site plans**

drawings, life
USE **life drawings**

drawings, line
USE **line drawings**

drawings, lines
USE **lines drawings**

drawings, master
USE **master drawings**

drawings, measured
USE **measured drawings**

drawings, mechanical
USE **mechanical drawings**

drawings, mechanical (building systems drawings)
USE **mechanical drawings (building systems drawings)**

drawings, minor assembly
USE **minor assembly drawings**

drawings, multiview
USE **multiview drawings**

drawings, oblique
USE **oblique drawings**

drawings, old master
USE **master drawings**

drawings, operational
USE **construction drawings**

drawings, ornament
USE **ornament drawings**

drawings, orthogonal
USE **orthographic drawings**

drawings, orthographic
USE **orthographic drawings**

drawings, outline
USE **outline drawings**

drawings, paraline
USE **axonometric drawings**

drawings, pastel
USE **pastels**

drawings, pattern
USE **pattern drawings**

drawings, perspective
USE **perspective drawings**

drawings, photogenic
USE **photogenic drawings**

drawings, pictorial
USE **pictorial drawings**

drawings, plan
USE **plans**

drawings, plan oblique
USE **plan oblique drawings**

drawings, plumbing
USE **plumbing drawings**

drawings, preliminary
USE **preliminary drawings**

drawings, preliminary (underdrawings)
USE **underdrawings**

drawings, preparatory
USE **preparatory drawings**

drawings, presentation
USE **presentation drawings**

drawings, presentation (gifts)
USE **presentation drawings (gifts)**

drawings, production
USE **working drawings**

drawings, record
USE **record drawings**

drawings, scale
USE **scale drawings**

drawings, schematic
USE **schematic drawings**

drawings, section
USE **sections**

drawings, ships
USE **ships plans**

drawings, shop
USE **shop drawings**

drawings, single-view
USE **pictorial drawings**

drawings, standard detail
USE **standard detail drawings**

drawings, structural
USE **structural drawings**

drawings, student
USE **student drawings**

drawings, subassembly
USE **subassembly drawings**

drawings, subcomponent
USE **subassembly drawings**

drawings, subcontractors'
USE **shop drawings**

drawings, survey
USE **measured drawings**

drawings, technical
USE **technical drawings**

drawings, theoretical
USE **theoretical drawings**

drawings, thesis
USE **student drawings**

drawings, three-tone
USE **three-tone drawings**

drawings, tone
USE **tone drawings**

drawings, trimetric
USE **trimetric drawings**

drawings, value
USE **tone drawings**

drawings, working
USE **working drawings**

drawknives
TB.900 (N)
ALT **drawknife**
SN Two-handled curved knives used in woodworking which is utilized by pulling it toward the user. (MEANS)
UF draft shaves
drawshaves
knives, shaving
shaves, draft
shaving knives
CN V.TB.AFU.BCW.CFS.ALO.AFU.DOI.ARI

drawknives, backing
USE **backing drawknives**

drawknives, barking
USE **barking drawknives**

drawknives, heading
USE **heading drawknives**

drawknives, hollowing
USE **hollowing drawknives**

drawknives, hollowing cooper's
USE **hollowing drawknives**

drawknives, mast
USE **mast drawknives**

drawn glass
MT.260
SN Glass that is made by continuous drawing of the molten glass by a series of rolls on automatic machinery. (W)
UF glass, drawn
CN M.MT.AFU.AFU.AFU.BIQ.AFU.ARI.BIQ

drawplates
TB.658
ALT **drawplate**
SN Plates with holes through which wire is drawn and shaped. (HAND)
UF plates, wire
wire plates
CN V.TB.AFU.BCW.BIQ.AFU.ALO.AXC

draws
USE **gullies**

drawshaves
USE **drawknives**

dread
USE **fear**

dredges
TB.40 (L,N)
ALT **dredge**
SN Floating excavators for removing earth or rock from under water, usually accomplished by clamshell buckets or power shovels combined with a suction line. (DAC)
CN V.TB.AFU.ARI.AFU.ARI.ARI.ALO

dredging
KT.607 (L)
SN Digging or pulling out with a dredge, especially for the purpose of deepening a body of water, searching for foreign objects in a body of water, or for keeping waterways clean.
CN K.KT.AFU.ALO.FUA.BIQ

dress design (costume design)
USE **costume design**

dress design (fashion design)
USE **fashion design**

dress designers (costume designers)
USE **costume designers**

dress designers (fashion designers)
USE **fashion designers**

dressed lumber
MT.1425
SN Lumber machined and surfaced at a mill. (PUTNAM)
UF lumber, dressed
lumber, surfaced
surfaced lumber
CN M.MT.AFU.AFU.ALO.BIQ.DCU.ALO.BOK.ALO.AFU.AFU

dressed stone
MT.902
SN Dimension stone with a smooth exposed face.
UF stone, dressed
CN M.MT.AFU.AFU.AFU.DCU.ARI.AFU.AFU.ALO

dressers
TG.507
ALT **dresser**
UF armoires dressoirs
dish dressers
dressers, dish
CN V.TG.AFU.AFU.AXC.ALO.BUE.BUE

dressers (chests of drawers)
USE **chests of drawers**

dressers (leatherworkers)
HG.487
ALT **dresser (leatherworker)**
SN Persons that finish leather. (W)
CN H.HG.AFU.AXC.BUE.ARI.BZY.ALO

dressers (sideboards)
USE **sideboards**

dressers, cheval
USE **cheval dressers**

dressers, corner dish
USE **corner cupboards**

dressers, dish
USE **dressers**

dressers, window
USE **window dressers**

dressing (leather)
KT.775
ALT **dressed**
CN K.KT.AFU.ALO.HOE.AXC.ALO

dressing bureaux
USE **dressing tables**

dressing chairs
TG.179
ALT **dressing chair**
UF chairs, dressing
CN V.TG.AFU.AFU.ALO.AFU.AFU.ALO.BZY

dressing chests (chests of drawers)
USE **chests of drawers**

dressing chests, French commode
USE **commode dressing tables**

dressing chests, Rudd
USE **Rudd dressing chests**

dressing drawers
TG.882
ALT **dressing drawer**
SN Term used by Hepplewhite for a specially designed top drawer equipped with compartments for such items as combs, powders, and essences. (MONTGO)
UF drawers, dressing
CN V.TG.ALO.DCU.AFU.ALO.ARI

dressing rooms
RM.67 (A,B)
ALT **dressing room**
UF changing rooms
rooms, changing
rooms, dressing
CN V.RM.AFU.DIO.ALO.ALO.ALO

dressing stands
TG.635
ALT **dressing stand**
UF stands, dressing
CN V.TG.AFU.AFU.BIQ.BCW.ALO.BCW

dressing stands, gentleman's
USE **gentleman's dressing stands**

dressing stands, lady's
USE **lady's dressing stands**

dressing stools
TG.256
ALT **dressing stool**
SN Stools designed as seats at dressing tables; introduced in the 18th century.
UF stools, dressing
stools, vanity
vanity stools
CN V.TG.AFU.AFU.ALO.AFU.ALO.ALO.AFU

dressing tables
TG.730 (N)
ALT **dressing table**
SN Generally applied to a variety of tables used for dressing, usually fitted with a mirror and having drawers to hold toilet articles such as brushes and combs.
UF bureaux, dressing
dressing bureaux
tables, dressing
tables, toilet
toilet tables
vanities
CN V.TG.AFU.AFU.BIQ.BOK.ALO.CLM

dressing tables and desks, combined
USE **bureau tables**

dressing tables, Beau-Brommel
USE **Beau-Brummel dressing tables**

dressing tables, bureau
USE **bureau tables**

dressing tables, commode
USE **commode dressing tables**

dressing tables, gentleman's
USE **gentleman's dressing tables**

dressing tables, lady's
USE **lady's dressing tables**

dressing tables, lady's cabinet
USE **lady's cabinet dressing tables**

dressing tables, reflecting
USE **Rudd tables**

dressing tables, Rudd
USE **Rudd tables**

dressmakers
HG.536 (L)
ALT **dressmaker**
CN H.HG.AFU.AXC.BUE.ARI.CXA.CFS.AFU

dressmaking
KT.522 (L)
CN K.KT.AFU.ALO.ELK.BOK

driers
MT.2310 (L)
SN Materials, such as metal compounds of some metals including lead, iron, manganese, and cobalt used for increasing the rapidity of the drying of paints and varnishes. (MH)
UF siccatives
CN M.MT.AFU.ARI.ALO.BZY

drift pins
USE **driftpins**

drift punches
TB.672 (N)
ALT **drift punch**
SN Tapered punches used to align holes for bolting and riveting.
UF aligning punches
punches, aligning
punches, drift
CN V.TB.AFU.BCW.BIQ.AFU.ALO.BZY.AXC

drift, continental
USE **continental drift**

driftpins
TF.460 (N)
ALT **driftpin**
SN Tapered pins used in steel erection to align holes for bolting or riveting. (MEANS)
UF drift pins
pins, drift
CN V.TF.AFU.AFU.AFU.ALO.AFU.CXA.ARI

drifts (metalworking tools)
TB.659
ALT **drift (metalworking tool)**
SN Tools similar to punches; used to open up punched holes, smoothing and shaping them at the same time. (ALMEID)
CN V.TB.AFU.BCW.BIQ.AFU.ALO.BCW

driftwood
MT.1410
CN M.MT.AFU.AFU.ALO.BIQ.DCU.AFU.ALO.ALO

drill bits
USE **bits**

drill braces
USE **hand drills**

drill clamps
TB.216
ALT **drill clamp**
SN Clamp-shaped tools used to put pressure on a drill when boring through metal.
UF clamp drills
clamps, drill
drills, clamp
drills, smith's
smith's drills
CN V.TB.AFU.ARI.CFS.AFU.ALO

drill halls
RK.876 (A,B)
ALT **drill hall**
UF halls, drill
CN V.RK.AFU.ALO.ALO.DIO.AXC.ALO

drill presses
TB.177 (L,N)
ALT **drill press**
SN Rotary drills, mounted on a permanent stand, that operate along a vertical shaft. (MEANS)
UF presses, drill
CN V.TB.AFU.ARI.BIQ.AFU.ALO

drillers
HG.592
ALT **driller**
CN H.HG.AFU.AXC.BZY.AFU.CFS

drilling
KT.608 (L,B)
ALT **drilled**
SN Use for the making of holes in metal, wood, or other materials, and for making holes in the earth, as for drilling a well or for oil.
UF boring
CN K.KT.AFU.ALO.FUA.BOK

drilling machinery
TB.175 (L)
UF machinery, drilling
CN V.TB.AFU.ARI.BIQ.AFU

drilling platforms, offshore
USE **offshore drilling platforms**

drilling rigs
RK.601
ALT **drilling rig**
UF rigs, drilling
CN V.RK.AFU.ALO.ALO.CLM.AFU.AFU

drills
TB.179 (N)
ALT **drill**
SN Large machines or hand tools used for making holes in a variety of materials.
CN V.TB.AFU.ARI.BIQ.ALO.AFU

drills, air
USE **pneumatic drills**

drills, automatic
USE **push drills**

drills, barrel
USE **barrel drills**

drills, bow
USE **bow drills**

drills, breast
USE **breast drills**

drills, clamp
USE **drill clamps**

drills, corner
USE **hand drills**

drills, electric
USE **electric drills**

drills, electric portable
USE **electric drills**

drills, fiddle
USE **bow drills**

drills, gimlet
USE **gimlets**

drills, hammer
USE **hammer drills**

drills, hand
USE **hand drills**

drills, percussive
USE **jackhammers**

drills, plugging
USE **plugging chisels**

drills, pneumatic
USE **pneumatic drills**

drills, pump
USE **pump drills**

drills, push
USE **push drills**

drills, reciprocating
USE **push drills**

drills, rock
USE **rock-drills**

drills, smith's
USE **drill clamps**

drills, star
USE **plugging chisels**

drills, thong
USE **bow drills**

drills, twist
USE **twist drills**

drink stands
USE **drinking stands**

drink tables
USE **drinking tables**

drinking fountains
RT.1481 (L,N,B)
ALT **drinking fountain**
UF fountains, drinking
CN V.RT.ALO.BCW.ALO.ARI.CFS.ARI

drinking stands
TG.638
ALT **drinking stand**
SN Stands fitted for bottles and glasses. (MONTGO)
UF drink stands
social tables
stands, drinking
tables, social
tables, toddy
tables, wine
toddy tables
wine tables
CN V.TG.AFU.AFU.BIQ.BCW.ALO.BIQ

drinking tables
TG.748
ALT **drinking table**
SN Small plank top tables supported on a triangular frame with three legs. (COMMFR)
UF drink tables
tables, drinking
CN V.TG.AFU.AFU.BIQ.BOK.ALO.DCU.AFU

drinking tables (slab tables)
USE **slab tables**

drinking water
MT.322 (L)
UF potable water
water, drinking
water, potable
CN M.MT.AFU.AFU.AFU.BOK.BOK.ALO.ALO

drip painting
KT.223
SN Includes both the technique whereby paint is dripped directly onto a canvas, and the printing technique of dripping ink on metal plates or transfer paper. (THDAT)
UF drip technique
dripping
painting, drip
CN K.KT.AFU.ALO.DUC.CXA.ALO.AFU.ARI

drip technique
USE **drip painting**

dripping
USE **drip painting**

dripstones
USE **hood moldings**

drive anchors
TF.294
ALT **drive anchor**
UF anchors, drive
CN V.TF.AFU.AFU.AFU.ALO.AFU.AFU.BIQ

drive-in banks
RK.129 (A,B)
ALT **drive-in bank**
UF banks, drive-in
drive-through banks
CN V.RK.AFU.ALO.ALO.ALO.ALO.AFU.ALO

drive-in cinemas
USE **drive-in theaters**

drive-in restaurants
RK.118 (B)
ALT **drive-in restaurant**
UF drive-ins
restaurants, drive-in
CN V.RK.AFU.ALO.ALO.ALO.AFU.AXC.BIQ.AFU

drive-in theaters
RK.939 (A,L,B)
ALT **drive-in theater**
UF cinemas, drive-in
drive-in cinemas
theaters, drive-in
CN V.RK.AFU.ALO.ALO.EFQ.ARI.BCW.ALO.AFU.AFU

drive-ins
USE **drive-in restaurants**

drive screws
USE **drivescrews**

drive-through banks
USE **drive-in banks**

drive type hangers
TF.344
ALT **drive type hanger**
UF hangers, drive type
CN V.TF.AFU.AFU.AFU.ALO.AFU.BOK.ALO.ALO.ALO

driven piles
RT.162
ALT **driven pile**
SN Use for piles driven into position at the site.
UF piles, driven
CN V.RT.AFU.AFU.AFU.AXC.BUE.ALO.ALO.AFU.ALO

driven wells
RK.597 (L)
ALT **driven well**
UF tube wells
wells, driven
wells, tube
CN V.RK.AFU.ALO.ALO.CFS.ALO.BCW.CXA.ALO.ARI

drivers, pile
USE **pile drivers**

drivers, stud
USE **stud drivers**

drives
USE **driveways**

drivescrew nails
USE **drivescrews**

drivescrews
TF.424
ALT **drivescrew**
SN Screws that are driven with a hammer and removed with a screwdriver. (MEANS)
UF drive screws
drivescrew nails
nails, screw
screw nails
screws, drive
CN V.TF.AFU.AFU.AFU.ALO.AFU.CFS.AFU.DIO.BCW

driveways
RK.1551 (A,L,B)
ALT **driveway**
UF drives
CN V.RK.ALO.ALO.BIQ.ARI.ALO.AXC

driving machines
RT.1324
ALT **driving machine**
UF machines, driving
CN V.RT.ALO.ALO.ALO.AFU

driving punches
USE **nail sets**

driving ranges
RK.1489 (A)
ALT **driving range**
SN Areas equipped with distance markers, clubs, balls, and tees for practicing golf drives. (W)
UF driving ranges, golf
golf driving ranges
ranges, driving
CN V.RK.ALO.ALO.BCW.AXC

driving ranges, golf
USE **driving ranges**

driving, pile
USE **pile driving**

droleries
USE **drolleries**

drolleries
DG.18
ALT **drollery**
SN Humorous designs in the margins of Medieval manuscripts or in inconspicuous parts of wood or stone carving in Medieval buildings. (THDAT)
UF droleries
CN D.DG.AFU.AFU.AXC

dromoi
RM.386
ALT **dromos**
SN Long, narrow passages leading into chamber tombs and tholoi.
CN V.RM.AFU.DIO.AXC.BCW.ALO

drop arches
RT.224
ALT **drop arch**
SN Use for pointed arches with the curves struck from centers below the springing line. (RS)
UF angle arches, obtuse
arches, depressed
arches, drop
arches, obtuse angle
depressed arches
obtuse angle arches
CN V.RT.AFU.AFU.AFU.BCW.AFU.AFU.AFU.BIQ

drop black
USE **bone black**
vine black

drop bow compasses
TB.239
ALT **drop bow compass**
UF compasses, drop bow
CN V.TB.AFU.ARI.CLM.AFU.ALO.ARI.ALO

drop ceilings
USE **suspended ceilings**

drop chutes
TB.546
ALT **drop chute**
UF chutes, drop
CN V.TB.AFU.BCW.ALO.ALO

drop drawer pulls
USE **drop pulls**

drop escutcheons
TF.265
ALT **drop escutcheon**
SN Key plates with a pivoting pendant attached that drops to cover the keyhole. (DITTRI)
UF drop key plates
eschutcheons, drop
key plates, drop
plates, drop key
CN V.TF.AFU.AFU.AFU.AFU.DZW.ALO.ARI

drop forges
USE **drop hammers**

drop-front cabinets
USE **fall-front desks**

drop-front desks
USE **fall-front desks**

drop-front secrétaires
USE **secrétaires à abattant**

drop hammers
TB.458 (N)
ALT **drop hammer**
SN Heavy weights for driving piles into the ground; dropped by gravity along a set of guide rails onto the head of the pile. (DAC)
UF board hammers
drop forges
forges, drop
hammers, board
hammers, drop
CN V.TB.AFU.ARI.ELK.AFU.AFU

drop handles
USE **drop pulls**

drop handles, pear
USE **pear drop handles**

drop hangers
TF.361
ALT **drop hanger**
UF hangers, drop
CN V.TF.AFU.AFU.AFU.ALO.AFU.BOK.ARI.ARI.AFU.AFU

drop-in seats
USE **slip seats**

drop key plates
USE **drop escutcheons**

drop keys
TF.532
ALT **drop key**
SN Keys having a bow or handle pivoted to the shank so that it may drop or fall parallel with the surface of the door. (STEIN)
UF keys, drop
CN V.TF.AFU.ALO.ARI.AFU.BCW

drop moldings
RT.801
ALT **drop molding**
SN Panel moldings recessed below the surface of the surrounding stiles and rails. (DAC)
UF moldings, drop
CN V.RT.AFU.ALO.AFU.BOK.AFU.ALO.BOK

drop ornament
USE **drops**

drop panels
RT.36
ALT **drop panel**
SN The stuctural portion of a flat slab which is thickened (by lowering the form) throughout an area surrounding a column, column capital, or bracket. (PUTNAM)
UF panels, drop
CN V.RT.AFU.AFU.AFU.ALO.ARI.ALO.ALO.AFU

drop pigment
MT.1804
UF pigment, drop
CN M.MT.AFU.AFU.ARI.AFU.AFU.ALO.ARI.ALO

drop pulls
TF.74
ALT **drop pull**
SN In furniture making, any type of handle, or drawer pull, which hangs like a pendant. (PUTNAM)
UF drawer pulls, drop
drop drawer pulls
drop handles
handles, drop
pulls, drop

CN V.TF.AFU.AFU.AFU.AFU.CFS.BCW.
AFU.BCW

drop testers
TG.859
ALT **drop tester**
SN Folding testers, such as those found on a press bed. (GILBR2)
UF testers, drop
CN V.TG.ALO.BIQ.CRG.AFU

drop tracery
RT.1024
SN Tracery hanging from the soffits of an arch. (HAS)
UF tracery, drop
CN V.RT.AFU.ARI.ALO.BZY.AFU.ARI

dropleaf tables
TG.670 (N)
ALT **dropleaf table**
SN Generic term for various types of space-saving tables with leaves hinged to the top so that they can be raised to extend the surface. (DDA)
UF fall-leaf tables
flap tables
tables à abattant
tables, dropleaf
tables, fall-leaf
tables, flap
CN V.TG.AFU.AFU.BIQ.BOK.AFU.AXC

dropped seats
USE **hollowed seats**

drops
RT.1055
ALT **drop**
SN Use for pendant ornament, such as on a furniture apron or rail, or within an arch and more loosely hanging than drop tracery.
UF drop ornament
ornament, drop
CN V.RT.AFU.BCW.BIQ

drops, newel
USE **newel drops**

drought
BM.746 (L,B)
CN B.BM.CFS.ALO.AXC.ALO.ARI

drought-resistant gardens
USE **xeriscapes**

drought-tolerant gardens
USE **xeriscapes**

drugstores
RK.157 (A,L,B,R)
ALT **drugstore**
UF apothecaries
chemist's shops
pharmacies
shops, chemist's
CN V.RK.AFU.ALO.ALO.ALO.ARI.
BIQ.AFU.BOK

druid stone
USE **sarsen**

drum sanders
USE **sanding disks**

drum tables
USE **capstan tables**
rent tables

drumlins
RD.183 (L)
ALT **drumlin**
SN Use for long, smooth, cigar-shaped hills of glacial origin.
CN V.RD.ARI.AFU.AXC.AFU.AFU.
ALO.AFU

drums (column components)
RT.146 (R)
ALT **drum (column component)**
SN Use for the cylinders of stone which form a column.
CN V.RT.AFU.AFU.AFU.AXC.BIQ.
ALO.AXC.ALO.ARI

drums (walls)
RT.593
ALT **drum (wall)**
SN The vertical wall, circular or polygonal in plan, which carries a dome.
CN V.RT.AFU.AFU.AFU.BIQ.BUE.
AFU.ARI.AFU

drunken saws
TB.999
ALT **drunken saw**
SN Circular saws designed to operate with a built-in wobble so that the kerf it makes is greater than the thickness of the saw; used for grooving and for other special purposes in carpentry. (MEANS)
UF saws, drunken
saws, wobble
wobble saws
CN V.TB.AFU.BCW.CFS.ALO.AFU.
EWY.AXC.AFU

dry-air filters
USE **dry filters**

dry-brush painting
KT.224
SN The technique of creating a broken or mottled effect with paint or ink on a relatively dry brush, allowing traces of the paper or underpainting to show through. (MAYER)
UF painting, dry-brush
CN
K.KT.AFU.ALO.DUC.CXA.ALO.AFU.
AXC

dry collodion process
KT.322
SN A type of collodion process in which the binder was dried before exposure or contained a hygroscopic agent to retain sufficient moisture to allow processing after an extended period of time; an improvement on the wet collodion process because it alleviated the need for a portable darkroom. Used to produce negatives and lantern slides.
UF collodion dry-plate process
dry-plate process (collodion)
CN K.KT.AFU.ALO.DUC.DIO.ALO.
BCW.ALO

dry color
MT.1805
UF color, dry
pigment, powdered
powdered pigment
CN M.MT.AFU.AFU.ARI.AFU.AFU.
ALO.ARI.ARI

dry construction
USE **drywall construction**

dry docks
RK.1316 (A,L,B)
ALT **dry dock**
UF docks, dry
docks, graving
graving docks
CN V.RK.AFU.ALO.ALO.GLI.ARI.ARI.
ALO

dry filters
RT.1436
ALT **dry filter**
SN Devices for removing pollutants from the air in a system by passing it through various screens and dry porous materials. (MEANS)
UF dry-air filters
dry-type filters
filters, dry
filters, dry-air
filters, dry-type
CN V.RT.ALO.BCW.AFU.ALO.ARI.
AXC.AFU

dry fresco
USE **secco**

dry kilns
TB.99
ALT **dry kiln**
SN Ovens for drying and seasoning cut lumber. (DAC)
UF kilns, dry
CN V.TB.AFU.ARI.ALO.ARI.ALO.
ALO.AXC

dry laid walls
RT.577 (B)
ALT **dry laid wall**
SN Masonry walls constructed without mortar.
UF dry stone walls
dry walls
mortarless walls
walls, dry
walls, dry laid
walls, dry stone
walls, mortarless
CN V.RT.AFU.AFU.AFU.BIQ.BUE.
AFU.AFU.BIQ

dry lumber
USE **air-dried lumber**

dry mortar
MT.2609
SN In masonry, mortar which contains enough moisture to cause it to set properly but is not wet enough to cause it to be sticky. (PUTNAM)
UF mortar, dry
CN M.MT.AFU.ARI.DZW.ARI.ARI.AFU

dry mounting
KT.654
ALT **dry-mounted**
SN Attaching a drawing, print, photograph, or other work of art done on paper to a cardboard or other backing by using a thermoplastic tissue as an adhesive. (RHDEL2)
UF mounting, dry
CN K.KT.AFU.ALO.GLI.AFU.BIQ.AFU.AFU

dry-mounting tissue
USE **mounting tissue**

dry plate negatives, gelatin
USE **gelatin dry plate negatives**

dry-plate process (collodion)
USE **dry collodion process**

dry plate process (gelatin)
USE **gelatin dry plate process**

dry plate, gelatin
USE **gelatin dry plate process**

dry plate, silver gelatin
USE **gelatin dry plate process**

dry sgraffito
KT.479
SN The technique of scratching designs or images into a dry plaster surface which has been covered with a thin or moderately thick lime wash layer. (WEHLTE)
UF sgraffito, dry
CN K.KT.AFU.ALO.DUC.DZW.AFU

dry sinks
TG.508
ALT **dry sink**
SN Wooden kitchen sinks, especially of the 19th century, not connected to an external water supply, with a shallow zinc or tin-lined well on top in which a dishpan can be placed, and usually a cupboard below. (RHDEL2)
UF sinks, dry
CN V.TG.AFU.AFU.AXC.ALO.BUE.BZY

dry stone walls
USE **dry laid walls**

dry-type filters
USE **dry filters**

dry wall
USE **wallboard**

dry walls
USE **dry laid walls**

dry wood
USE **air-dried lumber**

dryers
TB.86 (L,N)
ALT **dryer**
UF apparatus, drying
drying apparatus
CN V.TB.AFU.ARI.ALO.ALO

dryers (film)
USE **film dryers**

dryers, film
USE **film dryers**

dryers, print
USE **print dryers**

drying
KT.609 (A,L)
ALT **dried**
CN K.KT.AFU.ALO.FUA.BUE

drying apparatus
USE **dryers**

drying cabinets
USE **print dryers**

drying oil
MT.2006 (L)
SN Any oil that will solidify to a tough, leathery film when spread out in thin layers, either alone or with the assistance of a drier. (MAYER)
UF oil, drying
oil, paint
paint oil
CN M.MT.AFU.AFU.ARI.ARI.AXC.AFU

drying racks
USE **clotheshorses**

drying sheds
RK.1215
ALT **drying shed**
SN Use for structures of various designs erected to aid in the drying by flowing air of, for example, paper and textiles.
UF sheds, drying
CN V.RK.AFU.ALO.ALO.GFO.BIQ.ARI

drypoint
KT.452 (L,R)
SN Intaglio technique in which a sharp needle scratches the plate creating a burr that yields a characteristically soft and velvety line in the final print. (SAFF)
CN K.KT.AFU.ALO.DUC.DUC.ALO.BCW.AFU.ARI.AFU

drywall
USE **wallboard**

drywall (construction)
USE **drywall construction**

drywall construction
KT.30 (L)
SN Use for a construction technique that employs dry materials such as wallboard, plywood, or other prefabricated materials, without the use of plaster or mortar. (DAC)
UF construction, drywall
dry construction
drywall (construction)
CN K.KT.AFU.ALO.BCW.ARI.AFU.ARI

dual highways
USE **divided highways**

dual-pitched roofs
USE **curb roofs**

Duala
FL.425 (L)
CN F.FL.ALO.AFU.AXC.ALO.AFU.BIQ.AFU

dualism
BM.509 (L)
SN Doctrine that the universe is under the dominion of two opposing principles, one of which is good and the other evil. (WCOL)
CN B.BM.BIQ.AXC.BIQ

dubbing adzes
USE **lipped adzes**

ducal palaces
RK.342
ALT **ducal palace**
SN Use for the official residences of sovereigns bearing the title of duke.
UF palaces, ducal
CN V.RK.AFU.ALO.ALO.AXC.ALO.BOK.BOK.ALO.AXC.AFU

duchesse beds
USE **lits à la duchesse**

duchesses
TG.49
ALT **duchesse**
SN French chaise longues whose foot end is surrounded on three sides by a low curving back. (PC)
CN V.TG.AFU.AFU.ALO.AFU.AFU.AFU.DUC.AFU

duchesses (people)
HG.694
ALT **duchess (person)**
CN H.HG.AFU.AXC.CFS.CRG.AXC

duchesses avec encoignures
USE **canapés à confident**

duchesses brisées
TG.50
ALT **duchesse brisée**
SN Duchesses made in two or three parts, each of which can be used separately as a seat. (PC)
UF duchesses en trois
CN V.TG.AFU.AFU.ALO.AFU.AFU.AFU.DUC.AFU.AFU

duchesses en trois
USE **duchesses brisées**

duck (cloth)
MT.1865 (L)
SN Durable, plain, closely woven fabrics, now usually of cotton, made in various weights. (W)
CN M.MT.AFU.AFU.ARI.ALO.ALO.ALO.ALO.BUE

duck bill nails
TF.425
ALT **duck bill nail**
UF nails, duck bill
CN V.TF.AFU.AFU.AFU.ALO.AFU.CFS.AFU.DIO.BIQ

duck feet
USE **trifid feet**

duckboards
USE **catwalks**

ductile iron
MT.338 (L)
UF iron, ductile
iron, nodular
nodular iron
CN M.MT.AFU.AFU.AFU.BZY.AFU.AFU.AFU.AFU.AFU.AFU

ductility
BM.951 (L)
ALT **ductile**
SN The property of being permanently deformed by tension without rupture, that is, the ability to be drawn from a large to a small size. (MH)
CN B.BM.CFS.AXC.BZY.BOK.AXC

ducts, air
USE **air ducts**

dude ranches
RG.165 (L)
ALT **dude ranch**
UF guest ranches
ranches, dude
ranches, guest
CN V.RG.AFU.AFU.DOI.BIQ

Dufay's screen plate process
USE **Dufaycolor**

Dufaycolor
KT.315
UF Dufay's screen plate process
screen plate process, Dufay's
CN K.KT.AFU.ALO.DUC.DIO.ALO.AFU.ALO.AFU

dug-out chests
TG.463
ALT **dug-out chest**
UF chests, dug-out
CN V.TG.AFU.AFU.AXC.ALO.AXC.CXA

dug wells
RK.598
ALT **dug well**
SN Wells excavated by hand tools or dredging machinery as distinguished from ones put down by drills or augers. (STEIN)
UF wells, dug
CN V.RK.AFU.ALO.ALO.CFS.ALO.BCW.CXA.ALO.AXC

dukes
HG.695
ALT **duke**
CN H.HG.AFU.AXC.CFS.CRG.BCW

dull blackish green
USE **dark grayish green**

dull blue
USE **blackish blue**
dark bluish gray
dark grayish blue
deep blue
grayish blue
grayish purplish blue
moderate blue
pale blue
pale purplish blue
strong blue

dull blue green black
USE **blackish blue**
bluish black
dark grayish blue

dull blue violet
USE **brilliant violet**
moderate violet
strong purplish blue
strong violet

dull bluish green
USE **blackish green**
dark grayish green
grayish green
pale green
very pale green

dull bluish red
USE **dark purplish red**
moderate purplish red
very dark purplish red

dull bluish violet
USE **blackish purple**
brilliant violet
dark grayish purple
grayish violet
light violet
pale purple
pale violet
strong violet
very pale purple
very pale violet

dull bluish violet, dark
USE **dark purple**

dull bluish violet, deep
USE **grayish purplish blue**

dull bluish violet, light
USE **light violet**

dull brown
USE **brownish pink**
dark grayish brown
grayish brown
light grayish brown

dull brownish olive
USE **dark olive brown**

dull buff
USE **grayish yellowish pink**
moderate orange yellow
pale orange yellow
pale yellowish pink

dull dark purple
USE **deep reddish purple**
strong reddish purple

dull gold
USE **light olive**
light olive brown
moderate olive

dull green
USE **blackish green**
dark grayish green
dark yellowish green
grayish green
grayish olive green
light bluish green
light green
light yellowish green
pale green
very pale green

dull greenish black
USE **dark gray**
dark greenish gray

dull greenish blue
USE **blackish blue**
dark grayish blue
grayish blue
pale blue
very pale blue

dull greenish yellow
USE **grayish greenish yellow**
light olive
pale greenish yellow

dull lavender
USE **grayish purplish pink**

dull lilac
USE **grayish purplish red**
moderate violet
pale purple

dull magenta purple
USE **strong reddish purple**

dull orange
USE **moderate yellowish pink**

dull red
USE **dark red**
deep reddish brown
grayish red
moderate red
moderate reddish brown

strong reddish orange
very dark red

dull reddish blue
USE **blackish blue**
dark grayish blue
grayish blue
grayish purplish blue
pale blue
pale purplish blue
very pale blue
very pale purplish blue

dull reddish brown
USE **blackish red**
dark grayish red
dark grayish reddish brown
dark red
dark reddish brown
grayish red
grayish reddish brown
light grayish reddish brown
light reddish brown
very dark red

dull reddish orange
USE **grayish reddish orange**

dull reddish violet
USE **blackish purple**
dark grayish purple
grayish purple
grayish reddish purple
pale purple
pale reddish purple

dull reddish yellow
USE **dark grayish yellow**
grayish yellow
pale orange yellow
pale yellow

dull rose
USE **light grayish red**
moderate purplish pink

dull vermilion
USE **moderate reddish orange**

dull violet
USE **blackish purple**
dark grayish purple
dark purplish red
grayish purple
grayish purplish red
grayish reddish purple
light grayish purplish red
pale purple
very pale purple

dull violet black
USE **black**
dark bluish gray
dark gray
dark grayish blue
dark grayish purple
dark purplish gray

dull violet blue, dark
USE **grayish purplish blue**

dull yellow
USE **dark grayish yellow**
grayish yellow
light orange yellow
pale yellow

dull yellow green, dark
USE **grayish olive green**

dull yellow green, deep
USE **dark yellowish green**

dull yellowish brown
USE **dark grayish yellowish brown**
dark yellowish brown
grayish yellowish brown
light grayish yellowish brown
light yellowish brown
moderate yellowish brown

dull yellowish green
USE **grayish yellow green**
pale yellow green

dull yellowish orange
USE **pale orange yellow**

dull yellowish red
USE **grayish reddish orange**

Duma
FL.413 (L)
UF Aduma
CN F.FL.ALO.AFU.AXC.ALO.AFU.AXC.AFU

dumb
USE **mutes**

dumb waiters
USE **dumbwaiters (stands)**

dumbbell tenements
RK.366
ALT **dumbbell tenement**
SN Use for apartment houses offering an improvement over standard long, narrow tenements by including air and light shafts between adjacent buildings resulting in characteristic dumbbell-shaped plans; common in New York City between 1879 and 1901, when their construction was banned.
UF tenements, dumbbell
CN V.RK.AFU.ALO.ALO.AXC.AXC.ALO.ARI.AFU

Dumbo
FL.675
UF Wadumbo
CN F.FL.ALO.AFU.AXC.AXC.BOK.ARI

dumbwaiters
RT.1304 (L,N)
ALT **dumbwaiter**
CN V.RT.ALO.ALO.AFU.ARI.AFU

dumbwaiters (stands)
TG.621
ALT **dumbwaiter (stand)**
SN Term used by Sheraton for three-tiered stands intended for use in the dining room on which to place glasses and plates, both clean and used. (MONTGO)
UF dumb waiters
serviteurs-muets
tables servantes
CN V.TG.AFU.AFU.BIQ.BCW.AFU.ARI.AFU

dummies (mallets)
TB.589 (N)
ALT **dummy (mallet)**
SN Small mallets with heads of malleable iron. (HAND)
CN V.TB.AFU.BCW.BCW.ALO.CRG

dummy knobs
TF.61
ALT **dummy knob**
UF dummy levers
knobs, dummy
levers, dummy
CN V.TF.AFU.AFU.AFU.AFU.CFS.AXC.AFU.AFU

dummy levers
USE **dummy knobs**

dumont blue
USE **smalt**

dumping-grounds
USE **dumps**

dumps
RK.1468
ALT **dump**
UF dumping-grounds
dumps, garbage
dumps, rubbish
dumpsites
garbage dumps
rubbish dumps
CN V.RK.ALO.ALO.AXC.AFU

dumps, ash
USE **ashpits**

dumps, garbage
USE **dumps**

dumps, rubbish
USE **dumps**

dumpsites
USE **dumps**

dunes
RD.198 (L,R)
ALT **dune**
UF sand dunes
CN V.RD.ARI.AFU.AXC.AFU.AFU.AXC.AFU

dung
MT.919
CN M.MT.AFU.AFU.ALO.AFU.BOK

dung, cow
USE **cow manure**

Dunhuang
USE **Tun-huang**

Dunn County sandstone
USE **Dunville sandstone**

Dunville sandstone
MT.726
UF Dunn County sandstone
sandstone, Dunn County
sandstone, Dunville
CN M.MT.AFU.AFU.AFU.DCU.AFU.
ALO.AFU.ARI.AFU.ALO.BIQ.ARI

duochromatic processes
USE **two-color processes**

duodecagons
USE **dodecagons**

duplex apartments
RM.265 (B)
ALT **duplex apartment**
SN Use for apartments with rooms on two levels.
UF apartments, duplex
CN V.RM.AFU.DIO.ARI.ALO.BIQ.
AFU.AFU

duplex houses
RK.368 (A,N)
ALT **duplex house**
SN Use for houses with separate dwelling units for two individual families placed one above the other. When the units are placed side-by-side use **double houses.**
UF duplexes, vertical
houses, duplex
houses, two-family
two-family houses
vertical duplexes
CN V.RK.AFU.ALO.ALO.AXC.AXC.AXC

duplex locks
TF.206
ALT **duplex lock**
UF locks, duplex
CN V.TF.AFU.AFU.AFU.AFU.DIO.BIQ.
AFU.CLM.AFU

duplex nails
USE **double-headed nails**

duplexes, horizontal
USE **double houses**

duplexes, vertical
USE **duplex houses**

duplicates
VB.115
ALT **duplicate**
SN In the context of a collection of images or printed matter, use for additional copies in the same format and medium.
CN V.VB.ALO.BZY.AFU.AFU

duplicating
USE **copying**

duplicating processes
USE **copying**

duplicating, fluid
USE **spirit duplicating**

duplicating, offset
USE **offset printing**

duplicating, spirit
USE **spirit duplicating**

duplicating, stencil
USE **stencil duplicating**

dural
USE **duralumin**

duralumin
MT.366 (L)
SN An alloy consisting of 95.5 parts of aluminum to 3 parts of copper, 1 of manganese, and 0.5 of magnesium that after age-hardening is comparable in strength and hardness to soft steel. (W)
UF dural
CN M.MT.AFU.AFU.AFU.BZY.AFU.
AFU.AFU.ALO.AFU.ARI

durmast oak
MT.1239 (L)
UF oak, durmast
Quercus petraea
CN M.MT.AFU.AFU.ALO.BIQ.DCU.
AFU.AFU.AFU.IRA.BUE

Durour
USE **Aua**

Duruma
FL.604
CN F.FL.ALO.AFU.AXC.AXC.ALO.
BOK.ARI

dust
MT.2249 (L)
CN M.MT.AFU.ALO.DOI.AFU.AFU

dust masks
TB.409
ALT **dust mask**
UF masks, dust
CN V.TB.AFU.ARI.DUC.ARI.AFU

dust, marble
USE **marble dust**

dust, stone
USE **stone dust**

dustboards
TG.890
ALT **dustboard**
SN Horizontal boards between drawers. (FAIRB)
CN V.TG.ALO.DIO

Dustin
FL.815
CN F.FL.ALO.ALO.ALO.AFU.ALO.
ALO.AFU.ALO

dusting brushes
TB.350 (A,N,B)
ALT **dusting brush**
SN Flat brushes with long coarse bristles set in a wood handle; used by artists and draftsmen to sweep away eraser crumbs from work being done on a drawing board. (MAYER)
UF brushes, dusting
CN V.TB.AFU.ARI.CRG.ALO.ALO.AFU

dusting-on
USE **dusting-on process**

dusting-on process
KT.351
SN A process in which the image is formed by dusting a pigment onto a surface of bichromated colloid that has been exposed through a transparency. Areas exposed to light lose their tackiness and hold less pigment. Generally for prints on glass or ceramic, where the pigment is fired as a glaze.
UF dusting-on
powder process
CN K.KT.AFU.ALO.DUC.DIO.ALO.
DIO.AFU.ALO

dustproof strikes
TF.517
ALT **dustproof strike**
SN Strikes with a spring plunger that completely fills the hole when the door is open. (BROWNL)
UF strikes, dustproof
CN V.TF.AFU.ALO.AFU.ALO.ALO

duststorms
KM.119 (L)
CN K.KM.AFU.CXA.BIQ.ARI

Dutch
FL.3051 (L,B)
CN F.FL.ALO.BCW.AFU.CRG.AFU

Dutch arches
RT.254
ALT **Dutch arch**
SN Use for flat arches in which the joints of the voussoirs do not radiate but all slope outward at the same sharp angle.
UF arches, Dutch
arches, French
French arches
CN V.RT.AFU.AFU.AFU.BCW.AFU.
AFU.AFU.ELK.AXC.ALO

Dutch barns
RK.45
ALT **Dutch barn**
SN Designates squarish barns found in the northeast United States and characterized by one main floor, steeply pitched gables, primary entrances located under each gable end, wide central interior spaces spanned by massive anchor beams,

and narrow flanking aisles.
UF barns, Dutch
barns, New World Dutch
New World Dutch barns
CN V.RK.AFU.ALO.ALO.AFU.AFU.
AFU.AFU.ALO

Dutch brick
USE **clinker brick**

Dutch clinker
USE **clinker brick**

Dutch Colonial
FL.3236 (A)
UF Colonial, Dutch
CN F.FL.ALO.BCW.ALO.ARI.BIQ.
BIQ.BIQ.AFU

Dutch-door bolts
TF.166
ALT **Dutch-door bolt**
SN Devices for locking together upper and lower leaves of a Dutch door. (STEIN)
UF bolts, Dutch-door
CN V.TF.AFU.AFU.AFU.AFU.DIO.ARI.
ARI

Dutch-door quadrants
TF.185
ALT **Dutch-door quadrant**
UF quadrants, Dutch-door
CN V.TF.AFU.AFU.AFU.AFU.DIO.
BCW.ALO.ARI

Dutch doors
RT.847
ALT **Dutch door**
SN Doors consisting of two separate leaves, one above the other; the leaves may operate independently or together. (HAS)
UF doors, Dutch
hatchet doors
CN V.RT.AFU.ARI.AFU.AFU.AFU.ALO.
ARI.AFU.AFU.ALO

Dutch feet
USE **pad feet**
trifid feet

Dutch gables
RT.638
ALT **Dutch gable**
SN Gables with curving sides and surmounted by a pediment. (HAS)
UF gables, Dutch
CN V.RT.AFU.AFU.AFU.BIQ.BUE.
ALO.AFU.AXC.AFU.AXC

Dutch metal
USE **leaf**

Dutch mordant
MT.2722
SN A compound solution of potassium chlorate and hydrochloric acid used as a mordant in etching. (MAYER)
UF mordant, Dutch
CN M.MT.AFU.ARI.IFM.ARI.ALO

Dutch New Guinea
USE **Irian Jaya**

Dutch pink
MT.1762
UF brown pink
English pink
Italian pink
pink, brown
pink, Dutch
pink, English
pink, Italian
stil de grain brun
stil de grain vert
CN M.MT.AFU.AFU.ARI.AFU.AFU.
ALO.ALO.BUE.ALO.ALO

Dutch process white lead
MT.1739
UF white lead, Dutch process
CN M.MT.AFU.AFU.ARI.AFU.AFU.
ALO.ALO.BOK.AFU.BZY.AFU

Dutch vermilion
USE **vivid reddish orange**

Dutch white metal
MT.414
UF metal, Dutch white
white metal, Dutch
CN M.MT.AFU.AFU.AFU.BZY.AFU.
AFU.AFU.ALO.BUE.ALO.ARI

Dutch, Pennsylvania
USE **Pennsylvania Dutch**

Dvaravati
FL.2405
CN F.FL.ALO.ARI.BCW.BOK.AFU.ARI

dwarf birch
MT.1116
UF Betula nana
birch, dwarf
CN M.MT.AFU.AFU.ALO.BIQ.DCU.
AFU.AFU.AFU.BIQ.ALO

dwarf bookcases
TG.402
ALT **dwarf bookcase**
SN Low bookcases deliberately designed so as to leave the wall above free for paintings or pier glasses; generally having open shelves or doors with open grilles, instead of solid or silk-paneled doors.
UF bookcases, dwarf
CN V.TG.AFU.AFU.AXC.ALO.ALO.AXC

dwarf buckeye
MT.1089
UF Aesculus pavia
buckeye, dwarf
CN M.MT.AFU.AFU.ALO.BIQ.DCU.
AFU.AFU.AFU.AFU.AFU.ALO

dwarf galleries
RM.35
ALT **dwarf gallery**
SN Passages located on the external surface of a wall and screened by a small-scale arcade. (HAS)
UF galleries, dwarf
CN V.RM.AFU.DIO.AFU.AXC.ALO

dwelling terraces
USE **terrace houses**

dwellings
RK.216 (A,L,N,R)
ALT **dwelling**
SN Buildings or portions of a building designed exclusively for residential occupancy by one family, but not including hotels or other buildings intended for use by transients. (DDT)
UF architecture, domestic
buildings, residential
domestic architecture
domestic facilities
domiciles
facilities, domestic
facilities, residential
habitations
homes
housing, residential
residences
residential buildings
residential facilities
residential housing
CN V.RK.AFU.ALO.ALO.AXC

dwellings, beehive
USE **beehive houses**

dwellings, cave
USE **cave dwellings**

dwellings, cliff
USE **cliff dwellings**

dwellings, double
USE **double houses**

dwellings, lake
USE **lake dwellings**

dwellings, log
USE **log cabins**
log houses

dwellings, multiple
USE **multiple dwellings**

dwellings, pit
USE **pit dwellings**

dwellings, row
USE **row houses**

dwellings, seasonal
USE **seasonal dwellings**

dwellings, single-family
USE **single-family dwellings**

dwellings, slave
USE **slave quarters**

DWV piping
RT.1470
UF drainage, waste and vent piping
piping drainage, waste and vent

piping, DWV
CN V.RT.ALO.BCW.ALO.ARI.BZY.ARI

dye
MT.1513 (L,R)
SN Use for colored substances that dissolve in liquids and impart their color effects to materials by staining or by being absorbed.
CN M.MT.AFU.AFU.ARI.AFU.AFU.AFU

dye bleach process
USE **silver-dye bleach process**

dye bleaching process
USE **silver-dye bleach process**

dye coupler processes
USE **chromogenic processes**

dye coupling processes
USE **chromogenic processes**

dye destruction process
USE **silver-dye bleach process**

dye diffusion transfer
USE **dye diffusion transfer process**

dye diffusion transfer photoprints
USE **dye diffusion transfer prints**

dye diffusion transfer prints
VJ.33
ALT **dye diffusion transfer print**
SN Color instant camera photographs. (GMGPC)
UF diffusion transfer prints, dye
dye diffusion transfer photoprints
Kodak (TM) instant color photoprints
Kodak (TM) instant prints
photographs, Polaroid (TM) instant color
photoprints, dye diffusion transfer
Polaroid (TM) instant color photographs
prints, dye diffusion transfer
prints, Kodak (TM) instant
transfer prints, dye diffusion
CN V.VJ.AFU.AFU.ARI.AFU.AXC.AFU

dye diffusion transfer process
KT.327
SN Diffusion transfer process that uses dye couplers rather than silver and produces color instant camera photographs.
UF diffusion transfer, dye
dye diffusion transfer
CN K.KT.AFU.ALO.DUC.DIO.ALO.BOK.AFU

dye diffusion transfer process, internal
USE **internal dye diffusion transfer process**

dye imbibition process
USE **dye transfer process**

dye mordant process
USE **dye toning**

dye mordanting
USE **dye toning**

dye toning
KT.421
ALT **dye-toned**
UF dye mordant process
dye mordanting
mordant dye process
mordanting
toning, dye
CN K.KT.AFU.ALO.DUC.DIO.ARI.AXC.DOI.AFU

dye transfer
USE **dye transfer process**

dye transfer photoprints
USE **dye transfer prints**

dye transfer prints
VJ.17
ALT **dye transfer print**
SN Use for prints made by the dye transfer process.
UF dye transfer photoprints
photoprints, dye transfer
prints, dye transfer
transfer prints, dye
CN V.VJ.AFU.AFU.ALO.AFU

dye transfer process
KT.424 (L)
SN Photomechanical process in which gelatin relief matrices are made by a bichromate process from color separation negatives or positives; a full-color print is then made by transferring dye from the matrices, in register, to a support.
UF dye imbibition process
dye transfer
imbibition printing
imbibition process
imbibition process, dye
printing, imbibition
transfer process, dye
CN K.KT.AFU.ALO.DUC.DOI.AFU

dye, aniline
USE **aniline dye**

dye, coal-tar
USE **synthetic organic pigment**

dye, methyl
USE **methyl dye**

dye, natural
USE **natural dye**

dye, synthetic
USE **synthetic dye**

dye, vegetable
USE **vegetable dye**

dyehouses
USE **dyeworks**

dyeing
KT.77 (L,R)
ALT **dyed**
CN K.KT.AFU.ALO.BOK.ALO

dyeing, resist
USE **resist dyeing**

dyers
HG.526
ALT **dyer**
CN H.HG.AFU.AXC.BUE.ARI.CXA.AFU

dyes, oil soluble
USE **oil soluble dyes**

dyes, water soluble
USE **water soluble dyes**

dyestuff, natural
USE **natural dye**

dyeworks
RK.661 (B)
UF dyehouses
CN V.RK.AFU.ALO.ALO.CLM.ALO.ALO.AFU.AXC.DZW.ALO

dykes
USE **dikes**

dynamic symmetry
USE **approximate symmetry**

dynamics
BM.889 (L)
SN Physical forces which affect the motion or equilibrium of material bodies.
UF structural dynamics
CN B.BM.CFS.AXC.BIQ.AFU

dynamism
BM.190
SN A key concept for Futurist artists concerning the representation of movement and the persistence of images.
UF universal dynamism
CN B.BM.AFU.AFU.AXC.CLM.AXC

dynamite
MT.2587 (L)
CN M.MT.AFU.ARI.DIO.ALO.AFU

dynamos
USE **generators**

Dynasties, Southern
USE **Southern Dynasties**

Dynasty, Eighteenth
USE **Eighteenth Dynasty**

Dynasty, Eighth
USE **Eighth Dynasty**

Dynasty, Eleventh
USE **Eleventh Dynasty**

Dynasty, Fifteenth
USE **Fifteenth Dynasty**

Dynasty, Fifth
USE **Fifth Dynasty**

Dynasty, First
USE **First Dynasty**

Dynasty, Fourteenth
USE **Fourteenth Dynasty**

Dynasty, Fourth
USE **Fourth Dynasty**

Dynasty, Nineteenth
USE **Nineteenth Dynasty**

Dynasty, Ninth
USE **Ninth Dynasty**

Dynasty, Second
USE **Second Dynasty**

Dynasty, Seventeenth
USE **Seventeenth Dynasty**

Dynasty, Seventh
USE **Seventh Dynasty**

Dynasty, Sixteenth
USE **Sixteenth Dynasty**

Dynasty, Sixth
USE **Sixth Dynasty**

Dynasty, Tenth
USE **Tenth Dynasty**

Dynasty, Third
USE **Third Dynasty**

Dynasty, Thirteenth
USE **Thirteenth Dynasty**

Dynasty, Thirtieth
USE **Thirtieth Dynasty**

Dynasty, Thirty-first
USE **Thirty-first Dynasty**

Dynasty, Twelfth
USE **Twelfth Dynasty**

Dynasty, Twentieth
USE **Twentieth Dynasty**

Dynasty, Twenty-eighth
USE **Twenty-eighth Dynasty**

Dynasty, Twenty-fifth
USE **Twenty-fifth Dynasty**

Dynasty, Twenty-first
USE **Twenty-first Dynasty**

Dynasty, Twenty-fourth
USE **Twenty-fourth Dynasty**

Dynasty, Twenty-ninth
USE **Twenty-ninth Dynasty**

Dynasty, Twenty-second
USE **Twenty-second Dynasty**

Dynasty, Twenty-seventh
USE **Twenty-seventh Dynasty**

Dynasty, Twenty-sixth
USE **Twenty-sixth Dynasty**

Dynasty, Twenty-third
USE **Twenty-third Dynasty**

Dzhanbas-Kala
FL.1770
CN F.FL.ALO.ARI.AFU.ALO.ALO

Dzhebel Cave
FL.1771
UF Djebel
CN F.FL.ALO.ARI.AFU.ALO.ARI

Dzheytun
FL.1772
UF Djeitun
CN F.FL.ALO.ARI.AFU.ALO.AXC

e-mail
USE **electronic mail**

eagle bracket tables
USE **eagle console tables**

eagle console tables
TG.695
ALT **eagle console table**
SN Console tables supported by an eagle bracket.
UF bracket tables, console
console tables, eagle
eagle bracket tables
eagle tables
tables, eagle
tables, eagle bracket
tables, eagle console
CN V.TG.AFU.AFU.BIQ.BOK.AFU.DUC.AFU.AFU

eagle tables
USE **eagle console tables**

eagle's feet
USE **claw-and-ball feet**

Early American
USE **American Colonial**

Early American Hunter
USE **Paleo-Indian**

Early Andra
FL.2197
UF Andra, Early
CN F.FL.ALO.ARI.AXC.ALO.AFU.ARI.AXC.AFU

Early Archaic
FL.2574
UF Archaic, Early
CN F.FL.ALO.AXC.ALO.AFU.AFU.ARI.AXC.AFU

Early Babylonian
USE **Old Babylonian**

Early Baroque
FL.3173
UF Baroque, Early
CN F.FL.ALO.BCW.ALO.ARI.AXC.AFU

Early Benin
FL.94
UF Benin, Early
Ogiso period
CN F.FL.ALO.AFU.ALO.AFU.BUE.AFU.AFU

Early Bronze Age
FL.27
UF Bronze Age, Early
CN F.FL.AFU.BCW.ARI.AFU

Early Byzantine
FL.3069
UF Byzantine, Early
CN F.FL.ALO.BCW.ALO.AFU.ALO.AFU

Early Chalcolithic
FL.21
UF Chalcolithic, Early
CN F.FL.AFU.BCW.ALO.ALO.AFU

early childhood education
KD.121
SN Includes activities and experiences that are intended to effect developmental changes in children from birth through the early years of elementary school.
UF education, early childhood
education, nursery school
nursery school education
CN K.KD.AFU.ALO.BOK.AFU.AFU

Early Chiripa
FL.1137
UF Chiripa, Early
CN F.FL.ALO.ALO.ALO.ARI.AXC.AFU.ALO.AFU

Early Christian
FL.3067 (A,L,B,R)
UF Christian, Early
CN F.FL.ALO.BCW.ALO.AFU.AFU

Early Classic
FL.968
UF Classic, Early
CN F.FL.ALO.ALO.ALO.ALO.AFU.AFU.AXC.AFU

Early Classical
FL.2578
UF Classical, Early
CN F.FL.ALO.AXC.ALO.AFU.AFU.ARI.BCW.AFU

Early Cocle
USE **Conte Polychrome**

Early Corinthian
FL.2627
UF Corinthian, Early
CN F.FL.ALO.AXC.ALO.AFU.ALO.AXC.ALO.BCW.AFU.ALO

Early Cycladic
FL.2537
UF Cycladic, Early
CN F.FL.ALO.AXC.ALO.AFU.AFU.ALO.AFU.AFU

Early Cypriote
FL.2892
UF Cypriote, Early
CN F.FL.ALO.AXC.ARI.ARI.AFU.AFU

Early Decorated
FL.3125
UF Decorated, Early
Decorated, Geometrical
Geometrical Decorated
CN F.FL.ALO.BCW.ALO.ALO.AFU.
BOK.ARI.ALO.AXC.AFU.AFU

Early Dilmun
FL.2883
UF Dilmun, Early
CN F.FL.ALO.AXC.ARI.ALO.AFU.AFU.
AFU

Early Dynastic
FL.2965
CN F.FL.ALO.AXC.ARI.BCW.AFU.ARI

Early Dynastic (Egyptian)
FL.2792
UF Archaic period (Egyptian)
Semainean period
CN F.FL.ALO.AXC.ALO.ARI.AFU.AXC

Early Edo
FL.1983
UF Early Tokugawa
Edo, Early
Tokugawa, Early
CN F.FL.ALO.ARI.ALO.ALO.AFU.
BCW.AFU.AFU

Early Elamite
USE **Old Elamite**

Early English
FL.3127 (B)
UF Early English Gothic
English Gothic, Early
English, Early
First Pointed
Gothic, Early English
Lancet
Pointed, First
CN F.FL.ALO.BCW.ALO.ALO.AFU.
BOK.ARI.ALO.AXC.ALO

Early English Gothic
USE **Early English**

Early Etruscan
FL.2708
UF Etruscan, Early
CN F.FL.ALO.AXC.ALO.ALO.AFU.
ARI.AFU

Early Formative
USE **Early Preclassic**

Early Free Style
FL.2616
UF Free Style, Early
CN F.FL.ALO.AXC.ALO.AFU.ALO.
AXC.ALO.AXC.AFU.AFU.AFU

Early Geometric
FL.2565
UF Geometric, Early
CN F.FL.ALO.AXC.ALO.AFU.AFU.ARI.
ALO.AFU

Early Gerzean
FL.2782
UF Gerzean, Early
CN F.FL.ALO.AXC.ALO.ARI.AFU.AFU.
ALO.ARI.AFU

Early Gothic
FL.3094 (L,B)
UF 1200 Style
Gothic, Early
Primaire
Style 1200
Transitional Style
CN F.FL.ALO.BCW.ALO.ALO.AFU.
ARI.AFU

Early Han
USE **Western Han**

Early Heian
FL.1979
UF Heian, Early
Jogan
Konin
CN F.FL.ALO.ARI.ALO.ALO.AFU.
AXC.ARI.AFU

Early Helladic
FL.2549
UF Helladic, Early
CN F.FL.ALO.AXC.ALO.AFU.AFU.
ALO.ALO.AFU

Early horizon
FL.1139
CN F.FL.ALO.ALO.ALO.ARI.AXC.
AFU.ARI

Early Imperial
FL.2717
UF Imperial, Early
CN F.FL.ALO.AXC.ALO.ALO.AFU.
AXC.ALO.AFU

Early Intermediate period
FL.1150
UF Intermediate period, Early
CN F.FL.ALO.ALO.ALO.ARI.AXC.
AFU.AXC

Early Iron Age
FL.31
UF Iron Age, Early
CN F.FL.AFU.BCW.AXC.AFU

Early Jomon
FL.1961
UF Jomon, Early
CN F.FL.ALO.ARI.ALO.ALO.AFU.
.ALO.ALO

Early Kerma
FL.158
UF Kerma, Early
CN F.FL.ALO.AFU.ALO.AXC.AXC.
AFU.AFU.AFU

Early Khmer
USE **Pre-Angkorean**

Early Malla
FL.2163
UF Malla, Early
CN F.FL.ALO.ARI.AXC.AFU.AXC.AFU.
BCW.AFU

Early Mediaeval
USE **Early Medieval**

Early Medieval
FL.3088 (A)
UF Early Mediaeval
Medieval, Early
CN F.FL.ALO.BCW.ALO.ALO.AFU.AFU

Early Minoan
FL.2556
UF Minoan, Early
CN F.FL.ALO.AXC.ALO.AFU.AFU
ALO.ARI.AFU

Early Naqada
USE **Amratian**

Early Nara
FL.1976
UF Hakuho
Nara, Early
CN F.FL.ALO.ARI.ALO.ALO.AFU.
AXC.ALO.AFU

Early Neolithic
FL.15
UF Neolithic, Early
CN F.FL.AFU.BCW.AFU.ARI.AFU

Early Nomads Age
FL.2126
UF Nomads Age, Early
CN F.FL.ALO.ARI.ARI.AFU.BIQ

Early Orientalizing
FL.2570
UF Orientalizing, Early
CN F.FL.ALO.AXC.ALO.AFU.AFU.
ARI.ARI.AFU

Early Palace period
USE **Old Palace period**

Early Palaeologan
FL.3078
UF Palaeologan, Early
CN F.FL.ALO.BCW.ALO.AFU.ALO.
AXC.AFU.AFU

Early period Californian
FL.771
UF Californian, Early period
CN F.FL.ALO.ALO.ALO.AFU.AFU.
BCW.AFU.AFU

Early period Plateau
FL.777
UF Plateau, Early period
CN F.FL.ALO.ALO.ALO.AFU.AFU.
BCW.ARI.AFU

Early Postclassic
FL.972
UF Postclassic, Early
CN F.FL.ALO.ALO.ALO.ALO.AFU.
AFU.BCW.AFU

Early Preclassic
FL.963
UF Early Formative
Formative, Early
Preclassic, Early
CN F.FL.ALO.ALO.ALO.ALO.AFU.
AFU.ALO.AFU

early red ware
FL.3026
UF red ware (Persian pottery)
red ware, early
ware, early red
ware, red (Persian pottery)
CN F.FL.ALO.AXC.ARI.BIQ.ALO.
AXC.AXC

Early Renaissance
FL.3167
UF Renaissance, Early
CN F.FL.ALO.BCW.ALO.ARI.AFU.AFU

Early Style
FL.2524
CN F.FL.ALO.AXC.AFU.BOK.ALO.
ALO.AFU

Early Tokugawa
USE **Early Edo**

Early Victorian
FL.3318
UF Victorian, Early
CN F.FL.ALO.BCW.ALO.AXC.DIO.
ALO.BCW.ALO.AFU

ears (furniture components)
TG.833
ALT **ear (furniture component)**
SN Up-curved ends of a crest rail; usually on Chippendale chairs. (CTSB)
CN V.TG.ALO.AXC.ALO.ARI

earth
MT.2056
SN Use for soil as a building material.
UF dirt
CN M.MT.AFU.AFU.ARI.BOK.AFU.ARI

earth art
USE **land art**

earth color
USE **natural inorganic pigment**

earth dams
USE **earth-fill dams**

earth dams, reinforced
USE **zoned earth dams**

earth dams, zoned
USE **zoned earth dams**

earth-fill dams
RK.535 (L)
ALT **earth-fill dam**
SN Use for dams built of fine earth near the center, coarser earth or rock on the outside, and a waterproof core. (EAA)
UF dams, earth-fill
dams, hydraulic fill
earth dams
hydraulic fill dams
CN V.RK.AFU.ALO.ALO.GFS.AFU.
ARI.ARI.AFU

earth houses
USE **earth lodges**

earth lodges
RK.313 (A,L,B)
ALT **earth lodge**
SN Designates certain Native North American dwellings framed by heavy timbers and covered with earth or sod and a dome-shaped arrangement of branches.
UF earth houses
houses, earth
lodges, earth
CN V.RK.AFU.ALO.ALO.AXC.ALO.
BCW.AFU

earth movements
KM.103 (A,L)
SN Differential movements of the earth's crust or parts of its surface, or elevations or subsidences of land. (W)
UF movements, earth
CN K.KM.AFU.CXA.ALO

earth of cullen
USE **Van Dyke brown**

earth pressure
BM.933 (L)
UF pressure, earth
CN B.BM.CFS.AXC.BUE.ARI

earth red
USE **moderate brown**

earth sciences
KD.265 (L)
UF sciences, earth
CN K.KD.AFU.ARI.CLM.ARI

earth sheltered buildings
RK.1373 (A,L)
ALT **earth sheltered building**
UF buildings, earth sheltered
CN V.RK.AFU.ALO.AXC.AFU

earth stations
USE **satellite tracking stations**

earth wax, galician
USE **ozokerite**

earth yellow
USE **light yellowish brown**

earth, bituminous
USE **Van Dyke brown**

earth, Bohemian
USE **Bohemian earth**

earth, Cassel
USE **Van Dyke brown**

earth, Cologne
USE **Van Dyke brown**

earth, diatomaceous
USE **diatomaceous earth**

earth, green
USE **green earth**

earth, infusorial
USE **diatomaceous earth**

earth, Japan
USE **cutch**

earth, potter's
USE **potter's clay**

earth, rammed
USE **rammed earth**

earth, red
USE **moderate reddish brown**

earth, tamped
USE **rammed earth**

earth, yellow
USE **moderate orange yellow**
yellow ocher

earthenware
MT.149
CN M.MT.AFU.AFU.AFU.AXC.ALO.
ALO.AFU.ALO.AFU

earthenware, cream-colored
USE **creamware**

earthmovers
USE **earthmoving equipment**

earthmoving equipment
TB.32 (L)
UF earthmovers
equipment, earthmoving
CN V.TB.AFU.ARI.AFU.ARI

earthquake design
USE **seismic design**

earthquake loads
BM.1014
UF loads, earthquake
CN B.BM.CFS.AXC.CLM.ALO.ARI.
BZY.AFU

earthquake-resistant construction
KT.44 (L,B)
ALT **earthquake-resistant**
UF aseismic design
construction, earthquake-resistant
design, aseismic
design, earthquake-resistant
earthquake-resistant design
earthquake-resisting construction
CN K.KT.AFU.ALO.BCW.ARI.ALO.ALO

earthquake-resistant design
USE **earthquake-resistant construction**
seismic design

earthquake-resisting construction
USE **earthquake-resistant construction**

earthquake stations
USE **seismological stations**

earthquakes
KM.105 (L,B,R)
SN Occasions of shaking or trembling of earth, divisible into two major types, volcanic or tectonic, according to the major precipitating factor.
CN K.KM.AFU.CXA.ALO.ALO

earthworks
RK.1349 (A,L,N,B,R)
ALT **earthwork**
SN Use generally for the results of grading, trenching, or embanking earth, for utilitarian purposes.
CN V.RK.AFU.ALO.ARI.AXC.ARI

easels
TG.608 (L,N)
ALT **easel**
SN Stands or frames for supporting or displaying at an angle an artist's canvas, a blackboard, china plate, or other object. (RHDEL2)
CN V.TG.AFU.AFU.BIQ.ALO

easement
BM.447 (A,L,B)
SN Usually nonprofitable interest granted by deed or will that is held by one person in land owned by another and that entitles the holder to a specific limited use. (W)
UF servitude
CN B.BM.BCW.BCW

east
DC.46
CN D.DC.AFU.ALO.AXC.AFU

East African copal
MT.1482
UF anime
copal, East African
CN M.MT.AFU.AFU.ALO.BOK.ARI.ALO

East Asian
FL.1831 (L)
UF Asian, East
CN F.FL.ALO.ARI.ALO

East Gravettian
FL.2461
UF Gravettian, East
CN F.FL.ALO.AXC.AFU.ARI.AFU.AFU

East Greek
FL.2601
UF Greek, East
CN F.FL.ALO.AXC.ALO.AFU.ALO.AXC.ALO.ALO

East India porcelain
USE **Compagnie des Indes ware**

East India walnut
MT.1319
UF Albizia lebbeck
walnut, East India
CN M.MT.AFU.AFU.ALO.BIQ.DCU.AFU.AFU.AFU.MQW.ALO

East Indian rosewood
MT.1304 (L)
UF Dalbergia latifolia
Indian rosewood
rosewood, East Indian
rosewood, Indian
CN M.MT.AFU.AFU.ALO.BIQ.DCU.AFU.AFU.AFU.LCM.AXC.ARI

East Javanese
FL.2381
UF Javanese, East
CN F.FL.ALO.ARI.BCW.ARI.ALO.AXC.ALO

Easter
KM.81 (L,R)
CN K.KM.AFU.CFS.ARI.AXC

Easter cards
VW.569
ALT **Easter card**
SN Cards imprinted with greetings or messages and often suitable illustrations that are sent or given to celebrate Easter.
UF cards, Easter
CN V.VW.AFU.ALO.AFU.ARI.BOK.ARI

Easter Island
FL.3691 (L)
CN F.FL.ALO.BOK.AXC.ARI

Easter sepulchers
RT.1232
ALT **Easter sepulcher**
SN Recesses with tomb chests, usually in the north wall of the chancel, for the effigy of Christ used at Easter celebrations.
UF sepulchers, Easter
CN V.RT.AFU.BUE.ALO.ARI.BIQ

Eastern Apache
FL.1450
UF Apache, Eastern
CN F.FL.ALO.ALO.ARI.AFU.CFS.AFU.ALO

Eastern Archaic
FL.731
UF Archaic, Eastern
CN F.FL.ALO.ALO.ALO.AFU.AFU.ALO.AFU

Eastern Chin
USE **Eastern Jin**

Eastern Chou
USE **Eastern Zhou**

eastern cottonwood
MT.1272 (L)
UF cottonwood, eastern
Populus deltoides
CN M.MT.AFU.AFU.ALO.BIQ.DCU.AFU.AFU.AFU.KFK.AFU.ALO

Eastern Hamitic
FL.614
UF Hamitic, Eastern
Nilo-Hamitic
Nilotes
CN F.FL.ALO.AFU.AXC.AXC.ARI

Eastern Han
FL.1849
UF Han, Eastern
Han, Later (Eastern Han)
Later Han (Eastern Han)
CN F.FL.ALO.ARI.ALO.AFU.AFU.ALO.AFU.AFU

eastern hemlock
MT.1355 (L)
UF Canada hemlock
common hemlock
hemlock spruce
hemlock, Canada
hemlock, common
hemlock, eastern
hemlock, New England
New England hemlock
pine, spruce
spruce pine
spruce, hemlock
Tsuga canadensis
CN M.MT.AFU.AFU.ALO.BIQ.DCU.AFU.AFU.ALO.BOK.AFU

Eastern Indian
FL.2258
UF Indian, Eastern
CN F.FL.ALO.ARI.AXC.ALO.AFU.BZY.ALO

Eastern Jin
FL.1882
UF Chin, Eastern
Eastern Chin
Jin, Eastern
CN F.FL.ALO.ARI.ALO.AFU.AFU.ALO.BUE.ARI.AFU

Eastern Mono
FL.1310
UF Mono, Eastern
CN F.FL.ALO.ALO.ARI.AFU.AXC.ARI

Eastern Nahane
USE **Kaska**

Eastern Orthodox
USE **Orthodox Eastern**

Eastern Wei
FL.1871
UF Wei, Eastern
CN F.FL.ALO.ARI.ALO.AFU.AFU.ALO.BUE.AFU.AFU.AFU.AFU

Eastern Zhou
FL.1862
UF Chou, Eastern
Eastern Chou
Zhou, Eastern
CN F.FL.ALO.ARI.ALO.AFU.AFU.ALO.BIQ.AFU

Eastern, Orthodox
USE **Orthodox Eastern**

Eastlake
FL.1743
CN F.FL.ALO.ALO.BCW.AFU.BZY.ALO

Eastman Wash-off Relief (TM)
KT.425
UF relief process, wash-off
relief, Eastman wash-off
wash-off relief process
CN K.KT.AFU.ALO.DUC.DOI.AFU.AFU

easy chairs
TG.60 (N,B)
ALT **easy chair**
SN Armchairs with an upholstered frame and projecting wings for protection against drafts.
UF chairs, draught
chairs, easy
chairs, grandfather's
chairs, lug
chairs, saddle cheek
chairs, wing
chairs, wing-back
draught chairs
grandfather's chairs
lug chairs
saddle cheek chairs
wing-back chairs
wing chairs
CN V.TG.AFU.AFU.ALO.AFU.AFU.AFU.FZU

easy chairs, circular
USE **circular easy chairs**

easy chairs, egg
USE **egg chairs**

easy chairs, square
USE **square easy chairs**

easy chairs, straight-back
USE **square easy chairs**

easy chairs, swan
USE **swan chairs**

easy chairs, tub-back
USE **circular easy chairs**

eave troughs
USE **gutters (storm water systems)**

eaves
RT.459 (B,R)
SN Use for those horizontal portions of a sloping roof that project beyond the walls. For portions of the roof projecting beyond the gable, use **verges.**
CN V.RT.AFU.AFU.AFU.BIQ.ARI.ALO.AFU.ALO.AFU

eaves boards
RT.464
ALT **eaves board**
UF boards, eaves
fillets, tilting
tilting fillets
CN V.RT.AFU.AFU.AFU.BIQ.ARI.ALO.AFU.ALO.ALO.AFU

eaves fascias
RT.465
ALT **eaves fascia**
SN Boards that are nailed across the ends of roof rafters, sometimes supporting a gutter. (DAC)
UF boards, fascia
fascia boards
fascias, eaves
CN V.RT.AFU.AFU.AFU.BIQ.ARI.ALO.AFU.ALO.ALO.ALO

eaves gutters
RT.1462
ALT **eaves gutter**
UF gutters, eaves
CN V.RT.ALO.BCW.ALO.ARI.BCW.ARI

eaves tile
MT.184
CN M.MT.AFU.AFU.AFU.AXC.ALO.ALO.ALO.AFU.ALO.AXC.AFU.ARI.ALO

eaves, closed
USE **closed eaves**

eaves, flush
USE **flush eaves**

eaves, open
USE **open eaves**

ébano
USE **brazilwood**

ebenaceae
USE **ebony**

ébène, memuisiers en
USE **ébénistes**

ébénistes
HG.559
ALT **ébéniste**
SN Skilled French craftsmen of luxury furniture; also French cabinetmakers specializing in veneered furniture.
UF ébène, menuisiers en
ebonists
menuisiers-ébéniste
menuisiers en ébène
CN H.HG.AFU.AXC.BUE.AXC.BUE.AFU

Ebira
FL.257 (L)
UF Igbira
CN F.FL.ALO.AFU.AXC.AFU.ALO.ARI.AFU

ebonists
USE **ébénistes**

ebony
MT.1138 (R)
SN A hard, heavy, durable wood yielded by various trees of the genus diospyros in tropical Asia and Africa. (W)
UF Diospyros
ebenaceae
CN M.MT.AFU.AFU.ALO.BIQ.DCU.AFU.AFU.AFU.CXA

ebony (color)
USE **dark gray**
dark olive
olive gray

ebony brown
USE **dark gray**
dark reddish gray
reddish black

ebony, black
USE **black ebony**

ebony, Senegal
USE **African blackwood**

ebony, West Indian
USE **granadilla**

Ebrie
FL.295
UF Kyama
CN F.FL.ALO.AFU.AXC.AFU.ARI.AFU.ALO.AXC

EC
USE **ethyl cellulose**

eccentric loads
BM.1011 (L)
SN Load on a column or pile which is nonsymmetric with respect to the central axis, therefore producing a bending moment. (DAC)
UF loads, eccentric
loads, unsymmetrical
unsymmetrical loads
CN B.BM.CFS.AXC.CLM.ALO.ARI.BOK

ecclesiastical architecture
USE **religious buildings**

ecclesiastics
USE **clergy**

ecclesiology
KD.83 (R)
SN Study of the doctrines of the church, including the study of ecclesiastical art, antiquities, and the adornment and equipment of churches. (W)
CN K.KD.AFU.AFU.BUE.ALO.ARI

echauguettes
USE **bartizans**

echini
RT.137
ALT **echinus**
SN The convex projecting moldings of eccentric curve supporting the abaci of Doric capitals; hence corresponding features in capitals of other orders. (HAS)
CN V.RT.AFU.AFU.AFU.AXC.BIQ.ALO.ARI.ALO.BCW

echo
BM.996 (L,B)
UF sound reverberation
CN B.BM.CFS.AXC.CFS.ALO.AFU

Eclectic Style
USE **Settchuyo**

eclecticism
BM.173 (A,L,R)
SN Approach or practice of selecting the best elements from different doctrines, methods, or styles to apply them in a new creation. In the specific context of art or architectural criticism, use to mean borrowing from a variety of visual sources in the creation of a work. (PDAT)
CN B.BM.AFU.AFU.AXC.ALO

eco art
USE **land art**

ecological art
USE **land art**

ecologists
HG.338 (L)
ALT **ecologist**
CN H.HG.AFU.AXC.BIQ.AFU.AFU.BOK

ecology
KD.204 (A,L,B,R)
SN Study of mechanisms controlling the structure and functional processes of natural environmental systems. (PG)
CN K.KD.AFU.ARI.ARI.AXC

economic development
BM.1068 (L)
UF development, economic
CN B.BM.CLM.ALO.ALO

economic development, rural
USE **rural development**

economic rent
BM.408
SN Rate of rent which is sufficient to cover all costs of maintenance and operation of a building and, in addition, yield a reasonable return on the investment of the owner. (PUTNAM)
UF rent, economic
CN B.BM.ARI.EWY.AFU

economic value
USE **value**

economics
KD.118 (L,B,R)
SN Study concerned with the production, distribution, and consumption of goods and services. (RHDEL2)
CN K.KD.AFU.ALO.BIQ

economists
HG.259 (L)
ALT **economist**
CN H.HG.AFU.AXC.BCW.AFU.AXC

economy brick
USE **jumbo brick**

economy, fuel
USE **fuel economy**

écorché figures
USE **écorchés**

écorchés
VB.105 (R)
ALT **écorché**
SN Drawings, prints, or statues of flayed human or animal figures, used in the study of musculature. (MAYER)
UF écorché figures
figures, écorché
CN V.VB.ALO.BUE.ARI.AFU.AFU

écrans à pivot
TG.9
ALT **écran à pivot**
SN Pivoting fire screens adjusted in position by a thumbscrew on a rod.
CN V.TG.AFU.AFU.AFU.AFU.AXC.AFU

écrans à secrétaire
TG.13
ALT **écran à secrétaire**
SN Firescreens with a shelf or slide attached, to be used for writing before the fire. (WATSON)
UF écrans à secrétaire en pente
secrétaires en pente à écran
CN V.TG.AFU.AFU.AFU.AFU.BIQ.AFU

écrans à secrétaire en pente
USE **écrans à secrétaire**

ecru
USE **grayish yellow**
light grayish yellowish brown
pale yellow

Eden
FL.757
CN F.FL.ALO.ALO.ALO.AFU.AFU.ARI.ALO.ARI.ALO.AXC

edge (contour)
USE **contour**

edge (outline)
USE **outline**

edge planes
TB.916 (N)
ALT **edge plane**
SN Four- to 6-inch planes with the front edge open so that the iron can cut at the very nose of the plane; used for trimming in hard to reach places. (SALAM)
UF chisel planes
edge planes, piano maker's
piano maker's edge planes
planes, chisel
planes, edge
planes, piano maker's edge
CN V.TB.AFU.BCW.CFS.ALO.AFU.DUC.ALO.AXC

edge planes, piano maker's
USE **edge planes**

edge pulls, door
USE **door edge pulls**

edge reversal
USE **Sabattier effect**
solarization

edge rolls
USE **roll moldings**

edgers
TB.555
ALT **edger**
SN Finishing tools used on the edges of fresh concrete to provide a rounded corner. (STEIN)
CN V.TB.AFU.BCW.ALO.AXC.ALO

edicts
USE **decrees**

edicules
USE **aediculae**

editing
KG.89 (L)
CN K.KG.AFU.AFU.AXC.BZY

editions
VB.123
ALT **edition**
SN An arbitrarily set number of replicas of reproducible works, such as prints, photographs, or cast sculptures, done as a group.
CN V.VB.ALO.BZY.ALO

editions, limited
USE **limited editions**

editorial cartoons
VB.36 (L)
ALT **editorial cartoon**
SN Use for cartoons that express editorial opinions, usually by appearing on the editorial pages of a newspaper or periodical.
UF cartoons, editorial
CN V.VB.AFU.ALO.AFU.ALO

editorial writers
HG.287
ALT **editorial writer**
SN Persons who write comments on topics of reader interest to stimulate or mold public opinion, in accordance with viewpoints and policies of publication. (DOT)
UF writers, editorial
CN H.HG.AFU.AXC.BCW.ALO.AFU.ARI.ALO

editorials
VW.306 (L)
ALT **editorial**
SN Includes articles in publications expressing the opinions of their editors or publishers and commentaries on radio or television expressing the

opinions of a station or network. (AHD)
CN V.VW.AFU.AFU.ALO.BCW.ALO

editors
HG.199 (L)
ALT **editor**
SN Persons who revise, correct, or arrange the contents or style of literary, artistic, or musical work of others for publication or presentation. (W)
CN H.HG.AFU.AXC.AXC.ARI.ALO.AXC

Edo (African)
FL.249 (L)
CN F.FL.ALO.AFU.AXC.AFU.ALO.ALO.ALO

Edo (Japanese period)
FL.1982 (A,L)
UF Tokugawa
CN F.FL.ALO.ARI.ALO.ALO.AFU.BCW.AFU

Edo-e
FL.2085
CN F.FL.ALO.ARI.ALO.ALO.ALO.AXC.BZY.AFU

Edo, Early
USE **Early Edo**

Edo, Late
USE **Late Edo**

Edo, Middle
USE **Middle Edo**

educating
USE **teaching**

education
KD.119 (L,B,R)
CN K.KD.AFU.ALO.BOK

education buildings, physical
USE **physical education buildings**

education, architectural
USE **architectural education**

education, art
USE **art education**

education, continuing
USE **continuing education**

education, early childhood
USE **early childhood education**

education, elementary
USE **elementary education**

education, higher
USE **higher education**

education, lifelong
USE **continuing education**

education, nursery school
USE **early childhood education**
preschool education

education, preschool
USE **preschool education**

education, primary
USE **primary education**

education, secondary
USE **secondary education**

education, secondary school
USE **secondary education**

educational buildings
USE **schools**

educational complexes
RG.51 (L)
ALT **educational complex**
SN Groupings of educational buildings and other facilities; if possible, use a more specific term.
UF complexes, educational
complexes, school
educational facilities
facilities, educational
school complexes
CN V.RG.AFU.AFU.BIQ

educational facilities
USE **educational complexes**

educational media centers
USE **audiovisual centers**

educational parks
RG.53 (A,L)
ALT **educational park**
SN Complexes of schools, usually ranging from kindergarten through high school or two-year college, that draw students from a metropolitan area and are intended to minimize the effects of segregation. (ERIC)
UF parks, educational
CN V.RG.AFU.AFU.BIQ.ALO

educational societies
HG.898 (L)
ALT **educational society**
UF societies, educational
CN H.HG.ALO.DUC.BIQ

educators
HG.296 (L,R)
ALT **educator**
CN H.HG.AFU.AXC.BCW.ALO.ARI

Edwardian
FL.3321 (A,L,B,R)
CN F.FL.ALO.BCW.ALO.AXC.DIO.ALO.BCW.ARI

Edwards Plateau
FL.919 (L)
CN F.FL.ALO.ALO.ALO.AFU.ALO.ARI.AXC.ALO

eelgrass
MT.1030
SN A submerged marine plant with very long narrow leaves that is found in abundance along the North Atlantic coast. (W)
UF grass wrack
wrack, grass
CN M.MT.AFU.AFU.ALO.BIQ.AXC.ARI

effect, moiré
USE **moiré effect**

effect, Sabattier
USE **Sabattier effect**

efficiency apartments
USE **studio apartments**

efficiency, thermal
USE **thermal efficiency**

Effigy Mound
FL.816
CN F.FL.ALO.ALO.ALO.AFU.ALO.ALO.AFU.ARI

effigy mounds
RK.879
ALT **effigy mound**
SN Use for large earthworks formed in the likeness of birds and animals.
UF mounds, effigy
CN V.RK.AFU.ALO.ALO.DOI.AFU.AFU

Efik
FL.242 (L)
CN F.FL.ALO.AFU.AXC.AFU.ALO.AFU.BCW.ALO

Egba
FL.273 (L)
CN F.FL.ALO.AFU.AXC.AFU.ALO.BCW.ALO.AFU

egg
MT.922 (L,R)
CN M.MT.AFU.AFU.ALO.AFU.BUE

egg and anchor moldings
USE **egg and dart moldings**

egg and arrow moldings
USE **egg and dart moldings**

egg and dart moldings
RT.766
ALT **egg and dart molding**
SN Moldings enriched with egg-shaped ornaments alternating with dartlike ornaments.
UF egg and anchor moldings
egg and arrow moldings
egg and tongue moldings
moldings, egg and anchor
moldings, egg and arrow
moldings, egg and dart
moldings, egg and tongue
CN V.RT.AFU.ALO.AFU.BOK.AFU.AFU.ARI.BOK

egg and tongue moldings
USE **egg and dart moldings**

egg chairs
TG.66
ALT **egg chair**
UF chairs, egg

chairs, egg easy
easy chairs, egg
egg easy chairs
CN V.TG.AFU.AFU.ALO.AFU.AFU.AFU.GFO

egg easy chairs
USE **egg chairs**

egg-shaped
DC.115
CN D.DC.AFU.ARI.FCS.ARI

egg tempera
MT.2520
SN The traditional form of tempera paint consisting of pigments ground with pure egg yolk. (MAYER)
UF tempera, egg
CN M.MT.AFU.ARI.CRG.ALO.BCW.AFU.ALO.ARI.ALO

egg white
USE **albumen**

egg yolk
MT.923
SN Yolk of an egg, cleaned of white and separated from its sac, is a well known emulsion binder.
UF yolk, egg
CN M.MT.AFU.AFU.ALO.AFU.BZY

eggplant, dark
USE **blackish purple**

eggshell
USE **pale yellow**
yellowish white

eggshell ware
FL.2666
UF ware, eggshell
CN F.FL.ALO.AXC.ALO.AFU.ALO.AXC.BCW.ALO

églomisé
USE **verre églomisé**

Egnatian
USE **Gnathian**

Egun
USE **Gun**

Egyptian
FL.2770 (A,L,B,R)
CN F.FL.ALO.AXC.ALO.ARI

Egyptian blue
MT.1601
UF gyptischblau
Alexandria blue
bleu d'Egypte
blue frit
blue, Alexandria
blue, Egyptian
blue, Italian
blue, Pompeian
blue, Pozzuoli
blue, Venetian
blue, Vestorian
Italian blue
Pompeian blue
Pozzuoli blue
Venetian blue
Vestorian blue
CN M.MT.AFU.AFU.ARI.AFU.AFU.ALO.ALO.ALO.ARI.BIQ

Egyptian breccia marble
MT.754
SN A coarse breccia marble containing fragments of pophyry, basalt, quartz, and granite in a greenish or purplish ground. (RS)
UF breccia marble, Egyptian
marble, Egyptian breccia
CN M.MT.AFU.AFU.AFU.DCU.AFU.ARI.ARI.ALO.AFU.BOK

Egyptian brown
USE **mummy**

Egyptian crosses
USE **ankhs**

Egyptian Empire
USE **New Kingdom**

Egyptian gorges
USE **cavetto cornices**

Egyptian paper
USE **papyrus**

Egyptian Revival
FL.3267 (A,L,B,R)
UF Egyptian Taste
Neo-Egyptian
Revival, Egyptian
CN F.FL.ALO.BCW.ALO.AXC.CLM.AXC

Egyptian Taste
USE **Egyptian Revival**

eight-part vaults
USE **octopartite vaults**

eighteen-carat gold
MT.398
SN Gold which has 18 parts of gold to six parts of alloying elements. (OCDA)
UF 18-carat gold
gold, eighteen-carat
CN M.MT.AFU.AFU.AFU.BZY.AFU.AFU.AFU.ALO.AXC.ALO.AFU

Eighteenth Dynasty
FL.2815
UF 18th Dynasty
Dynasty, Eighteenth
CN F.FL.ALO.AXC.ALO.ARI.AFU.BUE.AFU

Eighth Dynasty
FL.2798
UF 8th Dynasty
Dynasty, Eighth
CN F.FL.ALO.AXC.ALO.ARI.AFU.BCW.ALO

Eile
FL.622
CN F.FL.ALO.AFU.AXC.AXC.ARI.BUE

Ejagham
FL.238 (L)
UF Ekoi
CN F.FL.ALO.AFU.AXC.AFU.ALO.AFU.AXC

Eket
FL.243
CN F.FL.ALO.AFU.AXC.AFU.ALO.AFU.BCW.ARI

ekistics
KD.132 (B)
SN Scientific study of human settlements. (RHDEL2)
CN K.KD.AFU.ALO.BUE

Ekiti
FL.274
CN F.FL.ALO.AFU.AXC.AFU.ALO.BCW.ALO.ALO

ekklesiasteria
RK.1196 (A)
ALT **ekklesiasterion**
SN Use for buildings housing the meeting places of the ekklesia or sovereign assembly of an ancient Greek city.
CN V.RK.AFU.ALO.ALO.FUA.BCW

Ekoi
USE **Ejagham**

ekphrasis
BM.20 (L,R)
SN Description of a work of art, real or imaginary, undertaken as a rhetorical exercise. (THDAT)
CN B.BM.AFU.AFU.AFU.CFS.ALO

Ektachrome (TM)
KT.368
SN A subtractive color reversal process using a film with an integral tripack, each layer containing dyes appropriate to the color sensitivity of the layer. The image is formed by the chromogenic process.
CN K.KT.AFU.ALO.DUC.DIO.ALO.DZW.AFU.ALO

El Arbolillo
FL.980
CN F.FL.ALO.ALO.ALO.ALO.AFU.ALO.AFU.AFU.ARI.AFU

El-Omari
FL.2776
CN F.FL.ALO.AXC.ALO.ARI.AFU.AFU.AFU.ARI

El Tajin
USE **Tajin**

Elamite
FL.3010 (L)
CN F.FL.ALO.AXC.ARI.BIQ.AFU.ALO

Elamite, Ancient
USE **Old Elamite**

Elamite, Early
USE **Old Elamite**

Elamite, Middle
USE **Middle Elamite**

Elamite, Old
USE **Old Elamite**

elastic buckling
KT.887
UF buckling, elastic
CN K.KT.ALO.AFU.AFU

elastic chairs
TG.67
ALT **elastic chair**
SN Term for the earliest type of bentwood chairs; patented by Samuel Gragg in 1808. (FAIRB)
UF chairs, elastic
CN V.TG.AFU.AFU.ALO.AFU.AFU.AFU.GLI

elastic knives
TB.612
ALT **elastic knife**
SN Plasterer's tools made of highly flexible carbon steel; used in trimming plaster. (PUTNAM)
UF knives, elastic
CN V.TB.AFU.BCW.BCW.ALO.FCS.AFU

elastic limit
BM.952
SN The greatest unit stress that a material is capable of withstanding without permanent deformation. (MH)
UF limit, elastic
CN B.BM.CFS.AXC.BZY.BOK.BCW

elasticity
BM.953 (L)
ALT **elastic**
CN B.BM.CFS.AXC.BZY.BOK.BIQ

elasticity, modulus of
USE **modulus of elasticity**

elastomer, epichlorohydrin
USE **epichlorohydrin elastomer**

elastomer, ethylene-propylene
USE **ethylene-propylene elastomer**

elastomer, fluorocarbon
USE **fluorocarbon elastomer**

elastomer, fluorosilicone
USE **fluorosilicone elastomer**

elastomer, isobutylene-isoprene
USE **butyl rubber**

elastomer, nitrile
USE **nitrile elastomer**

elastomer, polybutadiene
USE **polybutadiene elastomer**

elastomer, polyethylene
USE **polyethylene elastomer**

elastomer, polysulfide
USE **polysulfide elastomer**

elastomer, silicone
USE **silicone elastomer**

elastomer, sytrene-butadiene
USE **styrene-butadiene rubber**

elastomer, urethane
USE **urethane elastomer**

elastomers
MT.2080 (L)
SN Polymeric materials that will return to approximately their original length after stretching. (MH12)
UF artificial rubber
rubber, artificial
rubber, synthetic
synthetic rubber
CN M.MT.AFU.AFU.ARI.BUE.AFU

elbow chairs
TG.25
ALT **elbow chair**
SN Term applied to armchairs, particularly those with open arms and padded rests. (BEARD)
UF chairs, elbow
chairs, French (elbow chairs)
chairs, open-arm
French chairs (elbow chairs)
open-arm chairs
CN V.TG.AFU.AFU.ALO.AFU.AFU.AFU.ALO.ALO

elbow chairs, French
USE **French elbow chairs**

elbow pads
USE **arm pads**

elbow seams
TF.654
ALT **elbow seam**
UF seams, elbow
CN V.TF.ALO.ARI.ARI.BUE.BCW

elbows
USE **arms (furniture components)**

elbows (ancones)
USE **ancones**

elbows (crossettes)
USE **crossettes**

Elda 1005 upholstered chairs
TG.68
ALT **Elda 1005 upholstered chair**
UF chairs, Elda 1005 upholstered
CN V.TG.AFU.AFU.ALO.AFU.AFU.AFU.GRC

elder, box
USE **box elder**

elderly persons
USE **aged**

elderly, housing for the
USE **housing for the elderly**

elders
HG.224 (L)
ALT **elder**
SN Certain church officers or leaders. (W)
CN H.HG.AFU.AXC.AXC.BIQ.AFU.ARI.BZY

election ballots
USE **ballots**

election districts
RG.248 (L)
ALT **election district**
SN Districts created for the administration of elections. (W)
UF constituencies
districts, election
districts, voting
precincts, voting
voting districts
voting precincts
wards
CN V.RG.ALO.AFU.AFU.ARI

election returns
VW.774
ALT **election return**
SN Certified reports by election officers on the outcome vote in an election. (AHD)
UF returns, election
CN V.VW.AFU.ARI.AFU.ALO.BIQ

election tickets
USE **ballots**

elections
KM.52 (L)
CN K.KM.AFU.BIQ

electors' rolls
USE **voters' lists**

electors, registers of
USE **voters' lists**

electric arc welding
USE **arc welding**

electric cables
RT.1338 (L)
ALT **electric cable**
UF cables, electric
CN V.RT.ALO.ARI.ALO.ARI

electric circuit-breakers
USE **circuit breakers**

electric circuits
USE **circuits**

electric closets
RT.1339
ALT **electric closet**
UF closets, electric
CN V.RT.ALO.ARI.ALO.AXC

electric conductors
MT.2580 (L)
UF conductors, electric
CN M.MT.AFU.ARI.CXA.AFU

electric conduits
RT.1340 (L,B)
ALT **electric conduit**
UF conduits (electric)
conduits, electric
CN V.RT.ALO.ARI.ALO.BCW

electric drills
TB.189 (L,N)
ALT **electric drill**
SN Portable, hand-held, motor-driven tools used to turn a bit for boring holes in a material and powered either by direct or alternating current. (MEANS)
UF drills, electric
drills, electric-portable
electric-portable drills
portable drills, electric
CN V.TB.AFU.ARI.BIQ.ALO.AFU.ALO.AFU

electric elevators
RT.1318
ALT **electric elevator**
UF elevators, electric
CN V.RT.ALO.ALO.AFU.ARI.ALO.ARI.ALO

electric engineering
USE **electrical engineering**

electric eye cameras
TB.292 (L)
ALT **electric eye camera**
SN Automatic exposure meter cameras which directly control the lens aperture, in response to light falling on the photo cell. (FOCAL)
UF automatic cameras
cameras, automatic
cameras, electric eye
CN V.TB.AFU.ARI.CLM.ARI.AFU.AFU.AFU.ARI

electric fences
RM.436 (L)
ALT **electric fence**
SN Wire fences designed to give a shock upon touching. (W)
UF fences, electric
CN V.RM.ALO.AFU.BCW.ALO

electric furnaces
RT.1417 (L)
ALT **electric furnace**
UF furnaces, electric
CN V.RT.ALO.BCW.AFU.ALO.AFU.AXC.AFU.AFU

electric generating plants, tidal energy
USE **tidal power plants**

electric generators
USE **generators**

electric handsaws
USE **electric-portable saws**

electric hinges
TF.109
ALT **electric hinge**
SN Hinges designed to pass electric wires from the frame to the door for use in an electric-controlled lock. (MEANS)
UF electrically wired hinges
hinges, electric
hinges, electrically wired
CN V.TF.AFU.AFU.AFU.AFU.CLM.AFU.BZY

electric lighting
RT.1370 (A,L)
UF lighting, electric
CN V.RT.ALO.AXC.ARI.AFU

electric lines
USE **power lines**

electric metal-cutting
KT.827 (L)
UF metal-cutting, electric
CN K.KT.AFU.ALO.HOE.BCW.ALO.ARI.ALO

electric plants, tidal
USE **tidal power plants**

electric plants, water-power
USE **hydroelectric power plants**

electric-portable drills
USE **electric drills**

electric-portable saws
TB.1000 (N)
ALT **electric-portable saw**
UF circular saws, portable
electric handsaws
handsaws, electric
portable circular saws
saws, electric-portable
saws, portable circular
saws, skill
skill saws
CN V.TB.AFU.BCW.CFS.ALO.AFU.EWY.AXC.ALO

electric power plants
USE **power plants**

electric power production
BM.880 (L)
UF power production, electric
production, electric power
CN B.BM.CFS.AXC.ALO.ALO.AXC.AFU

electric power stations
USE **power plants**

electric power supply
USE **power supply**

electric power transmission lines
USE **power lines**

electric raceways
USE **raceways**

electric resistance heating
RT.1392 (L)
UF heating, electric resistance
heating, resistance
resistance heating
CN V.RT.ALO.BCW.AFU.AFU.ARI.AFU

electric resistance welding
USE **resistance welding**

electric stairways
USE **escalators**

electric substations
RK.671 (A,L,B)
ALT **electric substation**
UF stations, transformer
substations
substations, electric
transformer stations
CN V.RK.AFU.ALO.ALO.CLM.ALO.AXC.AFU

electric switch gear
USE **switchboards**

electric switches
RT.1341 (L)
ALT **electric switch**
UF switches
switches, electric
CN V.RT.ALO.ARI.ALO.BIQ

electric transformers
USE **transformers**

electric utilities
HG.863 (L)
ALT **electric utility**
SN Use for the public service organizations that provide electricity.
UF electricity supply industry
industry, electricity supply
utilities, electric
CN H.HG.ALO.DCU.AFU

electric welders
USE **arc welding machines**

electric welding
KT.800 (L)
SN Any of a number of methods of welding that use electricity as a source of power.
UF welding, electric
CN K.KT.AFU.ALO.HOE.BCW.ALO.AFU.ALO.ALO

electric wiring
RT.1342 (A,L,B)
UF electric wiring systems
systems, electric wiring
systems, wiring
wiring systems
wiring, electric
CN V.RT.ALO.ARI.ALO.BOK

electric wiring systems
USE **electric wiring**

electrical arc welding
USE **arc welding**

electrical conductivity
BM.945 (L)
UF conductivity, electrical
CN B.BM.CFS.AXC.BZY.BCW.AFU

electrical drawings
VD.152
ALT **electrical drawing**
SN Use for drawings of electrical systems or parts thereof. For scaled floor plans specifically, use **electrical plans.**
UF drawings, electrical
CN V.VD.AFU.BIQ.AXC

electrical engineering
KD.226 (L)
UF electric engineering
engineering, electrical
CN K.KD.AFU.ARI.BIQ.BCW

electrical engineers
HG.637 (L,B)
ALT **electrical engineer**
UF engineers, electrical
CN H.HG.AFU.AXC.BZY.BCW.BIQ

electrical installations
USE **electrical systems**

electrical insulation
MT.2404 (L)
UF insulation, electrical
CN M.MT.AFU.ARI.BZY.BCW.ALO

electrical plans
VD.54
ALT **electrical plan**
SN Use for scaled floor plans showing electrical layout; may include an adjacent small drawing of an elevation, or a riser diagram. For other drawings of electrical systems, use **electrical drawings.**
UF plans, electrical
CN V.VD.AFU.AFU.BIQ.ALO.AXC.ALO.BIQ.AFU

electrical power stations
USE **power plants**

electrical power systems
USE **electrical systems**

electrical properties
BM.944 (L)
UF properties, electrical
CN B.BM.CFS.AXC.BZY.BCW

electrical safety
BM.208
UF safety, electrical
CN B.BM.AFU.ALO.BOK.AFU

electrical supply lines
USE **power lines**

electrical supply stations
RT.1343
ALT **electrical supply station**
UF stations, electrical supply
supply stations, electrical
CN V.RT.ALO.ARI.ALO.BUE

electrical systems
RT.1332 (A,B)
ALT **electrical system**
UF electrical installations
electrical power systems
installations, electrical
power systems, electrical
systems, electrical
CN V.RT.ALO.ARI.AFU

electrically wired hinges
USE **electric hinges**

electricians
HG.593 (L)
ALT **electrician**
CN H.HG.AFU.AXC.BZY.AFU.CLM

electricity
BM.833 (L,R)
CN B.BM.CFS.AXC.AFU

electricity supply industry
USE **electric utilities**

electrochemical corrosion
KT.896 (L)
SN Corrosion that occurs when current flows between cathodic and anodic areas on metallic surfaces. (STEIN)
UF corrosion, electrochemical
corrosion, electrolytic
corrosion, galvanic
electrolytic corrosion
galvanic corrosion
CN K.KT.ALO.BCW.ALO.AFU

electrochemical cutting
KT.828 (L)
UF cutting, electrochemical
CN K.KT.AFU.ALO.HOE.BCW.ALO.ARI.ARI

electrogalvanizing
KT.818 (L)
SN Galvanizing by a process in which the zinc is deposited by an electroplating method. (DAC)
UF coating, zinc
plating, zinc
zinc coating
zinc plating
CN K.KT.AFU.ALO.HOE.BCW.ALO.ALO.ALO.AFU

electroless plating
KT.821 (L)
SN Deposition of a metallic coating by a controlled chemical reduction that is catalyzed by the metal or alloy being deposited. (STEIN)
UF plating, electroless
CN K.KT.AFU.ALO.HOE.BCW.ALO.ALO.ARI.AFU

electrolytic corrosion
USE **electrochemical corrosion**

electron beam welding
KT.809 (L)
UF welding, electron beam
CN K.KT.AFU.ALO.HOE.BCW.ALO.AFU.ALO.BCW.AFU

electronic data processing
USE **data processing**

electronic data processing departments
USE **computer centers**

electronic glue guns
TB.194
ALT **electronic glue gun**
SN Instantaneous curing glue guns for synthetic thermoset adhesives. (PUTNAM)
UF glue guns, electronic
guns, electronic glue
CN V.TB.AFU.ARI.BOK.AFU

electronic mail
VW.15 (L)
SN Messages from one individual to another sent via telecommunications links between computers or terminals. (RHDEL2)
UF e-mail
mail, electronic
CN V.VW.AFU.AFU.AFU.BIQ.AFU.ALO

electronic publishing
KG.103 (L)
SN Publishing text or images in electronic machine-readable formats such as online databases, magnetic tapes, or floppy disks.
UF online publishing
publishing, electronic
publishing, online
CN K.KG.AFU.AFU.AXC.DCU.AFU

electronic records
USE **machine-readable records**

electronics laboratories
RK.1167 (A,L,B)
ALT **electronics laboratory**
UF laboratories, electronics
CN V.RK.AFU.ALO.ALO.FIM.ALO.AFU.BUE

electrophotocopies
USE **electrostatic copies**

electrophotographic processes
USE **electrophotography**

electrophotography
KT.335 (L)
SN Creation of images by alteration to the electrical properties of the sensitive material as a result of the action of light. (LANG)
UF electrophotographic processes
CN K.KT.AFU.ALO.DUC.DIO.ALO.BZY

electroplate
MT.465
CN M.MT.AFU.AFU.AFU.BZY.AFU.ALO.AXC.ALO.AFU

electroplaters
HG.503
ALT **electroplater**
SN Persons who engage in electroplating.
UF platers
CN H.HG.AFU.AXC.BUE.ARI.CFS.ALO.AFU

electroplating
KT.822 (L)
ALT **electroplated**
SN Applying a protective or decorative coating of one metal to another by means of an electrolytic bath. (W)
CN K.KT.AFU.ALO.HOE.BCW.ALO.ALO.ARI.ALO

electropolishing
KT.689 (L)
SN Producing a smooth bright surface on a metal object by immersion as an anode in an electrolytic bath. (W)
CN K.KT.AFU.ALO.GRC.BCW.ARI.ALO

electrostatic copies
VW.686
ALT **electrostatic copy**
SN Copies produced by the process of electrostatic printing.
UF copies, electrostatic
electrophotocopies
CN V.VW.AFU.ALO.AFU.DZW.BIQ.BZY.AFU

electrostatic copying
USE **electrostatic printing**

electrostatic plotters
TB.161
ALT **electrostatic plotter**
SN Plotters in which paper passes under an array of fine metal teeth that deposit electrostatic charges which then attract toner.
UF plotters, electrostatic
CN V.TB.AFU.ARI.BCW.AXC.AXC.AFU.AFU

electrostatic printing
KT.181 (L)
SN A printing or dry photocopying process in which images are reproduced using electrostatic charges and a powdered toner. (RHDEL2)
UF copying, electrostatic
electrostatic copying
electrostatic processes
printing, electrostatic
CN K.KT.AFU.ALO.DUC.BOK.AFU.AFU

electrostatic processes
USE **electrostatic printing**

electrum
MT.393 (L)
CN M.MT.AFU.AFU.AFU.BZY.AFU.AFU.AFU.ALO.AXC.AFU.AFU

elegies
VW.67 (L)
ALT **elegy**
SN Mournful, melacholy, or plaintive poems, especially funeral songs or laments for the dead. (RHDEL2)
CN V.VW.AFU.AFU.AFU.EFQ.AFU

Elema
FL.3643 (L)
CN F.FL.ALO.BOK.ALO.BCW.ALO.AXC.AFU

Elementarist
FL.3351
ALT **Elementarism**
CN F.FL.ALO.BCW.ALO.AXC.DIO.AXC.ALO

elementary education
KD.123 (L)
SN Branch of education covering kindergarten or grade 1 through grades 6, 7, or 8. (ERIC)
UF education, elementary
CN K.KD.AFU.ALO.BOK.AFU.ALO

elementary schools
RK.837 (A,L,B)
ALT **elementary school**
UF grade schools
grammar schools
primary schools
schools, elementary
schools, grade
schools, grammar
schools, primary
CN V.RK.AFU.ALO.ALO.CXA.ARI.AXC.ALO

elements, architectural
USE **architectural elements**

elemi
MT.1491
SN Any of various fragrant oleoresins obtained from tropical trees and used chiefly in varnishes, lacquers, and printing inks. (WCOL)
CN M.MT.AFU.AFU.ALO.BOK.BIQ

elemi, Manila
USE **Manila elemi**

elephant enclosures
USE **elephant houses**

elephant houses
RK.374 (A)
ALT **elephant house**
UF elephant enclosures
elephant pavilions
elephant stockades
enclosures, elephant
houses, elephant
houses, pachyderm
pachyderm houses
pavilions, elephant
stockades, elephant
CN V.RK.AFU.ALO.ALO.BCW.AFU.ALO

elephant pavilions
USE **elephant houses**

elephant stockades
USE **elephant houses**

Eleusinian marble
MT.774
SN A fine, black marble from Attica, prized in ancient Greece, especially for friezes and interior decoration. (MAYER)
UF marble, Eleusinian
CN M.MT.AFU.AFU.AFU.DCU.AFU.ARI.ARI.ARI.AFU.ALO

elevated
DC.31
CN D.DC.AFU.ALO.ARI.BIQ

elevated freeways
USE **elevated roads**

elevated highways
USE **elevated roads**

elevated railroads
RD.111 (A,L,B)
ALT **elevated railroad**
SN Rail transit systems of any form that run above surface traffic, primarily for local transit in urban or interurban areas.
UF elevated railway systems
elevated railways
els
overhead railroads
railroads, elevated
railroads, overhead
railways, elevated
CN V.RD.ALO.ARI.AFU.ALO.ALO

elevated railway systems
USE **elevated railroads**

elevated railways
USE **elevated railroads**

elevated roads
RK.1560 (L,B)
ALT **elevated road**
UF elevated freeways
elevated highways
freeways, elevated
highways, elevated
roads, elevated
CN V.RK.ALO.ALO.BIQ.ARI.ARI.AFU

elevated walkways
USE **skywalks**

elevating
USE **lifting**

elevation drawings
USE **elevations**

elevation oblique drawings
VD.14

ALT **elevation oblique drawing**
SN Use for drawings in oblique projection in which the vertical plane is parallel to the plane of projection (drawing surface).
UF drawings, elevation oblique
drawings, facade oblique
facade oblique drawings
oblique drawings, elevation
oblique drawings, facade
CN V.VD.AFU.AFU.BIQ.AFU.ARI.AFU

elevation perspectives
USE **one-point perspectives**

elevation-sections
USE **sectional elevations**

elevations
VD.22 (A,B)
ALT **elevation**
SN Drawings showing the vertical elements of a building, either exterior or interior, as a direct projection to a vertical plane. (DAC)
UF drawings, elevation
elevation drawings
orthographs
CN V.VD.AFU.AFU.BIQ.ALO.ALO

elevations (building divisions)
RM.6 (B)
ALT **elevation (building division)**
SN Use for any of the sides or faces of a building or large interior space, however irregular, emphasizing their appearance; as distinct from **facades**, which usually constitute only those external faces which are substantially in one plane, and appear to have been designed with special regard to their conspicuousness or association with an entrance.
CN V.RM.AFU.BCW

elevations, back
USE **rear elevations**

elevations, end
USE **side elevations**

elevations, exterior
USE **exterior elevations**

elevations, flank
USE **side elevations**

elevations, front
USE **front elevations**

elevations, garden
USE **garden elevations**

elevations, half
USE **half elevations**

elevations, interior
USE **interior elevations**

elevations, laid-out
USE **laid-out elevations**

elevations, main
USE **front elevations**

elevations, partial
USE **partial elevations**

elevations, perspective
USE **exterior perspectives**

elevations, rear
USE **rear elevations**

elevations, sectional
USE **sectional elevations**

elevations, side
USE **side elevations**

elevations, street
USE **street elevations**

elevator doors
RT.876
ALT **elevator door**
UF doors, elevator
CN V.RT.AFU.ARI.AFU.AFU.AFU.ALO.ARI.AFU.AXC.AFU

elevators
RT.1305 (A,L,N,B,R)
ALT **elevator**
CN V.RT.ALO.ALO.AFU.ARI.ALO

elevators, automatic
USE **automatic elevators**

elevators, country
USE **grain elevators**

elevators, double-deck
USE **double-deck elevators**

elevators, electric
USE **electric elevators**

elevators, freight
USE **freight elevators**

elevators, grade-level
USE **grade-level elevators**

elevators, grain
USE **grain elevators**

elevators, hydraulic
USE **hydraulic elevators**

elevators, hydroelectric
USE **hydroelectric elevators**

elevators, inclined
USE **slant elevators**

elevators, observation car
USE **observation car elevators**

elevators, passenger
USE **passenger elevators**

elevators, plunger
USE **hydraulic elevators**

elevators, service
USE **service elevators**

elevators, sidewalk
USE **sidewalk elevators**

elevators, slant
USE **slant elevators**

elevators, traction
USE **traction elevators**

Eleventh Dynasty
FL.2804
UF 11th Dynasty
Dynasty, Eleventh
CN F.FL.ALO.AXC.ALO.ARI.AFU.BIQ.AFU

Elfenbeinschwarz
USE **ivory black**

elite directories
USE **social registers**

elitism
BM.348 (R)
SN Belief in and advocacy of leadership or rule by an elite. (W)
CN B.BM.ALO.ALO.CLM.BUE

Elizabethan
FL.3193 (L,B,R)
CN F.FL.ALO.BCW.ALO.ARI.BIQ.BIQ.AFU.AFU.AFU.AFU

Elizabethan Revival
FL.3323
UF Revival, Elizabethan
CN F.FL.ALO.BCW.ALO.AXC.DIO.ALO.BIQ.AFU

ellipses
BM.769 (L,B)
ALT **elliptical**
CN B.BM.CFS.ARI.AXC.BCW.AFU.ALO

ellipsographs
TB.247 (N,R)
ALT **ellipsograph**
SN Instruments used for drawing ellipses. (W)
CN V.TB.AFU.ARI.CLM.AFU.ALO.BIQ

elliptical arches
RT.225
ALT **elliptical arch**
SN Arches having the form of a semiellipse. (DAC)
UF arches, elliptical
arches, semielliptical
semielliptical arches
CN V.RT.AFU.AFU.AFU.BCW.AFU.AFU.AFU.BOK

ells
RM.427
ALT **ell**
SN Extensions that are at right angles to the length of buildings.
CN V.RM.AFU.ELK.AFU

elm
MT.1144 (L)
CN M.MT.AFU.AFU.ALO.BIQ.DCU.AFU.AFU.AFU.DCU

elm, American
USE **American elm**

elm, American white
USE **American elm**

elm, Chinese
USE **Chinese elm**

elm, English
USE **English elm**

elm, hickory
USE **rock elm**

elm, rock
USE **rock elm**

elm, slippery
USE **slippery elm**

elm, white
USE **American elm**

elm, wych
USE **wych elm**

els
USE **elevated railroads**

Elsner green
MT.1665
SN Composite pigment made with Bremen blue and a fustic lake; not used for permanent painting. (MAYER)
UF green, Elsner
CN M.MT.AFU.AFU.ARI.AFU.AFU.ALO.ALO.AXC.BCW.ALO

elvan
MT.620
SN Name applied in Cornwall, England to the local quartz-porphry. (PEB)
CN M.MT.AFU.AFU.AFU.DCU.AFU.AFU.AFU.ALO.AFU.AFU.AFU

email en ronde bosse
USE **en ronde bosse**

embankments
RK.1355 (L)
ALT **embankment**
SN Use for long ridges of earth, rocks, or gravel primarily constructed to carry a roadway; if built to retain water, use **levees** or **dikes**.
CN V.RK.AFU.ALO.ARI.AXC.ARI.ALO

embarcaderos
USE **landings (marine structures)**

embassy buildings
RK.972 (A,L,B,R)
ALT **embassy building**
SN Use for the official headquarters of foreign ministers called ambassadors appointed to transact international business with a foreign government; when such headquarters are for ministers appointed primarily to oversee and protect the home country's economic interests in a host country, use **consulates.** For the official residences of foreign ministers in general, use **legations.**
UF buildings, embassy
chancelleries
chanceries
CN V.RK.AFU.ALO.ALO.ERE.AFU.ALO.ALO

embattlements
USE **battlements**

emblem books
VW.499 (L,R)
ALT **emblem book**
UF books, emblem
CN V.VW.AFU.ALO.AFU.AFU.AFU.BUE

emblems
VW.705 (A,L,B,R)
ALT **emblem**
SN Objects, or representations of objects, symbolizing and suggesting other objects or ideas, especially by clear natural aptness or association, e.g., a balance as an emblem of justice.(W) For allegorical pictures with mottoes, use **emblems (allegorical pictures).**
CN V.VW.AFU.ALO.ALO.AFU.ALO

emblems (allegorical pictures)
VB.38 (L,R)
ALT **emblem (allegorical picture)**
SN Allegorical pictures, often inscribed with mottoes, common especially in the 17th century. Distinct from **emblems,** which are simpler symbolic representations of an object, or the object itself, standing for a concept.
CN V.VB.AFU.ALO.ALO

embossing
KT.675 (L,R)
ALT **embossed**
SN Process or technique of producing raised letters or designs on a surface, using a set of matched dies. (QUICK)
CN K.KT.AFU.ALO.GRC.ALO

embossing, imitation
USE **thermography**

embrasures (battlement components)
RT.1191
ALT **embrasure (battlement component)**
SN The open spaces between two merlons or solid portions of battlements or castellated parapets. (RS)
UF crenelets
crenels
CN V.RT.AFU.BUE.AFU.BCW.ALO.ARI.ALO.AFU

embrasures (openings)
RT.886
ALT **embrasure (opening)**
SN Openings in a wall with sides flaring outward, as for a door or window. (PUTNAM)
CN V.RT.AFU.ARI.AFU.AFU.ALO

embrittlement
KT.900 (L)
SN Process of becoming brittle; includes the loss of flexibilty or elasticity.
CN K.KT.ALO.BCW.BCW

embroiderers
HG.527
ALT **embroiderer**
CN H.HG.AFU.AXC.BUE.ARI.CXA.ALO

embroidery
KT.561 (L,R)
ALT **embroidered**
SN The art or process of stitching decorative designs into cloth, leather, or paper, by hand or machine.(W) Use **brocade** for the technique of weaving raised patterns into cloth.
CN K.KT.AFU.ALO.ELK.DUC.ALO.AXC

embuia
USE **imbuia**

embuya
USE **imbuia**

emerald
MT.492 (L,R)
CN M.MT.AFU.AFU.AFU.CFS.AFU.AXC.ALO

emerald (color)
USE **brilliant green**
brilliant yellowish green
deep yellowish green
light green
strong yellowish green
vivid green
vivid yellowish green

emerald green
MT.1653
UF English green
green, emerald
green, English
green, imperial
green, Mittis
green, Paris
green, Schweinfurt
green, Veronese
green, Vienna
imperial green
Mittis green
Paris green
Schweinfurt green
Schweinfurter Grün
Veronese green
vert anglais
vert émeraude
vert Paul Véronèse
Vienna green
CN M.MT.AFU.AFU.ARI.AFU.AFU.ALO.ALO.AXC.ARI.BIQ

emerald green (color)
USE **brilliant green**
brilliant yellowish green
moderate bluish green

moderate green
moderate yellowish green
strong bluish green
strong green
strong yellowish green
very light yellowish green

emerald green, bright
USE **brilliant green**
strong bluish green
strong green

emerald green, brilliant
USE **brilliant bluish green**

emerald green, dark
USE **deep green**
moderate bluish green

emerald green, deep
USE **moderate green**

emerald green, light
USE **brilliant green**
light bluish green
light green
very light bluish green

emerald green, pale
USE **very light green**

emerald green, vivid
USE **strong bluish green**

emergency electric power supply
USE **emergency power supply**

emergency exits
RT.987 (A)
ALT **emergency exit**
UF exits, emergency
exits, fire
fire exits
CN V.RT.AFU.ARI.AFU.ALO.ALO.AFU

emergency housing
RG.62 (A,L,B)
UF disaster housing
housing, disaster
housing, emergency
CN V.RG.AFU.AFU.BOK.ALO.AFU.AFU

emergency lighting
RT.1366 (A,L,B)
UF lighting, emergency
CN V.RT.ALO.AXC.ALO.ALO

emergency medical centers
RK.777 (A)
ALT emergency medical center
UF centers, emergency medical
emergency units
medical centers, emergency
units, emergency
CN V.RK.AFU.ALO.ALO.CXA.ALO.AFU.BOK.AFU

emergency power supply
RT.1333 (L)
UF emergency electric power supply
power supply, emergency
power supply, emergency electric
power systems, standby
standby power systems
CN V.RT.ALO.ARI.AFU.AFU

emergency rooms
RM.290 (L)
ALT **emergency room**
SN Hospital areas equipped and staffed for the prompt treatment of acute illness, trauma, or other medical emergencies. (RHDEL2)
UF rooms, emergency
CN V.RM.AFU.DIO.AXC.AFU.ALO

emergency services
HG.873
ALT **emergency service**
UF services, emergency
CN H.HG.ALO.DIO.ARI.AFU

emergency units
USE **emergency medical centers**

emery
MT.499 (L)
SN An impure corundum stone of a blackish or bluish gray color used as an abrasive. The stone is crushed and graded and made into emery paper, emery cloth, and emery wheels. (PUTNAM)
CN M.MT.AFU.AFU.AFU.CFS.AFU.BUE.AFU

emery cloth
TB.514
SN Finely abrasive cloth manufactured by sprinkling powdered emery or aluminum oxide onto a thin cloth coated with glue and used either wet or dry for polishing metallic surfaces. (MEANS)
UF cloth, emery
CN V.TB.AFU.ARI.EWY.ALO.BZY

emigration
BM.1049 (L,R)
SN Departure from a place of abode, natural home, or country for life or residence elsewhere. (W)
CN B.BM.CLM.AFU.ALO.AFU

eminent domain
BM.448 (L,B)
UF domain, eminent
expropriation
CN B.BM.BCW.BIQ

emotion
BM.571 (L,R)
UF feelings
CN B.BM.BUE.ARI

empathy
BM.489
SN The capacity for participating in, or a vicarious experiencing of, another's feelings, volitions, or ideas. (W)
CN B.BM.BIQ.AFU.ALO

emperors
HG.696 (L,R)
ALT **emperor**
SN Sovereigns or supreme monarchs of an empire. (W)
CN H.HG.AFU.AXC.CFS.CRG.BIQ

Empire
FL.3359 (A,B,R)
UF First Empire
CN F.FL.ALO.BCW.ALO.AXC.DIO.BCW.ALO.ALO

empires
HG.805
ALT **empire**
CN H.HG.ALO.ALO.AXC

employee housing
USE **industrial housing**

employees' buildings
RK.608 (A,L)
ALT **employees' building**
UF buildings, employees'
buildings, personnel
employees' facilities
employees' service buildings
facilities, employees'
personnel buildings
CN V.RK.AFU.ALO.ALO.CLM.ALO.AFU.ALO

employees' facilities
USE **employees' buildings**

employees' handbooks
USE **employees' manuals**

employees' manuals
VW.351 (L)
ALT **employee's manual**
UF employees' handbooks
handbooks, employees'
manuals, employees'
manuals, staff
staff manuals
CN V.VW.AFU.AFU.ALO.CXA.BIQ.ARI

employees' service buildings
USE **employees' buildings**

employees, government
USE **government employees**

employees, professional
USE **professionals**

employing
KG.151
SN Use for the ongoing activity of providing individuals with and paying them for work. For the action of engaging the services of a person or persons for wages or other payment, use **hiring**. For the concept of the degree or extent of the provision or availability of paid work to the population, use **employment**.
CN K.KG.AFU.AFU.BIQ.BUE.ALO

employment
BM.383 (L,B)
SN Use for the degree or extent to which paid work is provided or available to the population. For the ongoing activity of providing individuals with and paying them for work, use **employing.** For the action of engaging the services of a person or persons for wages or other payment, use **hiring.**
CN B.BM.ARI.BZY

employment agencies
RK.193 (L,B)
ALT **employment agency**
UF agencies, employment
employment exchanges
employment offices
exchanges, employment
exchanges, labor
labor exchanges
offices, employment
CN V.RK.AFU.ALO.ALO.ALO.AXC.BCW

employment exchanges
USE **employment agencies**

employment offices
USE **employment agencies**

empresses
HG.697 (L)
ALT **empress**
CN H.HG.AFU.AXC.CFS.CRG.BOK

emulsified asphalt
MT.981 (L)
SN An asphalt emulsion in water solution; uses include surfacing floors, painting pipes, and waterproofing concrete walls. (MH)
UF asphalt emulsion mixtures
asphalt, emulsified
CN M.MT.AFU.AFU.ALO.ALO.AFU.ALO.AFU.AFU

emulsifiers
MT.2311
SN Substances that promote the formation and stabilization of an emulsion. (WCOL)
UF agents, emulsifying
emulsifying agents
CN M.MT.AFU.ARI.ALO.CFS

emulsifying agents
USE **emulsifiers**

emulsion
MT.2493 (L)
SN The suspension of droplets of one liquid in another liquid in which the first liquid is not soluble.(MH) Also, an intimate mixture of a solid or semi-solid substance with a liquid, sometimes with the aid of an emulsifier.(W) In photography, the mixture of binder and final image material.
UF colloids, image-bearing
emulsion layer
image-bearing colloids
CN M.MT.AFU.ARI.CRG.ALO.AFU

emulsion ground
MT.2718
SN A ground made by combining or emulsifying gesso and oil. (MAYER)
UF ground, emulsion
CN M.MT.AFU.ARI.IFM.ALO.AFU

emulsion layer
USE **emulsion**

emulsion paint
MT.2517 (L,B)
SN Paint having water usually as the volatile phase with the various nonvolatile substances (as a linseed-oil varnish) in emulsion as the binder. (W)
UF paint, emulsion
CN M.MT.AFU.ARI.CRG.ALO.BCW.AFU.ALO.ALO

emulsion, oil-in-water
USE **oil-in-water emulsion**

emulsion, stripping
USE **stripping film**

en camaieu
USE **camaieu**

en face
USE **frontal**

en ronde bosse
KT.665
SN Enamel decoration characterized by an opaque coating of enamel. (DDA)
UF email en ronde bosse
ronde bosse, en
CN K.KT.AFU.ALO.GRC.AFU.ALO.BIQ

enacting
USE **legislation**

enamel
MT.2426 (L,B,R)
SN Composed chiefly of quartz, feldspar, clay, soda, and borax,(MH) a usually opaque, vitreous coating applied by fusion to surfaces especially of metal, ceramic, or glass; has a glossy appearance upon hardening.
CN M.MT.AFU.ARI.CRG.AFU.ALO

enamel paint
MT.2526 (L)
SN Use for paint made from oil, resin, varnish, or a combination of these, mixed with finely ground pigment; usually giving a glossy finish, but sometimes giving a semigloss or flat finish.
UF paint, enamel
CN M.MT.AFU.ARI.CRG.ALO.BCW.AFU.ARI

enamel process
USE **ceramic process**

enamel, porcelain
USE **porcelain enamel**

enamel, vitreous
USE **porcelain enamel**

enamelers
HG.473
ALT **enameler**
SN Persons who engage in enameling.
CN H.HG.AFU.AXC.BUE.ARI.ALO

enameling
KT.658 (L)
ALT **enameled**
SN The process of applying a vitreous glaze to metal or pottery objects and then fusing it to a smooth, hard surface in a kiln or furnace. (QUICK)
CN K.KT.AFU.ALO.GRC.AFU.ALO

enameling, copper
USE **copper enameling**

enameling, filigree
USE **filigree enameling**

Encabellado
FL.1579
CN F.FL.ALO.ALO.ARI.ARI.AFU.CRG

encaustic
USE **encaustic painting**

encaustic decoration
KT.866
SN Use for the technique of decorating clay in which the body material is inlaid with the clay of another color. For the technique of wax wall or panel painting, use **encaustic painting.**
UF decoration, encaustic
CN K.KT.AFU.ALO.HOE.BOK.AXC.ALO

encaustic painting
KT.241 (L,R)
SN Use for the technique of wax wall or panel painting. For the technique of decorating clay, use **encaustic decoration.**
UF cerography (wax painting)
encaustic
painting, encaustic
painting, wax
wax painting
CN K.KT.AFU.ALO.DUC.CXA.ALO.ALO.ALO

enceintes
RT.1182
ALT **enceinte**
SN Interior walls or ramparts that surround a place sometimes composed of bastions or curtains, either faced or lined with brick or stone, or made only of earth. (UMD)
CN V.RT.AFU.BUE.AFU.BCW.AFU.ARI

enclosed basin stands
TG.661
ALT **enclosed basin stand**
UF basin stands, enclosed
inclosed basin stands
stands, enclosed basin
stands, inclosed basin
CN V.TG.AFU.AFU.BIQ.BCW.ALO.FCS.AFU.ALO

enclosed basin stands, corner
USE **corner enclosed basin stands**

enclosed gardens
USE **walled gardens**

enclosed pier tables
TG.776
ALT **enclosed pier table**
UF pier tables, enclosed
tables, enclosed pier
CN V.TG.AFU.AFU.BIQ.BOK.ARI.AFU.ALO.AFU.AFU

enclosure walls
USE **curtain walls**

enclosures, chancel
USE **chancel screens**

enclosures, choir
USE **choir screens**

enclosures, elephant
USE **elephant houses**

encoignures
TG.504
ALT **encoignure**
SN Small triangular cupboards made to fit into a corner; usually made in pairs, often to match a commode. (PC)
UF armoires à encoignure
armoires d'encoignure
coins (encoignures)
corners (encoignures)
CN V.TG.AFU.AFU.AXC.ALO.BUE.BCW.AFU

Encrusted Style
USE **First Style**

encumbrances
BM.449 (L)
SN Any right or interest in land which diminishes the value of the fee but does not prevent the conveyance of the fee by the owner. Encumbrances such as taxes, mortgages, and judgements are known as liens; restrictions, reservations and easements are encumbrances but are not liens. (PUTNAM)
UF incumbrances
CN B.BM.BCW.BOK

encyclicals
VW.19 (L)
ALT **encyclical**
SN Letters intended for wide or general circulation. (RHDEL2)
CN V.VW.AFU.AFU.AFU.BIQ.AFU.ARI.ALO.AFU

encyclicals, papal
USE **papal encyclicals**

encyclopedias
VW.422 (L,B,R)
ALT **encyclopedia**
UF cyclopedias
CN V.VW.AFU.AFU.ALO.EWY.BCW

encyclopedists
HG.195 (L)
ALT **encyclopedist**
SN Persons who compile or assist in the compilation of an encyclopedia. (W)
CN H.HG.AFU.AXC.AXC.ARI.ALO.ALO.AFU

end
DC.16
SN Situated at or related to the extremity or terminal point or extent of something.
CN D.DC.AFU.ALO.ALO.ARI

end boards
TG.891
ALT **end board**
UF boards, end
CN V.TG.ALO.DOI

end-cut brick
MT.141
SN Brick having the end surfaces wire-cut. (W)
UF brick, end-cut
CN M.MT.AFU.AFU.AFU.AXC.ALO.AFU.AXC.ALO.AXC.AFU.AFU

end elevations
USE **side elevations**

end joints
USE **butt joints**

end lap joints
TF.686
ALT **end lap joint**
SN Angle joints involving two members, each having been cut to half its thickness and lapped over the other in such a manner as to result in a change of direction. (MEANS)
UF joints, end lap
CN V.TF.ALO.ARI.AXC.ARI.AXC.ALO

end tables
TG.679
ALT **end table**
SN Any small table used in relation to a couch or chair. (ARON)
UF tables, end
CN V.TG.AFU.AFU.BIQ.BOK.AFU.BCW

end users
HG.744
ALT **end user**
SN Use specifically for clients or patrons of a library, information center, or information retrieval service. For persons who themselves use products or services of the information industry to provide information services to clients or patrons, prefer **users.**
UF users, end
CN H.HG.AFU.BCW.HIK.AFU

endangered places
RG.210 (A,B)
ALT **endangered place**
SN Use for usually historic open spaces, buildings, or other structures that are threatened with development or demolition.
UF endangered sites
imperiled places
imperiled sites
places, endangered
places, imperiled
sites, endangered
sites, imperiled
CN V.RG.AFU.AFU.DZW.ARI

endangered sites
USE **endangered places**

endless saws
USE **band saws**

ends, astragal
USE **astragal ends**

ends, gable
USE **gable ends**

ends, hollow
USE **hollow ends**

ends, ovolo
USE **astragal ends**

Eneolithic
FL.24
UF Aeneolithic
CN F.FL.AFU.BCW.ALO.ARI

energy
BM.835 (A,L,B,R)
CN B.BM.CFS.AXC.ALO.AFU

energy conservation
BM.869 (A,L,B,R)
UF conservation, energy
CN B.BM.CFS.AXC.ALO.ALO.AFU

energy consumption
BM.870 (L)
UF consumption, energy
CN B.BM.CFS.AXC.ALO.ALO.ALO

energy conversion plants, ocean thermal
USE **ocean thermal energy conversion plants**

energy efficient buildings
RK.1374 (A,L,B)
ALT **energy efficient building**
UF buildings, energy efficient
buildings, low-energy

low-energy buildings
CN V.RK.AFU.ALO.AXC.ALO

energy resources
BM.873 (L)
UF energy sources
power resources
resources, energy
resources, power
sources, energy
CN B.BM.CFS.AXC.ALO.ALO.ARI

energy sources
USE **energy resources**

energy, ambient
USE **solar power**

energy, atomic
USE **nuclear power**

enfilade
BM.64
CN B.BM.AFU.AFU.ARI.AFU.BOK

enforcing
KG.147 (L)
SN Ensuring compliance with laws or regulations. (RLG7)
UF policing
CN K.KG.AFU.AFU.BIQ.BIQ

enforcing, law
USE **law enforcing**

engaged
DC.32
SN Partly embedded in or bonded to a supporting structure. (W)
CN D.DC.AFU.ALO.ARI.BOK

engaged columns
RT.105
ALT **engaged column**
SN Columns partially built into a surface, not freestanding. (HAS)
UF attached columns
columns, attached
columns, engaged
CN V.RT.AFU.AFU.AFU.AXC.BIQ.AFU.ALO.BCW

Engelmann spruce
MT.1404 (L)
UF spruce, Engelmann
CN M.MT.AFU.AFU.ALO.BIQ.DCU.AFU.AFU.ALO.DOI.BOK.AFU

engine houses
USE **fire stations**

engine houses (railway buildings)
USE **roundhouses**

engine houses, circular
USE **roundhouses**

engineering
KD.212 (A,L,B,R)
SN Science by which the properties of matter and the sources of energy in nature are made useful to humanity in structures, machines, and products. (W)
CN K.KD.AFU.ARI.BIQ

engineering brick
MT.97
UF brick, engineering
CN M.MT.AFU.AFU.AFU.AXC.ALO.AFU.ALO.BCW

engineering drawings
USE **technical drawings**

engineering maps
VW.163 (L)
ALT **engineering map**
SN Maps, usually maintained in the public works or engineering departments of a city, showing information such as street and rail rights of way, location of bridges, and grade separations; used for planning and executing engineering work in a locality. (ULANDU)
UF maps, engineering
CN V.VW.AFU.AFU.AFU.FZU.AXC.AFU.ARI.AFU.CXA.AXC.AFU

engineering physics
KD.284
SN Field concerned with the application of new concepts developed in the basic sciences, particularly physics, to engineering problems, and with the application of techniques developed in engineering disciplines to problems in physics. (PG)
UF physics, engineering
CN K.KD.AFU.ARI.CLM.AXC.ALO.AFU

engineering schools
RK.808 (L,B)
ALT **engineering school**
UF schools, engineering
CN V.RK.AFU.ALO.ALO.CXA.ARI.ALO.BIQ

engineering tolerances
USE **tolerances**

engineering, acoustical
USE **acoustical engineering**

engineering, aeronautical
USE **aeronautical engineering**

engineering, aerospace
USE **aerospace engineering**

engineering, architectural
USE **architectural engineering**

engineering, ceramic
USE **ceramic science**

engineering, chemical
USE **chemical engineering**

engineering, civil
USE **civil engineering**

engineering, electrical
USE **electrical engineering**

engineering, environmental
USE **environmental engineering**

engineering, geological
USE **geological engineering**

engineering, highway
USE **highway engineering**

engineering, human
USE **human factors**

engineering, human factors
USE **human factors**

engineering, hydraulic
USE **hydraulic engineering**

engineering, industrial
USE **industrial engineering**

engineering, management
USE **industrial engineering**

engineering, marine
USE **marine engineering**

engineering, mechanical
USE **mechanical engineering**

engineering, naval
USE **marine engineering**

engineering, plant
USE **plant engineering**

engineering, plastics
USE **polymer science**

engineering, road
USE **highway engineering**

engineering, sanitary
USE **sanitary engineering**

engineering, sonic
USE **acoustical engineering**

engineering, sound
USE **acoustical engineering**

engineering, structural
USE **structural engineering**

engineering, systems
USE **systems engineering**

engineering, textile
USE **textile science**

engineering, traffic
USE **traffic engineering**

engineering, transportation
USE **transportation engineering**

engineering, value
USE **cost benefit analysis**

engineers
HG.624 (L,B,R)
ALT **engineer**
SN Persons trained in a branch of engi-

neering. In some jurisdictions the designation is legally restricted in technical use to persons who have completed a prescribed course of study and complied with requirements concerning registration or licensing. (W)
CN H.HG.AFU.AXC.BZY.BCW

engineers, acoustical
USE **acoustical engineers**

engineers, aeronautical
USE **aeronautical engineers**

engineers, aerospace
USE **aerospace engineers**

engineers, biomedical
USE **biomedical engineers**

engineers, chemical
USE **chemical engineers**

engineers, civil
USE **civil engineers**

engineers, electrical
USE **electrical engineers**

engineers, hydraulic
USE **hydraulic engineers**

engineers, industrial
USE **industrial engineers**

engineers, marine
USE **marine engineers**

engineers, mechanical
USE **mechanical engineers**

engineers, military
USE **military engineers**

engineers, municipal
USE **municipal engineers**

engineers, naval
USE **marine engineers**

engineers, nuclear
USE **nuclear engineers**

engineers, product
USE **product engineers**

engineers, road
USE **transportation engineers**

engineers, safety
USE **safety engineers**

engineers, sanitary
USE **sanitary engineers**

engineers, sonic
USE **acoustical engineers**

engineers, sound
USE **acoustical engineers**

engineers, structural
USE **structural engineers**

engineers, traffic
USE **traffic engineers**

engineers, transportation
USE **transportation engineers**

engineers, water-supply
USE **water-supply engineers**

engines
TB.387 (L,N)
ALT **engine**
CN V.TB.AFU.ARI.DOI.ALO

engines, animal-powered
USE **animal-powered engines**

engines, dividing
USE **dividing engines**

engines, steam
USE **steam engines**

engines, winding
USE **windlasses**

English
FL.3040 (L,B)
CN F.FL.ALO.BCW.AFU.AXC.AFU

English barns
RK.46
ALT **English barn**
SN Rectangular, gable-roofed barns divided on the interior into three roughly equal bays, the center of which is a passageway entered from the center of the long sides. (WB&S)
UF 3-bay barns
barns, 3-bay
barns, Connecticut
barns, English
barns, New England
barns, three-bay
barns, Yankee
Connecticut barns
New England barns
three-bay barns
Yankee barns
CN V.RK.AFU.ALO.ALO.AFU.AFU.AFU.AFU.ARI

English bond
MT.2750
SN Bond composed of alternate courses of all headers and all stretchers with headers centered on stretchers and joints between stretchers. (PCMC)
UF bond, English
CN M.MT.AFU.AXC.BIQ.AFU.AFU.ALO

English britannia metal
MT.411
UF britannia metal, English
metal, English britannia
CN M.MT.AFU.AFU.AFU.BZY.AFU.AFU.AFU.ALO.BUE.ALO.ALO.AFU

English cherry
MT.1289
UF cherry, English
CN M.MT.AFU.AFU.ALO.BIQ.DCU.AFU.AFU.AFU.KLE.ARI.ALO

English elm
MT.1147
UF elm, English
Ulmus procera
CN M.MT.AFU.AFU.ALO.BIQ.DCU.AFU.AFU.AFU.DCU.ARI

English Gothic, Early
USE **Early English**

English green
USE **emerald green**

English I-houses
USE **I-houses**

English oak
MT.1240 (L)
UF British oak
oak, British
oak, English
Quercus pedunculata
Quercus robur
CN M.MT.AFU.AFU.ALO.BIQ.DCU.AFU.AFU.AFU.IRA.BZY

English ocher
USE **moderate orange yellow**

English pewter
MT.415
SN Pewter of the 16th century containing 91% tin and 9% antimony. (MH)
UF pewter, English
CN M.MT.AFU.AFU.AFU.BZY.AFU.AFU.AFU.ALO.BUE.ALO.AXC

English pink
USE **Dutch pink**

English poplar
USE **black poplar**

English vermilion
MT.1684
UF vermilion, English
CN M.MT.AFU.AFU.ARI.AFU.AFU.ALO.ALO.BCW.AFU.AXC.ARI

English vermilion (color)
USE **strong red**

English walnut
MT.1324 (L)
UF common Persian walnut
European walnut
Juglans regia
Persian walnut, common
walnut, common Persian
walnut, English
walnut, European
CN M.MT.AFU.AFU.ALO.BIQ.DCU.AFU.AFU.AFU.MQW.AXC.ARI

English white
USE **chalk**

English, Early
USE **Early English**

English, Old
USE **Old English**

engobe
MT.2572 (L)
SN A variety of slip used for decorating pottery; contains color oxides as well as clay, feldspar, and silica. (MAYER)
CN M.MT.AFU.ARI.CRG.ARI.ARI.AFU.ARI.BIQ.AFU

engravers
HG.126
ALT **engraver**
CN H.HG.AFU.AXC.AXC.AFU.AFU.ALO.AXC.DUC.AFU

engravers' marks
VW.748 (L)
ALT **engraver's mark**
UF marks, engravers'
CN V.VW.AFU.ALO.ALO.AFU.AXC.AXC.BUE

engravers, block
USE **wood engravers**

engravers, stipple
USE **stipple engravers**

engravers, wood
USE **wood engravers**

engravers, wood-cut
USE **wood engravers**

engraving on glass, reverse
USE **verre églomisé**

engraving operators
USE **photoengravers**

engraving (printmaking)
KT.451 (L,B,R)
ALT **engraved**
SN The process of incising an inscription or other design on a hard surface, usually metal or wood, with a sharp tool as preparation of a printing surface. (MAYER)
CN K.KT.AFU.ALO.DUC.DUC.ALO.BCW.AFU.ARI

engraving (surface decorating)
KT.677 (L,B,R)
ALT **engraved**
SN Use for the process of making a design on a hard surface, such as glass or metal, by inscribing it with a point.
CN K.KT.AFU.ALO.GRC.ARI

engraving, diamond-point
USE **diamond-point engraving**

engraving, line
USE **line engraving**

engraving, mezzotint
USE **mezzotint**

engraving, stipple
USE **stipple engraving**

engraving, wood
USE **wood engraving**

engravings, process line
USE **line photoengravings**

enlarged photographs
USE **enlargements**

enlargement
USE **enlarging**

enlargements
VJ.112
ALT **enlargement**
SN Refers to any photograph produced from a smaller photograph, usually a print from a negative. Distinct from **macrophotographs,** in which, specifically, the image is near life-size or larger.
UF blowups
enlarged photographs
macrophotographs (enlargements)
photographs, enlarged
CN V.VJ.AFU.ARI.ALO.BCW

enlargements, crayon
USE **crayon enlargements**

enlargements, frame
USE **frame enlargements**

enlargers
TB.331 (N)
ALT **enlarger**
SN Apparatuses for producing prints by projecting a negative or transparency onto sensitive paper; often allowing for the production of prints both larger and smaller than the original. (LANG)
UF enlargers, print
print enlargers
CN V.TB.AFU.ARI.CLM.ARI.ALO.BCW

enlargers, print
USE **enlargers**

enlarging
KT.412 (L)
ALT **enlarged**
SN Use for the darkroom procedure in which a photographic image is magnified by being projected through an optical system; generally used for making prints from small negatives.
UF enlargement
macrophotography (enlarging)
printing, projection
projection printing
CN K.KT.AFU.ALO.DUC.DIO.ARI.AXC.BUE

Enlightenment
BM.510 (L,R)
SN A philosophical movement of the late 18th century characterized by an untrammeled but frequently uncritical use of reason, a lively questioning of authority and traditional doctrines, a tendency toward individualism, and an emphasis on the idea of universal human progress. (W)
CN B.BM.BIQ.AXC.BOK

enlisting
USE **recruiting**

enneastyle
DC.88
CN D.DC.AFU.ARI.ERE.BIQ.BCW

enstatite
MT.503 (L)
SN A mineral of the pyroxene group consisting of magnesium silicate varying in color from grayish white to olive green and brown. (W)
CN M.MT.AFU.AFU.AFU.CFS.AFU.CFS

ensuring
USE **insuring**

entablatures
RT.328 (A,N,R)
ALT **entablature**
SN Use for the elaborated beam members carried by the columns in classical architecture, horizontally divided into architrave, frieze, and cornice. Use also for similar features in other contexts, such as the crown of a wall.
CN V.RT.AFU.AFU.AFU.BCW.BZY.AFU

Entartete Kunst
FL.3391 (R)
UF Degenerate art
CN F.FL.ALO.BCW.ALO.AXC.DIO.BIQ.BIQ.AFU

entasis
BM.78 (B)
SN The gently swelling convex curvature along the line of taper of columns, made to prevent the illusion of concavity in straight or regularly tapered columns. (A-Z)
CN B.BM.AFU.AFU.ARI.AFU.DOI.AFU

enterprises
USE **business enterprises**

enterprises, business
USE **business enterprises**

enterprises, commercial
USE **business enterprises**

entertainers
USE **performing artists**

entertaining
KG.218 (L)
SN Diverting or amusing someone; causing someone's time to pass agreeably. (W)
UF entertainment
CN K.KG.AFU.ALO.BOK.ALO

entertainment
USE **entertaining**

entertainment buildings
RK.1032 (A,B)
ALT **entertainment building**
UF buildings, entertainment
entertainment facilities
facilities, entertainment
CN V.RK.AFU.ALO.ALO.EWY.AXC.ARI

entertainment facilities
USE **entertainment buildings**

entomologists
HG.339 (L)
ALT **entomologist**
CN H.HG.AFU.AXC.BIQ.AFU.AFU.BUE

entrance halls
RM.134 (A,L,B,R)
ALT **entrance hall**
SN Use for passages or rooms just inside the entrance of a building, but sometimes with a vestibule between it and the outdoors. Prefer **lobbies** for such spaces in public buildings.
UF entries
entryways
foyers
halls, entrance
CN V.RM.AFU.DIO.ALO.BOK.ALO

entrance handles
TF.58
ALT **entrance handle**
UF handles, entrance
CN V.TF.AFU.AFU.AFU.AFU.CFS.ARI

entrance lodges
USE **gatehouses**

entrances
RT.984 (A,B)
ALT **entrance**
UF entries
CN V.RT.AFU.ARI.AFU.ALO.AFU

entrepreneurs
HG.415 (L,R)
ALT **entrepreneur**
SN Persons who organize, own, manage, and assume the risks of a business. (W)
CN H.HG.AFU.AXC.BOK.CXA

entresols
USE **mezzanines**

entretoises
USE **stretchers**

entries
USE **entrance halls**
entrances

entropy
BM.881 (L)
SN Includes both the quantity that is a measure of the amount of energy in a system not available for doing work, and the ultimate state in the degradation of matter and energy in the universe.
CN B.BM.CFS.AXC.ARI

entryways
USE **entrance halls**

enumerative bibiographies, systematic
USE **systematic enumerative bibliographies**

enumerative bibliographies
USE **systematic enumerative bibliographies**

envelope tables
USE **handkerchief tables**

envelopes, building
USE **building envelopes**

envelopes, bulk
USE **building envelopes**

environment
BM.421 (L,B,R)
CN B.BM.AXC.ALO

environment, state and
USE **environmental policy**

environmental art
BM.259 (R)
SN Artistic works that are planned, often on a grand scale, to surround or to involve the participation of the spectator. For works that use the land or natural forces, use **land art.**
UF ambiente
art, environmental
CN B.BM.AFU.ARI.BCW.FOG.BCW

environmental art (land art)
USE **land art**

environmental artists
HG.100
ALT **environmental artist**
UF artists, environmental
CN H.HG.AFU.AXC.AXC.AFU.AFU.ALO .AXC.BUE

environmental control
USE **environmental policy**

environmental engineering
KD.219 (L,B)
SN Professional application of scientific principles and technical practices to the management and optimum use of air, water, and land resources; also, the provision of facilities and the control of conditions for living, working, and recreation. (PG)
UF engineering, environmental
environmental management
management, environmental
CN K.KD.AFU.ARI.BIQ.AXC.ALO

environmental impact
BM.426
UF environmental risk
impact, environmental
risk, environmental
CN B.BM.AXC.ARI

environmental impact reports
USE **environmental impact statements**

environmental impact statements
VW.468 (A,L)
ALT **environmental impact statement**
SN Documents required by state and federal law that contain an analysis and report of the effects of major projects or programs on the quality of human, plant, or animal habitats.
UF environmental impact reports
impact statements, environmental
reports, environmental impact
statements, environmental impact
CN V.VW.AFU.AFU.ALO.FIM.BCW.AFU

environmental laboratories
RK.1168 (A,L)
ALT **environmental laboratory**
UF laboratories, environmental
CN V.RK.AFU.ALO.ALO.FIM.ALO.AFU.BZY

environmental law
KD.163 (A,L)
UF law, environmental
CN K.KD.AFU.ALO.DOI.ARI

environmental management
USE **environmental engineering**
environmental policy

environmental policy
BM.550 (A,L)
UF control, environmental
environment, state and
environmental control
environmental management
management, environmental
policy, environmental
state and environment
CN B.BM.BOK.BUE.AFU

environmental pollution
USE **pollution**

environmental protection
KG.113 (A,L,R)
UF protection, environmental
CN K.KG.AFU.AFU.BCW.ALO

environmental radioactivity
USE **radioactive pollution**

environmental risk
USE **environmental impact**

environmental sciences
KD.234
SN Interdisciplinary area of education and research for effective resource use, resource conservation, and environmental protection. (PG)
UF sciences, environmental
CN K.KD.AFU.ARI.BOK

envois
VD.143
SN Use for drawings required to be sent

yearly from Rome to the Académie des Beaux-Arts in Paris by winners of the Prix de Rome.
UF envois de rome
CN V.VD.AFU.BCW.ALO.AFU

envois (correspondence art)
USE **correspondence art**

envois de rome
USE **envois**

envy
BM.575 (L,R)
UF jealousy
CN B.BM.BUE.ARI.AXC

eolian landforms
USE **aeolian landforms**

Eolithic period
USE **Paleolithic**

Eotile
FL.296
CN F.FL.ALO.AFU.AXC.AFU.ARI.AFU.ALO.BCW

ephemera
VW.582 (L,N)
SN Documents considered to be of transitory value in some contexts, often preserved as samples or specimens.
UF ephemera, printed
printed ephemera
CN V.VW.AFU.ALO.AFU.BCW

ephemera, printed
USE **ephemera**

Ephyraean ware
FL.2656
UF ware, Ephyraean
CN F.FL.ALO.AXC.ALO.AFU.ALO.AXC.AXC.BCW

Epi-gravettian
FL.2478
CN F.FL.ALO.AXC.AFU.AXC.AXC

epichlorohydrin elastomer
MT.2083 (L)
UF elastomer, epichlorohydrin
CN M.MT.AFU.AFU.ARI.BUE.AFU.AFU.ALO

epidote
MT.504 (L)
SN A yellowish green mineral consisting of a silicate of calcium, aluminum, and iron and occurring massive or in grains, columns, and monoclinic crystals. (W)
CN M.MT.AFU.AFU.AFU.CFS.AFU.CLM

epigraphers
HG.270
ALT **epigrapher**
CN H.HG.AFU.AXC.BCW.AFU.BOK.ALO.ALO

epigraphs
VW.43 (L)
ALT **epigraph**
SN Inscriptions on statues, buildings, or other structures. (AHD)
CN V.VW.AFU.AFU.AFU.CRG.ALO

epigraphy
KD.148 (L,R)
SN Study and interpretation of ancient inscriptions, including writings, pictures, and random scratchings, incised on stone, clay, metal, or other hard surfaces. For the study of ancient modes of writing more generally, use **paleography.**
CN K.KD.AFU.ALO.CLM.ALO.AFU

epinaoi
USE **opisthodomoi**

Epipaleolithic
FL.12
CN F.FL.AFU.BCW.AFU.AFU.AXC

épis
RT.1056
ALT **épi**
SN Use for adornments or coverings found on the terminating points of roof ridges.
CN V.RT.AFU.BCW.BOK

episcaenia
RT.1273
ALT **episcenium**
SN The upper stories of the scene buildings in ancient Greek or Roman theaters. (HAS)
UF episkenia
CN V.RT.AFU.BUE.ARI.BIQ.ALO.AFU

Episcopal
BM.635 (L,B)
SN Use with reference to the Episcopal Church in America; with reference to the Church of England, use **Anglican.**
UF Anglican (Episcopal)
Episcopalian
Protestant Episcopal
CN B.BM.BZY.AFU.ALO.ARI.BCW

episcopal palaces
USE **bishops' palaces**

Episcopalian
USE **Episcopal**

episkenia
USE **episcaenia**

epistemology
KD.65 (L,R)
UF knowledge, theory of
theory of knowledge
CN K.KD.AFU.AFU.BOK.AXC

epistolaries
VW.546 (L)
ALT **epistolary**
CN V.VW.AFU.ALO.AFU.AFU.ALO.BUE.BUE.AFU

epistyles
USE **architraves**

epitaphs
VW.44 (L,R)
ALT **epitaph**
SN Inscriptions on sepulchral monuments in the memory of those buried in the tomb or grave. (AHD)
CN V.VW.AFU.AFU.AFU.CRG.ARI

epoxy
MT.2167 (L,B)
SN Synthetic resin used to produce strong cold-cured adhesives which set by chemical reaction and not through loss of solvent and coalescence. (TATEMT)
UF epoxy resin
resin, epoxy
CN M.MT.AFU.AFU.ARI.BUE.ALO.AXC.ALO.BCW

epoxy resin
USE **epoxy**

epoxy, basic liquid
USE **basic liquid epoxy**

epoxy, multifunctional
USE **multifunctional epoxy**

epoxy, silicone
USE **silicone epoxy**

EPR
USE **ethylene-propylene elastomer**

EPR rubber
USE **ethylene-propylene elastomer**

épures
USE **full-scale drawings**

equations
BM.759 (L)
SN Statements that each of two expressions is equal to the other. (MHDSTT)
CN B.BM.CFS.ARI.ALO

equestrian clubs
USE **riding clubs**

equilateral arches
RT.232
ALT **equilateral arch**
SN Use for pointed arches in which a line from the springing point to the pointed center equals the span between the springing points.
UF arches, equilateral
arches, equilateral pointed
equilateral pointed arches
pointed arches, equilateral
CN V.RT.AFU.AFU.AFU.BCW.AFU.AFU.AFU.CRG.ALO

equilateral pointed arches
USE **equilateral arches**

equilibrium
BM.1002 (L)

SN A state of balance between opposing forces that is either static or dynamic. (WCOL)
CN B.BM.CFS.AXC.CLM.ALO.AFU

equilibrium (composition)
USE **balance**

equipment
TB.1 (L,B)
CN V.TB.AFU

equipment, acoustic
USE **acoustic equipment**

equipment, arc-welding
USE **arc welding machines**

equipment, building
USE **construction equipment**

equipment, compacting
USE **compacting equipment**

equipment, construction
USE **construction equipment**

equipment, drafting
USE **drafting equipment**

equipment, earthmoving
USE **earthmoving equipment**

equipment, excavating
USE **excavating equipment**

equipment, firefighting
USE **firefighting equipment**

equipment, hydraulic
USE **hydraulic equipment**

equipment, mechanical
USE **mechanical equipment**

equipment, milling
USE **milling machinery**

equipment, photographic
USE **photographic equipment**

equipment, plumbing
USE **plumbing fixtures**

equipment, power producing
USE **power producing equipment**

equipment, sandblasting
USE **sandblasting equipment**

equipment, stage
USE **stage machinery**

equity
BM.385 (L)
SN An interest, commonly expressed in money, which an owner has in property over and above all liens against the property. (PUTNAM)
CN B.BM.ARI.CFS

era
USE **period**

erasers
TB.248 (N)
ALT **eraser**
SN Devices, such as pieces of rubber or cloth, for removing marks made with pen, pencil, chalk, or the like. (RHDEL2)
CN V.TB.AFU.ARI.CLM.AFU.ALO.BOK

erasing
KT.610
ALT **erased**
UF erasure
CN K.KT.AFU.ALO.FUA.BZY

erasing shields
TB.249
ALT **erasing shield**
SN Thin shields used when erasing to avoid erasing the surrounding work. (PUTNAM)
UF shields, erasing
CN V.TB.AFU.ARI.CLM.AFU.ALO.BUE

erasure
USE **erasing**

erection drawings
VD.119
ALT **erection drawing**
SN Shop drawings depicting components and relative positions, for process of erection of a structure. (DAC)
UF drawings, erection
CN V.VD.AFU.ALO.DCU.AXC.AFU

erectors
HG.594
ALT **erector**
SN Persons who work on a structure, such as a steel building or bridge, by assembling fabricated parts. (W)
CN H.HG.AFU.AXC.BZY.AFU.CRG

Eretrian
FL.2620
CN F.FL.ALO.AXC.ALO.AFU.ALO.AXC.ALO.AXC.AXC

ergastula
RK.715
ALT **ergastulum**
SN Use for ancient Roman domestic places of confinement for criminal offenders, usually slaves.
CN V.RK.AFU.ALO.ALO.CXA.AFU.AFU

ergonomics
USE **human factors**

Erh-li-t'ou
USE **Erlitou**

Eridu
FL.2957 (L)
UF Ubaid 1
CN F.FL.ALO.AXC.ARI.BCW.AFU.AFU.ALO.AFU

Erie
FL.1291 (L)
CN F.FL.ALO.ALO.ARI.AFU.ARI.AXC

Erimi ware
USE **red-on-white ware**

Erligang
FL.1856
CN F.FL.ALO.ARI.ALO.AFU.AFU.ALO.BCW.AFU.AFU

Erlitou
FL.1853
UF Erh-li-t'ou
Lo-yang
CN F.FL.ALO.ARI.ALO.AFU.AFU.ALO.AXC

eroding
USE **erosion**

erosion
KT.901 (L)
ALT **eroded**
SN Process whereby materials of the earth's surface are worn away and removed by natural causes including weathering, solution, corrosion, or transportation. (W)
UF eroding
CN K.KT.ALO.BCW.BIQ

erosion protection works
RK.554 (A)
UF water flow control works
works, erosion protection
works, water flow control
CN V.RK.AFU.ALO.ALO.CFS.ALO.ALO

erotica
BM.217 (L,R)
ALT **erotic**
SN Depiction or description of sexual love. For depiction or description of sexual activity in an exploitative, abusive, or violent context, use **pornography.**
CN B.BM.AFU.ARI.AFU

Ersari
FL.3590
CN F.FL.ALO.BIQ.AFU.IFM.ARI.ARI

Ertebølle
FL.2479
CN F.FL.ALO.AXC.AFU.AXC.BCW

Esa
USE **Ishan**

Esan
USE **Ishan**

escalator wells
RM.87
ALT **escalator well**
UF wells, escalator
wellways
CN V.RM.AFU.DIO.ALO.ARI.ARI

escalators
RT.1295 (A,L,B)
ALT **escalator**

UF electric stairways
moving staircases
staircases, moving
stairways, electric
CN V.RT.ALO.ALO.AFU.AFU.AFU

escallop shell
USE **scallop shell**

escapes, fire
USE **fire escapes**

escarpments
RT.1204 (L)
ALT **escarpment**
SN Steep slopes in front of a fortification. (W)
UF scarps
CN V.RT.AFU.BUE.AFU.BZY.AXC

escarpments (landform components)
RD.236 (L)
ALT **escarpment (landform component)**
UF scarps (landform components)
CN V.RD.ARI.AFU.AXC.ALO.AXC

eschatology
KD.84 (L,R)
CN K.KD.AFU.AFU.BUE.ALO.AXC

eschutcheons, drop
USE **drop escutcheons**

esconsons
USE **reveals**

escritoires
TG.565
ALT **escritoire**
SN Writing desks, especially of the small portable type, made since the 16th century and consisting of a nest of drawers enclosed in a box with a sloping front that is hinged along the bottom edge and may be let down to provide a writing platform. Term also applied to small, elegant desks patterned after the 18th century French form.
UF scritoires
CN V.TG.AFU.AFU.AXC.ALO.BZY.FOG.AFU

escritoires (desks and bookcases)
USE **desks and bookcases**

escritoires (secretaries)
USE **secretaries**

escritorios
USE **vargueños**

escrows
VW.913 (L)
ALT **escrow**
SN Any items, such as deeds, bonds, or monies, held in trust by a third party to be turned over to the grantee upon fulfillment of a condition. (WCOL)
CN V.VW.AFU.ARI.AFU.BOK.BOK.BOK

escutcheon pins
TF.461
ALT **escutcheon pin**
SN Small nails, usually brass and often ornamental, used to fix an escutcheon. (MEANS)
UF pins, escutcheon
CN V.TF.AFU.AFU.AFU.ALO.AFU.CXA.AXC

escutcheon plates
USE **escutcheons (hardware)**

escutcheon plates, combined
USE **combined escutcheon plates**

escutcheons (coats of arms)
VW.702 (L,R)
ALT **escutcheon (coat of arms)**
UF shields (heraldry)
CN V.VW.AFU.ALO.ALO.AFU.AFU.AFU.ALO.AFU

escutcheons (hardware)
TF.262 (L,N)
ALT **escutcheon (hardware)**
SN The protective plates that surround keyholes. For inserts or inlay surrounding keyholes, use **keyhole surrounds.**
UF escutcheon plates
key plates
lock plates
plates, escutcheon
plates, key
plates, lock
scutcheons
CN V.TF.AFU.AFU.AFU.AFU.DZW.ALO

escutcheons (keyhole surrounds)
USE **keyhole surrounds**

escutcheons, cup
USE **cup escutcheons**

escutcheons, thread
USE **thread escutcheons**

Eshira
USE **Shira**

Eshure
FL.98
CN F.FL.ALO.AFU.ALO.AFU.BUE.ARI

Esie
FL.99
CN F.FL.ALO.AFU.ALO.AFU.BUE.AXC

eskers
RD.184 (L)
ALT **esker**
SN Relatively long, narrow, winding ridges of mixed sand and gravel, deposited probably by streams of meltwater flowing through crevasses and tunnels in stagnant ice sheets. (WAYTA)
CN V.RD.ARI.AFU.AXC.AFU.AFU.ALO.ALO

Eskimo
FL.790 (A,L,R)
SN Use with reference to the native Arctic culture, prior to European contact. For names of specific native peoples of the present, use terms such as **Chugach, Inuit,** or **Katladlit.**
CN F.FL.ALO.ALO.ALO.AFU.ALO.AFU.ALO

Eskimo, Baffinland
USE **Baffin Island Inuit**

Eskimo, Caribou
USE **Caribou Inuit**

Eskimo, Greenlandic
USE **Katladlit**

Eskimo, Labrador
USE **Labrador Inuit**

Eskimo, North Alaskan
USE **Inupiaq**

Eskimo, Saint Lawrence Island
USE **Saint Lawrence Island Eskimo**

Esmeralda
FL.1660
CN F.FL.ALO.ALO.ARI.ARI.BCW.BUE

esonarthexes
RM.324
ALT **esonarthex**
SN Inner narthexes where there is also an outer narthex (the exonarthex).
CN V.RM.AFU.DIO.AXC.ALO.AFU.DCU.AFU

espagnolette bolts
TF.234
ALT **espagnolette bolt**
UF bolts, espagnolette
CN V.TF.AFU.AFU.AFU.AFU.DIO.BIQ.ALO.ALO.ARI.ALO

espagnolettes
DG.22
ALT **espagnolette**
SN Motifs of female masks having a ruff around the head and under the chin, popular in 18th-century French decorative arts, especially Régence. (LDDO)
CN D.DG.AFU.AFU.BCW.ARI

esparto
MT.1826 (L)
SN The fiber of either of two Spanish and Algerian grasses (Stipa tenacissima and Lygeum spartum) used especially to make cordage, shoes, and paper. (WCOL)
UF alfa
CN M.MT.AFU.AFU.ARI.ALO.AFU.AFU.ALO.AXC

Esperanza
FL.1018
CN F.FL.ALO.ALO.ALO.ALO.AFU.ALO.ARI.AFU.ALO.ALO

esplanades
USE **promenades**

esquisses
VB.9
ALT **esquisse**
SN Sketches representing an early step in the development of a pictorial composition or the design of a building, but more developed than a preliminary sketch. Used especially in the context of the École des Beaux-Arts.
CN V.VB.AFU.AFU.BCW.ALO

essayists
HG.184
ALT **essayist**
SN Writers of essays. (W)
CN H.HG.AFU.AXC.AXC.ARI.AFU.AFU.AXC

essays
VW.37 (L)
ALT **essay**
SN Short literary compositions on single subjects, often presenting the personal view of the author. (AHD)
UF literary sketches
sketches, literary
CN V.VW.AFU.AFU.AFU.BZY

essential oil
MT.1986 (L)
SN Aromatic oil found in uncombined form in various parts of plants and employed for flavors, perfumes, disenfectants and medicines. (MH)
UF oil, essential
CN M.MT.AFU.AFU.ARI.ARI.AFU.ARI.AFU

estancias
USE **haciendas**

estate administration records
VW.1017 (L)
ALT **estate administration record**
UF records, estate administration
CN V.VW.AFU.ARI.ALO.BCW.AFU.ALO.ALO.AFU.AFU.AFU

estate agents
USE **real estate agents**

estate inventories
VW.1018 (L)
ALT **estate inventory**
SN Lists, catalogs, accounts, or schedules, made by an estate executor or administrator of the tangible and intangible property of the estate, describing the items or classes of property so as to be identifiable and usually placing a value on each. (GAHLM)
UF household inventories
inventories of decedents' estates
inventories, estate
inventories, household
inventories, probate
probate inventories
CN V.VW.AFU.ARI.ALO.BCW.AFU.ALO.ALO.AFU.AFU.AFU.AFU

estate papers
USE **estate records**

estate records
VW.980
ALT **estate record**
SN Use broadly for any documents concerning the real or personal property of a person or group of persons.
UF estate papers
papers, estate
records, estate
CN V.VW.AFU.ARI.ALO.AXC

estates (country houses)
USE **country houses**

estates (law)
BM.461 (R)
SN Aggregate of property or liabilities of all kinds that a person leaves for his or her disposal at death. (W)
CN B.BM.BCW.CXA.AFU.ALO

estates, industrial
USE **industrial parks**

ester gum
MT.1507
UF ester, rosin
gum, ester
rosin ester
CN M.MT.AFU.AFU.ALO.BOK.DOI.AFU

ester, rosin
USE **ester gum**

esters
MT.2691 (L)
SN Any of a class of often fragrant compounds formed by the reaction between an acid and an alcohol usually with the elimination of water. (WCOL)
CN M.MT.AFU.ARI.HZS.AFU.BOK.ALO

esthetics
USE **aesthetics**

estilo desornamentado
USE **Herreran**

estimates
VW.820 (L,B)
ALT **estimate**
SN Rough or approximate calculations of cost or value, such as statements of price for which certain work will be done by one who is willing to undertake it. (GAHLM)
UF cost estimates
CN V.VW.AFU.ARI.AFU.BIQ.BOK

estimating
KG.56 (B)
CN K.KG.AFU.AFU.ARI.CFS

estipites
RT.92
ALT **estipite**
SN Use for pilasters that taper from top to base, as commonly encountered in Spanish post-Renaissance architecture, often with complicated ornament.
CN V.RT.AFU.AFU.AFU.AXC.BIQ.AFU.AFU.BUE

estrays
USE **animal shelters**

Estridentismo
FL.1758 (R)
ALT **Stridentism**
UF Stridenist
CN F.FL.ALO.ALO.BCW.ALO.ALO

estuaries
RD.158 (L)
ALT **estuary**
SN Water passages where tides meet the currents of streams. (W)
CN V.RD.ARI.AFU.AFU.ALO.ALO

étagères
TG.604 (N)
ALT **étagère**
SN Open-tiered shelves for displaying small objects; often with a mirrored back and sometimes having drawers or a cabinet below. (PC)
UF parlor cabinets
whatnots
CN V.TG.AFU.AFU.AXC.AXC

etages, beaux
USE **piani nobili**

Etchaottine
USE **Slave**

etched daguerreotype prints
VJ.18
ALT **etched daguerreotype print**
SN Photomechanical prints of the mid-19th century made by an etched daguerreotype process.
UF daguerreotype prints
daguerreotype prints, etched
etched daguerreotypes
prints, etched daguerreotype
CN V.VJ.AFU.AFU.ALO.ALO

etched daguerreotype process
KT.429
SN Use for various photomechanical processes that use a daguerreotype to make the printing plate.
CN K.KT.AFU.ALO.DUC.DOI.ARI.AFU

etched daguerreotypes
USE **etched daguerreotype prints**

Etchemin
USE **Malecite**

etchers
HG.129 (L,B,R)

ALT **etcher**
SN Artists who hand-etch copper or steel plates for use in printing. (W)
CN H.HG.AFU.AXC.AXC.AFU.AFU.ALO.AXC.DUC.ALO

etching (printmaking)
KT.456 (L,R)
ALT **etched**
SN Printmaking technique in which a design is scratched into a metal plate coated with an acid-restraint substance and is bitten into the metal upon immersion in acid.
CN K.KT.AFU.ALO.DUC.DUC.ALO.BCW.AFU.AXC

etching (surface decorating)
KT.681
ALT **etched**
SN Use for the process of forming a design on a hard surface, such as glass or metal, by the action of acid.
CN K.KT.AFU.ALO.GRC.AXC

etching, deep
USE **deep etching**

etching, fire
USE **pyrography**

etching, lift-ground
USE **lift-ground**

etching, soft-ground
USE **soft-ground etching**

etching, zinc
USE **anastatic printing**

ethanoic acid
USE **acetic acid**

ether, cellulose
USE **cellulose ether**

ether, ethylene glycol monoethyl
USE **ethylene glycol monoethyl ether**

ethics
BM.497 (L,B,R)
SN System of moral principles or rules of conduct. (RHDEL2)
CN B.BM.BIQ.ALO

ethics (philosophy)
KD.66 (L,B,R)
SN Use for the branch of philosophy dealing with values relating to human conduct, with respect to the rightness and wrongness of certain actions, and to the goodness and badness of the motives and ends of such actions.
UF moral philosophy
philosophy, moral
CN K.KD.AFU.AFU.BOK.BCW

ethics, professional
USE **professional ethics**

ethics, religious
USE **religious ethics**

ethics, social
USE **social ethics**

ethnic art
BM.242 (L,R)
UF art, ethnic
CN B.BM.AFU.ARI.BCW.CXA

ethnic groups
HG.778 (L,R)
ALT **ethnic group**
SN Use for groups within a society that are distinguished from the majority by their common ties of ancestry and culture. For groups that are the objects of prejudice or discrimination from the majority, use **minorities**.
CN H.HG.AFU.BOK.ARI

ethnic museums
USE **ethnological museums**

ethnoarchaeology
KD.105 (L)
SN Study of contemporary societies from a materialistic perspective, focusing on variability rather than typical and categorical behavior, (AJA) with the purpose of interpreting the past of those societies.
CN K.KD.AFU.ALO.ALO.AXC

ethnocentrism
BM.349 (L)
SN Tendency toward viewing alien cultures with disfavor; also the resulting sense of inherent superiority. (W)
CN B.BM.ALO.ALO.CLM.BZY

ethnographic photography
KT.298 (L)
UF photography, ethnographic
CN K.KT.AFU.ALO.DUC.DIO.AFU.BOK

ethnography
KD.92 (L,R)
SN Direct observation and descriptive study of the culture and way of life of particular societies. (TSIT)
CN K.KD.AFU.ALO.AFU.ALO

ethnography museums
USE **ethnological museums**

ethnological museums
RK.414 (A,L,B)
ALT **ethnological museum**
UF ethnic museums
ethnography museums
folk museums
museums, ethnic
museums, ethnological
museums, folk
CN V.RK.AFU.ALO.ALO.BCW.AXC.ARI.CFS.AFU.AFU

ethnologists
HG.252 (L)
ALT **ethnologist**
CN H.HG.AFU.AXC.BCW.AFU.AFU.AFU

ethnology
KD.93 (L,R)
SN Scientific, historic, or comparative study of the origins, characteristics, and functions of human cultures and societies. (TSIT)
CN K.KD.AFU.ALO.AFU.ARI

ethnomusicologists
HG.168 (L)
ALT **ethnomusicologist**
SN Persons who study music in a sociocultural context, especially that outside the European tradition. (WCOL)
CN H.HG.AFU.AXC.AXC.AFU.ALO.BCW.AFU

ethnomusicology
KD.28 (L)
CN K.KD.AFU.AFU.AFU.ALO.BIQ.AFU

ethnopsychology
KD.181 (L)
UF anthropology, psychological
cross-cultural psychology
psychological anthropology
psychology, cross-cultural
CN K.KD.AFU.ALO.EFQ.AFU.AFU

ethyl acetate
MT.2694
UF acetate, ethyl
CN M.MT.AFU.ARI.HZS.AFU.BOK.ALO.ARI

ethyl alcohol
MT.2686 (L)
UF alcohol, ethyl
alcohol, grain
Cologne spirits
grain alcohol
spirits, Cologne
CN M.MT.AFU.ARI.HZS.AFU.BOK.AFU.AXC

ethyl cellulose
MT.2131
SN A colorless, odorless ester of cellulose resulting from the reaction of ethyl chloride and cellulose; forms durable alkali-resistant coatings. (MH)
UF cellulose, ethyl
EC
CN
M.MT.AFU.AFU.ARI.BUE.ALO.AXC.AFU.BCW.ALO.AFU

ethylene glycol monoethyl ether
MT.2665
UF cellosolve
ether, ethylene glycol monoethyl
CN M.MT.AFU.ARI.HZS.AFU.BCW

ethylene-propylene elastomer
MT.2084 (L)
UF elastomer, ethylene-propylene
EPR
EPR rubber
ethylene-propylene rubber
rubber, EPR
rubber, ethylene-propylene
CN M.MT.AFU.AFU.ARI.BUE.AFU.AFU.ARI

ethylene-propylene rubber
USE **ethylene-propylene elastomer**

etiquette
BM.330 (L,R)
SN The forms required by good breeding or prescribed by authority to be observed in social or official life. (W)
CN B.BM.ALO.ALO.ALO.AFU

Etowah
FL.891
UF Etowah-Lamar
CN F.FL.ALO.ALO.ALO.AFU.ALO.ALO.BOK.BCW

Etowah-Lamar
USE **Etowah**

Etruscan
FL.2707 (A,L,B,R)
CN F.FL.ALO.AXC.ALO.ALO.AFU.ARI

Etruscan Style
FL.3268
CN F.FL.ALO.BCW.ALO.AXC.CLM.BCW

Etruscan, Early
USE **Early Etruscan**

Etruscan, Late
USE **Late Etruscan**

Etrusco-Greek
USE **Greco-Etruscan**

Etrusco-Italic
FL.2729
CN F.FL.ALO.AXC.ALO.ALO.ALO.AFU

Etrusco-Roman
FL.2730
CN F.FL.ALO.AXC.ALO.ALO.ALO.ALO

Etsako
FL.250 (L)
UF Kukuruku
CN F.FL.ALO.AFU.AXC.AFU.ALO.ALO.ARI

études
USE **studies**

etymological dictionaries
VW.393 (L)
ALT **etymological dictionary**
UF dictionaries, etymological
CN V.VW.AFU.AFU.ALO.EWY.ARI.AFU.AFU

etymology
KD.49 (A,L)
SN Study of the history of a particular word or element of a word, or of historical linguistic change. (RHDEL1)
CN K.KD.AFU.AFU.AXC.ALO.AFU

Euboean
FL.2621
CN F.FL.ALO.AXC.ALO.AFU.ALO.AXC.ALO.AXC.BCW

eucalyptus
MT.1151 (L)
CN M.MT.AFU.AFU.ALO.BIQ.DCU.AFU.AFU.AFU.DIO

Eucalyptus globulus
USE **blue gum**

Eucalyptus paniculata
USE **gray ironbark**

Eucalyptus pilulares
USE **blackbutt**

Eucalyptus regnans
USE **mountain ash**

eucharistic windows
USE **squints**

euchrome
USE **burnt umber**

eulogies
VW.325 (L)
ALT **eulogy**
SN Laudatory speeches or written tributes. (AHD)
CN V.VW.AFU.AFU.ALO.BZY

eurhythmy
USE **concinnity**

European
FL.3034 (L,B)
CN F.FL.ALO.BCW

European ash
MT.1101
UF ash, common
ash, European
common ash
Fraxinus excelsior
CN M MT AFU AFU ALO BIQ DCU AFU.AFU.AFU.ARI.AFU

European beech
MT.1107 (L)
UF beech, common
beech, European
common beech
Fagus sylvatica
CN M.MT.AFU.AFU.ALO.BIQ.DCU.AFU.AFU.AFU.BCW.ARI

European birch
MT.1117 (L)
UF Betula pubescens
birch, European
maple, Russian
Russian maple
CN M.MT.AFU.AFU.ALO.BIQ.DCU.AFU.AFU.AFU.BIQ.ARI

European black poplar
USE **black poplar**

European box
USE **boxwood**

European boxwood
USE **boxwood**

European chestnut
MT.1134 (L)
UF Castanea sativa
Castanea vesca
chestnut, European
chestnut, Italian
chestnut, Spanish
chestnut, sweet
Italian chestnut
Spanish chestnut
sweet chestnut
CN M.MT.AFU.AFU.ALO.BIQ.DCU.AFU.AFU.AFU.CLM.ARI

European green alder
MT.1097 (L)
UF alder, European green
Alnus viridis
CN M.MT.AFU.AFU.ALO.BIQ.DCU.AFU.AFU.AFU.ALO.BCW

European hackberry
MT.1169
UF Celtis australis
hackberry, European
CN M.MT.AFU.AFU.ALO.BIQ.DCU.AFU.AFU.AFU.DZW.ALO

European hop hornbeam
MT.1185
UF hop hornbeam, European
hornbeam, European hop
Ostrya carpinofolia
CN M.MT.AFU.AFU.ALO.BIQ.DCU.AFU.AFU.AFU.EWY.ALO.ALO

European hornbeam
MT.1182 (L)
UF Carpinus betulus
common hornbeam
hornbeam, common
hornbeam, European
ironwood (European hornbeam)
CN M.MT.AFU.AFU.ALO.BIQ.DCU.AFU.AFU.AFU.EWY.AFU

European larch
MT.1363 (L)
UF larch, European
Larix decidua
Larix europaea
CN M.MT.AFU.AFU.ALO.BIQ.DCU.AFU.AFU.ALO.BZY.AFU

European spruce
USE **common spruce**

European turkey oak
MT.1241 (L)
UF oak, European turkey
Quercus catesbaei
Quercus cerris
Quercus laevis
turkey oak, European
CN M.MT.AFU.AFU.ALO.BIQ.DCU.AFU.AFU.AFU.IRA.CFS

European walnut
USE **English walnut**

evaluating
KG.19 (A,L)
SN Determining qualitative or quantitative worth or significance. (RLG7)
CN K.KG.AFU.AFU.AFU.CFS

evaluation, building
USE **post-occupancy evaluation**

evaluation, post-occupancy
USE **post-occupancy evaluation**

evaluations, personnel
USE **personnel evaluations**

evaluators
USE **appraisers**

evangeliaries
VW.547 (L,R)
ALT **evangeliary**
UF gospel lectionaries
lectionaries, gospel
CN V.VW.AFU.ALO.AFU.AFU.ALO.BUE.BUE.ALO

evangelists
HG.225 (L,R)
ALT **evangelist**
SN Occasional preachers having no fixed pastoral charge. (W)
UF revivalists
CN H.HG.AFU.AXC.AXC.BIQ.AFU.ARI.CFS

events
KM.1
CN K.KM.AFU

evergreens
RD.276 (L)
ALT **evergreen**
CN V.RD.ARI.AFU.BCW.ALO.ALO.ALO.ARI.AFU.ALO

evicting
KG.195 (L)
SN Legally removing a person or persons from the premises.
CN K.KG.AFU.ALO.BCW.ALO

eviction control
USE **rent control**

evolute scrolls
USE **wave scrolls**

evolute spirals
USE **wave scrolls**

evolution
BM.720 (L,R)
SN Use for the gradual development of living organisms over successive generations, from lower to higher forms, especially as articulated in Darwinian theory or in alternatives to or modifications of Darwinian theory.
UF Darwinism
CN B.BM.CFS.AFU.ALO

Ewe
FL.302 (L)
CN F.FL.ALO.AFU.AXC.AFU.ARI.ALO.ALO

ex libris
USE **bookplates**

examination study guides
VW.336 (L)
ALT **examination study guide**
UF guides, examination study
study guides, examination
CN V.VW.AFU.AFU.ALO.CXA.AFU

examinations
VW.326 (L)
ALT **examination**
SN Written questions or exercises testing knowledge, aptitude, or skills. (AHD)
UF tests
CN V.VW.AFU.AFU.ALO.CFS

excavating
USE **excavation**

excavating equipment
TB.38 (L)
SN Equipment used in the removal of earth.
UF equipment, excavating
excavating machinery
machinery, excavating
CN V.TB.AFU.ARI.AFU.ARI.ARI

excavating machinery
USE **excavating equipment**

excavation
KT.611 (L,B)
ALT **excavated**
UF digging
excavating
CN K.KT.AFU.ALO.FUA.CFS

excavations
RK.1353 (A,L,B,R)
ALT **excavation**
UF digs
CN V.RK.AFU.ALO.ARI.AXC.ARI.AFU.ALO

excavators, trench
USE **trenching machines**

excelsior
MT.1416 (L)
SN Continuous, curly, fine wood shavings employed as a packing material for breakable articles. (MH)
CN M.MT.AFU.AFU.ALO.BIQ.DCU.ALO.ARI

exceptional persons
HG.782 (L)
ALT **exceptional person**
SN Persons atypical due to disabilities or giftedness. (ERIC)
CN H.HG.AFU.BOK.AXC

excerpts
VW.38
ALT **excerpt**
SN Passages reproduced verbatim from a printed work or a manuscript. (GAHLM)
UF selections
CN V.VW.AFU.AFU.AFU.CFS

exchangers, heat
USE **heat exchangers**

exchanges
RK.133 (B)
ALT **exchange**
UF bourses
lonjas
CN V.RK.AFU.ALO.ALO.ALO.ALO.ALO

exchanges, commodity
USE **commodity exchanges**

exchanges, employment
USE **employment agencies**

exchanges, labor
USE **employment agencies**

exchanges, military post
USE **post exchanges**

exchanges, post
USE **post exchanges**

exchanges, produce
USE **commodity exchanges**

exchanges, stock
USE **stock exchanges**

exchanges, telephone
USE **telephone exchanges**

excise marks
VW.718
ALT **excise mark**
UF marks, excise
CN V.VW.AFU.ALO.ALO.AFU.AXC.ALO.BIQ

excommunications
KM.145 (L)
CN K.KM.AFU.DZW.ARI

excursuses
VW.40
ALT **excursus**
SN Appendixes or digressions that contain further exposition on some point or topic from other works. (W)
CN V.VW.AFU.AFU.AFU.CLM

executing
KG.202 (L)
SN Taking human life under judicial order. (RLG7)
CN K.KG.AFU.ALO.BCW.BOK.ALO

execution
BM.34
SN Use for the actual activity of making something or carrying out a plan.
CN B.BM.AFU.AFU.ALO.BCW

executions
KM.136 (L,R)
CN K.KM.AFU.DOI.ALO.AFU

executive orders
VW.986 (L)
ALT **executive order**
SN Orders or regulations issued by the President, or some administrative authority under his direction, for the purpose of interpreting, implementing, or giving administrative effect to a provision of the Constitution or of some law or treaty. May also include similar state documents issued by governors or upper level management in business. (BLACKS)
UF orders, executive
CN V.VW.AFU.ARI.ALO.BCW.AFU.AFU.AFU.ALO

executive records
VW.983
ALT **executive record**
UF records, executive
CN V.VW.AFU.ARI.ALO.BCW.AFU.AFU

executives
HG.651 (L)
ALT **executive**
SN Persons who hold a position of administrative or managerial responsibility in a business. (W)
CN H.HG.AFU.AXC.CFS.AFU.AFU

exedrae
RM.272 (A)
ALT **exedra**
SN Use for niches, recesses, or other sheltered spaces, often semicircular and lined with seats; primarily in Roman architecture.
UF exhedrae
CN V.RM.AFU.DIO.ARI.ALO.BOK

exedrae (site elements)
RM.433
ALT **exedra (site element)**
SN Use for semicircular outdoor seats, usually of stone or concrete.
CN V.RM.ALO.AFU.AXC

exegesis
BM.310 (R)
SN Exposition or explanation, especially critical interpretation of a portion of Scripture or other text. (W)
CN B.BM.AFU.AXC.EFQ.ALO

exercises
VB.101
ALT **exercise**
SN Works of art made chiefly in order to practice or display a specific technical point or aspect. (W)
CN V.VB.ALO.BUE.AFU

exercising chairs
USE **chamber horses**

exercising machines, horse
USE **chamber horses**

exhaust ventilation
RT.1405
SN Ventilation that allows fresh air to enter a space through available or controlled openings and employs mechanical means such as fans to remove foul air from the same space. (MEANS)
UF ventilation, exhaust
CN V.RT.ALO.BCW.AFU.AFU.AXC.AFU

exhedrae
USE **exedrae**

exhibit cases
TG.584
ALT **exhibit case**
UF cases, exhibit
CN V.TG.AFU.AFU.AXC.ALO.CLM

exhibit scripts
VW.1056
ALT **exhibit script**
UF exhibition texts
scripts, exhibit
texts, exhibition
CN V.VW.AFU.ARI.ALO.BUE.AFU.AFU

exhibiting
KG.90
ALT **exhibited**
SN Showing or presenting to public view. (W)
UF displaying
CN K.KG.AFU.AFU.AXC.CFS

exhibition booths
RM.260 (A,L)
ALT **exhibition booth**
UF booths, exhibition
CN V.RM.AFU.DIO.ARI.ALO.AXC.AFU

exhibition buildings
RK.370 (A,L,B,R)
ALT **exhibition building**
UF buildings, exhibition
buildings, exposition
buildings, fair
exhibition facilities
exhibition halls
exposition buildings
facilities, exhibition
fair buildings
halls, exhibition
CN V.RK.AFU.ALO.ALO.BCW

exhibition catalogs
VW.115 (L)
ALT **exhibition catalog**
UF catalogs, exhibition
CN V.VW.AFU.AFU.AFU.FZU.ALO.ALO.AXC

exhibition designers
HG.153
ALT **exhibition designer**
UF designers, exhibition
exhibition preparators
preparators, exhibition
CN H.HG.AFU.AXC.AXC.AFU.AFU.ALO.BCW.AXC

exhibition facilities
USE **exhibition buildings**

exhibition grounds
USE **fairgrounds**

exhibition halls
USE **exhibition buildings**

exhibition preparators
USE **exhibition designers**

exhibition records
VW.1055
ALT **exhibition record**
UF records, exhibition
CN V.VW.AFU.ARI.ALO.BUE.AFU

exhibition reviews
VW.309
ALT **exhibition review**
UF reviews, exhibition
CN V.VW.AFU.AFU.ALO.BCW.ARI.ALO

exhibition texts
USE **exhibit scripts**

exhibitions
KM.64 (A,L,B,R)
SN Organized displays, especially of works of art or objects of manufacture. (W)
UF expositions
shows (exhibitions)
CN K.KM.AFU.BUE

exhibitions, garden
USE **garden shows**

exhibitions, traveling
USE **traveling exhibitions**

existentialism
BM.511 (L,R)
CN B.BM.BIQ.AXC.BUE

existing light photography
USE **available light photography**

exit devices, panic
USE **panicproof locks**

exit lights
RT.1367
ALT **exit light**
UF lights, exit
CN V.RT.ALO.AXC.ALO.ARI

exits
RT.986 (A,B)
ALT **exit**
SN Openings used solely to leave a building, room, or other enclosed area.
CN V.RT.AFU.ARI.AFU.ALO.ALO

exits, emergency
USE **emergency exits**

exits, fire
USE **emergency exits**

exodus, rural
USE **rural-urban migration**

exonarthexes
RM.325
ALT **exonarthex**
SN The outer narthexes where there is also an inner narthex (the esonarthex).
CN V.RM.AFU.DIO.AXC.ALO.AFU.DCU.ALO

exoticism
BM.350 (A,L,R)
SN Interest in or adoption of the exotic. (W)
CN B.BM.ALO.ALO.CLM.CFS

expandable dining tables
USE **extension dining tables**

expandable structures
USE **air-supported structures**

expanded glass
USE **cellular glass**

expanded metal
MT.475 (L)
UF metal, expanded
CN M.MT.AFU.AFU.AFU.BZY.ALO.AXC

expanded metal lath, flat
USE **diamond mesh lath**

expanded plastic
USE **plastic foam**

expanded views
USE **exploded drawings**

expanding cement
MT.40 (L)
SN Cement which when mixed with water forms a paste that tends to increase in volume after setting to a significantly greater degree than portland cement paste does; used to compensate for volume decrease due to shrinkage or to induce tensile stress in reinforcement. (DAC)
UF cement, expanding
cement, expansive
cement, sulfoaluminate
expansive cement
sulfoaluminate cement
CN M.MT.AFU.AFU.AFU.ALO.AFU.ALO.ARI

expanding concrete
USE **expansive concrete**

expanding tables, capstan
USE **capstan tables**

expanding vaults
RT.544
ALT **expanding vault**
SN Vaults that are larger at one end than at the other. (RS)
UF conical vaults
vaults, conical
vaults, expanding
CN V.RT.AFU.AFU.AFU.BIQ.BOK.AFU.ALO.ALO

expansion
KT.914 (L,B)
ALT **expanded**
SN The increase in length or volume of a material, or a body, caused by temperature, moisture, or other environmental condition. (DAC)
UF expansion, heat
expansion, thermal
heat expansion
thermal expansion
CN K.KT.ALO.BUE.ALO

expansion bits
TB.1104
ALT **expansion bit**
SN Drilling bits whose blade can be adjusted to bore holes of different diameters. (MEANS)
UF bits, expansion
CN V.TB.ALO.ARI.BIQ

expansion bolts
TF.311
ALT **expansion bolt**
SN Anchoring or fastening devices used in masonry, which expand within a predrilled hole as a bolt is tightened. (MEANS)
UF bolts, expansion
CN V.TF.AFU.AFU.AFU.ALO.AFU.ALO.AFU.AXC

expansion bolts, star
USE **star expansion bolts**

expansion joints
TF.605 (L,B)
ALT **expansion joint**
SN Joints that allow for expansion of two adjacent parts of a structure.
UF joints, expansion
CN V.TF.ALO.ALO.ARI

expansion, heat
USE **expansion**

expansion, thermal
USE **expansion**

expansive cement
USE **expanding cement**

expansive concrete
MT.222 (A,L)
UF concrete, expanding
concrete, expansive
expanding concrete
CN M.MT.AFU.AFU.AFU.BCW.AFU.AXC.AFU

expatriates
HG.790
ALT **expatriate**
SN Use for persons who have withdrawn voluntarily from their native country, especially those who have renounced allegiance to it. For persons who have fled their native country or country of residence to escape danger or persecution, use **refugees.**
CN H.HG.AFU.BOK.BCW

expatriation
BM.535 (L,R)
CN B.BM.BOK.BCW

expeditions
KM.92 (R)
CN K.KM.AFU.CLM.AFU

experiment stations
RK.1169 (L)
ALT **experiment station**
SN Use for buildings or outdoor facilities where research and experiments are carried out in a specific field, such as agriculture or mining, where practical applications are tested, and from where the results are disseminated. Distinct from **research stations** which are primarily for the observation of natural phenomena.
UF stations, experiment
CN V.RK.AFU.ALO.ALO.FIM.ALO.AFU.CFS

experimental buildings
RK.1375
ALT **experimental building**
UF buildings, experimental
CN V.RK.AFU.ALO.AXC.ARI

experimental plants
USE **pilot plants**

experimenting
KG.21 (L)
SN Testing an hypothesis or model systematically under controlled conditions to discover its qualities, behavior, or effects.
CN K.KG.AFU.AFU.AFU.CLM

expertizing
KG.20 (L,R)
SN Giving an expert or professional opinion, usually after careful study or examination.
CN K.KG.AFU.AFU.AFU.CFS.AFU

experts
HG.764

ALT **expert**
SN People with the special skill or knowledge representing mastery of a particular subject. (WCOL)
CN H.HG.AFU.BIQ.ARI

exploded drawings
VD.5
ALT **exploded drawing**
SN Use for drawings that show the components of a structure or object disassembled and spaced apart, but remaining in their proper relation with respect to their assembled positions.
UF drawings, exploded
expanded views
exploded views
views, expanded
views, exploded
CN V.VD.AFU.AFU.ARI

exploded views
USE **exploded drawings**

explorers
HG.718 (L,R)
ALT **explorer**
CN H.HG.AFU.BCW.CFS

explosive actuated guns
USE **stud guns**

explosives
MT.2584 (L,R)
CN M.MT.AFU.ARI.DIO

export porcelain, Chinese
USE **Chinese export porcelain**

exporters
HG.416
ALT **exporter**
CN H.HG.AFU.AXC.BOK.DCU

exporting
KG.167 (R)
CN K.KG.AFU.ALO.AFU.ARI

exposed hinges
TF.141
ALT **exposed hinge**
UF hinges, exposed
CN V.TF.AFU.AFU.AFU.AFU.CLM.ARI.ALO

exposed joints
TF.638
ALT **exposed joint**
UF joints, exposed
CN V.TF.ALO.ARI.ALO.ALO.AXC

exposition buildings
USE **exhibition buildings**

expositions
USE **exhibitions**

expositions, industrial
USE **industrial expositions**

exposure meters
USE **light meters**

express highways
USE **expressways**

express roads
USE **expressways**

expression
BM.35
CN B.BM.AFU.AFU.ALO.BIQ

Expressionist
FL.3254 (A,L,B,R)
ALT **Expressionism**
CN F.FL.ALO.BCW.ALO.AXC.AXC

Expressionist, Abstract
USE **Abstract Expressionist**

Expressionist, New
USE **Neo-Expressionist**

expressways
RK.1520 (L,B)
ALT **expressway**
SN Use for divided multilane highways with a minimum of traffic signals where grades are separated at important intersections, although there may be some grade crossings; can be freeways or turnpikes.
UF express highways
express roads
highways, express
roads, express
skyways
speedways
CN V.RK.ALO.ALO.BIQ.ARI.AFU.AFU.ARI.AFU.AFU

expropriation
USE **eminent domain**

extended care facilities
RK.749 (L)
ALT **extended care facility**
UF care facilities, extended
care facilities, long-term
facilities, extended care
facilities, long-term care
long-term care facilities
CN V.RK.AFU.ALO.ALO.CXA.ALO.AFU.AXC

extender white pigment
USE **transparent white pigment**

extenders
MT.2593
CN M.MT.AFU.ARI.DZW.ALO

extending tables
USE **extension dining tables**

extension bolts
USE **extension flush bolts**

extension dining tables
TG.724
ALT **extension dining table**
SN Dining tables with extending frames whose tops can be lengthened by inserting loose leaves.
UF dining-room tables
dining tables, expandable
dining tables, extension
dining tables, imperial
expandable dining tables
extending tables
extension tables
imperial dining tables
tables, dining-room
tables, expandable dining
tables, extension dining
tables, imperial dining
CN V.TG.AFU.AFU.BIQ.BOK.ALO.BZY.AFU

extension fire screens
TG.6
ALT **extension fire screen**
UF fire screens, extension
screens, extension fire
CN V.TG.AFU.AFU.AFU.AFU.ALO

extension flush bolts
TF.167
ALT **extension flush bolt**
SN Flush bolts whose heads connect to the operating mechanism via a rod which is inserted through a hole bored in the door. (MEANS)
UF bolts, extension
bolts, extension flush
extension bolts
flush bolts, extension
CN V.TF.AFU.AFU.AFU.AFU.DIO.ARI.AXC

extension keys
USE **adjustable keys**

extension ladders
TB.481
ALT **extension ladder**
SN Ladders comprising more than one section, each of which slides within the other and locks on the other, thus allowing lengthening. (MEANS)
UF ladders, extension
CN V.TB.AFU.ARI.ERE.ALO.ARI

extension tables
USE **extension dining tables**

extensions (additions)
USE **additions**

extensions (building divisions)
USE **wings (building divisions)**

exterior
DC.33 (B)
SN Connected with or situated at the outside or outer part of something. (W)
UF outside
CN D.DC.AFU.ALO.ARI.BUE

exterior elevations
VD.23
ALT **exterior elevation**
UF elevations, exterior
external elevations

CN V.VD.AFU.AFU.BIQ.ALO.ALO.AFU

exterior lighting
RT.1374 (A,L)
UF lighting, exterior
lighting, outdoor
outdoor lighting
CN V.RT.ALO.AXC.AXC.AFU

exterior perspectives
VD.80
ALT **exterior perspective**
UF elevations, perspective
perspective elevations
perspectives, exterior
CN V.VD.AFU.AFU.BIQ.ARI.AFU

exterior profiles (ships)
USE **outboard profiles**

exterior views
VB.24
ALT **exterior view**
SN Use for photographs or other representations of the exterior of a building or other structure.
UF external views
views, exterior
CN V.VB.AFU.AFU.BOK.ALO.BCW

exterior walls
RT.594 (A,L,B)
ALT **exterior wall**
SN Walls which are part of the building envelope, thereby having one face exposed to the weather or to earth. (DAC)
UF external walls
periphery walls
walls, exterior
walls, external
walls, periphery
CN V.RT.AFU.AFU.AFU.BIQ.BUE.AFU.
ARI.ALO

external elevations
USE **exterior elevations**

external views
USE **exterior views**

external walls
USE **exterior walls**

extinguishers, fire
USE **fire extinguishers**

extra-rapid-hardening cement
USE **high-early-strength cement**

Extra Terramaricolan
USE **Apennine**

extractors, staple
USE **staple pullers**

extraditing
KG.196 (L)
SN Turning over a criminal suspect to another state or province in the country, the national government, or a foreign country. (RLG7)
CN K.KG.AFU.ALO.BCW.ARI

extradosed arches
RT.251
ALT **extradosed arch**
SN Use for arches with a clearly marked extrados more or less parallel to the intrados.
UF arches, extradosed
CN V.RT.AFU.AFU.AFU.BCW.AFU.AFU.
AFU.ELK.ARI

extradoses
RT.682
ALT **extradose**
SN The outer surfaces of vaults or arches.
CN V.RT.AFU.AFU.ALO.AFU.AFU

extraterrestrial bases
RK.1360 (L)
ALT **extraterrestrial base**
SN Use only for manned installations established on natural extraterrestrial bodies for specific functions. For larger communites established in space or on natural extraterrestrial bodies use **space colonies.** For manned artificial satellites set to revolve in a fixed orbit and serving as a base for specific functions, use **space stations.**
UF bases, extraterrestrial
bases, space
space bases
CN V.RK.AFU.ALO.ARI.AXC.AXC.AFU

extraterrestrial structures
RK.1359 (B)
ALT **extraterrestrial structure**
UF structures, extraterrestrial
CN V.RK.AFU.ALO.ARI.AXC.AXC

extreme unction
KM.37 (L,R)
SN Formal religious act consisting of anointment with oil and the recitation of prayer, administered by a priest to a person in imminent danger of dying. (RHDEL2)
UF unction, extreme
CN K.KM.AFU.ARI.AXC.BUE

extruded plastic
MT.2108
UF plastic, extruded
CN M.MT.AFU.AFU.ARI.BUE.ALO.ARI.
AFU

extruding
USE **extrusion**

extrusion
KT.141 (L)
ALT **extruded**
SN The process of shaping a heated or unheated material, such as plastic or metal, by forcing or pressing it through a dye or other shaping device.
UF extruding
CN K.KT.AFU.ALO.DOI.BUE

extrusion blown plastic
MT.2109
UF plastic, extrusion blown
CN M.MT.AFU.AFU.ARI.BUE.ALO.ARI.
AFU.AFU

extrusive rock
USE **volcanic rock**

exurbs
RD.61
ALT **exurb**
SN Small, usually prosperous, communities situated beyond the suburbs of a city. (RHDEL2)
CN V.RD.AFU.BCW.AFU

Eyak
FL.1341 (L)
CN F.FL.ALO.ALO.ARI.AFU.BIQ.BUE

eye bolts
TF.313 (N)
ALT **eye bolt**
SN Anchoring devices comprising a threaded shank with a lopped head designed to accept a hook, cable, or rope. (MEANS)
UF bolts, eye
CN V.TF.AFU.AFU.AFU.ALO.AFU.ALO.
AFU.BCW

eye-catchers
RK.1332
ALT **eye-catcher**
SN Use for decorative features often seen in silhouette and generally placed on a distant eminence as part of an overall landscape design.
CN V.RK.AFU.ALO.ARI.AFU.ALO

eye hospitals
RK.765 (A,L,B)
ALT **eye hospital**
UF hospitals, eye
hospitals, opthalmic
ophthalmic hospitals
CN V.RK.AFU.ALO.ALO.CXA.ALO.AFU.
BCW.ALO.AXC

eye-level views
VB.25
ALT **eye-level view**
UF street-level views
views, eye-level
views, street-level
CN V.VB.AFU.AFU.BOK.ALO.BIQ

eye tongs
USE **hammer tongs**

eyebrow dormers
RT.478
ALT **eyebrow dormer**
SN Low dormers in a roof over which the roof is carried in a wavy line. (PUTNAM)
UF dormers, eyebrow

dormers, swept
swept dormers
CN V.RT.AFU.AFU.AFU.BIQ.ARI.ALO.AFU.BUE.AXC.ARI

eyelets (grommets)
USE **grommets**

eyelets (windows)
USE **loopholes**

eyesight
USE **sight**

fables
BM.271 (L,R)
CN B.BM.AFU.ARI.BIQ.AXC.AFU

fabric
USE **cloth**
textiles

fabricated chalk
MT.46
UF chalk, fabricated
CN M.MT.AFU.AFU.AFU.ARI.ALO

fabrics, textile
USE **textiles**

fabulists
HG.185
ALT **fabulist**
SN Writers of fables, especially those that carry a moral lesson. (W)
CN H.HG.AFU.AXC.AXC.ARI.AFU.AFU.BCW

facade oblique drawings
USE **elevation oblique drawings**

facade pavilions
USE **pavilions (building divisions)**

facades
RT.596 (A,L,B,R)
ALT **facade**
SN Use for those exterior faces of a building which are substantially in one plane and seem to have been designed with special regard to their conspicuousness or association with entrance. Distinct from **elevations (building divisions)**, which may constitute any side or face of a building or large interior space.
UF fronts (facades)
CN V.RT.AFU.AFU.AFU.BIQ.BUE.AFU.ARI.ALO.AFU.AFU

facades, flying
USE **false fronts**

facades, screen
USE **screen facades**

face brick
MT.99 (L)
UF brick, face
brick, facing
facing brick
CN M.MT.AFU.AFU.AFU.AXC.ALO.AFU.ALO.BIQ

face hammers
TB.605 (N)
ALT **face hammer**
SN Heavy hammers having flat faces, with one blunt end and one cutting end; used for rough dressing of blocks of quarried stone. (PUTNAM)
UF hammers, face
CN V.TB.AFU.BCW.BCW.ALO.EFQ.AXC

face joints
TF.639
ALT **face joint**
SN Visible joints on the surface of a masonry wall. (MEANS)
UF joints, face
CN V.TF.ALO.ARI.ALO.ALO.BCW

face strings
RT.1125
ALT **face string**
SN Outer strings on stairs, usually of better material or finish than the carriage pieces which they cover; may be part of the actual construction or applied to the face of the supporting member. (HAS)
UF finish strings
outer strings
stringboards
strings, face
strings, finish
strings, outer
CN V.RT.AFU.BIQ.AXC.ALO.BOK.AFU

faced walls
RT.578
ALT **faced wall**
SN Combination walls in which the masonry facing and the backing are so bonded as to exert a common reaction under load. (PUTNAM)
UF walls, faced
CN V.RT.AFU.AFU.AFU.BIQ.BUE.AFU.AFU.BOK

faces (lock components)
TF.564
ALT **face (lock component)**
SN Parts of mortise locks that show at the edge of a door through which a latch bolt or dead bolt projects. (DIT-TRI)
CN V.TF.AFU.ALO.AXC.BCW

Facet Cubist
USE **Analytical Cubist**

facilities management
USE **facility management**

facilities, administrative
USE **administration buildings**

facilities, agricultural
USE **agricultural buildings**

facilities, assembly
USE **assembly halls**

facilities, athletic
USE **sports complexes**

facilities, business
USE **commercial buildings**

facilities, commercial
USE **commercial buildings**

facilities, communications
USE **communications buildings**

facilities, conference
USE **convention centers**

facilities, congress
USE **convention centers**

facilities, correctional
USE **correctional institutions**

facilities, desalination
USE **desalination plants**

facilities, detention
USE **detention centers**

facilities, domestic
USE **dwellings**

facilities, educational
USE **educational complexes**

facilities, employees'
USE **employees' buildings**

facilities, entertainment
USE **entertainment buildings**

facilities, exhibition
USE **exhibition buildings**

facilities, extended care
USE **extended care facilities**

facilities, health
USE **health facilities**

facilities, horticultural
USE **horticultural buildings**

facilities, industrial
USE **industrial buildings**

facilities, long-term care
USE **extended care facilities**

facilities, medical
USE **health facilities**

facilities, mental health
USE **mental health facilities**

facilities, mercantile
USE **mercantile buildings**

facilities, military
USE **military buildings**

facilities, recreation
USE **recreation areas**
recreation buildings

facilities, religious
USE **religious buildings**

facilities, research
USE **research buildings**

facilities, residential
USE **dwellings**

facilities, resource recovery
USE **resource recovery facilities**

facilities, school
USE schools

facilities, sports
USE **sports buildings**
sports complexes

facilities, storage
USE **storage facilities**

facilities, teaching
USE **schools**

facilities, terminal care
USE **terminal care facilities**

facilities, transportation
USE **transportation buildings**

facilities, vocational education
USE **vocational schools**

facilities, welfare
USE **welfare buildings**

facility management
KG.140 (A,L)
SN Use for the practice of coordinating the physical workplace with the workflow of an organization.
UF facilities management
FM
management, facility
CN K.KG.AFU.AFU.BIQ.AFU.AFU

facing
KT.48
ALT **faced**
CN K.KT.AFU.ALO.BCW.AXC

facing brick
USE **face brick**

facing tile
USE **wall tile**

facsimiles
VB.120 (L,R)
ALT **facsimile**
SN Use for precise reproductions, usually in the same dimensions as the original, especially of books, documents, prints, and drawings. Today often reproduced photographically, in the past, by engravings or other prints.
CN V.VB.ALO.BZY.AFU.AXC.AFU

factitious negatives
USE **clichés-verre**

factories
RK.613 (A,L,N,B,R)
ALT **factory**
UF buildings, factory
factory buildings
industrial plants
mills (factories)
plants (factories)
plants, industrial
works (factories)
CN V.RK.AFU.ALO.ALO.CLM.ALO.ALO

factories, automobile
USE **automobile factories**

factories, food
USE **food processing plants**

factories, furniture
USE **furniture factories**

factories, glass
USE **glass factories**

factories, leather
USE **tanneries**

factories, sugar
USE **sugar refineries**

factories, textile
USE **textile mills**

factories, wine
USE **wineries**

factors, human
USE **human factors**

factors, shape
USE **shape factors**

factory buildings
USE **factories**

factory lumber
MT.1441
UF lumber, factory
lumber, shop
shop lumber
CN M.MT.AFU.AFU.ALO.BIQ.DCU.ALO.BOK.ARI.ARI

factory marks
VW.719
ALT **factory mark**
UF marks, factory
CN V.VW.AFU.ALO.ALO.AFU.AXC.ALO.BOK

factory outlets
USE **outlet stores**

factory sites
USE **industrial sites**

factory towns
USE **industrial towns**

factory villages
RD.53
ALT **factory village**
SN Designates industrial settlements purposely built by factory owners to attract workers to isolated or otherwise undesirable locations with a minimum of services.
UF villages, factory
CN V.RD.AFU.AXC.BIQ.AFU

faculty
USE **teachers**

faculty clubhouses
USE **faculty clubs**

faculty clubs
RK.1197
ALT **faculty club**
UF clubhouses, faculty
clubs, faculty
faculty clubhouses
CN V.RK.AFU.ALO.ALO.FUA.BIQ

faculty papers
VW.1066
ALT **faculty paper**
UF papers, faculty
CN V.VW.AFU.ARI.ALO.CRG.ARI

fading
faded
ALT **fade**
CN K.KT.ALO.BIQ.ALO

Fagus
USE **beech**

Fagus crenata
USE **Siebold's beech**

Fagus englerana
USE **Chinese beech**

Fagus grandifolia
USE **American beech**

Fagus japonica
USE **Japanese beech**

Fagus orientalis
USE **Oriental beech**

Fagus sylvatica
USE **European beech**

faience
MT.152 (A,L,B)
CN M.MT.AFU.AFU.AFU.AXC.ALO.ALO.AFU.ALO.AFU.ARI

faïence and porcelain, Strasbourg
USE **Strasbourg faïence**

faience tile
MT.191 (L)
UF tile, faience
CN M.MT.AFU.AFU.AFU.AXC.ALO.ALO.ALO.AFU.ARI.ALO

faïence, Gurgan
USE **Gurgan ware**

faïence, Haguenau
USE **Haguenau pottery**

faïence, Strasbourg
USE **Strasbourg faïence**

failures, bridge
USE **bridge failures**

failures, building
USE **building failures**

failures, structural
USE **structural failures**

fair buildings
USE **exhibition buildings**

fairgrounds
RK.1490 (A,B)
ALT **fairground**
UF exhibition grounds
CN V.RK.ALO.ALO.BCW.BCW

fairs
KM.65 (L,R)
CN K.KM.AFU.BUE.AFU

fairs, trade
USE **trade shows**

fairs, world's
USE **world's fairs**

faith
BM.683 (L,R)
SN Act or state of wholeheartedly and steadfastly believing in the existence, power and benevolence of a supreme being. (W)
CN B.BM.BZY.ALO.AFU.ARI

Faiyum Neolithic
USE **Fayum A**

fakes
USE **forgeries**

Falasha
FL.638 (L)
CN F.FL.ALO.AFU.AXC.AXC.AXC.ALO

faldesteuils (pliants)
USE **pliants**

faldistoria
USE **faldstools**

faldstools
TG.268
ALT **faldstool**
SN Folding stools, such as those used by a bishop or other prelate. Term also applied to small desks at which one kneels during devotions and to desks from which the litany is read or sung.
UF faldistoria
CN V.TG.AFU.AFU.ALO.AFU.ALO.AXC.AFU.ARI

faldstools (pliants)
USE **pliants**

faldyn tables
USE **occasional tables**

Fali
FL.368 (L)
CN F.FL.ALO.AFU.AXC.AFU.AXC.ALO.ALO

Faliscan ware
FL.2746 (L)
UF ware, Faliscan
CN F.FL.ALO.AXC.ALO.ALO.ALO.BUE.AFU.ARI

fall
USE **autumn**

fall-front desks
TG.534 (N)
ALT **fall-front desk**
SN Desks with a hinged cover that may be lowered to form the writing surface or table. (FAIRB)
UF bureau-cabinets
cabinets, drop-front
desks, drop-front
desks, fall-front
desks, straight-front
drop-front cabinets
drop-front desks
straight-front desks
CN V.TG.AFU.AFU.AXC.ALO.BZY.BUE

fall-leaf tables
USE **dropleaf tables**

fallout shelters
USE **nuclear bomb shelters**

falls
USE **waterfalls**

false Acacia
USE **black locust**

false ceilings
USE **suspended ceilings**

false doors
RT.848
ALT **false door**
SN Representations of doors, inserted to complete a series of doors, or to baffle intruders, or to deceive.
UF blank doors
doors, blank
doors, false
doors, sham
sham doors
CN V.RT.AFU.ARI.AFU.AFU.AFU.ALO.ARI.AFU.AFU.ARI

false fronts
RT.597
ALT **false front**
SN Use for facades extending beyond and especially above the dimensions of a building with the specific purpose of giving a more imposing appearance; for facades which exceed the height or width of buildings but not with that intention, use **screen facades.**
UF facades, flying
flying facades
fronts, false
CN V.RT.AFU.AFU.AFU.BIQ.BUE.AFU.ARI.ALO.AFU.AFU.AFU

false perspective
BM.150
UF perspective, false
CN B.BM.AFU.AFU.ARI.BOK.BZY.ALO

false thatched roofs
RT.425
ALT **false thatched roof**
SN Use for shingled roofs with inward curvature at the eaves and other features causing them to resemble thatched roofs; popular in the early 20th century.
UF roofs, false thatched
thatched roofs, false
CN V.RT.AFU.AFU.AFU.BIQ.ARI.AFU.AFU.AFU.BOK.ALO

false windows
RT.921 (B)
ALT **false window**
SN Representations of windows inserted to complete a series of windows. (HAS)
UF blank windows
blind windows
windows, blank
windows, blind
windows, false
CN V.RT.AFU.ARI.AFU.AFU.BOK.AFU.AFU.BZY

falsework
TB.18 (B)
SN Use for the temporary framework used to support a structure under construction until it is self-supporting. Distinct from **scaffolds** which are temporary structures for holding workers and materials.
CN V.TB.AFU.ARI.AFU.AFU.AFU

families
HG.881 (L,R)
ALT **family**
SN Groups of individuals related by blood, marriage, adoption, or cohabitation. (ERIC)
CN H.HG.ALO.DOI.AFU.ALO

family archives
USE **family papers**

family histories
VW.331 (L)
ALT **family history**
SN Histories of groups of persons sharing a common lineage. (GAHLM)
UF histories, family
CN V.VW.AFU.AFU.ALO.CRG.ARI

family papers
VW.1060 (L)
ALT **family paper**
SN Group of the personal papers of several and various members of a single family; usually of parents and their children, but sometimes including

papers of spouses and their families as well. (GAHLM)
UF archives, family
family archives
family records
papers, family
records, family
CN V.VW.AFU.ARI.ALO.CFS.AFU

family planning clinics
USE **birth control clinics**

family records
USE **family papers**

family rooms
RM.171 (L)
ALT **family room**
SN Informal living rooms, often adjacent to the kitchen, where a family may gather.
UF rooms, family
CN V.RM.AFU.DIO.ALO.CXA.BIQ

family trees
USE **genealogical tables**

fan-back chairs
TG.130
ALT **fan-back chair**
SN Descriptive term for a type of common chair, presumably with a fan-shaped splat. (GILBER)
UF chairs, fan-back
CN V.TG.AFU.AFU.ALO.AFU.AFU.AFU.NIE.BCW

fan-back Windsor chairs
TG.100
ALT **fan-back Windsor chair**
SN Windsor side chairs having a back of medium height, approximating a partailly opened fan, with the back spindles crowned by a crest rail curved laterally to follow the outside curve of the seat back and supported at the ends by heavy turned back posts. The form sometimes has an extended back and arms terminating in the back post. Such chairs usually have a back brace. (EVANS)
UF chairs, fan-back Windsor
Windsor chairs, fan-back
CN V.TG.AFU.AFU.ALO.AFU.AFU.AFU.MLC.AXC

fan Fink trusses
RT.363
ALT **fan Fink truss**
UF fan trusses
Fink trusses, fan
trusses, fan
trusses, fan Fink
CN V.RT.AFU.AFU.AFU.BCW.CLM.AFU.AFU.AFU.AXC.AFU

fan groining
USE **fan vaults**

fan-shaped
DC.65
CN D.DC.AFU.ARI.BZY

fan trusses
USE **fan Fink trusses**

fan vaults
RT.551 (A)
ALT **fan vault**
SN Vaults consisting or solid concave-sided semi-cones, meeting or nearly meeting at the apex of the vault, the areas between cones being flat, and the whole being given a highly decorative treatment with ribs that fan out from the vault's springing. (PDARC)
UF fan groining
groining, fan
vaults, fan
CN V.RT.AFU.AFU.AFU.BIQ.BOK.AFU.ARI.AFU.ALO.AFU

fan windows
USE **fanlights**

Fancy
FL.1744
SN Use with reference to 19th-century American painted furniture decorated in imitation of imported Neoclassical models.
UF Chamber (Fancy)
CN F.FL.ALO.ALO.BCW.AFU.BZY.ARI

fancy backsaws
USE **bead saws**

fanes
USE **temples**

Fang (Pahouin)
FL.411 (L)
CN F.FL.ALO.AFU.AXC.ALO.AFU.ARI.ARI

fanlights
RT.959 (A,N,B)
ALT **fanlight**
SN Semicircular windows over the opening of a door, with radiating bars in the form of an open fan. (HAS)
UF fan windows
lights, sunburst
sunburst lights
windows, fan
CN V.RT.AFU.ARI.AFU.AFU.BOK.AFU.ARI.ALO

fans, alluvial
USE **alluvial fans**

fantail tools
USE **fishtail tools**

fantastic architecture
BM.223 (A,B,R)
UF architecture, fantastic
architecture, imaginary
imaginary architecture
CN B.BM.AFU.ARI.AXC.ALO

fantastic art
BM.243 (R)
UF art, fantastic
art, visionary
visionary art
CN B.BM.AFU.ARI.BCW.DCU

Fantastic Realist
FL.3725 (R)
ALT **Fantastic Realism**
UF Phantastischer Realismus
Realist, Fantastic
CN F.FL.ALO.BUE.ARI.CFS

fantasy
BM.30 (L,R)
CN B.BM.AFU.AFU.ALO.ARI.AFU.AFU

fantasy finishes
USE **faux finishes**

Fanti
FL.290 (L)
CN F.FL.ALO.AFU.AXC.AFU.ARI.AFU.AFU.BCW

farm buildings
RK.58 (A,L,N,B,R)
ALT **farm building**
SN Use for buildings on farms, not limited to agricultural buildings.
UF buildings, farm
CN V.RK.AFU.ALO.ALO.AFU.AFU.ARI

farm complexes
USE **farms**

farm museums
USE **agriculture museums**

farmers
HG.361 (L,R)
ALT **farmer**
CN H.HG.AFU.AXC.BIQ.ALO.AXC.AFU.AFU

farmers' markets
KM.151
UF markets, farmers'
CN K.KM.AFU.ELK.ARI.AFU

farmers, nursery
USE **nurserymen**

farmhouses
RK.296 (A,L,B)
ALT **farmhouse**
CN V.RK.AFU.ALO.ALO.AXC.ALO.AXC.AFU.AFU.ALO

farming villages
USE **agricultural settlements**

farmland
RD.286
CN V.RD.ARI.ALO.AFU.AFU.AXC

farms
RG.4 (A,L,R)
ALT **farm**
UF farm complexes
farmsteads
CN V.RG.AFU.AFU.AFU.AFU

farms, abandoned
USE **abandoned farms**

farms, collective
USE **collective farms**

farms, dairy
USE **dairy farms**

farms, health
USE **health resorts**

farms, historic
USE **historic farms**

farms, poor
USE **almshouses**

farms, school
USE **school farms**

farms, sheep
USE **sheep farms**

farms, tank
USE **tank farms**

farms, tree
USE **tree farms**

farms, wind
USE **wind power plants**

farmsteads
USE **farms**

farmyards
RK.1603 (B)
ALT **farmyard**
UF bartons
CN V.RK.ALO.ARI.CRG.ARI

farrier's pincers
TB.219 (N)
UF carpenter's pincers
pincers, carpenter's
pincers, farrier's
CN V.TB.AFU.ARI.CFS.ARI.AFU

farriers
HG.498
ALT **farrier**
SN Persons who shoe horses or make horseshoes. (OED)
UF ferrers
CN H.HG.AFU.AXC.BUE.ARI.CFS.AFU.BCW.AFU.AFU

farthingale chairs
TG.33
ALT **farthingale chair**
SN Modern name for a type of Elizabethan chair with a wide but not very deep seat, low back, and no arms. Erroneously assumed that they were made to accommodate the fashionable wide hooped dresses called farthingales.
UF backstools, upholstered joined
chairs, farthingale
joined backstools, upholstered
upholstered joined backstools
CN V.TG.AFU.AFU.ALO.AFU.AFU.AFU.AXC.AFU

fascia boards
USE **eaves fascias**

fascia rafters
USE **bargeboards**

fascias
RT.734 (B,R)
ALT **fascia**
SN Use for the flat strips on Ionic and Corinthian friezes. For boards nailed across the ends of rafters in wood construction, use **eaves fascias.**
CN V.RT.AFU.ALO.AFU.AXC

fascias, eaves
USE **eaves fascias**

fascism
BM.557 (L,R)
SN Any regime with severely nationalistic policies exercising regimentation of industry, commerce, and finance, rigid censorship, and oppression of opposition. (W)
CN B.BM.BOK.BZY.AXC

fashion
BM.331 (L,R)
SN A prevailing usually short lived custom, usage, or style. (W)
CN B.BM.ALO.ALO.ARI

fashion artists
USE **fashion illustrators**

fashion design
KT.100 (L)
SN Designing clothing, accessories, and ensembles for personal wear. For the design of clothing, accessories, and ensembles intended to create an appearance characteristic of a particular period, person, place, or thing, especially (but not exclusively) for theatrical performances, use **costume design.**
UF design, dress (fashion design)
design, fashion
dress design (fashion design)
CN K.KT.AFU.ALO.CFS.BCW

fashion designers
HG.154 (L)
ALT **fashion designer**
SN Persons engaged in fashion design.
UF clothes designers
couturiers
designers, clothes
designers, dress (fashion designers)
designers, fashion
dress designers (fashion designers)
CN H.HG.AFU.AXC.AXC.AFU.AFU.ALO.BCW.BCW

fashion drawing
USE **fashion illustration**

fashion illustration
KT.205 (L,R)
SN The activity of drawing or painting illustrations of apparel and accessories, especially for advertisement. (DOT)
UF drawing, fashion
fashion drawing
illustration, fashion
CN K.KT.AFU.ALO.DUC.CLM.ARI

fashion illustrations
VB.48 (L,R)
ALT **fashion illustration**
UF illustrations, fashion
CN V.VB.AFU.ALO.AXC.ALO.ALO

fashion illustrators
HG.146 (L)
ALT **fashion illustrator**
SN Persons who engage in fashion illustration.
UF artists, fashion
fashion artists
illustrators, fashion
CN H.HG.AFU.AXC.AXC.AFU.AFU.ALO.BCW.AFU.ALO.ALO.ALO

fashion photography
KT.299 (L,R)
UF photography, fashion
CN K.KT.AFU.ALO.DUC.DIO.AFU.BUE

fast blue, Monastral
USE **phthalocyanine blue**

fast food restaurants
RK.117 (A,L,B)
ALT **fast food restaurant**
UF quick-service restaurants
restaurants, fast food
restaurants, quick-service
CN V.RK.AFU.ALO.ALO.ALO.AFU.AXC.BIQ

fast-pin hinges
TF.110
ALT **fast-pin hinge**
SN Hinges each having a pin fixed permanently in place. (MEANS)
UF hinges, fast-pin
hinges, tight pin
tight pin hinges
CN V.TF.AFU.AFU.AFU.AFU.CLM.AFU.CFS

fastener nails, hoop
USE **hoop fastener nails**

fasteners
TF.287 (A,L)
ALT **fastener**
SN Mechanical devices for holding together two or more pieces, parts, or members. (DAC)
CN V.TF.AFU.AFU.AFU.ALO.AFU

fasteners, casement-window
USE **casement-window fasteners**

fasteners, chain door
USE **chain door fasteners**

fasteners, hammer
USE **hammer fasteners**

fasteners, hook-and-eye
USE **hook-and-eye fasteners**

fasteners, sash
USE **window locks**

fasteners, skotch
USE **skotch fasteners**

fastening
KT.49
ALT **fastened**
CN K.KT.AFU.ALO.BCW.BCW

Fastnacht
USE **Carnival**

fasts
KM.70 (L,R)
CN K.KM.AFU.BZY

fasts, sash
USE **window locks**

fat
MT.1004 (L)
CN M.MT.AFU.AFU.ALO.AXC.BOK.AFU

fat boards
USE **hawks**

fat lime
MT.330
UF lime, fat
lime, rich
rich lime
CN M.MT.AFU.AFU.AFU.BUE.ALO.AFU

fat mortar
MT.2601
UF mortar, fat
mortar, rich
rich mortar
CN M.MT.AFU.ARI.DZW.ARI.AFU.AXC.AFU

fat over lean technique
KT.225
SN The practice of applying layers of color rich in oil over an underpainting that contains less oil and is therefore less flexible. (MAYER)
CN K.KT.AFU.ALO.DUC.CXA.ALO.AFU.BCW

fathers
HG.13 (L,R)
ALT **father**
CN H.HG.AFU.ALO.ALO.AFU

fatigue of materials
USE **fatigue strength**

fatigue strength
BM.960 (L)
SN Highest stress that a material can withstand for a given number of cycles without breaking. (W)
UF fatigue of materials
strength, fatigue
CN B.BM.CFS.AXC.BZY.BOK.CLM.ALO

Fatimid
FL.3442 (A,R)
CN F.FL.ALO.BIQ.AFU.BUE

fatty acid
MT.297 (L)
UF acid, fatty
CN M.MT.AFU.AFU.AFU.BOK.AFU.ARI

faubourgs
USE **suburbs**

fauces
RM.91
ALT **faux**
SN Ancient Roman entrance passages leading from the street into buildings, usually houses.
CN V.RM.AFU.DIO.ALO.ARI.AXC.ARI

faucets
TF.53 (N)
ALT **faucet**
UF bib taps
bibcocks
bibs
taps, bib
taps, water
water taps
CN V.TF.AFU.AFU.AFU.AFU.BUE

Faulkner
FL.834
CN F.FL.ALO.ALO.ALO.AFU.ALO.ALO.ARI.AFU.ALO

faults
RD.180 (L)
ALT **fault**
CN V.RD.ARI.AFU.AXC.AFU.AFU.AFU.ALO

Fauresmith
FL.53
CN F.FL.ALO.AFU.AFU.ALO.ALO.AFU

fauteuils
TG.26
ALT **fauteuil**
SN French chairs with open arms.
CN V.TG.AFU.AFU.ALO.AFU.AFU.AFU.ALO.ALO.AFU

fauteuils à joues
USE **fauteuils à orielles**

fauteuils à la reine
TG.135
ALT **fauteuil à la reine**
SN Fauteuils with flat backs; distinct from **fauteuils en cabriolet**, which have concave backs.
CN V.TG.AFU.AFU.ALO.AFU.AFU.AFU.NIE.BOK.ARI

fauteuils à orielles
TG.62
ALT **fauteuil à oreilles**
UF fauteuils à joues
fauteuils à oriellettes
fauteuils en confessional
CN V.TG.AFU.AFU.ALO.AFU.AFU.AFU.FZU.ALO

fauteuils à oriellettes
USE **fauteuils à orielles**

fauteuils à panneaux
USE **bergères**

fauteuils de bidet
USE **commode chairs**

fauteuils de bureau
TG.177
ALT **fauteuil de bureau**
SN Desk chairs with deeply coved backs and usually, but not always, with a projecting central front leg; may have four or five legs. Very often carved. (PC)
UF chaises de table
fauteuils de cabinet
CN V.TG.AFU.AFU.ALO.AFU.AFU.ALO.BUE.AFU

fauteuils de cabinet
USE **fauteuils de bureau**

fauteuils en bergère
USE **bergères**

fauteuils en cabriolet
TG.129
ALT **fauteuil en cabriolet**
SN Fauteuils with concave backs; distinct from **fauteuils à la reine**, which have flat backs.
CN V.TG.AFU.AFU.ALO.AFU.AFU.AFU.NIE.AXC.ARI

fauteuils en confessional
USE **fauteuils à orielles**

fauteuils en encoignures
USE **corner chairs**

Fauve
FL.3374 (L,R)
ALT **Fauvism**
UF Fauvist
CN F.FL.ALO.BCW.ALO.AXC.DIO.BCW.BCW.ARI

Fauvist
USE **Fauve**

faux finishes
MT.2554
ALT **faux finish**
UF fantasy finishes
finishes, fantasy
finishes, faux
CN M.MT.AFU.ARI.CRG.ARI.ALO.AFU

faux finishing
KT.256

ALT **faux finished**
UF finishing, faux
CN K.KT.AFU.ALO.DUC.CXA.ALO.BCW.ALO

favelas
RG.282
ALT **favela**
SN Use for shantytowns in or near cities in Brazil.
CN V.RG.ALO.AFU.ALO.BCW.ALO.ARI

Fayum A
FL.2774 (L)
UF Faiyum Neolithic
Fayum Neolithic
CN F.FL.ALO.AXC.ALO.ARI.AFU.AFU.AFU.AFU

Fayum Neolithic
USE **Fayum A**

fazendas
USE **haciendas**

fear
BM.576 (L,R)
UF dread
CN B.BM.BUE.ARI.BCW

feasibility studies
KG.25 (L)
SN Investigations to determine the practicability of instituting a larger study, program, or other proposed activity. (ERIC)
UF studies, feasibility
CN K.KG.AFU.AFU.AFU.DCU.AFU

Feast of Dedication
USE **Hanukkah**

Feast of Lights
USE **Hanukkah**

Feast of Tabernacles
USE **Sukkot**

Feast of the Maccabees
USE **Hanukkah**

feasts
KM.8 (L,R)
SN Celebratory occasions, either joyous or solemn, at which elaborate or ritual meals are a central feature.
CN K.KM.AFU.ALO.ALO

feather
MT.924 (L,R)
CN M.MT.AFU.AFU.ALO.AFU.CFS

feather banding
DG.109
SN Decorative inlaid border of contrasting woods cut diagonally across the grain, generally used to finish edges and rims of furniture. (DDA)
UF banding, feather
banding, herringbone
herringbone banding
CN D.DG.AFU.ARI.ALO.ARI.AFU.ALO

feather joints
TF.675
ALT **feather joint**
SN Joints between two squared, closely butted boards made by plowing a groove along the length of each and fitting them with a common tongue. (MEANS)
UF joints, feather
CN V.TF.ALO.ARI.AXC.ALO.ARI

featheredge brick
USE **compass brick**

featheredge rules
TB.590
ALT **featheredge rule**
SN Straight-edged devices used to shape and define angles in plastering. (MEANS)
UF rules, featheredge
CN V.TB.AFU.BCW.BCW.ALO.CXA

feathers (tools)
TB.591 (N)
ALT **feather (tool)**
SN Metal rods used to split rock by driving it into the surface.
CN V.TB.AFU.BCW.BCW.ALO.DCU

featherwork
MT.2742 (L)
CN M.MT.AFU.AXC.ARI

Federal
FL.1727 (A,B,R)
UF American Federal
Classical Revival (North American)
Federal, American
Revival, Classical (North American)
CN F.FL.ALO.ALO.BCW.AFU.BCW

federal aid
BM.392 (A,L)
UF aid, federal
CN B.BM.ARI.CRG.ALO.AFU

federal government
BM.548 (L)
UF government, federal
CN B.BM.BOK.BOK.ALO.AXC

federal government records
VW.1049 (L)
ALT **federal government record**
UF government records, federal
records, federal government
CN V.VW.AFU.ARI.ALO.BCW.ALO.ARI.AFU

federal penitentiaries
USE **federal prisons**

federal prisons
RK.727
ALT **federal prison**
UF federal penitentiaries
penitentiaries, federal
prisons, federal
CN V.RK.AFU.ALO.ALO.CXA.AFU.AXC.ALO.AFU

Federal Reserve banks
RK.130 (L)
ALT **Federal Reserve bank**
UF banks, Federal Reserve
CN V.RK.AFU.ALO.ALO.ALO.ALO.AFU.ARI

Federal, American
USE **Federal**

feed rooms
RM.342
ALT **feed room**
SN Rooms in barns or stables with provisions for feeding horses or other animals.
UF rooms, feed
CN V.RM.AFU.DIO.AXC.ARI.AFU

feeling
USE **sensation**
touch

feelings
USE **emotion**

fees
BM.373 (A,L,B)
SN Compensation often in the form of a fixed charge for professional services or requested exercise of talent or skill. (W)
UF charges
CN B.BM.ARI.AXC.AFU

feet
TG.896
ALT **foot**
SN Terminal elements used on the legs of furniture.
CN V.TG.ALO.DZW.AFU

feet, arrow
USE **therm feet**

feet, ball
USE **ball feet**

feet, ball-and-claw
USE **claw-and-ball feet**

feet, bar
USE **runner feet**

feet, block
USE **block feet**

feet, bootjack
USE **bootjack feet**

feet, bracket
USE **bracket feet**

feet, bulbous
USE **bun feet**

feet, bun
USE **bun feet**

feet, Chinese
USE **bracket feet**

feet, claw
USE **claw feet**

feet, claw-and-ball
USE **claw-and-ball feet**

feet, cloven
USE **hoof feet**

feet, club
USE **club feet**

feet, colt
USE **colt feet**

feet, common bracket
USE **French feet**

feet, connelly
USE **therm feet**

feet, deer-hoof
USE **hoof feet**

feet, disk
USE **pad feet**

feet, dog's paw
USE **dog's paw feet**

feet, dolphin
USE **dolphin feet**

feet, dragon
USE **dragon feet**

feet, drake
USE **trifid feet**

feet, duck
USE **trifid feet**

feet, Dutch
USE **pad feet**
trifid feet

feet, eagle's
USE **claw-and-ball feet**

feet, flared
USE **French feet**

feet, flaring bracket
USE **French feet**

feet, French
USE **French feet**

feet, French scroll
USE **scroll feet**

feet, French (scroll feet)
USE **scroll feet**

feet, Goddard
USE **bracket feet**

feet, haines
USE **therm feet**

feet, hairy paw
USE **hairy paw feet**

feet, hoof
USE **hoof feet**

feet, knulled
USE **scroll feet**

feet, knurl
USE **scroll feet**

feet, knurl toe
USE **scroll feet**

feet, lion's paw
USE **lion's paw feet**

feet, melon
USE **melon feet**

feet, ogee bracket
USE **ogee bracket feet**

feet, onion
USE **bun feet**

feet, pad
USE **pad feet**

feet, paintbrush
USE **Spanish feet**

feet, paw
USE **paw feet**

feet, plinth
USE **therm feet**

feet, pointed shod
USE **pointed shod feet**

feet, Portuguese
USE **Spanish feet**

feet, rat claw
USE **rat claw feet**

feet, retracted claw
USE **retracted claw feet**

feet, runner
USE **runner feet**

feet, scroll
USE **scroll feet**

feet, scrolled toe
USE **scroll feet**

feet, slipper
USE **slipper feet**

feet, snake
USE **snake feet**

feet, spade
USE **therm feet**

feet, Spanish
USE **Spanish feet**

feet, talon and ball
USE **claw-and-ball feet**

feet, tassel
USE **Spanish feet**

feet, tern
USE **scroll feet**

feet, therm
USE **therm feet**

feet, toupie
USE **toupie feet**

feet, trifid
USE **trifid feet**

feet, triphid
USE **trifid feet**

feet, turned spade
USE **therm feet**

feet, turnip
USE **turnip feet**

feet, web
USE **trifid feet**

feet, whorl
USE **scroll feet**

feet, winged claw
USE **winged claw feet**

feldspar
MT.505 (L)
SN A general name for a group of abundant minerals used for vitreous enamels, pottery, tile, and glass in fertilizers, fluxes, for roofing granules, and as an abrasive in soaps and cleaning compounds. (MH)
CN M.MT.AFU.AFU.AFU.CFS.AFU.CRG

feldspar, plagioclase
USE **plagioclase**

feldspathic sandstone
MT.716
UF arkose
sandstone, feldspathic
CN M.MT.AFU.AFU.AFU.DCU.AFU.ALO .AFU.ARI.AFU.ALO.ARI

Fellata
USE **Fulani**

felling axes
TB.839 (N)
ALT **felling ax**
UF axes, felling
CN V.TB.AFU.BCW.CFS.ALO.AFU.AXC. AXC

fellmongers
HG.488
ALT **fellmonger**
SN Persons who remove animal hair, especially wool, from hides in preparation for leathermaking. (W)
CN H.HG.AFU.AXC.BUE.ARI.BZY.ARI

felloe saws
TB.1009 (N)
ALT **felloe saw**
SN Large frame saws used to cut straight or slightly curved pieces of wood; often used by wheelwrights and furniture workers.
UF betty saws
donkey saws
Jesus saws
saws, betty

saws, donkey
saws, felloe
saws, Jesus
saws, up-and-down
up-and-down saws
CN V.TB.AFU.BCW.CFS.ALO.AFU.EWY.BCW.AXC

fellowships
BM.393 (L)
CN B.BM.ARI.CRG.ALO.ALO

felsite
MT.585
CN M.MT.AFU.AFU.AFU.DCU.AFU.AFU.AFU.AFU.AFU.ALO

felt
MT.1866 (L,B,R)
SN Cloth constructed usually of wool and fur fibers often mixed with natural or synthetic fibers by the interlocking of the loose fibers through the action of heat, moisture, chemicals, and pressure without spinning, weaving, or knitting. (W)
CN M.MT.AFU.AFU.ARI.ALO.ALO.ALO.ALO.BZY

felt paper
MT.1928
SN Sheathing papers used on roofs and side walls of buildings as protection against dampness; also used as insulation. Felt paper applied to roofs are usually infused with tar, asphalt, or chemical compounds. (PUTNAM)
UF paper, felt
CN M.MT.AFU.AFU.ARI.ALO.ALO.AXC.ARI.ALO.AFU

felt pens
USE **felt-tip pens**

felt-tip pens
TB.273 (N)
ALT **felt-tip pen**
SN Pens with pointed or blunt felt or nylon tips which make possible a great flexibility of line and ease in control. (MAYER)
UF felt pens
pens, felt
pens, felt-tip
CN V.TB.AFU.ARI.CLM.AFU.ALO.DOI.AXC.AFU

felt, rag
USE **rag felt**

feltwork
MT.2743 (L)
CN M.MT.AFU.AXC.AXC

Felup
FL.339
UF Flup
CN F.FL.ALO.AFU.AXC.AFU.ARI.BIQ.AXC

feminism
BM.353 (L,R)
ALT **feminist**
SN Social and political critical theory and movement asserting the inherent value of women and female characteristics, and working to protect and promote women's rights and interests.
UF movement, women's
movement, women's liberation
rights, women's
women's liberation movement
women's movement
women's rights
CN B.BM.ALO.ALO.CLM.CLM

feminists
HG.752 (L)
ALT **feminist**
CN H.HG.AFU.BCW.HZS.BCW

fences
RM.434 (A,L,N,B,R)
ALT **fence**
CN V.RM.ALO.AFU.BCW

fences, chain link
USE **chain link fences**

fences, electric
USE **electric fences**

fences, picket
USE **picket fences**

fences, rail
USE **rail fences**

fences, snow
USE **snow fences**

fences, sunken
USE **ha-has**

fencing nails
TF.433
ALT **fencing nail**
UF nails, fencing
CN V.TF.AFU.AFU.AFU.ALO.AFU.CFS.ALO.BCW

fender stools
TG.263 (N)
ALT **fender stool**
UF curbs, seat
hearth stools
seat curbs
stools, fender
stools, hearth
CN V.TG.AFU.AFU.ALO.AFU.ALO.ARI.ARI

fenestellas
RT.922
ALT **fenestella**
SN Small glazed openings in a shrine to afford a view of the relics. (HAS)
UF foramina
CN V.RT.AFU.ARI.AFU.AFU.BOK.AFU.AFU.CFS

fenestrae bifores
USE **French doors**

fenestrals
RT.923
ALT **fenestral**
SN Casement or window sashes closed with cloth or translucent paper instead of glass. (W)
CN V.RT.AFU.ARI.AFU.AFU.BOK.AFU.AFU.CLM

fengshui
KT.17 (A,L)
SN Chinese site analysis method that employs geomantic techniques; used especially in determining the placement and design of houses, graves, and gardens.
CN K.KT.AFU.ALO.AXC.AXC.AFU

fens
RD.172 (L)
ALT **fen**
SN Designates waterlogged areas with pondweeds, reeds, and rushes and in which peat is accumulating but the water remains alkaline. Distinct from bogs, in which the peat has reached a higher acidity.
CN V.RD.ARI.AFU.ARI.AXC

feretories
RM.321
ALT **feretory**
SN Use for shrines, often in the form of small chapels, situated behind the altar, where saints' relics are kept.
CN V.RM.AFU.DIO.AXC.ALO.AFU.CRG

fermes ornées
USE **cottages ornés**

ferneries
TG.648
ALT **fernery**
UF planters
CN V.TG.AFU.AFU.BIQ.BCW.ALO.DIO.AFU

ferns
RD.260 (L)
ALT **fern**
UF filicales
CN V.RD.ARI.AFU.BCW.ALO.ALO.AFU.ALO

Ferolia guianensis
USE **satinee**

ferrers
USE **farriers**

ferric processes
USE **iron processes**

ferris wheels
RK.1004 (L,N,R)
ALT **ferris wheel**
SN Amusement devices consisting of a large power-driven wheel made in two parallel sections having seats

suspended between them, the seats maintaining a horizontal position while the wheel rotates in a vertical plane. (W)
UF wheels, ferris
CN V.RK.AFU.ALO.ALO.EWY.AFU.AFU.AFU

ferrite
USE **Mars yellow**

ferrite yellow
USE **Mars yellow**

ferro-concrete
USE **reinforced concrete**

ferro-tannic
USE **ferrogallic process**

ferrogallic process
KT.343
SN An iron process largely used for reproducing technical drawings; produces an image in black. The image is developed out with gallic acid and is fixed by washing in water.
UF blackline process
ferro-tannic
ink process
CN K.KT.AFU.ALO.DUC.DIO.ALO.CRG.ALO

ferroginous bauxite
USE **laterite**

ferroprussiate process
USE **blueprint process**

ferrotype
USE **tintype**

ferrotypes
USE **tintypes**

ferrotyping
KT.413
ALT **ferrotyped**
SN Use for a photographic processing procedure in which a print having a gelatin emulsion layer is dried in contact with a polished surface so that the gelatin retains a highly glazed surface.
CN K.KT.AFU.ALO.DUC.DIO.ARI.AXC.BZY

ferrous alloys
USE **iron alloys**

ferrous metal
USE **iron**

ferrox
USE **Mars yellow**

ferruginous limestone
MT.683
UF limestone, ferruginous
CN M.MT.AFU.AFU.AFU.DCU.AFU.ALO.AFU.ALO.ALO.AFU.ALO.ARI

ferruginous sandstone
MT.717
UF ironstone
red sandstone
redstone
sandstone, ferruginous
sandstone, red
CN M.MT.AFU.AFU.AFU.DCU.AFU.ALO.AFU.ARI.AFU.ALO.AXC

fertilizers
MT.2589 (L,N)
ALT **fertilizer**
CN M.MT.AFU.ARI.DOI

festival marketplaces
RG.41
ALT **festival marketplace**
SN Use for complexes of shops, restaurants, kiosks, and pushcarts featuring music and other entertainment, generally built downtown to revitalize an urban center; coined in the 1970s.
UF marketplaces, festival
CN V.RG.AFU.AFU.AXC.AFU.ALO

festivals
KM.9 (A,L,B,R)
SN Gala occasions devoted to community observances, such as harvests or anniversaries of notable persons; also cultural events consisting typically of a series of performances of works in the arts. (W)
CN K.KM.AFU.ALO.ARI

festoon lamps
USE **festoon lighting**

festoon lighting
RT.1356
SN Use for lighting in which the light sources occur at intervals along a suspended strand.
UF festoon lamps
lamps, festoon
lighting, festoon
CN V.RT.ALO.AXC.AFU.ARI

festoons
DG.55
ALT **festoon**
SN Use for motifs of garlands of flowers, fruit, or foliage hung loosely from two points. Distinct from **swags**, which refers to cloth similarly hung.
UF garlands
CN D.DG.AFU.AFU.DIO.AXC

Festschriften
VW.327 (L,R)
ALT **festschrift**
SN Volumes of learned articles or essays by colleagues and admirers, serving as tributes or memorials, especially to scholars. (AHD)
UF memorial volumes
volumes, memorial
CN V.VW.AFU.AFU.ALO.CLM

fêtes
KM.55
SN Outdoor entertainments on a lavish scale. (W)
CN K.KM.AFU.BOK.ALO

feudalism
BM.559 (L,R)
SN Any social system in which great landlords or overlords exact revenue from the land and also exercise the functions of government in their domain. (W)
CN B.BM.BOK.BZY.BCW

Fia
FL.188
UF Bafia
CN F.FL.ALO.AFU.AXC.AFU.AFU.AFU.ALO.ARI

fiber
MT.1813 (L)
CN M.MT.AFU.AFU.ARI.ALO.AFU

fiber artists
HG.101
ALT **fiber artist**
SN Artists who use fibrous materials to create pictorial or sculptural works of art.
UF artists, fiber
CN H.HG.AFU.AXC.AXC.AFU.AFU.ALO.AXC.BZY

fiber building board
USE **fiberboard**

fiber paper, plant
USE **bark cloth**

fiber reinforced plastic
USE **reinforced plastic**

fiber V
USE **Dacron (TM)**

fiber, animal
USE **animal fiber**

fiber, bast
USE **bast**

fiber, kenaf
USE **kenaf**

fiber, natural
USE **natural fiber**

fiber, palm
USE **palm fiber**

fiber, plant
USE **plant fiber**

fiber, polyester
USE **polyester fiber**

fiber, ramie
USE **ramie**

fiber, sisal
USE **sisal**

fiber, synthetic
USE **synthetic fiber**

fiberboard
MT.1889 (A,L,B)
UF beaverboard
board, fiber
board, fiber building
building board, fiber
fiber building board
CN M.MT.AFU.AFU.ARI.ALO.ALO.ARI

fiberwork
MT.2744 (L,R)
CN M.MT.AFU.AXC.BCW

Fibonacci numbers
BM.820 (L)
UF numbers, Fibonacci
CN B.BM.CFS.ARI.CLM.ALO

fibre, Manila
USE **Manila hemp**

fibro-concrete
MT.202 (A,B)
CN M.MT.AFU.AFU.AFU.BCW.AFU.AFU.BIQ

fibrous plaster
MT.2437
SN Plaster reinforced with fiber (as manila hemp or sisal) or provided with a cloth backing and used chiefly as sheeting, cornice molding, and cover strips. (W)
UF plaster, fibrous
CN M.MT.AFU.ARI.CRG.AFU.AXC.AFU.ALO

fiche
USE **microfiche**

fiction
BM.268 (L)
CN B.BM.AFU.ARI.BIQ.ARI

fiction, science
USE **science fiction**

fictive architecture
BM.225 (R)
SN Use for painted simulation of architectural features in an actual built work.
UF architecture feinte
architecture, fictive
architecture, trompe-l'oeil
trompe-l'oeil architecture
CN B.BM.AFU.ARI.AXC.ARI

Ficus carica
USE **fig**

fiddle-back chairs
TG.131
ALT **fiddle-back chair**
SN Chairs with a single back splat which resembles the outline of a violin. (FAIRB)
UF chairs, fiddle-back
Hudson River valley chairs
York chairs
CN V.TG.AFU.AFU.ALO.AFU.AFU.AFU.NIE.BIQ

fiddle drills
USE **bow drills**

fids
TB.783 (N)
ALT **fid**
SN Long tapering cones used to stretch holes in rushwork. (HAND)
CN V.TB.AFU.BCW.BUE.AFU

field beds
TG.358 (N)
ALT **field bed**
SN Use for high-post beds with arched, or in the Federal period often serpentine, as opposed to straight canopies and whose posts are generally less than six feet in height.
UF beds, camp
beds, cant
beds, field
beds, slope
beds, tent
bedsteads, field
bedsteads, tent
brigantins
camp beds
cant beds
field bedsteads
lits brisés
lits d'armée
lits de camp
lits de campagne
lits de chasse
lits de voyage
slope beds
tent beds
tent bedsteads
CN V.TG.AFU.AFU.ARI.AFU.AFU.BZY.ALO.ALO

field bedsteads
USE **field beds**

field books
USE **field notes**

field cameras
USE **view cameras**

field fortifications
RK.442 (L)
ALT **field fortification**
SN Fortifications for more or less temporary use constructed in the field. (W)
UF fortifications, field
CN V.RK.AFU.ALO.ALO.BIQ.BCW

field guides
VW.511
ALT **field guide**
SN Manuals that identify objects in particular classes, especially natural objects. (W)
UF guides, field
CN V.VW.AFU.ALO.AFU.AFU.AFU.BZY.ARI.ALO

field hockey fields
USE **hockey fields**

field houses
RK.1061 (A,L,B)
ALT **field house**
SN Use for buildings providing enclosed and unobstructed space adaptable for various physical education and recreation activities, such as track events and basketball; often located at or near athletic fields.
UF houses, field
CN V.RK.AFU.ALO.ALO.EWY.AXC.BIQ.ALO.ARI

field notes
VW.63
ALT **field note**
SN Notes, often in books, kept by researchers or surveying parties while on site. (GAHLM)
UF books, field
field books
notes, field
CN V.VW.AFU.AFU.AFU.DZW.AFU

field studies
USE **fieldwork**

field tile
USE **draintile**

field work
USE **fieldwork**

fielded panels
RT.823
ALT **fielded panel**
SN Boards shaped to a tapered edge set into a frame and with a raised center section, field, or panel. (FAIRB)
UF panels, fielded
CN V.RT.AFU.ALO.ALO.ALO.AFU

fields, absorption
USE **leaching fields**

fields, athletic
USE **athletic fields**

fields, baseball
USE **baseball fields**

fields, cricket
USE **cricket fields**

fields, disposal
USE **leaching fields**

fields, field hockey
USE **hockey fields**

fields, football
USE **football fields**

fields, hockey
USE **hockey fields**

fields, lacrosse
USE **lacrosse fields**

fields, landing
USE **airfields**

fields, leaching
USE **leaching fields**

fields, oil
USE **oil fields**

fields, playing
USE **athletic fields**

fields, polo
USE **polo fields**

fields, rugby
USE **rugby fields**

fields, soccer
USE **soccer fields**

fields, softball
USE **softball fields**

fieldstone
MT.885 (L)
CN M.MT.AFU.AFU.AFU.DCU.ALO.AXC

fieldwork
KG.27 (L)
SN Studying or investigating a particular subject in its natural setting.
UF field studies
field work
CN K.KG.AFU.AFU.AFU.DIO.AFU

Fifteenth Dynasty
FL.2809
UF 15th Dynasty
Dynasty, Fifteenth
CN F.FL.ALO.AXC.ALO.ARI.AFU.BOK.ARI

Fifth Dynasty
FL.2790
UF 5th Dynasty
Dynasty, Fifth
CN F.FL.ALO.AXC.ALO.ARI.AFU.ARI.ARI

fig
MT.1165 (L)
UF common fig
Ficus carica
fig-tree
fig, common
CN M.MT.AFU.AFU.ALO.BIQ.DCU.AFU.AFU.AFU.DOI

fig bark paper
USE **bark cloth**

fig-tree
USE **fig**

fig, common
USE **fig**

fighters, fire
USE **fire fighters**

figuration
USE **figurative art**

Figuration, New
USE **New Figuration**

figurative art
BM.244 (L)
SN Includes both representations of the human figure, and art which portrays, in however altered or distorted form, things perceived in the visual world.
UF art, figurative
art, objective
art, representational
figuration
objective art
representational art
CN B.BM.AFU.ARI.BCW.DIO

figure drawings
VD.153
ALT **figure drawing**
UF drawings, figure
CN V.VD.AFU.BIQ.BCW

figure-ground perception
BM.144 (L)
SN In an image, the way in which an object or shape is related to the background against which it is seen. (THDAT)
UF perception, figure-ground
CN B.BM.AFU.AFU.ARI.BOK.BIQ

figure studies
VB.61
ALT **figure study**
UF studies, figure
CN V.VB.AFU.ALO.BOK.ARI

figured glass
MT.271 (L,B)
SN Use generally for glass used in architecture that is cut, embossed, sandblasted, or otherwise embellished.
UF decorative glass
figured rolled glass
glass, decorative
glass, figured
glass, figured rolled
glass, ornamental
glass, patterned
glass, rolled patterned
ornamental glass
patterned glass
rolled patterned glass
CN M.MT.AFU.AFU.AFU.BIQ.AFU.AXC.AFU.ALO

figured rolled glass
USE **figured glass**

figures, écorché
USE **écorchés**

figures, plane
USE **plane figures**

Fijian
FL.3619 (L)
CN F.FL.ALO.BOK.ALO.AFU

Fikellura
FL.2611
CN F.FL.ALO.AXC.ALO.AFU.ALO.AXC.ALO.ARI.AXC.AFU

filament
MT.2226
CN M.MT.AFU.ALO.CRG

filbert
MT.1348 (L)
UF hazel
hazelnut
CN M.MT.AFU.AFU.ALO.BIQ.DCU.AFU.AFU.ALO.BCW

file brushes
TB.351 (N)
ALT **file brush**
SN Brushes used to clean saw dust from the teeth of rasps and files.
UF brushes, file
brushes, rasp
rasp brushes
CN V.TB.AFU.ARI.CRG.ALO.ALO.ALO

file-cutting hammers
TB.661 (N)
ALT **file-cutting hammer**
SN Hammers whose head is a distinctively shaped truncated cone which is set off balance on the narrow end of its handle; used to cut teeth in files. (ARBOR)
UF hammers, file-cutting
CN V.TB.AFU.BCW.BIQ.AFU.ALO.BIQ.AFU

film, Mylar (TM)
USE **Mylar (TM)**

files
VW.583 (L,B)
ALT **file**
SN Organized units of documents grouped together in an overall arrangement or plan. (SAA)
CN V.VW.AFU.ALO.AFU.BIQ

files (tools)
TB.515 (L,N)
ALT **file (tool)**
SN Steel hand tools with teeth or raised oblique ridges; used for scraping, redressing, or smoothing metal or wood. (MEANS)
CN V.TB.AFU.ARI.EWY.ALO.CFS

files, accession
USE **accession records**

files, authority
USE **authority files**

files, biographical
USE **biography files**

files, cabinet
USE **cabinet files**

files, card
USE **card files**

files, case
USE **case files**

files, clipping
USE **clippings files**

files, clockmaker's
USE **clockmaker's files**

files, corporate
USE **corporation records**

files, cuttings
USE **clippings files**

files, data
USE **databases**

files, flat
USE **flat files**

files, float
USE **float files**

files, history
USE **organization files**

files, job
USE **project files**

files, joint
USE **joint files**

files, knife
USE **knife files**

files, leaning
USE **joint files**

files, legal
USE **legal files**

files, map
USE **map files**

files, master
USE **project files**

files, media
USE **clippings files**

files, mousetail
USE **round files**

files, name authority
USE **name authority files**

files, needle
USE **needle files**

files, office
USE **office files**

files, order
USE **order files**

files, organization
USE **organization files**

files, pamphlet
USE **vertical files**

files, personnel
USE **personnel records**

files, project
USE **project files**

files, rat tail
USE **round files**

files, riffler
USE **riffler files**

files, rough
USE **rough files**

files, round
USE **round files**

files, round-edge equalling
USE **joint files**

files, subject authority
USE **subject authority files**

files, thinning
USE **joint files**

files, vertical
USE **vertical files**

files, ward
USE **flat files**

files, watchmaker's
USE **clockmaker's files**

files, woodcarver's
USE **riffler files**

filicales
USE **ferns**

filigrains
USE **watermarks**

filigree enameling
KT.662
SN Variant of cloisonné, in which the design is worked in wire soldered to a base. Powdered enamel is put into spaces formed by wire and when it is contracted after fusing, the outlines of wire show above the surface of the enamel.
UF enameling, filigree
CN K.KT.AFU.ALO.GRC.AFU.ALO.ARI.AFU

filigree, paper
USE **paper quillwork**

filing
KT.614
ALT **filed**
CN K.KT.AFU.ALO.FUA.CLM

filing blocks
TB.654
ALT **filing block**
SN Hardened steel cylindrical blocks with different sized grooves for supporting wire while it is being filed. (WATCH)
UF blocks, filing
CN V.TB.AFU.BCW.BIQ.AFU.ALO.ARI.ALO

filing cabinets
TG.430 (N)
ALT **filing cabinet**
UF cabinets, filing
CN V.TG.AFU.AFU.AXC.ALO.ARI.ALO.BIQ

fill
MT.2590 (L)
SN Soil, crushed stone, or waste materials, used to raise an existing grade or as a manmade deposit. (DAC)
CN M.MT.AFU.ARI.DUC

fill insulation
MT.2407
SN Consists of loose, granulated materials such as rock wool, cork, or other material poured or packed between framing members.
UF fill-type insulation
granular-fill insulation
insulation, fill
insulation, fill-type
insulation, granular-fill
insulation, loose fill
loose fill insulation
CN M.MT.AFU.ARI.BZY.BCW.ARI.AFU.AFU

fill-type insulation
USE **fill insulation**

filled plastic
MT.2103
UF plastic, filled
CN M.MT.AFU.AFU.ARI.BUE.ALO.ALO.AFU

fillers
MT.2591 (L)
SN Use for any material added to another, usually to cheapen or adulterate it. (MAYER)
CN M.MT.AFU.ARI.DZW

fillet moldings
RT.775
ALT **fillet molding**
SN Moldings consisting of a narrow flat band, often square in section. (DAC)
UF moldings, fillet
CN V.RT.AFU.ALO.AFU.BOK.AFU.AFU.AXC.AXC

fillets, cover
USE **cover moldings**

fillets, sunk
USE **sunk fillets**

fillets, tilting
USE **eaves boards**

filling
KT.121
ALT **filled**
SN Inserting material into a hole, crack, or cavity.
CN K.KT.AFU.ALO.DCU

filling stations
USE **service stations**

filling, hydraulic
USE **hydraulic filling**

fillistered joints
TF.596
ALT **fillistered joint**
UF joints, fillistered
CN V.TF.ALO.AFU.ELK.ALO

fillisters
TB.917 (N)
ALT **fillister**
SN Planes used for cutting the angled portion of a wooden panel. (KEBABI)
CN V.TB.AFU.BCW.CFS.ALO.AFU.DUC.ALO.BCW

film
MT.2228 (N)
SN A thin coating or thin sheet of material. (DAC)
CN M.MT.AFU.ALO.CXA

film color
BM.111
SN A colored expanse that appears to be at a certain, though somewhat indefinite distance from the observer, nontransparent, but not on the surface of an object, such as the blue of the sky.
UF color, film
CN B.BM.AFU.AFU.ARI.BOK.ALO.AFU.ARI

film dryers
TB.332 (N)
ALT **film dryer**
UF dryers (film)
dryers, film
CN V.TB.AFU.ARI.CLM.ARI.ALO.BIQ

film formers
MT.2312
UF formers, film
CN M.MT.AFU.ARI.ALO.CLM

film librarians
USE **audiovisual librarians**

film (performing arts)
KD.9 (L,B,R)
UF cinema
motion pictures (performing arts)
CN K.KD.AFU.AFU.AFU.AFU.AFU.ALO

film (photographic)
USE **photographic film**

film producers
USE **filmmakers**

film production specialists
USE **filmmakers**

film reviews
VW.310 (L)
ALT **film review**
UF motion-picture reviews
movie reviews
moving-picture reviews
reviews, film
reviews, motion-picture
reviews, movie
reviews, moving-picture
CN V.VW.AFU.AFU.ALO.BCW.ARI.ARI

film scripts
USE **screenplays**

film splicers
TB.333 (N)
ALT **film splicer**
SN Devices used to hold two sections of film or recording tape in proper alignment while they are being spliced together. (RHDEL2)
UF splicers
splicers, film
CN V.TB.AFU.ARI.CLM.ARI.ALO.BOK

film-stencil method
KT.753
SN A silk-screen technique in which the stencils are cut from a paperbacked stopping-out film. (MAYER)
CN K.KT.AFU.ALO.HCQ.ALO.BUE.AFU

film stills
VJ.127
ALT **film still**
SN Still photographs of the action, actors, or production of a motion picture. For prints produced from a frame of motion picture film, use **frame enlargements.**
UF motion picture stills
movie stills
scene stills
stills (photographs)
stills, film
CN V.VJ.AFU.AXC.ALO

film studios
USE **motion-picture studios**

film theaters
USE **movie theaters**

film washers
TB.334 (N)
ALT **film washer**
SN Devices used for washing film.
UF washers, film
CN V.TB.AFU.ARI.CLM.ARI.ALO.BUE

film, American
USE **American film**

film, black-and-white
USE **black-and-white film**

film, color
USE **color film**

film, cut
USE **cut film**

film, disk
USE **disk film**

film, non-flam
USE **safety film**

film, panchromatic
USE **panchromatic film**

film, photographic
USE **photographic film**

film, Polaroid Land (TM)
USE **Polaroid (TM) film**

film, Polaroid (TM)
USE **Polaroid (TM) film**

film, reversal
USE **reversal film**

film, roll
USE **roll film**

film, safety
USE **safety film**

film, safety-base
USE **safety film**

film, sheet
USE **cut film**

film, stripping
USE **stripping film**

filmmakers
HG.64 (L)
ALT **filmmaker**
UF film producers
film production specialists
motion picture producers
moviemakers
producers
producers, film
producers, motion picture
production specialists, film
specialists, film production
CN H.HG.AFU.AXC.AXC.AFU.AFU.AFU.BCW

films
USE **motion pictures**

films, children's
USE **children's films**

films, strip
USE **filmstrips**

filmstrips
VW.639 (L)
ALT **filmstrip**
SN Strips of 16mm or 35mm film varying in length up to about fifty frames and bearing pictures, text, or captions. (LG)
UF films, strip
strip films
CN V.VW.AFU.ALO.AFU.DZW.AFU.ALO.AFU

filter paper
MT.1940 (N)
UF paper, filter
CN M.MT.AFU.AFU.ARI.ALO.ALO.AXC.ARI.BCW

filtering
USE **filtration**

filters
MT.2613 (L,N)
ALT **filter**
SN Any pourous material (as of paper or sand) through which a gas or liquid is passed to separate out matter in suspension. (WCOL)
CN M.MT.AFU.ARI.EFQ

filters, air
USE **air filters**

filters, color
USE **light filters**

filters, dry
USE **dry filters**

filters, dry-air
USE **dry filters**

filters, dry-type
USE **dry filters**

filters, light
USE **light filters**

filters, viscous impingement
USE **viscous impingement filters**

filtration
KT.640 (L)
ALT **filtered**
UF filtering
CN K.KT.AFU.ALO.GFO.AXC

filtration plants
RK.586 (A,L)
ALT **filtration plant**
UF plants, filtration
CN V.RK.AFU.ALO.ALO.CFS.ALO.BCW.CRG.ALO

fin de siècle
FL.3255
CN F.FL.ALO.BCW.ALO.AXC.BCW

final image material
MT.2633
UF image material
image material, final
material, final image
material, image
CN M.MT.AFU.ARI.GWW.AFU

Final Jomon
FL.1964
UF Jomon, Final
CN F.FL.ALO.ARI.ALO.ALO.AFU.AFU.ALO.BCW

Final Neolithic
FL.25
UF Neolithic, Final
CN F.FL.AFU.BCW.ALO.AXC

finance
BM.386 (L,B)
SN The management or use of funds by a government, business, or individual. (W)
CN B.BM.ARI.CLM

finance, municipal
USE **municipal finance**

financial aid, student
USE **student aid**

financial institutions
RK.126 (L)
ALT **financial institution**
UF institutions, financial
CN V.RK.AFU.ALO.ALO.ALO.ALO

financial records
VW.813
ALT **financial record**
UF records, financial
CN V.VW.AFU.ARI.AFU.BIQ

financial statements
VW.821 (L)
ALT **financial statement**
SN Reports summarizing the financial condition of an organization on any date or for any period. (BLACKS)
UF statements, financial
CN V.VW.AFU.ARI.AFU.BIQ.BUE

financiers
HG.417 (L)
ALT **financier**
SN Large-scale investors; also persons who undertake to secure large funds for government or business. (W)
CN H.HG.AFU.AXC.BOK.DIO

finding aids
VW.337
ALT **finding aid**
SN Documents, published or unpublished, listing or describing a body of records within a records center or archives, making them more readily accessible and comprehensible to the user. (ICA)
UF aids, finding
archival finding aids
CN V.VW.AFU.AFU.ALO.CXA.ALO

fine aggregate
MT.2299
UF aggregate, fine
CN M.MT.AFU.ARI.ALO.ALO.AFU.ARI

fine arts
KD.20 (L,R)
SN Traditional Western designation for those arts involving the creation of works as aesthetic or intellectual expressions intended primarily for visual contemplation or enjoyment.
UF arts, fine
CN K.KD.AFU.AFU.AFU.AFU.ALO.ALO.ALO

fine arts museums
USE **art museums**

fine-grain materials
MT.2248
UF materials, fine-grain
CN M.MT.AFU.ALO.DOI.AFU

Fine Orange
FL.1043
UF Orange, Fine
CN F.FL.ALO.ALO.ALO.ALO.AFU.ALO.ARI.ALO.ALO.AFU

fine solder
MT.421
UF solder, fine
CN M.MT.AFU.AFU.AFU.BZY.AFU.AFU.AFU.ALO.BUE.ARI.AFU

fine stuff
MT.2438
SN Material (as plasterer's putty or a mixture of fine sand with plasterer's putty) used for the final coat of a plastered wall. (W)
UF stuff, fine
CN M.MT.AFU.ARI.CRG.AFU.AXC.AFU.ARI

finger joints
TF.676
ALT **finger joint**
UF joints, finger
CN V.TF.ALO.ARI.AXC.ALO.AXC

finger painting
KT.249 (L)
UF painting, finger
CN K.KT.AFU.ALO.DUC.CXA.ALO.AXC.AFU

finger planes
TB.944
ALT **finger plane**
SN Very small wood planes.
UF planes, finger
CN V.TB.AFU.BCW.CFS.ALO.AFU.DUC.ARI.AXC

finials
RT.1057 (A,L,N,B,R)
ALT **finial**
SN Ornaments which terminate the point of a spire, pinnacle, or other vertical member. Common on furniture as well as architecture.
UF guglias (finials)
CN V.RT.AFU.BCW.BUE

finish builders' hardware
USE **finish hardware**

finish flooring
USE **flooring**

finish hardware
TF.4
SN Use for visible, functional hardware that has a finished appearance and is often treated as part of the decorative scheme on objects and in buildings and other structures.
UF architectural hardware
builders' finish hardware
builders' hardware
finish builders' hardware
hardware, architectural
hardware, builders'

hardware, finish
CN V.TF.AFU.AFU.AFU.AFU

finish lumber
MT.1447
UF lumber, finish
CN M.MT.AFU.AFU.ALO.BIQ.DCU.ALO.BOK.ARI.BIQ.AFU

finish strings
USE **face strings**

finishers, wood-type
USE **wood engravers**

finishes
MT.2553 (A,L,B)
ALT **finish**
SN Use for substances that serve as the final treatment or coating of a surface. (WCOL)
CN M.MT.AFU.ARI.CRG.ARI.ALO

finishes (building materials)
USE **finishings**

finishes, fantasy
USE **faux finishes**

finishes, faux
USE **faux finishes**

finishing
KT.683 (A,L,R)
ALT **finished**
CN K.KT.AFU.ALO.GRC.BCW

finishing horses
USE **sawhorses**

finishing machines, concrete
USE **concrete finishing machines**

finishing nails
TF.434
ALT **finishing nail**
SN Slender nails, each having a narrow head, that may be driven entirely into a wood surface leaving a small hole that can be filled with putty or a similar compound. (MEANS)
UF nails, finishing
CN V.TF.AFU.AFU.AFU.ALO.AFU.CFS.ALO.BIQ

finishing schools
USE **preparatory schools**

finishing varnish
MT.2479
UF floor varnish
varnish, finishing
varnish, floor
CN M.MT.AFU.ARI.CRG.AFU.BOK.AFU.BCW.AFU

finishing, barrel
USE **barreling**

finishing, faux
USE **faux finishing**

finishings
MT.2389 (A,L)
SN The final treatment of all surfaces in a building, such as the addition of veneers, woodwork, flooring, paint.
UF finishes (building materials)
CN M.MT.AFU.ARI.BZY.AXC

Fink trusses
RT.362
ALT **Fink truss**
SN Symmetrical trusses, especially used in supporting large sloping roofs, in the form of three isoceles triangles; one truss in the center with its base along the horizontal tie and each of the outer two having its base along the sloping side of an upper chord. (DAC)
UF Belgian trusses
French trusses
trusses, Belgian
trusses, Fink
trusses, French
W-trusses
CN V.RT.AFU.AFU.AFU.BCW.CLM.AFU.AFU.AFU.AXC

Fink trusses, fan
USE **fan Fink trusses**

Finlay process
USE **Finlaycolor**

Finlaycolor
KT.316
SN A photographic process patented by Clare L. Finlay. An additive color process for producing transparencies on a panchromatic, black-and-white emulsion by using a color screen of red and green circles on a blue-violet background.
UF Finlay process
Finlaycolor process
CN K.KT.AFU.ALO.DUC.DIO.ALO.AFU.ALO.ALO

Finlaycolor process
USE **Finlaycolor**

Finnish
FL.3059 (L,B)
CN F.FL.ALO.BCW.AFU.DUC.ALO

Finnish baths
USE **saunas**

fiords
RD.147 (L)
ALT **fiord**
SN Designates inlets of the sea that are long, deep, and narrow and have steep walls; usually formed by glacial erosion.
CN V.RD.ARI.AFU.AFU.AFU.ALO.ALO.ARI

fiore di Persico
MT.809
UF marmor Molossium
CN M.MT.AFU.AFU.AFU.DCU.AFU.ARI.ARI.ARI.BIQ.BIQ

fiorto di persico
USE **fiorto marble**

fiorto marble
MT.810
UF fiorto di persico
marble, fiorto
CN M.MT.AFU.AFU.AFU.DCU.AFU.ARI.ARI.ARI.BIQ.BOK

Fipa
FL.584 (L)
CN F.FL.ALO.AFU.AXC.AXC.AFU.ALO

fir
MT.1349 (L)
UF Abies
CN M.MT.AFU.AFU.ALO.BIQ.DCU.AFU.AFU.ALO.BIQ

fir, archangel
USE **Scotch pine**

fir, balsam
USE **balsam fir**

fir, cascadis
USE **silver fir**

fir, Danzig
USE **Scotch pine**

fir, Douglas
USE **Douglas fir**

fir, Fraser's balsam
USE **Fraser's balsam fir**

fir, Frazer
USE **Fraser's balsam fir**

fir, gray
USE **western hemlock**

fir, larch
USE **western larch**

fir, memel
USE **Scotch pine**

fir, Prince Albert
USE **western hemlock**

fir, red
USE **Douglas fir**

fir, red silver
USE **silver fir**

fir, Scotch
USE **Scotch pine**

fir, Scots
USE **Scotch pine**

fir, silver
USE **silver fir**

fir, spruce
USE **common spruce**

fir, spruce (Norway spruce)
USE **Norway spruce**

fir, white
USE **common spruce**

fir, white (Norway spruce)
USE **Norway spruce**

fir, yellow
USE **Douglas fir**

fire
BM.883 (L,R)
CN B.BM.CFS.AXC.AXC.AFU

fire alarm boxes
USE **manual stations**

fire alarm stations, manual
USE **manual stations**

fire alarm systems
RT.1505 (L,N,B)
ALT **fire alarm system**
SN Electrical or mechanical systems, installed in a building that sound a blast or bell when smoke or flames are detected; certain alarms are engineered to trigger sprinkler systems for added protection. (MEANS)
UF alarm systems, fire
fire alarms
systems, fire alarm
CN V.RT.ALO.BIQ.AFU.AFU.AFU

fire alarm systems, auxiliary
USE **auxiliary fire alarm systems**

fire alarm systems, local
USE **local fire alarm systems**

fire alarm systems, proprietary
USE **proprietary fire alarm systems**

fire alarm systems, remote-station
USE **remote-station fire alarm systems**

fire alarms
USE **fire alarm systems**

fire altars
RK.1086
ALT **fire altar**
SN Use for open-air structures, usually with stepped bases, constructed for the maintenance and worship of the sacred fire in Zoroastrianism and like religions.
UF altars, fire
CN V.RK.AFU.ALO.ALO.FCS.AFU.ARI

fire axes
TB.405 (N)
ALT **fire ax**
SN Axes found primarily in public buildings, with part of the head and sometimes the heft painted red; to be used in case of fire. (BLACKB)
UF axes, fire
axes, fireman's
fireman's axes
CN V.TB.AFU.ARI.DUC.ALO.AFU

fire barriers
USE **fire walls**

fire brick
MT.102 (L,B)
SN Bricks made of refractory ceramic material which will resist high temperatures; used to line furnaces, fireplaces, and chimneys. (DAC)
UF brick, fire
brick, refractory
refractory brick
CN M.MT.AFU.AFU.AFU.AXC.ALO.AFU.ALO.BOK

fire curtains
USE **asbestos curtains**

fire detection systems
USE **fire detectors**

fire detectors
RT.1511 (A,L,B)
ALT **fire detector**
UF detection systems, fire
detectors, fire
fire detection systems
systems, fire detection
CN V.RT.ALO.BIQ.AFU.AFU.ALO.AFU

fire-door latches
TF.186
ALT **fire-door latch**
SN Spring latches or deadlocking latches that have a 3/4-inch throw and an antifriction retractor. (STEIN)
UF latches, fire-door
CN V.TF.AFU.AFU.AFU.AFU.DIO.BCW.ALO.AXC

fire doors
RT.853 (B)
ALT **fire door**
SN Fire-resistant door assemblies, which are capable of providing a specified degree of fire protection when closed. (DAC)
UF doors, fire
doors, fire-resistant
fire-resistant doors
CN V.RT.AFU.ARI.AFU.AFU.AFU.ALO.ARI.AFU.AFU.BOK.AFU

fire escapes
RT.1092 (L,N,B)
ALT **fire escape**
SN Stairs, usually of steel, attached to the outside of buildings to provide means of escape in case of fire. Use **fire stairs** for fire-secure stairs within buildings.
UF escapes, fire
CN V.RT.AFU.BIQ.AXC.AFU.ALO.AFU

fire etching
USE **pyrography**

fire exit bolts
USE **panic bolts**

fire exits
USE **emergency exits**

fire extinguishers
TB.406 (A,L,N,B)
ALT **fire extinguisher**
SN Portable devices for immediate and temporary use in putting out a fire. (DAC)
UF extinguishers, fire
CN V.TB.AFU.ARI.DUC.ALO.ALO

fire extinguishing systems
RT.1519 (L,B)
ALT **fire extinguishing system**
UF systems, fire extinguishing
CN V.RT.ALO.BIQ.AFU.ALO.AFU

fire fighters
HG.42 (L,R)
ALT **fire fighter**
UF fighters, fire
firemen
CN H.HG.AFU.AXC.ARI.BCW

fire gilding
USE **amalgam-gilding**

fire halls
USE **fire stations**

fire hydrants
RM.497 (L,N)
ALT **fire hydrant**
UF fireplugs
hydrants, fire
CN V.RM.ALO.ALO.ALO.ALO.DUC.AFU

fire insurance maps
VW.165 (L)
ALT **fire insurance map**
SN Maps prepared primarily for fire insurance underwriters, showing information, such as type of construction, about structures in a given area.
UF atlases, insurance
insurance atlases
insurance maps
maps, fire insurance
maps, insurance
maps, Sanborn
Sanborn maps
CN V.VW.AFU.AFU.AFU.FZU.AXC.AFU.ARI.ALO.AFU

fire irons
USE **firesets**

fire marble
USE **shell marble**

fire polishing
KT.763
CN K.KT.AFU.ALO.HOE.ALO.AFU

fire prevention
KG.115 (A,L,B)
UF prevention, fire
CN K.KG.AFU.AFU.BCW.ALO.ALO

fire protection systems
RT.1503
ALT **fire protection system**
UF protection systems, fire
systems, fire protection
CN V.RT.ALO.BIQ.AFU

fire resistance
BM.984 (A,B)
ALT **fire-resistant**
CN B.BM.CFS.AXC.BZY.CFS.ALO

fire-resistant doors
USE **fire doors**

fire-resistant materials
MT.2793 (A,L,B)
UF inflammable materials
materials, fire-resistant
materials, inflammable
materials, noncombustible
noncombustible materials
CN M.MT.AFU.BCW.BCW

fire-resistive construction
KT.45 (B)
ALT **fire-resistive**
SN Method of construction that prevents or retards the passage of hot gases or flames. (STEIN)
UF construction, fire-resistive
construction, fireproof
fireproof construction
CN K.KT.AFU.ALO.BCW.ARI.ALO.ARI

fire resistive walls
USE **fire walls**

fire-retardant paint
MT.2542
UF paint, fire-retardant
CN M.MT.AFU.ARI.CRG.ALO.BCW.ARI.AXC

fire safety
BM.209 (L)
UF safety, fire
CN B.BM.AFU.ALO.BOK.ALO

fire sanctuaries
USE **fire temples**

fire screens
TG.4 (N,R)
ALT **fire screen**
SN Screens used to shelter the face or legs from the fire.
UF guards, spark
screens, fire
spark guards
CN V.TG.AFU.AFU.AFU.AFU

fire screens, cheval
USE **cheval fire screens**

fire screens, extension
USE **extension fire screens**

fire screens, folding
USE **folding fire screens**

fire screens, gentleman's writing
USE **gentleman's writing fire screens**

fire screens, horse
USE **cheval fire screens**

fire screens, lady's writing
USE **lady's writing fire screens**

fire screens, pole
USE **pole screens**

fire screens, sliding
USE **sliding fire screens**

fire screens, tripod
USE **pole screens**

fire screens, writing
USE **writing fire screens**

fire sprinklers
RT.1521 (A,L)
ALT **fire sprinkler**
SN Sprinklers installed inside buildings to extinguish fires.
UF sprinklers, fire
CN V.RT.ALO.BIQ.AFU.ALO.ALO.AFU

fire stairs
RT.1093
ALT **fire stair**
SN Stairs within buildings so designed that they are relatively secure from the effects of fire in a building and thus are designated as an emergency escape. Use **fire escapes** for stairs located on the outside of buildings to provide a means of escape in case of fire.
UF stairs, fire
CN V.RT.AFU.BIQ.AXC.AFU.ALO.ALO

fire stations
RK.990 (A,L,N,B,R)
ALT **fire station**
UF engine houses
fire halls
firehouses
halls, fire
houses, engine
stations, fire
CN V.RK.AFU.ALO.ALO.ERE.AFU.BZY.AFU

fire temples
RK.1134
ALT **fire temple**
SN Use for buildings constructed for the maintenance and worship of the sacred fire in Zoroastrianism.
UF fire sanctuaries
sanctuaries, fire
temples, fire
CN V.RK.AFU.ALO.ALO.FCS.BIQ.BZY.ALO.ALO

fire towers
RK.38 (A,B)
ALT **fire tower**
SN Towers, as on a mountain, from which a watch for fires is kept.
UF towers, fire
CN V.RK.AFU.ALO.AFU.ALO.DCU.AXC.AFU

fire towers (building divisions)
RM.12
ALT **fire tower (building division)**
UF towers, fire (building divisions)
CN V.RM.AFU.BIQ

fire walls
RT.582
ALT **fire wall**
SN In building construction, fire-resisting walls, enclosed stairways, and other similar obstructions for preventing the spread of fires in buildings. (PUTNAM)
UF barriers, fire
fire barriers
fire resistive walls
firewalls
walls, fire
walls, fire resistive
CN V.RT.AFU.AFU.AFU.BIQ.BUE.AFU.ALO.AFU

fire welding
USE **forge welding**

firebacks
RT.1153 (L,N)
ALT **fireback**
UF backs, chimney
chimney backs
CN V.RT.AFU.BOK.ALO.ALO.ALO

fireclay
MT.63 (L)
UF clay, refractory
refractory clay
CN M.MT.AFU.AFU.AFU.AXC.AFU.ALO.AFU

fired brick
MT.117
UF baked brick
brick, baked
brick, burned
brick, burnt
brick, fired
brick, kiln-burned
burned brick
burnt brick
kiln-burned brick
later coctilis
later coctus
CN M.MT.AFU.AFU.AFU.AXC.ALO.AFU.AXC.AFU.AFU

firefighting equipment
TB.404 (L)
UF equipment, firefighting
CN V.TB.AFU.ARI.DUC.ALO

firehoses
TB.407 (L,N)
ALT **firehose**
UF hoses, fire
CN V.TB.AFU.ARI.DUC.ALO.ARI

firehouse Windsor chairs
USE **low-back Windsor chairs**

firehouses
USE **fire stations**

fireman's axes
USE **fire axes**

firemen
USE **fire fighters**

fireplace cheeks
RT.1154
ALT **fireplace cheek**
UF cheeks, fireplace
CN V.RT.AFU.BOK.ALO.ALO.ARI

fireplace systems
USE **fireplaces**

fireplace throats
USE **chimney throats**

fireplace tools
USE **firesets**

fireplace utensils
USE **firesets**

fireplaces
RT.1150 (A,L,N,B,R)
ALT **fireplace**
SN Openings at the bases of chimneys, usually open recesses in walls, in which fires may be built. (HAS)
UF fireplace systems
ingles
systems, fireplace
CN V.RT.AFU.BOK.ALO.AFU

fireplugs
USE **fire hydrants**

fireproof construction
USE **fire-resistive construction**

fireproofing
KT.595 (A,L,B,R)
ALT **fireproofed**
UF flameproofing
CN K.KT.AFU.ALO.FOG.AFU

fireproofing agents
MT.2614 (L)
UF agents, fireproofing
flame retardants
flameproof materials
materials, flameproof
retardants, flame
CN M.MT.AFU.ARI.ELK

fireproofing tile
MT.169
UF tile, fireproofing
CN M.MT.AFU.AFU.AFU.AXC.ALO.ALO.ALO.AFU.ALO.ARI.AFU

fires
KM.109 (L,R)
CN K.KM.AFU.CXA.ARI

fires, forest
USE **forest fires**

firesets
TB.204 (N,B,R)
ALT **fireset**
UF fire irons
fireplace tools
fireplace utensils
irons, fire
tools, fireplace
utensils, fireplace
CN V.TB.AFU.ARI.BUE.AFU

firestone
USE **calcareous sandstone**

firewalls
USE **fire walls**

firewood
MT.2619 (L,R)
CN M.MT.AFU.ARI.FIM.AFU

firing
KG.152 (L)
SN Act of dismissing an employee from a position. (WCOL)
CN K.KG.AFU.AFU.BIQ.BUE.ARI

firing (ceramics)
KT.862
ALT **fired**
CN K.KT.AFU.ALO.HOE.BOK.ARI

firing ranges
RG.145 (L)
ALT **firing range**
SN Use only for military weapons testing; for small arms target ranges, use **shooting ranges** or a more specific term.
UF bombing and gunnery ranges
ranges, firing
weapons ranges
CN V.RG.AFU.AFU.DIO.AFU

firing, bonfire
USE **bonfire firing**

firm price contracts
USE **fixed-price contracts**

firmer gouges
TB.885 (N)
ALT **firmer gouge**
SN Long narrow gouges used for cutting grooves;(MEANS) generally beveled on the outside, although they may also be ground on the inside. (BLACKB)
UF gouges, firmer
CN V.TB.AFU.BCW.CFS.ALO.AFU.CXA.AXC

firmers
USE **forming chisels**

firms
HG.845 (L)
ALT **firm**
SN Partnerships of two or more persons who carry on business under a common name.
CN H.HG.ALO.BOK.AFU.ALO.AFU

firms, architectural
USE **architectural firms**

first asylum camps
USE **refugee camps**

first communion records
USE **communion records**

first drafts
VW.36
ALT **first draft**
SN Rough or preliminary proposed texts of documents, not yet in definitive form, usually subject to review, revision, rejection, approval, or adoption. (GAHLM)
UF drafts, first
drafts, rough
rough drafts
CN V.VW.AFU.AFU.AFU.BUE.AFU

First Dynasty
FL.2793
UF 1st Dynasty
Dynasty, First
CN F.FL.ALO.AXC.ALO.ARI.AFU.AXC.AFU

First Dynasty of Babylon
FL.2973
CN F.FL.ALO.AXC.ARI.BCW.AFU.BIQ.AFU

First Empire
USE **Empire**

First Golden Age (Byzantine)
USE **Justinianic**

First Intermediate period
FL.2796
UF Intermediate period, First
CN F.FL.ALO.AXC.ALO.ARI.AFU.BCW

first performances
USE **premieres**

First Persian period
USE **Twenty-seventh Dynasty**

First Plateresque
FL.3245
UF Gothic Plateresque
Plateresque, First
Plateresque, Gothic
CN F.FL.ALO.BCW.ALO.ARI.BIQ.BIQ.BUE.ALO.AFU

First Pointed
USE **Early English**

First Pompeian Style
USE **First Style**

First Romanesque
FL.3153
UF le premier art roman
Lombard-Catalan
premier art roman
Romanesque, First
CN F.FL.ALO.BCW.ALO.ALO.AFU.BOK.AXC.AFU

First Style
FL.2766
UF Encrusted Style
First Pompeian Style
Incrustation Style
Masonry Style
Pompeian Style, First

CN F.FL.ALO.AXC.ALO.ALO.ALO.CFS.AFU.AFU

fish breeding stations
USE **fish hatcheries**

fish glue
MT.2348
UF glue, fish
CN M.MT.AFU.ARI.ARI.AFU.ALO.ALO.AFU.AXC

fish hatcheries
RG.9 (L,B)
ALT **fish hatchery**
SN Facilities where fish eggs are hatched and the fry raised, especially to stock lakes, streams, and ponds. (RHDEL2)
UF fish breeding stations
hatcheries, fish
CN V.RG.AFU.AFU.AFU.AFU.ARI.ALO

fish ladders
USE **fishways**

fish oil
MT.2009 (L)
UF oil, fish
CN M.MT.AFU.AFU.ARI.ARI.AXC.AFU.ARI

fish passages
USE **fishways**

fish scale pattern
USE **scale pattern**

fish scales
MT.950
ALT **fish scale**
UF scales, fish
CN M.MT.AFU.AFU.ALO.AFU.DZW.AFU

fished joints
TF.682
ALT **fished joint**
SN Butted timber joints made using fishplates. (MEANS)
UF joints, fished
CN V.TF.ALO.ARI.AXC.ARI.ALO

Fisher
FL.835
CN F.FL.ALO.ALO.ALO.AFU.ALO.ALO.ARI.AFU.ARI

fisheries
RK.632 (L,R)
ALT **fishery**
CN V.RK.AFU.ALO.ALO.CLM.ALO.ALO.AFU.AXC.BCW.ARI

fishermen
HG.371 (L,R)
ALT **fisherman**
CN H.HG.AFU.AXC.BIQ.ALO.AXC.ALO

fishery museums
RK.424 (B)
ALT **fishery museum**
UF fishing museums
museums, fishery
CN V.RK.AFU.ALO.ALO.BCW.AXC.ARI.CLM.AFU

fisheye lenses
TB.317
ALT **fisheye lens**
SN Extremely wide-angle lenses, covering a field of about 180 degrees and reproducing a circular image with pronounced barrel distortion. (SWED)
UF lenses, fisheye
CN V.TB.AFU.ARI.CLM.ARI.AFU.ALO.BOK.ALO

fishing camps
USE **fishing lodges**

fishing houses
USE **fishing lodges**

fishing lodges
RK.960 (L,B)
ALT **fishing lodge**
UF angling lodges
camps, fishing
fishing camps
fishing houses
houses, fishing
lodges, angling
lodges, fishing
CN V.RK.AFU.ALO.ALO.ELK.BOK.AFU

fishing museums
USE **fishery museums**

fishing stools
TG.269
ALT **fishing stool**
SN Portable stools with joined legs which, when opened, are bound by girth webbing which serves as a seat. (CABDIC)
UF stools, fishing
CN V.TG.AFU.AFU.ALO.AFU.ALO.AXC.AFU.AXC

fishing villages
RD.51 (L,B)
ALT **fishing village**
UF villages, fishing
CN V.RD.AFU.AXC.BCW

fishponds
RD.135 (L)
ALT **fishpond**
CN V.RD.ARI.AFU.AFU.AFU.AFU.ALO.ALO.AFU

fishskin
MT.951
CN M.MT.AFU.AFU.ALO.AFU.DZW.ALO

fishtail chisels
USE **fishtail tools**

fishtail tools
TB.861
ALT **fishtail tool**
SN Chisels with straight sides which flare rapidly at the blade, forming a fan shape. (BLACKB)
UF chisels, fishtail
fantail tools
fishtail chisels
tools, fantail
tools, fishtail
CN V.TB.AFU.BCW.CFS.ALO.AFU.BUE.ARI

fishways
RM.461 (L)
ALT **fishway**
SN Contrivances for enabling fish to pass around a fall or dam in a stream. (W)
UF fish ladders
fish passages
ladders, fish
passages, fish
CN V.RM.ALO.ALO.AFU.AFU

fission track dating
KT.504 (L)
SN Method of dating glassy materials or objects based on the known rate of spontaneous fission of uranium 233 atoms, which leave detectable damage trails, called fission tracks. (HOLHZR)
UF dating, fission track
CN K.KT.AFU.ALO.EFQ.AFU.BCW.AFU

fissuring
USE **cracking**

fitching
MT.2740
CN M.MT.AFU.AXC.AFU.AFU

fits (engineering)
USE **tolerances**

fitted furniture
USE **built-in furniture**

fitters, pipe
USE **pipe fitters**

fitting axes
USE **beginning axes**

fitting, gas
USE **gas fitting**

fittings
USE **hardware**

fittings, door
USE **door hardware**

fittings, sanitary
USE **plumbing fixtures**

fittings, window
USE **window hardware**

five-and-dimes
USE **variety stores**

five-and-ten-cent stores
USE **variety stores**

five-and-tens
USE **variety stores**

five-color porcelain
USE **Wucai**

Five Dynasties
FL.1886 (L)
CN F.FL.ALO.ARI.ALO.AFU.AFU.ALO.CLM

Five Nations
USE **Iroquois**

five senses
USE **senses**

fives courts
RK.1015 (B)
ALT **fives court**
SN Use for courts of three or four walls prepared for the game of fives, a form of handball, largely British.
UF court, fives
CN V.RK.AFU.ALO.ALO.EWY.ALO.BIQ.AFU

fixation
USE **fixing**

fixatives
MT.2615
SN Substances that fix or set something, such as a varnish on a crayon drawing. (WCOL)
CN M.MT.AFU.ARI.ERE

fixed-focus lenses
TB.318
ALT **fixed-focus lens**
SN Lenses set at one fixed distance from the film and offering no method of focusing adjustment; most common on inexpensive cameras. (LANG)
UF lenses, fixed-focus
CN V.TB.AFU.ARI.CLM.ARI.AFU.ALO.BOK.ARI

fixed-guideway transit
USE **rail transit systems**

fixed joints
USE **rigid joints**

fixed lights
USE **fixed windows**

fixed-price contracts
VW.892
ALT **fixed-price contract**
SN Types of contracts in which the buyer agrees to pay the seller a definite, predetermined price. (BLACKS)
UF contracts, firm price
contracts, fixed-price
contracts, lump sum
firm price contracts
lump sum contracts
CN V.VW.AFU.ARI.AFU.BOK.BOK.ALO.ALO.ALO.ARI

fixed windows
RT.937
ALT **fixed window**
SN Windows or portions of window units that are designed not to open. (MEANS)
UF deadlights
fixed lights
lights, fixed
windows, fixed
CN V.RT.AFU.ARI.AFU.AFU.BOK.AFU.AFU.EWY.AFU

fixer masons
HG.600
ALT **fixer mason**
SN Masons who place the great blocks of stone accurately into position in a building. (W)
UF masons, fixer
CN H.HG.AFU.AXC.BZY.AFU.DIO.ARI

fixing
KT.126
SN Making a material or object firm, stable, or stationary. (W)
UF fixation
CN K.KT.AFU.ALO.DIO

fixture drains
RT.1457
ALT **fixture drain**
SN Drains that lead from the trap of a fixture to another drain pipe. (MEANS)
UF drains, fixture
CN V.RT.ALO.BCW.ALO.ARI.AXC.ALO

fixture traps
RT.1497
ALT **fixture trap**
UF traps, fixture
CN V.RT.ALO.BCW.ALO.ARI.DCU.AFU

fixtures, door
USE **door hardware**

fixtures, plumbing
USE **plumbing fixtures**

flagging irons
TB.419 (N)
ALT **flagging iron**
SN Prying tools with a double-hooked head used in caulking barrels with flags or for removing barrel heads. (W)
UF irons, flagging
irons, rush
levers, rushing
prying rods
rods, prying
rush irons
rushing levers
stave wrenches
wrenches, stave
CN V.TB.AFU.ARI.DZW.ARI

flagpoles
RM.441 (N,R)
ALT **flagpole**
UF flagstaffs
CN V.RM.ALO.AFU.BIQ

flagstaffs
USE **flagpoles**

flagstone
MT.886 (B)
CN M.MT.AFU.AFU.AFU.DCU.ALO.BCW

flagstone, Arizona
USE **Arizona flagstone**

flake
MT.2252
CN M.MT.AFU.ALO.DOI.ALO.AFU

flake board
USE **particle board**

flake white
USE **white lead**

flaking
KT.923
ALT **flaked**
SN Separating into thin flattened pieces or layers. (W)
CN K.KT.ALO.BZY.AXC.ALO

Flamboyant
FL.3140 (A,B,R)
UF Flamboyant Gothic
Gothic, Flamboyant
Tertiaire
CN F.FL.ALO.BCW.ALO.ALO.AFU.BOK.ARI.BIQ.ALO.ALO

Flamboyant Gothic
USE **Flamboyant**

flame black
USE **carbon black**

flame detectors
RT.1512
ALT **flame detector**
UF detectors, flame
flame sensors
sensors, flame
CN V.RT.ALO.BIQ.AFU.AFU.ALO.AFU.AFU

flame retardants
USE **fireproofing agents**

flame sensors
USE **flame detectors**

flame spread ratings
BM.885
SN Numerical values given to materials that designate their resistance to fire. (MEANS)
UF ratings, flame spread
CN B.BM.CFS.AXC.AXC.ALO.AFU

flameproof materials
USE **fireproofing agents**

flameproofing
USE **fireproofing**

flames
DG.43

ALT **flame**
SN Use for motifs of a conventionalized depiction of flames, usually wavy, peaked forms.
CN D.DG.AFU.AFU.CXA.ALO

flaming hearts
DG.35
ALT **flaming heart**
UF hearts, flaming
CN D.DG.AFU.AFU.BUE.AFU

flammable materials
MT.2794 (L)
UF materials, flammable
CN M.MT.AFU.BCW.BIQ

flammards
USE **froes**

flamming irons
USE **froes**

flange dovetail seams
TF.655
ALT **flange dovetail seam**
UF dovetail seams, flange
seams, flange dovetail
CN V.TF.ALO.ARI.ARI.BUE.BIQ

flange hangers
TF.362
ALT **flange hanger**
UF hangers, flange
CN V.TF.AFU.AFU.AFU.ALO.AFU.BOK.ARI.ARI.AFU.ALO

flank
USE **side**

flank elevations
USE **side elevations**

flanked columns
RT.106
ALT **flanked column**
SN Use for engaged columns flanked by half-pilasters.
UF columns, flanked
CN V.RT.AFU.AFU.AFU.AXC.BIQ.AFU.ALO.BCW.AFU

flanking windows
USE **side lights**

flannel
MT.1867 (L)
SN Includes soft, twilled cloth with a slightly napped surface, made in various weights of wool or worsted yarns, often in combination with cotton or synthetic yarns and napped cotton cloth of soft yarns which simulate the texture of wool flannel. (W)
CN M.MT.AFU.AFU.ARI.ALO.ALO.ALO.ALO.CFS

flap hinges
USE **backflap hinges**
strap hinges

flap tables
USE **dropleaf tables**

flaps
VB.93
ALT **flap**
CN V.VB.ALO.BOK.AXC

flare header
USE **glazed header**

flared feet
USE **French feet**

flaring bracket feet
USE **French feet**

flash attachments
TB.309 (N)
ALT **flash attachment**
SN Light sources which attach to the camera and coordinate with the shutter mechanism to provide a brief intense flash of light. (SWED)
UF attachments, flash
flash units
units, flash
CN V.TB.AFU.ARI.CLM.ARI.AFU.ALO.ALO

flash cubes
TB.310
ALT **flash cube**
UF cubes, flash
CN V.TB.AFU.ARI.CLM.ARI.AFU.ALO.ALO.AFU

flash point
BM.985
SN The minimum temperature in degrees Fahrenheit at which a material or its vapor will ignite or explode. (MH)
UF point, flash
CN B.BM.CFS.AXC.BZY.CFS.ARI

flash units
USE **flash attachments**

flashing
RT.735 (A,B)
SN Thin, impervious material placed in construction to prevent water penetration and/or provide water drainage; generally located between a roof and a wall and over exterior door openings and windows. (DAC)
CN V.RT.AFU.ALO.AFU.BCW

flashing (glassworking)
KT.764
ALT **flashed**
SN A method of coloring glass by dipping clear glass, while still pliant, into a bath of molten glass of a deep color, or by fusing a thin piece of dark glass to a thicker one of clear glass. (OCDA)
CN K.KT.AFU.ALO.HOE.ALO.ALO

flashing, base
USE **base flashing**

flashing, counter
USE **counter flashing**

flashing, cover
USE **counter flashing**

flashing, cap
USE **counter flashing**

flashing, stepped
USE **stepped flashing**

flashover
BM.886
CN B.BM.CFS.AXC.AXC.ALO.ALO

flasks (founding tools)
TB.692
ALT **flask (founding tool)**
SN Wooden or metal frames that hold the sand forming the mold used in a foundry. (W)
CN V.TB.AFU.BCW.BIQ.ALO.AFU

flat
DC.66 (R)
ALT **flatness**
SN Having a continuous surface without significant curvature, inclination, elevations, or depressions. Refers also to two-dimensional images lacking spatial qualities, and to areas of color without variations. To refer to a surface finish without gloss or luster, use **matte.**
CN D.DC.AFU.ARI.CFS

flat arches
RT.252
ALT **flat arch**
SN Use for arches of little or no curvature.
UF arches, flat
arches, jack
arches, straight
jack arches
straight arches
CN V.RT.AFU.AFU.AFU.BCW.AFU.AFU.AFU.ELK.AXC

flat bits
USE **flat tongs**

flat expanded metal lath
USE **diamond mesh lath**

flat files
TB.516 (N)
ALT **flat file**
SN General-purpose tapered steel files used essentially in metalwork but also in working hardwood surfaces.
UF files, flat
files, ward
ward files
CN V.TB.AFU.ARI.EWY.ALO.CFS.AFU

flat-head nails
TF.410

ALT **flat-head nail**
UF nails, flat-head
CN V.TF.AFU.AFU.AFU.ALO.AFU.CFS.AFU.DCU.BUE

flat-head wire brads
TF.403
ALT **flat-head wire brad**
UF brads, flat-head wire
wire brads, flat-head
CN V.TF.AFU.AFU.AFU.ALO.AFU.CFS.AFU.DCU.AFU.AFU

flat joints
USE **rough-cut joints**

flat (matte)
USE **matte**

flat nails, rose
USE **rose flat nails**

flat paint
MT.2543
SN Paint that dries to a surface substantially free from gloss or sheen. (GCT)
UF paint, flat
CN M.MT.AFU.ARI.CRG.ALO.BCW.ARI.BCW

flat plate construction, waffle
USE **waffle slabs**

flat plate systems
RT.31 (B)
ALT **flat plate system**
SN Use for structural systems based on two-way concrete slabs employing no beams, drop panels, or column capitals.
UF flat plate systems, two-way
systems, flat plate
systems, two-way flat plate
two-way flat plate systems
CN V.RT.AFU.AFU.AFU.ALO.ARI.ALO.AFU.ALO.AFU

flat plate systems, one-way
USE **one-way solid slab systems**

flat plate systems, two-way
USE **flat plate systems**

flat roofs
RT.415 (A,L,B)
ALT **flat roof**
SN Includes roofs with no slope and roofs with only sufficient slope to effect drainage.
UF roofs, flat
CN V.RT.AFU.AFU.AFU.BIQ.ARI.AFU.AFU.AFU.ARI

flat-sawed lumber
USE **plain-sawed lumber**

flat slab and beam systems
USE **two-way beam and slab systems**

flat slab and drop panel systems
USE **flat slab systems**

flat slab construction
USE **flat slab systems**

flat slab construction, two-way
USE **flat slab systems**

flat slab systems
RT.32
ALT **flat slab system**
SN Use for structural systems based on two-way concrete slabs with drop panels and often with capitals but without beams.
UF construction, flat slab
flat slab and drop panel systems
flat slab construction
flat slab construction, two-way
flat slab systems, two-way
flat slabs
slabs, flat
systems, flat slab
systems, flat slab and drop panel
two-way flat slab construction
two-way flat slab systems
CN V.RT.AFU.AFU.AFU.ALO.ARI.ALO.AFU.ALO.ALO

flat slab systems, two-way
USE **flat slab systems**

flat slabs
USE **flat slab systems**

flat stitching
USE **side sewing**

flat tongs
TB.754 (N)
SN Tongs whose jaws have flat straight faces.
UF bits, flat
flat bits
straight-lip tongs
tongs, flat
tongs, straight-lip
CN V.TB.AFU.BCW.BIQ.AXC.ALO.AXC.BCW

flat varnish
MT.2489
UF matte varnish
varnish, flat
varnish, matte
CN M.MT.AFU.ARI.CRG.AFU.BOK.ARI.AFU

flatbed cameras
USE **view cameras**

Flathead
FL.1407 (L)
UF Salish (Flathead)
CN F.FL.ALO.ALO.ARI.AFU.BUE.ARI

flats
RM.266 (A,L,B,R)
ALT **flat**
SN In American usage, one-floor apartments, usually modest, each having an outside entrance; use also for any building having a small number of such units and usually dating from the late 19th or early 20th century.
CN V.RM.AFU.DIO.ARI.ALO.BIQ.AFU.ALO

flats (landforms)
RD.215
SN Low-lying flat or level ground, usually associated with wetlands and river valleys.
CN V.RD.ARI.AFU.AXC.AFU.ALO.ARI.AFU

flats (theater elements)
RT.1279 (N)
ALT **flat (theater element)**
SN Usually rectangular units of scenery consisting of a framework of lightweight lumber and covered with canvas, linen, or other fabric.
CN V.RT.AFU.BUE.ARI.BUE.ALO.AFU

flats, blocks of
USE **apartment houses**

flats, coldwater
USE **coldwater flats**

flats, railroad
USE **railroad flats**

flats, salt
USE **salt flats**

Flavian
FL.2720 (R)
CN F.FL.ALO.AXC.ALO.ALO.AFU.AXC.ALO.AXC

flavine lake
USE **quercitron lake**

flax
MT.1827 (R)
CN M.MT.AFU.AFU.ARI.ALO.AFU.AFU.ALO.BCW

flea markets
KM.152 (L)
UF markets, flea
CN K.KM.AFU.ELK.ARI.ALO

fleches
RM.405
ALT **flech**
SN Use for slender spires rising from the ridge of a roof, most commonly from the roof intersection over the crossing of a church; use **crossing towers** for more substantial structures such as a lantern between spire and roof.
CN V.RM.AFU.DOI.ALO.AFU.ALO

Flemish
FL.3052 (L,B)
CN F.FL.ALO.BCW.AFU.CRG.ALO

Flemish bond
MT.2751
SN Bond in which headers and stretchers alternate horizontally and verti-

cally, each header being centered with regard to the stretcher above and below. (RS)
UF bond, Flemish
CN M.MT.AFU.AXC.BIQ.AFU.AFU.ARI

Flemish brick
MT.107
SN Hard, yellowish paving brick. (W)
UF brick, Flemish
CN M.MT.AFU.AFU.AFU.AXC.ALO.AFU.ALO.CFS.AFU

Flemish yellow
USE **massicot**

flesh
USE **pale orange yellow**

flesh pink
USE **light yellowish pink**
moderate yellowish pink
pale yellowish pink

fletton
MT.134
CN M.MT.AFU.AFU.AFU.AXC.ALO.AFU.AXC.ALO.ALO.AFU

fleurons
DG.56 (L)
ALT **fleuron**
SN Small decorative flowerlike elements; a term used loosely in reference to architecture and furniture and more specifically in reference to printers' type ornaments.
UF flowers, printer's
fonts, vignettes de
printer's flowers
Röslein
vignettes de fonts
CN D.DG.AFU.AFU.DIO.BCW

fleurs-de-lis
DG.57 (L,R)
ALT **fleur-de-lis**
SN A decorative motif in the form of a stylized lily, usually with three curled petals, but occasionally with five. (IDO)
CN D.DG.AFU.AFU.DIO.BIQ

flexibility
BM.201
ALT **flexible**
CN B.BM.AFU.ALO.ALO.AFU

flexible curves
TB.434 (N)
ALT **flexible curve**
SN Flexible guides that may be bent to fit the desired curve; used for drawing long curves. (PUTNAM)
UF curve tracers
curves, flexible
curves, snake
snake curves
tracers, curve
CN V.TB.AFU.ARI.EFQ.ALO.AFU.ALO

flexible insulation
MT.2406
UF insulation, flexible
CN M.MT.AFU.ARI.BZY.BCW.ARI.AFU

flexible materials
MT.2795
UF materials, flexible
CN M.MT.AFU.BCW.BOK

flexible pavements
RT.813
ALT **flexible pavement**
UF pavements, flexible
CN V.RT.AFU.ALO.AFU.BZY.AFU.AFU

flexible structures
USE **nonrigid structures**

fliers
RT.1114
ALT **flier**
SN Steps in a straight flight of stairs, each tread of which is of uniform width. (HAS)
UF flyers (steps)
CN V.RT.AFU.BIQ.AXC.ALO.BIQ.AFU.ALO

fliers, advertising
USE **advertising fliers**

flies
USE **fly lofts**

flights
RT.1101
ALT **flight**
SN Continuous series of steps with no intermediate landings. (HAS)
CN V.RT.AFU.BIQ.AXC.ALO.ARI

flights, straight
USE **straight stairs**

flint
MT.554 (L,N,B,R)
SN Type of quartz used in ceramic glazes and ceramic bodies.
CN M.MT.AFU.AFU.AFU.CFS.AFU.GRC.AFU.AXC

flint glass
MT.239 (R)
UF glass, flint
CN M.MT.AFU.AFU.AFU.BIQ.AFU.AFU.ALO

flint, potter's
USE **potter's flint**

flinting picks
TB.422 (N)
ALT **flinting pick**
UF picks, flinting
CN V.TB.AFU.ARI.DZW.BCW.AFU

flip-top tables
TG.703
ALT **flip-top table**
SN Double-top dining or card tables which unfold like a book, supported by pivoting about to the opposite axis, by a swing leg, or by a runner. (ARONS)
UF fold-over top tables
folding top tables
tables, flip-top
tables, fold-over top
tables, folding top
CN V.TG.AFU.AFU.BIQ.BOK.AFU.DZW.AFU

flipper-floppers
USE **rope ladders**

flit plows
USE **plow planes**

flitch beams
RT.295 (L)
ALT **flitch beam**
SN Beams built up of structural timbers which are bolted together with a steel plate sandwiched between them. (DAC)
UF beams, flitch
beams, flitch plate
beams, sandwich
flitch girders
flitch plate beams
girders, flitch
sandwich beams
CN V.RT.AFU.AFU.AFU.BCW.ALO.AFU.ARI.AFU

flitch girders
USE **flitch beams**

flitch plate beams
USE **flitch beams**

float files
TB.875
ALT **float file**
SN Coarse rounded single-cut files used for cleaning out mortises and for shaping the bed and throat of a plane.
UF files, float
floats (files)
CN V.TB.AFU.BCW.CFS.ALO.AFU.CFS.ALO

float glass
MT.261
UF glass, float
CN M.MT.AFU.AFU.AFU.BIQ.AFU.ARI.BOK

floating bridges
USE **pontoon bridges**

floating buildings
RK.1376 (A,B)
ALT **floating building**
UF buildings, floating
CN V.RK.AFU.ALO.AXC.AXC

floating docks
RK.1317 (N,B)
ALT **floating dock**
SN Docks that float on the water and

can be partly submerged to permit a ship to enter it and afterward floated to raise the ship high and dry as in a dry dock. (W)
UF docks, floating
floating dry docks
CN V.RK.AFU.ALO.ALO.GLI.ARI.ARI.ARI

floating dry docks
USE **floating docks**

floating floors
RT.742 (B)
ALT **floating floor**
SN Floor slabs or floor assemblies which are completely separated from (and mechanically isolated from) the structural floor by a resilient underlayment or resilient mounting devices; used to isolate the vibration of machinery from the building structure. (DAC)
UF floors, floating
CN V.RT.AFU.ALO.AFU.BIQ.AFU.ALO

floating hotels
RK.953 (A)
ALT **floating hotel**
UF hotels, floating
CN V.RK.AFU.ALO.ALO.ELK.BCW.AFU

floating houses
USE **houseboats**

floating (surface finishing)
KT.685
ALT **floated**
SN Surface finishing process for concrete and mortar that embeds aggregate, removes slight imperfections, humps, and voids to produce a level surface, and consolidates material rising to the surface. (STEIN)
CN K.KT.AFU.ALO.GRC.BCW.ALO

Floating-world
USE **Ukiyo-e**

floats
TB.592 (N)
ALT **float**
SN Tools, usually of wood, aluminum, or magnesium, used in concrete finishing operations to impart a relatively even but still open texture to an unformed fresh concrete surface. (MEANS)
CN V.TB.AFU.BCW.BCW.ALO.DIO

floats (files)
USE **float files**

floats, angle
USE **angle floats**

floats, bull
USE **bull floats**

floats, devil
USE **devil floats**

floats, hand
USE **hand floats**

floats, long
USE **darbies**

floats, nail
USE **devil floats**

floats, texture
USE **texture floats**

floatstones
TB.598
ALT **floatstone**
SN Stones used in bricklaying to rub the rough spots and ax marks from curved work. (MEANS)
UF rubbing stones
rubstones
stones, rubbing
CN V.TB.AFU.BCW.BCW.ALO.DOI

flock printing
USE **flocking**

flock spraying
USE **flocking**

flocking
KT.667
ALT **flocked**
SN The creation of a textured effect similar to suede or felt by blowing fibers of cotton, silk, nylon, or other material onto a tacky surface. (DAC)
UF flock printing
flock spraying
printing, flock
spraying, flock
CN K.KT.AFU.ALO.GRC.AFU.ARI

floggers, bung
USE **bungstarts**

flood control
KG.116 (L,B,R)
UF control, flood
flood damage protection
flood protection
protection, flood
protection, flood damage
CN K.KG.AFU.AFU.BCW.ALO.ARI

flood control dams
USE **flood dams**

flood control works
USE **flood protection works**

flood damage protection
USE **flood control**

flood dams
RK.530 (A,L)
ALT **flood dam**
SN Use for dams constructed to store floodwaters temporarily or to supply a surge of water, as for clearing a channel of logs. (W)
UF dams, flood
flood control dams
CN V.RK.AFU.ALO.ALO.CFS.AFU.ARI.ALO.BCW

flood plains
RD.194 (L)
ALT **flood plain**
UF plains, flood
CN V.RD.ARI.AFU.AXC.AFU.AFU.ARI.BIQ

flood-prone-area maps
VW.186
ALT **flood-prone-area map**
UF maps, flood-prone-area
CN V.VW.AFU.AFU.AFU.FZU.AXC.AFU.ARI.AXC.BCW.ALO

flood protection
USE **flood control**

flood protection works
RK.565
UF flood control works
waterflow control works
works, flood protection
works, waterflow control
CN V.RK.AFU.ALO.ALO.CFS.ALO.ARI

flood walls
USE **levees**

floodgates
USE **sluice gates**

floodlighting
RT.1357 (A,L,B)
CN V.RT.ALO.AXC.AFU.AXC

floods
KM.111 (L,R)
SN Risings and overflowings of bodies of water, covering land not usually underwater. (W)
CN K.KM.AFU.CXA.AXC

floor and roof systems, one-way
USE **one-way structural systems**

floor and roof systems, two-way
USE **two-way structural systems**

floor brick
MT.104
UF brick, floor
CN M.MT.AFU.AFU.AFU.AXC.ALO.AFU.ALO.BUE

floor chisels
TB.862
ALT **floor chisel**
SN Steel chisels having a broad blade and a long shank; especially used for ripping up floor boards. (DAC)
UF chisels, floor
CN V.TB.AFU.BCW.CFS.ALO.AFU.BUE.AXC

floor constructions, beam-and-slab
USE **one-way beam and slab systems**

floor hinges
TF.135
ALT **floor hinge**

UF hinges, floor
CN V.TF.AFU.AFU.AFU.AFU.CLM.ALO.ARI

floor hinges, checking
USE **checking floor hinges**

floor joists
RT.305 (N)
ALT **floor joist**
SN Joists which carry a floor. (DAC)
UF joists, floor
CN V.RT.AFU.AFU.AFU.BCW.ALO.AFU.BOK.ALO.ALO

floor planes
TB.945 (N)
ALT **floor plane**
SN Long planes, up to 36 inches, used in making floorboards; distinct from **jointer planes** in their size and use.
UF planes, floor
CN V.TB.AFU.BCW.CFS.ALO.AFU.DUC.ARI.BCW

floor plans
VD.46 (A,L)
ALT **floor plan**
SN Drawings that represent a horizontal section through a building taken above a floor.
UF plans, floor
CN V.VD.AFU.AFU.BIQ.ALO.AXC.ALO.AFU

floor plans, typical
USE **typical floor plans**

floor to ceiling windows
RT.924 (B)
ALT **floor to ceiling window**
UF windows, floor to ceiling
CN V.RT.AFU.ARI.AFU.AFU.BOK.AFU.AFU.CRG

floor varnish
USE **finishing varnish**

flooring
MT.2390 (A,L,B)
SN Any material used in laying a floor. (DAC)
UF finish flooring
flooring, finish
planching
CN M.MT.AFU.ARI.BZY.AXC.AFU

flooring awls
USE **bradawls**

flooring brad nails
USE **flooring nails**

flooring cement
USE **gypsum cement**

flooring hammers
USE **clench hammers**

flooring nails
TF.435
ALT **flooring nail**
SN Steel nails each having a deformed shank, often helically threaded, having a countersunk head and a short diamond-shaped point. (MEANS)
UF brad nails, flooring
flooring brad nails
nails, flooring
nails, plancher
plancher nails
CN V.TF.AFU.AFU.AFU.ALO.AFU.CFS.ALO.BOK

flooring plaster
USE **gypsum cement**

flooring sand
MT.2070
UF sand, flooring
CN M.MT.AFU.AFU.ARI.BOK.ALO.BOK.AFU.AFU

flooring systems, raised
USE **access floors**

flooring, finish
USE **flooring**

flooring, tile
USE **tile flooring**

floors
RT.740 (A,L,B,R)
ALT **floor**
CN V.RT.AFU.ALO.AFU.BIQ.AFU

floors (stories)
USE **stories**

floors, access
USE **access floors**

floors, floating
USE **floating floors**

floors, sprung
USE **sprung floors**

floors, stage
USE **stage floors**

floors, suspended
USE **suspended floors**

flophouses
RK.964 (L)
ALT **flophouse**
CN V.RK.AFU.ALO.ALO.ELK.BUE.AFU

floppy disks
VW.648
ALT **floppy disk**
SN Thin, round, flexible disks with magnetic surfaces for storing and retrieving data. (RHDEL2)
UF diskettes
disks, floppy
CN V.VW.AFU.ALO.AFU.DZW.ALO.ARI.AFU

floral designers
HG.155
ALT **floral designer**
SN Persons who design and fashion live, cut, dried, and artificial floral and foliar arrangements. (DOT)
UF designers, floral
CN H.HG.AFU.AXC.AXC.AFU.AFU.ALO.BCW.BIQ

floral ornament
USE **floral patterns**

floral patterns
DG.120 (L)
ALT **floriated**
floral pattern
UF floral ornament
floreation
floriated ornament
floriation
flower patterns
ornament, floral
ornament, floriated
patterns, floral
patterns, flower
CN D.DG.AFU.ARI.ALO.AXC

Floral Style
FL.2667
CN F.FL.ALO.AXC.ALO.AFU.ALO.AXC.BCW.ARI

floreation
USE **floral patterns**

Florentine arches
RT.226
ALT **Florentine arch**
SN Use for round arches in which the voussoirs increase in length as they approach the center, so that the curve of the extrados is more vertical in proportion than the curve of the intrados. For similar arches when pointed, use **Italian pointed arches.**
UF arches, Florentine
CN V.RT.AFU.AFU.AFU.BCW.AFU.AFU.AFU.BUE

Florentine lake
USE **carmine**
crimson lake

Flores
FL.2376 (L)
CN F.FL.ALO.ARI.BCW.ARI.ALO.ARI

floriated ornament
USE **floral patterns**

floriation
USE **floral patterns**

floriculture
KD.198 (L)
CN K.KD.AFU.ARI.ALO.AFU.AFU

Florid Style
FL.2646
CN F.FL.ALO.AXC.ALO.AFU.ALO.AXC.ARI.AXC.AFU

Florida rooms
USE **solariums**

florist shops
RK.158 (A,L,B,R)
ALT **florist shop**
UF florists
flower shops
shops, florist
shops, flower
CN V.RK.AFU.ALO.ALO.ALO.ARI.BIQ.AFU.BUE

florists
USE **florist shops**

flour mills
RK.633 (A,L,B,R)
ALT **flour mill**
UF gristmills
mills, flour
CN V.RK.AFU.ALO.ALO.CLM.ALO.ALO.AFU.AXC.BCW.AXC

flour, marble
USE **marble dust**

flow diagrams
USE **flowcharts**

flow-line maps
VW.146
ALT **flow-line map**
SN Maps showing movement of materials, the direction or route followed being indicated by a line representing the railway, waterway, or other route concerned, while the width of the line represents the quantity of material conveyed. (LG)
UF maps, flow-line
CN V.VW.AFU.AFU.AFU.FZU.AXC.AFU.ARI.AFU.BOK

flow, heat
USE **heat transmission**

flowcharts
VW.239 (L,N)
ALT **flowchart**
UF diagrams, flow
flow diagrams
CN V.VW.AFU.AFU.AFU.FZU.AXC.ALO.AXC

flower boxes
USE **window boxes**

flower gardens
RK.1432 (N)
ALT **flower garden**
UF gardens, flower
CN V.RK.ALO.AFU.AFU.AXC.AFU

flower patterns
USE **floral patterns**

flower shops
USE **florist shops**

flower stands
USE **plant stands**

flower tables
USE **plant stands**

flowers
RD.268 (L,B,R)
ALT **flower**
SN Designates both the reproductive shoots of seed-bearing plants and entire flowering plants.
UF angiospermae
CN V.RD.ARI.AFU.BCW.ALO.ALO.ALO.AFU.AXC

flowers, printer's
USE **fleurons**

flowers, Tudor
USE **Tudor flowers**

flowing tracery
RT.1018
UF curvilinear tracery
tracery, curvilinear
tracery, flowing
tracery, undulating
undulating tracery
CN V.RT.AFU.ARI.ALO.BZY.AFU.AFU.AFU

flue linings
RT.1146 (L)
ALT **flue lining**
UF chimney linings
linings, flue
CN V.RT.AFU.BOK.AFU.ALO.CFS

flue pipes
USE **flues**

flues
RT.1147 (A,L,N,B)
ALT **flue**
UF chimney flues
flue pipes
flues, chimney
pipes, flue
smoke-pipes
CN V.RT.AFU.BOK.AFU.ALO.CLM

flues, chimney
USE **flues**

fluid copying processes
USE **spirit duplicating**

fluid duplicating
USE **spirit duplicating**

flumes
RK.515 (L,N)
ALT **flume**
SN Artificial channels or troughs for conducting water, as for transporting logs or providing water power. (RHDEL2)
CN V.RK.AFU.ALO.ALO.CFS.AFU.AFU.AFU

fluorescence
BM.968 (L)
ALT **fluorescent**
SN Emission of or the property of emitting electro-magnetic radiation usually as visible light resulting from and occurring only during the absorption of radiation from some other source. (W)
CN B.BM.CFS.AXC.BZY.BUE.AFU

fluorescent lighting
RT.1371 (L,B)
UF lighting, fluorescent
CN V.RT.ALO.AXC.ARI.ALO

fluorescent paint
MT.2546 (B)
SN Luminous paint containing a pigment that stores light.
UF day-glow paint
paint, day-glow
paint, fluorescent
paint, phosphorescent
phosphorescent paint
CN M.MT.AFU.ARI.CRG.ALO.BCW.ARI.BOK.AFU

fluorine dating
KT.498
SN Method of relative dating by measuring the amount of flourine absorbed by groundwater percolation into the crystal lattice of the mineral component of buried bone. (FOFDA)
UF dating, fluorine
CN K.KT.AFU.ALO.EFQ.AFU.AFU.AFU

fluorine plastic
USE **fluoroplastic**

fluorite
MT.517 (L)
SN Transparent or translucent mineral of many different colors and containg calcium fluoride, occuring commonly in crystalline cubes with perfect octahedral cleavage and in massive form, and being used as a flux, as a source of fluorine compounds and in preparation of opalescent and opaque glasses and of vitreous enamels. (W)
UF fluorspar
CN M.MT.AFU.AFU.AFU.CFS.AFU.DCU

fluorocarbon elastomer
MT.2085
SN Highest in resistance to oxidation, chemicals, oils, solvents, and heat; typical applications are brake seals, O rings, diaphragms, and hose. (MH)
UF elastomer, fluorocarbon
CN M.MT.AFU.AFU.ARI.BUE.AFU.AFU.AXC

fluorocarbon plastic
USE **fluoroplastic**

fluorocarbon resin
USE **fluoroplastic**

fluorohydrocarbon
USE **fluoroplastic**

fluoroplastic
MT.2136 (L)

SN Class of plastics characterized by resistance to aggressive environments, including extremes of weather, and temperatures ranging from near zero to 260 degrees C. (DIETZ)
UF fluorine plastic
fluorocarbon plastic
fluorocarbon resin
fluorohydrocarbon
plastic, fluorine
plastic, fluorocarbon
resin, fluorocarbon
CN M.MT.AFU.AFU.ARI.BUE.ALO.AXC.AFU.BIQ

fluorosilicone elastomer
MT.2094
UF elastomer, fluorosilicone
CN M.MT.AFU.AFU.ARI.BUE.AFU.AFU.CLM.AFU

fluorspar
USE **fluorite**

Flup
USE **Felup**

flush and rodded joints
TF.626
ALT **flush and rodded joint**
UF joints, flush and rodded
CN V.TF.ALO.ARI.ALO.AFU.ARI.AXC.ALO

flush bolts
TF.168
ALT **flush bolt**
SN Door bolts or other bolts mounted on a surface. (MEANS)
UF bolts, flush
CN V.TF.AFU.AFU.AFU.AFU.DIO.ARI.BCW

flush bolts, extension
USE **extension flush bolts**

flush-cup pulls
TF.76
ALT **flush-cup pull**
SN Door pulls for a sliding door that are mortised flush into the door and have a curved recess serving as a finger grip. (MEANS)
UF flush pulls
pulls, flush-cup
CN V.TF.AFU.AFU.AFU.AFU.CFS.BCW.AFU.BIQ

flush doors
RT.854 (B)
ALT **flush door**
SN Smooth surfaced doors having faces which are plane and conceal their rails and stiles or other structures. (DAC)
UF doors, flush
CN V.RT.AFU.ARI.AFU.AFU.AFU.ALO.ARI.AFU.AFU.BOK.ALO

flush eaves
RT.461
SN Eaves in which the eaves fascias are fixed directly against the wall face. (MARSH)
UF eaves, flush
CN V.RT.AFU.AFU.AFU.BIQ.ARI.ALO.AFU.ALO.AFU.ALO

flush joints
TF.587
ALT **flush joint**
SN Any joints that are flush with the adjacent surfaces. (MEANS)
UF joints, flush
CN V.TF.ALO.AFU.CXA

flush joints (mortar joints)
USE **rough-cut joints**

flush masonry joints
USE **rough-cut joints**

flush pulls
USE **flush-cup pulls**

flush ring pulls
USE **flush rings**

flush rings
TF.77
ALT **flush ring**
SN Door pulls mortised into a door, each having a pulling ring that folds flat into a recess when not in use. (MEANS)
UF flush ring pulls
pulls, flush ring
rings, flush
CN V.TF.AFU.AFU.AFU.AFU.CFS.BCW.AFU.BOK

flush top hangers
TF.373
ALT **flush top hanger**
UF hangers, flush top
top hangers, flush
CN V.TF.AFU.AFU.AFU.ALO.AFU.BOK.ARI.ARI.AXC.ALO.ALO

flush valves
TF.281
ALT **flush valve**
SN Valves installed in the bottom of a toilet tank to discharge the water needed to flush the fixture. (MEANS)
UF valves, flush
CN V.TF.AFU.AFU.AFU.AFU.EWY.ARI

flute reamers
TB.719
ALT **flute reamer**
SN Tools used for removing burrs from pipes. (PUTNAM)
UF reamers, flute
CN V.TB.AFU.BCW.BIQ.ARI.ALO.AXC

Fluted, Cumberland
USE **Cumberland Fluted**

fluters
TB.886
ALT **fluter**
SN Gouges with a deep channel; used for making flutings.
UF fluting gouges
gouges, fluting
CN V.TB.AFU.BCW.CFS.ALO.AFU.CXA.BCW

flutes (surfacing pattern)
USE **fluting**

fluting
DG.112
ALT **fluted**
SN Closely spaced parallel grooves used to ornament columns and pilasters and in the decorative arts in woodwork, metalwork, glass, and ceramics. (THDAT)
UF flutes (surfacing pattern)
CN D.DG.AFU.ARI.ALO.ARI.ARI

fluting gouges
USE **fluters**

fluting, cabled
USE **cabled fluting**

fluting, ribbed
USE **cabled fluting**

flutter
BM.1003 (L)
CN B.BM.CFS.AXC.CLM.ALO.ALO

fluvial deposits
USE **fluvial landforms**

fluvial landforms
RD.187
ALT **fluvial landform**
UF deposits, fluvial
fluvial deposits
landforms, fluvial
CN V.RD.ARI.AFU.AXC.AFU.AFU.ARI

flux
MT.2616
SN A substance added to a solid to increase its fusibility. (TATEMT)
CN M.MT.AFU.ARI.EWY

Fluxus
FL.3726 (R)
CN F.FL.ALO.BUE.ARI.CLM

fly ash
USE **ash (residue)**

fly chairs
USE **rout chairs**

fly legs
USE **swing legs**

fly lofts
RM.360
ALT **fly loft**
SN The spaces above the stage behind the proscenium, out of view of the audience, used during a performance for the storage of hanging scenery. (TL)
UF flies

lofts, fly
lofts, stage
stage lofts
CN V.RM.AFU.DIO.AXC.AXC.ALO.AFU

fly rafters
USE **bargeboards**

fly tables
TG.672
ALT **fly table**
SN Small tables with extending flaps supported on slender legs, or hinged brackets. (BEARD)
UF tables, fly
CN V.TG.AFU.AFU.BIQ.BOK.AFU.AXC.ALO

flyers (flying buttresses)
USE **flying buttresses**

flyers (steps)
USE **fliers**

flying bridges
USE **skybridges**

flying buttresses
RT.77 (A,B,R)
ALT **flying buttress**
SN Arches or half-arches transmitting the thrust of a vault or roof from the upper part of a wall to an outer support or buttress. (PDARC)
UF arch buttresses
arched butments
arched buttresses
butments, arched
buttresses, arch
buttresses, arched
buttresses, flying
flyers (flying buttresses)
CN V.RT.AFU.AFU.AFU.AXC.AXC.ALO

flying facades
USE **false fronts**

flying ribs
RT.686
ALT **flying rib**
SN Use for ceiling ribs that are partly or entirely detached from the surface of the vault, thus forming an aerial network; found in German and English Late Gothic architecture.
UF ribs, flying
CN V.RT.AFU.AFU.ALO.AFU.ARI.ALO

flying stairs
RT.1071
ALT **flying stair**
SN Stairs cantilevered from the stairwell without a newel. (NICH)
UF cantilevered stairs
stairs, cantilevered
stairs, flying
CN V.RT.AFU.BIQ.AXC.AFU.AFU.ALO

flying testers
TG.860
ALT **flying tester**
SN Rooflike components generally cantilevered from the headboard as opposed to being supported by posts, and which extend over the whole area of the bed. Use **half-testers** for similar forms which only extend over the head half.
UF testers, flying
CN V.TG.ALO.BIQ.CRG.ALO

FM
USE **facility management**

Fo
USE **Bafo**
Fon

foam
MT.2245 (A,L)
CN M.MT.AFU.ALO.DCU

foam rubber
MT.2098 (L)
UF rubber, foam
rubber, sponge
sponge rubber
CN M.MT.AFU.AFU.ARI.BUE.AFU.ALO.AFU

foam, plastic
USE **plastic foam**

foam, structural
USE **structural foam**

foamed concrete
MT.212 (B)
UF concrete, foamed
CN M.MT.AFU.AFU.AFU.BCW.AFU.ARI.ALO

foamed glass
USE **cellular glass**

foamed plastic
USE **plastic foam**

foamed sand concrete
MT.213 (B)
UF concrete, foamed sand
sand concrete, foamed
CN M.MT.AFU.AFU.AFU.BCW.AFU.ARI.ALO.AFU

foamed slag concrete
MT.214 (B)
UF concrete, foamed slag
slag concrete, foamed
CN M.MT.AFU.AFU.AFU.BCW.AFU.ARI.ALO.ALO

foaming agents
MT.2313
SN Chemical additives that release a gas to expand the material by forming closed bubbles; also used to cause a froth as in detergents or fire-fighting foams. (MH)
UF agents, foaming
CN M.MT.AFU.ARI.ALO.CRG

focal point
BM.58
SN The area or feature of a composition, whether pictorial, sculptural, or architectural, to which the eye is especially drawn.
UF point, focal
CN B.BM.AFU.AFU.ARI.AFU.BCW.ALO.ARI

fog
BM.927 (L,B)
CN B.BM.CFS.AXC.BOK.AFU.ALO

fogous
RK.1369 (A,L)
ALT **fogou**
SN Designates partially or mostly underground structures or series of rooms and passages, of unclear function, found associated with English Iron Age settlements.
CN V.RK.AFU.ALO.ARI.AXC.BUE.AFU

foil
MT.455 (L)
SN Very thin sheet metal used chiefly for wrapping, insulation, electrical applications, and as an ornamental surface treatment. (MH12)
UF foil, metal
metal foil
CN M.MT.AFU.AFU.AFU.BZY.AFU.ALO.AFU

foil back insulation
USE **reflective insulation**

foil underengraving, glass
USE **verre églomisé**

foil, metal
USE **foil**

foiled arches
USE **cusped arches**

foils
RT.1028
ALT **foil**
SN In tracery, any of several lobes, circular or nearly so, tangent to the inner side of a larger arc, as of an arch, or meeting each other in cusps projecting inward from the arch, or circle. (HAS)
UF lobes
CN V.RT.AFU.ARI.ALO.BZY.ALO.ALO

fold joints, dog-eared
USE **dog-eared fold joints**

fold-over top tables
USE **flip-top tables**

folded-arm type
FL.2678
CN F.FL.ALO.AXC.ALO.AFU.ALO.BCW.AFU.ALO

folded plate structures
RT.23 (A,L)

ALT **folded plate structure**
SN Use for structural systems based on one-way plates given additional stiffness by folding into a series of long, narrow planes, the typical sections resembling a series of interconnected Ws or splay-sided Us.
UF folded plates
folded structures
plates, folded
structures, folded
structures, folded plate
CN V.RT.AFU.AFU.AFU.ALO.ARI.AFU

folded plates
USE **folded plate structures**

folded structures
USE **folded plate structures**

folding armchairs, Plona
USE **Plona folding armchairs**

folding beds
TG.338 (N)
ALT **folding bed**
UF beds, folding
beds, turn-up
turn-up beds
CN V.TG.AFU.AFU.ARI.AFU.AFU.BIQ

folding beds, chiffonier
USE **chiffonier beds**

folding beds, piano
USE **piano beds**

folding chairs
TG.218 (L,N)
ALT **folding chair**
UF chairs, folding
CN V.TG.AFU.AFU.ALO.AFU.AFU.AXC.AFU

folding chairs, Plia
USE **Plia folding chairs**

folding cribs
TG.335
ALT **folding crib**
UF cribs, folding
cribs, portable
portable cribs
CN V.TG.AFU.AFU.ARI.AFU.AFU.AXC.ARI.AFU

folding doors
RT.865 (N,B)
ALT **folding door**
SN Doors of two or more hinged leaves which open by bringing the leaves into parallel positions.
UF accordion doors
concertina doors
doors, accordion
doors, concertina
doors, folding
CN V.RT.AFU.ARI.AFU.AFU.AFU.ALO.ARI.AFU.ARI.AFU

folding fire screens
TG.7
ALT **folding fire screen**
SN Fire screens designed with two hinged leaves. (GILBR2)
UF fire screens, folding
screens, folding fire
CN V.TG.AFU.AFU.AFU.AFU.ARI

folding furniture
TG.793
UF convertible furniture
furniture, folding
CN V.TG.AFU.ARI.BCW

folding partitions
RT.607 (B)
ALT **folding partition**
SN Any partition that can be withdrawn into a relatively compact position by folding, coiling, or stacking its component parts.
UF movable partitions
partitions, folding
partitions, movable
CN V.RT.AFU.AFU.AFU.BIQ.BUE.AFU.ARI.AXC.AFU.ALO

folding screens
TG.16 (R)
ALT **folding screen**
UF draught screens
screens, draught
screens, folding
CN V.TG.AFU.AFU.AFU.ALO

folding shutters
RT.1010
ALT **folding shutter**
SN Window shutters which can be folded into the boxing or recess at the side. (HAS)
UF boxing shutters
shutters, boxing
shutters, folding
CN V.RT.AFU.ARI.ALO.BIQ.AFU

folding stools
TG.265 (N)
ALT **folding stool**
UF cross-legged stools
folding X-stools
stools, cross-legged
stools, folding
X-stools, folding
CN V.TG.AFU.AFU.ALO.AFU.ALO.AXC.AFU

folding top tables
USE **flip-top tables**

folding X-stools
USE **folding stools**

foldouts
VB.94
ALT **foldout**
CN V.VB.ALO.BOK.BCW

foliage
USE **leaves**

foliage scrolls
USE **scrolling foliage**

foliate decoration
USE **foliation**

foliate patterns
USE **foliation**

foliate scrolls
USE **leaf scrolls**

foliation
DG.121 (L)
ALT **foliated**
UF decoration, foliate
foliate decoration
foliate patterns
patterns, foliate
CN D.DG.AFU.ARI.ALO.BCW

folk architecture
USE **vernacular architecture**

folk art
BM.245 (L,B,R)
UF art, folk
art, peasant
peasant art
CN B.BM.AFU.ARI.BCW.DOI

folk art museums
RK.386 (A)
ALT **folk art museum**
UF art museums, folk
folk museums
museums, folk art
CN V.RK.AFU.ALO.ALO.BCW.AXC.ARI.AFU.ARI

folk artists
HG.102 (L)
ALT **folk artist**
UF artists, folk
CN H.HG.AFU.AXC.AXC.AFU.AFU.ALO.AXC.CFS

folk museums
USE **ethnological museums**
folk art museums

Folk Style, Kuba
USE **Kuba Folk Style**

folk tales
BM.272 (L,R)
UF tales, folk
CN B.BM.AFU.ARI.BIQ.AXC.ALO

folklore
BM.270 (L,R)
SN Study of culture through its traditional and expressive forms, such as song, story, dance, ritual, handicraft, art, food ways, costume, custom, religion, architecture, and work skills, and of the processes and meanings that underlie them. (PG)
CN B.BM.AFU.ARI.BIQ.AXC

follies
RK.1333 (A,L,B,R)

ALT **folly**
SN Use for garden structures characterized by a certain excess in terms of eccentricity, cost, or conspicuous inutility.
UF architectural follies
CN V.RK.AFU.ALO.ARI.AFU.ARI

Folsom
FL.747 (L)
CN F.FL.ALO.ALO.ALO.AFU.AFU.ARI.ALO.ALO

Fon
FL.303 (L)
UF Fo
CN F.FL.ALO.AFU.AXC.AFU.ARI.ALO.ARI

fonts
RT.1233 (A,L,N,B,R)
ALT **font**
UF baptismal fonts
CN V.RT.AFU.BUE.ALO.ARI.BOK

fonts, vignettes de
USE **fleurons**

food cupboards
USE **livery cupboards**

food factories
USE **food processing plants**

food lockers
USE **livery cupboards**

food processing plants
RK.629 (A,L,B)
ALT **food processing plant**
UF factories, food
food factories
plants, food processing
processing plants, food
CN V.RK.AFU.ALO.ALO.CLM.ALO.ALO.AFU.AXC.BCW

food products
MT.2617
UF foodstuffs
products, food
CN M.MT.AFU.ARI.FCS

food safes
USE **kitchen safes**

foodstuffs
USE **food products**

fool's gold
USE **pyrite**

fools
USE **jesters**

foot bolts
TF.314
ALT **foot bolt**
SN Bolts applied at the bottom of a door and arranged for foot operation; held up by a spring when door is unbolted. (STEIN)
UF bolts, foot
CN V.TF.AFU.AFU.AFU.ALO.AFU.ALO.AFU.BIQ

foot pedal valves
TF.282
ALT **foot pedal valve**
UF pedal valves, foot
valves, foot pedal
CN V.TF.AFU.AFU.AFU.AFU.EWY.AXC

foot sockets
TF.54
ALT **foot socket**
SN Use for cups or covers attached to the feet of furniture, to protect as well as to allow easy movement. Distinguished from **castors** which are wheels set in a swivel and added to the feet on furniture to allow easy movement.
UF sockets, foot
CN V.TF.AFU.AFU.AFU.AFU.BZY

foot streets
USE **pedestrian streets**

foot, bear's
USE **acanthus**

football fields
RK.1480
ALT **football field**
UF fields, football
gridirons
CN V.RK.ALO.ALO.BCW.AFU.ARI

football pitches
USE **soccer fields**

football stadiums
RK.1056
ALT **football stadium**
UF stadiums, football
CN V.RK.AFU.ALO.ALO.EWY.AXC.BIQ.AFU.BCW.ALO

footboards
TG.854
ALT **footboard**
SN Boards forming the end of anything, especially a bed.
CN V.TG.ALO.BIQ.BZY

footbridges
RK.1287 (A,L,B,R)
ALT **footbridge**
SN Use for generally narrow bridges for people and animals to cross on foot. (NTBOFB)
UF bridges, pedestrian
overpasses, pedestrian
pedestrian bridges
pedestrian overpasses
pedestrian walkways
walkways, pedestrian
CN V.RK.AFU.ALO.ALO.GLI.ALO.AFU.ALO.AFU

Foothill Yokuts
USE **Yokuts**

foothills
RD.204
ALT **foothill**
SN Hills or hilly regions at the base of a mountain or mountain range.
CN V.RD.ARI.AFU.AXC.AFU.ALO.AFU.ALO.AFU

footings
RT.171 (A,B)
ALT **footing**
SN Portions of the foundations of some structures which transmit loads directly to the soil; used to spread the load over a greater area to prevent or reduce settlings. (DAC)
CN V.RT.AFU.AFU.AFU.AXC.BUE.ARI.ALO.AFU

footings, cantilevered
USE **cantilevered footings**

footings, combined
USE **combined footings**

footings, continuous
USE **continuous footings**

footings, strap
USE **continuous footings**

footings, strip
USE **continuous footings**

footpaces
USE **footrests**

footpaths
RK.1575 (A,L,B)
ALT **footpath**
SN Narrow paths for pedestrians. (W)
CN V.RK.ALO.ALO.BUE.AXC.ARI

footposts
TG.848
ALT **footpost**
SN Posts at the foot of a bed.
CN V.TG.ALO.BIQ.AXC.AFU

footrails
USE **footrests**

footrests
TG.936
ALT **footrest**
SN Supports for a person's feet, as an attachment to a barber's or a reclining chair.
UF footpaces
footrails
footstools (footrests)
CN V.TG.ALO.EFQ

footstones
USE **kneelers (gable components)**

footstools
TG.243 (N)
ALT **footstool**
SN Small, low stools, to support one's feet.
UF tabourets de pied
threnys

CN V.TG.AFU.AFU.ALO.AFU.ALO.AFU.BIQ

footstools (footrests)
USE **footrests**

footstools, ottoman
USE **ottoman footstools**

fora
USE **forums**

foramina
USE **fenestellas**

forbidden arts
KD.295
SN One of the three ancient categories of learning, along with the seven liberal and the seven mechanical arts; included magic, divination, and thievery. (DMA)
UF arts, forbidden
CN K.KD.AFU.BCW.AFU

force
BM.904 (L,R)
SN An agency or influence (as a push or pull) that, if applied to a free body, results chiefly in an acceleration of the body and sometimes in elastic deformation and other effects. (W)
CN B.BM.CFS.AXC.BIQ.ALO.AFU

force cups
USE **plungers**

force, centrifugal
USE **centrifugal force**

force, centripetal
USE **centripetal force**

forced air heating
RT.1402
SN Systems that use motor driven fans or blowers to distribute heated air.
UF forced-air heating systems
heating, forced air
systems, forced-air heating
CN V.RT.ALO.BCW.AFU.AFU.ARI.BIQ.AFU

forced-air heating systems
USE **forced air heating**

forces, armed
USE **armed forces**

forces, task
USE **task forces**

forcing houses
RK.64
ALT **forcing house**
SN Greenhouses in which plants are brought to maturity out of season, especially in quantities for market.
UF hotbeds
CN V.RK.AFU.ALO.ALO.AFU.AFU.BOK.AFU.AFU

fore choirs
USE **antechoirs**

fore planes
USE **jack planes**

fore punches
TB.673 (N)
ALT **fore punch**
SN Punches used for making square holes in horeshoes. (SMITH)
UF punches, fore
CN V.TB.AFU.BCW.BIQ.AFU.ALO.BZY.BCW

foreclosing
KG.197 (L)
ALT **foreclosed**
SN Proceeding against a property owner who has failed to meet the obligation of a mortgage loan or other liens like tax liens; used to force the sale of the property to pay the debt. (STEIN)
CN K.KG.AFU.ALO.BCW.AXC

forecourts
RM.45 (A)
ALT **forecourt**
SN Courts forming an entrance plaza for a single building or several buildings in a group. (HAS)
UF antecourts
cours d'honneur
CN V.RM.AFU.DIO.AFU.BCW.ARI.ARI

foreground
BM.59
SN That part of a pictorial composition that appears to be closest to the viewer. (MAYER)
CN B.BM.AFU.AFU.ARI.AFU.BCW.ALO.AXC

foreign correspondents
HG.290 (L)
ALT **foreign correspondent**
UF correspondents, foreign
CN H.HG.AFU.AXC.BCW.ALO.AFU.ARI.ARI.AFU.AFU

foreign-language dictionaries
VW.399 (L)
ALT **foreign-language dictionary**
UF bilingual dictionaries
dictionaries, bilingual
dictionaries, foreign-language
CN V.VW.AFU.AFU.ALO.EWY.ARI.ALO.ARI

foremen
HG.659 (L)
ALT **foreman**
SN Specially trained workers who work with and commonly lead a crew. (W)
UF chargehands
CN H.HG.AFU.AXC.CFS.AFU.ALO.AFU.AFU

forensic jurisprudence
USE **forensic medicine**

forensic medicine
KD.292 (L)
UF forensic jurisprudence
jurisprudence, forensic
jurisprudence, medical
legal medicine
medical jurisprudence
medicine, forensic
medicine, legal
CN K.KD.AFU.AXC.AFU

fores
USE **door leaves**

foreshortening
KT.264 (R)
ALT **forshortened**
SN In pictorial representation, the diminishing of certain dimensions of an object or figure in order to indicate its recession into the pictorial space. (MAYER)
CN K.KT.AFU.ALO.DUC.DCU.ALO

forest fires
KM.110 (L)
UF fires, forest
CN K.KM.AFU.CXA.ARI.AFU

forest green
USE **dark green**

forest marble
MT.759
SN A pale-colored marble whose surface, when polished, displays dark markings that suggest the profile of woodlands or fields and streams. (MAYER)
UF landscape marble
marble, forest
marble, landscape
CN M.MT.AFU.AFU.AFU.DCU.AFU.ARI.ARI.ALO.ALO

forest reserves
RD.299 (L)
ALT **forest reserve**
UF reserves, forest
CN V.RD.ARI.ALO.ALO.BIQ.ALO.AFU

forestages
RM.372
ALT **forestage**
SN Parts of theater stages nearest the audience and usually projecting beyond the curtain. (W)
UF apron stages
aprons (stages)
stages, apron
CN V.RM.AFU.DIO.AXC.AXC.ALO.BIQ.ALO.AFU

foresters
HG.372 (L)
ALT **forester**
SN Persons who supervise the development, care, and management of forests or forest parks. (W)
CN H.HG.AFU.AXC.BIQ.ALO.AXC.ARI

forestry
KD.235 (L,B)
CN K.KD.AFU.ARI.BOK.AFU

forestry maps
VW.182 (L)
ALT **forestry map**
UF maps, forestry
CN V.VW.AFU.AFU.AFU.FZU.AXC.AFU.ARI.AXC.AXC

forestry, city
USE **urban forestry**

forestry, urban
USE **urban forestry**

forests
RD.298 (A,L,B,R)
ALT **forest**
SN Historically, refers to wilderness areas outside the scope of common law but within the legislation of kings and reserved for royal activities; more recently, used to designate extensive wooded areas, whether maintained for the production of timber or unmanaged and preserving a wilderness of dense growth and wild animal habitats.
CN V.RD.ARI.ALO.ALO.BIQ.ALO

forests, boreal
USE **taigas**

forests, national
USE **national forests**

forests, rain
USE **rain forests**

forests, tropical
USE **jungles**

forests, urban
USE **urban forests**

forge shops
USE **smithies**

forge welding
KT.806 (L)
SN The uniting of two pieces of hot metal by hammering them together on an anvil. (W)
UF fire welding
welding, fire
welding, forge
CN K.KT.AFU.ALO.HOE.BCW.ALO.AFU.ALO.ARI

forgeries
VB.116 (L,R)
ALT **forgery**
SN Use for valued objects or documents that are made or altered with intent to deceive; may range in falsehood from counterfeiting of whole works to altering of signatures or other deliberate misrepresentations.(OCA) Distinguished from copies by the intention of deception.
UF fakes
CN V.VB.ALO.BZY.AFU.ALO

forgers
HG.714 (L)
ALT **forger**
CN H.HG.AFU.BCW.BOK.ALO

forgery
BM.1097 (L)
SN Creating or altering valued objects or documents with intent to deceive.
CN B.BM.CRG.BCW.ALO.AFU.AFU

forges
TB.643 (N,R)
ALT **forge**
SN Furnaces where metal is heated before shaping. (RHDEL2)
CN V.TB.AFU.BCW.BIQ.AFU.AFU.AFU

forges (smithies)
USE **smithies**

forges, drop
USE **drop hammers**

forging
KT.846 (L,B)
ALT **forged**
SN Forming metal by heating and hammering. (W)
UF hot-working
CN K.KT.AFU.ALO.HOE.BCW.ALO.BIQ.ALO

forging, upset
USE **upset forging**

forgings
MT.476
CN M.MT.AFU.AFU.AFU.BZY.ALO.BCW

fork stail planes
USE **forkstaffs**

forks, kiln
USE **kiln forks**

forkstaffs
TB.958
ALT **forkstaff**
SN Hollow planes which produce smooth long cylindrical surfaces; used to make stair rails, carriage-wheel spokes, large furniture moldings for case pieces, and tool handles.
UF fork stail planes
planes, fork stail
planes, rounding (forkstaffs)
rounding planes (forkstaffs)
CN V.TB.AFU.BCW.CFS.ALO.AFU.DUC.AXC.AFU.BIQ.AFU

form
BM.65 (L,R)
SN Use with reference to works of art and architecture to mean the arrangement of visual elements such as line, mass, shape, or color.
CN B.BM.AFU.AFU.ARI.AFU.BUE

form board
USE **form lumber**

form letters
VW.21 (L)
ALT **form letter**
SN Letters, memorandums, or postcards which are printed and stocked in advance of actual use and usually contain prepared spaces for insertion of information. (GAHLM)
UF letters, form
CN V.VW.AFU.AFU.AFU.BIQ.AFU.ARI.ARI

form liner
USE **form lumber**

form lumber
MT.1422
UF board, form
form board
form liner
liner, form
lumber, form
CN M.MT.AFU.AFU.ALO.BIQ.DCU.ALO.BOK.AFU.AFU

form nails
USE **double-headed nails**

form oil
MT.2629
SN Oil with which concrete forms, especially those of metal, are sometimes treated to prevent sticking of the concrete upon removal. (W)
UF oil, form
CN M.MT.AFU.ARI.GLI.AFU.AFU

form, significant
USE **significant form**

formal French gardens
USE **French gardens**

formal gardens
RK.1399 (A,L,B)
ALT **formal garden**
SN Gardens whose plantings, walks, pools, fountains, and other features follow a definite, recognizable plan, frequently symmetrical, emphasizing geometrical forms. (HAS)
UF gardens, formal
CN V.RK.ALO.AFU.AFU.AFU.ARI

formaldehyde
MT.1001
UF methylene oxide
CN M.MT.AFU.AFU.ALO.AXC.BCW

formaldehyde, melamine
USE **melamine**

formaldehyde, urea
USE **urea-formaldehyde resin**

formalism
BM.174 (R)
SN Use when referring to the critical attitude which places emphasis on

analysis of form and the use of formal elements rather than on context or content.
CN B.BM.AFU.AFU.AXC.ARI

Formative
USE **Preclassic**

Formative Angkor
USE **Transitional**

Formative, Early
USE **Early Preclassic**

Formative, Late
USE **Late Preclassic**

Formative, Middle
USE **Middle Preclassic**

formed piles, in situ
USE **cast-in-place piles**

formed ridge hangers
TF.370
ALT **formed ridge hanger**
UF hangers, formed ridge
ridge hangers, formed
CN V.TF.AFU.AFU.AFU.ALO.AFU.BOK.ARI.ARI.AXC.AFU

formed seat hangers
TF.374
ALT **formed seat hanger**
UF hangers, formed seat
seat hangers, formed
CN V.TF.AFU.AFU.AFU.ALO.AFU.BOK.ARI.ARI.AXC.ALO.ARI

Former Han
USE **Western Han**

formerets
USE **wall ribs**

formers
USE **forming chisels**

formers, film
USE **film formers**

Formica (TM)
MT.2111
CN M.MT.AFU.AFU.ARI.BUE.ALO.ARI.ALO.AFU

forming
KT.127
ALT **formed**
UF shaping
CN K.KT.AFU.ALO.DOI

forming chisels
TB.856 (N)
ALT **forming chisel**
SN Long narrow chisels used for mortising. (MEANS)
UF cant chisels
chisels, cant
chisels, forming
firmers
formers
CN V.TB.AFU.BCW.CFS.ALO.AFU.BUE.ALO.ARI

forming, vacuum
USE **vacuum forming**

Formosa marble
MT.789
UF marble, Formosa
CN M.MT.AFU.AFU.AFU.DCU.AFU.ARI.ARI.ARI.ALO.BOK

Formosan alder
USE **seaside alder**

forms
VW.116 (A,L)
ALT **form**
SN Printed or typed documents with blank spaces for insertion of requested information. (WCOL)
UF forms, printed
printed forms
CN V.VW.AFU.AFU.AFU.FZU.ARI

forms (benches)
TG.282
ALT **form (bench)**
CN V.TG.AFU.AFU.ALO.ALO.AFU.AFU.BCW

forms, application
USE **application forms**

forms, bid
USE **bid forms**

forms, order
USE **order forms**

forms, printed
USE **forms**

forms, racing
USE **racing forms**

forms, tax
USE **tax returns**

formulas
BM.757 (L)
CN B.BM.CFS.ARI.AFU.AFU

forstner bits
TB.1105
ALT **forstner bit**
SN Bits used to sink blind holes in timber. (PUTNAM)
UF bits, forstner
CN V.TB.ALO.ARI.BOK

Fort Ancient
FL.879 (L)
CN F.FL.ALO.ALO.ALO.AFU.ALO.ALO.BCW.ALO

Fort Walton
FL.892
CN F.FL.ALO.ALO.ALO.AFU.ALO.ALO.BOK.BIQ

fortification marble
MT.760
UF marble, fortification
CN M.MT.AFU.AFU.AFU.DCU.AFU.ARI.ARI.ALO.ARI

fortifications
RK.434 (A,L,B,R)
ALT **fortification**
SN General term for any works made to oppose a small number of troops against a greater. (HOGG)
CN V.RK.AFU.ALO.ALO.BIQ

fortifications, coastal
USE **coastal fortifications**

fortifications, field
USE **field fortifications**

fortifications, plant
USE **plant fortifications**

fortifications, vegetation
USE **plant fortifications**

fortified cities
USE **fortified towns**

fortified towns
RD.31 (B)
ALT **fortified town**
UF cities, fortified
fortified cities
towns, fortified
CN V.RD.AFU.ALO.ALO.AFU

fortlets
RK.449
ALT **fortlet**
CN V.RK.AFU.ALO.ALO.BIQ.BOK.ALO

fortresses
RK.443 (B,R)
ALT **fortress**
UF strongholds
CN V.RK.AFU.ALO.ALO.BIQ.BIQ

forts
RK.447 (A,L,N)
ALT **fort**
CN V.RK.AFU.ALO.ALO.BIQ.BOK

forts, bastioned
USE **bastioned forts**

Forum ware
FL.3156 (R)
UF ware, Forum
CN F.FL.ALO.BCW.ALO.ALO.AFU.BOK.AXC.ALO.AFU.AFU

forums
RK.1584 (A,L,B)
ALT **forum**
UF fora
CN V.RK.ALO.ARI.AXC

fosses
RK.1352
ALT **fossa**
SN Use for moats or defensive ditches, wet or dry, used in association with fortifications.
CN V.RK.AFU.ALO.ARI.AXC.ARI.AFU.AFU.AFU

fossil fuels
MT.2620 (L)

UF fuels, fossil
CN M.MT.AFU.ARI.FIM.ALO

fossil resin
MT.1493 (L)
UF resin, fossil
CN M.MT.AFU.AFU.ALO.BOK.BOK

Fostat lustre ware
USE **Fostat ware**

Fostat ware
FL.3444
UF Fostat lustre ware
Fustat ware
lustre ware, Fostat
ware, Fostat
ware, Fustat
CN F.FL.ALO.BIQ.AFU.BUE.AFU.AFU

Foulah
USE **Fula**

foundation bolts
USE **anchor bolts**

foundation buildings
USE **societies' buildings**

foundation plans
VD.49
ALT **foundation plan**
UF masonry plans
plans, foundation
plans, masonry
CN V.VD.AFU.AFU.BIQ.ALO.AXC.ALO.ALO

foundation walls
RT.603
ALT **foundation wall**
UF walls, foundation
CN V.RT.AFU.AFU.AFU.BIQ.BUE.AFU.ARI.ARI

foundations
RT.149 (A,L,B)
ALT **foundation**
CN V.RT.AFU.AFU.AFU.AXC.BUE

foundations (organizations)
HG.854 (A,L,B)
ALT **foundation (organization)**
SN Organizations or institutions established by endowment or otherwise established with provision for future maintenance. (W)
UF trusts
CN H.HG.ALO.CFS

foundations, boat
USE **raft foundations**

foundations, caisson
USE **pier foundations**

foundations, mat
USE **mat foundations**

foundations, pier
USE **pier foundations**

foundations, pile
USE **pile foundations**

foundations, raft
USE **raft foundations**

foundations, slab
USE **slab foundations**

foundations, spread
USE **spread foundations**

founders
HG.719 (R)
ALT **founder**
CN H.HG.AFU.BCW.CLM

founders (metalworkers)
HG.504 (R)
ALT **founder (metalworker)**
CN H.HG.AFU.AXC.BUE.ARI.CFS.ALO.ALO

founding
KT.848 (L,R)
SN Use generally for the melting and casting of metals.
CN K.KT.AFU.ALO.HOE.BCW.ALO.BIQ.ARI

foundling hospitals
USE **orphanages**

foundries
USE **ironworks**
steel mills

foundries, iron
USE **ironworks**

foundry ladles
USE **melting ladles**

foundry sand
MT.2073 (L)
UF molding sand
sand, foundry
sand, molding
CN M.MT.AFU.AFU.ARI.BOK.ALO.BOK.ALO

foundrymen
HG.444 (L)
ALT **foundryman**
CN H.HG.AFU.AXC.BUE.ALO.BCW

fountain brushes
TB.506
ALT **fountain brush**
SN Brushes with a reservoir in their handle for ink or paint. (W)
UF brushes, fountain
CN V.TB.AFU.ARI.EWY.ALO.ALO.AFU.AFU

fountain-houses
RK.573 (R)
ALT **fountain-house**
CN V.RK.AFU.ALO.ALO.CFS.ALO.BCW.ARI

fountain pens
TB.269 (L,N)
ALT **fountain pen**
SN Pens containing a reservoir that automatically feeds the split writing point the ink, making a variable line. (MCFAD)
UF pens, fountain
CN V.TB.AFU.ARI.CLM.AFU.ALO.DOI.ALO

fountains
RK.574 (A,L,N,B,R)
ALT **fountain**
CN V.RK.AFU.ALO.ALO.CFS.ALO.BCW.AXC

fountains, ablution
USE **ablution fountains**

fountains, drinking
USE **drinking fountains**

four-centered arches
RT.269
ALT **four-centered arch**
SN Arches in which the intrados is struck from four centers.
UF arches, composite
arches, four-centered
composite arches
CN V.RT.AFU.AFU.AFU.BCW.AFU.AFU.AFU.EWY.AXC

four-centered pointed arches
USE **Tudor arches**

four-centered Tudor arches
USE **Tudor arches**

four-iwan mosques
RK.1119
ALT **four-iwan mosque**
UF mosques, four-iwan
CN V.RK.AFU.ALO.ALO.FCS.BIQ.BIQ.AFU.AFU

four-part vaults
USE **quadripartite vaults**

four-posted beds
USE **tester beds**

four-poster beds
USE **high-post beds**

four-posters
USE **high-post beds**
tester beds

fourteen-carat gold
MT.399
UF 14-carat gold
gold, fourteen-carat
CN M.MT.AFU.AFU.AFU.BZY.AFU.AFU.AFU.ALO.AXC.ALO.ALO

Fourteenth Dynasty
FL.2808
UF 14th Dynasty
Dynasty, Fourteenth
CN F.FL.ALO.AXC.ALO.ARI.AFU.BOK.ALO

Fourth Dynasty
FL.2789
UF 4th Dynasty
Dynasty, Fourth
CN F.FL.ALO.AXC.ALO.ARI.AFU.ARI.A LO

Fourth Pompeian Style
USE **Fourth Style**

Fourth Style
FL.2769
UF Composite Style
Fourth Pompeian Style
Intricate Style
Pompeian Style, Fourth
CN F.FL.ALO.AXC.ALO.ALO.ALO.CFS. AFU.AXC

fowlhouses
USE **poultry houses**

Fox
FL.1323 (L)
UF Meskwaki
Mesquakie
Outagami
CN F.FL.ALO.ALO.ARI.AFU.BCW.AFU

foxing
KT.909
SN Yellowish or brown spots and splotches which appear on paper or other surfaces in a scattered pattern caused by a species of mold which is encouraged by dampness. (MAYER)
CN K.KT.ALO.BIQ.ARI

foyers
USE **entrance halls**
lobbies

fractals
BM.758 (L)
CN B.BM.CFS.ARI.AFU.ALO

fragments
VB.95 (R)
ALT **fragment**
CN V.VB.ALO.BOK.BIQ

fraileros
TG.180
ALT **frailero**
SN Spanish Renaissance type of armchair with a rectangular leather hung seat and with a leather or velvet back; generally having a broad front stretcher, which is often carved. Sometimes hinged to allow for folding and easy transportation.
UF chairs, friars'
chairs, monk's (sillónes fraileros)
friars' chairs
monk's chairs (sillónes fraileros)
sillónes de frailero
sillónes fraileros
CN V.TG.AFU.AFU.ALO.AFU.AFU.ALO. CFS

frame chairs, Turkish
USE **Turkish chairs**

frame construction
KT.31 (A,L,B)
SN Types of construction in which walls, partitions, floors, and roof are wholly or partly made of wood. (BCMTC)
UF construction, frame
construction, wood frame
framing
wood frame construction
CN K.KT.AFU.ALO.BCW.ARI.AFU.AXC

frame construction, balloon
USE **balloon frames**

frame enlargements
VJ.128
ALT **frame enlargement**
SN Photographs produced from a frame of motion picture film. For other photographs of the action, actors, or production of a motion picture, use **film stills.**
UF enlargements, frame
CN V.VJ.AFU.AXC.ARI

frame pit saws
TB.1013
ALT **frame pit saw**
SN Large pit saws supplied with frames; used to cut logs into boards or planks.
UF pit saws, frame
saws, frame pit
CN V.TB.AFU.BCW.CFS.ALO.AFU.EWY. BCW.BIQ.AFU

frame saws
TB.1004 (N)
ALT **frame saw**
SN Saws which are set within a wood frame.
UF saws, frame
CN V.TB.AFU.BCW.CFS.ALO.AFU.EWY. BCW

frames (structural frames)
USE **structural frames**

frames, balloon
USE **balloon frames**

frames, box
USE **box frames**

frames, braced
USE **braced frames**

frames, card
USE **card frames**

frames, cellular
USE **box frames**

frames, chests of drawers on
USE **chests on frames**

frames, chests on
USE **chests on frames**

frames, door
USE **doorframes**

frames, doorway
USE **doorframes**

frames, grid space
USE **space frames**

frames, platform
USE **platform frames**

frames, portal
USE **rigid frames**

frames, rigid
USE **rigid frames**

frames, seat
USE **seat frames**

frames, slab
USE **slab tables**

frames, space
USE **space frames**

frames, structural
USE **structural frames**

frames, western
USE **platform frames**

frames, window
USE **window frames**

framing
USE **frame construction**

framing chisels
TB.857 (N)
ALT **framing chisel**
SN Heavier versions of forming chisels; used for harder work and generally fitted with an iron band on the handle to prevent it from splitting. (BLACKB)
UF chisels, framing
CN V.TB.AFU.BCW.CFS.ALO.AFU.BUE. ALO.ARI.AFU

framing hammers
TB.1081 (N)
ALT **framing hammer**
SN Large hammers, weighing as much as 32 ounces, with a long handle and a claw which is relatively straight; used in house framing and construction work.
UF coach framing hammers
coachbuilder's framing hammers
double-faced hammers
framing hammers, coach
framing hammers, coachbuilder's
hammers, coach framing
hammers, coachbuilder's framing
hammers, double-faced
hammers, framing
mashes
massies
CN V.TB.AFU.BCW.CFS.ALO.ARI.AFU. ARI

framing hammers, coach
USE **framing hammers**

framing hammers, coachbuilder's
USE **framing hammers**

framing plans
VD.50
ALT **framing plan**
UF plans, framing
CN V.VD.AFU.AFU.BIQ.ALO.AXC.ALO.ARI

framing squares
USE **carpenter's squares**

framing, post-and-beam
USE **post-and-beam structures**

frammers
USE **froes**

franchises
VW.914 (L)
ALT **franchise**
SN Includes documents expressing special privileges conferred by government on individuals or corporations, any privileges granted or sold, such as to use a name or to sell products or services, and rights given by a manufacturer or supplier to a retailer to use his products or name, on terms and conditions mutually agreed upon. (BLACKS)
CN V.VW.AFU.ARI.AFU.BOK.BOK.BUE

Francis I
USE **François I**

Franciscan
BM.657 (A,L)
CN B.BM.BZY.AFU.ALO.BCW.BIQ

Franco-Flemish
FL.3135
CN F.FL.ALO.BCW.ALO.ALO.AFU.BOK.ARI.BCW

Franco-Saxon
FL.3132
CN F.FL.ALO.BCW.ALO.ALO.AFU.BOK.ARI.ARI.AFU

François I
FL.3213 (R)
UF Francis I
CN F.FL.ALO.BCW.ALO.ARI.BIQ.BIQ.ARI.ALO.ARI.AFU

Frankfort black
USE **bone black**

Frankfurt school of sociology
USE **critical theory**

Frankish
FL.3107 (A,R)
CN F.FL.ALO.BCW.ALO.ALO.AFU.BOK.ALO.ALO.ARI

Fraser fir
USE **Fraser's balsam fir**

Fraser's balsam fir
MT.1351
UF Abies Fraseri
Abies humilis
fir, Fraser's balsam
fir, Frazer
Fraser fir
Frazer fir
CN M.MT.AFU.AFU.ALO.BIQ.DCU.AFU.AFU.ALO.BIQ.AFU.AFU

fraternal buildings
USE **fraternal lodges**

fraternal lodges
RK.1203 (B)
ALT **fraternal lodge**
UF buildings, fraternal
fraternal buildings
lodges (fraternal buildings)
lodges, fraternal
CN V.RK.AFU.ALO.ALO.FZU.ALO

fraternity houses
RK.221 (B)
ALT **fraternity house**
UF houses, fraternity
CN V.RK.AFU.ALO.ALO.AXC.AFU.AXC

fraud
BM.1096 (L,R)
SN Action or instance of deceit, trickery, or breach of confidence used to acquire unfair or dishonest advantage or material gain. (RHDEL2)
CN B.BM.CRG.BCW.ALO.AFU

Fraxinus americana
USE **white ash**

Fraxinus excelsior
USE **European ash**

Frazer fir
USE **Fraser's balsam fir**

free schools
RK.798 (L)
ALT **free school**
UF alternative schools
schools, alternative
schools, free
CN V.RK.AFU.ALO.ALO.CXA.ARI.AFU.AXC

Free Style (architecture)
FL.3332
CN F.FL.ALO.BCW.ALO.AXC.DIO.ALO.BOK.AFU

Free Style (pottery)
FL.2615
CN F.FL.ALO.AXC.ALO.AFU.ALO.AXC.ALO.AXC.AFU.AFU

Free Style, Early
USE **Early Free Style**

free time
USE **leisure**

freedom
BM.536 (L,R)
SN A right or liberty guaranteed by a constitution or fundamental law assuring exemption or liberation from slavery, imprisonment, or restraint by a despotic power. (W)
UF liberty
CN B.BM.BOK.BIQ

freehand drawing
KT.198 (B)
SN Drawing executed without the aid of mechanical devices. (MAYER)
UF drawing, freehand
CN K.KT.AFU.ALO.DUC.BZY.ALO.BOK

freehand drawings
VD.127
ALT **freehand drawing**
UF drawings, freehand
CN V.VD.AFU.AXC.AXC

freehold
USE **ownership**

freehouses
USE **pubs**

freestanding
DC.34
SN Standing alone, usually on a foundation or base. (W)
CN D.DC.AFU.ALO.ARI.BZY

freestone
MT.887
SN Stone, as sandstone, that may be cut freely in any direction without fracture or splitting. (STEIN)
CN M.MT.AFU.AFU.AFU.DCU.ALO.BIQ

freeways
RK.1523 (A,L,B)
ALT **freeway**
SN Use for tax-supported, high-speed, multilane highways; can be expressways or throughways.
CN V.RK.ALO.ALO.BIQ.ARI.AFU.AFU.ARI.ALO.AFU

freeways, elevated
USE **elevated roads**

freezing
KT.729 (L)
ALT frozen
CN K.KT.AFU.ALO.GWW.ALO.AFU

freezing point
BM.986 (L)
UF point, freezing
CN B.BM.CFS.AXC.BZY.CFS.AXC

freight elevators
RT.1311
ALT **freight elevator**
UF elevators, freight
CN V.RT.ALO.ALO.AFU.ARI.ALO.ALO.AFU

freight houses
RK.1239
ALT **freight house**
SN Facilities owned and operated by a railroad for receiving, delivering, or dispatching freight. (W)
UF houses, freight
CN V.RK.AFU.ALO.ALO.GLI.AFU.ALO.AFU.AFU

freight terminals
RK.1265
ALT **freight terminal**
UF terminals, freight
CN V.RK.AFU.ALO.ALO.GLI.AFU.BCW.AFU

Fremont
FL.933 (L)
CN F.FL.ALO.ALO.ALO.AFU.ALO.ARI.BIQ.ARI

French
FL.3045 (L,B,R)
CN F.FL.ALO.BCW.AFU.BOK

French arches
USE **Dutch arches**

French beds
TG.352
ALT **French bed**
SN Beds with a simple wooden framework, which supports the bed hangings so as to form a plain, rectangular box; no wooden components are visible, even the posts are encased in cloth.(THORN2) Use **sleigh beds** for beds with two ends of equal height.
UF beds, French
dome beds, French
French dome beds
CN V.TG.AFU.AFU.ARI.AFU.AFU.BOK

French beds (sleigh beds)
USE **sleigh beds**

French berry
USE **buckthorn berry**

French blue
USE **artificial ultramarine blue**
light purplish blue
strong purplish blue
vivid purplish blue

French chairs (cabriole chairs)
USE **cabriole chairs**

French chairs (elbow chairs)
USE **French elbow chairs**
elbow chairs

French chalk
MT.564
UF chalk, French
CN M.MT.AFU.AFU.AFU.CFS.AFU.HCQ.ALO

French Colonial
FL.3208 (A)
UF Colonial, French
CN F.FL.ALO.BCW.ALO.ARI.BIQ.BIQ.ARI.AFU

French commode dressing chests
USE **commode dressing tables**

French commode tables
USE **commodes**

French curves
TB.435
ALT French curve
SN Thin, rigid pieces of clear plastic or some other material, cut in a continuously curved or scroll shape; used as a guide for ruling curves through a series of points that are not on the arc of a circle. (MAYER)
UF curves, French
curves, irregular
irregular curves
CN V.TB.AFU.ARI.EFQ.ALO.AFU.ARI

French dome beds
USE **French beds**

French-door locks
TF.232
ALT **French-door lock**
UF French-window locks
locks, French-door
locks, French-window
CN V.TF.AFU.AFU.AFU.AFU.DIO.BIQ.ALO.ALO.ARI

French doors
RT.849 (B)
ALT **French door**
SN Doors in which the top rail, bottom rail, and stiles all have glass panes throughout (or nearly throughout) their entire length; often used in pairs. (HAS)
UF casement doors
door windows
doors, casement
doors, French
fenestrae bifores
French windows
windows, door
windows, French
CN V.RT.AFU.ARI.AFU.AFU.AFU.ALO.ARI.AFU.AFU.AXC

French elbow chairs
TG.27
ALT **French elbow chair**
SN Term used during the mid-18th century for armchairs with upholstered seats and backs, carved frames and cabriole legs. (BEARD)
UF chairs, French elbow
chairs, French (elbow chairs)
elbow chairs, French
French chairs (elbow chairs)
CN V.TG.AFU.AFU.ALO.AFU.AFU.AFU.ALO.ALO.ALO

French feet
TG.902
ALT **French foot**
SN Slender, outward-curving bracket feet. (TOMLIN)
UF bracket feet, common
bracket feet, flaring
common bracket feet
feet, common bracket
feet, flared
feet, flaring bracket
feet, French
flared feet
flaring bracket feet
CN V.TG.ALO.DZW.AFU.AXC.AFU

French feet (scroll feet)
USE **scroll feet**

French formal gardens
USE **French gardens**

French gardens
RK.1402 (L)
ALT **French garden**
UF formal French gardens
French formal gardens
gardens, formal French
gardens, French
CN V.RK.ALO.AFU.AFU.AFU.ARI.ALO

French mattresses
TG.857
ALT **French mattress**
SN Trade term for mattresses made of half wool and half hair. (GILBR2)
UF mattresses, French
CN V.TG.ALO.BIQ.CLM.AFU

French ocher
USE **moderate orange yellow**

French process zinc oxide
USE **zinc white**

French Protestant
USE **Huguenot**

French red marble
USE **Languedoc marble**
griotte marble

French roofs
RT.424
ALT **French roof**
SN Use for mansard roofs in which the lower slope is nearly vertical, the upper slope nearly horizontal.
UF roofs, French
CN V.RT.AFU.AFU.AFU.BIQ.ARI.AFU.AFU.AFU.BOK.AFU.ALO.AFU

French scroll feet
USE **scroll feet**

French stools (window seats)
USE **window seats**

French tile
MT.174
SN Type of interlocking roof tile, heavily corrugated and formed with interlocking side joints and a rounded bull nose butt edge to engage the

corrugations of the course immediately below.
UF tile, French
CN M.MT.AFU.AFU.AFU.AXC.ALO.ALO.ALO.AFU.ALO.AXC.AFU.AFU.AFU

French tissues
USE **tissue stereographs**

French trusses
USE **Fink trusses**

French ultramarine
USE **artificial ultramarine blue**
strong blue
strong purplish blue

French upholsterer's hammers
USE **cabriolet hammers**

French vermilion
USE **vivid reddish orange**

French-window locks
USE **French-door locks**

French windows
USE **French doors**

French, Old
USE **Rococo Revival**

Freon (TM)
USE **chlorofluorocarbons**

fresco à secco
USE **secco**

fresco painting
KT.226 (L,B)
SN Mural painting technique in which permanent limeproof pigments, dispersed in water, are painted on freshly laid lime plaster. (MAYER)
UF buon fresco
fresco, buon
painting, fresco
CN K.KT.AFU.ALO.DUC.CXA.ALO.AFU.BIQ

fresco-secco
USE **secco**

fresco, buon
USE **fresco painting**

fresco, dry
USE **secco**

fresh water
MT.316 (L)
UF water, fresh
CN M.MT.AFU.AFU.AFU.BOK.BOK.AFU.AFU

fresqueras
TG.512
ALT **fresquera**
SN Tall, three-storied cabinets decorated with inlay and consisting of a desk between two cupboards, built in Spain during the 17th century. The spindled top story forms a ventilated food cupboard for fruit, cheese, and bread. (BURR)
CN V.TG.AFU.AFU.AXC.ALO.BUE.CRG.AFU

Fresson
KT.353
UF Fresson process
Fresson quadrichromie
quadrichrome
CN K.KT.AFU.ALO.DUC.DIO.ALO.DIO.AFU.ARI

Fresson process
USE **Fresson**

Fresson quadrichromie
USE **Fresson**

fret-back chairs
TG.136
ALT **fret-back chair**
UF chairs, fret-back
CN V.TG.AFU.AFU.ALO.AFU.AFU.AFU.NIE.BUE

fret bands
USE **frets**

fret tables
USE **china tables**

frets
DG.124 (L)
ALT **fret**
SN Use for patterns consisting of repeated, linear, geometrical shapes, usually angular, in a continuous band. For similar patterns not confined to a band, especially openwork, use **fretwork.**
UF bands, fret
fret bands
fretwork (band pattern)
labyrinth pattern (frets)
pattern, labyrinth (frets)
CN D.DG.AFU.ARI.ALO.BIQ.ALO

frets, Chinese
USE **Chinese frets**

frets, Greek
USE **key pattern**

frets, stepped
USE **stepped frets**

fretsaw machines
USE **jigsaws**

fretsaws
TB.1010 (N)
ALT **fretsaw**
SN Saws with extremely fine blades, as narrow as 1/32 inch, set in a frame or a file-style handle. (DISSTO)
UF bracket saws
saws, bracket
CN V.TB.AFU.BCW.CFS.ALO.AFU.EWY.BCW.BCW

fretwork
DG.127 (A,L)
SN Carved geometrical patterns of intersecting lines, either pierced or in relief; in the late 19th century applied especially to openwork patterns carved out of thin pieces of wood with a fretsaw. (DDA)
CN D.DG.AFU.ARI.ALO.BIQ.ARI

fretwork (band pattern)
USE **frets**

fretwork, Chinese
USE **Chinese fretwork**

friaries
RG.198 (B)
ALT **friary**
CN V.RG.AFU.AFU.DUC.BIQ.AXC

friars
USE **monks**

friars' chairs
USE **fraileros**

friction catches
TF.47
ALT **friction catch**
SN Any catches held in position by friction when engaged with their strikes. (MEANS)
UF catches, friction
CN V.TF.AFU.AFU.AFU.AFU.BCW.BOK

friction hinges
TF.111
ALT **friction hinge**
SN Hinges that use internal friction to hold a door or window in a selected position. (MEANS)
UF hinges, friction
CN V.TF.AFU.AFU.AFU.AFU.CLM.AFU.CLM

friction tape
MT.2358
UF tape, friction
CN M.MT.AFU.ARI.ARI.ALO.AFU.AFU

friction welding
KT.807 (L)
SN A process by which thermoplastic materials are softened and welded together with heat produced by friction. (MEANS)
UF welding, friction
CN K.KT.AFU.ALO.HOE.BCW.ALO.AFU.ALO.AXC

Friendly Island
USE **Tongan**

Friends' meeting houses
USE **Quaker meeting houses**

friends, plumber's
USE **plungers**

frieze band windows
RT.960

ALT **frieze band window**
SN Windows externally located in a frieze.
UF frieze windows
windows, frieze
windows, frieze band
CN V.RT.AFU.ARI.AFU.AFU.BOK.
AFU.ARI.ARI

frieze windows
USE **frieze band windows**

friezes (entablature components)
RT.346 (A,L,B,R)
ALT **frieze (entablature component)**
SN Middle horizontal members of a classical entablature, above the architrave and below the cornice.
CN V.RT.AFU.AFU.AFU.BCW.BZY.
ALO.ARI.AFU

friezes (ornamental bands)
DG.89 (A,L,B,R)
ALT **frieze (ornamental band)**
SN Use for extended horizontal bands decorating architecture, furniture, or other objects and containing figures, scenes, or ornamental motifs. For the specific parts of classical entablatures, use **friezes (entablature components)**.
CN D.DG.AFU.ALO.ARI

friezes, cushioned
USE **pulvinated friezes**

friezes, pulvinated
USE **pulvinated friezes**

friezes, swelled
USE **pulvinated friezes**

frigidaria
RM.75
ALT **frigidarium**
SN The cold sections of Roman baths, sometimes including a swimming pool. (HAS)
CN V.RM.AFU.DIO.ALO.ALO.BOK. ARI

fringes, urban
USE **urban fringes**

froe clubs
TB.1092 (N)
ALT **froe club**
SN Mallets used in conjunction with froes.
UF clubs, froe
clubs, frow
cudgels
frow clubs
CN V.TB.AFU.BCW.CFS.ALO.ARI.
ALO.BIQ

froe horses
TB.473 (N)
ALT **froe horse**
SN Supports in the form of a forked log or a straight log with two short legs on one end and resting on a larger wooden support at the other end.
UF frow horses
horses, froe
horses, frow
CN V.TB.AFU.ARI.ERE.AFU.AFU

froe knives
USE **knife froes**

froes
TB.878 (N)
ALT **froe**
SN Cleaving tools whose handles are at a right angle to the blade; used in conjunction with a froe club for splitting wood.
UF axes, dill
axes, lath
axes, pole (froes)
axes, rending
axes, split
chits
cleaving irons
dill axes
dividers (froes)
flammards
flamming irons
frammers
fromards
frows
frummers
helpmates
irons, cleaving
irons, flamming
knives, side
lath axes
lath rivers
pole axes (froes)
ramheads
rending axes
rivers, lath
side knives
split axes
throwers
CN V.TB.AFU.BCW.CFS.ALO.AFU.CLM

froes, knife
USE **knife froes**

froes, lathmaker's
USE **knife froes**

frog perspective
USE **sotto in su**

frog perspectives
USE **worm's-eye perspectives**

fromards
USE **froes**

frond, palm
USE **palm leaf**

front
DC.17
SN Use in the sense of being situated at or relating to the front or forward part of something. For the sense of facing the viewer, use **frontal.**
UF main (front)
CN D.DC.AFU.ALO.ALO.AXC

front-door locks
TF.235
ALT **front-door lock**
UF locks, front-door
CN V.TF.AFU.AFU.AFU.AFU.DIO.BIQ.
ALO.ALO.AXC

front elevations
RM.7
ALT **front elevation**
UF elevations, front
elevations, main
main elevations
CN V.RM.AFU.BCW.AFU

front-gabled houses
USE **gable-front houses**

front hearths
RT.1157
ALT **front hearth**
UF hearths, front
hearths, outer
outer hearths
CN V.RT.AFU.BOK.ALO.ALO.AXC.
ALO

front locks, guarded
USE **guarded front locks**

frontage roads
USE **service roads**

frontages
BM.482 (B)
SN The lengths of lot lines or building sites adjacent to a street or other public way, or to a body of water forming a boundary. (DAC)
CN B.BM.BCW.DUC.ARI

frontal
DC.8
SN Use in relation to something that is facing the viewer. For the sense of being situated at or relating to the front or forward part of something, use **front.**
UF en face
full-face
head-on
CN D.DC.AFU.ALO.AFU.ALO

frontal perspectives
USE **one-point perspectives**

frontality
BM.66
SN The quality possessed by a sculpture that is designed to be viewed from directly in front; in pictorial compositions, the quality possessed by figures that face directly out of the picture.
CN B.BM.AFU.AFU.ARI.AFU.BZY

frontals
USE **altar frontals**

frontals, altar
USE **altar frontals**

frontispieces (facade components)
RT.601
ALT **frontispiece (facade component)**
SN Use for the central portions or features of entrance facades, given emphasis by a more elaborate architectural treatment.
CN V.RT.AFU.AFU.AFU.BIQ.BUE.AFU.ARI.ALO.AFU.ALO.AFU

frontons
USE **canchas**

fronts (facades)
USE **facades**

fronts (furniture components)
TG.937
ALT **front (furniture component)**
CN V.TG.ALO.ELK

fronts, false
USE **false fronts**

fronts, shop
USE **storefronts**

frost
BM.928 (L,B)
CN B.BM.CFS.AXC.BOK.AFU.ARI

frost heaves
KM.106 (L,B)
SN Upthrusts of ground caused by freezing of moist soil. (WCOL)
UF heaves, frost
CN K.KM.AFU.CXA.ALO.ARI

frost horseshoe nails
TF.440
ALT **frost horseshoe nail**
UF horseshoe nails, frost
nails, frost horseshoe
CN V.TF.AFU.AFU.AFU.ALO.AFU.CFS.ALO.CLM.AFU

frost-proof paint
MT.2544 (B)
UF paint, frost-proof
CN M.MT.AFU.ARI.CRG.ALO.BCW.ARI.BIQ

frost-resistant concrete
MT.223 (A,L)
UF concrete, frost-resistant
CN M.MT.AFU.AFU.AFU.BCW.AFU.AXC.ALO

frostproofing
KT.596 (B)
ALT **frostproof**
CN K.KT.AFU.ALO.FOG.ALO

frottage
KT.742 (L,R)
SN The technique of making an impression of the texture of wood, stone, fabric, or other material by placing paper over the object and rubbing the paper with a crayon or pencil. (MAYER)
CN K.KT.AFU.ALO.HCQ.ALO.ARI

frow clubs
USE **froe clubs**

frow horses
USE **froe horses**

frows
USE **froes**

fruit
MT.1023 (L,R)
CN M.MT.AFU.AFU.ALO.BIQ.ARI

fruit and vegetable stands
USE **produce stands**

fruit stands
USE **produce stands**

fruit stone black
MT.1571
UF black, fruit stone
CN M.MT.AFU.AFU.ARI.AFU.AFU.ALO.ALO.AFU.AFU.AFU.ALO.AFU

fruitwood
MT.1166
SN Wood from any fruit-bearing tree. Use a more specific term, if possible.
CN M.MT.AFU.AFU.ALO.BIQ.DCU.AFU.AFU.AFU.DUC

frummers
USE **froes**

fuchsia
USE **strong purplish red**
strong red
vivid purplish red
vivid reddish purple

fuchsia pink
USE **deep purplish pink**
moderate purplish pink

fuchsia purple
USE **dark reddish purple**
deep purplish red
moderate reddish purple
strong reddish purple
vivid purplish red

fuchsia purple, bright
USE **deep purplish red**
deep reddish purple
strong reddish purple

fuchsia purple, light
USE **strong reddish purple**

fuchsia red
USE **deep purplish red**
moderate purplish red

fuchsia rose
USE **moderate purplish red**
strong purplish red
vivid purplish red

fuchsia rose, bright
USE **moderate purplish red**

fuchsia, dark
USE **strong reddish purple**

fuchsine
USE **magenta**

fuel
MT.2618 (L,B)
SN Material used to produce heat or power by burning. (WCOL)
CN M.MT.AFU.ARI.FIM

fuel consumption
BM.871 (L)
UF consumption, fuel
CN B.BM.CFS.AXC.ALO.ALO.ALO.AFU

fuel economy
BM.872 (B)
UF economy, fuel
CN B.BM.CFS.AXC.ALO.ALO. ALO.AFU.AFU

fuels, fossil
USE **fossil fuels**

Fujiwara
USE **Late Heian**

Fula
FL.393 (L)
UF Foulah
Fulbe
CN F.FL.ALO.AFU.AXC.AFU.AXC.AXC.ALO.ALO

Fulani
FL.391 (L)
UF Fellata
Fulbe
Peul
CN F.FL.ALO.AFU.AXC.AFU.AXC.AXC.ALO

Fulbe
USE **Fula**
Fulani

full beds
USE **double beds**

full-face
USE **frontal**

full mold casting
USE **lost-wax process**

full mortise hinges
TF.112
ALT **full mortise hinge**
UF hinges, full mortise
mortise hinges, full
CN V.TF.AFU.AFU.AFU.AFU.CLM.AFU.CRG

full-scale drawings
VD.8
ALT **full-scale drawing**
UF drawings, full-scale
drawings, full-size
épures
full-size drawings
CN V.VD.AFU.AFU.BCW.AFU

full sections
USE **sections**

full size beds
USE **double beds**

full-size drawings
USE **full-scale drawings**

full-surface hinges
TF.113
ALT **full-surface hinge**
SN Hinges that may be installed on the surface of a door and jamb without need of mortising. (MEANS)
UF hinges, full-surface
CN V.TF.AFU.AFU.AFU.AFU.CLM.AFU.CXA

full-turn stairs
USE **one-turn stairs**

full views
USE **general views**

fulling mills
RK.662 (N)
ALT **fulling mill**
UF mills, fulling
CN V.RK.AFU.ALO.ALO.CLM.ALO.ALO.AFU.AXC.DZW.ARI

Fulse
USE **Kurumba**

Fulton Caddo
FL.853
UF Caddo, Fulton
CN F.FL.ALO.ALO.ALO.AFU.ALO.ALO.ARI.ARI.AFU.AFU

Fum
FL.197
UF Bafum
Fut
CN F.FL.ALO.AFU.AXC.AFU.AFU.AFU.ARI.ARI

fumage
KT.201 (R)
SN Image-making technique that uses smoke as a medium. Paper is held above candle flame and carbon deposits are allowed to collect on the paper, creating a smooth, slick texture. (BETTI)
CN K.KT.AFU.ALO.DUC.CFS

fumigating
KT.72 (L)
ALT **fumigated**
SN Treating with a gas for the purpose of disinfecting or of destroying pests. (W)
UF fumigation
CN K.KT.AFU.ALO.BIQ.BCW

fumigation
USE **fumigating**

Fumu
FL.462
UF Bafumungu
Mfinu
CN F.FL.ALO.AFU.AXC.ALO.ALO.ARI.ALO

fun houses
RK.1041 (A)
ALT **fun house**
UF houses, fun
CN V.RK.AFU.ALO.ALO.EWY.AXC.ARI.BIQ

Funan
FL.2318
CN F.FL.ALO.ARI.BCW.ALO.AFU.AFU

function, theory of
USE **functionalism**

functionalism
BM.175 (A,B,R)
SN Doctrine or practice that emphasizes practical utility or functional relations in the design and construction of structures, objects, and systems. Use also when referring to the 20th-century design philosophy, relating chiefly to architecture and furnishings, holding that form should be adapted to use, material, and structure.
UF function, theory of
theory of function
CN B.BM.AFU.AFU.AXC.AXC

functions
KG.1
SN Areas of responsibility in which activities are conducted in order to accomplish a purpose. (PC)
CN K.KG.AFU

functions (mathematics)
BM.760 (L)
SN Mathematical rules between two sets which assign to each member of the first set exactly one member of the second. (MHDSTT)
CN B.BM.CFS.ARI.ARI

fund raising
KG.57 (L)
UF money raising
CN K.KG.AFU.AFU.ARI.CLM

funding
KG.47
ALT **funded**
UF allocating
granting
CN K.KG.AFU.AFU.ARI.ALO.AFU

funding agencies
HG.813
ALT **funding agency**
SN Foundations, government agencies, institutions, or other organizations which give funds for a specific purpose. (ERIC)
UF agencies, funding
agencies, granting
funding resource centers
granting agencies
resource centers, funding
CN H.HG.ALO.ARI.AFU

funding resource centers
USE **funding agencies**

fundos
USE **haciendas**

funeral chapels
RM.307 (A)
ALT **funeral chapel**
SN Use for rooms devoted to funeral services in funeral homes. For small chapels containing individual or family tombs, use **sepulchral chapels.**
UF chapels, funeral
CN V.RM.AFU.DIO.AXC.ALO.AFU.AXC.ARI

funeral homes
RK.464 (B)
ALT **funeral home**
SN Distinguished from **mortuaries** by having more complete facilities for preparing the dead for burial or cremation.
UF funeral parlors
homes, funeral
parlors, funeral
CN V.RK.AFU.ALO.ALO.BOK.ARI.AFU.ALO

funeral parlors
USE **funeral homes**

funeral registers
VW.971
ALT **funeral register**
UF registers, funeral
CN V.VW.AFU.ARI.ALO.ALO.AFU.BCW.ARI

funerals
KM.21 (L,R)
CN K.KM.AFU.ARI.ARI.AXC

funerary art
BM.246 (R)
SN Use for art produced for rituals commemorating the dead and for art produced as an individual expression of grief.
UF art, funerary
art, mourning
mourning art
CN B.BM.AFU.ARI.BCW.DUC

funerary buildings
RK.459 (A,B)
ALT **funerary building**
UF buildings, funerary
CN V.RK.AFU.ALO.ALO.BOK.ARI

fungi
RD.261 (L)
ALT **fungus**
UF mycophyta
CN V.RD.ARI.AFU.BCW.ALO.ALO.

AFU.ARI

fungicides
MT.2377 (L)
ALT **fungicide**
CN M.MT.AFU.ARI.BOK.ARI

funicular lines
BM.906
UF lines, funicular
CN B.BM.CFS.AXC.BIQ.ALO.ALO.AFU

funicular polygons
BM.907
SN Force diagrams showing a string hung from two points from which weights are suspended at various points in which the forces are represented by a series of adjacent triangles. (MHDSTT)
UF polygons, funicular
CN B.BM.CFS.AXC.BIQ.ALO.ALO. ALO

funicular railroads
RD.101 (L,B)
ALT **funicular railroad**
SN Use for light rail transit in which cable cars or short trains are used to climb a steep incline by having vehicles raised or lowered by cables, simultaneously lowering or raising a second train on a parallel track in such a way that the two are counterbalanced.
UF funicular railways
funiculars
railroads, funicular
railways, funicular
CN V.RD.ALO.ARI.AFU.AFU.ALO.
AFU.AFU.AFU

funicular railways
USE **funicular railroads**

funiculars
USE **funicular railroads**

Funk
FL.3727 (R)
CN F.FL.ALO.BUE.ARI.CRG

Funnel Beaker
FL.2506 (L)
UF Beaker
TRB
TRBK
Trichterbecher
Trichterrandbecher
CN F.FL.ALO.AXC.AFU.BCW.DCU.ARI

fur
MT.926 (L,R)
CN M.MT.AFU.AFU.ALO.AFU.CLM

furan
MT.2137 (L)
UF copolymer, tetrole
furfuranes
tetrole copolymer
tetroles
CN M.MT.AFU.AFU.ARI.BUE.ALO.

AXC.AFU.BOK

furfuranes
USE **furan**

furnace brazing
KT.793
SN Brazing method whereby the entire assembly, including brazing alloy and flux set correctly in place, is raised to brazing temperature in a furnace. (HORNB)
UF brazing, furnace
CN K.KT.AFU.ALO.HOE.BCW.ALO.
AFU.AFU.AFU.ARI

furnacemen
HG.505
ALT **furnaceman**
SN Persons who install and repair furnaces or who tend them. (W)
CN H.HG.AFU.AXC.BUE.ARI.CFS.
ALO.ARI

furnaces
RT.1415 (L,N,B,R)
ALT **furnace**
CN V.RT.ALO.BCW.AFU.ALO.AFU.
AXC

furnaces (kilns)
USE **kilns**

furnaces, atomic
USE **nuclear reactors**

furnaces, blast
USE **blast furnaces**

furnaces, electric
USE **electric furnaces**

furnaces, oil
USE **oil furnaces**

furnaces, warm-air
USE **warm-air furnaces**

furniture
TG.1 (A,L,B,R)
CN V.TG.AFU

furniture drawers
USE **drawers**

furniture factories
RK.617 (A,B)
ALT **furniture factory**
UF factories, furniture
CN V.RK.AFU.ALO.ALO.CLM.ALO.
ALO.AFU.AFU.ALO

furniture hardware
TF.507 (A,L)
UF brasses (furniture hardware)
hardware, furniture
CN V.TF.AFU.AFU.ALO.BCW

furniture locks
TF.246
ALT **furniture lock**
UF locks, furniture
CN V.TF.AFU.AFU.AFU.AFU.DIO.BIQ.

ALO.ARI

furniture makers
USE **furniture workers**

furniture making
KT.523 (L)
CN K.KT.AFU.ALO.ELK.BUE

furniture marks
VW.730 (R)
ALT **furniture mark**
UF marks, furniture
CN V.VW.AFU.ALO.ALO.AFU.AXC.
ARI.AXC

furniture showrooms
RM.101 (A)
ALT **furniture showroom**
UF showrooms, furniture
CN V.RM.AFU.DIO.ALO.AXC.ARI.ALO

furniture stores
RK.159 (A,B)
ALT **furniture store**
UF stores, furniture
CN V.RK.AFU.ALO.ALO.ALO.ARI.
BIQ.AFU.BZY

furniture workers
HG.557 (A,L)
ALT **furniture worker**
UF furniture makers
makers, furniture
workers, furniture
CN H.HG.AFU.AXC.BUE.AXC.BUE

furniture, adaptable
USE **adjustable furniture**

furniture, adjustable
USE **adjustable furniture**

furniture, air-supported
USE **inflatable furniture**

furniture, architect-designed
USE **architectural furniture**

furniture, architectural
USE **architectural furniture**

furniture, art
USE **art furniture**

furniture, blow-up
USE **inflatable furniture**

furniture, built-in
USE **built-in furniture**

furniture, camp
USE **camp furniture**

furniture, campaign
USE **campaign furniture**

furniture, carcase
USE **case furniture**

furniture, case
USE **case furniture**

furniture, crate

USE **crate furniture**

furniture, fitted
USE **built-in furniture**

furniture, folding
USE **folding furniture**

furniture, inflatable
USE **inflatable furniture**

furniture, interchangeable
USE **sectional furniture**

furniture, KD
USE **knock-down furniture**

furniture, knock-down
USE **knock-down furniture**

furniture, mechanical
USE **mechanical furniture**

furniture, multi-functional
USE **multipurpose furniture**

furniture, multipurpose
USE **multipurpose furniture**

furniture, nomadic
USE **portable furniture**

furniture, outdoor
USE **outdoor furniture**

furniture, package
USE **knock-down furniture**

furniture, patent
USE **patent furniture**

furniture, pneumatic
USE **inflatable furniture**

furniture, portable
USE **portable furniture**

furniture, seat
USE **seating furniture**

furniture, seating
USE **seating furniture**

furniture, sectional
USE **sectional furniture**

furniture, street
USE **street furniture**

furniture, unit
USE **unit furniture**

furniture, utility
USE **utility furniture**

furniture, window
USE **window hardware**

furriers
HG.528 (L)
ALT **furrier**
SN Persons who buy and sell furs or fur products; also persons who make, repair, alter, or clean fur garments. (W)
CN H.HG.AFU.AXC.BUE.ARI.CXA.ARI

furring
KT.720
SN In wall plastering, the creating of an insulating space of a few inches between an exterior wall of a building and the lath of the plaster wall. (MAYER)
CN K.KT.AFU.ALO.GRC.CXA.AFU

furring anchors
USE **slot anchors**

furring brick
MT.105
UF brick, furring
CN M.MT.AFU.AFU.AFU.AXC.ALO.AFU.ALO.BZY

furring inserts
TF.381
ALT **furring insert**
UF inserts, furring
CN V.TF.AFU.AFU.AFU.ALO.AFU.BZY.AXC

furring strips
MT.1417
UF strips, furring
CN M.MT.AFU.AFU.ALO.BIQ.DCU.ALO.AXC

fusain
MT.1047 (L)
CN M.MT.AFU.AFU.ALO.BIQ.BUE.ARI.AFU.AFU

fusaroles
RT.802
ALT **fusarole**
SN Rounded usually beaded convex moldings placed under the echini of capitals in the Doric, Ionic, and Corinthian orders. (W)
CN V.RT.AFU.ALO.AFU.BOK.AFU.ALO.BUE

fused quartz
USE **fused silica glass**

fused silica glass
MT.242
UF fused quartz
glass, fused silica
glass, quartz
glass, silica
quartz glass
quartz, fused
silica glass
silica glass, fused
CN M.MT.AFU.AFU.AFU.BIQ.AFU.AFU.ARI

fusibility
BM.987
CN B.BM.CFS.AXC.BZY.CFS.BCW

fusion welding
KT.808
SN The welding of metals in a molten state without mechanical pressure or pounding. (W)
UF welding, fusion
CN K.KT.AFU.ALO.HOE.BCW.ALO.AFU.ALO.BCW

Fustat ware
USE **Fostat ware**

fustet
USE **young fustic**

fustian
MT.1850
SN Any of a variety of linen-and-cotton or all-cotton cloth, in a variety of patterns, used for bedding and clothing; common in the 18th and early 19th centuries.
CN M.MT.AFU.AFU.ARI.ALO.ALO.ALO.AFU.ALO.ARI

fustic
MT.1763
SN Wood of the tree chlorophora tinctoria; the liquid extract produces the yellow dystuff morin. (MH)
UF fustic, old
old fustic
CN M.MT.AFU.AFU.ARI.AFU.AFU.ALO.ALO.BUE.ALO.ARI

fustic, old
USE **fustic**

fustic, young
USE **young fustic**

Fut
USE **Fum**

future cities
RD.81
ALT **future city**
SN Use especially with reference to the urban designs of the Futurists of the early 20th century; may also be used in general for projected forms or lifestyles of settlements in the future.
UF cities of the future
cities, future
futurist cities
CN V.RD.AFU.BUE.AFU

Futurist
FL.3396 (A,L,B,R)
ALT **Futurism**
CN F.FL.ALO.BCW.ALO.AXC.DIO.BOK.AFU

futurist cities
USE **future cities**

futuristic architecture
USE **visionary architecture**

fylfots
USE **swastikas**

Fyzabad
FL.2262
CN F.FL.ALO.ARI.AXC.ALO.AFU.BZY.ARI.AFU

G-clamps
USE **C-clamps**

Gä
FL.306 (L)
UF Gan
CN F.FL.ALO.AFU.AXC.AFU.ARI.ALO.
AXC

Ga'anda
FL.228 (L)
UF Gabin
Kabin
Kanda
Mokar
CN F.FL.ALO.AFU.AXC.AFU.AFU.
ALO.ARI.AXC

Gabbra
FL.623 (L)
CN F.FL.ALO.AFU.AXC.AXC.ARI.BZY

gabbro
MT.610 (L)
SN Igneous rock similar to diorite, predominantly composed of ferromagnetic minerals with crystals visible to the eye; has the same mineral composition as basalt. (DAC)
CN M.MT.AFU.AFU.AFU.DCU.AFU
.AFU.AFU.AFU.ALO.ARI

Gabin
USE **Ga'anda**

gabions
RK.559 (A)
ALT **gabion**
SN Baskets or cages filled with earth or rocks and used generally for support or abutment, especially for erosion protection; may also be used for military works, flood control, harbor works, dams, and foundations.
CN V.RK.AFU.ALO.ALO.CFS.ALO.
ALO.ALO

gable ends
RT.602
ALT **gable end**
SN End walls having a gable. (HAS)
UF ends, gable
gable walls
walls, gable
CN V.RT.AFU.AFU.AFU.BIQ.BUE.
AFU.ARI.ALO.ALO

gable-front houses
RK.272
ALT **gable-front house**
UF front-gabled houses
houses, front-gable
houses, gable-front
CN V.RK.AFU.ALO.ALO.AXC.ALO.
AFU.CXA.AFU

gable-on-hip roofs
RT.426
ALT **gable-on-hip roof**
SN Use for roofs in which one or more of the hipped sides (usually two) are surmounted by gables.
UF roofs, gable-on-hip
CN V.RT.AFU.AFU.AFU.BIQ.ARI.AFU.
AFU.AFU.BOK.ARI

gable posts
RT.645
ALT **gable post**
SN Short posts located at the peak of a gable into which the bargeboards are fixed. (HAS)
UF posts, gable
CN V.RT.AFU.AFU.AFU.BIQ.BUE.
ALO.AFU.AXC.ALO.ARI

gable roofs
RT.427 (B)
ALT **gable roof**
SN Roofs with two sloping sides meeting at a ridge, and gables at one or both ends.
UF double pitch roofs
roofs, double pitch
roofs, gable
CN V.RT.AFU.AFU.AFU.BIQ.ARI.AFU.
AFU.AFU.BOK.AXC

gable roofs, clipped
USE **jerkinhead roofs**

gable roofs, hipped
USE **jerkinhead roofs**

gable roofs, parallel
USE **double-gable roofs**

gable shoulders
RT.646
ALT **gable shoulder**
SN Projecting brickwork or masonry supporting the foot of a gable. (HAS)
UF shoulders, gable
CN V.RT.AFU.AFU.AFU.BIQ.BUE.
ALO.AFU.AXC.ALO.AXC

gable springers
USE **kneelers (gable components)**

gable walls
USE **gable ends**

gableboards
USE **bargeboards**

gabled dormers
RT.479
ALT **gabled dormer**
SN Dormers with a roof terminating in a gable.
UF dormers, gabled
CN V.RT.AFU.AFU.AFU.BIQ.ARI.ALO.
AFU.BUE.AXC.AXC

gables
RT.634 (A,L,B,R)
ALT **gable**
SN Vertical triangular portions of the ends of buildings having double-sloping roofs. Includes similar ends which are not triangular in shape, as of a gambrel roof. (HAS)
CN V.RT.AFU.AFU.AFU.BIQ.BUE.
ALO.AFU.AXC.AFU

gables, bell
USE **bellcotes**

gables, catsup
USE **crow-stepped gables**

gables, corbel
USE **crow-stepped gables**

gables, corbie
USE **crow-stepped gables**

gables, corbiestepped
USE **crow-stepped gables**

gables, cross
USE **cross gables**

gables, crow-stepped
USE **crow-stepped gables**

gables, Dutch
USE **Dutch gables**

gables, shaped
USE **shaped gables**

gables, side
USE **side gables**

gables, side-facing
USE **side gables**

gables, step
USE **crow-stepped gables**

gablets
RT.639
ALT **gablet**
SN Small ornamental gables, usually not roof gables but rather a decoration over a buttress or opening.
CN V.RT.AFU.AFU.AFU.BIQ.BUE.
ALO.AFU.AXC.AFU.BCW

Gabri ware
FL.3597
UF ware, Gabri
CN F.FL.ALO.BIQ.AFU.ILG.AFU.AFU

Gabrieliño
FL.1253 (L)
UF Kizh
Tobikhar
CN F.FL.ALO.ALO.ARI.AFU.ALO.BOK

gadrooning
DG.115
ALT **gadrooned**
SN A decorative pattern formed of a series of convex ridges. (IGA)
UF decoration, knulled
decoration, lobed
decoration, nulled
knulled decoration
lobed decoration
lobing
moldings, thumb
nulled decoration
nulling
thumb moldings

CN D.DG.AFU.ARI.ALO.ARI.AXC

gain, heat
USE **heat gain**

galas
KM.131
CN K.KM.AFU.DIO.ALO

Galconda
USE **Golconda**

Galibi
FL.1580 (L)
CN F.FL.ALO.ALO.ARI.ARI.AFU.CXA

galician earth wax
USE **ozokerite**

galipot
MT.1496
CN M.MT.AFU.AFU.ALO.BOK.BUE

Galla
USE **Arusi**

galleried tables
USE **china tables**

galleries
RM.33 (A,L,R)
ALT **gallery**
SN Use to designate substantial interior platforms at the level of an upper story that overlook the level below and usually extend the full length or width of a room. For railed platforms projecting from the exterior walls of buildings or small, similar interior features, use **balconies.** For gallery stories in a church above the aisles and open to the nave, use **tribunes** or **triforiums.**
UF lofts (galleries)
CN V.RM.AFU.DIO.AFU.AXC

galleries (art galleries)
USE **art galleries**

galleries (art museums)
USE **art museums**

galleries (furniture components)
TG.938
ALT **gallery (furniture component)**
SN Decorative, raised borders of wood or metal extending around the back and sides of a shelf or on the top of a piece of furniture. (KETCH)
CN V.TG.ALO.ERE

galleries (long galleries)
USE **long galleries**

galleries (shopping arcades)
USE **shopping arcades**

galleries, art
USE **art galleries**

galleries, art (museums)
USE **art museums**

galleries, auction
USE **auction houses**

galleries, dwarf
USE **dwarf galleries**

galleries, long
USE **long galleries**

galleries, minstrel
USE **minstrel galleries**

galleries, music
USE **minstrel galleries**

galleries, picture
USE **art museums**

galleries, roof
USE **widow's walks**

galleries, shooting
USE **shooting galleries**

galleries, shooting (theaters)
USE **nickelodeons**

gallery directors
HG.653
ALT **gallery director**
UF directors, gallery
CN H.HG.AFU.AXC.CFS.AFU.AFU.AFU.AFU

gallery graves
RK.486
ALT **gallery grave**
SN Distinguished from **passage graves** by the lack of internal distinction between burial chamber and access passage.
UF allées couvertes
graves, gallery
CN V.RK.AFU.ALO.ALO.BOK.BUE.AFU.ALO.ALO.AFU

galletted joints
TF.622
ALT **galletted joint**
SN Joints filled with chips of rock, stone, or masonry, either for appearance or to minimize the required amount of mortar. (MEANS)
UF joints, galletted
CN V.TF.ALO.ARI.ALO.AFU.ARI.ALO

galley proofs
VW.602
ALT **galley proof**
SN Proofs made from type before final printing.
UF proofs, galley
CN V.VW.AFU.ALO.AFU.BOK

Gallinazo
FL.1153
UF Negativo
CN F.FL.ALO.ALO.ALO.ARI.AXC.AFU.AXC.ARI

Gallo-Roman
FL.2734 (A,L,R)
CN F.FL.ALO.AXC.ALO.ALO.ALO.BCW.AFU

Galoa
USE **Galwa**

galvanic corrosion
USE **electrochemical corrosion**

galvanizing
KT.817 (L)
ALT **galvanized**
SN The process whereby a protective coat of zinc is applied to steel or iron to protect it from corrosion. (HORNB)
CN K.KT.AFU.ALO.HOE.BCW.ALO.ALO.ALO

galvanizing, hot-dip
USE **hot-dip galvanizing**

Galwa
FL.400 (L)
UF Galoa
CN F.FL.ALO.AFU.AXC.ALO.AFU.ALO.AFU

Gam
USE **Bagam**

gambier
MT.1621
CN M.MT.AFU.AFU.ARI.AFU.AFU.ALO.ALO.ARI.ALO.BCW.AFU

Gambier Island
FL.3692
CN F.FL.ALO.BOK.AXC.AXC

gambling casinos
RK.1038 (A,B,R)
ALT **gambling casino**
SN Use for recreation buildings equipped with gambling devices and often providing other forms of entertainment and restaurant facilities; for similar buildings but which lack gambling devices, use **casinos.**
UF casinos, gambling
CN V.RK.AFU.ALO.ALO.EWY.AXC.ARI.ARI.AFU

gamboge
MT.1497
UF gomme gutte
gummigutt
guti ambar
gutto gumbo
CN M.MT.AFU.AFU.ALO.BOK.BZY

gamboge (color)
USE **strong yellow**

gambrel roofs
RT.422 (B)
ALT **gambrel roof**
SN Curb roofs with only the two opposite sides sloping. (RS)
UF roofs, gambrel
CN V.RT.AFU.AFU.AFU.BIQ.ARI.AFU.AFU.AFU.BOK.AFU.AFU

game parks
USE **safari parks**

game reeves
USE **game wardens**

game rooms
RM.127 (L)
ALT **game room**
SN Use for recreation rooms devoted entirely to table games.
UF rooms, game
CN V.RM.AFU.DIO.ALO.BIQ.BCW. AFU

game tables
USE **gaming tables**

game wardens
HG.373 (L)
ALT **game warden**
UF game reeves
reeves, game
wardens, game
CN H.HG.AFU.AXC.BIQ.ALO.AXC.AXC

games
KM.43 (L,B,R)
CN K.KM.AFU.AXC.ALO

games tables
USE **gaming tables**

gaming rooms
RM.124 (B,R)
ALT **gaming room**
SN Use for rooms devoted to gambling.
UF rooms, gaming
CN V.RM.AFU.DIO.ALO.BIQ.ARI

gaming tables
TG.742 (N)
ALT **gaming table**
SN Use for tables with tops marked as a board for playing chess, backgammon, or other games. Distinct from **card tables** which have a smooth, undecorated top.
UF game tables
games tables
tables à jouer
tables de jeu
tables, gaming
CN V.TG.AFU.AFU.BIQ.BOK.ALO.CRG

gamis
USE **jamis**

gampi
MT.1963
SN Vegetable fiber used in papermaking.
CN M.MT.AFU.AFU.ARI.ALO.ALO.AXC.AXC.AFU.AFU

Gan
USE **Gä**

Ganda
FL.676 (L)
UF Baganda
CN F.FL.ALO.AFU.AXC.AXC.BOK.AXC

Gandharan
FL.2200 (L)
UF Greco-Buddhist
CN F.FL.ALO.ARI.AXC.ALO.AFU.ARI.BCW.AFU

gang mills
USE **gang sawmills**

gang sawmills
TB.803 (N)
ALT **gang sawmill**
SN Machines that utilizes several parallel saw blades which can cut all of the boards of a log in one pass. (KNIGHT)
UF gang mills
mills, gang
sawmills, gang
CN V.TB.AFU.BCW.CFS.AFU.BCW.AFU

Ganga
FL.2209 (L)
CN F.FL.ALO.ARI.AXC.ALO.AFU.AXC.ARI

gangaw
MT.1188
UF chestnut, Indian rose
Indian rose chestnut
Mesua ferra
rose chestnut, Indian
CN M.MT.AFU.AFU.ALO.BIQ.DCU.AFU.AFU.AFU.FIM.AFU

gangers
HG.660
ALT **ganger**
SN Foremen of gangs of laborers. (RHDEL2)
CN H.HG.AFU.AXC.CFS.AFU.ALO.AFU.AFU.AFU

gangways
RT.1064
ALT **gangway**
SN Platforms or boardwalks erected over unfinished building sections to provide access for workers and material carriers. (DAC)
CN V.RT.AFU.BIQ.ALO

ganister
MT.848
SN A natural refractory mineral used for furnace linings; in compact form it was used for furnace hearths. (MH)
CN M.MT.AFU.AFU.AFU.DCU.AFU.ARI.BCW.AFU

ganosis
KT.535
SN Use for the process of toning down the glare of marble sculpture.
CN K.KT.AFU.ALO.ELK.DIO.ALO.ALO

Gansu
FL.1845
UF Kansu
CN F.FL.ALO.ARI.ALO.AFU.AFU.AFU.ARI.ALO.ALO

gantries
TB.19 (B)
ALT **gantry**
SN Frameworks or overhead structures of beam or timber; used as a working platform or as a means of support equipment. (MEANS)
CN V.TB.AFU.ARI.AFU.AFU.ALO

gantries (railroads)
USE **signal gantries**

gantries, signal
USE **signal gantries**

gantry cranes
TB.66 (L)
ALT **gantry crane**
SN Revolving cranes situated atop a heavy framework which moves along the ground on tracks. (MEANS)
UF bridge cranes (gantry cranes)
cranes, bridge (gantry cranes)
cranes, gantry
CN V.TB.AFU.ARI.AFU.BCW.AXC.BCW

Gaô
FL.121 (L)
CN F.FL.ALO.AFU.ALO.AFU.CFS.AFU

gaols
RK.717 (A,L,B)
ALT **gaol**
SN Designates local places of detention for the poor, vagrants, or those awaiting trial, used in Britain between the 11th and 18th centuries.
CN V.RK.AFU.ALO.ALO.CXA.AFU.ALO.AFU

garage doors
RT.877 (L,B)
ALT **garage door**
UF doors, garage
CN V.RT.AFU.ARI.AFU.AFU.AFU.ALO.ARI.AFU.AXC.ALO

garage sales
KM.149 (L)
UF sales, garage
sales, tag
sales, yard
tag sales
yard sales
CN K.KM.AFU.ELK.ALO

garages
RK.1225 (A,L,N,B,R)
ALT **garage**
CN V.RK.AFU.ALO.ALO.GFO.BUE.ALO

garages, multistory
USE **parking garages**

garages, parking
USE **parking garages**

garages, roof parking
USE **roof parking garages**

garbage chutes

USE **refuse chutes**

garbage dumps
USE **dumps**

garden apartments
RK.364 (A,L)
ALT **garden apartment**
SN Use for ground-floor apartments with access to gardens, or the two- or three-story apartment buildings with communal gardens generally located in the suburbs. (AVERY)
UF apartments, garden
CN V.RK.AFU.ALO.ALO.AXC.AXC.ALO.ALO

garden benches
USE **garden seats**

garden chairs
USE **garden machines**

garden cities
RD.85 (A,L,B,R)
ALT **garden city**
SN Use for cities or sections of cities newly planned to incorporate large tracts of green spaces, to control internal growth and development, and to separate industrial and non-industrial activities. Distinguished from **garden suburbs** by their larger size and urban location.
UF cities, garden
CN V.RD.AFU.BUE.AXC.AFU

garden clubs
HG.820 (A,L)
ALT **garden club**
UF botanical societies (garden clubs)
clubs, garden
garden societies
societies, botanical (garden clubs)
societies, garden
CN H.HG.ALO.BCW.AFU.AFU

garden elevations
RM.8
ALT **garden elevation**
UF elevations, garden
CN V.RM.AFU.BCW.ALO

garden exhibitions
USE **garden shows**

garden houses
RK.1183 (A,B)
ALT **garden house**
SN Open shelters in gardens used for dining, viewing, or relaxation. (DLA)
UF houses, gardens
CN V.RK.AFU.ALO.ALO.FOG.ALO

garden lattices
USE **trellises**

garden machines
TG.182 (N)
ALT **garden machine**
SN Chairs used for wheeling the elderly and the infirm through large gardens. (RUSTIC)
UF chairs, garden
garden chairs
machines, garden
CN V.TG.AFU.AFU.ALO.AFU.AFU.ALO.CLM.AFU

garden paths
USE **garden walks**

garden seats
TG.288 (N)
ALT **garden seat**
UF benches, garden
garden benches
seats, garden
CN V.TG.AFU.AFU.ALO.ALO.AFU.ALO.AFU

garden shows
KM.67 (A)
UF exhibitions, garden
garden exhibitions
shows, garden
CN K.KM.AFU.BUE.ALO

garden societies
USE **garden clubs**

garden structures
RK.1328 (A,L,R)
ALT **garden structure**
UF structures, garden
CN V.RK.AFU.ALO.ARI.AFU

garden suburbs
RD.65 (A,B)
ALT **garden suburb**
SN Use for suburbs designed to incorporate large tracts of green spaces and to control internal growth and development with an emphasis on residential communities. Distinguished from **garden cities** by their smaller size and location outside urban centers.
UF suburbs, garden
CN V.RD.AFU.BCW.AXC.AFU

garden walks
RK.1570 (A,L)
ALT **garden walk**
UF garden paths
paths, garden
walks, garden
CN V.RK.ALO.ALO.BUE.ALO

gardeners
HG.374 (A,L)
ALT **gardener**
CN H.HG.AFU.AXC.BIQ.ALO.AXC.BCW

gardening
KT.489 (A,L)
CN K.KT.AFU.ALO.DZW.AFU

gardening, greenhouse
USE **greenhouse gardening**

gardening, indoor
USE **indoor gardening**

gardening, landscape
USE **landscape gardening**

gardens
RK.1395 (A,L,B,R)
ALT **garden**
CN V.RK.ALO.AFU.AFU

gardens, allotment
USE **allotment gardens**

gardens, beer
USE **beer gardens**

gardens, botanical
USE **botanical gardens**

gardens, children's
USE **children's gardens**

gardens, children's zoological
USE **children's zoos**

gardens, Chinese
USE **Chinese gardens**

gardens, cloister
USE **cloister gardens**

gardens, community
USE **community gardens**

gardens, drought-resistant
USE **xeriscapes**

gardens, drought-tolerant
USE **xeriscapes**

gardens, enclosed
USE **walled gardens**

gardens, flower
USE **flower gardens**

gardens, formal
USE **formal gardens**

gardens, formal French
USE **French gardens**

gardens, French
USE **French gardens**

gardens, hanging
USE **hanging gardens**

gardens, herb
USE **herb gardens**

gardens, historic
USE **historic gardens**

gardens, informal
USE **landscape gardens**

gardens, kitchen
USE **kitchen gardens**

gardens, knot
USE **knot gardens**

gardens, labyrinth
USE **maze gardens**

gardens, landscape
USE **landscape gardens**

gardens, low-water input
USE **xeriscapes**

gardens, market
USE **market gardens**

gardens, maze
USE **maze gardens**

gardens, miniature
USE **miniature gardens**

gardens, neighborhood
USE **community gardens**

gardens, paradise
USE **paradise gardens**

gardens, peat
USE **peat gardens**

gardens, pleasure
USE **pleasure gardens**

gardens, private
USE **private gardens**

gardens, public
USE **public gardens**

gardens, rock
USE **rock gardens**

gardens, roof
USE **roof gardens**

gardens, rope-knot
USE **knot gardens**

gardens, sculpture
USE **sculpture gardens**

gardens, secret
USE **giardini segreti**

gardens, tea
USE **tea gardens**

gardens, vegetable
USE **vegetable gardens**

gardens, victory
USE **victory gardens**

gardens, walled
USE **walled gardens**

gardens, water
USE **water gardens**

gardens, water-conserving
USE **xeriscapes**

gardens, winter
USE **winter gardens**

gardens, working-men's
USE **community gardens**

gardens, xeriscape
USE **xeriscapes**

garderobes
USE **wardrobes (rooms)**

garderobes (wardrobes)
USE **wardrobes**

gardes du vin
USE **cellerets**

gargoyles
RT.466 (A,N,B,R)
ALT **gargoyle**
SN Waterspouts projecting from the roof gutter of a building, often carved grotesquely. (HAS)
CN V.RT.AFU.AFU.AFU.BIQ.ARI.ALO.AFU.ARI

garlands
USE **festoons**

garlands, husk
USE **husks (motifs)**

garm-mulamma
KT.714
SN Technique of laying gold leaf on articles made of inferior metals by covering the parts to be gilded with mercury and pressing the gold leaf into place. (SCHNEI)
CN K.KT.AFU.ALO.GRC.CRG.ALO.ALO

garnet
MT.518 (L,R)
SN A general name for a group of minerals varying in color and hardness; used for coating abrasive paper and cloth, for bearing pivots in watches, for electronics, and the finer specimens for gemstones. Garnets are trisilicates of alumina, magnesia, calcia, ferrous oxide, manganese oxide, or chrome oxide. (MH)
CN M.MT.AFU.AFU.AFU.CFS.AFU.DIO

garnet brown
USE **dark red**
deep red

garnet (color)
USE **dark purplish red**
dark red
deep reddish brown
very dark red

garnet paper
TB.502
SN Finishing and polishing paper whose abrasive is powdered garnet. (MEANS)
UF paper, garnet
CN V.TB.AFU.ARI.EWY.ALO.AFU.ALO

garnet red
USE **dark red**
deep red

garnet, light
USE **dark red**

garrets
USE **attics (interior spaces)**

garrison houses
RK.249
ALT **garrison house**
SN Houses whose second story projects beyond the first story, usually on the facade.
UF houses, garrison
CN V.RK.AFU.ALO.ALO.AXC.ALO.AFU.CLM.ARI

garrisons
USE **military bases**

Garrus ware
FL.3564
UF Garuz ware
ware, Garrus
CN F.FL.ALO.BIQ.AFU.HIK.BCW.ALO

garths
USE **cloister garths**

garths, cloister
USE **cloister garths**

Garuz ware
USE **Garrus ware**

Garwhal
FL.2275
CN F.FL.ALO.ARI.AXC.ALO.AFU.BZY.BCW.ARI.BCW

gas black
USE **carbon black**

gas fitting
KT.581 (L)
SN The installation or repairing of gas pipes and appliances. (W)
UF fitting, gas
CN K.KT.AFU.ALO.ERE.ALO.ARI.AFU

gas-lighting
RT.1372 (A,L)
UF gaslight
CN V.RT.ALO.AXC.ARI.ARI

gas masks
TB.410 (L,N,R)
ALT **gas mask**
UF masks, gas
CN V.TB.AFU.ARI.DUC.ARI.ALO

gas pipelines
RM.510 (L)
ALT **gas pipeline**
UF natural gas pipelines
pipelines, gas
pipelines, natural gas
CN V.RM.ALO.ALO.ARI.AFU

gas-turbine power plants
RG.109 (L)
ALT **gas-turbine power plant**
UF plants, gas-turbine power
power plants, gas-turbine
CN V.RG.AFU.AFU.BUE.ARI.AFU

gas turbines
TB.397 (L)
ALT **gas turbine**
UF turbines, gas
CN V.TB.AFU.ARI.DOI.BUE.AFU

gas welding
KT.810 (L)
SN Any method of welding that uses burning gas as a source of heat. (DAC)
UF welding, gas
CN K.KT.AFU.ALO.HOE.BCW.ALO.AFU.ALO.BCW.ALO

gas wells
RK.591 (L)
ALT **gas well**
UF wells, gas
CN V.RK.AFU.ALO.ALO.CFS.ALO.BCW.CXA.AFU.AFU

gas, bottled
USE **liquefied petroleum gas**

gas, liquefied petroleum
USE **liquefied petroleum gas**

gas, natural
USE **natural gas**

gases
MT.2287 (L)
ALT **gas**
CN M.MT.AFU.ALO.JCO.AFU

gaslight
USE **gas-lighting**

gaslight paper
MT.1945
SN Photographic papers that could be both exposed and processed indoors by the light of gas illuminators. (REILLY)
UF paper, gaslight
CN M.MT.AFU.AFU.ARI.ALO.ALO.AXC.ARI.BOK.ARI

gasoline
MT.1010 (L,B)
SN A colorless, liquid hydrocarbon obtained in the fractional distillation of petroleum; used chiefly as a motor fuel but also as a solvent. (MH)
UF petrol
CN M.MT.AFU.AFU.ALO.BCW.ALO.AFU

gasoline service stations
USE **service stations**

gasoline stations
USE **service stations**

gasoline tanks
RK.1221 (B)
ALT **gasoline tank**
UF liguid gas storage tanks
petrol tanks
storage tanks, liquid gas
tanks, gasoline
tanks, liquid gas storage
tanks, petrol
CN V.RK.AFU.ALO.ALO.GFO.BOK.AFU

Gasparcolor
KT.373
SN A subtractive color process using the silver-dye bleach process for making photographic prints; also used in cinematography.
CN K.KT.AFU.ALO.DUC.DIO.ALO.DZW.ALO.ALO

gasworks
RK.640 (A,L,B)
CN V.RK.AFU.ALO.ALO.CLM.ALO.ALO.AFU.AXC.BIQ

gatch
MT.2456
SN Plaster as used in Persia for decorative purposes. (HAS)
CN M.MT.AFU.ARI.CRG.AFU.AXC.ARI.ALO

gate hardware
TF.508
UF hardware, gate
CN V.TF.AFU.AFU.ALO.BIQ

gate latches, secret
USE **secret gate latches**

gate-leg tables
TG.673
ALT **gate-leg table**
SN Tables whose flaps are supported by jointed gates which swing out from the central section. (BEARD)
UF tables, gate-leg
CN V.TG.AFU.AFU.BIQ.BOK.AFU.AXC.ARI

gate legs
TG.957
ALT **gate leg**
SN Use for hinged legs with a stretcher, which swing out to support the drop leaf of a table, such as found on gate-leg tables. For similar legs without a stretcher, use **swing legs.**
UF legs, gate
CN V.TG.ALO.FIM.AFU.ALO.ALO.AFU

gate nails
TF.436
ALT **gate nail**
UF nails, gate
CN V.TF.AFU.AFU.AFU.ALO.AFU.CFS.ALO.BUE

gate piers
USE **hanging posts**

gate posts
USE **hanging posts**

gate saws
TB.804 (N)
ALT **gate saw**
SN Saws used in large mills in which a heavy blade is tensioned in a sash frame. (HUMMEL)
UF gate-type sawmills
sawmills, gate-type
saws, gate
CN V.TB.AFU.BCW.CFS.AFU.BCW.ALO

gate towers
RM.420
ALT **gate tower**
SN Use to designate towers containing gates to fortresses.
UF towers, gate
CN V.RM.AFU.DZW.ALO

gate-type sawmills
USE **gate saws**

gatehouses
RK.1341 (A,N,B,R)
ALT **gatehouse**
UF entrance lodges
lodges (gatehouses)
lodges, entrance
CN V.RK.AFU.ALO.ARI.ALO

gates
RT.892 (A,L,N,B,R)
ALT **gate**
SN Swinging or sliding barriers used to fill or close a gateway between two exterior spaces, often made of a grating or open framework or forming a heavy or rough structure.(W) Also, interior barriers resembling these. For barriers of more solid and finished construction and usually leading to interior spaces, use **doors.**
CN V.RT.AFU.ARI.AFU.AFU.ARI.ALO.AFU.AFU

gates, city
USE **city gates**

gates, dog
USE **dog gates**

gates, hydraulic
USE **hydraulic gates**

gates, postern
USE **posterns**

gates, sluice
USE **sluice gates**

gates, water
USE **water gates**

gateways
RT.888 (A,N,B)
ALT **gateway**
SN Passages through fences or walls separating two exterior spaces, or the structures or ornamental constructions enclosing such a passage.
CN V.RT.AFU.ARI.AFU.AFU.ARI.AFU

Gato
FL.625
CN F.FL.ALO.AFU.AXC.AXC.ARI.CFS.AFU

gaude yellow
USE **weld**

gauffering
USE **goffering**

gauffering machines
USE **goffering machines**

gauged arches
RT.256
ALT **gauged arch**
SN Use for arches built of bricks that are slightly wedge-shaped, so that the joints radiate.
UF arches, gauged
CN V.RT.AFU.AFU.AFU.BCW.AFU.AFU.AFU.ELK.BCW

gauged brick
MT.131
SN Brick that has been ground or otherwise produced to accurate dimensions. (DAC)
UF brick, gauged
CN M.MT.AFU.AFU.AFU.AXC.ALO.AFU.AXC.ALO.AFU.ALO

gauges, right-angle
USE **try squares**

gauging plaster
MT.2441
SN Special gypsum plaster mixed with lime putty for use in finishing plastered surfaces. (W)
UF plaster, gauging
CN M.MT.AFU.ARI.CRG.AFU.AXC.AFU.AXC.ALO

gauze
MT.1868
SN A lighter grade of cheesecloth with very open weave; used especially for surgical dressings and for backings for paper and maps. (MH)
CN M.MT.AFU.AFU.ARI.ALO.ALO.ALO.ALO.CLM

Gawra period
FL.2961
CN F.FL.ALO.AXC.ARI.BCW.AFU.ALO.AFU

gazebos
RK.1335 (A,N,B,R)
ALT **gazebo**
SN Use for small structures, usually roofed and open-sided, located in gardens or parks from which one may gaze out over the surrounding grounds.
UF belvederes (gazebos)
CN V.RK.AFU.ALO.ARI.AFU.AXC

gazetteers
VW.401 (L)
ALT **gazetteer**
SN Geographical dictionaries with varying amounts of descriptive, geographical, historical, or statistical information. (LG)
CN V.VW.AFU.AFU.ALO.EWY.ARI.ALO.AXC

gazetteers (guidebooks)
USE **guidebooks**

gazettes
VW.615 (L)
ALT **gazette**
SN Records of public events published periodically. (LG)
UF gazettes, official
official gazettes
CN V.VW.AFU.ALO.AFU.CXA.AFU.ALO

gazettes, official
USE **gazettes**

Gbande
FL.323 (L)
UF Bandi
CN F.FL.ALO.AFU.AXC.AFU.ARI.BCW.ALO

Gbanya
USE **Gonja**

Gbari
USE **Gwari**

Gbaya
USE **Ngbaka**

Gbundi
FL.324
CN F.FL.ALO.AFU.AXC.AFU.ARI.BCW.ARI

Ge, Central
USE **Central Ge**

gean
USE **sweet cherry**

gearing braces
USE **hand drills**

gears
TB.1122 (L)
ALT **gear**
SN Toothed wheels, cones, or cylinders, or other machined elements that are designed to mesh with other similarly toothed elements for purposes which include the transmission of power and the change of speed or direction. (MEANS)
UF cogwheels
CN V.TB.ALO.BZY

gebrannte grüne Erde
USE **transparent brown**

gebrannte Siena
USE **burnt sienna**

gebrannter Ocker
USE **burnt ocher**

Gedankenmalerei
FL.3392
UF Thought painting
CN F.FL.ALO.BCW.ALO.AXC.DIO.BIQ.BIQ.ALO

gee clamps
USE **C-clamps**

geelums
USE **rabbet planes**

Geelvinck Bay
FL.3632 (L)
CN F.FL.ALO.BOK.ALO.BCW.AFU.ALO.AFU

gel
MT.2246 (L)
SN Type of thick and viscous collodion dispersion of granules of water-soluble gums. (MH)
UF colloid
CN M.MT.AFU.ALO.DIO

gelatin
MT.927 (L)
SN A water-soluble, tasteless colloidal hemicellulose obtained from bones or from skins and used as a dispersing agent, sizing medium, coating for photographic films, and stabilizer for foodstuffs and pharmaceutical preparations. (MH)
CN M.MT.AFU.AFU.ALO.AFU.CRG

gelatin dry plate
USE **gelatin dry plate process**

gelatin dry-plate negative process
USE **gelatin dry plate process**

gelatin dry plate negatives
VJ.13
ALT **gelatin dry plate negative**
SN Use for negatives that have a gelatin layer as a binder on a glass support.
UF dry plate negatives, gelatin
gelatin dry plate photonegatives
negatives, gelatin dry plate
plate negatives, gelatin dry
CN V.VJ.AFU.AFU.AFU.BCW.ALO.AFU

gelatin dry plate photonegatives
USE **gelatin dry plate negatives**

gelatin dry plate process
KT.337
SN A photographic process employing silver in a gelatin binder on a glass photographic plate.
UF dry plate process (gelatin)
dry plate, gelatin
dry plate, silver gelatin
gelatin dry plate
gelatin dry-plate negative process
negative process, gelatin dry-plate
silver gelatin dry plate
CN K.KT.AFU.ALO.DUC.DIO.ALO.CFS.AFU

gelatin photonegatives
USE **gelatin silver negatives**

gelatin prints
USE **gelatin silver prints**

gelatin process
USE **gelatin silver process**

gelatin silver negatives
VJ.12
ALT **gelatin silver negative**
SN Use for negatives having gelatin as the binder, holding silver as the final image material; may be on glass (**gelatin dry plate negatives**) or on film.
UF gelatin photonegatives
negatives, gelatin silver
negatives, silver gelatin
silver gelatin negatives
silver gelatin photonegatives
silver negatives, gelatin
CN V.VJ.AFU.AFU.AFU.BCW.ALO

gelatin silver photoprints
USE **gelatin silver prints**

gelatin silver phototransparencies
USE **gelatin silver transparencies**

gelatin silver prints
VJ.50
ALT **gelatin silver print**
SN Use for photographic prints having gelatin as the binder, holding silver as the final image material; always black-and-white, though they may be toned to a monochrome hue.
UF gelatin prints
gelatin silver photoprints
photoprints, gelatin silver
prints, gelatin
prints, gelatin silver
prints, silver gelatin
silver gelatin photoprints
silver gelatin prints
silver prints, gelatin
CN V.VJ.AFU.AFU.ARI.ARI.AXC.BIQ

gelatin silver process
KT.336
SN Use for photographic processes that use gelatin as the binder and silver as the final image material. May employ a glass plate (in which case use **gelatin dry plate process**) or film as the support.
UF gelatin process
silver gelatin process
CN K.KT.AFU.ALO.DUC.DIO.ALO.CFS

gelatin silver transparencies
VJ.68
ALT **gelatin silver transparency**
SN Use for positive transparencies having gelatin as the binder, holding silver as the final image material.
UF gelatin silver phototransparencies
gelatin transparencies
silver gelatin phototransparencies
silver gelatin transparencies
silver transparencies, gelatin
transparencies, gelatin silver
CN V.VJ.AFU.AFU.ARI.AXC.BCW.ALO

gelatin transparencies
USE **gelatin silver transparencies**

gelb Ocker
USE **yellow ocher**

Gellert green
USE **cobalt green**

gem carving
USE **lapidary**

gem cutting
USE **lapidary**

gem photographs
VJ.83
ALT **gem photograph**
SN Use for small tintypes, sometimes mounted in jewelry.
UF gem tintypes
gems (photographs)
photographs, gem
tintypes, gem
CN V.VJ.AFU.AFU.BCW.ALO

Gem Style
USE **Polychrome Style**

gem tintypes
USE **gem photographs**

gemel windows
USE **coupled windows**

Gemini symbols
DG.78
ALT **Gemini symbol**
CN D.DG.AFU.AFU.ERE.BCW

gems
MT.570 (L,R)
ALT **gem**
SN Minerals of crystalline structure that have great beauty, durability, and value, depending on rarity and perfection of color, structure, and finished form. (W)
UF gemstones
jewels
CN M.MT.AFU.AFU.AFU.CFS.ALO

gems (photographs)
USE **gem photographs**

gemstones
USE **gems**

genealogical tables
VW.333 (L)
ALT **genealogical table**
SN Documents representing the lineage of a person or persons in tabular or diagrammetrical form. (LG)
UF family trees
tables, genealogical
trees, family
CN V.VW.AFU.AFU.ALO.CRG.ARI.AFU.AFU

genealogies
VW.332
ALT **genealogy**
SN Accounts or histories of the descent of persons, families, or other groups, from an ancestor or ancestors; enumerations of ancestors and their descendants in the natural order of succession. (GAHLM)
CN V.VW.AFU.AFU.ALO.CRG.ARI.AFU

genealogists
HG.271 (L)
ALT **genealogist**
CN H.HG.AFU.AXC.BCW.AFU.BOK.ALO.ARI

genealogy
KD.149 (L,R)
CN K.KD.AFU.ALO.CLM.ALO.ALO

general contractors
HG.617
ALT **general contractor**
SN Contractors who are responsible for most of the work at the construction site, including that performed by the subcontractors. (DAC)
UF contractors, general
contractors, main
main contractors
CN H.HG.AFU.AXC.BZY.ALO.AFU

general diffuse lighting
RT.1358
SN Lighting from units that direct 40 to 60% of their emitted light upward, and the remainder downward. (MEANS)
UF diffuse lighting, general
lighting, general diffuse
CN V.RT.ALO.AXC.AFU.BCW

general hospitals
USE **hospitals**

general lighting
RT.1359
UF lighting, general
CN V.RT.ALO.AXC.AFU.BIQ

general oblique drawings
VD.17
ALT **general oblique drawing**
SN Use for oblique drawings in which a vertical plane is parallel to the plane of projection, and receding planes are drawn at a scale that is somewhere between the same scale as and one-half the scale of that vertical plane.
UF drawings, general oblique
oblique drawings, general
CN V.VD.AFU.AFU.BIQ.AFU.ARI.AFU.ARI

general plans
USE **comprehensive plans**

general records schedules
VW.292

ALT **general records schedule**
SN Records schedules governing specified series of records common to several or all government agencies. (ICA)
UF general schedules
schedules, general
schedules, general records
CN V.VW.AFU.AFU.AFU.FZU.BOK.AFU.AFU

general schedules
USE **general records schedules**

general sections
USE **sections**

general stores
RK.177 (A,L)
ALT **general store**
UF country stores
stores, country
stores, general
CN V.RK.AFU.ALO.ALO.ALO.ARI.BIQ.ALO.BOK

general views
VB.17
ALT **general view**
UF full views
overall views
views, full
views, general
views, overall
views, whole
whole views
CN V.VB.AFU.AFU.BOK.AFU.AFU

generating stations
USE **power plants**

generative systems (copy art)
USE **copy art**

generators
TB.390 (L,N)
ALT **generator**
SN Mechanical or electromechanical devices that convert mechanical energy into electrical power, as alternators producing alternating current or dynamos producing direct current. (MEANS)
UF dynamos
electric generators
generators, electric
CN V.TB.AFU.ARI.DOI.ARI

generators, electric
USE **generators**

genetics
KD.205 (L)
SN Biological science which deals with the phenomena of heredity and the variation between progenitors and offspring. (ERIC)
CN K.KD.AFU.ARI.ARI.BCW

genius
BM.37 (L,R)
CN B.BM.AFU.AFU.ALO.BOK

genre
VB.72 (L,R)
SN Use for pictorial representations, which may be in various media, that represent scenes or events from everyday life.
UF genre scenes
genre works
scenes, genre
works, genre
CN V.VB.AFU.AXC.ARI

genre scenes
USE **genre**

genre works
USE **genre**

gentian
USE **light purplish blue**

gentian blue
USE **moderate purplish blue**

gentleman's dressing stands
TG.636
ALT **gentleman's dressing stand**
UF dressing stands, gentleman's
stands, gentleman's dressing
CN V.TG.AFU.AFU.BIQ.BCW.ALO.BCW.AFU

gentleman's dressing tables
TG.733
ALT **gentleman's dressing table**
SN English and American 18th-century tables made to provide the facilities of the modern bathroom, with provisions for a basin, bottles, bidet, and other toilet equipment. (MONTGO)
UF dressing tables, gentleman's
tables, gentleman's dressing
CN V.TG.AFU.AFU.BIQ.BOK.ALO.CLM.ARI

gentleman's portable desks
USE **portable desks**

gentleman's repositories
TG.403
ALT **gentleman's repository**
UF repositories, gentleman's
CN V.TG.AFU.AFU.AXC.ALO.ALO.BCW

gentleman's secretaries
TG.552
ALT **gentleman's secretary**
UF secretaries, gentleman's
CN V.TG.AFU.AFU.AXC.ALO.BZY.DUC.AFU

gentleman's writing fire screens
TG.14
ALT **gentleman's writing fire screen**
UF fire screens, gentleman's writing
writing fire screens, gentleman's
CN V.TG.AFU.AFU.AFU.AFU.BIQ.ALO

gentleman's writing tables
TG.574
ALT **gentleman's writing table**
UF tables, gentleman's writing
writing tables, gentleman's
CN V.TG.AFU.AFU.AXC.ALO.BZY.FUA.BOK

gentrification
BM.1072 (A,L)
SN The renovation and settlement of decaying urban areas by middle- and high-income people. (COLENC)
CN B.BM.CLM.ALO.ALO.AFU.ALO.AFU

genuine ultramarine
USE **ultramarine blue**

genuine ultramarine blue
USE **strong blue**
vivid blue

genuineness
USE **authenticity**

geochemistry
KD.266 (L)
SN Application of the principles of chemistry to earth and planetary sciences, having two main categories, organic and inorganic. (PG)
CN K.KD.AFU.ARI.CLM.ARI.AFU

geodesic domes
RT.392 (A,L,B,R)
ALT **geodesic dome**
SN Structures consisting of numerous similar, light, straight-line elements (usually in tension) which form a grid in the shape of a dome. (DAC)
UF domes, geodesic
CN V.RT.AFU.AFU.AFU.BIQ.AFU.AFU.ARI

geodesy
KD.267 (L,R)
SN Science that determines the size and shape of the earth or other celestial bodies, and carries out measurements and computations necessary for accurate mapping of the surface. (PG)
UF geodetic sciences
sciences, geodetic
CN K.KD.AFU.ARI.CLM.ARI.ALO

geodetic sciences
USE **geodesy**

geographers
HG.260 (L)
ALT **geographer**
CN H.HG.AFU.AXC.BCW.AFU.BCW

geography
KD.133 (L,R)
SN Science dealing with the earth and its life, especially the description of land, sea, air, and the distribution of plant and animal life, including

human beings, their activities and territorial organizations. (W)
CN K.KD.AFU.ALO.BZY

geography, physical
USE **physical geography**

geography, population
USE **population geography**

geography, urban
USE **urban geography**

Geokysur
FL.1773
CN F.FL.ALO.ARI.AFU.ALO.BCW

geological engineering
KD.227
SN Application of geology to engineering works such as highway and dam construction, building foundation investigations, mining, and petroleum production. (PG)
UF engineering, geological
CN K.KD.AFU.ARI.BIQ.BIQ

geological maps
VW.183 (L)
ALT **geological map**
SN Maps showing the structure and composition of the earth's crust. (DOD)
UF maps, geological
CN V.VW.AFU.AFU.AFU.FZU.AXC.AFU.ARI.AXC.BCW

geological museums
USE **geology museums**

geologists
HG.340 (L)
ALT **geologist**
CN H.HG.AFU.AXC.BIQ.AFU.AFU.BZY

geology
KD.268 (L,B,R)
SN Science that deals with the physical history of the earth, the rocks of which it is composed, and the physical changes which it has undergone and is undergoing. (RHDEL2)
CN K.KD.AFU.ARI.CLM.ARI.ARI

geology museums
RK.418 (L,B)
ALT **geology museum**
UF geological museums
museums, geology
CN V.RK.AFU.ALO.ALO.BCW.AXC.ARI.CFS.AXC

geology, structural
USE **structural geology**

Geometric
FL.2564 (A)
CN F.FL.ALO.AXC.ALO.AFU.AFU.ARI.ALO

geometric abstraction
BM.187 (R)
UF abstraction, classical
abstraction, geometric
classical abstraction
CN B.BM.AFU.AFU.AXC.CLM.AFU.ALO

geometric designs
USE **geometric patterns**

geometric ornament
USE **geometric patterns**

geometric patterns
DG.122
ALT **geometric pattern**
UF designs, geometric
geometric designs
geometric ornament
ornament, geometric
patterns, geometric
CN D.DG.AFU.ARI.ALO.BIQ

Geometric, Early
USE **Early Geometric**

Geometric, Late
USE **Late Geometric**

Geometric, Middle
USE **Middle Geometric**

Geometrical Decorated
USE **Early Decorated**

geometrical stairs
RT.1072
ALT **geometrical stair**
SN Stairs constructed without the use of newels at the angles or turning points. (RS)
UF stairs, geometrical
stairs, wreathed
wreathed stairs
CN V.RT.AFU.BIQ.AXC.AFU.AFU.ARI

geometrical tile
USE **mathematical tile**

geometry
KD.256 (L,B,R)
CN K.KD.AFU.ARI.CFS.BIQ

geomorphologists
HG.341
ALT **geomorphologist**
CN H.HG.AFU.AXC.BIQ.AFU.AFU.BZY.AFU

geomorphology
KD.272 (L)
SN Science that deals with the land and submarine relief features of the earth's surface and seeks a generic interpretation of them using the principles of physical geography in its descriptive aspects and of structural geology in its explanatory phases. (W)
CN K.KD.AFU.ARI.CLM.ARI.AXC

geophysics
KD.273 (L)
SN Study of the physics of the earth. (PG)
CN K.KD.AFU.ARI.CLM.ARI.BCW

Georgetown Mogollon
FL.937
UF Mogollon, Georgetown
CN F.FL.ALO.ALO.ALO.AFU.ALO.ARI.BIQ.BCW.ALO

Georgia marble
MT.825
UF marble, Georgia
CN M.MT.AFU.AFU.AFU.DCU.AFU.ARI.ARI.ARI.BOK.BCW

Georgia pine
USE **longleaf pine**
southern yellow pine

Georgian
FL.3199 (A,L,B,R)
CN F.FL.ALO.BCW.ALO.ARI.BIQ.BIQ.AFU.AFU.ARI

Georgian Revival
FL.3324 (A,R)
UF Neo-Georgian
Revival, Georgian
CN F.FL.ALO.BCW.ALO.AXC.DIO.ALO.BIQ.ALO

geothermal power
BM.874
UF power, geothermal
CN B.BM.CFS.AXC.ALO.ALO.ARI.AFU

geothermal power plants
RG.117 (L)
ALT **geothermal power plant**
UF plants, geothermal power
power plants, geothermal
CN V.RG.AFU.AFU.BUE.ARI.AXC.ALO

geranium lake
USE **geranium red**
vivid red

geranium red
MT.1704
UF geranium lake
lake, geranium
red, geranium
CN M.MT.AFU.AFU.ARI.AFU.AFU.ALO.ALO.BCW.AXC.ALO

geranium red (color)
USE **strong red**

geranium rose
USE **moderate red**
strong red

Gere
USE **Wee**

German
FL.3046 (L,B)
CN F.FL.ALO.BCW.AFU.BUE

German bank barns
USE **Pennsylvania bank barns**

German black
USE **vine black**

German silver
MT.402 (L)
SN Nickel alloy used as a base metal for plated silverware, for springs and contacts in electrical equipment, and for corrosion-resistant parts. (MH)
UF silver, German
CN M.MT.AFU.AFU.AFU.BZY.AFU.AFU.AFU.ALO.BIQ.AFU

German, Pennsylvania
USE **Pennsylvania Dutch**

Germanic
FL.3104 (L,B,R)
CN F.FL.ALO.BCW.ALO.ALO.AFU.BOK.ALO.ALO

germicides
USE **disinfectants**

gerontologists
HG.263 (L)
ALT **gerontologist**
CN H.HG.AFU.AXC.BCW.AFU.BIQ

gerontology
KD.138 (L)
SN Study of aging and the special problems and capabilities of the elderly.
CN K.KD.AFU.ALO.CFS

Gerzean
FL.2781
UF Late Naqada
Naqada II
CN F.FL.ALO.AXC.ALO.ARI.AFU.AFU.ALO.ARI

Gerzean, Early
USE **Early Gerzean**

Gerzean, Late
USE **Late Gerzean**

Gesamtkunstwerk
BM.295 (A,R)
SN Creative work in which is sought the unification of many art forms, including those from the visual, decorative, and performing arts, into a single total work.
CN B.BM.AFU.AXC.BOK

gesso
MT.2714 (L,B,R)
SN A white fluid or plastic coating material made by mixing chalk or whiting with a glue solution (or occasionally casein). It is used as a ground on wood or hardboard supports in painting, gilding, and other decorative processes. (MAYER)
CN M.MT.AFU.ARI.IFM.AFU

gesso grosso
MT.2715
SN Coarse gesso. (MAYER)
CN M.MT.AFU.ARI.IFM.AFU.AFU

gesso sottile
MT.2716
SN Fine gesso. (MAYER)
CN M.MT.AFU.ARI.IFM.AFU.ALO

gesso, polymer
USE **polymer primer**

gestural drawing
USE **gesture drawing**

Gestural painting
USE **Action painting**

gesture
BM.145 (L,R)
SN Use of motion of limbs or body as means of intentional expression. (W)
CN B.BM.AFU.AFU.ARI.BOK.BOK

gesture drawing
KT.199
SN Capturing in a few strokes the major forms of a figure, object, or composition. A method of drawing in which the artist responds to the action, gesture and movement of the subject, not the details of structure.
UF drawing, gesture
gestural drawing
CN K.KT.AFU.ALO.DUC.BZY.ALO.BUE

gesture drawings
VD.128
ALT **gesture drawing**
UF drawings, gesture
CN V.VD.AFU.AXC.BCW

GFCIs
USE **ground-fault circuit interruptors**

Ghana Kingdom
FL.78 (L)
CN F.FL.ALO.AFU.ALO.AFU.ALO

Ghassulian
FL.2923
UF Beersheba-Ghassulian
CN F.FL.ALO.AXC.ARI.AXC.AFU.ALO.BOK

ghats
RT.1094 (A)
ALT **ghat**
SN Use for flights of steps, found in India, that lead down to the banks of rivers or other bodies of water.
CN V.RT.AFU.BIQ.AXC.AFU.ALO.ARI

Ghaznavid
FL.3445 (L)
CN F.FL.ALO.BIQ.AFU.BZY

ghettos
RG.276 (A,L)
ALT **ghetto**
SN Districts of cities in which members of a minority racial or cultural group live, especially because of social, legal, and economic pressure. (W)
CN V.RG.ALO.AFU.ALO.BCW.AFU.ARI

Ghiyath-al-Din Kaykhusraw I, first reign
FL.3556
CN F.FL.ALO.BIQ.AFU.HIK.ARI.AXC

Ghiyath-al-Din Kaykhusraw I, second reign
FL.3559
CN F.FL.ALO.BIQ.AFU.HIK.ARI.BOK

Ghiyath-al-Din Kaykhusraw II
FL.3560
CN F.FL.ALO.BIQ.AFU.HIK.ARI.BUE

Ghorid
USE **Ghurid**

ghost photographs
USE **spirit photographs**

ghost towns
RD.37 (A,L,B)
ALT **ghost town**
SN Designates once-flourishing settlements recently abandoned due primarily to dramatic economic decline or exhaustion of local natural resources; generally the buildings remain standing but in a state of deterioration.
UF towns, ghost
CN V.RD.AFU.ARI.AFU

Ghurid
FL.3446 (L)
UF Ghorid
CN F.FL.ALO.BIQ.AFU.CFS

giallo antico
USE **Numidian marble**

giallo di Siena
USE **Siena marble**

giallo tigrato
MT.811
UF marmor corinthium
CN M.MT.AFU.AFU.AFU.DCU.AFU.ARI.ARI.ARI.BIQ.BUE

giallolino
USE **Naples yellow**
massicot

giallolino di Fiandra
USE **massicot**

giallorino
USE **Naples yellow**

giant sequoia
MT.1393 (L)
UF redwood, sierra
sequoia, giant
Sequoidendron giganteum
sierra redwood
CN M.MT.AFU.AFU.ALO.BIQ.DCU.AFU.AFU.ALO.DCU.ALO

giardini segreti
RK.1429
ALT **giardino segreto**
SN Use for small private gardens, primarily, but not restricted to, those found accompanying Italian

Renaissance villas, discreetly hidden, but not secret, set near the house and designed as intimate places for entertaining and pensive reflection away from the public gaze.
UF gardens, secret
secret gardens
CN V.RK.ALO.AFU.AFU.ARI.ALO

gib doors
USE **jib doors**

gibbets
USE **gimlets**

Gibson Caddo
FL.854
UF Caddo, Gibson
CN F.FL.ALO.ALO.ALO.AFU.ALO.ALO.ARI.ARI.AFU.ALO

gifted
HG.783 (L)
CN H.HG.AFU.BOK.AXC.AFU

gifts
BM.462 (L)
SN Gratuitous grants or transfers of property. (OCLD)
CN B.BM.BCW.CXA.AFU.ARI

gig sticks
USE **radius tools**

giggers
USE **jiggers**

Gilbert Island
USE **Kiribati**

gilders
HG.474 (R)
ALT **gilder**
CN H.HG.AFU.AXC.BUE.ARI.ARI

gilders red clay
USE **red bole**

gilders' marks
VW.749
ALT **gilder's mark**
UF marks, gilders'
CN V.VW.AFU.ALO.ALO.AFU.AXC.AXC.BZY

gilding
KT.712 (L,R)
ALT **gilded**
SN The art of adhering thin gold leaf to a surface to approximate the effect of solid or inlaid metal. (MAYER)
UF gilding, mercury
gilt
mercury gilding
CN K.KT.AFU.ALO.GRC.CRG.ALO

gilding, amalgam
USE **amalgam-gilding**

gilding, fire
USE **amalgam-gilding**

gilding, mercury
USE **gilding**

gilding, mordant
USE **mordant gilding**

gilding, water
USE **water gilding**

gilds
USE **guilds**

gilead, balm of
USE **balm of gilead**

gilsonite
MT.976 (L)
SN A natural asphalt used for roofing, paving, floor tiles, storage-battery cases, in coatings and for adding to heavy fuel oils. (MH)
CN M.MT.AFU.AFU.ALO.ALO.AFU.AFU.ALO.ALO

gilt
USE **gilding**

gimlet bits
TB.1106 (N)
ALT **gimlet bit**
SN Bits with spiral flutes and sharp threaded points; used for boring small holes in wood. (W)
UF bits, gimlet
CN V.TB.ALO.ARI.BUE

gimlet drills
USE **gimlets**

gimlets
TB.880 (N)
ALT **gimlet**
SN T-shaped tools with a steel shank and a wood head, used to make small holes in wood so that it is easier to start nails or screws. (QUICK)
UF drills, gimlet
gibbets
gimlet drills
nailsins
screw starters
starters, screw
CN V.TB.AFU.BCW.CFS.ALO.AFU.CRG

gimp nails
TF.437
ALT **gimp nail**
UF nails, gimp
CN V.TF.AFU.AFU.AFU.ALO.AFU.CFS.ALO.BZY

gin pole derricks
TB.77
ALT **gin pole derrick**
SN Derricks without a boom whose mast can lean in any direction. Loads are raised and lowered by ropes threaded through the top of the mast. (STEIN)
UF derricks, gin pole
CN V.TB.AFU.ARI.AFU.BCW.BCW.AFU.ALO.AFU

gin wheels
USE **gins**

ginger pine
USE **Port Orford cedar**

Gingerbread
FL.1728 (B)
UF Spindlework
CN F.FL.ALO.ALO.BCW.AFU.BIQ

gingerbread stone
USE **carstone**

gins
TB.81 (L,N)
ALT **gin**
SN Simple lifting devices consisting of a vertical pole, tripod, or other frame. (MEANS)
UF gin wheels
hoists, mine
mine hoists
wheels, gin
CN V.TB.AFU.ARI.AFU.BCW.BCW.ALO.ARI

Gio
USE **Dan**

girder bridges
RK.1298
ALT **girder bridge**
UF bridges, girder
CN V.RK.AFU.ALO.ALO.GLI.ALO.AFU.ARI.AXC

girders
RT.298 (A,L,B)
ALT **girder**
SN Large or principal beams used to support concentrated loads at isolated points along their length. (HAS)
CN V.RT.AFU.AFU.AFU.BCW.ALO.AFU.BIQ

girders, box
USE **box beams**

girders, continuous
USE **continuous girders**

girders, flitch
USE **flitch beams**

girders, plate
USE **plate girders**

girders, Vierendeel
USE **Vierendeel trusses**

girders, Warren
USE **Warren trusses**

Giriama
FL.605 (L)
UF Kiriama
CN F.FL.ALO.AFU.AXC.AXC.ALO.BOK.AXC

girt strips
USE **ledger boards**

girts
RT.311 (N)
ALT **girt**
SN Use for horizontal structural members at an intermediate level, spanning between studs or columns, and serving as stiffeners or as supports for joists.
CN V.RT.AFU.AFU.AFU.BCW.ALO.ALO.AXC

Gishu
USE **Gisu**

Gisu
FL.677 (L)
UF Gishu
CN F.FL.ALO.AFU.AXC.AXC.BOK. BCW

Gitksan
FL.1342 (L)
UF Kitksan
CN F.FL.ALO.ALO.ARI.AFU.BIQ.BZY

Givaro
USE **Jivaro**

Gizii
USE **Gusii**

Glacial Kame
FL.817
CN F.FL.ALO.ALO.ALO.AFU.ALO.ALO.AFU.AXC

glacial landforms
RD.182 (L)
ALT **glacial landform**
UF landforms, glacial
CN V.RD.ARI.AFU.AXC.AFU.AFU.ALO

glaciers
RD.153 (L,R)
ALT **glacier**
CN V.RD.ARI.AFU.AFU.AFU.ARI.AFU

glacis
RT.1205
SN Slopes used for defense against attack; may be natural or artificial. (W)
CN V.RT.AFU.BUE.AFU.BZY.BCW

glare
BM.855 (B)
SN Harsh, uncomfortably brilliant, usually reflected light.
CN B.BM.CFS.AXC.ALO.AFU.ALO.ALO.ARI

glare-reducing glass
MT.274
UF glass, glare-reducing
CN M.MT.AFU.AFU.AFU.BIQ.AFU.AXC.ALO

glass
MT.235 (A,L,B,R)
CN M.MT.AFU.AFU.AFU.BIQ.AFU

glass block
MT.290 (L,B)
SN A hollow block of glass, usually translucent with textured faces; has relatively low thermal-insulation and low fire-resistant value; used in non-load bearing walls. (DAC)
UF block, glass
CN M.MT.AFU.AFU.AFU.BIQ.ALO. AFU

glass-collodion positives
USE **ambrotypes**

glass factories
RK.641 (A,L,B,R)
ALT **glass factory**
UF factories, glass
glass works
works, glass
CN V.RK.AFU.ALO.ALO.CLM.ALO.ALO.AFU.AXC.BOK

glass foil underengraving
USE **verre églomisé**

glass holders
USE **tumbler holders**

glass marks
VW.731 (R)
ALT **glass mark**
UF marks, glass
CN V.VW.AFU.ALO.ALO.AFU.AXC.ARI.BCW

glass negatives, wet-collodion
USE **wet collodion negatives**

glass photoprints
USE **clichés-verre**

glass positives, collodion
USE **ambrotypes**

glass prints
USE **clichés-verre**

glass reinforced cement
MT.20 (B)
UF cement, glass reinforced
CN M.MT.AFU.AFU.AFU.ALO.AFU.AFU.AXC

glass reinforced plastic
MT.2114 (A,L,B)
UF plastic, glass reinforced
reinforced plastic, glass
CN M.MT.AFU.AFU.ARI.BUE.ALO.ARI.ARI.AFU

glass sand
MT.2074 (L)
SN Sand employed in glassmaking. (MH)
UF sand, glass
CN M.MT.AFU.AFU.ARI.BOK.ALO.BOK.ARI

glass silk
USE **glass wool**

glass technique
USE **glassworking**

glass underengraving
USE **verre églomisé**

glass underpainting
USE **reverse painting on glass**

glass wool
MT.247 (B)
SN A glass fiber, .001 inches in diameter. (MH)
UF glass silk
silk, glass
wool, glass
CN M.MT.AFU.AFU.AFU.BIQ.AFU.ALO.AFU

glass works
USE **glass factories**

glass, architectural
USE **architectural glass**

glass, basalt
USE **tachylite**

glass, blown
USE **blown glass**

glass, borosilicate
USE **borosilicate glass**

glass, broad
USE **cylinder glass**

glass, bullet-resistant
USE **bullet-resistant glass**

glass, bulletproof
USE **bullet-resistant glass**

glass, Carrara structural
USE **Carrara structural glass**

glass, cased
USE **cased glass**

glass, cast plate
USE **rolled glass**

glass, cellular
USE **cellular glass**

glass, cellulated
USE **cellular glass**

glass, crown
USE **crown glass**

glass, crystal
USE **crystal**

glass, cylinder
USE **cylinder glass**

glass, decorative
USE **figured glass**

glass, disc-blown
USE **crown glass**

glass, double strength window
USE **double strength window glass**

glass, drawn
USE **drawn glass**

glass, expanded
USE **cellular glass**

glass, figured
USE **figured glass**

glass, figured rolled
USE **figured glass**

glass, flint
USE **flint glass**

glass, float
USE **float glass**

glass, foamed
USE **cellular glass**

glass, fused silica
USE **fused silica glass**

glass, glare-reducing
USE **glare-reducing glass**

glass, greenhouse
USE **greenhouse glass**

glass, ground
USE **ground glass**

glass, heat-absorbing
USE **heat-absorbing glass**

glass, heat-resisting
USE **heat-resisting glass**

glass, heat-strengthened
USE **heat-strengthened glass**

glass, heavy sheet
USE **sheet glass**

glass, high-lead crystal
USE **crystal**

glass, insulating
USE **insulating glass**

glass, laminated
USE **safety glass**

glass, lead
USE **lead glass**

glass, lead-alkali
USE **lead glass**

glass, lead silicate
USE **lead glass**

glass, leaded
USE **leaded glass**

glass, lime
USE **soda lime glass**

glass, lime soda
USE **soda lime glass**

glass, mercury
USE **silvered glass**

glass, mirrored
USE **reflective glass**

glass, muff
USE **cylinder glass**

glass, muscovy
USE **mica**

glass, nonreflective
USE **nonreflective glass**

glass, nonshattering
USE **safety glass**

glass, opal
USE **opal glass**

glass, opalescent
USE **opal glass**

glass, optical
USE **optical glass**

glass, ornamental
USE **figured glass**

glass, patterned
USE **figured glass**

glass, photosensitive
USE **photosensitive glass**

glass, plate
USE **plate glass**

glass, pot
USE **pot glass**

glass, prismatic
USE **prismatic glass**

glass, quartz
USE **fused silica glass**

glass, reflective
USE **reflective glass**

glass, rolled
USE **rolled glass**

glass, rolled patterned
USE **figured glass**

glass, safety
USE **safety glass**

glass, shatterproof
USE **safety glass**

glass, sheet
USE **sheet glass**

glass, silica
USE **fused silica glass**

glass, silvered
USE **silvered glass**

glass, single strength window
USE **single strength window glass**

glass, soda lime
USE **soda lime glass**

glass, soluble
USE **water glass**

glass, spandrel
USE **spandrel glass**

glass, stained
USE **stained glass**

glass, Venetian
USE **Venetian glass**

glass, volcanic
USE **obsidian**

glass, volcanic (white pigment)
USE **pumice (white pigment)**

glass, water
USE **water glass**

glass, window
USE **sheet glass**

glass, wired
USE **wired glass**

glass, x-ray absorbing
USE **x-ray protective glass**

glass, x-ray protective
USE **x-ray protective glass**

glass, x-ray rejecting
USE **x-ray protective glass**

glass, x-ray resistant
USE **x-ray protective glass**

glassblowers
HG.477
ALT glassblower
CN H.HG.AFU.AXC.BUE.ARI.AXC.AFU

glassblowing
KT.765 (L)
CN K.KT.AFU.ALO.HOE.ALO.ARI

glasshouses
USE **greenhouses**

glassine
MT.1905
SN A transparent thin paper used especially for envelope windows and for sanitary wrapping. (MH)
CN M.MT.AFU.AFU.ARI.ALO.ALO.AXC.ALO.ALO

glassmakers
HG.478
ALT glassmaker
CN H.HG.AFU.AXC.BUE.ARI.AXC. ALO

glassware
MT.291 (L)
SN Articles made of glass; especially tableware of glass used in serving food and drink. (W)
CN M.MT.AFU.AFU.AFU.BIQ.ALO.ALO

glassworkers
HG.476 (L)
ALT glassworker
CN H.HG.AFU.AXC.BUE.ARI.AXC

glassworking
KT.762 (L,R)
SN Includes the making of or working on or with glass or glass articles. (W)
UF glass technique
CN K.KT.AFU.ALO.HOE.ALO

Glastonbury chairs
TG.220
ALT **Glastonbury chair**
SN Collector's term for early 17th-century English folding chairs having legs crossed front to back and having arms connected to the back and to the front seat rail; supposedly based on a chair used by the last Abbot of Glastonbury at Wells cathedral.
UF abbots' chairs
chairs, abbots'
chairs, Glastonbury
CN V.TG.AFU.AFU.ALO.AFU.AFU.AXC.AFU.ALO

glauconite
USE **green earth**

glauns
USE **clamps**

glaze
MT.2555 (L,N,R)
SN Thin, usually glossy surface coating.
CN M.MT.AFU.ARI.CRG.ARI.ARI

glaze, alkaline
USE **alkaline glaze**

glaze, ash
USE **ash glaze**

glaze, blister
USE **blister glaze**

glaze, Bristol
USE **Bristol glaze**

glaze, ceramic
USE **ceramic glaze**

glaze, clear
USE **clear glaze**

glaze, crystalline
USE **crystalline glaze**

glaze, mat
USE **matte glaze**

glaze, matt
USE **matte glaze**

glaze, salt
USE **salt glaze**

glaze, slip
USE **slip glaze**

glazed header
MT.2762
SN In masonry, a header of darker color than the field of the wall. (DAC)
UF dark header
flare header
header, flare
header, glazed
header, vitrified
vitrified header
CN M.MT.AFU.AXC.BIQ.ALO.ALO.ALO

glazier's putty
MT.2655
SN Any caulking compound used to hold window glass in place. (DAC)
UF painter's putty
putty, glazier's
putty, painter's
CN M.MT.AFU.ARI.HTY.ALO.AFU

glaziers
HG.479
ALT **glazier**
SN Persons whose work is cutting and setting glass, such as window panes. (W)
CN H.HG.AFU.AXC.BUE.ARI.AXC.ARI

glazing
KT.867 (L)
ALT **glazed**
SN The fusing of a thin, vitreous coating of a ceramic body by firing in a kiln. (MAYER)
CN K.KT.AFU.ALO.HOE.BOK.AXC.ARI

glazing (glass)
KT.579 (A,L,B)
SN Use for the installation of glass in building openings.
CN K.KT.AFU.ALO.ERE.ALO.ALO

glazing bars
USE **muntins**

glazing, sealed double
USE **double windows**

Gleditsia triacanthos
USE **honey locust**

gliders
TG.296
ALT **glider**
SN Seats suspended from a steel framework by links or springs; generally used on porches.
CN V.TG.AFU.AFU.ALO.ALO.AXC

globe stands
TG.639
ALT **globe stand**
SN Stands for terrestrial and celestial globes. (MONTGO)
UF stands, globe
CN V.TG.AFU.AFU.BIQ.BCW.ALO.BOK

globes
VW.135 (L,N,R)
ALT **globe**
SN Representations of the earth or heavens in the form of a ball. (AHD)
CN V.VW.AFU.AFU.AFU.FZU.AXC.AFU.ALO

globes, celestial
USE **celestial globes**

globes, terrestrial
USE **terrestrial globes**

glossarial indexes
VW.427
ALT **glossarial index**
SN Book indexes which give descriptions or definitions of the words indexed as well as their page numbers. (LG)
UF indexes, glossarial
CN V.VW.AFU.AFU.ALO.EWY.BOK.AFU.ALO

glossaries
VW.423 (L,B)
ALT **glossary**
SN Alphabetical lists of words and their meanings, usually in a specialized subject area and often part of a larger work; generally exclude pronunciation and etymological information.
CN V.VW.AFU.AFU.ALO.EWY.BIQ

glossy
DC.135
ALT **gloss**
SN Having a brilliant, highly reflective surface, giving a more mirrorlike reflected image than a lustrous finish or a finish having a sheen.
CN D.DC.AFU.BCW.AFU

glovers
HG.564
ALT **glover**
CN H.HG.AFU.AXC.BUE.AXC.BZY

glue
MT.2343 (L,B)
CN M.MT.AFU.ARI.ARI.AFU.ALO.ALO

glue guns, electronic
USE **electronic glue guns**

glue paint
USE **distemper paint**

glue, albumin
USE **albumin glue**

glue, animal
USE **animal size**

glue, bone
USE **bone glue**

glue, casein
USE **casein glue**

glue, fish
USE **fish glue**

glue, hide
USE **hide glue**

glue, marine
USE **marine glue**

glue, soya
USE **soybean glue**

glue, soybean
USE **soybean glue**

glue, vegetable
USE **vegetable glue**

gluing
KT.23 (L)
ALT glued
CN K.KT.AFU.ALO.BCW.AFU.AFU

gluts
USE **wedges**

glycerine development
USE **glycerine process**

glycerine process
KT.414
SN A technique for localized development of platinum prints by application of glycerine to only certain areas of a print to resist image formation.
UF glycerine development
CN K.KT.AFU.ALO.DUC.DIO.ARI.AXC.CFS

glyceryl trinitrate
USE **nitroglycerin**

glyptics
KT.770 (L)
SN The art or process of carving or engraving gems. (W)
CN K.KT.AFU.ALO.HOE.ARI.AFU

Gmelin's blue
USE **artificial ultramarine blue**

Gmelina leichhardti
USE **white beech**

Gnathian
FL.2633
UF Egnatian
CN F.FL.ALO.AXC.ALO.AFU.ALO.AXC.ALO.BIQ.AFU.AFU

gneiss
MT.740 (L)
SN A laminated or foliated metamorphic rock. (W)
CN M.MT.AFU.AFU.AFU.DCU.AFU.ARI.AFU

gnosticism
BM.698 (L,R)
CN B.BM.BZY.ALO.ARI.BCW

Goan
FL.2245 (L,B)
CN F.FL.ALO.ARI.AXC.ALO.AFU.BOK.ALO.AFU

goat hair
MT.932
UF hair, goat
CN M.MT.AFU.AFU.ALO.AFU.CXA.AFU.AFU.ALO

Gobelins
FL.3211 (L,R)
CN F.FL.ALO.BCW.ALO.ARI.BIQ.BIQ.ARI.ALO.ALO

Gobu
FL.528
CN F.FL.ALO.AFU.AXC.ALO.ALO.BIQ.ALO.ARI

Goddard feet
USE **bracket feet**

godowns
RK.1207
ALT **godown**
SN Denotes Far Eastern storehouses, especially those in India, China, and Japan.
CN V.RK.AFU.ALO.ALO.GFO.AFU

Goemai
FL.229
UF Ankwe
CN F.FL.ALO.AFU.AXC.AFU.AFU.ALO.ARI.BCW

goffering
KT.676
ALT **goffered**
SN Decorating a surface by indenting or embossing it, as in stamping of linen book bindings or gold leaf surfaces. (MAYER)
UF gauffering
CN K.KT.AFU.ALO.GRC.ALO.AFU

goffering machines
TB.428 (L,N)
ALT **goffering machine**
SN Machines used in goffering.
UF gauffering machines
machines, gauffering
machines, goffering
CN V.TB.AFU.ARI.EFQ.AFU.ALO

Gogo
FL.585 (L)
CN F.FL.ALO.AFU.AXC.AXC.AFU.ARI

Gola
FL.340 (L)
CN F.FL.ALO.AFU.AXC.AFU.ARI.BIQ.BCW

Golconda
FL.2256
UF Galconda
CN F.FL.ALO.ARI.AXC.ALO.AFU.BZY.AFU.BCW

gold
MT.435 (L,R)
SN A soft, yellow metal, known since ancient times as a precious metal on which all material trade values are based. It is so chemically inactive that it is found mostly in its native state. (MH)
UF 24-carat gold
gold, 24-carat
gold, twenty-four carat
twenty-four carat gold
CN M.MT.AFU.AFU.AFU.BZY.AFU.AFU.ARI.BIQ

gold (color)
USE **moderate yellow**
vivid yellow

gold alloys
MT.391 (L)
UF alloys, gold
CN M.MT.AFU.AFU.AFU.BZY.AFU.AFU.AFU.ALO.AXC

gold brown
USE **brownish orange**
strong brown

gold mines
RG.101 (L)
ALT **gold mine**
UF mines, gold
CN V.RG.AFU.AFU.BUE.AFU.ALO.AXC

gold ocher
USE **moderate orange**

gold ocher, transparent
USE **transparent gold ocher**

gold ocher, transparent (color)
USE **brownish orange**
strong yellowish brown

gold plate
MT.460 (L)
SN Much used for jewelry, ornaments, and for chemical resistance, but the gold is so soft that thin plates wear off easily. (MH)
UF plate, gold
CN M.MT.AFU.AFU.AFU.BZY.AFU.ALO.AXC.AFU.AFU

gold size
MT.2730
SN In gilding, the adhesive that holds the metal leaf to the ground. (MAYER)
UF size, gold
CN M.MT.AFU.ARI.IFM.BOK.ALO

gold size, red burnish
USE **red bole**

gold solder
USE **chrysocolla**

gold varnish
MT.2472
UF varnish, gold
CN M.MT.AFU.ARI.CRG.AFU.BOK.AFU.AFU

gold yellow
USE **moderate orange yellow**
strong orange yellow

gold, 24-carat
USE **gold**

gold, amber
USE **grayish yellow**

light yellowish brown

gold, bright
USE deep yellow
vivid yellow

gold, bronze
USE strong yellow

gold, dull
USE light olive
light olive brown
moderate olive

gold, eighteen-carat
USE eighteen-carat gold

gold, fool's
USE pyrite

gold, fourteen-carat
USE fourteen-carat gold

gold, green
USE green gold

gold, light
USE brilliant yellow
moderate yellow
strong yellow

gold, mustard
USE light olive brown

gold, rose
USE rose gold

gold, twenty-four carat
USE gold

gold, white
USE white gold

golden age
BM.354 (L,R)
SN The most flourishing period in the history of something, the time of highest achievement or greatest development.
UF age, golden
CN B.BM.ALO.ALO.CLM.CRG

golden beryl
MT.493
UF beryl, golden
CN M.MT.AFU.AFU.AFU.CFS.AFU.AXC.ARI

golden brown
USE deep yellowish brown
moderate yellowish brown

Golden Horde
USE Kipchak Khanate

golden mean
USE golden section

golden ocher
MT.1787
UF brown, ocher
chrome ocher
Goldocker
ocher brown
ocher, chrome
ocher, golden
ocher, Roman
ocre d'or
Roman ocher
CN M.MT.AFU.AFU.ARI.AFU.AFU.ALO.ALO.BUE.ARI.CFS.AFU

golden ocher (color)
USE moderate orange

golden ratio
USE golden section

golden section
BM.86 (L,R)
SN Canon of proportion based on the ratio between two unequal parts of a whole when the proportion of the smaller to the larger is equal to that of the larger to the whole. (MAYER)
UF golden mean
golden ratio
mean, golden
ratio, golden
section, golden
CN B.BM.AFU.AFU.ARI.AFU.ELK.AFU

golden yellow
USE dark orange yellow
moderate orange yellow
strong orange yellow
vivid yellow

Goldi
FL.2142 (L)
CN F.FL.ALO.ARI.ARI.ALO.AFU.ALO

Goldocker
USE golden ocher

goldsmithing
KT.781 (L,R)
CN K.KT.AFU.ALO.HOE.BCW.AFU.AXC

goldsmiths
HG.495 (L,R)
ALT goldsmith
CN H.HG.AFU.AXC.BUE.ARI.CFS.AFU.AXC

goldsmiths' marks
VW.750
ALT goldsmith's mark
UF marks, goldsmiths'
CN V.VW.AFU.ALO.ALO.AFU.AXC.AXC.CFS

goldwork
MT.2768 (L,R)
CN M.MT.AFU.AXC.BOK.ARI

golf courses
RK.1491 (A,L,B)
ALT golf course
UF courses, golf
golf links
links, golf
CN V.RK.ALO.ALO.BCW.BIQ

golf courses, miniature
USE miniature golf courses

golf driving ranges
USE driving ranges

golf links
USE golf courses

Gombroon ware
FL.3539
UF Gombrun ware
ware, Gombroon
CN F.FL.ALO.BIQ.AFU.GRC.ALO.AFU

Gombrun ware
USE Gombroon ware

gomme gutte
USE gamboge

gondola beds
USE sleigh beds

gondola chairs
TG.69 (N)
ALT gondola chair
SN Chairs whose backs gently curve forward and downward to form the arms; so called because of their resemblance to 18th-century gondolas.
UF chairs, gondola
curved-back chairs en gondola
gondola-shaped chairs
CN V.TG.AFU.AFU.ALO.AFU.AFU.AFU.GWW

gondola-shaped beds
USE sleigh beds

gondola-shaped chairs
USE gondola chairs

Gongan
FL.1930
CN F.FL.ALO.ARI.ALO.AFU.AFU.AXC.ALO.BCW

Gongen
FL.1994
UF Ishi-no-ma
Yatsumune
CN F.FL.ALO.ARI.ALO.ALO.ALO.AFU.ALO

Gonja
FL.80 (L)
UF Gbanya
Ngbanya
Ngbanyito
CN F.FL.ALO.AFU.ALO.AFU.ARI

Good Friday
KM.82 (L,R)
CN K.KM.AFU.CFS.ARI.BCW

Goodall
FL.818
CN F.FL.ALO.ALO.ALO.AFU.ALO.ALO.AFU.BCW

goods, capital
USE capital

goosewing axes
TB.838 (N)
ALT **goosewing ax**
SN Side axes with a long blade shaped like a bird's wing with the eye or socket near the lower, wider end. (SALAM)
UF axes, goosewing
CN V.TB.AFU.BCW.CFS.ALO.AFU.AXC.ARI.AFU

gopuras
RK.500
ALT **gopura**
SN Use for gateways or gate towers of South Indian temples or temple enclosures.
CN V.RK.AFU.ALO.ALO.BUE.ALO

gores
RT.401
ALT **gore**
SN Use for the triangular segments of a dome, especially those between ribs.
UF lunes
CN V.RT.AFU.AFU.AFU.BIQ.AFU.ALO.AFU

gorge cornices
USE **cavetto cornices**

gorge moldings
USE **cavetto moldings**

gorgerins
USE **hypotrachelia**

gorges
RD.195 (L)
ALT **gorge**
SN Deep, rocky land depressions with steep sides, larger than ravines, with a river or stream at the bottom; distinct from **canyons,** which tend to be larger and less rocky.
CN V.RD.ARI.AFU.AXC.AFU.AFU.ARI.BOK

gorges (bastion components)
RT.1175
ALT **gorge (bastion component)**
SN Use for the entrances into bastions or other outworks of fortifications.
CN V.RT.AFU.BUE.AFU.ALO.ALO.ARI

gorges (scotias)
USE **scotias**

gorges, Egyptian
USE **cavetto cornices**

Gosiute
FL.1311 (L)
CN F.FL.ALO.ALO.ARI.AFU.AXC.AXC

gospel lectionaries
USE **evangeliaries**

gossiping chairs
USE **voyeuses**

Gossypiospermum praecox
USE **Maracaibo boxwood**

Gothic
FL.3093 (A,L,B,R)
UF Pointed Style
CN F.FL.ALO.BCW.ALO.ALO.AFU.ARI

Gothic arches
USE **pointed arches**

Gothic (Migration period)
FL.3109 (L)
CN F.FL.ALO.BCW.ALO.ALO.AFU.BOK.ALO.ALO.AXC

Gothic Plateresque
USE **First Plateresque**

Gothic Revival
FL.3269 (A,L,B,R)
UF Gothic, Strawberry Hill
Gothic, Victorian
High Victorian Gothic
Neo-Gothic
Revival, Gothic
Strawberry Hill Gothic
Victorian Gothic
CN F.FL.ALO.BCW.ALO.AXC.CLM. BIQ

Gothic, Angevin
USE **Angevin Gothic**

Gothic, Backstein
USE **Backsteingotik**

Gothic, Carpenter's
USE **Carpenter's Gothic**

Gothic, Early
USE **Early Gothic**

Gothic, Early English
USE **Early English**

Gothic, Flamboyant
USE **Flamboyant**

Gothic, High
USE **High Gothic**

Gothic, International
USE **International Gothic**

Gothic, Late
USE **Late Gothic**

Gothic, Perpendicular
USE **Perpendicular Style**

Gothic, Rayonnant
USE **Rayonnant**

Gothic, Strawberry Hill
USE **Gothic Revival**

Gothic, Victorian
USE **Gothic Revival**

gouache
MT.2525
UF opaque watercolor
watercolor, opaque
CN M.MT.AFU.ARI.CRG.ALO.BCW.AFU.ALO.AXC.ALO

gouache drawings
USE **gouaches**

gouache paintings
USE **gouaches**

gouaches
VD.162
ALT **gouache**
UF drawings, gouache
gouache drawings
gouache paintings
paintings, gouache
CN V.VD.ARI.AFU

gouge adzes
USE **hollowing adzes**

gouge bits
TB.1107
ALT **gouge bit**
SN Scooped-out bits with a rounded end.
UF bits, gouge
split-quills
CN V.TB.ALO.ARI.BZY

gouge slips
TB.738
ALT **gouge slip**
SN Curved stones used for sharpening gouges with an inside or an outside bevel. (HAND)
UF slips, gouge
CN V.TB.AFU.BCW.BIQ.ARI.ALO.BZY.AFU

gouges
TB.121 (L,N)
ALT **gouge**
SN Cutting chisels having a long, curved blade; used for hollowing out wood, or for making holes, channels, or grooves in wood or stone. (MEANS)
CN V.TB.AFU.ARI.AXC.ALO.BCW

gouges, bent
USE **bent gouges**

gouges, bowl
USE **bowl gouges**

gouges, carving
USE **carving gouges**

gouges, firmer
USE **firmer gouges**

gouges, fluting
USE **fluters**

gouges, paring
USE **paring gouges**

gouges, spade
USE **bent gouges**

gouges, spoon
USE **bent gouges**

gouges, turning
USE **turning gouges**

gourd
MT.1025 (L)
CN M.MT.AFU.AFU.ALO.BIQ.ARI.ALO

Gouro
USE **Guro**

gout chairs
USE **gouty chairs**

goût grec
FL.3367
SN Use for the 18th-century fashion in decoration, often having little to do with historical Greek styles. For more historicist architecture and other work, use **Greek Revival.**
UF Greek Taste
le goût grec
CN F.FL.ALO.BCW.ALO.AXC.DIO.BCW.AXC.AFU

gout stools
TG.244 (N)
ALT **gout stool**
SN Footstools with a padded top which may be adjusted to support a gouty foot at the least uncomfortable angle. Made mainly in 18th-century England. (DDA)
UF gouty stools
stools, gout
CN V.TG.AFU.AFU.ALO.AFU.ALO.AFU.BIQ.AFU

gouty chairs
TG.183
ALT **gouty chair**
UF chairs, gouty
gout chairs
CN V.TG.AFU.AFU.ALO.AFU.AFU.ALO.CLM.ALO

gouty stools
USE **gout stools**

governing boards
USE **boards of trustees**

government
BM.537 (L,B,R)
CN B.BM.BOK.BOK

government architects
HG.85 (A,L,B)
ALT **government architect**
UF architects, government
architects, official
architects, public
official architects
public architects
CN H.HG.AFU.AXC.AXC.AFU.AFU.ALO.ALO.ALO

government buildings
USE **public buildings**

government contracts
VW.896 (L)
ALT **government contract**
UF contracts, government
contracts, public
public contracts
CN V.VW.AFU.ARI.AFU.BOK.BOK.ALO.ALO.ARI.ARI

government employees
HG.665 (L)
ALT **government employee**
UF civil servants
employees, government
public servants
servants, civil
servants, public
CN H.HG.AFU.AXC.CFS.BIQ

government housing
USE **public housing**

government librarians
HG.311 (L)
ALT **government librarian**
UF librarians, government
CN H.HG.AFU.AXC.BCW.ALO.BCW.ALO.BCW.AFU

government office buildings
RK.973 (B)
ALT **government office building**
UF buildings, government office
office buildings, government
CN V.RK.AFU.ALO.ALO.ERE.AFU.ARI

government officials
USE **public officers**

government ownership
USE **nationalization**

government policy
BM.549 (L)
UF policy, government
CN B.BM.BOK.BUE

government records
VW.981 (L)
ALT **government record**
SN Records made or received by an agency of government and maintained in the conduct of government business.
UF documents, public
official records
public documents
public records
records, government
records, official
records, public
CN V.VW.AFU.ARI.ALO.BCW

government records, federal
USE **federal government records**

government records, local
USE **local government records**

government records, municipal
USE **municipal government records**

government records, national
USE **national government records**

government records, state
USE **state government records**

government, comparative
USE **comparative government**

government, federal
USE **federal government**

government, municipal
USE **municipal government**

government, provincial
USE **provincial government**

government, state
USE **state government**

governments, local
USE **local government**

Governor Winthrop desks
TG.539
ALT **Governor Winthrop desk**
SN Popular term for American slant-front desks.
UF desks, Governor Winthrop
desks, Winthrop
Winthrop desks
CN V.TG.AFU.AFU.AXC.ALO.BZY.BUE.ALO.ARI

governors
HG.675 (L,R)
ALT **governor**
CN H.HG.AFU.AXC.CFS.CFS.AXC

governors general
HG.688
ALT **governor general**
CN H.HG.AFU.AXC.CFS.CFS.CRG.AFU

governors, lieutenant
USE **lieutenant governors**

GR-S
USE **styrene-butadiene rubber**

grab bars
TF.274
ALT **grab bar**
SN Bars attached to the wall in a shower or near a bathtub that may be grasped to steady the bather.
UF bars, grab
CN V.TF.AFU.AFU.AFU.AFU.ELK.AFU

grab buckets
TB.59
ALT **grab bucket**
SN Bucket-like devices with hinged lower halves or jaws hydraulically or cable-operated from a crane. (MEANS)
UF buckets, grab
CN V.TB.AFU.ARI.AFU.BCW.ALO.AXC

grade books
VW.1067
ALT **grade book**
SN Books used by teachers to record marks indicating students' levels of

accomplishment or quality of academic work. (AHD)
UF books, grade
CN V.VW.AFU.ARI.ALO.CRG.AXC

grade crossings
RM.505 (L)
ALT **grade crossing**
SN Use for the intersections of two thoroughfares, such as at highways, railroad tracks, or pedestrian walks, that cross at the same level.
UF crossings (grade crossings)
crossings, level
level crossings
CN V.RM.ALO.ALO.ALO.ARI.AFU

grade-level elevators
RT.1312
ALT **grade-level elevator**
SN Freight elevators whose hoistways are located partially outside the building and have no openings into the building at the upper terminal landing. (STEIN)
UF elevators, grade-level
CN V.RT.ALO.ALO.AFU.ARI.ALO.ALO.AFU.AFU

grade schools
USE **elementary schools**

grade separations
RM.473 (L)
ALT **grade separation**
SN Crossings of two highways, or of highways and pedestrian paths or railroads, utilizing an underpass or overpass. (W)
UF separations, grade
CN V.RM.ALO.ALO.ALO.ALO.AXC

graders
TB.43 (L,N)
ALT **grader**
SN Multipurpose earthworking machines having a single, centrally located blade that can be lifted from either end and angles so as to cast to either side; used mostly for leveling and crowning. (MEANS)
UF blades (graders)
graders, motor
grading machinery
machinery, grading
motor graders
CN V.TB.AFU.ARI.AFU.ARI.AXC

graders, motor
USE **graders**

grading
KT.612
ALT **graded**
SN The earthmoving required to create a surface of desired grade elevation. (NBCT)
CN K.KT.AFU.ALO.FUA.CFS.AFU

grading machinery
USE **graders**

grading plans
VD.41
ALT **grading plan**
UF plans, grading
CN V.VD.AFU.AFU.BIQ.ALO.AXC.AFU.ALO.ALO

graduals
VW.543 (L,R)
ALT **gradual**
SN Service books containing the musical portion of the mass sung by the choir. (W)
CN V.VW.AFU.ALO.AFU.AFU.ALO.BUE.BIQ

graduations
USE **commencements**

graffiato
USE **sgraffito**

graffiti
VB.67 (A,L,B,R)
SN In archaeology, casual scribbles or pictographs on ancient walls, stones, or other surfaces. In recent times applied to humorous, satiric, or obscene writings or drawings executed anonymously in public places. (MAYER)
CN V.VB.AFU.ARI.AFU

graffito decoration
USE **sgraffito**

grain
MT.1069 (L)
CN M.MT.AFU.AFU.ALO.BIQ.CFS.AFU.ARI

grain alcohol
USE **ethyl alcohol**

grain bins
RK.98 (A,L,B)
ALT **grain bin**
UF bins, grain
CN V.RK.AFU.ALO.ALO.AFU.ARI.ALO

grain elevators
RK.59 (A,L,N,B,R)
ALT **grain elevator**
SN Use for buildings comprised of large, deep, and narrow storage bins and mechanical conveying systems for the receiving, weighing, storing, and discharging of large quanitities of grain.
UF country elevators
elevators, country
elevators, grain
CN V.RK.AFU.ALO.ALO.AFU.AFU.AXC

grain lake
USE **kermes**

grain silos
USE **silos**

grainers
HG.111
ALT **grainer**
SN Artisans who paint surfaces in imitation of woodgrain.
CN H.HG.AFU.AXC.AXC.AFU.AFU.ALO.AXC.CXA.ALO.AFU

graining
KT.258 (L,B,R)
ALT **grained**
SN Painting that imitates wood or stone. (W)
UF brush graining
graining, brush
CN K.KT.AFU.ALO.DUC.CXA.ALO.BCW.ALO.ALO

graining, brush
USE **graining**

graminae
USE **grasses**

grammar
USE **syntax**

grammar schools
USE **elementary schools**

grammar, discourse
USE **pragmatics**

grammarians
HG.171
ALT **grammarian**
CN H.HG.AFU.AXC.AXC.ALO.AFU.AFU

gramophone records
USE **phonograph records**

granadilla
MT.1303
UF Brya ebenus
cocoacood
cocus wood
ebony, West Indian
West Indian ebony
wood, cocus
CN M.MT.AFU.AFU.ALO.BIQ.DCU.AFU.AFU.AFU.LCM.AXC.ALO.AFU

granaries
RK.60 (A,L,B,R)
ALT **granary**
SN Storehouses or other repositories for grain, especially after it has been threshed or husked.
CN V.RK.AFU.ALO.ALO.AFU.AFU. BCW

Grand Rapids
FL.1745
SN Use for the type of mass-produced American furniture produced in Grand Rapids, Michigan, particularly between the 1850s and 1920s. (THDAT)
CN F.FL.ALO.ALO.BCW.AFU.BZY.AXC

grand tours
KM.95 (R)

SN Extended European tours especially through France, Germany, Italy, and Switzerland; formerly taken by youth of the aristocracy as part of their education. (W)
UF tours, grand
CN K.KM.AFU.CLM.ARI.AFU

grandeur
BM.490
SN The quality of being majestic, magnificent, splendid, stately, or imposing in an awe-inspiring way. (W)
CN B.BM.BIQ.AFU.ARI

grandfather's chairs
USE **easy chairs**

grandstands
RK.1022 (A,L,N,B)
ALT **grandstand**
SN Structures, often with roofs and tiered platforms, for spectators to sit or stand on while viewing sporting events or other spectacles or performances.
UF stands (grandstands)
CN V.RK.AFU.ALO.ALO.EWY.ARI

granges
HG.824 (R)
ALT **grange**
SN Associations of farmers joined to further their interests and particularly to bring producers and consumers, farmers, and manufacturers into direct commercial relations. (W)
CN H.HG.ALO.BCW.BCW

granges (farms)
RG.18 (R)
ALT **grange (farm)**
SN Use for farm complexes, including living quarters and outbuildings, belonging to a monastery or a feudal lord.
CN V.RG.AFU.AFU.AFU.AFU.AXC.ALO

graniflora, magnolia
USE **magnolia graniflora**

granite
MT.586 (A,L,B,R)
UF moorstone
CN M.MT.AFU.AFU.AFU.DCU.AFU.AFU.AFU.AFU.AFU.ARI

granite (color)
USE **purplish gray**

granite blue
USE **light gray**

granite grafico
USE **graphic granite**

granite-powder cement
MT.21
SN Used in making floors of enclosures (huts) in Southern Africa. (WALTON)
UF cement, granite-powder
CN M.MT.AFU.AFU.AFU.ALO.AFU.AFU.BCW

granite, Barre
USE **Barre granite**

granite, black
USE **diabase**
diorite

granite, Cornish
USE **Cornish granite**

granite, graphic
USE **graphic granite**

granite, gray
USE **gray granite**

granite, Hebrew
USE **graphic granite**

granite, Milford
USE **Milford granite**

granite, Minnesota
USE **Minnesota granite**

granite, pink
USE **pink granite**

granite, red
USE **red granite**

granite, shap
USE **shap granite**

granite, Wicklow
USE **Wicklow granite**

granodiorite
MT.604 (L)
CN M.MT.AFU.AFU.AFU.DCU.AFU.AFU.AFU.AFU.AFU.AXC

grant proposals
VW.386 (L)
ALT **grant proposal**
UF proposals, grant
CN V.VW.AFU.AFU.ALO.ELK.AFU

granting
USE **funding**

granting agencies
USE **funding agencies**

grants
BM.389 (L,B,R)
SN Use broadly for funds allocated by a government or organization usually for a specific purpose.
UF grants-in-aid
CN B.BM.ARI.CRG.AFU

grants-in-aid
USE **grants**

grants, land
USE **land grants**

granular-fill insulation
USE **fill insulation**

granular materials
MT.2247 (L)
UF materials, granular
materials, particulate
particulate materials
CN M.MT.AFU.ALO.DOI

granulation (metal finishing)
KT.836 (R)
ALT **granulated**
CN K.KT.AFU.ALO.HOE.BCW.ALO.AXC.ARI

granules, roofing
USE **roofing granules**

graph paper
MT.1934
UF cross-section paper
paper, cross-section
paper, graph
CN M.MT.AFU.AFU.ARI.ALO.ALO.AXC.ARI.AXC.ALO

graphemics
KD.36 (L)
SN Study of writing systems and of their relation to speech. (RHDEL2)
CN K.KD.AFU.AFU.AXC.AFU.AFU.ARI

graphic artists (draftsmen)
USE **draftsmen**

graphic artists (printmakers)
USE **printmakers**

graphic arts (drawing)
USE **drawing**

graphic arts (illustration)
USE **illustration**

graphic arts (printmaking)
USE **printmaking**

graphic design
KT.101 (B,R)
SN Preparing and creating words and images for commercial applications such as book production, posters, advertising, and packaging.(A-Z) Includes creating graphs, charts, and other methods of displaying data.
UF design, graphic
CN K.KT.AFU.ALO.CFS.BIQ

graphic designers
HG.142 (B)
ALT **graphic designer**
SN Persons who design and create artwork and copy layouts, including both words and images, for presentation by visual media such as books, magazines, newspapers, posters, television, and packaging.
UF designers, graphic
CN H.HG.AFU.AXC.AXC.AFU.AFU.ALO.BCW.AFU.ALO

graphic diagrams
USE **diagrams**

graphic granite
MT.590
UF granite grafico
granite, graphic
granite, Hebrew
Hebrew granite
lapis judaicus
CN M.MT.AFU.AFU.AFU.DCU.AFU.AFU.AFU.AFU.AFU.ARI.AFU.ALO.AFU

graphic statics
BM.905 (L)
UF statics, graphic
CN B.BM.CFS.AXC.BIQ.ALO.ALO

graphics tablets
TB.152
ALT **graphics tablet**
SN Flat surfaces, usually consisting of a grid of wire set in a substrate, that can be placed on a desk and used together with a mouse or stylus for the input of data to a computer graphics system.
UF digitizing tablets
tablets, digitizing
tablets, graphics
CN V.TB.AFU.ARI.BCW.AXC.AFU.ALO

graphics, computer
USE **computer graphics**

graphite
MT.519 (L)
CN M.MT.AFU.AFU.AFU.CFS.AFU.DOI

graphite (black pigment)
MT.1574
UF black lead
lead, black
plumbago
CN M.MT.AFU.AFU.ARI.AFU.AFU.ALO.ALO.AFU.AFU.AFU.ARI

graphite (color)
USE **black**
dark grayish blue
dark grayish purple
grayish blue

graphite blue
USE **blackish blue**
dark grayish blue
dark purplish blue
grayish purplish blue

graphite pencils
TB.264
ALT **graphite pencil**
UF lead pencils
pencils, graphite
pencils, lead
CN V.TB.AFU.ARI.CLM.AFU.ALO.DIO.ARI

graphologists
HG.302 (L)
ALT **graphologist**
SN People who study handwriting, especially for the purpose of character analysis. (WCOL)
UF analysts, handwriting
handwriting analysts
CN H.HG.AFU.AXC.BCW.ALO.AXC

graphophone records
VW.636
ALT **graphophone record**
UF records, graphophone
CN V.VW.AFU.ALO.AFU.DZW.AFU.AFU.ARI.AFU

graphs
VW.245 (L)
ALT **graph**
SN Representations of any sort of data by means of dots, lines, or bars; usually to illustrate relationships.
CN V.VW.AFU.AFU.AFU.FZU.AXC.AXC

graphs, bar
USE **bar graphs**

graphs, circular
USE **circular graphs**

graphs, line
USE **line graphs**

graphs, pie
USE **circular graphs**

grass
MT.1026 (L,B,R)
CN M.MT.AFU.AFU.ALO.BIQ.AXC

grass wrack
USE **eelgrass**

grass, China
USE **ramie**

grass, marrum
USE **sea reed**

grass, pampas
USE **pampas grass**

grass, quitch
USE **cutch-grass**

grasses
RD.269 (L,R)
ALT **grass**
UF graminae
CN V.RD.ARI.AFU.BCW.ALO.ALO.ALO.AFU.BCW

grassland
RD.244 (L)
SN Use for the natural, uncultivated regions of the world in which the characteristic plants are grasses.
CN V.RD.ARI.AFU.BCW.ALO.AFU.AFU

grates
RT.1042 (A,L,B,R)
ALT **grate**
SN Frames of parallel or crossed bars blocking an opening or passage; also, similar elements used for cooking over a fire or in fireplaces.
CN V.RT.AFU.AXC.ALO.ALO

gratings
USE **grilles**

grattage
KT.229
SN The removal of granulation by scraping or friction; in painting refers especially to the creation of forms and textures by scraping a wet painted surface.
CN K.KT.AFU.ALO.DUC.CXA.ALO.AFU.BOK

gravel
MT.888 (L,B)
CN M.MT.AFU.AFU.AFU.DCU.ALO.BOK

gravel pits
RG.96 (A)
ALT **gravel pit**
UF pits, gravel
CN V.RG.AFU.AFU.BUE.AFU.AFU

gravel, pea
USE **pea gravel**

gravers
TB.122 (N)
ALT **graver**
SN Any of a class of rod-shaped steel engraving tools with variously shaped points and a wood handle that is generally rounded to fit against the palm. (MAYER)
UF burins
CN V.TB.AFU.ARI.AXC.ALO.BIQ

graves
RK.473 (L,R)
ALT **grave**
SN Excavations in the earth used for burial;(W) for constructions raised over or around burial sites, use **tombs.**
CN V.RK.AFU.ALO.ALO.BOK.AXC

graves, cist
USE **cist graves**

graves, gallery
USE **gallery graves**

graves, passage
USE **passage graves**

graves, pit
USE **shaft graves**

graves, shaft
USE **shaft graves**

gravestones
USE **tombstones**

Gravettian
FL.2467 (L)
CN F.FL.ALO.AXC.AFU.ARI.ALO.ARI

Gravettian, East
USE **East Gravettian**

graveyard lanterns
USE **lanterns of the dead**

graveyards
USE **cemeteries**

graveyards, automobile
USE **automobile graveyards**

graving docks
USE **dry docks**

gravity dams
RK.524 (L)
ALT **gravity dam**
SN Dams that resist water pressure by their own weight.
UF dams, gravity
CN V.RK.AFU.ALO.ALO.CFS.AFU.ARI.AFU.ARI

gravity door hinges
USE **rising hinges**

gravity heating
RT.1403 (B)
SN Central warm air heating systems through which air is circulated by gravity. (ACME)
UF gravity warm air systems
heating, gravity
systems, gravity warm air
warm air systems, gravity
CN V.RT.ALO.BCW.AFU.AFU.ARI.BIQ.ALO

gravity retaining walls
USE **gravity walls**

gravity walls
RT.589
ALT **gravity wall**
SN Use for retaining walls prevented from overturning by their own weight.
UF gravity retaining walls
mass retaining walls
retaining walls, gravity
walls, gravity
walls, mass retaining
CN V.RT.AFU.AFU.AFU.BIQ.BUE.AFU.ALO.AXC.ALO

gravity warm air systems
USE **gravity heating**

gravity, specific
USE **specific gravity**

gravure
USE **photogravure**

gravure printing
USE **photogravure**

gravure prints (photomechanical)
USE **photogravures**

gravures (photomechanical)
USE **photogravures**

gray
DL.301 (L)
UF grey
CN D.DL.AFU.ALO.ALO

gray birch
MT.1118 (L)
UF Betula populifolia
birch, gray
CN M.MT.AFU.AFU.ALO.BIQ.DCU.AFU.AFU.AFU.BIQ.AXC

gray bistre
USE **light grayish yellowish brown**
light olive brown
light yellowish brown

gray black
USE **greenish gray**
light brownish gray
light olive gray
medium gray
olive gray

gray-black ware, Syrian
USE **Syrian gray-black ware**

gray blue
USE **light bluish gray**
light purplish gray
moderate blue
pale blue
pale purplish blue
pale violet

gray blue, light
USE **grayish blue**
pale blue

gray brown
USE **light brownish gray**
light grayish reddish brown
light olive brown
light olive gray

gray burnished ware
FL.2992
UF burnished ware, gray
ware, gray burnished
CN F.FL.ALO.AXC.ARI.BCW.ALO.BCW.ARI

gray burnished ware (Syrian)
USE **Syrian gray-black ware**

gray dawn
USE **purplish gray**

gray fir
USE **western hemlock**

gray granite
MT.593
UF granite, gray
CN M.MT.AFU.AFU.AFU.DCU.AFU.AFU.AFU.AFU.AFU.ARI.ALO.AFU

gray green
USE **grayish yellow green**
light bluish green
light olive gray
moderate green
moderate yellow green
moderate yellowish green

gray green, bluish
USE **grayish green**
pale green

gray green, dark bluish
USE **dark bluish green**
dark grayish green
grayish green
moderate bluish green

gray green, deep bluish
USE **grayish green**

gray green, pale
USE **pale yellow green**

gray iron
MT.339
SN Pig or cast-iron containing much graphite iron. (W)
UF iron, gray
CN M.MT.AFU.AFU.AFU.BZY.AFU.AFU.AFU.AFU.AFU.ALO

gray ironbark
MT.1154
UF Eucalyptus paniculata
ironbark
ironbark, gray
CN M.MT.AFU.AFU.ALO.BIQ.DCU.AFU.AFU.AFU.DIO.ARI

gray light
USE **light gray**

gray lilac
USE **light brownish gray**
light purplish gray
reddish gray
very pale purple

gray marble
MT.780
UF marble, gray
CN M.MT.AFU.AFU.AFU.DCU.AFU.ARI.ARI.ARI.ALO

Gray Minyan ware
FL.2660
UF Minyan ware, Gray
ware, Gray Minyan
CN F.FL.ALO.AXC.ALO.AFU.ALO.AXC.AXC.BOK.ALO

gray poplar
MT.1278
UF poplar, gray
Populus canescens
CN M.MT.AFU.AFU.ALO.BIQ.DCU.AFU.AFU.AFU.KFK.ALO.BCW

gray slate
MT.863
UF slate, gray
CN M.MT.AFU.AFU.AFU.DCU.AFU.ARI.BUE.AFU.AFU

gray teak
USE **white beech**

gray ultramarine ash
USE **light greenish gray**

gray violet
USE **purplish gray**

gray ware
FL.2749
UF ware, gray
CN F.FL.ALO.AXC.ALO.ALO.ALO.
BUE.ALO.ALO

gray wether
USE **sarsen**

gray, aqua
USE **bluish gray**
grayish blue
light bluish gray
pale green

gray, beige
USE **medium gray**
yellowish gray

gray, blue
USE **bluish gray**
medium gray

gray, bluish
USE **bluish gray**

gray, brownish
USE **brownish gray**

gray, celadon
USE **grayish yellow green**
pale green

gray, charcoal
USE **dark gray**

gray, dark
USE **dark gray**

gray, dark bluish
USE **dark bluish gray**

gray, dark greenish
USE **dark greenish gray**

gray, dark jade
USE **dark bluish green**

gray, dark neutral
USE **dark gray**

gray, dark olive
USE **grayish olive green**
olive gray

gray, dark Payne's
USE **dark bluish gray**
dark grayish blue

gray, dark purplish
USE **dark purplish gray**

gray, dark reddish
USE **dark reddish gray**

gray, deep green blue
USE **grayish blue**

gray, deep navy
USE **dark gray**

gray, deep neutral
USE **dark gray**

gray, deep Payne's
USE **grayish blue**

gray, greenish
USE **greenish gray**

gray, iron
USE **dark gray**
olive gray

gray, jade
USE **pale green**

gray, lavender
USE **pale purplish blue**
pale violet
very pale purplish blue
very pale violet

gray, lead
USE **dark gray**
reddish gray

gray, light
USE **light gray**

gray, light bluish
USE **light bluish gray**

gray, light brownish
USE **light brownish gray**

gray, light greenish
USE **light greenish gray**

gray, light navy
USE **medium gray**

gray, light neutral
USE **medium gray**

gray, light olive
USE **light olive gray**

gray, light Payne's
USE **bluish gray**
pale blue

gray, light purplish
USE **light purplish gray**

gray, lilac
USE **brownish pink**
grayish purple
light purplish gray

gray, mauve
USE **grayish purple**

gray, medium
USE **medium gray**

gray, medium dark
USE **dark gray**

gray, medium light
USE **medium gray**

gray, medium navy
USE **medium gray**

gray, metallic
USE **purplish gray**

gray, mineral
USE **ultramarine blue**

gray, navy
USE **dark gray**

gray, neutral
USE **medium gray**

gray, olive
USE **olive gray**

gray, oyster
USE **light gray**

gray, pale green blue
USE **pale blue**

gray, pale neutral
USE **medium gray**

gray, pale Payne's
USE **pale blue**

gray, pale purplish
USE **purplish gray**

gray, pastel
USE **grayish yellow**

gray, Payne's
USE **dark grayish blue**
grayish blue

gray, peach
USE **pale yellowish pink**

gray, pearl
USE **light bluish gray**
light gray
pale blue
very pale blue

gray, pinkish
USE **pinkish gray**

gray, purplish
USE **purplish gray**

gray, reddish
USE **reddish gray**

gray, rose
USE **brownish gray**
grayish red

gray, silver
USE **light brownish gray**
light olive brown
medium gray

gray, steel
USE **dark gray**

gray, taupe
USE **dark purplish gray**
purplish gray

gray, teal
USE **dark bluish gray**
dark gray

gray, very dark
USE **brownish gray**
dark gray

gray, very light
USE **light gray**

gray, warm
USE **grayish yellow**

gray, yellowish
USE **yellowish gray**

grayish black
USE **black**

grayish blue
DL.223
UF Antwerp blue (color)
aqua gray
azurite blue
blue, Antwerp (color)
blue, azurite
blue, dark cerulean
blue, dark steel
blue, deep delft
blue, delft
blue, dull
blue, dull greenish
blue, dull reddish
blue, grayish
blue, indigo
blue, light gray
blue, pastel
blue, slate
blue, steel
centroid color 186
cerulean blue, dark
dark cerulean blue
dark navy
dark steel blue
dark teal
dark violet slate
deep delft blue
deep green blue gray
deep Payne's gray
deep slate blue
delft blue
delft blue, deep
dull blue
dull greenish blue
dull reddish blue
graphite (color)
gray blue, light
gray, aqua
gray, deep green blue
gray, deep Payne's
gray, Payne's
green blue gray, deep
green blue slate
greenish blue, dull
indigo blue
light gray blue
navy, dark
pastel blue
Payne's gray
Payne's gray, deep
pewter (color)
reddish blue, dull
slate blue
slate blue, deep
slate, dark violet
slate, green blue
steel blue
steel blue, dark
teal, dark
violet slate
violet slate, dark
CN D.DL.AFU.AFU.BZY.BZY

grayish blue green
USE **grayish green**
moderate bluish green

grayish blue green, dark
USE **dark gray**
dark greenish gray

grayish blue green, deep
USE **grayish green**

grayish blue violet
USE **light purplish blue**
moderate purplish blue
moderate violet
strong purplish blue
strong violet

grayish blue violet, dark
USE **grayish violet**

grayish blue violet, light
USE **light purplish blue**

grayish blue violet, pale
USE **very pale purplish blue**

grayish blue, dark
USE **dark grayish blue**

grayish blue, pale
USE **very pale blue**
very pale purplish blue

grayish brown
DL.82
UF bistre
black brown
brown, black
brown, dull
brown, grayish
brown, mummy
brown, taupe
brown, umber
brown, Van Dyke(color)
centroid color 61
dull brown
mummy brown
rose taupe
taupe brown
taupe, rose
umber brown
Van Dyke brown(color)
CN D.DL.AFU.AFU.AXC.BIQ

grayish brown, dark
USE **dark grayish brown**

grayish brown, light
USE **light grayish brown**

grayish brown, very dark
USE **dark grayish yellowish brown**
moderate olive brown

grayish green
DL.175
UF blue green, deep grayish
blue green, grayish
bluish gray green
bluish gray green, dark
bluish gray green, deep
bluish green, dull
centroid color 150
dark bluish gray green
dark terre verte
deep bluish gray green
deep grayish blue green
dull bluish green
dull green
gray green, bluish
gray green, dark bluish
gray green, deep bluish
grayish blue green
grayish blue green, deep
green, dull
green, dull bluish
green, grayish
green, slate
slate green
slate green
terre verte
terre verte, dark
CN D.DL.AFU.AFU.BUE.BZY

grayish green, dark
USE **dark grayish green**

grayish greenish yellow
DL.143
UF centroid color 105
citron
citron green
dull greenish yellow
green, citron
green, lime
greenish yellow, grayish
lime green
yellow, grayish greenish
CN D.DL.AFU.AFU.BCW.CRG.ALO. BZY

grayish lavender
USE **pale purple**

grayish lavender, dark
USE **pale violet**

grayish lavender, deep
USE **pale purple**
pale violet

grayish lilac
USE **blackish red**

grayish olive
DL.148
UF black brown
brown, black
centroid color 110

dark greenish olive
dark olive gray
deep olive
drab, olive
greenish olive, dark
olive drab
olive gray, dark
olive, dark greenish
olive, deep
olive, grayish
CN D.DL.AFU.AFU.BIQ.AXC

grayish olive green
DL.210
UF bluish olive
centroid color 127
dark dull yellow green
dark olive gray
dull green
dull yellow green, dark
gray, dark olive
green, dull
green, grayish olive
green, ivy
green, jade
ivy green
jade green
olive gray, dark
olive green, grayish
olive, bluish
peridot
yellow green, dark dull
CN D.DL.AFU.AFU.BUE.DCU.ARI.BCW

grayish olive green, dark
USE **dark grayish olive green**

grayish olive, dark
USE **dark grayish olive**

grayish olive, deep
USE **olive gray**

grayish olive, light
USE **light grayish olive**

grayish orange
USE **light yellowish brown**

grayish orange pink
USE **grayish yellowish pink**

grayish pink
DL.11
UF centroid color 8
pink, grayish
pink, silver
silver pink
CN D.DL.AFU.AFU.AFU.BUE

grayish purple
DL.279
UF amethyst (color)
bluish violet, dark
brown purple
brown, purple
brown, violet
centroid color 228
dark bluish violet
dark slate violet
deep slate violet
dull reddish violet
dull violet
gray, lilac
gray, mauve
grayish red purple
light purple drab
lilac
lilac gray
litho purple
mauve gray
mauve, rose
orchid gray
orchid taupe
orchid, slate
purple brown
purple drab
purple drab, light
purple, brown
purple, grayish
purple, grayish red
purple, litho
purple, slate
red purple, grayish
reddish violet, dull
rose mauve
rose taupe
slate orchid
slate purple
slate violet
slate violet, dark
slate violet, deep
taupe, orchid
taupe, rose
violet brown
violet, dark bluish
violet, dull
violet, dull reddish
violet, slate
CN D.DL.AFU.AFU.CFS.BZY

grayish purple, dark
USE **dark grayish purple**

grayish purplish blue
DL.253
UF blue, delft
blue, dull
blue, dull reddish
blue, graphite
blue, grayish purplish
blue, indigo
blue, medium
blue, navy
bluish violet, deep dull
centroid color 204
dark dull violet blue
deep dull bluish violet
delft blue
dull blue
dull bluish violet, deep
dull reddish blue
dull violet blue, dark
graphite blue
indigo blue
light navy
medium blue
navy blue
navy, light
periwinkle
purplish blue, grayish
reddish blue, dull
slate blue
slate (color)
ultramarine
violet blue, dark dull
violet, deep dull bluish
CN D.DL.AFU.AFU.BZY.DCU.ALO.BZY

grayish purplish pink
DL.23
UF bluish pink
centroid color 253
dull lavender
lavender, dull
lilac
orchid
pale purple drab
pink, bluish
pink, grayish purplish
purple drab, pale
purplish pink, grayish
red violet
violet, red
CN D.DL.AFU.AFU.AFU.CLM.AFU.BUE

grayish purplish red
DL.58
UF artificial vermilion
bright rose
brown violet
centroid color 262
dull lilac
dull violet
lake, rose
lilac
lilac, dull
lilac, red
lilac, rose
magenta (color)
mauve taupe
plum, rose
purplish red, grayish
red lilac
red violet
red, grayish purplish
rose
rose lake
rose lilac
rose plum
rose, bright
taupe, mauve
vermilion, artificial
violet, brown
violet, dull
violet, red
CN D.DL.AFU.AFU.ALO.CFS.AFU.BIQ

grayish purplish red, light
USE **light grayish purplish red**

grayish red
DL.42
UF brick red
brown red
brown, dull reddish
brown, light rose
brown, red
brown, rose

brown, violet
carmine (color)
carmine rose
centroid color 19
dark Indian red
dragon's blood (color)
dull red
dull reddish brown
gray, rose
haematite red
Indian red (color)
Indian red, dark
light rose brown
Pompeian red (color)
red brown
red, brick
red, brown
red, dark Indian
red, dull
red, grayish
red, haematite
red, Indian (color)
red, Pompeian (color)
reddish brown, dull
rose
rose brown
rose brown, light
rose gray
rose taupe
rose, carmine
taupe brown
taupe, rose
vermilion (color)
violet brown
CN D.DL.AFU.AFU.ALO.BIQ

grayish red purple
USE **grayish purple**

grayish red, dark
USE **dark grayish red**

grayish red, light
USE **light grayish red**

grayish reddish brown
DL.95
UF brown red
brown, deep red
brown, dull reddish
brown, grayish reddish
brown, rose
brown, taupe
burnt umber (color)
centroid color 46
dark red brown
deep red brown
dull reddish brown
haematite red
maroon
red brown, deep
red, brown
red, haematite
reddish brown, dull
reddish brown, grayish
rose brown
rose taupe
taupe brown
taupe, rose
umber, burnt (color)
CN D.DL.AFU.AFU.AXC.BZY.AFU.BIQ

grayish reddish brown, light
USE **light grayish reddish brown**

grayish reddish orange
DL.74
UF brown orange
brown, orange
centroid color 39
copper (color)
dull reddish orange
dull yellowish red
lake (color)
light red
orange brown
orange, brown
orange, dull reddish
orange, grayish reddish
Pompeian red (color)
red, dull yellowish
red, light
red, pompeian (color)
reddish orange, dull
reddish orange, grayish
terra cotta (color)
yellowish red, dull
CN D.DL.AFU.AFU.ARI.BOK.AFU.BIQ

grayish reddish purple
DL.298
UF amethyst (color)
centroid color 245
dull reddish violet
dull violet
plum, rose
purple, grayish reddish
reddish purple, grayish
reddish violet, dull
rose plum
slate purple
violet, dull
violet, dull reddish
CN D.DL.AFU.AFU.CFS.DCU.AFU.BUE

grayish violet
DL.265
UF blackish violet
blue plum
blue violet, dark grayish
blue, diamin azo
bluish violet, dark
bluish violet, dark dull
bluish violet, dull
centroid color 215
dark bluish violet
dark dull bluish violet
dark dull violet blue
dark grayish blue violet
diamin azo blue
dull bluish violet
grayish blue violet, dark
plum, blue
violet blue, dark dull
violet, blackish
violet, dark bluish
violet, dark dull bluish
violet, dull bluish
violet, grayish
CN D.DL.AFU.AFU.BZY.DCU.ARI.BZY

grayish violet blue
USE **light violet**

grayish violet blue, light
USE **brilliant purplish blue**

grayish violet blue, pale
USE **light purplish blue**

grayish yellow
DL.120
UF amber gold
beige
beige, light
bisque
bistre
buff
buff, yellow
centroid color 90
chamois (color)
dull reddish yellow
dull yellow
ecru
gold, amber
gray, pastel
gray, warm
ivory (color)
light beige
Naples yellow (color)
parchment (color)
pastel gray
putty (color)
reddish yellow, dull
warm gray
yellow buff
yellow, dull
yellow, dull reddish
yellow, grayish
yellow, Naples (color)
CN D.DL.AFU.AFU.BCW.BZY

grayish yellow green
DL.162
UF celadon gray
celadon green
centroid color 122
dull yellowish green
gray green
gray, celadon
green, celadon
green, dull yellowish
green, gray
green, grayish yellow
green, pastel
pastel green
peridot
putty (color)
yellow green, grayish
yellowish green, dull
CN D.DL.AFU.AFU.BOK.BUE

grayish yellow, dark
USE **dark grayish yellow**

grayish yellowish brown
DL.104
UF beige brown

bistre
brown, beige
brown, dull yellowish
brown, grayish yellowish
brown, mummy
centroid color 80
dull yellowish brown
mummy brown
yellowish brown, dull
yellowish brown, grayish
CN D.DL.AFU.AFU.AXC.BZY.ALO.BIQ

grayish yellowish brown, light
USE **light grayish yellowish brown**

grayish yellowish pink
DL.32
UF beige, light rose
bisque
brown, red
buff, dull
centroid color 32
dull buff
grayish orange pink
light rose beige
orange pink, grayish
pink, grayish orange
pink, grayish yellowish
red brown
rose
rose beige, light
yellowish pink, grayish
CN D.DL.AFU.AFU.AFU.CLM.ALO.BUE

graywacke
MT.713 (L)
CN M.MT.AFU.AFU.AFU.DCU.AFU.ALO.AFU.ARI.AFU.ALO.AFU.ALO

graywether sandstone
USE **sarsen**

grease
MT.1993 (L)
CN M.MT.AFU.AFU.ARI.ARI.ALO.ALO

grease crayons
USE **grease pencils**

grease pencils
TB.265
ALT **grease pencil**
SN Black or colored crayons, usually in stick form, with peel-off paper casing. (MAYER)
UF crayons, grease
grease crayons
pencils, grease
CN V.TB.AFU.ARI.CLM.AFU.ALO.DIO.AXC

great armchairs
USE **great chairs**

great brick
MT.75
UF brick, great
CN M.MT.AFU.AFU.AFU.AXC.ALO.AFU.AFU.AFU.BOK

Great Buddha Style
USE **Daibutsuyo**

great chairs
TG.28 (N)
ALT **great chair**
SN Period term for large armchairs in 17th-century America.
UF armchairs, great
chairs, great
chairs, Harvard
chairs, turned three-square great
great armchairs
great chairs, turned three-square
Harvard chairs
turned three-square great chairs
CN V.TG.AFU.AFU.ALO.AFU.AFU.AFU.ALO.ARI

great chairs, turned three-square
USE **great chairs**

great halls
USE **halls**

great houses
USE **plantation houses**

Great Khans
USE **Qarakhanid**

Great Seljuk
FL.3550
UF Seljuk, Great
CN F.FL.ALO.BIQ.AFU.HIK.AFU

Great Silla
USE **Unified Silla Kingdom**

great tables
USE **refectory tables**

Great Tombs period
USE **Kofun**

Great Vehicle
USE **Mahayana**

great wheel lathes
TB.794
ALT **great wheel lathe**
SN Large lathes used for turning heavy work such as locomotive and railroad car wheels.
UF lathes, great wheel
CN V.TB.AFU.BCW.CFS.AFU.AFU.AFU

Great Zimbabwe
USE **Karanga**

Greater Indian
USE **Southeast Asian**

Grebo
FL.319 (L)
CN F.FL.ALO.AFU.AXC.AFU.ARI.AXC.ALO

grechetto duro
USE **porino**

Grecian beds
USE **sleigh beds**

Grecian couches
TG.389 (N)
ALT **Grecian couch**
SN Term used during the Greek Revival era to describe the form of couch with scrolled ends reminiscent of Roman and Greek furniture designs.
UF couches, Grecian
Grecian sofas
recamier sofas
recamiers
sofas, Grecian
sofas, recamier
CN V.TG.AFU.AFU.ARI.ALO.ARI

Grecian cross legs
USE **curule legs**

Grecian purple
USE **Tyrian purple**

Grecian rocking chairs
USE **Lincoln rockers**

Grecian sofas
USE **Grecian couches**

Greco-Bactrian
FL.1791 (A,L)
UF Hellenistic-Bactrian
CN F.FL.ALO.ARI.AFU.AXC.AXC.AFU

Greco-Buddhist
USE **Gandharan**

greco duro
USE **Parian marble**

Greco-Etruscan
FL.2731
UF Etrusco-Greek
CN F.FL.ALO.AXC.ALO.ALO.ALO.ARI

greco fino
USE **Pentelic marble**

greco giallognolo
USE **lesbio**

greco livido
USE **tasio**

greco rigato
USE **Hymettian marble**

Greco-Roman
FL.2761 (L)
CN F.FL.ALO.AXC.ALO.ALO.ALO.BZY.AFU.ALO

greco turchiniccio
USE **tirio**

Greek
FL.2562 (A,L,B,R)
UF Hellenic
CN F.FL.ALO.AXC.ALO.AFU.AFU.ARI

Greek cross-plan
DC.80
UF plan, Greek cross
CN D.DC.AFU.ARI.ERE.ARI

Greek crosses
DG.9
ALT **Greek cross**
SN Crosses whose vertical and horizontal arms are of equal length. (THDAT)
UF crosses, Greek
CN D.DG.AFU.AFU.ARI.AXC

Greek frets
USE **key pattern**

Greek keys
USE **key pattern**

Greek pitch
USE **rosin**

Greek Revival
FL.3266 (A,L,B,R)
UF Neo-Greek
Revival, Greek
CN F.FL.ALO.BCW.ALO.AXC.CLM.ARI.AFU

Greek Taste
USE **goût grec**

Greek, East
USE **East Greek**

green
DL.163 (L)
CN D.DL.AFU.AFU.BUE

green alder, American
USE **American green alder**

green bice
USE **green earth**

green black
USE **dark grayish green**
dark greenish gray

green blue gray, deep
USE **grayish blue**

green blue gray, pale
USE **pale blue**

green blue slate
USE **grayish blue**

green blue slate, dark
USE **dark blue**
dark grayish blue

green blue, blackish
USE **dark greenish blue**

green copper ore
USE **malachite**

green dull
USE **blackish green**

green earth
MT.1637
UF bice, green
celadon green
earth, green
glauconite
green bice
green sand
green, celadon
green, holly
green, stone
grüne Erde
holly green
sand, green
stone green
terre verte
verdeterra
verdetta
CN M.MT.AFU.AFU.ARI.AFU.AFU.ALO.ALO.AXC.AFU.ALO

green earth, burnt
USE **transparent brown**

green earth, Cyprian
USE **Cyprian green earth**

green gold
MT.394
UF gold, green
CN M.MT.AFU.AFU.AFU.BZY.AFU.AFU.AFU.ALO.AXC.AFU.ALO

green gray, blackish
USE **black**

Green Kutani
USE **Ao Kutani**

green lumber
MT.1435
UF lumber, green
CN M.MT.AFU.AFU.ALO.BIQ.DCU.ALO.BOK.ALO.ARI.ALO

green marble
MT.791
UF marble, green
CN M.MT.AFU.AFU.AFU.DCU.AFU.ARI.ARI.ARI.ARI

green pigment
MT.1634
UF pigment, green
CN M.MT.AFU.AFU.ARI.AFU.AFU.ALO.ALO.AXC

green pigment, artificial inorganic
USE **artificial inorganic green pigment**

green pigment, artificial organic
USE **synthetic organic green pigment**

green pigment, composite
USE **composite green pigment**

green pigment, inorganic
USE **inorganic green pigment**

green pigment, organic
USE **organic green pigment**

green pigment, synthetic inorganic
USE **artificial inorganic green pigment**

green pigment, synthetic organic
USE **synthetic organic green pigment**

green rooms
RM.361
ALT **green room**
SN Off-stage lounges for performers, also serving as a place where they may receive visitors. (IDTL)
UF rooms, green
CN V.RM.AFU.DIO.AXC.AXC.ALO.ALO

green rouge
MT.2578
UF rouge, green
CN M.MT.AFU.ARI.CRG.AXC.ALO. AFU

green sand
USE **green earth**

green slate
MT.866
UF slate, green
CN M.MT.AFU.AFU.AFU.DCU.AFU.ARI.BUE.AFU.ALO

green smalt
USE **cobalt green**

green soap, tincture of
USE **soft soap**

green yellow
USE **brilliant greenish yellow**

green yellow, bright
USE **vivid yellow green**

green yellow, light
USE **light greenish yellow**

green yellow, pale
USE **light greenish yellow**
pale greenish yellow

green, anthracene
USE **moderate bluish green**

green, aqua
USE **light bluish green**
light greenish blue

green, aquamarine
USE **moderate bluish green**

green, Arnaudon's
USE **chromium oxide green**

green, blackish
USE **blackish green**

green, bladder
USE **sap green**

green, blue
USE **light yellowish green**

green, bluish
USE **bluish green**

green, bright
USE **brilliant bluish green**
brilliant green
deep green
deep yellowish green
moderate green
strong bluish green
strong green

strong yellowish green
vivid green
vivid yellowish green

green, bright aqua
USE **brilliant bluish green**
light bluish green
very light bluish green

green, bright bluish
USE **vivid bluish green**

green, bright emerald
USE **brilliant bluish green**
brilliant green
strong bluish green
strong green

green, bright jade
USE **brilliant bluish green**
strong bluish green
strong green

green, bright kelly
USE **brilliant green**
strong green
strong yellowish green
vivid yellowish green

green, bright lime
USE **brilliant yellow green**
brilliant yellowish green
strong yellow green
vivid yellow green

green, bright olive
USE **light olive**
moderate olive
moderate olive green
moderate yellow green

green, bright turquoise
USE **brilliant bluish green**
light bluish green
moderate bluish green
strong bluish green

green, bright yellowish
USE **vivid yellow green**
vivid yellowish green

green, brilliant
USE **brilliant green**

green, brilliant bluish
USE **brilliant bluish green**

green, brilliant yellow
USE **brilliant yellow green**

green, brilliant yellowish
USE **brilliant yellowish green**

green, bronze
USE **chrome green**

green, Brunswick
USE **Brunswick green**

green, cadmium
USE **cadmium green**

green, Casali's
USE **viridian**

green, cedar
USE **chrysocolla**

green, celadon
USE **grayish yellow green**
green earth
moderate yellowish green
pale green

green, chartreuse
USE **brilliant yellow green**
dark greenish yellow
vivid yellow green

green, Chinese
USE **lokao**

green, chrome
USE **chrome green**

green, chrome (color)
USE **moderate green**
strong green
very dark yellowish green

green, chromium oxide
USE **chromium oxide green**

green, chrysocolla
USE **brilliant green**
strong green

green, cinnabar
USE **chrome green**

green, citron
USE **grayish greenish yellow**
moderate greenish yellow

green, cobalt
USE **cobalt green**

green, cobalt (color)
USE **moderate yellowish green**

green, dark
USE **dark green**

green, dark bluish
USE **dark bluish green**

green, dark emerald
USE **deep green**
moderate bluish green

green, dark grayish
USE **dark grayish green**

green, dark grayish olive
USE **dark grayish olive green**

green, dark hunter
USE **dark green**
very dark yellowish green

green, dark jade
USE **dark bluish green**
dark green
light bluish green

green, dark olive
USE **dark olive green**

green, dark slate
USE **blackish green**
dark grayish green
dark green
very dark green

green, dark teal
USE **dark bluish green**

green, dark viridian
USE **moderate green**

green, dark yellowish
USE **dark yellowish green**

green, deep
USE **deep green**

green, deep bluish
USE **deep bluish green**

green, deep chrome
USE **dark yellowish green**

green, deep emerald
USE **moderate green**

green, deep malachite
USE **moderate yellowish green**

green, deep olive
USE **deep olive green**

green, deep teal
USE **dark bluish green**

green, deep turquoise
USE **deep bluish green**

green, deep yellow
USE **deep yellow green**

green, deep yellowish
USE **deep yellowish green**

green, Dingler's
USE **chromium oxide green**

green, dull
USE **dark grayish green**
dark yellowish green
grayish green
grayish olive green
light bluish green
light green
light yellowish green
pale green
very pale green

green, dull blackish
USE **dark grayish green**

green, dull bluish
USE **blackish green**
dark grayish green
grayish green
pale green
very pale green

green, dull yellowish
USE **grayish yellow green**
pale yellow green

green, Elsner
USE **Elsner green**

green, emerald
USE **emerald green**

green, emerald (color)
USE **brilliant green**
brilliant yellowish green
moderate bluish green
moderate green
moderate yellowish green
strong bluish green
strong green
strong yellowish green
very light yellowish green

green, English
USE **emerald green**

green, forest
USE **dark green**

green, Gellert
USE **cobalt green**

green, gray
USE **grayish yellow green**
light bluish green
light olive gray
moderate green
moderate yellow green
moderate yellowish green

green, grayish
USE **grayish green**

green, grayish blue
USE **moderate bluish green**

green, grayish olive
USE **grayish olive green**

green, grayish yellow
USE **grayish yellow green**

green, Guignet's
USE **viridian**

green, hemlock
USE **dark grayish green**
very dark bluish green
very dark green

green, holly
USE **green earth**

green, Hooker's
USE **Hooker's green**

green, Hungarian
USE **malachite green**

green, hunter
USE **dark green**
moderate green
very dark yellowish green

green, hunter's
USE **very dark yellowish green**

green, imperial
USE **emerald green**

green, intense
USE **phthalocyanine green**

green, iris
USE **sap green**

green, ivy
USE **dark grayish olive green**
grayish olive green

green, jade
USE **grayish olive green**
moderate bluish green
moderate green
moderate olive green
moderate yellowish green
strong bluish green

green, kelly
USE **deep yellowish green**
strong green
strong yellowish green

green, light
USE **light green**

green, light aqua
USE **pale green**
very light bluish green

green, light blue
USE **light bluish green**

green, light bluish
USE **light bluish green**

green, light chrome
USE **dark yellowish green**

green, light emerald
USE **brilliant green**
light bluish green
light green
very light bluish green

green, light jade
USE **light bluish green**

green, light lime
USE **brilliant yellowish green**
strong yellow green

green, light mint
USE **light green**
very light green

green, light olive
USE **moderate yellow green**

green, light Paris
USE **light yellowish green**

green, light turquoise
USE **very light bluish green**

green, light yellow
USE **light yellow green**

green, light yellowish
USE **light yellowish green**

green, lily
USE **lily green**

green, lime
USE **dark greenish yellow**
grayish greenish yellow
light olive
moderate greenish yellow
strong yellow green

green, malachite
USE **malachite green**

green, malachite (color)
USE **light yellowish green**

green, medium chrome
USE **dark green**
dark yellowish green

green, mineral
USE **malachite green**

green, Ming
USE **strong green**

green, mint
USE **light green**

green, Mittis
USE **emerald green**

green, Mittler's
USE **viridian**

green, moderate
USE **moderate green**

green, moderate blue
USE **moderate bluish green**

green, moderate bluish
USE **moderate bluish green**

green, moderate olive
USE **moderate olive green**

green, moderate yellow
USE **moderate yellow green**

green, moderate yellowish
USE **moderate yellowish green**

green, Monastral
USE **phthalocyanine green**

green, Montpellier
USE **verdigris**

green, mountain
USE **malachite green**

green, nitrate
USE **chrome green**

green, oil
USE **chrome green**

green, olive
USE **olive green**

green, pale
USE **pale green**

green, pale aqua
USE **very light bluish green**
very pale green

green, pale blue
USE **pale green**

green, pale emerald
USE **very light bluish green**
very light green

green, pale gray
USE **pale yellow green**

green, pale jade
USE **very pale green**

green, pale mint
USE **very light green**
very pale green

green, pale olive
USE **moderate yellow green**

green, pale turquoise
USE **very light bluish green**

green, pale yellow
USE **pale yellow green**

green, pale yellowish
USE **pale green**

green, Pannetier's
USE **viridian**

green, pansy
USE **pansy green**

green, Paris
USE **brilliant green**
brilliant yellowish green
emerald green
light yellowish green
strong yellowish green
vivid yellowish green

green, pastel
USE **grayish yellow green**
moderate yellow green
pale green
very pale green

green, pastel turquoise
USE **very light bluish green**

green, permanent
USE **permanent green**

green, phthalocyanine
USE **phthalocyanine green**

green, pistachio
USE **light yellowish green**
moderate yellow green
moderate yellowish green

green, Plessy's
USE **chromium oxide green**

green, Prussian
USE **Brunswick green**
deep bluish green
deep greenish blue
moderate bluish green

green, Reading
USE **chromium oxide green**

green, Rinman's
USE **cobalt green**

green, royal
USE **chrome green**

green, sap
USE **sap green**

green, Saxony
USE **cobalt green**

green, Scheele's
USE **Scheele's green**

green, Scheele's (color)
USE **moderate yellow green**
strong yellow green
strong yellowish green

green, Schnitzer's
USE **chromium oxide green**

green, Schweinfurt
USE **emerald green**

green, slate
USE **dark grayish green**
grayish green
greenish gray
light grayish olive
light olive gray
moderate green
moderate olive green
strong olive green

green, stone
USE **green earth**

green, strong
USE **strong green**

green, strong bluish
USE **strong bluish green**

green, strong olive
USE **strong olive green**

green, strong yellow
USE **strong yellow green**

green, strong yellowish
USE **strong yellowish green**

green, teal
USE **dark bluish green**
moderate bluish green

green, transparent chromium oxide
USE **viridian**

green, turquoise
USE **brilliant bluish green**
light bluish green
light greenish blue
moderate bluish green
strong bluish green
vivid bluish green

green, Tyrolean
USE **Tyrolean green**

green, ultramarine
USE **ultramarine green**

green, Van Eyck
USE **verdigris**

green, verdigris
USE **light green**

green, verditer
USE **moderate yellowish green**

green, Verona
USE **Verona green**

green, Veronese
USE **emerald green**

green, very dark
USE **very dark green**

green, very dark bluish
USE **very dark bluish green**

green, very dark yellowish
USE **very dark yellowish green**

green, very deep yellowish
USE **very deep yellowish green**

green, very light
USE **very light green**

green, very light bluish
USE **very light bluish green**

green, very light yellowish
USE **very light yellowish green**

green, very pale
USE **very pale green**

green, Victoria
USE **chrome green**

green, Vienna
USE **emerald green**

green, viridian
USE **brilliant green**
strong green

green, vivid
USE **vivid green**

green, vivid bluish
USE **vivid bluish green**

green, vivid emerald
USE **strong bluish green**

green, vivid turquoise
USE **strong bluish green**

green, vivid yellow
USE **vivid yellow green**

green, vivid yellowish
USE **vivid yellowish green**

green, yellow
USE **yellow green**

green, yellowish
USE **yellowish green**

green, zinc
USE **cobalt green**

green, zinc chrome
USE **zinc chrome green**

green, zinnober
USE **chrome green**

greenbelts
RK.1585 (A,L,B,R)
ALT **greenbelt**
SN Use for permanently reserved zones of land around and between cities.
UF jneins
CN V.RK.ALO.ARI.BCW

greenhouse gardening
KT.490 (A,L)
UF gardening, greenhouse
CN K.KT.AFU.ALO.DZW.AFU.AFU

greenhouse glass
MT.252
UF glass, greenhouse
CN M.MT.AFU.AFU.AFU.BIQ.AFU.ALO.AXC.AFU.AFU

greenhouses
RK.63 (A,L,N,B,R)
ALT **greenhouse**
SN Structures enclosed by glass and devoted to the cultivation and protection of plants out of season. (W)
UF conservatories (greenhouses)
glasshouses
hothouses
stoves (greenhouses)
CN V.RK.AFU.ALO.ALO.AFU.AFU.BOK.AFU

greenhouses, solar
USE **solar greenhouses**

greenhouses, solar-heated
USE **solar greenhouses**

greenhouses, sun-heated
USE **solar greenhouses**

greenish black
DL.182
UF black, greenish
centroid color 157
CN D.DL.AFU.AFU.BUE.CXA

greenish black, dull
USE **dark gray**
dark greenish gray

greenish blue
DL.232
UF blue, greenish
CN D.DL.AFU.AFU.BZY.DCU.AFU

greenish blue, bright
USE **vivid greenish blue**

greenish blue, brilliant
USE **brilliant greenish blue**

greenish blue, dark
USE **dark greenish blue**

greenish blue, deep
USE **deep greenish blue**

greenish blue, dull
USE **blackish blue**
dark grayish blue
grayish blue
pale blue
very pale blue

greenish blue, light
USE **light greenish blue**

greenish blue, moderate
USE **moderate greenish blue**

greenish blue, strong
USE **strong greenish blue**

greenish blue, very dark
USE **very dark greenish blue**

greenish blue, very light
USE **very light greenish blue**

greenish blue, vivid
USE **vivid greenish blue**

greenish gray
DL.179
UF black, gray
centroid color 155
gray black
gray, greenish
green, slate
slate (color)
slate green
CN D.DL.AFU.AFU.BUE.CRG

greenish gray, light
USE **light greenish gray**

greenish navy
USE **blackish blue**
dark blue

greenish olive, dark
USE **grayish olive**
moderate olive

greenish slate black
USE **black**
dark gray
dark greenish gray

greenish white
DL.178
UF centroid color 153
white, greenish
CN D.DL.AFU.AFU.BUE.CLM

greenish yellow
DL.134
UF yellow, greenish
CN D.DL.AFU.AFU.BCW.CRG.ALO

greenish yellow, bright
USE **vivid greenish yellow**

greenish yellow, dark
USE **dark greenish yellow**

greenish yellow, deep
USE **deep greenish yellow**

greenish yellow, dull
USE **light olive**
pale greenish yellow

greenish yellow, grayish
USE **grayish greenish yellow**

greenish yellow, light
USE **light greenish yellow**

greenish yellow, moderate
USE **moderate greenish yellow**

greenish yellow, pale
USE **pale greenish yellow**

greenish yellow, strong
USE **strong greenish yellow**

greenish yellow, vivid
USE **vivid greenish yellow**

Greenlandic Eskimo
USE **Katladlit**

greens
RK.1586 (R)
ALT **green**
SN Use for grassy, public open spaces near the center of a town and used for a variety of community functions; found especially in New England and Mid-Atlantic states.
UF greens, village
lots, meeting house
meeting house lots
village greens
CN V.RK.ALO.ARI.BIQ

greens, bowling
USE **bowling greens**

greens, village
USE **greens**

greensand
MT.2076 (L)
SN Consists largely of glauconite (a greenish granular mineral containing up to 25% iron) with a large percentage of silica, and some potash and aluminum, used especially as a water softener(MH) and as a source of potash. (W)
CN M.MT.AFU.AFU.ARI.BOK.ALO.BOK.AXC

greenstone, Virginia
USE **Virginia greenstone**

greeting cards
VW.566 (L,N,R)
ALT **greeting card**
SN Cards that are imprinted with messages and often suitable illustrations and are sent or given on special occasions or holidays. (AHD)
UF cards, greeting
CN V.VW.AFU.ALO.AFU.ARI.BOK

greige
USE **light grayish olive**

light olive brown
light olive gray

grenier houses
USE **Creole cottages**

grey
USE **gray**

grid plan
BM.83 (A)
UF chessboard plan
gridiron plan
orthogonal plan
plan, chessboard
plan, grid
plan, orthogonal
CN B.BM.AFU.AFU.ARI.AFU.EFQ.AFU

grid space frames
USE **space frames**

gridiron plan
USE **grid plan**

gridirons
USE **football fields**

gridirons (theater elements)
RT.1265
ALT **gridiron (theater element)**
SN Use for open frameworks of beams over a stage, below the roof but with working room between the grid and the roof, used principally for the suspension of drapery and scenery.
CN V.RT.AFU.BUE.ARI.AFU

grief
BM.577 (L,R)
UF sorrow
CN B.BM.BUE.ARI.BIQ

griffes
RT.70
ALT **griffe**
SN Ornaments resembling a claw that projects from the round base of an architectural column upon the angle formed by a corner of the plinth. (W)
UF spurs (griffes)
CN V.RT.AFU.AFU.AFU.AXC.ARI.ALO.ALO

Griffith's patent zinc white
USE **lithopone**

grillages
RT.175 (L)
ALT **grillage**
SN Frameworks of heavy timbers, steel, or reinforced concrete beams laid longitudinally and crossed by similar members laid on them to spread a heavy load over a larger area; includes similar structures used to distribute a concentrated load over the top of the footing. (DAC)
CN V.RT.AFU.AFU.AFU.AXC.BUE.ARI.ALO.ALO

grilles
RT.1043 (A,L,B,R)
ALT **grille**
SN Grating or openwork barriers, often of metal, used to cover, conceal, decorate, or protect an opening; common also on furniture.
UF gratings
grillwork
CN V.RT.AFU.AXC.ALO.ARI

grillwork
USE **grilles**

grinders
TB.210 (L,N)
ALT **grinder**
SN Machines or tools which grind with abrasives; used to cut hardened or tempered metals and to develop a smooth finish as on metal, wood, stone, or concrete.
CN V.TB.AFU.ARI.BZY.ALO.AFU

grinders (metalworkers)
HG.506
ALT **grinder (metalworker)**
SN Persons who sharpen tools by grinding.
CN H.HG.AFU.AXC.BUE.ARI.CFS.ALO.AXC

grinders, mower-knife
USE **mower-knife grinders**

grinding
KT.615 (L)
ALT **ground**
CN K.KT.AFU.ALO.FUA.CRG

grinding wheels
TB.1133 (L,N)
ALT **grinding wheel**
SN Abrasive wheels or disks used for cutting or smoothing materials such as metal, glass, plastics, or clay.
UF abrasive wheels
wheels, abrasive
wheels, grinding
CN V.TB.ALO.DUC.AFU

grindstones
TB.1134 (L,N)
ALT **grindstone**
SN Flat sandstone wheels which are rotated on an axle; used to sharpen implements and to shape and smooth objects.
CN V.TB.ALO.DUC.ALO

griotte marble
MT.798
UF French red marble
marble, French red
marble, griotte
red marble, French
CN M.MT.AFU.AFU.AFU.DCU.AFU.ARI.ARI.ARI.BCW.AFU

grips (handles)
USE **handles**

grisaille
KT.255 (L,R)
SN Painting in gray or grayish monochrome sometimes heightened in gold. (THDAT)
CN K.KT.AFU.ALO.DUC.CXA.ALO.BCW.AFU.ALO

gristmills
USE **flour mills**

grit, millstone
USE **gritstone**

gritstone
MT.704
UF grit, millstone
millstone grit
CN M.MT.AFU.AFU.AFU.DCU.AFU.ALO.AFU.ARI.AFU.AFU.AFU

gritty buff ware
FL.2871
UF buff ware, gritty
ware, gritty buff
CN F.FL.ALO.AXC.ARI.AFU.ALO.ARI.BIQ

grizzle
MT.121
CN M.MT.AFU.AFU.AFU.AXC.ALO.AFU.AXC.AFU.AFU.ALO.AFU

groceries
USE **grocery stores**

grocery shops
USE **grocery stores**

grocery stores
RK.160 (B)
ALT **grocery store**
UF groceries
grocery shops
shops, grocery
stores, grocery
CN V.RK.AFU.ALO.ALO.ALO.ARI.BIQ.AFU.CFS

groin ribs
USE **diagonal ribs**

groined vaults
RT.531
ALT **groined vault**
SN Compound vaults in which barrel vaults intersect forming ridges called groins. (HAS)
UF cross vaults
vaults, cross
vaults, groined
CN V.RT.AFU.AFU.AFU.BIQ.BOK.AFU.AFU.AFU.ALO.ALO

groining, fan
USE **fan vaults**

groins
RT.563
ALT **groin**
SN The ridges or edges formed by the intersection of the surfaces of two or

more intersecting vaults. (DAC)
CN V.RT.AFU.AFU.AFU.BIQ.BOK.ALO.ALO

groins (erosion protection works)
RK.560 (L)
ALT **groin (erosion protection work)**
SN Use for long, narrow, permeable or impermeable protective structures built out from a seashore to check or increase erosion. For similar structures located along a river or stream bank, use **wing dams**; when such structures are built to control shoaling, use **jetties**.
UF groynes
CN V.RK.AFU.ALO.ALO.CFS.ALO.ALO.ARI

grommets
TF.333 (L)
ALT **grommet**
SN Metal or plastic eyelets that provide a reinforced hole in a material, such as cloth or leather, that might otherwise tear from the stress on the hole when a fastener or other device is passed through it or attached to it. (MEANS)
UF eyelets (grommets)
CN V.TF.AFU.AFU.AFU.ALO.AFU.AXC

grooved seams
TF.656
ALT **grooved seam**
UF seams, grooved
CN V.TF.ALO.ARI.ARI.BUE.BOK

groovers
TB.599
ALT **groover**
SN Tools used for creating grooved joints in unhardened concrete slabs. (MEANS)
CN V.TB.AFU.BCW.BCW.ALO.DUC

grooving planes
TB.912 (N)
ALT **grooving plane**
SN Includes any of a variety of planes intended to make grooves in wood. (SALAM)
UF planes, grooving
CN V.TB.AFU.BCW.CFS.ALO.AFU.DUC.ALO

grooving planes, carcase
USE **dado planes**

grooving planes, dado
USE **dado planes**

grooving saws
USE **stairbuilder's saws**

Gros Ventre
USE **Atsina**

Gros Ventres of the Missouri
USE **Hidatsa**

grotesques
DG.33 (R)
ALT **grotesque**
SN Ornamental motifs including fanciful human and animal forms and floral ornament, based on the decoration of Nero's Domus Aurea in Rome, discovered in 1488.
UF grotteschi
CN D.DG.AFU.AFU.BOK

Grotta-Pelos
FL.2539
CN F.FL.ALO.AXC.ALO.AFU.AFU.ALO.AFU.AFU.ALO

grotteschi
USE **grotesques**

grotto architecture
USE **cave architecture**

grotto chairs
TG.138
ALT **grotto chair**
SN Design which originally appeared in Chippendale's Director for chairs with a back in the form of an open scallop shell; often decorated in silver gilt or painted to look like mother of pearl. (RUSTIC)
UF chairs, grotto
CN V.TG.AFU.AFU.ALO.AFU.AFU.AFU.NIE.BZY

grotto tables
TG.680
ALT **grotto table**
SN Design which originally appeared in Chippendale's Director for garden tables with a top carved in the form of an open scallop shell; often silver gilt or painted to look like mother of pearl. (RUSTIC)
UF tables, grotto
CN V.TG.AFU.AFU.BIQ.BOK.AFU.BIQ

grottoes
RK.1336 (A,L,B,R)
ALT **grotto**
SN Use only for the artificially constructed garden features, common since the 16th century in French and English landscapes; for the natural features, use **caves** or **caverns**.
CN V.RK.AFU.ALO.ARI.AFU.BCW

ground (material)
MT.2717 (R)
SN Substance, such as gesso for paintings or acid-resistant wax for etchings, used to prepare the surface on which or from which an image is made.
CN M.MT.AFU.ARI.IFM.ALO

ground beams
USE **sill plates**

ground-fault circuit interruptors
RT.1344
ALT **ground-fault circuit interruptor**
SN Special devices to interrupt electrical current where a weak electrical loss or ground occurs. (PBCD)
UF circuit interruptors, ground-fault
GFCIs
CN V.RT.ALO.ARI.ALO.BZY

ground glass
MT.262
SN Double strength glass that has one side ground to a frosted finish, thus transforming the clear glass to an obscure glass. (STEIN)
UF glass, ground
CN M.MT.AFU.AFU.AFU.BIQ.AFU.ARI.BUE

ground plans
VD.47
ALT **ground plan**
SN Floor plans taken near ground level and showing the foundation and ground floor of the building.
UF ground plots
plans, ground
plots, ground
CN V.VD.AFU.AFU.BIQ.ALO.AXC.ALO.AFU.AFU

ground plates
USE **sill plates**

ground plots
USE **ground plans**

ground rent
BM.409 (L)
SN A price per year or term of years paid for the right to occupy and improve a piece of land. (W)
UF rent, ground
CN B.BM.ARI.EWY.ALO

ground stations
USE **satellite tracking stations**

ground, emulsion
USE **emulsion ground**

ground, middle
USE **middle ground**

grounded paper
USE **prepared paper**

grounded systems
RT.1334
ALT **grounded system**
SN Systems of electric conductors, at least one of which is intentionally grounded, either solidly or by means of a device that limits currents. (MEANS)
UF systems, grounded
CN V.RT.ALO.ARI.AFU.ALO

grounds
RK.1587 (A,L,B)
ALT **ground**
SN The gardens, lawn, and planted areas immediately surrounding and

belonging to a house or other building. (W)
CN V.RK.ALO.ARI.BOK

grounds, burial
USE **cemeteries**

grounds, cricket
USE **cricket fields**

grounds, dance
USE **dance grounds**

grounds, picnic
USE **picnic areas**

grounds, pleasure
USE **pleasure gardens**

grounds, polo
USE **polo fields**

grounds, proving
USE **proving grounds**

grounds, rugby
USE **rugby fields**

grounds, sports
USE **athletic fields**

groundsills
USE **sill plates**

groundwood paper
USE **wood pulp paper**

group foster homes
USE **group homes**

group homes
RK.788 (A,L)
ALT **group home**
SN Use for residential dwellings that are single housekeeping units, provide care for small groups of unrelated residents requiring supervision, and are intended to reproduce the circumstances of family life. (LCSH)
UF community based residences
group foster homes
homes, group
homes, group foster
residences, community based
CN V.RK.AFU.ALO.ALO.CXA.ALO.ALO.AXC

group portraits
VB.75 (L,R)
ALT **group portrait**
UF portraits, group
CN V.VB.AFU.AXC.BCW.AFU

grouped columns
RT.108
ALT **grouped column**
SN Use for three or more closely spaced columns which form a distinct group.
UF columns, grouped
CN V.RT.AFU.AFU.AFU.AXC.BIQ.AFU.ALO.BIQ

grouped domestic architecture
USE **cluster housing**

groups, civic
USE **community organizations**

groups, user
USE **user groups**

grout
MT.2606 (L,B)
SN Mortar whose watery consistency allows it to be placed or pumped into small joints or cavities, as between pieces of ceramic clay, slate, or floor tile. (MEANS)
CN M.MT.AFU.ARI.DZW.ARI.ALO.AFU

grouting
KT.122 (L,B)
SN Filling or finishing with a grout. (W)
CN K.KT.AFU.ALO.DCU.AFU

Grove
FL.885
CN F.FL.ALO.ALO.ALO.AFU.ALO.ALO.BIQ.ALO

groves
RD.256
ALT **grove**
SN Use for groups of trees, often of a single species, smaller than forests in extent, growing naturally or planted in formation, and generally with little or no undergrowth.
CN V.RD.ARI.AFU.BCW.ALO.AFU.BIQ.AFU

groves (orchards)
USE **orchards**

growers, nursery
USE **nurserymen**

growth
BM.723 (A,L)
CN B.BM.CFS.AFU.AXC.AFU

growth areas
USE **growth centers**

growth centers
RG.300 (A)
ALT **growth center**
SN Use for cities or parts of cities which have the potential for rapid and successful development, have begun to attract businesses and population, and have the capability of becoming local focal points.
UF areas, growth
centers, growth
growth areas
growth points
points, growth
CN V.RG.ALO.ARI.ALO

growth points
USE **growth centers**

growth, population
USE **population growth**

growth, suburban
USE **suburban growth**

groynes
USE **groins (erosion protection works)**

grozing irons
TB.123
ALT **grozing iron**
SN Hot irons used by plumbers for finishing soldered joints; also the name of tools used to cut glass.
UF irons, grozing
CN V.TB.AFU.ARI.AXC.ALO.BOK

grub saws
TB.623
ALT **grub saw**
SN Hand-operated saws used for cutting stone, especially marble, into useable slabs. (MEANS)
UF saws, grub
CN V.TB.AFU.BCW.BCW.ALO.GLI.AFU

Grubenhäuser
USE **sunken huts**

Grünblauoxid
USE **blue-green oxide**

grüne Erde
USE **green earth**

Grunshi
FL.353 (L)
CN F.FL.ALO.AFU.AXC.AFU.AXC.AFU.AXC

Grunshi (Voltaic people)
USE **Gurunsi**

Grünspan
USE **verdigris**

Guacamayo
FL.1100
CN F.FL.ALO.ALO.ALO.ALO.ALO.ALO.ALO.AXC.AFU

Guadalupe
FL.1053
CN F.FL.ALO.ALO.ALO.ALO.AFU.ALO.AXC.AFU.ALO

Guahibo
FL.1581 (L)
CN F.FL.ALO.ALO.ARI.ARI.AFU.DCU

guaiacum
USE **lignum vitae**

Guaicura
FL.1281
CN F.FL.ALO.ALO.ARI.AFU.ALO.FZU.ALO.AFU

Guaicurian
FL.1280 (L)
CN F.FL.ALO.ALO.ARI.AFU.ALO.FZU.ALO

Guaitacá
FL.1678
CN F.FL.ALO.ALO.ARI.ARI.BIQ.BIQ

Guajajara
USE **Tembé**

Guaná
FL.1643 (L)
CN F.FL.ALO.ALO.ARI.ARI.AXC.BUE

Guanahatabey
FL.1565
CN F.FL.ALO.ALO.ARI.ALO.BUE.AXC

Guang
FL.297
CN F.FL.ALO.AFU.AXC.AFU.ARI.AFU.ARI

Guangala
FL.1118
CN F.FL.ALO.ALO.ALO.ARI.ALO.AXC

Guangxu
FL.1918 (L)
UF Kuang-hsu
CN F.FL.ALO.ARI.ALO.AFU.AFU.ALO.DOI.BZY

guano
MT.921 (L)
SN A substance that is found on some coasts or islands frequented by sea fowl, is composed chiefly of their partially decomposed excrement, is rich in phosphates, nitrogenous matter, and other material for plant growth, and has been used extensively as a fertilizer. (W)
CN M.MT.AFU.AFU.ALO.AFU.BOK.ALO

Guaraní
FL.1679 (L)
CN F.FL.ALO.ALO.ARI.ARI.BIQ.BOK

guarantees
VW.897
ALT **guarantee**
SN Agreements by which one person undertakes to secure another in the possession or enjoyment of something, such as an expressed or implied assurance of the quality or performance of goods purchased. (W)
CN V.VW.AFU.ARI.AFU.BOK.BOK.ALO.ARI

guard rails
RM.476 (B)
ALT **guard rail**
SN Barriers placed at dangerous points, as along the edges of roads or on stair landings.
UF rails, guard
CN V.RM.ALO.ALO.ALO.ALO.BCW

guarded front locks
TF.200
ALT **guarded front lock**
SN Locks designed and constructed with the front and strike protected, thus preventing the latchbolt from being tampered with through the crevice between the door and the jamb. (MEANS)
UF front locks, guarded
locks, guarded front
locks, recessed front
recessed front locks
CN V.TF.AFU.AFU.AFU.AFU.DIO.BIQ.AFU.BIQ

guardhouses
RK.865
ALT **guardhouse**
CN V.RK.AFU.ALO.ALO.DIO.ALO.ARI

guardivines
USE **cellerets**

guards, roof
USE **snow guards**

guards, security
USE **security guards**

guards, snow
USE **snow guards**

guards, spark
USE **fire screens**

guards, window
USE **window guards**

Guarpe
USE **Huarpe**

Guastavino vaults
RT.558
ALT **Guastavino vault**
SN Use for the tile timbrel vaults erected by the Guastavino family between about 1800 and 1950.
UF vaults, Guastavino
CN V.RT.AFU.AFU.AFU.BIQ.BOK.AFU.ARI.AFU.AXC.AFU

Guatemalan
FL.705 (L,B)
CN F.FL.ALO.ALO.AFU.AFU.AFU

guayacan
USE **lignum vitae**

guayacum
USE **lignum vitae**

Guaymí
FL.1552 (L)
CN F.FL.ALO.ALO.ARI.ALO.BOK.ARI

Guere
USE **Wee**

guéridons
TG.631
ALT **guéridon**
SN French term of uncertain derivation denoting decorative candlestands; original type had a circular top and a central standard, often in the form of a Moor, or, as the taste for exoticism increased, of a negress or Indian. In Louis XV and Louis XVI periods guéridons became small movable tables. (OCDA)
UF blackamoors
guéridons-luminaire
guéridons porte lumière
guéridons porte-luminaire
guéridons-table
guéridons-torchère
tables en guéridon
CN V.TG.AFU.AFU.BIQ.BCW.ALO.ALO.AFU

guéridons-luminaire
USE **guéridons**

guéridons porte lumière
USE **guéridons**

guéridons porte-luminaire
USE **guéridons**
torchères

guéridons-table
USE **guéridons**

guéridons-torchère
USE **guéridons**
torchères

guerilla warfare
BM.1121 (L)
UF warfare, guerilla
CN B.BM.CRG.BCW.CLM.ARI.ALO

Guerrero
USE **Mezcala**

Guerze
USE **Kpelle**

guest books
USE **guest registers**

guest ranches
USE **dude ranches**

guest registers
VW.277
ALT **guest register**
SN Books usually of printed forms, soliciting information about visitors, such as date of visit, name, address, and comments. (GAHLM)
UF books, guest
guest books
registers, guest
CN V.VW.AFU.AFU.AFU.FZU.BCW.ALO.ARI

guesthouses
RK.332 (A,B)
SN Use for separate residences for guests, as a house on a private estate or a monastery building specifically for receiving visitors.
CN V.RK.AFU.ALO.ALO.AXC.ALO.BOK.AXC

Guetar
FL.1553 (L)

UF Huetar
CN F.FL.ALO.ALO.ARI.ALO.BOK.AXC

Guge
FL.2178
CN F.FL.ALO.ARI.AXC.AFU.BOK.AFU.ALO

guglias
USE **obelisks**

guglias (finials)
USE **finials**

guglias (pinnacles)
USE **pinnacles**

guidance, vocational
USE **vocational guidance**

guidebooks
VW.500 (A,L,B,R)
ALT **guidebook**
SN Handbooks of directions and information, as for travelers. (GAHLM)
UF gazetteers (guidebooks)
guides
CN V.VW.AFU.ALO.AFU.AFU.AFU.BZY

guidebooks, architectural
USE **architectural guidebooks**

guidebooks, city
USE **city guidebooks**

guidebooks, national
USE **national guidebooks**

guidebooks, pilgrimage
USE **pilgrimage guidebooks**

guidebooks, state
USE **state guidebooks**

guidebooks, travel
USE **travel guidebooks**

guided missile bases
RG.127 (L,B)
ALT **guided missile base**
UF bases, guided missile
bases, missile
missile bases
CN V.RG.AFU.AFU.BZY.AFU.ARI

guided missile ranges
RG.146 (L)
ALT **guided missile range**
UF missile ranges
missile ranges, guided
ranges, guided missile
CN V.RG.AFU.AFU.DIO.ALO

guided missile silos
RK.857 (L)
ALT **guided missile silo**
UF missile silos
silos, guided missile
silos, missile
CN V.RK.AFU.ALO.ALO.DIO.AFU.ALO

guidelines
VW.343
ALT **guideline**
UF directives
CN V.VW.AFU.AFU.ALO.CXA.ARI

guidelines, design
USE **design guidelines**

guides
USE **guidebooks**

guides (docents)
USE **docents**

guides, archival
USE **archival guides**

guides, builders'
USE **builders' guides**

guides, buyers'
USE **buyers' guides**

guides, collectors'
USE **collectors' guides**

guides, examination study
USE **examination study guides**

guides, field
USE **field guides**

guides, holiday
USE **travel guidebooks**

guides, shippers'
USE **shippers' guides**

Guignet's green
USE **viridian**

guildhalls
RK.1205 (A,B,R)
ALT **guildhall**
UF company halls
halls, company
halls, livery
livery halls
CN V.RK.AFU.ALO.ALO.FZU.ARI

guilds
HG.825 (L,B,R)
ALT **guild**
UF gilds
CN H.HG.ALO.BCW.BIQ

guilloche
DG.135
SN A pattern of interlaced curving bands, sometimes giving the effect of a braid, but most often in smooth curves forming circles. Sometimes considered a type of fret or a type of interlace.
UF water-pattern
CN D.DG.AFU.ARI.ALO.BOK

guillotines (shears)
USE **sheet shears**

guinea corn stalk
MT.1075
UF corn stalk, guinea
CN M.MT.AFU.AFU.ALO.BIQ.CLM.AFU.AFU

Gujarati
USE **Western Indian**

Guler
FL.2276 (L)
CN F.FL.ALO.ARI.AXC.ALO.AFU.BZY.BCW.ARI.BIQ

Gulf of Papua
USE **Papuan Gulf**

gulf red
MT.1671
UF oxide, Persian Gulf
Persian Gulf oxide
red, gulf
CN M.MT.AFU.AFU.ARI.AFU.AFU.ALO.ALO.BCW.AFU.ALO.AFU

gulfs
RD.148 (L)
ALT **gulf**
SN Large inlets of the sea, usually more enclosed and more deeply indented than bays. (DNE)
CN V.RD.ARI.AFU.AFU.AFU.ALO.ALO.AXC

gullies
RD.212
ALT **gully**
SN Small, commonly v-shaped channels carved in the land by fluvial action and through which water flows only occasionally or seasonally.
UF draws
CN V.RD.ARI.AFU.AXC.AFU.ALO.ALO.ALO

gum
MT.1048 (L)
SN Hardened sap or exudation from any of various trees and shrubs; used especially in vehicles or binders for aqueous paints, in tempera emulsions, and as adhesives, sizes, and stiffeners. (MH)
CN M.MT.AFU.AFU.ALO.BIQ.BUE.AXC

gum accroides
USE **acaroid resin**

gum arabic
MT.1051 (L)
UF Acacia gum
arabic, gum
babool gum
babul gum
gum, Acacia
gum, babool
gum, babul
CN M.MT.AFU.AFU.ALO.BIQ.BUE.AXC.ARI

gum arabic tree
USE **Acacia**

gum bichromate
USE **gum bichromate process**

gum bichromate photoprints
USE **gum bichromate prints**

gum bichromate prints
VJ.54
ALT **gum bichromate print**
SN Use for photographic prints made by the gum bichromate process.
UF bichromate prints, gum
gum bichromate photoprints
gum prints
photoprints, gum bichromate
prints, gum
prints, gum bichromate
CN V.VJ.AFU.AFU.ARI.ARI.AXC.BUE.ALO

gum bichromate process
KT.354
SN A process to make photographic prints using a colloid emulsion of bichromated gum arabic as the binder and pigment as the final image material. The image is formed as the emulsion hardens in relation to exposure and is developed by washing away the unhardened emulsion to reveal the support, forming the highlights and midtones.
UF bi-gum
bichromate, gum
gum bichromate
gum-pigment process
gum printing
gum process
printing, gum
CN K.KT.AFU.ALO.DUC.DIO.ALO.DIO.AFU.AXC

gum damar
USE **damar**

gum hog
USE **gum karaya**

gum karaya
MT.1052
UF gum hog
hog, gum
karaya, gum
CN M.MT.AFU.AFU.ALO.BIQ.BUE.AXC.AXC

gum-pigment process
USE **gum bichromate process**

gum printing
USE **gum bichromate process**

gum prints
USE **gum bichromate prints**

gum process
USE **gum bichromate process**

gum resin
MT.1498 (L)
UF resin, gum
CN M.MT.AFU.AFU.ALO.BOK.CFS

gum spirits
USE **gum turpentine**

gum tempera
MT.2521
SN Artist's material consisting of pigments ground in an emulsion medium in which the oily ingredient is linseed oil, stand oil, or most often, a mixture of stand oil and damar varnish; emulsified with gum arabic solution and glycerin. (MAYER)
UF tempera, gum
CN M.MT.AFU.ARI.CRG.ALO.BCW.AFU.ALO.ARI.ARI

gum thus
MT.1053
SN The oleoresin or balsam from pine trees of the southern United States, from which turpentine and rosin are obtained;(MAYER) used especially in oil paints. (MH)
UF thus, gum
CN M.MT.AFU.AFU.ALO.BIQ.BUE.AXC.BCW

gum tragacanth
MT.1054
SN A gum that is obtained as a dried exudate from various Asiatic or East European plants; swells to a gel in water; used chiefly as an emulsifying, suspending, or thickening agent. (W)
UF tragacanth, gum
CN M.MT.AFU.AFU.ALO.BIQ.BUE.AXC.BIQ

gum turpentine
MT.2706
SN Obtained by the distillation from turpentine oleoresins, it is used chiefly as a solvent and thinner, as a raw material of certain chemicals, such as synthetic camphor, and in medicine.
UF gum spirits
spirits of turpentine
spirits, gum
turpentine, gum
turpentine, spirits of
CN M.MT.AFU.ARI.HZS.AFU.BZY.ARI.AFU

gum, Acacia
USE **gum arabic**

gum, apricot
USE **apricot gum**

gum, babool
USE **gum arabic**

gum, babul
USE **gum arabic**

gum, black
USE **black gum**

gum, blue
USE **blue gum**

gum, Botany Bay
USE **acaroid resin**

gum, British
USE **British gum**

gum, cherry
USE **cherry gum**

gum, cherry-tree
USE **cherry gum**

gum, cotton
USE **tupelo**

gum, ester
USE **ester gum**

gum, kauri
USE **kauri**

gum, plum
USE **cherry gum**

gum, red
USE **red gum**

gum, sour
USE **tupelo**

gum, starch
USE **dextrine**

gum, swamp
USE **tupelo**

gum, sweet
USE **sweet gum**

gum, tupelo
USE **tupelo**

gum, water
USE **swamp tupelo**

gum, yacca
USE **acaroid resin**

gumbads
RK.470
ALT **gumbad**
SN Mausoleums in tower form, particularly in Indian, Persian, and Turkish regions.
UF tomb towers
towers, tomb
CN V.RK.AFU.ALO.ALO.BOK.ARI.ALO.AFU.AFU

gummigutt
USE **gamboge**

gumwood
MT.1155 (L)
CN M.MT.AFU.AFU.ALO.BIQ.DCU.AFU.AFU.AFU.DIO.AXC

Gun
FL.307 (L)
UF Egun
Popo
CN F.FL.ALO.AFU.AXC.AFU.ARI.ALO.BCW

gun cabinets
TG.431 (N)
ALT **gun cabinet**

UF cabinets, gun
CN V.TG.AFU.AFU.AXC.ALO.ARI.
ALO.BOK

gun rooms
RM.199
ALT **gun room**
UF rooms, gun
CN V.RM.AFU.DIO.ALO.DCU.BZY

guncrete
USE **gunite**

gunflint
MT.555 (L,R)
CN M.MT.AFU.AFU.AFU.CFS.AFU.
GRC.AFU.AXC.AFU

gunite
MT.215 (L,B)
SN A construction material composed of cement, sand, or crushed slag and water forced through a pneumatic gun. (PUTNAM)
UF concrete, sprayed
guncrete
shotcrete
sprayed concrete
CN M.MT.AFU.AFU.AFU.BCW.AFU.
ARI.ARI

gunmetal
MT.381
SN Includes the copper alloy formerly used for making cannon and any of several metals or alloys treated to resemble gunmetal. (W)
CN M.MT.AFU.AFU.AFU.BZY.AFU
.AFU.AFU.ALO.ARI.BCW.ARI

gunmetal (color)
USE **dark gray**

gunmetal, light
USE **dark gray**

gunny
USE **burlap**

gunports
RT.988
ALT **gunport**
SN Openings through which a gun can be fired, as in a fortification or on the side of a ship.
CN V.RT.AFU.ARI.AFU.ALO.ARI

gunpowder
MT.2585 (L,R)
CN M.MT.AFU.ARI.DIO.AFU

guns, electronic glue
USE **electronic glue guns**

guns, explosive actuated
USE **stud guns**

guns, plug-driving
USE **stud guns**

guns, soldering
USE **soldering guns**

guns, staple
USE **staple guns**

guns, stud
USE **stud guns**

gunsmithing
KT.525 (L,R)
CN K.KT.AFU.ALO.ELK.BZY

gunsmiths
HG.514 (L)
ALT **gunsmith**
CN H.HG.AFU.AXC.BUE.ARI.CFS.ARI.
BCW

gunstock Windsor chairs
TG.101
ALT **gunstock Windsor chair**
SN Windsor chairs with sawn back posts of gunstock shape; common in the mid-19th century. (EVANS)
UF chairs, gunstock Windsor
Windsor chairs, gunstock
CN V.TG.AFU.AFU.ALO.AFU.AFU.
AFU.MLC.BCW

Gupta
FL.2201 (A,L)
CN F.FL.ALO.ARI.AXC.ALO.AFU.ARI.
BIQ

Gurage
FL.639 (L)
CN F.FL.ALO.AFU.AXC.AXC.AXC.ARI

Gurgan faïence
USE **Gurgan ware**

Gurgan ware
FL.3565
UF faïence, Gurgan
Gurgan faïence
ware, Gurgan
CN F.FL.ALO.BIQ.AFU.HIK.BCW.ARI

Gurjara-Partihara
FL.2216 (L)
UF Gurjara-Pratihara
Pratihara
CN F.FL.ALO.ARI.AXC.ALO.AFU.
AXC.CFS

Gurjara-Pratihara
USE **Gurjara-Partihara**

Gurkha
FL.2165 (L)
UF Shah Period
CN F.FL.ALO.ARI.AXC.AFU.AXC.AFU.
BIQ

Guro
FL.325 (L)
UF Gouro
Kweni
CN F.FL.ALO.AFU.AXC.AFU.ARI.
BCW.AXC

Gurunsi
FL.383 (L)
UF Grunshi (Voltaic people)
CN F.FL.ALO.AFU.AXC.AFU.AXC.ARI.
ARI.ALO

Gusii
FL.678 (L)
UF Gizii
Kisii (Gusii)
Kosova
CN F.FL.ALO.AFU.AXC.AXC.BOK.BIQ

gusset plates
USE **gussets**

gussets
TF.334
ALT **gusset**
SN Plates fastened across a joint, as in wood or steel framework members. (MEANS)
UF gusset plates
plates, gusset
CN V.TF.AFU.AFU.AFU.ALO.AFU.BCW

guti ambar
USE **gamboge**

guttae
RT.342
ALT **gutta**
SN Pendant ornaments, usually found on the underside of mutules and regulae of Doric entablatures. (HAS)
CN V.RT.AFU.AFU.AFU.BCW.BZY.
ALO.ALO.ALO.BCW

gutter bolts
TF.323
ALT **gutter bolt**
UF bolts, gutter
CN V.TF.AFU.AFU.AFU.ALO.AFU.
ALO.ALO.ARI

gutter planes
USE **guttering planes**

gutter spikes
TF.488
ALT **gutter spike**
UF spikes, gutter
CN V.TF.AFU.AFU.AFU.ALO.AFU.
DUC.ALO

guttering adzes
TB.816 (N)
ALT **guttering adz**
SN Adzes with a rounded, lipped cutting surface.
UF adzes, guttering
adzes, spout
spout adzes
CN V.TB.AFU.BCW.CFS.ALO.AFU.
AFU.BIQ.AFU

guttering planes
TB.956 (N)
ALT **guttering plane**
SN Planes with convex soles; used for planing out wooden gutters. (BLACKB)
UF convex planes
gutter planes

planes, convex
planes, gutter
planes, guttering
planes, round (guttering planes)
planes, spout
round planes (guttering planes)
spout planes
CN V.TB.AFU.BCW.CFS.ALO.AFU.DUC.AXC.AFU.BCW

gutters (roadside elements)
RM.477 (A,L,B)
ALT **gutter (roadside element)**
SN Channels at the side or in the middle of a road or street, for leading off surface water. (RHDEL2)
CN V.RM.ALO.ALO.ALO.ALO.BIQ

gutters (storm water systems)
RT.1459 (A,L,B)
ALT **gutter (storm water system)**
SN Shallow channels of wood, metal, or polyvinyl chloride positioned just below and following along the eaves of a building for the purpose of collecting and diverting water from a roof. (MEANS)
UF eave troughs
troughs, eave
CN V.RT.ALO.BCW.ALO.ARI.BCW

gutters, arris
USE **arris gutters**

gutters, back
USE **back gutters**

gutters, eaves
USE **eaves gutters**

gutters, valley
USE **valley gutters**

gutto gumbo
USE **gamboge**

guy derricks
TB.75
ALT **guy derrick**
SN A derrick whose mast is held upright by guy cables attached to the top. (W)
UF derricks, guy
CN V.TB.AFU.ARI.AFU.BCW.BCW.AFU.AFU

guyed masts
USE **masts**

guys
RT.213
ALT **guy**
SN Ropes, cables, or wires which are anchored at one end and tied to an object or structure in order to stabilize it. (DAC)
CN V.RT.AFU.AFU.AFU.AXC.DOI.ALO

Gwandara
FL.230 (L)
CN F.FL.ALO.AFU.AXC.AFU.AFU.ALO.ARI.BIQ

Gwari
FL.208 (L)
UF Gbari
CN F.FL.ALO.AFU.AXC.AFU.AFU.ALO.ALO.ALO

gymnasiums
RK.1063 (A,L,B)
ALT **gymnasium**
UF gyms
CN V.RK.AFU.ALO.ALO.EWY.AXC.BIQ.ALO.AXC.AFU

gymnasteria
USE **apodyteria**

gymnosperm
USE **softwood**

gyms
USE **gymnasiums**

gynaecea
RM.390
ALT **gynaeceum**
SN Womens' apartments in ancient Greek or Roman houses. (W)
CN V.RM.AFU.DIO.BCW.ALO

gypboard
USE **gypsum board**

gypsum
MT.520 (A,L,B)
SN A mineral, hydrous sulfate of calcium, commonly used as a core in sheets of wallboard;(PUTNAM) also used as a white pigment.
UF calcium sulphate
mineral white
sulphate, calcium
terra alba
white, mineral
CN M.MT.AFU.AFU.AFU.CFS.AFU.DUC

gypsum board
MT.2215 (B)
UF board, gypsum
gypboard
gypsum lath
gypsum plaster board
gypsum wallboard
lath, gypsum
lath, rock
plaster board, gypsum
plasterboard
rock lath
sheetrock
wallboard, gypsum
CN M.MT.AFU.ALO.ARI.AFU.AFU.AFU

gypsum board nails
TF.438
ALT **gypsum board nail**
SN Nails which come in 1-inch and 1 3/4-inch lengths; used primarily for applying gypsum board or rock lath. (PUTNAM)
UF board nails, gypsum
nails, gypsum board
nails, wallboard
wallboard nails
CN V.TF.AFU.AFU.AFU.ALO.AFU.CFS.ALO.CFS

gypsum cement
MT.22
UF cement, flooring
cement, gypsum
flooring cement
flooring plaster
hard-finish plaster
plaster, flooring
plaster, hard-finish
plaster, tiling
tiling plaster
CN M.MT.AFU.AFU.AFU.ALO.AFU.AFU.BIQ

gypsum lath
USE **gypsum board**

gypsum mortar
MT.2599
UF mortar, gypsum
CN M.MT.AFU.ARI.DZW.ARI.AFU.ARI

gypsum plaster
MT.2439
SN Any of the common wall plasters in general use, all of which contain various amounts of gypsum. (MAYER)
UF plaster, gypsum
CN M.MT.AFU.ARI.CRG.AFU.AXC.AFU.AXC

gypsum plaster board
USE **gypsum board**

gypsum plaster, anhydrous
USE **anhydrous gypsum plaster**

gypsum plaster, class B
USE **retarded hemihydrate plaster**

gypsum plaster, class C
USE **anhydrous gypsum plaster**

gypsum plaster, class D
USE **Keene's cement**

gypsum wallboard
USE **gypsum board**

gypsum, calcined
USE **calcined gypsum**

gypsum, uncalcined
USE **uncalcined gypsum**

gypsy wagons
USE **caravans**

gyration, radius of
USE **radius of gyration**

H and L hinges
USE **H/L hinges**

H-beams
RT.711
ALT **H-beam**
SN Beams with an H-shaped section, with wider flanges in relation to the depth of the web than in I-beams.

CN V.RT.AFU.AFU.ALO.ARI.ARI

H hinges
TF.114
ALT **H hinge**
UF hinges, H
CN V.TF.AFU.AFU.AFU.AFU.CLM.
AFU.DCU

H/L hinges
TF.115
ALT **H/L hinge**
UF H and L hinges
hinges, H and L
hinges, H/L
CN V.TF.AFU.AFU.AFU.AFU.CLM.
AFU.DIO

Ha
FL.586
CN F.FL.ALO.AFU.AXC.AXC.AFU.AXC

ha-has
RM.452 (A,R)
ALT **ha-ha**
SN Barriers in the form of trenches or sunken fences; usually used to prevent livestock from crossing. (HAS)
UF fences, sunken
haw-haws
sunk fences
sunken fences
CN V.RM.ALO.AFU.CFS.ARI

Haarlem blue
USE **Antwerp blue**

Habaner ware
FL.3206 (L,R)
UF ware, Habaner
CN F.FL.ALO.BCW.ALO.ARI.BIQ.
BIQ.ALO.AFU.ALO

Habe
USE **Dogon**

habitations
USE **dwellings**

habitats, wildlife
USE **wildlife refuges**

Haboku
FL.2051
CN F.FL.ALO.ARI.ALO.ALO.ALO.
ARI.ARI

HAC
USE **aluminous cement**

Hachiman
FL.1995
CN F.FL.ALO.ARI.ALO.ALO.ALO.
AFU.ARI

Hachiroemon Kutani
USE **Saiko Kutani**

haciendas
RG.19 (A,L)
ALT **hacienda**
SN Large Spanish-American landed estates, farms, or ranches; may also be used for the main building of such a complex.
UF estancias
fazendas
fundos
CN V.RG.AFU.AFU.AFU.ALO

hack irons
USE **hardies**

hackberry
MT.1167 (L)
UF celtis
CN M.MT.AFU.AFU.ALO.BIQ.DCU.
AFU.AFU.AFU.DZW

hackberry, Chinese
USE **Chinese hackberry**

hackberry, European
USE **European hackberry**

hackberry, Mississippi
USE **Mississippi hackberry**

hackia
MT.1189
UF Ixora ferrea
CN M.MT.AFU.AFU.ALO.BIQ.DCU.
AFU.AFU.AFU.FIM.ALO

hackmatack, western
USE **western larch**

hacksaws
TB.136 (L,N)
ALT **hacksaw**
SN Lightweight metal-cutting hand saws with a narrow fine-toothed blade retained in an adjustable metal frame. (MEANS)
CN V.TB.AFU.ARI.AXC.ALO.CLM.ARI

Hadra
FL.2840
CN F.FL.ALO.AXC.ALO.ARI.ALO.
AFU.ARI

Hadrianic
FL.2722 (R)
CN F.FL.ALO.AXC.ALO.ALO.AFU.
AXC.ALO.BIQ

haematite red
USE **dark grayish red**
dark red
grayish red
grayish reddish brown

Hafsid
FL.3447 (L)
CN F.FL.ALO.BIQ.AFU.CLM

hafts
TB.1123
ALT **haft**
SN Handles of cutting tools. (MEANS)
CN V.TB.ALO.CFS

hafts (helves)
USE **helves**

Hagi
FL.2020 (L)
CN F.FL.ALO.ARI.ALO.ALO.ALO.
ALO.ALO.BCW

hagiographers
HG.181
ALT **hagiographer**
CN H.HG.AFU.AXC.AXC.ARI.AFU.
AFU.AFU.AFU

hagiography
BM.279 (L,R)
CN B.BM.AFU.ARI.BIQ.BOK.AFU.ALO

Haguenau faïence
USE **Haguenau pottery**

Haguenau pottery
FL.3220 (R)
UF faïence, Haguenau
Haguenau faïence
pottery, Haguenau
CN F.FL.ALO.BCW.ALO.ARI.BIQ.
BIQ.ARI.ALO.AXC.AFU

Haida
FL.1343 (L)
CN F.FL.ALO.ALO.ARI.AFU.BIQ.CFS

hail
BM.750 (L,B)
UF hailstorms
CN B.BM.CFS.ALO.AXC.ALO.BIQ.AFU

hailstorms
USE **hail**

haines feet
USE **therm feet**

hair
MT.929 (L,R)
SN The fibrous covering of the skins of various animals, used for making coarse fabrics and for stuffing purposes. (MH)
CN M.MT.AFU.AFU.ALO.AFU.CXA.
AFU

hair, camel
USE **camel hair**

hair, goat
USE **goat hair**

hair, human
USE **human hair**

hairdressers
USE **beauty shops**

hairdressing salons
USE **beauty shops**

hairpin lace
MT.1873 (L)
SN Lace with looped edges made by crocheting around the prongs of a U-shaped needle. (W)
UF lace, hairpin
CN M.MT.AFU.AFU.ARI.ALO.ALO.
ALO.ALO.CXA.ALO

hairy paw feet
TG.928
ALT **hairy paw foot**
UF feet, hairy paw
CN V.TG.ALO.DZW.AFU.DCU.BIQ.ALO

Haisla
FL.1344 (L)
UF Kitamat
Kitimat
Kitlope
CN F.FL.ALO.ALO.ARI.AFU.BIQ.CLM

Haitian
FL.709 (L,B)
CN F.FL.ALO.ALO.AFU.ALO.ALO

Hajji Muhammed
FL.2958
UF Ubaid 2
CN F.FL.ALO.AXC.ARI.BCW.AFU.AFU.ALO.ALO

Hakataya
USE **Patayan**

Hakuho
USE **Early Nara**

Halaf
FL.2955
CN F.FL.ALO.AXC.ARI.BCW.AFU.AFU.AFU.AXC

Halchidhoma
FL.1254
CN F.FL.ALO.ALO.ARI.AFU.ALO.BUE

half barrel vaults
RT.539
ALT **half barrel vault**
SN Vaults of approximately quarter-circle profile, such as would cover an aisle in a church.
UF vaults, half barrel
CN V.RT.AFU.AFU.AFU.BIQ.BOK.AFU.ALO.AFU.ALO

half-baths
USE **lavatories (rooms)**

half-breadth plans
VD.64
ALT **half-breadth plan**
SN Drawings representing one longitudinal half of a ship as viewed from above and emphasizing the ship's lines. When appearing with a body plan and a sheer plan, use **lines drawings** for the set.
UF half-breadths
plans, half-breadth
CN V.VD.AFU.AFU.BIQ.ALO.AXC.BOK.AFU.AFU

half-breadths
USE **half-breadth plans**

half canopies
USE **half-testers**

half chests
USE **low chests**

half columns
RT.107
ALT **half column**
SN Use for engaged columns which project approximately half their diameter.
UF columns, half
demicolumns
semicolumns
CN V.RT.AFU.AFU.AFU.AXC.BIQ.AFU.ALO.BCW.ALO

half domes
USE **semidomes**

half elevations
VD.27
ALT **half elevation**
UF elevations, half
CN V.VD.AFU.AFU.BIQ.ALO.ALO.AXC.AFU

half hatchets
TB.600
ALT **half hatchet**
SN Heavy-duty combinations of hatchet and hammer with a broad blade with a notched under part for pulling nails; used to chop off hardened plaster and to do other heavy work.
UF hatchets, half
CN V.TB.AFU.BCW.BCW.ALO.DZW

half-headed beds
USE **half-tester beds**

half-headed testers
USE **half-testers**

half-lap joints
TF.687
ALT **half-lap joint**
SN Transverse joints formed at the intersection of two equally thick pieces of wood, both having been notched to half their original depth, so as to form a joint with flush faces. (MEANS)
UF halved joints
halved splices
joints, half-lap
joints, halved
splices, halved
CN V.TF.ALO.ARI.AXC.ARI.AXC.ARI

half-mortise hinges
TF.116
ALT **half-mortise hinge**
SN Door hinges each having one plate surface-mounted on the jamb and the other plate mortised into the door stile; the opposite of half-surface hinges. (MEANS)
UF hinges, half-mortise
CN V.TF.AFU.AFU.AFU.AFU.CLM.AFU.DOI

half plans
VD.63
ALT **half plan**
UF plans, half
CN V.VD.AFU.AFU.BIQ.ALO.AXC.BOK.AFU

half plate
DC.127
SN A photographic plate size, usually 6 1/2 by 4 3/4 inches.
CN D.DC.AFU.AXC.BIQ.ALO

half-rabbeted locks
TF.211
ALT **half-rabbeted lock**
SN Mortise locks each having a front turned into two perpendicular planes, used on a door with a rabbeted edge. (MEANS)
UF locks, half-rabbeted
CN V.TF.AFU.AFU.AFU.AFU.DIO.BIQ.AFU.CRG.ALO.AFU

half-ripsaws
TB.1029
ALT **half-ripsaw**
SN Lighter or shorter ripsaws, with teeth that are more closely spaced.
CN V.TB.AFU.BCW.CFS.ALO.AFU.EWY.BUE.BIQ.AFU

half-round cabinet rasps
USE **cabinet rasps**

half-round chairs
USE **corner chairs**

half-round moldings
RT.783
ALT **half-round molding**
SN Convex strips or moldings of semicircular profile. (HAS)
UF moldings, half-round
CN V.RT.AFU.ALO.AFU.BOK.AFU.AFU.AXC.BCW

half-round pliers
USE **combination pliers**

half sections
VD.70
ALT **half section**
SN Use for orthographic drawings in which a symmetrical object is cut away so that one half of it is shown as an exterior elevation and the other as a section. For buildings thus represented, use **sectional elevations**. For drawings of an incomplete section alone, use **partial sections**.
UF sections, half
CN V.VD.AFU.AFU.BIQ.ALO.BIQ.ARI

half-serpentine
DC.107
CN D.DC.AFU.ARI.EWY.BOK

half-space stairs
USE **halfpace stairs**

half-span roofs
USE **shed roofs**

half-surface hinges
TF.117
ALT **half-surface hinge**
SN Door hinges each having one plate surface-mounted onto the door leaf, and the other plate mortised into the jamb; the opposite of half-mortise hinges. (MEANS)
UF hinges, half-surface
CN V.TF.AFU.AFU.AFU.AFU.CLM.AFU.DUC

half-tester beds
TG.353 (N)
ALT **half-tester bed**
SN Beds with testers which only cover the head half of the bed. (THORN2)
UF beds, half-tester
half-headed beds
CN V.TG.AFU.AFU.ARI.AFU.AFU.BUE

half-testers
TG.861 (N)
ALT **half-tester**
SN Rooflike components, generally cantilevered from the head posts, which extend over the head half of the bed.
UF canopies, half
half canopies
half-headed testers
testers, half-headed
CN V.TG.ALO.BIQ.CRG.ARI

half-timber construction
KT.32 (B)
ALT **half-timber**
SN Use both for the vernacular building technique in which the spaces between the heavy supporting timbers are filled with brick, wattle and daub, or other material, and to describe buildings with a false-timber frame attached to the outside wall to give the appearance of half-timber construction.
UF construction, half-timber
half-timbering
CN K.KT.AFU.ALO.BCW.ARI.AFU.BCW

half-timbering
USE **half-timber construction**

half-turn stairs
RT.1087
ALT **half-turn stair**
SN Stairs which turn 180 degrees as they progress from bottom to top.
UF stairs, half-turn
CN V.RT.AFU.BIQ.AXC.AFU.AFU.BZY.ALO

halfpace stairs
RT.1083
ALT **halfpace stair**
SN Stairs with landings at which the stair turns 180 degrees.
UF half-space stairs
stairs, half-space
stairs, halfpace
CN V.RT.AFU.BIQ.AXC.AFU.AFU.BUE.ALO

halftone negatives
VJ.5
ALT **halftone negative**
SN Negatives exposed through a line screen so that the image appears as a pattern of dots or squares of varying sizes. Used to make photomechanical prints. (GMGPC)
UF halftone photonegatives
negatives, halftone
CN V.VJ.AFU.AFU.AFU.ALO

halftone photomechanical prints
USE **relief halftones**

halftone photonegatives
USE **halftone negatives**

halftone process
USE **relief halftone**

halftone, letterpress
USE **relief halftone**

halftone, relief
USE **relief halftone**

halftones
USE **relief halftones**

halftones, letterpress
USE **relief halftones**

halftones, relief
USE **relief halftones**

halfway houses
RK.789 (A,L)
ALT **halfway house**
UF houses, halfway
CN V.RK.AFU.ALO.ALO.CXA.ALO.ALO.BCW

halide
MT.307 (L)
SN A two-element crystalline compound of a halogen and a metal; it is named by the metal and the stem of the halogen plus -ide (such as, gold chloride). (ICPEP)
CN M.MT.AFU.AFU.AFU.BOK.AXC

halide, silver
USE **silver halide**

hall chairs
TG.212 (N)
ALT **hall chair**
SN Chairs with elaborately carved or painted backs, frequently bearing emblems and coats of arms, and having solid wood seats often with hinged lids to reveal a storage compartment. Intended for use in halls and corridors.
UF chairs, hall
CN V.TG.AFU.AFU.ALO.AFU.AFU.ARI.AXC.ALO

hall churches
RK.1097 (R)
ALT **hall church**
SN Use for churches with side aisles as high or nearly as high as the nave; popular in Germany.
UF churches, hall
hallenkirchen
CN V.RK.AFU.ALO.ALO.FCS.BIQ.ALO.AFU.ALO

hall racks
USE **hat racks**

hall seats
TG.289
ALT **hall seat**
SN Benches, generally without padding and upholstery, often made en suite with chairs or hall glasses and intended for use in halls and galleries.
UF seats, hall
CN V.TG.AFU.AFU.ALO.ALO.AFU.ALO.ALO

hall stands
TG.640 (N)
ALT **hall stand**
UF hall trees
hat and umbrella stands
stands, hall
trees, hall
CN V.TG.AFU.AFU.BIQ.BCW.ALO.BUE

hall tables
USE **refectory tables**

hall trees
USE **hall stands**

hallenkirchen
USE **hall churches**

hallmarks
VW.720 (L,R)
ALT **hallmark**
SN Official stamps originally affixed by goldsmiths upon articles made of gold or silver as evidence of genuineness; hence, used to signify any mark of genuineness. (BLACKS)
CN V.VW.AFU.ALO.ALO.AFU.AXC.ALO.BUE

halls
RM.273 (A,L,B,R)
ALT **hall**
SN Use generally for rooms very large in proportion to rooms for sleeping and individual or family use; use also for the principal rooms of a Medieval house and for large central rooms in certain 19th- and 20th-century English and American houses.
UF great halls
halls, great
living-halls

CN V.RM.AFU.DIO.ARI.ALO.BUE

halls (assembly halls)
USE **assembly halls**

halls (corridors)
USE **corridors**

halls of fame
RK.376 (A,L)
ALT **hall of fame**
SN Buildings set aside to honor outstanding individuals as in a profession, locality, or nation. (RHDEL2)
CN V.RK.AFU.ALO.ALO.BCW.ARI

halls, assembly
USE **assembly halls**

halls, audience
USE **presence chambers**

halls, banking
USE **banking rooms**

halls, banquet
USE **banquet halls**

halls, beer
USE **beer halls**

halls, billiard
USE **pool halls**

halls, bingo
USE **bingo halls**

halls, church
USE **parish houses**

halls, city
USE **city halls**

halls, company
USE **guildhalls**

halls, concert
USE **concert halls**

halls, convention
USE **convention centers**

halls, county
USE **county halls**

halls, dance
USE **dance halls**

halls, dining
USE **dining halls**

halls, drill
USE **drill halls**

halls, entrance
USE **entrance halls**

halls, exhibition
USE **exhibition buildings**

halls, fire
USE **fire stations**

halls, great
USE **halls**

halls, hypostyle
USE **hypostyle halls**

halls, juvenile
USE **reformatories**

halls, lecture
USE **lecture halls**

halls, livery
USE **guildhalls**

halls, market
USE **market halls**

halls, mess
USE **mess halls**

halls, music
USE **music halls**

halls, parish
USE **parish houses**

halls, pool
USE **pool halls**

halls, public
USE **assembly halls**

halls, residence
USE **dormitories**

halls, riding
USE **riding halls**

halls, servants'
USE **servants' halls**

halls, sports
USE **sports buildings**

halls, symphony
USE **concert halls**

halls, synodal
USE **chapter houses**

halls, town
USE **town halls**

halls, village
USE **town halls**

Hallstatt
FL.2510 (L)
CN F.FL.ALO.AXC.AFU.BIQ.AFU.ALO

hallways
USE **corridors**

halved joints
USE **half-lap joints**

halved splices
USE **half-lap joints**

Ham
USE **Jaba**

Hamburgian
FL.2480
CN F.FL.ALO.AXC.AFU.AXC.BIQ

Hamdanid
FL.3448 (L)
CN F.FL.ALO.BIQ.AFU.CRG

Hamilton
FL.893
CN F.FL.ALO.ALO.ALO.AFU.ALO.ALO.BOK.BOK

Hamitic, Eastern
USE **Eastern Hamitic**

hamlets
RD.6 (A,B)
ALT **hamlet**
SN Use for small rural centers which contain basic community, education, and religious facilities and which generally do not exceed 250 residents;(LOC) may also refer to the smallest incorporated units of a municipal government. (W)
CN V.RD.AFU.AFU.ALO.AFU

hamlets, market
USE **market towns**

hammams
USE **Turkish baths**

hammer-beam roofs
RT.451 (A,B)
ALT **hammer-beam roof**
SN Roofs supported by hammer beams. (DAC)
UF roofs, hammer-beam
CN V.RT.AFU.AFU.AFU.BIQ.ARI.AFU.ALO.ARI.ARI

hammer-beam trusses
RT.364
ALT **hammer-beam truss**
SN Trusses of the type utilized in hammer-beam roofs, with a combination of hammer beams, hammer posts, and braces taking the place of the beam at the base of the roof.
UF trusses, hammer-beam
CN V.RT.AFU.AFU.AFU.BCW.CLM.AFU.AFU.AFU.BCW

hammer beams
RT.312
ALT **hammer beam**
SN Short, horizontal members attached to the foot of a principal rafter in a roof, in place of a tie beam. (HAS)
UF beams, hammer
CN V.RT.AFU.AFU.AFU.BCW.ALO.ALO.BCW

hammer drills
TB.586
ALT **hammer drill**
SN Pneumatically powered mechanisms using percussion to penetrate rock. (MEANS)
UF drills, hammer
CN V.TB.AFU.BCW.BCW.ALO.CLM.ALO

hammer fasteners
TF.335

ALT **hammer fastener**
UF fasteners, hammer
CN V.TF.AFU.AFU.AFU.ALO.AFU.BIQ

hammer posts
USE **pendant posts**

hammer tongs
TB.755 (N)
SN Blacksmith's tongs having projecting lugs for engaging holes of hammer-heads during forging. (W)
UF eye tongs
tongs, eye
tongs, hammer
CN V.TB.AFU.BCW.BIQ.AXC.ALO.AXC.BIQ

hammering
KT.840
ALT **hammered**
CN K.KT.AFU.ALO.HOE.BCW.ALO.BCW.ALO

hammermen
HG.595
ALT **hammerman**
CN H.HG.AFU.AXC.BZY.AFU.CXA

hammers
TB.457 (L,N)
ALT **hammer**
SN Hand tools with the handle perpendicular to the head; used for driving nails or other applications involving pounding or striking. (MEANS)
CN V.TB.AFU.ARI.ELK.AFU

hammers, air
USE **jackhammers**

hammers, ball-peen
USE **ball-peen hammers**

hammers, board
USE **drop hammers**

hammers, bush
USE **bushhammers**

hammers, cabriolet
USE **cabriolet hammers**

hammers, claw
USE **claw hammers**

hammers, clench
USE **clench hammers**

hammers, coach framing
USE **framing hammers**

hammers, coach trimmer's cabriolet
USE **cabriolet hammers**

hammers, coachbuilder's framing
USE **framing hammers**

hammers, crandall
USE **crandall hammers**

hammers, cross-peen
USE **cross-peen hammers**

hammers, double-faced
USE **framing hammers**

hammers, drop
USE **drop hammers**

hammers, face
USE **face hammers**

hammers, file-cutting
USE **file-cutting hammers**

hammers, flooring
USE **clench hammers**

hammers, framing
USE **framing hammers**

hammers, French upholsterer's
USE **cabriolet hammers**

hammers, helve
USE **helve hammers**

hammers, Lancashire pattern riveting
USE **Warrington-pattern hammers**

hammers, lath
USE **lathing hatchets**

hammers, lathing
USE **lathing hatchets**

hammers, patent
USE **patent hammers**

hammers, peen
USE **peen hammers**

hammers, planishing
USE **planishing hammers**

hammers, plow
USE **plow hammers**

hammers, pneumatic
USE **jackhammers**

hammers, power
USE **power hammers**

hammers, roofing
USE **clench hammers**

hammers, scabbling
USE **scabbling hammers**

hammers, set
USE **set hammers**

hammers, ship's mauls
USE **top maul hammers**

hammers, slating
USE **zaxes**

hammers, straight-peen
USE **straight-peen hammers**

hammers, striking
USE **sledgehammers**

hammers, tack
USE **tack hammers**

hammers, Thor's
USE **swastikas**

hammers, tilt
USE **helve hammers**

hammers, top maul
USE **top maul hammers**

hammers, veneer
USE **veneer hammers**

hammers, Warrington-pattern
USE **Warrington-pattern hammers**

hammerstones
TB.467 (N)
ALT **hammerstone**
SN Prehistoric hammering implements consisting of rounded stones. (W)
CN V.TB.AFU.ARI.ELK.ALO

hammock chairs
TG.71
ALT **hammock chair**
SN Canvas chairs suspended from a tree limb, roof, or other structure; of a type made in the late 19th and early 20th centuries. (PC)
UF chairs, hammock
CN V.TG.AFU.AFU.ALO.AFU.AFU.AFU.HCQ

hammocks
TG.393 (L)
ALT **hammock**
SN Swinging couches or beds usually made of netting or canvas and slung by cords from supports at each end. (W)
CN V.TG.AFU.AFU.ARI.AXC

Hamza
FL.3580
CN F.FL.ALO.BIQ.AFU.IFM.AFU.ALO

Han (Chinese)
FL.1848 (L)
CN F.FL.ALO.ARI.ALO.AFU.AFU.ALO.AFU

Han (Native American)
FL.1232
CN F.FL.ALO.ALO.ARI.AFU.AFU.ARI.BUE

Han, Eastern
USE **Eastern Han**

Han, Later
USE **Later Han**

Han, Later (Eastern Han)
USE **Eastern Han**

Hanabusa School
FL.2086
CN F.FL.ALO.ARI.ALO.ALO.ALO.AXC.BZY.ALO

Hanau pottery
FL.3227 (R)
UF Hanau ware

pottery, Hanau
ware, Hanau
CN F.FL.ALO.BCW.ALO.ARI.BIQ.BIQ.AXC.AFU.ALO

Hanau ware
USE **Hanau pottery**

hand braces
USE **braces (woodworking tools)**

hand-bronzing
USE **bronzing**

hand clamps
USE **screw clamps**

hand coloring
KT.82
ALT **hand-colored**
UF coloring, hand
hand tinting
tinting, hand
CN K.KT.AFU.ALO.BOK.ARI

hand drills
TB.190 (N)
ALT **hand drill**
SN Hand-operated boring devices made up of a central steel tube containing a shaft. At one end is a handle and at the other a bit-holding chuck. (MEANS)
UF angle braces (hand drills)
braces, angle (hand drills)
braces, drill
braces, gearing
corner drills
drill braces
drills, corner
drills, hand
gearing braces
CN V.TB.AFU.ARI.BIQ.ALO.AFU.ALO.ALO

hand floats
TB.596
ALT **hand float**
SN Wooden tools used to lay on and to smooth or texture a finish coat of plaster or concrete. (MEANS)
UF floats, hand
CN V.TB.AFU.BCW.BCW.ALO.DIO.AXC

hand lever punches
TB.674
ALT **hand lever punch**
SN Hand tools for punching holes in sheetmetal. (PUTNAM)
UF punches, hand lever
CN V.TB.AFU.BCW.BIQ.AFU.ALO.BZY.BIQ

hand saws
TB.1015 (N)
ALT **hand saw**
SN Name given to a group of saws which have a handle at one end and a wide blade which tapers in width from handle to toe; hand saws are never power saws.
UF saws, hand
CN V.TB.AFU.BCW.CFS.ALO.AFU.EWY.BIQ

hand screws
USE **screw clamps**

hand spinning
KT.571 (L)
ALT **hand spun**
UF spinning, hand
CN K.KT.AFU.ALO.ELK.DUC.AXC.AFU

hand tinting
USE **hand coloring**

hand tools
TB.12 (L)
ALT **hand tool**
SN Any tools which are operated by and guided by hand. (PUTNAM)
UF tools, hand
CN V.TB.AFU.ALO.ARI.AFU

hand towel dispensers
TF.144
ALT **hand towel dispenser**
UF dispensers, hand towel
towel dispensers, hand
CN V.TF.AFU.AFU.AFU.AFU.CRG.AFU

hand vises
TB.226
ALT **hand vise**
SN Vises used in metal- and woodworking for holding small objects or for grasping nuts or bolts. (SALAM)
UF vises, hand
CN V.TB.AFU.ARI.CFS.BOK.ALO

hand weaving
KT.554 (L)
ALT **handwoven**
UF weaving, hand
CN K.KT.AFU.ALO.ELK.DUC.AFU.BOK.ALO

handball courts
RK.1014 (B)
ALT **handball court**
UF courts, handball
CN V.RK.AFU.ALO.ALO.EWY.ALO. BIQ

handbills
VW.603 (L,N)
ALT **handbill**
SN Small printed sheets usually containing an advertisement, to be distributed by hand and often doubling as posters. (GAHLM)
UF handouts
leaflets
CN V.VW.AFU.ALO.AFU.BUE

handbills, advertising
USE **advertising fliers**

handbooks
USE **manuals**

handbooks, carpenters'
USE **builders' guides**

handbooks, employees'
USE **employees' manuals**

handbooks, sign and symbol
USE **sign and symbol handbooks**

handgrips
USE **handholds**

handholds
TG.823
ALT **handhold**
UF handgrips
CN V.TG.ALO.ALO.ALO.AXC

handicapped
HG.784 (L,B,R)
UF disabled
CN H.HG.AFU.BOK.AXC.ALO

handicapped access
USE **barrier-free design**

handicapped, housing for the
USE **housing for the handicapped**

handicapped, mentally
USE **mentally handicapped**

handicapped, physically
USE **physically handicapped**

handicapped, speech
USE **mutes**

handicrafts
USE **crafts**

handkerchief tables
TG.674 (N)
ALT **handkerchief table**
SN Tables with triangular tops intended to stand in corners. (MONTGO)
UF corner tables
envelope tables
tables, corner
tables, envelope
tables, handkerchief
tables, triangular dropleaf
triangular dropleaf tables
CN V.TG.AFU.AFU.BIQ.BOK.AFU.AXC.AXC

handkerchief vaults
USE **pendentive domes**

handlers, air
USE **air-handling units**

handles
TF.55 (L)
ALT **handle**
UF grips (handles)
CN V.TF.AFU.AFU.AFU.AFU.CFS

handles (tool components)
TB.1124 (L)
ALT **handle (tool component)**
CN V.TB.ALO.CLM

handles, bar
USE **bar handles**

handles, drop
USE **drop pulls**

handles, entrance
USE **entrance handles**

handles, lion and ring
USE **lion and ring handles**

handles, loop
USE **ring handles**

handles, pear drop
USE **pear drop handles**

handles, ring
USE **ring handles**

handles, store-door
USE **store-door handles**

handmade brick
MT.129 (B)
UF brick, handmade
CN M.MT.AFU.AFU.AFU.AXC.ALO.
AFU.AXC.ALO.AFU

handmade paper
MT.1962 (L)
UF paper, handmade
CN M.MT.AFU.AFU.ARI.ALO.ALO.
AXC.AXC.AFU

handouts
USE **handbills**

handrail bolts
TF.324
ALT **handrail bolt**
UF bolts, handrail
bolts, joint
bolts, rail
joint bolts
rail bolts
CN V.TF.AFU.AFU.AFU.ALO.AFU.
ALO.ALO.AXC

handrail brackets
TF.37
ALT **handrail bracket**
UF brackets, handrail
CN V.TF.AFU.AFU.AFU.AFU.ARI.AFU

handrail planes
TB.963 (N)
ALT **handrail plane**
SN Molding planes made with an ogee profile, usually made in sets of two for the two sides of a handrail. (SALAM)
UF banister planes
capping planes (handrail planes)
planes, banister
planes, capping (handrail planes)
planes, handrail
planes, stairbuilder's
stairbuilder's planes
CN V.TB.AFU.BCW.CFS.ALO.AFU.
DUC.AXC.ALO.ALO

handrail punches
TB.975 (N)
ALT **handrail punch**
SN Short steel bars, square in section, with one end tapered to a chisel point and bent slightly backwards; used for tightening the nuts of handrail bolts. (SALAM)
UF punches, handrail
CN V.TB.AFU.BCW.CFS.ALO.AFU.
DZW.ALO

handrails
RT.1041 (A,L,B)
ALT **handrail**
SN Use for railings that are intended to be grasped by the hand in order to serve as a support; may also refer to the top members of balustrades or railings.
UF banisters
rails (handrails)
CN V.RT.AFU.AXC.ALO.AFU.ARI.ALO

hands
USE **assistants**

hands, stone
USE **makeup arrangers**

handsaws, electric
USE **electric-portable saws**

handscrew clamps
USE **screw clamps**

handworked photographs
USE **manipulated photographs**

handwriting analysts
USE **graphologists**

hangars
RK.1236 (A,L,B)
ALT **hangar**
SN Structures for the shelter, service, and repair of aircraft. (DAC)
UF aircraft hangars
hangars, aircraft
CN V.RK.AFU.ALO.ALO.GLI.AFU.
AFU.ARI

hangars, aircraft
USE **hangars**

hanger bolts
TF.315
ALT **hanger bolt**
UF bolts, hanger
CN V.TF.AFU.AFU.AFU.ALO.AFU.ALO.
AFU.BOK

hangers (rough hardware)
TF.336
ALT **hanger (rough hardware)**
SN Hardware used in supporting or connecting members of similar or different material as, for instance, a beam hanger for supporting the end of a beam or joist at a masonry wall. (MEANS)
CN V.TF.AFU.AFU.AFU.ALO.AFU.BOK

hangers, adjustable pipe
USE **adjustable pipe hangers**

hangers, barn-door
USE **barn-door hangers**

hangers, beam
USE **beam hangers**

hangers, bottom and flange bend
USE **bottom and flange bend hangers**

hangers, bottom bend
USE **bottom bend hangers**

hangers, channel saddle
USE **channel saddle hangers**

hangers, clip
USE **clip hangers**

hangers, cut and straight
USE **cut and straight hangers**

hangers, double style
USE **double style hangers**

hangers, drive type
USE **drive type hangers**

hangers, drop
USE **drop hangers**

hangers, flange
USE **flange hangers**

hangers, flush top
USE **flush top hangers**

hangers, formed ridge
USE **formed ridge hangers**

hangers, formed seat
USE **formed seat hangers**

hangers, hook-over
USE **hook-over hangers**

hangers, joist
USE **joist hangers**

hangers, metal-to-wood wire
USE **metal-to-wood wire hangers**

hangers, nicked hanging wire
USE **nicked hanging wire hangers**

hangers, nook type
USE **nook type hangers**

hangers, plate saddle
USE **plate saddle hangers**

hangers, pocket style
USE **pocket style hangers**

hangers, saddle style
USE **saddle style hangers**

hangers, snap-tie
USE **snap-tie hangers**

hangers, standard coil
USE **standard coil hangers**

hangers, steel-to-steel beam
USE **steel-to-steel beam hangers**

hangers, tie
USE **tie hangers**

hangers, variable
USE **variable hangers**

hangers, wood-to-masonry
USE **wood-to-masonry hangers**

hangers, wood-to-steel joist
USE **wood-to-steel joist hangers**

hangers, wood-to-wood
USE **wood-to-wood hangers**

hanging buttresses
RT.78
ALT **hanging buttress**
SN Use for elements resembling buttresses, but supported by corbels rather then having separate foundations and therefore not serving as true structural buttresses.
UF buttresses, hanging
CN V.RT.AFU.AFU.AFU.AXC.AXC.ARI

hanging cabinets
TG.415
ALT **hanging cabinet**
UF cabinets, hanging
CN V.TG.AFU.AFU.AXC.ALO.ARI.AFU.AXC

hanging cupboards
TG.509 (N,R)
ALT **hanging cupboard**
UF armoires, mural
cupboards, hanging
cupboards, wall
hanging shelves (cupboards)
mural armoires
shelves, hanging (cupboards)
wall cupboards
CN V.TG.AFU.AFU.AXC.ALO.BUE.CFS

hanging gardens
RK.1408 (A)
ALT **hanging garden**
UF gardens, hanging
CN V.RK.ALO.AFU.AFU.AFU.AXC

hanging posts
RT.898
ALT **hanging post**
SN Posts on which a gate is hung. (DAC)
UF gate piers
gate posts
hinge posts
piers, gate
posts, gate
posts, hanging
posts, hinge
posts, swinging
swinging posts
CN V.RT.AFU.ARI.AFU.AFU.ARI.ALO.AFU.ALO.AFU

hanging roofs
USE **suspension roofs**

hanging scaffolds
USE **suspended scaffolding**

hanging shelves (cupboards)
USE **hanging cupboards**

hanging steps
RT.1115
ALT **hanging step**
SN Flights of steps, usually of stone, that are built into a wall at one end and have no other support except what they may derive by slightly overlapping the stone step next below. (RS)
UF steps, hanging
CN V.RT.AFU.BIQ.AXC.ALO.BIQ.AFU.ARI

hanging stiles
USE **hinge stiles**

hanging wire hangers, nicked
USE **nicked hanging wire hangers**

Haniwa
USE **Kofun**

Hanover white metal
MT.416
UF metal, Hanover white
white metal, Hanover
CN M.MT.AFU.AFU.AFU.BZY.AFU.AFU.AFU.ALO.BUE.ALO.BCW

Hansa yellow
MT.1799
UF Hansagelb
jaune solide
monolite yellow
yellow, Hansa
yellow, monolite
CN M.MT.AFU.AFU.ARI.AFU.AFU.ALO.ALO.BUE.AXC.ALO

Hansagelb
USE **Hansa yellow**

Hanukkah
KM.83 (L,R)
UF Chanukah
Dedication, Feast of
Feast of Dedication
Feast of Lights
Feast of the Maccabees
Lights, Feast of
Maccabees, Feast of
CN K.KM.AFU.CFS.ARI.BIQ

Hanukkah cards
VW.570
ALT **Hanukkah card**
UF cards, Chanukah
cards, Hanukkah
Chanukah cards
CN V.VW.AFU.ALO.AFU.ARI.BOK.AXC

Haoussa
USE **Hausa**

Harappa
USE **Harappan**

Harappan
FL.2188 (L)
UF Harappa
CN F.FL.ALO.ARI.AXC.ALO.AFU.AFU.AFU

harbors
RD.149 (A,L,B,R)
ALT **harbor**
SN Designates well-sheltered inlets of water affording protection from wind and sea and sufficient depth to allow anchorage for vessels.
CN V.RD.ARI.AFU.AFU.AFU.ALO.ALO.BCW

hard brick
USE **hard-burned brick**

hard-burned brick
MT.118
UF brick, hard
brick, hard-burned
brick, stone
brick, well-burned
hard brick
stone brick
well-burned brick
CN M.MT.AFU.AFU.AFU.AXC.ALO.AFU.AXC.AFU.AFU.AFU

Hard-edge
FL.3728 (L,R)
CN F.FL.ALO.BUE.ARI.CXA

hard-finish plaster
USE **gypsum cement**

hard-line drawings
USE **mechanical drawings**

hard maple
USE **sugar maple**

hard paste porcelain
MT.146 (R)
UF porcelain, hard paste
CN M.MT.AFU.AFU.AFU.AXC.ALO.ALO.AFU.AFU.AFU

hard pine
USE **longleaf pine**
southern yellow pine

hard solder
MT.422
UF solder, hard
CN M.MT.AFU.AFU.AFU.BZY.AFU.AFU.AFU.ALO.BUE.ARI.ALO

Hard Style
FL.2762
CN F.FL.ALO.AXC.ALO.ALO.ALO.BZY.AFU.ARI

hard water
MT.317 (L)
UF water, hard
CN M.MT.AFU.AFU.AFU.BOK.BOK.AFU.ALO

Hardaway
FL.740
CN F.FL.ALO.ALO.ALO.AFU.AFU.
ARI.AFU.AXC

hardboard
MT.1461 (L,B)
SN Any firm, dense, rigid board; (MAYER) often manufactured from fibers consolidated under heat and pressure in a hot press. (HORNB)
CN M.MT.AFU.AFU.ALO.BIQ.DCU.
ALO.DOI.AXC

hardenable stainless steel
USE **martensitic stainless steel**

hardeners
MT.2314
SN Materials added to paint or varnish to increase gum or resin content or to increase rate of oxidation so as to cause an increase in hardness of the drying film. (DAC)
CN M.MT.AFU.ARI.ALO.CXA

hardening, surface
USE **surface hardening**

hardies
TB.650 (N)
ALT **hardy**
SN Metal components having a square shank for insertion into a hole in an anvil.
UF anvil cutters
cutters, anvil
hack irons
irons, hack
CN V.TB.AFU.BCW.BIQ.AFU.ALO.
AFU.ALO.AFU

hardness
BM.961
SN Property of materials indicating solidity and firmness in substance or outline. (MH)
CN B.BM.CFS.AXC.BZY.BOK.CLM.ARI

Hardoy chairs
TG.88
ALT **Hardoy chair**
UF butterfly chairs
chairs, butterfly
chairs, Hardoy
Hardoy lounge chairs 198
CN V.TG.AFU.AFU.ALO.AFU.AFU.
AFU.KQY.AFU

Hardoy lounge chairs 198
USE **Hardoy chairs**

hardware
TF.2 (A,L,B,R)
SN Large and small items that are necessary to attach, anchor, hold, or join materials and components of structures, furniture, and other objects. Also, items used in the finishing of buildings and objects, such as hinges and knobs.
UF fittings
ironmongery
CN V.TF.AFU.AFU

hardware (computers)
USE **computers**

hardware (peripherals)
USE **peripherals**

hardware stores
RK.161 (L,B)
ALT **hardware store**
UF stores, hardware
CN V.RK.AFU.ALO.ALO.ALO.ARI
.BIQ.AFU.CLM

hardware, architectural
USE **finish hardware**

hardware, awning
USE **awning hardware**

hardware, bathroom
USE **bathroom hardware**

hardware, builders'
USE **finish hardware**

hardware, closet
USE **closet hardware**

hardware, door
USE **door hardware**

hardware, finish
USE **finish hardware**

hardware, furniture
USE **furniture hardware**

hardware, gate
USE **gate hardware**

hardware, plumbing
USE **plumbing hardware**

hardware, rough
USE **rough hardware**

hardware, shelf
USE **shelf hardware**

hardware, shutter
USE **window hardware**

hardware, window
USE **window hardware**

hardwood
MT.1085 (A,L,B)
SN Wood produced from trees that have broad leaves. Distinct from **softwood** which is produced from trees having needle like leaves.
UF angiosperm
CN M.MT.AFU.AFU.ALO.BIQ.DCU.
AFU.AFU.AFU

Hare
FL.1233 (L)
UF Kawchottine
CN F.FL.ALO.ALO.ARI.AFU.AFU.ARI.
BZY

harems
RM.391 (R)
ALT **harem**
UF zenanas
CN V.RM.AFU.DIO.BCW.ARI

haricots
USE **kidney tables**

Haripunjaya
FL.2410
CN F.FL.ALO.ARI.BCW.BOK.AFU.BCW

Harlem Renaissance
FL.1729 (L,R)
UF Negro Movement, New
Negro Renaissance
New Negro Movement
Renaissance, Harlem
Renaissance, Negro
CN F.FL.ALO.ALO.BCW.AFU.BOK

harlequin Pembroke tables
USE **harlequin tables**

harlequin tables
TG.676
ALT **harlequin table**
SN A more elaborate version of the pembroke table, with a small nest of drawers which is concealed in the body and may be made to rise from the top by means of weights; of a type made in late 18th-century England. (DDA)
UF harlequin Pembroke tables
Pembroke tables, harlequin
tables, harlequin
tables, harlequin Pembroke
CN V.TG.AFU.AFU.BIQ.BOK.AFU.
AXC.BCW.AFU

harling
USE **roughcast**

harmon hinges
TF.118
ALT **harmon hinge**
UF hinges, harmon
CN V.TF.AFU.AFU.AFU.AFU.CLM.
AFU.DZW

harmonic proportions
USE **harmony**

harmony
BM.100 (L,B,R)
SN Use generally to mean a pleasingly orderly and consistent arrangement of the parts of a whole. With reference specifically to art and architecture, use for the concept of aesthetic description in which architectural proportion or artistic design displays congruity.
UF concord
harmonic proportions
proportions, harmonic
CN B.BM.AFU.AFU.ARI.ARI

harness rooms
USE **tack rooms**

harnesses, safety
USE **safety belts**

harp-back chairs
USE **lyre-back chairs**

harp banister-back chairs
USE **lyre-back chairs**

harpsicord chairs
USE **music chairs**

Harrison's red
USE **lithol red**

Harshavarman III
FL.2340
CN F.FL.ALO.ARI.BCW.ALO.ARI.AFU.BUE

hart's-tongue
USE **water leaf**

hartshorn, spirit of
USE **ammonia water**

Harvard chairs
USE **great chairs**

Hasegawa School
FL.2052
CN F.FL.ALO.ARI.ALO.ALO.ALO.ARI.AXC

Hasidism
BM.699 (L)
UF Chasidism
CN B.BM.BZY.ALO.ARI.BIQ

hasp locks
TF.240
ALT **hasp lock**
SN Devices permanently secured to the hasp on a door which causes the hasp to be locked as soon as the door is closed; often used in prisons. (MEANS)
UF locks, hasp
CN V.TF.AFU.AFU.AFU.AFU.DIO.BIQ.ALO.ALO.BUE.AFU

hasps
TF.565 (N)
ALT **hasp**
SN Use for hinged strips, each with a slot on the free end so that it may be thrown over a staple and be secured there by means of a hook or lock.
CN V.TF.AFU.ALO.AXC.BIQ

hassocks
TG.245 (N)
ALT **hassock**
SN Large stuffed cushions that serve as seats or leg rests. (W)
CN V.TG.AFU.AFU.ALO.AFU.ALO.AFU.BIQ.ALO

Hassuna
FL.2953
CN F.FL.ALO.AXC.ARI.BCW.AFU.AFU.AFU.ALO

Hassuna Archaic ware
FL.2993
UF Archaic painted ware
Archaic ware, Hassuna
painted ware, Archaic
ware, Archaic painted
ware, Hassuna Archaic
CN F.FL.ALO.AXC.ARI.BCW.ALO.BCW.AXC

Hassuna standard ware
FL.2994
UF standard ware
standard ware, Hassuna
ware, Hassuna standard
CN F.FL.ALO.AXC.ARI.BCW.ALO.BCW.BCW

hasters
TG.510
ALT **haster**
SN Open front cupboards on wheels, used in front of a fire to warm plates of food. (BACKST)
CN V.TG.AFU.AFU.AXC.ALO.BUE. CLM

hat and cloak stands
USE **hat stands**

hat and coat stands
USE **hat stands**

hat and umbrella stands
USE **hall stands**

hat racks
TG.613 (N)
ALT **hat rack**
UF hall racks
racks, hall
racks, hat
CN V.TG.AFU.AFU.BIQ.AXC.ALO

hat stands
TG.641
ALT **hat stand**
UF hat and cloak stands
hat and coat stands
stands, hat
stands, hat and cloak
stands, hat and coat
CN V.TG.AFU.AFU.BIQ.BCW.ALO.BZY

hatch davits
USE **davits**

hatcheries, chicken
USE **chicken hatcheries**

hatcheries, fish
USE **fish hatcheries**

hatches
RT.901
ALT **hatch**
SN Use for openings in horizontal positions, as between the decks of a ship, and for doors horizontally divided, the upper part being opened for ventilation or so that articles may be passed over the lower part.
UF hatchways
CN V.RT.AFU.ARI.AFU.AFU.AXC

hatches, buttery
USE **buttery hatches**

hatchet-adzes
TB.814
ALT **hatchet-adz**
SN Two-bladed tools having the larger blade in the form of an adz and the smaller in the form of a hatchet; distinguished from **adze-hatchets** in which the hatchet blade is larger.
UF hatchet, adzes
CN V.TB.AFU.BCW.CFS.ALO.AFU.AFU.BCW

hatchet doors
USE **Dutch doors**

hatchet stakes
TB.686 (N)
ALT **hatchet stake**
SN Sharp-edged stakes on which to bend sheet metal. (W)
UF stakes, hatchet
CN V.TB.AFU.BCW.BIQ.AFU.ALO.CXA.AXC

hatchet, adzes
USE **hatchet-adzes**

hatchets
TB.890 (N)
ALT **hatchet**
SN Wood-handled tools having a steel head flattened at one end suitable for striking or driving; formed at the other end into a wide sharp blade used for chopping. The underpart of the blade may be notched for pulling nails. (MEANS)
CN V.TB.AFU.BCW.CFS.ALO.AFU.DCU

hatchets, claw
USE **claw hatchets**

hatchets, half
USE **half hatchets**

hatchets, hewing
USE **hewing hatchets**

hatchets, lathing
USE **lathing hatchets**

hatchets, shingling
USE **shingling hatchets**

hatching
KT.265
SN Shading or modeling with fine, closely laid parallel lines. (TATEMT)
CN K.KT.AFU.ALO.DUC.DCU.ARI

hatchways
USE **hatches**

hate
BM.578 (L)

CN B.BM.BUE.ARI.BOK

hatters
HG.537 (L)
ALT **hatter**
SN Persons who make, sell, clean, and repair hats. (W)
CN H.HG.AFU.AXC.BUE.ARI.CXA.CFS.ALO

haulms
USE **helms**

haunches
RT.287
ALT **haunch**
SN The middle part between the crown and the springing of an arch or vault. (HAS)
CN V.RT.AFU.AFU.AFU.BCW.AFU.ALO.ALO

haunted houses
RK.333 (A,L)
ALT **haunted house**
UF houses, haunted
CN V.RK.AFU.ALO.ALO.AXC.ALO.BOK.BCW

Hausa
FL.395 (A)
UF Haoussa
CN F.FL.ALO.AFU.AXC.AFU.AXC.AXC.ARI

Havana Hopewellian
FL.836
UF Hopewellian, Havana
CN F.FL.ALO.ALO.ALO.AFU.ALO.ALO.ARI.AFU.AXC

Havasupai
FL.1457 (L)
UF Supai
CN F.FL.ALO.ALO.ARI.AFU.CFS.AXC

havens, temporary
USE **refugee camps**

haw-haws
USE **ha-has**

Hawaiian
FL.3694 (L)
UF Sandwich Island
CN F.FL.ALO.BOK.AXC.BCW

Hawaiian obsidian
USE **tachylite**

hawks
TB.608 (N)
ALT **hawk**
SN Flat pieces of metal or wood held by a wood handle on the underside; used by plasterers to carry plaster or mortar. (DAC)
UF boards, fat
boards, spot
fat boards
holders, mud
mud holders
spot boards
CN V.TB.AFU.BCW.BCW.ALO.ELK

hawksbeak moldings
USE **beak moldings**

hawthorn
MT.1171 (L)
UF common hawthorn
Crataegus
Crataegus monogyna
hawthorn, common
CN M.MT.AFU.AFU.ALO.BIQ.DCU.AFU.AFU.AFU.EFQ

hawthorn, common
USE **hawthorn**

Haya
FL.679 (L)
UF Ziba
CN F.FL.ALO.AFU.AXC.AXC.BOK. BOK

haylofts
RM.343
ALT **hayloft**
CN V.RM.AFU.DIO.AXC.ARI.ALO

hazardous substances
MT.2796 (L)
ALT **hazardous substance**
UF substances, hazardous
substances, toxic
toxic substances
CN M.MT.AFU.BCW.BUE

hazel
USE **filbert**

hazelnut
USE **filbert**

head joints
TF.640
ALT **head joint**
SN Joints between two adjacent masonry units in the same course. (MEANS)
UF heading joints (masonry joints)
joints, head
CN V.TF.ALO.ARI.ALO.ALO.BIQ

head moldings
USE **hood moldings**

head-on
USE **frontal**

headache balls
USE **wrecking balls**

headboards
TG.855 (R)
ALT **headboard**
SN Boards forming the head of anything, especially a bed. (RHDEL2)
UF chevets (headboards)
CN V.TG.ALO.BIQ.CFS

header joists
USE **headers (frame components)**

header, bull
USE **bull header**

header, flare
USE **glazed header**

header, glazed
USE **glazed header**

header, snap
USE **brickbat**

header, vitrified
USE **glazed header**

headers
MT.2760
SN A masonry unit, laid so that its ends are exposed, overlapping two or more adjacent wythes of masonry and tying them together. (DAC)
CN M.MT.AFU.AXC.BIQ.ALO.ALO

headers (frame components)
RT.699
ALT **header (frame component)**
SN Framing members that cross and support the ends of joists or rafters. (DAC)
UF header joists
joists, header
CN V.RT.AFU.AFU.ALO.ALO.AFU

headers, nail
USE **nail headers**

headhouses
RM.183
ALT **headhouse**
SN Parts of railroad passenger terminals providing accommodations for persons waiting for trains. (W)
CN V.RM.AFU.DIO.ALO.CXA.DIO.AFU

heading chisels
USE **mortise chisels**

heading drawknives
TB.904 (N)
ALT **heading drawknife**
SN Large flat blades up to 2 1/4 inches wide and 16 inches long; used to smooth and trim barrel heads to the proper angle to fit into the staves. (SALAM)
UF drawknives, heading
heading knives
knives, heading
CN V.TB.AFU.BCW.CFS.ALO.AFU.DOI.ARI.AXC

heading joints
TF.683
ALT **heading joint**
SN Joints formed between two pieces of timber connected end-to-end, in a straight line. (MEANS)
UF joints, heading
CN V.TF.ALO.ARI.AXC.ARI.ARI

heading joints (masonry joints)
USE **head joints**

heading knives
USE **heading drawknives**

headlands
USE **promontories**

headless nails
TF.411
ALT **headless nail**
UF nails, headless
CN V.TF.AFU.AFU.AFU.ALO.AFU.CFS.AFU.DCU.BZY

headposts
TG.849
ALT **headpost**
CN V.TG.ALO.BIQ.AXC.ALO

headquarters, corporate
USE **corporate headquarters**

heads, chimney
USE **chimney pots**

heads, leader
USE **leader heads**

heads, rainwater
USE **leader heads**

heads, window
USE **window heads**

headstones
USE **tombstones**

health
BM.721 (L,B,R)
CN B.BM.CFS.AFU.ARI

health boards
HG.837 (L)
ALT **health board**
UF boards of health
boards, health
boards, public health
public health boards
CN H.HG.ALO.BIQ.BCW

health buildings
USE **health facilities**

health care buildings
USE **health facilities**

health care facilities
USE **health facilities**

health care institutions
USE **health facilities**

health centers
USE **health facilities**
medical centers

health centers, adult day
USE **adult day care centers**

health clubs
USE **athletic clubs**

health facilities
RK.734 (A,L,N,B)
ALT **health facility**
UF buildings, health care
centers, health
facilities, health
facilities, medical
health buildings
health care buildings
health care facilities
health care institutions
health centers
institutions, health care
medical facilities
CN V.RK.AFU.ALO.ALO.CXA.ALO. AFU

health facilities, mental
USE **mental health facilities**

health farms
USE **health resorts**

health resorts
RG.169 (A,L,B,R)
ALT **health resort**
UF farms, health
health farms
resorts, health
watering places
CN V.RG.AFU.AFU.DOI.BZY.AFU

health sciences
KD.237 (L)
UF sciences, health
CN K.KD.AFU.ARI.BUE

health, public
USE **public health**

heaps, slag
USE **slag heaps**

heaps, spoil
USE **spoil banks**

hearing
BM.725 (L,R)
CN B.BM.CFS.AFU.BCW.AFU

hearings
KM.99 (L)
SN Meetings or sessions in which testimony, arguments, or evidence is presented in a formal setting, usually before an official.
CN K.KM.AFU.CRG.ALO

heart and shield back chairs
USE **heart-back chairs**

heart-back chairs
TG.139
ALT **heart-back chair**
SN Late 18th-century American chairs, with heart-shaped backs; especially popular in New England.
UF chairs, heart and shield back
chairs, heart-back
heart and shield back chairs
CN V.TG.AFU.AFU.ALO.AFU.AFU.AFU.NIE.CFS

heart pulls
TF.78
ALT **heart pull**
UF pulls, heart
CN V.TF.AFU.AFU.AFU.AFU.CFS.BCW.AFU.BUE

hearth stools
USE **fender stools**

hearths
RT.1155 (B,R)
ALT **hearth**
CN V.RT.AFU.BOK.ALO.ALO.AXC

hearths, back
USE **back hearths**

hearths, front
USE **front hearths**

hearths, inner
USE **back hearths**

hearths, outer
USE **front hearths**

hearthstones
RT.1158
ALT **hearthstone**
CN V.RT.AFU.BOK.ALO.ALO.BCW

hearts
DG.34 (L)
ALT **heart**
SN Use for the highly conventionalized figure based on the shape of the human heart.
CN D.DG.AFU.AFU.BUE

hearts and crown chairs
TG.124
ALT **hearts and crown chair**
SN 18th-century American turned baluster-back chairs whose crest rail has cutouts of these shapes; the period name for these chairs is not known. (TRENT)
UF chairs, hearts and crown
CN V.TG.AFU.AFU.ALO.AFU.AFU.AFU.NIE.ALO.AFU

hearts, flaming
USE **flaming hearts**

hearts, pierced
USE **pierced hearts**

heat
BM.837 (L,B,R)
CN B.BM.CFS.AXC.ALO.AFU.AFU.AFU

heat-absorbing glass
MT.275
UF glass, heat-absorbing
CN M.MT.AFU.AFU.AFU.BIQ.AFU.AXC.ARI

heat bridges
USE **thermal bridges**

heat copying
USE **thermography**

heat-distributing units
RT.1427
ALT **heat-distributing unit**
UF units, heat-distributing
CN V.RT.ALO.BCW.AFU.ALO.ALO

heat exchangers
RT.1419 (L)
ALT **heat exchanger**
SN Devices that transfer heat between two physically separated fluids; generally consists of a cylindrical shell with longitudinal tubes; one fluid flows inside, the other outside. (DAC)
UF exchangers, heat
CN V.RT.ALO.BCW.AFU.ALO.AFU.BCW

heat expansion
USE **expansion**

heat flow
USE **heat transmission**

heat gain
BM.839 (B)
SN The net increase in heat within a space. (DAC)
UF gain, heat
CN B.BM.CFS.AXC.ALO.AFU.AFU.ALO.AFU

heat insulation
USE **thermal insulation**

heat insulation windows
USE **double windows**

heat loss
BM.840 (B)
SN The net decrease in heat within a space. (DAC)
UF loss, heat
CN B.BM.CFS.AXC.ALO.AFU.AFU.ALO.ALO

heat pollution
USE **thermal pollution**

heat pumps
RT.1425 (L,B)
ALT **heat pump**
UF pumps, heat
CN V.RT.ALO.BCW.AFU.ALO.AFU. BIQ

heat pumps, solar-assisted
USE **solar-assisted heat pumps**

heat-resistant concrete
MT.224 (A,L)
UF concrete, heat-resistant
CN M.MT.AFU.AFU.AFU.BCW.AFU.AXC.ARI

heat-resistant materials
MT.2797 (L)
UF materials, heat-resistant
CN M.MT.AFU.BCW.BZY

heat-resisting glass
MT.276
UF glass, heat-resisting
CN M.MT.AFU.AFU.AFU.BIQ.AFU.AXC.AXC

heat-sealing
KT.672
ALT **heat-sealed**
SN A method of joining plastic sheets or films by the simultaneous application of heat and pressure to the areas in contact. (DAC)
CN K.KT.AFU.ALO.GRC.AFU.BIQ.AFU

heat stabilizers
MT.2329
UF stabilizers, heat
CN M.MT.AFU.ARI.ALO.FIM.AFU

heat-strengthened glass
MT.277
SN Glass used in the curtain wall design as spandrel glazing of multistoried buildings. It is usually polished plate glass or patterned glass on one surface of which is fused a colored enamel. (STEIN)
UF glass, heat-strengthened
CN M.MT.AFU.AFU.AFU.BIQ.AFU.AXC.BCW

heat transmission
BM.841 (L,B)
SN Transfer of heat from one point to another due to the tendency of heat to flow from an area of higher temperature to an area of lower temperature. (STEIN)
UF flow, heat
heat flow
transmission, heat
CN B.BM.CFS.AXC.ALO.AFU.AFU.ALO.ARI

heat, specific
USE **specific heat**

heaters, baseboard
USE **baseboard units**

heaters, solar water
USE **solar water heaters**

heaters, water
USE **water heaters**

heathenism
USE **paganism**

heathstone
USE **sarsen**

heating
KT.731 (A,L,B,R)
CN K.KT.AFU.ALO.GWW.ARI

heating (systems)
USE **heating systems**

heating and cooling plans
USE **HVAC plans**

heating coils
RT.1423
ALT **heating coil**
UF air-heating coils
coils, air heating
coils, heating
CN V.RT.ALO.BCW.AFU.ALO.AFU.BCW.AFU.ARI

heating plans
VD.56
ALT **heating plan**
UF plans, heating
CN V.VD.AFU.AFU.BIQ.ALO.AXC.ALO.BIQ.ALO.AFU

heating plants
USE **heating systems**

heating systems
RT.1391 (A,L,B,R)
ALT **heating system**
UF building heating systems
heating (systems)
heating plant
heating systems, building
systems, heating
CN V.RT.ALO.BCW.AFU.AFU.ARI

heating systems, building
USE **heating systems**

heating systems, passive solar
USE **passive solar heating**

heating systems, warm air
USE **warm air heating**

heating, baseboard
USE **baseboard units**

heating, electric resistance
USE **electric resistance heating**

heating, forced air
USE **forced air heating**

heating, gravity
USE **gravity heating**

heating, hot air
USE **warm air heating**

heating, hot water
USE **hot water heating**

heating, panel
USE **panel heating**

heating, passive solar
USE **passive solar heating**

heating, radiant
USE **radiant heating**

heating, radiant panel
USE **panel heating**

heating, resistance
USE **electric resistance heating**

heating, solar
USE **solar heating**

heating, steam
USE **steam heating**

heating, vacuum
USE **vacuum heating**

heating, ventilation, and air conditioning
USE **HVAC**

heating, ventilation, and air conditioning drawings
USE **HVAC drawings**

heating, ventilation, and air conditioning plans
USE **HVAC plans**

heating, warm air
USE **warm air heating**

heaves, frost
USE **frost heaves**

heavy
USE **heavyweight**

heavy sheet glass
USE **sheet glass**

heavy spar
USE **blanc fixe**

heavyweight
DC.146
UF heavy
CN D.DC.AFU.BOK.AFU

heavyweight aggregate
MT.2303
UF aggregate, heavyweight
CN M.MT.AFU.ARI.ALO.ALO.ALO.ALO

Hebrew granite
USE **graphic granite**

Hebrew schools
RK.809 (L)
ALT **Hebrew school**
SN Use for elementary and secondary schools teaching Jewish subject matter only, usually supplementary to secular schools, and operated under Conservative or Reform Jewish auspices.
UF Jewish religious schools
schools, Hebrew
schools, Jewish religious
CN V.RK.AFU.ALO.ALO.CXA.ARI.ALO.BOK

hedge mazes
RK.1406
ALT **hedge maze**
UF mazes, hedge
CN V.RK.ALO.AFU.AFU.AFU.ARI.ARI.ALO.AFU

hedgerows
USE **hedges**

hedges
RM.453 (A,L,B)
ALT **hedge**
SN Plantings of bushes or woody plants in a row, usually as fences, dividers, or windbreaks. (STEIN)
UF hedgerows
CN V.RM.ALO.AFU.CFS.AXC

heel planes
USE **compass planes**

heel stones
RT.899
ALT **heel stone**
SN Stones at the bottom of a gate pier used to mount the bottom hinge pin for the gate. (DAC)
UF stones, heel
CN V.RT.AFU.ARI.AFU.AFU.ARI.ALO.AFU.ALO.ALO

Hehe
FL.587 (L)
UF Wahehe
CN F.FL.ALO.AFU.AXC.AXC.AFU.BCW

Heian
FL.1978 (A,L)
CN F.FL.ALO.ARI.ALO.ALO.AFU.AXC.ARI

Heian, Early
USE **Early Heian**

Heian, Late
USE **Late Heian**

height
BM.806 (B)
CN B.BM.CFS.ARI.AXC.BUE.BCW

height restrictions
BM.483 (A,L,B)
UF restrictions, height
CN B.BM.BCW.DUC.AXC

heightening
KT.267
ALT **heightened**
SN Use for the painting or drawing technique in which the rendition of forms is completed by raising the value of appropriate areas with white or pale color. (MAYER)
CN K.KT.AFU.ALO.DUC.DCU.AXC

Heiltsuk
FL.1345 (L)
CN F.FL.ALO.ALO.ARI.AFU.BIQ.CRG

helical nails
TF.394
ALT **helical nail**
UF nails, helical
CN V.TF.AFU.AFU.AFU.ALO.AFU.CFS.AFU.BOK

helical stairs
USE **spiral stairs**

heliochromy
KT.332
SN Use for the variant of the daguerreotype process devised by Claude-Abel Niépce de St. Victor, distinguished by the use of silver chloride to produce natural color. The image cannot be fixed, and therefore is impermanent. In the early 20th century, sometimes used to mean color photography in general.
UF photochromy
CN K.KT.AFU.ALO.DUC.DIO.ALO.BUE.ALO.AFU

heliochromy (color photography)
USE **color photography**

Heliogenblau
USE **phthalocyanine blue**

heliography
KT.333
SN Use for the process invented by J.N. de Niépce around 1825 in which bitumen that had been coated on glass or metal hardened in relation to exposure; by washing with oil of lavender left only the hardened image area.
UF bitumen process
Niépceotype
CN K.KT.AFU.ALO.DUC.DIO.ALO.BUE.ARI

heliogravure
USE **photogravure**

heliotrope
USE **bloodstone**

helipads
RK.1505 (A)
ALT **helipad**
SN Designates helicopter takeoff and landing surfaces, usually without commercial facilities.
CN V.RK.ALO.ALO.BIQ.AFU.ALO

heliports
RG.219 (A,L,B)
ALT **heliport**
CN V.RG.AFU.AFU.EFQ.AFU.AFU.AFU

Helladic
FL.2548
CN F.FL.ALO.AXC.ALO.AFU.AFU.ALO.ALO

Helladic, Early
USE **Early Helladic**

Helladic, Late
USE **Late Helladic**

Helladic, Middle
USE **Middle Helladic**

Hellenerne
FL.3348 (R)
CN F.FL.ALO.BCW.ALO.AXC.DIO.ARI.AFU

Hellenic
USE **Greek**

Hellenism
BM.355 (L,R)
SN Use to refer to the influences of Greek culture as it spread to new areas following the conquests of Alexander the Great; use also for devotion to Greek culture and ideals in any later period.

CN B.BM.ALO.ALO.CLM.CXA

Hellenistic
FL.2581 (A,R)
CN F.FL.ALO.AXC.ALO.AFU.AFU.ARI.BIQ

Hellenistic-Bactrian
USE **Greco-Bactrian**

Hellenistic, Late
USE **Late Hellenistic**

helm roofs
RM.406
ALT **helm roof**
SN Roofs of four steeply pitched faces, forming a spire; the four ridges rise from the peaks of four gables, the roof faces being set diagonally in relation to the gable faces. (HAS)
UF roofs, helm
CN V.RM.AFU.DOI.ALO.AFU.ARI

helms
RK.1208 (A,R)
ALT **helm**
SN Use for vernacular British structures of uncertain construction and purpose, possibly temporary and made of wood with an earthen floor and used for storage of produce, equipment, or animals, popular from the 16th to the 19th century.
UF haulms
CN V.RK.AFU.ALO.ALO.GFO.ALO

helpers
USE **assistants**

helpers, plumber's
USE **plungers**

helpmates
USE **froes**

helve hammers
TB.662 (N)
ALT **helve hammer**
SN Power hammers consisting essentially of a heavy head at one end of a lever lifted by power and dropped by its own weight on work that rests on an anvil. (W)
UF hammers, helve
hammers, tilt
tilt hammers
CN V.TB.AFU.BCW.BIQ.AFU.ALO.BIQ.ALO

helves
TB.1125
ALT **helve**
SN Tool handles, such as those of axes, hatchets, or hammers. (MEANS)
UF hafts (helves)
CN V.TB.ALO.CLM.AFU

hematite
MT.511 (L)
CN M.MT.AFU.AFU.AFU.CFS.AFU.CXA.AFU

hematite, brown
USE **limonite**

Hemba
FL.497 (L)
UF Buye
CN F.FL.ALO.AFU.AXC.ALO.ALO.BCW.BCW.ALO

hembras
TG.461
ALT **hembra**
SN 15th- and 16th-century brides' chests constructed in the Catalina region of Spain. At one side of its face is a door which concealed a set of drawers to hold small articles. Both inner and outer sides of the lid are decorated, the inner usually with religious scenes. (BURR)
CN V.TG.AFU.AFU.AXC.ALO.AXC.CRG.AFU

hemicycles
RM.275
ALT **hemicycle**
SN Use for rooms or divisions of rooms that are semicircular in plan.
CN V.RM.AFU.DIO.ARI.ALO.BZY

hemiglyphs
RT.350
ALT **hemiglyph**
SN Use for the half channels on either side of a triglyph.
CN V.RT.AFU.AFU.AFU.BCW.BZY.ALO.ARI.ALO.AFU

hemihydrate plaster
USE **Plaster of Paris**

hemihydrate plaster, retarded
USE **retarded hemihydrate plaster**

hemispheres
BM.792
ALT **hemispherical**
CN B.BM.CFS.ARI.AXC.BCW.ALO.ARI

hemlock
MT.1354 (L)
UF Tsuga
CN M.MT.AFU.AFU.ALO.BIQ.DCU.AFU.AFU.ALO.BOK

hemlock (color)
USE **blackish green**

hemlock green
USE **dark grayish green**
very dark bluish green
very dark green

hemlock spruce
USE **eastern hemlock**

hemlock, black
USE **mountain hemlock**

hemlock, Canada
USE **eastern hemlock**

hemlock, common
USE **eastern hemlock**

hemlock, eastern
USE **eastern hemlock**

hemlock, mountain
USE **mountain hemlock**

hemlock, New England
USE **eastern hemlock**

hemlock, Pacific
USE **western hemlock**

hemlock, western
USE **western hemlock**

hemp
MT.1828 (L,B)
SN A fiber from the stalk of the plant Cannabis sativa, valued chiefly for cordage, sacking, packings, and as a fiber for plastic filler. (MH)
CN M.MT.AFU.AFU.ARI.ALO.AFU.AFU.ALO.BIQ

hemp, Manila
USE **Manila hemp**

hemp, sisal
USE **sisal**

hempseed oil
MT.2010
UF oil, hempseed
CN M.MT.AFU.AFU.ARI.ARI.AXC.AFU.AXC

hen houses
USE **chicken houses**

henequen
MT.1830 (L)
SN A strong yellowish or reddish hard fiber derived from the leaves of a tropical American agave. (W)
UF Mexican sisal
sisal, Mexican
sisal, Yucatan
Yucatan sisal
CN M.MT.AFU.AFU.ARI.ALO.AFU.AFU.ALO.BOK

henge monuments
USE **henges**

henges
RK.891
ALT **henge**
SN Designates circular areas bounded by a ditch and an enclosing embankment, the whole usually surrounding a circle or circles of standing stones or wood posts.
UF henge monuments
monuments, henge
CN V.RK.AFU.ALO.ALO.DOI.AFU.ARI.ALO

Henri Deux
USE **Henri II**

Henri II
FL.3214
UF Henri Deux
CN F.FL.ALO.BCW.ALO.ARI.BIQ.
BIQ.ARI.ALO.ARI.ALO

Hepplewhite
FL.3338 (R)
CN F.FL.ALO.BCW.ALO.AXC.DIO
.ALO.BUE.ALO

heptane
MT.2678 (L)
SN A constituent hydrocarbon of gasoline. (MH)
CN M.MT.AFU.ARI.HZS.AFU.BIQ.AXC

Heracleopolitan period
FL.2801
CN F.FL.ALO.AXC.ALO.ARI.AFU.
BCW.BCW

heraldic achievements
USE **coats of arms**

heraldic dictionaries
VW.402 (L)
ALT **heraldic dictionary**
UF dictionaries of heraldry
dictionaries, heraldic
CN V.VW.AFU.AFU.ALO.EWY.ARI.
ALO.BCW

heraldic motifs
DG.37
ALT **heraldic motif**
UF charges (heraldic motifs)
motifs, heraldic
CN D.DG.AFU.AFU.BZY

heraldry
KD.150 (L,B,R)
CN K.KD.AFU.ALO.CLM.ALO.ARI

Herat School
FL.3573
CN F.FL.ALO.BIQ.AFU.HTY.AFU.AFU

herb gardens
RK.1433 (A,L)
ALT **herb garden**
UF gardens, herb
CN V.RK.ALO.AFU.AFU.AXC.ALO

herbaceous plants
RD.264
ALT **herbaceous plant**
UF plants, herbaceous
CN V.RD.ARI.AFU.BCW.ALO.ALO.
ALO.AFU

herbaria
RK.417 (L)
ALT **herbarium**
SN Use for rooms or buildings containing a systematically ordered collection of preserved plants;(OCG) for gardens of herbs, use **herb gardens**.
CN V.RK.AFU.ALO.ALO.BCW.AXC.
ARI.CFS.ARI.AFU

herbicides
MT.2378 (L)
ALT **herbicide**
UF killers, weed
weed killers
CN M.MT.AFU.ARI.BOK.AXC

herbs
RD.262 (L,B)
ALT **herb**
CN V.RD.ARI.AFU.BCW.ALO.ALO.
AFU.AXC

herdsmen
HG.362 (L,R)
ALT **herdsman**
CN H.HG.AFU.AXC.BIQ.ALO.AXC.
AFU.ALO

Herero
FL.577 (L)
CN F.FL.ALO.AFU.AXC.ARI.BIQ.ALO

heritage buildings
USE **historic buildings**

heritage property
USE **cultural property**

heritage trails
RG.184 (A)
ALT **heritage trail**
SN Use for organized and labeled trails laid out to follow points of interest concerning the local history of a region.
UF archaeological trails
trails, archaeological
trails, heritage
CN V.RG.AFU.AFU.DOI.CLM.AFU

hermeneutics
BM.296 (L,R)
SN The study and application of the methodological principles of interpretation and explanation; specifically the general principles of Biblical interpretation. (W)
UF interpretation
CN B.BM.AFU.AXC.BUE

hermetism
BM.356 (L,R)
SN A system of ideas based on hermetic teachings. (W)
CN B.BM.ALO.ALO.CLM.DCU

hermitages
RG.191 (A,L,R)
ALT **hermitage**
CN V.RG.AFU.AFU.DUC.ARI

heroa
RK.1141
ALT **heroum**
SN Use for shrines or small chapels dedicated to a hero, demigod, or person of great dignity; may or may not be located over a grave.
CN V.RK.AFU.ALO.ALO.FCS.BOK.ALO

Herrera
FL.1092
CN F.FL.ALO.ALO.ALO.ALO.ALO.
ALO.AFU.BOK

Herrera beds
TG.359
ALT **Herrera bed**
UF beds, Herrera
CN V.TG.AFU.AFU.ARI.AFU.AFU.BZY.
ALO.ARI

Herreran
FL.3249
UF estilo desornamentado
CN F.FL.ALO.BCW.ALO.ARI.BIQ.
BIQ.BUE.AXC.AFU

herringbone
DG.129
SN A pattern consisting of adjoining vertical rows of slanting lines, forming Vs or inverted Vs; used in masonry, textiles, and other work. (RHDEL2)
CN D.DG.AFU.ARI.ALO.BIQ.AXC

herringbone banding
USE **feather banding**

herringbone perspective
USE **axial perspective**

herringbone strutting
USE **cross bridging**

Hertfordshire spikes
USE **needle spires**

Hervey Island
USE **Cook Island**

hessian
USE **burlap**

heterosexuality
BM.603
SN Sexuality characterized by romantic love or sexual desire toward members of the opposite sex.
CN B.BM.BUE.CXA.ALO

hewing axes
USE **broadaxes**

hewing hatchets
TB.892 (N)
ALT **hewing hatchet**
SN Small straight-handled broadaxes. (SLOANE)
UF hatchets, hewing
CN V.TB.AFU.BCW.CFS.ALO.AFU.
DCU.ALO

hexagon clamps
USE **universal clamps**

hexagons
BM.782 (L)
ALT **hexagonal**
CN B.BM.CFS.ARI.AXC.BCW.AFU.
BIQ.AXC

hexane
MT.2679 (L)
CN M.MT.AFU.ARI.HZS.AFU.BIQ.BCW

hexapartite vaults
USE **sexpartite vaults**

hexastyle
DC.89
CN D.DC.AFU.ARI.ERE.BIQ.BIQ

hexone
USE **methyl isobutyl ketone**

HFE
USE **human factors**

Hiberno-Saxon
FL.3121 (R)
CN F.FL.ALO.BCW.ALO.ALO.AFU.
BOK.ARI.ALO.ALO

Hibiscus elatus
USE **mahoe**

hick joints
USE **rough-cut joints**

hickory
MT.1172 (L)
UF Carya
CN M.MT.AFU.AFU.ALO.BIQ.DCU.
AFU.AFU.AFU.ELK

hickory elm
USE **rock elm**

hickory, big shellbark
USE **big shellbark hickory**

hickory, bitternut
USE **bitternut hickory**

hickory, black
USE **black hickory**

hickory, king nut
USE **big shellbark hickory**

hickory, mockernut
USE **mockernut hickory**

hickory, pecan
USE **pecan**

hickory, pignut
USE **pignut hickory**

hickory, shagbark
USE **shagbark hickory**

hickory, shellbark
USE **shagbark hickory**

hickory, white
USE **mockernut hickory**

Hidatsa
FL.1382 (L)
UF Gros Ventres of the Missouri
Minnetaree
CN F.FL.ALO.ALO.ARI.AFU.BOK.BZY

Hidden Valley
FL.837
CN F.FL.ALO.ALO.ALO.AFU.ALO.
ALO.ARI.AFU.BCW

hide
MT.953 (L,B)
CN M.MT.AFU.AFU.ALO.AFU.DZW.
ARI

hide glue
MT.2350
SN Made from impure gelatin from animal hide, used chiefly to mount textile or papers on artists' supports, often in weak solution.
UF glue, hide
CN M.MT.AFU.ARI.ARI.AFU.ALO.
ALO.AFU.BCW

hideaway beds
TG.349
ALT **hideaway bed**
UF beds, hideaway
CN V.TG.AFU.AFU.ARI.AFU.AFU.BIQ.
ALO

Hie
FL.1996
CN F.FL.ALO.ARI.ALO.ALO.ALO.
AFU.AXC

hiera
USE **temene**

high-alloy iron
MT.340
UF iron, high-alloy
CN M.MT.AFU.AFU.AFU.BZY.AFU.
AFU.AFU.AFU.AFU.ARI

high altars
RT.1215
ALT **high altar**
SN Primary altars in churches. (HAS)
UF altars, high
altars, main
main altars
CN V.RT.AFU.BUE.ALO.ALO.AFU.AFU

high alumina cement
USE **aluminous cement**

high-back Windsor chairs
TG.102
ALT **high-back Windsor chair**
SN Tall Windsor armchairs with a horizontal U-shaped armrail and long back spindles crowned by a crest rail curved laterally to follow the outside curve of the seat back. (EVANS)
UF chairs, comb-back Windsor
chairs, high-back Windsor
chairs, pillow back Windsor
comb-back Windsor chairs
pillow back Windsor chairs
Windsor chairs, comb-back
Windsor chairs, high-back
Windsor chairs, pillow back
CN V.TG.AFU.AFU.ALO.AFU.AFU.
AFU.MLC.BIQ

High Baroque
FL.3174
UF Baroque, High
CN F.FL.ALO.BCW.ALO.ARI.AXC.ALO

high buildings
USE **skyscrapers**

high-carbon steel
MT.347
UF steel, high-carbon
CN M.MT.AFU.AFU.AFU.BZY.AFU.
AFU.AFU.AFU.ALO.AFU.AFU.ARI

high cases
USE **high chests of drawers**

high chairs (tall chairs)
USE **tall chairs**

high chests
USE **high chests of drawers**

high chests of drawers
TG.492 (N,R)
ALT **high chest of drawers**
SN Tall case pieces generally having seven or more drawers, and divided by a cornice into two sections, consisting of a lower case resembling an enlarged dressing table and an upper case resembling a chest of drawers. For equivalent English pieces use **tallboys.**
UF cases, high
chests of drawers, high
chests, high
drawers, high chests of
high cases
high chests
highboys
highdaddys
CN V.TG.AFU.AFU.AXC.ALO.BCW.CFS

High Classical
FL.2579
UF Classical, High
CN F.FL.ALO.AXC.ALO.AFU.AFU.ARI.
BCW.ALO

high-early cement
USE **high-early strength cement**

high-early-strength cement
MT.12
UF cement, extra-rapid-hardening
cement, high-early
cement, high-early-strength
cement, type III
cement, type III portland
extra-rapid-hardening cement
high-early cement
portland cement, type III
type III cement
type III portland cement
CN M.MT.AFU.AFU.AFU.ALO.AFU.
AFU.ARI.AFU.AFU

High Edwardian Baroque
USE **Baroque Revival**

high energy physics
KD.285 (L)
UF physics, high energy
CN K.KD.AFU.ARI.CLM.AXC.ARI

High Gothic
FL.3095 (L,B)
UF Gothic, High
CN F.FL.ALO.BCW.ALO.ALO.AFU.ARI.ALO

high-lead crystal glass
USE **crystal**

High Palaeologan
FL.3079
UF Palaeologan, High
CN F.FL.ALO.BCW.ALO.AFU.ALO.AXC.AFU.ALO

high-post beds
TG.354 (N)
ALT **high-post bed**
SN Beds with two or four posts approximately six feet in height which often, but not always, support a tester.
UF beds, high-post
beds, post
beds, tall-post
bedsteads, high-post
four-poster beds
four-posters
high-post bedsteads
post beds
tall-post beds
CN V.TG.AFU.AFU.ARI.AFU.AFU.BZY

high-post bedsteads
USE **high-post beds**

high relief
KT.539
SN Sculptural relief technique in which half or more than half of the natural circumference of the modeled form projects from the surrounding surface. (W)
UF relief, high
CN K.KT.AFU.ALO.ELK.DIO.ALO.AXC.ALO

High Renaissance
FL.3168 (L)
UF Renaissance, High
CN F.FL.ALO.BCW.ALO.ARI.AFU.ALO

high-rise buildings
RK.11 (A,L,B,R)
ALT **high-rise building**
SN Use for buildings over nine or ten stories and served by elevators, especially when such buildings stand out in a skyline.
UF buildings, high-rise
high-rises
CN V.RK.AFU.ALO.AFU.AFU.AFU.ARI

high-rises
USE **high-rise buildings**

high schools
RK.840 (A,L,B)
ALT **high school**
UF colleges, sixth-form
lycees
schools, high
schools, secondary
secondary schools
sixth-form colleges
CN V.RK.AFU.ALO.ALO.CXA.ARI.AXC.BCW

high schools, junior
USE **junior high schools**

high-security prisons
USE **maximum-security prisons**

high speed cement
USE **aluminous cement**

high-speed photography
KT.384 (L)
UF photography, high-speed
CN K.KT.AFU.ALO.DUC.DIO.ARI.ARI.ALO

high-strength concrete
MT.225 (L,B)
UF concrete, high-strength
CN M.MT.AFU.AFU.AFU.BCW.AFU.AXC.AXC

high-strength low-alloy steel
MT.354
UF alloy constructional steel
constructional steel, alloy
HSLA steel
low-alloy steel
steel, alloy constructional
steel, high-strength low-alloy
steel, HSLA
steel, low-alloy
CN M.MT.AFU.AFU.AFU.BZY.AFU.AFU.AFU.AFU.ALO.AFU.ALO.ALO

High-Tech
FL.3709 (A,R)
CN F.FL.ALO.BUE.ALO.AXC

high tombs
USE **altar tombs**

High Victorian
FL.3319
UF Victorian, High
CN F.FL.ALO.BCW.ALO.AXC.DIO.ALO.BCW.ALO.ALO

High Victorian Gothic
USE **Gothic Revival**

highboys
USE **high chests of drawers**

highchair and carriages, combination
USE **carriage chairs**

highchairs
TG.171 (N)
ALT **highchair**
SN Children's chairs with long legs, a feeding tray, and a footrest. (RHDEL2)
UF chairs, child's table
child's table chairs
table chairs, child's
CN V.TG.AFU.AFU.ALO.AFU.AFU.ALO.BCW.AFU

highdaddys
USE **high chests of drawers**

higher education
KD.126 (L)
UF education, higher
CN K.KD.AFU.ALO.BOK.AFU.AXC

Highland, Provincial
USE **Provincial Highland**

highlights
BM.856
SN Use for the points of brightest reflection of light off of an object; use also for the areas of brightest value in a picture, whether achieved by brightening or by leaving white areas of the support.
CN B.BM.CFS.AXC.ALO.AFU.ALO.ALO.AXC

highway access roads
USE **access roads**

highway beautification
USE **roadside improvement**

highway engineering
KD.225 (L)
SN Branch of civil engineering dealing with the planning, design, and operation of facilities and systems used for the movement of persons and goods. (PG)
UF engineering, highway
engineering, road
road engineering
CN K.KD.AFU.ARI.BIQ.AXC.BIQ.AFU

highway maps
USE **road maps**

highway planning
KD.174 (L)
UF planning, highway
CN K.KD.AFU.ALO.DUC.BCW.AFU

highway shoulders
USE **shoulders (roads)**

highway tunnels
RK.1305
ALT **highway tunnel**
UF tunnels, highway
CN V.RK.AFU.ALO.ALO.GLI.ALO.ALO.AFU

highways
RK.1515 (A,L,B,R)
ALT **highway**
SN Use for major, high-speed, high-capacity roads between urban areas, often laid out to take advantage of pleasant countryside.
UF thoroughfares

CN V.RK.ALO.ALO.BIQ.ARI.AFU.AFU

highways, belt
USE **beltways**

highways, circumferential
USE **beltways**

highways, controlled access
USE **limited access highways**

highways, divided
USE **divided highways**

highways, dual
USE **divided highways**

highways, elevated
USE **elevated roads**

highways, express
USE **expressways**

highways, limited access
USE **limited access highways**

hill pine
USE **longleaf pine**
southern yellow pine

hill towns
RD.68 (A)
ALT **hill town**
UF towns, hill
CN V.RD.AFU.BCW.BCW.ALO

hillforts
RK.450 (L)
ALT **hillfort**
SN Defensive enclosures comprised of ramparts and ditches encircling a fortified structure on a central prominence; common in Bronze Age and Iron Age Europe.
CN V.RK.AFU.ALO.ALO.BIQ.BOK.ARI

hillocks
RD.205
ALT **hillock**
UF hummocks
knolls
CN V.RD.ARI.AFU.AXC.AFU.ALO.
AFU.ALO.ALO

Hillotype
KT.334 (L)
SN Early color photographic process announced by Levi L. Hill in 1856 but thought until recently to be spurious, and still not fully understood.
CN K.KT.AFU.ALO.DUC.DIO.ALO.
BUE.AXC

Hillotypes
VJ.31
ALT **Hillotype**
SN Direct positive photographs produced by the process called Hillotype.
CN V.VJ.AFU.AFU.ARI.AFU.ARI

hills
RD.203 (L)
ALT **hill**
CN V.RD.ARI.AFU.AXC.AFU.ALO.
AFU.ALO

hillside architecture
RK.1363 (L,B)
UF alpine architecture
architecture, alpine
architecture, hillside
architecture, mountain
mountain architecture
CN V.RK.AFU.ALO.ARI.AXC.BCW

Himalayan
FL.2152 (L)
CN F.FL.ALO.ARI.AXC.AFU

Himalayan birch
MT.1119
UF Betula utilis
birch, Himalayan
CN M.MT.AFU.AFU.ALO.BIQ.DCU.
AFU.AFU.AFU.BIQ.BCW

Himalayan cedar
USE **deodar**

Hinayana
BM.611 (L)
UF Buddhism, Hinayana
Hinayana Buddhism
Lesser Vehicle
Small Vehicle
Vehicle, Lesser
Vehicle, Small
CN B.BM.BZY.AFU.AFU.AFU

Hinayana Buddhism
USE **Hinayana**

Hinduism
BM.660 (A,L,B,R)
ALT **Hindu**
CN B.BM.BZY.AFU.AXC

Hindur
FL.2277
CN F.FL.ALO.ARI.AXC.ALO.AFU.BZY.
BCW.ARI.BOK

hinge chisels
TB.863
ALT **hinge chisel**
SN Grooved or tooth-ended chisels used to cut the channels for hinge fittings. (HAND)
UF chisels, hinge
CN V.TB.AFU.BCW.CFS.ALO.AFU.
BUE.BCW

hinge pins
USE **pins (hinge components)**

hinge plates
USE **hinge straps**

hinge posts
USE **hanging posts**

hinge stiles
RT.826
ALT **hinge stile**
UF butt stiles
hanging stiles
stiles, butt
stiles, hanging
stiles, hinge
CN V.RT.AFU.ALO.ALO.AXC.AFU

hinge straps
TF.522
ALT **hinge strap**
SN Ornamental straps fastened to the surface of a door to render the appearance of a strap hinge. (MEANS)
UF hinge plates
plates, hinge
straps, hinge
CN V.TF.AFU.ALO.ALO.AFU

hinged doors
RT.866
ALT **hinged door**
UF doors, hinged
CN V.RT.AFU.ARI.AFU.AFU.AFU.ALO.
ARI.AFU.ARI.ALO

hinged latch bolts
USE **swinging latch bolts**

hinged windows
RT.938
ALT **hinged window**
SN Windows that swing on hinges, fixed to the sides, top, or bottom of the frame; the sash can open inward or outward.
UF windows, hinged
CN V.RT.AFU.ARI.AFU.AFU.BOK.
AFU.AFU.EWY.ALO

hinges
TF.93 (L,N,B)
ALT **hinge**
SN Flexible plates or leaves joined by a pin so as to allow swinging motion in a single plane of one of the members to which they are attached, such as a door or gate. (MEANS)
CN V.TF.AFU.AFU.AFU.AFU.CLM

hinges, adjustable ball
USE **adjustable ball hinges**

hinges, anchor
USE **anchor hinges**

hinges, backflap
USE **backflap hinges**

hinges, ball-bearing
USE **ball-bearing hinges**

hinges, blind
USE **concealed hinges**

hinges, butt
USE **butt hinges**

hinges, butterfly
USE **butterfly hinges**

hinges, capped butt
USE **capped butt hinges**

hinges, casement
USE **casement hinges**

hinges, checking floor
USE **checking floor hinges**

hinges, concealed
USE **concealed hinges**

hinges, continuous
USE **continuous hinges**

hinges, cotter pin
USE **cotter pin hinges**

hinges, double-acting
USE **double-acting hinges**

hinges, double-acting spring
USE **double-acting spring hinges**

hinges, electric
USE **electric hinges**

hinges, electrically wired
USE **electric hinges**

hinges, exposed
USE **exposed hinges**

hinges, fast-pin
USE **fast-pin hinges**

hinges, flap
USE **strap hinges**

hinges, floor
USE **floor hinges**

hinges, friction
USE **friction hinges**

hinges, full mortise
USE **full mortise hinges**

hinges, full-surface
USE **full-surface hinges**

hinges, gravity door
USE **rising hinges**

hinges, H
USE **H hinges**

hinges, H and L
USE **H/L hinges**

hinges, H/L
USE **H/L hinges**

hinges, half-mortise
USE **half-mortise hinges**

hinges, half-surface
USE **half-surface hinges**

hinges, harmon
USE **harmon hinges**

hinges, hydraulic
USE **hydraulic hinges**

hinges, ice box
USE **ice box hinges**

hinges, invisible
USE **invisible hinges**

hinges, jamb spring
USE **jamb spring hinges**

hinges, lift-off
USE **lift-off hinges**

hinges, loose-joint
USE **loose-joint hinges**

hinges, loose-joint butt
USE **loose-joint hinges**

hinges, loose-pin
USE **loose-pin hinges**

hinges, offset
USE **offset hinges**

hinges, oilite bearing
USE **oilite bearing hinges**

hinges, olive knuckle
USE **olive knuckle hinges**

hinges, paumelle
USE **paumelle hinges**

hinges, pivot-reinforced
USE **pivot-reinforced hinges**

hinges, plastic
USE **plastic hinges**

hinges, pocket butt
USE **pocket butt hinges**

hinges, rattail
USE **rattail hinges**

hinges, rising
USE **rising hinges**

hinges, rising butt
USE **rising hinges**

hinges, secret
USE **invisible hinges**

hinges, shutter
USE **shutter hinges**

hinges, snipe
USE **cotter pin hinges**

hinges, snipe-bill
USE **cotter pin hinges**

hinges, spring
USE **spring hinges**

hinges, strap
USE **strap hinges**

hinges, surface
USE **surface hinges**

hinges, T
USE **T hinges**

hinges, tight pin
USE **fast-pin hinges**

hip jacks
USE **jack rafters**

hip-joint chairs
USE **X-chairs**

hip knobs
RT.1058
ALT **hip knob**
SN Use for finials which surmount roof hips or gables.
UF knobs, hip
CN V.RT.AFU.BCW.BUE.AFU

hip rafters
RT.499
ALT **hip rafter**
UF angle rafters
angle ridges
rafters, angle
rafters, hip
ridges, angle
CN V.RT.AFU.AFU.AFU.BIQ.ARI.ALO.ALO.AFU.ALO

hip rolls
RT.467
ALT **hip roll**
SN Rounded strips of wood, tile, metal, or composition material used to cover and finish the hip of a roof. (DAC)
UF ridge rolls
rolls, hip
rolls, ridge
CN V.RT.AFU.AFU.AFU.BIQ.ARI.ALO.AFU.AXC

hip roofs
RT.430 (A)
ALT **hip roof**
SN Use for roofs, usually four-sided, in which sloping sides, rather than gables, abut each other, therefore requiring a hip rafter at the angles of intersection.
UF roofs, hip
CN V.RT.AFU.AFU.AFU.BIQ.ARI.AFU.AFU.AFU.BOK.BCW

hip tile
MT.185
UF tile, hip
CN M.MT.AFU.AFU.AFU.AXC.ALO.ALO.ALO.AFU.ALO.AXC.AFU.ARI.ARI

hip tile, bonnet
USE **bonnet hip tile**

hip tile, cone
USE **bonnet hip tile**

hipped dormers
RT.481
ALT **hipped dormer**
SN Dormers with hip roofs. (FGAH)
UF dormers, hipped

CN V.RT.AFU.AFU.AFU.BIQ.ARI.ALO.
AFU.BUE.AXC.BCW

hipped gable roofs
USE **jerkinhead roofs**

hipped knees
TG.962
ALT **hipped knee**
SN Knees with carved ornament on cabriole chair legs.
UF hipped legs
knees, hipped
legs, hipped
CN V.TG.ALO.FIM.ALO.ALO.AFU.AFU

hipped legs
USE **hipped knees**

hipped roofs, pyramidal
USE **pyramidal roofs**

hippodromes
RK.1049 (A,L,B)
ALT **hippodrome**
SN Use for ancient Greek oblong enclosures curved at one end and built for horse and chariot racing; for similar ancient Roman structures, use **circuses (Roman arenas).**
CN V.RK.AFU.ALO.ALO.EWY.AXC.
BIQ.AFU.ARI

Hirado
FL.2021 (L)
CN F.FL.ALO.ARI.ALO.ALO.ALO.
ALO.ALO.BIQ

hiring
KG.153
SN Use for the activity of engaging the services of a person or persons for wages or other payment. For the ongoing activity of providing individuals with and paying them for work, use **employing.** For the concept of the degree or extent of the provision or availability of paid work to the population, use **employment.**
CN K.KG.AFU.AFU.BIQ.BUE.AXC

Hiroshige School
FL.2087
CN F.FL.ALO.ARI.ALO.ALO.ALO.
AXC.BZY.ARI

Hishigawa School
FL.2088
UF Hishikawa School
CN F.FL.ALO.ARI.ALO.ALO.ALO.
AXC.BZY.AXC

Hishikawa School
USE **Hishigawa School**

Hispanic
USE **Latin American**

Hispanic Americans
USE **Latinos**

Hispano-Flemish
FL.3160
CN F.FL.ALO.BCW.ALO.ALO.AFU.
BOK.AXC.AXC.AFU

Hispano-Islamic
USE **Hispano-Moresque**

Hispano-Moresque
FL.3161 (L,R)
UF Hispano-Islamic
CN F.FL.ALO.BCW.ALO.ALO.AFU.
BOK.AXC.AXC.ALO

Hissar
FL.1782
CN F.FL.ALO.ARI.AFU.ARI.ARI

historians
HG.265 (A,L)
ALT **historian**
CN H.HG.AFU.AXC.BCW.AFU.BOK.
AFU

historians of religion
HG.246 (L)
ALT **historian of religion**
UF religion historians
CN H.HG.AFU.AXC.AXC.BIQ.ALO.
ALO

historians of science
HG.357 (L)
ALT **historian of science**
UF science historians
CN H.HG.AFU.AXC.BIQ.ALO.ALO

historians, architectural
USE **architectural historians**

historians, art
USE **art historians**

historians, church
USE **church historians**

historians, literary
USE **literary historians**

historians, urban
USE **urban historians**

historic areas
USE **historic districts**

historic buildings
RK.509 (A,L,B)
ALT **historic building**
UF buildings, heritage
buildings, historic
heritage buildings
CN V.RK.AFU.ALO.ALO.BZY

historic districts
RG.270 (A,L)
ALT **historic district**
UF areas, historic
districts, historic
districts, historic preservation
districts, preservation
historic areas
historic preservation districts
preservation districts
CN V.RG.ALO.AFU.ALO.ARI

historic farms
RG.6 (L)
ALT **historic farm**
UF farms, historic
CN V.RG.AFU.AFU.AFU.AFU.ALO

historic gardens
RK.1420 (A,L)
ALT **historic garden**
UF gardens, historic
CN V.RK.ALO.AFU.AFU.ALO.AXC

historic homes
USE **historic houses**

historic house museums
RK.395
ALT **historic house museum**
UF museums, historic house
CN V.RK.AFU.ALO.ALO.BCW.AXC.
ARI.AXC.ARI

historic houses
RK.510 (L)
ALT **historic house**
UF historic homes
homes, historic
houses, historic
CN V.RK.AFU.ALO.ALO.BZY.AFU

historic listed buildings
USE **landmark buildings**

historic monuments
USE **historical monuments**

historic preservation
KG.131 (A,L)
SN Actions taken to promote the protection and continued use of the built environment for cultural, aesthetic, or historic reasons. For actions taken specifically to return an object, site, or structure to a state of historical correctness, use **restoration.** For actions taken generally to prevent further changes or deterioration in objects, sites, or structures, use **preservation.** For actions taken to return an already deteriorated structure to sound condition, use **rehabilitating.**
UF preservation, historic
CN K.KG.AFU.AFU.BCW.ARI.AFU

historic preservation districts
USE **historic districts**

historic preservationists
HG.732 (A)
ALT **historic preservationist**
UF preservationists, historic
CN H.HG.AFU.BCW.FCS.AFU

historic sites
RG.211 (A,L,R)
ALT **historic site**
UF sites, historic

CN V.RG.AFU.AFU.DZW.AXC

historic structure surveys
USE **architectural surveys**

historical atlases
VW.125 (L)
ALT **historical atlas**
UF atlases, historical
CN V.VW.AFU.AFU.AFU.FZU.AXC.AFU.AFU.AFU.AFU

historical bibliography
USE **analytical bibliography**

historical criticism
USE **historiography**

historical linguistics
KD.40 (L)
UF linguistics, historical
CN K.KD.AFU.AFU.AXC.AFU.ALO.AFU

historical maps
VW.193
ALT **historical map**
UF maps, historical
CN V.VW.AFU.AFU.AFU.FZU.AXC.AFU.ARI.AXC.BIQ

historical monuments
RK.906 (L,B,R)
ALT **historical monument**
UF historic monuments
monuments, historical
CN V.RK.AFU.ALO.ALO.DOI.ALO.ALO

historical museums
USE **history museums**

historical societies
HG.899
ALT **historical society**
UF societies, historical
CN H.HG.ALO.DUC.BOK

historical society museums
RK.396
ALT **historical society museum**
UF museums, historical society
CN V.RK.AFU.ALO.ALO.BCW.AXC.ARI.AXC.AXC

historical sociology
KD.189 (L)
SN Branch of sociology concerned with study of the origins, stages, and laws of social life and social institutions. (W)
UF sociology, historical
CN K.KD.AFU.ALO.ELK.AFU

historicism
BM.176 (A,L,R)
SN General theory that emphasizes the importance of history as a standard of value or as a determinant of events.(WCOL) Also refers specifically to the self-conscious revival of or reliance upon historical styles in art and architecture.
UF storicismo
CN B.BM.AFU.AFU.AXC.BCW

histories
VW.328
ALT **history**
SN Use to designate chronological records of events, as of the life or development of a people, country, or institution.
CN V.VW.AFU.AFU.ALO.CRG

histories, case
USE **case histories**

histories, family
USE **family histories**

historiographers
HG.266 (L)
ALT **historiographer**
SN Persons who engage in historiography; also, persons officially appointed to write a history or to record the continuing history of a country, group, or institution. (W)
CN H.HG.AFU.AXC.BCW.AFU.BOK.AFU.AFU

historiography
KD.151 (A,L,R)
SN The study and writing of history based on the critical examination of sources, the selection of particulars from authentic material, and the synthesis of particulars into a narrative that will stand the test of critical methods. (W)
UF criticism, historical
historical criticism
CN K.KD.AFU.ALO.CLM.ALO.AXC

history
KD.140 (A,L,B,R)
CN K.KD.AFU.ALO.CLM.AFU

history files
USE **organization files**

history museums
RK.392 (A,L)
ALT **history museum**
UF historical museums
museums, history
CN V.RK.AFU.ALO.ALO.BCW.AXC.ARI.AXC

history of architecture
USE **architectural history**

history of art
USE **art history**

history of cities
USE **urban history**

history of religion
KD.85 (L)
UF religion, history of
CN K.KD.AFU.AFU.BUE.ALO.BCW

history, architectural
USE **architectural history**

history, art
USE **art history**

history, church
USE **church history**

history, industrial
USE **industrial history**

history, intellectual
USE **intellectual history**

history, literary
USE **literary history**

history, local
USE **local history**

history, oral
USE **oral history**

history, social
USE **social history**

history, urban
USE **urban history**

Hitchcock chairs
TG.72
ALT **Hitchcock chair**
UF chairs, Hitchcock
CN V.TG.AFU.AFU.ALO.AFU.AFU.AFU.HIK

hitches
TB.1126 (L)
ALT **hitch**
SN Connections between an implement and a detachable source of motive power, as a tractor or a crane. (W)
CN V.TB.ALO.CRG

hitching posts
RM.447 (N,B,R)
ALT **hitching post**
SN Fixed posts to which horses can be fastened to prevent straying. (W)
UF posts, hitching
posts, tethering
tethering posts
CN V.RM.ALO.AFU.BUE

Hittite
FL.2854
CN F.FL.ALO.AXC.ARI.AFU.AFU.ARI

Hittite Empire
FL.2857
UF Hittite New Kingdom
CN F.FL.ALO.AXC.ARI.AFU.AFU.ARI.ARI

Hittite Kingdom, Middle
USE **Middle Hittite Kingdom**

Hittite Kingdom, Old
USE **Old Hittite Kingdom**

Hittite New Kingdom
USE **Hittite Empire**

Hittite Old Kingdom
USE **Old Hittite Kingdom**

Hoa Lai
FL.2444
CN F.FL.ALO.ARI.BCW.BUE.ALO.ALO.AFU.BCW

Hoabinhian
FL.1839
CN F.FL.ALO.ARI.ALO.AFU.AFU.AFU.ALO.ALO

hoardings
RM.437 (B,R)
ALT **hoarding**
SN Use for temporary board fences erected around construction sites.
CN V.RM.ALO.AFU.BCW.ARI

hobby rooms
USE **recreation rooms**

hobs
RT.1159
ALT **hob**
SN Flat projecting shelves at the side of fireplaces where pots or pans may be placed to keep warm. (DAC)
CN V.RT.AFU.BOK.ALO.ALO.BIQ

hockey fields
RK.1481 (B)
ALT **hockey field**
UF field hockey fields
fields, field hockey
fields, hockey
CN V.RK.ALO.ALO.BCW.AFU.AXC

hockey rinks
USE **ice hockey rinks**

hockey rinks, ice
USE **ice hockey rinks**

hods
TB.609 (N)
ALT **hod**
SN Wood or metal containers, usually V-shaped with a long handle and having one end open, used in masonry work to carry plaster or lime putty to the mortarboard. (DAC)
CN V.TB.AFU.BCW.BCW.ALO.ERE

hog, gum
USE **gum karaya**

hogans
RK.314 (N,B)
ALT **hogan**
CN V.RK.AFU.ALO.ALO.AXC.ALO.BCW.ALO

Hogarth chairs
USE **bended-back chairs**

Hogarth's line
BM.70
UF beauty, line of
line of beauty
line, Hogarth's
CN B.BM.AFU.AFU.ARI.AFU.CLM.ALO

hoghouses
USE **pig houses**

hognut
USE **mockernut hickory**

Hohokam
FL.934 (L)
CN F.FL.ALO.ALO.ALO.AFU.ALO.ARI.BIQ.AXC

hoisting
USE **lifting**

hoisting machinery
TB.73 (L)
UF machinery, hoisting
CN V.TB.AFU.ARI.AFU.BCW.BCW

hoists
TB.78 (N,B)
ALT **hoist**
SN Any mechanical devices for lifting loads. (MEANS)
CN V.TB.AFU.ARI.AFU.BCW.BCW.ALO

hoists, mine
USE **gins**

hoists, ratchet
USE **come-alongs**

hoistways
RT.1330
ALT **hoistway**
SN Use for vertical passages through which dumbwaiters, lifts, or similar contrivances move from level to level.
UF shaftways
CN V.RT.ALO.ALO.ALO.ARI.ALO

Hokusai School
FL.2089 (L)
UF Katsushika School
CN F.FL.ALO.ARI.ALO.ALO.ALO.AXC.BZY.BCW

Holbein
FL.3525
CN F.FL.ALO.BIQ.AFU.FOG.ARI.AFU

hold-down bolts
USE **anchor bolts**

holdbacks, drapery
USE **drapery holdbacks**

holdbacks, shutter
USE **shutter dogs**

holders, card
USE **card frames**

holders, chalk
USE **portcrayons**

holders, crayon
USE **portcrayons**

holders, door
USE **door holders**

holders, glass
USE **tumbler holders**

holders, Koran
USE **Koran stands**

holders, mechanical pencil
USE **pencil holders**

holders, mud
USE **hawks**

holders, overhead door
USE **overhead door holders**

holders, paper
USE **toilet paper holders**

holders, pencil
USE **pencil holders**

holders, sash
USE **window locks**

holders, stair carpet
USE **stair carpet holders**

holders, toilet paper
USE **toilet paper holders**

holders, toothbrush
USE **toothbrush holders**

holders, towel
USE **towel bars**

holders, tumbler
USE **tumbler holders**

holdfasts
TB.1065 (N)
ALT **holdfast**
SN Devices for securing anything in its place, as a hook, bolt, or spike. (DAC)
CN V.TB.AFU.BCW.CFS.ALO.ALO.BUE

holding blocks
TB.655
ALT **holding block**
SN Wood blocks used to hold metal-working stamps.
UF blocks, holding
CN V.TB.AFU.BCW.BIQ.AFU.ALO.ARI.ARI

hole saws
USE **crown saws**

holes, Judas
USE **peepholes**

holes, shot
USE **loopholes**

holiday guides
USE **travel guidebooks**

holiday houses
USE **vacation houses**

holiday resorts
USE **resorts**

holidays
KM.71 (L,R)
CN K.KM.AFU.CFS

holidays, legal
USE **legal holidays**

hollow
DC.143
SN Having an empty space or cavity within; not filled in with matter. (W)
CN D.DC.AFU.BIQ.AFU

hollow-bit tongs
TB.757 (N)
SN Tongs with two rounded jaws. (RICHAR)
UF tongs, hollow-bit
tongs, V-lip
V-lip tongs
CN V.TB.AFU.BCW.BIQ.AXC.ALO.AXC.BOK

hollow block
MT.2211 (B)
UF block, hollow
CN M.MT.AFU.ALO.ALO.AFU

hollow brick
MT.88 (L)
UF brick, hollow
CN M.MT.AFU.AFU.AFU.AXC.ALO.AFU.AFU.ALO.ALO

hollow-core doors
RT.855
ALT **hollow-core door**
SN Flush doors with a space between the facings that is occupied by a structure of air- or insulation-filled cells, made of wood, plastic, or other suitable material. (PUTNAM)
UF doors, hollow-core
CN V.RT.AFU.ARI.AFU.AFU.AFU.ALO.ARI.AFU.AFU.BOK.ALO.AFU

hollow corners
TG.869
ALT **hollow corner**
UF corners, hollow
CN V.TG.ALO.CRG.ALO

hollow ends
TG.894
ALT **hollow end**
UF ends, hollow
CN V.TG.ALO.DUC.ALO

hollow-mandrel stakes
TB.687 (N)
ALT **hollow-mandrel stake**
SN Stakes having long rounded mandrels without a taper; used for sheet metal work, particularly hollow work.
UF stakes, hollow-mandrel
CN V.TB.AFU.BCW.BIQ.AFU.ALO.CXA.BCW

hollow masonry walls
USE **cavity walls**

hollow moldings
USE **cavetto moldings**

hollow newel stairs
RT.1077
ALT **hollow newel stair**
SN Spiral stairs built around a hollow central cylinder, sometimes containing another stair.
UF hollow newels
newels, hollow
stairs, hollow newel
CN V.RT.AFU.BIQ.AXC.AFU.AFU.BIQ.ALO

hollow newels
USE **hollow newel stairs**

hollow planes
TB.957 (N)
ALT **hollow plane**
SN Planes with a concave sole for cutting rounded moldings; usually paired with round planes in a set. (MERCER)
UF planes, hollow
CN V.TB.AFU.BCW.CFS.ALO.AFU.DUC.AXC.AFU.BIQ

hollow shaves
USE **hollowing drawknives**

hollow tile
USE **structural clay tile**

hollow volumes
USE **negative space**

hollow walls
USE **cavity walls**

hollowed arms
TG.811
ALT **hollowed arm**
UF arms, hollowed
CN V.TG.ALO.ALO.AFU.AFU.AFU

hollowed seats
TG.972
ALT **hollowed seat**
SN 18th-century term for seats in which the middle and front are lower than the sides.
UF concave seats
dipped seats
dropped seats
seats, concave
seats, dipped
seats, dropped
seats, hollowed
CN V.TG.ALO.GLI.AFU.ALO

hollowing adzes
TB.815 (N)
ALT **hollowing adz**
SN Adzes with a blade gouge-shaped in cross section and designed for hollowing. (SALAM)
UF adzes, dished
adzes, gouge
adzes, hollowing
adzes, saucer
dished adzes
gouge adzes
saucer adzes
CN V.TB.AFU.BCW.CFS.ALO.AFU.AFU.BIQ

hollowing drawknives
TB.905 (N)
ALT **hollowing drawknife**
SN Small drawknives used to make hollows in wood.
UF belly knives
cooper's hollowing drawknives
drawknives, hollowing
drawknives, hollowing cooper's
hollow shaves
hollowing drawknives, cooper's
knives, belly
shaves, hollow
CN V.TB.AFU.BCW.CFS.ALO.AFU.DOI.ARI.BCW

hollowing drawknives, cooper's
USE **hollowing drawknives**

hollows
RD.211
ALT **hollow**
SN Small valleys. (W)
CN V.RD.ARI.AFU.AXC.AFU.ALO.ALO.AFU.AFU

holly
MT.1180 (L,R)
UF Ilex
CN M.MT.AFU.AFU.ALO.BIQ.DCU.AFU.AFU.AFU.ERE

holly green
USE **green earth**

hollywood beds
TG.381
ALT **hollywood bed**
SN Beds consisting of metal frames, box springs, mattresses, and headboards, but lacking footboards; of a type made in America about 1945. (RHDEL2)
UF beds, hollywood
CN V.TG.AFU.AFU.ARI.AFU.ALO.AFU.AFU

Holo
FL.463
CN F.FL.ALO.AFU.AXC.ALO.ALO.ARI.ARI

holograms
VJ.35 (R)
ALT **hologram**
UF holographs (photographs)
CN V.VJ.AFU.AFU.ARI.ALO

holograms, reflection
USE **reflection holograms**

holograms, transmission
USE **transmission holograms**

holographs
VW.8
ALT **holograph**
SN Use for documents wholly written in the hand of the author. (LG)
CN V.VW.AFU.AFU.AFU.ARI.AFU

holographs (photographs)
USE **holograms**

holography
KT.339 (L,R)
SN A method of forming three-dimensional appearing images by laser light. When properly viewed, the interference pattern recreates the pattern of light originally reflected by the subject. Allows multiple perspectives such that images in the background are obscured and revealed by those in the foreground as the angle of view changes.
CN K.KT.AFU.ALO.DUC.DIO.ALO.CLM.AFU

Holoholo
FL.491
UF Baholoholo
CN F.FL.ALO.AFU.AXC.ALO.ALO.BCW.AFU

holy arks
USE **arks**

holy lofts
USE **rood lofts**

holy places
USE **shrines**

holy water stoups
USE **stoups**

holy wells
RK.1088 (L)
ALT **holy well**
UF wells, holy
CN V.RK.AFU.ALO.ALO.FCS.ALO

holystone
MT.705
SN A block of close-grained sandstone usually used for rubbing down furniture and concrete work. (MH)
CN M.MT.AFU.AFU.AFU.DCU.AFU.ALO.AFU.ARI.AFU.AFU.ALO

home computers
USE **microcomputers**

home economics
KD.155 (L,B,R)
SN Study of home management, including such skills as budgeting, child care, nutrition, cooking, and sewing. (ERIC)
UF domestic science
science, domestic
CN K.KD.AFU.ALO.CRG

home ownership
BM.473 (A,L)
UF ownership, home
CN B.BM.BCW.CXA.ALO.ALO.AFU.AFU

homeless persons
HG.791 (A,L,B)
ALT **homeless person**
CN H.HG.AFU.BOK.BIQ

homelessness
BM.1109 (A,L)
CN B.BM.CRG.BCW.AXC

homemakers
USE **housewives**

homemakers, men
USE **househusbands**

homes
USE **dwellings**

homes (institutions)
USE **asylums**

homes for the aged
USE **old age homes**

homes for the elderly
USE **housing for the elderly**

homes, animal
USE **animal shelters**

homes, architects'
USE **architects' houses**

homes, boarding
USE **rest homes**

homes, children's
USE **orphanages**

homes, convalescent
USE **convalescent hospitals**

homes, country
USE **country houses**

homes, detention
USE **detention centers**

homes, funeral
USE **funeral homes**

homes, group
USE **group homes**

homes, group foster
USE **group homes**

homes, historic
USE **historic houses**

homes, juvenile
USE **reformatories**

homes, juvenile detention
USE **detention centers**

homes, mobile
USE **mobile homes**

homes, motor
USE **motor homes**

homes, nursing
USE **nursing homes**

homes, old age
USE **old age homes**

homes, old peoples
USE **old age homes**

homes, remand
USE **reformatories**

homes, rest
USE **rest homes**

homes, retirement
USE **retirement homes**

homes, second
USE **second homes**

homes, sheltered care
USE **rest homes**

homes, stately
USE **mansions**

homes, suburban
USE **suburban houses**

homes, summer
USE **summer houses**

homes, vacation
USE **vacation houses**

homesites
RG.208 (L)
ALT **homesite**
CN V.RG.AFU.AFU.DZW.ALO.AFU

homesteads
RG.57
ALT **homestead**
SN Designates the dwelling, land, and outbuildings, if any, where a family lives.
CN V.RG.AFU.AFU.BOK.AFU.ALO

homilies
USE **sermons**

homosexuality
BM.604 (L,R)
SN Sexuality characterized by romantic love or sexual desire toward members of one's own sex.
CN B.BM.BUE.CXA.ARI

Honduran rosewood
USE **cocobolo**

Honduras mahogany
USE **South American mahogany**

hones
USE **whetstones**

honey locust
MT.1203 (L)
UF Gleditsia triacanthos
locust, honey
CN M.MT.AFU.AFU.ALO.BIQ.DCU.AFU.AFU.AFU.HCQ.AXC

honeycomb materials
MT.2221
UF materials, honeycomb
CN M.MT.AFU.ALO.BOK.AFU

honeycomb work
USE **muqarnas**

honeysuckle motifs
USE **anthemions**

Hongwe
FL.414
UF Hungwe
Mahoungoue
CN F.FL.ALO.AFU.AXC.ALO.AFU.AXC.ALO

Hongwu
FL.1898
UF Hung-wu
CN F.FL.ALO.ARI.ALO.AFU.AFU.ALO.DIO.AFU

Hongxian
FL.1921
UF Hung-hsien
CN F.FL.ALO.ARI.ALO.AFU.AFU.ARI.AFU

Hongzhi
FL.1902
UF Hung-chih
CN F.FL.ALO.ARI.ALO.AFU.AFU.ALO.DIO.BCW

honing
KT.165 (L)
ALT **honed**
SN Sharpening edged tools with or as if with a whetstone. (W)
CN K.KT.AFU.ALO.DOI.ERE.AFU

honorific arches
USE **memorial arches**

hood moldings
RT.803
ALT **hood molding**
SN Moldings having the form of a miniature hood; especially the moldings which, in Medieval architecture, are often carried in projection above the opening of a door or window, and which commonly follow and are parallel to the lines of the opening. (RS)
UF dripstones
head moldings
moldings, head
moldings, hood
CN V.RT.AFU.ALO.AFU.BOK.AFU.ALO.BZY

hooded settles
TG.285
ALT **hooded settle**
SN Settles with boards across the tops of the side boards. (FORMAN)
UF dossiers (benches)
settles, hooded
CN V.TG.AFU.AFU.ALO.ALO.AFU.AFU.BIQ.ALO

hooded tops
USE **bonnet tops**

hoods (furniture components)
TG.939
ALT **hood (furniture component)**
SN Shaped tops on cabinet pieces.
UF domes (furniture components)
CN V.TG.ALO.EWY

hoods (roofs)
RT.417
ALT **hood (roof)**
SN Includes small projecting covers, usually of wood or metal, over doors and windows; also covers serving to carry off the fumes from stoves or laboratory benches.
CN V.RT.AFU.AFU.AFU.BIQ.ARI.AFU.AFU.AFU.AXC

hoods, chimney
USE **chimney hoods**

hoods, door
USE **doorheads**

hoods, lens
USE **lens hoods**

hoof feet
TG.925
ALT **hoof foot**
SN Terminal for chair legs in the form of a cloven hoof; first used by ancient Egyptians, and popular in 17th- and 18th-century Europe. (DDA)
UF cloven feet
cloven-hoof feet
deer-hoof feet
feet, cloven
feet, deer-hoof
feet, hoof
pieds de biche
CN V.TG.ALO.DZW.AFU.DCU.BCW

hook-and-butt joints
TF.588
ALT **hook-and-butt joint**
SN Scarf joints between timbers with their ends fashioned to lock together positively and resist tension. (MEANS)
UF joints, hook-and-butt
CN V.TF.ALO.AFU.DCU

hook-and-eye fasteners
TF.376
ALT **hook-and-eye fastener**
UF fasteners, hook-and-eye
CN V.TF.AFU.AFU.AFU.ALO.AFU.BUE

hook ladders
TB.482
ALT **hook ladder**
SN Firemen's scaling ladders consisting of a pole with crossbars for rungs and a hook at one end. (W)
UF ladders, hook
ladders, pompier
pompier ladders
CN V.TB.AFU.ARI.ERE.ALO.AXC

hook nails
TF.395
ALT **hook nail**
UF nails, hook
CN V.TF.AFU.AFU.AFU.ALO.AFU.CFS.AFU.BUE

hook-over hangers
TF.367
ALT **hook-over hanger**
UF hangers, hook-over
CN V.TF.AFU.AFU.AFU.ALO.AFU.BOK.ARI.ARI.ARI.AFU

hookaroons
USE **pickaroons**

Hooke's modulus
USE **modulus of elasticity**

hooked reamers
TB.984
ALT **hooked reamer**
SN Curved, tapered cone-shaped blades with a handle and a hook on the tapered end; used to enlarge the hub-holes of wheels. (SLOANE)
UF reamers, hooked
CN V.TB.AFU.BCW.CFS.ALO.AFU.ELK.AFU

Hooker's green
MT.1666
UF green, Hooker's
CN M.MT.AFU.AFU.ARI.AFU.AFU.ALO.ALO.AXC.BCW.ARI

hooking
KT.544 (L)
ALT **hooked**
SN The process of making a rug, or similar object, by drawing loops of thread, yarn, or cloth into a pattern. (W)
CN K.KT.AFU.ALO.ELK.DUC.AFU.ALO

hooks
TB.217 (L,N)
ALT **hook**
CN V.TB.AFU.ARI.CFS.ALO

hooks (hardware)
TF.150 (L,N)
ALT **hook (hardware)**
SN Any bent or curved devices used for holding, pulling, catching, or attaching. (MEANS)
CN V.TF.AFU.AFU.AFU.AFU.CXA

hooks, bathroom
USE **bathroom hooks**

hooks, bench
USE **bench hooks**

hooks, cabin
USE **cabin hooks**

hooks, cabin door
USE **cabin door hooks**

hooks, cant
USE **cant hooks**

hooks, ceiling
USE **ceiling hooks**

hooks, chimney
USE chimney hooks

hooks, ladder
USE **ladder hooks**

hooks, side
USE **bench hooks**

hooks, steps and
USE **stepped frets**

hooks, utility
USE **utility hooks**

hooks, wardrobe
USE **wardrobe hooks**

hoop-back Windsor chairs
USE **sack-back Windsor chairs**

hoop fastener nails
TF.412
ALT **hoop fastener nail**
UF fastener nails, hoop
nails, hoop fastener
CN V.TF.AFU.AFU.AFU.ALO.AFU.CFS.AFU.DCU.CFS

hoop-notching knives
TB.908 (N)
ALT **hoop-notching knife**
SN Knives used to cut V-shaped notches in both ends of a split hazel rod so that the notches interlock with one another to form a complete wooden hoop. (SALAM)
UF cooper's whittles
knives, hoop-notching
whittles, cooper's
CN V.TB.AFU.BCW.CFS.ALO.AFU.DOI.AXC

hoop tongs
TB.758 (N)
SN Tongs whose jaws are bent at a right angle.
UF tongs, hoop
CN V.TB.AFU.BCW.BIQ.AXC.ALO.AXC.BUE

hooped stretchers
USE **saltire stretchers**

Hoosier cabinets
TG.434
ALT **Hoosier cabinet**
SN Popular term for tall kitchen cabinets mass-produced during the early 20th century; usually oak, with such features as an enameled work surface, storage bins, and a flour sifter. (RHDEL2)
UF cabinets, Hoosier
CN V.TG.AFU.AFU.AXC.ALO.ARI.ALO.BZY.AFU

hop barns
RK.61 (A)
ALT **hop barn**
SN Structures built for the drying, baling, and storing of hops.
UF barns, hop
hop houses
hop sheds
houses, hop
sheds, hop
CN V.RK.AFU.ALO.ALO.AFU.AFU.BIQ

hop hornbeam
MT.1183
UF hornbeam, hop
Ostrya
CN M.MT.AFU.AFU.ALO.BIQ.DCU.AFU.AFU.AFU.EWY.ALO

hop hornbeam, American
USE **American hop hornbeam**

hop hornbeam, European
USE **European hop hornbeam**

hop houses
USE **hop barns**

hop sheds
USE **hop barns**

hope chests
USE **dower chests**

Hopea
USE **merawan**

Hopewell
FL.880 (L)
UF Hopewellian
CN F.FL.ALO.ALO.ALO.AFU.ALO.ALO.BCW.ARI

Hopewell, Baehr
USE **Baehr Hopewell**

Hopewell, Trempealeau
USE **Trempealeau**

Hopewellian
USE **Hopewell**

Hopewellian, Havana
USE **Havana Hopewellian**

Hopi
FL.1481 (L,R)
UF Moki
Tusayan
CN F.FL.ALO.ALO.ARI.AFU.CFS.CRG.ALO.AFU

hopper joints
TF.580
ALT **hopper joint**
UF joints, hopper
CN V.TF.ALO.AFU.BOK.AFU

hopper lights
USE **hopper windows**

hopper windows
RT.942
ALT **hopper window**
SN Windows in which each sash opens inward on hinges placed at the bottom of each sash. (PUTNAM)
UF hopper lights
lights, hopper
windows, hopper
CN V.RT.AFU.ARI.AFU.AFU.BOK.AFU.AFU.EWY.ALO.ALO.ALO

hoppers
RK.1209 (B)
ALT **hopper**
SN Top-loading, bottom-discharging funnels or storage bins, as for crushed stone, sand, or food stuffs. (MEANS)
CN V.RK.AFU.ALO.ALO.GFO.ARI

hopsitals, veterans'
USE **veterans' hospitals**

horizon line
BM.154
SN Use with reference to perspective systems for the line in which the horizontal plane containing the eye meets the picture plane and for the line containing the vanishing points of horizontal planes in the picture.
UF line, horizon
CN B.BM.AFU.AFU.ARI.BOK.CFS.ALO

horizontal duplexes
USE **double houses**

horizontality
BM.67
ALT **horizontal**
SN Use for parallel relationships to a horizontal axis in designs for graphic works, objects, and structures.
CN B.BM.AFU.AFU.ARI.AFU.CFS

horn
MT.940 (L,R)
CN M.MT.AFU.AFU.ALO.AFU.DCU

hornbeam
MT.1181
CN M.MT.AFU.AFU.ALO.BIQ.DCU.AFU.AFU.AFU.EWY

hornbeam, American hop
USE **American hop hornbeam**

hornbeam, common
USE **European hornbeam**

hornbeam, European
USE **European hornbeam**

hornbeam, European hop
USE **European hop hornbeam**

hornbeam, hop
USE **hop hornbeam**

hornbooks
VW.358 (L)
ALT **hornbook**
SN Children's primers consisting typically of a sheet of parchment or layer of paper mounted on a thin wooden board and protected by a sheet of transparent horn and having on it the alphabet and other rudiments such as the digits and often the Lord's Prayer. (W)
UF battledores
CN V.VW.AFU.AFU.ALO.CXA.BOK.AFU

horned rabbets
TB.924
ALT **horned rabbet**
SN Rabbet planes with a horn-shaped front handle.
UF rabbets, horned
CN V.TB.AFU.BCW.CFS.ALO.AFU.DUC.ALO.BUE.ALO

hornfels
MT.741
SN Fine-grain silicate rock produced by contact metamorphism. (W)
CN M.MT.AFU.AFU.AFU.DCU.AFU.ARI.ALO

hornworkers
HG.480
ALT **hornworker**
CN H.HG.AFU.AXC.BUE.ARI.BCW

hornworks
RT.1206
ALT **hornwork**
SN In military architecture, outworks of two demi-bastions connected by a curtain and joined to the main work by two parallel wings. (PDARC)
CN V.RT.AFU.BUE.AFU.BZY.BIQ

horrea
RK.1230
ALT **horreum**
SN Designates ancient Roman storage buildings or warehouses, commonly used as granaries or for wine storage.
CN V.RK.AFU.ALO.ALO.GFO.BZY.ALO

Horse and Camel sub-period
FL.74
CN F.FL.ALO.AFU.AFU.ARI.AXC.ARI

horse barns
RK.50
ALT **horse barn**
SN Distinguished from **stables** by their barnlike appearance and their use as housing primarily for farm stock and feed.
UF barns, horse
CN V.RK.AFU.ALO.ALO.AFU.AFU.AFU.ALO.ALO

horse breeders
HG.368 (L)
ALT **horse breeder**
UF breeders, horse
CN H.HG.AFU.AXC.BIQ.ALO.AXC.AFU.AXC.AFU

horse chestnut
MT.1135 (L)
UF Aesculus hippocastanum
chestnut, common horse
chestnut, horse
common horse chestnut
horse chestnut, common
CN M.MT.AFU.AFU.ALO.BIQ.DCU.AFU.AFU.AFU.CLM.AXC

horse chestnut, American
USE **buckeye**

horse chestnut, common
USE **horse chestnut**

horse exercising machines
USE **chamber horses**

horse fire screens
USE **cheval fire screens**

horse nails
USE **horseshoe nails**

Horse phase
FL.71
UF Caballine phase
CN F.FL.ALO.AFU.AFU.ARI.AXC

horse racetracks
RG.180 (L,B,R)
ALT **horse racetrack**
UF horse tracks
racetracks, horse
CN V.RG.AFU.AFU.DOI.CFS.ALO.ARI

horse tracks
USE **horse racetracks**

horseback riding clubs
USE **riding clubs**

horsehair
MT.933 (L)
SN From the manes and tails of horses, used chiefly as a brush fiber and for making haircloth. (MH)
CN M.MT.AFU.AFU.ALO.AFU.CXA.AFU.AFU.ARI

Horseman sub-period
FL.73
CN F.FL.ALO.AFU.AFU.ARI.AXC.ALO

horses
TB.472
ALT **horse**
SN Framework functioning as a temporary support. (MEANS)
UF trestles (equipment)
CN V.TB.AFU.ARI.ERE.AFU

horses (stair components)
USE **carriage pieces**
strings

horses, chamber
USE **chamber horses**

horses, finishing
USE **sawhorses**

horses, froe
USE **froe horses**

horses, frow
USE **froe horses**

horses, saw
USE **sawhorses**

horses, saw filing
USE **saw-sharpening horses**

horses, saw-sharpening
USE **saw-sharpening horses**

horses, towel
USE **towel racks**

horseshoe arches
RT.227
ALT **horseshoe arch**
SN Arches in which the curves are carried below the springing line so that the opening at the bottom of the arch is less than its greatest span. (RS)
UF Arabic arches
arches, Arabic
arches, Byzantine
arches, crescent
arches, horseshoe
arches, Moorish
Byzantine arches
crescent arches
Moorish arches
CN V.RT.AFU.AFU.AFU.BCW.AFU.AFU.AFU.BZY

horseshoe dining tables
TG.726
ALT **horseshoe dining table**
UF dining tables, horseshoe
tables, horseshoe dining
CN V.TG.AFU.AFU.BIQ.BOK.ALO.BZY.ALO

horseshoe nails
TF.439 (N)
ALT **horseshoe nail**
UF horse nails
nails, horseshoe
CN V.TF.AFU.AFU.AFU.ALO.AFU.CFS.ALO.CLM

horseshoe nails, frost
USE **frost horseshoe nails**

horseshoe seats
USE **compass seats**

horseshoe tables
TG.681
ALT **horseshoe table**
UF hunt tables
tables, horseshoe
tables, hunt
CN V.TG.AFU.AFU.BIQ.BOK.AFU.BOK

horticultural buildings
RK.62 (B)
ALT **horticultural building**
UF buildings, horticultural
facilities, horticultural
horticultural facilities
CN V.RK.AFU.ALO.ALO.AFU.AFU.BOK

horticultural facilities
USE **horticultural buildings**

horticultural societies
HG.900 (L)
ALT **horticultural society**
UF botanical societies
societies, botanical
societies, horticultural
CN H.HG.ALO.DUC.BUE

horticulture
KD.197 (L,B,R)
SN Intensive and extensive cultivation of garden plants including fruits, vegetables, flower crops, and landscape and nursery crops. (PG)
CN K.KD.AFU.ARI.ALO.AFU

horticulture, ornamental
USE **ornamental horticulture**

horticulturists
HG.364 (L)
ALT **horticulturist**
CN H.HG.AFU.AXC.BIQ.ALO.AXC.AFU.ARI

hoses
TB.380 (L)
ALT **hose**
CN V.TB.AFU.ARI.DCU.ALO.AFU

hoses, fire
USE **firehoses**

hospices
RK.947 (A,R)
ALT **hospice**
SN Use for lodging places providing a variety of amenities for travelers and often maintained by a religious order.
UF hospitia
CN V.RK.AFU.ALO.ALO.ELK.ARI

hospices (terminal care)
USE **terminal care facilities**

hospital beds
TG.362 (L,B)
ALT **hospital bed**
SN Beds with frames in three sections equipped with mechanical spring parts that permit raising the head, foot, or middle as required. (W)
UF beds, hospital
infirmary beds
CN V.TG.AFU.AFU.ARI.AFU.AFU.CFS

hospital latches
TF.188
ALT **hospital latch**
UF latches, hospital
CN V.TF.AFU.AFU.AFU.AFU.DIO.BCW.ALO.BCW

hospital records
VW.1052 (L)
ALT **hospital record**
UF records, hospital
CN V.VW.AFU.ARI.ALO.BIQ

hospital-training schools
USE **nursing schools**

hospital units
USE **hospital wards**

hospital wards
RM.291 (A,B)
ALT **hospital ward**
UF hospital units
wards, hospital
CN V.RM.AFU.DIO.AXC.AFU.ARI

hospitals
RK.757 (A,L,N,B,R)
ALT **hospital**
UF general hospitals
hospitals, general
polyclinics
spitals
CN V.RK.AFU.ALO.ALO.CXA.ALO.AFU.BCW

hospitals, animal
USE **veterinary hospitals**

hospitals, aural
USE **aural hospitals**

hospitals, children's
USE **children's hospitals**

hospitals, convalescent
USE **convalescent hospitals**

hospitals, cottage
USE **cottage hospitals**

hospitals, eye
USE **eye hospitals**

hospitals, foundling
USE **orphanages**

hospitals, general
USE **hospitals**

hospitals, leprosy
USE **leprosariums**

hospitals, maternity
USE **maternity hospitals**

hospitals, mental
USE **psychiatric hospitals**

hospitals, military
USE **military hospitals**

hospitals, mobile
USE **mobile hospitals**

hospitals, opthalmic
USE **eye hospitals**

hospitals, pediatric
USE **children's hospitals**

hospitals, psychiatric
USE **psychiatric hospitals**

hospitals, teaching
USE **teaching hospitals**

hospitals, VA
USE **veterans' hospitals**

hospitals, veterinary
USE **veterinary hospitals**

hospitia
USE **hospices**

hostages
HG.795 (L,R)
ALT **hostage**
SN Persons given or kept as a pledge pending the fulfillment of an agreement, demand, or treaty. (W)
CN H.HG.AFU.BOK.BZY.AFU

hostels
RK.950 (A,L,B)
ALT **hostel**
CN V.RK.AFU.ALO.ALO.ELK.AXC

hostels, children's
USE **orphanages**
youth hostels

hostels, youth
USE **youth hostels**

hot air heating
USE **warm air heating**

hot chisels
TB.706 (N)
ALT **hot chisel**
SN Long chisels, ground to a cutting edge of 30 degrees, which are not hardened or tempered and can be used in work on heated metal.
UF chisels, hot
CN V.TB.AFU.BCW.BIQ.ARI.ALO.AFU.ALO

hot-dip galvanizing
KT.819
SN The application of a protective coating to ferrous metal by dipping it in a bath of molten zinc. (DAC)
UF galvanizing, hot-dip
CN K.KT.AFU.ALO.HOE.BCW.ALO.ALO.ALO.ALO

hot-rolling
KT.849
ALT **hot-rolled**
CN K.KT.AFU.ALO.HOE.BCW.ALO.BIQ.AXC

hot water boilers
RT.1412
ALT **hot water boiler**
SN Any heating unit in a hot water heating system in which water is heated before being circulated through

pipes to radiators or baseboards. (MEANS)
UF boilers, hot water
CN V.RT.ALO.BCW.AFU.ALO.AFU.ALO.AFU

hot water heating
RT.1393 (L)
UF heating, hot water
CN V.RT.ALO.BCW.AFU.AFU.ARI.ALO

hot-working
USE **forging**

hotbeds
USE **forcing houses**

hotel locks
TF.207
ALT **hotel lock**
UF locks, hotel
CN V.TF.AFU.AFU.AFU.AFU.DIO.BIQ.AFU.CLM.ALO

hotel managers
USE **hotelkeepers**

hotel registers
VW.278
ALT **hotel register**
UF motel registers
registers, hotel
registers, motel
CN V.VW.AFU.AFU.AFU.FZU.BCW.ALO.ARI.AFU

hoteliers
USE **hotelkeepers**

hotelkeepers
HG.418 (L)
ALT **hotelkeeper**
SN Proprietors or managers of hotels. (W)
UF hotel managers
hoteliers
hotelmen
managers, hotel
CN H.HG.AFU.AXC.BOK.DOI

hotelmen
USE **hotelkeepers**

hôtels
RK.302
ALT **hôtel**
SN Use for French town houses, especially of the 18th century, generally more elegant, ornate, and larger than other houses.
CN V.RK.AFU.ALO.ALO.AXC.ALO.AXC.AFU.ARI.AFU

hotels
RK.952 (A,L,N,B,R)
ALT **hotel**
CN V.RK.AFU.ALO.ALO.ELK.BCW

hôtels de ville
RK.996
ALT **hôtel de ville**
UF mairies
CN V.RK.AFU.ALO.ALO.ERE.ALO.AFU.ARI

hotels, apartment
USE **apartment hotels**

hotels, floating
USE **floating hotels**

hotels, motor
USE **motels**

hotels, railway
USE **railway hotels**

hotels, residential
USE **apartment hotels**

hothouses
USE **greenhouses**

Hottentots
USE **KhoiKhoi**

hours, books of
USE **books of hours**

house agents
USE **real estate agents**

house inscriptions
USE **house marks**

house journals
USE **house organs**

house magazines
USE **house organs**

house marks
VW.732 (L)
ALT **house mark**
UF house inscriptions
inscriptions, house
marks, house
CN V.VW.AFU.ALO.ALO.AFU.AXC.ARI.BIQ

House of Commons bills
VW.1040
ALT **House of Commons bill**
UF bills, House of Commons
CN V.VW.AFU.ARI.ALO.BCW.AFU.ARI.ALO.ALO.AFU.AFU

House of Commons papers
VW.1039
ALT **House of Commons paper**
UF papers, House of Commons
CN V.VW.AFU.ARI.ALO.BCW.AFU.ARI.ALO.ALO.AFU

House of Lords bills
VW.1042
ALT **House of Lords bill**
UF bills, House of Lords
CN V.VW.AFU.ARI.ALO.BCW.AFU.ARI.ALO.ALO.ALO.AFU

House of Lords papers
VW.1041
ALT **House of Lords paper**
UF papers, House of Lords
CN V.VW.AFU.ARI.ALO.BCW.AFU.ARI.ALO.ALO.ALO

House of Representatives records
VW.1036 (L)
ALT **House of Representatives record**
UF records, House of Representatives
CN V.VW.AFU.ARI.ALO.BCW.AFU.ARI.ALO.AFU.ALO

House of Representatives, Members of the
USE **Members of the House of Representatives**

house organs
VW.621 (L)
ALT **house organ**
SN Periodicals produced by an organization, especially a commercial or industrial enterprise, and intended for primarily internal dissemination, or for distribution to customers.
UF house journals
house magazines
journals, house
magazines, house
organs, house
plant publications
publications, plant
CN V.VW.AFU.ALO.AFU.CXA.AFU.BCW.ALO

house paint
MT.2537
SN Paint designed for outdoors, having high-grade pigment in linseed oil with a small amount of thinner and drier, or in a synthetic resin. (STEIN)
UF paint, house
CN M.MT.AFU.ARI.CRG.ALO.BCW.ALO.ARI

house traps
RT.1498
ALT **house trap**
UF traps, house
CN V.RT.ALO.BCW.ALO.ARI.DCU.ALO

houseboats
RK.353 (A,L,B,R)
ALT **houseboat**
UF floating houses
houses, floating
shantyboats
CN V.RK.AFU.ALO.ALO.AXC.ARI.ARI

housebooks
VW.51 (R)
ALT **housebook**
SN Documents in which are recorded household expenditures such as for food, utilities, and domestic help, maintained in a journal or other book; also includes classed or chronological files of the bills and receipts for household goods and services. (GAHLM)
UF account books, household
books, household account
household account books

CN V.VW.AFU.AFU.AFU.DCU.ARI

housed joints
TF.666
ALT **housed joint**
SN Usually perpendicular joints formed where the full thickness of one member's edge or end is accepted into a corresponding housing, groove, or dado in another member. (MEANS)
UF joints, housed
joints, sliding
sliding joints
CN V.TF.ALO.ARI.AXC.AFU

household account books
USE **housebooks**

household inventories
USE **estate inventories**

househusbands
HG.43 (L)
ALT **househusband**
SN Married men who manage their own households, especially as their principle occupation.
UF homemakers, men
men homemakers
CN H.HG.AFU.AXC.ARI.BIQ

housekeeping records
USE **administrative records**

houses
RK.226 (A,L,N,B,R)
ALT **house**
CN V.RK.AFU.ALO.ALO.AXC.ALO

houses of correction
USE **correctional institutions**
workhouses

houses of ill repute
USE **brothels**

houses of prostitution
USE **brothels**

houses, A-frame
USE **A-frame houses**

houses, Acadian
USE **Creole cottages**

houses, apartment
USE **apartment houses**

houses, architect-designed
USE **architect-designed houses**

houses, architects'
USE **architects' houses**

houses, artists'
USE **artists' houses**

houses, atrium
USE **atrium houses**

houses, attiring
USE **tiring houses**

houses, auction
USE **auction houses**

houses, bastel
USE **bastel houses**

houses, beach
USE **beach houses**

houses, bee
USE **apiaries**

houses, beehive
USE **beehive houses**

houses, bell
USE **bell towers**

houses, bettering
USE **workhouses**

houses, big
USE **plantation houses**

houses, boarding
USE **lodging houses**

houses, boiler
USE **boiler houses**

houses, bone
USE **ossuaries**

houses, bridewell
USE **workhouses**

houses, builder-designed
USE **builder-designed houses**

houses, carriage
USE **carriage houses**

houses, cat
USE **brothels**

houses, catslide
USE **saltbox houses**

houses, cave
USE **cave dwellings**

houses, chaise
USE **carriage houses**

houses, chapter
USE **chapter houses**

houses, charnel
USE **ossuaries**

houses, chicken
USE **chicken houses**

houses, church
USE **parish houses**

houses, circular engine
USE **roundhouses**

houses, coach
USE **carriage houses**

houses, continental log
USE **log houses**

houses, corn
USE **corncribs**

houses, country
USE **country houses**

houses, courtyard
USE **courtyard houses**

houses, Creole
USE **Creole cottages**

houses, demonstration
USE **model houses**

houses, detached
USE **detached houses**

houses, discount
USE **discount houses**

houses, dogtrot
USE **dogtrot houses**

houses, double
USE **double houses**

houses, double-pen
USE **double-pen houses**

houses, double-pile
USE **double-pile houses**

houses, duplex
USE **duplex houses**

houses, earth
USE **earth lodges**

houses, elephant
USE **elephant houses**

houses, engine
USE **fire stations**

houses, field
USE **field houses**

houses, fishing
USE **fishing lodges**

houses, floating
USE **houseboats**

houses, fraternity
USE **fraternity houses**

houses, freight
USE **freight houses**

houses, Friends' meeting
USE **Quaker meeting houses**

houses, front-gable
USE **gable-front houses**

houses, fun
USE **fun houses**

houses, gable-front
USE **gable-front houses**

houses, gardens
USE **garden houses**

houses, garrison
USE **garrison houses**

houses, great
USE **plantation houses**

houses, grenier
USE **Creole cottages**

houses, halfway
USE **halfway houses**

houses, haunted
USE **haunted houses**

houses, hen
USE **chicken houses**

houses, historic
USE **historic houses**

houses, holiday
USE **vacation houses**

houses, hop
USE **hop barns**

houses, ice
USE **ice houses**

houses, lazar
USE **lazarettos**

houses, lean-to
USE **saltbox houses**

houses, lockkeepers'
USE **lockkeepers' houses**

houses, lodging
USE **lodging houses**

houses, log
USE **log houses**

houses, manor
USE **manor houses**

houses, mansion
USE **mansions**

houses, meeting
USE **meeting houses**

houses, milk
USE **milk houses**

houses, model
USE **model houses**

houses, movie
USE **movie theaters**

houses, necessary
USE **outhouses**
privies

houses, one-family
USE **single-family dwellings**

houses, opera
USE **opera houses**

houses, owner-built
USE **owner-built houses**

houses, pachyderm
USE **elephant houses**

houses, packing
USE **packing plants**

houses, palm
USE **palm houses**

houses, panel
USE **brothels**

houses, parish
USE **parish houses**

houses, patio
USE **courtyard houses**

houses, penitentiary
USE **prisons**

houses, peristyle
USE **peristyle houses**

houses, picture
USE **movie theaters**

houses, pig
USE **pig houses**

houses, pigeon
USE **dovecotes**

houses, pit
USE **pit dwellings**

houses, pitcher
USE **wine cellars**

houses, plantation
USE **plantation houses**

houses, pool
USE **bathhouses**

houses, possum-trot plan
USE **dogtrot houses**

houses, poultry
USE **poultry houses**

houses, prototype
USE **model houses**

houses, public
USE **pubs**

houses, pump
USE **pumping stations**

houses, Quaker meeting
USE **Quaker meeting houses**

houses, rabbit
USE **rabbit hutches**

houses, ranch
USE **ranch houses**

houses, riding
USE **riding halls**

houses, rooming
USE **lodging houses**

houses, row
USE **row houses**

houses, saddlebag
USE **saddlebag houses**

houses, saltbox
USE **saltbox houses**

houses, sap
USE **sugar houses**

houses, semidetached
USE **double houses**

houses, shotgun
USE **shotgun houses**

houses, show
USE **decorators' show houses**

houses, single-family
USE **single-family dwellings**

houses, single-pen
USE **single-pen houses**

houses, slat
USE **lathhouses**

houses, slave
USE **slave quarters**

houses, solar
USE **solar houses**

houses, sorority
USE **sorority houses**

houses, speculative
USE **speculative houses**

houses, split-level
USE **split-level houses**

houses, sporting
USE **brothels**

houses, stage
USE **stage houses**

houses, stilt
USE **stilt houses**

houses, suburban
USE **suburban houses**

houses, sugar
USE **sugar houses**

houses, summer
USE **summer houses**

houses, tenement
USE **tenement houses**

houses, terrace
USE **terrace houses**

houses, tiring
USE **tiring houses**

houses, town
USE **town houses**

houses, tract
USE **tract houses**

houses, tree
USE **tree houses**

houses, triple-decker
USE **three-deckers**

houses, two-family
USE **double houses**
duplex houses

houses, tyreing
USE **tiring houses**

houses, urban
USE **town houses**

houses, vacation
USE **vacation houses**

houses, wash
USE **laundries**

houses, weekend
USE **vacation houses**

houses, well
USE **well houses**

housewives
HG.44 (L)
ALT **housewife**
SN Married women who manage their own households, especially as their principal occupation. (RHDEL1)
UF homemakers
CN H.HG.AFU.AXC.ARI.BOK

housing
RG.54 (A,L,B)
SN When possible use a more specific term.
UF housing complexes
shelter
CN V.RG.AFU.AFU.BOK

housing complexes
USE **housing**

housing developments
RG.77 (A,R)
ALT **housing development**
SN Use for commercially developed real estate tracts commonly consisting of one- to four-unit dwellings.
UF developments
developments, housing
CN V.RG.AFU.AFU.BOK.AXC.ALO

housing discrimination
BM.1106 (A,L)
UF discrimination in housing
discrimination, housing
CN B.BM.CRG.BCW.ARI.ARI

housing for disabled
USE **housing for the handicapped**

housing for low income persons
USE **low income housing**

housing for physically handicapped
USE **housing for the handicapped**

housing for the aged
USE **housing for the elderly**

housing for the elderly
RG.82 (A,L)
UF aged, housing for the
elderly, housing for the
homes for the elderly
housing for the aged
CN V.RG.AFU.AFU.BOK.BCW.AFU

housing for the handicapped
RG.83 (A,B)
UF disabled, housing for
handicapped, housing for the
housing for disabled
housing for physically handicapped
physically handicapped, housing for
CN V.RG.AFU.AFU.BOK.BCW.ALO

housing planes
USE **dado planes**

housing projects
RG.69 (A,L,R)
ALT **housing project**
SN Use for planned residential developments, generally publicly built and operated, intended for low- and moderate-income tenants.
UF projects, housing
CN V.RG.AFU.AFU.BOK.AXC.AFU.AFU

housing security
USE **burglary protection**

housing, affordable
USE **affordable housing**

housing, animal
USE **animal housing**

housing, cattle
USE **cattle barns**

housing, cluster
USE **cluster housing**

housing, college
USE **student housing**

housing, communal
USE **communal housing**

housing, company
USE **industrial housing**

housing, cooperative
USE **cooperative housing**

housing, council
USE **public housing**

housing, disaster
USE **emergency housing**

housing, emergency
USE **emergency housing**

housing, employee
USE **industrial housing**

housing, government
USE **public housing**

housing, industrial
USE **industrial housing**

housing, infill
USE **infill**

housing, low cost
USE **low cost housing**

housing, low income
USE **low income housing**

housing, low rent
USE **low cost housing**

housing, low-rise
USE **low-rise housing**

housing, military
USE **military housing**

housing, moderate income
USE **moderate income housing**

housing, public
USE **public housing**

housing, rental
USE **rental housing**

housing, residential
USE **dwellings**

housing, rural
USE **rural housing**

housing, scattered-site
USE **scattered-site housing**

housing, self-help
USE **self-help housing**

housing, student
USE **student housing**

housing, temporary
USE **temporary housing**

housing, trade-in
USE **trade-in housing**

housing, worker's
USE **industrial housing**

Hova
USE **Merina**

hovels
RK.238 (R)
ALT **hovel**
SN Use for small, poorly constructed, or very humble dwellings.
CN V.RK.AFU.ALO.ALO.AXC.ALO.AFU.BOK.ALO

hoverports
RG.225 (B)
ALT **hoverport**
CN V.RG.AFU.AFU.EFQ.ARI.ALO

Howe trusses
RT.365

ALT **Howe truss**
SN Trusses having upper and lower horizontal members, between which are vertical and diagonal members: the vertical members of the web take tension, and the diagonal members are under compression. (DAC)
UF trusses, Howe
CN V.RT.AFU.AFU.AFU.BCW.CLM.AFU.AFU.AFU.BIQ

howell planes
TB.946 (N)
ALT **howell plane**
SN Planes with a broad curved blade; used to smooth the inside of barrels. (MERCER)
UF box chivs
chaifs
cheves
chiv planes
chives
chivs, box
howells
howels, stock
planes, chiv
planes, howell
stock howels
CN V.TB.AFU.BCW.CFS.ALO.AFU.DUC.ARI.BIQ

howells
USE **howell planes**

howels, stock
USE **howell planes**

Hoysala
FL.2218 (A,L)
CN F.FL.ALO.ARI.AXC.ALO.AFU.AXC.CRG

hoyuks
USE **hüyüks**

Hsia
USE **Xia**

Hsiao-t'un
USE **Xiaotun**

Hsien-feng
USE **Xianfeng**

Hsing ware
USE **Xing ware**

HSLA steel
USE **high-strength low-alloy steel**

Hsuan-t'ung
USE **Xuantong**

Hsuan-te
USE **Xuande**

Hualapai
USE **Walapai**

Huamachuco
FL.1169
CN F.FL.ALO.ALO.ALO.ARI.AXC.AFU.BIQ.BIQ

Huana
FL.464 (L)
UF Bahuana
Hungana
CN F.FL.ALO.AFU.AXC.ALO.ALO.ARI.AXC

Huanca
USE **Huari**

Huancavilca
FL.1661 (L)
CN F.FL.ALO.ALO.ARI.ARI.BCW.BZY

Huari
FL.1157 (L)
UF Huanca
Wari
CN F.FL.ALO.ALO.ALO.ARI.AXC.AFU.AXC.BOK

Huarpe
FL.1620 (L)
UF Guarpe
CN F.FL.ALO.ALO.ARI.ARI.ALO.ALO.AXC

Huastec
FL.1500 (L)
CN F.FL.ALO.ALO.ARI.ALO.ARI.ALO

Huave
FL.1516 (L)
CN F.FL.ALO.ALO.ARI.ALO.AXC.BOK

hubs (lock components)
TF.566
ALT **hub (lock component)**
SN Lock parts through which spindles pass to actuate the mechanism. (BROWNL)
CN V.TF.AFU.ALO.AXC.BOK

hubs, compensating
USE **compensating hubs**

huches
USE **cupboards**

Huchiti
FL.1282
CN F.FL.ALO.ALO.ARI.AFU.ALO.FZU.ALO.ALO

hucksters
USE **peddlers**

Hudson bluestone
MT.710
UF bluestone, Hudson
CN M.MT.AFU.AFU.AFU.DCU.AFU.ALO.AFU.ARI.AFU.ALO.AFU.AFU.AFU

Hudson River valley chairs
USE **fiddle-back chairs**

hue
BM.131
SN The property or characteristic of a color which refers to its position in the spectrum. (AFTP)
CN B.BM.AFU.AFU.ARI.BOK.ALO.ALO.ALO.ALO

Huetar
USE **Guetar**

Huguenot
BM.636 (L,R)
UF French Protestant
Reformed French Protestant
CN B.BM.BZY.AFU.ALO.ARI.BIQ

Huichol
FL.1490 (L)
CN F.FL.ALO.ALO.ARI.ALO.AFU.ALO

Huilliche
FL.1621 (L)
CN F.FL.ALO.ALO.ARI.ARI.ALO.ALO.BCW

Hum
FL.465
UF Bawumbu
CN F.FL.ALO.AFU.AXC.ALO.ALO.ARI.BCW

human behavior
BM.582 (L,R)
UF behavior, human
CN B.BM.BUE.AXC

human beings
USE **people**

human engineering
USE **human factors**

human factors
KD.156 (A,L,B)
SN Study of human physiological and psychological capacities, limitations, and needs in relation to the human environment, particularly the workplace, and the application of this knowledge to the design and creation of the spaces, objects, and systems that people use.
UF engineering, human
engineering, human factors
ergonomics
factors, human
HFE
human engineering
human factors engineering
CN K.KD.AFU.ALO.CXA

human factors engineering
USE **human factors**

human hair
MT.934
UF hair, human
CN M.MT.AFU.AFU.ALO.AFU.CXA.AFU.AFU.AXC

human settlements
USE **settlements**

human territoriality
USE **territoriality**

humanism
BM.357 (A,L,R)
SN A philosophy that asserts the essential dignity and worth of humanity and its capacity to achieve self-realization through reason; also (capitalized), the Renaissance movement characterized by the revival of classical letters. (W)
CN B.BM.ALO.ALO.CLM.DIO

humanities
KD.2 (L,R)
SN Branches of learning regarded as having primarily a cultural character, such as languages, literature, and philosophy. (W)
CN K.KD.AFU.AFU

humans
USE **people**

Humayun
FL.2230
CN F.FL.ALO.ARI.AXC.ALO.AFU.BIQ.ALO.AFU.ARI

Humber ware
FL.3130 (R)
UF ware, Humber
CN F.FL.ALO.BCW.ALO.ALO.AFU.BOK.ARI.ALO.BCW.AFU

Humboldt Bay
FL.3633
CN F.FL.ALO.BOK.ALO.BCW.AFU.ALO.ALO

Humboldt Bay Indians
USE **Wiyot**

Humboldt redwood
MT.1394
UF coast redwood
redwood, coast
redwood, Humboldt
Sequoia sempervirens
CN M.MT.AFU.AFU.ALO.BIQ.DCU.AFU.AFU.ALO.DCU.ARI

humidifiers
TB.109 (L,N)
ALT **humidifier**
SN Devices for supplying or maintaining humidity. (WCOL)
CN V.TB.AFU.ARI.ALO.AXC

humidity
BM.747 (L,B)
CN B.BM.CFS.ALO.AXC.ALO.AXC

humidity control
KG.117 (L)
UF control, humidity
CN K.KG.AFU.AFU.BCW.ALO.AXC

hummocks
USE **hillocks**

humor
BM.5 (L,R)
CN B.BM.AFU.AFU.AFU.ALO

humor concretions
USE **biomorphic abstraction**

humorists
HG.186 (L)
ALT **humorist**
SN Persons who write humorous material for publication or performance. (DOT)
CN H.HG.AFU.AXC.AXC.ARI.AFU.AFU.BIQ

hump yards
USE **marshalling yards**

humus
MT.2063 (L)
CN M.MT.AFU.AFU.ARI.BOK.ALO.ALO

hunebedden
USE **megalithic chamber tombs**

Hung-chih
USE **Hongzhi**

Hung-hsien
USE **Hongxian**

Hung-wu
USE **Hongwu**

Hungana
USE **Huana**

Hungarian
FL.3047 (L,B)
CN F.FL.ALO.BCW.AFU.BZY

Hungarian green
USE **malachite green**

Hungarian yellow wood
USE **young fustic**

Hungary blue
USE **cobalt blue**
smalt

Hungwe
USE **Hongwe**

Huno
USE **Uru**

hunt tables
USE **horseshoe tables**
huntboards

huntboards
TG.593 (N)
ALT **huntboard**
SN Sideboard tables without drawers, or with a single row of drawers under the top; of a type made in the southern states of North America. (MONTGO)
UF boards, hunting
hunt tables
hunter's tables
hunting boards
hunting tables
tables, hunt
CN V.TG.AFU.AFU.AXC.ALO.CRG.BOK

hunter green
USE **dark green**
moderate green
very dark yellowish green

hunter green, dark
USE **dark green**
very dark yellowish green

Hunter period
USE **Bubalus phase**

hunter planes
USE **roughing planes**

hunter's green
USE **very dark yellowish green**

hunter's tables
USE **huntboards**

hunters
HG.375 (L)
ALT **hunter**
CN H.HG.AFU.AXC.BIQ.ALO.AXC.BIQ

hunting boards
USE **huntboards**

hunting camps
USE **hunting lodges**

hunting chairs
TG.73
ALT **hunting chair**
SN Armchairs stuffed all over, except the legs, which are of mahogany. (CABDIC)
UF chairs, hunting
CN V.TG.AFU.AFU.ALO.AFU.AFU.AFU.HOE

hunting lodges
RK.961 (A,L,B,R)
ALT **hunting lodge**
UF camps, hunting
hunting camps
lodges, hunting
CN V.RK.AFU.ALO.ALO.ELK.BOK.ALO

hunting museums
RK.425 (L)
ALT **hunting museum**
UF museums, hunting
CN V.RK.AFU.ALO.ALO.BCW.AXC.ARI.CLM.ALO

hunting tables
USE **huntboards**

Huon Gulf
FL.3637
UF Huon Peninsula
CN F.FL.ALO.BOK.ALO.BCW.ALO.ALO

Huon Peninsula
USE **Huon Gulf**

Hupa
FL.1255 (L)
CN F.FL.ALO.ALO.ARI.AFU.ALO.BZY

hurdle nails
TF.396
ALT **hurdle nail**
UF nails, hurdle
CN V.TF.AFU.AFU.AFU.ALO.AFU.CFS.AFU.BZY

Huron
FL.1324 (L)
UF Wyandot
CN F.FL.ALO.ALO.ARI.AFU.BCW.ALO

Huron-Iroquois
FL.869
CN F.FL.ALO.ALO.ALO.AFU.ALO.ALO.AXC.AXC

Hurrian ware
USE **Atchana ware**

hurricanes
KM.116 (L,B)
CN K.KM.AFU.CXA.BIQ.ALO.AFU

husbands
HG.16 (L)
ALT **husband**
CN H.HG.AFU.ALO.ARI.AFU

husk
MT.1037
CN M.MT.AFU.AFU.ALO.BIQ.BCW

husk garlands
USE **husks (motifs)**

husks (motifs)
DG.58
ALT **husk (motif)**
SN Stylized budlike motifs popular in late 18th-century Neoclassical work, nearly always used in a string, often like a festoon. (LDDO)
UF bell flower motifs
bellflowers
garlands, husk
husk garlands
motifs, bell flower
CN D.DG.AFU.AFU.DIO.BOK

hutches
USE **cupboards**

hutches, rabbit
USE **rabbit hutches**

huts
RK.236 (L,B,R)
ALT **hut**
CN V.RK.AFU.ALO.ALO.AXC.ALO.AFU.BOK

huts, beehive
USE **beehive houses**

huts, nissen
USE **quonset huts**

huts, quonset
USE **quonset huts**

huts, sunken
USE **sunken huts**

huun
USE **bark cloth**

hüyüks
RD.42
ALT **hüyük**
SN Tells (artificial mounds resulting from layers of human habitation) in Turkey.
UF hoyuks
CN V.RD.AFU.ARI.ARI.AFU.AFU.AFU

HVAC
RT.1382 (A)
UF heating, ventilation, and air conditioning
indoor climate control
CN V.RT.ALO.BCW.AFU.AFU

HVAC drawings
VD.147
ALT **HVAC drawing**
SN Use for drawings of HVAC systems or parts thereof. For scaled floor plans specifically, use a more specific term, e.g., **plumbing plans.**
UF drawings, HVAC
heating, ventilation, and air conditioning drawings
CN V.VD.AFU.BIQ.AFU.AFU.AFU

HVAC plans
VD.55
ALT **HVAC plan**
SN Use for scaled floor plans showing HVAC layout; may include an adjacent small drawing of an elevation. For other drawings of HVAC systems, use **HVAC drawings.**
UF heating and cooling plans
heating, ventilation, and air conditioning plans
plans, HVAC
CN V.VD.AFU.AFU.BIQ.ALO.AXC.ALO.BIQ.ALO

hyacinth
MT.569 (L)
CN M.MT.AFU.AFU.AFU.CFS.AFU.HZS.AFU

hyalotypes
USE **lantern slides**

hybrid balsam
USE **balm of gilead**

Hyderabad
FL.2257
CN F.FL.ALO.ARI.AXC.ALO.AFU.BZY.AFU.BIQ

hydrants, fire
USE **fire hydrants**

hydrated lime
MT.328
UF lime, hydrated
lime, slaked
slaked lime
CN M.MT.AFU.AFU.AFU.BUE.AFU

hydration ring dating
USE **obsidian hydration dating**

hydraulic cement
USE **natural cement**

hydraulic construction works
USE **hydraulic structures**

hydraulic elevators
RT.1319 (L)
ALT **hydraulic elevator**
SN Elevators powered by the action of a liquid under pressure in a cylinder equipped with a plunger or piston. (STEIN)
UF elevators, hydraulic
elevators, plunger
plunger elevators
CN V.RT.ALO.ALO.AFU.ARI.ALO.ARI.ARI

hydraulic engineering
KD.221 (L)
UF engineering, hydraulic
CN K.KD.AFU.ARI.BIQ.AXC.ARI

hydraulic engineers
HG.631 (L)
ALT **hydraulic engineer**
UF engineers, hydraulic
CN H.HG.AFU.AXC.BZY.BCW.BCW.AFU

hydraulic equipment
TB.9 (L)
SN Equipment powered by hydraulics.
UF equipment, hydraulic
CN V.TB.AFU.ALO.AFU

hydraulic fill dams
USE **earth-fill dams**

hydraulic filling
KT.123 (L)
SN The placing of fill composed of solids, liquids, and usually water. After placement, the liquid eventually drains, leaving the solid fill.
UF filling, hydraulic
CN K.KT.AFU.ALO.DCU.ALO

hydraulic gates
RK.561 (L,R)
ALT **hydraulic gate**
UF gates, hydraulic
CN V.RK.AFU.ALO.ALO.CFS.ALO.ALO.AXC

hydraulic hinges
TF.119
ALT **hydraulic hinge**
UF hinges, hydraulic
CN V.TF.AFU.AFU.AFU.AFU.CLM.AFU.EFQ

hydraulic jacks
TB.372 (L)
ALT **hydraulic jack**
UF jacks, hydraulic
CN V.TB.AFU.ARI.DCU.AFU.ALO.AFU

hydraulic lime cement
USE **natural cement**

hydraulic limestone
MT.680
SN Limestone containing silica and alumina and yielding a lime that will harden under water. (W)
UF cement stone
limestone, hydraulic
stone, cement
CN M.MT.AFU.AFU.AFU.DCU.AFU.ALO.AFU.ALO.ALO.AFU.ALO.AFU.AFU

hydraulic machinery
TB.4 (L)
UF machinery, hydraulic
CN V.TB.AFU.AFU.AFU.AFU

hydraulic mortar
MT.2607
SN Mortar that is capable of setting and hardening under water. (DAC)
UF mortar, hydraulic
CN M.MT.AFU.ARI.DZW.ARI.ALO.ALO

hydraulic motors
TB.392 (L)
ALT **hydraulic motor**
UF motors, hydraulic
CN V.TB.AFU.ARI.DOI.AXC.AFU

hydraulic structures
RK.512 (L)
ALT **hydraulic structure**
UF hydraulic construction works
structures, hydraulic
works, hydraulic construction
CN V.RK.AFU.ALO.ALO.CFS

hydraulic turbines
TB.398 (L,N)
ALT **hydraulic turbine**
UF turbines, hydraulic
CN V.TB.AFU.ARI.DOI.BUE.ALO

hydraulics
KD.286 (L,R)
SN Science that deals with practical applications of water or other liquids in motion, such as the transmission of energy or the effects of flow. (W)
CN K.KD.AFU.ARI.CLM.AXC.AXC

hydrocal
MT.2453 (L)
CN M.MT.AFU.ARI.CRG.AFU.AXC.ALO.ALO.AFU

hydrocarbons, aliphatic
USE **aliphatic hydrocarbons**

hydrocarbons, aromatic
USE **aromatic hydrocarbons**

hydrocarbons, chlorinated
USE **chlorinated hydrocarbons**

hydrochloric acid
MT.298 (L)
UF acid, hydrochloric
acid, muriatic
muriatic acid
salt, spirits of
spirits of salt
CN M.MT.AFU.AFU.AFU.BOK.AFU.AXC

hydroelectric dams
RK.531
ALT **hydroelectric dam**
SN Dams built on rivers to harness the energy of waterpower to produce electricity.
UF dams, hydroelectric
dams, power
power dams
CN V.RK.AFU.ALO.ALO.CFS.AFU.ARI.ALO.BIQ

hydroelectric elevators
RT.1320
ALT **hydroelectric elevator**
UF elevators, hydroelectric
CN V.RT.ALO.ALO.AFU.ARI.ALO.ARI.ARI.AFU

hydroelectric plants
USE **hydroelectric power plants**

hydroelectric power
BM.875 (L)
UF power, hydroelectric
water-power
CN B.BM.CFS.AXC.ALO.ALO.ARI.ALO

hydroelectric power plants
RG.110 (A,L,B)
ALT **hydroelectric power plant**
UF electric plants, water-power
hydroelectric plants
plants, hydroelectric power
power plants, hydroelectric
water-power electric plants
CN V.RG.AFU.AFU.BUE.ARI.ALO

hydrofluoric acid
MT.300 (L)
SN A highly corrosive, caustic, and toxic water solution of hydrogen fluoride that dissolves most metals, except gold, platinum, glass, ceramics, and organic material; used for etching glass and cleaning metals. (MH)
UF acid, hydrofluoric
CN M.MT.AFU.AFU.AFU.BOK.AFU.BCW

hydrographers
HG.345
ALT **hydrographer**
CN H.HG.AFU.AXC.BIQ.AFU.AFU.CFS

hydrographic charts
USE **nautical charts**

hydrographic maps
USE **nautical charts**

hydrography
KD.274 (L)
SN Description and study of seas, lakes, and other bodies of water. (W)
CN K.KD.AFU.ARI.CLM.ARI.BIQ

hydrologic maps
VW.187 (L)
ALT **hydrologic map**
UF maps, hydrologic
CN V.VW.AFU.AFU.AFU.FZU.AXC.AFU.ARI.AXC.BCW.ARI

hydromel
MT.2323 (L)
SN A mixture of honey and water, usually of equal proportions, used as a plasticizer in watercolor paints. (MAYER)
CN M.MT.AFU.ARI.ALO.EFQ.AFU

hydrostone
MT.2446
SN Ordinary casting plaster of 100 parts solid and 45 parts water.
CN M.MT.AFU.ARI.CRG.AFU.AXC.AFU.BCW

hydroxide, sodium
USE **sodium hydroxide**

Hyksos
FL.2812 (L)
CN F.FL.ALO.AXC.ALO.ARI.AFU.BOK.BIQ

Hymettian marble
MT.826
UF greco rigato
marble, Hymettian
marmor Hymmetium
marmor imezio
CN M.MT.AFU.AFU.AFU.DCU.AFU.ARI.ARI.ARI.BOK.BIQ

hymnals
VW.544 (N,R)
ALT **hymnal**
SN Books containing collections of church hymns. (AHD)
CN V.VW.AFU.ALO.AFU.AFU.ALO.BUE.BOK

hymns
VW.59 (L,R)
ALT **hymn**
SN Songs of praise to God. (W)
CN V.VW.AFU.AFU.AFU.DOI.ARI.AFU

hypaethral temples
RK.1128
ALT **hypaethral temple**
SN Use for temples whose sanctuary spaces are wholly or partly open to the sky.
UF temples, hypaethral
CN V.RK.AFU.ALO.ALO.FCS.BIQ.BZY.AFU.AFU

Hyper-realist
USE **Photorealist**

hyperbolas
BM.770 (L)
ALT **hyperbolic**

CN B.BM.CFS.ARI.AXC.BCW.AFU.ARI

hypermarkets
USE **supermarkets**

hyperthyra
RT.347
ALT **hyperthyrum**
SN Use for friezes above doorways.
CN V.RT.AFU.AFU.AFU.BCW.BZY.
ALO.ARI.AFU.AFU

hyphens
RM.17
ALT **hyphen**
SN Use to designate the elements connecting the central block with the outlying wings of a building of five-part Palladian form.
CN V.RM.AFU.BUE

hypocausts
RT.1161 (A)
ALT **hypocaust**
CN V.RT.AFU.BOK.ARI

hypogea
RK.484 (A,R)
ALT **hypogeum**
SN Includes underground tomb chambers or groups of such chambers and the vaults of those and similar underground structures.
CN V.RK.AFU.ALO.ALO.BOK.BUE.
AFU.ALO.AFU

hypostyle halls
RM.274 (L)
ALT **hypostyle hall**
UF halls, hypostyle
CN V.RM.AFU.DIO.ARI.ALO.BUE.AFU

hypostyle mosques
RK.1120
ALT **hypostyle mosque**
SN Use for mosques having a vast rectangular hall, generally a flat roof, and whose interior is divided by many rows of columns.
UF mosques, hypostyle
CN V.RK.AFU.ALO.ALO.FCS.BIQ.
BIQ.AFU.ALO

hypothecation certificates
VW.825
ALT **hypothecation certificate**
UF certificates, hypothecation
CN V.VW.AFU.ARI.AFU.BIQ.BZY.AFU

hypotrachelia
RT.138
ALT **hypotrachelium**
SN Use for the groove or grooves beneath the necking of Doric columns.
UF gorgerins
CN V.RT.AFU.AFU.AFU.AXC.BIQ.
ALO.ARI.ALO.BIQ

hypsographic maps
USE **relief maps**

hypsometric maps
USE **relief maps**

Hypurina
USE **Ipuriná**

I-beams
RT.712
ALT **I-beam**
CN V.RT.AFU.AFU.ALO.ARI.AXC

I-houses
RK.250
ALT **I-house**
UF English I-houses
I-houses, English
CN V.RK.AFU.ALO.ALO.AXC.ALO.
AFU.CLM.AXC

I-houses, English
USE **I-houses**

I.D. cards
USE **identity cards**

IAQ
USE **indoor air quality**

Iatmul
FL.3649 (L)
CN F.FL.ALO.BOK.ALO.BCW.ALO.
BCW.AFU.ARI

Ibibio
FL.240 (L)
CN F.FL.ALO.AFU.AXC.AFU.ALO.
AFU.BCW

IBM (TM) cards
USE **punched cards**

Ibo
USE **Igbo**

Ibrahim
FL.3500
CN F.FL.ALO.BIQ.AFU.FOG.AFU.EFQ

Ica
FL.1165
UF Rukana
CN F.FL.ALO.ALO.ALO.ARI.AXC.
AFU.BIQ.ALO

ice
MT.324 (L,B)
CN M.MT.AFU.AFU.AFU.BOK.BOK.
ARI.AFU

ice box hinges
TF.137
ALT **ice box hinge**
UF hinges, ice box
CN V.TF.AFU.AFU.AFU.AFU.CLM.
ALO.AXC

ice box latches
TF.189
ALT **ice box latch**
UF latches, ice box
CN V.TF.AFU.AFU.AFU.AFU.DIO.
BCW.ALO.BIQ

ice-cream parlor chairs
TG.213 (N)
ALT **ice-cream parlor chair**
SN Chairs made from looped and twisted iron wire, usually having circular oak seats. Chairs of this type were patented in the early 1900s. A number of manufacturers made such wire chairs; the name derives from their use in public restaurants and cafes.
UF bent-wire chairs
café chairs
chair, soda fountain
chairs, bent-wire
chairs, café
chairs, ice-cream parlor
chairs, iron-wire
chairs, soda
chairs, soda fountain
iron-wire chairs
soda chairs
soda fountain chairs
CN V.TG.AFU.AFU.ALO.AFU.AFU.
ARI.AXC.ARI

ice cream parlors
RK.119 (A,L,B)
ALT **ice cream parlor**
UF parlors, ice cream
CN V.RK.AFU.ALO.ALO.ALO.AFU.
AXC.BOK

ice-cream tables
TG.779
ALT **ice-cream table**
UF café tables
tables, café
tables, ice-cream
CN V.TG.AFU.AFU.BIQ.BOK.ARI.
ALO.AFU

ice hockey rinks
RK.1052 (B)
ALT **ice hockey rink**
UF hockey rinks
hockey rinks, ice
rinks, hockey
rinks, ice hockey
CN V.RK.AFU.ALO.ALO.EWY.AXC.
BIQ.AFU.AXC.AFU.AFU

ice houses
RK.71 (A,L,B,R)
ALT **ice house**
SN Specially insulated and ventilated agricultural buildings, increasingly popular after the mid-19th-century rise in dairy production, for the storing of ice blocks. (W)
UF houses, ice
CN V.RK.AFU.ALO.ALO.AFU.AFU.BUE

ice packs
USE **pack ice**

ice palaces
RK.1385 (L,R)
ALT **ice palace**
SN Use for structures built of ice, often

elaborately decorated, furnished, and lit, erected for festivals, exhibitions, and sporting events; popular in 18th-century Russia and then throughout the northern latitudes during the mid-20th century.
UF palaces, ice
CN V.RK.AFU.ALO.AXC.CFS.AFU.AFU

ice rinks
USE **ice-skating rinks**

ice-skating rinks
RK.1051 (A,L,B)
ALT **ice-skating rink**
UF ice rinks
rinks, ice-skating
CN V.RK.AFU.ALO.ALO.EWY.AXC.BIQ.AFU.AXC.AFU

ice stations
RK.1175 (L)
ALT **ice station**
SN Camps or bases in an isolated part of the Arctic or Antartic, manned by specialists to monitor such things as the weather, geologic formations, and wildlife. (RHDEL2)
UF stations, ice
CN V.RK.AFU.ALO.ALO.FIM.ALO.ALO.ALO.AFU

ice storage systems
RT.1389
ALT **ice storage system**
SN Use for supplemental cooling systems in buildings that utilize ice production and storage for the purpose of reducing utility loads.
UF storage systems, ice
systems, ice storage
CN V.RT.ALO.BCW.AFU.AFU.ALO.ALO

ice storms
KM.120
SN Storms in which falling rain freezes as soon as it touches any object. (W)
UF storms, ice
CN K.KM.AFU.CXA.BIQ.AXC

icebergs
RD.154 (L,R)
ALT **iceberg**
CN V.RD.ARI.AFU.AFU.AFU.ARI.ALO

ichnographic plans
VD.59
ALT **ichnographic plan**
SN Designates 16th- to 18th-century images, usually of cities, that are in plan view as opposed to bird's-eye view.
UF ichnographies
plans, ichnographic
CN V.VD.AFU.AFU.BIQ.ALO.AXC.AXC

ichnographic views
USE **plan views**

ichnographies
USE **ichnographic plans**

ichthyologists
HG.330 (L)
ALT **ichthyologist**
SN Persons who specialize in the study of fish.
CN H.HG.AFU.AXC.BIQ.AFU.AFU.ALO.ALO.AFU

iconoclasm
BM.358 (L,R)
ALT **iconoclastic**
SN Doctrine, practice, or attitude of one who destroys religious images or opposes their veneration. Use also for the specific period of Byzantine history. For opposition to the use of idols generally, use **aniconism.**
CN B.BM.ALO.ALO.CLM.DOI

iconography
BM.321 (A,L,R)
SN Includes both the art historical method of studying subject matter, and the imagery used in the art devoted to a particular subject, including its symbolic meaning.
CN B.BM.AFU.AXC.ELK.AXC

iconology
BM.322 (R)
SN A broader approach than iconography to analysis of meaning in the visual arts, taking account of the tradition of pictorial motifs and their historical, cultural, or social meaning. (OCA)
CN B.BM.AFU.AXC.ELK.BCW

iconostases
RT.1251 (A,L,R)
ALT **iconostasis**
SN Screens which, in Byzantine churches, separate the sanctuary from the nave, pierced by three doors and, since the 14th or 15th century, covered with icons. (ODCC)
CN V.RT.AFU.BUE.ALO.ARI.CXA.ALO.AFU

ICUs
USE **intensive care units**

Idea art
USE **Conceptual**

ideal cities
RD.82 (A,B,R)
ALT **ideal city**
SN Use for cities and towns designed and built to fulfill a specific political, military, economic, or pedagogic function and having a prescribed form imposed on them.
UF cities, ideal
ideal towns
towns, ideal
CN V.RD.AFU.BUE.ALO

ideal states
USE **utopias**

ideal towns
USE **ideal cities**

Ideal, the
BM.491
SN Use for the aesthetic quality of the permanent, essential, or eternal character of phenomena, rooted in the artist's or percipient's own idea of perfection.
UF the Ideal
CN B.BM.BIQ.AFU.AXC

idealism
BM.512 (L,R)
SN A theory that affirms that mind or the spiritual and ideal is of central importance in reality. (W)
CN B.BM.BIQ.AXC.BZY

ideism
BM.191
ALT **ideist**
SN A concept of art important to the Symbolist painters and opposed to academic idealism.
CN B.BM.AFU.AFU.AXC.CLM.BCW

identification cards
USE **identity cards**

identification photographs
VJ.89
ALT **identification photograph**
UF identity photographs
mugshots
photographs, identification
CN V.VJ.AFU.ALO.AFU

identifying
KG.22 (L)
SN Recognizing or establishing someone or something as being a particular person or thing. (W)
CN K.KG.AFU.AFU.AFU.CRG

identity cards
VW.572 (L,N)
ALT **identity card**
UF cards, I.D.
cards, identification
cards, identity
I.D. cards
identification cards
CN V.VW.AFU.ALO.AFU.ARI.BUE

identity photographs
USE **identification photographs**

idgahs
RK.1089
ALT **idgah**
SN Immense, open praying areas with nothing but a qibla wall with a mihrab and an open air pulpit. (AIW)
CN V.RK.AFU.ALO.ALO.FCS.ARI

Idjebu
USE **Ijebu**

Idoma
FL.258 (L)
CN F.FL.ALO.AFU.AXC.AFU.ALO.ARI.
ALO

Idrisid
FL.3449
CN F.FL.ALO.BIQ.AFU.CXA

Ife
FL.100
UF Ile-Ife
CN F.FL.ALO.AFU.ALO.AFU.BUE.BCW

Ife, Classical
USE **Classical Ife**

Ife, Postclassical
USE **Postclassical Ife**

Iga
FL.2022 (L)
CN F.FL.ALO.ARI.ALO.ALO.ALO.
ALO.ALO.BOK

Igala
FL.259 (L)
CN F.FL.ALO.AFU.AXC.AFU.ALO.ARI.
ARI

Igbira
USE **Ebira**

Igbo
FL.260 (L)
UF Ibo
CN F.FL.ALO.AFU.AXC.AFU.ALO.ARI.
AXC

Igbo Isaiah
FL.104
UF Isaiah, Igbo
CN F.FL.ALO.AFU.ALO.AFU.BUE.
BIQ.AFU

Igbo Jonah
FL.105
UF Jonah, Igbo
CN
F.FL.ALO.AFU.ALO.AFU.BUE.BIQ.
ALO

Igbo Laja
FL.114
UF Laja, Igbo
CN F.FL.ALO.AFU.ALO.AFU.BUE.
CLM.AFU

Igbo Richard
FL.106
UF Richard, Igbo
CN F.FL.ALO.AFU.ALO.AFU.BUE.
BIQ.ARI

Igbo-Ukwu
FL.103
CN F.FL.ALO.AFU.ALO.AFU.BUE.BIQ

Igbomina
FL.275
CN F.FL.ALO.AFU.AXC.AFU.ALO.
BCW.ALO.ARI

Igloolik
USE **Iglulik**

igloos
RK.315 (A,L,B,R)
ALT **igloo**
SN Eskimo houses usually made of sod, wood, or stone when permanent or of snow blocks in the shape of a dome when built for temporary purposes. (W)
CN V.RK.AFU.ALO.ALO.AXC.ALO.
BCW.ARI

Iglulik
FL.1210 (L)
UF Igloolik
Iglulirmiut
CN F.FL.ALO.ALO.ARI.AFU.AFU.AFU.
ALO.AFU.AXC

Iglulirmiut
USE **Iglulik**

Ignacieño
FL.1286 (L)
CN F.FL.ALO.ALO.ARI.AFU.ALO.FZU.
ARI.ALO

igneous rock
MT.580 (L)
SN Rock formed by the solidification of molten magma. (W)
UF rock, igneous
CN M.MT.AFU.AFU.AFU.DCU.AFU.AFU

igneous rock, acid
USE **acid igneous rock**

igneous rock, basic
USE **basic igneous rock**

igneous rock, intermediate
USE **intermediate igneous rock**

Ijaw
USE **Ijo**

Ijebu
FL.276 (L)
UF Idjebu
Yebu
CN F.FL.ALO.AFU.AXC.AFU.ALO.
BCW.ALO.AXC

Ijo
FL.266 (L)
UF Ijaw
CN F.FL.ALO.AFU.AXC.AFU.ALO.
AXC.AFU

Ikhshidid
FL.3450 (L)
UF Ilkshidid
CN F.FL.ALO.BIQ.AFU.DCU

Il-Khanid
FL.3451
UF Ilkhanid
CN F.FL.ALO.BIQ.AFU.DIO

Ile-Ife
USE **Ife**

Ilex
USE **holly**

Ilkhanid
USE **Il-Khanid**

Ilkshidid
USE **Ikhshidid**

ill, terminally
USE **terminally ill**

illegal buildings
RK.1391
ALT **illegal building**
SN Use for buildings that are constructed consciously in violation of building and zoning codes.
UF buildings, illegal
CN V.RK.AFU.ALO.BCW.ALO

illiberal arts
USE **mechanical arts**

Illinois
FL.1325 (L)
CN F.FL.ALO.ALO.ARI.AFU.BCW.ARI

illness, mental
USE **mental illness**

illuminated manuscripts
VW.657
ALT **illuminated manuscript**
SN Manuscripts adorned by hand with richly colored ornamental initial letters, decorative designs, or illustrations. (ALAG)
UF manuscripts, illuminated
CN V.VW.AFU.ALO.AFU.DZW.ARI.
AFU.ALO

illumination (lighting)
USE **lighting**

illumination, manuscript
USE **manuscript illumination**

illuminations
VB.39
ALT **illumination**
SN Includes both the ornamental decoration and the miniatures (small pictures) in manuscripts.
UF illuminations, manuscript
manuscript illuminations
CN V.VB.AFU.ALO.ARI

illuminations, manuscript
USE **illuminations**

illuminators
HG.103
ALT **illuminator**
SN Persons who practice the art of manuscript illumination.
CN H.HG.AFU.AXC.AXC.AFU.AFU.
ALO.AXC.CLM

illuminism
BM.359 (R)
SN Belief in or claim to personal intel-

lectual, cultural, or spiritual superiority not accessible to mankind in general. (W)
CN B.BM.ALO.ALO.CLM.DUC

illusion, optical
USE **optical illusion**

illusionism
BM.146 (R)
SN Use of pictorial techniques such as perspective and foreshortening to deceive the eye into taking that which is depicted for that which is real. (MURRAY)
CN B.BM.AFU.AFU.ARI.BOK.BUE

illustrated periodicals
VW.622 (L,R)
ALT **illustrated periodical**
UF periodicals, illustrated
CN V.VW.AFU.ALO.AFU.CXA.AFU.BCW.ARI

illustration
KT.202 (L)
ALT **illustrated**
UF graphic arts (illustration)
CN K.KT.AFU.ALO.DUC.CLM

illustration board
MT.1912
SN Laminated paper board that has paper layers glued to its surface; used commonly as temporary artists' supports.
UF board, illustration
CN M.MT.AFU.AFU.ARI.ALO.ALO.AXC.ALO.BIQ.AFU.ALO

illustration, anatomical
USE **anatomical illustration**

illustration, archaeological
USE **archaeological illustration**

illustration, biological
USE **biological illustration**

illustration, book
USE **book illustration**

illustration, botanical
USE **botanical illustration**

illustration, fashion
USE **fashion illustration**

illustration, magazine
USE **periodical illustration**

illustration, medical
USE **medical illustration**

illustration, newspaper
USE **newspaper illustration**

illustration, periodical
USE **periodical illustration**

illustration, scientific
USE **scientific illustration**

illustration, technical
USE **technical illustration**

illustration, zoological
USE **zoological illustration**

illustrations
VB.41
ALT **illustration**
SN Representations or diagrams that clarify, usually accompanying a text.
CN V.VB.AFU.ALO.AXC

illustrations, anatomical
USE **anatomical illustrations**

illustrations, biological
USE **biological illustrations**

illustrations, book
USE **book illustrations**

illustrations, botanical
USE **botanical illustrations**

illustrations, courtroom
USE **courtroom illustrations**

illustrations, fashion
USE **fashion illustrations**

illustrations, magazine
USE **periodical illustrations**

illustrations, medical
USE **medical illustrations**

illustrations, newspaper
USE **newspaper illustrations**

illustrations, periodical
USE **periodical illustrations**

illustrations, scientific
USE **scientific illustrations**

illustrations, technical
USE **technical illustrations**

illustrations, topographical
USE **topographical views**

illustrations, zoological
USE **zoological illustrations**

illustrators
HG.144 (L)
ALT **illustrator**
CN H.HG.AFU.AXC.AXC.AFU.AFU.ALO.BCW.AFU.ALO.ALO

illustrators, book
USE **book illustrators**

illustrators, fashion
USE **fashion illustrators**

illustrators, medical
USE **medical illustrators**

illustrators, scientific
USE **scientific illustrators**

Ilusiones
FL.1034
CN F.FL.ALO.ALO.ALO.ALO.AFU.ALO.ARI.AFU.ARI.BOK

image-bearing colloids
USE **binders**
emulsion

image cards
USE **aperture cards**

image material
USE **final image material**

image material, final
USE **final image material**

imagery
BM.6 (R)
CN B.BM.AFU.AFU.AFU.ARI

imagery, serial
USE **serial art**

imaginary architecture
USE **fantastic architecture**

imagination
BM.29 (L,R)
CN B.BM.AFU.AFU.ALO.ARI.AFU

imagism
BM.313 (L,R)
CN B.BM.AFU.AXC.EFQ.ARI.ALO

Imagist (Chicago Imagist)
USE **Chicago Imagist**

Imagist, Abstract
USE **Abstract Imagist**

Imagist, Chicago
USE **Chicago Imagist**

imams
HG.237 (L)
ALT **imam**
SN Prayer leaders and officiating priests of Islamic mosques. (W)
CN H.HG.AFU.AXC.AXC.BIQ.AFU.BCW

imarets
RK.948
ALT **imaret**
SN Use for Turkish hospices established for pilgrims and other travelers; in some contexts may also denote Turkish soup kitchens.
CN V.RK.AFU.ALO.ALO.ELK.ARI.AFU

Imari
FL.2015
CN F.FL.ALO.ARI.ALO.ALO.ALO.ALO.ALO.ALO.AFU

imbibition printing
USE **dye transfer process**

imbibition process
USE **dye transfer process**

imbibition process, dye
USE **dye transfer process**

imbrex
MT.163
SN A tile, semicircular in shape, which fits over the joints in a tile roof. (HAS)
CN M.MT.AFU.AFU.AFU.AXC.ALO.ALO.ALO.AFU.AFU.ARI

imbrication
DG.136
ALT **imbricated**
SN Use for the arrangement of forms, whether tiles, shingles, or a decorative pattern, in which rows of repeating elements successively overlap one another.
CN D.DG.AFU.ARI.ALO.BUE

imbuia
MT.1320
SN Brazilian wood resembling walnut, from the tree Nectandra villosa, valued for cabinet work, flooring, and furniture. (MH)
UF canella
embuia
embuya
imbuya
Phoebe porosa
CN M.MT.AFU.AFU.ALO.BIQ.DCU.AFU.AFU.AFU.MQW.ARI

imbuya
USE **imbuia**

imitation
USE **mimesis**

imitation embossing
USE **thermography**

imitations
USE **copies**

Immaculate
USE **Precisionist**

Immaculate Conception
BM.684 (L,R)
UF Conception, Immaculate
CN B.BM.BZY.ALO.AFU.AXC

immigrants
HG.792 (L,R)
ALT **immigrant**
CN H.HG.AFU.BOK.BOK

immigration
BM.1050 (L,R)
SN Going into a country for the purpose of permanent residence. (W)
CN B.BM.CLM.AFU.ALO.ALO

immigration records
VW.987
ALT **immigration record**
UF records, immigration
CN V.VW.AFU.ARI.ALO.BCW.AFU.AFU.AFU.ARI

immunization centers
USE **vaccination centers**

impact loads
BM.1012
UF loads, impact
loads, short term
short term loads
CN B.BM.CFS.AXC.CLM.ALO.ARI.BUE

impact printers
TB.167
ALT **impact printer**
SN Any devices that make use of mechanical impact to print characters onto paper. (DOC)
UF printers, impact
CN V.TB.AFU.ARI.BCW.AXC.AXC.ALO.ARI.AFU

impact statements, environmental
USE **environmental impact statements**

impact strength
BM.962
SN Resistance of a material to fracture by a blow expressed in terms of amount of energy absorbed before fracture. (W)
UF strength, impact
CN B.BM.CFS.AXC.BZY.BOK.CLM.AXC

impact wrenches
TB.776
ALT **impact wrench**
SN Electric or pneumatic wrenches whose adjustable torque is supplied to a nut or bolt in short, rapid impulses. (MEANS)
UF wrenches, impact
CN V.TB.AFU.BCW.BIQ.AXC.ALO.BIQ.BCW

impact, environmental
USE **environmental impact**

impasto
KT.230
UF impasto painting
loaded brush painting
painting, impasto
painting, loaded brush
painting, pastose
pastose painting
CN K.KT.AFU.ALO.DUC.CXA.ALO.AFU.BUE

impasto painting
USE **impasto**

impeaching
KG.198 (L)
SN Accusing a public official of misconduct in office before a competent tribunal, with the intent of removing that official.
CN K.KG.AFU.ALO.BCW.BCW

Imperial
FL.2716
UF Roman Empire
CN F.FL.ALO.AXC.ALO.ALO.AFU.AXC.ALO

imperial card photographs
USE **imperial prints**

imperial card photoprints
USE **imperial prints**

imperial dining tables
USE **extension dining tables**

imperial green
USE **emerald green**

imperial palaces
RK.343
ALT **imperial palace**
UF palaces, imperial
CN V.RK.AFU.ALO.ALO.AXC.ALO.BOK.BOK.ALO.AXC.ALO

imperial prints
VJ.79
ALT **imperial print**
SN Use for card photographs on mounts measuring about 7 by 10 inches.
UF card photographs, imperial
imperial card photographs
imperial card photoprints
imperials
photoprints, imperial card
prints, imperial
CN V.VJ.AFU.AFU.BCW.AFU.AXC

Imperial, Early
USE **Early Imperial**

Imperial, Late
USE **Late Antique**

impériales
USE **canopies (bed components)**

imperials
USE **imperial prints**

imperiled places
USE **endangered places**

imperiled sites
USE **endangered places**

impervious material
USE **waterproof materials**

implements
USE **tools**

impluvia
RT.1464
ALT **impluvium**
SN Basins, usually rectangular, in the center of the atrium of Roman houses to receive rainwater from the surrounding roofs. (PDARC)
CN V.RT.ALO.BCW.ALO.ARI.BIQ

importers
HG.419
ALT **importer**
CN H.HG.AFU.AXC.BOK.DUC

importing
KG.168 (R)
ALT **imported**

CN K.KG.AFU.ALO.AFU.AXC

imposition process
KT.445 (L)
SN Process for printing a combination of forms on the same sheet by drawing or printing individual items on transfer paper, trimming, and affixing them to a larger backing sheet of transfer paper in positions corresponding to layout. (TBL)
CN K.KT.AFU.ALO.DUC.DUC.ALO.ARI

impost blocks
RT.288
ALT **impost block**
SN Stones, usually with the shape of a truncated inverted pyramid, placed between capitals and the arches that spring from them.
UF blocks, impost
dosserets
supercapitals
CN V.RT.AFU.AFU.AFU.BCW.AFU.ALO.ARI

imposts
RT.289
ALT **impost**
SN Projecting members, often molded, on which the ends of an arch rest.
CN V.RT.AFU.AFU.AFU.BCW.AFU.ALO.AXC

impregnated materials
MT.2805
UF materials, impregnated
CN M.MT.AFU.BCW.CLM

impregnated wood
MT.1418 (L)
SN Wood impregnated with thermosetting resin then subjected to heat and pressure to provide both resin curing and compression. (DAC)
UF compreg
compregnated wood
plastic-impregnated wood
resin-treated wood
wood, compregnated
wood, impregnated
wood, plastic-impregnated
wood, resin-treated
CN M.MT.AFU.AFU.ALO.BIQ.DCU.ALO.BCW

impresas
VW.703 (R)
ALT **impresa**
SN Use for devices, usually composed of a design and a motto, that signify an individual rather than a family or organization, popular especially in the Renaissance.
UF imprese
CN V.VW.AFU.ALO.ALO.AFU.AFU.ALO

imprese
USE **impresas**

impressed watermarks
VW.711
ALT **impressed watermark**
SN Watermarks produced by placing a stereo in bronze, rubber, or other substance, on the press roll of the papermaking machine and so leaving a design in the paper where it was more compressed. (LG)
UF watermarks, impressed
CN V.VW.AFU.ALO.ALO.AFU.AXC.AFU.ALO.AFU

impression printers
HG.460
ALT **impression printer**
UF printers, impression
CN H.HG.AFU.AXC.BUE.ALO.CFS.BUE.AFU

Impressionist
FL.3296 (L,R)
ALT **Impressionism**
CN F.FL.ALO.BCW.ALO.AXC.DCU.BCW

Impressionist, Abstract
USE **Abstract Impressionist**

imprisoning
USE **incarcerating**

imprisonment
USE **incarcerating**

improved land
RD.303
SN Land which has been provided with water systems, sewers, sidewalks, and other basic facilities in preparation for residential or industrial development. (DAC)
UF land, improved
land, serviced
serviced land
CN V.RD.ARI.ALO.ARI.AFU

improvement, civic
USE **civic improvement**

improvement, municipal
USE **civic improvement**

improvement, roadside
USE **roadside improvement**

impulse turbines
TB.399 (N)
ALT **impulse turbine**
SN Turbines in which the rotor is driven by fluid jets impinging directly against the blades. (W)
UF turbines, impulse
CN V.TB.AFU.ARI.DOI.BUE.ARI

in situ formed piles
USE **cast-in-place piles**

inaugurations
KM.22 (L,R)
CN K.KM.AFU.ARI.ARI.BCW

inboard profiles
VD.72
ALT **inboard profile**
SN Use for drawings of a full longitudinal section of a ship, showing internal arrangement.
UF interior profiles (ships)
profiles, inboard
profiles, interior (ships)
CN V.VD.AFU.AFU.BIQ.ALO.BIQ.AXC.AFU

Inca
FL.1170 (A,L,B,R)
UF Inka
CN F.FL.ALO.ALO.ALO.ARI.AXC.AFU.BIQ.BOK

Inca horizon
FL.1177
UF Tahuantinsuyo
CN F.FL.ALO.ALO.ALO.ARI.AXC.ALO.ALO.ARI

incarcerating
KG.203 (L)
UF imprisoning
imprisonment
CN K.KG.AFU.ALO.BCW.BOK.ARI

incense cedar
MT.1337 (L)
UF bastard cedar
cedar, bastard
cedar, incense
Libocendrus decurrens
CN M.MT.AFU.AFU.ALO.BIQ.DCU.AFU.AFU.ALO.ALO.AXC

incentives, tax
USE **tax incentives**

incinerators
TB.344 (L,B)
ALT **incinerator**
SN Apparatuses in which solid, semisolid, or gaseous combustible wastes are ignited or burned. (DAC)
CN V.TB.AFU.ARI.CRG.AFU.AFU

Incised and Punctate horizon
FL.1126
CN F.FL.ALO.ALO.ALO.ARI.ARI.AFU.AXC

Incised Banded ware
USE **Stichbandkeramik**

Incised Rim horizon
FL.1124
CN F.FL.ALO.ALO.ALO.ARI.ARI.AFU.ALO

incised ware, dark-faced
USE **dark-faced incised ware**

incising
KT.690
ALT **incised**
CN K.KT.AFU.ALO.GRC.BIQ

inclined barrel vaults
RT.540
ALT **inclined barrel vault**
SN Barrel vaults with a constant section but an inclined ridge, most commonly encountered as a ceiling for stairs.
UF barrel vaults, inclined
vaults, inclined barrel
CN V.RT.AFU.AFU.AFU.BIQ.BOK.AFU.ALO.AFU.ARI

inclined elevators
USE **slant elevators**

inclined lifts
RT.1296
ALT **inclined lift**
SN Use for devices, for raising and lowering passengers or freight on a car or platform, that travel on guide rails set on an angle, rather than being directly vertical.
UF lifts, inclined
CN V.RT.ALO.ALO.AFU.AFU.ALO

inclined planes
USE **ramps**

inclines (ramps)
USE **ramps**

inclosed basin stands
USE **enclosed basin stands**

incorporated companies
USE **corporations**

incorporation, articles of
USE **articles of incorporation**

incorporation, certificates of
USE **certificates of incorporation**

increase, population
USE **population growth**

incremental air conditioning
RT.1385
UF air conditioning, incremental
incremental air conditioning systems
incremental systems
systems, incremental air conditioning
CN V.RT.ALO.BCW.AFU.AFU.AFU.ALO

incremental air conditioning systems
USE **incremental air conditioning**

incremental systems
USE **incremental air conditioning**

Incrustation Style
USE **First Style**

incumbrances
USE **encumbrances**

indanthrone blue
MT.1606
UF blue, indanthrone
CN M.MT.AFU.AFU.ARI.AFU.AFU.ALO.ALO.ALO.AXC.AFU

indentures
VW.915 (L)
ALT **indenture**
SN Legally binding agreements between two or more parties in two or more originals or copies. Also, contracts binding one person to work for another for a given period of time.
CN V.VW.AFU.ARI.AFU.BOK.BOK.BZY

Independence Day
KM.74 (L)
CN K.KM.AFU.CFS.ALO.AFU

independent schools
USE **private schools**

indeterminate structures
USE **statically indeterminate structures**

index maps
VW.154 (L)
ALT **index map**
SN Small-scale maps keyed to an atlas or series of maps showing how the total area has been divided up by the individual maps. (LG)
UF key maps
maps, index
maps, key
CN V.VW.AFU.AFU.AFU.FZU.AXC.AFU.ARI.AFU.CLM.ALO

indexers
HG.304 (L)
ALT **indexer**
CN H.HG.AFU.AXC.BCW.ALO.BCW.AFU

indexes
VW.424 (L,R)
ALT **index**
SN Lists, usually in alphabetical order, of persons and/or subjects referred to in documents, with location of references thereto. (ICA)
UF indices
CN V.VW.AFU.AFU.ALO.EWY.BOK

indexes, annual
USE **annual indexes**

indexes, author
USE **author indexes**

indexes, card
USE **card indexes**

indexes, citation
USE **citation indexes**

indexes, cumulative
USE **cumulative indexes**

indexes, glossarial
USE **glossarial indexes**

indexes, key-word-and-context
USE **key-word-and-context indexes**

indexes, key-word-in-context
USE **key-word-in-context indexes**

indexes, key-word-out-of-context
USE **key-word-out-of-context indexes**

indexes, key-word-out-of-title
USE **key-word-out-of-title indexes**

indexes, newspaper
USE **newspaper indexes**

indexes, periodical
USE **periodical indexes**

indexes, permuted
USE **rotated indexes**

indexes, rotated
USE **rotated indexes**

indexes, subject
USE **subject indexes**

indexes, title
USE **title indexes**

indexing
KG.91 (L,B)
ALT **indexed**
SN Preparing indexes for books and other publications; analyzing the subject content of textual or visual documents and assigning terms or strings of terms representing that content.
CN K.KG.AFU.AFU.AXC.CLM

indexing and abstracting services
USE **abstracting and indexing services**

India chairs
TG.74
ALT **India chair**
UF chairs, India
CN V.TG.AFU.AFU.ALO.AFU.AFU.AFU.HTY

India ink
MT.2500 (L)
SN Inks made of carbon black pigment ground in water with water-dispersed resin used as a liquid drawing medium.
UF ink, India
CN M.MT.AFU.ARI.CRG.ALO.ALO.BCW

india ink (color)
USE **dark gray**

India paper
MT.1906
UF Bible paper
paper, Bible
paper, India
CN M.MT.AFU.AFU.ARI.ALO.ALO.AXC.ALO.ARI

Indian
FL.2185 (L,B)
CN F.FL.ALO.ARI.AXC.ALO

Indian (American)
USE **Native American**

Indian bean tree
USE **catalpa**

Indian blue
USE **indigo**

Indian boxwood
USE **boxwood**

Indian Knoll
FL.881
CN F.FL.ALO.ALO.ALO.AFU.ALO.ALO.BCW.AXC

Indian lake
USE **lac (red pigment)**

Indian madder
USE **madder**

Indian oak
USE **teak**

Indian red
MT.1699
UF caput mortuum
colcothar
red, Indian
rouge (Indian red)
CN M.MT.AFU.AFU.ARI.AFU.AFU.ALO.ALO.BCW.ARI.ARI

Indian red (color)
USE **dark reddish orange**
grayish red
strong reddish brown

Indian red (iron oxide red)
USE **iron oxide red**

Indian red, dark
USE **dark grayish red**
grayish red

Indian reservations
RD.72 (L)
ALT **Indian reservation**
UF reservations, Indian
CN V.RD.AFU.BIQ.ALO

Indian rose chestnut
USE **gangaw**

Indian rosewood
USE **East Indian rosewood**

Indian Style
USE **Daibutsuyo**

Indian Subcontinent
USE **South Asian**

Indian yellow
MT.1765
UF Indischgelb
jaune indien
pioury
piuri
puree
pwree
yellow, Indian
CN M.MT.AFU.AFU.ARI.AFU.AFU.ALO.ALO.BUE.ALO.AXC

Indian yellow (color)
USE **brilliant orange yellow**
light orange yellow
moderate orange yellow

Indian, Central
USE **Central Indian**

Indian, Eastern
USE **Eastern Indian**

Indian, Medieval
USE **Post-Gupta**

Indian, South
USE **South Indian**

Indian, Western
USE **Western Indian**

Indiana limestone
MT.668
UF limestone, Indiana
CN M.MT.AFU.AFU.AFU.DCU.AFU.ALO.AFU.ALO.ALO.AFU.AFU.ALO.BIQ

Indians, Humboldt Bay
USE **Wiyot**

indices
USE **indexes**

indicting
KG.204 (L)
UF indictment
CN K.KG.AFU.ALO.BCW.BOK.AXC

indictment
USE **indicting**

indictments
VW.917 (L)
ALT **indictment**
SN Formal written accusations originating with a prosecutor and issued by a grand jury against a party charged with a crime. (BLACKS)
CN V.VW.AFU.ARI.AFU.BOK.BOK.CFS

Indigenismo
FL.1759
ALT **Indigenism**
CN F.FL.ALO.ALO.BCW.ALO.ARI

indigenous architecture
USE **vernacular architecture**

indigo
MT.1523 (L,R)
UF blue, Indian
blue, indigo
blue, intense
Indian blue
indigo blue
indigofera
intense blue
CN M.MT.AFU.AFU.ARI.AFU.AFU.AFU.AFU.AFU.AXC.AXC

indigo (color)
USE **blackish blue**
dark blue
dark bluish gray
dark grayish blue
dark grayish purple
deep blue

indigo blue
USE **dark grayish blue**
grayish blue
grayish purplish blue
indigo

indigo, red
USE **orchil**

indigofera
USE **indigo**

indirect lighting
RT.1360 (B)
SN Lighting achieved by directing the light source toward a ceiling, wall, or other reflecting surface, rather than directly at the area to be illuminated. (MEANS)
UF lighting, indirect
CN V.RT.ALO.AXC.AFU.BOK

Indischgelb
USE **Indian yellow**

indiscrets
TG.302
ALT **indiscret**
SN Settees formed of three linked armchairs. (DDA)
UF chairs, three-seated
confidents à trois places
indiscrets à trois places
three-seated chairs
CN V.TG.AFU.AFU.ALO.ALO.BUE.ALO

indiscrets à trois places
USE **indiscrets**

individualism
BM.513 (L,R)
SN The ethical doctrine or principal that the interests of the individual are or ought to be paramount in determination of conduct. (W)
CN B.BM.BIQ.AXC.CFS

Individualist
FL.1931
CN F.FL.ALO.ARI.ALO.AFU.AFU.AXC.ALO.BIQ

Indonesian
FL.2368 (L,B)
CN F.FL.ALO.ARI.BCW.ARI

indoor air pollution
BM.431 (L)
UF air pollution, indoor
pollution, indoor air
CN B.BM.AXC.BCW.AFU.AFU.AFU

indoor air quality
BM.203

UF air quality, indoor
IAQ
quality, indoor air
CN B.BM.AFU.ALO.ARI.AFU

indoor climate control
USE **HVAC**

indoor courts
USE **indoor tennis courts**

indoor gardening
KT.491 (A,L,B)
UF gardening, indoor
CN K.KT.AFU.ALO.DZW.AFU.ALO

indoor lighting
USE **interior lighting**

indoor photography
KT.395 (L)
UF photography, indoor
CN K.KT.AFU.ALO.DUC.DIO.ARI.ARI.BZY.ARI

indoor running tracks
USE **indoor tracks**

indoor tennis courts
RK.1020 (B)
ALT **indoor tennis court**
UF courts, indoor tennis
indoor courts
tennis courts, indoor
CN V.RK.AFU.ALO.ALO.EWY.ALO.CFS.AFU

indoor tracks
RK.1501
ALT **indoor track**
UF indoor running tracks
tracks, indoor
CN V.RK.ALO.ALO.BCW.CFS.AFU

Indravarman I
FL.2333
CN F.FL.ALO.ARI.BCW.ALO.ARI.AFU.AFU

Indravarman II
FL.2348
CN F.FL.ALO.ARI.BCW.ALO.ARI.AFU.DOI

induction brazing
KT.794
SN Brazing method where heat is developed by electricity in a heating coil and induced into the parts to be brazed. (HORNB)
UF brazing, induction
CN K.KT.AFU.ALO.HOE.BCW.ALO.AFU.AFU.AFU.AXC

indulgence
BM.685 (L)
SN Remission of the punishment, including purgatorial atonement, due by divine justice for sins whose guilt has been pardoned by the reception of the sacrament of penance. (W)
CN B.BM.BZY.ALO.AFU.BCW

Indus
USE **Indus Valley**

Indus Valley
FL.2187 (L)
UF Indus
CN F.FL.ALO.ARI.AXC.ALO.AFU.AFU

industrial alcohol
USE **methyl alcohol**

industrial and labor relations
USE **industrial relations**

industrial arbitrators
HG.314 (L)
ALT **industrial arbitrator**
UF arbitrators, industrial
CN H.HG.AFU.AXC.BCW.ALO.BIQ.AFU.AFU

industrial archaeologists
HG.257
ALT **industrial archaeologist**
UF archaeologists, industrial
CN H.HG.AFU.AXC.BCW.AFU.ALO.ALO

industrial archaeology
KD.106 (A,L,B,R)
UF archaeology, industrial
CN K.KD.AFU.ALO.ALO.BCW

industrial architecture
USE **industrial buildings**

industrial areas
USE **industrial districts**

industrial buildings
RK.605 (A,L,N,B,R)
ALT **industrial building**
UF architecture, industrial
buildings, industrial
facilities, industrial
industrial architecture
industrial facilities
CN V.RK.AFU.ALO.ALO.CLM.ALO

industrial complexes
RG.94
ALT **industrial complex**
SN Use generally for any grouping of diversified industrial buildings and related facilities.
UF complexes, industrial
CN V.RG.AFU.AFU.BUE

industrial design
KT.102 (L,B,R)
SN Use broadly to refer to the design of machine-made consumer and commercial products. (PG)
UF design, industrial
CN K.KT.AFU.ALO.CFS.BOK

industrial designers
HG.156 (A,L,B)
ALT **industrial designer**
UF designers, industrial
CN H.HG.AFU.AXC.AXC.AFU.AFU.ALO.BCW.BOK

industrial development
USE **industrialization**

industrial districts
RG.271 (B)
ALT **industrial district**
UF districts, industrial
industrial areas
industrial zones
CN V.RG.ALO.AFU.ALO.AXC

industrial engineering
KD.228 (L)
SN Professional field applying principles of engineering and scientific management in industrial enterprises to maintain efficiency and high productivity. (W)
UF engineering, industrial
engineering, management
management engineering
CN K.KD.AFU.ARI.BIQ.BOK

industrial engineers
HG.638 (L)
ALT **industrial engineer**
UF engineers, industrial
CN H.HG.AFU.AXC.BZY.BCW.BOK

industrial estates
USE **industrial parks**

industrial expositions
KM.68 (L)
UF expositions, industrial
CN K.KM.AFU.BUE.ARI

industrial facilities
USE **industrial buildings**

industrial history
KD.141 (L,B)
UF history, industrial
CN K.KD.AFU.ALO.CLM.AFU.AFU

industrial history museums
USE **industrial museums**

industrial housing
RG.93 (A,L,R)
UF company housing
employee housing
housing, company
housing, employee
housing, industrial
housing, worker's
worker's housing
CN V.RG.AFU.AFU.BOK.BIQ.AXC

industrial jewels
MT.572
SN Hard stones, usually ruby and sapphire, used chiefly for bearings and impulse pins in instruments and for recording needles. (MH)
UF jewels, industrial
CN M.MT.AFU.AFU.AFU.CFS.ALO.ALO

industrial location
BM.1086 (A,L,B)
UF location of industries
location, industrial
location, plant
plant location
CN B.BM.CLM.ARI

industrial majolica
USE **majolica**

industrial museums
RK.397 (A,L)
ALT **industrial museum**
UF industrial history museums
museums, industrial
CN V.RK.AFU.ALO.ALO.BCW.AXC.
ARI.AXC.BCW

industrial painters
HG.596 (L)
ALT **industrial painter**
UF painters, industrial
CN H.HG.AFU.AXC.BZY.AFU.DCU

industrial parks
RG.107 (A,L,B)
ALT **industrial park**
SN Use for areas zoned and planned for so-called clean industries, developed and managed as a unit, where plots are offered fully equipped with transport and installation facilities, often already including a number of multi-use buildings.
UF estates, industrial
industrial estates
industrial research parks
parks, industrial
research parks, industrial
CN V.RG.AFU.AFU.BUE.ALO

industrial photography
KT.300 (L)
UF photography, industrial
CN K.KT.AFU.ALO.DUC.DIO.AFU.BZY

industrial plants
USE **factories**

industrial relations
KD.157 (L)
UF industrial and labor relations
labor and industrial relations
labor relations
relations, industrial
relations, labor
CN K.KD.AFU.ALO.DCU

industrial research parks
USE **industrial parks**

industrial sites
RG.209 (L)
ALT **industrial site**
SN Use for building sites upon which one or more industries are planned or located. For a grouping of industrial buildings use **industrial complexes** or **industrial parks.**
UF factory sites
sites, factory
sites, industrial
CN V.RG.AFU.AFU.DZW.ALO.ALO

industrial stores
USE **company stores**

industrial towns
RD.52 (A,B)
ALT **industrial town**
SN Designates settlements, built mostly since the Industrial Revolution, in which the primary employment is in factories. When the primary employment is in factories for the manufacture of paper, steel, or textiles, use **mill towns.** When settlements are purposely built by factory owners to attract workers to isolated locations, use **factory villages.**
UF factory towns
towns, factory
towns, industrial
CN V.RD.AFU.AXC.BIQ

industrial unions
USE **trade unions**

industrial zones
USE **industrial districts**

industrialists
HG.420 (L)
ALT **industrialist**
SN Persons owning or engaged in the management of an industry. (W)
CN H.HG.AFU.AXC.BOK.DZW

industrialization
BM.1081 (L,B,R)
SN The process of becoming or state of being industrialized. (W)
UF development, industrial
industrial development
CN B.BM.CLM.ALO.ARI

industries
HG.855 (L)
ALT **industry**
SN Groups of productive or profit-making enterprises or organizations that share a similar technological structure and that supply similar goods or services.
UF trades
CN H.HG.ALO.CLM

industries, cottage
USE **cottage industries**

industries, village
USE **cottage industries**

industry
BM.397 (L,R)
CN B.BM.ARI.CXA

industry, electricity supply
USE **electric utilities**

inelastic buckling
KT.888
UF buckling, inelastic
CN K.KT.ALO.AFU.ALO

inert materials
MT.2806
SN Materials, such as the aggregate in a concrete mixture, that do not enter into a chemical reaction. (PUTNAM)
UF materials, inert
CN M.MT.AFU.BCW.CRG

inert pigment
MT.1553
UF base
pigment, inert
CN M.MT.AFU.AFU.ARI.AFU.AFU.
ALO.AFU.AFU.ARI.AFU

inert white pigment
USE **transparent white pigment**

inertia
BM.897 (L)
SN Property of matter by which it remains at rest or in uniform motion in the same straight line unless acted upon by some external force. (W)
CN B.BM.CFS.AXC.BIQ.AFU.AXC.AXC

inertia, moment of
USE **moment of inertia**

infant schools
USE **nursery schools**

infill
BM.1073 (A,B)
SN Use for architectural design which attempts to maintain the character of an older area by adding new buildings which are architecturally similar.
UF development, infill
housing, infill
infill development
infill housing
CN B.BM.CLM.ALO.ALO.AFU.ALO.
ALO

infill development
USE **infill**

infill housing
USE **infill**

infinity
BM.812 (L)
CN B.BM.CFS.ARI.BCW

infirmaries
RK.775 (L,B)
ALT **infirmary**
SN Use for health care units which provide uncomplicated medical and nursing care for residents or members of an institution or other facility.
CN V.RK.AFU.ALO.ALO.CXA.ALO.
AFU.BIQ

infirmary beds
USE **hospital beds**

inflammable materials
USE **fire-resistant materials**

inflatable furniture
TG.794 (B)
UF air-supported furniture
blow-up furniture
furniture, air-supported
furniture, blow-up
furniture, inflatable
furniture, pneumatic
pneumatic furniture
CN V.TG.AFU.ARI.BIQ

inflatable structures
USE **air-inflated structures**

inflected arches
USE **inverted arches**

influence
BM.38 (L,B)
CN B.BM.AFU.AFU.ALO.BUE

influence lines
BM.908 (L)
SN Graphs of the shear stress, bending moment, or other effect of a movable load on a structural member versus the position of the load. (MHDSTT)
UF lines, influence
CN B.BM.CFS.AXC.BIQ.ALO.ARI

Informal art
USE **Art Informel**

informal gardens
USE **landscape gardens**

information bureaus
USE **information centers**

information centers
RK.689 (A,L,B)
ALT **information center**
SN Use for buildings or other structures erected for the dissemination to the public of such items as tourist brochures, shopping guides, travel maps, or other documents, or for structures on which such information is publicly displayed.
UF advice centers
bureaus, information
centers, advice
centers, information
centers, tourist information
information bureaus
tourist information centers
CN V.RK.AFU.ALO.ALO.CRG.ARI

information centers (organizations)
USE **information services**

information clearinghouses
USE **clearinghouses**

information management
KG.92
SN Use broadly for functions associated with the organization and control of information, including processing, storage, and retrieval. For the gathering and recording of information, use **documenting.**
UF management, information
CN K.KG.AFU.AFU.AXC.CRG

information retrieval
KG.94 (L)
SN Searching, locating, and retrieving data from a file or database. (ALAG)
UF data retrieval
retrieval, data
retrieval, information
CN K.KG.AFU.AFU.AXC.CRG.ALO

information retrieval services
HG.868
ALT **information retrieval service**
SN Automated information services which search for, locate, and retrieve data, either directly or in the form of citations to data sources, from electronically stored databases in response to users' queries. For specifically those services which provide direct answers to users' queries, or which provide direct access to sources of the needed information, prefer **online reference services.**
UF data search services
database search services, online
information storage and retrieval services
online database search services
online information retrieval services
online retrieval services
online search services
retrieval services, information
retrieval services, online
search services, data
search services, online
services, data search
services, information retrieval
services, information storage and retrieval
services, online search
storage and retrieval services, information
CN H.HG.ALO.DIO.AFU.ARI

information science
KD.158 (L)
SN Use for the study of the nature, collection, and management of data and information in automated environments. (PG)
UF science, information
CN K.KD.AFU.ALO.DIO

information scientists
HG.303 (L)
ALT **information scientist**
SN Persons who engage in the activities of information science or who design automated information systems.
UF scientists, information
CN H.HG.AFU.AXC.BCW.ALO.BCW

information services
HG.865 (L)
ALT **information service**
SN Organizations, either commercial or nonprofit, which provide information or documents (in any media), or facilitate access to them.
UF centers, information (organizations)
information centers (organizations)
services, information
CN H.HG.ALO.DIO.AFU

information storage
KG.98 (L)
SN Recording information in order to retain it for subsequent use. (DOC)
UF storage, information
CN K.KG.AFU.AFU.AXC.CRG.ARI

information storage and retrieval services
USE **information retrieval services**

information technology
BM.1136 (L)
SN Technology concerned with the use of microelectronics, computers, and telecommunication to acquire, process, store, and disseminate vocal, pictorial, textual, and numeric information. (LCSH)
UF IT
technology, information
CN B.BM.CXA.AFU.ARI

information vendors
USE **online vendors**

infrared photography
KT.401 (L,R)
UF photography, infrared
CN K.KT.AFU.ALO.DUC.DIO.ARI.ARI.CFS.ALO

infrastructure
BM.1140 (A)
SN Use for the underlying foundation or basic framework of a system or organization, especially the services and facilities which are an integral part of the life in an urban community.
UF capital plant
infrastructure, urban
plant, capital
urban infrastructure
CN B.BM.CXA.ALO.ALO

infrastructure, urban
USE **infrastructure**

infusing
KT.692
ALT **infused**
SN Introducing coating material into the voids of a porous paint, ground layer, or support. (BRAD)
CN K.KT.AFU.ALO.GRC.BOK

infusorial earth
USE **diatomaceous earth**

Ingalik
FL.1234 (L)
UF Tena
CN F.FL.ALO.ALO.ARI.AFU.AFU.ARI.CFS

inglenooks
RM.29 (A,R)
ALT **inglenook**
SN Recessed seating areas by a fire or hearth.
UF chimney corners
corners, chimney
ingles, roofed
roofed ingles
CN V.RM.AFU.DIO.AFU.AFU.ALO

ingles
USE **fireplaces**

ingles, roofed
USE **inglenooks**

Ingombe Ilede
FL.154
CN F.FL.ALO.AFU.ALO.AXC.ARI

ingots
MT.456 (L)
CN M.MT.AFU.AFU.AFU.BZY.AFU.ALO.ALO

inhabited scrolls
DG.146
ALT **inhabited scroll**
SN Scrollwork involving human and animal figures intertwined with the curving lines. (RAWS)
UF peopled scrolls
scrolls, inhabited
scrolls, peopled
CN D.DG.AFU.ARI.ALO.CRG.ALO

inhibitors
MT.2315 (L)
ALT **inhibitor**
UF chemical inhibitors
inhibitors, chemical
CN M.MT.AFU.ARI.ALO.DCU

inhibitors, chemical
USE **inhibitors**

inhibitors, corrosion
USE **corrosion inhibitors**

inhibitors, rust
USE **rust inhibitors**

Initial period
FL.1136
CN F.FL.ALO.ALO.ALO.ARI.AXC.AFU.ALO

initial sketches
USE **preliminary sketches**

initials
VW.46 (L,R)
ALT **initial**
CN V.VW.AFU.AFU.AFU.CRG.AXC.AFU

initials (motif)
USE **monograms**

initiations
KM.23 (L,R)
CN K.KM.AFU.ARI.ARI.BIQ

injection molding
KT.148 (L)
SN Plastic molding process whereby hot thermoplastic material is forced from a heating chamber through a small channel or sprue into a cooled mold under enough pressure and at a high enough speed to fill the mold while the charge is still soft. (DIETZ)
UF molding, injection
CN K.KT.AFU.ALO.DOI.CRG.ARI

Inju School
FL.3454
CN F.FL.ALO.BIQ.AFU.DIO.AFU.AFU.AFU

ink
MT.2495 (N,R)
SN A fluid medium used for drawings or tracings. An opaque, usually black, pigment is mixed with a vehicle such as water to produce a fluid which can be applied with a pen or stylus. Through the end of the 19th century, ink was supplied in dried form in sticks or blocks which were ground and mixed with water as needed. At the beginning of this century prepared inks became popular. (MCFAD)
CN M.MT.AFU.ARI.CRG.ALO.ALO

ink black
USE **dark bluish gray**

ink blue
USE **dark grayish blue**

ink jet printers
TB.171
ALT **ink jet printer**
SN Printers that form the required image by projecting droplets of ink onto the paper. (DOC)
UF printers, ink jet
CN V.TB.AFU.ARI.BCW.AXC.AXC.ALO.ARI.ALO.AFU

ink process
USE **ferrogallic process**

ink slabs
USE **inkstones**

ink, black carbon
USE **black carbon ink**

ink, Chinese
USE **Chinese ink**

ink, colored
USE **colored ink**

ink, cuttlefish
USE **sepia**

ink, India
USE **India ink**

ink, india (color)
USE **dark gray**

ink, invisible
USE **invisible ink**

ink, iron gall
USE **iron gall ink**

ink, Japanese
USE **Japanese ink**

ink, Roman
USE **atramentum**

ink, secret
USE **invisible ink**

ink, sympathetic
USE **invisible ink**

Inka
USE **Inca**

inkstones
TB.253 (L,N)
ALT **inkstone**
SN Stones with hollows or depressions deeper at one end than at the other; used for preparing calligrapher's ink. (HAND)
UF ink slabs
slabs, ink
CN V.TB.AFU.ARI.CLM.AFU.ALO.CFS

inlay
KT.700 (B,R)
ALT **inlaid**
SN Any process by which small pieces of one material are inserted into a larger piece of another so as to create a design. (THDAT)
CN K.KT.AFU.ALO.GRC.BZY

inlayers
HG.481
ALT **inlayer**
SN Persons who engage in inlay work.
CN H.HG.AFU.AXC.BUE.ARI.BIQ

inlaying saws
USE **buhl saws**

inner baileys
RT.1168
ALT **inner bailey**
SN Use for the spaces between an inner wall and a keep in a castle.
UF baileys, inner
CN V.RT.AFU.BUE.AFU.AFU.AFU

inner cities
RG.293 (B)
ALT **inner city**
SN Use for the usually older and more densely populated central sections of cities. (W)

UF center cities
cities, center
cities, inner
downtowns
CN V.RG.ALO.ALO.AXC

inner hearths
USE **back hearths**

inner-spring seats, coiled
USE **coil-spring seats**

inner stages
USE **chambers**

inns
RK.956 (A,L,N,B,R)
ALT **inn**
SN Use for public accommodations with an emphasis equally on good food and good drink.
UF pandokeia
CN V.RK.AFU.ALO.ALO.ELK.BIQ

inns, bed-and-breakfast
USE **bed-and-breakfasts**

inns, motor
USE **motels**

inorganic black pigment, artificial
USE **artificial inorganic black pigment**

inorganic black pigment, synthetic
USE **artificial inorganic black pigment**

inorganic blue pigment
MT.1581
UF blue pigment, inorganic
pigment, inorganic blue
CN M.MT.AFU.AFU.ARI.AFU.AFU.ALO.ALO.ALO.AFU

inorganic blue pigment, artificial
USE **artificial inorganic blue pigment**

inorganic blue pigment, synthetic
USE **artificial inorganic blue pigment**

inorganic brown pigment
MT.1612
UF brown pigment, inorganic
pigment, inorganic brown
CN M.MT.AFU.AFU.ARI.AFU.AFU.ALO.ALO.ARI.AFU

inorganic brown pigment, artificial
USE **artificial inorganic brown pigment**

inorganic brown pigment, synthetic
USE **artificial inorganic brown pigment**

inorganic chemistry
KD.263 (L)
UF chemistry, inorganic
CN K.KD.AFU.ARI.CLM.ALO.ALO

inorganic green pigment
MT.1635
UF green pigment, inorganic
pigment, inorganic green
CN M.MT.AFU.AFU.ARI.AFU.AFU.ALO.ALO.AXC.AFU

inorganic green pigment, artificial
USE **artificial inorganic green pigment**

inorganic green pigment, synthetic
USE **artificial inorganic green pigment**

inorganic pigment
MT.1549
UF mineral pigment
pigment, inorganic
pigment, mineral
CN M.MT.AFU.AFU.ARI.AFU.AFU.ALO.AFU.AFU

inorganic pigment, artificial
USE **artificial inorganic pigment**

inorganic pigment, natural
USE **natural inorganic pigment**

inorganic red pigment
MT.1668
UF pigment, inorganic red
red pigment, inorganic
CN M.MT.AFU.AFU.ARI.AFU.AFU.ALO.ALO.BCW.AFU

inorganic red pigment, artificial
USE **artificial inorganic red pigment**

inorganic red pigment, synthetic
USE **artificial inorganic red pigment**

inorganic violet pigment
MT.1711
UF pigment, inorganic violet
violet pigment, inorganic
CN M.MT.AFU.AFU.ARI.AFU.AFU.ALO.ALO.BIQ.AFU

inorganic violet pigment, artificial
USE **artificial inorganic violet pigment**

inorganic violet pigment, synthetic
USE **artificial inorganic violet pigment**

inorganic yellow pigment
MT.1758
UF pigment, inorganic yellow
yellow pigment, inorganic
CN M.MT.AFU.AFU.ARI.AFU.AFU.ALO.ALO.BUE.AFU

inorganic yellow pigment, artificial
USE **artificial inorganic yellow pigment**

inorganic yellow pigment, synthetic
USE **artificial inorganic yellow pigment**

inpainting
KT.627
SN In the conservation of paintings, coloring or painting an area that has been damaged or obliterated so that it blends with the surrounding colors. (MAYER)
CN K.KT.AFU.ALO.FZU.AFU.AFU

input devices
TB.150 (L)
ALT **input device**
SN Any devices that transfer data, programs, or signals into a processor system. (DOC)
UF devices, input
CN V.TB.AFU.ARI.BCW.AXC.AFU

insane asylums
USE **psychiatric hospitals**

insane, art of the
USE **art brut**

insanity
BM.718 (L,R)
CN B.BM.CFS.AFU.AFU.AFU.AFU

inscribers
HG.720
ALT **inscriber**
SN Persons who assign or address a work of art or literature, in a style less formal than that of a dedication; also, persons who mark a surface with words or characters, especially in a durable or conspicuous way.
CN H.HG.AFU.BCW.CRG

inscriptions
VW.41 (A,L,R)
ALT **inscription**
CN V.VW.AFU.AFU.AFU.CRG

inscriptions, house
USE **house marks**

insect wax
MT.2189
UF wax, insect
CN M.MT.AFU.AFU.ARI.BZY.AFU.AFU

insect wax, Chinese
USE **Chinese insect wax**

insecticides
MT.2379 (L)
ALT **insecticide**
UF pesticides
CN M.MT.AFU.ARI.BOK.BCW

insert bottom seams
TF.657
ALT **insert bottom seam**
UF bottom seams, insert
seams, insert bottom
CN V.TF.ALO.ARI.ARI.BUE.BUE

inserts
VB.97
ALT **insert**
SN Use for something inserted into a larger whole, as a piece of cloth to a garment or a replaced portion of a drawing.
CN V.VB.ALO.BOK.BOK

inserts (hardware)
TF.377
ALT **insert (hardware)**
SN Units of hardware embedded into concrete or masonry to provide a means of attaching something. (MEANS)
CN V.TF.AFU.AFU.AFU.ALO.AFU.BZY

inserts, adjustable
USE **adjustable inserts**

inserts, channel
USE **channel inserts**

inserts, concrete
USE **concrete inserts**

inserts, continuous
USE **channel inserts**

inserts, furring
USE **furring inserts**

inserts, nailer
USE **nailer inserts**

inserts, nut
USE **nut inserts**

inserts, reglet
USE **reglet inserts**

inserts, wedge
USE **wedge inserts**

inshaves
USE **scorpers**

inside
USE **interior**

inside corner trowels
TB.634
ALT **inside corner trowel**
SN Trowels used to finish inside corners. (PUTNAM)
UF corner trowels, inside
trowels, inside corner
CN V.TB.AFU.BCW.BCW.ALO.HCQ.ARI.AFU

inside-door locks
USE **room-door locks**

inside planes
USE **cooper's stoup planes**

inside shaves
USE **scorpers**

insignias
VW.704 (L,R)
ALT **insignia**
SN Use for devices that indicate rank, honor, or association with a large organized entity, such as a corps of the military.
CN V.VW.AFU.ALO.ALO.AFU.AFU.ARI

inspecting
KG.23 (A,L,B)
SN Examining or reviewing officially. (RLG7)
CN K.KG.AFU.AFU.AFU.CXA

inspiration
BM.31 (L)
CN B.BM.AFU.AFU.ALO.ARI.ALO

installations (military complexes)
USE **military installations**

installations, electrical
USE **electrical systems**

installations, military
USE **military installations**

installing
KT.577
CN K.KT.AFU.ALO.ERE.ALO

instant camera photographs
VJ.32
ALT **instant camera photograph**
SN Photographic prints made from film packets which contain their own developing chemicals and are exposed in a special camera. (GMGPC)
UF diffusion transfer prints
instant photographs
instant prints
photographs, instant camera
Polaroid (TM) instant photographs
prints, diffusion transfer
prints, instant
CN V.VJ.AFU.AFU.ARI.AFU.AXC

instant locks
TF.223
ALT **instant lock**
SN Automatic locks actuated by the closing of the door; also, time locks working on the same principle. (MEANS)
UF locks, instant
CN V.TF.AFU.AFU.AFU.AFU.DIO.BIQ.AFU.ERE.AFU

instant photographs
USE **instant camera photographs**

instant photography
USE **diffusion transfer process**

instant prints
USE **instant camera photographs**

instantaneous photographs
VJ.97
ALT **instantaneous photograph**
SN Use for early photographs (beginning about 1860) that did not need long exposure times, thus being able to capture figures in motion; often showing city street scenes.
UF photographs, instantaneous
CN V.VJ.AFU.ARI.AFU.ARI

institutes
HG.857 (L,B)
ALT **institute**
SN Organizations for the promotion of some estimable or learned cause, the welfare of some group, or that constitute a technical or professional authority in a field of work or study. (W)
CN H.HG.ALO.CRG

institutes, research
USE **research institutes**

institutions
HG.858
ALT **institution**
CN H.HG.ALO.CXA

institutions, charitable
USE **charities**
welfare buildings

institutions, correctional
USE **correctional institutions**

institutions, financial
USE **financial institutions**

institutions, health care
USE **health facilities**

institutions, juvenile
USE **reformatories**

institutions, maximum-security
USE **maximum-security prisons**

institutions, medium-security
USE **medium-security prisons**

institutions, mental
USE **psychiatric hospitals**

institutions, minimum-security
USE **minimum-security prisons**

institutions, penal
USE **correctional institutions**

institutions, public
USE **public institutions**

institutions, social
USE **social institutions**

instruction
USE **teaching**

instructional materials
VW.335 (L)
ALT **instructional material**
UF materials, instructional
CN V.VW.AFU.AFU.ALO.CXA

instructional materials centers
USE **audiovisual centers**
learning resource centers

instructions
VW.345
SN Information in the form of outlines of procedures, as directions or commands. (GAHLM)
CN V.VW.AFU.AFU.ALO.CXA.AXC

instructions to bidders
VW.810
ALT **instruction to bidders**
SN Documents outlining the procedures for preparing and submitting bids.
UF bid instructions
bidders, instructions to
instructions, bid
CN V.VW.AFU.ARI.AFU.AXC.AXC

instructions, bid
USE **instructions to bidders**

instructors
USE teachers

instructors, private
USE tutors

instrumentalists
HG.77
ALT instrumentalist
CN H.HG.AFU.AXC.AXC.AFU.AFU.AFU.BIQ.BIQ.BCW

instruments
TB.6 (L,B)
ALT instrument
SN Tools used for delicate or precision work. (W)
CN V.TB.AFU.AFU.ALO.AFU

instruments, drawing
USE drawing instruments

instruments, legal
USE legal instruments

instruments, meteorological
USE meteorological instruments

instruments, negotiable
USE negotiable instruments

instruments, optical
USE optical instruments

instruments, scientific
USE scientific instruments

instruments, statutory
USE statutes

instruments, writing
USE writing instruments

insulae
RK.369
ALT insula
SN Use only for ancient Roman tenement or apartment houses.
CN V.RK.AFU.ALO.ALO.AXC.AXC.BCW

Insular
FL.3122 (R)
CN F.FL.ALO.BCW.ALO.ALO.AFU.BOK.ARI.ALO.ARI

insulating concrete
MT.208
SN Concrete having low thermal conductivity and used as thermal insulation. (DAC)
UF concrete, insulating
CN M.MT.AFU.AFU.AFU.BCW.AFU.ALO.AFU

insulating glass
MT.278
UF glass, insulating
thermopane
CN M.MT.AFU.AFU.AFU.BIQ.AFU.AXC.BIQ

insulating materials
USE insulation

insulating materials, acoustic
USE acoustical insulation

insulating materials, thermal
USE thermal insulation

insulation
MT.2402 (L,R)
UF insulating materials
materials, insulating
CN M.MT.AFU.ARI.BZY.BCW

insulation, acoustical
USE acoustical insulation

insulation, batt
USE batt insulation

insulation, blanket
USE batt insulation

insulation, board
USE rigid insulation

insulation, electrical
USE electrical insulation

insulation, fill
USE fill insulation

insulation, fill-type
USE fill insulation

insulation, flexible
USE flexible insulation

insulation, foil back
USE reflective insulation

insulation, granular-fill
USE fill insulation

insulation, heat
USE thermal insulation

insulation, loose fill
USE fill insulation

insulation, reflective
USE reflective insulation

insulation, rigid
USE rigid insulation

insulation, roll
USE roll insulation

insulation, slab
USE rigid insulation

insulation, sound
USE acoustical insulation
soundproofing

insulation, thermal
USE thermal insulation

insurance
BM.399 (A,L,B,R)
SN Coverage by contract whereby for a stipulated consideration one party undertakes to indemnify or guarantee another against loss by a specified contingency or peril. (W)
CN B.BM.ARI.DCU

insurance agents
HG.409 (L)
ALT insurance agent
SN Agents of an insurer authorized to negotiate contracts of insurance. (W)
UF agents, insurance
CN H.HG.AFU.AXC.BOK.BZY.ALO

insurance atlases
USE fire insurance maps

insurance claims
VW.857
ALT insurance claim
UF claims, insurance
CN V.VW.AFU.ARI.AFU.BIQ.CXA.ARI.AFU

insurance maps
USE fire insurance maps

insurance policies
VW.858 (L)
ALT insurance policy
SN Documents by which one party (the insurer) in consideration of a premium, engages to indemnify another (the insured) against a contingent loss, by making a payment in compensation. (BLACKS)
UF polices, insurance
CN V.VW.AFU.ARI.AFU.BIQ.CXA.ARI.ALO

insurance records
VW.856
ALT insurance record
UF records, insurance
CN V.VW.AFU.ARI.AFU.BIQ.CXA.ARI

insurance surveys
VW.859 (L)
ALT insurance survey
UF surveys, insurance
CN V.VW.AFU.ARI.AFU.BIQ.CXA.ARI.ARI

insuring
KG.58 (L)
ALT insured
SN Assuring against a loss by a contingent event on certain stipulated conditions or at a given rate or premium. (W)
UF ensuring
underwriting
CN K.KG.AFU.AFU.ARI.CRG

intaglio printing
KT.448 (L,R)
SN A printing process by which the design is etched or engraved onto the plate, which is then covered with ink. The surface is wiped clean and the print is made from these lines directly on the paper. (THDAT)
UF printing, intaglio
CN K.KT.AFU.ALO.DUC.DUC.ALO.BCW.AFU

intakes
RT.989 (L)
ALT **intake**
SN Use for openings through which air or a fluid enters a plenum, pipe, or system.
CN V.RT.AFU.ARI.AFU.ALO.AXC

intarsia
KT.708 (L,R)
SN Italian type of wood inlay characterized especially by representational motifs.
UF tarsia
CN K.KT.AFU.ALO.GRC.CLM.ALO

integral bipacks
MT.2235
SN Color film formed from an integral, two-layer emulsion. For film with two separate emulsions bound together, use **bipacks.**
UF bipacks, integral
monopacks
CN M.MT.AFU.ALO.CXA.ALO.ARI.ALO

integral joints
TF.589
ALT **integral joint**
UF joints, integral
CN V.TF.ALO.AFU.DIO

integral latches
USE **integral locks**

integral locks
TF.209
ALT **integral lock**
SN Mortise locks in which the cylinder is contained in the knob. (MEANS)
UF integral latches
latches, integral
locks, integral
CN V.TF.AFU.AFU.AFU.AFU.DIO.BIQ.AFU.CRG.AFU

integral tripacks
MT.2236
SN Color film formed of an integral, three-layer emulsion. For film with three separate emulsions bound in register, use **tripacks.**
UF monopacks
tripacks, integral
CN M.MT.AFU.ALO.CXA.ALO.ARI.ARI

intellectual history
KD.142 (L)
SN Branch of history that deals with the evolution of ideas, how these ideas were influenced by various factors, and what happens to these ideas or thoughts among people in a given society. (ERIC)
UF history, intellectual
CN K.KD.AFU.ALO.CLM.AFU.ALO

intellectual property
BM.465 (L)
UF property, intellectual
CN B.BM.BCW.CXA.AFU.AXC

intelligent buildings
RK.1377 (A)
ALT **intelligent building**
SN Use for buildings that incorporate computerized building management systems which automatically control HVAC, security, and other systems.
UF buildings, intelligent
buildings, smart
smart buildings
CN V.RK.AFU.ALO.AXC.BCW

intense blue
USE **indigo**
phthalocyanine blue

intense green
USE **phthalocyanine green**

intensification
KT.415
SN Use for the photographic processing procedure used to increase the density of a processed negative or print to enhance overall density or contrast.
CN K.KT.AFU.ALO.DUC.DIO.ARI.AXC.CLM

intensity
BM.132
SN Use for the strength or purity of a color, determined by the quality of light reflected from it; a vivid color is of high intensity, a dull color of low intensity. (AFTP)
UF chroma
saturation
CN B.BM.AFU.AFU.ARI.BOK.ALO.ALO.ALO.ARI

intensive care units
RM.292 (L,B)
ALT **intensive care unit**
UF critical care units
ICUs
CN V.RM.AFU.DIO.AXC.AFU.AXC

intent, letters of
USE **letters of intent**

intercepting sewers
RK.550
ALT **intercepting sewer**
SN Sewers into which empty the dry-weather flows from several branch sewers or outlets and which also may receive a certain amount of storm water. (MEANS)
UF sewers, intercepting
CN V.RK.AFU.ALO.ALO.CFS.ALO.FU.ALO.ALO.ARI

interchangeable furniture
USE **sectional furniture**

interchanges
RM.479 (L,B)
ALT **interchange**
SN Road junctions that permit vehicles to pass from one road to another by a system of separate levels.
CN V.RM.ALO.ALO.ALO.ALO.BOK.AFU

intercom systems
RT.1286 (L,N)
ALT **intercom system**
UF intercommunication systems
intercoms
systems, intercom
systems, intercommunication
CN V.RT.ALO.AFU.AFU.ARI

intercommunication systems
USE **intercom systems**

intercoms
USE **intercom systems**

interference processes
KT.338
CN K.KT.AFU.ALO.DUC.DIO.ALO.CLM

intergovernmental records
VW.1050
ALT **intergovernmental record**
SN Use for records in which documents from various governmental jurisdictions are represented.
UF records, intergovernmental
CN V.VW.AFU.ARI.ALO.BCW.ALO.AXC

interim reports
USE **progress reports**

interior
DC.35
SN Existing or situated within the limiting surface or boundary of something. (W)
UF inside
internal
CN D.DC.AFU.ALO.ARI.CFS

interior decoration
KT.103 (A,L,B,R)
SN Selecting and organizing the surface coverings, draperies, furniture, and furnishings of architectural interiors.
UF decoration, interior
CN K.KT.AFU.ALO.CFS.BUE

interior decorators
HG.158 (L)
ALT **interior decorator**
SN Persons engaged in interior decoration.
UF decorators, interior
CN H.HG.AFU.AXC.AXC.AFU.AFU.ALO.BCW.BUE

interior design
KT.104 (A,L,B)
SN Design specializing in interiors, including space planning, construction, building systems, acoustics, lighting, heating, and air conditioning, as well as aesthetic or decorative schemes and spatial arrangements.

UF design, interior
CN K.KT.AFU.ALO.CFS.BZY

interior designers
HG.159 (A,L,B)
ALT **interior designer**
SN Persons engaged in interior design.
UF designers, interior
CN H.HG.AFU.AXC.AXC.AFU.AFU.ALO.BCW.BZY

interior elevations
VD.24
ALT **interior elevation**
UF elevations, interior
internal elevations
CN V.VD.AFU.AFU.BIQ.ALO.ALO.ALO

interior lighting
RT.1375 (A,L)
UF indoor lighting
lighting, indoor
lighting, interior
CN V.RT.ALO.AXC.AXC.ALO

interior perspectives
VD.81
ALT **interior perspective**
UF perspectives, interior
CN V.VD.AFU.AFU.BIQ.ARI.ALO

interior profiles (ships)
USE **inboard profiles**

interior views
VB.26
ALT **interior view**
SN Use for photographs or other representations of the interior of a building or other structure.
UF internal views
views, interior
CN V.VB.AFU.AFU.BOK.ALO.BOK

interior walls
RT.604 (A,L,B)
ALT **interior wall**
SN Walls having two interior faces and existing entirely within the exterior walls. (MEANS)
UF internal walls
walls, interior
walls, internal
CN V.RT.AFU.AFU.AFU.BIQ.BUE.AFU.ARI.AXC

interlace
DG.138 (R)
SN Various types of patterns that consist of interweaving lines or bands. If these are rectilinear, use **frets** or **fretwork**; if they form a very regular series of near circles, use **guilloche.**
UF interlacement
interlacing
labyrinth pattern (interlace)
pattern, labyrinth (interlace)
CN D.DG.AFU.ARI.ALO.BZY

interlaced splat-back chairs
USE **ribbon-back chairs**

interlacement
USE **interlace**

interlacing
USE **interlace**

interlacing arcades
RT.49
ALT **interlacing arcade**
SN Arches resting on alternate supports in one row, the arches overlapping in series where they cross. (HAS)
UF arcades, interlacing
CN V.RT.AFU.AFU.AFU.ARI.ALO.ALO

interlacing circles
USE **interlocking circles**

interlocking
FL.1178
CN F.FL.ALO.ALO.ALO.ARI.AXC.ALO.ALO.AXC

interlocking circles
DG.27
UF circles, interlocking
interlacing circles
CN D.DG.AFU.AFU.BIQ.AXC

interlocking joints
TF.648
ALT **interlocking joint**
SN In sheet metal, the joints between two parts whose preformed edges engage to form a continuous locked splice. (MEANS)
UF joints, interlocking
joints, side locking
side locking joints
CN V.TF.ALO.ARI.ARI.BOK

intermediate igneous rock
MT.611
UF igneous rock, intermediate
rock, intermediate igneous
CN M.MT.AFU.AFU.AFU.DCU.AFU.AFU.AFU.AFU.ARI

Intermediate period, Early
USE **Early Intermediate period**

Intermediate period, First
USE **First Intermediate period**

Intermediate period, Late
USE **Late Intermediate period**

Intermediate period, Second
USE **Second Intermediate period**

intermediate rafters
USE **common rafters**

intermediate ribs
USE **tiercerons**

intermediate technology
USE **appropriate technology**

intermediate varnish
MT.2473
UF varnish, intermediate
CN M.MT.AFU.ARI.CRG.AFU.BOK.AFU.ALO

intermediate ware
FL.2872
UF ware, intermediate
CN F.FL.ALO.AXC.ARI.AFU.ALO.ARI.BOK

intermediates, sepia
USE **sepia prints**

intermission alarm systems
RT.1287
ALT **intermission alarm system**
UF alarm systems, intermission
systems, intermission alarm
CN V.RT.ALO.AFU.AFU.AXC

interns' quarters
USE **interns' residences**

internal
USE **interior**

internal dye diffusion transfer process
KT.328
SN Diffusion transfer process in which color dyes migrate from the negative to a sealed film unit and residual materials used in the internal development are rendered harmless and invisible once processing is complete. Generic name for the Polaroid SX-70 (TM) process. (SHADOW)
UF diffusion transfer process, internal dye
dye diffusion transfer process, internal
Polaroid SX-70 (TM) process
SX-70 (TM) process
CN K.KT.AFU.ALO.DUC.DIO.ALO.BOK.AFU.AFU

internal elevations
USE **interior elevations**

internal migration
BM.1051 (L)
SN Use to designate population movement within a country for purposes of permanent settlement.
UF migration, internal
mobility
CN B.BM.CLM.AFU.ALO.ARI

internal shear force
USE **shear stress**

internal views
USE **interior views**

internal walls
USE **interior walls**

international affairs
USE **international relations**

international agreements
VW.899 (L)
ALT **international agreement**
SN Treaties and other agreements of a contractual character between different countries. (BLACKS)

UF agreements, international
CN V.VW.AFU.ARI.AFU.BOK.BOK.
ALO.AXC

international directories
VW.421
ALT **international directory**
UF directories, international
CN V.VW.AFU.AFU.ALO.EWY.AXC.
AFU.BOK.BOK

International Gothic
FL.3099 (R)
UF Gothic, International
International Style (Gothic)
Soft Style
Weicher Stil
CN F.FL.ALO.BCW.ALO.ALO.AFU.BIQ

international law
KD.164 (L)
UF law, international
CN K.KD.AFU.ALO.DOI.AXC

International Modern
USE **International Style**

international museums
RK.431 (L)
ALT **international museum**
UF museums, international
CN V.RK.AFU.ALO.ALO.BCW.AXC.
AXC.ARI

international organizations
HG.908 (L)
ALT **international organization**
UF organizations, international
CN H.HG.ALO.ELK.ALO

international relations
KD.177
UF international affairs
relations, international
CN K.KD.AFU.ALO.DZW.ALO

International Style
FL.3279 (A,L,B,R)
UF International Modern
CN F.FL.ALO.BCW.ALO.AXC.CRG.ALO

International Style (Gothic)
USE **International Gothic**

internegatives
VJ.6
ALT **internegative**
SN Negatives made from positive transparencies or prints (or by reversal from original negatives) for use in printing copies. (ICPEP)
CN V.VJ.AFU.AFU.AFU.ARI

internment camps
USE **concentration camps**

interns
HG.765 (L)
ALT **intern**
SN Advanced students or recent graduates in a professional field who are getting practical experience under the supervision of experienced practitioners. (W)
CN H.HG.AFU.BIQ.AXC

interns' residences
RK.222
ALT **intern's residence**
UF interns' quarters
quarters, interns'
residences, interns'
CN V.RK.AFU.ALO.ALO.AXC.AFU.BCW

interoceanic canals
RK.519 (L)
ALT **interoceanic canal**
UF canals, interoceanic
canals, sea level
sea level canals
CN V.RK.AFU.ALO.ALO.CFS.AFU.
ALO.AFU

interpositives
VJ.61
ALT **interpositive**
SN Positive photographic transparencies used as an intermediate step in making copies of negatives.
CN V.VJ.AFU.AFU.ARI.AXC.ALO

interpretation
USE **hermeneutics**

interpreters
HG.294 (L)
ALT **interpreter**
CN H.HG.AFU.AXC.BCW.ALO.AFU.
BCW.AFU

interpreters (docents)
USE **docents**

intersecting
DC.36
CN D.DC.AFU.ALO.ARI.CLM

intersections
RM.478 (L,B)
ALT **intersection**
SN Use for places where two or more roads, streets, or highways join or cross.
UF carrefours
crossroads
junctions
road junctions
CN V.RM.ALO.ALO.ALO.ALO.BOK

interviews
VW.47 (L)
ALT **interview**
SN Statements, transcripts, or recordings of conversations in which one person obtains information from another such as for research purposes, publication, or broadcast. (GAHLM)
CN V.VW.AFU.AFU.AFU.CXA

Intimist
FL.3375 (R)
ALT **Intimism**
CN F.FL.ALO.BCW.ALO.AXC.DIO.
BCW.BCW.AXC

intonaco
MT.2457
SN In fresco, the final coat of plaster on which the painter actually works, while it is still wet. (PDAT)
UF scialbo
CN M.MT.AFU.ARI.CRG.AFU.AXC.
ARI.ARI

intradoses
RT.683
ALT **intrados**
SN Inner curves or faces of arches or vaults forming the concave underside. (HAS)
CN V.RT.AFU.AFU.ALO.AFU.ALO

Intricate Style
USE **Fourth Style**

introduction, letters of
USE **letters of introduction**

Intrusive Mound
FL.882
CN F.FL.ALO.ALO.ALO.AFU.ALO.
ALO.BCW.BCW

intrusive rock
USE **plutonic rock**

intuition
BM.589 (L)
SN The act or process of coming to direct knowledge or certainty without reasoning or inferring. (W)
CN B.BM.BUE.BOK.AFU

Inuit
FL.1206 (A,L)
CN F.FL.ALO.ALO.ARI.AFU.AFU.AFU.
ALO.AFU

Inuit, Baffin Island
USE **Baffin Island Inuit**

Inuit, Caribou
USE **Caribou Inuit**

Inuit, Copper
USE **Copper Inuit**

Inuit, Labrador
USE **Labrador Inuit**

Inuit, Mackenzie
USE **Western Arctic Inuit**

Inuit, Québec
USE **Ungava**

Inuit, Western Arctic
USE **Western Arctic Inuit**

Inupiaq
FL.1200
UF Alaskan Eskimo, North
Eskimo, North Alaskan
North Alaskan Eskimo
CN F.FL.ALO.ALO.ARI.AFU.AFU.AFU.
AFU.ALO

inustion
USE **burning in (painting)**

Inuvialuit
USE **Western Arctic Inuit**

invalid's chairs
TG.181 (N)
ALT **invalid's chair**
SN Term applied to a variety of mid-19th-century chairs for invalids, many of which were patented, with ratchet mechanisms for raising and lowering the arms, back, or footrest or with large wheels for ease of motion.
UF chairs, invalid's
CN V.TG.AFU.AFU.ALO.AFU.AFU.ALO.CLM

invention
BM.39 (R)
SN The quality of original and productive creativity. Use with reference specifically to art theory, especially during the Renaissance, to mean the selection and utilization of subject matter.
UF invenzione
CN B.BM.AFU.AFU.ALO.BZY

inventories
VW.363 (A,L,N,R)
ALT **inventory**
SN Detailed lists of things in one's view or possession, especially a periodic survey of all goods and materials on hand. (AHD)
UF surveys (inventories)
CN V.VW.AFU.AFU.ALO.DCU

inventories of decedents' estates
USE **estate inventories**

inventories, archival
USE **archival inventories**

inventories, estate
USE **estate inventories**

inventories, household
USE **estate inventories**

inventories, merchandise
USE **merchandise inventories**

inventories, parish
USE **parish inventories**

inventories, probate
USE **estate inventories**

Inventories, retail
USE **merchandise inventories**

inventories, room-by-room
USE **room-by-room inventories**

inventories, stock
USE **merchandise inventories**

inventors
HG.721 (L,R)
ALT **inventor**
SN Persons who by creative imagination create a new device or process. (W)
CN H.HG.AFU.BCW.CXA

inventory control
USE **inventorying**

inventorying
KG.80 (L)
SN Listing items on hand. (RLG7)
UF control, inventory
inventory control
listing
CN K.KG.AFU.AFU.AXC.AXC.CFS

invenzione
USE **invention**

inverted arches
RT.228
ALT **inverted arch**
SN Use for arches turned upside down, so that the intrados is below the springing; a form used to distribute loads in foundations.
UF arches, inflected
arches, inverted
countervaults
inflected arches
CN V.RT.AFU.AFU.AFU.BCW.AFU.AFU.AFU.CFS

inverted perspective
KT.272
SN Use for the pictorial device of making parallel lines diverge, rather than converge, to suggest recession into depth.
UF perspective, inverted
perspective, reverse
reverse perspective
CN K.KT.AFU.ALO.DUC.DCU.BIQ.ARI

investigating
KG.24 (L)
SN Examining the particulars in an attempt to learn the facts about something hidden, unique, or complex. (RHDEL2)
CN K.KG.AFU.AFU.AFU.DCU

investing
KG.59 (L)
SN Committing funds to a project or enterprise in order to promote that project or to earn a return.
UF investment
CN K.KG.AFU.AFU.ARI.CXA

investing (metal casting)
USE **lost-wax process**

investment
USE **investing**

investment advisors
HG.422 (L)
ALT **investment advisor**
UF advisors, investment
counselors, investment
investment counselors
CN H.HG.AFU.AXC.BOK.EFQ

investment casting
USE **lost-wax process**

investment counselors
USE **investment advisors**

investments
BM.400 (L)
SN Expenditures of money for income or profit or to purchase something of extrinsic value. (W)
CN B.BM.ARI.DIO

investors
HG.423 (L)
ALT **investor**
SN Persons who seek to commit funds for profitable return.
CN H.HG.AFU.AXC.BOK.ELK

invisible hinges
TF.142
ALT **invisible hinge**
SN Use for door hinges which are completely concealed when the door is either open or closed. Distinguished from **concealed hinges** which are invisible only when the door is closed.
UF hinges, invisible
hinges, secret
secret hinges
CN V.TF.AFU.AFU.AFU.AFU.CLM.ARI.ARI

invisible ink
MT.2501
UF ink, invisible
ink, secret
ink, sympathetic
secret ink
sympathetic ink
CN M.MT.AFU.ARI.CRG.ALO.ALO.BIQ

invitations
VW.369 (N,R)
ALT **invitation**
SN Engraved, printed, or written expressions soliciting or requesting a person's company at a certain time and place. (GAHLM)
CN V.VW.AFU.AFU.ALO.DIO

invitations to bid
USE **bidding announcements**

invitations, bid
USE **bidding announcements**

invitations, wedding
USE **wedding invitations**

invoices
VW.862 (L,N)
ALT **invoice**
SN Documents showing items supplied, together with the prices charged for each; also, itemized bills or accounts. (LG)

UF bills (invoices)
CN V.VW.AFU.ARI.AFU.BIQ.CXA.AXC.ALO

iodide, silver
USE **silver iodide**

iodine scarlet
MT.1705
UF brilliant scarlet
pure scarlet
royal scarlet
scarlet, brilliant
scarlet, iodine
scarlet, pure
scarlet, royal
CN M.MT.AFU.AFU.ARI.AFU.AFU.ALO.ALO.BCW.AXC.ARI

ion plating
KT.823 (L)
UF plating, ion
CN K.KT.AFU.ALO.HOE.BCW.ALO.ALO.ARI.ARI

Iona crosses
USE **Celtic crosses**

Iona marble
MT.793
UF marble, Iona
CN M.MT.AFU.AFU.AFU.DCU.AFU.ARI.ARI.ARI.ARI.ALO

Ionian
FL.2603 (L)
CN F.FL.ALO.AXC.ALO.AFU.ALO.AXC.ALO.ALO.ALO

Ionian Island Style
FL.2686
CN F.FL.ALO.AXC.ALO.AFU.ALO.BCW.ALO.AXC

Ionic
FL.2590
CN F.FL.ALO.AXC.ALO.AFU.ALO.ARI.AXC

Ionic order
RT.54 (A,B,R)
UF order, Ionic
CN V.RT.AFU.AFU.AFU.ARI.ARI.AXC

ionization detectors
RT.1516
ALT **ionization detector**
SN Detectors of fire and smoke that work by detecting ionized particles in the air.
UF detectors, ionization
CN V.RT.ALO.BIQ.AFU.AFU.ALO.ARI.AFU

ionomer polymer
MT.2138 (L)
UF polymer, ionomer
CN M.MT.AFU.AFU.ARI.BUE.ALO.AXC.AFU.BUE

IOUs
USE **promissory notes**

Iowa
FL.1383 (L)
CN F.FL.ALO.ALO.ARI.AFU.BOK.CFS

Ipitinere
USE **Amahuaca**

Ipiutak
FL.799
CN F.FL.ALO.ALO.ALO.AFU.ALO.AFU.ALO.ALO.AFU.ALO

Ipuriná
FL.1582 (L)
UF Hypurina
Jupurina
Kangutu
Kankiti
CN F.FL.ALO.ALO.ARI.ARI.AFU.DIO

irgazin blue
MT.1607
UF blue, irgazin
CN M.MT.AFU.AFU.ARI.AFU.AFU.ALO.ALO.ALO.AXC.ALO

Irian Barat
USE **Irian Jaya**

Irian Jaya
FL.3627 (L)
UF Barat, Irian
Dutch New Guinea
Irian Barat
Jaya, Irian
New Guinea, Dutch
CN F.FL.ALO.BOK.ALO.BCW.AFU

iridescence
BM.969 (L)
ALT **iridescent**
CN B.BM.CFS.AXC.BZY.BUE.ALO

iris green
USE **sap green**

Irish
FL.3048 (L,B,R)
CN F.FL.ALO.BCW.AFU.CFS

Irish black marble
MT.775
UF black marble, Irish
Kilkenny marble
marble, Irish black
marble, Kilkenny
CN M.MT.AFU.AFU.AFU.DCU.AFU.ARI.ARI.ARI.AFU.ARI

Irish crosses
USE **Celtic crosses**

iroko
MT.1186
UF Chlorophora excelsa
CN M.MT.AFU.AFU.ALO.BIQ.DCU.AFU.AFU.AFU.FCS

iron
MT.427 (A,L,B,R)
UF ferrous metal
metal, ferrous
CN M.MT.AFU.AFU.AFU.BZY.AFU.AFU.ALO

iron (color)
USE **black**

Iron Age
FL.30 (A,L,R)
UF Age, Iron
CN F.FL.AFU.BCW.AXC

Iron Age, Early
USE **Early Iron Age**

Iron Age, Late
USE **Late Iron Age**

Iron Age, Middle
USE **Middle Iron Age**

iron alloys
MT.336 (L)
UF alloys, ferrous
alloys, iron
ferrous alloys
CN M.MT.AFU.AFU.AFU.BZY.AFU.AFU.AFU.AFU

iron blue
USE **Prussian blue**
dark gray

iron brown
USE **black**

iron foundries
USE **ironworks**

iron gall ink
MT.2502
SN Drawing material prepared by binding carbon particles in gall extract. (A-L)
UF ink, iron gall
CN M.MT.AFU.ARI.CRG.ALO.ALO.BOK

iron gray
USE **dark gray**
olive gray

iron mines
RG.102 (L)
ALT **iron mine**
UF mines, iron
CN V.RG.AFU.AFU.BUE.AFU.ALO.BCW

iron ore, bog
USE **limonite**

iron ore, magnetic
USE **magnetite**

iron ore, spathic
USE **siderite**

iron oxide red
MT.1670
UF Indian red (iron oxide red)
lead, red (iron oxide red)
Mars red
oxide, red
Oxidrot
red iron oxide

red lead (iron oxide red)
red oxide
red, Indian (iron oxide red)
red, iron oxide
red, Mars
CN M.MT.AFU.AFU.ARI.AFU.AFU.ALO.ALO.BCW.AFU.ALO

iron oxide red (color)
USE **strong brown**
strong reddish brown

iron oxide, black
USE **Mars black**

iron oxide, brown
USE **brown iron oxide**

iron printing processes
USE **iron processes**

iron process prints
USE **blueprints**

iron processes
KT.341
SN Photographic processes based on the photosensitivity of certain iron compounds. Usually require intense light and thus employ contact printing. Do not use when iron sulfate is used to develop a silver image.
UF ferric processes
iron printing processes
iron salt processes
printing processes, iron
salt processes, iron
CN K.KT.AFU.ALO.DUC.DIO.ALO.CRG

iron pyrite
USE **pyrite**

iron salt processes
USE **iron processes**

iron-wire chairs
USE **ice-cream parlor chairs**

iron yellow
USE **Mars yellow**

iron, ductile
USE **ductile iron**

iron, gray
USE **gray iron**

iron, high-alloy
USE **high-alloy iron**

iron, nodular
USE **ductile iron**

iron, structural
USE **structural iron**

iron, white
USE **white iron**

iron, wrought
USE **wrought iron**

iron, yellow oxide of
USE **Mars yellow**

ironbark
USE **gray ironbark**

ironbark, gray
USE **gray ironbark**

ironing boards
TG.746 (N)
ALT **ironing board**
UF boards, ironing
ironing tables
tables, ironing
CN V.TG.AFU.AFU.BIQ.BOK.ALO.CXA

ironing tables
USE **ironing boards**

ironmongery
USE **hardware**

irons, angle
USE **angles (rolled sections)**

irons, barking
USE **barking irons**

irons, beak
USE **beak irons**

irons, bick
USE **beak irons**

irons, branding
USE **brands**

irons, caulking
USE **caulking irons**

irons, channel
USE **channel beams**

irons, chincing
USE **chincing irons**

irons, cleaving
USE **froes**

irons, dog
USE **dogs (woodworking tools)**

irons, fire
USE **firesets**

irons, flagging
USE **flagging irons**

irons, flamming
USE **froes**

irons, grozing
USE **grozing irons**

irons, hack
USE **hardies**

irons, knocking-up
USE **jumpers**

irons, peeling
USE **barking irons**

irons, raising
USE **jumpers**

irons, rinding
USE **barking irons**

irons, rush
USE **flagging irons**

irons, snarling
USE **snarling irons**

irons, soldering
USE **soldering irons**

irons, tacking
USE **tacking irons**

irons, wrong
USE **barking irons**

ironsmiths
HG.496
ALT **ironsmith**
CN H.HG.AFU.AXC.BUE.ARI.CFS.AFU.BCW

ironstone
USE **ferruginous sandstone**
siderite

ironwood
MT.1187
SN Exceptionally tough or hard wood from any of numerous trees and shrubs, such as ebony, hornbeam, or acacia. (W)
CN M.MT.AFU.AFU.ALO.BIQ.DCU.AFU.AFU.AFU.FIM

ironwood (American hop hornbeam)
USE **American hop hornbeam**

ironwood (European hornbeam)
USE **European hornbeam**

ironwood, Persian
USE **Persian ironwood**

ironwork
MT.2769 (A,L,R)
SN Use for architectural finishings or any decorative forms in wrought or cast iron.
CN M.MT.AFU.AXC.BOK.AXC

ironworking
KT.782 (B)
SN The process of fashioning things from iron. (W)
CN K.KT.AFU.ALO.HOE.BCW.AFU.BCW

ironworks
RK.643 (A,L,B,R)
SN Mills or other buildings where iron or steel is smelted or heavy iron or steel products are made. (W)
UF foundries
foundries, iron
iron foundries
CN V.RK.AFU.ALO.ALO.CLM.ALO.ALO.AFU.AXC.BUE.AFU

irony
BM.21 (L,R)
CN B.BM.AFU.AFU.AFU.CFS.ARI

Iroquois
FL.1292 (L,R)
UF Five Nations
Six Nations
CN F.FL.ALO.ALO.ARI.AFU.ARI.BCW

irregular
DC.67
CN D.DC.AFU.ARI.CLM

irregular curves
USE **French curves**

irrigation networks
USE **irrigation systems**

irrigation systems
RD.120 (A,L,B)
ALT **irrigation system**
SN Artificial systems that water land to supply moisture for plant growth.
UF irrigation networks
irrigation works
networks, irrigation
systems, irrigation
CN V.RD.ALO.AXC.ARI.AFU

irrigation works
USE **irrigation systems**

Isabelline
FL.3162
CN F.FL.ALO.BCW.ALO.ALO.AFU.BOK.AXC.AXC.ARI

Isaiah, Igbo
USE **Igbo Isaiah**

Isala
USE **Sisala**

Isfahan School
FL.3533
CN F.FL.ALO.BIQ.AFU.GRC.AFU.AFU

Ishan
FL.251
UF Esa
Esan
CN F.FL.ALO.AFU.AXC.AFU.ALO.ALO.AXC

Ishaq
FL.3470
CN F.FL.ALO.BIQ.AFU.DUC.BUE

Ishi-no-ma
USE **Gongen**

Ishizuri-e
FL.2077
CN F.FL.ALO.ARI.ALO.ALO.ALO.AXC.ALO

Isin-Larsa
FL.2974
CN F.FL.ALO.AXC.ARI.BCW.AFU.BIQ.ALO

isinglass
MT.2349 (L)
SN A gelatin made from the dried swimming bladders, or fish sounds, of sturgeon and other fishes. (MH)
CN M.MT.AFU.ARI.ARI.AFU.ALO.ALO.AFU.AXC.AFU

Islam
BM.664 (A,L,B,R)
ALT **Islamic**
UF Mohammedan
Moslem
Muhammadanism
Muslim
CN B.BM.BZY.AFU.BCW

Islamic Revival
FL.3270 (A,R)
UF Moorish Revival
Revival, Islamic
Revival, Moorish
CN F.FL.ALO.BCW.ALO.AXC.CLM.BOK

islands
RD.220 (A,L)
ALT **island**
UF isles
CN V.RD.ARI.AFU.AXC.AFU.ALO.AXC.ALO

islands, artificial
USE **artificial islands**

islands, traffic
USE **traffic islands**

Isle of Man tables
USE **pillar and claw tables**

isles
USE **islands**

Ismailabad ware
FL.3027
UF ware, Ismailabad
CN F.FL.ALO.AXC.ARI.BIQ.ALO.AXC.BCW

Isnik pottery
USE **Iznik ware**

isobutylene-isoprene elastomer
USE **butyl rubber**

isogonic charts
VW.189
ALT **isogonic chart**
SN Charts having lines that connect places of equal magnetic declination or variation. (LG)
UF charts, isogonic
CN V.VW.AFU.AFU.AFU.FZU.AXC.AFU.ARI.AXC.BCW.AXC

isographs
TB.429 (N)
ALT **isograph**
SN Sets of two parallel rulers joined by a circular joint, marked with degrees, that combine the functions of a protractor and a set square. (W)
CN V.TB.AFU.ARI.EFQ.AFU.ARI

Isoko
FL.252 (L)
CN F.FL.ALO.AFU.AXC.AFU.ALO.ALO.BCW

isolating varnish
MT.2474
SN A dilute varnish for spray application in a very thin layer over dry oil paintings in order to prevent the paint from being disturbed or picked up by the solvent action of another coat of paint. (MAYER)
UF varnish, isolating
CN M.MT.AFU.ARI.CRG.AFU.BOK.AFU.ALO.AFU

isolation joints
TF.606
ALT **isolation joint**
SN Joints between two adjacent structures which are not in physical contact. (DAC)
UF joints, isolation
CN V.TF.ALO.ALO.AXC

isoline maps
VW.148
ALT **isoline map**
UF isopleth maps
maps, isoline
maps, isopleth
CN V.VW.AFU.AFU.AFU.FZU.AXC.AFU.ARI.AFU.BUE

isometric drawings
VD.12 (L)
ALT **isometric drawing**
SN Use for drawings in which all three spatial axes are equally inclined to the plane of projection (drawing surface).
UF drawings, isometric
isometric projections
projections, isometric
CN V.VD.AFU.AFU.BIQ.AFU.ALO

isometric projection
KT.283
SN Axonometric projection in which the three spatial axes are equally inclined to the plane of projection (drawing surface).
UF projection, isometric
CN K.KT.AFU.ALO.DUC.DCU.BOK.ALO.AFU.ALO

isometric projections
USE **isometric drawings**

isopleth maps
USE **isoline maps**

isoprene
USE **polyisoprene**

isopropyl acetate
MT.2695
UF acetate, isopropyl
CN M.MT.AFU.ARI.HZS.AFU.BOK.ALO.AXC

isopropyl alcohol
MT.2689
UF alcohol, isopropyl
CN M.MT.AFU.ARI.HZS.AFU.BOK.
AFU.BCW

Issaquena
FL.856
CN F.FL.ALO.ALO.ALO.AFU.ALO.
ALO.ARI.ARI.ARI

issues, social
USE **social issues**

issuing
KG.199
SN Sending out official or legal instruments and documents such as warrants, writs, and licenses.
CN K.KG.AFU.ALO.BCW.BIQ

isthmuses
RD.222 (L)
ALT **isthmus**
CN V.RD.ARI.AFU.AXC.AFU.ALO.
AXC.ARI

Istrian marble
MT.827
UF marble, Istrian
CN M.MT.AFU.AFU.AFU.DCU.AFU.
ARI.ARI.ARI.BOK.BOK

IT
USE **information technology**

Italian
FL.3049 (L,B)
CN F.FL.ALO.BCW.AFU.CLM

Italian blue
USE **Egyptian blue**

Italian chalk
USE **black chalk**

Italian chestnut
USE **European chestnut**

Italian earth
USE **burnt sienna**
raw sienna

Italian ocher
USE **yellow ocher**

Italian pink
USE **Dutch pink**

Italian pointed arches
RT.233
ALT **Italian pointed arch**
SN Use for pointed arches in which the length of the voussoirs increases toward the center, so that the arch of the extrados has more vertical proportions than the arch of the intrados. For similar arches when rounded use **Florentine arches.**
UF arches, Italian pointed
pointed arches, Italian
CN V.RT.AFU.AFU.AFU.BCW.AFU.
AFU.AFU.CRG.ARI

Italian Villa Style
FL.1734
SN A version of the Italianate style, usually restricted to domestic architecture and including a tall tower.
UF Bracketed mode
Tuscan Villa Style
Villa Style, Italian
Villa Style, Tuscan
CN F.FL.ALO.ALO.BCW.AFU.BUE.
ARI.AFU

Italian, South
USE **South Italian**

Italianate
FL.1733 (A,R)
SN A mid-19th-century North American residential architecture style, often featuring a low-pitched hipped roof topped by a belvedere. (THDAT)
CN F.FL.ALO.ALO.BCW.AFU.BUE.ARI

Italianate (Romanist)
USE **Romanist**

Italianizing
USE **Romanist**

Italic
FL.2732 (L)
UF Italiote
CN F.FL.ALO.AXC.ALO.ALO.ALO.AXC

Italiote
USE **Italic**
South Italian

Italo-Byzantine
FL.3082
UF Maniera greca
CN F.FL.ALO.BCW.ALO.AFU.ALO.
BCW.ALO

itaùba
MT.1191
SN Greenish yellow Brazilian wood, formerly prized for ship building.
CN M.MT.AFU.AFU.ALO.BIQ.DCU.
AFU.AFU.AFU.FOG

Iteso
USE **Teso**

itineraries
VW.942
ALT **itinerary**
SN Documents outlining a proposed journey.
CN V.VW.AFU.ARI.AFU.CRG.AFU

Itsekiri
FL.253 (L)
UF Jekri
Warri
CN F.FL.ALO.AFU.AXC.AFU.ALO.
ALO.BIQ

Itzá
FL.1527 (L)
CN F.FL.ALO.ALO.ARI.ALO.BCW.AFU

ivory
MT.965 (L,R)
SN The material that composes the tusks of elephant and some other large mammals; a medium for carving since ancient times. (MAYER)
CN M.MT.AFU.AFU.ALO.AFU.ELK.
AFU.AFU

ivory (color)
USE **grayish yellow**
light yellow
pale yellow
yellowish white

ivory black
MT.1568
UF black, ivory
Elfenbeinschwarz
noire d'ivoire
CN M.MT.AFU.AFU.ARI.AFU.AFU.
ALO.ALO.AFU.AFU.AFU.AFU.AFU

ivory board
MT.1914
SN Highly finished cardboard that is clay-coated on both sides; used chiefly for menus and printed material. (MH)
UF board, ivory
CN M.MT.AFU.AFU.ARI.ALO.ALO.
AXC.ALO.BIQ.AFU.ARI

ivory white
USE **pale yellow**

ivory yellow
USE **pale yellow**

ivory, artificial
USE **artificial ivory**

ivory, light
USE **pale yellow**

ivorytypes
VJ.114
ALT **ivorytype**
SN Use for photographic prints made, by various procedures, to resemble miniature paintings on ivory.
UF American ivorytypes
artificial ivorytypes
ivorytypes, American
ivorytypes, artificial
CN V.VJ.AFU.ARI.ALO.BIQ

ivorytypes, American
USE **ivorytypes**

ivorytypes, artificial
USE **ivorytypes**

ivy
USE **dark greenish gray**

ivy green
USE **dark grayish olive green**
grayish olive green

ivy, dark
USE **dark greenish gray**

iwans
RM.246
ALT **iwan**
SN Large vaulted halls having one side open to a court; prevalent in Parthian, Sassanian, and Islamic architecture. (HAS)
UF aiwans
CN V.RM.AFU.DIO.ARI.AFU.AXC

Ixil
FL.1533 (L)
CN F.FL.ALO.ALO.ARI.ALO.BIQ.AFU.ALO

Ixora ferrea
USE **hackia**

Ixtlán
FL.1072
CN F.FL.ALO.ALO.ALO.ALO.AFU.ALO.BCW.BCW.AFU

Izapa
FL.1033
CN F.FL.ALO.ALO.ALO.ALO.AFU.ALO.ARI.AFU.ARI.BIQ

Izcatec
FL.1517
CN F.FL.ALO.ALO.ARI.ALO.AXC.BUE

Iznik pottery, Abraham of Kütahya style
USE **Kütahya ware**

Iznik pottery, Damascus style
USE **Damascus ware**

Iznik pottery, Rhodian style
USE **Rhodian ware**

Iznik ware
FL.3520
UF Isnik pottery
pottery, Iznik
ware, Iznik
CN F.FL.ALO.BIQ.AFU.FOG.ALO.ALO

Izumo Taisha
FL.1997
UF Taisha
CN F.FL.ALO.ARI.ALO.ALO.ALO.AFU.BCW

`Izz-ad-Din Qilich Arslan III
FL.3558
CN F.FL.ALO.BIQ.AFU.HIK.ARI.BIQ

Jaba
FL.209
UF Djaba
Ham
CN F.FL.ALO.AFU.AXC.AFU.AFU.ALO.ALO.ARI

Jabrudian
FL.2912
CN F.FL.ALO.AXC.ARI.AXC.AFU.AFU.AFU

jacaranda
USE **Brazilian rosewood**

jacaranda brown
USE **burnt umber**

jacaranda wood
USE **Brazilian rosewood**

jack arches
USE **flat arches**

jack pine
MT.1374 (L)
UF pine, jack
Pinus banksiana
CN M.MT.AFU.AFU.ALO.BIQ.DCU.AFU.AFU.ALO.CXA.AXC

jack planes
TB.934 (N)
ALT **jack plane**
SN Bench planes with a slightly curved blade; used for smoothing flat surfaces of rough boards.
UF fore planes
planes, fore
planes, jack
CN V.TB.AFU.BCW.CFS.ALO.AFU.DUC.ARI.AFU.ALO

jack rafters
RT.500
ALT **jack rafter**
UF cripple rafters
hip jacks
jacks, hip
rafters, cripple
rafters, jack
CN V.RT.AFU.AFU.AFU.BIQ.ARI.ALO.ALO.AFU.ARI

jack trusses
RT.382
ALT **jack truss**
SN Roof trusses which are smaller in size than the others, usually because of location, as in a hip roof. (DAC)
UF trusses, jack
CN V.RT.AFU.AFU.AFU.BCW.CLM.AFU.ALO.ALO.AFU

jacked piles
RT.163
ALT **jacked pile**
SN Piles (usually sections of pipe spliced together) which are forced into the ground to a bearing stratum, jacking it against a building or structure above, used primarily for underpinning. (DAC)
UF piles, jacked
CN V.RT.AFU.AFU.AFU.AXC.BUE.ALO.ALO.AFU.ARI

jackhammers
TB.464 (N)
ALT **jackhammer**
SN Hand-held pneumatically powered drills which hammer and rotate a bit or chisel; used for drilling rock or breaking up concrete, asphalt, or paving. (MEANS)
UF air hammers
drills, percussive
hammers, air
hammers, pneumatic
percussive drills
pneumatic hammers
CN V.TB.AFU.ARI.ELK.AFU.ARI.AFU

jacking up
USE **shoring**

jackknives
TB.127 (L)
ALT **jackknife**
SN Large pocket knives. (RHDEL2)
CN V.TB.AFU.ARI.AXC.ALO.BUE.AFU.ALO

jacks
TB.371 (L,N)
ALT **jack**
SN Portable mechanisms used for moving loads short distances by means of force applied with a lever, screw, hydraulic press, or air pressure. (MEANS)
UF jacks, lifting
lifting jacks
CN V.TB.AFU.ARI.DCU.AFU.ALO

jacks, door
USE **door jacks**

jacks, hip
USE **jack rafters**

jacks, hydraulic
USE **hydraulic jacks**

jacks, lifting
USE **jacks**

jacks, screw
USE **jackscrews**

jacks, trench
USE **trench jacks**

jacks, valley
USE **valley jacks**

jackscrews
TB.373
ALT **jackscrew**
SN Jacks in which a screw is used for lifting and carrying a plate which bears on the load. (DAC)
UF jacks, screw
screw jacks
CN V.TB.AFU.ARI.DCU.AFU.ALO.ALO

Jacob's ladders
USE **rope ladders**

Jacobean
FL.3195 (A,L,B,R)
CN F.FL.ALO.BCW.ALO.ARI.BIQ.BIQ.AFU.AFU.ALO.AFU

Jacobean Revival
FL.3325 (A,R)
UF Revival, Jacobean
CN F.FL.ALO.BCW.ALO.AXC.DIO.ALO.BIQ.ARI

Jacobethan
FL.3326
CN F.FL.ALO.BCW.ALO.AXC.DIO.
ALO.BIQ.AXC

Jacobite
BM.644 (L)
SN Use with reference to the Syrian Monophysite Christian church.
CN B.BM.BZY.AFU.ALO.AXC.ALO

jade
MT.525 (L)
CN M.MT.AFU.AFU.AFU.CFS.AFU.DZW

jade gray
USE **pale green**

jade gray, dark
USE **dark bluish green**

jade green
USE **grayish olive green**
light bluish green
moderate bluish green
moderate green
moderate olive green
moderate yellowish green
strong bluish green

jade green, bright
USE **brilliant bluish green**
strong bluish green
strong green

jade green, dark
USE **dark bluish green**
dark green
light bluish green

jade green, light
USE **light bluish green**

jade green, pale
USE **very pale green**

jadeite
MT.527 (L)
SN Monoclinic mineral found chiefly in Burma that consists of a sodium aluminum silicate and when cut constitutes a valuable variety of jade. (W)
CN M.MT.AFU.AFU.AFU.CFS.AFU.EFQ

Jahangir
FL.2232
CN F.FL.ALO.ARI.AXC.ALO.AFU.BIQ.
ALO.AFU.BCW

jai alai courts
USE **canchas**

jails
RK.716 (A,L,N,B,R)
ALT **jail**
SN Use for places of confinement operated by a local government both for temporary detention of sentenced and unsentenced individuals and for persons serving sentences of less than one year; for longer periods of confinement amd more secure than lockups, but less confining and for shorter confinements than prisons.
CN V.RK.AFU.ALO.ALO.CXA.AFU.ALO

Jainism
BM.668 (A,L)
ALT **Jaina**
CN B.BM.BZY.AFU.BIQ

Jaipur
USE **Amber (painting style)**

Jala-irid
USE **Jalairid**

Jalairid
FL.3461
UF Jala-irid
Jalayirid
CN F.FL.ALO.BIQ.AFU.DOI

Jalayirid
USE **Jalairid**

Jalisco
FL.1068
CN F.FL.ALO.ALO.ALO.ALO.AFU.
ALO.BCW.ARI

jalousie windows
RT.949
ALT **jalousie window**
SN Windows consisting of a series of overlapping horizontal glass louvers that pivot simultaneously in a common frame. (DAC)
UF windows, jalousie
CN V.RT.AFU.ARI.AFU.AFU.BOK.
AFU.AFU.EWY.AXC.AFU

jalousies
RT.1011 (B)
ALT **jalousie**
SN Shutters or blinds with fixed or adjustable slats which exclude rain and provide ventilation, shade, and visual privacy. (DAC)
CN V.RT.AFU.ARI.ALO.BIQ.ALO

jam pikes
TB.1071 (N)
ALT **jam pike**
SN Long-handled tools which terminate in an iron spike; used by lumbermen to pry logs. Later combined with the cant hook to become a peavey.
UF pikes, jam
CN V.TB.AFU.BCW.CFS.ALO.ALO.CFS

Jamaican
FL.710 (L,B)
CN F.FL.ALO.ALO.AFU.ALO.ARI

jamb locks
TF.241
ALT **jamb lock**
SN Prison-type locks designed to be built into the masonry of the door jamb, the bolt when locked being projected from the jamb and engaging with the door. (STEIN)
UF locks, jamb
CN V.TF.AFU.AFU.AFU.AFU.DIO.BIQ.
ALO.ALO.BUE.ALO

jamb posts
RT.200
ALT **jamb post**
SN Use for upright timbers at the sides of openings.
UF posts, jamb
CN V.RT.AFU.AFU.AFU.AXC.DCU.
ALO.AFU

jamb shafts
RT.98
ALT **jamb shaft**
SN Use for small columns with capital and base placed against the jambs of doors or windows, especially found in Medieval architecture.
UF shafts, jamb
CN V.RT.AFU.AFU.AFU.AXC.BIQ.
AFU.AFU.CXA.AFU

jamb spring hinges
TF.128
ALT **jamb spring hinge**
UF hinges, jamb spring
spring hinges, jamb
CN V.TF.AFU.AFU.AFU.AFU.CLM.
AFU.FOG.ALO

jamba oil
MT.2034
UF oil, jamba
CN M.MT.AFU.AFU.ARI.ARI.AXC.ARI.
ARI

Jambeli
FL.1116
CN F.FL.ALO.ALO.ALO.ARI.ALO.ARI.
AFU

jambs
RT.1002 (B)
ALT **jamb**
SN Vertical members at either side of doorframes, window frames, or the like. (DAC)
UF casings
postis
CN V.RT.AFU.ARI.ALO.ALO

jambs, door
USE **door jambs**

Jamdat Nasr
FL.2963
UF Djemdet Nasr
Protoliterate C-D
CN F.FL.ALO.AXC.ARI.BCW.AFU.
ALO.ARI

jamis
RK.1122
ALT **jami**
SN Places of prayer, usually mosques, for congregations.
UF camis
djamis
gamis
CN V.RK.AFU.ALO.ALO.FCS.BIQ.
BIQ.ALO.AFU

Jammu
FL.2278
UF Jasrota
CN F.FL.ALO.ARI.AXC.ALO.AFU.
BZY.BCW.ARI.BUE

janitors
HG.46 (L)
ALT **janitor**
SN Persons employed in keeping the premises of an apartment building, office, or other building clean and free of refuse, tending the heating system, and making minor repairs. (W)
CN H.HG.AFU.AXC.ARI.BUE.AFU

janus-face locks
TF.201
ALT **janus-face lock**
UF locks, janus-face
CN V.TF.AFU.AFU.AFU.AFU.DIO.BIQ.
AFU.BOK

Japan earth
USE **cutch**

japan (enamel)
MT.2427 (L)
SN Black baking enamel. (MH)
CN M.MT.AFU.ARI.CRG.AFU.ALO.AFU

Japan wax
MT.2207
SN Wax obtained from a variety of the sumac tree native to Japan; used as an adhesive. (GOTTS)
UF wax, Japan
CN M.MT.AFU.AFU.ARI.BZY.AXC.ARI

Japanese
FL.1955 (A,L,B,R)
CN F.FL.ALO.ARI.ALO.ALO

Japanese beech
MT.1108
UF beech, Japanese
Fagus japonica
CN M.MT.AFU.AFU.ALO.BIQ.DCU.
AFU.AFU.AFU.BCW.AXC

Japanese binding
KT.516
SN Bookbinding in which sheets are folded and bound as double leaves with the folds at the fore-edges of the book, opposite the binding.
UF binding, Chinese
binding, Japanese
Chinese binding
CN K.KT.AFU.ALO.ELK.ARI.AFU

Japanese chestnut
MT.1136
UF Castanea crenata
chestnut, Japanese
CN M.MT.AFU.AFU.ALO.BIQ.DCU.
AFU.AFU.AFU.CLM.BCW

Japanese ink
MT.2503
UF black watercolor
ink, Japanese
sumi
watercolor, black
CN M.MT.AFU.ARI.CRG.ALO.ALO.BUE

Japanese larch
MT.1364 (L)
UF larch, Japanese
CN M.MT.AFU.AFU.ALO.BIQ.DCU.
AFU.AFU.ALO.BZY.ALO

Japanese maple
MT.1222 (L)
UF Acer mono
maple, Japanese
CN M.MT.AFU.AFU.ALO.BIQ.DCU.
AFU.AFU.AFU.IFM.BCW

Japanese paper
MT.1907 (L)
UF paper, Japanese
CN M.MT.AFU.AFU.ARI.ALO.ALO.
AXC.ALO.AXC

Japanese paper folding
USE **origami**

Japanese stone pine
MT.1375 (L)
UF pine, Japanese stone
Pinus pumila
stone pine, Japanese
CN M.MT.AFU.AFU.ALO.BIQ.DCU.
AFU.AFU.ALO.CXA.BCW

Japanese Style
USE **Nihonga**

Japanese tung oil
MT.2023
UF oil, Japanese tung
tung oil, Japanese
CN M.MT.AFU.AFU.ARI.ARI.AXC.
AFU.CXA.AFU

Japanese white pine
MT.1376 (L)
UF pine, Japanese white
white pine, Japanese
CN M.MT.AFU.AFU.ALO.BIQ.DCU.
AFU.AFU.ALO.CXA.BIQ

Japanese willow
MT.1328
UF Salix melanostach
willow, Japanese
CN M.MT.AFU.AFU.ALO.BIQ.DCU.
AFU.AFU.AFU.MWQ.ALO

Japanism
USE **Japonism**

japanners
HG.483
ALT **japanner**
CN H.HG.AFU.AXC.BUE.ARI.BOK.AFU

japanning
KT.669 (L,R)
ALT **japanned**
SN The hard-finish lacquering technique which utilizes many coats of varnish composed of shellac dissolved in spirit, then polished and decorated, usually Oriental in style and subject matter. Originally developed as a substitute for genuine Oriental lacquer which was popular during the second half of the 17th century. (OCDA)
CN K.KT.AFU.ALO.GRC.AFU.AXC.AFU

Japonaiserie
FL.3284 (R)
UF Anglo-Japanese
CN F.FL.ALO.BCW.ALO.AXC.CXA.ALO

Japonism
BM.352 (R)
UF Japanism
CN B.BM.ALO.ALO.CLM.CFS.AFU.AFU

Jarawa
FL.210
CN F.FL.ALO.AFU.AXC.AFU.AFU.
ALO.ALO.AXC

jardinières
TG.649 (N,R)
ALT **jardinière**
UF meubles jardinières
tables à fleurs
CN V.TG.AFU.AFU.BIQ.BCW.ALO.
DIO.ALO

Jarmo
FL.2952
CN F.FL.ALO.AXC.ARI.BCW.AFU.
AFU.AFU.AFU

jasper
MT.553 (L)
CN M.MT.AFU.AFU.AFU.CFS.AFU.
GRC.AFU.ARI.BCW

Jasrota
USE **Jammu**

Jastorf
FL.2519
CN F.FL.ALO.AXC.AFU.BOK.AFU.AFU

jaune antique dore
USE **Numidian marble**

jaune brillant
USE **Naples yellow**

jaune d'arsenic
USE **orpiment**

jaune d'oxyde
USE **Mars yellow**

jaune de baryte
USE **barium yellow**

jaune de cadmium
USE **cadmium yellow**

jaune de cadmium citron
USE **lemon cadmium yellow**

jaune de cadmium clair
USE **pale cadmium yellow**

jaune de cadmium foncé
USE **deep cadmium yellow**

jaune de cadmium moyen
USE **middle cadmium yellow**

jaune de chrome
USE **chrome yellow**

jaune de cobalt
USE **cobalt yellow**

jaune de Naple
USE **Naples yellow**

jaune de strontium
USE **strontium yellow**

jaune de zinc
USE **zinc yellow**

jaune indien
USE **Indian yellow**

jaune solide
USE **Hansa yellow**

jaune titane de nickel
USE **nickel-titanium yellow**

Jaunpur
FL.2263
CN F.FL.ALO.ARI.AXC.ALO.AFU.BZY.ARI.ALO

java cotton
USE **kapok**

Javanese
FL.2377 (L)
CN F.FL.ALO.ARI.BCW.ARI.ALO.AXC

Javanese period (Balinese)
FL.2374
CN F.FL.ALO.ARI.BCW.ARI.ALO.AFU.AFU

Javanese, Central
USE **Central Javanese**

Javanese, East
USE **East Javanese**

Jaya, Irian
USE **Irian Jaya**

Jayavarmadiparamesvara
FL.2352
CN F.FL.ALO.ARI.BCW.ALO.ARI.AFU.ELK

Jayavarman I
FL.2327
CN F.FL.ALO.ARI.BCW.ALO.AFU.ARI.ALO

Jayavarman II
FL.2329
CN F.FL.ALO.ARI.BCW.ALO.ALO.AFU

Jayavarman III
FL.2330
CN F.FL.ALO.ARI.BCW.ALO.ALO.ALO

Jayavarman IV
FL.2336
CN F.FL.ALO.ARI.BCW.ALO.ARI.AFU.AXC

Jayavarman V
FL.2338
CN F.FL.ALO.ARI.BCW.ALO.ARI.AFU.BIQ

Jayavarman VI
FL.2341
CN F.FL.ALO.ARI.BCW.ALO.ARI.AFU.BZY

Jayavarman VII
FL.2347
CN F.FL.ALO.ARI.BCW.ALO.ARI.AFU.DIO

Jayavarman VIII
FL.2349
CN F.FL.ALO.ARI.BCW.ALO.ARI.AFU.DUC

Jazz Modern
USE **Art Deco**

jealousy
USE **envy**

Jebba
FL.116
CN F.FL.ALO.AFU.ALO.AFU.BUE.CRG.AFU

Jebel Uri
FL.169
CN F.FL.ALO.AFU.ALO.BCW.AFU.AFU

jedding axes
USE **cavils**

Jeffrey pine
MT.1377 (L)
UF pine, Jeffrey
Pinus jeffreyi
CN M.MT.AFU.AFU.ALO.BIQ.DCU.AFU.AFU.ALO.CXA.BOK

Jekri
USE **Itsekiri**

Jellinge Style
FL.3147
CN F.FL.ALO.BCW.ALO.ALO.AFU.BOK.ARI.BUE.AFU

jelly, petroleum
USE **petroleum jelly**

Jemez
FL.1469 (L)
CN F.FL.ALO.ALO.ARI.AFU.CFS.CRG.AFU.ARI

Jenne
FL.86
UF Djenne
CN F.FL.ALO.AFU.ALO.AFU. BOK.AFU.AFU

Jenny Lind beds
USE **spool beds**

Jericho Pottery Neolithic A
USE **Yarmukian**

Jericho Pottery Neolithic B
FL.2921
CN F.FL.ALO.AXC.ARI.AXC.AFU.ALO.BCW

jerkinhead roofs
RT.432
ALT **jerkinhead roof**
SN Use for pitched roofs in which the gables are truncated, being surmounted by hips.
UF clipped gable roofs
gable roofs, clipped
gable roofs, hipped
hipped gable roofs
roofs, clipped gable
roofs, hipped gable
roofs, jerkinhead
roofs, shreadhead
shreadhead roofs
CN V.RT.AFU.AFU.AFU.BIQ.ARI.AFU.AFU.AFU.BOK.BIQ

Jersey Bluff
FL.838
CN F.FL.ALO.ALO.ALO.AFU.ALO.ALO.ARI.AFU.BIQ

Jersey lily white
USE **lithopone**

Jersey pine
USE **scrub pine**

jesters
HG.70 (L,R)
ALT **jester**
UF fools
CN H.HG.AFU.AXC.AXC.AFU.AFU.AFU.BIQ.BCW

jesting beams
RT.313
ALT **jesting beam**
SN Use for nonstructural beams, introduced for appearance.
UF beams, jesting
CN V.RT.AFU.AFU.AFU.BCW.ALO.ALO.BIQ

Jesuit
BM.658 (A,L,B)
CN B.BM.BZY.AFU.ALO.BCW.BOK

Jesuit porcelain
USE **Jesuit ware**

Jesuit ware
FL.1944
SN Porcelain from China made during the Qing dynasty and decorated with Christian subjects taken from European engravings. (SAVAGE)
UF Jesuit porcelain
porcelain, Jesuit
ware, Jesuit

CN F.FL.ALO.ARI.ALO.AFU.AFU.AXC.
ARI.AFU.ALO

Jesus saws
USE **felloe saws**

jet
MT.528 (L,R)
SN A very compact velvet-black mineral, similar to coal, that is often used for jewelry. (W)
CN M.MT.AFU.AFU.AFU.CFS.AFU.ELK

jet black
USE **black**

jetties
RK.562 (A,L,B)
ALT **jetty**
SN Use for structures extending from the shore into a body of water and built to influence current or protect the entrance to a harbor or river from shoaling. For similar structures built to control or direct seashore erosions, use **groins (erosion protection works)**; use **wing dams** when such erosion control structures occur along banks of rivers or streams.
CN V.RK.AFU.ALO.ALO.CFS.ALO.
ALO.BCW

jetties (building divisions)
RM.18
ALT **jetty (building division)**
SN Parts of a building that project beyond the rest. (W)
UF jutties
CN V.RM.AFU.BZY

jewel cabinets
TG.432
ALT **jewel cabinet**
SN French 17th- and 18th-century cabinets on stands used to store jewels; often heavily adorned with inlay. (HAYWAR)
UF cabinets, jewel
coffre à bijoux
jewel-caskets on stands
serres-bijoux
CN V.TG.AFU.AFU.AXC.ALO.ARI.
ALO.BUE

jewel-caskets on stands
USE **jewel cabinets**

jeweler's cloth
TB.518
UF cloth, jeweler's
CN V.TB.AFU.ARI.EWY.ALO.CLM

jewelers
HG.565 (L,R)
ALT **jeweler**
CN H.HG.AFU.AXC.BUE.AXC.CFS

jewelry making
KT.526 (L,R)
CN K.KT.AFU.ALO.ELK.CFS

jewelry shops
USE **jewelry stores**

jewelry stores
RK.162 (A,L,B)
ALT **jewelry store**
UF jewelry shops
shops, jewelry
stores, jewelry
CN V.RK.AFU.ALO.ALO.ALO.ARI.
BIQ.AFU.CRG

jewels
USE **gems**
precious stones

jewels, industrial
USE **industrial jewels**

Jewish day schools
USE **yeshivas**

Jewish New Year
USE **Rosh Hashanah**

Jewish religious schools
USE **Hebrew schools**

Jewish temples
USE **synagogues**

Jewish theological seminaries
USE **rabbinical seminaries**

Jiajing
FL.1904
UF Chia-ching
CN F.FL.ALO.ARI.ALO.AFU.AFU.
ALO.DIO.BOK

Jiang Hmai
USE **Chiang Mai**

Jiaqing
FL.1914 (L)
UF Chia-ch'ing
CN F.FL.ALO.ARI.ALO.AFU.AFU.
ALO.DOI.BCW

jib doors
RT.850
ALT **jib door**
SN Doors that are flush with and treated in the same manner as the surrounding wall so as to be concealed and have no visible hardware. (HAS)
UF concealed doors
doors, concealed
doors, gib
doors, jib
gib doors
CN V.RT.AFU.ARI.AFU.AFU.AFU.ALO.
ARI.AFU.AFU.BCW

jib-headed windows
RT.945
ALT **jib-headed window**
SN Sash windows which slide into a cavity above the head of the window frame, leaving the aperture unobstructed. (BARNST)
UF box-head windows
windows, box-head
windows, jib-headed
CN V.RT.AFU.ARI.AFU.AFU.BOK.
AFU.AFU.EWY.ARI.ALO

Jibana
FL.597
CN F.FL.ALO.AFU.AXC.AXC.ALO.ARI

Jibu
FL.212
UF Djibu
Djubu
Jubu
CN F.FL.ALO.AFU.AXC.AFU.AFU.
ALO.ALO.BCW

Jicaque
FL.1554 (L)
CN F.FL.ALO.ALO.ARI.ALO.BOK.BCW

Jicarilla Apache
FL.1451 (L)
UF Apache, Jicarilla
CN F.FL.ALO.ALO.ARI.AFU.CFS.AFU.
ARI

Jie
FL.680 (L)
CN F.FL.ALO.AFU.AXC.AXC.BOK.BUE

jiffler mixers
TB.561
ALT **jiffler mixer**
SN Apparatuses for mixing drywall mud and exposed aggregate materials, consisting of two bladed wheels, an upper which cuts the material downward and a lower which cuts it upward. (PUTNAM)
UF mixers, jiffler
CN V.TB.AFU.BCW.BCW.AFU.AFU.AFU

jiggers
TB.906 (N)
ALT **jigger**
SN Drawknives which combine a straight and a hollow blade.
UF giggers
CN V.TB.AFU.BCW.CFS.ALO.AFU.DOI.
ARI.BIQ

jigsaws
TB.1016 (L,N)
ALT **jigsaw**
SN Electrically powered saws, having a narrow blade which moves with a reciprocating motion in a vertical direction; used especially for cutting curves and ornamental designs. (DAC)
UF fretsaw machines
machines, fretsaw
CN V.TB.AFU.BCW.CFS.ALO.AFU.EWY.
BOK

Jiji
FL.492
CN F.FL.ALO.AFU.AXC.ALO.ALO.BCW.
ALO

Jin
FL.1851
UF Chin
CN F.FL.ALO.ARI.ALO.AFU.AFU.ALO.
ALO

Jin (Six Dynasties)
FL.1881
UF Chin (Six Dynasties)
CN F.FL.ALO.ARI.ALO.AFU.AFU.ALO.
BUE.ARI

Jin, Eastern
USE **Eastern Jin**

Jin, Later
USE **Later Jin**

Jin, Western
USE **Western Jin**

jinjas
RK.1142
ALT **jinja**
SN Shinto shrines. (PAINE3)
CN V.RK.AFU.ALO.ALO.FCS.BOK.ARI

Jirajara
FL.1631
CN F.FL.ALO.ALO.ARI.ARI.ARI.AXC

Jivaro
FL.1583 (L)
UF Givaro
Shuara
CN F.FL.ALO.ALO.ARI.ARI.AFU.DOI

jneins
USE **greenbelts**

job applications
VW.779 (L)
ALT **job application**
UF applications, job
CN V.VW.AFU.ARI.AFU.ALO.BZY.ALO

job files
USE **project files**

job lists
VW.280
ALT **job list**
SN Comprehensive records of projects undertaken by architectural, and other firms.
UF lists, job
CN V.VW.AFU.AFU.AFU.FZU.BCW.
ALO.AXC

job manuals
USE **project manuals**

job printers
HG.461
ALT **job printer**
SN Persons who set type according to copy and operate a cylinder or automatic platen press to print complete job orders. (DOT)
UF country printers
printers, country
printers, job
CN H.HG.AFU.AXC.BUE.ALO.CFS.
BUE.ALO

job resumes
USE **resumes**

jobbers
USE **wholesalers**

jobent nails
TF.397
ALT **jobent nail**
UF nails, jobent
CN V.TF.AFU.AFU.AFU.ALO.AFU.
CFS.AFU.CFS

Jocho
FL.2100
CN F.FL.ALO.ARI.ALO.ALO.ALO.
BCW.ALO

Jocotal
FL.1030
CN F.FL.ALO.ALO.ALO.ALO.AFU.
ALO.ARI.AFU.ARI.ARI

Jodhpur
FL.2291
CN F.FL.ALO.ARI.AXC.ALO.AFU.BZY.
BCW.BCW.BIQ

Jodo
BM.622 (L)
UF Jodo Shinsu
Jodo-shu'
Pure Land sect (Japan)
CN B.BM.BZY.AFU.AFU.BIQ.AFU

Jodo Shinsu
USE **Jodo**

Jodo-shu'
USE **Jodo**

Jogan
USE **Early Heian**

joggle joints
TF.618
ALT **joggle joint**
SN In masonry or stonework, joints which employ joggles in the adjacent members so as to prevent their later movement. (MEANS)
UF joints, joggle
CN V.TF.ALO.ARI.ALO.AFU.ALO

joined backstools, upholstered
USE **farthingale chairs**

joined stools
USE **joint stools**

joined tables (refectory tables)
USE **refectory tables**

joiner's chisels
USE **paring chisels**

joiner's clamps
TB.1052 (N)
ALT **joiner's clamp**
SN Long bar-type clamps either of wood or metal with an adjustable stop at one end, and a screw-type stop at the other. (SALAM)
UF bar clamps
clamps, bar
clamps, joiner's
CN V.TB.AFU.BCW.CFS.ALO.ALO.
BCW.AXC

joiners
HG.561 (A,L,R)
ALT **joiner**
SN Persons who join wood, especially in the construction of doors, window sashes, paneling, and other permanent woodwork. (RHDEL2)
CN H.HG.AFU.AXC.BUE.AXC.BUE.ARI

joinery
MT.2785 (A,L,B,R)
SN Includes the lighter forms of woodwork in a building, i.e., doors, window frames, staircases, cupboards, etc., which may be carved or painted with decoration. Excludes the heavier structural timber members of a building.
UF cabinetwork
CN M.MT.AFU.AXC.DOI.AFU

joinery, nailed
USE **nailed joinery**

joining
KT.56
SN Use especially with reference to the construction of articles made of wood.
CN K.KT.AFU.ALO.BCW.BIQ

joint bolts
USE **handrail bolts**

joint cement
USE **Spackle (TM)**

joint files
TB.716
ALT **joint file**
SN Files with rounded edges and tapered or parallel sides; used to clean and shape the spaces between gear wheel teeth and pinions.
UF files, joint
files, leaning
files, round-edge equalling
files, thinning
leaning files
round-edge equalling files
thinning files
CN V.TB.AFU.BCW.BIQ.ARI.ALO.ARI.
ALO

joint occupancy
BM.206 (A,L)
UF occupancy, joint
CN B.BM.AFU.ALO.BIQ

joint pointing, tuck
USE **pointing**

joint stools
TG.247
ALT **joint stool**
SN Early backless seating forms of stout mortise and tenon construction and with turned legs joined by stretchers.
UF coffin stools
joined stools
joint tables (stools)
joyned stools
low stools
stools, coffin
stools, joint
stools, joyned
stools, low
tables, joint (stools)
CN V.TG.AFU.AFU.ALO.AFU.ALO.AFU.BOK

joint tables (stools)
USE **joint stools**

joint ventures
BM.401 (L)
SN Partnerships or cooperative agreements between two or more persons restricted to specified undertakings. (W)
UF ventures, joint
CN B.BM.ARI.DOI

jointer planes
TB.935 (N)
ALT **jointer plane**
SN The longest of the bench planes, ranging from 2 to 3 feet; used to level long boards that are to be joined together.
UF planes, jointer
CN V.TB.AFU.BCW.CFS.ALO.AFU.DUC.ARI.AFU.ARI

jointer planes, cooper's
USE **cooper's jointer planes**

jointers
TB.610 (L,N)
ALT **jointer**
SN Offset metal tools used to smooth or indent mortar joints in masonry. (MEANS)
CN V.TB.AFU.BCW.BCW.ALO.EWY

jointing materials
USE **sealing compounds**

joints
TF.571 (A,L,B)
ALT **joint**
SN Use for the apparatus used or the manner of joining two or more parts of an object or structure.
UF connections
CN V.TF.ALO

joints, abutting
USE **abutting joints**

joints, angle
USE **angle joints**

joints, ball
USE **ball joints**

joints, batten
USE **batten joints**

joints, beaded
USE **beaded joints**

joints, beaking
USE **beaking joints**

joints, bed
USE **bed joints**

joints, bell-and-spigot
USE **bell-and-spigot joints**

joints, beveled butt
USE **oblique joints**

joints, blind
USE **blind joints**

joints, blind dovetail
USE **blind dovetail joints**

joints, blown
USE **blown joints**

joints, bolted
USE **bolted joints**

joints, break
USE **break joints**

joints, bridle
USE **bridle joints**

joints, broken
USE **break joints**

joints, butt
USE **butt joints**

joints, butterfly
USE **butterfly joints**

joints, calk
USE **calk joints**

joints, cogged
USE **cogged joints**

joints, cold
USE **cold joints**

joints, collar
USE **collar joints**

joints, concave
USE **concave joints**

joints, construction
USE **construction joints**

joints, contraction
USE **contraction joints**

joints, control
USE **control joints**

joints, coopered
USE **coopered joints**

joints, coped
USE **coped joints**

joints, covered
USE **covered joints**

joints, crosslap
USE **crosslap joints**

joints, cup
USE **cup joints**

joints, curb
USE **knuckle joints**

joints, dado
USE **dado joints**

joints, dado and rabbet
USE **dado and rabbet joints**

joints, dado, tongue and rabbet
USE **dado, tongue and rabbet joints**

joints, dap
USE **dap joints**

joints, deformed
USE **deformed joints**

joints, dog-eared fold
USE **dog-eared fold joints**

joints, double rabbet
USE **double rabbet joints**

joints, dovetail
USE **dovetail joints**

joints, end
USE **butt joints**

joints, end lap
USE **end lap joints**

joints, expansion
USE **expansion joints**

joints, exposed
USE **exposed joints**

joints, face
USE **face joints**

joints, feather
USE **feather joints**

joints, fillistered
USE **fillistered joints**

joints, finger
USE **finger joints**

joints, fished
USE **fished joints**

joints, fixed
USE **rigid joints**

joints, flat
USE **rough-cut joints**

joints, flush
USE **flush joints**

joints, flush (mortar joints)
USE **rough-cut joints**

joints, flush and rodded
USE **flush and rodded joints**

joints, galletted
USE **galletted joints**

joints, half-lap
USE **half-lap joints**

joints, halved
USE **half-lap joints**

joints, head
USE **head joints**

joints, heading
USE **heading joints**

joints, hick
USE **rough-cut joints**

joints, hook-and-butt
USE **hook-and-butt joints**

joints, hopper
USE **hopper joints**

joints, housed
USE **housed joints**

joints, integral
USE **integral joints**

joints, interlocking
USE **interlocking joints**

joints, isolation
USE **isolation joints**

joints, joggle
USE **joggle joints**

joints, keyed
USE **keyed joints**

joints, knuckle
USE **knuckle joints**

joints, lap
USE **lap joints**

joints, locking
USE **locking joints**

joints, matched
USE **matched joints**

joints, miter
USE **miter joints**

joints, mortise-and-tenon
USE **mortise-and-tenon joints**

joints, oblique
USE **oblique joints**

joints, oblique butt
USE **oblique joints**

joints, overlapping
USE **lap joints**

joints, pinned
USE **pinned joints**

joints, plain cut
USE **rough-cut joints**

joints, rabbet
USE **rabbet joints**

joints, rabbeted ledge and miter
USE **rabbeted ledge and miter joints**

joints, raked
USE **raked joints**

joints, random
USE **random joints**

joints, rebated
USE **rabbet joints**

joints, recessed
USE **recessed joints**

joints, reveal
USE **recessed joints**

joints, rigid
USE **rigid joints**

joints, rodded
USE **concave joints**

joints, roller
USE **roller joints**

joints, rough-cut
USE **rough-cut joints**

joints, round mortise-and-tenon
USE **round mortise-and-tenon joints**

joints, rubbed
USE **rubbed joints**

joints, rule
USE **rule joints**

joints, rust
USE **rust joints**

joints, rustic
USE **rustic joints**

joints, saddle
USE **water joints**

joints, sawed
USE **sawed joints**

joints, scarf
USE **scarf joints**

joints, scarfed
USE **scarf joints**

joints, scarped
USE **scarf joints**

joints, scribed
USE **coped joints**

joints, seismic
USE **seismic joints**

joints, shadow
USE **recessed joints**

joints, shift
USE **break joints**

joints, shiplap
USE **covered joints**

joints, shouldered dovetail
USE **shouldered dovetail joints**

joints, shoved
USE **shoved joints**

joints, side locking
USE **interlocking joints**

joints, simple
USE **simple joints**

joints, sliding
USE **housed joints**

joints, slip
USE **slip joints**

joints, spigot-and-socket
USE **bell-and-spigot joints**

joints, spline
USE **spline joints**

joints, spline miter
USE **spline joints**

joints, squeezed
USE **squeezed joints**

joints, staggered
USE **break joints**

joints, starved
USE **starved joints**

joints, stripped
USE **stripped joints**

joints, struck
USE **struck joints**

joints, T and G
USE **tongue-and-groove joints**

joints, tongue-and-groove
USE **tongue-and-groove joints**

joints, tongue-and-lip
USE **tongue-and-lip joints**

joints, tooled
USE **tooled joints**

joints, topping
USE **topping joints**

joints, V-shaped
USE **V-shaped joints**

joints, water
USE **water joints**

joints, weather-struck
USE **weather-struck joints**

joints, weathered
USE **weather-struck joints**

joist anchors
TF.295
ALT **joist anchor**
UF anchors, joist
CN V.TF.AFU.AFU.AFU.ALO.AFU.AFU.BOK

joist anchors (beam anchors)
USE **beam anchors**

joist hangers
TF.371
ALT **joist hanger**
UF hangers, joist
CN V.TF.AFU.AFU.AFU.ALO.AFU.BOK.ARI.ARI.AXC.ALO

joist hangers, wood-to-steel
USE **wood-to-steel joist hangers**

joists
RT.301 (B)
ALT **joist**
SN Parallel beams used to support floor and ceiling loads, and supported in turn by larger beams, girders, bearing walls, or other members. (HAS)
CN V.RT.AFU.AFU.AFU.BCW.ALO.AFU.BOK

joists, bar
USE **open web joists**

joists, binding
USE **binding joists**

joists, bridging
USE **common joists**

joists, ceiling
USE **ceiling joists**

joists, common
USE **common joists**

joists, floor
USE **floor joists**

joists, header
USE **headers (frame components)**

joists, open web
USE **open web joists**

joists, trimming
USE **trimmers (frame components)**

joists, trussed
USE **open web joists**

Jokwe
USE **Chokwe**

Jolof
USE **Wolof**

Jomon
FL.1959 (L)
CN F.FL.ALO.ARI.ALO.ALO.AFU.AFU.ALO

Jomon, Early
USE **Early Jomon**

Jomon, Final
USE **Final Jomon**

Jomon, Late
USE **Late Jomon**

Jomon, Middle
USE **Middle Jomon**

Jompre
USE **Zumper**

Jonah, Igbo
USE **Igbo Jonah**

journalism
KD.113 (L,B,R)
CN K.KD.AFU.ALO.ARI.ARI

journalistic photographs
USE **news photographs**

journalistic photography
USE **photojournalism**

journalists
HG.285 (L)
ALT **journalist**
SN Persons employed to collect, write, or edit the subject matter of a news medium. (W)
UF newswriters
CN H.HG.AFU.AXC.BCW.ALO.AFU.ARI

journals
VW.48 (N,R)
ALT **journal**
SN Use for books containing impersonal accounts of an individual's or organization's daily occurrences or transactions. Use **diaries** when referring to personal accounts of the writer's experiences, attitudes, or observations.
CN V.VW.AFU.AFU.AFU.DCU

journals (bookkeeping records)
VW.846
ALT **journal (bookkeeping record)**
SN Daily records of financial transactions. (ICA)
CN V.VW.AFU.ARI.AFU.BIQ.CXA.AFU.BOK

journals (periodicals)
USE **periodicals**

journals, cash
USE **cashbooks**

journals, house
USE **house organs**

journeymen
HG.766 (L)
ALT **journeyman**
SN Artists or craftsmen who have completed apprenticeship but have not attained master status in a guild. (MURRAY)
CN H.HG.AFU.BIQ.BCW

journeys
KM.91 (L,R)
UF trips
CN K.KM.AFU.CLM

joy
BM.579 (L)
CN B.BM.BUE.ARI.BUE

joyned stools
USE **joint stools**

joysticks
TB.153
ALT **joystick**
SN Devices consisting of a vertically mounted shaft that can be pushed in any direction; used for generating signals that can cause the cursor or some other symbol to be moved rapidly about on a display screen. (DOC)
CN V.TB.AFU.ARI.BCW.AXC.AFU.ARI

Ju Chou ware
USE **Ru ware**

Ju ware
USE **Ru ware**

Jubu
USE **Jibu**

Judaism
BM.669 (L,R)
ALT **Jewish**
CN B.BM.BZY.AFU.BOK

Judas holes
USE **peepholes**

Judas windows
USE **peepholes**

judgements
USE **decisions**

judges
HG.315 (L)
ALT **judge**
SN Persons who arbitrate disputes, advise counsel, jury, litigants, or court personnel, and administer judicial systems. (DOT)
CN H.HG.AFU.AXC.BCW.ALO.BIQ.ALO

judicial records
VW.1008 (L)
ALT **judicial record**
SN Records of a tribunal established for the administration of justice. (GAHLM)
UF court records
court rolls
records, court
records, judicial

rolls, court
CN V.VW.AFU.ARI.ALO.BCW.AFU.ALO

Jugendstil
FL.3382 (A,L,B,R)
UF Bandwurmstil
Belgischestil
Schnörkelstil
Studio-Stil
Veldesche
CN F.FL.ALO.BCW.ALO.AXC.DIO.BIQ.ALO

Juglans nigra
USE **black walnut**

Juglans regia
USE **English walnut**
walnut

Jukun
FL.213 (L)
UF Djukun
CN F.FL.ALO.AFU.AXC.AFU.AFU.ALO.ALO.BIQ

Julio-Claudian
FL.2719 (R)
CN F.FL.ALO.AXC.ALO.ALO.AFU.AXC.ALO.ARI

jumble sales
USE **rummage sales**

jumbo brick
MT.77
SN Brick fired at the nominal dimensions of 4 by 4 by 8 inches. (DLA)
UF brick, economy
brick, jumbo
economy brick
CN M.MT.AFU.AFU.AFU.AXC.ALO.AFU.AFU.AFU.BUE

jumpers
TB.896 (N)
ALT **jumper**
SN Heavy, round iron rods about 3 to 6 inches long, curved round at one end nearly at a right angle; used by coopers. (SALAM)
UF billys
devil's tails
devils (jumpers)
irons, knocking-up
irons, raising
knocking-up irons
raising irons
tails, devil's
CN V.TB.AFU.BCW.CFS.ALO.AFU.DIO

jumping up
USE **upset forging**

jumps, ski
USE **ski jumps**

Jun ware
FL.1946 (L)
UF Chun ware
ware, Chun
ware, Jun
CN F.FL.ALO.ARI.ALO.AFU.AFU.AXC.ARI.ARI

junctions
USE **intersections**

jungle zoos
USE **open-air zoos**

jungles
RD.250
ALT **jungle**
SN Denotes generally impenetrable tropical forests with dense tangled undergrowth of grasses, vines, shrubs, and trees.
UF forests, tropical
tropical forests
CN V.RD.ARI.AFU.BCW.ALO.AFU.ALO

Junín
FL.1133
CN F.FL.ALO.ALO.ALO.ARI.AXC.AFU.AFU.AFU

junior colleges
RK.844 (L,B)
ALT **junior college**
SN Post-high school institutions which offer a two-year program of study of a terminal nature or in preparation for continued college studies. (DAC)
UF colleges, junior
CN V.RK.AFU.ALO.ALO.CXA.ARI.AXC.BIQ.AFU.ALO

junior high schools
RK.839 (L,B)
ALT **junior high school**
SN Use for schools in the United States usually covering grades 7 through 9. Distinguished from Middle schools by their scope and their general restriction to schools in the United States.
UF high schools, junior
schools, junior high
CN V.RK.AFU.ALO.ALO.CXA.ARI.AXC.AXC

junior museums
USE **children's museums**

juniper
MT.1358 (L)
UF juniper, red
red juniper
savin
CN M.MT.AFU.AFU.ALO.BIQ.DCU.AFU.AFU.ALO.BUE

juniper resin
MT.1501
UF resin, juniper
CN M.MT.AFU.AFU.ALO.BOK.CLM

juniper, mountain
USE **mountain juniper**

juniper, red
USE **juniper**

Juniperus montana
USE **mountain juniper**

Juniperus procera
USE **African cedar**

Juniperus virginiana
USE **red cedar**

junk playgrounds
USE **adventure playgrounds**

junkyards
RK.1469
ALT **junkyard**
UF scrap yards
yards, scrap
CN V.RK.ALO.ALO.AXC.AFU.AFU

junkyards, automobile
USE **automobile graveyards**

Jupurina
USE **Ipuriná**

Jura turpentine
MT.1474
UF turpentine, Jura
CN M.MT.AFU.AFU.ALO.BOK.AFU.AXC

juridical manuscripts
USE **legal manuscripts**

juries
KM.49
SN Use for occasions when a preselected group passes judgement on the work of artists, architects, and architectural or other students.
CN K.KM.AFU.BCW.ARI

jurisprudence, forensic
USE **forensic medicine**

jurisprudence, medical
USE **forensic medicine**

jurors
HG.722
ALT **juror**
UF jurymen
jurywomen
CN H.HG.AFU.BCW.DCU

jurts
USE **yurts**

jurymen
USE **jurors**

jurywomen
USE **jurors**

justices of the peace
HG.316 (L)
ALT **justice of the peace**
UF peace, justices of the
CN H.HG.AFU.AXC.BCW.ALO.BIQ.ARI

Justinianic
FL.3071
UF First Golden Age (Byzantine)
CN F.FL.ALO.BCW.ALO.AFU.ALO.AFU.ALO

jut windows
USE **bay windows**

jute
MT.1831 (L,B)
SN The glossy fiber of either of two East Indian plants (Corchorus olitorius and C. capsularis) used chiefly for sacking, burlap, and cheaper varieties of twine. (W)
CN M.MT.AFU.AFU.ARI.ALO.AFU.AFU.ALO.BUE

jute board
MT.1890
SN A strong plyboard containing no jute fiber but made typically from sulfate and wastepaper pulps and used especially for shipping containers. (W)
UF board, jute
CN M.MT.AFU.AFU.ARI.ALO.ALO.ARI.AFU

jutties
USE **jetties (building divisions)**

juvenile detention centers
USE **detention centers**

juvenile detention homes
USE **detention centers**

juvenile halls
USE **reformatories**

juvenile homes
USE **reformatories**

juvenile institutions
USE **reformatories**

juvenilia
BM.274
SN Works, particularly written or artistic works, produced by persons in their childhood or youth. (AHD)
CN B.BM.AFU.ARI.BIQ.BCW

K-Ar dating
USE **potassium-argon dating**

K'ana-chu
USE **Sogdian**

K'ang-hsi
USE **Kangxi**

Kabin
USE **Ga'anda**

Kabre
FL.384 (L)
CN F.FL.ALO.AFU.AXC.AFU.AXC.ARI.ARI.ARI

Kabyle
FL.697 (L)
CN F.FL.ALO.AFU.AXC.BCW.AXC.AFU

Kachemak
FL.787
CN F.FL.ALO.ALO.ALO.AFU.ALO.AFU.AFU.ARI.AFU

Kadam School
FL.2179
UF Atisha Style
Bka'gdams
Kadampa Style
CN F.FL.ALO.ARI.AXC.AFU.BOK.AFU.ARI

Kadampa Style
USE **Kadam School**

Kadmiumgelb
USE **cadmium yellow**

Kadmiumgelb dunkel
USE **deep cadmium yellow**

Kadmiumgelb hell
USE **pale cadmium yellow**

Kadmiumgelb mittel
USE **middle cadmium yellow**

Kadmiumgelb orange
USE **cadmium orange**

Kadmiumgelb zitron
USE **lemon cadmium yellow**

Kadmiumrot
USE **cadmium red**

kaesten
USE **kassen**

Kafuan
FL.49
CN F.FL.ALO.AFU.AFU.ALO.AFU.AFU.AFU

Kahlur
USE **Bilaspur**

Kaigetsudo School
FL.2090
CN F.FL.ALO.ARI.ALO.ALO.ALO.AXC.BZY.BIQ

Kaiho School
FL.2053
CN F.FL.ALO.ARI.ALO.ALO.ALO.ARI.BCW

Kainah
USE **Blood (Native American)**

Kaingua
USE **Caingang**

Kainji Dam Area
USE **Yelwa**

Kairak-Kum
USE **Kayrakkum**

Kajar
USE **Qajar**

kaki
MT.1142 (L)
SN Japanese ebony from the tree Dalbergia kaki.
CN M.MT.AFU.AFU.ALO.BIQ.DCU.AFU.AFU.AFU.CXA.ARI

Kakiemon
FL.2016
CN F.FL.ALO.ARI.ALO.ALO.ALO.ALO.ALO.ALO.ALO

Kalaallit
USE **Katladlit**

Kalabari
FL.268 (L)
CN F.FL.ALO.AFU.AXC.AFU.ALO.AXC.AFU.ALO

Kalai
USE **Ngom**

Kalapuya
FL.1346 (L)
UF Calapooya
CN F.FL.ALO.ALO.ARI.AFU.BIQ.CXA

Kaleri
FL.214 (L)
CN F.FL.ALO.AFU.AXC.AFU.AFU.ALO.ALO.BOK

Kalighat
FL.2259
CN F.FL.ALO.ARI.AXC.ALO.AFU.BZY.ALO.AFU

Kalimantan
USE **Bornean**

Kalispel
FL.1408 (L)
UF Pend d'Oreille
CN F.FL.ALO.ALO.ARI.AFU.BUE.AXC

Kalkblau
USE **blue verditer**

kallitype
KT.344 (L)
SN An iron process for making prints using a light-sensitive emulsion of a ferric salt and silver nitrate. When developed, a metallic silver image is formed; various developers can produce black, brown, purple, or maroon tones.
UF argentotype
callitype
CN K.KT.AFU.ALO.DUC.DIO.ALO.CRG.ARI

kalsomine
USE **calcimine**

Kamakura
FL.1966 (A,L)
CN F.FL.ALO.ARI.ALO.ALO.AFU.ALO.AFU

Kamares ware
FL.2668

UF ware, Kamares
CN F.FL.ALO.AXC.ALO.AFU.ALO.AXC.BCW.AXC

Kamba
FL.646 (L)
UF Akamba
CN F.FL.ALO.AFU.AXC.AXC.BCW.BCW

Kambe
FL.598
CN F.FL.ALO.AFU.AXC.AXC.ALO.AXC

Kameirian
USE **Rhodian**

Kamenny Log phase
FL.2125
CN F.FL.ALO.ARI.ARI.AFU.BCW

kames
RD.185 (L)
ALT **kame**
SN Use only for mounds, knobs, or hillocks of poorly stratified drift left by retreating ice sheets. For sinuous ridges of fluvio-glacial origin, use **eskers**; for elongated hills of glacial origin, use **drumlins.**
CN V.RD.ARI.AFU.AXC.AFU.AFU.ALO.ARI

Kami
FL.599
CN F.FL.ALO.AFU.AXC.AXC.ALO.BCW

Kamia
FL.1276 (L)
UF Comeya
Kumeyaay
CN F.FL.ALO.ALO.ARI.AFU.ALO.FZU.AFU.ALO

Kamigata-e
FL.2078
CN F.FL.ALO.ARI.ALO.ALO.ALO.AXC.ARI

Kamirian
USE **Rhodian**

kanats
USE **qanats**

Kanda
USE **Ga'anda**

Kande
FL.415 (L)
UF Okanda
CN F.FL.ALO.AFU.AXC.ALO.AFU.AXC.ARI

kane stone
USE **Caen stone**

Kanem-Bornu
FL.81
CN F.FL.ALO.AFU.ALO.AFU.AXC

Kangra
FL.2279
CN F.FL.ALO.ARI.AXC.ALO.AFU.BZY.BCW.ARI.BZY

kangs
RT.1162 (A)
ALT **kang**
SN Includes Chinese heated masonry beds and similar Chinese heating systems employing ducts in walls.
CN V.RT.AFU.BOK.AXC

Kangutu
USE **Ipuriná**

Kangxi
FL.1911 (L)
UF K'ang-hsi
CN F.FL.ALO.ARI.ALO.AFU.AFU.ALO.DOI.ALO

Kaniagmiut
USE **Koniag**

Kanioka
FL.493
UF Bena Kanioka
Kanyoka
CN F.FL.ALO.AFU.AXC.ALO.ALO.BCW.ARI

Kankiti
USE **Ipuriná**

Kankju
USE **Sogdian**

Kano School
FL.2054 (L)
CN F.FL.ALO.ARI.ALO.ALO.ALO.ARI.BIQ

Kansa
FL.1384 (L)
UF Kaw
CN F.FL.ALO.ALO.ARI.AFU.BOK.CLM

Kansu
USE **Gansu**

Kanuri
FL.107 (L)
CN F.FL.ALO.AFU.ALO.AFU.BUE.BOK

Kanyoka
USE **Kanioka**

kaolin
MT.56 (L)
SN A pure form of hydrated aluminum silicate clay; used for making porcelain for china and chemical porcelain for valves, tubes, and fittings, as a pigment and filler in paints and plastics, an abrasive powder, and in paper to yield a glossy surface. (MH)
UF China-clay
clay, Devonshire
Devonshire clay
bole, white
China clay
clay, China
clay, pipe
pipe clay
white bole
CN M.MT.AFU.AFU.AFU.AXC.AFU.AFU.AXC

kaolinite
MT.1751 (L)
CN M.MT.AFU.AFU.ARI.AFU.AFU.ALO.ALO.BOK.ALO.BZY

kapa
USE **bark cloth**

kapok
MT.1832 (L)
UF ceika
cotton, java
cotton, silk
java cotton
silk cotton
CN M.MT.AFU.AFU.ARI.ALO.AFU.AFU.ALO.BZY

kapok oil
MT.2029
UF oil, kapok
CN M.MT.AFU.AFU.ARI.ARI.AXC.ALO.AXC

Kapriman
FL.3650
CN F.FL.ALO.BOK.ALO.BCW.ALO.BCW.AFU.AXC

Kara Depe
FL.1774 (L)
UF Kara-Tepe
CN F.FL.ALO.ARI.AFU.ALO.BIQ

Kara-e
FL.2055
CN F.FL.ALO.ARI.ALO.ALO.ALO.ARI.BOK

Kara-Tepe
USE **Kara Depe**

Karagwe
FL.681
CN F.FL.ALO.AFU.AXC.AXC.BOK.BZY

Karajá
USE **Carajá**

Karakhanid
USE **Qarakhanid**

Karakoyunlu
FL.3586
CN F.FL.ALO.BIQ.AFU.IFM.ALO

Karaman
USE **Karamanid**

Karaman b. Nura Sufi
FL.3463
UF Qaraman b. Nura Sufi
CN F.FL.ALO.BIQ.AFU.DUC.AFU

Karamanid
FL.3462
UF Karaman
Qaramanid
CN F.FL.ALO.BIQ.AFU.DUC

Karamojong
FL.682 (L)
CN F.FL.ALO.AFU.AXC.AXC.BOK.CFS

Karanga
FL.129 (L,B)
UF Great Zimbabwe
Ma Karanga
Zimbabwe
CN F.FL.ALO.AFU.ALO.ARI.AFU

Karankawa
FL.1436 (L)
UF Carancahua Indians
CN F.FL.ALO.ALO.ARI.AFU.BZY.BOK

Karasuk
FL.2124
CN F.FL.ALO.ARI.ARI.AFU.AXC

Karatau
FL.1765
CN F.FL.ALO.ARI.AFU.AFU.ALO

Karatsu
FL.2023
CN F.FL.ALO.ARI.ALO.ALO.ALO.
ALO.ALO.BUE

karaya, gum
USE **gum karaya**

Karayo
FL.1924
CN F.FL.ALO.ARI.ALO.AFU.AFU.AXC.
AFU.AFU

karez
USE **qanats**

Karim Shaharian
FL.3003
CN F.FL.ALO.AXC.ARI.BIQ.AFU.AFU.
AXC

Karinye
USE **Carib**

Karma Gardri School
FL.2180
UF Karma sgar bris
CN F.FL.ALO.ARI.AXC.AFU.BOK.
AFU.AXC

Karma sgar bris
USE **Karma Gardri School**

Karmin
USE **carmine**

Karminlack
USE **carmine**

Karok
FL.1256 (L)
CN F.FL.ALO.ALO.ARI.AFU.ALO.CFS

kasai velvet
USE **cut-pile cloth**

Kashan ware
FL.3457
UF ware, Kashan
CN F.FL.ALO.BIQ.AFU.DIO.ALO.AFU

Kashmiri
FL.2154 (L)
CN F.FL.ALO.ARI.AXC.AFU.ALO

Kasim
USE **Qasim**

Kasingo
FL.510
UF Basikasingo
CN F.FL.ALO.AFU.AXC.ALO.ALO.
BIQ.AFU.AFU.AXC

Kaska
FL.1235 (L)
UF Eastern Nahane
Nahane, Eastern
CN F.FL.ALO.ALO.ARI.AFU.AFU.ARI.
CLM

kasrs
USE **qasrs**

kassen
TG.600 (N)
ALT **kas**
SN Use with reference to the American version of the 17th-century Netherlandish kast or large cupboard; made by Dutch settlers in the Hudson and Delaware valleys about 1675-1750 and more widely into the 19th century. Generally have two raised paneled doors, and a heavy overhanging cornice with a drawer or drawers below; sometimes decoratively painted with grisaille panels and fruit.
UF cases (kassen)
kaesten
CN V.TG.AFU.AFU.AXC.ALO.CXA.ALO

Kassite
FL.2976
UF Cassite
CN F.FL.ALO.AXC.ARI.BCW.AFU.BOK

Kassler yellow
USE **Turner's yellow**

Kasslerbraun
USE **Van Dyke brown**

Kastri group
FL.2542
CN F.FL.ALO.AXC.ALO.AFU.AFU.
ALO.AFU.AFU.BCW

Kasuga
FL.1998
CN F.FL.ALO.ARI.ALO.ALO.ALO.
AFU.BIQ

Kasuga School
FL.2056
CN F.FL.ALO.ARI.ALO.ALO.ALO.ARI.
BUE

katechu
USE **cutch**

Kathmandu
FL.2168
UF Katmandu
CN F.FL.ALO.ARI.AXC.AFU.AXC.
ALO.ALO

Katladlit
FL.1216
UF Eskimo, Greenlandic
Greenlandic Eskimo
Kalaallit
CN F.FL.ALO.ALO.ARI.AFU.AFU.AFU.
ARI.AFU

Katmandu
USE **Kathmandu**

Katsugawa School
USE **Katsukawa School**

Katsukawa School
FL.2091 (L)
UF Katsugawa School
CN F.FL.ALO.ARI.ALO.ALO.ALO.
AXC.BZY.BOK

Katsushika School
USE **Hokusai School**

Katunga
USE **Old Oyo**

kauri
MT.1502 (L)
UF copal, kauri
gum, kauri
kauri copal
kauri gum
kauri resin
resin, kauri
CN M.MT.AFU.AFU.ALO.BOK.CRG

kauri copal
USE **kauri**

kauri gum
USE **kauri**

kauri resin
USE **kauri**

Kavirondo
USE **Bantu Kavirondo**

Kaw
USE **Kansa**

Kawaiisu
FL.1312 (L)
CN F.FL.ALO.ALO.ARI.AFU.AXC.BCW

Kawchottine
USE **Hare**

Kawia
USE **Cahuilla**

Kayapo
USE **Cayapó**

Kayrak Kum
USE **Kayrakkum**

Kayrakkum
FL.1783
UF Kairak-Kum

Kayrak Kum
CN F.FL.ALO.ARI.AFU.ARI.AXC

Kazvin School
FL.3534
UF Qazwin
CN F.FL.ALO.BIQ.AFU.GRC.AFU.ALO

KD furniture
USE **knock-down furniture**

Keaka
FL.239
CN F.FL.ALO.AFU.AXC.AFU.ALO.AFU.AXC.AFU

Kebaran
FL.2914
CN F.FL.ALO.AXC.ARI.AXC.AFU.AFU.ARI

keel arches
USE **ogee arches**

Keene's cement
MT.23
SN A cement made by the addition of alum to gypsum burned at high temperature; used for areas exposed to moisture because of its dense, hard quality.
UF cement, Keene's
class D gypsum plaster
gypsum plaster, class D
Keene's plaster
plaster, class D gypsum
plaster, Keene's
CN M.MT.AFU.AFU.AFU.ALO.AFU.AFU.BIQ.AFU

Keene's plaster
USE **Keene's cement**

keepers
USE **strikes**

keepers (curators)
USE **curators**

keeping rooms
RM.172
ALT **keeping room**
SN Rooms (often rectangular) at the back of colonial New England houses, which served as a combination kitchen, living room, and workroom. (HAS)
UF rooms, keeping
CN V.RM.AFU.DIO.ALO.CXA.BOK

keeps
RT.1198 (A,B)
ALT **keep**
SN The strongest and securest parts of castles, often used as residences. (W)
UF donjons
kepes
maiden towers
towers, maiden
CN V.RT.AFU.BUE.AFU.BOK

keepsakes
USE **souvenirs**

Kekchi
FL.1534 (L)
CN F.FL.ALO.ALO.ARI.ALO.BIQ.AFU.ARI

Kel'teminar
USE **Kelteminar**

Kele
FL.435 (L)
CN F.FL.ALO.AFU.AXC.ALO.ALO.AFU.AFU.AXC.AFU

kellastone
MT.2462
CN M.MT.AFU.ARI.CRG.AFU.AXC.ARI.BOK.AFU

kelly green
USE **deep yellowish green**
strong green
strong yellowish green

kelly green, bright
USE **brilliant green**
strong green
strong yellowish green
vivid yellowish green

Kelsterbach porcelain
FL.3388 (R)
UF porcelain, Kelsterbach
CN F.FL.ALO.BCW.ALO.AXC.DIO.BIQ.BCW.ALO

Kelteminar
FL.1775
UF Kel'teminar
CN F.FL.ALO.ARI.AFU.ALO.BOK

Keltic
USE **Celtic**

Kemant
FL.640 (L)
UF Qement
CN F.FL.ALO.AFU.AXC.AXC.AXC.AXC

Kemerian
FL.2852
CN F.FL.ALO.AXC.ARI.AFU.AFU.AFU.ARI

kenaf
MT.1833 (L)
UF fiber, kenaf
kenaf fiber
CN M.MT.AFU.AFU.ARI.ALO.AFU.AFU.ALO.CFS

kenaf fiber
USE **kenaf**

Kennebec
USE **Abnaki**

kennels
RK.86 (A,L,N,B,R)
ALT **kennel**
UF dog kennels
kennels, dog
CN V.RK.AFU.ALO.ALO.AFU.ALO.BOK

kennels, dog
USE **kennels**

kente
MT.1869
UF cloth, kente
kente cloth
CN M.MT.AFU.AFU.ARI.ALO.ALO.ALO.ALO.CRG

kente cloth
USE **kente**

Kentish ragstone
USE **ragstone**

kepes
USE **keeps**

Kerala
FL.2298 (L)
CN F.FL.ALO.ARI.AXC.ALO.AFU.BZY.BIQ.AFU

keramics
USE **ceramics**

Kerch Style
FL.2647
CN F.FL.ALO.AXC.ALO.AFU.ALO.AXC.ARI.AXC.ALO

Keremian
FL.43
CN F.FL.ALO.AFU.AFU.AFU.ALO.ALO

Kerewe
FL.683 (L)
UF Bakerewe
Wakerewe
CN F.FL.ALO.AFU.AXC.AXC.BOK.CLM

kerfing
KT.883
ALT **kerfed**
SN Use for the process of making deep cuts in wood so that it may be bent.
CN K.KT.AFU.ALO.HOE.BUE.ALO.AFU

Kerma
FL.156 (A)
CN F.FL.ALO.AFU.ALO.AXC.AXC.AFU

Kerma, Classic
USE **Classic Kerma**

Kerma, Early
USE **Early Kerma**

Kerma, Middle
USE **Middle Kerma**

Kerman ware
USE **Kirman ware**

kermes
MT.1516
SN A red natural dyestuff obtained from an insect found in the kermes oak. (MAYER)
UF grain lake

kermes lake
lake, grain
lake, kermes
CN M.MT.AFU.AFU.ARI.AFU.AFU.AFU.AFU.AFU.AFU

kermes (color)
USE **vivid red**

kermes lake
USE **kermes**

kernel black
USE **peach black**

kernel oil
MT.2035
UF oil, kernel
CN M.MT.AFU.AFU.ARI.ARI.AXC.ARI.AXC

Keros-Syros
FL.2540
CN F.FL.ALO.AXC.ALO.AFU.AFU.ALO.AFU.AFU.ARI

kerosene
MT.2668 (L)
UF coal oil
oil, coal
CN M.MT.AFU.ARI.HZS.AFU.BIQ.AFU.AFU

kerosene torches
TB.106 (N)
ALT **kerosene torch**
UF torches, kerosene
CN V.TB.AFU.ARI.ALO.ARI.BCW.ARI

kersantite
USE **mica diorite**

Kete
FL.431 (L)
UF Bakete
Tukete
CN F.FL.ALO.AFU.AXC.ALO.ALO.AFU.AFU.ALO

ketone, dimethyl
USE **acetone**

ketone, methyl ethyl
USE **methyl ethyl ketone**

ketone, methyl isobutyl
USE **methyl isobutyl ketone**

ketones
MT.2696 (L)
SN Group of organic solvents used in paint and varnish removers, and as solvents for lacquer and plastics. (GOTTS)
CN M.MT.AFU.ARI.HZS.AFU.BOK.ARI

kettle (bombé)
USE **bombé**

kettle stands
TG.642
ALT **kettle stand**
SN Stands made to support a hot-water kettle or urn. (BEARD)
UF stands, kettle
stands, tea kettle
stands, tined kettle
stands, urn
tables, urn
tea kettle stands
tined kettle stands
urn stands
urn tables
CN V.TG.AFU.AFU.BIQ.BCW.ALO.CFS

kettle stands, tea
USE **tea tables**

Ketton stone
MT.670
UF stone, Ketton
CN M.MT.AFU.AFU.AFU.DCU.AFU.ALO.AFU.ALO.ALO.AFU.AFU.ALO.BOK

Ketu
FL.277
CN F.FL.ALO.AFU.AXC.AFU.ALO.BCW.ALO.BCW

kevils
USE **cavils**

kevlar
MT.2142
SN Synthetic fiber produced from long-chain polyamides (nylons) suitable for ropes, cables, webbings, and tapes. (MH)
CN M.MT.AFU.AFU.ARI.BUE.ALO.AXC.AFU.CFS.AFU.AFU

key (color)
BM.133
SN The prevailing range of color values and tonal quality in an artwork, structure, object, or design.
CN B.BM.AFU.AFU.ARI.BOK.ALO.ALO.ALO.AXC

key bits
USE **bits (key components)**

key blocks
USE **keystones**

key brick
USE **compass brick**

key changing locks
TF.202
ALT **key changing lock**
UF locks, key changing
CN V.TF.AFU.AFU.AFU.AFU.DIO.BIQ.AFU.BUE

key consoles
RT.696
ALT **key console**
SN Consoles which act as the keystone of an arch.
UF consoles, key
CN V.RT.AFU.AFU.ALO.AFU.AXC.AFU.AFU

Key-Kobad-Shakh
FL.1794
CN F.FL.ALO.ARI.AFU.AXC.BOK

key locks, bit
USE **bit key locks**

key maps
USE **index maps**

key pattern
DG.126
SN Use for frets consisting of a relatively continuous series of rectilinear hook shapes, sometimes crossing each other.
UF frets, Greek
Greek frets
Greek keys
keys, Greek
pattern, key
CN D.DG.AFU.ARI.ALO.BIQ.ALO.ALO

key plans
VD.60
ALT **key plan**
SN Use for plans designed for locating details that appear on other drawings.
UF plans, key
CN V.VD.AFU.AFU.BIQ.ALO.AXC.BCW

key plates
USE **escutcheons (hardware)**

key plates, drop
USE **drop escutcheons**

key-word-and-context indexes
VW.429 (L)
ALT **key-word-and-context index**
SN Indexes in which each significant word in the entry is brought to the beginning, in alphabetical order, followed by the remaining words which follow it, and then followed by that part of the original title which came before the significant word. (LG)
UF indexes, key-word-and-context
KWAC indexes
CN V.VW.AFU.AFU.ALO.EWY.BOK.AFU.ARI.AFU

key-word-in-context indexes
VW.430
ALT **key-word-in-context index**
SN Indexes in which each significant word in the entry appears in a fixed position within the entry and is arranged with other entries in alphabetical order in a column.
UF indexes, key-word-in-context
KWIC indexes
CN V.VW.AFU.AFU.ALO.EWY.BOK.AFU.ARI.ALO

key-word-out-of-context indexes
VW.431
ALT **key-word-out-of-context index**
SN Indexes in which each significant word in an entry is separated from

the entry on separate lines of their own, with the full entry in original order under them.
UF indexes, key-word-out-of-context
KWOC indexes
CN V.VW.AFU.AFU.ALO.EWY.BOK.AFU.ARI.ARI

key-word-out-of-title indexes
VW.432
ALT **key-word-out-of-title index**
UF indexes, key-word-out-of-title
KWOT indexes
CN V.VW.AFU.AFU.ALO.EWY.BOK.AFU.ARI.AXC

keyboards
TB.154 (L,N)
ALT **keyboard**
SN Assemblages of systematically arranged keys by which a machine is operated. (WCOL)
CN V.TB.AFU.ARI.BCW.AXC.AFU.AXC

keyed joints
TF.590
ALT **keyed joint**
SN Joints between two timbers that are located or secured by a wedge or insert that prevents movement. (DAC)
UF joints, keyed
CN V.TF.ALO.AFU.DOI

keyhole saws
TB.1020 (N)
ALT **keyhole saw**
SN Compass saws having especially narrow blades and fine teeth. (DAC)
UF pad saws
saws, keyhole
saws, pad
CN V.TB.AFU.BCW.CFS.ALO.AFU.EWY.BUE.ALO.AFU

keyhole surrounds
TF.159
ALT **keyhole surround**
SN Use for inserts or inlay surrounding keyholes. For larger plates surrounding keyholes, use **escutcheons (hardware)**.
UF escutcheons (keyhole surrounds)
CN V.TF.AFU.AFU.AFU.AFU.DCU

keys
TF.527 (A,L,N,R)
ALT **key**
SN The removable actuating devices of a lock. (MEANS)
CN V.TF.AFU.ALO.ARI.AFU

keys of life
USE **ankhs**

keys, adjustable
USE **adjustable keys**

keys, barred
USE **pipe keys**

keys, barrel
USE **pipe keys**

keys, bed
USE **bed wrenches**

keys, card
USE **card keys**

keys, change
USE **master keys**

keys, detachable
USE **detachable keys**

keys, double-bitted
USE **double-bitted keys**

keys, drop
USE **drop keys**

keys, extension
USE **adjustable keys**

keys, Greek
USE **key pattern**

keys, master
USE **master keys**

keys, night
USE **night keys**

keys, pass
USE **master keys**

keys, pipe
USE **pipe keys**

keys, push
USE **push keys**

keys, round
USE **round keys**

keys, skeleton
USE **skeleton keys**

keys, sliding-door
USE **sliding-door keys**

keys, stop
USE **stop keys**

keys, submaster
USE **submaster keys**

keys, thrust
USE **push keys**

keys, warded
USE **warded keys**

keys, wing
USE **wing keys**

keystones
RT.695 (A,B,R)
ALT **keystone**
SN The central wedge-shaped voussoir in an arch or vault; also, similar elements used as ornaments on the heads of doors or windows. (IGA)
UF key blocks
CN V.RT.AFU.AFU.ALO.AFU.AXC.AFU

Khabur ware
FL.2938
UF ware, Khabur
CN F.FL.ALO.AXC.ARI.AXC.ALO.BIQ.BIQ

khaki
USE **light olive brown**
light yellowish brown
moderate yellowish brown

Khalchayan
FL.1795
CN F.FL.ALO.ARI.AFU.AXC.BUE

Khalji
FL.3473 (L)
UF Khiliji
CN F.FL.ALO.BIQ.AFU.DZW

Khami
FL.139
CN F.FL.ALO.AFU.ALO.ARI.BCW.ALO

khaya
USE **African mahogany**

Khaya anthotheca
USE **white mahogany**

Khaydarabad-Tepe
FL.1796
CN F.FL.ALO.ARI.AFU.AXC.BZY

Khazineh
FL.3007
CN F.FL.ALO.AXC.ARI.BIQ.AFU.AFU.BUE

Khiliji
USE **Khalji**

Khirbet Kerak ware
FL.2939
UF burnished ware, red-black
red-black burnished ware
ware, Khirbet Kerak
ware, red-black burnished
CN F.FL.ALO.AXC.ARI.AXC.ALO.BIQ.BOK

Khmer
FL.2408
CN F.FL.ALO.ARI.BCW.BOK.AFU.AXC

Khmer (Angkorean)
USE **Angkorean**

Khocho
FL.1814
UF Koco
Qoco
CN F.FL.ALO.ARI.AFU.AXC.ELK.AXC

KhoiKhoi
FL.552 (L)
UF Hottentots
CN F.FL.ALO.AFU.AXC.ARI.ALO.ALO

Khorezm
FL.1776 (L)
UF Chorasmia
Khwarezm

Kwarasm
CN F.FL.ALO.ARI.AFU.ALO.BUE

Khotan
FL.1815
CN F.FL.ALO.ARI.AFU.AXC.ELK.BCW

Khwarezm
USE **Khorezm**

Ki Seto
FL.2037
UF Seto, Ki
Seto, Yellow
Yellow Seto
CN F.FL.ALO.ARI.ALO.ALO.ALO.ALO.ALO.DUC.AFU

kibbutzim
RD.79 (L,B)
ALT **kibbutz**
CN V.RD.AFU.BOK.AFU.ALO

kick plates
USE **kickplates**

Kickapoo
FL.1326 (L)
CN F.FL.ALO.ALO.ARI.AFU.BCW.AXC

kickplates
TF.19
ALT **kickplate**
SN Metal strips or plates attached to the bottom rail of a door for protection against marring, as by shoes; also, plates, usually metal, used to create a lip or ridge at the open edge of a stair platform or floor, or at the back edge or open ends of a stair tread. (MEANS)
UF kick plates
plates, kick
CN V.TF.AFU.AFU.AFU.AFU.AFU.CFS.ARI

kidney library writing tables
USE **kidney tables**

kidney tables
TG.682
ALT **kidney table**
SN Use for kidney-shaped tables, generally used as writing or dressing tables, which were first made in France during the Louis XV period and later introduced in England and America.
UF haricots
kidney library writing tables
library writing tables, kidney
tables, kidney
writing tables, kidney library
CN V.TG.AFU.AFU.BIQ.BOK.AFU.BUE

Kikuyu
FL.647 (L)
UF Akikuyu
CN F.FL.ALO.AFU.AXC.AXC.BCW.BIQ

Kiliwa
FL.1277 (L)
CN F.FL.ALO.ALO.ALO.ARI.AFU.ALO.FZU.AFU.ARI

Kilkenny marble
USE **Irish black marble**

killers, weed
USE **herbicides**

kiln-burned brick
USE **fired brick**

kiln-dried lumber
MT.1436
UF lumber, kiln-dried
CN M.MT.AFU.AFU.ALO.BIQ.DCU.ALO.BOK.ALO.ARI.ARI

kiln forks
TB.88
ALT **kiln fork**
SN Long-handled forks used for placing glass in kilns. (HAND)
UF forks, kiln
CN V.TB.AFU.ARI.ALO.ARI.AFU

kilns
TB.89 (A,L,N,B,R)
ALT **kiln**
SN Furnaces, ovens, or heated enclosures for drying, charring, hardening, baking, or burning various materials. (MEANS)
UF furnaces (kilns)
ovens (kilns)
CN V.TB.AFU.ARI.ALO.ARI.ALO

kilns, beehive
USE **beehive ovens**

kilns, brick
USE **brick kilns**

kilns, cartunnel
USE **tunnel kilns**

kilns, cement
USE **cement kilns**

kilns, chamber
USE **chamber kilns**

kilns, continuous
USE **tunnel kilns**

kilns, dry
USE **dry kilns**

kilns, lime
USE **lime kilns**

kilns, rotary
USE **rotary kilns**

kilns, tunnel
USE **tunnel kilns**

Kilwa
FL.151
CN F.FL.ALO.AFU.ALO.AXC.ALO.AFU

Kimberly
FL.3616 (L)
CN F.FL.ALO.BOK.AFU.ALO.ALO

Kincaid
FL.839
CN F.FL.ALO.ALO.ALO.AFU.ALO.ALO.ARI.AFU.BOK

kindergartens
RK.834 (A,L,B)
ALT **kindergarten**
CN V.RK.AFU.ALO.ALO.CXA.ARI.AXC.AFU.ALO

kinematics
BM.891 (L)
CN B.BM.CFS.AXC.BIQ.AFU.ALO

Kinetic
FL.3729 (L,R)
UF Art in motion
CN F.FL.ALO.BUE.ARI.DCU

kinetics
BM.892 (L,R)
SN The effects of forces upon the motions of material bodies. (W)
CN B.BM.CFS.AXC.BIQ.AFU.ARI

king closer
MT.112
UF beveled closer
closer, beveled
closer, king
closer, three-quarter
closure, king
king closure
three-quarter closer
CN M.MT.AFU.AFU.AFU.AXC.ALO.AFU.ARI.AFU.AFU

king closure
USE **king closer**

king nut hickory
USE **big shellbark hickory**

king-post roofs
RT.452
ALT **king-post roof**
SN Roofs supported by a king-post truss.
UF roofs, king-post
CN V.RT.AFU.AFU.AFU.BIQ.ARI.AFU.ALO.ARI.AXC

king-post trusses
RT.366
ALT **king-post truss**
SN Triangular frames formed by two inclined members joined at their apex and a horizontal tie beam that connects their lower ends; a vertical central strut (the king post) extends from apex to tie beam. (DAC)
UF trusses, king-post
CN V.RT.AFU.AFU.AFU.BCW.CLM.AFU.AFU.AFU.BOK

king posts
RT.512
ALT **king post**
SN Vertical members connecting the apex of a triangular truss, as in a roof, with the base. (WCOL)

UF posts, king
CN V.RT.AFU.AFU.AFU.BIQ.ARI.ALO.ALO.ARI.AFU.AFU

king-size beds
TG.385
ALT **king-size bed**
UF beds, king-size
CN V.TG.AFU.AFU.ARI.AFU.ALO.BCW

king-tables
RT.624
ALT **king-table**
SN In Medieval architecture, a string-course with ballflower ornaments sometimes found under parapets. (HAS)
CN V.RT.AFU.AFU.AFU.BIQ.BUE.ALO.AFU.ALO.CFS.ALO

king's blue
USE **cobalt blue**

king's yellow
USE **orpiment**

Kingdom, Middle
USE **Middle Kingdom**

Kingdom, New
USE **New Kingdom**

Kingdom, Old
USE **Old Kingdom**

kingfisher
USE **dark blue**

kingfisher blue
USE **strong greenish blue**

kings
HG.698 (L,R)
ALT **king**
SN Male monarchs who reign over a major territorial unit. (W)
CN H.HG.AFU.AXC.CFS.CRG.BUE

kinship
BM.1129 (L)
CN B.BM.CRG.BUE.ARI

Kintampo
FL.82
CN F.FL.ALO.AFU.ALO.AFU.BCW

Kioko
USE **Chokwe**

Kiokwe
USE **Chokwe**

kiosks
RK.20 (A,L,B,R)
ALT **kiosk**
SN Small, freestanding structures either open or partially enclosed, where merchandise is displayed, advertised, or sold. (MEANS)
CN V.RK.AFU.ALO.AFU.ALO.ARI

Kiowa
FL.1385 (L,R)
CN F.FL.ALO.ALO.ARI.AFU.BOK.CRG

Kiowa Apache
FL.1386 (L)
UF Apache, Kiowa
CN F.FL.ALO.ALO.ARI.AFU.BOK.CXA

Kipchak Khanate
FL.3607 (L,R)
UF Golden Horde
CN F.FL.ALO.BIQ.AXC.AFU

Kipsigis
FL.648 (L)
CN F.FL.ALO.AFU.AXC.AXC.BCW.BOK

Kiriama
USE **Giriama**

Kiribati
FL.3682 (L)
UF Gilbert Island
CN F.FL.ALO.BOK.ARI.ARI

kirks
USE churches

Kirlian photography
KT.385 (L)
SN A process to record the surface conduction characteristics of an object or material by placing it on photographic film, which is then exposed by the blue and ultraviolet light of a corona generated by a high-voltage, high-frequency power.
UF corona discharge photography
discharge photography, corona
photography, corona discharge
photography, Kirlian
CN K.KT.AFU.ALO.DUC.DIO.ARI.ARI.ARI

Kirman ware
FL.3540
UF Kerman ware
ware, Kerman
ware, Kirman
CN F.FL.ALO.BIQ.AFU.GRC.ALO.ALO

Kishangarh
FL.2292
CN F.FL.ALO.ARI.AXC.ALO.AFU.BZY.BCW.BCW.BOK

Kisi
USE **Kissi**

Kisii (Gusii)
USE **Gusii**

Kissi
FL.326 (L)
UF Kisi
CN F.FL.ALO.AFU.AXC.AFU.ARI.BCW.BCW

Kitagawa School
FL.2092
CN F.FL.ALO.ARI.ALO.ALO.ALO.AXC.BZY.BUE

Kitamat
USE **Haisla**

Kitao School
FL.2093
CN F.FL.ALO.ARI.ALO.ALO.ALO.AXC.BZY.BZY

kitchen cabinets
TG.433
ALT **kitchen cabinet**
UF cabinets, kitchen
CN V.TG.AFU.AFU.AXC.ALO.ARI.ALO.BZY

kitchen chairs
TG.214
ALT **kitchen chair**
UF chairs, kitchen
CN V.TG.AFU.AFU.ALO.AFU.AFU.ARI.AXC.AXC

kitchen gardens
RK.1421 (A,L)
ALT **kitchen garden**
SN Use for private gardens established primarily for growing vegetables and herbs for domestic consumption.
UF gardens, kitchen
CN V.RK.ALO.AFU.AFU.ALO.BCW

kitchen middens
USE **middens**

kitchen safes
TG.435 (N)
ALT **kitchen safe**
SN Kitchen cabinets with a ventilated front, generally of pierced tin and sometimes of screening or cloth, in which food is stored.
UF food safes
safes, food
safes, kitchen
CN V.TG.AFU.AFU.AXC.ALO.ARI.ALO.CFS

kitchen tables
TG.780
ALT **kitchen table**
UF tables, kitchen
CN V.TG.AFU.AFU.BIQ.BOK.ARI.ALO.ALO

kitchenettes
RM.229
ALT **kitchenette**
SN Small rooms or alcoves fitted with the essential conveniences of a kitchen. (DAC)
CN V.RM.AFU.DIO.ALO.DOI.BIQ.AFU

kitchens
RM.228 (A,L,B,R)
ALT **kitchen**
SN Rooms intended for the preparation and cooking of food. (DAC)
CN V.RM.AFU.DIO.ALO.DOI.BIQ

kitchens, soup
USE **soup kitchens**

kitemaking
KT.527
CN K.KT.AFU.ALO.ELK.CLM

Kitimat
USE **Haisla**

Kitksan
USE **Gitksan**

Kitlope
USE **Haisla**

kits, learning
USE **learning modules**

kitsch
BM.297 (A,L,R)
SN Designation applied to artistic or literary material, produced to appeal to popular taste, and marked especially by sentimentalism, sensationalism, or slickness. (W)
CN B.BM.AFU.AXC.BZY

Kitunaha
USE **Kutenai**

kivas
RK.1114 (A,L,N)
ALT **kiva**
SN Pueblo Indian buildings used as men's clubhouses and for ceremonial and social activities.
CN V.RK.AFU.ALO.ALO.FCS.BIQ.AXC

Kiwai
FL.3644 (L)
CN F.FL.ALO.BOK.ALO.BCW.ALO.AXC.ALO

Kizh
USE Gabrieliño

Kizil
FL.1816
UF Ming-öi
Qizil
Qyzyl
CN F.FL.ALO.ARI.AFU.AXC.ELK.BIQ

Klallam
FL.1347 (L)
UF Clallam
CN F.FL.ALO.ALO.ARI.AFU.BIQ.DCU

Klamath
FL.1409 (L)
CN F.FL.ALO.ALO.ARI.AFU.BUE.BCW

Klikitat
FL.1410 (L)
CN F.FL.ALO.ALO.ARI.AFU.BUE.BIQ

klinkart
USE **clinker brick**

klismoi
TG.75 (N)
ALT **klismos**
SN Ancient Greek chairs having a deep top rail curving forward from the back and sabre legs; usually undecorated. Imitated during various classical revivals, especially in the 19th century.
UF chairs, klismos
klismos chairs
klysmos chairs
CN V.TG.AFU.AFU.ALO.AFU.AFU.AFU.HZS

klismos chairs
USE **klismoi**

klysmos chairs
USE **klismoi**

Knaiakhotana
USE **Tanaina**

knee braces
RT.207
ALT **knee brace**
SN Members placed across the inside of an angle in a framework to add stiffness to the framework, especially at the angle between the roof and wall of a building. (PUTNAM)
UF braces, knee
CN V.RT.AFU.AFU.AFU.AXC.DOI.AFU.AFU.ALO

knee brackets
TG.964
ALT **knee bracket**
UF brackets, knee
CN V.TG.ALO.FIM.ALO.ALO.ALO.AFU

kneehole chests
USE **kneehole desks**

kneehole chests of drawers
USE **kneehole desks**

kneehole desks
TG.541
ALT **kneehole desk**
SN Desks or chests with a recessed center front which is usually flanked on each side by a set of drawers.
UF bureaux (kneehole desks)
chests of drawers, kneehole
chests, kneehole
desks, kneehole
drawers, kneehole chests of
kneehole chests
kneehole chests of drawers
kneehole writing tables
writing tables, kneehole
CN V.TG.AFU.AFU.AXC.ALO.BZY.BZY

kneehole desks (bureau tables)
USE **bureau tables**

kneehole tables (bureau tables)
USE **bureau tables**

kneehole writing tables
USE **kneehole desks**

kneelers
RT.1234 (L)
ALT **kneeler**
SN Cushions, stools, or boards for kneeling, often attached to pews.
CN V.RT.AFU.BUE.ALO.ARI.BUE

kneelers (gable components)
RT.647
ALT **kneeler (gable component)**
UF blocks, skew
butts, skew
footstones
gable springers
kneestones
skew blocks
skew butts
skews
springers, gable
CN V.RT.AFU.AFU.AFU.BIQ.BUE.ALO.AFU.AXC.ALO.BCW

knees
TG.961
ALT **knee**
SN The outward upper portion of a furniture leg, especially of a cabriole leg. (FAIRB)
CN V.TG.ALO.FIM.ALO.ALO.AFU

knees, hipped
USE **hipped knees**

kneestones
USE **kneelers (gable components)**

knife files
TB.876
ALT **knife file**
SN Files having a blade-like cross section, with a sharp edge; used to finish narrow grooves. (DAC)
UF files, knife
CN V.TB.AFU.BCW.CFS.ALO.AFU.CFS.ARI

knife froes
TB.879 (N)
ALT **knife froe**
SN Froes shaped like a knife; usually about 1 foot long. (SLOANE)
UF froe knives
froes, knife
froes, lathmaker's
knives, froe
lathmaker's froes
CN V.TB.AFU.BCW.CFS.ALO.AFU.CLM.AFU

knife sharpeners
USE **whetstones**

knitters
HG.529
ALT **knitter**
CN H.HG.AFU.AXC.BUE.ARI.CXA.AXC

knitting
KT.545 (L,R)
ALT **knitted**
CN K.KT.AFU.ALO.ELK.DUC.AFU.ARI

knives
TB.124 (L,N)
ALT **knife**

CN V.TB.AFU.ARI.AXC.ALO.BUE

knives, belly
USE **hollowing drawknives**

knives, bench
USE **bench knives**

knives, block
USE **block knives**

knives, board
USE **utility knives**

knives, chamfer
USE **chamfer knives**

knives, clasp
USE **clasp knives**

knives, craft
USE **utility knives**

knives, elastic
USE **elastic knives**

knives, froe
USE **knife froes**

knives, heading
USE **heading drawknives**

knives, hoop-notching
USE **hoop-notching knives**

knives, mortising
USE **twivels**

knives, pen
USE **penknives**

knives, picking
USE **picking knives**

knives, plaster
USE **plaster knives**

knives, pocket
USE **pocket knives**

knives, putty
USE **putty knives**

knives, race
USE **race knives**

knives, shaving
USE **drawknives**

knives, side
USE **froes**

knives, sloyd
USE **sloyd knives**

knives, stock
USE **block knives**

knives, stopping (putty knives)
USE **putty knives**

knives, utility
USE **utility knives**

knives, willow
USE **willow knives**

knob bolts
USE **knob latches**

knob latches
TF.175
ALT **knob latch**
SN Door latches whose spring bolts are operated by one or more knobs, but whose dead bolts are actuated by a key. (MEANS)
UF bolts, knob
knob bolts
latches, knob
CN V.TF.AFU.AFU.AFU.AFU.DIO.BCW.AFU.ALO

knob locks
TF.203
ALT **knob lock**
SN Door locks whose spring bolts are operated by one or more knobs, but whose dead bolts are actuated by a key. (MEANS)
UF locks, knob
CN V.TF.AFU.AFU.AFU.AFU.DIO.BIQ.AFU.BZY

knobbed ware
FL.2873
UF Buckelkeramik
ware, knobbed
CN F.FL.ALO.AXC.ARI.AFU.ALO.ARI.BUE

knobs
TF.59
ALT **knob**
SN Small rounded ornaments or handles. (WCOL)
CN V.TF.AFU.AFU.AFU.AFU.CFS.AXC

knobs, cabinet
USE **cabinet knobs**

knobs, closet
USE **closet knobs**

knobs, cupboard
USE **cabinet knobs**

knobs, door
USE **doorknobs**

knobs, drawer
USE **cabinet knobs**

knobs, dummy
USE **dummy knobs**

knobs, hip
USE **hip knobs**

knobs, screwless
USE **screwless knobs**

knobs, shutter
USE **shutter knobs**

knobs, thru-screw
USE **thru-screw knobs**

knock-down furniture
TG.801
SN Furniture sold in units which can be packed flat and easily assembled with a screwdriver.
UF furniture, K D
furniture, knock-down
furniture, package
K D furniture
package furniture
CN V.TG.AFU.ARI.BZY.ARI

knockers
USE **door knockers**

knockers, door
USE **door knockers**

knocking-up irons
USE **jumpers**

Knole settees
TG.303
ALT **Knole settee**
SN Settees with high backs and hinged arms that may be upright or sloped out from the seat, named after the unique early specimen at Knole Park, Kent; popular for rich suburban furnishings in England in the 1920s and 1930s. (DDA)
UF settees, Knole
CN V.TG.AFU.AFU.ALO.ALO.BUE.ARI

knolls
USE **hillocks**

Knorpelwork
USE **Auricular**

knot gardens
RK.1404 (A,L)
ALT **knot garden**
SN Use for intricately designed gardens in which ground coves, low shrubs, or colored earths are arranged in interlacing patterns resembling knots.
UF gardens, knot
gardens, rope-knot
rope-knot gardens
CN V.RK.ALO.AFU.AFU.AFU.ARI.ARI.AFU

knot pattern, linked
USE **knotwork**

knots
DG.38
ALT **knot**
SN Use for ornamental motifs resembling cords which are interlaced. (HAS)
CN D.DG.AFU.AFU.CFS

knotted columns
RT.93
ALT **knotted column**
SN Use for two columns with shafts intertwined as if tied in a knot.
CN V.RT.AFU.AFU.AFU.AXC.BIQ.AFU.AFU.BZY